S0-CFI-964

SEVENTH EDITION

POLICE ADMINISTRATION

Structures, Processes, and Behavior

CHARLES R. SWANSON

University of Georgia

LEONARD TERRITO

Saint Leo University

ROBERT W. TAYLOR

University of North Texas

Upper Saddle River, New Jersey
Columbus, Ohio

Library of Congress Cataloging-in-Publication Data

Swanson, Charles R.
Police administration: structures, processes, and behavior / Charles R. Swanson, Leonard Territo, Robert W. Taylor.—7th ed.
p. cm.
ISBN-13: 978-0-13-158933-9
ISBN-10: 0-13-158933-4
1. Police administration. I. Territo, Leonard, II. Taylor, Robert W. III. Title.
HV7935.S95 2008
363.2068—dc22 2007015913

Editor in Chief: Vernon R. Anthony
Senior Acquisitions Editor: Tim Peyton
Editorial Assistant: Alicia Kelly
Production Coordination: Emily Bush, S4Carlisle Publishing Services
Project Manager: Holly Shufeldt
Design Coordinator: Christy Mahon
Cover Designer: Christopher Weigand
Cover Image: Getty Images, Inc.—Stockbyte
Senior Operations Supervisor: Pat Tonneman
Director of Marketing: David Gesell
Marketing Manager: Adam Kloza
Marketing Coordinator: Alicia Dysert

This book was set in Berkeley Book by S4Carlisle Publishing Services. It was printed and bound by Courier Kendallville. The cover was printed by Phoenix Color Corp.

Pearson Education Ltd.
Pearson Education Singapore, Pte. Ltd.
Pearson Education Canada, Ltd.
Pearson Education—Japan
Pearson Education Australia PTY, Limited
Pearson Education North Asia Ltd.
Pearson Educación de Mexico, S.A. de C.V.
Pearson Education Malaysia, Pte. Ltd.

10 9 8 7 6 5
ISBN-13 978-0-13-158933-9
ISBN-10 0-13-158933-4

DEDICATION

For my wife, Paige, for her endless cheer and support; the kids, Ben, Cole, Colin, Kellie, Maggie, and Traci; my good friends and critics Russ Abernathy, Bob Miller, Mark Foster, and Joe Markham; and the men and women out there, 24-7-365.

— C. R. "Mike" Swanson

To Elena, the kindest and sweetest women I have ever known, and our children Lorraine, Kseniya, Ilia, and grandchildren Matthew and Branden.

—Leonard Territo

For my good friend and colleague, Dr. Tory J. Caeti who tragically died in Kenya (2006) while on a mission for the U.S. Department of State. He was a wonderful man that leaves behind a beautiful wife (Melinda) and two children (Anthony 7 and Lauren 4). He always wanted to be the "next author" on this book.

—Bob Taylor

BRIEF CONTENTS

Part I The Evolution of American Policing 1

1 Historical Development 3

2 Policing Today 37

3 Intelligence, Terrorism, and Homeland Security 69

4 Politics and Police Administration 107

Part II The Organization and the Leader 159

5 Organizational Theory 161

6 Organizational Design 223

7 Leadership 267

8 Planning and Decision Making 299

Part III The Management of Police Organizations 345

9 Organizational Communication 347

10 Human Resource Management 385

11 Labor Relations 457

12 Financial Management 493

Part IV Organizational Issues 527

13 Stress and Police Personnel 529

14 Legal Aspects of Police Administration 581

15 Organizational Change and the Future 653

CONTENTS

Preface **xvii**
Acknowledgments **xx**
About the Authors **xxiii**

Part I The Evolution of American Policing 1

1 Historical Development 3

Politics and Administration 5
Police Professionalization 7
    Profession and Professional 7
    August Vollmer 8
    The Pendleton Act of 1883 to the Military Model 10
Prohibition to 1940 11
World War II and the 1950s 15
The Turbulent 1960s 17
    Renewed Interest in Professionalization 18
The Call for Research and Other Developments 20
    The Trilogy 21
    Other Major Developments 23
The 1980s and Beyond 23
    Community Oriented Policing 24
    Private Security 24
    Investigative Technology 25
    Terrorism 25
America Responds to September 11 30
Chapter Review 32
Key Terms 34
Notes 35

2 Policing Today 37

Community Policing 40
    Newport News, Virginia 40
    Chicago, Illinois 42
Compstat and Community Policing 47
    Minneapolis, Minnesota 48
    Merging Strategies 49
Policing and New Information Technologies 51
    Crime Analysis 52
    Geographic Information Systems 56
    Artificial Intelligence and Expert Systems 56
    Fax Machines, Websites, and the Internet 59
    The Impact of New Technologies 61

Chapter Review 63
Key Terms 65
Notes 66

3 Intelligence, Terrorism, and Homeland Security 69

Terrorism, Intelligence, and Intelligence-Led Policing 72
Defining Intelligence 73
The Intelligence Process and Cycle 74
Fusion Centers 75
Homeland Security 79
Political Violence and Terrorism 82
Defining Terrorism 84
Radical Islamic Terrorism 87
Jamaah Islamiyah 90
Hamas 93
Other International Threats 95
Right-Wing Extremism 95
Ecoterrorists and Animal Rights Groups 99
Chapter Review 100
Key Terms 102
Notes 103

4 Politics and Police Administration 107

Police Accountability 109
Federal Influence in Law Enforcement 110
Supreme Court Decisions Affecting Law Enforcement: 1961 to 1966 110
More Recent Supreme Court Decisions 112
Traffic Stops and Arrest 112
Self-Incrimination 113
Age-Old Problems in Policing: Brutality and Scandal 114
Racial and Ethnic Profiling 118
Training and Police Ethics 122
Commission on Accreditation for Law Enforcement Agencies 124
The Roles of State and Local Government in Law Enforcement 125
Local Political Forces 127
Strong Mayor 128
City Manager 128
City Councils 129
Politics and the Police Chief 131
The Police Chief and External Incidents 132
Tenure and Contracts for Police Chiefs 135
Politics and the County Sheriff 137
The Sheriff's Role 138
State Prosecutor 140
The Judiciary 141
Citizen Involvement 142
Senior Citizen Organizations 143
Chambers of Commerce and Service Clubs 144
Churches 145
News Media 145
School Violence 148
School Resource Officers 150
Chapter Review 152
Key Terms 154
Notes 154

Part II The Organization and the Leader 159

5 Organizational Theory 161

Traditional Organizational Theory 163
Taylor: Scientific Management 164
Weber: The Bureaucratic Model 168
Administrative Theory 170
Critique of Traditional Theory 172
Open Systems Theory 176
Human Relations 176
Behavioral Systems Theory 185
Organizations as Open Systems 194
Newer Paradigms of Administration 199
Critique of Open Systems Theory 203
Bridging Theories 206
General Bridging Theories 206
Contingency Theory 208
Ouchi's Theory Z 208
Critique of Bridging Theories 209
Synthesis and Prognosis 209
Chapter Review 210
Key Terms 215
Notes 217

6 Organizational Design 223

Organizing: An Overview 224
Specialization in Police Agencies 224
The Principle of Hierarchy 228
Span of Control vs. Span of Management 228
Graicunas Theory 12 229
Organizational Structure and Design 230
Top-Down vs. Bottom-Up Approaches 232
Types of Organizational Design 238
Line Structure 238
Line and Staff Structure 239
Functional Structure 240
Matrix Structure 243
Some Unique Organizational Features of Sheriff's Offices 244
Organizational Structure and Community Policing 247
Decentralizaton vs. Centralization 247
Community Policing Units vs. Departmental Philosophy 247
Traditional Design vs. Structural Change 250
Line and Staff Relationships in Police Agencies 251
The Line Point of View 252
The Staff Point of View 253
Solutions 253
The Informal Organization 255
Expanding the Law Enforcement Personnel Pool 256
Citizen Police Academies 256
Citizens on Patrol 257
Reserves 258
Volunteers 259
Chapter Review 262
Key Terms 264
Notes 264

7 Leadership 267

Leadership and Performance 269
The Nature of Leadership, Authority, and Power 271
The Power Motivation of Police Managers 273
The Leadership Skill Mix 275
Human Relations Skills 275
Conceptual Skills 276
Technical Skills 276
Theories of Leadership 277
Styles of Leadership 278
Lewin, Lippitt, and White: Authoritarian, Democratic, and Laissez-Faire 278
Tannenbaum and Schmidt: The Authoritarian–Democratic Leadership Continuum 279
Downs: Leadership Styles in Bureaucratic Structures 280
Van Maanen: Station House Sergeants and Street Sergeants 281
Blake and Mouton: The Managerial Grid 282
Hersey and Blanchard: Situational Leadership Theory 283
Transactional and Transformational Leaders 285
Total Quality Leadership 289
The Leader and Conflict 290
Leadership and Organizational Control 291
Chapter Review 293
Key Terms 295
Notes 296

8 Planning and Decision Making 299

Planning 300
Definitions of Planning 302
Planning Approaches 302
Synoptic Planning 302
Summation of the Synoptic Planning Approach 310
Incremental Planning 310
Transactive Planning 310
Advocacy Planning 311
Radical Planning 312
Types of Plans 312
Effective Plans 313
Decision Making 315
Decision-Making Models 315
Decision Making during Crisis Events 322
The Branch Davidians, Waco, Texas (1993) 322
The Weaver Family, Ruby Ridge, Idaho (1992) 324
Crisis Events in the Future 327
Group Decision Making 329
Group Assets 329
Ethics and Decision Making 335
Common Errors in Decision Making 336
Cognitive Nearsightedness 336
Assumption That the Future Will Repeat Itself 336
Oversimplification 336
Overreliance on One's Own Experience 337
Preconceived Notions 337
Unwillingness to Experiment 337
Reluctance to Decide 337

Chapter Review 338
Key Terms 340
Notes 340

Part III The Management of Police Organizations 345

9 Organizational Communication 347

The Communication Process 349
Steps in the Communication Process 349
Communication Barriers 350
Organizational Systems of Communication 352
Downward Communication 352
Upward Communication 353
Interpersonal Communication 356
Speaking and Writing 356
Nonverbal Communication 359
Group vs. Interpersonal Communication 361
Size of the Group 361
Group Interaction 361
Cross-Gender Communications 362
Male/Female Conversation Is Cross-Culture Communication 365
Styles in Conflict Resolution 366
Communication with Other Cultures 367
Methods of Responding in Language Differences 368
Other Multicultural Issues 369
Oral or Written Communication 374
Suiting the Medium to the Recipient 374
Written Communication 374
Oral Communication 375
Electronic Media (E-mail) 376
Personal Tactics 376
Organizational Strategies 378
Chapter Review 380
Key Terms 382
Notes 382

10 Human Resource Management 385

Functions of the Human Resource Management Unit 387
Police Personnel Selection and the Americans with Disabilities Act 388
The Courts and the ADA 394
Supreme Court Limits on State Workers' ADA Access 396
The Police Personnel Selection Process 397
The Entrance Examination: The Written Test 397
Reverse Discrimination 400
Physical Ability Testing 401
The Polygraph Test in Pre-Employment Screening 403
The Character Investigation 405
Interviews and Oral Boards 406
Psychological Testing of Police Applicants 407
The Recruit Academy, Probationary Period, and Career Status 409
Field Training Officer 410
Special Gender Issues 410
Possible Solutions 415
College Education for Police Officers 418

The Fair Labor Standards Act 420
The Family Medical Leave Act 422
Performance Evaluation 423
Legal Standards 424
Common Rater Errors 425
Salary Administration 425
Organization of a Pay Plan 426
Police Salary Schedule 426
Assessment Centers 426
Historical Development of Assessment Centers 427
Developmental Simulation Exercises 427
The Value of Assessment Center Testing 429
The Administration of Discipline 430
Determining Factors 431
Profile of Violence-Prone Officers 432
Early Warning Systems 434
The Internal Affairs Unit 436
Time Limits 438
Investigation by Line Supervisors 439
Proactive Enforcement Operations 439
Investigations by Another Agency 440
Use of the Polygraph or Voice Stress Detection Equipment 440
Chemical Tests 440
Photo and Physical Lineups 442
Financial Records 442
Use of Covert Collection Techniques 442
Retirement Counseling 442
Psychological Losses 443
Family Input and Adjustments 444
The Need for Financial Planning 445
Chapter Review 446
Key Terms 451
Notes 451

11 Labor Relations 457

The Unionization of the Police and Its Impact 458
The Needs of Labor Organizations 458
The Reduction of Legal Barriers 458
Police Frustration with Support for the War on Crime 459
Personnel Practices 459
Salaries and Benefits 460
The General Structure of Laws Governing Collective Bargaining for Law Enforcement Officers 462
Binding Arbitration Model 463
Meet and Confer Model 463
Bargaining Not Required Model 464
Unfair Labor Practices 464
Mandatory Subjects for Bargaining 466
Establishing the Bargaining Relationship 469
The Process 469
The Opportunity for Conflict 471
Negotiations 471
Selection of the Management and Union Teams 471
Preparing for Negotiations 473
The Negotiating Sessions 473

Grievances 476
Why Grievances Are Inevitable 476
The Definition of a Grievance 477
The Grievance Procedure 477
Arbitration Issues and Decision Making 478
Job Actions 479
The Vote of Confidence 479
Work Slowdowns 480
Work Speedups 480
Work Stoppages 480
Police Unions: The Political Context 482
Administrative Reaction to Job Actions 484
Chapter Review 487
Key Terms 489
Notes 489

12 Financial Management 493

Politics and Financial Management 496
Federal, State, and Local Financial Management 496
Key Budget Terms 497
The Budget Cycle 498
Step One: Budget Preparation in the Police Department 500
Step Two: Budget Review and Approval 501
Step Three: Budget Execution 503
Step Four: The Audit 510
Budget Formats 511
The Line Item Budget 512
The Program Budget 512
The Performance Budget 514
The Zero-Based Budget (ZBB) 517
The Hybrid Budget 518
Supplementing the Police Budget:Tactics and Strategies 520
Federal and Private Foundation Grants 520
Donation and Fundraising Programs 521
Forfeiture Laws 522
User Fees and Police Taxes 522
Chapter Review 524
Key Terms 525
Notes 525

Part IV Organizational Issues 527

13 Stress and Police Personnel 529

What Is Stress? 530
Biological Stress and the General Adaptation Syndrome 532
Psychological Stress 532
Reactions to Stress 533
Stress and Personality Type 533
Stress in Law Enforcement 535
Police Stressors 535
Alcoholism and Police Officers 537
Departmental Programs 537
Drug Use by Police Officers 539
Anabolic Steroids 539

Police Suicide 542
Why Police Officers Commit Suicide 543
Access to Firearms 546
Alcohol Abuse 546
Fear of Separation from the Police Subculture 547
Recognizing the Warning Signs 547
Supervisory Responsibility in Suicide Prevention 547
Sources of Work Satisfaction as a Stress Reducer 548
Providing Assistance to Citizens 549
Exercising Interpersonal Skills 549
Getting Feedback 550
Receiving Peer-Group Support 550
Suicide by Cop 551
Case Studies 551
Indicators of an SbC 554
Police Officers as Victims 555
Critical Incident Stress 555
Posttraumatic Stress Disorder 556
Emotional Response to Critical Incidents 558
Critical Incident Debriefing 558
Stress and the Female Police Officer 559
Studies of Male and Female Officers 560
Female Law Enforcement Officer Stress Today 561
Police Domestic Violence 562
Early Warning and Intervention 563
Zero Tolerance Policy 563
Department Responsibilities 564
Supervisory Responsibilities 564
Police Officer Responsibilities 565
Incident Response Protocols 565
Responding to Stress 568
Employee Assistance Programs 568
Benefits of Employee Assistance Programs 569
Benefits to the Employee 569
Chapter Review 573
Key Terms 577
Notes 577

14 Legal Aspects of Police Administration 581

Liability for Police Conduct 582
Basic Types of Police Tort Actions 582
Title 42, U.S. Code, Section 1983 584
Bivens Action 584
Who Can Be Sued? 585
Negligent Hiring 586
Negligent Assignment, Retention, and Entrustment 586
Negligent Direction and Supervision 586
Negligent Training 587
Scope of Liability 589
Trends in Tort Liability for Police Supervisors and Administrators 592
Administrative Discipline: Due Process for Police Officers 594
Liberty and Property Rights of Police Officers 594
Procedural Due Process 596
Substantive Due Process 598
Damages and Remedies 599

Constitutional Rights of Police Officers 599
Free Speech 599
Other First Amendment Rights 601
Searches and Seizures 604
Right Against Self-Incrimination 605
Other Grounds for Disciplinary Action 606
Conduct Unbecoming an Officer 607
Sexual Conduct 607
Residency Requirements 609
Religious Belief or Practice 609
Moonlighting 610
Misuse of Firearms and Deadly Force 610
Tennessee v. Garner (1985) 611
Evaluation of Written Directives 612
Familiarization with the Department's Policy 615
Police Liability and High-Speed Pursuit 616
Duty Owed 616
Proximate Cause 618
Federal Civil Rights Act 619
Factors Determining Liability 619
Departmental Responsibility for Liability Reduction 621
Liability and Emotionally Disturbed Persons 623
Testing in the Work Environment 625
Alcohol and Drug Testing 625
Terms and Conditions of Employment 627
Wage and Hour Regulations 627
Age-Based Hiring and Retirement Policies 628
Sexual Harassment 629
Sexual Harassment: A Definition 629
Sexual and Racial Harassment: Theories of Liability 630
Unwelcome Sexual Harassment 632
Harrassment Based on Gender 633
Harassment Affecting a Condition of Employment 634
Grounds for Sexual Harassment Claims 634
Liability for Sexual Harassment 636
Prevention of Workplace Harassment 637
Chapter Review 639
Key Terms 641
Notes 642

15 Organizational Change and the Future 653

Why Change Occurs 655
When Change Should Not Be Made 658
Two Organizational Change Models 659
Kurt Lewin's Three-Step Model 661
Traditional Action Research Model 662
Politics and Organizational Change 664
Resistance to Change 665
Levels of Change 667
Police Futures Research 668
Establishing a Futures Research Unit/Capability 669
Chapter Review 670
Key Terms 672
Notes 672

Index 675

PREFACE

The field of police administration is dynamic and ever changing. Laws are modified, new problems occur, and administrative practices that were once accepted as gospel are challenged, modified, and in some cases, discarded. For instance, in the early morning hours of September 11, 2001, our country was attacked in a manner that will forever change the way we look at police and security in this country. The terrorist attacks of the World Trade Center and the Pentagon have hailed the development of a completely new federal branch—the Department of Homeland Security. Local police officers now have a significant role in the detection and prevention of terrorist attacks through expanded yet controversial roles posed by the Patriot Act. The primary mission of police in local communities has become somewhat blurred as community policing efforts from the last decade fade to the emergence of security checks, intelligence gathering, and participation in joint terrorism task forces. In this edition, as with the previous six editions, we have tried to provide the most current and useful information to readers in an effort to help them deal with these dynamic changes. This edition has posed significant challenges as local, state, and federal governments try to cope with the new threats of terrorism while still addressing the core issues of increasing crime rates and expanding social disorder in many of our largest urban areas.

Collectively, the three authors of this text have been police officers, detectives, administrators, and educators for nearly one hundred years. We have studied, practiced, researched, taught, and consulted on police administration, and an inevitable by-product of these experiences is the development of certain perspectives. It is these perspectives that form the rationale for this book.

NEW TO THIS EDITION

We have significantly changed the format of this book from that of previous editions. Working together, the authors and editors have developed new pedagogical aids to help students maximize their learning experience and to simplify the understanding of complex issues. For instance, the book has been redesigned with a host of new photographs, updated tables and figures, and innovative learning tools. The book is now divided into four parts, each devoted to an important element of police administration: The Evolution of American Policing; The Organization and the Leader; The Management of Police Organizations; and Organizational Issues. Each chapter begins with a ***Chapter Outline*** and ***Chapter Objectives,*** which highlight and amplify important parts of the text. Boldface key terms within the text emphasize core concepts and ideas. Each chapter includes new special boxed features that ***Focus on Policies, Programs, and People,*** as well as a variety of ***Quick Facts*** and ***In the News*** briefs that present interesting and contemporary information designed to retain the student's interest. We are especially excited about our end-of-the-chapter review sections that include a ***Summary by Chapter Objectives*** and list of ***Key Terms***. These provide excellent study guides for each chapter.

There is much new information in this book that students will find informative and useful. For example, Chapter 1 addresses the historical development of policing in the United States with a special emphasis on some of the key individuals, such as August Vollmer and O. W. Wilson, who were so important in the evolution of police administration. An entirely new Chapter 2 focuses on Policing Today and discusses the merging of community policing philosophies with high-tech Compstat models observed in many of our largest metropolitan areas. Chapter 3 concentrates on the impact of terrorism and homeland security on police administration, with specific descriptions of Middle Eastern groups (for example, al-Qaeda, Hamas, and Hezbollah), domestic hate groups (for example, Aryan Nations, National Alliance, and the World Church of the Creator), and single-issue anarchists groups (for example, Earth Liberation Front and Animal Liberation Front) that continue to threaten the United States. In Chapter 6, we have included a discussion on the unique organizational features of sheriff's offices, as well as some of the organizational differences that typically exist between municipal police departments and sheriff's departments. We also talk extensively about the informal organization that affects almost every police department today. In Chapter 8, Planning and Decision-Making, we explore the various theories associated with decision-making and provide a series of case studies focusing on the use of force during incidents of protracted conflict. These case studies highlight the myraid of problems and issue associated with decision-making in the police arena. In Chapter 10, Human Resource Management, we discuss the issues of gender bias and racial/ethnic discrimination within law enforcement and provide a self-assessment questionnaire for administrators to determine the level of multi-cultural participation reflected within their departments. In addition, we have expanded our discussion of the early warning system as it relates to problem officers and the use of new psychological testing of police applicants designed to reveal potential problems in the future. In Chapter 13, Stress and Police Personnel, we pay particular attention to critical incident stress as reflected in the NYPD study on police suicide and add an entirely new section on the topic of "suicide by cop (SbC)" which examines the phenomenon from both the officer's perspective and the offender's motivation. Chapter 14, Legal Aspects of Police Administration, includes a new section on police responses to emotionally disturbed persons and theories of liability relating to sexual and racial harassment in the workplace. There is also expanded discussion of recent Supreme Court decisions that limit liability for injuries and deaths associated with high-speed police pursuits and officer-involved shootings. And, in Chapter 15, we have focused on the important events that have shaped the past three years of policing and have provided new content on addressing the challenges and stress often associated with organizational change and the future.

As with all previous editions, we have attempted to provide case studies and vignettes from our own experience. These are scattered throughout to illustrate points discussed in the narrative in order to make them more informative. Along with the new pedagogical tools introduced in this edition and mentioned earlier, we have found that these items pique student interest and learning.

Finally, the mention of any product, firm, or agency in this book is intended for illustrative purposes only and does not necessarily constitute a direct criticism, an endorsement, or a recommendation by the authors or the publisher.

SUPPLEMENTS

The following supplements will accompany this textbook:

- Instructor's Manual
- PowerPoint
- TestGen
- Companion Website

To access supplementary materials online, instructors need to request an instructor access code. Go to **www.prenhall.com**, click the **Instructor Resource Center** link, and then click **Register Today** for an instructor access code. Within 48 hours after registering you will receive a confirming e-mail including an instructor access code. Once you have received your code, go to the site and log on for full instructions on downloading the materials you wish to use.

ACKNOWLEDGMENTS

Although it is insufficient compensation for their gracious assistance, we wish to recognize here the individuals and organizations who helped to make this book a reality. Unless asked to do otherwise, we have indicated their organizational affiliation at the time they made their contribution.

We would like to thank the following reviewers for their comments and suggestions for the sixth and seventh editions: Brian G. Onieal and James Albrecht, John Jay College of Criminal Justice, New York City; David Wedlick, Westchester Community College, Valhalla, New York; Donna Nicholson, Manchester Community College, Manchester, Connecticut; Jonathan W. McCombs, Tri-County Technical College, Pendleton, South Carolina; Rulette Armstead, San Diego State University, San Diego, California; William Bourns, California State University–Stanislaus, Turlock, California; and Charles Brawner, Heartland Community College, Normal, Illinois.

Sal Territo, Maryellin Territo, Sharon Ostermann, Jeannie Griffin, Linda Pittman, Dwayne Shumate, and Donna McKnight provided typing and research assistance and made innumerable contributions, not only for this edition but for many previous ones as well. Dr. John Liederbach, Bowling Green State University, was responsible for developing the extensive instructor's manual and accompanying learning tools for this edition.A special thanks to these individuals.

Those who supplied photographs and written material and made suggestions about how to strengthen the book include Charlie Rinkevich and Peggy Hayward, Federal Law Enforcement Training Center, Glynco, Georgia; Scott Wofford, Radio Shack, Fort Worth, Texas; the Drug Enforcement Administration; our colleague of 20 years, Jim Campbell, East Carolina University; Chief John Kerns, Sacramento, California, Police Department; U.S. Secret Service; Bureau of Alcohol, Tobacco, Firearms and Explosives; Deputy Superintendent Jim Finley, Illinois State Police; Drs. Walter Booth and Chris Hornickj, Multidimensional Research Association, Aurora, Colorado; Lieutenant Rick Frey, Broward County, Florida, Sheriff's Office; Captain Lawrence Akley, St. Louis, Missouri, Metro Police Department; Chief Lee McGehee and Captain Glenn Whiteacre, Ocala, Florida, Police Department; the Maricopa, Arizona, Sheriff's Office; Inspector Vivian Edmond, Michelle Andonian, and Commander Dorothy Knox, Detroit, Michigan, Police Department; Major Herman Ingram, Baltimore, Maryland, Police Department; Commissioner Morgan Elkins and Captain Dennis Goss, Kentucky State Police; St. Paul, Minnesota, Police Department; Thomas J. Deakin, John E. Ott, editor of the *FBI Law Enforcement Bulletin*, all three with the Federal Bureau of Investigation; our good friend, Bill Tafoya, the "father" of futuristics in policing; our lifelong friend, Ron Lynch, University of North Carolina; the California Highway Patrol; Norma Kane, the Kansas City, Missouri, Police Department; the San Diego, California, Police Department; the Texas Department of Public Safety: the Philadelphia Police Department; Sergeant Maurice McGough, St Petersburg, Florida, Police Department; National Tactical Officers Association; Lieutenant James B. Bolger, Michigan State Police; the Denver Police Department; Colonel Carroll D. Buracker and Scott Boatright, Fairfax County, Virginia, Police Department; Major Dave Sturtz, Ohio State Patrol; the National Consortium for Justice Information and Statistics. Sacramento, California; Phoenix, Arizona, Police and Fire Departments; Deputy Chief Troy McClain, Captain Terry Haucke, Dr. S. A. Somodevilla, and Sergeant Mark Stallo, Dallas, Texas, Police Department; Mary Ann Wycoff, Police Foundation; Don Fish, Florida Police Benevolent Association; Captain Keith Bushey, Los Angeles, California, Police Department; Deputy Chief Kevin Stoeher, Mt. Lebanon, Pennsylvania, Police Department; Karen Anderson and Lisa Bird, LAN Publications Group; Lieutenant Rex Splitt, Craig, Colorado, Police Department; Chief R. E. Hansen and Cynthia Shaw, Fayetteville, North Carolina, Police Department; Officer David Hoffman, Anchorage, Alaska, Police Department; LaNell Thornton, Chief Paul Annee, and Lieutenant Michael Spears, Indianapolis, Indiana, Police Department; Lexington-Fayette, Kentucky, Urban County Police Department; Environmental Systems Research Institute, Redlands, California; Nancy Brandon, Metro Software, Park City, Utah; Sheriff Jim Roache and Sara Brooks, San Diego, California, Sheriff's Department; Larry Yium, Director of Budget and Finance, Houston, Texas; Lois Roethel and Leslie Doak, Las Vegas, Nevada, Police Department; the Knox County, Maine, Sheriff's Department; Chief Jim Wetherington, a mentor, and Assistant Chief Sam Woodall, Semper, Fi, Columbus, Georgia, Police Department; Sergeant Mike Parker, Los Angeles County Sheriff's Office; Major John F. Meeks, Baltimore, Maryland, Police Department; Mary Foss and Chief Randall Gaston, Anaheim, California, Police Department; Captain Tom Brennan, Newark, New Jersey, Police Department; Lieutenant Robert O'Toole, Boston, Massachusetts, Police Department; Commander Tim McBride, Los Angeles, California, Police Department; Superintendent Richard Pennington, New Orleans, Louisiana, Police Department; Sergeant Patrick Melvin, Phoenix, Arizona, Police Department; Officer Matthew Rastovski, Birmingham, Alabama, Police Department; Lieutenant Doug Cain, Baton Rouge, Louisiana, Police Department; Sheriff Leroy D. Baca and Natalie Salazar Macias, Los Angeles County Sheriff's Office; Chief P. Thomas Shanahan and Sergeant James Cifala, Ann Arundel County Police Department, Maryland; Chief Harold L. Hurts, Assistant Police Chief Jack Harris, Phoenix, Arizona, Police Department; Chief R. Gill Kerlikowske and Amy M. Pich, Seattle, Washington, Police Department; Deputy Chief Raymond D. Schultz, Albuquerque, New Mexico, Police Department; Sheriff Cal Henderson and Detective Herb Metzger, Hillsborough County Sheriff's Office, Tampa, Florida; Chief T.N. Oettmeier, Houston, Texas, Police Department; Sergeant Robert J. Delaney, Chicago, Illinois, Police Department; Dr. Sergei Paromchik, Department of Criminology, University of South Florida, Tampa, Florida; a very special thanks to Dr. Eric Fritsch and Professor Peggy Tobolowsky, University of North Texas, for their continued support and willingness to review specific parts of this text; Sergeant Don Pahlke (retired), Portland, Oregon, Police Bureau, Bob's partner in a squad car, who taught Bob what real policing was all about; Chief David Kunkle, Lt. Ronald Thomasson, Sergeant Terry Cahill, and Mr. Michael Freeman, Dallas Police Department; retired Chief Lowell Canaday, Irving, Texas, Police Department; Chief Jimmy Perdue, North Richland Hills, Texas, Police Department; Chief David James, Carrollton, Texas, Police Department; former Commissioner Paul Evans, Boston Police Department; former Chief Bob Olsen, Minneapolis, Minnesota, Police Department; Mr. Dan Carlson and Greg Smith, Institute for Law Enforcement Administration, Dallas, Texas; Sheriff Jerry Keller (retired), Las Vegas Metropolitan Police Department; Dean Victor Strecher (retired), Sam Houston State University; Warden Chuck Keeton, Dawson State Jail Facility, Dallas, Texas, Chief Ed O'Bara and Assistant Chief Chuck Barr, Highland Village, Texas, Police Department; Mr. Bill Hill, former Dallas County District Attorney, Dallas Texas; Chief

Richard Wiles, Assistant Chief Diana Kirk, and Mr. Stuart Ed, El Paso, Texas, Police Department; Mr. Doug Bodrero, Dr. Richard Holden, and Dr. Jonathan White, Institute for Intergovernmental Research, Tallahassee, Florida; Dr. David Carter, Michigan State University; Dr. Larry Gaines, California State University–San Bernadino; and Mr. Jeffrey Higgenbotham, a special agent in the Legal Division, FBI Academy, Quantico, Virginia, who contributed to the discussion on sexual harassment.

Lieutenant Stephen Hartnett of the Tampa, Florida, Police Department provided us with material on the psychological testing of police applicants. Chief of Police Ronald Miller and Major Roger Villanueva of the Kansas City, Kansas, Police Department provided us with information on their agency's college incentive and college tuition assistance programs. Chief of Police Bill McCarthy of the City of Des Moines, Iowa, Police Department provided us with information on the agency's salary schedule. Cynthia Brown, publisher of *American Police Beat*, Cambridge, Massachusetts, gave us permission to use numerous articles and photographs in several of our chapters. Melonie Hamilton with *Police Magazine*, Torrence, California, assisted us in obtaining photos in relation to our discussion of assessment centers, as well as our discussion of Internal Affairs investigations. We wish to thank Will Aitchison for his extensive contributions to Chapter 11, Labor Relations. He allowed us to draw from his previous works, and for this we are greatly indebted.

We would also like to thank Chief Joe Lumpkin of the Athens Clarke County, Georgia, Police Department for his continued good counsel and information on the subject of police administration and Chief Dwayne Orrick of the Cordele, Georgia, Police Department for his continued work as the president of the Georgia Association of Chiefs of Police. We also wish to thank Deanette L. Palmer, Ph.D., a psychologist with the Spokane, Washington, Police Department. We wish to thank Meredith A. Bowman of the Southeastern Public Safety Institute, St. Petersburg College, St. Petersburg, Florida, and our colleague Jim Sewell, Florida Department of Law Enforcement, who has also contributed to this book. And a very special thanks to Jennifer Davis, University of North Texas, Denton, Texas for her outstanding research and energy on this project. She was largely responsible for reformatting the book to a more user-friendly, student-oriented text. We would like to thank Mayda Bosco, Ann Pulido, Holly Shufeldt, and Emily Bush for their patience and encouragement throughout the duration of the textbook revision process. Lastly, we would like to thank our editor, Tim Peyton, for his continued guidance, support, patience, and encouragement. It has been a pleasure working with him.

Charles R. "Mike" Swanson
Leonard Territo
Robert W. Taylor

ABOUT THE AUTHORS

Charles R. "Mike" Swanson provides promotional testing services to police departments through his firm Swanson and Bracken (Promotionaltesting.com) and has more than 30 years of experience in designing police promotional systems, conducting job analysis, preparing written tests and assessment centers, and training assessors. He has provided promotional consulting services to state police, state patrol, sheriffs, and county and municipal law enforcement agencies.

Mike enlisted in the Marine Corps when he was 17 years old, subsequently working as a patrol officer and detective in the Tampa Police Department. He served in the Florida Governor's Office as a senior police planner and later as deputy director of the Council on Law Enforcement and Criminal Justice. He taught at East Carolina University before accepting a faculty position in the University of Georgia's Carl Vinson Institute of Government, where he rose through the administrative ranks, retiring in 2001 as its interim director.

In addition to co-writing this book, Mike has co-authored four others, including *Criminal Investigation*, and has authored or co-authored numerous conference papers, articles, monographs, and book chapters on various aspects of policing. He holds bachelor's and master's degrees in criminology from Florida State University and a Ph.D. in public administration from the University of Georgia. In addition to other recognition, he is the 2001 recipient of the O. W. Wilson Award for Distinguished Police Scholarship.

Leonard Territo is presently a visiting distinguished professor in the Department of Criminal Justice at Saint Leo University, Saint Leo, Florida, and professor emeritus in the Department of Criminology at the University of South Florida, Tampa, Florida. He was previously the chief deputy (undersheriff) of the Leon County Sheriff's Office in Tallahassee, Florida. He also served for almost nine years with the Tampa Police Department as a patrol officer, motorcycle officer, and homicide detective. He is the former chairperson of the Department of Police Administration and director of the Florida Institute for Law Enforcement at St. Petersburg Junior College, St. Petersburg, Florida.

In addition to writing nearly 50 articles, book chapters, and technical reports, he has authored and co-authored nine books, including *Criminal Investigation,* which is in its tenth edition; *Crime and Justice in America,* which is in its sixth edition; *Stress Management in Law Enforcement,* which is in its second edition; *Police Civil Liability; College Crime Prevention and Personal Safety Awareness; Stress and Police Personnel; The Police Personnel Selection Process;* and *Hospital and College Security Liability.* His books have been used in more than a thousand colleges and universities in all 50 states, and his writings have been used and referenced by both academic and police departments in 14 countries, including Australia, Barbados, Canada, Chile, China, Czechoslovakia, England, France, Germany, Israel, the Netherlands, Poland, Saudi Arabia, South Korea, and Spain.

His teaching awards include being selected from among 200 criminal justice educators from the state of Florida as the Outstanding Criminal Justice Educator of the

Year by the College of Social and Behavioral Sciences at the University of South Florida. He has been given awards by both the Florida Police Chiefs Association and the Tampa Police Academy for his years of teaching and meritorious service; he was given an award for Distinguished Scholarly Publications by Saint Leo University, Saint Leo, Florida; and he has been selected for inclusion in *Who's Who in American Law Enforcement.*

Robert W. Taylor is currently professor and chair of the Department of Criminal Justice at the University of North Texas in Denton, Texas. For the past 25 years, Dr. Taylor has studied police administration, police tactics and strategies, and police responses to terrorism. He has traveled extensively throughout the Middle East and Southeast Asia, meeting several heads of state and acting as a consultant to numerous federal agencies on intelligence analysis and terrorism, hostage negotiations, Middle Eastern groups, and Palestinian-Israeli conflict. Since September 11, 2001, Dr. Taylor has been a consultant to the U.S. Department of Justice, working with the Institute for Intergovernmental Research. He acts as a lead instructor in the State and Local Anti-Terrorism Training (SLATT) program and is responsible for training all law enforcement and other related criminal justice professionals. He also contracts with the U.S. Department of State, Anti-Terrorism Assistance Program.

Dr. Taylor has authored or co-authored over 150 articles, books, and manuscripts. Most of his publications focus on international and domestic terrorism, police administration and management, police procedures, drug trafficking, and criminal justice policy. Dr. Taylor is the senior author of *Juvenile Justice: Policies, Practices and Programs*, second edition, Glencoe/McGraw-Hill, 2006; and *Digital Crime, Digital Terrorism*, Prentice Hall, 2005. Further, Dr. Taylor is co-author of the landmark text *Criminal Investigation*, published by McGraw-Hill (2006), currently in its ninth edition. Dr. Taylor continues to conduct research in policing and is the recipient of numerous grants and contracts (over $8 million in funded projects). His latest work has concentrated in four areas: (1) international terrorism, especially Middle-Eastern groups, and the spread of radical Islam into Southeast Asia; (2) intelligence analysis and decision making, particularly during protracted conflict or crisis situations; (3) quality improvement in police agencies through advanced leadership and management practices; and (4) evaluation of community policing, Compstat, and intelligence-led policing strategies in the United States. In 2004, Dr. Taylor was asked by the International Justice Mission in Washington, D.C., to assist in the training of the Cambodian National Police on child sex slavery and human trafficking as part of a large project funded through the U.S. Department of State. His interest and research in this area has led to a leadership role in designing and developing training efforts in the United States aimed at raising awareness of the human trafficking tragedy for American law enforcement officers, funded through the U.S. Department of Justice. Dr. Taylor focuses on the nexus among human trafficking, drug trafficking, and the financing of terrorist incidents internationally and domestically.

Dr. Taylor has been a consultant to the U.S. Army; U.S. Air Force; U.S. Marine Corps; U.S. Department of Homeland Security; U.S. Department of Treasury; Federal Law Enforcement Training Center; U.S. Secret Service; Bureau of Alcohol, Tobacco, and Firearms; U.S. Department of Justice; Federal Bureau of Investigation; Drug Enforcement Administration; Police Foundation; and Police Executive Research Forum (PERF); as well as numerous state and local municipalities and private corporations. He has also conducted significant training in the United States protectorates of the U.S. Virgin Islands, Guam, and Saipan and the countries of England, France,

Switzerland, Thailand, Cambodia, Barbados, Northern Cyprus, Bahrain, United Arab Emirates, Kenya, and Turkey. He is an active member of the Academy of Criminal Justice Sciences (elected national chair of the Police Section—2002) and the American Society of Criminology.

Dr. Taylor has an extensive background in academic and professional criminal justice, having taught at four major universities and serving as a sworn police officer and major crimes detective (in Portland, Oregon) for over six years. Dr. Taylor is a graduate of Michigan State University (Master of Science—1973) and Portland State University (Doctor of Philosophy—1981).

PART I

THE EVOLUTION OF AMERICAN POLICING

THE FOLLOWING CHAPTERS ARE COVERED IN PART I:

1 Historical Development

2 Policing Today

3 Intelligence, Terrorism, and Homeland Security

4 Politics and Police Administration: External Influences and Controls

OVERVIEW

What is the primary role of police in our society? What do we expect them to do? And how has this role changed over time, particularly considering the impact of 9/11 and the war on terrorism? These are the pressing questions facing today's police administrators as they attempt to cope with rising crime rates, the threat of foreign attacks, drug and gang escalation, and school violence amid dwindling resources. In this part, we look at the historical development of the police from traditional methods of dealing with crime to more innovative community policing ventures that blend the use of information technologies and management accountability to law enforcement.

(Corbis/Bettmann)

The police at all times should maintain a relationship with the public that gives reality to the historic tradition that the police are the public and that the public are the police.

—Sir Robert Peel

CHAPTER 1

HISTORICAL DEVELOPMENT

CHAPTER OUTLINE

Introduction

Politics and Administration

Police Professionalization

Prohibition to 1940

World War II and the 1950s

The Turbulent 1960s

The Call for Research and Other Developments

The 1980s and Beyond

America Responds to September 11

Chapter Review

Key Terms

Notes

OBJECTIVES

1. Identify the primary responsibility of policing in America.
2. Define "politics" and explain whether it is a positive or a negative.
3. Identify the "conceptual cornerstone" of the good government reformation period of 1900–1926.
4. Describe the paradigm which replaced the politics–administration dichotomy in the late 1920s.
5. Explain what "profession" means.
6. Discuss the contributions of Chief Vollmer to the police profession.
7. State the purpose of the federal Pendleton Act of 1883.
8. Explain the use of the military model in policing.
9. Describe how prohibition was harmful to policing in this country.
10. Explain how World War II affected law enforcement.
11. Explain the meaning of the "turbulent 1960s."
12. Explain the impact of the call for research on policing and related developments.
13. Identify and briefly discuss four major themes which have dominated policing since 1980.

INTRODUCTION

If the many different purposes of the American police service were narrowed to a single focus, what would emerge is the obligation to preserve the peace in a manner consistent with the freedoms secured by the Constitution.[1] It does not follow from this assertion that our police alone bear the responsibility for maintaining a peaceful society; this responsibility is shared by other elements of society, beginning with each individual and spreading to each institution and each level of government—local, state, and federal. However, because crime is an immediate threat to our respective communities, the police have a highly visible and perhaps even primary role in overcoming the threat and fear of crime.

The preservation of peace is more complex than simply preventing crimes, making arrests for violations of the law, recovering stolen property, and providing assistance in the prosecution of persons charged with acts of criminality. In all likelihood, the police only spend something on the order of 15 percent of their time enforcing the law. The most substantial portion of their time goes toward providing less glamorous services that are utterly essential to maintaining the public order and well-being. Illustrative of these services are providing directions to motorists, mediating conflicts, evacuating neighborhoods threatened or struck by natural disasters, and serving as a bridge between other social service agencies and persons who come to the attention of the police, such as the mentally disturbed.

The degree to which any society achieves some amount of public order through police action depends in part on the price that society is willing to pay to obtain it. This price can be measured in the resources dedicated to the police function and in the extent to which citizens are willing to tolerate a reduction in the number, kinds, and extent of liberties they enjoy. In this regard, totalitarian and democratic governments reflect very different choices. This point underscores the fact that the American police service cannot be understood properly if it is examined alone, as an island in a lake. A more appropriate and persuasive analogy is that policing is like a sandbar in a river, subject to being changed continuously by the currents in which it is immersed. As a profoundly significant social institution, policing is subject to, and continuously shaped by, a multitude of forces at work in our larger society. Indeed, that is the single most important lesson of this chapter.

The year 1890 is the date normally associated with the **closing of the frontier** and a milestone in our transition from a rural, agrarian society to one that is highly urbanized and industrialized (see Figures 1.1 and 1.2). This period of time is a long one to have lived by current expectancies, but as a period of history, it is brief. Still, in this historically short time span, the changes that have taken place in this country are staggering.

Inevitably, any attempt to highlight this period will have some deficits. However, the balance of this chapter does so to achieve two objectives: (1) to demonstrate the impact of social forces on policing and (2) to identify and set the stage for some of the content treated in subsequent chapters. These two objectives will be met by presenting material organized under the headings of (1) politics and administration, (2) police professionalization, (3) prohibition to 1940, (4) World War II and the 1950s, (5) the turbulent 1960s, (6) the call for research and other developments, and (7) the 1980s and beyond.

FIGURE 1.1

Native American Ute tribal police officers wearing badges circa 1890.
(Uintah County Library Regional History Center, Dick DeJournette Collection)

FIGURE 1.2

The entire Denver Police Department poses for an annual picture, 1900.
(Courtesy of the Denver, Colorado, Police Department)

POLITICS AND ADMINISTRATION

Politics, stated simply, is the exercise of power. As such, it is value free, its "goodness" or "badness" stemming from its application rather than from some inherent character. Although police executives can occasionally be heard avowing to "keep politics out of the department," this unqualified posture is unrealistic. Personal politics exist in every

FIGURE 1.3

Children were still being exploited as a source of labor at the beginning of the twentieth century. Here, "coal breaker boys" circa 1890–1910 take a break from separating chunks of coal in the mines, where they labored 14 hours a day. Note the lunch pails in the foreground.

(Courtesy of the Library of Congress)

organization, and democratic control of the policing mechanism is fundamental to our society. However, policing and partisan party politics have had a long and not entirely healthy relationship in this country.

In New York City, at the middle of the nineteenth century, the approval of the ward's **alderman** was required before appointment to the police force, and the Tammany Hall corruption of the same period depended in part on the use of the police to coerce and collect graft and to control elections.[2] During this same time, the election of a new mayor—particularly if from a party different from the incumbent's—signaled the coming dismissal of the entire police force and the appointment of one controlled by the new mayor.

At the beginning of the 20th century, our cities were staggering under the burden of machine politics, corruption, crime, poverty, and the exploitation of women and children by industry (see Figure 1.3).[3] The federal government, too, was not without its woes, as illustrated by the somewhat later Teapot Dome scandal, which stained Warren G. Harding's administration.

Central to the **Reformation period** of 1900–1926 was the need to arouse the public and establish a conceptual cornerstone. Steffens exposed the plight of such cities as St. Louis, Minneapolis, Pittsburgh, and Chicago in *The Shame of the Cities* (1906); novels such as Sinclair's *The Jungle* (1906) called attention to abuses in the meatpacking industry; and Churchill addressed political corruption in *Coniston* (1911). The conceptual cornerstone was supplied by Woodrow Wilson's 1887 essay calling for a separation of politics and administration.[4] However impractical that might now seem, it is important to understand that to the reformers "politics" meant "machine politics" and all the ills associated with it.[5]

With an aroused public and a conceptual touchstone, rapid strides were made. In 1906, the New York Bureau of Municipal Research was formed, and by 1910, the city manager movement was under way. In 1911, the Training School for Public Service was established in New York, and by 1914, the University of Michigan was offering a degree in municipal administration. Further strengthening the reform movement—whose center was the desire to separate politics (in the worst sense) and administration—was the issuance in 1916 of a model city charter by the National Municipal League that called for a strict separation of these two elements.

Politics and administration continues to this day to be an important item on policing's agenda. However, with the publication of White's *Public Administration* in 1926 and Willoughby's *Principles of Public Administration* the following year, there was an important paradigm shift in which the politics–administration dichotomy was supplanted as the dominant focus of public administration by administrative/management theorists who sought to identify universal principles and methods of administration (see Chapter 5, Organizational Theory). Parenthetically, although White's and Willoughby's books serve as a convenient marker for the beginning of the paradigm shift, both of them endorsed the 1924 city managers' code of political neutrality.

These events combined to produce movement toward reducing corruption, waste, fraud, and abuse in government; the desire to create a professionally qualified cadre of people committed to careers in public service; the rise of the civil service; an emphasis on proper recruitment, selection, and training of public employees; the freeing of government from the influence of machine politics; and the development of new theories, techniques, and models related to organizations. In short, these events were not only historical milestones; they unleashed a process of improvement that is still in progress today.

Critical Thinking Question

1. Politics, in the sense of democratic control or guidance of our law enforcement agencies, is something which is expected and appropriate. Our system of government is one with many checks and balances. What are some specific examples of how a city council or county commission exercises control over law enforcement agencies?

POLICE PROFESSIONALIZATION

Profession and Professional

The terms "profession" and "professional" are tossed around with great abandon and a conspicuous lack of definition. The general absence of attention to definition has produced endless and futile debates as to whether policing is, in fact, a **profession**. The term "profession" is derived from the Latin *pro* (forth) and *fateri* (confess), meaning to "announce a belief"; at its early use, the word referred to public or open avowals of faith.[6] Cogan[7] notes that the earliest recorded use of the word "profession" as a learned vocation was in 1541 and that by 1576 the meaning had been generalized to mean any calling or occupation by which a person habitually earned his or her living. By 1675, a refinement of the secular use of the term had occurred when it was associated with the act of professing to be duly qualified.[8]

Most of the serious work on professions has centered on specifying what criteria must be met to constitute a profession. The result is not a single definition but rather a collection of similar definitions that usually approximate the following: (1) an organized body of theoretically grounded knowledge, (2) advanced study, (3) a code of ethics, (4) prestige, (5) standards of admission, (6) a professional association, and (7) a service ideal, which may also be stated alternatively as altruism.[9] Merton[10] reduced the values that make up a profession to (1) knowing (systematic knowledge), (2) doing (technical skill and trained capacity), and (3) helping (the joining of knowing and doing). Becker[11] has reduced the argument further to the pithy observation that, in a debate as to whether a particular type of work can be called a profession, if the work group is successful in getting itself called a profession, it is one.

August Vollmer

The rise of "professional" policing is associated initially with the paid, full-time body of police that stemmed from England's Peelian Reform of 1829. Despite the existence of similar bodies in this country from 1845 onward, the genesis of American professional policing is associated with the initiatives of August **Vollmer,** who was chief of police in Berkeley, California, from 1905 to 1932 (see Figure 1.4).

Without detracting one bit from Vollmer's genius, note that his tenure as chief parallels closely the reformation movement of 1900–1926, which, in addition to its politics–administration dichotomy concern, also had a heavy orientation toward good, progressive government. Carte summarizes the work of this giant by noting,

> *The image of professional policing as we know it today is largely the creation of one man, August Vollmer. Vollmer was a tireless crusader for the reform of policing through*

FIGURE 1.4

August Vollmer, seated third from the left, at work in the Berkeley, California, Police Department about 1914.

(Courtesy of the Berkeley Police Department)

Quick Facts

"Gus" Vollmer (1876–1955) is often referred to as the father of modern law enforcement. Born to German immigrant parents in New Orleans, he served in the Marine Corps. Although his first interest was in fire departments, he was elected Berkeley Town Marshall in 1905; the job title was changed to Police Chief in 1909. In 1921, he was elected president of the International Association of Chiefs of Police and retired from the Berkeley Police Department in 1932 due to failing eyesight Stricken with both Parkinson's disease and cancer, he ended his own life at 79.

Source: Wikipedia, The Free Encyclopedia.

technology and higher personnel standards. Under his direction the Berkeley department became a model of professional policing—efficient, honest, scientific. He introduced into Berkeley a patrolwide police signal system, the first completely mobile patrol—first on bicycles, then in squad cars—modern records systems, beat analysis and modus operandi. The first scientific crime laboratory in the United States was set up in Berkeley in 1916, under the direction of a full-time forensic scientist. The first lie detector machine to be used in criminal investigation was built in the Berkeley department in 1921.

However, Vollmer's department was better known for the caliber of its personnel. He introduced formal police training in 1908, later encouraging his men to attend classes in police administration that were taught each summer at the University of California. Eventually he introduced psychological and intelligence testing into the recruitment process and actively recruited college students from the University, starting around 1919. This was the beginning of Berkeley's "college cops," who set the tone for the department throughout the 1920s and 30s and came to be accepted by police leaders as the ultimate model of efficient, modern policemen.[12]

Focus on Policy

Orlando Winfield Wilson

Certainly, the most well known and influential protégé of August Volmer was O. W. Wilson. Born in 1900 in South Dakota, Wilson enrolled at the University of California at Berkeley and completed his degree in 1924. In order to pay his tuition, Wilson took a job as a patrolman with the Berkeley Police Department under Chief August Vollmer, also a professor at UC-Berkeley. Shortly after graduation, at the age of 25, Wilson became chief of police of the Fullerton Police Department. Three years later, at the age of 28, he became the chief of police in Wichita, Kansas, where he served until 1939. In Wichita, he led reforms to reduce corruption and instituted the concept of professionalism by requiring new recruits to have a college education. He was a major leader during the reform movement in policing, introducing innovations and technology, including the use of police cars for patrol, mobile radios, crime laboratories and accurate records systems, and the efficient deployment of police personnel to fight crime and reduce corruption.

In 1960, Mayor Richard J. Daley appointed Wilson as superintendent of police for the Chicago Police Department. Wilson continued his efforts to professionalize the police, establishing non-partisan police boards to help oversee the force, a strict merit system for promotions within the department, a nationally visible recruiting effort for hiring new officers, and higher police salaries to attract qualified officers.

O. W. Wilson was also a successful academic; he taught at Harvard University in the 1930s and was dean at UC-Berkeley's School of Criminology from 1950 to 1960. He authored several books, including *Police Records, Police Planning,* and the highly influential *Police Administration,* first published in 1943, wherein he detailed much of his ideas on police professionalism. His work certainly influenced the formative years of the authors of this book while they served as police officers under the professional model. Interestingly, many of Wilson's concepts continue to flourish today as police officers and organizations become much more technically educated in their mission to protect and serve individual communities across America.

The Pendleton Act of 1883 to the Military Model

The **Pendleton Act** of 1883 sought to eliminate the ills of the political spoils system in the federal government. Many states and local governments passed parallel legislation over the next 30 years, establishing civil service systems designed to protect government employees from political interference. Although these measures were intuitively attractive, their application was questioned early by one observer of the police, Fosdick, who wrote in 1920,

> *In its application to a police department civil service has serious limitations. In the endeavor to guard against abuse of authority, it frequently is carried to such extremes that rigidity takes the place of flexibility in administration, and initiative in effecting essential changes in personnel is crippled and destroyed. Too often . . . civil service is a bulwark for neglect and incompetence, and one of the prime causes of departmental disorganization. Too often does the attempt to protect the force against the capricious play of politics compromise the principle of responsible leadership, so that in trying to nullify the effects of incompetence and favoritism, we nullify capacity and intelligence too.*
>
> *As a result of this divided responsibility between police executives and civil service commissions, there are in most large departments many men whose continuance in office is a menace to the force and to the community, but who cannot be dismissed because the proof of incompetence or dishonesty does not satisfy the requirements of the civil service law.*[13]

It is a matter of some irony that there is a basic tension between Vollmer's trained and educated "professional" police officer and the early administration of civil service acts. The reason was that Vollmer was highly concerned with competence and performance—his notion of merit—whereas the measure of merit for many of the initial years of civil service was simply the degree to which political influence was kept out of appointments and promotion.[14]

Of significant consequence to the very structure of police organizations were the continuing efforts during the reformation period to separate politics and administration. One mechanism for doing so was to change the political structure; thus, in Los Angeles a council elected at large was substituted for the ward system.[15] Other reformers, persuaded that America was besieged by crime and that the police were our first line of defense, saw the police as analogous to the military. A second mechanism, therefore, was giving chiefs expanded powers, large and competent staffs, and the capability to control their departments.[16] In many cities, the precincts had previously operated largely or totally autonomously, and this second mechanism required centralization, which meant consolidating or eliminating precincts, as in New York City and elsewhere,[17] a further blow to ward boss control. The military analogy was so potent that its logical extension—recruiting military officers as police commissioners or chiefs—became a common practice for some years. Illustrative of this practice was the appointment in 1923 in Philadelphia of Marine Corps General Smedley Butler as director of public safety.

The highly centralized military analogy model (see Figure 1.5 and Chapter 5) that became widely adopted and remains today as the dominant force of police organization is technically a bureaucratic structure that has been subjected to a number of criticisms. At the time of its adoption in American policing, it may have been an essential part of promoting police professionalism. Whatever its weaknesses, it brought with it an emphasis on discipline, inspections, improved record keeping, supervision, close-order drill, improved accountability, and other bits and pieces that contributed to the transformation of the police from semiorganized ruffians operating under the mantle of law into something entirely different.

FIGURE 1.5

The **military model** at work in policing. A 1906 Pennsylvania State Police barracks inspection. (Courtesy of the Pennsylvania State Police)

Critical Thinking Question

1. Explain your reasoning as to whether policing is a profession. Of what importance is it whether or not policing is one?

PROHIBITION TO 1940

In 1869, the Prohibition Party was formed as a political party whose primary goal was to abolish liquor. It offered candidates for president of the United States for many decades thereafter. The Woman's Christian Temperance Union (WCTU) was founded in 1874 by women who were opposed to the problems that alcohol and its associated ills were causing in their homes. Shortly thereafter, in 1893, the Anti-Saloon League was initiated. The year 1903 saw Howard Russell's Lincoln Legion swing into action as a pledge of abstinence from alcohol program (see Figure 1.6). In 1912, it was renamed the Lincoln–Lee Legion to honor both the assassinated president and the late Confederate General Robert E. Lee, who had a substantial reputation as a gentleman.

Primarly through the efforts of the WCTU and organizations and programs with allied interests, the 18th Amendment to the U.S. Constitution was ratified in 1919. It prohibited the manufacture, sale, transportation, exportation, and importation of intoxicating liquors. The same year, Congress passed the National Prohibition Act, more commonly known as the Volstead Act, as the statutory means of enforcing the 18th Amendment. The federal Volstead Act of 1919 is possibly the worst piece of legislation ever enacted because it was never workable and because it produced such negative unintended consequences. Its purpose was to establish **prohibition** nationally,

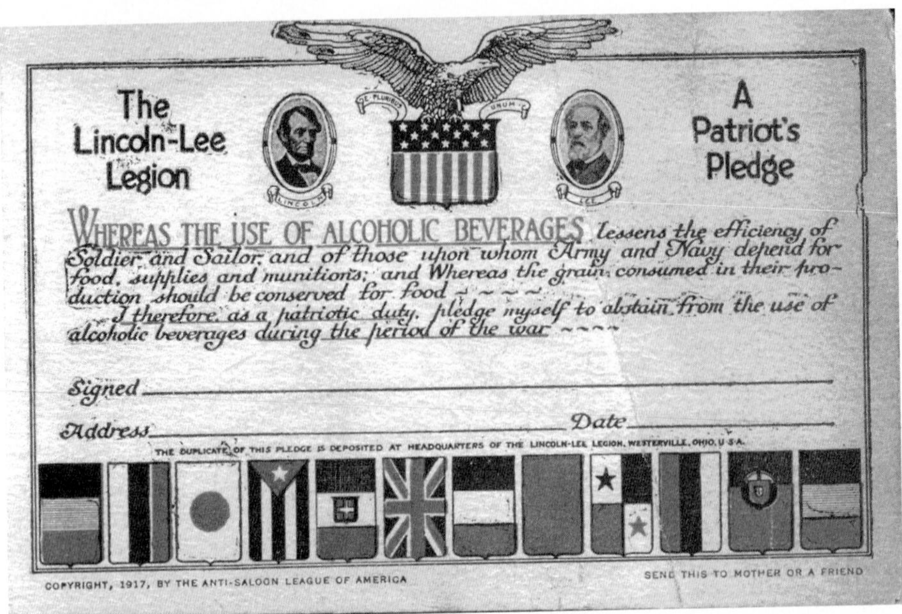

The Lincoln-Lee Legion

A Patriot's Pledge

WHEREAS THE USE OF ALCOHOLIC BEVERAGES lessens the efficiency of Soldier and Sailor, and of those upon whom Army and Navy depend for food, supplies and munitions; and Whereas the grain consumed in their production should be conserved for food ~ ~ ~

I therefore, as a patriotic duty, pledge myself to abstain from the use of alcoholic beverages during the period of the war ~ ~ ~ ~

Signed __________

Address __________ Date __________

THE DUPLICATE OF THIS PLEDGE IS DEPOSITED AT HEADQUARTERS OF THE LINCOLN-LEE LEGION, WESTERVILLE, OHIO, U.S.A.

COPYRIGHT, 1917, BY THE ANTI-SALOON LEAGUE OF AMERICA

SEND THIS TO MOTHER OR A FRIEND

FIGURE 1.6

A Lincoln-Lee pledge card. Girls who signed the pledges were called "Willards" and boys "Lincolns."
(Courtesy Westerville Public Library, Ohio)

but instead it created a large illicit market that gangsters rushed to fill. "Booze boats" smuggled whiskey from Canada and other countries into the United States, and illegal breweries quickly sprang up. Using a portion of their enormous profits, gangsters bribed police officers to "look the other way" as they established "speakeasies" in which to satisfy the public's thirst. These were so named because, to enter such an establishment, one quietly said the password at the entrance. The corruption of officers gave policing a lingering black eye. Gangsters fought violently over the lucrative markets, and assassinations and shoot-outs between rival factions became common during the "Roaring '20s" (see Figure 1.7). In this wild-and-woolly era, which extended through the **Depression** of 1929 and into the 1930s, bank robberies and kidnapings flourished, and bandits and other gangsters achieved celebrity status in some circles, their names often festooned with colorful monikers such as "Pretty Boy" Floyd, "Creepy" Karpis, "Machine Gun" Kelly, "Scarface" Capone, "Handsome Harry" Pierpont, "Baby Face" Nelson, and Clyde "Texas Rattlesnake" Barrow.[18] Recognizing the widespread disobedience to the Volstead Act and the many ills it created, Congress abolished it in 1931, and the 21st Amendment abolished prohibition in 1933.

The Ku Klux Klan (KKK) was formed in Pulaski, Tennessee, in 1866 by former members of the Confederate Army who were bored and wanted to create a "buzz" around town. To make it seem mysterious, they conjured up names that had no real meaning to them, such as Grand Cyclops and Imperial Wizard. At first they simply rode around town in sheets and masks made by the wife of one of the founding members, causing a stir and appearing at social functions, asking ladies to dance while everyone tried to guess who they were. Quickly, however, the KKK began opposing the rights being granted by Congress to former slaves, using scare tactics against them. These tactics rapidly gave way to the use of violence. Former Confederate General Nathan Bedford Forrest, who had earlier associated with the KKK, soon disavowed the Klan and ordered it to disband. When this did not occur, he sent selected members of his former cavalry units to ride against the most notorious KKK units.

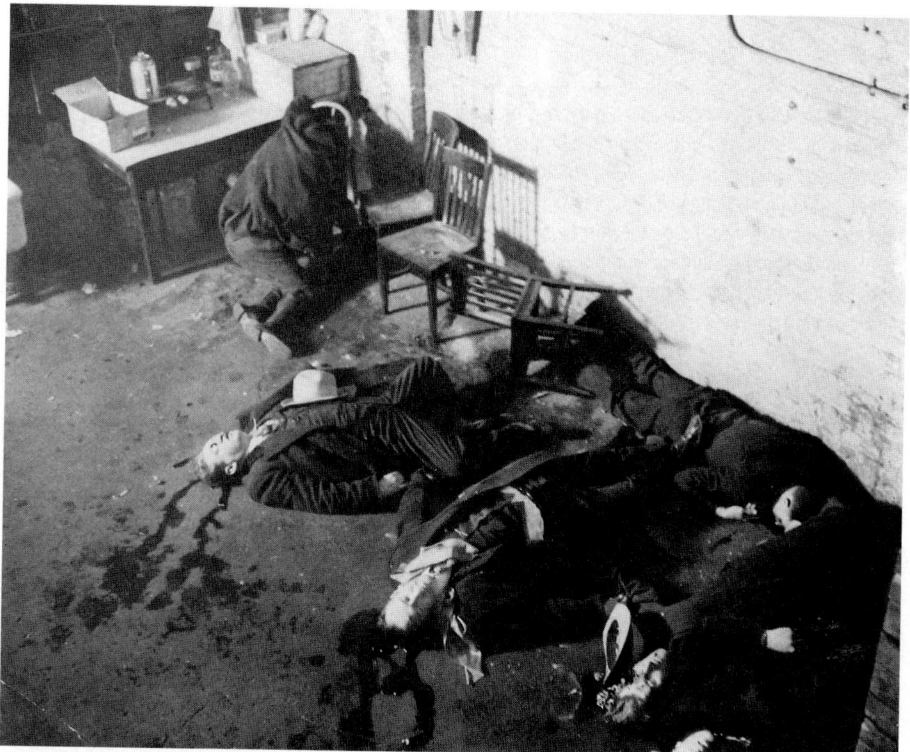

FIGURE 1.7

Members of bootlegger "Bugs" Moran's gang were killed at 2122 North Clarke Street in Chicago in the infamous 1929 St. Valentine's Day Massacre. Rival gangsters posing as police officers lined the men up against a wall and shot them to death using Thompson machine guns.

(© Chicago Historical Museum)

The 1920s and 1930s were also years during which the KKK was strong nationally and often at the forefront of one of America's most ugly episodes: the lynching of African Americans. "Lynching" is derived from the name of Charles Lynch (1736–1796) of Virginia, who led a group that took the law into its own hands during the tumultuous American Revolution. In the early years, lynching was "rough justice" and often involved only a severe beating. Over time, lynching came to mean that people without any legal authority to do so would execute someone. Although we associate lynching with hanging, death was also inflicted in some horrifying cases by chaining African Americans to trees and burning them to death. In many cases, the reasons for lynching were based on mistaken information, rumors, or social offenses. Favorite targets for the KKK over the years have been African Americans, immigrants, Catholics, and Jews. Over the years some law enforcement officers have been active members of the KKK and participated in shameful events, including lynchings and the harassment and killing of civil rights workers. The power of the KKK was broken largely by the work of federal agencies with the assistance of evenhanded state and local law enforcement officers. Movement away from participating in extremist groups was an essential condition for police to continue their march toward professionalization.

The 1930s was a pivotal period in which the police began to shed their tarnished image and move toward an increased legitimacy and authority in society.[19] Starting in 1931, the National Commission on Law Observance and Law Enforcement—popularly named after its chairman, the Wickersham Commission—presented a number of reforms for the police. Central to the commission's recommendations were provisions for civil service classification for police and enhanced support for education and training. Radelet[20]

In The News

While the Ku Klux Klan was once America's pre-eminent terrorist organization, today it is a fragmented, amorphous collection of independent groups and individuals fighting over diminishing memberships and limited resources. The Anti-Defamation League estimates that there are a little over 100 independent groups of the KKK in the United States. For the most part, they act alone and have virtually no national organization. Young white supremacists consider the Klan to be ineffectual and past its time, and they forgo the ritual of hooded anonymity to the openness and power of militia groups, Christian Identity churches, the Aryan Nations, and the National Alliance (neo-Nazis). Even though the Klan appears to be far less of a threat to public order than at any time in the past century, it continues to be a specter that haunts the American psyche, and the sight of a burning cross or a hooded rider can still inspire both horror and terror. In Chapter 3, we will address the growth of the "new right" and the potential violence that this movement poses to our country.

KKK symbol.

Source: Anti-Defamation League: *Extremism in America 2006.* See www.adl.org/learn/ext_us/KKK.asp?xpicked=4&item=18.

reports that "Take the police out of politics," a common slogan of the era, represented an important first step in gaining respectability. This step was a continuation of the separation of politics and administration, which first arose during the reformation period discussed earlier in this chapter.

The emphasis on **law enforcement** in American society was timely, as crime was perceived to be dramatically increasing. Stimulated by high-profile cases, such as the kidnaping of Charles Lindbergh's baby in 1932, the Federal Bureau of Investigation (FBI), under the direction of J. Edgar Hoover, began to emerge as a dominant entity in American policing. In 1935, the FBI created the National Police Academy, where local police leaders and officials were educated in the "professional" and "scientific" aspects of law enforcement.[21] This move was concurrent with the first major university programs (at the University of California at Berkeley, Michigan State University, and Northwestern University) devoted to the academic study of police practices. According to Kelling and Stewart, the decade that followed concretized the "reform" period from political "patsies" to professional agencies:

> *Police departments nationwide had come to embrace an integrated and coherent organizational strategy that sought authority in criminal law; narrowed police function to crime control; emphasized classical organizational forms; relied on preventive patrol, rapid response to calls for service, and criminal investigation as its primary tactics; and measured its success by crime, arrest, and clearance data. . . . Indeed, with rare exception police defined themselves as professional organizations that should be kept out of the purview of citizens, academics and researchers, and other persons with an interest in police. Police business was just that: police business.*[22]

Although the police began to make some headway in improving their image during the 1930s, times remained economically hard because of the continuing effects of the Depression and years of drought that created the "dust bowl" in the Midwest. Enormous numbers of families lost their homes because they could not pay their mortgages. Often they ended up in makeshift shanty towns called "Hoovervilles," using newspapers as blankets during the winter. These towns derived their name from President Herbert Hoover (1874–1964), whom many people blamed for their losses. Once in a Hooverville, families found it difficult to improve their situations (see Figure 1.8).

Residency requirements for municipal jobs became popular as a means of ensuring that any available jobs went to local citizens. People fleeing the dust bowl and economic hard times were unwelcome in other locations because it was believed they

FIGURE 1.8

A "Hooverville" in Circleville, Ohio, 1938. Note the gaunt condition of the man and that a woman is standing just inside the door.

(Courtesy of the Library of Congress)

would be a drain on resources, create social unrest, or commit crimes. In 1936, the Los Angeles chief of police ordered his officers to man "bum blockades" to prevent "invasion" by those fleeing the devastation of the dust bowl. Such practices were a drag on efforts to improve the image of policing.

Critical Thinking Question

1. Can you make arguments for and against the proposition "Current drug control laws are the 'New Prohibition'?"

WORLD WAR II AND THE 1950s

World War II (1941–1945) affected the composition and role of policing in this country. No occupational group, including police officers, received a blanket exemption from conscription during this war, although many rushed out and joined voluntarily. Thus, departments were often stripped of their most physically able officers and left increasingly understaffed as the war years continued. In addition to hiring some women, police auxiliary units were formed and staffed by those who were too old to serve in the military, those who were rejected as being physically unfit for such service, and those who had received draft deferments for other reasons (see Figure 1.9). In addition to their role in combating traditional crimes, the police were faced with new challenges, including ferreting out subversive activities, potential saboteurs, and the forging of war ration books. These books limited the amount of certain commodities, such as butter, gas, and meat, that people could purchase because of the great need to supply the rapidly growing armed forces.

During the 1950s, the pace of change in America quickened. The veterans of World War II were home and quickly found jobs in an expanding economy. Americans were past the pain of the Depression and the war, finding that economic security

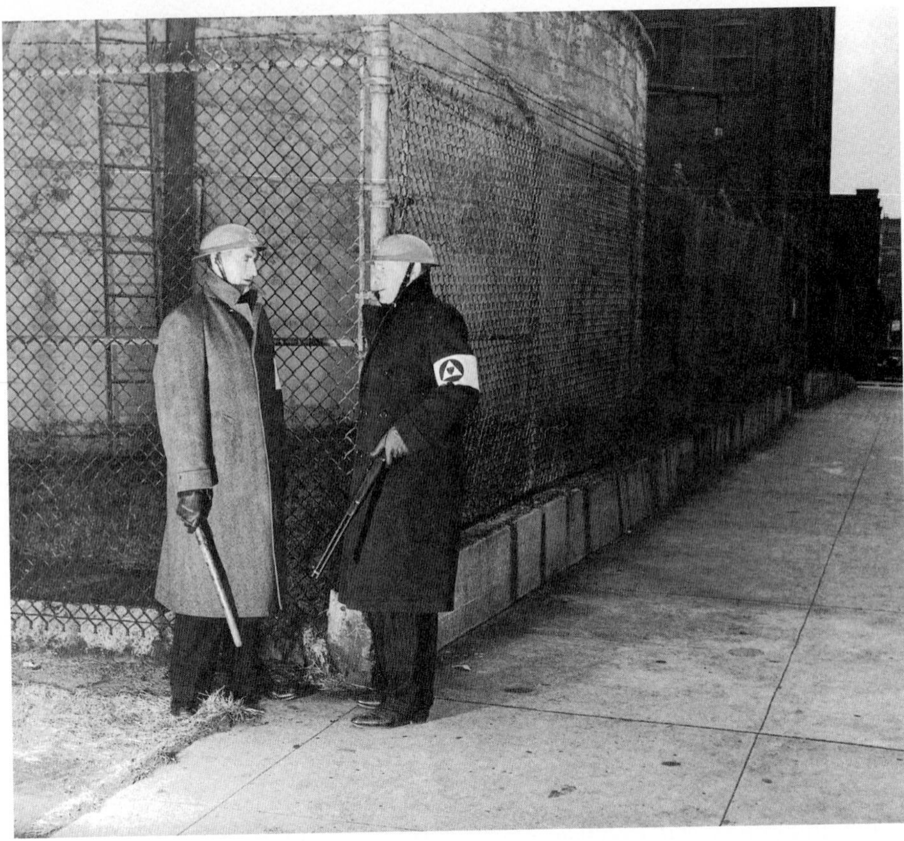

FIGURE 1.9

Police auxiliary officers patrolling in December 1941. Note they are equipped only with helmets, armbands, and nightsticks. The location of this photograph is not recorded.

(Courtesy of the Library of Congress)

Quick Facts

Victory Gardens

The resources of our whole nation were mobilized during World War II. Because food was needed to feed the armed forces, families were encouraged to grow their own vegetables in "victory gardens," which met 40 percent of the domestic needs. Children took aluminum-cooking pots to school, so they could be collected and used to make airplanes.

was within their grasp. New highways and interstates were constructed; factories that had built tanks for use in World War II returned to their prewar vocation and produced millions of new cars. As a result of these twin factors, the police began to put more emphasis on enforcing drinking and driving laws. Continuing the movement started in the late 1940s, many people who were suddenly becoming middle class left the inner cities for the rapidly growing suburbs. These suburbs were occasionally referred to generically as "Levitt Towns," after the brothers who specialized in building quality, cost-efficient homes there. For many families, their first homes were purchased with veterans' benefits. A novelty in the late 1940s, television rapidly expanded in the 1950s, and the New York City Police Department used closed-circuit television to broadcast lineups of suspects to police precincts conveniently located for witnesses. The Cold War was a dominant foreign policy focus, and the Korean War raged from

1950 to 1953. The Rosenbergs were executed in 1953 for revealing atomic bomb secrets to the Russians, and Senator Joseph McCarthy ran roughshod, searching everywhere for communists until he was discredited. More women entered law enforcement, althought the numbers were not very large. Often their opportunities were limited to working with juvenile delinquents, the shoplift detail, and other out-of-the-mainstream jobs. At the end of the decade, police officers in some large cities were questioning the reasoning used to prevent them from engaging in collective bargaining (see Chapter 11, Labor Relations).

Following World War II, interest in the police seemed to wane as economic development and social mobility gave rise to new issues—urban congestion, decaying values, and ethnic/racial unrest. It was not until the 1960s that significant attention was once again brought to bear on the functions and duties of the police.

Critical Thinking Questions

1. Many police officers voluntarily joined the military during World War II. After being discharged, they resumed their law enforcement careers and joined National Guard and Reserve units to build a second pension inasmuch as they had already accumulated some years of military service. During the Korean War (1950–1953), many of these units were recalled to active duty. What effect might those facts have had on their police careers?
2. Although there are laws to protect the jobs of people called to such active duty, do they "forfeit" the opportunity to develop a mentor relationship with a police superior who can get them good assignments in the department and favorable promotional consideration?
3. Can you see how this might apply to law enforcement officers today who have been in National Guard or Reserve units and served several tours in Iraq?

THE TURBULENT 1960s

The 1960s were a staggering decade for society and the police as smoldering racial, social, and economic tensions erupted. During 1965, these tensions boiled over in the Watts neighborhood in Los Angeles when a majority police officer stopped a minority, Marquette Fry, for drunk driving. Other African Americans congregated at the scene, police reinforcements were dispatched, and violence quickly followed. In the six days of looting, sniping, and arson that followed, 34 people were killed, most of them minorities, and losses amounted to more than $200 million before peace was restored. Over the next three years, similar riots struck more than two dozen major cities. Among the causes cited for these riots were a lack of jobs and other opportunities, anger at white shopkeepers in minority districts, a segregated and unequal society, and largely white police departments that were increasingly viewed as hostile and repressive.

In the wake of the riots, two significant federal commissions issued their reports. In 1967, President Johnson's Commission on Law Enforcement and Criminal Justice released its summary report, *The Challenge of Crime in a Free Society*, which was supplemented by *Task Force Reports* on specific subjects, including the police and organized crime. These volumes essentially summarized certain conditions and made recommendations for the future, including that police officers should have college degrees. The following year, the National Advisory Commission on Civil Disorders, often referred to as the Kerner Commission from the name of its chair, Governor Otto Kerner (1908–1976), published its findings, among which was this statement:

> *The policeman in the ghetto is a symbol of increasingly bitter social debate over law enforcement. One side, disturbed and perplexed by sharp increases in crime and urban violence, exerts extreme pressure on police for tougher law enforcement. Another group, inflamed against police as agents of repression, tend toward defiance of what it regards as order maintained at the expense of justice.*[23]

This role conflict also called into question the legitimacy of policing as a profession. Were the police viable agents capable of controlling crime and disorder or simply bullies who attempted to control a culturally divided American society? Such questions led to the identification of several conflicting and ambiguous roles for the police.

As a result of the previous "crime-fighting" era, police officers were considered law enforcers, charged with fighting crime, arresting criminals, and maintaining order. This image remains today and is reinforced by the popular media and continued community perception. At the same time, the police were touted as conflict managers, keepers of the peace, crime prevention specialists, and, to some degree, social service agents. In other words, the police were also supposed to *assist* citizens rather than *arrest* law violators.[24] To a large extent, this role ambiguity still exists as law enforcement agencies and their communities strive to define more accurately the evolving nature of policing.

Meanwhile, other events during the 1960s were also rapidly changing the worldview of police officers. There were yippies, hippies, psychedelic drugs, massive demonstrations against the Vietnam War and for the civil rights movement, draft evaders and deserters, freedom riders and sit-ins, the beginning of open emergence by gays, the burgeoning women's rights movement, the passage of the 1964 Civil Rights Act of 1964 and its subsequent amendments, Cesar Chavez's (1927–1993) efforts to provide better conditions and earnings for farmworkers (many of whom were Mexicans), Supreme Court decisions (such as the *Miranda* decision) that seemed to favor criminals and make law enforcement more difficult, Native Americans who sought more control over their land and resources, and other conditions that policing was ill prepared to handle. For example, in 1968 at the Democratic National Convention in Chicago, the police and protestors clashed violently (see Figure 1.10), with some of the former using excess force in some instances and some of the latter fueling the clashes by throwing at officers containers of urine and apples into which razor blades had been partially inserted. Further evidence to the police of an unraveling society during the 1960s were the assassinations of President John Kennedy (1917–1963), Senator Robert Kennedy (1925–1968), and the Reverend Martin Luther King, Jr. (1929–1968).

A new world was unfolding that the police did not understand and in which they felt isolated and unsupported. In this milieu, police professionalization took on new urgency.

Renewed Interest in Professionalization

Major interest in police professionalization was renewed once again in the 1960s. During this time, a high school diploma or a general equivalency degree became the minimum educational requirement for appointment. Character and background investigations became standard practice and increasingly more thorough. The use of the polygraph and psychological instruments to screen applicants became more widespread. All together, such factors signaled a shift from screening out the undesirable and hiring the rest to identifying and hiring those believed to be most able. At the state level, Police Officer Standards and Training Commissions (POSTs) were created, often with the incentive of

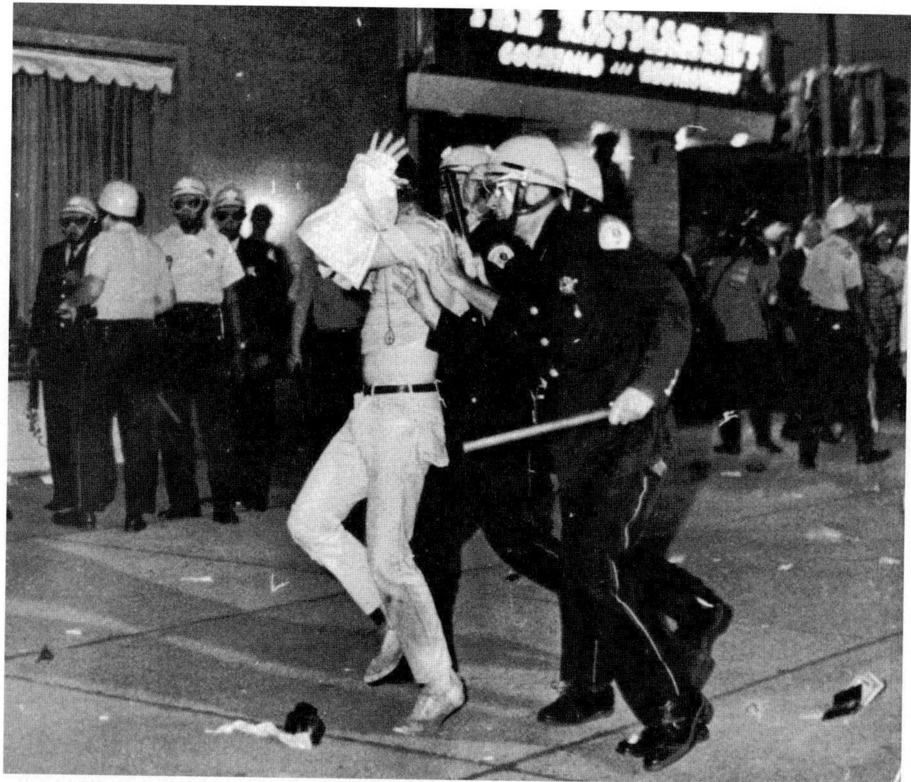

FIGURE 1.10

A demonstrator is led by Chicago police down Michigan Avenue on the night of August 28, 1968, during a confrontation with police and National Guardsmen who battled demonstrators near Conrad Hilton Hotel, headquarters for the Democratic National Convention.

(AP/Wide World Photos)

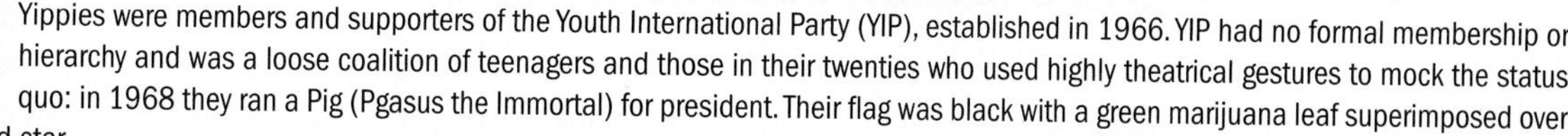

Yippies and Hippies

Yippies were members and supporters of the Youth International Party (YIP), established in 1966. YIP had no formal membership or hierarchy and was a loose coalition of teenagers and those in their twenties who used highly theatrical gestures to mock the status quo: in 1968 they ran a Pig (Pgasus the Immortal) for president. Their flag was black with a green marijuana leaf superimposed over a five-point red star.

Hippies emerged in the 1960s as a free speech, free love, anti-war movement composed almost entirely of whites between the ages of 15 and 25. In the 1970s, hippies declined to the point of almost vanishing altogether. Society was seen as corrupt and having too much power over their lives; thus, there was resistance to "the man," "big brother," and "the establishment." As we move into the twenty-first century there is somewhat of a neo-hippie movement with beliefs similar to those of the 1960s.

Source: Wikipedia, The Free Encyclopedia.

Law Enforcement Assistance Administration (LEAA) grants to initiate operations and to ensure that uniform minimum standards—including training—were met.

Training academies proliferated, and a few departments began to require a college degree as an entry-level educational requirement. More numerous, however, were the departments that required a few college credits, such as 6 or 12, and the departments that required as a condition of employment that officers agree to obtain a certain number of college hours within a specified time after appointment. Written promotional tests gained in prominence, although many rank-and-file members objected to them, favoring seniority instead. Even some chiefs complained that written tests interfered with their ability to promote the most able persons. The length of recruit academy curricula increased steadily, and social science subjects were introduced. From 1965 on, the number of junior colleges, colleges, and universities offering police administration or criminal justice degrees grew steadily, if not exponentially, initially because of the availability of seed money to start such programs from the Office of Law Enforcement Assistance (OLEA), LEAA's predecessor. Law Enforcement Education Program (LEEP) funds from LEAA were offered to induce and support the studies of students with career interests in criminal justice. Parenthetically, these agencies no longer exist; LEAA was abolished in 1982.

Further impetus to the movement to educate in-service officers and infuse college graduates into police departments was gained by providing incentive pay for college credits, which is a supplement above the regular salary based on the number of college credits earned. "Professionalization" of the police and "education" became virtually synonymous in the eyes of many observers. Illustratively, while conspicuously failing to define professionalization, the 1967 President's Commission on Law Enforcement and Administration of Justice nonetheless clearly equated professionalism with education.

Thus, despite a variety of practices designed to foster a higher caliber of personnel, the hallmark from 1950 to 1970—particularly after 1965—was the attempt to promote police professionalism through education. Education was seen as a means by which to improve community relations, which had suffered and had contributed to the urban riots of 1965–1968; to reduce police use of violence; to promote more judicious use of police discretionary powers; to counter the problem of corruption; and to accurately define the role of police in society.[25]

Critical Thinking Question

1. Assume that you were a uniformed police officer during the turbulent 1960s. In a world that was rapidly changing and in an occupation under great stress, how would you have felt and what options would you have considered?

THE CALL FOR RESEARCH AND OTHER DEVELOPMENTS

As the 1960s drew to a close, there were calls for more research, and massive grants became available from the LEAA both to conduct research and to allow criminal justice agencies to make enhancements that they otherwise could not afford. Both of these events influenced policing during the 1970s.

The previously mentioned *Challenge of Crime in a Free Society* (1967) noted that "there was virtually no subject connected with crime or criminal justice into which further research is unnecessary."[26] The following year, Doig buttressed this stance, calling the police a "terra incognita," an unknown land.[27] The federal Omnibus Crime Control and Safe Streets Act (1968), which created LEAA and LEEP, created a national system for improving criminal justice agencies and for conducting research on them. It also created a need for police, courts, corrections planners, and program evaluators, occupations that were virtually nonexistent at that time. The LEAA was structurally part of the U.S. Department of Justice and was headquartered in Washington, D.C. It was administered on the federal side largely by regional offices, each of which was responsible for a number of states. At the state level, State Planning Agencies (SPAs) were created by governors, as were subordinate multicounty regional offices. The LEAA made multi-million-dollar block grants to the states that programmed the money annually in plans for use according to broad LEAA guidelines. There were always considerable tensions in the state administration of LEAA funds. More than occasionally, governors wanted funds for projects to go to politicians and jurisdictions that had supported their election. Sometimes the projects that funded in this manner were of dubious merit. If such projects were not in the state plan, then SPA staff were often pressured to solicit an approval for a deviation from the LEAA. Occasionally, such requests created friction between the planners and LEAA regional offices because the latter were responsive to the governor and the state board that oversaw its activities; likewise, its nominally subordinate regional offices had their local boards to satisfy. Thus, there was always an implicit struggle as to whether the dominant planning model was to be top-down, with the SPAs setting priorities, or bottom-up by the subordinate regional offices. In practice, neither of these two planning models purely dominated. The local boards were more inclined to support the purchase of police vehicles, the construction of firing ranges, the improvement of the radio systems, and kindred projects. In contrast, the SPAs tried to foster more substantial programs, such as real-time criminal justice information systems and research programs.

The Trilogy

In the 1970s, three major experiments rocked policing: (1) the **Kansas City Preventive Patrol Experiment,** whose findings challenged long-held tenets about the effects of patrol by marked units; (2) the **RAND Criminal Investigation Study,** which confirmed what most uniformed patrol officers of that era believed, that the first officer on the scene makes a substantial contribution to solving cases and that follow-up investigations by detectives are often not productive; and (3) the team policing experiments, which introduced new structures and processes and set the stage for other evolutionary police delivery concepts, such as community policing (see Chapter 2, Policing Today).

The Kansas City Preventive Patrol Experiment (1972–1973)

This experiment was a large-scale test of one of policing's most cherished doctrines: conspicuous and aggressive patrol in all areas of the community at all times prevents crime and reduces the public's fear of crime. Funded with a Police Foundation grant, this 12-month experiment divided 15 geographical areas or beats covering 32 square miles into reactive (no preventive patrol), proactive (received two to three times the amount of normal patrol), and control (which were operated normally) beats to test the doctrine of conspicuous and aggressive patrol. The findings were controversial and included such data as no significant deviations in reported crime or arrests across the three types of beats and no significant differences in security measures taken by citizens and businesses; nor was there any correlation between level of patrolling, the number of traffic accidents, and citizens' fear of crime or attitudes toward the police. As local leaders learned of the study, a few were inclined to deny requests for additional officers. Police leaders quickly countered the situation by pointing out that patrol was only one of a number of programs designed to control crime and that even the reactive beats received some patrol service as cars entered them in response to calls for service. Moreover, they claimed it would be precipitous to cut funding based on a lone study with "methodological flaws."

The RAND Criminal Investigation Study

Essentially, this study attempted to determine what factors contribute to the success of investigations and just what it is that detectives do. Funded in 1973 by the National Institute of Law Enforcement and Criminal Justice and conducted by the RAND

Corporation, this study looked at serious crimes, murder, aggravated assault, rape, robbery, burglary, grand larceny, and vehicle theft. A national sample of police agencies was surveyed and interviews were conducted in 25 police departments. The study concluded that most clearances of crimes were achieved through the contributions of the patrol officers who conducted the preliminary investigation, information volunteered by the public, and routine police procedures, as opposed to advanced investigative procedures used by detectives, whose time was often encumbered by administrative paperwork. Among the recommendations made were improving crime scene processing capabilities and expanding the role of uniformed officers in the original investigation. The study generated instant controversy; some officials said it confirmed their suspicions about the value of detectives; others said that, like the Kansas City study, the results had not been replicated and detectives became a budget issue in some jurisdictions.

Team Policing

The final part of the trilogy is **team policing**, an innovation in which a single team commander, of perhaps 20 to 30 officers has 24-hour responsibility for one geographical area and makes all decisions as to the delivery of police services. In its pure form, the role of patrol officers is expanded dramatically and they worked in uniform or plainclothes investigative assignments on an as needed basis (see Figure 1.11). Although a number of jurisdictions adopted team policing, it never swept the country in the manner in which community policing has. While its use had almost vanished by the late 1970s, it left important legacies. Team policing resulted in a renewed appreciation for the capabilities of patrol officers and helped set the stage for community-oriented policing. Its demise was caused by a variety of factors: (1) planning prior to

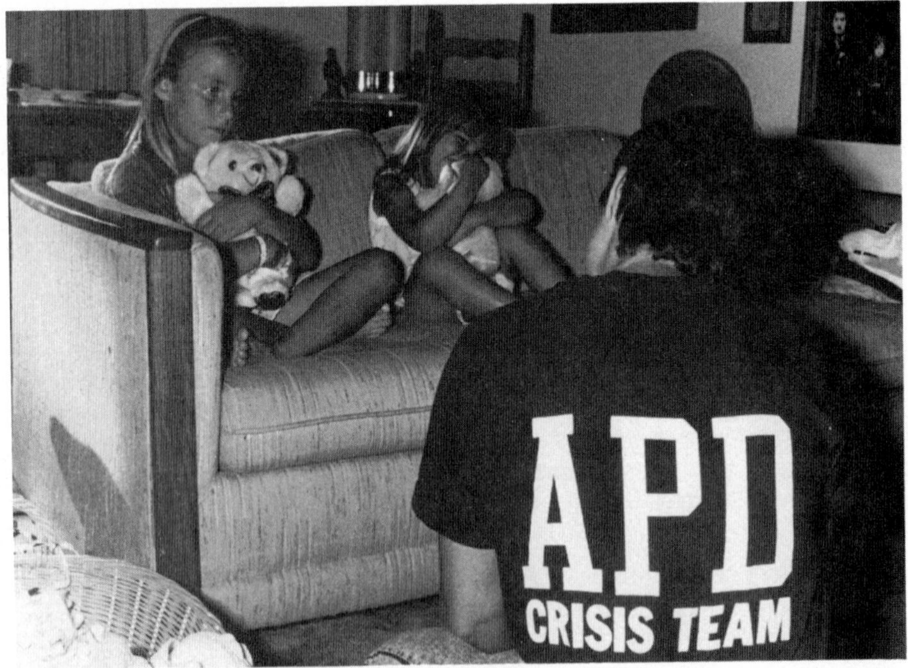

FIGURE 1.11

Based in part on the RAND Criminal Investigation Study, some departments used a team approach to solve crimes. Here members of a crisis team help children cope with the traumatic aspects of a family crime while maintaining their roles as detectives.

(Courtesy of the Austin, Texas, Police Department)

implementation was often not thorough and resulted in problems, (2) too little importance was attached to the opinions of lower-ranking officers, (3) organizational policies were not changed to accommodate the new processes associated with team policing, and (4) its use of team leaders lessened the importance of mid-level police managers, who came to oppose it for that reason.

Other Major Developments

In 1972, the National Criminal Justice Reference Service (NCJRS) was formed to archive and disseminate the rapidly growing body of criminal justice knowledge being generated by research. Today, both older and cutting-edge research crime- and justice-related research can be accessed for free at NCJRS via the Internet (www.ncjrs.org). It is an important source of information for practitioners, scholars, and students.

Police executives from the 10 largest cities met in 1975 to have informal discussions about common problems confronting their agencies. As an outgrowth of this experience, the Police Executive Research Forum (**PERF**; www.policeforum.org) was incorporated in 1977 as a national organization of progressive police executives from larger city, county, and state law enforcement organizations. PERF is dedicated to improving policing through research and public policy debates. Its primary sources of income are from grants and contracts, as well as partnerships with private foundations and other organizations.

The Commission on Accreditation for Law Enforcement Agencies, Inc. (**CALEA**; www.calea.org) was established in 1979 as an independent accrediting authority by the four major law enforcement member associations: the International Association of Chiefs of Police (IACP; www.theiacp.org) the National Organization of Black Law Enforcement Executives (**NOBLE**; www.noblenatl.org), the National Sheriffs' Association (NSA; www.sheriffs.org), and PERF. Accreditation is a voluntary process in terms of entering into it. However, there are hundreds of mandatory standards that agencies must meet through an inspection in order to be recognized as accredited. Every three years, CALEA offers an accredited agency the opportunity to be reaccredited through another inspection process.

CALEA accreditation offers significant advantages:

1. It can be an important part of the economic development program for a jurisdiction because employers seeking to relocate their businesses from one city to another always consider the quality of government.
2. Liability insurance costs can be reduced.
3. Community pride and confidence in the agency are stimulated.
4. The comprehensive written directive system provides greater accountability.

Critical Thinking Question

1. You have been given $25 million to conduct research on what you think are the top five to ten issues facing policing today. What projects do you fund and why?

THE 1980S AND BEYOND

Over the past several decades, some important themes have dominated law enforcement in this country: (1) the rise of community oriented policing, (2) the growth of private security, (3) substantial advances in investigative technology, and (4) terrorism.

Community Oriented Policing

At its simplest, community oriented policing (COP) involves delivering police services which are tailored to the needs of the respective neighborhoods. While team policing enjoyed only a brief period of visibility and was never widely used, COP has swept across this and other countries with breathtaking speed and still is gaining in popularity since its beginning in the early 1980s. Several factors account for this: (1) sharp increases in crimes created an awareness that the traditional philosophy of simply responding to incidents (R2I) was not working and a new approach was needed, (2) a key part of COP doctrine is forging relationships with the multiple groups that constitute a community (such as neighborhoods and businesses), so that what the police do is to some degree shaped by the input they receive and are democratically responsive to the community, and (3) while never straying from its basic tenets, COP has grown and evolved. In Chapter 2, Policing Today, COP receives further discussion and a critique, including the growing use of intelligence-led policing and fusion centers within the COP philosophy.

The shift from R2I to COP is not complete and probably never will be because some agencies prefer the traditional policing model. Moreover, the implementation of COP often is accompanied by a period of turbulence; in part this is due to the natural resistance to major changes in most organizations. It is also caused by officers who see themselves as "crime fighters" and view the shift in philosophy and additional meetings as antithetical to why they got into law enforcement in the first place; predictably, after a period of being vocally unhappy, some of these officers will leave for "greener (R2I) pastures."

Private Security

Private security includes uniformed guards, private investigators, protection services to business leaders and others, the manufacturing and sale of security/alarm systems, and other related activities. Policing at the three levels of government employs some 1 million people[28], with about \$65 billion in expenditures.[29] Private security dwarfs these figures with at least 2 million workers and more than \$100 billion in expenditures for it.[30] These figures underscore the reality that private security, in terms of employees and expenditures, is the nation's primary protective service.[31] In particular, private security has played a key role in preventing financial crimes and espionage against businesses, providing a sense of security in the home, and preventing violence in the workplace.[32]

There are a number of informal and formal ways in which private security and the police establish effective partnerships. In recent years, there has been a growth in security–police conferences at which partnering has been a significant or main topic. Private security is increasingly making the police aware of its resources and expertise and is learning the same about the police. Often, private security does a substantial portion of investigations before contacting the police, especially in the areas of credit card fraud, embezzlement, fraud, computer hacking, and information theft. Conversely, some businesses do not report many crimes officially because they do not want to publicize their crime problems. Particularly in a weak economy, such reports may undermine confidence in management and further spook investors. Perhaps the most frequent type of cooperation by security is providing the police with videotapes of crimes recorded on the seemingly ubiquitous surveillance cameras.

As the private security industry has grown increasingly sophisticated and as its markets change, so, too, do the needs to staff the industry. One of the little-recognized effects of private security is that increasingly over the past several years it has raided police agencies, taking away highly trained and experienced personnel. In New York City, Mayor Bloomberg stated, "I think the private sector is going after lots of members of the NYPD . . . and one of my jobs is to try and retain as many as we possibly can."[33]

While high-ranking police officials have always had opportunities in private security, the current hiring away of police officers is extending further down agencies than ever before. To illustrate, one security firm alone hired six officers from the New York City Police Department's elite Bomb Squad. From a personnel standpoint, turnover, or a "little bloodletting," is good because the replacements may bring a sense of excitement and energy to their new jobs that is higher than that of their predecessors. But when the bloodletting turns to hemorrhages, losing many skilled people quickly, it is hard to replace them quickly enough, creating disruptions in police agencies.[34]

Clearly, some of this raiding was directly fueled by the events of September 11, 2001, as private security clients clamored for more, specialized kinds of services, such as bomb technicians. A related change is the security industry's increasing shift from unarmed to armed personnel who often are recruited from police agencies. While some of this need is being met by retiring officers, it is also draining away experienced officers who are approaching their peak years of productivity.

Further complicating this situation is that police officers belonging to military reserve units have been called up more frequently and for longer periods of time over the past decade, leaving agencies shorthanded and depriving the officers of training and experience they need to be competitive for promotions in their agencies. Both the personnel raiding by security companies and the personnel shortages caused by military reserve call-ups underscore the need for an effective human resource management program.

Investigative Technology

The single most important development in personal identification since fingerprints is deoxyribonucleic acid (DNA) typing. The first use of it in a criminal case was in 1987 and involved the rape and murder of two teenage girls in the English village of Enderby. Within a year, it was also successfully used in Orlando, Florida, helping to win the conviction of a man who had committed a series of rapes. In 1988, the FBI became the first public sector crime laboratory to accept DNA evidence for analysis. In addition to being compelling prosecution evidence, DNA analysis has been used to free people who were not actually responsible for the crimes for which they were convicted. Table 1.1 summarizes many of the institutional and systems initiatives in criminal investigation from 1990 to 2001.

While these developments collectively are staggering in their capabilities, they have also produced challenges for law enforcement administrators. In addition to having to learn about the capabilities of these developments, police leaders have also had to seek funding from state legislatures, county commissions, and city councils to train investigative personnel and to cover costs not funded by the limited grants associated with some of the initiatives identified in Table 1.1. The management of fiscal resources is covered in Chapter 12.

Terrorism

The senseless and horrorifying murders at Virginia Tech illustrate the difference between events which are terrifying and terrorism. The FBI divides terrorism into two broad categories: domestic and international. Over a 20-year period the FBI recorded 335 suspected or actual incidents of terrorism. Of these, 247 were domestic and the remaining 88 international.[35]

TABLE 1.1 Major Institutional and System Initiatives, 1990–2007

YEAR	INNOVATION	DESCRIPTION
1990	Combined DNA Index System (CODIS)	Began as an FBI pilot project to combine forensic science and computer technology into a tool for combating violent crime; includes major databases, such as the Offender Index (profiles of convicted violent-crime offenders contributed by states) and the Forensic Index (DNA evidence recovered at crime scenes). CODIS consists of the National DNA Index System (NDIS), State DNA Information System (SDIS), and Local DNA Information System (LDIS). CODIS software can be used to link together in the Forensic Index, revealing the existence of a predatory violent offender. When such profiles are run against the Offender Index, identification of the offender may be established.
1992	Jewelry and Germ (JAG) database	Created by the FBI to combat increasing jewelry and gem thefts by organized criminal enterprises working across jurisdictional lines; provides information about modus operandi, descriptions and images of stolen property, and case analysis and coordination for cases submitted by other agencies nationally
1992	Exceptional Case Study Project (ECSP)	A five-year project run by the Secret Service, National Institute of Justice, and Bureau of Prisons; covered 83 subjects who in the previous 50 years had attacked or come close to attacking a U.S. government official
1995	Justice Prisoner and Alien Transport System (JPATS)	Created by combining the air fleets of the Marshals Service and Immigration and Naturalization Service; moves criminals and aliens between judicial districts, correctional facilities, and foreign countries
1997	National Drug Pointer Index (NDPIX)	Run by the DEA; uses the National Law Enforcement Telecommunications System (NLETS) as its communication backbone. Participating local, state, and federal agencies submit active case data and get back "pointer" information, so agencies know of common targets and can enhance safety of undercover operatives. By mid-2000, 86,000 cases were in the system.
1998	National Instant Criminal Background Check System (NICS)	Mandated by the Brady Handgun Prevention Act of 1994; requires that federal firearms licensees request background checks on individuals and refuse sales to those not eligible under the Brady Act. In 1998, the FBI, in cooperation with the Bureau of Alcohol, Tobacco, and Firearms (ATF) implemented the permanent provisions of the Brady Act.
1998	National Infrastructure Protection Center (NIPC)	Established within the FBI, with support from other agencies and the private sector; designed for threat assessment, warning, investigation, and response to threats or attacks against energy and water systems, banking and finance, and government operation systems
1998	Child Abduction and Serial Murder Investigative Resources (CASMIRC)	Authorized by Congress; provides investigative support, training, assistance, and coordination to federal, state, and local agencies in matters involving child abductions, disappearances of children, and child violence and serial homicides
1999	National Crime Center (NCIC)	The FBI's much enhanced, online information center. NCIC has been operational since 1967.
1999	Safe School Initiative (SSI)	Conducted by the Secret Service's National Threat Assessment Center, in partnership with the Department of Education; uses threat assessment to help prevent incidents of school-based violence
2000	National Threat Assessment Center (NTAC)	Officially mandated by Congress, although already operational for more than a year. Part of the impetus for the Secret Service's creation of NTAC was the final ECSP report.
2000	Internet Fraud Complaint Center (IFCC)	A joint venture between the FBI and the National White Collar Crime Center (NW3C); addresses fraud committed over the Internet
2001	National Integrated Ballistic Information Network (NIBIN)	A joint venture between the ATF and the FBI; NIBIN was intended to enhance the use of firearms evidence conducted in a few regions of the country in 2001

TABLE 1.1 Continued

YEAR	INNOVATION	DESCRIPTION
2001	Trade Partnerships Against Terrorism (TPAT)	A U.S. Customs program developed in response to the events of September 11, 2001; designed to fight terrorism by establishing a cooperative relationship with carriers, manufacturers, exporters, importers, and others. Cooperators receive benefits, such as priority services and processing.
2001	Missing Persons Index (MPI)	Became a CODIS database; contains DNA from skeletal remains and DNA reference samples from maternal relatives of missing persons in order to match known remains with missing persons reports.
2002	New crime lab	The Washington State Patrol's new crime lab opened in December 2002, but without sufficient funds to fully staff it.
2003	New crime labs	Federal Alcohol, Tobacco, and Firearms (ATF) opened a $135 million lab in Ammendale, Maryland; Minnesota's Bureau of Criminal Identification dedicated a 224,000-square-foot $83 million facility, and the FBI's new $135 million lab operates from three buildings on its campus in Quantico, Virginia.
2004	i2 Visual Notebook	i2 has developed investigative software for 20 years. Its visual notebook allows investigators to enter data and the software diagrams known or possible relationship between people and events.
2007	New crime lab	The Phoenix Police Department's $34 million, 104,000-square-foot facility opened in 2007 facing a significant backlog in cases.

SOURCE: Charles Swanson, Neil Chamelin, and Leonard Territo, *Criminal Investigation*, 9th ed. (Boston: McGraw-Hill, 2006), p. 18.

Domestic terrorism is the unlawful use, or threatened use, of violence by a group or individual based and operating entirely within the United States or its territories without foreign direction committed against persons or property to intimidate or coerce a government, the civilian population, or any segment thereof, in furtherance of political or social objectives.[36] Examples of domestic terrorism include extreme-right-wing hate groups (such as the Aryan Nations), those using violence to promote the full independence of Puerto Rico from the United States, and the Oklahoma City bombing (Figure 1.12).[37]

International terrorism transcends national boundaries and may be state sponsored, part of the radical jihad movement, and sponsored by formal terrorist organizations.[38] Of these, the most significant threat is opposed by radical Sunni extremists, including Osama bin Laden and his associates in al-Qaeda ("the base"). There are perhaps several hundred such associates in the United States waiting to wreak havoc on this country.

Since the murderous bombing of the Marine barracks in Beirut, Lebanon, in 1983, which killed 295 people, there has been a growth in large-scale attacks against Americans, including the 1988 bombing of Pan Am Flight 103 over Lockerbie, Scotland; the bombing of the World Trade Center in 1993; the Khobar Towers bombing in Saudi Arabia, which killed 19 members of the U.S. Air Force; the bombings of American embassies in Kenya and Tanzania in 1998; the USS *Cole* bombing in 2000; the murderous attacks on the World Trade Center and the Pentagon in 2001 (Figures 1.13, 1.14, and 1.15); and Richard Reid's failed attempt to ignite explosives in his shoes on an American Airlines flight in 2001. Al-Qaeda is responsible for many of these attacks. Moreover, Osama bin Laden has issued fatwahs (rulings by Muslim clerics) calling it the "religious duty" of all Muslims to kill American civilians—men, women, and children—and military members and to acquire weapons of mass destruction, which

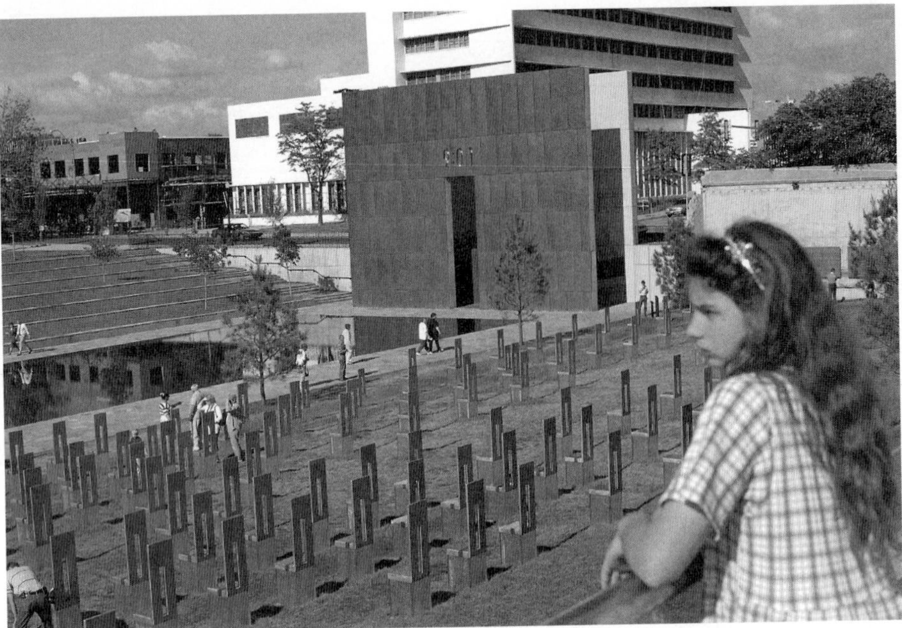

FIGURE 1.12

A young visitor looks over the Oklahoma City National Memorial, built on the site of the Alfred P. Murrah Federal Building.

(© David Butow/CORBIS SABA)

FIGURE 1.13

New York City, September 13, 2001. Urban search-and-rescue teams inspect the wreckage at the World Trade Center.

(Photo by Andrea Booher/FEMA News Photo)

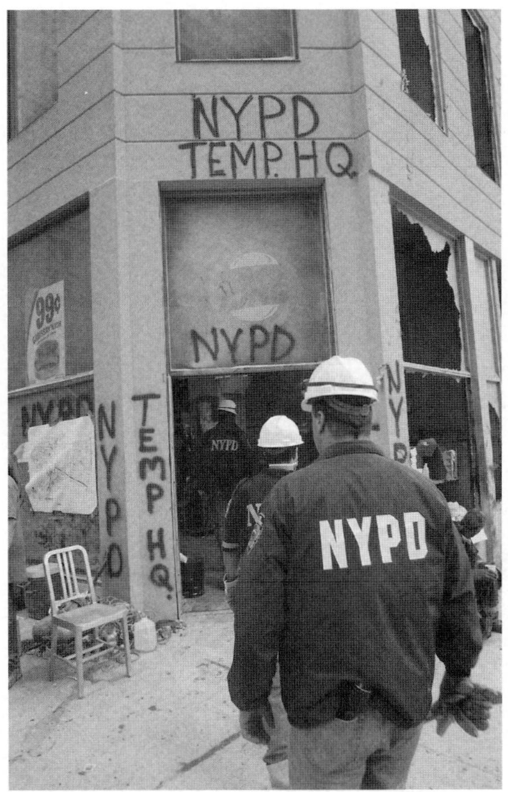

FIGURE 1.14

Immediately following the September 11, 2001, airplane attacks, the New York Police Department (NYPD) set up a temporary headquarters near ground zero.

(Photo by Andrea Booher/FEMA News Photo)

FIGURE 1.15

Aerial view, September 14, 2001, of the destruction caused when a hijacked commercial jetliner crashed into the Pentagon on September 11. The terrorist attack caused extensive damage to the Pentagon and followed similar attacks on the twin towers of the World Trade Center in New York City.

(Department of Defense photo by Tech. Sgt. Cedric H. Rudisill/U.S. Department of Defense Visual Information Center) include chemical, biological, radiological, and nuclear weapons. A "dirty bomb," often mentioned by media sources as a possible weapon, means a bomb that spreads radiological materials through the use of conventional explosives or weapons.

Radical Muslims hate the United States because, in their view, the U.S. presence in Arab countries violates the holy land, the United States supports "infidel" regimes and is one such regime, and it is our intention to plunder the riches of Arab countries. Moreover, our arrest, conviction, and imprisonment of those who plan, coordinate, and execute attacks against us further aggrieves them.[39] The intention of the radical Muslim movement goes well beyond driving us back to our shores; ultimately, they would like to destroy our way of life. These attacks on our nation are not anomalies; they are a window to our future. The fight against terrorism will be long and difficult. It is a fight that we must not only be in but also win. However, totally stamping out terrorist attacks on us here and abroad is not achievable. Therefore, based on what we now know, some degree of terrorism will be a continuing reality for Americans.

AMERICA RESPONDS TO SEPTEMBER 11

The cruel attack of September 11 produced horrendous losses for families and businesses. It was also gutwrenching for the rest of the nation, which recognized it as a pivotal moment in the nation's history and which stirred memories of the attack on Pearl Harbor. Two key responses to these attacks were the passage of the USA Patriot Act in October 2001 and, in late 2002, congressional legislation creating the Department of Homeland Security (www.dhs.gov/dhspublic).

In the aftermath of September 11, several studies were conducted to assess shortcomings that may exist in the nation's ability to collect and analyze important intelligence information on terrorist groups. Several weaknesses were identified in counterterrorism efforts led by the FBI, the Central Intelligence Agency (CIA), and the National Security Agency. These included communication problems among agencies, a shortage of linguists, and a failure by these agencies to correctly analyze relevant intelligence information to potential terrorist threats. Several of the issues identified as potential problems existing within the U.S. intelligence community were (1) a failure to place an emphasis on traditional human intelligence gathering and analysis, hence relying too much on technology tools, such as spy satellites and expert system programs, to gain intelligence advantages; (2) a failure to provide timely, accurate, and specific intelligence information to law enforcement agencies and U.S. policymakers; (3) an overly bureaucratic and decentralized structure (particularly within the FBI) that hindered counterterrorism efforts and the efficient use of intelligence information; (4) outdated and obsolete computer systems that were not compatible with other systems and were unable to provide accurate and timely sharing of critical information nationally; and (5) overly restrictive guidelines and laws that hindered the effective use of informants and the general collection of intelligence information.[40]

In an effort to improve these conditions and provide sweeping new powers to both domestic law enforcement and traditional intelligence agencies, President George W. Bush signed into law the USA Patriot Act on October 26, 2001. The USA Patriot Act (**P**rovide **A**ppropriate **T**ools **R**equired to **I**ntercept and **O**bstruct **T**errorism) changed over 15 different statutes with little or no external review. The law not only addressed terrorism and intelligence issues but also focused on more traditional money laundering, computer abuse and crime, immigration processes, and fraud. The act even provided compensation for victims of terrorism and access for local law enforcement to regional cybercrime labs. However, the most substantial part of the act is

In The News

2001 Patriotic Act

Some 16 provisions of the Patriot Act were originally to expire at the end of 2005; the expiration was temporarily extended for several months as Congress decided what to do. In 2006, Congress sent President Bush legislation, which he signed into law, renewing the Patriot Act. The tension between civil liberties and the control of crime and the fight against terrorism has been highlighted by the Patriot Act. Since its passage in 2001, 8 states and almost 400 cities and counties have passed resolutions which characterize this legislation as an attack on civil liberties.

that it expanded all four traditional tools of surveillance used by law enforcement with significantly reduced checks and balances—that is, wiretaps, search warrants, pen/trap and trace orders, and court orders and subpoenas.

Law enforcement and intelligence agencies can now more easily and more surreptitiously monitor the communication of individuals using the Internet, conduct nationwide roving wiretaps on cell and line telephones, and build profiles on the reading habits of people visiting public libraries. Under the act, police can now force Internet Service Providers (ISPs), such as America Online, AT&T Worldnet, and Prodigy to "voluntarily" hand over information on customer profiles and Web-surfing habits without a warrant or court order.

The expanded scope of the act has raised concerns from a variety of sources.[41] Most agree that intelligence gathering and analysis have to improve in order to prevent future terrorist attacks. However, the act may well go too far. The act increases information sharing between domestic law enforcement departments and traditional intelligence agencies, such as the FBI and the CIA. In such a state, the line between intelligence gathering and public law enforcement becomes blurred. Critics are quick to point out the civil rights abuses that have occurred in the past whenever police agencies have become too involved in intelligence gathering. Most major cities, including New York, Chicago, Denver and Los Angeles have had recent litigation aimed at limiting the role of police in this function. Arguments against an expanded police role in intelligence gathering cite the potential for collecting irrelevant information, such as web-surfing habits and sexual orientation. In advancing these arguments, opponents note that some police agencies already have previous history of abusing intelligence gathering capabilities. In one case, an intelligence officer in Portland, Oregon, developed boxes of information on over 500 community groups and over 3,000 well-noted citizens of the city and stored them at his own residence. Over 20 years of police intelligence records were discovered by family members after the officer died. The dusty reports and pictures not only focused on private meetings and information on local politicians but also revealed that the officer himself had been an active member of the John Birch Society, a right wing organization often under scrutiny by government intelligence agencies itself.[42] Some argue that the expanded role of police in intelligence gathering under the act will only provide a significant threat to the personal and civil liberties of all Americans and do very little to thwart terrorism.[43] Clearly, this role will not come without controversy.

Two other relatively quick responses to the September 11 attacks were the passage of the Homeland Security Act (2002) and the creation of a Terrorist Threat Integration Center (TTIC, 2003). This latter entity was superceded the following year when its functions were transferred to the National Counterterrorism Center (NCTC), created by an executive order issued by President Bush. TTIC's mandate was essentially to share terrorism related information across departmental lines, closing the "seam" between domestic and foreign intelligence. NCTC's mission is "to inform, empower and help shape the national and international counterterrorism effort to diminish the ranks, capabilities and activities of current and future terrorists." The topic of protecting our country from such persons and groups is discussed in Chapter 3, "Intelligence, Terrorism, and Homeland Security."

Critical Thinking Questions

1. At least one city has enacted a local ordinance which prohibits its municipal employees from assisting with any activity associated with the Patriot Act which would infringe on civil liberties.
2. As police chief, you have sworn an oath of office to uphold the laws of the land; still, you are also a city employee and subject to its direction and discipline. What would you do if conformed by a request to help implement provisions of the Patriot Act which might be in conflict with your local ordinance? What would the policy you write say to guide the actions of your officers in such situations?

CHAPTER REVIEW

1. Identify the primary responsibility of policing in America.
It is the responsibility of policing to preserve the peace in a manner which is consistent with the freedoms secured by the Constitution.
2. Define politics and explain whether it is a positive or a negative.
Politics is the exercise of power and is free of any inherent value of "goodness or badness"; its character depends on how that power is used.
3. Identify the "conceptual cornerstone" of the good government reformation period of 1900–1926.
It was articulated by Woodrow Wilson in 1887 and required the separation of "politics" (in the worse sense) from administration.
4. Describe the paradigm which replaced the politics–administration dichotomy in the late 1920s.
Several books on public administration were published; the dominant focus became finding universal principles and methods of administration, meaning ones which were applicable in all governmental departments.
5. Explain what "profession" means.
The term comes from the latin pro (forth) and fateri (confess), meaning to announce a belief and first meant a public vow of faith. In 1541, the term was first used to mean a learned occupation and by 1576 the term had become generalized to mean any calling by which a person made his or her living.
6. Discuss the contributions of Chief Vollmer to the police profession.
His many innovations—include the first scientific crime laboratory; the first use of mobile patrol, including bikes and cars; his insistence on hiring the highest possible caliber of personnel and the first lie detector machine was built in 1921 in the Berkeley Police Department.
7. State the purpose of the federal Pendleton Act of 1883.
It was to protect government employees from the ills associated with the spoils system; it was common when an election was won by the party which had not been in power to fire all employees and give the jobs to party supporters. By eliminating such practices, public employees would be stable in their employment, developing additional knowledge and expertise over time. Over the decades following 1883, many local governments enacted similar measures, often creating civil service systems to recruit, select, and protect employees from gross political interference with their employment.

8. Explain the use of the military model in policing.
   From roughly around the beginning of the twentieth century, the military model became the dominant one in American policing. Reformers saw this country as under attack by crime and criminals and the first line of defense was police departments. Even today, politicians occasionally use the phrase "the war on crime."
9. Describe how prohibition was harmful to policing in this country.
   Police officers widely accepted bribes to "look the other way" as alcohol was sold and speakeasies operated. This corruption gave policing a terrible reputation.
10. Explain how World War II affected law enforcement.
    No occupation, including policing, was exempt from the draft during this war and many police officers hurried to join branches of the armed service voluntarily. Police departments were left understaffed and were stripped of physically able officers. Older officers and those rejected by the draft as being physically unfit were left. Part time volunteer auxiliary police officers were often used and more women found police employment. Beyond their traditional crime-fighting role, the police were also tasked with helping to look for possible saboteurs. New crimes were also created, such as forging ration books, which limited the amount of certain things which could be purchased, including, gasoline, butter, and meat.
11. Explain the meaning of the "turbulent 1960s."
    Smoldering racial, economic, and social tensions boiled over. From 1965 to 1968, there were race riots in many cities, often in reaction to an arrest or the shooting of a minority by officers. The deeper causes were a lack of jobs; a segregated, repressive, and unequal society; white store owners in minority areas who took advantage of customers; and largely white police departments which were viewed as hostile and unfair to minorities. The role of the police was increasingly ambiguous, shifting from crime-fighting enforcers to a responsibility to help citizens. Everyone seemed to be demonstrating about something, from the increasingly unpopular Vietnam War to rights for migrant farmworkers. The Supreme Court passed a series of decisions, beginning with the Miranda decision, making police work increasingly more difficult. A new world was unfolding which perplexed and frightened officers; within this context, the professionalization of the police took on a new urgency and its foundation was education. Police academies became more numerous and longer.
12. Explain the impact of the call for research on policing and related developments.
    As the 1960s drew to a close, it was clear that for the most part policing had escaped the interest of researchers; one observer noted that policing was an "unknown land." The creation of the federal grant awarding LEAA brought both massive grants to criminal justice agencies and a responsibility to evaluate them. Grants were also given to study virtually all aspects of the criminal justice system, creating new knowledge and new occupations, such as police planner. A trilogy challenged fundamental doctrines: (1) the Kansas City Preventive Patrol Project, (2) the RAND Criminal Investigation Study, (3) team policing experimentation. The Creation of NCJRS in 1972 established a major repository, or library, to disseminate and house knowledge about criminal justice. Important new organizations interested in research professionalization were created, including PERF, NOBLE, and CALEA.
13. Identify and briefly discuss four major themes which have dominated policing since 1980.
    These themes are (1) the rise of community policing, with its emphasis on input from the community and the delivery of custom-tailored police services, (2) the growth of private security, which dwarfs public law enforcement in terms of numbers of employees and expenditures, (3) substantial advances in investigative technology, including the advent of DNA, the rise of numerous automated data bases and the continuing construction of crime laboratories due to the increased importance of forensic evidence in criminal

trials, and (4) terrorism, which the FBI divides into international and domestic categories. Within this structure, the most significant international threat presently comes from radical, fundamentalist Islamic groups. Attacks by international terrorists in this country and abroad are far less numerous than attacks by domestic terror groups, but they are more catastrophic with respect to causalities and damage. Examples of domestic terror groups include extreme groups, such as the Aryan Nations and the Animal Liberation Front (ALF).

KEY TERMS

Alderman: a person elected to serve on a city council, which is the municipal legislative branch of government.

CALEA: Commission of Accreditation of Police Agencies, established in 1979.

Closing the frontier: in 1890, the federal Census Bureau announced that there could no longer be a frontier; most people lived in cities. It marked a milestone in the movement from a rural, agrarian society to an industrialized society.

Great Depression: the economic turmoil in this country which began in 1929 with the crash of the stock market and lasted roughly 10 years.

Kansas City Preventive Patrol Experiment: a major study which questioned the traditional police doctrine of the importance of preventive patrol and which was instantly controversial.

Law enforcement: the enforcement of criminal laws, an activity on which the police spend only 15 percent of their time.

Military model: a concept which gained currency around the turn of the 20th century; the police were seen as the first line of defense in the war against a crime. It is also associated with the use of staffs to help run departments professionally.

NOBLE: National Organization of Black Law Enforcement Executives, founded in 1976 at a three-day symposium on crime in low-income areas.

Pendleton Act: federal legislation designed to take the ills of machine politics out of government. Many local governments enacted similar laws establishing civil service systems designed to protect employees from gross political inteference.

PERF: Police Executive Research Forum, a national organization dedicated to fostering research and debate to examining traditional police practices. It was created in 1976 by leaders from 10 of the largest police agencies in America.

Politics: stated simply, the exercise of power. It is neither "good" nor "bad"; its character springs from how it is used.

Profession: from the Latin *pro* (forth) and *fateri* (confess); at its earliest, it meant the public declaration of faith. It has come to mean a learned calling in which a person earns his or her living.

Prohibition: the 18th Amendment to the United States Constitution, ratified in 1919, prohibited the manufacture, sale, transportation, exportation, or importation of intoxicating liquors. The same year, the National Prohibition Act (also called the Volstead Act) was passed as the federal law by which the amendment was implemented. Gangsters quickly paid the police to "look the other way" as they sold liquor and operated speakeasies, giving the police a reputation for corruption. Congress abolished the law in 1931 and the 21st Amendment abolished prohibition in 1933.

RAND Criminal Investigation Study: a highly controversial project which questioned the importance of detectives in solving cases.

Reformation period: as used in this country in public administration, it refers to the period of roughly 1900–1926 when a great deal of emphasis was put on improving government. The conceptual cornerstone of the movement was the separation of politics (in the worst sense) and administration.

Residency requirement: a measure, which gained popularity during the Great Depression, which required that those who were hired by a local government had lived in the community for a period of time, which ensured that those who paid taxes got the local jobs and not "outsiders."

Team policing: a form of policing in which a commander of small team of 20 to 30 officers makes all decisions about what police services a neighborhood receives over a 24-hour period. It was never widespread in its use and failed for a number of reasons, including inadequate planning prior to implementation and opposition by police middle managers who lost power to the team commanders. Still, it can be argued that it helped to prepare departments for the use of community policing.

Turbulent 1960s: a decade marked by social upheaval, including race riots, whose catalysts were long-simmering anger over inequality and prejudice, demonstrations for farmworkers and against the war in Vietnam, the emergence of the counterculture "hippie lifestyle," and the use of drugs, then passage of the sweeping Civil Rights Act of 1964, and the series of Supreme Court decisions, which started with the *Miranda* decision, which left the police feeling isolated and unsupported.

Vollmer: one of the giant figures in police history; during his tenure as police chief in Berkeley, California, he introduced such innovations as mobile patrol, the signal system used on police radios, and the hiring of the most able people.

World War II: in this country, the war lasted from late 1941 until the late spring of 1945, when Japan surrendered, the European Axis powers having surrendered some months prior.

NOTES

1. This section draws on and extends material found in the National Advisory Commission on Criminal Justice Standards and Goals, *Police*, Russell W. Peterson, chairman (Washington, D.C.: U.S. Government Printing Office, 1973), p. 13.
2. Thomas A. Reppetto, *The Blue Parade* (New York: Free Press, 1978), pp. 41–42.
3. Alice B. Stone and Donald C. Stone, "Early Development of Education in Public Administration," in *American Public Administration: Past, Present, and Future*, ed. Frederick C. Mosher (Tuscaloosa: University of Alabama Press, 1975), pp. 17–18. The themes in this and the subsequent paragraph are reflected in Stone and Stone's "Early Development" and sounded repeatedly in the literature. See Howard E. McCurdy, *Public Administration: A Synthesis* (Menlo Park, Calif.: Cummings, 1977), pp. 19–21; William L. Morrow, *Public Administration: Politics and the Political System* (New York: Random House, 1975), p. 25; and Lynton K. Caldwell, "Public Administration and the Universities: A Half-Century of Development," *Public Administration Review* 25 (March 1965): 52–60.
4. Woodrow Wilson, "The Study of Administration," *Political Science Quarterly* 2 (June 1887): 197–222.
5. Edwin O. Stene, "The Politics–Administration Dichotomy," *Midwest Review of Public Administration* 9 (April–July 1975): 84.
6. E. W. Roddenbury, "Achieving Professionalism," *Journal of Criminal Law, Criminology, and Police Science* 44 (May 1953–1954): 109.
7. Morris L. Cogan, "Toward a Definition of Profession," *Harvard Educational Review* 23 (winter 1953): 34.
8. Everette Hughes, "Professions," in *The Professions in America*, ed. K. S. Lynn (Cambridge, Mass.: Riverside Press, 1965), pp. 1–14.
9. See, for example, Ernest Greenwood, "Attributes of a Profession," *Social Work* 2, no. 3 (1957): 45.
10. Robert K. Merton, "Some Thoughts on the Professions in American Society" (address before the Brown University graduate convocation, Providence, R.I., June 6, 1960).
11. Howard Becker, "The Nature of a Profession," in the *Sixty-First Yearbook of the National Society for the Study of Education* (Chicago: National Society for the Study of Education 1962). See also Harold L. Wilensky, "The Professionalization of Everyone?" *American Journal of Sociology* 70, no. 2 (1964): 137–58.
12. Gene Edward Carte, "August Vollmer and the Origins of Police Professionalism," *Journal of Police Science and Administration* 1, no. 3 (1973): 274.
13. Raymond B. Fosdick, *American Police Systems* (Montclair, N.J.: A 1969 Patterson Smith Reprint of a Century Company Work), pp. 284–285.
14. Ibid., p. 271.
15. Robert M. Fogelson, *Big-City Police* (Cambridge, Mass.: Harvard University Press, 1975), p. 76.
16. Extended treatment of this line of thinking is found in Fogelson, "The Military Analogy," in *Big-City Police*, pp. 40–66.
17. Ibid., p. 77.
18. For more details on the gangster era, see William B. Breuer, *J. Edgar Hoover and His G-Men* (Westport, Conn.: Praeger, 1995).
19. George L. Kelling and James K. Stewart, "The Evolution of Contemporary Policing," in *Local Government Police Management*, ed. William A. Gellar (Washington, D.C.: International City Management Association, 1991), p. 7.
20. Louis A. Radelet, *The Police and the Community*, 3rd ed. (Encino, Calif.: Glencoe, 1980), p. 8.
21. See Kelling and Stewart, "The Evolution of Contemporary Policing," for an excellent historical brief on the police.

22. Ibid., p. 9.
23. U.S. National Advisory Commission on Civil Disorders, *Reports of the National Advisory Commission on Civil Disorders* (Washington, D.C.: U.S. Government Printing Office, 1968), p. 157.
24. Conflicting role expectations for police have been a historical issue. See Radelet, *The Police and the Community*; James Q. Wilson, *Varieties of Police Behavior: The Management of Law and Order in Eight Communities* (Cambridge, Mass.: Harvard University Press, 1968); Michael Banton, *Policeman in the Community* (New York: Basic Books, 1964); Jerome H. Skolnick, *Justice without Trial: Law Enforcement in Democratic Society* (New York: John Wiley & Sons, 1966); and Peter K. Manning and John Van Maanen, eds., *Policing: A View from the Street* (Santa Monica, Calif.: Goodyear Publishing, 1978).
25. James Q. Wilson, "The Police and Their Problems," *Public Policy* 12 (1963): 189–216.
26. Nicholas deB Katzenback, *The Challenge of Crime in a Free Society* (Washington, D.C.: U.S. Government Printing Office, 1967), p. 12.
27. Jameson W. Doig, "Police Problems, Proposals, and Strategies for Change," *Public Administration Review* 28 (September/October 1968): 393.
28. U.S. Department of Justice, *Sourcebook of Criminal Justice Statistics 2001* (Washington, D.C.: Bureau of Justice Statistics, 2002), table 1.19, p. 26.
29. Ibid., table 1.3, p. 5.
30. William C. Cunningham, "U.S. Private Security Trends Abstract," Hallcrest Systems, Inc., December 12, 2002 (www.lcc.gc.ca/en/ress/conf/conf_ flyer /speakers_abstract/Cunningham.asp).
31. Ibid., p. 1.
32. Ibid., with the added mention by the authors of the home.
33. Al Baker, "Private Security's Gain Is Public Safety's Loss Police Say," *New York Times*, December 26, 2001. At the time of this article, Bloomberg was actually the mayor-elect.
34. Ibid.
35. Dale L. Watson, executive assistant director, FBI, "Statement for the Record on the Terrorist Threat Confronting the United States," before the Senate Select Committee on Intelligence, February 6, 2002, p. 1.
36. Ibid., p. 2.
37. Ibid., pp. 3–4.
38. Ibid., p. 4.
39. J. T. Caruso, deputy executive assistant director, FBI, "Statement for the Record on Al-Qaeda," before the Senate Subcommittee on International Operations and Terrorism, December 18, 2001, pp. 1–2.
40. Summary of classified report to the U.S. Congress, House of Representatives Intelligence Subcommittee, *Report on Intelligence Gathering and Analysis pre September 11, 2001*, July 16, 2002.
41. Electronic Frontier Foundation, *EFF Analysis of the Provisions of the USA PATRIOT ACT*, October 31, 2001.
42. "Terrorism Forces Renewed," *Portland Observer*, September 25, 2002, p. 1.
43. Ibid.

As society changes, so must policing change to address social, economic, and technological conditions.

—William F. Walsh

CHAPTER 2

POLICING TODAY

CHAPTER OUTLINE

Introduction

Community Policing

Compstat and Community Policing

Policing and New Information Technologies

Chapter Review

Key Terms

Notes

OBJECTIVES

1. Define community policing.
2. Describe the four-step problem-solving model called SARA.
3. Identify the problems commonly associated with traditional policing.
4. Define the concept of a problem as defined by Herman Goldstein in his book *Problem-Oriented Policing*.
5. Define the CAPS program.
6. Define Compstat and identify the core principles of Compstat as presented in the New York City model.
7. List the advantages of merging fundamental community policing philosophies with the Compstat process.
8. List and briefly describe some of the more common crime analysis techniques.
9. Describe a geographic information system and how such a system enhances police service.
10. Explain the impact of technology on the police.

INTRODUCTION

The failure of traditional law enforcement methods to curb rising crime rates during the 1970s and 1980s and to reintegrate the police with society gave rise to a new movement, generally referred to as **community policing.** One of the first major critics of the traditional policing model was Herman Goldstein.[1] In his classic work *Policing a Free Society,* Goldstein questioned the effectiveness of traditional police methods in safeguarding the constitutional rights and privileges celebrated in American society (e.g., freedom of speech and expression, due process, the right to privacy) versus the control of crime and the decay of social order. Goldstein pointed out that these two goals may be incompatible under the traditional police model and called for a closer link between the police and the community.

During the same time period, Wilson and Kelling's "broken windows" thesis emerged as a dominant theme in American policing debate.[2] Arguing that crime seemed to increase dramatically in neighborhoods where visible signs of social decay were present (e.g., graffiti on bridge structures, unkept lots with overgrown weeds, warehouses with broken windows), Wilson and Kelling suggested that the police needed to do more than just "crime control." Indeed, they argued that other functions of the police were as important, and maybe more important, than strictly enforcing the law and maintaining order. Police should focus more on a service orientation, building key partnerships with churches, youth centers, and other neighborhood groups in an effort to forge new alliances with the community. Crime was seen not as the sole purview of the police but rather an entire community responsibility. Police administrators began to look for new techniques and operational strategies that emphasized more service than arrest. Decentralization of services, characterized by storefront operations and neighborhood centers, began to be commonplace in police organizations. Old programs, such as the horse patrol and the "walking beat" officer, were reintroduced to American policing as ways to bring the police and the community closer together (see Figure 2.1).

Although Braiden[3] argues that community policing was "nothing new under the sun" because it only echoed the ideas expressed by Sir Robert Peel in the early 1800s, community policing did represent a refreshing approach to earlier problems. Community policing embraced the Peelian principle of police as members of the public giving full-time attention to community welfare and existence. Therefore, policing was linked to a myriad of social issues other than simply crime, including poverty, illiteracy, racism, teenage pregnancy, and the like.[4]

Although precise definitions of community policing are hard to find, it generally is an operational and management philosophy that is uniquely identifiable. Primarily, community policing was characterized by ongoing attempts to promote greater community involvement in the police function. For the most part, the movement focused on programs that fostered five elements: (1) a commitment to crime prevention, (2) public scrutiny of the police, (3) accountability of police actions to the public, (4) customized police service, and (5) community organization.[5]

Community policing advocates argue that **traditional policing** is a system of response; that is, the police respond to calls for services *after* the activity occurs. Police response is then reactive and incident driven rather than proactive and preventive. Further, a randomized motor patrol neither lowers crime nor increases the chances of catching suspects. Increasing the number of police, then, has limited impact on the crime rate because improving response time on calls for service has little relevance to preventing the original incident.[6] In addition, the role of the individual police officer is largely limited within the confines of patrol and response.

FIGURE 2.1

Officers interact with community functions in order to provide customized police services appropriate to the city area. In this case, an officer on horseback provides visible patrol for the congested areas of Manhattan.

(Mark Mainz/Getty Images)

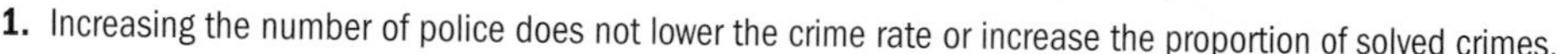

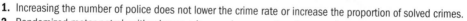

Quick Facts

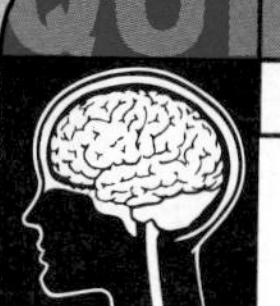

Review of Research on Traditional Policing

1. Increasing the number of police does not lower the crime rate or increase the proportion of solved crimes.
2. Randomized motor patrol neither lowers crime nor increases the chances of catching suspects.
3. Two-person patrol cars are not more effective than one-person cars in lowering crime rates or catching criminals; they are also no safer.
4. Saturation patrol does not reduce crime; instead, it displaces crime.
5. The kind of crime that terrifies Americans most (mugging, rape, robbery, burglary, and homicide) is rarely encountered by police on patrol.
6. Improving response time on calls has no effect on the likelihood of arresting criminals or even in satisfying involved citizens.
7. Crimes are not solved through criminal investigations conducted by police–they are solved because suspects are immediately apprehended or someone identifies them (name or license number).

Source: Adapted with permission of the Free Press, a Division of Simon & Schuster Adult Publishing Group, from *New Blue Line: Police Innovation in Six American Cities* by Jerome H. Skolnick and David H. Bayley.

Though community policing has *not* had the drastic effects its supporters had hoped, the premise behind the philosophy has in turn led to the quality movement within policing: making the police be more efficient and effective. Today most ambitious police methodology focuses on precisely that concept—Compstat. The word **Compstat** is derived from "comp," stemming from the word "computer," and "stat," which originates from "statistics." The process was originally developed in New York City by then-Commissioner William Bratton in the mid 1990s.[7] Compstat is a process that looks at the individual needs of the community and then designs proactive strategies to stop or prevent crime. To accomplish this goal, Bratton required his department to analyze crime data weekly and required New York police administrators to meet regularly to share information between divisions and precincts. A key component of Compstat is to force police administrators to address crime and social problems in their areas of responsibility and to address them immediately. Police administrators are then held accountable for the success or failure of their plans and decisions. Combining the two strategies of in-depth analysis with management accountability is the heart of the process.

Compstat focuses on using the most accurate and timely information and data available to the police, opening lines of communication both horizontally and vertically within the organization, activating the community at large, and improving the overall efficiency and effectiveness of the police. The long-term effectiveness of the Compstat process is promising, as communities such as New York and Los Angeles (now headed by William Bratton) have implemented the process and witnessed significant drops in crime.

COMMUNITY POLICING

Many cities have implemented a blend of community policing strategies with Compstat. To understand the merger of these important movements and the evolution of policing today, three historical case studies that highlight the evolution of the community policing philosophy are presented.

Newport News, Virginia

In 1983, under the direction of a new chief, Darrel Stephens, the Newport News Police Department developed a "problem-oriented" approach to policing. This innovative style of community policy focused on the department's traditional response to major, recurring problems. Its goal was to reassess the traditional, incident-driven aspects of police work and fundamentally change the way the Newport News Police Department viewed its mission. The resulting self-analysis yielded an important four-step, problem-solving methodology (commonly referred to as **SARA**) that has become an integral part of daily operations (see Figure 2.2).

Scanning: Instead of relying on broad, law-related concepts, such as robbery, burglary, and auto theft, officers are encouraged to group individual related incidents that come to their attention as "problems" and define these problems in more precise and useful terms. For example, an incident that typically would be classified simply as a "robbery" might be seen as part of a pattern of prostitution-related robberies committed by transvestites in center-city hotels. In essence, officers are expected to look for possible problems and accurately define them as part of their daily routine.

Analysis: Officers working on a well-defined problem then collect information from a variety of public and private sources, not just traditional police data, such as criminal records and past offense reports. Officers rely on problem analysis guides that direct officers to examine offenders, victims, the social and physical environment, and

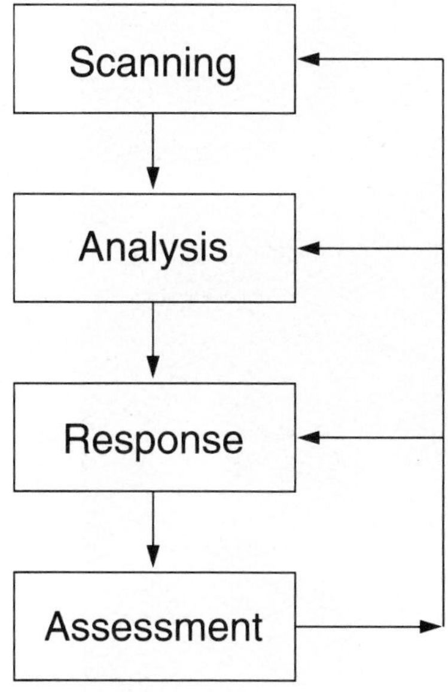

FIGURE 2.2

The problem-solving system used in Newport News, Virginia, Police Department.

(*Source:* William Spelman and John E. Eck, "Problem Oriented Policing," in *Research in Brief* [Washington, D.C.: National Institute of Justice, October 1986], p. 4)

previous responses to the problem. The goal is to understand the scope, nature, and causes of the problem and formulate a variety of options for its resolution.

Response: The knowledge gained in the analysis stage is then used to develop and implement solutions. Officers seek the assistance of citizens, businesses, other police units, other public and private organizations, and anyone else who can help develop a program of action. Solutions may go well beyond traditional police responses to include other community agencies and/or municipal organizations.

Assessment: Finally, officers evaluate the impact and the effectiveness of their responses. Were the original problems actually solved or alleviated? They may use the results to revise a response, to collect more data, or even to redefine the problem.[8]

Goldstein[9] further explains this systematic process in his book *Problem-Oriented Policing*. Destined to become a classic in the field, Goldstein's work attempts to give meaning to each of the four steps. For instance, a *problem* is expanded to mean a cluster of similar, related, or recurring incidents rather than a single incident. The assumption is that few incidents are isolated, as all are part of a wider set of urban social phenomena. Examples of such community problems are the following:

- Disorderly youth who regularly congregate in the parking lot of a specific convenience store
- Street prostitutes and associated "jack roll" robberies of patrons that continually occur in the same area
- Drunk and drinking drivers around the skid-row area of the city

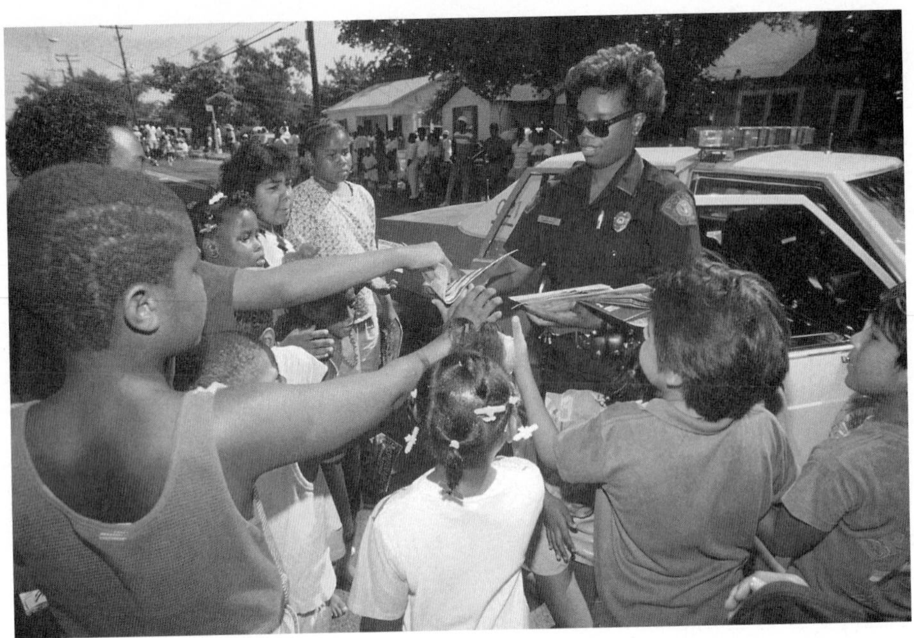

FIGURE 2.3

Officers focus on problem solving in traditionally high crime areas, such as low-income, densely populated urban settings. Providing quality policing and an improved image are important parts of the community policing movement.

(Larry Kolvoord/The Image Works)

- Panhandlers, vagrants, and other displaced people living on the sidewalk in a business district
- Juvenile runaways, prostitutes, and drug dealers congregating at the downtown bus depot
- Robberies of commercial establishments at major intersections of a main thoroughfare of a suburban area that is a corridor leading out of a large central city[10]

Note that each of these problems incorporates not only a potential or real crime but also a wider community/social issue. Further, each problem has been identified with a specific location. Goldstein[11] emphasizes that the traditional functions of crime analysis under the problem-solving methodology take on much wider and deeper importance. The pooling of data and subsequent analysis provide the basis for problem identification and response strategies. Therefore, the accuracy and timeliness of such information becomes a necessity for the department. However, the ultimate challenge in problem-oriented policing is not the identification of problems but rather the integration of the community with the police in developing effective ways of dealing with them (Figure 2.3).

Chicago, Illinois

In January 1993, Mayor Richard Daley and then–Police Superintendent Matt L. Rodriguez announced the first major operational changes to set in place community policing in the city of Chicago. The new program, the **Chicago Alternative Policing Strategy (CAPS)**, was designed to move the department from a traditional, reactive, incident-driven agency to a more proactive and community-oriented department. At first, CAPS was hailed as a method to combat crime, drugs, and gang activity in the

Quick Facts

The Newport News PD Website

The community policing movement stresses the integration of police with the community. Most departments, including the Newport News Police Department, utilize the Internet to encourage community participation.

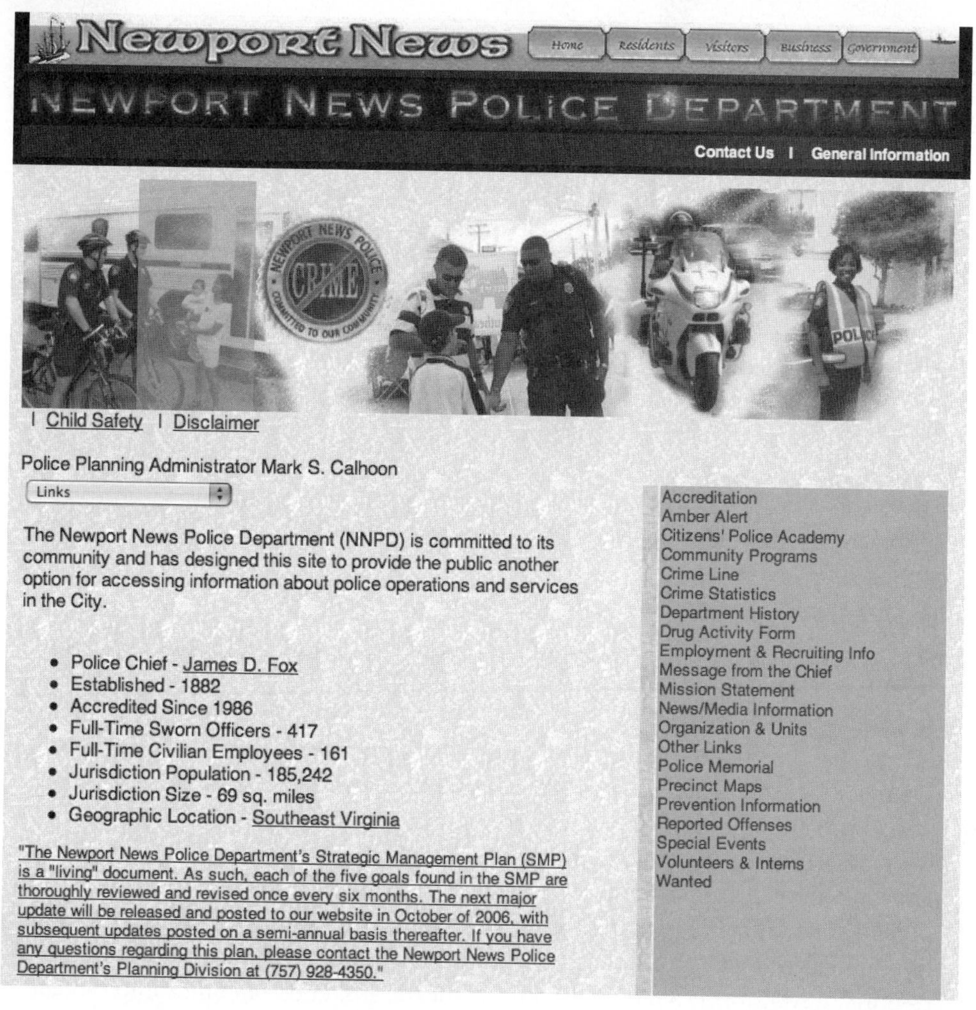

Newport News
Home
Residents
Visitors
Business
Government
NEWPORT NEWS POLICE DEPARTMENT
Contact Us I General Information
NEWPORT NEWS POLICE
CRIME
COMMITTED TO OUR COMMUNITY
POLICE
I Child Safety I Disclaimer
Police Planning Administrator Mark S. Calhoon
Links
The Newport News Police Department (NNPD) is committed to its community and has designed this site to provide the public another option for accessing information about police operations and services in the City.
• Police Chief - James D. Fox
• Established - 1882
• Accredited Since 1986
• Full-Time Sworn Officers - 417
• Full-Time Civilian Employees - 161
• Jurisdiction Population - 185,242
• Jurisdiction Size - 69 sq. miles
• Geographic Location - Southeast Virginia
"The Newport News Police Department's Strategic Management Plan (SMP) is a "living" document. As such, each of the five goals found in the SMP are thoroughly reviewed and revised once every six months. The next major update will be released and posted to our website in October of 2006, with subsequent updates posted on a semi-annual basis thereafter. If you have any questions regarding this plan, please contact the Newport News Police Department's Planning Division at (757) 928-4350."
Accreditation
Amber Alert
Citizens' Police Academy
Community Programs
Crime Line
Crime Statistics
Department History
Drug Activity Form
Employment & Recruiting Info
Message from the Chief
Mission Statement
News/Media Information
Organization & Units
Other Links
Police Memorial
Precinct Maps
Prevention Information
Reported Offenses
Special Events
Volunteers & Interns
Wanted

Source: www.newport-news.va.us/police/index.htm.

inner city. However, as the implementation plan unfolded, a much broader mission statement evolved that focused on a combined effort with the community to "identify and solve problems of crime and disorder and to improve the quality of life in all of Chicago's neighborhoods."[12]

As in many large cities implementing community policing in the past five years, Chicago developed five prototype districts to serve as "laboratories" for testing new police ideas, innovations, and strategies (see Figure 2.4).

These districts could then refine the successful new programs and hence improve the CAPS model. Essentially, the new CAPS program echoed the methodology for implementing community policing in several other large metropolitan cities. For instance, in Houston, Texas, and New York City, under the direction of then-Commissioner Lee P. Brown, the transition to community policing occurred only in

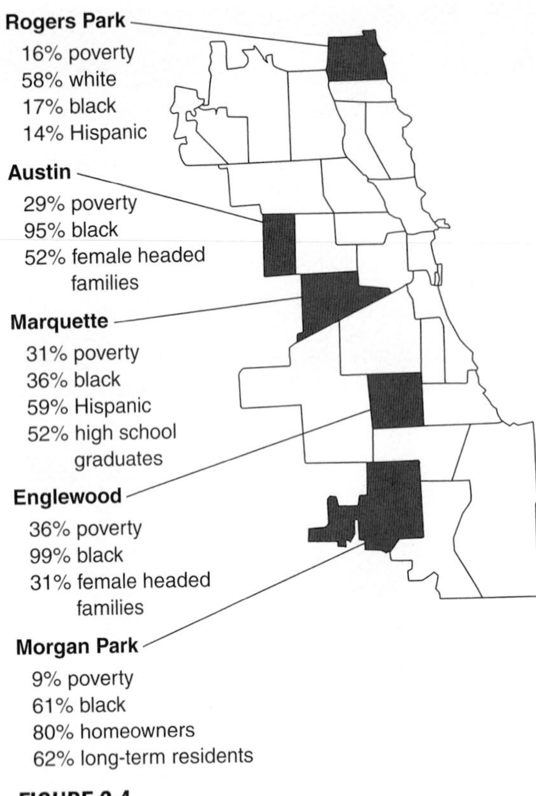

FIGURE 2.4

Chicago's five experimental districts.

(*Source:* Susan M. Harnett and Wesley G. Skogan, "Community Policing: Chicago's Experience," *NIJ Journal* [April 1999]: 3)

select neighborhoods or districts. Similar programs evolved in Phoenix, Arizona; Miami, Florida; Philadelphia, Pennsylvania; and Newark, New Jersey. Only a few cities have attempted to implement community policing strategies on a department-wide basis (Portland, Oregon, and Baltimore, Maryland). Most cities, and particularly large metropolitan communities, have realized that the implementation of community policing demands dramatic modification in the existing philosophy, structure, operation, and deployment of police.[13] The gradual evolution toward full-scale adoption essentially continues to redefine both the means and ends of community policing.[14]

CAPS has a number of key features aimed at improving and expanding the overall quality of police services in the city of Chicago, as well as reducing crime.[15] These key features are the following:

Crime control and prevention—CAPS emphasizes both crime control and crime prevention. Vigorous and impartial enforcement of the law, rapid response to serious crimes and life-threatening emergencies, and proactive problem solving with the community are the foundations of the city's policing strategy.

Neighborhood orientation—CAPS gives special attention to the residents and problems of specific neighborhoods, which demands that officers know their beats (i.e., crime trends, hot spots, and community organizations and resources) and develop partnerships with the community to solve problems. Beat officers work the same beat on the same watch every day, so they can more intimately know the beat's residents, its chronic crime problems, and the best strategies for solving those problems.

Increased geographic responsibility—CAPS involves organizing police services so that officers are responsible for crime control in a specific area or beat. A new district organizational structure using rapid-response cars to handle emergency calls allows newly created beat teams to engage in community policing activities. The beat teams share responsibility for specific areas under the leadership of a supervisory beat sergeant.

Structured response to calls for police service—A system of differential responses to citizen calls frees beat team officers from the continuous demands of 911 calls. Emergency calls are handled primarily by rapid-response sector cars, whereas non-emergency and routine calls are handled by beat officers or by telephone callback contacts. Sector officers also attend to community matters, and sector and beat teams rotate, so that all officers participate in community policing.

Proactive, problem-solving approach—CAPS focuses on the causes of neighborhood problems rather than on discrete incidents of crime or disturbances. Attention is given to the long-term prevention of these problems and to the signs of community disorder and decay that are associated with crime (e.g., drug houses, loitering youth, and graffiti).

Combined community and city resources for crime prevention and control—CAPS assumes that police alone cannot solve the crime problem and that they depend on the community and other city agencies to achieve success. Hence, part of the beat officer's new role is to broker community resources and to draw on other city agencies to identify and respond to local problems. Mayor Daley has made CAPS a priority of all city agencies. Hence, the mayor's office ensures that municipal agencies are responsive to requests for assistance from beat officers.

Emphasis on crime and problem analysis—CAPS requires more efficient data collection and analysis to identify crime patterns and to target areas that demand police attention. Emphasis is placed on crime analysis at the district level, and beat information is recorded and shared among officers and across watches or shifts. To accomplish such a task, each district has implemented a local area network of advanced computer workstations employing a crime analysis system called ICAM (Information Collection for Automated Mapping). This new technology allows beat officers and other police personnel to analyze and map crime hot spots, to track other neighborhood problems, and to share this information with the community.

Training—The Chicago Police Department has made a significant commitment to training police personnel and the community in the CAPS philosophy and program. Intensive training on problem solving and community partnerships is being provided to district patrol officers and their supervisors. Innovative classroom instruction for the community and a program of joint police–community training have also been developed.

Communication and marketing—The Chicago Police Department is dedicated to communicating the CAPS philosophy to all members of the department and the community. This is a fundamental strategy of the CAPS program. To ensure such communication, an intensive marketing program has been adopted that includes a newsletter, roll-call training, a regular cable television program, information exchanges via computer technology (Internet and fax machines), and various brochures and videos. Feedback is collected through personal interviews, focus groups, community surveys, a CAPS hotline, and several suggestion boxes. The information collected through this marketing program assists in the refinement and development of the CAPS program.

Evaluation, strategic planning, and organizational change—The CAPS program is undergoing one of the most thorough evaluations of any community policing initiative in the United States. A consortium of four major Chicago-area universities

(Northwestern, DePaul, Loyola, and the University of Illinois at Chicago) is conducting an evaluation of the process and results in the prototype districts.

CAPS represents one of the largest and most comprehensive community policing initiatives in the country (see Figure 2.5). During its first year of operation, preliminary

Chicago's community policing effort is more extensive and more organized than programs in most other jurisdictions, and it permeates the city to a greater extent than in most others. Below is an "at a glance" description of a typical, more limited program compared to Chicago's program.

Chicago's Community Policing Model

Police

- The entire patrol division is involved.
- The program is fully staffed with permanent officers on regular shifts.
- Extensive training is given to both officers and supervisors.
- All districts and all shifts are involved.
- Program activities are supervised through the regular chain of command and through standard patrol operations.

Residents

- Residents are expected to take an active role in solving problems.
- Residents are encouraged to meet with police regularly to exchange information and report on actions taken.
- Public priorities play an important role in setting beat team priorities.
- Residents receive training in Chicago's problem-solving model.

Municipal Services

- Management systems are in place to trigger a rapid response to service requests.
- Agencies are held accountable by the mayor for the effectiveness of their response.
- Community policing is the entire city's program, not the police department's program.

More Limited Community Policing Model

Police

- Small units are staffed by officers who have volunteered for a community policing assignment.
- Officers work overtime and are usually paid with temporary federal funding.
- Officers work on evening shift only.
- Little training is provided; officers' personal motivation propels the program.
- Officers are assigned only to selected areas.
- Program activities are supervised by the chief's office or from outside the routine command structure.

Residents

- Residents are asked to be the police department's "eyes and ears."
- Surveys or postcards are distributed to residents as a way of gathering information.
- Residents are called to meet occasionally, to publicize the program.
- Residents have no role in setting police priorities or operations.

Municipal Services

- Service agencies have no special responsibility to police or citizen groups.
- Service agencies believe community policing is the police department's program and should be funded by the police department's budget.

FIGURE 2.5

Chicago community policing at a glance.

(Source: Susan M. Harnett and Wesley G. Skogan, "Community Policing: Chicago's Experience," *NIJ Journal* [April 1999]: p. 8)

evaluation findings indicated that major crime and neighborhood problems were reduced, drug and gang problems were reduced, and public perception of the quality of police services were improved. Under this orientation, the community is viewed as a valuable resource from which powerful information and ties can be gathered. It aims "to increase the interaction and cooperation between local police and the people and neighborhoods they serve" to combat crime.[16] Hence, the major goals of community policing are not only to reduce crime but, more significantly, to increase feelings of safety among residents.[17] These two goals appear to be separate but are actually very closely linked in the community policing process. This approach attempts to increase the visibility and accessibility of police to the community. Through this process, police officers are no longer patrol officers enforcing the laws of the state but rather neighborhood officers. These officers infiltrate local neighborhoods, targeting specific areas in need of improvement. By involving themselves within the community, the officers are more available to meet and discuss the specific problems and concerns of each neighborhood and work to develop long-term solutions.[18] These solutions are the root of the proactive approach to policing. By listening to the public, the police will be better informed of the specific problems in each area. As cooperation between police and citizens in solving neighborhood problems increases, residents feel more secure.[19]

Critical Thinking Question

1. Discuss the concept of a problem as defined by Herman Goldstein in his book *Problem-Oriented Policing*. Do you think it is helpful for the police to think beyond the concept of a crime when discussing a specific neighborhood?

COMPSTAT AND COMMUNITY POLICING

Misunderstanding of the community policing philosophy has led some administrators to believe that community policing is somehow "soft" on crime. Nothing could be further from the truth, as community policing advocates argue that making police agencies more efficient and more understanding of quality-of-life issues increases arrest of violent predators and reduces overall crime. This is especially true with the application of new technology with the community policing philosophy.

Compstat is one such application. Originally started in the New York Police Department under Commissioner William Bratton, Compstat was a central theme of the Jack Maple novel *The Crime Fighter*, set in New Orleans.[20] Essentially, Compstat is a collection of modern management practices, military-like deployment efforts, and strong enforcement strategies all based on the availability of accurate and timely statistical crime data. Four core principles highlight the police department's model of Compstat:

1. Accurate and timely intelligence and statistical crime information based on geographical settings and/or areas. High-tech computer systems and geographical mapping programs are most helpful in providing the aggregate and individual data often required for effective Comstat efforts. However, more rudimentary aspects of visual crime analysis can be accomplished through daily pin mapping and bulletins.
2. Rapid deployment of resources, particularly combining the immediate presence of uniform patrol working in concert with directed undercover operations. Rapid deployment of other city and governmental resources, such as nuisance and abatement personnel, sanitation workers, and alcoholic beverage and licensing enforcement, is an additional aspect of this principle.

3. Effective tactics and strategies of enforcement that focus on visible street crimes or "quality-of-life" crimes, such as loitering, drinking in public, street prostitution, or even jumping subway turnstiles.
4. Relentless follow-up and assessment, which include placing accountability and responsibility not only on the individual police officer on the beat but also on individual police managers of traditionally defined areas, such as division heads or precinct captains.[21]

Minneapolis, Minnesota

Comparing the core principles of Compstat with the problem-solving model of Newport News, presented earlier, reveals a significant amount of similarity. Indeed, Compstat may well be the natural evolution of the problem-solving model in today's more sophisticated cities. While a number of jurisdictions, including Los Angeles, Philadelphia, New Oreleans, Albuquerque, Sacramento, Boston, and Dallas, continue to refine the Compstat principles, none has been more successful in implementing the process than the Minneapolis Police Department.

In Minneapolis, the Compstat program is referred to as **CODEFOR** (**C**omputer **O**ptimized **DE**ployment—**F**ocus **O**n **R**esults). This strategy is designed specifically to reduce crime and involves every geographical and structural unit within the Minneapolis Police Department. CODEFOR combines the latest technology in computer applications and geographical mapping with field-proven police techniques, such as directed patrol, safe streets, and "hot-spot" policing. Computer-generated maps identify high-intensity crime areas, and police resources are coordinated to such locations in a timely manner. Each week, police managers gather together and ask very directed questions regarding the crime rates in each of their areas. Colorful crime maps are projected on large screens, and computer-generated bulletins are passed out at the meeting.

Departmental executives and commanders grill precinct captains on the crimes in their areas. Precinct captains, while not expected to be able to eliminate crime entirely, are expected to articulate a sensible strategy for reversing a trend or eliminating a hot spot. In many cases, those leaders who repeatedly fail to rise to the occasion—not unlike what might happen to the manager of a struggling department in a corporation—have found themselves promptly reassigned. The process works, as police managers are held accountable for reducing crime in their areas. A more enlightened understanding of why the process works is that it gets the top police managers involved with crime once again. In addition to the solution of internal problems, attendance at community meetings, scheduling, and a myriad of other administrative tasks, managers are forced to direct their efforts to addressing crime in their geographical districts of responsibility. This emphasis on crime awareness and crime fighting has sparked renewed feelings of self-worth among managers as well as an increase in communication between the beat officer and the precinct captain. Everyone realizes that individual performance and success is dependent on their relationship and their interconnectiveness in addressing crime within the precinct. Obviously, a more team-oriented spirit naturally arises that increases morale and supports the primary goals of Compstat under the CODEFOR program (see Figure 2.6).[22]

The Minneapolis Police Department is one of the few departments not only to generate specific crime statistics each week by geographical area but also to use a much more refined process of tabulating success or failure. Interestingly, the reports are also provided over the Internet on a monthly basis for public consumption and evaluation.[23]

FIGURE 2.6

Officers work as a team to reduce problems in specific neighborhoods while other members of the community (such as the media) become integral partners in addressing overall crime issues.
(Chris Gregerson)

In The News

Today's News

The Impact of Compstat on Crime

The use of Compstat has been a very successful evolution in the community policing philosophy. Almost every jurisdiction experimenting with the Compstat innovation has witnessed dramatic decreases in crime. For instance, in 1993 the number of murder cases in New York City approached 2,000 (1,946). However after implementing Compstat in 1998, the number decreased to 629. In Philadelphia, the impact was also dramatic, reflecting murder rates that plummeted by more than 15 percent in the first year of Compstat implementation. In New Orleans, the city observed an unprecedented 24 percent decline in all violent crime after implementing Compstat. The pattern appears to be continuing as other cities initiate the Compstat model:

New York City (10 years, 1993 to 2003)	64 percent drop in crime
Philadelphia (7 years, 1995 to 2003)	24 percent drop in crime
Baltimore (5 years, 1995 to 2000)	31 percent drop in crime
Newark (6 years, 1995 to 2001)	51 percent drop in crime
Minneapolis (10 years, 1996 to 2006)	12 percent drop in crime

However, after several years of decline, the number of *violent* crimes (especially murder) appears to be rising nationally, reaching the highest level in a decade in some places. In 2006 in New York City the number of homicides (520) rose nearly 10 percent from the year before, and in Chicago homicides were up nearly 4 percent, reversing a four-year decline. Some cities such as Cincinnati, Oakland, and Philadelphia, recorded the highest murder numbers in their history. Houston attributed its 15 percent increase in homicides to displaced Katrina evacuees from the Gulf Coast. Interestingly, New Orleans had a decline in the number of homicides, down nearly 8 percent. Similarly, Los Angeles, San Francisco, and Dallas (all cities that have vigorous Compstat programs) reported lower homicide numbers as well.

Source: John M. Shane and John E. Ott, "Compstat Implementation," *FBI Law Enforcement Bulletin* (Washington, D.C.: FBI, June 2004), pp. 13–21; Associated Press, "Cities Report Rise in Murders," *Dallas Morning News*, December 28, 2006, p. 5A.

Merging Strategies

The major case studies presented (Newport News, Chicago, and Minneapolis) represent only three attempts to develop community policing and Compstat initiatives in the United States. Policing continues to develop and change; it is organic. As such, cities large and small are experimenting with best practices in attempts to improve the quality of life within the community. Compstat represents a natural evolution in the community policing philosophy. Essentially, the merging of Compstat with fundamental community policing methodologies maximizes the efficiency and effectiveness of a police organization.[24] Several advantages from this merging of strategies can be summarized as follows:

- *Compstat enhances communication between the police and the community.* The desire to bring the community and the police together is a common goal for both Compstat and community policing advocates. Information exchange is often the product of community policing efforts, especially focusing on quality-of-life issues as well as crime. Statistical exchange of information via Compstat provides a transparent and public view of just "how well" the police are doing on curbing crime in specific areas or citywide. Improving communication between the police and the community can only aid the police in acquiring accurate information and in implementing effective crime prevention and control policies.
- *Compstate improves communication within the police organization and between other organizations and agencies.* Compstat and community policing methodologies require that the police work hand-in-hand with other governmental agencies, non-profit organizations, and organizations in the private sector to address crime and disorder problems. An important part of the Compstat process is the sharing of information with other criminal justice agencies, at all levels (i.e., federal, state, county). Compstat meetings are attended by commanders of support units, local prosecutors, federal agents, and representatives of other criminal justice agencies, allowing information to disseminate widely to appropriate parties.[25] In addition, the sharing of information between organizations allows for more thorough and accurate data collection, which in turn helps accomplish the primary goal of Compstat—again, making the police more efficient and effective. In addition to improving communication between organizations, Compstat meetings are designed to open lines of communication with the police organization as well. The meetings are designed to flow in a vertical direction between managers, supervisors, and officers in a two-way direction. William Bratton describes this process as a "seamless web" which facilitates brainstorming, innovative problem solving, and the development of effective strategies and plans that *every* individual, unit, and function within the department participates.[26] This structure allows for all people at the meeting to contribute. Ideas and strategies formed in the meetings are products of a team approach and not the sole decision of a single administrator. Assignments and evaluation projects can then be assigned for future review and accountability.
- *Compstat is problem-oriented and preventive.* The problem-orientation requirements of Compstat stress the need to focus on problems rather than past incidents. In this manner, Compstat significantly departs from the traditional police model by taking a preventive approach rather than a more reactive, incident-driven approach. Hence, Compstat meetings tend to focus on an individual area or a community's problems with an eye toward remedying the situation or preventing future crime.
- *The Compstat process highlights managerial accountability.* Weekly Compstat meetings present an opportunity for police administrators to assess those in charge and the tactics or strategies that have been implemented to solve specific problems. Compstat meetings provide a forum for creating short- and long-term objectives and for holding area commanders (as well as individual police officers) accountable for crime levels, case clearance rates, and other crime and

quality-of-life indicators.[27] Certainly, the police are not the only element in reducing crime and improving the quality of life in a specific area. However, Compstat meetings provide a mechanism of peer review and reflection that quickly determines what works and what does not in achieving specific objectives in a given neighborhood. This process reflects a relatively new paradigm in policing: accountability and evaluation at all levels within the police organization.

- *Compstat is flexible and adaptive, with a focus on effectiveness.* If a specific tactic or strategy is not working, or as new problems become apparent and demands change, Compstat allows for adaptation. The focus of Compstat is on efficiency and effectiveness: collect and analyze accurate and timely data and information in order to identify specific problems in a specific geographical area, develop solutions to the problems, implement the tactics and strategies devised, and review/evaluate the results.

The Compstat process is not limited to large, metropolitan agencies. Indeed, Compstat can be implemented in cities of all sizes with diverse populations and varying crime rates. The process helps police executives clarify their agency's mission and focus its efforts on the most important issues first, identifying problems early and developing effective strategies for remediation and prevention. Most importantly, the Compstat process allows the organization to learn quickly what works and what does not, while providing a flexible methodology to try innovative programs and promising strategies.[28]

Critical Thinking Questions

1. Identify the core principals of the Compstat process. Why do you think the process appears to work—that is, reduce crime in most major cities where the program has been implemented?
2. Discuss the impact that William Bratton has had on Compstat. Search the Web to find out more about his career and the implementation of Compstat methodologies in the Los Angeles Police Department.

POLICING AND NEW INFORMATION TECHNOLOGIES

The evolution of community policing and as Compstat new methodologies for the police has included the development of sophisticated information technologies. Before the community policing movement, information technologies were best left to highly skilled technicians, separated from the day-to-day operations of the police. For the most part, information technologies were relegated to the collection and maintenance of vast amount of data. However, this role has changed as the tenets of community policing have emerged and the need to analyze crime data have become a priority. As Sparrow writes,

> *Now, information systems are the essential circuitry of modern [police] organizations, often determining how problems are defined and how progress is evaluated. They frequently help determine how work gets done, often who does it, and sometimes what the work is.*[29]

Information technologies have assumed a new and more vital role not only because of the development of community policing but also because of the passage of several federal initiatives, which often provided the financial assistance and support for such technologies at the local level. These new technologies—crime analysis, geographic information systems, artificial intelligence and expert systems, and Internet communication—are now central to the support of community policing and Compstat.

Crime Analysis

The statistical analysis of data and the organization of information into manageable summaries provide law enforcement with meaningful tools with which to combat crime. The crime problem has continued to grow in terms of quantity, sophistication, and complexity, thereby forcing police officers and investigators to seek additional help in enforcement techniques. The purpose of crime analysis is to organize massive quantities of raw information from data bases used in automated records systems and to forecast specific future events from the statistical manipulation of these data. In theory, **crime analysis** provides a thorough and systematic analysis of data on which to make rational decisions regarding past, present, and future actions.[30]

Crime analysis is not limited solely to reported crime information. Attention has also been given to the statistical analysis of intelligence information. Kinney[31] reports that criminal intelligence analysis can support investigators, decision makers, and policymakers in their attempts to prevent and control crime. The following are some of the more common crime analysis techniques:

- *Tactical crime analysis or crime-specific analysis*—a tabular or graphic display of reported crimes with a given pattern of time and/or location. It is often used to detect patterns of crime (e.g., robberies, burglaries, auto thefts) that cluster in specific locations during various time periods. The focus of tactical crime analysis is on recent criminal incidents through the examination of characteristics such as how, when, and where the activity has occurred in order to aid suspect identification and case clearance.[32]
- *Strategic crime analysis*—the study of crime and/or social problems in a specific area in an effort to determine long-term patterns of activity as well as to evaluate police responses and organizational procedures.[33] Strategic crime analysis is often used to determine the effectiveness of police over a given period of time.
- *Link analysis*—a graphic portrayal of associations and relationships among people, organizations, events, activities, and locations from a given point in time. This technique is a powerful analytic tool used to reveal the hidden connections among criminals and the structure of clandestine, organized criminal entities often found in street gangs, La Cosa Nostra families, white-collar crime syndicates, large drug trafficking cartels, and terrorist organizations. Link analysis is invaluable in complex investigations, particularly those that have a "conspiracy" aspect, as is often found in racketeering and continuing criminal enterprise cases.
- *Telephone toll analysis*—computerized reports derived from court-ordered long-distance telephone billings of suspects in illegal narcotics trafficking. Reports indicate the number and frequency of calls displayed in numerical, chronological, and geographical order. Link analysis can be used to show the relationship between billing numbers and the numbers called.[34]
- *Visual investigative analysis (VIA)*—charting that depicts key events of criminal activity in chronological order. VIA is used to show the degree of involvement of subjects. This method is especially convincing in conspiracy cases and can also be used as a planning tool to focus the resources of an investigative effort.[35] At a conference focusing on school shootings, a graphical VIA was presented on the

Virginia Tech University shooting incident.[36] Interestingly, the VIA effort displayed a horizontal graph, over 60 feet long, with over 1,200 entries.

- *Case analysis and management system (CAMS)*—computerized case management in which large amounts of data are compiled and indexed for each retrieval of specific items. This system is used to clarify relationships and to calculate the probability of associations.[37]
- *Intelligence analysis*—the identification of networks of offenders and criminal activity, often associated with organized crime, gangs, drug traffickers, prostitution rings, and terrorist organizations. Recent interest in intelligence analysis has given rise to the development of large, centralized intelligence processing hubs, referred to as fusion centers. The national focus on terrorism has produced significant interest in this process, forming the base of what is commonly called "intelligence-led policing," discussed much more thoroughly in Chapter 3, Intelligence, Terrorism and Homeland Security.

Crime analysis is a flexible and dynamic process designed primarily to identify trends and patterns associated with crime and social problems. It is designed to be a perpetual and continuous process and to assist law enforcement executives in making more informed decisions in their response to crime. The technology of crime analysis

Focus on Policy

Crime Analysis and Compstat—Dallas, Texas

A vital part of the Compstat process is the ability to continually monitor crime and other problems in a specific geographical region. This task requires the ongoing ability to assess reported crime in comparison to previous time periods at the smallest reporting districts or beats within a division.

The Dallas Police Department continually monitors all patrol areas for the entire city, as well as for each of its six operational divisions—Central, North Central, Northeast, Northwest, Southeast, and Southwest—on a monthly basis, tracking the following variables:

- Emergency calls and response time in minutes
- Victimization rates
- Investigative clearance rates
- Violent crimes
- Property crimes
- Arrests
- Drug and prostitution arrests
- Risk
- Complaints
- Field activities
- Division strength

Mandatory Compstat meetings are held once a week (Thursday mornings) for commanders and shift supervisors, where commanders are often asked direct questions relating to the rise or fall of these variables in their division. Often, a special focus and review is placed on one division and one area that may be composed of several beats.

In this example, for the week of 12/07/05 to 01/03/06, note the significant increase in violent crime (up 20 percent) and the corresponding increase in aggravated assaults (up 50 percent), the increase in shots fired calls (up 46 percent) and the number of firearms seizures (up 120 percent) from the previous year. During the Compstat meeting, the division commander was asked to explain the sudden increase. Her answer corresponded with significant research showing that the number of domestic assaults (usually categorized as aggravated assaults) dramatically rise during the Christmas and New Year holiday season as families come together for celebration, sometimes engaging in significant alcohol and drug abuse. In such cases, the police have very little impact in terms of prevention.

Compstat
Northwest Operations Division
12/07/05 - 01/03/06

		City Council Districts		Division Demographics
Bureau Commander Rank: Division Commander Rank:	Daniel Garcia Assistant Chief Cynthia Villarreal Deputy Chief	District 2 Pauline Medrano District 3 Ed Oakley District 6 Steve Salazar	District 13 Mitchell Rasansky District 14 Angela Hunt	Population: 127,761 Area: 48.64 sq. mi.

EMERGENCY CALLS - Average Response Time to Citizen in Minutes

	12/07/05 TO 1/3/2006	11/09/05 TO 12/6/2005	% Change	YTD 2006	YTD 2005	% Change
Division	8.5	8.1	4%	8.9	10.0	-11%
Bureau	8.5	8.1	6%	9.4	10.8	-13%
City	8.4	8.4	1%	8.6	9.7	-11%

Investigative Unit Clearance Rates

	DEC, 2005	NOV, 2005	YTD 2005	YTD 2004
Residence Burg	0.00%	8.93%	7.78%	9.54%
Business Burg	0.00%	8.26%	5.89%	6.08%
Burg of Motor Veh	0.00%	5.90%	8.59%	8.67%
Theft	0.00%	36.99%	31.05%	31.84%

Victimization Rates-Crimes per 1000 population (adjusted for annual comparison)

	12/07/05- 1/3/2006	11/09/05- 12/6/2005	% Change	YTD 2006	YTD 2005	% Change
Violent	17.4	14.5	20%	28.6	32.4	-12%
Property	94.1	93.0	1%	89.5	91.4	-2%

	Hot Beats - Period Ending 01/03/06	Hot Beats - Period Ending 12/06/05
Violent	1. Beat 536- 17 Crimes	1. Beat 554- 12 Crimes
	2. Beat 537- 17 Crimes	2. Beat 535- 11 Crimes
	3. Beat 541- 14 Crimes	3. Beat 541- 11 Crimes
Property	1. Beat 541- 101 Crimes	1. Beat 541- 105 Crimes
	2. Beat 542- 68 Crimes	2. Beat 542- 69 Crimes
	3. Beat 535- 43 Crimes	3. Beat 535- 50 Crimes

CRIME STATISTICS for Period ending 01/03/06

VIOLENT CRIMES	12/07/05 TO 1/3/2006	11/09/05 TO 12/6/2005	% Change	11/09/05 TO 12/6/2005	10/12/05 TO 11/8/2005	% Change	YTD 2006	YTD 2005	% Change	YTD 2006	YTD 2004	% Change
HOMICIDE	3	1	200%	1	2	-50%	0	0	N.C.*	0	0	N.C.*
SEXUAL ASSAULT	2	3	-33%	3	4	-25%	0	2	-100%	0	1	-100%
BUSINESS ROBBERY	17	19	-11%	19	11	73%	3	0	N.C.*	3	0	N.C.*
INDIVIDUAL ROBBERY	65	63	3%	63	73	-14%	12	12	0%	12	9	33%
AGGRAVATED ASSAULT	84	56	50%	56	81	-31%	15	20	-25%	15	21	-29%
TOTAL VIOLENT	171	142	20%	142	171	-17%	30	34	-12%	30	31	-3%

PROPERTY CRIMES	12/07/05 TO 1/3/2006	11/09/05 TO 12/6/2005	% Change	11/09/05 TO 12/6/2005	10/12/05 TO 11/8/2005	% Change	YTD 2006	YTD 2005	% Change	YTD 2006	YTD 2004	% Change
BUSINESS BURGLARY	134	102	31%	102	123	-17%	13	18	-28%	13	20	-35%
RESIDENCE BURGLARY	90	98	-8%	98	83	18%	9	13	-31%	9	8	13%
SHOPLIFT	61	66	-8%	66	65	2%	8	6	33%	8	9	-11%
BMV & AUTO ACC	311	295	5%	295	289	2%	36	32	13%	36	58	-38%
OTHER THEFT	136	182	-25%	182	149	22%	12	16	-25%	12	27	-56%
AUTO THEFT	190	168	13%	168	176	-5%	16	11	45%	16	23	-30%
TOTAL PROPERTY	922	911	1%	911	885	3%	94	96	-2%	94	145	-35%
TOTAL PART I	1093	1053	4%	1053	1056	0%	124	130	-5%	124	176	-30%

SHOTS FIRED CALLS	131	90	46%	90	94	-4%	27	34	-21%	27	33	-18%
CRIMES INVOLVING FIREARMS	77	60	28%	60	72	-17%	22	13	69%	22	8	175%
FIREARMS SEIZURES	11	5	120%	5	8	-38%	3	2	50%	3	0	N.C.*
WEAPON ARRESTS(POSSESSION)	18	23	-22%	23	7	229%	3	1	200%	3	0	N.C.*

Data in this report is gathered from several D. P. D. databases and the accuracy of the report is dependent upon the accuracy of those databases

Crime data is based on date of occurrence

*N.C. - Not Calculable

This Report is prepared for COMPSTAT purposes only

Date: 1/4/2006

Northwest Operations Division
Page 2

ARREST STATISTICS for period ending 01/03/06

ARRESTS	12/07/05 TO 1/3/2006	11/09/05 TO 12/6/2005	% Change	11/09/05 TO 12/6/2005	10/12/05 TO 11/8/2005	% Change	YTD 2006	YTD 2005	% Change	YTD 2006	YTD 2004	% Change
HOMICIDE	0	0	N.C.*	0	0	N.C.*	0	0	N.C.*	0	0	N.C.*
SEXUAL ASSAULT	0	0	N.C.*	0	1	-100%	0	0	N.C.*	0	0	N.C.*
ROBBERY	1	8	-88%	8	3	167%	0	1	-100%	0	0	N.C.*
AGGRAVATED ASSAULT	9	8	13%	8	8	0%	2	2	0%	2	3	-33%
BURGLARY	3	4	-25%	4	3	33%	1	2	-50%	1	1	0%
THEFT	36	29	24%	29	25	16%	6	1	500%	6	1	500%
AUTO THEFT	9	15	-40%	15	17	-12%	1	3	-67%	1	0	N.C.*
TOTAL VIOLENT	10	16	-38%	16	12	33%	2	3	-33%	2	3	-33%
TOTAL PART I	58	64	-9%	64	57	12%	10	9	11%	10	5	100%
TOTAL ALL ARRESTS	576	711	-19%	711	687	3%	47	73	-36%	47	45	4%

RISK MANAGEMENT

	12/07/05-01/03/06	11/09/05-12/06/05	% Change	YTD 2006	YTD 2005	% Change
Pursuits	1	3	-67%	0	1	-100%
Traffic Accidents	0	1	-100%	0	0	N.C.*
Officer Shootings	1	0	N.C.*	0	0	N.C.*

FIELD ACTIVITIES

	11/09/05-12/06/05	10/12/05-11/08/05	% Change	YTD 2006	YTD 2005	% Change
Traffic Citations**	3091	3593	-14%	0	186	-100%
City Citations**	1061	1132	-6%	1	87	-99%
Traffic Stops	1682	1931	-13%	141	50	182%

COMPLAINTS

	12/07/05-01/03/06	11/09/05-12/06/05	% Change	YTD 2006	YTD 2005	% Change
Division Referral	2	2	0%	0	0	N.C.*
Phy Abuse/Ex Force	0	1	-100%	0	0	N.C.*
Alleged Criminal Activity	0	0	N.C.*	0	0	N.C.*
Administrative Inquiry	0	0	N.C.*	0	0	N.C.*
Accidental Discharge	0	0	N.C.*	0	0	N.C.*
Alleged Racial Profiling	0	0	N.C.*	0	0	N.C.*
External	0	0	N.C.*	0	0	N.C.*
Summary Discipline	0	0	N.C.*	0	0	N.C.*
Other	1	1	0%	0	0	N.C.*
Total Number	3	4	-25%	0	0	N.C.*

TOTAL DIVISION SWORN PERSONNEL

	PATROL	INVEST	ADMIN	ICP	OTHER	TOTAL
Assigned	**177**	**14**	**9**	**13**	**58**	**271**
First Watch	56	0	2	0	6	64
Second Watch	58	14	6	8	25	111
Third Watch	63	0	1	5	27	96
A-Time	0	0	0	0	0	0
Injured	1	0	0	0	0	1
Maternity	0	0	0	0	0	0
Temporary	17	0	0	0	13	30
Military	3	0	0	0	2	5
Total Deployed	156	14	9	13	43	235
Light Duty	0	0	0	0	0	0

TOTAL CIVILIAN STAFFING

Total Civilians Assigned to Patrol	9
Total Civilians Assigned to Investigative Unit	0

SICK/IOD/OT

	12/07/05-01/03/06	11/09/05-12/06/05	% Change	YTD 2006	YTD 2005	% Change
Number of Sick Hours	1426	1630.7	-13%		117	-100%
Injured on Duty Hours	0	0	N.C.*	0	0	N.C.*
Overtime Hours	1033.6	1734.9	-40%		124	-100%

Drug and Prostitution Arrests

	12/07/05-01/03/06	11/09/05-12/06/05	% Change	YTD 2006	YTD 2005	% Change
Drug	268	336	-20%	9	24	-63%
Prostitution	222	279	-20%	8	17	-53%

** Citations are compared for older periods because of database entry delay
Data in this report is gathered from several D. P. D. databases and the accuracy of the report is dependant upon the accuracy of those databases
Data on this page is based on employees of this division

*N.C. - Not Calculable

This Report is prepared for COMPSTAT purposes only

Date: 1/4/2006

takes advantage of research and statistical methodologies, often in an automated process. It does not necessarily have to be relegated to advanced statistical techniques, but it can be accomplished quite well with a basic understanding of Microsoft Office programs, such as Word and Excel. Indeed, Mark Stallo's inviting work focuses on developing a relatively sophisticated crime analysis model based solely on the application of Microsoft Office products to reported police data.[38]

Geographic Information Systems

The past decade has given rise to the integration of automated database operations, crime analysis, and high-level mapping. The merger of these powerful programs is commonly referred to as **geographic information systems (GIS)**.[39] Traditionally, map data and tabular data describing pieces of land, such as police beats, have been stored separately, but computer technology provides the opportunity to merge the two yet preserves their independent natures. Several PC-based mapping programs are making significant advances in the crime analysis field.

The technology of desktop mapping allows the display of geographical information (spatial data) on computer monitors—topography, natural resources, transportation hubs, highways, utilities, political boundaries, and police beats. Geographic information systems combine these spatial representations with almost any other type of data an analyst wishes to enter. Textual and tabular data (attribute data), such as population density, crime locations, traffic patterns, demographic profiles, and voting patterns can be displayed and manipulated against map backgrounds. From this type of analysis, it is possible to overlay multiple map sets, so that police researchers and executives can pictorially view the interrelationships among several variables. Thus, GIS technologies differ from previous types of crime analysis techniques and/or information systems in that their primary purpose is *not* purely cartographic, with emphasis on display and graphics, but rather the analysis, manipulation, and management of spatial data.

Geographic information system technologies have far-reaching implications not only in police operations as defined by crime analysis but also as management and communications tools. For instance, by integrating the mapping of GIS with the navigational properties of global positioning systems (GPS), a powerful vehicle tracking system can be developed. Using a PC-based software package, real-time tracking can be accomplished for under $1,000.

Police agencies can use GIS in dispatching police units by providing directions to locations; address histories; and locations of nearby fire and waste hazards, fire hydrants, alarm boxes, high power lines, water lines, and the like. Police managers can use GIS to provide graphic analysis of specific crime patterns, evaluate new policing strategies, and even track individual officer performance by area.[40] Not surprisingly, GIS have emerged as powerful tools helping police executives make better informed decisions (see Figure 2.7).

Artificial Intelligence and Expert Systems

Another type of information system having direct applications in law enforcement is **artificial intelligence (AI)**. Most definitions of AI vary to emphasize the interdisciplinary nature of the subject. Artificial intelligence is a science and a technology based on disciplines such as computer science, biology, psychology, linguistics, mathematics, and engineering. The goal of AI is to develop computers that can think as well as see, hear, walk, talk, and feel.[41] Basically, artificial intelligence can be defined as a shift

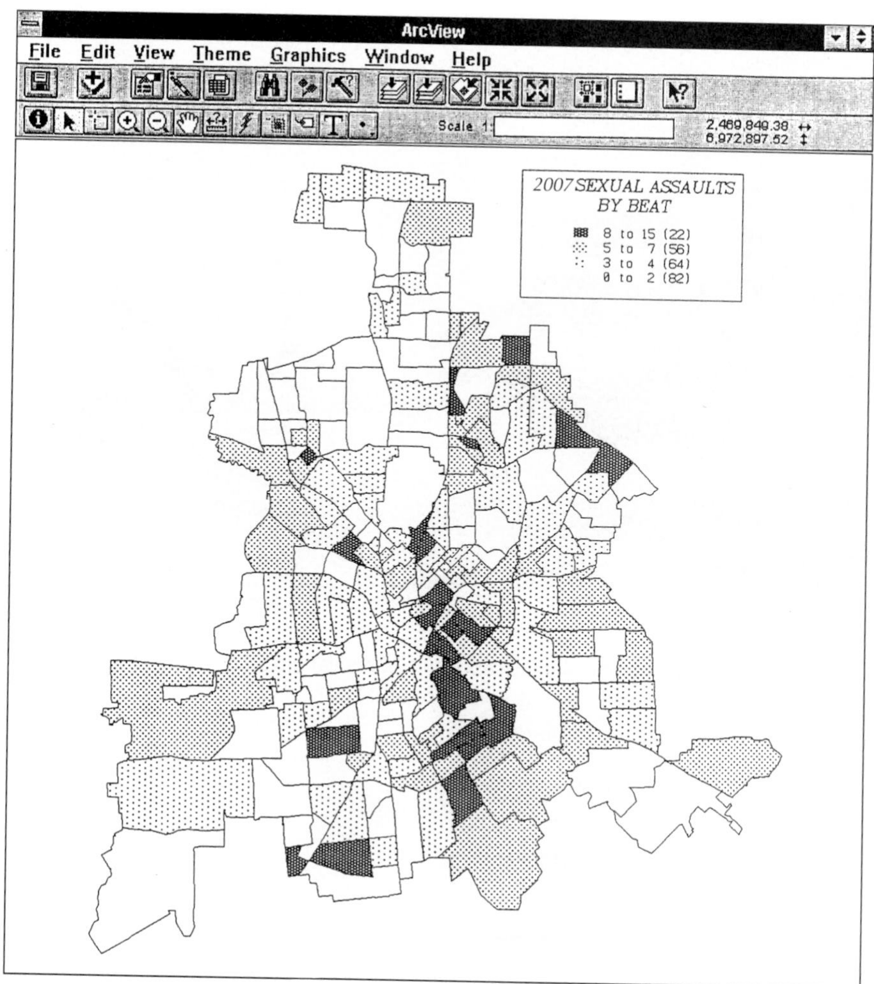

FIGURE 2.7

Geographic information systems (GIS) provide a wide array of maps and diagrams useful for crime analysis and decision making.

(Courtesy of the Dallas Police Department, Cpl. Chad Smith, Sgt. Terry Hill, and Lt. Todd Thomasson, 2007)

from mere data processing to an intelligent processing of knowledge. The model for such development is the human body and brain. Artificial intelligence focuses on four major areas of research:

- *Natural language applications*—systems that translate ordinary human commands into language that computer programs can understand and execute; computer programs that read, speak, and understand human languages
- *Robotic applications*—machines that move and relate to objects as humans do; programs that focus on developing visual, tactile, and movement capabilities in machines (see Figure 2.8)
- *Computer science applications*—development of more advanced, fifth-generation computers and the replication of physical brain functioning, such as that found in the human cell–computer interfacing and neural networks
- *Cognitive science applications*—programs that mimic the decision-making logic of the human brain, such as that found in expert systems, knowledge-based systems, and logic systems

Figure 2.9 provides a schematic view of the major application domains of AI.

FIGURE 2.8

One of the application domains of artificial intelligence (AI) (robotics) produces robots often used in law enforcement for special operations, such as bomb disposal.

(Photo courtesy of the Denver, Colorado, Police Department)

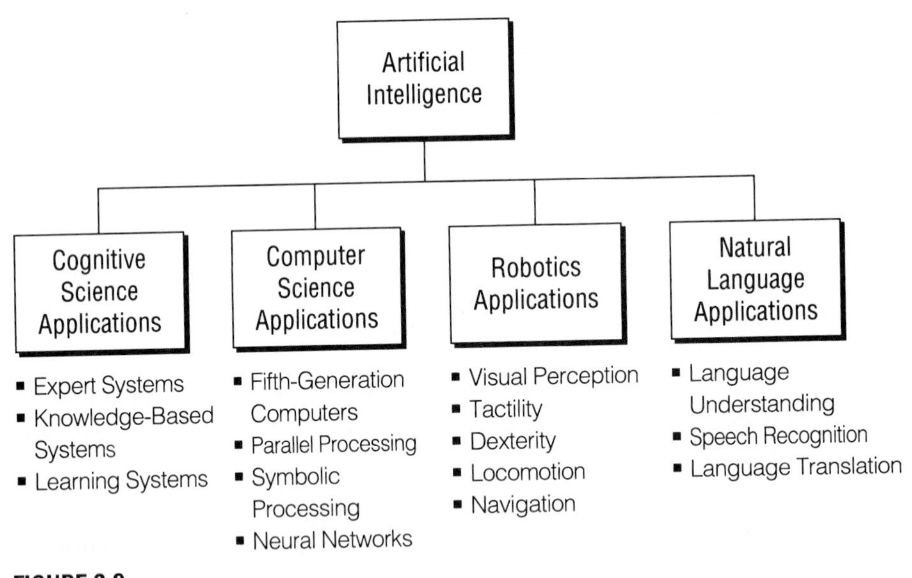

FIGURE 2.9

The major application domains of artificial intelligence.

(*Source:* J. A. O'Brien, *Management Information Systems: A Managerial End User Perspective* [Homewood, Ill: Irwin, 1990], p. 357)

It is this last area of cognitive science applications involving expert systems that police managers find most promising. Basically, expert systems attempt to supplant rather than supplement human efforts in arriving at solutions to complex problems. For instance, the state of Washington used a case analysis expert system to provide suspect profiles in the Green River homicide investigation. The Baltimore, Maryland, Police Department uses an expert system (known as ReBES—Residential Burglary Expert System) to assist in solving burglary cases.[42] The system correlates past suspect

In The News

Police Use of Expert Systems

New expert systems are being used in Phoenix, Arizona, to solve violent crimes. An expert system's matching and ranking capabilities, combined with the power of enlarging or narrowing the geographical scope of an inquiry, provide powerful tools for investigative analysis. In a crime scene scenario, for instance, with little or no evidence, an expert system can generate a demographic profile of a suspect based on variables such as type of crime, location, time of day, and method of entry (if applicable). The demographic profile can then be used to generate suspect lists while expanding or narrowing a geographical search based on similar criteria. In a like manner, the modus operandi (MO) of a particular crime can be used by the expert system to identify the set of solved and unsolved crimes with similar MOs. It is the expert system's ability to match the MO of crimes based on similarity that is so powerful, because it can take into account conflicting or incomplete information that conventional computer programs are hard-pressed to deal with effectively.

Source: Kevin J. Lynch and Frank J. Rogers, "Development of Integrated Criminal Justice Expert System Applications" (2006). See http://ai.arizona.edu/COPLINK/publications/develop/developm.html.

methods of operation with current burglary events to determine potential trends. About 25 specific items of information relating to a burglary are entered into the AI system, which provides a list of possible suspects, ranked in order of probability.[43] The Los Angeles Sheriff's Department uses a comprehensive data base called CHIEFS to aid in homicide investigations. Other expert systems are being developed within the FBI's Behavioral Science Unit in Quantico, Virginia, to support investigations of organized crime, narcotics, arson, and terrorism.[44]

AI development is not limited to traditional criminal investigations. For instance, in Chicago an artificial intelligence program is used to identify traits or behavior patterns shared by officers who have been fired for disciplinary reasons. The program, called Brainmaker, is being used by the department as an automated "early warning system" intended to flag at-risk officers before they commit acts that could get them fired or arrested.[45]

On a more mundane level, expert systems are also being used to assist local police managers with complex planning and task scheduling. However, their greatest benefit may be in changing the way organizations behave by promoting a different perspective on problem solving. In law enforcement, this approach requires creative and innovative police executives who challenge traditional assumptions concerning the police function and mission. Indeed, with the development of expert systems that attempt to combine textbook guesses about a specific problem, executives need no longer rely on their own intuition or inspiration. What may have worked well in the past may appear foolish when contrasted to solutions based on expert systems.[46]

The future of expert systems and other AI applications holds great promise for law enforcement as the price and power of computer hardware improve and the sophistication of software development increases. The trend is clear. Police administrators will be using more AI-based technology as decision support systems in both operations and management.

Fax Machines, Websites, and the Internet

Clearly, one of the most important technological advantages of the information age is the improvement of communication through the use of varied electronic media, such as fax machines and computers. This improvement can be directly linked to the vast improvements in the speed, processing, and access capabilities of the personal computer and various network technologies.

The simplest digital device capable of transmitting electronic information from point to point is the fax machine. When the fax machine was first introduced into policing, it was relegated to special transmissions involving the communication of suspect photographs and fingerprints between and within agencies. Now the fax machine is used in almost every aspect of police communication, from the standard transmission of police reports between precincts to the wide dispersal of suspect information. The FBI commonly uses fax transmissions of fingerprints for analysis in its lab. Local police agencies fax latent prints found at crime scenes to be compared to the vast inventory of prints held by the FBI in Washington, D.C.

In a survey exploring police computer websites and other online electronic services, several agencies reported extensive use of such systems.[47] For instance, three agencies (Alaska Department of Public Safety; Marin County, California, Sheriff's Office; and Newport News, Virginia, Police Department) reported frequent use of several different national services. The online websites most often used by police agencies are the National Criminal Justice Reference Service (NCJRS) sponsored by the National Institute of Justice, the International Association of Chiefs of Police (IACP) Net, the Search website, Partnership Against Violence Network (PAVNET), the FBI website, and the Metapol website operated by the Police Executive Research Forum (PERF). The NCJRS home page (www.ncjrs.org) acts as a gateway to various criminal justice agencies, shared information exchanges, other websites, and a host of research articles focusing on various aspects of the criminal justice system. In addition to these specialized websites, a number of "generic" online services (e.g., America Online) are also used by police agencies. These services are most commonly used for research on policies, trends, and other issues related to policing. Other applications include information exchange, electronic mail, data base access, downloading of software, online software support, legal research, file exchange, posting of information, and collaboration/networking with other agencies.

However, the electronic system used most widely by police to communicate more effectively on a global scale is the **Internet.**[48] The Internet is a worldwide network of computer systems and other computer networks that offers the opportunity for sending information to and receiving information from a vast audience from around the world. The unique benefits of the Internet are speed and efficiency combined with global reach. There are essentially no barriers to sending information and receiving information from as close as next door to around the world. Of particular importance to police agencies is the ease and speed with which information can be kept current. With the introduction of the World Wide Web, finding information on the Internet is very easy and user friendly. Several features of the Internet make it an ideal network technology for police and other criminal justice system practitioners:

1. The Internet acts as a gateway to a vast and varied array of information resources that may be physically located in distant repositories. Police agencies can access this information as well as establish worldwide communication links with other agencies.
2. The Internet facilitates dialogue among users and groups of users. Police agencies, for example, can "talk" to each other over the Internet, either directly or in dialogue structured and mediated by a third party. The Internet offers the capability of worldwide e-mail exchange.
3. Information can be downloaded (or transferred) directly to a user's personal computer, eliminating printing and distribution costs often associated with hard paper copies.

4. Relatively easy searches of vast amounts of data can be accomplished on a worldwide basis, providing immediate access to important information. For instance, electronic publications and research bulletins focusing on the police and the criminal justice system are now commonplace on the Internet. New research and findings are available online from the National Institute of Justice and from prestigious research facilities, such as RAND, Harvard University, and the Ford Foundation.
5. The Internet promotes communication and information exchange between criminal justice agencies and practitioners, a problem that has traditionally plagued criminal justice coordination. Users can engage in electronic discussions with one another, one on one or in groups.

Local police agencies have capitalized on the use of the Internet, with many departments establishing their own home pages. Several departments have encouraged their communities to keep abreast of police activities through the Internet. A list of emergency services and phone numbers, names and descriptions of the most "wanted" fugitives in the community, periodic updates on a specific (usually high-profile) case, employment announcements and opportunities within the department, residential and commercial crime alerts, and even online crime reporting are now available through various departments on the Internet. The home page of the Kansas City, Missouri, Police Department (www.kcpd.org) offers many of these services.

As worldwide communication and global reach via the Internet expand, policing will likely experience dramatic changes. As more agencies and individuals gain access, wider communication opportunities will exist. The United Nations recently linked various criminal justice research institutes from different countries, allowing for the first time a free exchange of information among countries on issues impacting the world community (e.g., international terrorism, environmental crime, gangs, and computer fraud). New and combined training sessions, various telecommunication partnerships, and interactive information exchanges will become commonplace on the Internet. The Internet should not be viewed merely as a "tool of the information age," however; in the past, some tools have been the catalysts for major changes in society. The greater access to information provided by the Internet has made a major difference in the future not only for police agencies and researchers but also for individual communities addressing wider criminal justice issues.

The Impact of New Technologies

Clearly, information technologies in policing have assumed a new and more vital role. They have taken on a new dimension, one that is central to the support of a new police strategy embraced in the tenets of community policing and Compstat.

Herman Goldstein, in *Problem-Oriented Policing,* described the wide range of "problems" that should receive police attention.[49] He made it clear that problems may or may not be crime-related. He also pointed out that varied dimensions of a problem must be identified by the police—geographical location, time, offender class, victim profile, behavior type, weapon, and other modus operandi elements (see Figure 2.10). The new task for information technologies is analysis, in addition to the storage and maintenance of information. The analytic support for community policing, however, must permeate the entire organizational structure and not be just a function of the crime analysis division. Information technology functionality must be much more flexible—ranging from support for quick, officer-level field inquiries to longitudinal mapping of a specific neighborhood to specific managerial performance measurements.

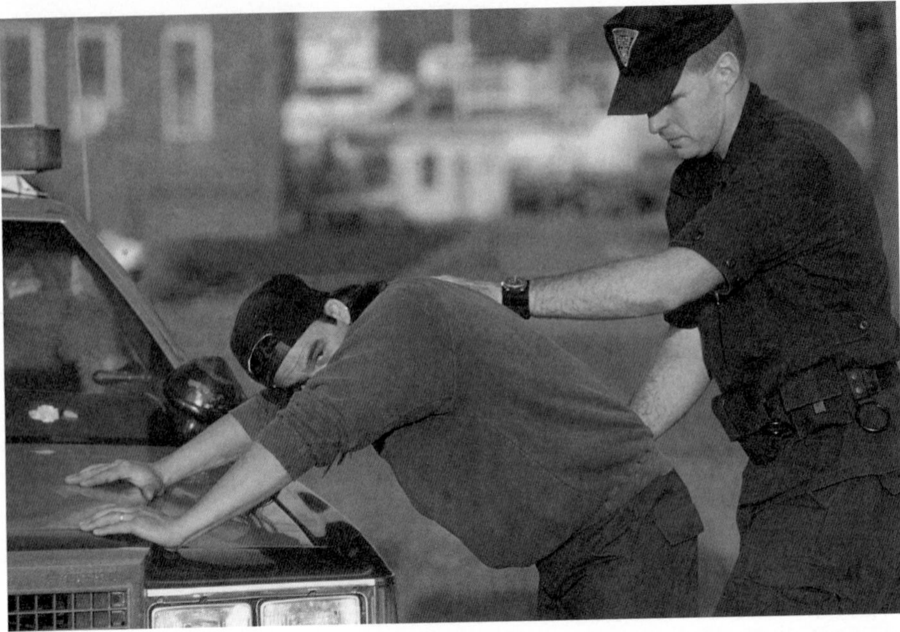

FIGURE 2.10

Officers patrol neighborhoods, focusing on crime control and high-order maintenance activities.
(Dorothy Littell Greco/The Image Works)

Information technologies can no longer be separated from the integral parts of police management. They can no longer be relegated solely to the storage, maintenance, and retrieval of vast amounts of police data. Compstat and community policing are information-based and information-intensive and require the ability to identify problems, suggest specific police responses, and evaluate their effectiveness. This function cannot follow the same information-processing path as before.

Today's police officers must be equipped with information and training. The job still requires the ability to relate to various people under strained conditions in often hostile environments. Compstat and community policing involves new strategies that call for individual judgment and skill in relating to problems that are both criminal and non-criminal. The police officer of the future must be able to relate to diverse groups of people in ways that stretch the imagination. To meet this challenge, police executives must ensure that three conditions exist. First, information technology development and design must support the emerging strategies in policing, particularly meeting the analytic demands embraced in community policing. Second, police officers and executives must manage technology rather than allow themselves to be managed by it. Finally, individual police officers must understand their role in the community as aided by, but not controlled by, the technological marvels of automation.

Critical Thinking Questions

1. What do you think the differences are between tactical and strategic crime analysis techniques? Do you think that Compstat emphasizes one type of technique? Why or why not?
2. Discuss the impact of crime analysis and geographic information systems on the Compstat process. What do you think has generally been the impact of such technologies on crime reduction? If you think that these technologies have helped the police reduce crime in major cities, why have crime rates been rising since the beginning of 2006?

CHAPTER REVIEW

1. Define community policing.
   Community policing was a relatively new movement in policing during the 1990s, focusing on a service orientation characterized by building key partnerships within the community and addressing a variety of social problems (e.g., poverty, illiteracy, racism, unemployment, teenage pregnancy) within a neighborhood other than just crime. Crime was not viewed as the sole purview of the police but rather an entire community responsibility. For the most part, the movement focused on programs that fostered five elements: (1) a commitment to crime prevention, (2) public scrutiny of the police, (3) accountability of police actions to the public, (4) customized and decentralized police service, and (5) community organization. Community policing is preventive, proactive, and information driven.
2. Describe the four-step problem-solving model commonly referred to as SARA.
   SARA is a continuous self-analysis model utilized in the problem-solving methodology. It is composed of four distinct parts:
   1. **S***canning: Identifying and defining "problems" in a specific neighborhood or beat*
   2. **A***nalysis: An examination of the problem in an effort to understand the scope, nature, and causes of the problem and formulate options for its resolution*
   3. **R***esponse: The development and implementation of solutions that are community-based and that may include other community agencies or governmental organizations*
   4. **A***ssessment: An evaluation of the impact and the effectiveness of the response*

SARA is reflective and cyclical, often leading to a refinement of the problem and reprocessing through the model.

3. Identify the problems commonly associated with traditional policing.
   The research on traditional policing has yielded the following problems:
   1. *Increasing the number of police does not lower the crime rate or increase the proportion of solved crimes.*
   2. *Randomized motor patrol neither lowers crime nor increases the chances of catching suspects.*
   3. *Two-person patrol cars are not more effective than one-person cars in lowering crime rates or catching criminals, and they are no safer for the officers.*
   4. *Saturation patrol does not reduce crime; instead, it displaces crime.*
   5. *The kind of crime that terrifies Americans most (violent crimes, such as muggings, rape, robberies, and homicide) is rarely encountered by police on patrol.*
   6. *Improving response time on calls has no effect on the likelihood of arresting criminals or even in satisfying involved citizens.*
   7. *Crimes are not solved through criminal investigations conducted by police—they are solved because suspects are immediately apprehended or someone identifies them.*
4. Define the concept of a problem as defined by Herman Goldstein in his book *Problem-Oriented Policing*.
   According to Goldstein, a problem is expanded to mean a cluster of similar, related, or recurring incidents rather than a single incident or reported crime. The assumption is that few incidents are isolated and they are part of a wider set of urban social phenomena. Hence, most problems incorporate not only a potential or real crime but also a wider community or social issue. Further, problems are associated with a specific location.

5. What was the CAPS program?
   The Chicago **A***lternative* **P***olicing* **S***trategy was the largest and most comprehensive community policing initiative in the United States. It represented a full-scale adoption of community policing with the following features:*
   - *Crime control and prevention through vigorous and impartial enforcement of the law, rapid response to serious crime and life-threatening emergencies, and proactive problem solving within the community*
   - *Special attention to building and identifying neighborhoods*
   - *Organizing police services so that officers were responsible for crime control in a specific neighborhood or geographical area*
   - *A system of differential and structured response to calls for police service*
   - *A proactive and problem-solving approach toward community disorder and decay that are often associated with crime*
   - *Combined community and city resources for crime prevention and control*
   - *More efficient data collection and analysis to identify crime patterns and target areas of concern*
   - *A commitment to training police personnel and the community on the community policing philosophy*
   - *A dedication to communication and marketing of the community policing philosophy*
   - *A commitment to evaluation, strategic planning, and organizational change needed to fulfill the community policing philosophy*
6. Define Compstat and identify the core principles of Compstat as presented in the New York City model.
   The application of technology to the community policing philosophy gave way to a process commonly referred to as Compstat. It is a collection of modern management practices, military-like deployment efforts, and strong enforcement strategies, all based on the availability of accurate and timely statistical crime data. The focus of Compstat is on making the police more effective and more efficient. The following are the core principles of Compstat:
   - *Analysis and manipulation of accurate and timely intelligence and statistical crime information based on geographical settings and/or areas, utilizing high-tech computers and systems*
   - *Rapid deployment of resources, particularly combining patrol with non-uniform agents within a specific area aimed at a specific target*
   - *Tactics and strategies of enforcement that focus on visible street crime or "quality-of-life" crimes.*
   - *Relentless follow-up and assessment that include placing accountability and responsibility on all levels within the organization (from individual officer to division commander)*
7. List the advantages of merging fundamental community policing philosophies with the Compstat process.
   - *The following are the advantages of merging the community policing philosophy with the Compstat process:*
   - *Enhanced communication between the police and the community*
   - *Improved communication with the police organization and between other organizations and agencies*
   - *A more problem-oriented and preventive focus on crime*
   - *A highlighted focus on managerial accountability within the police organization*
   - *A more flexible and adaptive process that focuses on effectiveness and efficiency*
8. List and briefly describe some of the more common crime analysis techniques.
   Some of the more common crime analysis techniques are the following:

- *Tactical crime analysis or crime-specific crime analysis's designed to detect patterns of crime that cluster in specific locations during various time periods; it is more concerned with recent criminal incidents in order to identify suspects and clear cases*
- *Strategic crime analysis studies crime and/or social problems in a specific area in an effort to determine long-term patterns and potential solutions.*
- *Link analysis is a graphic representation of associations and relationships between people, organizations, events, activities, and locations from a given point in time.*
- *Telephone toll analysis involves computerized reports on the number and frequency of calls to or from a specific telephone number.*
- *Visual investigative analysis includes charting the key events of a crime or criminal activity in a chronological order.*
- *Case analysis and management system analysis helps to clarify relationships and to calculate the probability of associations between people and events.*
- *Intelligence analysis includes the identification of networks of offenders and criminal activity, often associated with organized crime, gangs, drug traffickers, prostitution rings, and terrorist organizations.*

9. What is a geographic information system and how does such a system enhance police service?
The integration of automated data base operations, crime analysis, and high-level mapping programs is commonly referred to as geographic information systems (GIS). These new technologies allow the display of geographical information with police beats. The focus of GIS technologies is not purely cartographic, with emphasis on display and graphics, but rather the analysis, manipulation, and management of spatial data.
10. What has been the impact of technology on the police?
Information technologies have assumed a vital role in support of new policing strategies, such as community policing and Compstat. The merger of these two concepts has required a demand for accurate and timely data relating to crime and neighborhood problems. Information technologies can no longer be separated from the integral parts of police management. They can no longer be relegated solely to the storage, maintenance, and retrieval of vast amounts of police data. Fax machines, websites, and the Internet have vastly improved communication among criminal justice agencies. In addition, new developments in artificial intelligence, including expert systems and robotics, hold great promise for law enforcement application as the demand for decision support systems in both operations and management increases.

KEY TERMS

Artificial Intelligence (AI): Computer software systems focused on the intelligent processing of knowledge versus mere data processing; based on scientific disciplines.

CAPS: Chicago Alternative Policing Strategy; one of the largest and most comprehensive community policing initiatives in the United States, conducted by the Chicago Police Department during the 1990s.

CODEFOR: Computer Optimized DEployment—Focus On Results; one of the first experiments in the Compstat process, used in Minneapolis, Minnesota, designed specifically to reduce crime and improve the efficiency and effectiveness of the police department.

Community policing: a policing philosophy that focuses on general neighborhood problems as a source of crime; community policing is preventive, proactive, and information-based.

Compstat: a police methodology using the most accurate and timely information to identify crime and social problems within a given geographic area and then to develop strategies designed to stop or prevent them from occurring in the future; Compstat holds police administrators accountable for their decisions, tactics, and strategies aimed at reducing crime.

Crime analysis: the organization of massive quantities of raw data and information relating to reported crime in an effort to identify trends and patterns and then to forecast specific events from the statistical manipulation of these data.

Geographic information systems (GIS): the integration of automated data base operations and high-level mapping to analyze, manipulate, and manage spatial data, particularly relevant to crime analysis and forecasting.

Internet: a worldwide network of computer systems and other computer networks that offers the opportunity for sending information to and receiving information from a vast audience from around the world.

SARA: a cyclical, four-step problem-solving methodology designed to enhance community policing: **S**canning, **A**nalysis, **R**esponse, and **A**ssessment.

Traditional policing: a style of policing based on response to calls for service after the activity has occurred; traditional policing is reactive and incident driven.

NOTES

1. See Herman Goldstein, *Policing in a Free Society* (Cambridge, Mass.: Ballinger, 1977).
2. See James Q. Wilson and George Kelling, "The Police and Neighborhood. Safety: Broken Windows," *Atlantic Monthly,* no. 249 (1982): 29–38.
3. Chris Braiden, "Community Policing: Nothing New under the Sun" (Edmonton, Alberta: Edmonton Police Department, 1987).
4. Ibid. See Peel's Principle 7, as expressed on p. 2.
5. Jerome H. Skolnick and David H. Bayley, *Community Policing: Issues and Practices around the World* (Washington, D.C.: U.S. Department of Justice, 1988), pp. 67–70.
6. A number of researchers have documented the failures of traditional policing methods. Most notably, see A. J. Reiss, *The Police and the Public* (New Haven, Conn.: Yale University Press, 1971); G. L. Kelling, T. Pate, D. Dickman, and C. Brown, *Kansas City Preventive Patrol Experiment* (Washington, D.C.: Police Foundation, 1975); M. T. Farmer, ed., *Differential Police Response Strategies* (Washington, D.C.: Police Executive Research Forum, 1981); L. W. Sherman, P. R. Gartin, and M. E. Buerger, "Hot Spot of Predatory Crime: Routine Activities and the Criminology of Place," *Criminology* 27 (1989): 27–55; and W. H. Bieck, W. Spelman, and T. J. Sweeney, "The Patrol Function," in *Local Government Police Management,* ed. William A. Geller (Washington, D.C.: International City Management Association), pp. 59–95.
7. For a discussion of Compstat as a new police strategy to reduce crime, see William Bratton and Peter Knobler, *Turnaround: How America's Top Cop Reversed the Crime Epidemic* (New York: Random House, 1998); William Bratton and William Edwards, "What We Have Learned about Policing," *City Journal* (spring 1999): William F. Walsh, "Compstat: An Analysis of an Emerging Police Managerial Paradigm," *Policing: An International Journal of Police Strategies and Management,* 24, no. 3, (2001): 347–362; William F. Walsh and Gennaro F. Vito, "The Meaning of Compstat," *Journal of Contemporary Criminal Justice,* 20, no. 1 (2004): 51–69; John E. Conklin, *Why Crime Rates Fell* (Boston, Mass.: Pearson Education 2003).
8. The SARA methodology was adapted from William Spelman and John E. Eck, *Newport News Tests Problem-Oriented Policing* (Washington, D.C.: National Institute of Justice, SNI 201, January/February 1987), pp. 2–3, and Spelman and Eck, "Police and Delivery," p. 61.
9. Herman Goldstein, *Problem-Oriented Policing* (New York: McGraw-Hill, 1990).
10. This list was adapted, in part, from Goldstein, *Problem-Oriented Policing,* pp. 66–67.
11. Ibid., pp. 36–37.
12. City of Chicago, Department of Police, "Fact Sheet—the Chicago Alternative Policing Strategy (CAPS)," July 1995.
13. Arthur J. Lurigio and Wesley G. Skogan, "Winning the Hearts and Minds of Police Officers: An Assessment of Staff Perceptions of Community Policing in Chicago," *Crime and Delinquency* 40, no. 3 (July 1994): 319.
14. Mark Moore, "Problem-Solving and Community Policing," in *Modern Policing,* ed. M. Tonry and N. Morris (Chicago: University of Chicago Press, 1992), pp. 99–158.
15. The key features of the CAPS program presented in this text are adapted from Lurigio and Skogan, "Winning the Hearts and Minds of Police Officers;" p. 318, and Chicago Police Department, "Fact Sheet," pp. 1–2.

16. Stephen Mastrofski, Roger Parks, and Robert E. Worden, "Community Policing in Action: Lessons from an Observational Study," *Research Preview* (Washington, D.C.: National Institute of Justice, June 1998).
17. Ibid.
18. Quint C. Thurman and Jihong Zhao, "Community Policing: Where Are We Now?" *Crime and Delinquency* 43, no. 3 (July 1997): 554–564.
19. Mastrofski et al., "Community Policing in Action," p. 7.
20. Jack Maple, *The Crime Fighter* (New York: Doubleday, 1999).
21. Much of this section has been adapted from Raymond Dussault, "Maps and Management: Comstat Evolves," *Government Technology*, April 2000, pp. 1–2.
22. Interview with Chief Robert K. Olsen, October 7, 2002.
23. Refer to www.ci.minneapolis.mn.us/citywork/police/index.html.
24. For more information on the success of the Comstat program, refer to Raymond Dussault, "Maps and Management: Comstat Evolves," p. 2, and Marc Moore, "Best Practices in Performance Measurement Systems: A Review and Critique of the Original Version of COMSTAT," in *Recognizing Value in Policing: The Challenge of Measuring Police Performance* (Washington, D.C.: Police Executive Research Forum, 2002), pp. 175–80.
25. Vincent E. Henry, *The Compstat Paradigm: Management Accountability in Policing, Business and the Public Sector* (Flushing, N.Y.: Loose Leaf Law Publications, 2003).
26. Ibid.
27. U.S. Department of Justice, Office of Community-Oriented Policing Services, *Police Department Information Systems Technology Enhancement Project (ISTEP): Phase II Case Studies* (Washington, D.C.: Abt, 2003).
28. William F. Walsh and Gennero F. Vito, "The Meaning of Compstat," *Journal of Contemporary Criminal Justice* 20, no. 1 (2004): 51–69.
29. Malcolm K. Sparrow, "Information Systems and the Development of Policing," in *Perspectives on Policing* (Washington, D.C.: National Institute of Justice, March 1993), p. 1.
30. Several scholars have provided definitions of crime analysis. See J. B. Howlett, "Analytical Investigative Techniques," *Police Chief* 47 (December 1980): 42; Rachel Boba, *Crime Analysis and Crime Mapping* (Thousand Oaks, Calif.: Sage, 2005), p. 5; S. Gottlieb, S. Arenberg, and R. Singh, *Crime Analysis: From First Report to Final Arrest* (Monclair, Calif.: alpha, 1994); Mark A. Stallo, *Using Microsoft Office to Improve Law Enforcement Operations: Crime Analysis, Community Policing, and Investigations* (Dallas, Tex.: Act, Now, 2005).
31. J. A. Kinney, "Criminal Intelligence Analysis: A Powerful Weapon," *International Cargo Crime Prevention,* (April 1984): p. 4.
32. Boba, *Crime Analysis and Crime Mapping,* p. 14
33. Ibid., pp. 15–16.
34. D. M. Ross, "Criminal Intelligence Analysis," *Police Product News*, (June 1983): p. 45.
35. Ibid.
36. Incident occurring on Virginia Tech University, April 16, 2007 resulting in over 30 deaths from gunman, Seung-Hui Cho.
37. Ross, "Criminal Intelligence Analysis," p. 49.
38. Mark A. Stallo, *Using Microsoft Office to Improve Law Enforcement Operations.*
39. For background material on the development of GIS, see Roger F. Tomlinson and A. Raymond Boyle, "The State of Development of Systems for Handling Natural Resources Inventory Data," *Cartographica* 18 (1988): 65–95; Donna Peuguet and John O'Callaghan, eds., *Design and Implementation of Computer-Based Geographic Information Systems* (Amherst, N.Y.: IGU Commission on Geographical Data Sensing and Processing, 1983); Robert C. Maggio and Douglas F. Wunneburger, "A Microcomputer-Based Geographic Information System for Natural Resource Managers," unpublished manuscript, Texas A&M University, Department of Forest Science, 1988; Robert Rogers, "Geographic Information Systems in Policing," *Police Computer Review* 4, no. 2 (1995): 8–13; Mark A. Stallo and Jim Rogers, *Using Geographic Information Systems in Law Enforcement: Crime Analysis and Community Policing* (Washington, D.C.: COPS Office, 2004); Spencer Chainey and Jerry Ratcliffe, *GIS and Crime Mapping* (Washington, D.C.: COPS Office, 2005); Keith Harries, *Mapping Crime, Principles and Practice* (Washington, D.C.: NIJ, 2000).
40. For more information relating to the applications of GIS technology to policing, see Nancy G. La Vigne and Julie Wartell, *Mapping across Boundaries: Regional Crime Analysis* (Washington, D.C.: Police Executive Research Forum, 2001).

41. James A. O'Brien, *Management Information Systems: A Managerial End User Perspective* (Homewood, Ill.: Irwin, 1990), p. 356.
42. W. Coady, "Automated Link Analysis: Artificial Intelligence–Based Tools for Investigators," *Police Chief* 52 (1985): 22–23.
43. Edward C. Ratledge and Joan E. Jacoby, *Handbook on Artificial Intelligence and Expert Systems in Law Enforcement* (Westport, Conn.: Greenwood, 1989), chap. 8.
44. R. Krause, "The Best and the Brightest," *Law Enforcement Technology* 3 (1986): 25–27.
45. See "Artificial Intelligence Tackles a Very Real Problem—Police Misconduct Control," *Law Enforcement News,* (September 30): 1994, p. 1.
46. For more detailed information on this subject, refer to Robert W. Taylor, "Managing Police Information," in *Police and Policing: Contemporary Issues,* ed. Dennis J. Kenney (New York: Praeger, 1989), pp. 257–70.
47. The findings of this survey were reported by Gary Cordner, "Bulletin Boards," *Police Computer Review* 4, no. 3 (1995): 19–20.
48. Much of the section focusing on the Internet was adapted from G. Martin Lively and Judy A. Reardon, "Justice on the Net: The National Institute of Justice Promotes Internet Services," *NIJ Research in Action Bulletin* (Washington, D.C.: U.S. Government Printing Office, March 1996), pp. 1–7.
49. Herman Goldstein, *Problem-Oriented Policing* (New York: McGraw-Hill, 1990).

There is no priority higher than the prevention of terrorism.

—John Ashcroft

CHAPTER 3

INTELLIGENCE, TERRORISM, AND HOMELAND SECURITY

OUTLINE

Introduction

Terrorism, Intelligence, and Intelligence-Led Policing

Homeland Security

Political Violence and Terrorism

Chapter Review

Key Terms

Notes

OBJECTIVES

1. Explain the concept of a paradigm shift. What factors or events have caused the paradigm shift in policing?
2. Describe intelligence-led policing.
3. Define intelligence.
4. Describe the Intelligence Cycle as presented in the *National Criminal Intelligence Sharing Plan (NCISP)*.
5. Define a fusion center and briefly list its four primary goals.
6. List the four primary areas of responsibility within the Department of Homeland Security.
7. Define terrorism.
8. Briefly describe the concept of jihad and name some of the more radical groups active in the Middle East.
9. Define a hate crime.
10. Define an ecoterrorist.

INTRODUCTION

By the late 1960s, the decades-long movement to reform and professionalize police had reached a crossroads. The movement that began at the turn of the twentieth century with upper-class elites demanding an end to endemic patronage and political corruption had continued unabated through the middle of the century with the likes of O. W. Wilson and other police reformers who successfully centralized police organizational structures, improved the quality of police personnel, and implemented new and more efficient crime control tactics.[1] However, in the midst of spiraling crime rates and the violent rioting that had erupted within many of the nation's large cities, it became clear that the movement to reform and professionalize police had gone awry.

Calls from researchers and community leaders to "halt reform in its tracks" began with the growing recognition that, while the movement to reform police had worked to increase the status of the profession and to sever ties that had promoted political corruption, the process of reform had *also* resulted in a burgeoning rift between police and the communities they were supposed to protect and serve.[2] For example, reform and professionalization had resulted in police forces that had become unrepresentative and largely unresponsive to community concerns, and the costs associated with reforms in terms of rising salaries and growing benefits had become burdensome to inflation-weary taxpayers and budget-conscious city administrators. Communities—especially those within the nation's urban minority areas—had become increasingly alienated from the professionalized police.

Over the course of the ensuing three to four decades since community alienation initially became an issue, contemporary law enforcement administration has been engaged in an ongoing, evolutionary process of change toward strategies that seek to increase collaboration between communities and the police. Changes began to emerge during the 1970s with experiments in what was then referred to as "team policing," an attempt to mitigate street-level corruption and bridge the growing rift between officers and the general public (refer to Chapter 1, Historical Development).[3] By the early 1980s, police agencies were experimenting with foot patrol as a means of capturing some of the attributes of the old-style pre-reform "beat cop" who personally knew members of the public and was intimately tied to the precincts they patrolled.[4]

Likewise, during this period researchers and law enforcement administrators began to use the term "community policing" to describe a wide range of philosophies and tactics that challenged police to enact strategies intended to engage citizens and communities in the effort to control crime and community disorder (see Chapter 2, Policing Today). As the community policing movement took hold among researchers and police administrators, the belief that law enforcement could do more than simply react to ongoing problems and respond to citizen calls for service became accepted and proactive crime prevention and fear reduction strategies began to emerge (see Figure 3.1). Individual officers were being challenged with designing methodologies that identified neighborhood problems and providing innovative, holistic means of solving them. Businesses and residents became partners in the effort to curtail crime in any given neighborhood.

By the early 1990s, the widespread acceptance of the community policing model seemed beyond dispute, given survey results that indicated a strong willingness on the part of police executives to adhere to the model's dominant tenets and to implement strategies consistent with the philosophy (see Chapter 2, Policing Today). The new ideas of decentralizing services to neighborhoods, using storefront mini-stations, focusing on broader social problems and crime prevention, and holding the police accountable for their actions appeared to be working—crime in many of the largest cities began to drop. Indeed, the community policing philosophy became so pervasive that

DALLAS POLICE DEPARTMENT
Departmental Goals and Missions

- Continue to reduce crime: focus on guns, gangs, and drugs; year-over-year overall crime reduction of 10%
- Ensure Departmental integrity, accountability, and performance
- Ensure officer morale, safety, and training
- Become a leader in the use of technology for investigations, crime analysis, and criminal intelligence
- Reduce crime and prevent acts of terrorism via intelligence-led policing
- Continue to increase community partnerships and community involvement: the police do not act alone but must work in concert with the community and the rest of the criminal justice system
- Increase citizen satisfaction with public safety
- The protection of life and property of all citizens is the primary duty of the police
- Improve the quality of life for citizens, businesses, and visitors

FIGURE 3.1

These goals and missions are paraphrased from a number of sources within the Dallas Police Department. Like other large metropolitan police agencies, the department reflects the progressive shift in strategies, missions, and goals. Note the merging of traditional policing efforts (e.g., reduce crime, ensure officer safety) with community policing philosophies (e.g., ensure departmental integrity and accountability, increase community partnerships, increase citizen satisfaction, and improve quality of life) with a new focus on preventing terrorism via intelligence-led policing.

(Courtesy of the Dallas Police Department, Dallas, Texas)

police administrators who even suggested a different type of reform or concept were labeled stagnant and non-progressive.[5] Community policing became overly politicized and big business. Rather than calming the proverbial waters of debate concerning how the police should operate on the street, however, the emergence and wide-scale acceptance of the model seemed to have prompted *more* new ideas and additional strategies, including such things as the use of Compstat, directed patrol, hot spot patrol, and zero tolerance policing. While some have argued that a number of these newer strategies represent a shift away from the larger community policing model, the fact that new ideas continue to appear regarding how police should be managed and the manner in which they should engage citizens lends credence to the notion that policing is currently engaged in what organizational theorists refer to as a **paradigm shift**, or a period in which operational experimentation is challenging the established beliefs of a profession.[6]

If what has been occurring over the course of the past 30 years in policing can properly be referred to as a paradigm shift, then we need to consider how the wide variety of new philosophies, strategies, and tactics have or likely will impact police administration today.[7] This is particularly important, given the impact of September 11, 2001, and the critical mandate given to all police: prevent the next terrorist attack on our homeland.

TERRORISM, INTELLIGENCE, AND INTELLIGENCE-LED POLICING

The 9/11 attacks and the ongoing war on terror have demonstrated that terrorism respects no jurisdictional boundaries, whether these attacks take the form of aircraft hijackings, the use of biological agents, or more sophisticated attempts to infiltrate crucial infrastructures. This realization has forced local police administrators to focus considerable attention on the need to improve law enforcement intelligence operations. The notion that state and local law enforcement agencies must enhance their intelligence gathering and analysis capabilities represents a fundamental shift in the strategic dimension of local policing that involves making these agencies "intelligence-led" organizations reminiscent of the military model used for gathering, assessing, and distributing critical information.[8]

While much of the effort to reform intelligence operations after 9/11 focused on the need to restructure and better coordinate the intelligence infrastructure and model at the federal level, there has also been a significant effort to define the role state and local law enforcement agencies play in homeland security. **Intelligence-led policing** represents a collaborative enterprise based on improved intelligence operations stemming from community policing and problem-solving strategies. The concept is relatively simple: improving intelligence operations and capabilities at the local level enhances the proactive strategies of law enforcement agencies to respond to crime, as well as provides a mechanism for the discovery of potential terrorist plots to harm the United States. For intelligence to be effective, it should support an agency's entire operations. Crime detection, investigation, prevention, and deterrence must be based on all-source information gathering and analysis.[9] Good policing, then, is good terrorism prevention.

The introduction of intelligence-led policing in the United States has been somewhat problematic, as agencies wrestle with understanding their new role in collecting and analyzing intelligence relevant at a larger level while managing crime in their own jurisdictions. As a result, David L. Carter published *Law Enforcement Intelligence: A Guide for State, Local, and Tribal Law Enforcement Agencies* in 2004 to address some of these important issues. His work represents the state of the art in reflecting the thoughts of several federal and local initiatives, including the work of the Global Intelligence Working Group (GIWG) and the Major City Chief's Intelligence Commanders Working Group. One of the most important points of Carter's guide is that it stresses the *integration* of community policing philosophies, Compstat processing, and law enforcement intelligence gathering and analysis[10] (see Figure 3.2).

BOTH COMMUNITY POLICING AND ILP RELY ON:

- Information Management
  - Community policing–information gained from citizens helps define the parameters of community problems.
  - ILP–information input is the essential ingredient for intelligence analysis.
- Two-way Communications with the Pubic
  - Community policing–information sought from the public about offenders. Communicating critical information to the public aids in crime prevention and fear reduction.
  - ILP–communications from the public can provide valuable information for the intelligence cycle. When threats are defined with specific information, communicating critical information to citizens may help prevent a terrorist attack and, like community policing, will reduce fear.
- Scientific Data Analysis
  - Community policing–crime analysis is a critical ingredient in the CompStat process.
  - ILP–intelligence analysis is the critical ingredient of threat management.

Comparison of CompStat and Intelligence-Led Policing		
CompStat	Commonalities	Intelligence-Led Policing
■ Single jurisdiction	■ Each has a goal of prevention	■ Multi-jurisdiction
■ Incident driven	■ Each requires	■ Threat driven
■ Street crime and burglary	- Organizational flexibility	■ Criminal enterprises and terrorism
■ Crime mapping ■ Time sensitive (24-hour feedback and response)	- Consistent information input - A significant analytical component	■ Commodity flow, input trafficking and transiting logistics ■ Strategic
■ Disrupt crime series (e.g., burglary ring)	■ "Bottom-up" driven with respect to operational needs	■ Disrupt enterprises ■ Drives operations:
■ Drives operations: - Patrol - Tactical unit - Investigators		- JTTF Joint Terrorism Task Force - Organized crime investigations - Task forces
■ Analysis of offender Mos		■ Analysis of enterprise Mos
Correlated goals and methodologies make both concepts complement each other.		

- Problem Solving
  - Community policing–problem solving is used to reconcile community conditions that are precursors to crime and disorder.
  - ILP–the same process is used for intelligence to reconcile factors related to vulnerable targets and trafficking of illegal commodities.

FIGURE 3.2

Commonalities among community policing, Compstat, and intelligence-led policing (ILP).

(*Source:* David L. Carter, *Law Enforcement Intelligence: A Guide for State, Local, and Tribal Law Enforcement Agencies* [Washington, D.C.: U.S. Department of Justice, COPS Office, October 2004], pp. 41–43)

Defining Intelligence

Historically, the missing dimension in quality intelligence has been analysis.[11] The transformation of raw data, whether acquired through human, technical, or open sources, must be collated, scrutinized, and processed accurately and quickly. The ultimate goal of this analytical process is a finished product more intelligible, accurate, and usable than the data and information drawn on to prepare it. Herein is the definition of **intelligence**—data and information that has been evaluated, analyzed, and produced with careful conclusions and recommendations. Intelligence, then, is a *product* created from systematic and thoughtful examination, placed in context, and provided to law enforcement executives, with facts and alternatives that can inform critical decisions.[12]

There are three major perspectives on the purpose of intelligence and analysis. Each voices a different focus on the ability of intelligence officers and agents to provide sound information on which responsible decision making can be based. The first perspective is associated with the writings of Sherman Kent; it holds that the role of intelligence is to limit surprise from national security policymaking.[13] In other words, the analysis of data (or the making of intelligence) should render facts and figures, identify trends and patterns, and provide statistical support on *past* events. There are no follow-up investigations, postaudits, or continued evaluations concerning the policy implemented in response to the data provided. In essence, this type of analysis provides the facts and leaves the decisions to decision makers.

In the second perspective, analysts not only should be responsible for providing historical data but also should force policymakers and decision makers to confront alternative views of specific events, potential threats, and/or foreign situations. The emphasis is on connecting the political ends with the course of events. Analysts cannot limit themselves simply to giving situational reports and briefings; they must inherently focus on the dynamics of the political arena in order to give meaning to data. This may be particularly true regarding threats (such as terrorism) from foreign sources, in which state and local police executives may be relatively naïve to the geo-global dimensions of a specific region outside the United States. Most important, analysts need to place intelligence into the relevance and perspective of state and local governments. For instance, increased violence in the West Bank may be of little consequence to rural areas in the United States but much more meaningful to areas outside Detroit, Michigan, where nearly 300,000 Palestinians reside.

The final and sharply contrasting perspective concerning the purpose of analysis is somewhat latent. Its emphasis is not on providing past data on which to base decisions or policy; rather, the focus is squarely on the *prediction* of future events. This shift in emphasis can be viewed as an outgrowth of the second perspective as more technological advances have come to pass. With the advent of advanced analytical software and artificial intelligence systems, more robust records management systems, and relatively easy access to huge data banks (see Chapter 2, Policing Today), it should now be possible to provide accurate and reliable predictions concerning specific events.[14] The ultimate goal is twofold: (1) provide accurate information concerning the future in order to avoid decision and policy pitfalls and bureaucratic blunderings and (2) chart out courses of action directly aimed at achieving specific objectives. This, of course, requires a new way of thinking about policing—one that emphasizes prediction and prevention rather than detection and apprehension.

The Intelligence Process and Cycle

The *National Criminal Intelligence Sharing Plan (NCISP)*, released in 2003, contained 28 specific recommendations for major changes in local policing.[15] However, the key concept from the document emphasized the strategic integration of intelligence into the overall mission of the police organization—intelligence-led policing. Rather than react and respond to past calls for service, the NCISP placed much more emphasis on predictive analysis derived from the discovery of hard facts, information, patterns, intelligence, and good crime analysis. By concentrating on key criminal activities, problems, and individuals targeted through analysis, significant attention could be directed to alleviate the crime problem. In order to protect the civil liberties of all individuals, the intelligence process was developed with key evaluation points aimed at verifying source reliability and validity at the beginning of the collection cycle. The goal was to develop a universal process that would integrate both law enforcement and national security intelligence agendas, while providing mechanisms for securing individual freedoms and allowing law enforcement agencies to be proactive in preventing and deterring crime and terrorism. The end result was the "Intelligence Cycle," presented by the FBI in an effort to bring varied pieces of information together in an effort to draw logical conclusions from a thorough and systematic process (see Figure 3.3). As important, the Intelligence Cycle also provides a means of communicating and sharing intelligence between individuals and agencies through the dissemination process.

Fusion Centers

The transformation of local police agencies into intelligence-led organizations involves four key objectives: (1) the creation of a task and coordination process, (2) the development of core intelligence products to lead the operation, (3) the establishment of standardized training practices, and (4) the development of protocols to facilitate intelligence capabilities. This approach is intended to improve the capability of local law enforcement in regard to responding to terror threats and traditional anti-crime efforts. Intelligence-led policing blends community partnerships with crime fighting and police accountability in an effort to maximize police efficiency and effectiveness in terrorism prevention and crime reduction. There is evidence to suggest that this initiative has started to alter the face of traditional policing in the United States. A recent national survey found that a majority of responding local and state police agencies have conducted terrorism threat assessments since 9/11, and about one-third of these agencies have collaborated with the FBI's joint terrorism task force to assist in local crime investigations.[16] The movement toward intelligence-led policing has also been pushed by the creation of **fusion centers** (see Figure 3.4), inside local and state police agencies, which serve as clearinghouses for all potentially relevant homeland security information that can be used to assess local terror threats and aid in the apprehension of more traditional criminal suspects.

Originally launched in New York City under the direction of Raymond Kelly in 2002, the concept of a fusion center blended the power of information technology with terrorism prevention and crime fighting. With a price tag exceeding $11 million, the Real Time Crime Center (RTCC) in New York City combs through tens of millions of criminal complaints, arrest and parole records, and 911 call records dating back a decade in an effort to provide NYPD officers with the information tools necessary to stop a terrorist event or investigate a crime.[17] Fusion centers distribute relevant, actionable, and timely information and intelligence, incorporating a simultaneously vertical (i.e., federal, state, and local) and horizontal (i.e., within the agency, with other local agencies, and across disciplines such as fire, EMS, public works, and private partners) approach within a given jurisdiction. Fusion centers are composed of talented and trained individuals using sophisticated application software in crime analysis and mapping to manage and manipulate information and intelligence into a usable product. The resulting analysis acts as a basis for the deployment of police resources and directed operations in a real-time format—that is, almost immediately. The fusion center not only acts as a centralized host for intelligence information and analysis but also serves as a conduit for passing out critical information to other regional, state, and national authorities.

Directorate of Intelligence

The Intelligence Cycle

The intelligence cycle is the process of developing unrefined data into polished intelligence for the use of policymakers. The intelligence cycle consists of six steps, described below. The graphic below shows the circular nature of this process, although movement between the steps is fluid. Intelligence uncovered at one step may require going back to an earlier step before moving forward.

Requirements are identified information needs—what we must know to safeguard the nation. Intelligence requirements are established by the Director of National Intelligence according to guidance received from the President and the National and Homeland Security Advisors. Requirements are developed based on critical information required to protect the United States from National Security and criminal threats. The Attorney General and the Director of the FBI participate in the formulation of national intelligence requirements.

Planning and Direction is management of the entire effort, from identifying the need for information to delivering an intelligence product to a consumer. It involves implementation plans to satisfy requirements levied on the FBI, as well as identifying specific collection requirements based on FBI needs. Planning and direction also is responsive to the end of the cycle, because current and finished intelligence, which supports decision-making, generates new requirements. The Executive Assistant Director for the National Security Branch leads intelligence planning and direction for the FBI.

Collection is the gathering of raw information based on requirements. Activities such as interviews, technical and physical surveillances, human source operation, searches, and liaison relationships result in the collection of intelligence.

Processing and Exploitation involves converting the vast amount of information collected into a form usable by analysts. This is done through a variety of methods including decryption, language translations, and data reduction. Processing includes the entering of raw data into databases where it can be exploited for use in the analysis process.

Analysis and Production is the conversion of raw information into intelligence. It includes integrating, evaluating, and analyzing available data, and preparing intelligence products. The information's reliability, validity, and relevance is evaluated and weighed. The information is logically integrated, put in context, and used to produce intelligence. This includes both "raw" and finished intelligence. Raw intelligence is often referred to as "the dots"—individual pieces of information disseminated individually. Finished intelligence reports "connect the dots" by putting information in context and drawing conclusions about its implications.

Dissemination—the last step—is the distribution of raw or finished intelligence to the consumers whose needs initiated the intelligence requirements. The FBI disseminates information in three standard formats: Intelligence Information Reports (IIRs), FBI Intelligence Bulletins, and FBI Intelligence Assessments. FBI intelligence products are provided daily to the Attorney General, the President, and to customers throughout the FBI and in other agencies. These FBI intelligence customers make decisions—operational, strategic, and policy—based on the information. These decisions may lead to the levying of more requirements, thus continuing the FBI intelligence cycle.

FIGURE 3.3

The Intelligence Cycle

(*Source:* Federal Bureau of Investigation)

FIGURE 3.4

Fusion centers are high-tech, information-intensive operational centers that analyze and disseminate intelligence relating to terrorism and crime to police officers on the street.
(Jason DeCrow/AP Wide World Photos)

This is a particularly important point that fulfills the National Criminal Intelligence Sharing Plan in protecting the homeland.

Almost every state and several large metropolitan cities have undertaken the development of fusion centers with significant funding assistance from the Department of Homeland Security. For instance, the Chicago Police Department Deployment Operations Center (DOC) was one of the first centers to combine real-time intelligence analysis with the deployment process. In Los Angeles, both the city and the county have well-developed fusion centers, and in Dallas, Texas, the Metropolitan Operations and Analytical Intelligence Center (MOSAIC) provides real-time tactical information to officers on the street 24/7.

The goals of a fusion center are fourfold:

1. Fusion centers support the broad range of activities undertaken by a police department relating to the detection, examination, and investigation of a potential terrorist and/or criminal activity. Ideally, the center serves as a hub of anti-terrorist and anti-crime operations in a specific region, focusing on the recognition of patterns, indications and warnings, source development, interdiction, and the coordination of critical criminal justice resources. These are critical activities for any police agency attempting to be proactive and intelligence-led—to be successful in deterring, detecting, disrupting, investigating, and apprehending suspects involved in terrorist and criminal activity directly related to homeland security. Figure 3.4 represents one of several information technology solutions that are commonly used in fusion centers to help identify patterns and indicators associated with terrorism and/or crime.
2. Fusion centers support operations that protect **critical infrastructure and key resources (CI/KRs)** in a given region, support major incident operations,

support specialized units charged with interdiction and investigative operations, and assist in emergency operations and planning. The aim of a fusion center is to reduce the vulnerability of the high-value and high-risk targets identified within a jurisdiction. For example, in any major city there are several important CI/KRs—bank buildings, corporate headquarters, bridges and overpasses, water supply tanks and systems, electronic switching hubs, rail and subway stations, and a myriad of other important infrastructure entities. Fusion centers maintain huge data bases, which are immediately retrievable for use in thwarting an attack or dealing with an emergency. For instance, the Los Angeles Police Department has implemented the "Archangel Project," aimed at developing a large data base for all CI/KRs in the region. Its primary purpose is to maintain as much accessible and critical data as possible on any one given piece of critical infrastructure, so that during an emergency or a potentially threatening event police resources can be directed appropriately. Hence, building schematics and event histories, alternative road and highway routes, and maps of water supply mains, electrical grids, switching stations, and the like are maintained and accessible within the fusion center. Fusion centers are **all-hazard** in scope—that is, they are developed to support operations during an emergency that is either human-made, such as a terrorist event, or natural, such as a hurricane, flood, or tornado.

3. Fusion centers often maintain public "tip lines," which gives them the capability to promote more public involvement in and awareness of terrorist threats. The goal is to identify and recognize warning signs and potential threats in a timely manner in order to pre-empt potential terrorist attacks and reduce the vulnerability of the CI/KRs in a given region. Fusion centers accomplish this task on a daily basis, focusing on the analysis of crimes that are often linked to terrorist cells and activity for funding, such as narcotics trafficking, credit card abuse, armament and gun theft, prostitution, and human trafficking, by distributing information relating to these linkages to all agencies within a given region. The timeliness of gathering, analyzing, and disseminating information is vital to successfully preventing acts of violence and threats to homeland security.
4. Fusion centers assist police executives in making better-informed decisions, especially during emergencies or critical incidents. Fusion centers are ongoing deployment operations centers with the real-time ability to monitor critical resources. This includes real-time status monitoring of major events, communicating with area medical facilities and trauma units, coordinating the allocation and deployment of multi-agency personnel resources (including military reserve units), monitoring changing weather conditions, and directing all support services through a centralized operations center.

Clearly, the 9/11 attacks transformed the role of police in our country. Police executives need to recognize that the public, and federal officials, will increasingly expect local police to take a broader and more important role in safeguarding their communities against terrorists.[18] Refer to the Quick Facts box item on Application Programs.

Critical Thinking Questions

1. What are the commonalities between community and intelligence-led policing?
2. Discuss the potential problems of protecting the constitutional rights of individuals while practicing intelligence-led policing. How might a balance be maintained between protecting the homeland and protecting the individual?

Quick Facts

Application Programs

Since 1990, **i2 Corporation** has been a worldwide leader of visual investigative analysis software for law enforcement, intelligence, military, and Fortune 500 organizations. The application software performs an array of sophisticated analytical techniques, including social network analysis, commodity flow, telephone record analysis, link analysis, and the like, often used in real-time fusion centers to convey analytical findings in intuitive charts that organize support data. Refer to Chapter 2, Policing Today for a more thorough discussion on crime and intelligence analysis techniques used in law enforcement.

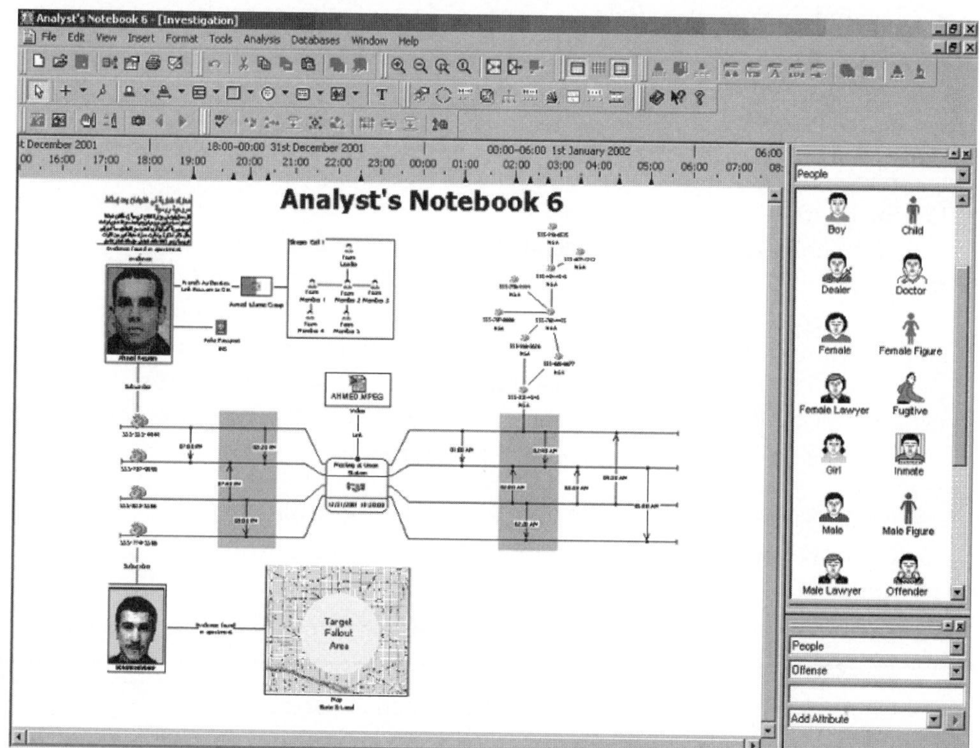

Courtesy of i2 Corporation, McLean, Virginia, 2007. Visit www.i2inc.com.

Analyst's Notebook 6 is designed for a wide range of investigations, including:

- Counterterrorism
- Drug Trafficking
- Money Laundering
- Securities Fraud
- Credit Card Fraud
- Insurance Fraud
- Forensic Accounting
- Organized Crime
- Major Incident
- Immigration Control
- Identify Theft
- Corporate Security
- Threat Assessment

3. Explain the role of a fusion center in the day-to-day operations of a large, metropolitan police agency. Do you think that fusion centers would be very helpful to smaller agencies as well, considering the cost-benefit ratio?
4. Name some of the CI/KRs in your area and discuss their importance to your community. Do you think they are major targets for terrorists?

HOMELAND SECURITY

In November 2002, President George W. Bush ushered in the largest federal bureaucratic shuffle in 55 years to create the cabinet-level Department of Homeland Security (DHS). Headed by the former governor of Pennsylvania, Tom Ridge, the new department focused the anti-terrorism effort in the United States, absorbing many of the enforcement agencies within the Departments of Treasury and Transportation

(Transportation Security Administration; U.S. Coast Guard; U.S. Customs; Bureau of Alcohol, Tobacco, and Firearms; U.S. Secret Service; and Federal Emergency Management Administration [FEMA]). In addition, the department created a division to analyze intelligence gathered by the FBI, CIA, and other police and military agencies. There are four primary areas of responsibility within the Department of Homeland Security:

- Border security and transportation
- Emergency preparedness and response
- Chemical, biological, radiological, and nuclear countermeasures
- Intelligence analysis and infrastructure protection

The building of the department has been slow, with a variety of changes and setbacks coming from different leadership and severe criticism stemming from the poor departmental response to the City of New Orleans during Hurricane Katrina in 2005.

On February 15, 2005, Judge Michael Chertoff was sworn in as the second Secretary of Homeland Security. His methodical leadership has attempted to define six primary agenda points for improving Homeland Security (announced in July 2006) and to ensure that the department's policies, operations, and structures are aligned in the best way to address the potential threats—both present and future—that face our nation. The six-point agenda is structured to guide the department in the near term and to result in changes that will do the following:

1. Increase overall preparedness, particularly for catastrophic events
2. Create better transportation security systems to move people and cargo more securely and efficiently
3. Strengthen border security and interior enforcement and reform immigration processes
4. Enhance information sharing with departmental partners
5. Improve DHS financial management, human resource development, procurement, and information technology
6. Realign the DHS organization to maximize mission performance

The Department of Homeland Security is the third-largest department with the ninth largest budget in the federal government, boasting over 180,000 employees and a budget in 2005 that exceeded $38 billion, with an additional $11 billion earmarked for grants aimed at funding anti-terror and border security initiatives at the state and local levels (see Figure 3.5). Much of this money will be provided to local and state law enforcement agencies for the development of programs that address one of the six-point agenda items.

Beyond the ultimate mission of ensuring the nation's safety and preventing terrorism, DHS is responsible for immigration policy, airport security, and the protection of the president. Immigration reform is a major hot topic of discussion as it relates to homeland security. During summer 2006, large rallies and protests in support of immigration reform and increased border security, especially concerning the border with Mexico, were observed across the country. In the middle of the controversy were the individual agencies within the Department of Homeland Security tasked with both internal immigration/citizenship issues and the security of homeland borders. While much of the absorbing and restructuring of individual agencies has been completed within DHS since early 2007, the department will continue to

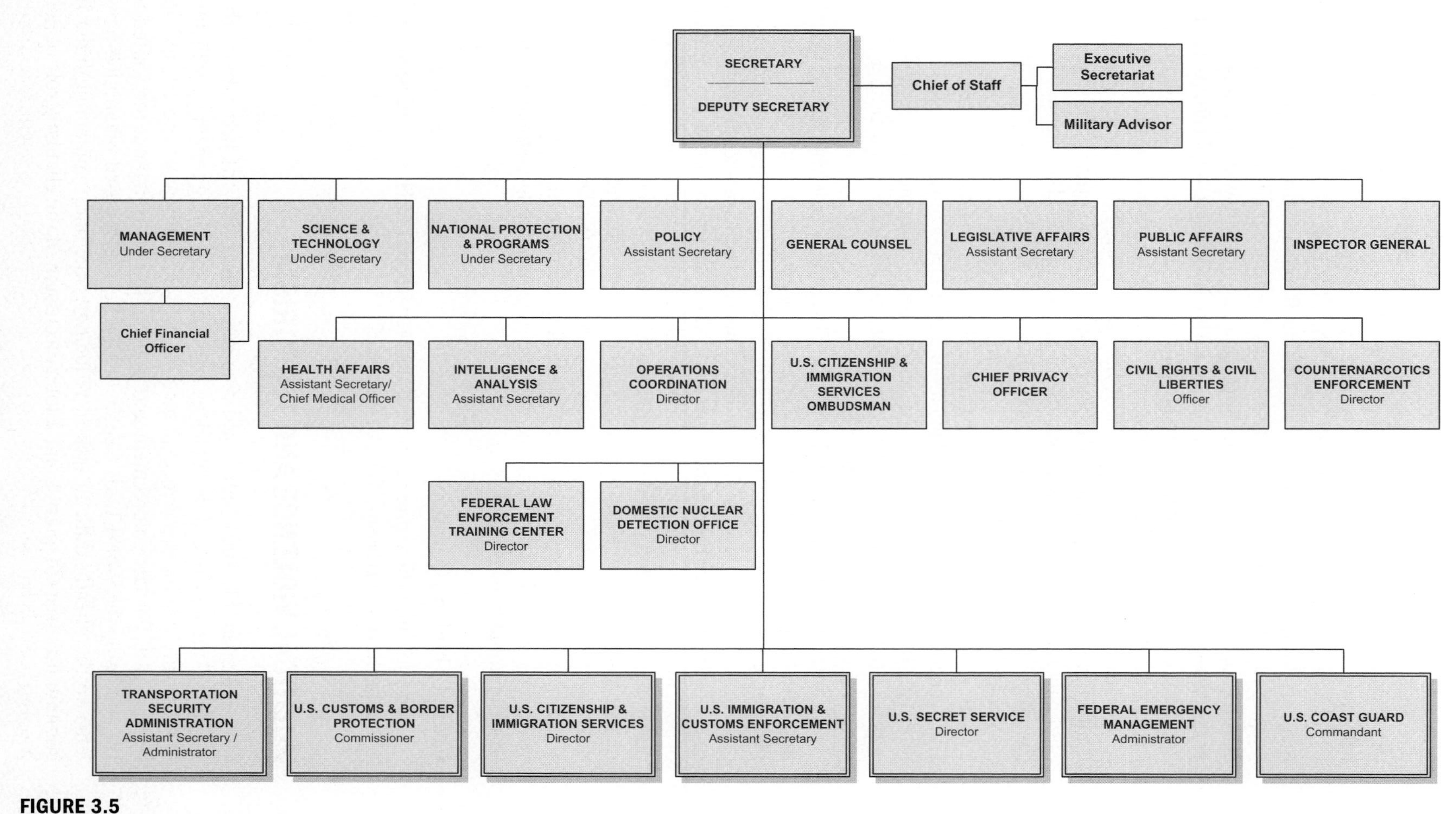

FIGURE 3.5

U.S. Department of Homeland Security.

(*Source:* U.S. Department of Homeland Security)

move in accordance with political issues and responses to actual events. For instance, the Federal Emergency Management Agency (FEMA) assumes the task of responding to national emergencies, including potential nuclear and biological attacks by terrorists. FEMA's response to Hurricane Katrina in August 2005 resulted in some of the harshest criticisms of DHS to date. The effect of Hurricane Katrina on New Orleans and the gulf coast of Louisiana and Mississippi was catastrophic. The storm, which was certainly one of the most costly and deadliest natural disasters in U.S. history, left 80 percent of the city of New Orleans flooded, with some parts over 20 feet deep. Four of the primary protective levees were breached, isolating stranded citizens throughout the city and in the Louisiana Superdome, which became the "refuge of last resort" for many residents. The disaster had major implications for the Department of Homeland Security, as FEMA was criticized for its inability to evacuate the city in a timely manner, and more importantly, for its poor response to the entire region immediately after the storm. It has been a struggle for the agency to exist. Funds have been raided, staff have been transferred into other DHS functions without being replaced, slowdowns because of added layers of bureaucracy for nearly all functions have dramatically increased, and there has been a constant threat of reprogramming appropriated funds[19] Then, too, the agency's director, Michael D. Brown, resigned under pressure just three days after losing onsite command of the Hurricane Katrina relief effort. Many argued that DHS's misguided concentration on terrorism and its overly bureaucratic restructuring of agencies had come at a huge expense, the loss of the federal government's ability to respond properly to emergencies presented by natural disasters.[20]

Quite interestingly, the FBI and the CIA remain independent agencies, apart from the Department of Homeland Security, in the war on terrorism. Interestingly, these were the primary agencies most criticized for their failure to coordinate intelligence information in the pre-9/11 world. However, both agencies are now required to share the intelligence they gather with DHS. The analysis and further communication of such intelligence information have been relegated to the independent Office of National Intelligence, composed of representatives from 16 agencies assigned the monumental task of effectively integrating foreign, domestic, and military intelligence in defense of the homeland of the United States. Like the Department of Homeland Security, it is an entirely new entity, stemming from the aftermath of 9/11 and the sweeping governmental reforms recommended by joint congressional inquiry and the 911 Commission (see Figure 3.6).

Critical Thinking Question

1. Do you think the reorganization of the Department of Homeland Security will help prevent terrorism? Why or why not?

POLITICAL VIOLENCE AND TERRORISM

On September 11, 2001, our world changed forever. For the first time in the past 50 years, America came under attack by an outside and foreign enemy (see Figure 3.7). Our security weaknesses were exploited, our vulnerability was exposed, and our fear became real. For law enforcement and police officers throughout the United States, the attacks on the World Trade Center and the Pentagon posed yet another new challenge to the already difficult task of reducing crime and maintaining order in our communities (see Chapters 1 and 2 for a discussion of the changing role of police in America).

FIGURE 3.6

Judge Michael Chertoff became the second Secretary of the Department of Homeland Security. Under his leadership, the department has refined its role in preventing, detecting, and investigating terrorist threats.

(US Department of Homeland Security)

The impact on federal and local law enforcement agencies has been profound, as police administrators are confronted with the most pressing and significant external issue of their careers: how to investigate, interdict, and prevent terrorism. Police departments around the country have had to address new threats of violence that are sometimes the result of federal actions or international foreign policy actions in which they have no authority. For instance, since September 11, virtually every large metropolitan police department has been placed on the highest alert. Operational demands required police agencies to perform new activities, including increasing infrastructure security around critical buildings and airports, building anti-terrorism barriers, beefing up intelligence gathering and analysis functions, monitoring activity in Middle Eastern communities, and participating in joint terrorism task forces. Even though an extensive federal structure has been developed to counter the terrorist threat, the first level of prevention (and response) remains with uniformed police officers on the street.

The federal structure came under considerable criticism before September 11 for failing to coordinate anti-terrorism activity, assess and analyze accurate intelligence information, and act quickly to prevent terrorist activities. Since that horrible day, the

FIGURE 3.7

September 11, 2001, represented a day of infamy, dramatically changing the role of American law enforcement in preventing similar acts of terrorism.

(Doug Kanter/Agence France Presse/Getty Images)

pressure to reorganize federal efforts has been the focus of national debate and action.[21] At the center of the controversy was the FBI. FBI agent Coleen Rowley went before Congress to blow the whistle on an agency she described as too big, too slow, and too set in its ways to effectively combat terrorism.[22] According to Rowley, the structure of the FBI was archaic and in need of significant repair. However, it was the closed subculture that existed within the FBI that Rowley hammered during her testimony before Congress, focusing not only on the top-heavy and cumbersome bureaucratic structure but also on the close-minded, egotistical, and non-cooperative attitude that existed throughout the ranks of the FBI.[23] Accordingly, FBI Director Robert Mueller has promised to reform the organization. However, criticism aimed at the FBI continues to grab the headlines of most major news agencies.[24] In 2004 a blistering report from a bipartisan presidential commission faulted the FBI for being too ambitious, directly leading to unnecessary new turf battles with the CIA. And a Justice Department report (in 2005) cited "rapid turnover" among counterterrorism managers at FBI headquarters and a failure to retain knowledgable experts about terrorism as central issues still confounding the FBI's ability to deal effectively with the terrorist threat. The largest blow to the bureau may still be unfolding, as a newly $170 million computerized case-management system—Virtual Case File (VCF)—developed by Science Applications International Corporation (SAIC) has been scraped due to its inoperability. Much of the criticism has been laid at the door of Director Robert Mueller, who has taken full responsibility for the debacle.

Defining Terrorism

In the popular mind, terrorism is viewed as the illegitimate and violent actions of specific groups that violate the authority of rightfully established governments. **Terrorism** encompasses the threat of and/or use of violence to achieve a specific set of political objectives or goals.[25] Historically, defining terrorism has been a very difficult venture, shaped and altered by a number of factors, including our own national interests, government interpretations, the news media, hidden political agendas, and emotional human rights rhetoric.[26] Such phrases as "guerrilla warfare," "revolutionary movement," "communist-supported terrorism," and "radical fundamentalist" only heighten ideological sentiment and play to emotion rather than intellect. Hence, we find the cliché that one person's terrorist is another person's freedom fighter to be truly an observation based on perspective and perception.[27] This is certainly the case in the United States, as some actions, such as the attacks of September 11, the first attack on the World Trade Center (1993), the bombing of the Alfred P. Murrah Federal Building in Oklahoma City (1995), and the downing of TWA flight 800 (1996), are "terrorist," while the sporadic bombings at abortion centers or mosques across the country are not.

Large, high-profile terrorist events greatly impact how members of society interact. Random acts of terrorism upset the framework of society, leaving only futile questions without rational answers. Essentially, terrorism tests the basic social structure of dependence and trust. If random bombings and acts of violence occur on a frequent basis at the most secure institutions of a society (e.g., federal buildings, police departments, churches, synagogues, and hospitals), then people tend to lose faith in the existing social and government structure. Safety and security are severely compromised and questioned. Terrorism destroys the solidarity, cooperation, and interdependence on which social functioning is based and substitutes insecurity and distrust.

Terrorism, then, plays to emotion not intellect.[28] It strikes at the very heart of who we are as Americans. For the first time in modern history (9/11), the United States was rocked by an attack on its own land. People were afraid as their daily lives were impacted and changed forever. The privileges and lifestyle that we so enjoyed in this country appeared to be jeopardized. The ability to travel freely was restricted. Few of us can recall where we were on September 2, 2001, but almost all of us can give vivid details of where we were and what we were doing in the morning hours of September 11, 2001.

The overwhelming question plaguing so many of us was, why? We are a great nation that has helped almost every other nation in need. We give billions of dollars away each year in foreign aid. And we consistently stand for the human rights of all people, emphasizing the dignity of the human spirit and integrity of all people to live free, so why were we the victims of such rage on September 11, 2001, from a group that few of us even knew?

Interestingly, the answer may be found in the question. We knew little about the Middle East, dare we suggest that law enforcement still knows very little about the Middle East. In part, Osama bin Laden and the al-Qaeda group stated to the world that one of the primary reasons for the attack was our lack of knowledge about the true political and economic conditions of the Middle East. Indeed, bin Laden made it very clear that they believed our goals in the Middle East were much more motivated by our own self-interest and quest for oil than in safeguarding the human rights of the people in that land. These may be particularly stinging remarks, considering the War in Iraq. He maintained that the stationing of American troops in the Middle East—in particular, near the holy city of Mecca (in Saudi Arabia)—was an egregious affront to his religion. He maintained that the people of the Middle East suffer under puppet governments supported by the United States and that these governments practice state terrorism against their own people.

Here we see quite profoundly the perspective that terrorism can be different things to different people. Theoretically, scholars have been debating the definition of terrorism for the past 25 years.[29] The goal here is to provide a conceptual framework on which to classify and understand terrorism, particularly in the Middle East. The work of Edward Mickolus provides such a framework.[30]

Terrorism is situationally defined—that is, a number of factors play on the difficulty of defining terrorism, including competing political agendas, national interests, economic security, the news media, fundamental cultural and religious beliefs, and the use of misinformation. By exploiting any one of these, it is possible to distort the facts. Even more disturbing and most compromising is the moral judgment passed on those who are labeled terrorists, for we in America assume that terrorism is "what the bad guys do." Hence, what better way is there to distort the sovereign interest of people than to associate them with illegitimate action or sources? In the Middle East, all of these factors are at play, making for a very complicated and difficult analysis. Those perpetrating terrorism against the United States do not view themselves as criminals. Indeed, many are at war and may well be agents provocateur and within the employ of a foreign government. This is an audience that American law enforcement has had little experience with, and they pose special challenges to the everyday police officer now charged with thwarting attacks against our homeland and with securing our infrastructure. Conceptualizing terrorism from a different perspective provides us with an opportunity to learn our adversaries and hopefully exploit their weaknesses. Mickolus conceptualizes terrorism in four distinct typologies, based on actors:

- *International terrorism*—Actions conducted in the international arena by individuals that are members of a nation state. This usually includes members of intelligence and secret services employed by governments, such as the Cuban DGI, the old Soviet KGB, the Syrian Secret Police, the British M-9, the Israili Mousad, and even the CIA.
- *Transnational terrorism*—Actions conducted in the international arena by individuals that have no nation-state. The predominate groups for the past 50 years are associated with the Palestinian cause (e.g., Popular Front for the Liberation of Palestine [PFLP], al-Fatah, Black June, Black September Organization, and Abu Nidal). However, other groups have also been active in the Middle East, such as the Kurdish Workers Party (PKK), the Armenians, and various groups from the breakaway lands of the former Soviet Union. The radical Islamic groups, such as al-Qaeda, HAMAS, and Hezbollah, are also classified in this typology.
- *Domestic terrorism*—Actions conducted by groups within a nation, usually against the government or specific groups within the nation-state. This may be one of the most difficult aspects of attempting to define the concept of terrorism. When do the rights of a government to control splinter elements within its own country end and the rights of the people to rebel become legitimate? This is a difficult question and one most often "flavored" by the myriad of factors already discussed. In any event, within the United States, groups associated with an extremist perspective (whether from the far left, the far right, or single issue) often fall within this typology. This includes groups such as the Weather Underground, the Earth Liberation Front, the Animal Liberation Front, the Ku Klux Klan, the Neo-Nazis, the National Alliance, many of the state militias, and a myriad of anarchist groups sprouting up in our largest cities. In the Middle East, Israel commonly refers to the Palestinian elements as terrorists acting within Israel's borders, and the Egyptian government has been plagued by radical Islamic extremists influenced by Sheik Abdul Omar Rahman (the Muslim Brotherhood) and Osama bin Laden.
- *State terrorism*—Actions conducted by governments against their own population. Unfortunately, history is replete with suppressive governments that victimize their own populations. Certainly, the regimes of Adolph Hitler, Joseph Stalin,

Quick Facts

Terrorist Attacks

According to U.S. government figures, the number of serious international terrorist incidents more than tripled in 2005. Overall, the number of what the U.S. government considers "significant" attacks grew to about 655, up from the record of around 175 in 2003. Terrorist incidents in Iraq also dramatically increased, from 22 attacks to 198, or nine times the previous year's total—a sensitive subset of the tally, given the Bush administration's assertion that the situation there stabilized significantly after the installation of a new Iraqi government.

Source: U.S. State Department, National Counterterrorism Center (NCTC), 2005.

and Pol Pot represent these types of regimes, often characterized by ethnic and political cleansing. More recently, we have seen these types of activities in smaller countries throughout the Far East and Latin America. In the Middle East, Saddam Hussein in Iraq and Haffez Assad in Syria represented these types of entities. Interestingly, many (including Osama bin Laden) in the Middle East refer to the governments of Israel, Jordan, Kuwait, Egypt, and Saudi Arabia as suppressive regimes controlled by rich elites that suppress the legitimate rights of their people through the use of kidnaping, death squads, and brutal police tactics. By proxy, the same people also argue that the United States is guilty of state terrorism as it financially and militarily supports these governments. They are quick to point to the military use of power against the Palestinian people in the West Bank and Gaza by the Israelis, the use of armed soldiers in Jordan and Egypt to quell mass demonstrations, and the huge differential between classes in Saudi Arabia. Again, and to re-emphasize, the Middle East is a hodge-podge of cultural, religious, and ethnic groups, all struggling for power and recognition. Precisely defining the terrorist and placing moral judgment is a very difficult task, at best.[31]

From a law enforcement perspective, it is important to understand this conceptualization of terrorism. It provides a framework on which to understand the motivations behind people's actions, particularly in the Middle East. Further, it provides a basis on which to develop a conversation or an interview with members of Middle Eastern communities living within the United States, some of which may be sympathetic to the causes of specific Middle Eastern groups.

Radical Islamic Terrorism

The list of potential international terrorist threats against the United States is almost unlimited, considering the numerous political conflicts continuing in the international arena. Many of these threats are fueled by political, religious, and/or ideologically motivated causes. Certainly, terrorism from various Middle Eastern groups has posed significant problems to American law enforcement. Historically, the root of conflict in the Middle East was the establishment of Israel in 1948 and the subsequent U.S. support provided to that country. While peace between the two major groups (Israelis and Palestinians) was formally established in 1995, both sides still have major radical movements opposing the process. These groups often act out in the international arena, with the United States being a potential target. Confirmed activities by members of the Jewish Defense League (JDL), the Popular Front for the Liberation of Palestine (PFLP), the Fatah Revolutionary Council, and a host of other

In The News

Jewish Extremism

When most Americans think of terrorism generated from conflict in the Middle East, their thoughts are generally focused on the myriad of groups and actors associated with radical Islamic movements, such as al-Qaeda, Hamas, and Hezbollah. However, there are also significant Jewish movements and extremists that are active internationally as well as domestically within the United States. For instance, the Jewish Defense League (JDL), Eyal, Kach, and Kahane Lives are all active, far-right Jewish extremist groups. The JDL was founded in 1968 by Rabbi Meir Kahane and has a long track record of political violence and anti-Arab hatred inside the United States. Some of the activities linked to these groups are the following:

- Attempting to kidnap a Soviet diplomat and shooting rounds into the Soviet Embassy, as well as firebombing the Iraqi Embassy in Washington, D.C. (1975)
- Firebombing the Egyptian Tourist Agency in Rockefeller Center in New York City (1981)
- Attacking and killing numerous Palestinians in the West Bank and plotting to blow up the al-Aqsa Mosque in Jerusalem (1980s)
- Slaughtering 29 Palestinian Muslims praying at a mosque in Hebron (in the West Bank), known as the Cave of Patriarchs massacre (1994)
- Assassinating Prime Minister Yitzhak Rabin in Israel (1995)
- Plotting to attack the offices of Arab-American Congressman Darrell Issa in Los Angeles, California (2001)
- Devising bombing plots and activities on Palestinians in the West Bank (2002–2005)

Attacks by Jearit Extremist Groups to the United States

1968–Present

Incidents	Injuries	Fatalities
73	40	5

Targets:	
Government	2%
Airports and airlines	10%
Business	23%
Diplomatic	45%
Journalists and media	1%
Terrorists/former terrorists	5%
Other	6%
Maritime	1%
Religious figures/institutions	2%

*Data for 1968–1997 cover only International Incidents. Data for 1998–present cover both domestic and International Incidents.

Source: Courtesy of the National Memorial Institute for the Prevention of Terrorism (MIPT), Oklahoma City, Oklahoma, www.MIPT.org.

splinter groups have caused concern to law enforcement. As if these groups were not enough, mercenary terrorists from the Abu Nidal organization still foment activity in support of the highest bidder. Although the leader of this rogue outfit, Sabri al-Banna, was found dead in Iraq in August 2002, many scholars suspect that his followers have been enlisted to the ranks of foreign intelligence services or state-sponsored groups active in the Middle East and not friendly to the United States.[32]

However, the most significant activities against the United States in the past 10 years have been led by fundamental Islamic groups acting from clandestine areas in Afghanistan, Iraq, Lebanon, and Iran. The first major incident witnessed in the United States connected to fundamental Islam was the bombing of the World Trade Center on February 26, 1993, which killed five people. FBI experts contend that, if the bomb had

been just slightly larger and more skillfully placed, the entire building may have collapsed, causing untold devastation and death. Unfortunately, this was just a preview of the horrible events to come just eight years later. Linkages to Islamic fundamentalist groups in Egypt were developed, resulting in several indictments of Arab nationals living in the United States. One of those convicted was the blind cleric Sheik Abdul Omar Rahman, a spiritual leader and scholar who helped spawn a number of other groups.

The most infamous of these groups is the **al-Qaeda** organization, led by Osama bin Laden and Ayman al-Zawarahi. It is actually a network of many different fundamental Islamic groups in diverse countries. Their ideology is based primarily on the writings of Sayyid Muhammad Qubt and Ibn Wahhab, two early Islamic scholars calling for a violent purification movement throughout the Middle East and the greater Islamic world. This religious movement is commonly called "Wahhabism" and can be traced back to the early 1920s in Egypt. According to these radical philosophers, the Middle East must be purged of Western influence. To this end, leaders call for a "holy war," or **jihad**, calling on everyday Muslims to join in their fight against the West. Bin Laden and other members of the al-Qaeda network pervert parts of the Koran to justify their philosophy and do not represent mainstream Islam. It is important to understand that Islam is the world's second-largest religion, with over 1 billion peaceful followers, living primarily in Africa, Asia, and Europe. The actions of radical fundamentalists such as Rahman and bin Laden represent not the true path of Islam but rather only a fraction (less than one-tenth of 1 percent) of all Islam.

Unfortunately, the movement has flourished in Egypt and Saudi Arabia for the past 20 years, countries where American influence is easily observed. Members of the al-Qaeda organization are politically motivated to overthrow the "heretic governments" that they see as puppets of Western influence and replace them with Islamic governments based on the rule of the Shariah (the first book of the Koran, strictly regulating all aspects of life).

Osama bin Laden (b. 1957), the son of a wealthy building contractor in Saudi Arabia, rose to power within the fundamental Islamic movement as a student of Ayman al-Zawarahi (see Figure 3.10). However, it was not until the 1979–1989 Soviet–Afghan War that bin Laden actually took a recognized leadership role in the organization. Triumphant over the Soviets and enlisting the aid of American interests in Afghanistan, bin Laden amassed a number of hardened mujahideen (holy warriors) fighters. He became obsessed with Western influence in the Middle East and declared a holy war on the United States in 1996.[33] Fueled by Middle Eastern oil wealth and an increasing radicalization of Islam, bin Laden set out to destroy those entities that he believes have adulterated his homeland. The activities of al-Qaeda have been significant and numerous, culminating on September 11, with the attacks on the World Trade Center and the Pentagon. Their activities include the following:

1996: Bin Laden issues a declaration of war against the "Great Satan" (the United States).

1998: Suicide bombings of the U.S. embassies in Kenya and Tanzania kill 224 people.

2000: Suicide bombing of the USS *Cole* in Yemen kills 17 American sailors.

2001: Attacks on the World Trade Center and the Pentagon kill more than 2,800.

Since Operation Enduring Freedom, which sent troops to Afghanistan (2001) and the War in Iraq (2003), most scholars and government officials have believed that the stability and operational capability of al-Qaeda has been diminished in the

FIGURE 3.8

Osama bin Laden was the mastermind behind several terrorist attacks against the United States both domestically and abroad. Most notably, his group, known as al-Qaeda ("The Base"), was responsible for the bombing of the World Trade Center Towers and the Pentagon on September 11, 2001.

(AFP Photo Files/Agence France Presse/Getty Images)

international arena. Certainly, the leadership has been dismantled and most are on the run. Much of the operational capability of al-Qaeda as a single group has also been destroyed. However, al-Qaeda continues to flourish as a *movement* rather than a single group. American soldiers are being attacked in Iraq on a daily basis by those fighting the "holy jihad." Indeed, the number of deaths attributed to terrorism for the past several years continues to double each year due primarily to the explosion of violence in Iraq.[34] Suicide bombers expressing the same sentiment have conducted attacks in Riyadh, Istanbul, Madrid, and London with the hallmarks of previous al-Qaeda attacks. The movement adapted from targeting aviation to hitting softer targets, such as mass transit hubs (subway systems) and bus terminals.

Although al-Qaeda may be diminished as a single group, their movement continues to be successful in recruiting new members. From website announcements and flyers to the recruitment of new fighters in the Middle East, the movement continues to grow in sustained acts of violence against Western interests. The future portends that the movement will continue for some time, particularly given the instability of the Middle East and other areas of the world.

Jamaah Islamiyah

The largest concentration of Islamic people in the world is not in the Middle East. The fastest-growing area of Islam is also not in the Middle East. Indeed, the country of Indonesia, and the Southeast Asian region in general, have witnessed a rapid expansion of Islam over the past decade. The vast majority of this increase in Islam has not been

Focus on Policies, Programs, and People

The Memorial Institute for the Prevention of Terrorism

The Memorial Institute for the Prevention of Terrorism (MIPT), located in Oklahoma City, Oklahoma, is a non-profit, nationally recognized think tank, creating state-of-the-art knowledge bases on terrorism. MIPT was established out of the experiences of the bombing of Oklahoma City's Alfred P. Murrah Federal Building on April 19, 1995. Those who survived and the family members of those lost believed it important to create an institute to actively engage in research and study, programs, and reporting, to help policymakers and leaders have the best and most complete information in their hands to avert terrorism and/or lessen the impact of a terrorist event. The MIPT mission is to inform the public about terrorism prevention and responder preparedness. MIPT sponsors training for both law enforcement and the general public; however, most important resources are the powerful and robust knowledge bases developed and maintained via its online resource center. Three very impressive knowledge bases compose the MIPT online resources:

- **Lessons Learned Information Sharing Database** (www.LLIS.gov) is a central repository for sharing lessons learned among the nation's emergency responder community.
- **Responder Knowledge Base** (www.rkb.mipt.org) has been designed to provide emergency responders with a single source for integrated information on current equipment, including organizing information, such as the Inter Agency Board's Standardized Equipment List (SEL) and the Authorized Equipment List from the Office for Domestic Preparedness, two important lists for state and local agencies attempting to purchase equipment through federal grants and initiatives.
- **Terrorism Knowledge Base** (www.tkb.org) is one of the most exhaustive, open source knowledge bases on terrorism in the country. It aids responders, researchers, academicians, executives, and others in their understanding of individual terrorist group histories, attacks, motive, structures, tactics, and ideologies. It represents the most advanced, most interactive, and most comprehensive site about global terrorism on the Web.

Source: The National Memorial Institute for the Prevention of Terrorism, Oklahoma City, Oklahoma, www.MIPT.org.

anti-Western or fundamental in nature, but one group has emerged as a leading radical group—**Jemaah Islamiyah (JI).** The group began in the 1960s in Indonesia, when two radical clerics, named Abdullah Sungkar and Abu Bakar Bashir, established a pirate radio station in secular Indonesia, advocating the imposition of strict Muslim law. The two found themselves in disfavor with the Indonesian government, continuing to draw negative attention with the establishment of their Islamic boarding school, which taught a hard-line and radical version of Islam, following the principles of Qubt. While both men were temporarily imprisoned, their movement began to spread, with active cells in Malaysia, Singapore, southern Thailand, the Philippines, and Indonesia. These cells operated fairly independently of each other. The Malaysian cell was easily the largest and was the primary link between JI and al-Qaeda during the 1990s. The cell was also responsible for establishing "front" companies used to channel funds and weapons into both al-Qaeda and JI.

The cells established throughout Southeast Asia did little but build capacity until after the collapse of the Indonesian dictatorship in 1998. At that time, most of the senior leadership relocated to Indonesia and began actively planning terrorist attacks for the first time. In December 2000, there were a series of bombings carried out in Indonesia.[35] These attacks were aimed at Christian churches that had voiced support for Christian paramilitary groups organizing around Indonesia's islands. There were also several bombings in Manila, killing 22 people. There were also plans for large-scale attacks against the United States in Singapore. JI and al-Qaeda had procured mass amounts of explosives and ammunition with the help of the Lebanese group **Hezbollah** in order to attack U.S. ships in Singaporean waters, as well as the U.S., British, and Israeli embassies and several American companies based there.

On October 12, 2002, members of Jemaah Islamiyah attacked a nightclub in Bali, a small Indonesian island popular with U.S., British, and Australian tourists, killing 202 people and devastating the Indonesian tourist economy (see Figure 3.9). The incident marked one of the bloodiest single events since 9/11. The Indonesian government immediately sought the arrest of the responsible parties. Bashir and his associate, Riduan Isamuddin, also known as Hambali, were arrested after the attacks. The arrests of the key JI leaders has not quashed the organization itself or limited its dangerousness. On August 5, 2003, a bomb ripped through the Marriott Hotel in Jakarta, Indonesia, killing 13 people. Additionally, there continues to be violent attacks in southern Thailand and through Malaysia and Indonesia aimed at destabilizing local governments. It appears that the networks established by JI throughout Southeast Asia have resulted in a strong backbone of radical Islamic terrorists attempting to build what is commonly referred to as the "New Kingdom of Islam," an area expressed as beginning at the Great Wall of China and extending to the southern tip of Australia. These are particularly troubling

FIGURE 3.9

The bombing of a nightclub in Bali represents a new wave of terrorist attacks against the West and Muslim regimes friendly to the West. Using indigenous people and groups throughout the Middle East and Asia sympathetic to Islamic fundamental beliefs, al-Qaeda facilitates suicide bombing attacks to maximize civilian casualties. Similar attacks have been observed in Indonesia, Saudi Arabia, Egypt, the Philippines, and Turkey.

(AFP Photo/Weda/Agence France Presse/Getty Images)

statements, considering that Abu Bakar Bashir was released from his Indonesian prison in late 2006 and has again taken a visible leadership in the JI movement.

Hamas

Hamas is the largest and most influential Palestinian militant movement today. Its ideology is focused on Israeli–Palestinian conflict and expresses an escalation of armed conflict and terrorism against Israel and its allies (e.g., the United States). Hamas represent an outgrowth of the Muslim Brotherhood and Wahhabism as expressed by earlier revolutionary writers. It has been a legally registered group in Israel since 1978 and was originally founded by Sheik Ahmed Yassin, the movement's spiritual leader. Yassin was assassinated by the Israeli government as he left prayer service from a mosque in Jerusalem on March 22, 2004, sparking significant violence yet a quell in suicide bombing.

The image of Hamas in the Middle East is unique in that the group has attempted to rebuild much of the destroyed infrastructure of the Palestinian community while being responsible for 90 percent of the suicide bombings throughout Israel for the past several years. It is an interesting dichotomy: building roads, schools, and social services in the territories of the West Bank and Gaza and wreaking havoc with random suicide bombings against Israel. Hamas has developed strong financial support from unofficial bodies in Saudi Arabia and Iran. In addition, Hamas makes use of an extensive network of charity associations developed throughout the world, including the United States. This network often serves as a facade for covert activities, including worldwide association with other radical leaders, the transfer of funds to field operatives, and the identification of potential recruits for suicide bombings and other acts of terrorism. Several of these charities operate in larger cities throughout the United States (e.g., New York, Portland, Detroit, Chicago, and Dallas) and have come under the scrutiny of law enforcement. For instance, in late 2002, local police officers and federal agents raided an organization in Richardson, Texas (a suburb of Dallas), seizing records and financial documents, freezing bank accounts, and arresting leaders within the organization.

In January 2006, the group won the Palestinian Authority's (PA's) general legislative elections, defeating Fatah, the party of the PA's president, Mahmoud Abbas, and setting the stage for a power struggle. Since attaining power, Hamas has continued its refusal to recognize the state of Israel, leading to severe economic sanctions against the Palestinian Authority. In Arabic, the word "hamas" means zeal. But it is also an Arabic acronym for "Harakat al-Muqawama al-Islamiya," or Islamic Resistance Movement. It is primarily located in the Gaza Strip and the West Bank.

Hezbollah

Historically, Arab and Iranian (formerly Persian) factions have not collaborated well on issues of political debate. Each sees the other as a major threat in the Middle East. For instance, several wars have been fought between Iran and its neighbors (e.g., Iraq) over border disputes. However, common enemies and philosophies have unfortunately united several radical terrorist groups. Their ideology expresses the destruction of Israel and the liberation of Jerusalem as a religious obligation for all Muslims. It justifies the use of terror as a weapon in the hands of the weak and oppressed against the strong, aggressive, and imperialistic activities of Israel and the United States.

Hezbollah, or "Party of God," is based primarily in Lebanon, Syria, and Iran. The basis of Hezbollah is to develop a pan-Islamic republic throughout the Middle East

FIGURE 3.10

Hassan Nasrallah has effectively led Hezbollah since the first Israeli invasion into Lebanon in 1982. He continues to rise in popularity among the Lebanese people.

heated by religious clerics in Iran. The group rose to international prominence in 1983 with its involvement in the bombing of the U.S. Marine barracks in Beirut, Lebanon, killing 241 soldiers. For the most part, Hezbollah has been very active throughout the Middle East, targeting U.S. interests abroad. To date, the group has not conducted direct attacks on American soil.

However, since August 2006, Hezbollah has become much more active in the international arena and in the United States. Stemming from its emotionally charged leader, Hassan Nasrallah, and its "victory" over Israel in Lebanon (2006), Hezbollah has garnered significant financial support from Iran (see Figure 3.10). In addition, there have been several cases in the United States indicating that profits garnered through illegal activities (e.g., fraud, narcotic trafficking) as well as legitimate business operations have been funneled to the terrorist organization. Several of these cases have arisen in areas of the United States where large concentrations of Lebanese Shiite Muslims reside, such as Charlotte, North Carolina; New York City; and Detroit/Dearborn, Michigan.

In the coming decade, Middle Eastern politics will continue to be combustible and relations with the West more severely strained. As Islamic populations continue to grow in the countries of the former Soviet Union, China, India, Europe, and the United States, it will become more imperative to deal with political realities dispassionately and to transcend stereotypes.[36] Islam is not synonymous with violence, and thus not every Muslim is a terrorist.[37]

Other International Threats

Certainly, the Middle East is not the only area ripe with terrorist activity aimed at the United States. Historical conflict in Northern Ireland has spawned the Provisional Irish Republican Army (PIRA), reportedly having significant financial contacts with groups in large East Coast cities (e.g., Boston, Philadelphia, and New York).[38] Incidents in Germany, Italy, and France have indicated a "reawakening" of the Red Brigades, the Greens, and other cell groups expressing a left-wing, Marxist orientation.[39]

Then, too, a relatively new phenomenon called "narco-terrorism" continues to plague American police agencies as well as the international community. The most illustrative cases are seen in South America surrounding the highly lucrative cocaine business. Drug lords in the Medellin and Cali cartels have allied with the M-19 group in Colombia and Sendero Luminoso (Shining Path) in Peru for protection in cultivating and trafficking cocaine to the United States. Similar arrangements between drug dealers and anti-Western political groups (or states) have been observed in Cuba, Nicaragua, Panama, Bulgaria, and Burma.[40] One of the most successful of these collaborations is the development of the notorious street gang Mara Salvatrucha (MS-13). Originally composed of former soldiers and fighters from civil wars in El Salvador and Honduras during the 1970s and 1980s, MS-13 has become a violent and sophisticated gang associated with drug and human trafficking from Latin America. More problematic to local police agencies is the connection between ethnic drug dealers (Haitians, Jamaicans, and Cubans) and foreign governments, which results in significant financing and armament supplying in support of drug trafficking to the United States.[41]

Right-Wing Extremism

The resurgence of right-wing, white supremacist groups across the country was highlighted in the bombing of the Alfred P. Murrah Federal Building in Oklahoma City on April 19, 1995. The blast killed 169 people, including 19 children, and injured more than 500 others. Convicted and sentenced to death, Timothy James McVeigh held "extreme right-wing views and hated the federal government."[42] According to the FBI, the former army sergeant often wore military fatigues, sold weapons at gun shows, and attended militia meetings.[43] The incident focused attention on a number of right-wing groups and state militias that have traditionally expressed strong

Quick Facts

Linking Traditional Crime with Terrorism

In September 2004, Chechen rebels raided a school in Beslan, Russia, killing 331 men, women, and children. Two years later, in February 2006, the Los Angeles Police Department arrested 8 people for fraud in connection with an international car-theft ring and an alleged charity scam claiming to send aid to Russia, Georgia, Armenia, and Jordan. While at first glance the two incidents appear to be unconnected, the arrest in Los Angeles was a major setback to financing of the international Chechen terrorist group. Police agencies today are using a low-key strategy to concentrate on traditional criminal activity (such as credit card abuse, identity theft, marital fraud, fencing operations, prostitution, and narcotics trafficking) associated with terrorist groups. By focusing on criminal activity to finance terrorism, police are finding success in arresting known actors and preventing domestic acts of terrorism against the homeland. The old investigative adage "Follow the money" appears to be working well in law enforcement's efforts to prevent terrorism.

Source: Robert Block, "An LA Police Bust Shows New Tactics for Fighting Terror," *Wall Street Journal*, December 29, 2006, p. 2C.

anti-government and white-supremacist propaganda. These groups have also supported violence against minorities (African Americans, Asians, and Jews), homosexuals, and members of the U.S. government (Bureau of Alcohol, Tobacco and Firearms and the Internal Revenue Service). While the number of members of each of these groups is relatively small, they pose a significant threat because of their ability to communicate and coordinate activities. The groups have multiple names and members, publish regular newsletters, maintain websites, and operate automated bulletin board systems. In some cases, documented collusion between these groups and local law enforcement officials has posed a significant threat. Many people are attracted to these groups because they identify themselves with fundamentalist Christianity. Much of their rhetoric focuses on patriotism as interpreted by their leaders, usually using a perversion of the Constitution or the Bible. These groups consist of well-armed ideologues who possess the potential for increased terrorism, at least in geographical pockets throughout the United States.[44]

Quick Facts

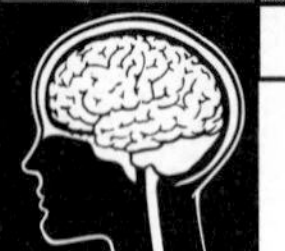

Major Right-Wing Militant Groups in the United States

Aryan Nation—This is a white-supremacist organization with strong separatist ideology, led by Richard Butler of Hayden Lake, Idaho, a major figure in the Christian Identity Church, a pseudoreligious justification for white supremacy. The Nations recruits members from white prison gangs. Their goal is to develop an all-white homeland, to be called the "Northwest Mountain Republic," in Washington, Oregon, Idaho, Montana, and Wyoming.

Covenant, Sword and Arm of the Lord—This paramilitary group operated primarily in Texas, Arkansas, and Missouri. Eight members were arrested with illegal weapons, explosives, land mines, and an anti-tank rocket launcher in 1985. High Christian fundamentalist with survivalist mentality.

Ku Klux Klan (KKK)—This is primarily a southern states organization, with the largest memberships in Alabama, Georgia, North Carolina, and Mississippi. Several of the chapters have forgone the traditional cross burning and hooded robes in favor of automatic weapons, paramilitary training camps, and camouflage uniforms. In 1997, members of the KKK were indicted in a plot to blow up a natural gas plant in Texas, covering the planned armed robbery of an armored car. The group still maintains the white-supremacist and anti-Semitic beliefs prominently characterizing the KKK historically.

Minutemen—This paramilitary organization was strongest during the 1960s. Small enclaves still exist that express strong anti-communist rhetoric and violence against liberals. Their insignia of the crosshairs of a rifle scope usually earmarks this group from other right-wing extremists.

National Alliance—This is a Neo-Nazi group led by William L. Pierce, who started a new white enclave in rural West Virginia. Pierce is the author of *The Turner Diaries,* the saga of a family that survives the impending race war against African Americans and retreats to the mountains for safety.

Posse Comitatus—This is a loose-knit group attracting rural farmers. Strong anti-government sentiment claims that the Federal Reserve System and income tax are unconstitutional. Posse leaders have fused tax-protest doctrine with virulent anti-Semitism. Leader Gordon Kahl murdered two U.S. marshals in North Dakota and was subsequently killed in a shootout in 1983.

Skinheads—This is a violence-prone, Neo-Nazi youth gang whose members are noted for their shaved heads. They express a strong white-supremacist, racist, and anti-Semitic ideology with close linkages to the Ku Klux Klan.

The Order—This is the most violent of the Neo-Nazi groups, with several ties to the Aryan Nations. It is responsible for the murder of a Jewish radio personality in Denver in 1984; at least two armored car robberies totaling $4 million in Seattle, Washington, and Ukiah, California; and a large bombing attempt in Coeur d'Alene, Idaho.

White Aryan Resistance (WAR)—This is the main white-supremacist group in California, headed by Tom Metzger, former Grand Dragon of the California Ku Klux Klan. It currently produces *Race and Reason*, a white-supremacist program shown on public access cable television.

State militias—Active paramilitary organizations exist in almost every state (e.g., the Michigan Militia, the Republic of Texas Militia, and the Arizona Vipers), expressing a strong white, Protestant, local constitutionalist perspective of government. They conduct a variety of paramilitary camps and are preparing for an "impending race war." Many groups have legitimate firearms licenses allowing automatic weapons and explosives. One group in Arizona is known to have purchased a World War II-era tank. Strong linkages to local police agencies have been documented. Members are strong gun owner advocates with a superpatriotism and anti-federal government sentiment.

Source: Adapted from several law enforcement intelligence reports. See also Cheryl Sullivan, "New Extremists Exceed 'Jim Crowism' of KKK," *Christian Science Monitor*, January 12, 1992, p. 2.

Hate Crimes

Right-wing extremist groups represent a movement that promotes whites, especially northern Europeans and their descendants, as intellectually and morally superior to other races.[45] It is not coincidental that, as these groups have grown in strength, so have the number of reported hate crimes. **Hate crimes** are harms inflicted on a victim by an offender whose motivation derives primarily from hatred directed at a perceived characteristic of the victim (e.g., the person's race, religion, ethnicity, gender, and/or sexual orientation). They are particularly heinous because of their unique impact on victims as well as on the community. Victims often suffer from the suspect's underlying criminal behavior, such as the physical injury caused by violence or the property damage associated with vandalism. In addition, they are victims by the thought that such acts were *not* random, that at least some people in our society detest them because of who they are: African-American, Jewish, Islamic, Catholic, Irish, lesbian, and so on. Hate crimes are often brutal and injurious, and victims are not only physically hurt but also emotionally traumatized and terrified. Others in the community who share the victim's characteristic may also feel vulnerable, and this may escalate the conflict as they attempt to retaliate for the original offense.

In the past, police officers have not been adequately trained to handle such incidents, treating them as routine assaults or vandalism. However, with new federal legislation has come the development of the National Institutes Against Hate, located at the Simon Wiesenthal Center in Los Angeles, California. The institute provides training for teams of criminal justice professionals from the same jurisdiction to combat hate crimes. Its goal is to provide new strategic approaches to combatting hate crimes based on an understanding of the unique elements that differentiate such crimes from other acts. The center has been highly successful in training over 500 participants and providing an ongoing support center for follow-up communication, program evaluation, and professional development via website updates and videoconferences.[46]

Legal definitions of hate crimes vary. The federal definition addresses civil rights violations under 18 U.S.C. Section 245. A hate crime is a criminal offense committed against persons, property, or society that is motivated, in whole or in part, by an offender's bias against an individual's or a group's perceived race, religion, ethnic/national origin, gender, age, disability, or sexual orientation.[47] Most states have a hate crime statute that provides enhanced penalties for crimes in which victims are selected because of the perpetrator's bias against the victims' perceived race, religion, or ethnicity. Some states also classify as hate crimes those in which a victim is selected on the basis of a perception of his or her sexual orientation, gender, or disability. In some states, the passage of hate crime statutes has been controversial as politicians have debated the constitutionality of enhanced penalties based on a suspect's association with an extremist group or the inclusion of homosexuality as a protected class.

Digital Hate

Many white-supremacist groups have used the Internet to recruit potential members and spread their message of hate. Over 1,500 websites can be identified and attributed to extremist organizations that incite racial hatred and religious intolerance as well as terrorism and bomb making. More disturbing is the directed effort by many of these groups to attract young people into their ranks. Based in part on links to other social youth movements involving music and dress (e.g., Skinheads, black cults, and heavy-metal music), aggressive recruitment on college campuses and the development of webpages designed to attract young people are now quite common. In addition, white-power rock concerts are often sponsored by extremist groups, such as the

In The News

The Internet: Selected Hate Sites

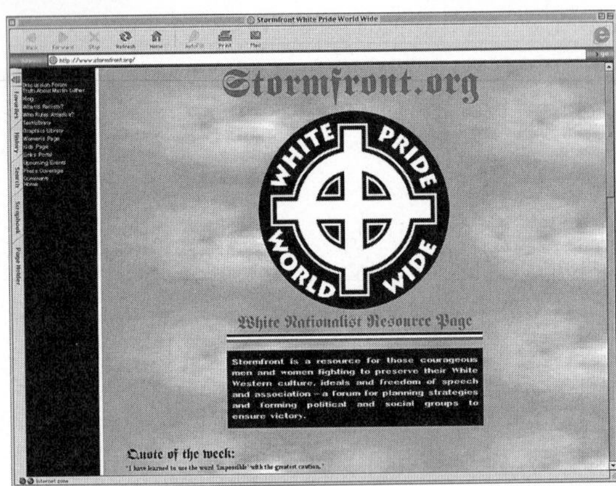

Stormfront maintains libraries for both text and graphics, foreign language sections, and a large list of links to other Internet sites.

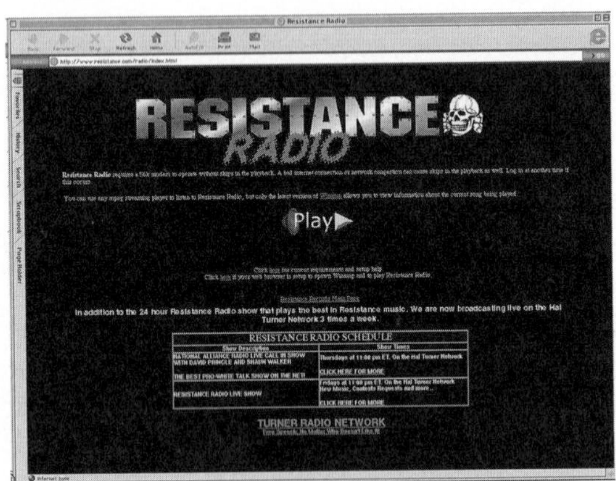

Resistance Radio promotes and sells the music of hate. Its success has unified many Skinhead bands and has given them their first opportunity to target millions of young people.

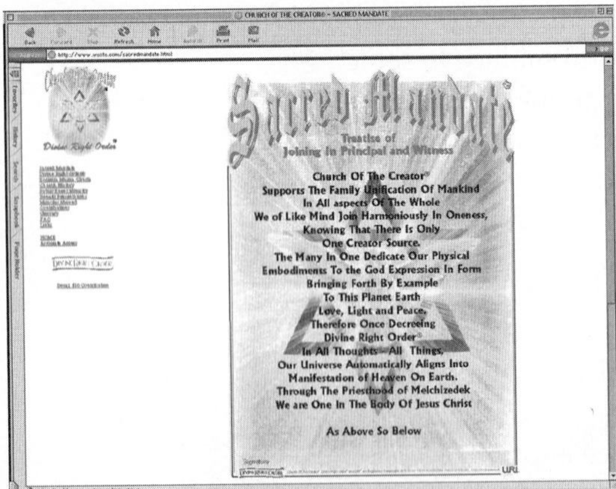

World Church of the Creator and other racist groups attempt to recruit younger and younger followers via the Internet.

Source: The New Lexicon of Hate: The Changing Tactics, Language and Symbols of America's Extremists (Los Angeles: Simon Wiesenthal Center, 1999), www.wiesenthal.com, for updated information on Wiesenthal Center's *Digital Terrorism and Hate 2003*. See also Robert W. Taylor, Tory J. Caeti, D. Kall Loper, Eric J. Fritsch, and John Liederbach, *Digital Crime and Digital Terrorism* (Upper Saddle River, N.J.: Pearson Prentice Hall, 2006).

National Alliance and the World Church of the Creator. These concerts provide face-to-face opportunities for meeting and recruitment.

White-supremacist groups have also created sophisticated computer games aimed at attracting teenagers. *Ethnic Cleansing*, the most high-tech game of its kind, encourages players to kill blacks, Jews, and Hispanics as they run through urban ghettos and subway environments. In the game, players can dress in Ku Klux Klan robes and carry a noose. Every time a black enemy is shot, he emits a monkeylike squeal, while Jewish characters shout, "Oy vey!" when they are killed.[48] Quite predictably, the game has spurred significant controversy between game developers and censor advocates. However, very little can be done to ban the game, since many other video games are designed to allow enthusiasts to create new levels and characters, while free software tools enable programmers to build new platforms easily.

These types of games and directed recruitment efforts have been effective tools in swelling the ranks of some extremist organizations.[49] According to one Skinhead source, young people represent the future—"they are the frontline warriors in the battle for white supremacy."[50]

Ecoterrorists and Animal Rights Groups

Many of the single-issue terrorist groups, such as the **Earth Liberation Front (ELF)** and the **Animal Liberation Front (ALF)**, arose from relatively peaceful movements and call for a renewal of the planet's geophysical and biological environment. The notable difference between the terrorist group and the more passive movements (e.g., Earth First and People for the Ethical Treatment of Animals [PETA]) is in the advocacy of violence and destruction to accomplish their ends. Single-issue groups, such as ELF and ALF, pose one of the most significant new threats in domestic terrorism. Both organizations work in small groups with no central hierarchy. They have no formal membership lists, and they work independently in a cell-structured manner similar to other violent groups. To date, most of their activity has been aimed at the destruction of property and vandalism.

Both groups began in England and migrated to the United States during the 1980s. Like so many other groups, ELF was inspired by the fictional writings of one author. *The Monkey Wrench Gang*, a 1975 novel by Edward Abbey, told the story of a group of ecologists who were fed up with industrial development in the West. In the novel, environmental activists travel through the western United States spiking trees, burning billboards, sabotaging bulldozers, and damaging the property of people they deem to be destroying the environment. This type of low-level activity has become so popular that, among activists, the term "monkey wrenching" has become a key touchstone for ecoterrorism.[51] The FBI designated ELF a terrorist organization in January 2001. This action was based primarily on the arson attack of a ski resort under construction near Vail, Colorado, in 2001. ELF burned three buildings and caused the destruction of four ski lifts. The group quickly claimed responsibility for the attack, which caused an estimated $12 million in damages. Ironically, the fire almost swept through the adjoining forest and would have destroyed the very habitat ELF was attempting to "save" for the preservation of wildlife. Of course, this was not the only attack from ELF, but it does represent one of the most financially destructive incidents directly attributed to the group.

ALF grew substantially during the 1990s and took on a much more destructive perspective. Instead of just tossing blood or spray-painting individuals wearing furs, the group began a campaign to "free" animals from cages and destroy animal-linked farms, business, and laboratories. Breeding companies were attacked when the animals

In The News

Eco Terrorists Arrested

In January 2006, after a nine-year investigation, the FBI indicted 11 people in connection with a five-year wave of arson and sabotage claimed by the Earth Liberation Front and the Animal Liberation Front. Detailing nearly 20 attacks from 1996 to 2001, causing no deaths but nearly $25 million in damage to lumber companies, a Vail ski resort, meat plants, and electric towers throughout the Pacific Northwest, the "vast ecoterrorism conspiracy" has been dealt a very severe blow, one which will place a significant dent in the movement.

Source: Blaine Harden, "11 Indicted in 'Eco-Terrorism' Case," *Washington Post*, January 21, 2006, p. A-3.

were released from their cages and the surrounding areas destroyed by fire and/or vandalism. Several of the targets were major research universities in Michigan and California, which not only suffered significant physical damage to buildings but also lost years of research findings and records.[52]

Certainly, the face of terrorism in the United States has changed in the past five years. More and more terrorist activities are characterized by random bombings and shootings not aimed at political agendizing or ransom delivery but done for "effect." That is, they are specific acts of violence aimed at causing significant death, destruction, and widespread pandemonium throughout our communities, leaving the larger society helplessly asking, "Why?"

Critical Thinking Questions

1. How do you define terrorism? Explain the myriad of problems associated with defining this term and discuss the concept that one person's terrorist is another person's freedom fighter.
2. Discuss some of the active terrorist groups in the Middle East. Do you think that there will ever be peace in the Middle East? Why or why not?
3. What is a hate crime? Give examples and discuss relevant current events in your community that might be labeled hate crimes.

CHAPTER REVIEW

1. Explain the concept of a paradigm shift. What factors or events have caused the paradigm shift in policing?
   Paradigm shifts are periods of time in which operational experimentation challenges the established beliefs of a profession. In the case of policing, the past 30 years have been marked by significant changes in the fundamental role police play in society. Beginning with the first movements toward team policing in the 1970s, police have become more integrated into society and the larger community, not just focusing on crime control but also attempting to address wider social issues related to the crime problem (e.g., poverty, unemployment, health care, schools, teenage pregnancy, and gangs). Community police partnerships became the hallmarks of progressive police departments, revealing an engaged and active police agency willing to work with the greater community, particularly youth, minority, and decayed parts of the city. This 20-year period (1980s–1990s) witnessed a major shift toward more proactive, community-oriented approaches to crime

rather than the reactive responses to calls for service indicative of traditional policing efforts. And in the early part of the twenty-first century, the United States government and hence, policing, were forever changed by the terrorist attacks of September 11, 2001. The new role given police has now moved in another direction; not only should police prevent and solve crime, but they should also be much more active in preventing the next terrorist attack on this country.

2. Describe intelligence-led policing.
   Intelligence-led policing represents a collaborative enterprise between the police and the community based on improved intelligence operations stemming from community policing and problem-solving strategies. Improving intelligence operations throughout a police organization assists the department in crime detection, investigation, prevention, and deterrence, as well as helps identify and prevent potential acts of terrorism within a community. Good policing is good terrorism prevention.
3. Define intelligence.
   Intelligence can be defined as raw data and information that has been evaluated, analyzed, and produced with careful conclusions and recommendations. It is a product of a systematic and thoughtful examination, placed in context, and provided to law enforcement executives with facts and alternatives that can inform critical decisions.
4. Describe the Intelligence Cycle as presented in the *National Criminal Intelligence Sharing Plan (NCISP)*.
   The Intelligence Cycle is a process applied to policing that integrates both law enforcement and national security intelligence agendas, while providing mechanisms for insuring and safeguarding individual constitutional rights and freedoms. The model consists of six sequential steps: (1) requirements; (2) planning and direction; (3) collection; (4) processing and exploitation; (5) analysis and production; and (6) dissemination.
5. Define a fusion center. Briefly list its four primary goals.
   Fusion centers are located within state and local police agencies; they act as clearinghouses for all potentially relevant homeland security information that can be used to assess local terror threats and aid in the apprehension of more traditional criminal suspects. They are the centralized hub of intelligence and crime analysis supporting the basic elements of operations and investigations. The following are the four primary goals of a fusion center:
   1. *To act as a centralized hub of intelligence and crime analysis supporting the basic elements of anti-terror and anti-crime operations and investigations*
   2. *To provide support for operations designed to protect critical infrastructure and key resources during an all-hazard event within a specific community or region*
   3. *To reduce the vulnerability of critical infrastructure and key resources within a community by improving public awareness relating to terrorism and concentrating on criminal activities often associated with terrorist organizations*
   4. *To assist police executives in making better-informed decisions, especially during emergencies or critical incidents, relating to critical resource deployment and multi-agency coordination*
6. List the four primary areas of responsibility within the Department of Homeland Security.
   The four primary areas of responsibility within the Department of Homeland Security are (1) border security and transportation; (2) emergency preparedness and response; (3) chemical, biological, radiological, and nuclear countermeasures; and (4) intelligence analysis and infrastructure protection.

7. Define terrorism.
   Terrorism can be defined as the threat of and/or use of violence for the purpose of achieving a specific set of political objectives or goals. There are four specific and distinct typologies of terrorism, based on actors:
   1. *International terrorism: actions conducted in the international arena by individuals that are members of a nation-state*
   2. *Transnational terrorism: actions conducted in the international arena by individuals that have no nation-state*
   3. *Domestic terrorism: actions conducted by groups within a nation, usually against the government or against other specific ethnic or tribal groups within that nation-state*
   4. *State terrorism: actions conducted by governments against their own population*
8. Briefly describe the concept of "jihad," and name some of the more radical groups active in the Middle East.
   The concept of "jihad," or "holy war," is derived from the revolutionary writings of Sayyid Muhammad Qubt and Ibn al-Wahhab, who called on everyday Muslims to join in their fight against the West. The physical manifestation of a jihad is a corruption of the Holy Koran and is used to justify the radicalization of the Islamic religion. It does not *represent mainstream Islam.*
9. Define a hate crime.
   Hate crimes (usually violent crimes) are harms committed against an individual by an offender whose motivation derives primarily from hatred directed at a perceived characteristic of the victim (e.g., the person's race, religion, gender, sexual orientation). These crimes are particularly heinous because, aside from the physical injury, they also cause victims to be emotionally traumatized and terrified. Victims are not random, and they often feel that at least some people detest them because of who they are (e.g., African-American, Jewish, Muslim, gay).
10. Define an ecoterrorist.
    Ecoterrorists are groups of individuals advocating and conducting violence and destruction for a single-issue cause, such as the Earth Liberation Front and the Animal Liberation Front. While the causes stem from a renewal of the planet's geophysical and biological environment, these groups often resort to violence, arson, and vandalism to achieve their ends.

KEY TERMS

Al-Qaeda: a radical Islamic Middle Eastern terrorist organization led by Osama bin Laden and Ayman al-Zawarahi; it was responsible for the attacks against the United States on September 11, 2001.

All-hazard: able to support operations during an emergency that is either human-made or natural.

Critical infrastructure and key resources (CI/KRs): the important facilities, buildings, and installations that provide basic services within a community, such as transportation and telecommunications systems, water and power lines, electronic data systems, key bridges and waterways, emergency facilities, and private sector industries and businesses, that are essential for the defense and security of the United States.

Earth Liberation Front (ELF), Animal Liberation Front (ALF): the two most infamous single-issue, ecoterrorist groups active in the United States; they are responsible for significant destruction of property caused by arson and vandalism and sometimes resort to more violent means to express their message.

Fusion centers: data centers within police agencies that serve as intelligence hubs and clearninghouses for all potentially relevant homeland security and crime information that can be used to assess local terror threats and aid in more traditional anti-crime operations.

Hamas: the Islamic Resistance Movement of Palestine, representing an outgrowth of the Muslim Brotherhood and Wahhabism, focused on escalating armed conflict and terrorism against Israel.

Hate crimes: harms (usually violent crimes) committed against an individual because of his or her perceived race, religion, ethnicity, gender, and/or sexual orientation.

Hezbollah: the "Party of God" terrorist organization primarily based in Lebanon, Syria, and Iran, currently very active in the international arena and responsible for the bombing of the U.S. Marine barracks in Beirut in 1983, killing 241 soldiers.

Intelligence: data and information that have been evaluated, analyzed, and produced with careful conclusions and recommendations for future decision makers and policymakers.

Intelligence-led policing: a type of policing stemming from the post–9/11 era, representing a collaborative enterprise of improved intelligence operations with community policing and problem-solving strategies.

Jemaah Islamiyah (JI): a radical Islamic group active in Southeast Asia (Indonesia, Thailand, and Malaysia) responsible for attacks on Australian, European, and American tourists in Bali after 9/11.

Jihad: a "holy war," a concept perverted by radical Islamists to justify a physical war against the West; a perversion of the concept proscribed in the Holy Koran and *not* representative of mainstream Islam.

Paradigm shift: a period in which operational experimentation challenges the established beliefs of a profession.

Terrorism: the threat of and/or use of violence to achieve a specific set of political objectives or goals.

NOTES

1. See Robert M. Fogelson, *Big City Police* (Cambridge, Mass.: Harvard University Press, 1977), and George L. Kelling and Mark H. Moore, "The Evolving Strategy of Police," *Perspectives on Policing* (Washington, D.C.: National Institute of Justice, 1988).
2. Ibid.
3. William G. Gay, H. Talmadge Day, and Jane P. Woodward, *Neighborhood Team Policing* (Washington, D.C.: USGPO, 1977).
4. See Robert Trojanowicz, *An Evaluation of the Neighborhood Foot Patrol Program in Flint, Michigan* (E. Lansing: Michigan State University Press, 1979).
5. See Robert W. Taylor, Eric J. Fritsch, and Tory J. Caeti, "Core Challenges Facing Community Policing: The Emperor Still Has No Clothes," *ACJS Today,* May/June 1988.
6. See Thomas Kuhn, *The Structure of Scientific Revolutions*, 2nd ed. (Chicago: University of Chicago Press, 1970), and William F. Walsh, "Compstat: An Analysis of an Emerging Police Managerial Paradigm," *Policing: An International Journal of Police Strategies and Management* 24 (3): 347–62.
7. For a more thorough discussion on the impact of new strategies on police operations, refer to Eric J. Fritsch, John Liederbach, and Robert W. Taylor, *Police Patrol Allocation and Deployment* (Upper Saddle River, N.J.: Pearson Prentice Hall, 2007).
8. Marilyn Peterson, *Intelligence-Led Policing: The New Intelligence Architecture* (Washington, D.C.: U.S. Department of Justice, BJA, September 2005) NCJ 210681, and K. Riley, G. Terverton, J. Wilson, and L. Davis, *State and Local Intelligence in the War on Terror* (Washington, D.C.: The RAND Corporation, 2005).
9. Peterson, *Intelligence-Led Policing: The New Intelligence Architecture*, p. 1.
10. David L. Carter, *Law Enforcement Intelligence: A Guide for State, Local, and Tribal Law Enforcement Agencies* (Washington, D.C.: U.S. Department of Justice, COPS Office, October 2004).
11. For a more thorough discussion of the role of intelligence in combatting terrorism, see Robert W. Taylor, "Terrorism and Intelligence," *Defense Analysis* 3, no. 2 (1987): 165–75.
12. Peterson, *Intelligence-Led Policing: The New Intelligence Architecture*, p. 3.
13. For a more thorough discussion of the first two schools of thought, refer to R. Godson, ed., *Intelligence Requirements for the 1980s: Analysis and Estimates* (Washington, D.C.: National Strategy Information Center, 1983).
14. Early models of predictive intelligence are discussed in R. Hever, *Quantitative*

Approaches to Political Intelligence (Boulder, Colo.: Westview Press, 1978).

15. *National Criminal Intelligence Sharing Plan* (Washington, D.C.: U.S. Department of Justice, 2003).
16. Riley, et. al., *State and Local Intelligence in the War on Terror.*
17. Joseph D' Amico, "Stopping Crime in Real Time," *Police Chief,* September 2006, pp. 20–24.
18. Samuel Walker and Charles M. Katz, *The Police in America,* 5th ed. (Boston: McGraw-Hill, 2005).
19. Jon Elliston, "Disaster in the Making," *The Independent Weekly,* September 24, 2004.
20. Ibid.
21. Bill Gertz, *Breakdown: How America's Intelligence Failures Led to September 11* (Washington, D.C.: Regnery, 2002).
22. Toni Locy, "FBI Too Top-Heavy, Whistleblower Tells Panel," *USA Today,* June 7, 2002, p. 4A.
23. Ibid.
24. Several news agencies have reported on continued problems with the FBI. See Dan Eggen and Griff Witte, "The FBI's Upgrade That Wasn't," *Washington Post,* August 18, 2006; Terry Frieden, "Report Examines FBI's Focus on Terrorism," *CNN,* October 4, 2004; Bill Gertz, "WMD Panel Fires FBI Agent," *Washington Times,* January 13, 2005; and Alfred Cummings and Todd Masse, *FBI Intelligence Reform Since September 11, 2001: Issues and Options for Congress* (Washington, D.C.: CRS Report to Congress, August 4, 2004).
25. Richard Schultz, "Conceptualizing Political Terrorism: A Typology," *Journal of International Affairs* 4, no. 8 (spring/summer 1978): p. 8.
26. Robert W. Taylor and Harry E. Vanden, "Defining Terrorism in El Salvador: La Matanza," *Annals of the American Academy of Political and Social Science* (September 1982): 106–17.
27. Ibid., p. 109.
28. Ibid.
29. For a discussion on the various definitions of terrorism, see Richard Schultz, "Conceptualizing Political Terrorism: A Typology," *Journal of International Affairs* 4, no. 8 (spring 1978); Martha Crenshaw Hutchinson, *Revolutionary Terrorism* (Stanford, Calif.: Hoover Institute Press, 1978); Brian Jenkins, *The Study of Terrorism: Definitional Problems* (Santa Monica, Calif.: The RAND Corporation, 1980); James M. Poland, *Understanding Terrorism: Groups, Strategies, and Responses* (Upper Saddle River, N.J.: Prentice Hall, 1988); Paul Wilkinson, *Political Terrorism* (New York: Wiley Press, 1974); Bruce Hoffman, *Inside Terrorism* (New York: Columbia University Press, 1998); and Jonathan R. White, *Terrorism: An Introduction* (Belmont, Calif.: West/Wadsworth, 2003).
30. The conceptualization of terrorism is presented in a number of works. See Edward Mickolus, "Statistical Approaches to the Study of Terrorism," in *Terrorism: Interdisciplinary Perspectives,* ed. Yonah Alexander and Maxwell Finger (New York: McGraw-Hill, 1977), pp. 209–69. For additional reading on this subject, see David Milbank, *International and Transnational Terrorism: Diagnosis and Prognosis* (Washington, D.C.: CIA, 1976), and Richard Schultz, Jr., and Stephen Sloan *Responding to the Terrorist Threat: Security and Crisis Management* (New York: Pergamon Press, 1980).
31. Ibid.
32. "Notorious Terrorist Reportedly Dead," *USA Today,* August 20, 2002, p. A2.
33. For detailed information on the life of Osama bin Laden, see Yossef Bodansky, *Bin Laden: The Man Who Declared War on America* (Rocklin, Calif.: Prima, 1999).
34. RAND Corporation, RAND Terrorism Incident Data Base. See www.rand.org/ise/projects/terrorismdatabase/.
35. Council on Foreign Relations. "Terrorism Q and A: Jemaah Islamayiah," www.terrorismanswers.com/groups/jemaah_print.html.
36. John L. Esposito, *The Islamic Threat: Myth or Reality?* (Oxford: Oxford University Press, 1992), p. ix.
37. See A. M. Rosenthal, "As You Sow," *New York Times,* December 22, 1992, p. A21; E. McQuaid, "By Peace or the Sword," *Jerusalem Post,* December 16, 1992; D. Pipes, "Fundamental Questions about Muslims," *Wall Street Journal,* October 30, 1992, p. A11; and A. Permutter, "Wishful Thinking about Islamic Fundamentalism," *Washington Post,* January 19, 1991, p. 16.
38. Scott S. Smith, "The Anglo-Irish Accord: Diverting Attention from the Real Issues," *Christian Science Monitor*, December 14, 1988, p. 15.
39. See Robert Kupperman and Jeff Kamen, "A New Outbreak of Terror Is Likely," *New York Times,* April 19, 1988, p. 6, and Alan Riding, "Rifts Threaten Plan to Remove Borders," *CJ Internaitonal* 6, no. 5 (September/October 1990): 3.
40. David W. Balsiger, "Narco-Terrorism 'Shooting Up' America," in *Annual Edition: Violence and Terrorism 1990/91* (Guilford, Conn.: Dushkin, 1990), pp. 164–66.

41. Ibid.
42. "Families Scoff at Suspect's New Images," *Sunday Oklahoman,* July 2, 1995, p. 24.
43. Ibid.
44. Louis A. Radelet and David Carter, *Police and the Community*, 5th ed. (New York: Macmillan, 1994), p. 248.
45. *The New Lexicon of Hate: The Changing Tactics, Language and Symbols of America's Extremists* (Los Angeles: Simon Wiesenthal Center, 1999).
46. For more information, see the National Institutes Against Hate Crimes website: www.wiesenthal.com.
47. *Responding to Hate Crimes: A Police Officer's Gluide to Investigation and Prevention* (Washington, D.C.: U.S. Department of Justice and International Association of Chiefs of Police, 1999).
48. Victor Godinez, "Hate Group Wooing Teens by Making a Game Out of Racism," *Dallas Morning News,* March 14, 2002, p. A2.
49. R. W. Taylor, E. J. Fritsch, and T. J. Caeti, *Juvenile Justice: Policies, Programs, and Practices* (New York: Glencoe/McGraw-Hill, 2002) pp. 518–20. See also Robert W. Taylor, Tory J. Caeti, K. Kall Loper, Eric J. Fritsch, and John Liederbach, *Digital Crime and Digital Terrorism* (Upper Saddle River, N.J.: Pearson Prentice Hall, 2006).
50. An interview with leader of the Texas Militia in Dallas (January 2006), reflecting much of the sentiments expressed by Tom Metzger, a leader of the White Aryan Resistance (WAR).
51. Johathan R. While, *Terrorism,* 3rd ed. (Belmont, Calif.: Wadsworth, 2002), p. 233.
52. Cindy C. Combs, *Terrorism in the Twenty-First Century,* 3rd ed. (Upper Saddle River, N.J.: Prentice Hall, 2003), pp. 164–66.

Terrifying are the weaknesses of power.
—Greek Proverb

CHAPTER 4

POLITICS AND POLICE ADMINISTRATION

OUTLINE

Introduction
Police Accountability
The Roles of State and Local Government in Law Enforcement
Local Political Forces
The Police Chief and External Incidents
Tenure and Contracts for Police Chiefs
Politics and the County Sheriff
State Prosecutor
The Judiciary
Citizen Involvement
News Media
School Violence
Chapter Review
Key Terms
Notes

OBJECTIVES

1. Explain the significance of the U.S. Supreme Court decisions in each of the following cases: *Mapp v. Ohio* (1966), *Gideon v. Wainwright* (1963), *Escobedo v. Illinois* (1964), and *Miranda v. Arizona* (1966).
2. Describe the impact of incidents such as the Abner Louima case and the Sean Bell shooting.
3. List the goals of the Commission on Accreditation for Law Enforcement Agencies.
4. Describe three styles of law enforcement as presented by James Q. Wilson.
5. Briefly describe the three major forms of local government found in the United States.
6. List the three political arenas of conflict.
7. Explain why police chiefs that are not protected from arbitrary and unjustified termination often resist setting new goals and instituting organizational change.
8. Describe the differences in status between a county sheriff and a police chief.
9. Explain how the state prosecutor impacts police practices.
10. Explain how citizens can be involved in the policymaking process of law enforcement agencies.
11. Describe some circumstances in which the police and the media might be in conflict.
12. Describe the function of a school resource officer (SRO).

INTRODUCTION

In discussing the relationship between politics and police administration, it is important to distinguish between "Politics" and "politics." **Politics** refers to attempts to impose external, partisan political influence on the operation of a department. For example, people are promoted because they know precinct committeepersons and ward chairpersons who have influence with the party in power. The department is manipulated for partisan, political advantage and forced to make financial contributions. Justice is not dispensed evenhandedly. This use of the word is negative. However, **politics** means governance of a city. Aristotle's original understanding of the word "politics" was "science of the polis," seeking the good of both citizen and city-state. The present-day police are its practitioners, as are politicians at their best. "Politics" with a small *p* avoids political leveraging and supports merit and job performance—all positive connotations. The art of governing a local community requires a commitment to take bad politics out of the police department and put the right kind back in.[1]

This chapter addresses a number of subjects involving the police that are often the focus of political debate and compromise. As such, these issues are often controversial and tend to become more or less influential, depending on the amount of attention expressed by specific individuals or parties in office. For instance, one of the most dynamic debates in Congress from 1993 to 1996 was over the development and refinement of the Violent Crime Control and Law Enforcement Act of 1994, commonly referred to as the crime bill (see Chapter 2, Policing Today). While the bill had almost unanimous support in providing federal money for an additional 100,000 local police officers under the COPS (Community-Oriented Policing Services) program, the bill also included stringent gun control measures—an issue that markedly divided Congress.

In November 1993, Congress passed the Brady Bill, which mandated a five-day waiting period for gun purchases, after overcoming a fierce lobbying effort mounted primarily by the National Rifle Association (NRA). The following year, in May 1994, the House of Representatives voted to ban 19 types of assault weapons and their look-alikes. And again, in 1994, Congress passed the entire crime bill inclusive of various gun control initiatives strongly supported by the Democratic Congress, President Clinton, and Attorney General Janet Reno. However, in 1995, touting a Republican majority, Congress initiated H.R. 2076, a $27.3 billion FY'96 Commerce, Justice, and State Appropriations Bill that dramatically cut over $4 billion in funding from the original deployment of 100,000 new police officers. Separate funding streams for community policing efforts were eliminated in the proposed bill. While President Clinton vowed to veto such a bill, one might believe that such a dramatic congressional change may be due to retaliation for the passage of rigorous gun control laws, which were part and parcel of the overall Crime Bill of 1994.[2]

The tragic events of September 11, 2001, prompted a renewed focus on the protection of America. President George W. Bush proposed the biggest reorganization of the federal bureaucracy in more than half a century to create a vast cabinet department overseeing homeland security. However, the bill stalled in the Senate in a dispute over workers' rights. President Bush wanted more authority to hire, fire, or transfer people in so sensitive a department, while opposing Democrats wanted to preserve the rights of dedicated employees finding themselves shuffled into a new bureaucracy. The issue became hotly contested in Congress as President Bush complained about Senate Democrats more interested in "special interests" than homeland security. The open debate covered any form of previous criticism against President Bush for not being prepared for such an event and focused on the Democratic-led Senate support of unions and individual workers' rights. The debate sparked a national interest in the American public and is credited for fueling the Republican takeover of the Senate in the November 5, 2002, elections. After the election, President Bush made the development of the Department of Homeland Security his top priority, and on November 19, 2002, the bill was overwhelmingly passed by the Senate. Interestingly, the original proposal for such a department was introduced on October 11, 2001, by Senator Joe Lieberman (D-Conn.) and was strongly supported by Democratic senators a month after the attacks on the World Trade Center and the Pentagon and well before the Bush administration recommended the agency. However, it is President Bush who has emerged as the leader in fusing nearly two dozen federal law enforcement organizations into a single megadepartment with one urgent mission: to stop terrorism.[3]

Clearly, the Department of Homeland Security represents the single largest federal reorganization since the modern Defense Department was created in 1947. The 170,000-employee department absorbed the Coast Guard; the Immigration and Naturalization Service; the Secret Service; much of the Bureau of Alcohol, Tobacco, and Firearms; the Federal Emergency Management Agency; the Border Patrol; and a host of other agencies. It represents one of the most dramatic and sweeping changes in law enforcement organization and one that will significantly change the impact and role of American police officers at all levels of government. This is not a new phenomenon to police executives who have had to manage agencies under such turbulent and dynamic environments. This chapter provides a thumbnail sketch of the political issues often confronting police administrators, including police accountability, state and local political forces, the state prosecutor, the judiciary, citizen involvement, the media, school violence, and terrorism.

POLICE ACCOUNTABILITY

Accountability of the police to other institutions conforms to the American notion of a system of checks and balances. There are, however, some questions about the actual means by which this accountability occurs and the degree to which it exists. It has been suggested that the degree of control over the police by political authority varies with the level of government at which the police functions take place. In this country, although cities and counties are legally creatures of the states under state constitutions, the states have traditionally divested themselves of much of their control over these jurisdictions and have allowed them to operate with considerable independence.[4] The existence of local autonomy has also been facilitated by the belief in home rule, which maintains that local government can manage its own affairs and that strong controls from the state capital or the federal government are neither desirable nor consistent with American political philosophy. Nevertheless, the influences and controls being exerted on local law enforcement from both the federal and the state level have increased since the turbulent period of the 1960s.

Some argue that this encroachment of local hegemony will eventually result in a significant shift of control and political power away from the local level. In reply, the proponents of this development argue that the traditionally strong local control of policing has resulted in a degree of parochialism that has retarded the growth of professionalism. They also maintain that the increased involvement in local law enforcement by the state and federal government has produced important qualitative improvements in such areas as personnel selection standards, training, crime laboratory capabilities, and labor–management relations.

As we discussed in Chapter 2, Policing Today, the movement toward community policing places a renewed emphasis on police accountability. Under community policing, outside review and citizen involvement in the day-to-day operations of the police department are highlighted. The police are accountable to the community they serve. To this end, several types of review or oversight vehicles have been implemented in cities across the nation. These include citizen complaint desks, neighborhood substations staffed by volunteers, police–community relations committees, and outside review commissions. The transition to more citizen and community involvement has not been an easy one, often fraught with conflicting political agendas and open confrontation.

A good example can be observed in the community review system developed by Sheriff Lee Baca in Los Angeles County in 2001. Beginning in 1998, Baca began to express a philosophy of policing that was radically different from anything that had ever come out of the Sheriff's Department or the Los Angeles Police Department. He spoke of his police force being an "enemy" of bigotry in all its forms and of the necessity for his deputies to revere the U.S. Constitution and particularly the Bill of Rights. According to Baca, communities should tell the police department the solutions to their problems, not the other way around. His community review plan embodied his unconventional approach to law enforcement. It called for civilian oversight and supervision of his department's investigation of officer-involved shootings, abuse, and misconduct cases—not the use of a traditional internal affairs division. What made Baca's proposal even more radical was that the civilians chosen to head and staff his new "Office of Independent Review" were civil rights attorneys—traditionally, the nemeses of overzealous police officers. While the board has been controversial, it is hailed as one of the most important changes in a major city police department in the country. Created in part as a response to the Los Angeles Police Department's Rampart corruption scandal, it is intended to add credence and confidence to the sheriff's internal investigations.[5] The Los Angeles Sheriff's Department is a force of over 13,000 deputies and civilian personnel who police roughly 2.5 million people and run the nation's largest urban jail system.

Federal Influence in Law Enforcement

Some authorities believe that trends occurring from the 1960s to the present have resulted in the partial nationalization of criminal justice. Up to the 1960s, it was safely said that criminal justice was almost completely the responsibility of state and local governments. Federal criminal statutes were limited in their coverage, federal assistance to local law enforcement was generally in the areas of training and the processing of evidence, and the U.S. Supreme Court concerned itself with only the most notorious violations of constitutional rights by state and local authorities.[6] This trend was reversed in no small measure by a series of opinions, rendered by the Supreme Court under the strong leadership of Chief Justice Earl Warren, that greatly strengthened the rights of accused persons in criminal cases. However, as the Supreme Court has become more conservative in the past two decades, an "erosion" of many of the landmark cases of the Warren era can be observed.

Supreme Court Decisions Affecting Law Enforcement: 1961 to 1966

Significant judicial review of local police actions has been a somewhat recent practice.[7] However, from 1961 to 1966—a period frequently referred to as the "due process revolution"—the Supreme Court took an activist role, becoming quite literally givers of the law rather than interpreters of it. The Warren court's activist role in the piecemeal extension of the provisions of the Bill of Rights, via the due process clause of the Fourteenth Amendment, to criminal proceedings in the respective states might have been a policy decision.[8] Normally, the Supreme Court writes opinions in about 115 cases during any particular term. During the 1938–1939 term, only five cases appeared under the heading of criminal law; a scant three decades later, during the height of the due process revolution, about one-quarter of each term's decisions related to criminal law.[9] The Supreme Court could scarcely have picked a worse period in which to undertake the unpopular role of policing the police; a burgeoning crime rate far outstripped population increases, and many politicians were campaigning on "law and order" platforms that all too often dissolved into rhetoric on their election. The problem of crime increasingly came to the public's eye through the media. In sum, the high court extended procedural safeguards to defendants in criminal cases precisely when the public's fear of crime was high and there was great social pressure to do something about crime.

Fundamentally, the Supreme Court's role in the due process revolution was a response to a vacuum in which the police themselves had failed to provide the necessary leadership. The era of strong social activism by various special-interest groups was not yet at hand, and neither the state courts nor the legislatures had displayed any broad interest in reforming the criminal law. What institution was better positioned to undertake this responsibility? The Court may even have felt obligated by the inaction of others to do so. Therefore, it became the Warren court's lot to provide the reforms so genuinely needed but so unpopularly received. The high court did not move into this arena until after it had issued warnings that, to responsive and responsible leaders, would have been a mandate for reform.

Several key decisions were made by a split vote of the Court and drew heavy criticism from law enforcement officers and others as handcuffing police in their struggle with lawlessness. These decisions included *Mapp v. Ohio* (1961), which banned the use of illegally seized evidence in criminal cases in the states by applying the Fourth Amendment guarantee against unreasonable searches and seizures; *Gideon v. Wainwright* (1963), which affirmed that equal protection under the Fourteenth Amendment requires that legal counsel be appointed for all indigent defendants in all criminal cases; *Escobedo v. Illinois* (1964), which affirmed that a suspect is entitled to confer with an attorney as soon as the focus of a police investigation of the suspect shifts from investigatory to accusatory; and *Miranda v. Arizona* (1966), which required police officers, before questioning suspects, to inform them of their constitutional right to remain silent, their right to an attorney, and their right to have an attorney appointed if they cannot afford to hire one. Although the suspect may knowingly waive these rights, the police cannot question anyone who, at any point, asks for a lawyer or indicates "in any manner" that he or she does not wish to be questioned.[10]

The impact of these decisions on police work was staggering. In an effort to curb questionable and improper tactics, the Supreme Court essentially barred the use of illegally obtained evidence in a criminal prosecution to prove guilt. This action, known as the *exclusionary rule,* rested primarily on the judgment that deterring police conduct that violates the constitutional rights of an individual outweighs the importance of securing a conviction of the specific defendant on trial. A need for new procedures in such areas as interrogations, lineups, and seizures of physical evidence was created.

Although the decisions of the due process revolution initially were criticized by many law enforcement officers, over the years that view has changed as new generations of law enforcement officers come along for whom those decisions are simply the correct way to do things. Also, time has seen the exodus of some officers from the police profession who simply could not or would not adapt to a new way of doing business. Finally, there was a growing willingness among law enforcement leaders to acknowledge not only that some of their tactics needed changing but also that *Miranda* and other decisions had accomplished it.

More Recent Supreme Court Decisions

In more recent years, appointments to the Supreme Court by Presidents Ronald Reagan and George Bush provided a conservative majority who generated decisions more favorable to law enforcement. Beginning in the early 1970s and continuing to today, the Supreme Court has systematically eroded the basic principles set forth in the *Mapp* and *Miranda* decisions.[11]

Exceptions to the exclusionary rule developed in *Mapp v. Ohio* started in 1984. In *Massachusetts v. Sheppard* and *United States v. Leon,* the Court held that evidence obtained by the police acting in "good faith," even if it is ultimately found to be illegally seized because of an error committed by the judge or magistrate, is still admissible in court.[12] In *Leon,* the Court reasoned that the exclusionary rule was designed to deter police misconduct rather than punish the police for the errors of judges. Therefore, the Fourth Amendment's exclusionary rule should not be applied to bar the prosecution from using evidence that had been obtained by police officers acting in reasonable reliance on a search warrant issued by a neutral magistrate, even if that warrant is found to be invalid substantively for lack of probable cause. Critics of the decision suggest that the "good faith" exception will encourage police to provide only the minimum of information in warrant applications and hence will undermine the integrity of the warrant process.[13]

Traffic Stops and Arrest

The original decision on automobile stops and searches was developed in 1925 in *Carroll v. United States* (see Figure 4.1).[14] As long as the vehicle was stopped because of reasonable and individualized suspicion (usually a traffic violation), the areas in plain view and the area around the driver were subject to search without a warrant. The mobility of the motor vehicle produced an exigent circumstance to the search warrant requirement. As long as the officer could develop probable cause that the vehicle was transporting contraband or other illegal substances, a warrant was not required. In 1990, the court expanded the right to stop and search a vehicle without violation or individualized suspicion by allowing sobriety checkpoints and roadblocks. The Court rejected the concept that sobriety checkpoints violated the Fourth Amendment and allowed police agencies to stop vehicles without individualized suspicion.[15]

In 2001, the Supreme Court, in *Atwater v. City of Lago Vista,* [16] ruled that the Fourth Amendment does not forbid warrantless arrests for minor criminal or traffic offenses. The case involved the arrest of a person for a seat belt violation, an offense punishable by a maximum $50 fine.

This line of reasoning was unanimously upheld by the Supreme Court in 2002, which ruled that, if an officer has reason to suspect a crime, he or she may stop a suspect vehicle without due cause. The case stemmed from a U.S. Border Patrol officer stopping a minivan that turned out to be carrying over 125 pounds of marijuana. The case involved a 1998 traffic stop in Arizona near the Mexican border. The Border Patrol officer observed the minivan on a back road frequently used by drug traffickers.

FIGURE 4.1

The landmark case involving automobile stops and searches was developed in 1925 in *Carroll v. United States.* Here, a New York motorcycle officer shows the correct technique in stopping vehicles in 1921.

(Courtesy of AP/Wide World Photos, New York, 1996)

The driver looked nervous and failed to wave at the officer, although children in the van were waving vigorously. According to the officer, the van was registered in a high-crime neighborhood, and minivans are often used in smuggling drugs. A California-based federal appeals court had ruled that the officer did not have enough reason to make the stop and had violated the owner's constitutional right to be free from unreasonable search and seizure. Chief Justice William Rehnquist wrote for the Court that the appropriateness of a police stop must be judged on the "totality of the circumstances" in each case. This process allows officers to draw on their own experience and specialized training; hence, the appeals court decision was overturned. This case was important to the enforcement of drug and immigration laws. Further, it could also apply to anti-terrorism efforts. As Justice Sandra Day O'Connor indicated, "We live in a perhaps more dangerous age today than when this traffic stop happened."[17]

Self-incrimination

Nowhere is the erosion of a Warren court decision more obvious than in the cases impacting the *Miranda v. Arizona* doctrine. During the past 25 years, the Court has systematically loosened the application of the Miranda warning, allowing evidence to be admitted under a variety of exceptions. The most controversial and complex of these cases occurred in 1991. In *Arizona v. Fulminante,* the Court ruled that an error made by the trial court in admitting illegally obtained evidence (in determining that a confession was coerced) does not require an automatic reversal of the conviction if the error is determined to be harmless—that is, if there is no reasonable possibility

Quick Facts

Atwater vs. City of Lago Vista: A Case Study

On March 26, 1997, in Lago Vista, Texas, Officer Bart Turek pulled over Gail Atwater after noticing that neither Atwater nor her two children were wearing seat belts as required by Texas law. Officer Turek approached the vehicle and recognized Atwater as someone he had previously pulled over for the same violation. In addition, Atwater did not have her driver's license or proof of insurance. He decided to arrest Ms. Atwater and, after placing her children in the care of a guardian, the officer transported her to the Lago Vista Police Department, where she was held for an hour and a half.

Atwater's offenses were all punishable by a fine only by Texas law. She argued that the Fourth Amendment protection against warrantless searches and seizures forbid a warrantless arrest for such a minor criminal offense. Atwater further claimed that, since her offenses did not involve any sort of violence, there was no Common Law precedent for her arrest. The Supreme Court disagreed, citing Common Law statutes that predated the founding of the United States allowing peace officers to make warrantless arrests for all sorts of relatively minor offenses unaccompanied by violence, including cursing and unlawful game playing.

The Court also cited the fact that statutes in all 50 states permit warrantless arrest for misdemeanors by some peace officers. The Court refused to create a new rule of law forbidding custodial arrest when conviction could not ultimately carry any jail time and stated that an officer may arrest an individual without violating the Fourth Amendment if there is probable cause to believe that the individual has committed even a minor criminal offense in the officer's presence. Ultimately, the Court felt that, although Atwater's arrest was probably humiliating, it was no more harmful to her interests than the normal custodial arrest.

Source: *Atwater v. City of Lago Vista*, 165 F. 3d 380 (5th Circuit 1999).

that a different result would have been reached without the illegally seized evidence.[18] Even though Fulminante's confession was ruled to be "harmful" and was subsequently reversed, the importance of the ruling was the establishment of a more conservative procedure for reversing cases, even when confessions have been coerced and, hence, illegally obtained.

In the foreseeable future, the Supreme Court will likely continue to expand police powers in such areas as search and seizure and interrogation. It is equally likely that the Court will produce rulings that will reverse some of the gains made since the due process revolution of the Warren court regarding misconduct by the police.[19]

Age-Old Problems in Policing: Brutality and Scandal

In an era of police reform characterized by significant Supreme Court decisions and sweeping programmatic changes (imbued in the new philosophy of community policing as described in Chapter 2, Policing Today), law enforcement continues to be plagued by the old problems of brutality and scandal. Celebrated cases (e.g., the Rodney King incident, the O. J. Simpson trial, and the Abner Louima case) have revealed only the tip of the iceberg. Police officers across the country have been accused of lying in court, falsifying or withholding of evidence, gross mishandling of case investigations, corruption, racism, physical abuse and violence, and even murder. The phenomenon has not been isolated, with several major cases highlighting police misconduct in rapid succession.[20]

Setting the stage in 1991, the beating of Rodney King by Los Angeles police exposed to the world the ugliness of police racism and brutality. However, Los Angeles is hardly the only place where police administer such "street justice" with disturbing regularity. Again in 1991, in New York City, five officers were indicted on murder charges in the death by suffocation of a 21-year-old Hispanic man suspected of car theft. The officers were accused of having hit, kicked, and choked Federico Pereira while he lay face down and "hog-tied"—his wrists cuffed behind his back while another set of cuffs bound his hands to one ankle. The case led to a sweeping investigation

FIGURE 4.2

Abner Louima was tortured in a Brooklyn police station in 1997.
(©Reuters NewMedia Inc./CORBIS)

into New York City police brutality and corruption. In a 1993 scandal, a New York state trooper was convicted of falsifying fingerprint evidence to get convictions. In 1995, the O. J. Simpson case highlighted the actions of Detective Mark Fuhrman. Fuhrman testified that he had found a bloody glove at Simpson's estate that matched one found 2 miles away near the bodies of Nicole Brown Simpson and Ronald L. Goldman. Such evidence, along with DNA matching of the blood on the glove, directly linked Simpson to the murder. Simpson's lawyers, however, were able to discredit Fuhrman as a liar and a racist who planted evidence, producing a tape-recorded conversation in which Fuhrman spoke of beating African-American suspects (commonly referred to by Fuhrman as the "n word") and repeatedly used other racial slurs and epithets.

On August 8, 1997, police in New York City arrested Abner Louima in one of the most infamous police abuse cases in recent history. At the time of his arrest, Louima had no bruises or injuries. Three hours after his arrest, Louima was rushed by ambulance to the hospital in critical condition. Internal affairs investigators confirmed that Louima had been severely beaten by officers during his arrest and subsequent transport to the jail. While in police custody, Louima was taken to a restroom and endured what one investigator described as "torture." Police officers removed Louima's pants and began to sodomize him with a toilet plunger. Medical doctors confirmed that Louima's internal injuries were the result of blunt force trauma. Two of the five officers indicted for the beating and torture were found guilty and sentenced to prison[21] (see Figure 4.2). Four years later, in July 2001, Louima settled his civil lawsuit against New York City and its main police union. The settlement called for the city to pay Louima $7.125 million and the union, the Patrolmen's Benevolent Association, to pay him $1.625 million. It was the most money that New York City had ever paid to settle a police brutality case and was the first time that a police union had to pay part of the claim. Further, Louima insisted that several policy changes be made to the New York Police Department, including a civilian panel for brutality case oversight, the prosecution of future department officers involved in brutality cases, and an increase in officer training involving ethics and the use of force.[22] The case has had a significant impact on the New York Police Department.

In 1999, again in New York City, four officers fired 41 shots, killing unarmed Amadou Diallo in the stairway of his apartment. Officers contend that they opened fire on Diallo because he "acted suspiciously" and they "thought he was armed with a gun." The internal affairs investigation revealed that four officers completely emptied their weapons (16 shots each) and that one officer fired five times. It appeared that one officer panicked and that the others followed suit in the shooting. Three of the officers had been involved in other shooting incidents, an anomaly for the New York City Police Department, where 90 percent of officers have never fired their weapon. The discrepancies in the officers' statements prompted a criminal investigation; all four officers were found not guilty of charges of second-degree murder.[23]

In 2000, an inquiry into the Los Angeles Police Department's Rampart station revealed an extensive and massive corruption scandal in that city. Allegations and the subsequent convictions of 3 officers revealed that over 70 officers had been involved in either committing crimes or covering up criminal activity. The police scandal centered on former members of the Community Resources Against Street Hoodlums (CRASH) anti-gang unit, charged with framing gang members, planting evidence, committing perjury, and even shooting innocent victims. The scandal was declared the worst in the department's history. About 100 criminal cases associated with the Rampart scandal were overturned after investigators found evidence of police abuses. Over 20 officers were relieved of duty, quit the department, were suspended, or were fired during the investigation. In the most notorious of the activities cited, one officer was charged with attempted murder when he shot a handcuffed suspect and left him paralyzed. In November 2006, citizens of New York City were forced to recall the shooting death of Amadou Diallo as members of the NYPD fired 50 shots at a group of unarmed men, killing one of them. Sean Bell, age 23, was leaving his bachelor party at a strip club when he was involved in an altercation with a plainclothes detective who was investigating the club for drug, weapons, and prostitution violations. The officer approached Bell's car, intending to question one of the passengers. Bell's car bumped the officer and then plowed into a minivan carrying additional officers. The car reversed and again struck the van. Officers opened fire on the vehicle after they thought one of the men in Bell's car was reaching for a weapon, shooting 50 rounds before discovering that none of the men were armed. Bell was killed, and two other men were wounded. Thousands of New Yorkers later marched in a series of protests organized by the NAACP and Reverend Al Sharpton, decrying the use of excessive force against Bell, whose wedding was to be held only hours after he was killed. Mayor Michael Bloomberg met with Bell's family after calling the shooting "unacceptable and inexplicable" (see Figure 4.3). In the aftermath of the shooting, the officers were placed on leave. The mayor bolstered the budget of a civilian review board designed to investigate claims of police abuse as a result of the shootings.

The problems of police deviance and misconduct have not been limited to local police. Federal agents and agencies have also come under attack, with the most embarrassing moments stemming from botched raids against the Branch Davidians in Waco, Texas, and white separatists in Idaho and revelations that agents of the FBI withheld evidence in the Timothy McVeigh Oklahoma City bombing case. As if these debacles were not enough, the events of September 11, 2001, cast a serious shadow

FIGURE 4.3

New York City Mayor Michael Bloomberg met with community leaders and elected officials in the aftermath of the Sean Bell shooting in November 2006.

(Kathy Wilens/AP Wide World Photos)

on whether the FBI could sustain one of its core missions—that of domestic intelligence. In early 2001, the bureau was rocked by the arrest of Agent Robert Hanssen, a 25-year counterintelligence agent accused of selling secrets to Moscow. The spy scandal was just one in a series of controversies facing the FBI, including a botched Chinese espionage investigation, persistent problems in the FBI crime lab, and questions concerning the FBI's failure to prevent the terrorist strikes of September 11.

These cases have not only marred the reputation of specific police agencies but have also raised serious questions about police accountability, autonomy, and ethics. Certainly, these are not new issues in American law enforcement. Historically, corruption has been a documented problem throughout the development of many East Coast departments. Police brutality, commonly accompanied by charges of racism, has been a constant complaint of many inner-city and ghetto residents. The riots of the 1960s, as well as the more recent riots in Miami and Los Angeles, were all ignited by episodes of perceived police brutality. More seriously, the rash of celebrated cases of police deviance have produced a wide-sweeping public apathy toward the police. As one Los Angeles resident indicated, "I don't even put quarters in parking meters anymore. After Fuhrman, police in this town couldn't get a conviction for a parking ticket."[24] Tensions between minority groups, especially in inner-city, low-income areas, are exceptionally high. Continued reports of police brutality and harassment focus on racism (see Figure 4.4). Some experts argue that these types of cases clearly undermine the public's confidence in the entire criminal justice system.[25]

As a result of these and similar incidents, serious questions concerning the ability of police internal affairs units to control police misconduct and deviance have been raised. Critics of the police argue that civil damage suits are a much more useful deterrent to police brutality than any type of internal disciplinary sanction.[26] Title 42 of the United States Code, Section 1983, titled *Civil Action for Deprivation of Rights,*

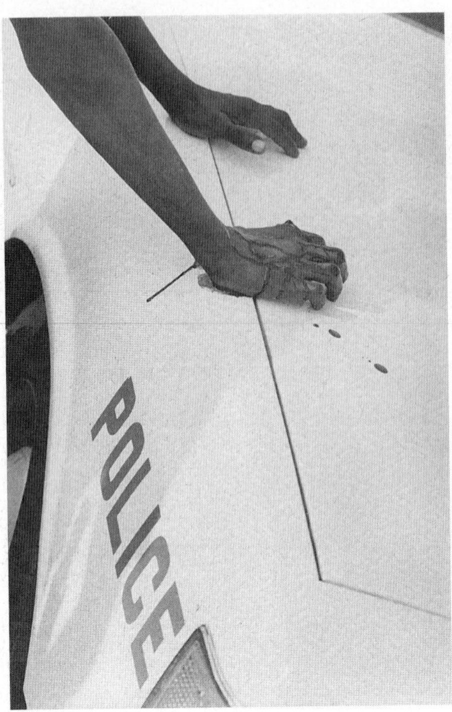

FIGURE 4.4

Even in routine arrests, some force is often required. However, the recent highlighted cases involving African Americans and the police have again raised issues of brutallty and racism.

(Courtesy of Michelle Andonian, Detroit, Michigan, 1996)

specifically provides a mechanism for filing a civil tort action against individual police officers for violation of a suspect's constitutional rights. Infliction of mental and emotional distress, assault, battery, and excessive use of force, including use of deadly force, are routinely the grounds for a 1983 action against police officers (see Chapter 14, Legal Aspects of Police Administration, for more detail on Title 42 U.S.C., Section 1983). The damages under this section can be punitive and general and cannot be limited by recent state "tort reform" movements. Rodney King brought a $56 million civil suit under this section against all the officers that were involved in the incident and the Los Angeles Police Department, reportedly $1 million for each blow against him. He was eventually awarded $3.5 million for sustained damages. In 2001, over $8.5 million was paid by the City of New York and the New York Police Department Union for just one case, the Abner Louima case. While the courts have ruled that police officers cannot be held individually liable for most actions undertaken on the job, taxpayer concern about the rising cost of lawsuits has revived the popularity of civilian review boards.[27] Such panels are at work in 26 of the nation's 50 largest cities (e.g., Los Angeles County, Philadelphia, New York, Kansas City, and Chicago).[28] Despite the increase in civil litigation and public scrutiny, brutality and scandal still persist as a major problem in policing.

Racial and Ethnic Profiling

Nothing has fueled the fire between police and minorities more than the use of race and ethnicity as criteria in police decision making during discretionary traffic and field interrogation stops, often described as "racial and ethnic profiling."[29] Weitzer and Tuch define **racial profiling** as "the use of race as a key factor in police decisions to stop and interrogate citizens."[30] The term has several meanings, most of which are associated

In The News

LAPD Gets Mixed Progress Report

The Los Angeles Police Department (LAPD) has failed to comply with several of the standards required by a federal consent decree for handling investigations into the use of force, according to a federal monitor. The consent decree between the U.S. Department of Justice and the LAPD was signed in 2000 in an effort to bring federal oversight to the department after a pattern of constitutional rights violations by officers, particularly in the wake of the Rampart Division scandal. The agreement was initially supposed to last for five years but has been extended to early 2008.

Since the decree was enacted, the LAPD has been required to enact a number of mandates, including provisions for dealing with officers suspected of using excessive use of force, recruitment of confidential informants, and a data base that tracks every LAPD officer's personnel history, including all complaints against that officer. The data base is one of the cornerstones of the agreement.

A report in 2006 showed that the department was still not in compliance with 38 mandates of the consent decree, including the data base. The federal monitor also found that the LAPD failed to address discrepancies in reports of uses of force in 13 cases. Additionally, the LAPD did not immediately initiate complaint investigations in five of the use-of-force incidents as required by the consent decree.

LAPD Chief William Bratton stated that he is pleased with the city's progress on the mandates. However, in the aftermath of an incident in November 2006 involving apparent excessive force caught on videotape, many citizens and civil leaders are questioning why nearly 30 percent of the consent decree has not been implemented after its initial five-year period. "Five years is a pretty long period of time," said Blair Taylor, president of the Urban League of Los Angeles.

Source: Patrick McGreevey, "LAPD Gets Mixed Progress Report," *Los Angeles Times*, November 16, 2006.

with law enforcement officers making the decision to stop an individual because of race or ethnicity. Officers often use the "pretext" or "suspicious vehicle stop" argument to justify their actions as legal (e.g., using a legal pretext, such as an illegal lane change or broken license plate light, to stop the vehicle and then gain a basis to search for illegal drugs). These actions are lawful under *Whren v. United States of America*[31] and were affirmed in *Brown v. City of Oneonta*. The U.S. Court of Appeals for the Second Circuit held that, where law enforcement officials possess a description of a criminal suspect that consists primarily of the suspect's race and gender and where they do not have other evidence of discriminatory intent, they can act on the basis of that description without violating the equal protection clause of the Fourteenth Amendment.[32] This includes the practice of issuing profiles of suspects or offenders in general offenses (e.g., drug traffickers and gang members) as well as more specific offender descriptions. For instance, if a specific crime occurs (e.g., a rape or a murder) and the suspect description by a witness includes race, gender, or ethnicity, the police are lawful to stop a citizen on the basis of how closely the individual resembles the characteristics or description within the "profile."

Racial profiling is a relatively recent phenomenon. The first racial profile originated with the attempt to interdict drug trafficking from Miami on Interstate 95 through the Northeast corridor in 1985.[33] The Florida Department of Highway Safety and Motor Vehicles issued guidelines for police in "The Common Characteristics of Drug Couriers," in which race and ethnicity were explicitly defined as characteristics.[34] On the sole basis of this profile, police officers were allowed to make "pretextual stops." Advocates of this policy argued that it produced more efficient crime control than random stops, measured in terms of detecting and seizing illegal drugs and arresting drug couriers.[35] Others challenged the factual basis for the drug courier profile and argued that profiles are a form of racial discrimination, creating a self-fulfilling prophecy because they result in higher rates of arrest, conviction, and imprisonment of minorities, particularly blacks.[36] The controversy set the stage for a flurry of methodological and empirical studies focusing on data collection and interpretation of research on racial profiling.[37] Some of the more interesting studies are presented here.

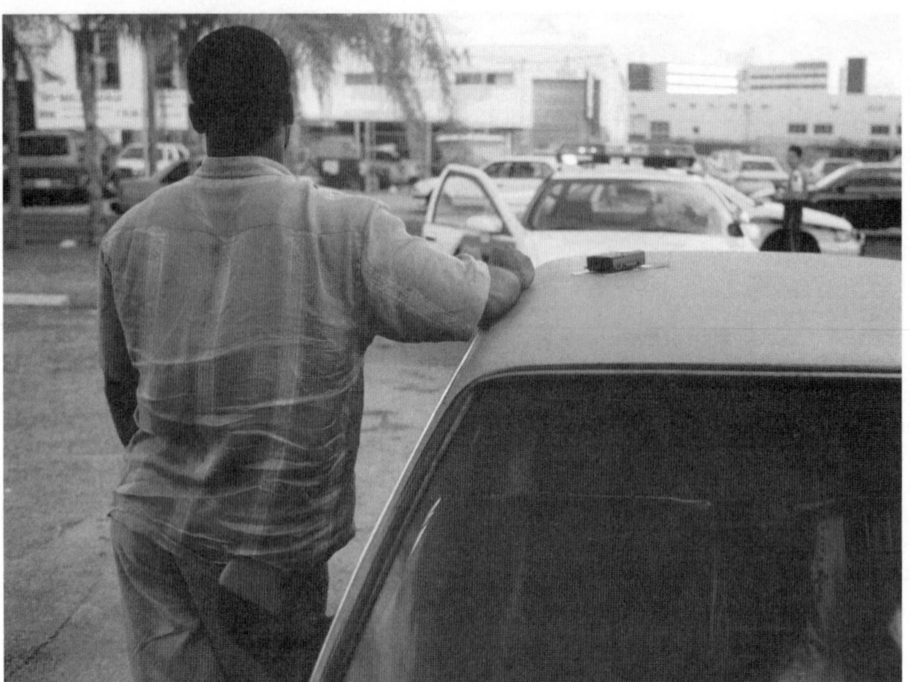

FIGURE 4.5

Racial profiling in traffic stops has become an increasingly controversial issue in police procedure. (Steve Lehman/CORBIS/SABA Press Photos, Inc.)

A study by Meehan and Ponder suggests that roadway composition plays an important role in analyzing existing police data on the occurrence of racial and ethnic profiling.[38] Police data alone reveal only the number and proportion of stops of specific groups, such as African-American, Hispanic, or white drivers, but does not relate these stops to the number within each racial/ethnic group of drivers traveling a specific roadway. They contend that, when police data alone are used to analyze profiling, it appears that police stop African-American drivers more frequently in high-crime areas of suburban communities that border communities composed predominantly of African Americans. However, when the same data are correlated with the distribution of African-American drivers on specific roadways in these same areas, it becomes apparent that the police show virtually no discriminatory practice. Indeed, African-American drivers are stopped at rates proportional to their numbers in the driving population. In the same study, Meehan and Ponder found that African Americans were indeed stopped two to three times greater in proportion to the number of other drivers in predominantly white areas. However, these numbers were proportional to the overall number of African Americans driving in these neighborhoods.[39] Unfortunately, the increase in stops in predominantly white areas seems to contribute to the perception formed erroneously by members of the African-American community that they are being treated unfairly (see Figure 4.5).

In an attempt to see how these perceptions are formed, Weitzer and Tuch conducted a study on the public's perception of racial profiling.[40] Not surprisingly, they found that both race and personal experience with being stopped are closely related to a person's attitude toward the issue. They found that social class was a much more important variable in developing specific perceptions on racial and ethnic profiling than race or ethnicity. Middle-class African Americans were more likely to feel that they had been victims of racial profiling (and discrimination) than were members of the lower class. This may be explained by the fact that members of the middle class tend to live in areas that are not populated predominantly by other African Americans and because they possess symbols of their affluence that are easily visible. People who believe that the police stopped them on the basis of their race alone were more likely to express dissatisfaction toward the police. Additionally, African Americans with higher levels of education were more likely than the less educated to disapprove of racial and ethnic profiling. This is an interesting phenomenon and may be explained again through personal experience. It appears that minorities with higher education are simply more aware of the problems associated with brutality, police discrimination, and racial/ethnic profiling. There is widespread media coverage of these topics, and highlighted cases (such as those previously mentioned, involving Rodney King, Abner Louima, and Amadou Diallo) keep these issues sharp in the minds of educated upper- and middle-class minorities. Additional studies seem to support this conclusion. Brueger and Farrell found that individuals choose to believe and interpret stories of discrimination and racial profiling incidents on the basis of their relationship to the storyteller (i.e., other members of the minority community).[41] That is, one is more likely to believe a story told by someone similar to oneself than to believe the story of the police officer or agency involved. Thus, in hearing the personal accounts of events affecting those with whom they most closely relate, individuals may perceive future police encounters in negative and stereotypic ways, expecting the worst, including violations of their rights.[42]

Notwithstanding the results of the Brueger and Farrell study, several court decisions suggest that racial profiling is discriminatory and therefore illegal. In the face of these decisions and in response to the widespread belief that there is a growing epidemic of racial profiling, hundreds of police departments have begun to voluntarily collect detailed records of traffic stops. Nine states have adopted legislation requiring their police departments to collect data, including the gender, race, and ethnicity of the person stopped, as well as whether a search was initiated and whether any warning or citation was issued.[43] The primary purpose for such activity begins to address the poignant issue how do law enforcement officials overcome the past experiences and feelings by minority communities that they are being treated unfairly? Weitzer and Tuch recommend that officers provide more information in justifying their traffic and investigatory stops.[44] By thoroughly explaining and providing the legal justification for the stop, citizens may be less likely to perceive the stop as racially motivated. The International Association of Chiefs of Police (IACP) provides further guidelines.[45] Racial profiling can be illegal and discriminatory and not an action that should be undertaken by professional police officers. Specific training in police ethics should be given to all police officers on the motivation for stopping motorists and civilians. Further, police officers should forever be cognizant of the need for embracing public and community support. This support is founded on mutual trust and respect, both of which are destroyed through incidents of racial and ethnic profiling, often leading to discrimination.

Unfortunately, the issue of racial profiling has become much more sensitive and controversial since the events of September 11, 2001. Renewed concerns have been raised by citizens of Middle Eastern dissent and the Muslim community who believe they have been singled out and harassed as potential terrorists. This situation has become acute in some cities having large Middle Eastern communities and few officers who are familiar with Islam and other aspects of Middle Eastern culture. Officers often base their assumptions on weakly supported ideas and facts that, unfortunately, are carried out in all-too-frequent, unfriendly contacts with members of the Middle Eastern community. To counter these incidents, training for police officers has been developed that focuses on understanding terrorism and the Middle East. Specifically, the State and

Local Anti-Terrorism Training Program (SLATT), funded through the U.S. Department of Justice and provided by the Institute for Intergovernmental Research in Tallahassee, Florida, concentrates on understanding the Middle East.[46] Courses focus on Islam and culture as well as the radical differences and non-traditional religious beliefs expressed by the al-Qaeda terrorist organization. Osama bin Laden does not represent Islam and the Arab world any more than David Koresh (from the Branch Davidians in Waco, Texas) represented Christianity and mainstream American society.

Training in ethics and other current issues confronting police officers will certainly help curtail the number of incidents involving racial profiling and discrimination. Providing the public with more information surrounding the reasons for a stop, showing an equal amount of respect and cooperation to *every* citizen stopped, and improving the public's trust in law enforcement agencies will help improve the community's overall perception of the police. Positively altering this perception of police motivation should result in a more trusting relationship and fewer feelings of victimization by members of minority communities.

Training and Police Ethics

In response to these issues or as a coincidence of the most sweeping changes in American policing, law enforcement has responded with reform through advanced training, education, and enhanced community policing efforts. A few cities have revamped their training and supervising to make abuses less likely. Since 1988, all police officers on the Metro Dade County force have undergone violence reduction training. Several new movements have entered the police training arena in an effort to raise the awareness of police ethics, particularly in wake of the issues surrounding racial profiling. One such program, partially funded by the Meadows Foundation, is located at the Institute for Law Enforcement Administration (ILEA), formerly the Southwestern Law Enforcement Institute, in Dallas, Texas. Intensive training seminars that apply classic ethical theories to more contemporary police problems are offered. Police officer trainers who teach courses on police ethics in law enforcement academies are particularly encouraged to attend seminars led by members of well-respected ethics centers, such as the Aspen Institute and the Josephson Institute.

To date, an estimated 5,000 police trainers have attended the seminars, resulting in over 250,000 officers from over 750 local and state jurisdictions in the United States, Canada, and Great Britain being instructed on police ethics, corruption, brutality, and racial profiling. The ILEA provides a bulletin titled *The Ethic Role Call* and a website, both of which provide officer reports and vignettes focusing on ethical constraints and problems confronted "on the job."

As observed by Radelet and Carter,[47] the importance of applied ethics is that they help officers develop a reasoned approach to decision making instead of making decisions by habit. As such, a solid ethical background provides a guide for officers making complex moral judgments about depriving people of their liberty and sometimes their lives. Given the largely unchecked discretion police officers exercise, it is incumbent that they be given an ethical foundation to ensure their decisions are just and legal. Many police agencies, especially those actively implementing a community policing philosophy, have emphasized the importance of maintaining police integrity and ethical decision making. For instance, many departments have written value statements that attempt to integrate ethics, departmental mission, professional responsibility, fairness, due process, and empathy[48] (see Figure 4.6). These statements clearly articulate managerial philosophy and behavioral expectations for officers. Again, as Radelet and Carter indicate,

Newport News, Virginia Police Department Statement of Values

Value #1
The Newport News Police Department is committed to protecting and preserving the rights of individuals as guaranteed by the Constitution.

Value #2
While the Newport News Police Department believes the prevention of crime is its primary responsibility, it aggressively pursues those who commit serious offenses.

Value #3
The Newport News Police Department believes that integrity and professionalism are the foundations for trust in the community.

Value #4
The Newport News Police Department is committed to an open and honest relationship with the community.

Value #5
The Newport News Police Department is committed to effectively managing its resources for optimal service delivery.

Value #6
The Newport News Police Department is committed to participating in programs which incorporate the concept of shared responsibility with the community in the delivery of police services.

Value #7
The Newport News Police Department actively solicits citizen participation in the development of police activities and programs which impact their neighborhood.

Value #8
The Newport News Police Department believes it achieves its greatest potential through the active participation of its employees in the development and implementation of programs.

Value #9
The Newport News Police Department recognizes and supports academic achievement of employees and promotes their pursuit of higher education.

FIGURE 4.6

Statement on values and integrity for the Newport News, Virginia, Police Department.

(Carter David L., and Radalet, Louis A., *Police and the Community*, 7th, © 2002. Reproduced by permission of Pearson Education Inc., Upper Saddle River, New Jersey)

> *These statements should leave no question in the minds of officers about the department's position and expectation concerning any form of improper behavior. Because of the "moral" implications of the values, proper behavior is urged, not out of the threat of discipline, but because this type of behavior is "right."*[49]

Additionally, community policing advocates have focused on changing the philosophy of police activity from order maintenance and arrest, which often encourages "street justice" scenarios, to a more dispute resolution, mediation, and service orientation. Some agencies have responded by sending officers into depressed neighborhoods in an attempt to protect, serve, and often befriend local residents. In many cases, the results have been positive, especially among minority youth groups (see Chapter 2). As one report indicates, "Episodes of police brutality are likely never to vanish entirely. But they could be significantly curtailed if more officers concluded that as long as their fellow police take the law into their own hands, *there is no law at all*."[50]

Commission on Accreditation for Law Enforcement Agencies

The Commission on Accreditation for Law Enforcement Agencies (**CALEA**) is a private, non-profit organization. It was formed in 1979 by the four major national law enforcement associations (International Association of Chiefs of Police [IACP], National Organization of Black Law Enforcement Executives [NOBLE], National Sheriffs' Association [NSA], and Police Executive Research Forum [PERF]). The commission has developed a national set of 900 law enforcement standards for all types and sizes of state and local agencies. In some ways, CALEA can be viewed as a direct product of the reform era to professionalize the police. Nowhere is this more apparent than in the stated goals of the commission. Its standards are designed to accomplish the following:

- Increase agency capabilities to prevent and control crime
- Enhance agency effectiveness and efficiency in the delivery of law enforcement services
- Improve cooperation and coordination with other law enforcement agencies and with other components of the criminal justice system
- Increase citizen and staff confidence in the goals, objectives, policies, and practices of the agency[51]

The accreditation process is a voluntary undertaking. In the past decade, significant movement toward accreditation has been spurred by two developments. First, because most of the standards identify topics and issues that must be covered by written policies and procedures, successful accreditation offers a viable defense or "liability shield" against civil litigation.[52] Second, CALEA provides a nationwide system for change.[53] One of the most important parts of the accreditation process is self-assessment. During this stage, agencies undergo a critical self-evaluation that addresses the complete gamut of services provided by law enforcement. The agency is also later assessed by an on-site team of law enforcement professionals to determine whether it has complied with the applicable standards for a department of its type and size.

CALEA enjoys wide support among police executives and community leaders. In particular, when a city manager is seeking to hire a new police chief from outside a troubled department, the candidates' experience with the accreditation process is a substantial plus. In one city, officers received information on Christmas Eve that a rapist who had beaten and cut his victims was in a house in a county outside their jurisdiction. Without any significant evaluation of the information, without a raid plan, with personnel who were untrained or had not previously trained together for conducting raids, and without a search warrant, the officers conducted a raid, killed a 74-year-old man in his own home who had no connection with the crime, and found out the rapist had never been there. In the aftermath, the community lost confidence in its police department. A member of the grand jury asked the police chief, "How do I know that your officers won't kill me or members of my family in my home tonight?" Departmental morale plunged to an all-time low. A management study of the department revealed that written policies and procedures were virtually non-existent and identified other deficiencies. The chief of police retired, and a new chief was brought in from the outside with orders from the city manager to get the department accredited. In the process of accomplishing accreditation, the department regained its esprit de corps and the support of the community. The city manager said he believed that "no other mechanism besides accreditation could have done so much good so quickly in turning the department around."

Despite similar accounts and the reduction of liability risks that typically accompanies accreditation, the process is not without its critics. Some see it as "window dressing . . . long on show and short on substance"—a reference to the fact that some departments allegedly develop the necessary policies to meet the standards and then fail to follow them. Some city managers are reluctant to authorize their police departments to enter a process that takes an average of 21 months to complete at an average cost of $73,708.[54] This cost includes the modest CALEA accreditation fee, which ranges from $3,800 for a department with up to 9 full-time employees to $14,700 for agencies with 3,000 or more full-time employees.[55] Other components of the average cost of accreditation include direct costs, such as purchases necessary to meet standards (e.g., first aid kits for all cars, body armor for special weapons, and tactics teams); modifications to facilities or capabilities, such as upgrading the evidence storage area and radio communication; and indirect costs, such as the cost of personnel actually doing the work necessary to meet standards (e.g., writing policies and procedures).[56] Others have maintained that the process is control-oriented and at odds with important values set forth in community policing, such as individual initiative, participatory management, and organizational democracy. (See Chapter 2, Policing Today, for a more thorough discussion of the perceived conflict between CALEA standards and community policing.)

In balance, however, it is clear that accreditation is an important national influence because it requires both self-scrutiny and external evaluation in determining the extent to which a law enforcement agency has met the 900 standards promulgated by experts in the field. It serves as a liability shield, promotes pride among employees, and stimulates confidence among the community. Moreover, it can play an important role in the economic development of a community. Businesspeople seeking to relocate evaluate the communities they are considering on the basis of transportation, taxation, recreational opportunities, and the ability of the local government to conduct its affairs professionally. In one instance, a well-managed city of 300,000 lost a major prospective employer to another city because of one salient factor: the police department in the other city was accredited. As soon as this fact became known, the mayor directed the police chief to pursue accreditation by CALEA as a "top priority."

Critical Thinking Questions

1. What is meant by the "erosion" of many of the landmark cases of the Warren Court?
2. What have police departments done to address police brutality and unethical conduct among officers? Which programs and policies do you think have been most successful at addressing these issues?
3. What are the harms inherent in racial profiling? Can you think of any situations in which racial profiling might be necessary?

THE ROLES OF STATE AND LOCAL GOVERNMENT IN LAW ENFORCEMENT

From the outset, most Americans had a firm belief that the police should be controlled by local officials organized along municipal lines. For them, a national police, such as the Italian *carabinieri,* was inconceivable, and a state police, such as the German *polizei*, was undesirable.[57] However, the history of state and local relations in the area of law enforcement has often been a rocky and tumultuous one. Fogelson, for example, has noted,

> *By the mid-nineteenth century, it was plain that for most police departments local control meant Democratic control. Hence the Republican leaders, who generally spoke for the upper middle and upper classes, demanded state control, arguing that it would remove the police from partisan politics and improve the quality of law enforcement. Their Democratic opponents countered that state control would merely shift the focus of political interference and plainly violate the principle of self-government. The issue erupted in one city after another, with the Republicans usually getting their way. They imposed state control of the police in New York City in 1857, Detroit in 1865, Cleveland in 1866, New Orleans in 1868, Cincinnati in 1877, Boston in 1885, and Omaha in 1887. They also established metropolitan police departments, with jurisdiction over the central city and adjacent territory, in New York City in 1857, Albany in 1865, and a few other places thereafter.*
>
> *Under these arrangements the state authorities appointed a board to manage, or at any rate to oversee, the big-city police. But the states did not contribute anything toward the upkeep of the police departments; nor, except in a few cases, did they authorize them to operate in the metropolitan area, much less throughout the entire state. Not until the early twentieth century did Pennsylvania, New York, and a few other states form statewide constabularies; and these forces, which patrolled mainly in small towns and rural districts, supplemented rather than supplanted the municipal police. Thus despite these changes, the American police remained decentralized to a degree unheard of anywhere in Western Europe. By the late nineteenth century, moreover, state control was well on the wane. The Democrats attacked it at every opportunity; and in the face of mounting evidence that the state boards had neither removed the police from partisan politics nor improved the quality of law enforcement, the Republicans were hard pressed to defend it. The issue was soon resolved, usually when the Democrats took office. The state authorities not only abolished metropolitan policing in New York and Albany in 1870 but also reestablished local control in Cleveland in 1868, New York in 1870, New Orleans in 1877, Cincinnati in 1880, Detroit in 1891, and Omaha in 1897. By 1900 the big-city police were controlled by local officials and organized along municipal lines everywhere in urban America except for Boston, Baltimore, St. Louis, Kansas City, and a few other places.*[58]

The type of direct takeover of local law enforcement by the states described by Fogelson will very likely not occur again, or at least not on the grand scale of the 1800s. However, we may see some isolated cases. For example, a decade ago some public officials in Georgia were urging the state to take over the administration of the Atlanta Police Department because of dramatic political upheavals that were affecting the morale and effectiveness of that department. A takeover by the state did not occur, but the political atmosphere was conducive to such a move.

Even if a state does not exercise its official political power to intervene in local police administration, it may be called on to exercise its influence in less apparent ways—in which case, the influence may not always be proper or appropriate:

> *Our department was going through a major reorganization and in the process was going to have to make about 50 promotions. One of the newly created positions was deputy chief. The only requirement for the position was that you had to have been a Major for one year. "Ed Hawks" had been a Major for about 8 months and he really wanted that deputy chief's position. Nobody believed that he even had a chance. He went to his cousin, who was close to the Governor, and talked to him. The Governor called the Mayor and expressed his "confidence" in what a great deputy chief Hawks would make. The Mayor's son sat as a political appointee of the Governor on one of the most important state boards. So, the Mayor sat on the reorganization plan until the day after Ed Hawks had a year in*

grade as a Major—which meant that 50 promotions were held up for about four months—and then approved the implementation of the plan . . . Hawks got promoted . . . crap like that is really demoralizing.[59]

In a positive vein, the impact of the state on the affairs of local law enforcement is continuing via the imposition of pre-employment and training standards, as well as through various funding formulas tied to these standards. The first state to impose minimum standards of training for police officers was California, in 1959. This move was soon followed by the states of New York, Oklahoma, and Oregon. In 1970, the LEAA did make available discretionary grants to those states that wanted to implement minimum standards programs. Today all 50 states have mandated training for law enforcement officers. It must be noted, however, that much of the impetus for the implementation of minimum standards on a statewide basis comes from the local law enforcement community. Requirements related to the minimum standards for employment as police officers are administered through state organizations, often termed Police Officers Standards and Training Commissions (POST), which generally operate under three broad mandates: (1) to establish minimum standards for employment in a state, county, or local law enforcement agency; (2) to articulate curricula of training for police officers; and (3) to conduct and encourage research designed to improve all aspects of law enforcement.[60]

In its assessment of the role of the states in criminal justice planning, in general the National Advisory Commission on Criminal Justice Standards and Goals suggested that the State Planning Agencies (SPAs), which were created by the Omnibus Crime Control and Safe Streets Act of 1968 as the state-level organizations through which federal funds were funneled from the LEAA, bear a special responsibility for the formation of minimum statewide standards.[61] However, with the demise of LEAA in 1982 there has been a reduction in or total dismantling of large state planning agencies.

LOCAL POLITICAL FORCES

The special dimension of police politics varies from community to community, but law enforcement activities are governed for the most part by the dominant values of the local political culture. James Q. Wilson, in his now classic study of the police in eight communities, identified three distinctly different styles of law enforcement, all of which were reflective of the political culture of the communities they served (1) the "watchman" style of law enforcement emphasizes order maintenance and is found in economically declining cities with traditional political machines; (2) the "legalistic" style of law enforcement is found in cities with heterogeneous populations and reform-oriented, professional governments (law enforcement of both a reactive and proactive nature characterizes this style); and (3) in the homogeneous suburban communities, the "service" style of law enforcement is oriented toward the needs of citizens.[62]

In Wilson's studies, these variations in the community political culture manifested themselves in a number of ways that subsequently affected both the qualitative and the quantitative enforcement action taken by the police. Significant enforcement variations emerged in the areas of vice, juvenile offenses, order maintenance, and traffic enforcement. Numerous variations, linked to the community's political culture, also emerged in the police department's personnel entry standards, promotional policies, extent of specialization, and level of managerial skills. These, in turn, affected the overall operations of the department, which in turn impacted the citizens' perception and confidence in its police department.

As indicated earlier, there is an unfailing, consistent, and close relationship between the type of law enforcement a community has and its dominant political culture.

This is not to suggest, however, that any community's political culture is unalterably fixed. In fact, the reform movements that have been a part of the American political scene throughout much of its history have corresponded with the emergence of new political cultures. Each new dominant political culture in time leaves its own unique mark on the unit of government within its sphere of control.

Strong Mayor

To some extent, the type of local government that a community has impacts the way police chiefs are selected, the freedom they enjoy in the performance of their status, and their tenure. For example, with a strong mayor form of government, the mayor is elected to office and serves as the chief executive of the city. The city council constitutes the chief legislative and policymaking body. The mayor nominates a candidate to serve as police chief, with majority approval needed from the city council. Once approved, the candidate assumes the position of police chief and serves at the discretion of the mayor.

Ideally, the person the mayor selects as police chief should possess the full range of managerial and administrative skills necessary to operate the police department. However, to a great extent, the kind of person selected to serve as police chief is determined by the mayor's professional qualifications, philosophy about the role of law enforcement, and political commitments. If the mayor is endowed with sound business or public administration skills and has a "good government" philosophy, then the chief of police will very likely be selected on the basis of professional abilities rather than extraneous political factors. Unfortunately, on too many occasions in the past, this appointment has been a method of repaying political favors. A classical case of the misuse of this appointing authority was illustrated by the Wickersham Commission in 1931:

> *A few years ago the mayor of Indianapolis was called upon to introduce the police chief of that city to an assemblage of police chiefs during one of their conferences. In the course of his introductory remarks, the mayor said, "I know that my man is going to be a good chief because he has been my tailor for 20 years. He knows how to make good clothes; he ought to be a good chief."*[63]

No big-city mayor would make the same choice today, but the choice will nevertheless be a reflection of the mayor's personal value system and abilities and of the political environment of the community.

In the strong mayor form of local government, the tenure of the chief of police is often linked directly to the mayor, and the nature of the relationship is such that the chief is quite dependent on the mayor for support and guidance on budgetary matters, enforcement practices, and a multitude of other areas essential to the overall success of the police department. If there is mutual respect between the police chief and the mayor, a strong professional and political bond will be formed. If the reverse holds true, however, significant antagonisms may begin to emerge. There are too many situations to enumerate positively or negatively that can affect the working relationship between a mayor and a police chief. The important differences that do emerge are frequently those that evolve out of philosophical and ethical differences rather than questions of legality. These are differences that can occur in any form of government (see Figure 4.7).

City Manager

There is no lack of supporters or detractors for every form of local government found in the United States. The proponents of the city manager form claim that it provides the most conducive atmosphere in which professional law enforcement can operate and

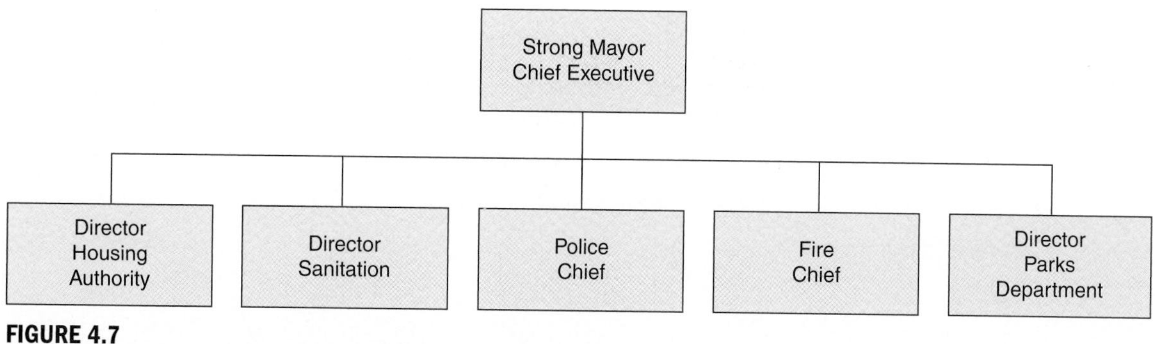

FIGURE 4.7

The strong mayor form of government. The mayor serves as the chief executive and appoints all department heads. The department heads serve at the pleasure of the mayor.

minimizes external interference. One of the reasons for this assessment is the balancing mechanisms developed over the years that are typically inherent in the city manager form of government: (1) the city manager is accountable to the elected members of the city council as a body rather than to any individual council member; (2) individual council members are prevented (by law of council rules) from giving administrative, operational, or policy direction to the city manager; (3) the council as a body may not give specific administrative direction to the city manager, who generally has exclusive executive authority over the city employees; (4) the city manager, consistent with civil service statutes and subject to employee appeals, has full authority to hire, promote, and discipline city personnel; (5) the city manager has broad authority within state municipal financial statutes to manage the budget and to depart from line item appropriations to meet unanticipated needs; and (6) the council as a body hires the city manager and may dismiss the city manager in its discretion without stating its cause. The city manager model is significant because it has been clearly successful in the American local political milieu and because its separation of the political policymaking body and the independent chief executive is realistically defined.[64]

The city manager more often than not is a professional administrator who is recruited for certain skills and training and appointed by the city council. A person with this background tends to make sincere efforts to select a competent individual to serve as police chief because the manager's professional reputation is tied inextricably to the effective management of the city departments.

It is significant that city managers have sought qualified police chiefs and that they have in most instances based their selection on the professional qualifications of the candidate rather than on political or other extraneous considerations that too often have governed appointments to this position in the past.[65] This does not mean that the city manager form of government removes the chief from local politics, but it does create more distance and insulation than the one-to-one political relationship commonly found in the strong mayor form of government (see Figure 4.8).

City Councils

The legally defined roles of city councils are fairly consistent throughout the United States; namely, they act as the chief legislative and policymaking body. Through its ordinance power, subject to constitutional and statutory provisions, including the city charter, the council carries out its legislative function; when within its authority, its enactments have the force of law and are binding on both administration and electorate. In addition to legislative and policymaking functions, the council, in common with

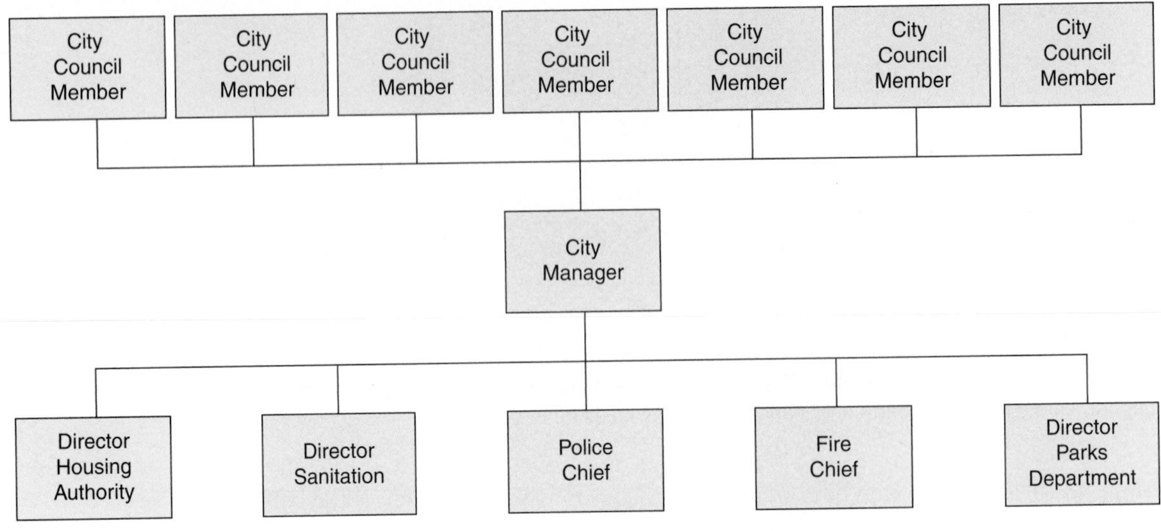

FIGURE 4.8

The city manager form of government. The city manager is appointed by the counsel (typically the majority), and the manager serves at the pleasure of the city council. The city manager in turn appoints all department heads, and they serve at the pleasure of the manager.

most legislative bodies, holds the purse strings and exercises control over appropriations.[66] Thus, the immediate impact of a council's actions on the operation of a law enforcement agency is considerable.

The record of involvement by council members and other elected officials in police operations to the detriment of both the efficiency and the effectiveness of the police establishment is a well-established fact. One observer of this problem has noted,

> *Local political leaders frequently promote more abuses of police power than they deter. In seeking favored treatment for a violator of the law or in exerting pressure for police assistance in the sale of tickets to a fund-raising dinner, the politician only encourages the type of behavior he is supposed to prevent. Although such political interference into police work is not as extensive as it once was, it still exists.*[67]

James F. Ahern, former chief of the New Haven, Connecticut, Police Department, discusses this issue at length in his book *Police in Trouble.* He describes the extent to which political forces negatively affected the New Haven Police Department and the course of action he took to nullify them:

> *There is nothing more degrading or demoralizing to a police department than the knowledge that every favor or promotion within it is controlled by hack politicians and outright criminals. And there is nothing more nearly universal. Five years ago, anyone with the most superficial knowledge of the workings of the New Haven Police Department could point to the political power behind every captain on the force. Every cop who wanted to get ahead had his "hook"—or, as they say in New York, his "rabbi." Everyone owed his success to a politician—from the Town Chairman on down—or to an influential underworld figure. Needless to say, in a situation like this there was no chance whatever of the department functioning in the public interest.*
>
> *A day after I had taken office, I closed the second-story back door to the Mayor's office and issued a renewal of a long-standing and long-ignored departmental order prohibiting any police officer from seeing the Mayor without the authorization of the chief.*
>
> *Given the incredible tangle of grimy politics that still existed in the lower levels of government and in the structures of the city's political parties, this action was largely symbolic. But as a gesture it was necessary. It would be immediately evident to everyone in the police department that if I would not permit the Mayor who had*

appointed me to influence departmental promotions or assignments, I certainly would allow no other politicians to influence them.

Mayor Lee was aware of the connections between politics and police and was himself capable of intervening in the affairs of the police department to advance cops whom he considered honest and effective who otherwise would have been buried. Riding home with the Mayor in a car one day, I showed him a draft of my order. He frowned slightly, nodded, and then approved.

But this order was only the opening shot in the war to end political interference in the police department. The far more substantive challenge was to make clear in every way possible, to every man in the department, that political influence of any kind was out. There was only one way to handle the problem, and it was somewhat heavy-handed. The men were made responsible for stopping interference themselves. They were warned that if politicians or underworld figures approached me with requests for promotions, transfers, or easy assignments for cops, the officers in question would be barred permanently from those positions.

The immediate reaction among the cops was total incredulity. Political maneuvering had been the basis for advancement in the department for so long that it was doubtful whether they believed there was another way to be promoted. I would not be surprised if they thought that promotions in the department would freeze until I resigned or retired. But they did believe me. And they did convey the message to their hooks. For the time being, political interference in the department all but stopped.[68]

To suggest that the experience of New Haven is typical of most communities would be an inaccurate generalization, but there is little doubt that the council's fiscal control over the police department's budget and its legislative powers make it a political force that is never taken lightly by chiefs of police. As a matter of fact, most police chiefs will go to great lengths to maintain the goodwill and support of their council members.

Politics and the Police Chief

A study conducted in California showed that the average tenure of a police chief in that state was less than three years before the chief was fired or resigned.[69] Even though the tenure of police chiefs across the nation has somewhat improved since that time, the national average is still only about five years.[70] Of course, the reasons for change are numerous, including movement to another (often larger) police department, resignation, retirement, and, of course, dismissal. Much has been written about the need for some type of protection for police chiefs against the arbitrary and unjustified removal from office by an elected or political officeholder.[71] In some states, such as Illinois, statutory protections have been implemented to protect police chiefs against such actions. Special boards or commissions have been created for the sole purpose of establishing recruitment, selection, and retention policies for chiefs of police. In Illinois, the law prohibits the removal or discharge of a member of the fire or police department (including the chief) without cause; the individual must also be given written charges and an opportunity to be heard in his or her defense. While this is a state mandate, these protections are available only when there is no local ordinance prescribing a different procedure. If such an ordinance exists, the statute requires the municipal appointing authority to file the reasons for the chief's removal but does not require a showing of cause or a hearing.

New Hampshire affords significant protection to police chiefs. It requires written notice of the basis for the proposed termination, a hearing on the charges, and a finding of cause before the dismissal can be effected. Minnesota, on the other hand, provides no mandatory protections for police chiefs but does require that they be included in any civil service system adopted by a municipality.

A few other states have attempted to provide police chiefs with at least some job security whenever they have been promoted from within the ranks of the police department. Both Illinois and Ohio allow chiefs who resign or who are removed from their positions to return to the ranks they held within their departments before being appointed chiefs. Most states, however, offer very little protection. Chiefs across the country are therefore forced to look for job protections in local civil service codes, local municipal ordinances, and such individual employment contracts as they are able to negotiate.[72]

However, for the most part, the ability to endure the realities of the position of chief of police requires a unique blend of talent, skill, and knowledge that is often not "guaranteed" in statute or law. The reality is that few protections exist for persons occupying the highest position of a police agency except for those developed in the person themselves. That is to say, the characteristics and qualities of excellent management and leadership imbued in the person are generally the reasons that a chief remains in office.

Critical Thinking Questions

1. Describe how each form of local government influences the selection of a police chief.
2. Discuss the advantages and disadvantages of statutory employment protection for police chiefs.

THE POLICE CHIEF AND EXTERNAL INCIDENTS

Being a chief of police is difficult enough in a normal situation in which both internal and external factors often make it hard for the police chief to discern the public interest.[73] However, it is tolerable only if time and effort are available to solve a problem. Some situations and conflicts, however, are outside the chief's control, yet their occurrence may cost the police chief his or her job. Mintzberg[74] refers to these conflicts as "political arenas" and divides them into three types based on their duration, intensity, and pervasiveness.

The first type of political arena is "confrontation." In this most common type, the situational conflict is intense but brief and confined. An obvious example is the Rodney King incident, which put an end to the contract of Daryl Gates as the Los Angeles chief of police. The second political arena is a "shaky alliance," in which conflict is less intense but still pervasive. A shaky alliance may be a sequel to a confrontational situation. Chief Willie Williams, Daryl Gates's successor and the first outsider appointed as chief in over 40 years, had to deal with both external pressures (i.e., the impact of the King incident on the public) and internal pressures (i.e., resentful feelings from his own police officers). This was a shaky alliance, and at the end of his term in 1997, Williams's contract was not renewed. The third type of political arena, a "politicized organization," features pervasive but muted conflict that is tolerable for a time. This kind of conflict is commonplace in American policing, and survival of the agency's police chief depends on external support. Examples include riots resulting from allegations of police brutality, such as those in 1996 in St. Petersburg, Florida, or the protracted JonBenet Ramsey homicide investigation in Boulder, Colorado. The "complete" political arena is the fourth situation in which the conflict is pervasive, intense, brief, and out of control. Fortunately, police chiefs seldom face this type of conflict. However, when it does occur, termination becomes a possibility.

Because of the common occurrence of the third type of political arena, the politicized organization arena, several expanded cases are offered. In the St. Petersburg example, riots began on Thursday night, October 25, 1996, after a white police officer shot and killed a black man driving a stolen car. Former Police Chief Darrel Stephens was considered by many within both the community and law enforcement to be an enlightened visionary leader. The front-page story on October 30 in the *St. Petersburg Times* reflected Stephens's philosophy:

> *I've always believed that we would be able to keep something like this from happening. Personally, you look at what's happening and you have lots of questions about what more we could have done in this situation to keep it from developing. . . . In many respects, his [Stephens's] actions at the scene reflect a policing philosophy and management style that have brought national attention to the St. Petersburg force, but have frustrated officers who prefer a tougher approach to crime or see the department as understaffed and overworked. Stephens now finds himself facing new scrutiny. Last Thursday's violence has been his administration's biggest crisis since he was hired in December 1992 to restore morale in a department troubled by racial friction and political factions.*[75]

An editorial titled "Help Stephens Succeed" in the *St. Petersburg Times,* on October 31, 1996, reported,

> *One casualty of the riot in south St. Petersburg could be the city's common sense approach to law enforcement community policing. That would be a shame and a setback for citizens, both black and white. In the aftermath of the fatal shooting . . . by a police officer and the ensuing chaos, some people are criticizing Police Chief Darrel Stephens' approach to law enforcement and his tempered reaction to rioters. Emotion rules such arguments and ignores history. Stephens was hired four years ago to return stability and respect to the police department after the firing of combative Chief Ernest "Curt" Curtsinger. An expert on community policing, Stephens took some officers out of their patrol cars and put them in neighborhoods to help residents solve their problems. . . . Community policing cannot be expected to resolve the broader problems in St. Petersburg's poor black neighborhoods, unemployment, broken families and the hopelessness of poverty. Those who hold the police responsible for such breaches in the nation's social fabric are misguided. Instead, St. Petersburg residents—both black and white—should be asking how they can help Stephens succeed. Black residents can invite police officers into their communities and offer their help. White residents can support measures that strengthen Stephens' work. We should not let the emotion of the moment stop progress toward a police force that serves all citizens.*[76]

It is interesting that, in the third arena of politicized support, not only did Stephens have the support of the *St. Petersburg Times* editorial staff, but he also had the mayor's continued political support. On reelection to a second term, the mayor asked Stephens to become the city administrator for St. Petersburg in June 1997. The mayor and newly promoted city administrator quickly named a new police chief, an African American with a Ph.D., from within the ranks of the department. This all occurred within the span of several days during June.

In the JonBenet Ramsey murder investigation in Boulder, Colorado, Police Chief Tom Koby, the Boulder Police Department, and the entire city of Boulder were under intense national media scrutiny after the murder of the six-year-old JonBenet Ramsey on December 26, 1996. Both of Denver's major newspapers, the *Denver Post* and the *Rocky Mountain News,* were openly critical of the investigation and of Chief Koby. On June 8, 1997, an article in the *Rocky Mountain News* was titled "Ramsey Case a Tragedy of Errors." Similarly, the *Denver Post* printed the following headlines: "Cops Grumpy with Koby," "DA Brushes Off Koby Problems," "Is the Trail Too Cold?" "Mute Leaders," "Cops' Vote on Koby Negative," and "It's Ludicrous." As a yet unproductive (as this debate was finalized) investigation in a city in which murder cases are rare—and an unsolved murder case unheard of—it would appear that this case has polarized the department and city politicians. As a May 30, 1997, column in the *Denver Post* noted,

> *Here is a glimpse into the inner workings of the city of Boulder: The troops, by a vote of 2 to 1 say they have lost confidence in Police Chief Tom Koby. Spense Havlik, deputy mayor of Boulder was "quite surprised" by the vote. Havlik must have spent most of April and May on Comet Hale-Bopp. Havlik's incredulous statement underscores a mystery as mystifying as JonBenet Ramsey's murder itself—where is the political and moral leadership in Boulder? Just like Chief Koby and District Attorney Alex Hunter—the two men supervising the investigation of the murder—Havlik doesn't have a clue. While the rank-and-file cops have no confidence in Koby, Councilman Havlik and most other political officers in the city are heartily endorsing the city's beleaguered police chief. Leading the parade for Koby are Mayor Leslie Durgin and City Manager Tim Honey, two people who also were surprised by the rank-and-file vote on Koby.*[77]

On May 29, members of Boulder's police union voted 78 to 31 that they had no confidence in Chief Tom Koby's leadership. The vote came amidst rumblings that Boulder's elected officials were displeased with Koby's boss, City Manager Tim Honey (*Denver Post*, May 30, 1997). On June 8, 1997, the *Rocky Mountain News* reported, "The night that Boulder City Manager Tim Honey tendered his forced resignation to the city council, he said, 'this investigation is going to lead to an arrest.' "

Chief Koby announced he would retire at the end of 1998, but his tenure as chief of police ended on June 28, 1998, when he was forced to step down by an acting city manager. He was terminated because of a combination of factors, including little or no support from the media, crumbling or divided political support within the city council, and support from less than 40 percent of the department's rank and file.

Without support from the mayor and the media, it is quite unlikely that Stephens would have been promoted to city administrator and may indeed have been in a situation similar to the one Koby experienced. Conversely, had Koby received positive editorials and strong political and rank-and-file support, it is likely his situation would have turned out differently.

In several cases, either police chiefs were terminated or their contracts were not renewed despite the lack of valid grounds. For example, the mayor of Cleveland, Ohio, ousted three police chiefs in a 4-year period for political reasons. In 1992, Police Chief Elizabeth Watson was terminated by the newly elected mayor in Houston, Texas, because of her advocacy of community-oriented policing. She was criticized for reducing the effectiveness of the police as crime fighters. In 1996, Police Chief Philip Arreola of Milwaukee, Wisconsin, was forced to resign because of his failure to satisfy all of the constituencies. Police Commissioner William Bratton of New York was forced to resign after only 27 months in the position, despite the fact that during his administration the city experienced the largest 2-year decline of crime in its history.

Being a police chief today is very difficult. Chiefs can be terminated or forced to resign either because they do things too progressively or quickly (as in the case of Chiefs Watson and Arreola) or because they are perceived as doing things too slowly (as in the case of Chief Williams). Chiefs can even be forced to resign when their tenure is considered successful, as in the case of Commissioner Bratton.[78]

Should police chiefs be allowed to keep their positions if there is no evidence that they are incompetent, unethical, or involved in illegal activities? Should chiefs be terminated only for cause and not for personal or political reasons? Unfortunately, terminating police chiefs has become the norm. A Los Angeles city charter change guaranteed that no one will ever again hold the position as long as Gates did. In other cities where chiefs serve at the mayor's pleasure, they are virtually assured of a brief stay. All the examples cited here occurred at a time when big-city police chiefs as a group were more educated, more skilled at public relations, and better trained in management than ever before. Even the most adroit police chief tends to run into political conflicts. Whether

Focus on Policy

Charles Ramsey

Celebrated Washington, D.C., Police Chief Charles Ramsey stepped down from his post effective January 2, 2007, after eight years of service. Ramsey left as a new mayor, Adrian Felty, was sworn into office. Felty, formerly a city council member, had long disagreed with Ramsey on deployment of police officers, saying that he wanted police to be more community-oriented. Felty had voted against giving Ramsey a raise three years previously, saying that he felt the department was headed in the wrong direction among citizen complaints that there were not enough officers on patrol in neighborhoods. Although Ramsey initially expressed a desire to stay through his contract, up in 2008, Felty was non-committal on his election regarding the fate of the chief and was said to be looking at candidates for the position.

The chief's resignation was a shock to many after a tenure that saw many successes. Ramsey first went to Washington, D.C., from the Chicago Police Department, where he was deputy superintendent of staff services. During his service there, Ramsey was instrumental in the design and implementation of the Chicago Area Policing Strategy (CAPS), a nationally acclaimed model of community policing. On his arrival in Washington, D.C., Ramsey initiated a Department of Justice review into shootings of civilians by officers in order to address the highest rate of such shootings in the country. He also mandated annual use-of-force training for officers, supplied new police cruisers and computers for officers, and built a state-of-the-art command and communications center, which has been a model for cities around the world. He targeted police patrols to areas classified as "crime emergencies" and organized massive police response to September 11 attacks in the city. Ramsey was also responsible for organizing security for the state funerals of former Presidents Ronald Reagan and Gerald Ford.

During Ramsey's tenure as chief, crime rates in the Washington, D.C., area fell to their lowest since the 1960s. Public confidence in the D.C. police also rose during Ramsey's term, and he enjoyed a national reputation as an expert on policing. No replacement for Ramsey has been named, and D.C. council members are concerned that his departure sends a negative signal to potential applicants for the job, one of the most high-profile law enforcement positions in the country. Ramsey, meanwhile, has said that he looks forward to serving in the private sector or in the U.S. Department of Homeland Security.

Source: Allison Klein and David Nakamura, "Chief Ramsey to Step Down, Sources Say." *Washington Post,* November 18, 2006, p. 1.

(Getty Images, Inc.)

by his or her own choice or by the mayor's or city manager's command, the chief is frequently terminated within a few years of a much publicized arrival.[79]

Organizationally, replacing chiefs every few years can leave a department in a seemingly never-ending spiral of change, as each new chief strives to remedy the problems he or she was hired to solve and to create a loyal and cohesive command staff. Worse is the possibility that meaningful progress is not attempted because the rank and file believe that it is futile to begin a project that will never be finished: just as progress is begun, there very likely will be another change.

Critical Thinking Question

1. Discuss how replacing police chiefs frequently impacts a municipal police department.

TENURE AND CONTRACTS FOR POLICE CHIEFS

Police chiefs who lack protection from arbitrary and unjustified termination cannot objectively and independently fulfill their responsibilities. The average **tenure** of most police chiefs is three to six years. For their contracts (an extremely limited number of formal contractual cases exist) to be renewed at the end of the term or their status as an at-will appointee to be continued, compromises of the chief's sense of responsibility may be necessary, especially if his or her decisions run counter to those of city officials. A discussion of the lack of a reappointment agreement for Milwaukee's former Chief Philip Arreola states,

> *He wasn't exactly fired, but months before his scheduled reappointment for a second term, word simply filtered out of City Hall that Mayor John O. Norquist no longer saw eye to eye with the chief. It was not a matter of scandal or of incompetence, it was a case of political failure—too many constituencies, all with clear-cut agendas, and no way to satisfy all of them at once. . . . It may seem curious for a city to can a respected police chief without any whiff of impropriety or misconduct, but in fact it is the norm these days, not the exception. The sacking of the police chief is part of the routine in urban America.*[80]

The advent of community policing as the evolving contemporary policing strategy emphasizes enhanced relations between the police and the public and demands that police chiefs possess new skills and attitudes and become effective visionary leaders. In other words, chiefs must not be reluctant to pioneer innovative programs geared toward community problem-solving policing goals. The inherent risks, however, are obvious, and the failure of these high-profile public projects may jeopardize the chief's position.

Consider where police chiefs come from. Most top police executives today, as in the past, reach their position as police chief in the twilight of their policing careers. Charles Gain, former chief of the Oakland, California, Police Department, argued that police chiefs in this twilight period tend to resist organizational change because they fear the loss of the position for which they have so long waited, and as they are in the final stages of their career, they engage in a "holding action."[81] Gain further commented that, when chiefs make it to the top, they are not going to jeopardize their position by setting new goals and moving ahead.[82]

One researcher cites another example as a demonstration of this bankrupt leadership style. Researchers of the Police Executive Development Project at Pennsylvania State University found that top police executives showed greater devotion for their personal moral standards than for the citizens they served. Their findings also indicated that top police executives showed greater submission to authority than did the general public. This subservient attitude is formed as a result of working in a rigid organizational structure that demands and rewards obedience to authority.[83] The results of the project indicated that the average police executive failed to possess initiative, self-reliance, and confidence because of a lifelong habit of submission and social conformity. The study concluded that these findings correlate to some extent with the suggestion that police chiefs tend to treat their job as a sinecure and are incapable of innovation at this late stage in their police careers.[84] Without some form of contract protection, it is difficult to expect any police chief to jeopardize his or her job by implementing a vision or a program that has any chance of failure.

In spite of the previous lack of job security for big-city police chiefs, there is some evidence in some cases that this may be changing, in part because of the recent dramatic decrease in crime, a strong economy, and the desire of local government to improve services to its citizens.

Critical Thinking Question

1. Why is job security for police chiefs becoming more stable?

POLITICS AND THE COUNTY SHERIFF

There are approximately 3,100 county sheriff's departments in the United States.[85] The county sheriff's office is unique among American law enforcement agencies in terms of both its role and its legal status.[86] However, in discussions about police administration, sheriff's offices are frequently overlooked. Historically, the tasks and roles of sheriff's departments and police departments have been fundamentally different.[87] Sheriff's law enforcement functions have often been relegated to jurisdictions of sparse populations that cannot support municipal police agencies. Sheriffs are typically elected, as opposed to their appointed counterpart police chiefs. In addition, sheriffs routinely have a custodial role in the detention of prisoners not common to municipal police functions. This all changed somewhat after World War II, when populations expanded into rural areas that eventually became the suburbs. This eliminated part of the distinction between sheriffs and chiefs when big-city problems came to these areas.[88]

The twentieth century brought a marked decline in the strength of sheriff's departments in many parts of the country. As law enforcement became more abundant, a curious academic neglect of the office of the sheriff resulted in serious breaks of understanding regarding the role of sheriff in the criminal justice system. Literature about policing and law enforcement analyzed the office as a jailer, court bailiff, process server, and county tax collector. Little, if any, emphasis was placed on the office in police literature, and if there was reference to the position, it was generally unfavorable. In 1925, Bruce Smith's book *The State Police* referred to the office as a "dying medieval" throwback. A later book by the same author, *Rural Crime Control,* alluded to county government in general as the "dark continent of American politics." A 1935 book by A. E. Parker and A. Vollmer, *Crime and the State Police,* stated that the sheriff was an outdated law enforcement institution.[89]

Patterns of academic neglect continued after mid-century, even as the nation's police interest was escalating. O. W. Wilson neglected to mention sheriffs in his 1950 book *Police Administration.* R. E. Clift neglected reference to the position in the 1956 edition of *A Guide to Modern Police Thinking* but did make small reference to the office in his third edition in 1970. George Felkenes devoted considerable discussion to the decrease and scope of the office in an inverse relationship with urbanization in his 1973 *The Criminal Justice System: Its Functions and Personnel.* He further observed that sheriffs were banished to only three modes of operation: (1) contract law enforcement for small or rural communities, (2) supervision of metropolitan police agencies along the East Coast only, (3) civil process functions, and (4) custodial functions as prescribed by law.[90] Many other law enforcement journals have noted that the sheriff's law enforcement functions lacked the professional standards of larger police departments.

A strong criticism of the position came from Dana B. Brammer and James E. Hurley, who wrote *A Study of the Office of Sheriff in the United States Southern Region* in 1968.[91] After they alluded to the sheriff as often the most important, if not the sole, law enforcement agency in many unincorporated areas of the South, they added,

> *The elected nature of the office has been cause for the most serious indictments of the office. Allegations regarding a sheriff being required to participate in partisan politics in order to hold his office is the most prevalent criticism. Yet in reality, all law enforcement executives are politicians in one form or another. Some may refute this assertion, but only out of misguided notions that politicians are evil or that an administrator cannot be a politician and a professional manager at the same time. Realistically, a politician is nothing more than a person accountable to the public for decisions made in the performance of duty. Certainly a police chief or police commissioner could fall into this category as easily as a sheriff.*[92]

The Sheriff's Role

Sheriffs have a unique role in that they typically serve all three components of the criminal justice system, acting in (1) law enforcement (e.g., in patrol, traffic, and criminal investigation), (2) the courts (e.g., as civil process servers and bailiffs), and (3) corrections (e.g., in county jails and probation). In many urban areas, civil process responsibilities consume more time and resources than criminal law enforcement. About 97 percent of all sheriff's departments are responsible for civil processing, such as serving warrants and subpoenas. Over 98 percent of sheriffs perform work related directly to the county or state court system, and about 87 percent of the sheriff's departments operate a county jail system.[93]

In a few states, the county jails are operated by state departments of corrections. In most big cities, responsibility for the jail system is in the hands of a separate agency, but not always. Not all sheriff's departments play this three-part role. Some offer no police services, while others are not responsible for jails. One author has described four models of sheriff's departments according to their responsibilities.[94] The full-service includes law enforcement and other police services, judicial processing, and correctional duties. The law enforcement model carries out only law enforcement duties, while other duties are assumed by separate civil process and correctional agencies. The civil–judicial model involves only court-related duties. Finally, the correction–judicial model involves all functions except law enforcement.

In terms of size, most sheriff's departments are small. Nearly two-thirds of them employ fewer than 25 sworn officers, and a third employ fewer than 10. About half serve a population of less than 25,000.[95]

The county sheriff's legal status is unique in two ways. First, in 37 states, it is specified by the state constitution. As a result, major changes in the office of sheriff require a constitutional amendment—a lengthy and difficult process.

Quick Facts

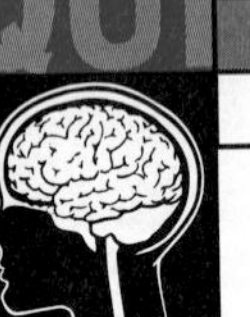

The Los Angeles County Sheriff's Department

The Los Angeles County Sheriff's Department is among the nation's largest and most diverse law enforcement agencies. Here's just a few interesting facts about the L.A.S.D.

- It is the largest sheriff's department and third largest police agency in the nation.
- It has more than 16,000 employees, including more than 8,400 full-time sworn.
- It staffs and operates the largest jail system in the free world, with more than 20,000 inmates.
- It provides municipal and superior court deputies for the largest county court system in the nation.
- It is the sole police agency for more than 2.5 million of the county's 9.5 million people. This includes nearly half of the county's 88 cities and all of the unincorporated areas, totaling over 75 percent of the county's 4,083 square miles.
- It is the mutual aid coordinator for the region, coordinating the response of federal, state, and local public safety resources during earthquakes, civil unrest, and other catastrophes.
- It patrols areas ranging from densely populated urban communities in South Central, East Los Angeles and West Hollywood to the beach city of Malibu, to the mountains of the Angeles National Forests, desert communities of the Antelope Valley, and many suburban communities.
- It has specialized units, such as Aero Bureau, Substance Abuse & Narcotics Education (S.A.N.E.), Special Enforcement Bureau (SWAT, K-9, Motors, etc.), Emergency Services Detail (Search & Rescue), Mounted Enforcement Detail, Organized Crime Unit, Arson/Explosives, Joint Regional Intelligence Center (JRIC), and the Terrorism Early Warning (TEW) group.

Source: Parker, Mike, "Big and Complicated: The LA County Sheriff's Department Operates the Largest Jail System in the Free World," *American Police Beat*, May 1996, p. 2, updated August 2007.

Second, unlike most law enforcement executives, sheriffs are elected in all but two states. (In Rhode Island, they are appointed by the governor; in Hawaii, they are appointed by the chief justice of the state supreme court.) As elected officials, sheriffs are important political figures. In many rural areas, the sheriff is the most powerful political force in the county. As a result, sheriffs are far more independent than appointed law enforcement executives because, as discussed earlier, police chiefs can be removed by the mayors or city managers who appoint them. However, this is not to suggest that because sheriffs enjoy greater independence than police chiefs they are not subject to powerful political forces within their communities. Indeed, because the office is usually an elected position (in 48 of the 50 states), there is considerable media scrutiny and state accountability. Individuals seeking the position of sheriff must run for public office the same as any other public official. In fact, the office of sheriff is the only local law enforcement position recognized and decreed by many state constitutions, a holdover from the days when local sheriffs were the only law of the land.

The extent to which politics, in the negative sense, enters into the sheriff's race and subsequently into the operations of the sheriff's department varies radically from community to community and even among sheriff's races. For example, in states in which sheriffs—because they are constitutional officers—are not bound by normal purchasing restrictions, some potential for abuse exists. If a candidate running for the office of sheriff has accepted a large donation from a certain business, there would be an expectation of reciprocity in return for such "support." This could result in purchases of cars from "loyal" car dealers, food for jail inmates from certain distributors, uniforms from a specific uniform company, and so forth. However, a sheriff who becomes too partisan in his or her purchasing risks disappointing other vendors. As such, a marshaling of support for the next candidate in the next election usually occurs. The "real politics" of such a situation is that, while more purchases will be made from key supporting organizations, the incumbent must "spread around" enough purchasing to appease other vendors.

Then, too, there are potentials in any political environment for dirty campaigns, and sheriff's races are no exception.

Several years ago, an incumbent sheriff who realized he might not be reelected because of strong opposition from a highly qualified opponent contacted one of his vice squad officers to see if he could create a situation that would be embarrassing to the opponent. The vice squad officer made contact with a young and exceptionally attractive prostitute, who also served as his informant. He asked her to approach the man running against the incumbent sheriff at his place of business and try to entice him into joining her in a nearby hotel to have sex. The preselected hotel room had been set up with audiovisual equipment, so that the entire event could be recorded. Once the planned act was recorded, the videotape would be sent to the candidate's wife, along with copies to his minister and other key people in his life. It was felt that such a tape in the hands of these people would be sufficiently disruptive to the candidate's personal life to make him ineffectual as a campaigner. The prostitute, as instructed, did go to the business of the candidate and attempted to entice the individual to join her. The candidate, who was a politically astute individual, saw through this transparent farce and told the woman to leave his business. However, as soon as she left, he very discreetly followed her for a couple of blocks and saw her getting into an unmarked sheriff's department vehicle, which was being driven by the vice squad officer, whom he recognized. When the election was held, the incumbent sheriff lost. Since this was only one of many "dirty tricks" attempted by a number of employees of the sheriff's department, the newly elected sheriff immediately "cleaned house" and fired everyone who he could prove (or suspected) was involved in the efforts to embarrass him.

Inside the sheriff's department, politics can also be a decisive factor in the operational effectiveness of the organization. It is no accident that increased enforcement activity by the local sheriff's office usually precedes an election. The activity usually focuses on highly visible suspects or signs of disorder. Characteristic events include the roundup of local prostitutes, the crackdown on street corner vagrants, and the closing of "X-rated" video stores, all of which just happen to ensure considerable positive media attention. The interpretation is obvious—that the incumbent sheriff is "tough" on crime.

One of the most important political processes that impact the internal organization is the absence of local or state civil service boards. In many states, employees of the county sheriff's office serve at the pleasure of the current sheriff. Therefore, if the incumbent sheriff either decides not to run for office or is defeated in the next election, the newly elected sheriff may decide to fire a high percentage of the employees currently working at the sheriff's department. Although a number of conflicting court cases have attempted to provide a sense of balance and order, this capability still exists in most states. As a result, most deputy sheriffs attempt to work in a politically neutral environment, trying not to favor one candidate over another. Such a condition results in a lack of continuity in the skill level of employees and affects the quality of service being delivered to the public. It also creates enormous job insecurity and provides a mechanism whereby unqualified persons may be elected to one of the highest positions of law enforcement in the community. Thus, the very nature of the electoral process and the enormous power inherent in the office can foster an environment in which politics prevails.

Critical Thinking Question

1. Why have many sheriff's departments lacked the professional standards of municipal police departments?

STATE PROSECUTOR

The **prosecutor,** state's attorney, or district attorney is the chief law enforcement officer under the statutes of some states. However, despite this designation, the state prosecutor does not have overall responsibility for the supervision of the police.[96] Even so, the prosecutor's enforcement policies, procedures for review of all arrests before their presentation in court, and overall supervision of the cases prepared by the police do have an observable effect on police practices and enforcement policies. The initial contact of police officers with prosecutors occurs when the former brings a complaint to be charged. This encounter may be critical because it is an important point for making decisions about the disposition of the case and whether the complaint will be dismissed or reduced to a lesser offense. This discretionary power given the prosecuting attorney has tremendous influence on the ways and extent to which certain laws are enforced or ignored. Police chiefs who perceive that the prosecutor consistently reduces or fails to vigorously enforce certain types of violations may very likely divert their enforcement efforts and resources elsewhere. Then again, some chiefs may decide to "go public" and try to mobilize community support for enforcing the ignored violations. However, few police chiefs take this course of action because it could result in a serious deterioration in the working relationship with the local prosecutor, a situation most would prefer to avoid.

From the prosecutor's perspective, a cordial relationship with the police is also a desired condition. This is not, however, always possible. For example, the prosecutor cannot ignore suspicions of corruption or other illegal activity by local police officers. When prosecutor-led investigations become public knowledge or lead to indictments, a prosecutor's rapport with the police can be severely strained, requiring years to recultivate. The resulting tension may become high if officers believe that the prosecutor is "sticking it to the police department by dragging the thing out" or by not allowing affected officers to plea bargain to lesser charges or if the prosecutor is suspected of furthering his or her career at the officers' expense.

Critical Thinking Question

1. How might the discretionary power given to prosecuting attorneys influence policies and procedures enforced by police chiefs?

THE JUDICIARY

Once the police have made an arrest and brought the arrestee before a judge, from pretrial release onward the case is within the domain of the **judiciary.** In its assessment of the relationships of the judiciary and the police, one government report noted that trial judges have acted as chief administrative officers of the criminal justice system, using their power to dismiss cases as a method of controlling the use of the criminal process. However, except in those rulings involving the admissibility of evidence, this has been done largely on an informal basis and has tended to be haphazard, often reflecting primarily the personal values of the individual trial judge.[97]

In contrast, the function of trial judges in excluding evidence that they determine to have been obtained illegally places them very explicitly in the role of controlling police practices. Trial judges have not viewed this role as making them responsible for developing appropriate police practices. However, many trial judges, when asked to explain their decisions, indicate that they have no more responsibility for explaining decisions to police than they have to private litigants.[98]

Occasionally, judges grant motions to suppress evidence to dismiss cases that they feel should not be prosecuted because the violation is too minor or for some other reason. The use of a motion to suppress evidence in this manner confuses the standards that are supposed to guide the police and has a disturbing, if not demoralizing, effect on them.[99]

If judges consistently interject their personal biases into the judicial process and make it very clear to police that they will dismiss certain categories of violations, the police may discontinue enforcing that law. This, in turn, may put the police on a collision course with certain segments of the community that favor the rigorous enforcement of those laws.

Skolnick, commenting on police–judiciary relationships, has noted,

> *When an appellate court rules that police may not in the future engage in certain enforcement activities, since these constitute a violation of the rule of law, the inclination of the police is typically not to feel* shame *but* indignation. *This response may be especially characteristic of "professional" police, who feel a special competence to decide, on their own, how to reduce criminality in the community. The police, for example, recognize the court's power to bar admission of illegally seized evidence if the police are discovered to have violated the constitutional rights of the defendant. They do not, however, feel morally blameworthy in having done so; nor do they even accept such injunctions with good grace and go about their business. On the contrary, the police typically view the court with hostility for having interfered with their capacities to practice their craft. Police tend to rest their moral position on the argument that the "independence" and social distance of the appellate judiciary constitutes a type of government—by the courts—without the consent*

of the governed—the police. Thus, the police see the court's affirmation of principles of due process as, in effect, the creation of harsh "working conditions." From their point of view, the courts are failing to affirm democratic notions of the autonomy and freedom of the "worker." Their political superiors insist on "production" while their judicial superiors impede their capacity to "produce." Under such frustrating conditions, the appellate judiciary inevitably comes to be seen as "traitor" to its responsibility to keep the community free from criminality.

Antagonism between the police and the judiciary is perhaps an inevitable outcome, therefore, of the different interests residing in the police as a specialized agency and the judiciary as a representative of wider community interests. Constitutional guarantees of due process of law do make the working life and conditions of the police more difficult. But if such guarantees did not exist, the police would of course engage in activities promoting self-serving ends, as does any agency when offered such freedom in a situation of conflicting goals. Every administrative agency tends to support policies permitting it to present itself favorably. Regulative bodies restricting such policies are inevitably viewed with hostility by the regulated. Indeed, when some hostility does not exist, the regulators may be assumed to have been "captured" by the regulated. If the police could, in this sense, "capture" the judiciary, the resulting system would truly be suggestive of a "police state."[100]

Critical Thinking Question

1. Describe how judicial bias can affect police enforcement of laws. What effect might this have on police–community relations?

CITIZEN INVOLVEMENT

Citizen involvement in the policymaking process of law enforcement agencies is frequently met with considerable resistance from members of the law enforcement community. Many police administrators feel that their effectiveness rests on a high degree of autonomy. They view attempts to alter the way in which the law is enforced as efforts to negate the effectiveness of and politicize the police. They argue further that, during the past quarter century, law enforcement agencies have slowly but surely been successful in freeing themselves of partisan political interference and that public involvement will result in the police becoming instruments of pressure group politics and avowedly partisan to the most vocal and disruptive segments of society.[101]

One national commission took strong exception to this traditional posture of opposition to citizen involvement in policymaking:

> *In some areas of government activity, there is increasing utilization of citizen advisory committees as a way of involving members of the community in the policy making process. In some cases, the group may be advisory only, the governmental agency being free to accept or reject its advice. In other instances, the group is official and policies are cleared through the committee as a regular part of the policy making process. The advantages of both methods are that they serve as an inducement for the police administrator to articulate important policies, to formulate them, and to subject them to discussion in the advisory group. How effective this is depends upon the willingness of the group and the police administrator to confront the basic law enforcement policy issues rather than being preoccupied with the much easier questions of the mechanics of running the department. Where there is a commitment to exploring basic enforcement policy questions, the citizens' advisory group or policy making board has the advantage of involving the community in the decision making process, thus giving a broader base than would otherwise exist for the acceptance and support of enforcement policies.*[102]

FIGURE 4.9

Former New York Mayor Rudy Giuliani was in the final months of his eight years in office. He had been a political maverick, his final years marked by a very public divorce, a battle with prostate cancer, and a decision not to run against Hillary Clinton for the U.S. Senate. But in a matter of moments, Giuliani's place in history was forever secured. He narrowly escaped disaster himself on September 11, 2001. His stalwart leadership after that terrible day earned him the nickname "Rudy the Rock," but to most people in the United States he best represented "America's mayor." It was his perseverance and charisma that brought the citizens of New York together and his hands-on style that helped calm the chaos and rebuild the city.

(AFP PHOTO/Timothy A. Clary/Agence France Presse/Getty Images)

Hurricanes, floods, tornadoes, and other large-scale disasters have a tendency to bring the police and citizenry closer together. Nowhere was this more evident than in the aftermath of the bombing of the Alfred P. Murrah Building in Oklahoma City (1995) and the terrorist attacks on the World Trade Center and Pentagon on September 11, 2001. Individual members of the community worked hand-in-hand with police and other rescue personnel to assist in the recovery. The ruthless attacks left police exhausted and frustrated, except for the genuine support and care shown to them by the citizens of their communities. The strong sense of community was most evident by Mayor Rudy Giuliani, who embodied effective leadership during a crisis (see Figure 4.9). Rallying thousands of New Yorkers to give of their time, energy, and finances, the City of New York paid high tribute to their embattled public service departments.

Senior Citizen Organizations

Older Americans make up the most rapidly growing segment of the American population. One in every eight Americans is age 65 or older, and according to the American Association of Retired Persons (AARP), people 85 or older constitute the fastest-growing segment of the senior citizen population.[103] By 2025, about one in five Americans is expected to be 65 or older. Increased life expectancy is leading to new issues and problems that not only challenge the nation's health-care and social service systems but also place new demands on the police.

More and more police officers often find themselves coming in contact with senior citizens on a regular basis. Many communities compete for attracting lucrative retirement resettlement markets and cater to retirement services. Unfortunately, with the concentration of retired persons and the shear increase in their numbers comes the targeting of this group by criminals who have traditionally found the elderly to be easy scores for fraudulent schemes, scams, and rip-offs. Police calls for service, crime patterns, and people who are victims of crimes differ today because of the concentration and number of older Americans living in our cities.[104]

One of the most important new programs to address the needs of older Americans is called Triad. This innovative agreement embodies the philosophy of community policing; it consists of individual three-way partnerships among the county sheriff, area police chiefs, and the AARP. The primary focus of the partnership is to work together to reduce the criminal victimization of older citizens and enhance the delivery of law enforcement services to this population. Triad focuses on reducing unwarranted fear of crime and improving the quality of life of older Americans. Each Triad is tailored to meet the needs of each town, city, or county and is governed by a senior advisory council, often called S.A.L.T. (Seniors And Law enforcement Together). In each community, the S.A.L.T. Council acts as an advocacy and advisory group that provides a forum for the exchange of information between seniors and law enforcement. Planning and needs assessment by each S.A.L.T. Council often provide innovative programming to address crime prevention, victim assistance, reassurance and check-in programs, training for law enforcement, and the involvement of volunteers within police agencies.[105]

In 1999, the National Association of Triads, Inc. (NATI) was formed in cooperation with the National Sheriff's Association. It acts as an umbrella organization to provide advice, support, technical assistance, and training to local Triads throughout the United States. Over 775 counties in the United States have Triad programs. Several (e.g., Cook County [Chicago] and Hampshire County, Massachusetts) have been very successful and serve as model Triad communities throughout the United States, England, and Canada.[106]

Citizen groups are varied, and they have different interests in police service. Chambers of commerce and service clubs generally promote police professionalism out of civic pride. Churches and church groups have historically campaigned against vice and corruption and for civil liberties and police–community relations.[107]

Chambers of Commerce and Service Clubs

Local chambers of commerce and service clubs typically are supportive of efforts that lead toward efficient and clean government. Although such groups are characterized as being apolitical, they can exercise considerable influence. Their support for improving the quality of law enforcement in the community is frequently heard in the chambers of city hall and is demonstrated through various community projects intended to assist local law enforcement. Attuned police chiefs realize the benefit to be gained from the support of such groups, encourage personnel to become active members in these clubs, and frequently join one or two themselves. Support from these groups is not surprising when one considers that many comprise men and women from the middle class who are well educated and deeply involved in many aspects of community leadership. Such groups often have mobilized behind a police chief to get much needed budget increases for salaries, additional personnel, and equipment.

Churches

The religious leaders and congregation of a community's church groups represent one of the most potentially powerful pressure groups in the community. Their influence can, and frequently does, extend into the voting booth, which assures a high degree of responsiveness from local elected officials. Church leaders and their congregations almost always find an open door and a receptive ear at the office of their local police chief when they present their concerns. The problems that are frequently of greatest concern to such groups are vice-related, such as prostitution, massage parlors, X-rated theaters, and adult bookstores. It is true that individual communities impose different standards and have varying levels of tolerance, but if the church leaders of a community mobilize and call on their police chief to eradicate or reduce what they perceive to be a serious problem, there is a high probability that they will receive some positive response. And if the police chief suggests that the police department cannot cope realistically with the problem because of limited personnel and resources, those church groups will likely begin applying pressure on the city officials to give the police chief the needed resources. Thus, the religious leaders of the community can be powerful allies of the police chief in certain types of enforcement efforts. On the other hand, this pressure group may force the chief to redirect resources away from areas that may have a higher priority.

Critical Thinking Question

1. How might the use of citizen advisory committees in policing have a positive effect on law enforcement policymaking?

NEWS MEDIA

It is the responsibility of the police department, and especially its top leadership, to establish and maintain a cordial association with all media representatives.[108] Both the electronic and the print news media can be powerful friends or devastating antagonists of a local police department, and to a great extent this is determined by the attitudes, policies, and working relationships among editors, news directors, and the police chief. When friction does occur between the police and the news media, as it invariably does in every community, it frequently emanates from the events surrounding a major crime or an unusual occurrence.

Often in the case of major crimes or incidents, police departments do not want to release information that will jeopardize the safety of the public or its officers, impair the right of a suspect to a fair and impartial trial, or impede the progress of an investigation. On the other hand, the news media have a different orientation and duty: to inform the public. Although their goals are often compatible, the police and the news media frequently disagree irreconcilably.

The three-week shooting spree of John Allen Muhammad (also known as John Allen Williams) and Lee Boyd Malvo (also known as John Lee Malvo) near Washington, D.C., during the first three weeks of October 2002 certainly exhibited this disagreement. After 22 days of investigation, the sniper case, involving the shooting of nine victims and the deaths of six, ended amid a rash of criticism aimed primarily at the media. Montgomery County Police Chief Charles Moose levied accusations that the media simply revealed too much information about the shootings and the suspect, confounding the police investigation (see Figure 4.10). Most notably, the media leaked details concerning a tarot card left near the homicide scene of a 13-year-old boy. The back of the card had a message from the killer stating, "Mister Policeman, I am God." Police also retrieved shell casings and other evidence at the scene that eventually led to the capture of the suspects

FIGURE 4.10

Montgomery County Police Chief Charles A. Moose fields questions on the sniper shootings.
(AP Wide World Photos)

through ballistic comparisons of the .223-caliber rifle used in the sniper shootings and similar killings in Alabama. In an emotional report to the media, an irate Chief Moose chastised the media for hampering the investigation. His forthright and honest personality won him the sincere accolades of the public after the arrest of the snipers. The community strongly supported his actions through the development of a website, a flurry of letters, and an outpouring of community support around the Washington, D.C., area. *Time* magazine even honored him as its "Person of the Week."

Another situation in which the police and other officials may be in conflict with the news media occurs when journalists uncover information that is of actual investigative or legal significance and, if police investigators, prosecuting attorneys, or defense attorneys want to confirm the information, the media decline to divulge from whom or how they got the information on the basis of protecting their sources. The argument of the news media is that failing to protect their sources could result in reduced information flowing to them, thus jeopardizing the public's right to know. However, a reporter's First Amendment right to protect sources is not absolute. Recognizing this, some states have enacted so-called shield laws. For both First Amendment rights and shield laws, the courts apply a "balancing test" to determine whether reporters can be required to release the identities of their sources: is there a compelling need for the information? That is, is the defendant's need for the information to make an effective defense greater than the need of a reporter to protect the identity of a source?

Other circumstances for potential tension or conflict in police–news media relationships include "off-the-record" police information appearing in the news media, the occasional claim by a police administrator that he or she was misquoted, and the

FIGURE 4.11

The media hover while members of the Los Angeles Police Department SWAT team prepare for action as a suspected gunman emerges from cover.

(Courtesy of *Police*, April 1988. Photograph by Mike Mullin)

involvement of press at the scenes of bank robberies, gangland killings, and hostage situations or in the sensitive investigations of kidnapings and drug rings. From a legal standpoint, the police may release relevant information about a defendant if it is not prejudicial to the defendant's right to a fair trial. Many police departments have policies that protect the defendant's rights, but those policies may obstruct the needs of reporters to gather images and information for the public. For example, with respect to pretrial suspects, Kentucky State Police policy prohibits personnel from doing the following:

1. Requiring the suspect to pose for photographers
2. Re-enacting the crime
3. Disclosing that the suspect told where weapons, the proceeds of a crime, or other materials were located
4. Referring to the suspect as a "depraved character," "a real no-good," "a sexual monster," or similar terms
5. Revealing that the suspect declined to take certain types of tests or that the suspect did take certain tests—for example, a blood alcohol test to determine the degree, if any, to which the suspect was under the influence of alcohol or other drugs
6. Telling the press the results of any tests to which the suspect submitted
7. Making statements as to the guilt or innocence of a suspect
8. Releasing the identities of prospective witnesses or commenting on the nature of their anticipated testimony or credibility
9. Making statements of a purely speculative nature about any aspect of the case[109]

On the other hand, with the move toward community policing, many officers conduct crime prevention classes, crime block meetings, and media interviews. Some departments have taken a very positive approach to this issue, viewing these interactions as opportunities to communicate with the general public on police affairs (see Figure 4.11).

Despite all potential and actual conflicting interests, the fact is that both the police and the news media have profoundly important duties in a free society. In the course of day-to-day activities, people of considerable conscience in both professions go about their jobs peacefully; police–news media clashes are atypical situations. Certainly, if the local news media believe that the police are being arbitrary, high handed, uncooperative, or, worst of all, untruthful, then their news stories will reflect that dissatisfaction. Moreover, their coverage may even accentuate negative stories. For example, the dismissal of a felony charge because of insufficient evidence may lead to headlines such as "Shoddy Police Work Lets Burglar Go Free," as opposed to "Attorney Successfully Defends Local Man." Another consequence of a strained relationship with the news media could be minor or no coverage of favorable stories about the police, such as an awards ceremony. Thus, police administrators should exert a great deal of effort in seeing that all personnel understand the role of the press, that the applicable police department policies are current, that those policies are followed, and that open lines of communication with the news media are maintained.

Critical Thinking Question

1. Why is it so important that police administrators establish and maintain good relationships with all media representatives?

SCHOOL VIOLENCE

Similar to acts of terrorism, the recent tragedies stemming from school shootings seem to have no logical explanations. Almost every state has suffered a tragic incident involving a school shooting or an episode of school violence in which students have lost their lives. Most of these incidents have not captured the nation's attention as did the shootings in Littleton, Colorado (April 20, 1999), or Jonesboro, Arkansas (March 24, 1998), in which several students were killed. Indeed, in these cases the nation stood, shocked, as innocent children and teachers were killed by random acts of irrational violence carried out by fellow students. In Littleton, the tragedy ended only when the young perpetrators committed suicide.

No other single incident has had such a profound impact on American feelings of safety and security than the shooting at Columbine High School in Littleton. Two heavily armed students dressed in black trench coats attacked fellow students with homemade bombs and automatic weapons. It remains the worst attack in an American school, with 15 students and teachers dead (including the 2 gunmen) and another 25 wounded. The 2 students were among a handful of students called the "Trench Coat Mafia." They wore long, black coats; kept to themselves; generally followed the "goth" culture; and professed strong white-supremacist ideals. More recently, two incidents illustrated that school security concerns aren't just internal. The tragic events, only a week apart, began in Bailey, Colorado, on September 29, 2006, when a 53-year-old man entered Platte County High School, claiming to be carrying a bomb. The man, later identified as Duane Roger Morrison, took six girls hostage and barricaded himself in a classroom for several hours, while police attempted to negotiate with him. The hostages were sexually assaulted during that time. After Morrison refused to release the hostages, a SWAT team burst into the room. Morrison fired his gun, killing 16-year-old Emily Keyes, then committed suicide. His family later found a suicide note in his home. School officials have since stepped up security practices at the school, including locking all but one entrance to the building during school hours. Seven days later, a man burst into an Amish schoolhouse in Nickel Mines, Pennsylvania, and took 10 girls hostage. Police attempted to negotiate with Carl

FIGURE 4.12

The Amish schoolhouse in Nickel Mines, Pennsylvania, where five schoolgirls were killed. (Willam Thomas Cain/Getty Images Inc.)

Charles Roberts IV, a 32-year-old milkman, through the PA systems in their patrol cars, but Roberts opened fire on the students only minutes after the police arrived. The girls were reportedly shot execution-style, killing 5 of them and wounding the rest. Roberts also shot and killed himself. Roberts's family members found suicide notes, but there is no clear motive for the rampage. The nation was shocked that something so violent could happen to a people known for their simple and peaceful lifestyle. The school building was later bulldozed (see Figure 4.12).

Following a rash of other school shootings, the Columbine episode brought immediate attention to school safety. The most recent research available on school violence shows that, although the rates of fatal school incidents have fallen overall since the 1990s, they have begun rising over the past few years. In 1990, there were 11 school homicides. In 2005, there were 21 such killings.[110] This number is likely to increase when 2006 statistics are available, based just on a cursory review of the news. Furthermore, almost 7 percent of school-age children reported taking a weapon to school with them.[111] These statistics, while not staggering, are frightening for many, especially those with a child in school, and are proof that violence is a continuing issue in our nation's schools. The Columbine shootings, along with the more recent incidents in Bailey, Colorado, and Nickel Mines, Pennsylvania, represent a breach of basic security in the conscience of the nation: these shootings have been in serene suburban and rural settings, far from the ghettos and inner cities, where such acts are more commonly expected.

So it was on April 16, 2007 when the nation was again shocked by the horrific massacre of 32 students at Virginia Tech University in Blacksburg, Virginia. A rural campus tucked away in the Blue Ridge Mountains of southwestern Virginia, the Virginia Tech campus became the site of the deadliest shooting in modern U.S. history. Beginning in the early morning hours on what appeared to be a "normal" class day, Seung-Hui Cho entered the dorm room of Emily Jane Hilsher, and killed her. The resident assistant at West Ambler Johnston Hall, Ryan Clark, hearing the shots went to investigate and was also killed by the assailant. Returning to his own dorm room on

FIGURE 4.13

Born in South Korea, Seung-Hui Cho displays his bizarre and violent behavior in this photograph sent to NBC News headquarters in New York, along with other photographs, videos, and text outlining the reasons for his horrific killings on the campus of Virginia Tech University.

(© Courtesy NBC)

the campus, the killer Seung-Hui Cho sent a rambling letter and video tape to NBC News depicting his psychotic and violent behavior (see Figure 4.13). Armed with a 9 mm and a .22 caliber semi-automatic pistol, South Korean-born student Seung-Hui Cho then calmly walked across campus and systematically killed 30 students and wounded another 30 on the second floor of Norris Hall attending classes. After the rampage, he committed suicide.

Allthough the Virginia Tech University shooting did not involve children attending K through 12 grades, the incident sparked a reflection on school safety and security, as well as a renewed debate on mental health and gun control similar to the aftermath of the Columbine shooting. Seung-Hui Cho had a history of mental illness and bizarre behavior. In 2005, he had been contacted by the police for stalking two female students on campus, and he had been reported to the police as possibly suicidal. Also in 2005, after interaction with a counselor, he was temporarily committed to a mental health facility. And in 2006, faculty members had reported him to campus police for the violence depicted in his course writing assignments. Indeed, Seung-Hui Cho had several contacts with the police and mental health professionals prior to his deadly actions on April 16, 2007, fitting the profile of other shooters in Columbine and Nickel Mines, Pennsylvania; estranged individuals with histories of isolating and psychotic behavior. Like other assailants, Cho purchased the handguns locally, just a few weeks before the shooting incident, and like many of the other school shooters, Seung-Hui Cho committed suicide after the attack (see Quick Facts box).

School Resource Officers

The escalating violence has led to the demand for permanently assigned police officers at school locations. The primary purpose of these **school resource officers**

Quick Facts

School Shooting Incidents

March 24, 1998: Two boys, 11 and 13, open fire from the woods on students conducting a fire drill at a middle school in Jonesboro, Arkansas. Four girls and a teacher are shot to death and 10 others wounded; both boys are convicted in juvenile court of murder and can be held up to age 21.

April 24, 1998: A science teacher is shot to death by a 14-year-old in front of students at an eighth-grade graduation dance in Edinboro, Pennsylvania.

May 19, 1998: Three days before his graduation, an 18-year-old honor student opens fire in the parking lot of his high school in Fayetteville, Tennessee, killing a classmate who was dating his ex-girlfriend.

May 21, 1998: A 15-year-old boy kills his parents and then opens fire on students at his high school in Springfield, Oregon. Two teenagers are killed and 20 others wounded.

April 20, 1999: Two heavily armed students attack students at Columbine High School in Littleton, Colorado, with homemade bombs and automatic weapons. 15 students and teachers (including the gunmen) are killed and another 25 wounded.

May 20, 1999: A student opens fire at Heritage High School near Conyers, Georgia, just east of Atlanta. While there are no life-threatening injuries, 6 schoolmates are hospitalized with gunshot injuries.

February 29, 2000: A six-year-old first-grade student shoots and kills his classmate, Kayla Rolland, at Buell Elementary School in Flint, Michigan. No charges against the shooter are filed, but the student's 19-year-old uncle, Jamelle James, is indicted for felony manslaughter, since he provided the shooter with easy access to a loaded firearm.

March 10, 2000: Two students were killed by Darrell Ingram, 19, while leaving a dance sponsored at Beach High School in Savannah, Georgia.

May 26, 2000: A teacher, Barry Gurnow, was shot and killed at Lake Worth Middle School in Lake Worth, Florida, by Nate Brazill, 13, with a .25-caliber semiautomatic pistol on the last day of school.

March 5, 2001: Two students were killed and 13 others wounded by Charles Williams, 15, firing a rifle from a bathroom at Santana High School in Santee, California.

March 22, 2001: One teacher and 3 students were wounded by Janson Hoffman, 18, at Granite Hills High School in Williamsport, Pennsylvania. The School Resource Officer (SRO) assigned to the school shot and wounded Hoffman, preventing further casualties.

January 15, 2002: A teenager wounded 2 students at Martin Luther King, Jr., High School in New York City.

April 14, 2003: One 15-year-old student is killed and 3 students are wounded at John McDonogh High School in New Orleans by gunfire from 4 teenagers, none of whom are students. The shooting is gang-related.

April 24, 2003: James Sheets, age 14, kills Principal Eugene Segro of Red Lion Area Junior High School in Red Lion, Pennsylvania, before killing himself.

September 24, 2003: Fifteen-year-old James Jason McLaughlin kills 2 students at Rocori High School in Cold Spring, Minnesota.

March 21, 2005: Jeff Weise, age 16, kills a teacher, a security guard, and 5 students before committing suicide at Red Lake High School in Red Lake, Minnesota. Weise also kills his grandfather and his grandfather's wife before arriving at school.

November 8, 2005: An assistant principal is killed and 2 other administrators shot by a 15-year-old at Campbell County High School in Jacksboro, Tennessee.

September 26, 2006: Duane Roger Morrison, age 53, holds 6 female students hostage at Platte County High School in Bailey, Colorado. After sexually assaulting them, he shoots and kills 16-year-old Emily Keyes, then himself.

September 29, 2006: In Cazenovia, Wisconsin, a 15-year-old student kills Weston Schools Principal John Klang after being reprimanded by him.

October 3, 2006: Thirty-two-year-old Carl Charles Roberts IV enters the one-room West Nickel Mines Amish School and shoots 7 schoolgirls ranging in age from 6 to 13. Five of the girls die. Roberts commits suicide at the scene.

January 3, 2007: Samnang Kok, a 17-year-old student at Henry Foss High School in Tacoma, Washington, is shot and killed by a fellow student, Douglas Chanthabouly.

April 16, 2007: On the campus of Virginia Tech University in Blacksburg, Virginia, Seung-Hui Cho kills 32 people (29 students and 3 faculty members) and wounds another 30 before killing himself in the deadliest shooting incident in U.S. history.

(SROs) is the safety and well-being of students. They contribute to an orderly environment in the school as on-site public safety specialists trained to provide immediate response to life-threatening situations and to ensure that laws are enforced when illegal activities occur (e.g., drug trafficking and abuse, gang activities, and theft).[112] Experience has shown that the presence of an SRO has a general deterrent effect on illegal and disruptive behavior, as well as a more specific effect on isolated and violent student outbursts.[113]

The SRO is most likely to be the first responder in the case of a critical incident, such as a school shooting. As such, SROs have become instrumental staff members for schools in developing school crisis and emergency management plans. In some cases, SROs have been invited to teach classes to students on criminal justice and policing. The School Resource Officer Program is a collaborative effort by law enforcement officers, educators, students, parents, and the community aimed at reducing crime, drug abuse, and violence and providing a safe school environment. This program has been highly successful, with over 9,000 SROs representing every state in the nation.

School shootings over the past decade have sent shockwaves through the American public. The result has been an intense debate on several highly controversial subjects, such as gun control, entertainment and media violence, and pop culture. School violence and random acts of terrorism leave us all with a sense of helplessness and desperation. These are phenomena that will be facing American police agencies throughout the foreseeable future. No place seems to be safe, and more intense demands are being made on the police to prevent and deter such acts of violence. Clearly, these external influences will continue to impact the role of the police in a highly political and dynamic manner.

Critical Thinking Questions

1. Why do you think that school shootings receive so much national attention when they account for a relatively small percentage of overall victimization?
2. Can we prevent random school shootings? What steps do you think society can take to reduce the potential of school shootings in the future?

CHAPTER REVIEW

1. Explain the significance of the U.S. Supreme Court decisions in each of the following cases: *Mapp v. Ohio* (1966), *Gideon v. Wainwright* (1963), *Escobedo v. Illinois* (1964), and *Miranda v. Arizona* (1966).
   Mapp v. Ohio *banned the use of illegally seized evidence in criminal cases in the states by applying the Fourth Amendment guarantee against unreasonable search and seizure.* Gideon v. Wainwright *affirmed that equal protection under the Fourteenth Amendment requires that legal counsel be appointed for all indigent defendants in all criminal cases.* Escobedo v. Illinois *affirmed that a suspect is entitled to confer with an attorney as soon as the focus of a police investigation of suspects becomes accusatory.* Miranda v. Arizona *required police to inform suspects of their constitutional right to remain silent, their right to an attorney, and their right to have an attorney even if they can't afford one. Although the suspect may knowingly waive these rights, police may not question anyone who asks for a lawyer or refuses to answer questions at any point.*
2. Describe the impact of incidents such as the Abner Louima case and the Sean Bell shooting.

These incidents have marred the reputation of police agencies and have raised questions about police accountability, ethics, and autonomy. These issues have also produced public apathy and resentment toward police.

3. List the goals of the Commission on Accreditation for Law Enforcement Agencies (CALEA).

   The goals of CALEA are to increase agency capabilities to prevent and control crime; to enhance agency effectiveness and efficiency in the delivery of law enforcement services; to improve cooperation and coordination with other law enforcement agencies and with other components of the criminal justice system; and to increase citizen and staff confidence in the goals, objectives, policies, and practices of the agency.

4. Describe three styles of law enforcement as presented by James Q. Wilson.

   The first style of law enforcement described by Wilson is the watchman style. This style emphasizes order maintenance and is found in cities that have traditional political machines and are in economic decline. Next, Wilson described the legalistic style, characterized by law enforcement that is both proactive and reactive. Legalistic style is found in cities with reform-minded, professional governments with a heterogeneous citizenry. Finally, the service style of law enforcement is oriented toward the needs of citizens and is found in homogenous suburban communities.

5. Briefly describe the three major forms of local government in the United States.

   The three major forms of local government are the strong mayor, where the mayor serves as the chief executive of the city; the city manager, where the city council entrusts an individual to make city personnel and budget decisions; and the city council structure, where the city council acts as the chief legislative and policymaking body.

6. List the three political arenas of conflict.

   The first type of political arena is confrontation, in which the situational conflict is intense but brief and confined. Next is the shaky alliance, in which conflict is less intense but still pervasive. This may be the aftermath of a confrontation. The third type of political arena is the politicized organization. This is the most common and features pervasive but muted conflict that is tolerable for a time. Finally, the complete political arena is a conflict that is pervasive, intense, brief, and out of control.

7. Explain why police chiefs that are not protected from arbitrary and unjustified termination often resist setting new goals and instituting organizational change.

   Chiefs who are afraid of jeopardizing their positions are less likely to pioneer innovative programs. The inherent risk of failure with new projects is often too risky for a chief who is not protected from arbitrary and unjustified termination.

8. Describe the differences in status between a county sheriff and a police chief.

   Sheriffs are typically elected to their posts, as opposed to police chiefs, who are appointed. Also, sheriffs have a custodial role in the detention of prisoners, a role not common to municipal police.

9. Explain how the state prosecutor impacts police practices.

   The state prosecutor affects police practices through enforcement policies, procedures for review of all arrests before their presentation in court, and overall supervision of cases prepared by police.

10. Explain how citizens can be involved in the policymaking process of law enforcement agencies.

    Easy ways in which citizens can be involved in the policymaking process of law enforcement agencies include participation in community groups, such as senior citizen organizations, service clubs, and religious organizations.

11. Describe some circumstances in which the police and the media might be in conflict.
Some circumstance in which the police and the media might be in conflict include situations in which the police do not want to release information that will jeopardize the safety of citizens or officers, that will impede an investigation, or that will impair the right of a suspect to a fair trial. Another situation in which conflict might arise is when the news media refuses to divulge the source of information that is of actual investigative or legal significance. Other situations are the inclusion in media reports of "off-the-record" information given by police, claims by police officials that they were misquoted, and press involvement at the scene of dangerous incidents or sensitive investigations.
12. Describe the function of a school resource officer (SRO).
The school resource officer is a police officer permanently assigned at a school location in order to protect students, contribute to an orderly environment, and provide immediate response to life-threatening situations.

KEY TERMS

Accountability: responsibility to someone or for an action or activity.

CALEA: the Commission on Accreditation for Law Enforcement Agencies; a private, non-profit organization that has developed laa enforcement standards for all types and sizes of state and local law enforcement agencies.

Judiciary: a system of courts of law that administer justice.

Politics: attempts to impose external, partisan political influence on the operation of a police department.

Politics: the governance of a city.

Prosecutor: a public officer within a jurisdiction representing the citizenry of a state or county that charges and prosecutes an individual for a crime.

Racial profiling: the consideration of race as a key factor in police decisions to stop and interrogate citizens.

School resource officers (SROs): police officers permanently assigned to a school.

Tenure: a period, or term, during which a position is held.

NOTES

1. W. H. Hudnut III, "The Police and the Polis: A Mayor's Perspective," in *Police Leadership in America: Crisis and Opportunity,* ed. William A. Geller (Westport, Conn.: Praeger, 1985), p. 20.
2. "Congress Clears Bill to Eliminate COPS Program," *Crime Prevention News* 95, no. 23 (December 13, 1995): 1.
3. See David Jackson, "Homeland Agency Gets Senate OK," *Dallas Morning News,* November 20, 2002, and "Bush Benefits from Homeland Shift," *Dallas Morning News,* November 26, 2002.
4. A. E. Bent, *The Politics of Law Enforcement* (Lexington, Mass.: D. C. Heath, 1974), p. 63.
5. Some of this material was excerpted from Joe Domanick, "County Sheriff Stacks His Values against a 'Self-Limiting' Legacy," *Los Angeles Times,* March 11, 2001, p. M3.
6. N. G. Holten and M. E. Jones, *The Systems of Criminal Justice* (Boston: Little, Brown, 1978), p. 416.
7. Treatment of the Supreme Court's influence has been drawn from Thomas Phelps, Charles Swanson, and Kenneth Evans, *Introduction to Criminal Justice* (Santa Monica, Calif.: Goodyear, 1979), pp. 128–31.
8. In a legal sense, the Supreme Court opted for a piecemeal application when it rejected the "shorthand doctrine" (i.e., making a blanket application of the federal Bill of Rights provisions binding on the states) in its consideration of *Hurtado v. California,*

110 U.S. 516 (1884); therefore, the statement should be read in the context that the activist role was a policy decision.

9. Fred P. Graham, *The Self-Inflicted Wound* (New York: Macmillan, 1970), p. 37. For a look at the police and due process, see A. T. Quick, "Attitudinal Aspects of Police Compliance with Procedural Due Process," *American Journal of Criminal Law* 6 (1978): 25–56.
10. T. R. Dye, *Politics in States and Communities* (Englewood Cliffs, N.J.: Prentice Hall, 1973), p. 214.
11. The concept of the "erosion" of the *Mapp* and *Miranda* decisions is commonly referred to in studies by Thomas Davies as cited in *The Oxford Companion to the Supreme Court of the United States*, ed. Kermit L. Hall (New York: Oxford University Press, 1992), p. 266; G. M. Caplan, *Modern Procedures for Police Interrogation* (Washington, D.C.: Police Executive Research Forum, 1992); and Rolando V. del Carmen, *Criminal Procedure: Law and Practice*, 3rd ed. (Belmont, Calif.: Wadsworth, 1995), pp. 317–36.
12. See *Massachusetts v. Shepard*, 468 U.S. 981 (1984), and *United States v. Leon*, 468 U.S. 897 (1984).
13. Justice William Brennan's dissent in *United States v. Leon*.
14. *Carroll v. United States*, 267 U.S. 132 (1925).
15. *Michigan Department of State Police v. Sitz*, 496 U.S. 444 (1990).
16. See *Atwater v. City of Lago Vista*, 532 U.S. 318 (2001), and S. M. Mamasis, "Fear of the Common Traffic Stop—'Am I Going to Jail?' The Right of Police to Arbitrarily Arrest or Issue Citations for Minor Misdemeanors in *Atwater v. City of Lago Vista*." *Thurgood Marshall Law Review* 27(2001): 85.
17. See *United States v. Arvizu*, 232 F. 3d, 1241.
18. *Arizona v. Fulminante*, 111 S. Ct. 1246 (1991).
19. "Supreme Court on Police Powers," *Law Enforcement News* 17, nos. 338, 339 (June 15/30, 1991): 1, 9, 10.
20. Edward Timms, "Scandal Leaving Some Leary of Nation's Law Enforcement," *Dallas Morning News*, September 25, 1995, p. 1.
21. Adapted from David Kocieniewski, "Injured Man Says Brooklyn Officers Tortured Him in Custody," *New York Times*, August 13, 1997, pp. B1, B3, and "New York Officer to Plead Guilty in Beating," *Dallas Morning News*, May 25, 1999, p. A3.
22. Alan Feuer and Jim Dwyer, "New York Settles in Brutality Case," *New York Times*, July 13, 2001, p. A1.
23. Michael Cooper, "Officers in Bronx Fire 41 Shots, and an Unarmed Man Is Killed," *New York Times*, February 4, 1999, pp. A1, B5.
24. Anonymous Los Angeles resident, *USA Today*, September 22, 1995, p. 1.
25. Cathy Booth, Sylvester Monroe, and Edwin M. Reingold, "Law and Disorder," *Time*, April 1, 1991, pp. 18–21.
26. Ibid., 21.
27. Ibid.
28. Louis A. Radelet and David Carter, *Police and the Community*, 5th ed. (New York: Macmillan, 1994), p. 46.
29. Special thanks to Brooke Nodeland for her assistance in developing this section on racial and ethnic profiling. See also Robin Engle, Jennifer Calnon, and Thomas Bernard, "Racial Profiling: Shortcomings and Future Directions in Research," *Justice Quarterly* 19, no. 2 (June 2002): 249–73.
30. Ronald Weitzer and Steven Tuch, "Perceptions of Racial Profiling: Race, Class, and Personal Experience," *Criminology* 40, no. 2 (2002).
31. See *Whren v. United States*, 517 U.S. 806 (1996).
32. See *Brown v. City of Oneonta*, 221 F. 3d (2d Cir. 2000), cert. denied, 122 S. Ct. 44 (2001), and Elliot B. Spector, "Stopping Suspects Based on Racial and Ethnic Descriptions," *Police Chief*, January 2002, pp. 10–12.
33. See note 1 and D. A. Harris, "'Driving While Black' and All Other Traffic Offenses: The Supreme Court and Pretextual Traffic Stops," *Journal of Criminal Law and Criminology* 87 (1997): 544–82.
34. See *The Common Characteristics of Drug Couriers* (Tallahassee: Florida Department of Highway Safety and Motor Vehicles, 1985).
35. See note 29.
36. See note 33 and R. Kennedy, *Race, Crime and the Law* (New York: Vintage Books, 1997).
37. For an excellent review of the research on racial profiling, see D. Ramirez, J. McDevitt, and A. Farrell, *A Resource Guide on Racial Profiling Data Collection Systems: Promising Practices and Lessons Learned* (Washington, D.C.: U.S. Department of Justice, 2000).
38. Albert Meehan and Michael Ponder, "How Roadway Composition Matters in Analyzing Police Data on Racial Profiling," *Police Quarterly* 5, no. 3 (September 2002): 401–32.
39. Ibid.
40. See note 30.
41. Michael Brueger and Amy Farrell, "The Evidence of Racial Profiling: Interpreting Documented and Unofficial Sources," *Police Quarterly* 5, no. 3 (September 2002): 327–46.
42. Ibid.

43. See Brandon Garrett, "Remedying Racial Profiling," *Columbia Human Rights Law Review* 33 (fall 2001): 107–40, and *U.S. v. Tapia,* 912 F. 2d 1367 (11th Cir. 1990); *U.S. v. Griffen,* 412 R. 2d 14060 (11th Cir. 1997); and *U.S. v. Bizier,* U.S. Dist. Ct., D. Ma 476 (1st Cir. 1997).
44. See the American Civil Liberties Union's articles on racial profiling at www.aclu.org. See also note 30.
45. International Association of Chiefs of Police, "Policies Help Gain Public Trust: Racial Profiling," August 21, 2002 (www.theiacp.org/documents).
46. See D. Douglas Bodrero, "Law Enforcement's New Challenge to Investigate, Interdict, and Prevent Terrorism," *Police Chief,* February 2002: 41–47.
47. Radelet and Carter, *Police and the Community,* pp. 91–92.
48. Ibid., p. 99.
49. Ibid., p. 100.
50. Booth et al., "Law and Disorder," p. 21 (italics added).
51. Commission on Accreditation for Law Enforcement Agencies, *Accreditation Program Overview* (Fairfax, Va.: CALEA, 1990), p. 4.
52. Gary W. Cordner, "Written Rules and Regulations: Are They Necessary?" *FBI Law Enforcement Bulletin* 58, no. 7 (1999): 18.
53. Russell Maas, "Written Rules and Regulations: Is the Fear Real?" *Law and Order,* May 1990, p. 36.
54. Gerald Williams, *Making the Grade: The Benefits of Law Enforcement Accreditation* (Washington, D.C.: Police Executive Research Forum, 1989), pp. xv, xvii.
55. Ibid.
56. Ibid., pp. xvii, xviii.
57. Robert M. Fogelson, *Big-City Police* (Cambridge, Mass: Harvard University Press, 1975), pp. 14–15.
58. Ibid., p. 14.
59. This vignette is based on one of the author's experiences while serving in law enforcement.
60. Information provided by the National Association of State Directors of Law Enforcement Training.
61. The National Advisory Commission on Criminal Justice Standards and Goals, *A National Strategy to Reduce Crime* (Washington, D.C.: U.S. Government Printing Office, 1972), p. 149.
62. James Q. Wilson, *Varieties of Police Behavior* (New York: Atheneum, 1973).
63. The President's Commission on Law Enforcement and Administration of Justice, *Task Force Report: The Police* (Washington, D.C.: U.S. Government Printing Office, 1967), p. 127.
64. A. H. Andrews, Jr., "Structuring the Political Independence of the Police Chief," in *Police Leadership in America: Crisis and Opportunity,* ed. William Geller (New York: Praeger, 1985), pp. 9, 10.
65. V. A. Leonard and H. W. Moore, *Police Organization and Management* (Mineola, N.Y.: Foundation Press, 1971), p. 21.
66. G. E. Berkeley et al., *Introduction to Criminal Justice* (Boston: Holbrook Press, 1976), p. 216.
67. Leonard and Moore, *Police Organization and Management,* p. 15.
68. J. F. Ahern, *Police in Trouble* (New York: Hawthorn Books, 1972), pp. 96–98.
69. J. J. Norton and G. G. Cowart, "Assaulting the Politics/Administration Dichotomy," *Police Chief* 45, no. 11 (1978): 26.
70. Interview with staff assistants at the International Association of Chiefs of Police, Washington, D.C., December 8, 1995.
71. One of the most comprehensive collections of articles and essays focusing on the role of the chief of police is found in Geller, *Police Leadership in America.*
72. Janet Ferris et al., "Present and Potential Legal Job Protections Available to Heads of Agencies," *Florida Police Chief* 14, no. 5 (1994): 43–45.
73. G. L. Williams and S. Cheurprakobkit, "Police Executive Contracts: Are They a Foundation for Successful Tenure?" In *Controversial Issues in Policing,* ed. J. D. Sewell (Boston: Allyn and Bacon, 1999), pp. 105–12. (This discussion was adapted with permission from this source.)
74. H. Mintzberg, *Power in and around Organizations.* (Englewood Cliffs, N.J.: Prentice Hall, 1983).
75. T. Roche, "Chief's Policy Thrust into Debate," *St. Petersburg Times,* October 30, 1996, p. A1.
76. "Help Stephens Succeed," *St. Petersburg Times,* October 31, 1996, editorial page.
77. C. Green, "Boulder Leadership Missing in Action," *Denver Post,* May 30, 1997.
78. C. Mahtesian, "Mission Impossible," *Governing,* January 1997, pp. 19–23.
79. Ibid.
80. Ibid.
81. J. Ruiz, "The Return of the Ultimate Outsider: A Civilian Administrator as the Top Cop" (unpublished paper, 1997).
82. Ibid.
83. Ibid.
84. Ibid.
85. See S. Walker, *The Police in America* (New York: McGraw-Hill, 1992), p. 44, and B. A.

Reaves, *Sheriff's Departments 1990* (Washington, D.C.: U.S. Department of Justice, Bureau of Justice Statistics), p. 1.
86. National Sheriff's Association, *County Law Enforcement: Assessment of Capabilities and Needs* (Washington, D.C.: National Sheriff's Association, 1995), p. 1.
87. Most of the following material has been excerpted from Harry C. Guffardi, "History of the Office of Sheriff," www.hostpc.com/Buffardi/htm.
88. B. L. Garmire, ed., *Local Police Management* (Washington, D.C.: Institute for Training in Municipal Administration, 1982, 2001).
89. D. R. Struckoff, *The American Sheriff* (Joliet, Ill.: Justice Research Institute, 1994), p. 43.
90. Ibid., pp. 44–45.
91. D. B. Brammer and J. E. Hurley, *A Study of the Office of Sheriff in the United States Southern Region* (Oxford, Miss.: University of Mississippi Bureau of Government Research, 1968), pp. 1–2.
92. R. N. Holden, *Modern Police Management* (Englewood Cliffs, N.J.: Prentice Hall Career and Technology, 1994), p. 13.
93. Reaves, *Sheriff's Departments 1990,* p. 1.
94. L. P. Brown, "The Role of the Sheriff," in *The Future of Policing,* ed. Alvin W. Cohn (Beverly Hills, Calif.: Sage, 1978), pp. 227–28.
95. Reaves, *Sheriff's Departments 1990,* p. 1.
96. The President's Commission, *Task Force Report,* p.30.
97. Ibid., p. 31.
98. Ibid.
99. Ibid.
100. J. H. Skolnick, *Justice without Trial: Law Enforcement in a Democratic Society* (New York: John Wiley & Sons, 1966), pp. 228–29.
101. H. W. More, Jr., ed., *Critical Issues in Law Enforcement* (Cincinnati: Anderson, 1972), p. 261.
102. The President's Commission, *Task Force Report,* p.34.
103. See American Association of Retired Persons, *A Profile of Older Americans* (Washington, D.C.: AARP, 1999).
104. See Debra C. Duncan, "Community Policing: Preserving the Quality of Life of Our Senior Citizens," *Police Chief,* March 2001, pp. 75–77.
105. For a more thorough discussion of TRIAD, sponsored by AARP, the International Association of Chiefs of Police, and the National Sheriff's Association, see www.sheriffs.org and click on "TRIAD."
106. Ibid.
107. Bent, *The Politics of Law Enforcement,* p. 72.
108. E. M. Davis, "Press Relations Guide for Peace Officers," *Police Chief* 39, no. 3 (1972): 67.
109. See General Order OM-F-4, "Release of Information to the News Media" issued by the Kentucky State Police, January 1, 1990.
110. "Indicators of School Crime and Safety 2006," National Center for Educational Statistics, Institute of Education Sciences, U.S. Department of Education.
111. Ibid.
112. For more information on SROs, see Anne J. Atkinson, "School Resource Officers: Making Schools Safer and More Effective," *Police Chief,* March 2001, pp. 55–63.
113. Ibid., p. 57.

PART II

THE FOLLOWING CHAPTERS ARE COVERED IN PART II:

5 Organizational Theory

6 Organizational Design

7 Leadership

8 Planning and Decision Making

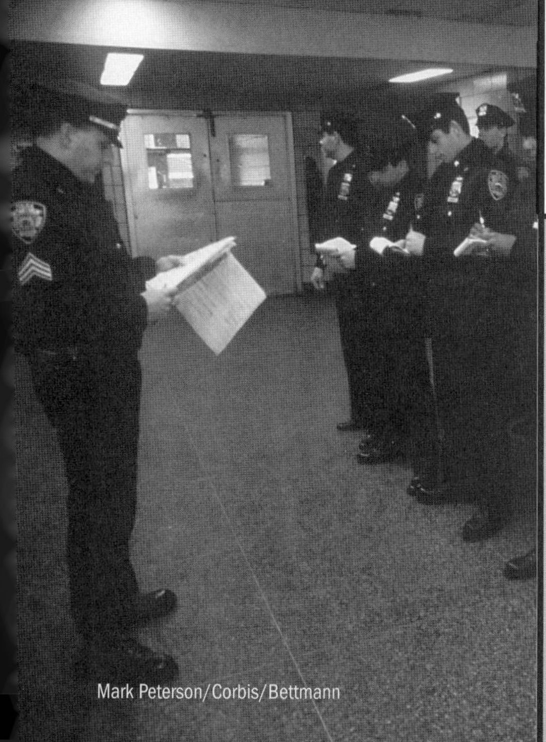

Mark Peterson/Corbis/Bettmann

OVERVIEW

Many theorists and popular management "gurus" maintain that people—in the form of employees—are an organization's most important asset. We can immediately think of two reasons why this may be true: 1) they are often the largest single expenditure in an organization's budget and 2) the way clients experience an organization and form opinions of it is through its employees. It is therefore surprising that some organizations adopt structures, policies, and practices which get in the way of developing officers to their fullest potential and taking advantage of their considerable talents. The chapters in this section deal with such matters as what assumptions about employees do different types of organizational structure make, how to motivate officers, and the way to make better decisions.

THE ORGANIZATION AND THE LEADER

Theory and practice are inseparable.

—Douglas McGregor

CHAPTER 5

OUTLINE

Introduction
Traditional Organizational Theory
Open Systems Theory
Bridging Theories
Synthesis and Prognosis
Chapter Review
Key Terms
Notes

OBJECTIVES

1. State why organizations exist.
2. Identify and give examples of the four types of organizations that result from asking the question of *cui bono*.
3. Identify the key issue for the police as a commonweal organization.
4. Define traditional organizational theory.
5. Discuss scientific management.
6. Describe how the exception principle operates.
7. Identify Henry Gantt's most important contribution.
8. Identify with whom the bureaucratic form of organization is most closely associated and state the reasons why this identification exists.
9. Discuss administrative theory.
10. Critique traditional organizational theory.
11. Define the human relations school.
12. Discuss open systems theory.
13. Explain the Hawthorne effect.
14. Describe Maslow's needs hierarchy.
15. Identify and define hygiene and motivation factors.
16. Discuss the relationship between the human relations school (in the Hawthorne studies tradition) and behavioral systems theory.
17. State why the work of Kurt Lewin is notable.
18. Explain what Homans meant when he used the terms "internal systems" and "external systems."
19. Describe the immaturity–maturity and the mix model.
20. Define theory X and theory Y.
21. Describe the relationship between Likert's four types of management systems and McGregor's theory X–theory Y.
22. Explain the concept of organizational development.
23. Discuss how chaos theory and quantum theory may help police administrators understand their environment.
24. Critique open systems theory.
25. Define bridging theories.

ORGANIZATIONAL THEORY

INTRODUCTION

Formal organizations are not a recent innovation.[1] Alexander the Great and Caesar used them to conquer, the pharaohs employed them to build pyramids, the emperors of China constructed great irrigation systems with them, and the first popes created an organization to deliver religion on a worldwide basis.[2] The extent to which contemporary America is an organizational society is such that

> we are born in organizations, educated by organizations, and spend most of our lives working for organizations. We spend much of our time . . . playing and praying in organizations. Most of us will die in an organization and when the time comes for burial, the largest organization of all—the state—must grant official permission.[3]

The basic rationale for the existence of organizations is that they do those things that people are unwilling or unable to do alone. Parsons notes that organizations are distinguished from other human groupings or social units in that to a much greater degree they are constructed and reconstructed to achieve specific goals; corporations, armies, hospitals, and police departments are included within this meaning, whereas families and friendship groups are not.[4] Schein defines an organization as

> the rational coordination of the activities of a number of people for the achievement of some common explicit purpose or goal, through division of labor and function, and through a hierarchy of authority and responsibility.[5]

Blau and Scott identify four types of formal organizations by asking the question of ***cui bono***, or who benefits: (1) mutual benefit associations, such as police labor unions, where the primary beneficiary is the membership; (2) business concerns, such as Microsoft, where the owners are the prime beneficiary; (3) service organizations, such as community mental health centers, where a specific client group is the prime beneficiary; and (4) commonweal organizations, such as the Department of Defense and police departments, where the beneficiary is the public at large.[6]

Each of these four types of formal organizations has its own central issues.[7] Mutual benefit associations, such as police unions, face the crucial problem of maintaining the internal democratic processes—providing for participation and control by their membership. For businesses, the central issue is maximizing profits in a competitive environment. Service organizations are faced with the conflict between administrative regulations and provision of the services judged by the professional to be most appropriate. In the case of a community mental health center, an illustration is that, following a reduction in funding, a regulation is placed into effect that requires

In The News

Today's News

Police, City at Impasse

Unions fight to get their members the best contract they can; that is the reason they exist. In Stamford, Connecticut, the police union and the city are so far apart in negotiating a new contract on wages, pensions, and other factors that they have reached an impasse in the bargaining and the conflict will have to be decided by an impartial outside arbitrator.

The city claims that the union's request for a 7 percent salary hike, reducing the retirement age from 55 to 50, and adding cost-of-living increases to police pensions would cost the city $10 million a year, possibly more. The union also balks at the city's desire to charge officers more for health insurance, as they do with members of other city departments. Union leaders say that they are not like other city departments because they are the only ones who come to work wearing bullet-proof vests.

Source: Zach Lowe, *The Stamford (Connecticut) Advocate*, "Political Feud Fuels Heated Police Contract Talks" September 24, 2006, with restatement.

In The News

Police Review Board Considered

In Eureka, California, 200 people appeared at a city council meeting to demand the creation of an independent police review board in the wake of Christopher Burgess's death. Burgess, who was 16 years old, was being pursued on foot in a gulley by a Eureka police officer when he turned toward the officer at a range of 4 to 6 feet and made a stabbing motion, which precipitated the fatal shot. Chief Dave Douglas asked for prayers for everyone involved and defended his officer, noting that it is not necessary for officers to be wounded before they can defend themselves.

One council member, Virginia Bass, who was at that time a candidate for mayor, announced she would host a forum on the Eureka Police Department's use of force policies. Within a week, a toxicology report revealed that Burgess had methamphetamine in his system when he brandished the knife at the police officer.

Source: Chris Durant, *The Eureka (California) Times Standard,* October 31, 2006, "Angry Citizens Demand Police Review Board."

all clients to be treated in group sessions when the psychiatric social worker believes that the only effective treatment for a particular client is to be seen individually. The core reason that police managers must have a working knowledge of organizational theory stems from the fact that police departments are commonweal organizations.

The key issue for a police department and other types of commonweal organizations is finding a way to accommodate pressures from two sources, external and internal. The public, through its elected and appointed representatives, must have a means of controlling its police department. This external democratic control feature also has the expectation that the internal workings of the police department will be bureaucratic, governed by the criterion of efficiency, and not also democratic. This is because democratic control by the members of a police department might be at the expense of lessening the police department's ability to affect the will of the community. Simultaneously, the large numbers of officers at the lower levels of the police department do not want to be treated like "cogs in a machine" and desire some voice in how the department operates. Thus, the challenge for police managers is how to maintain an organization that meets society's needs and the needs of the officers who work in it. This requires an understanding of such things as the different ways of organizing and the contrasting assumptions that various organizational forms make about the nature of people. Such knowledge is found within organizational theory.

This chapter consists of three major areas; each deals with different ways of thinking about how to organize work and work processes. Discussed more fully as they arise, the three major streams of thinking about work structures and processes to be treated are (1) traditional organizational theory, on which most police departments are based; (2) open systems theory, which represents a direct counterpoint to traditional theory; and (3) bridging theories, which to some greater or lesser degree show concern for the issues reflected in both traditional and open systems theories. Bridging theories do not fall neatly into either the traditional or the open systems category, yet they reflect consideration of each, thus constituting a distinctly unique category. Within each of the three major streams of thinking about work structures and processes are illustrations of some of the specific techniques associated with various theorists and examples cast in a police context.

TRADITIONAL ORGANIZATIONAL THEORY

Traditional theory is associated with organizations described as mechanistic, closed systems, bureaucratic, and stable. This body of knowledge evolved over centuries and crystallized between 1900 and 1940. The three stems of traditional organizational theory are (1) scientific management, (2) the bureaucratic model, and (3) administrative, or management, theory.

Taylor: Scientific Management

The father of **scientific management** was **Frederick W. Taylor** (1856–1915), and the thrust of his thinking was to find the "one best way" to do work (see Figure 5.1). In addition to its status as a theory of work organization, Taylor's scientific management is a theory of motivation in its belief that employees will be guided in their actions by what is in their economic self-interest.

A Pennsylvanian born of Quaker–Puritan parents, Taylor was so discontented with the "evils" of waste and slothfulness that he applied the same careful analysis to finding the best way of playing croquet and of taking a cross-country walk with the least fatigue that was to be the hallmark of his later work in factories.[8] From 1878 to 1890, Taylor worked at the Midvale Steel Company in Philadelphia, rising from the ranks of the laborers to chief engineer in just six years.[9] Taylor's experience at Midvale gave him insight into the twin problems of productivity and worker motivation. He saw workers as deliberately restricting productivity by "natural soldiering" and "systematic soldiering."

Natural soldiering came from the natural inclination of employees not to push themselves; *systematic soldiering* came from workers not wanting to produce so much as to see their quotas raised or other workers thrown out of their jobs.[10] To correct these deficiencies, Taylor called for a "complete mental revolution"[11] on the part of

FIGURE 5.1

Frederick W. Taylor.

(Courtesy of the Library of Congress)

both workers and managers, although it is certain that he faulted management more for its failure to design jobs properly and to give workers the proper economic incentives to overcome soldiering than he did workers for not producing.[12]

Taylor's scientific management was only loosely a theory of organization because its focus was largely on work at the bottom part of the organization rather than being a general model. Scientific management's method was to find the most physically and time-efficient way to sequence tasks and then to use rigorous and extensive controls to enforce the standards. Taylor's conversation with "Schmidt" illustrates this:

> *"Schmidt, you can keep making $1.15 a day like the rest of these workers or you can be a high price man and make $1.85 each and every day. Do you want to be a high price man?"*
> *"Vell yes, I vant to be high price man."*
> *"Good. When this man tells you to load pig iron on the car, you walk, pick up the pig and load it exactly like he tells you. Rest when he tells you to and never give him any backtalk. That's what a high price man does."*
> *"I vant to be a high price man and vill do what this man tells me."*[13]

For Taylor, authority was based not on position in a hierarchy but rather on knowledge; **functional supervision** meant that people were responsible for directing certain tasks despite the fact this meant that the authority of the supervisor might cut across organizational lines.[14] The **exception principle** meant that routine matters should be handled by lower-level managers or by supervisors and that higher-level managers should only receive reports of deviations above or below standard performances.[15] The integration of cost accounting into the planning process became part of some budgeting practices treated in Chapter 12, Financial Management.

Despite the success of scientific management in raising productivity and cutting costs, "Taylorism" was attacked from a variety of quarters. Union leaders saw it as a threat to their movement because it seemed to reduce, if not eliminate, the importance of unions. The management of Bethlehem Steel ultimately abandoned task management, as Taylor liked to refer to his system, because they were uncomfortable with such an accurate appraisal of their performance[16] and some liberals saw it as an exploitation of workers. Upton Sinclair charged that Taylor had given workers a 61 percent increase in wages while getting a 362 percent increase in work.[17] Taylor replied to this charge by saying that employees worked no harder, only more

In The News

Ticket Quotas Dropped

Quotas in law enforcement have traditionally been resisted by officers who maintain that no one really knows how many good cases they will see during a day, week, or month. Moreover, the number and types of offenses vary by geographical area and demographic characteristics; for example, older people commit fewer crimes. Moreover, officers are quick to point out that quotas force them to make marginal cases in order to get good evaluations, decreasing public goodwill and support.

The Ogden, Utah, City Council dropped a controversial police performance evaluation plan which included 18 factors, including a score for the number of traffic tickets given. This followed a period during which the wife of an officer drove a van displaying signs critical of the traffic quota and Mayor Godfrey. Within hours, the officer was placed on administrative leave, although the police chief maintains this was due to other alleged actions by the officer. A two-day "blue-flu" was also used, with officers calling in "sick" during it. The city's administration has agreed to meet with officers to identify and discuss issues; the meetings will be led by a professional mediator to keep them on track.

Source: "Ogden Rescinds Ticket Quota for Police," The Associated Press and Local Wire, August 16, 2006, with restatement.

Quick Facts

About Pravda

Pravda (Russian, "The Truth") was the official communist newspaper from 1918 until 1991, when President Yeltsin ordered it closed. A number of newspapers now operate using this name.

State Police Testing Project

Task Name	Duration	Start	End	2001 12/Sep	19/Sep	26/Sep	03/Oct	1
Order Project Equipment	18.0 d	13/Sep/01	06/Oct/02					
Write Request for Computer, Printer, and Software	2.0 d	13/Sep/01	14/Sep/02					
Obtain Administrative Approval for Equipment Request	3.0 d	15/Sep/01	17/Sep/02					
Order Equipment & Software through Procurement	3.0 d	20/Sep/01	22/Sep/02					
Equipment and Software on Order	8.0 d	23/Sep/01	04/Oct/02					
Receive and Configure Equipment	2.0 d	05/Oct/01	06/Oct/02					
Staff Project	14.0 d	13/Sep/01	30/Sep/02					
Develop Job Descriptions	2.0 d	13/Sep/01	14/Sep/02					
Announce Positions	3.0 d	15/Sep/01	17/Sep/02					
Screen Applicants	3.0 d	20/Sep/01	22/Sep/02					
Interview Finalists	2.0 d	23/Sep/01	24/Sep/02					
Make Hiring Decisions	1.0 d	27/Sep/01	27/Sep/02					
Train Staff	3.0 d	28/Sep/01	30/Sep/02					

FIGURE 5.2

A portion of a Gantt chart showing the start-up phase of a project. This figure was prepared using only the most basic capabilities of Microsoft's *Project* software. As set up for this application, the numbers of days listed in the "Duration" column count only weekdays as working days and does not include any weekend days.

efficiently. In hearings before the U.S. House of Representatives in 1912, Taylor's methods were attacked thoroughly, and he died three years later a discouraged man.

Scientific management did not disappear with Taylor, however. There remained a core of people devoted to its practice, including Henry L. Gantt (1861–1919); Watlington Emerson (1853–1931), also a promoter of the staff concept; Frank (1868–1924) and Lillian (1878–1972) Gilbreth; and Morris Cooke (1872–1960), who in *Our Cities Awake* (1918) called for the application of scientific management in municipal government. Gantt gained a measure of immortality by developing a basic planning chart, illustrated in Figure 5.2, that remains in wide use today and still bears his name. Developed during the summer of 1917 while Gantt worked at the Frankford Arsenal, the **Gantt chart** contained the then-revolutionary idea that the key factor in planning production was not quantity but time.[18] Some international interest in scientific management also remained after Taylor's death; in 1918, France's Ministry of War called for the application of scientific management, as did Lenin in an article in *Pravda*.[19] It is, of course, ironic that a communist society should call for the use of a management system based on the principle that economic self-interest guides the behavior of workers.

The fact that the period when scientific management was a dominant force has "come and gone" does not mean that it is all history. Many of the techniques associated with scientific management, such as time and motion studies and work flow

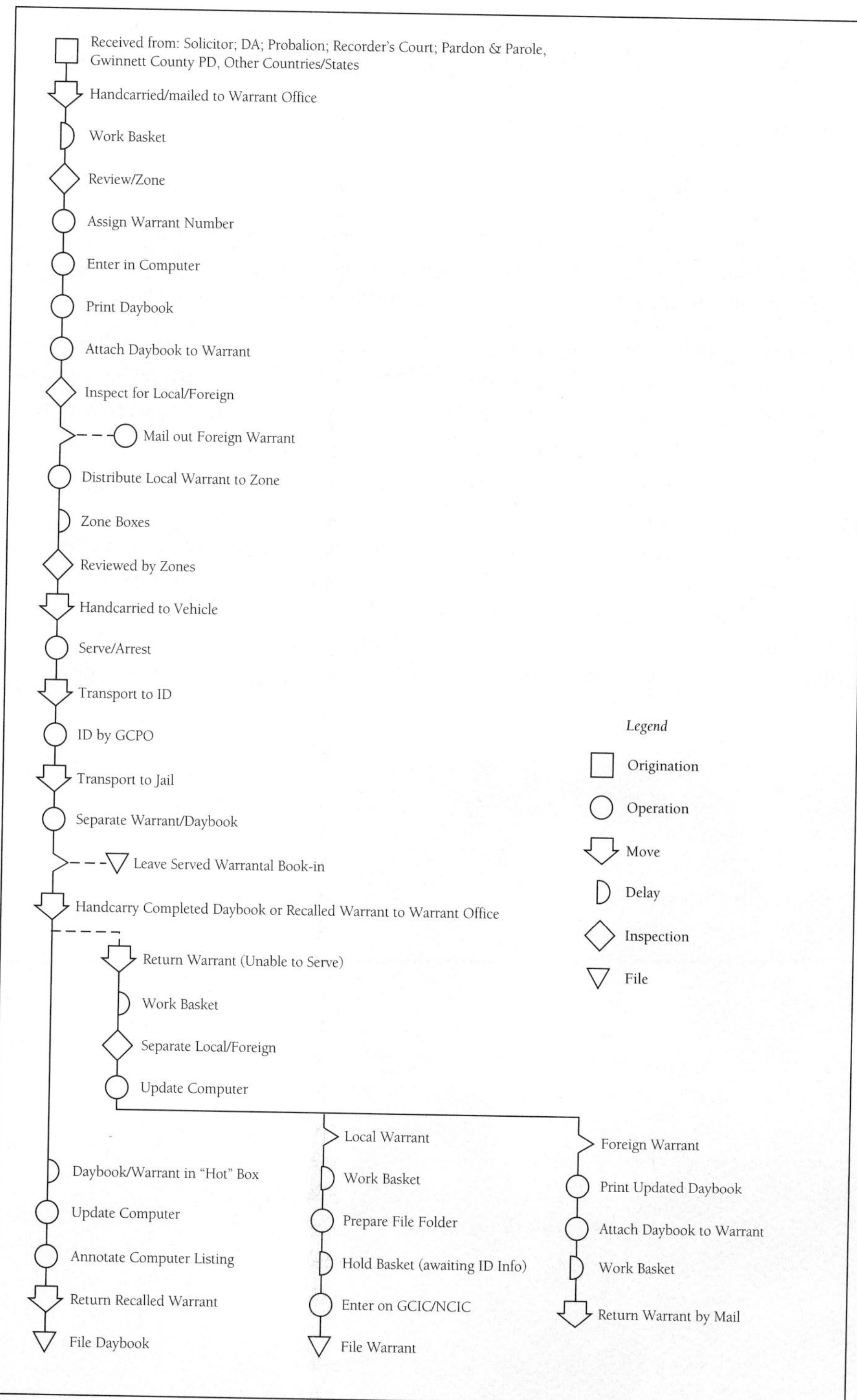

FIGURE 5.3

Analysis of sheriff's department criminal warrant work flow.

analysis (depicted in Figure 5.3), remain in use in what is generally called industrial engineering. Other modern successors to scientific management were developed during World War II to support the war effort, and the refinement and more general application of these techniques is a post-1945 movement. The new techniques have alternatively been referred to as management science and operations research (OR), and their central orientation has been the application of quantitative and technical analysis to decision making.[20]

Weber: The Bureaucratic Model

In popular usage, "bureaucracy" has come to mean

> *the slowness, the ponderous, the routine, the complication of procedures, and the maladapted responses of "bureaucratic" organizations to the needs which they should satisfy and the frustrations which their members, clients, or subjects consequently endure.*[21]

This meaning is far from the image of the ideal or pure bureaucracy developed by the towering German intellect **Max Weber** (1864–1920), the founder of modern sociology (see Figure 5.4). For Weber, the choice was "only that between bureaucracy and dilettantism in the field of administration."[22] In this regard, Weber claimed,

> *Experience tends universally to show that the purely bureaucratic type of administrative organization—that is, the monocratic variety of the bureaucracy—is, from a purely technical point of view, capable of attaining the highest degree of efficiency and is in this sense formally the most rational known means of carrying out imperative control over human beings. It is superior to any other form in precision, in stability, in the stringency of its discipline, and in its reliability. It thus makes possible a particularly high degree of calculability of results for the heads of the organization and*

FIGURE 5.4

Max Weber.

(Courtesy of the Library of Congress)

for those acting in relation to it. It is finally superior both in intensive efficiency and in the scope of operations, and is formally capable of application to all kinds of administrative tasks.[23]

Weber's **bureaucratic model** included the following characteristics:

1. The organization of offices follows the principle of hierarchy; that is, each lower office is under the control and supervision of a higher one. There is a right of appeal and of statement of grievances from the lower to the higher.
2. Specified areas of competence, meaning a division of labor, exist, in each of which the authority and responsibility of every organizational member is identified.
3. Official duties are bound by a system of rational rules, such as policies and procedures.
4. Administrative acts, decisions, and rules are recorded in writing.
5. The "rights" associated with a position are the property of the office or job and not of the officeholders.
6. Employees are appointed on the basis of qualifications, and specialized training is necessary.
7. Organizational members do not own the means of production.[24]

Critical Thinking Question

1. Take each of Weber's seven characteristics of the bureaucratic model and apply them to a public organization in your geographical area. How many of them are applicable?

Although not all the characteristics of Weber's bureaucratic model can be revealed by an organizational chart, Figure 5.5 does depict two important features: (1) the principle of hierarchy and (2) a division of labor that results in specialization.

Weber's bureaucratic model rested on what he called rational–legal authority. This he contrasted to (1) **traditional authority,** which rested on an established belief in the sanctity of immemorial traditions and the legitimacy of the status of people exercising authority under those traditions, illustrated by kings or queens, and (2) **charismatic authority,** which stemmed from the exceptional sanctity, heroism, or exemplary character of an individual.[25]

Two dimensions to Weber's work are often not considered. First, on the one hand, he considered bureaucracy as the most efficient form of organization, and, on the other

In The News

Two Views on Inefficient Bureaucracies

Bureaucracy has to be one of life's top frustrations. You place a call to your government and you can't get through, no one calls back, or nobody pays attention to you. In short, you are either ignored or treated like a pest.

Source: Jane Ann Morrison, "Bureaucracy Trumps Safety in Quest for Stoplight Near Highway Patrol Office," *Las Vegas Review-Journal,* August 14, 2006, with restatement.

Cleveland, Ohio, Mayor Frank Jackson said that his city's public safety forces are top-heavy, inefficient bureaucracies which need to be streamlined. He made 53 specific recommendations to improve the police, fire, emergency medical service, animal services, and corrections departments. Among them were close the 3rd Police District, reduce the number of police and fire supervisors through attrition, and turn over the city jail function to the Cuyahoga County Sheriff's Department.

Source: Gabriel Baird, "Jackson to Revamp City Safety Services; Plan Would Eliminate 3rd Police District," *Plain Dealer* (Cleveland, Ohio), October 6, 2006, with restatement.

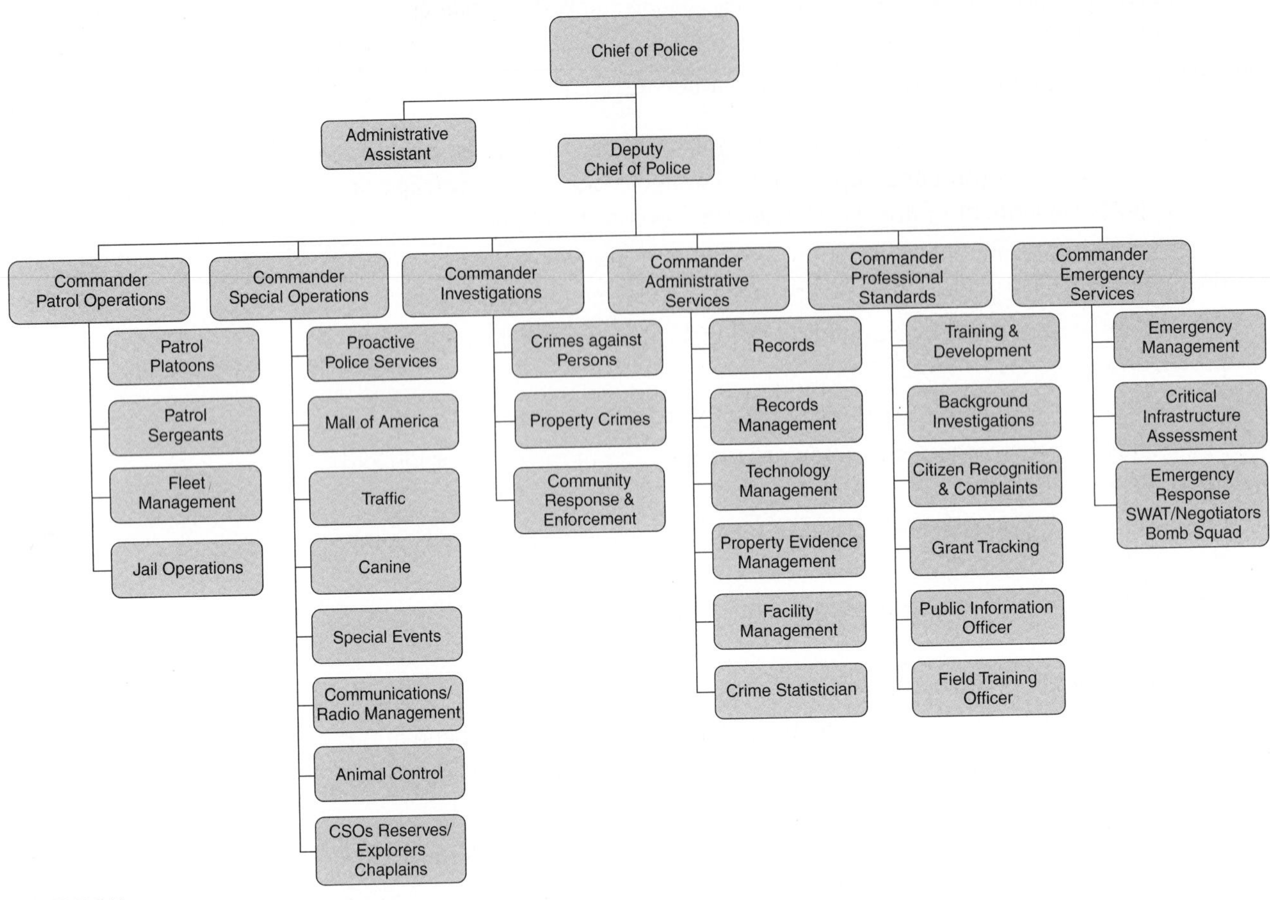

FIGURE 5.5

The organizational chart for the Bloomington, Minnesota, Police Department.

(Courtesy of the Bloomington, Minnesota Police Department)

hand, he feared that this very efficiency constituted a threat to individual freedom by its impersonal nature and oppressive routine.[26] Second, Weber deplored the career professional of moderate ambitions who craved security; Weber saw this type of person as lacking spontaneity and inventiveness, the modern-day "petty bureaucrat."[27]

Weber did not invent the bureaucratic model; it had existed for centuries. Thus, whereas Weber spawned the formal study of organizations, it scarcely seems fair to lay at his feet any real or fancied inadequacies of the model or its operation. Moreover, although it would be difficult to overstate Weber's contributions, it must be borne in mind that, although some people read him in the original German,[28] his work was not translated into English and was not generally available until 1947, long after the bureaucratic model was well entrenched.

Administrative Theory

Administrative, or management, **theory** sought to identify generic or universal methods of administration. Its benchmark is the 1937 publication of Luther Gulick (1892–1993) and Lyndall Urwick's (1891–1983) edited *Papers on the Science of Administration.*

In content, administrative theory is more compatible with the bureaucratic model than with scientific management because it concentrates on broader principles. Administrative theory, also referred to as the principles approach, is distinguished from the bureaucratic model by its "how-to" emphasis. At some risk of oversimplification, the principles both operationalize and reinforce features of the bureaucratic model. Consequently, because of the continuing pervasiveness of the bureaucratic model, the principles either explicitly or implicitly continue to play an important role in organizations, including police departments. The key contributors to this school are Henri Fayol (1841–1925), James Mooney (1884–1957), Alan Reiley (1869–1947), and Gulick and Urwick.

Henri Fayol graduated as an engineer at the age of 19 from France's National School of Mines at St. Etienne and began a 40-year career with the Commentary-Fourchambault Company.[29] His contributions are based on writings that were an outgrowth of his experiences as a manager. Fayol's fame rests chiefly on his *General and Industrial Management* (1916). The first English edition of this appeared in Great Britain in 1923, and although his "Administrative Theory of the State" appeared in *Papers on the Science of Administration,* his main work, *General and Industrial Management,* was not widely available in this country until 1949. Fayol's principles included the following:

1. A **division of work**—that is, specialization
2. Authority—namely, the right to give orders and the power to extract obedience—whoever exercises authority has responsibility
3. Discipline—in essence, the obedience, application, energy and behavior, and outward marks of respect in accordance with the standing agreement between the firm and its employees
4. Unity of command, with an employee receiving orders from only one supervisor on any one function or task
5. Unity of direction, with one head and one plan for a group of activities having the same objective—unity of command cannot exist without unity of direction
6. Subordination of individual interest to the general interest—the interest of an individual or a group of employees does not prevail over the concerns of the firm
7. Remuneration, or pay, of personnel—to be fair to the employee and employer
8. Centralization, a natural order of things—however, centralization or decentralization is a question of proportion, finding the optimum degree for the particular concern
9. Scalar chain—namely, the chain of superiors ranging from the ultimate authority to the lowest ranks, often referred to as the chain of command
10. Order—that is, a place for everyone and everyone in his or her place
11. Equity—namely, the combination of kindness and justice
12. Stability of tenure of personnel, which allows employees to become familiar with their jobs and productive—a mediocre manager who stays is infinitely preferable to outstanding managers who come and go
13. Initiative at all levels of the organization—this represents a great source of strength for business
14. Esprit de corps, harmony, and union of personnel—these constitute a great strength, and efforts should be made to establish them[30]

Fayol recognized that his scalar principle could produce disastrous consequences if it were followed strictly, since it would hamper swift action.[31] He therefore developed Fayol's gangplank, or horizontal bridge, as a means of combating this issue.

Fayol's belief that a mediocre manager who stays is better than outstanding ones who come and go refound currency in the late 1970s as many city managers retreated from hiring police chiefs from outside the organization. Although it can be argued with some validity that this movement was due to the increased qualifications of internal candidates, it is also true that the frequent recruitment, screening, and selection of "portable" police managers was an expensive, time-consuming, and, at least occasionally in terms of results, disappointing process.

Mooney and Reiley's *Onward Industry* (1931) was generally consistent with the work of Fayol, as were the subsequent revisions of this publication, which appeared in 1939 and 1947 under the title *The Principles of Organization.*[32]

In "Notes on the Theory of Organization," which was included in *Papers on the Science of Administration,* Gulick coined the most familiar and enduring acronym of administration, POSDCORB:

> **P***lanning, that is, working out in broad outline the things that need to be done and the methods for doing them to accomplish the purpose set for the enterprise;*
> **O***rganizing, that is, the establishment of the formal structure of authority through which work subdivisions are arranged, defined and co-ordinated for the defined objective;*
> **S***taffing, that is, the whole personnel function of bringing in and training the staff and maintaining favorable conditions of work;*
> **D***irecting, that is, the continuous task of making decisions and embodying them in specific and general orders and instructions and serving as the leader of the enterprise;*
> **Co***-ordinating, that is, the all important duty of interrelating the various parts of the work;*
> **R***eporting, that is, keeping those to whom the executive is responsible informed as to what is going on, which thus includes keeping himself and his subordinates informed through records, research and inspection;*
> **B***udgeting, with all that goes with budgeting in the form of fiscal planning, accounting and control.*[33]

Gulick acknowledged that his POSDCORB was adapted from the functional analysis elaborated by Fayol in *General and Industrial Management.* Urwick's "Organization as a Technical Problem," which appeared in *Papers on the Science of Administration,* also drew on the work of another Frenchman, A. V. Graicunas, for his treatment of the span of control. Urwick asserted,

> *Students of administration have long recognized that, in practice, no human brain should attempt to supervise directly more than five, or at the most six individuals whose work is interrelated.*[34]

Urwick, an Oxford-educated and military-career Englishman, also underscored management theory with his subsequent *Scientific Principles of Organization* (1938).

Critique of Traditional Theory

Scientific management is decried because of its "man as machine" orientation, and ample life is given to that argument by even a casual reading of the conversation

Quick Facts

Acronyms

An acronym is a word formed by using the first letter of each word in a list; it is a memory-enhancing device.

between Taylor and the legendary "Schmidt." On balance, although Taylor's emphasis was on task, he was not totally indifferent to the human element, arguing,

> *No system of management, however good, should be applied in a wooden way. The proper personal relations should always be maintained between the employers and men; and even the prejudices of the workmen should be considered in dealing with them.*[35]

The bureaucratic model has no shortage of critics. Humanist Warren Bennis levels the following specific criticisms:

1. Bureaucracy does not adequately allow for the personal growth and development of mature personalities.
2. It develops conformity and "group think."
3. It does not take into account the "informal organization" and emerging and unanticipated problems.
4. Its systems of control and authority are hopelessly outdated.
5. It has no adequate judicial process.
6. It does not possess adequate means for resolving differences and conflicts between ranks and, most particularly, between functional groups.
7. Communication and innovative ideas are thwarted or distorted due to hierarchical divisions.
8. The full human resources of bureaucracy are not utilized due to mistrust, fear of reprisals, and so on.
9. It cannot assimilate the influx of new technology entering the organization.
10. It modifies the personality structure such that each person becomes and reflects the full, gray, conditioned "organization person."[36]

Sociologist Robert K. Merton (1910–2003) noted the "dysfunction of bureaucracy" in his work *Social Theory and Social Structure.*[37] He stated that the structure of bureaucracy lends itself to an overbearing formality, causing overconformity, inflexibility, and impersonal interaction between bureaucrats, their employees, and customers. Weber's analysis of bureaucracy suggests that, if a bureaucracy is to attain its goals of accuracy, reliability, and efficiency, it requires that constant pressure be exerted on officials to maintain a very high degree of conformity with prescribed patterns of action. In other words, an organization needs rules, regulations, and procedures to accomplish its goals and objectives.

Merton believes that this conformity is underscored by a strict sense of discipline. Bureaucracy—or any other social structure, according to Weber—relies on its

Quick Facts

Warren Gameliel Bennis (1925-)

Warren G. Bennis's career is long and distinguished. He has authored more than 27 books and has been the adviser to four different Presidents of the United States. Dr. Bennis is widely regarded as having founded the modern study of leadership, which is one of his main interests. During World War II he received the Bronze Star and a Purple Heart for being wounded in action. Warren Bennis served as a faculty member at several institutions and later in his career as the President of the University of Cincinnati. He is the founder of the Leadership Institute at the University of Southern California.

In The News

Troubled Police Department

As this news article points out, Merton's notion of a "dysfunction of bureaucracy" is not some dusty theory with little utility or application to what is going on now; instead, it reveals the concept is as timely as ever.

A 2006 200-page consultant's report is highly critical of the Newport Police Department, calling its operation dysfunctional . . . deeply flawed . . . needing a complete shift in culture . . . and its treatment of citizens as rude and condescending." A large portion of the blame is attributed to ineffective leadership by the former chief, who led the department for five years.

The report, which pulled no punches, characterized the department as being mired in internal conflict, possessing poor employee morale throughout, and having pervasive micro management and an absence of clear direction.

Source: Richard Salit, "Consultants' Report Highly Critical of Police Department," *Providence* (Rhode Island) *Journal,* September 21, 2006, with restatement.

Quick Facts

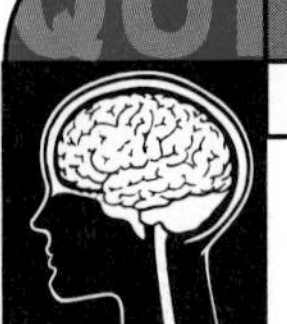

Merton Biography

Robert K. Merton was born Meyer R. Schkolnick to immigrant parents. After teaching at Harvard and Tulane, he spent the bulk of his career at Columbia University. Among his many other contributions, he coined such now-common phrases as "self-fulfilling prophecy," "role model," and "unintended consequences."

Source: Wikipedia Free Encyclopedia.

ability to imbue its members with intense sentiments related to discipline. According to Merton, these sentiments are often more intense than is technically necessary, allowing a transference of the sentiments from the aims of the organization onto the particular details of a behavior required by the rules.[38] Abiding by the rules, which are originally intended as a means to an end, becomes the desired product. This may become so pervasive that the attainment of perfect discipline and conformity begins to interfere with the organization's true goals. Those who adopt such an emphasis on rules and discipline are less accommodating when situations require change or flexibility. Merton suggests that in extreme cases this creates a "bureaucratic virtuoso, who never forgets a single rule" and hence is unable to accomplish the organization's mission. He uses the example of Bernt Balchen, a Norwegian who piloted the first American flight over the South Pole:

> *According to a ruling of the department of labor Bernt Balchen . . . cannot receive his citizenship papers. Balchen a native of Norway, declared his intention in 1927. It is held that he has failed to meet the condition of five years continuous residence in the United States. The Byrd Antarctic voyage took him out of the country, although he was on a ship carrying the American flag, was an invaluable member of the American expedition, and in a region to which there is an American claim because of the exploration and occupation of it by Americans, known as "Little America." The bureau of naturalization explains that it cannot proceed on the assumption that Little America is American soil. That would* trespass on international questions *where it has no sanction. So far as the bureau is concerned. Balchen was out of the country and technically has not complied with the law of naturalization.*[39]

Quick Facts

Simon Biography

Herbert Simon received a Ph.D. from Chicago University in 1936 and spent most of his career at Carnegie-Mellon University. He is best known for his work in the field of decision making, for which he won a Nobel Prize in 1978. Later in life, he had an interest in using computer technology to develop artificial intelligence.

Merton's criticisms of bureaucracy are to a degree validated by the way such structures operate. For example, bureaucrats who conform to expectations about how they should conduct themselves receive salary increases and promotions to more senior positions. Such rewards may lead to a preoccupation with adherence to rules, timidity in decision making, and a bias toward preserving the status quo. A central tenet of bureaucracies is that all clients are treated the same; they are all processed the same way under the same set of laws, policies, and procedures. However, people want their special situations and circumstances to be taken into account so they can "get a break." This is easily illustrated by complaints from some drivers who have been issued a traffic citation. Such complainants report that the officer did not raise her voice, was polite and even said "Have a nice day" after the driver returned the signed ticket to her." But, the complainants go on to say, "She never gave me a chance to explain why I was speeding" or "She didn't really consider my explanation of why I shouldn't have been charged with running the stop sign."

Herbert Simon (1916–2001) has mounted the most precise criticisms of the principles approach. He writes,

> *It is a fatal defect of the . . . principles of administration that, like proverbs, they occur in pairs. For almost every principle one can find an equally plausible and acceptable contradictory principle. Although the two principles of the pair will lead to exactly opposite organizational recommendations, there is nothing in the theory to indicate which is the proper one to apply.*[40]

To illustrate his point, Simon notes that administrative efficiency is enhanced by keeping at a minimum the number of organizational levels through which a matter must pass before it is acted on, yet a narrow span of control—say, of five or six subordinates—produces a tall hierarchy. To some extent, Simon's criticism is blunted by invoking Fayol's exception principle and the gangplank, but in the main, Simon's point that some of the principles contain logical contradictions is potent.

Less critical than both Bennis and Simon, Hage[41] describes bureaucracy in mixed terms and specifically as having the following:

1. High centralization
2. High formalization
3. High stratification
4. Low adaptiveness
5. Low job satisfaction
6. Low complexity
7. High production
8. High efficiency

In *Complex Organizations* (1972), Charles Perrow mounted a major and articulate defense of the bureaucratic model, concluding that

> *the extensive preoccupation with reforming, "humanizing," and decentralizing bureaucracies, while salutary, has served to obscure from organizational theorists the true nature of bureaucracy and has diverted us from assessing its impact on society. The impact on society in general is incalculably more important than the impact upon the members of a particular organization . . . bureaucracy is a form of organization superior to all others we know or can hope to afford in the near and middle future; the chances of doing away with it or changing it are probably non-existent in the rest in this century. Thus it is crucial to understand it and appreciate it.*[42]

Relatedly, in *The Case for Bureaucracy* (1985), Charles Goodsell notes that denunciations of the "common hate object are fashionable, appealing, and make us feel good; they invite no retaliation or disagreement since almost everybody agrees that bureaucracy is bad," but fashionable contentions are not necessarily solid ones.[43] Goodsell observes that

> *the attacks are almost always made in the tone of unremitting dogmatism. They are usually unqualified in portraying wicked behavior and inadequate outcomes. The pessimistic picture presented seems unbroken. The absolutism itself, it would seem, cannot help but strain our credulity. How can we believe that all public bureaucracies, all of the time, are inefficient, dysfunctional, rigid, obstructionist, secretive, oligarchic, conservative, undemocratic, imperialist, oppressive, alienating, and discriminatory? How could any single human creation be so universally terrible in so many ways?*[44]

Purely deductive models critical of bureaucracy abound, but they are—in the words of Alvin Gouldner—"a theoretical tapestry devoid of the plainest empirical trimmings."[45] Goodsell elaborates on this theme by observing that, when empirical study is taken, single cases illustrating the conclusions desired are selected, and by concentrating on the problems, disorders, and dysfunctions of bureaucracy rather than on what is working well, academics both confirm their own diagnoses and demonstrate the need for their own solutions.[46] Interestingly, Goodsell is able to muster a number of empirical studies that reveal positive evaluations of bureaucracies, including the police, by members of the public who have had direct contact with them; in general, these favorable evaluations are at least at the two-thirds level and many go beyond the 75 percent level.[47]

Despite philosophical criticisms and practical difficulties with the stems of traditional theory, in its entirety it must be appreciated for having formed the basic fund of knowledge on which the overwhelming majority of organizations in the world rest. Knowledge of traditional theory remains as an essential part of education and training for police leaders.

OPEN SYSTEMS THEORY

Organizations described as flexible, adaptive, and organic are associated with open systems theory. This line of thought began its development in the late 1920s and comprises three major divisions: (1) human relations, (2) behavioral systems theory, and (3) open systems theory.

Human Relations

The **human relations school** developed in reaction to the mechanistic orientation of traditional organizational theory, which was viewed as neglecting or ignoring the human element.

Quick Facts

Mayo Biography

An Australian by birth and a psychologist by education, Mayo did not become interested in sociology until he was 46 years old. However, his contributions to that field were so outstanding that he is rightly considered the father of the human relations school. He was a long-standing faculty member of Harvard's Business School.

Mayo: The Hawthorne Studies

In 1927, a series of experiments, which were to last five years, began near Chicago at the Western Electric Company's Hawthorne plant.[48] This work was guided by **Elton Mayo** (1880–1949), a professor in the Harvard School of Business, and his associate, Fritz Roethlisberger (1898–1974). Also involved in these studies was the plant manager, William Dickson.[49] From the perspective of organizational theory, the major contribution of the **Hawthorne experiments** is the view that organizations are social systems. Two research efforts, the telephone relay assembly study and the telephone switchboard wiring study,[50] were especially important to the development of the human relations school.

In the first study, five women assembling telephone relays were put into a room and subjected to varying physical work conditions.[51] Even when the conditions changed unfavorably, production increased. Mayo and his associates were puzzled by these results. Ultimately, they decided that (1) when the experimenters took over many of the supervisory functions the work environment became less strict and less formal; (2) the women behaved differently from what was expected because they were receiving attention, creating the "Hawthorne effect"; and (3) by placing the women together in the relay assembling test room, the researchers had provided the opportunity for them to become a closely knit group.[52] On the basis of these observations, the researchers concluded that an important influence on productivity is the interpersonal relations and spirit of cooperation that had developed among the women and between the women and their supervisors. The influence of these "human relations" was believed to be every bit as important as physical work conditions and financial incentives.[53]

In the telephone switchboard wiring study, 14 men were put on a reasonable piece rate; that is, without physically straining themselves, they could earn more if they produced more. The assumption was that the workers would behave as rational economic actors and produce more, since it was in their own best interest. To insulate these men from the "systematic soldiering" they knew to exist among the plant's employees, the researchers also placed these workers in a special room. The workers' output did not increase. The values of the informal group appeared to be more powerful than the allure of financial betterment:

1. Don't be a "**rate buster**" and produce too much.
2. If you turn out too little work, you are a "chisler."
3. Don't be a "squealer" to supervisors.
4. Don't be officious; if you are an inspector, don't act like one.[54]

Taken together, the relay assembly study and the switchboard wiring study raise an important question. Why did one group respond so favorably and the other not? The answer is that, in the relay assembly study, the values of the workers and the supervisors were mutually supportive, whereas in the switchboard wiring study, the objectives of the company and the informal group conflicted. The harder question is, Why was there mutuality in one situation and not the other? The basis of mutuality has already been discussed; the conflict is more difficult to account for, but it may have been the interplay of some things we know and some things we must speculate about:

1. The researchers did not involve themselves in the supervision of the switchboard wiring room workers as they had with the relay assembly room employees.[55] The wiring room workers and their supervisor developed a spirit of cooperation, but it was one in which the supervisor was coopted by the informal group, which was suspicious of what would happen if output actually increased.[56]
2. The way in which the subjects for both studies was selected is suspect and may have influenced the findings. The relay assembly women were experienced operators known to be friendly with each other and "willing and cooperative" participants, whereas the men were designated by the foreman.[57]
3. The relay assembly room workers were women, and the switchboard wiring study employees were men. This difference in gender may have influenced the character of the responses. The studies were going on during the Depression; the women may have tried to hold on to their jobs by pleasing their supervisors, while the men restricted their output, so that there would be work to do and nobody would lose his job. In this context, both groups of employees can be seen as rational economic actors.

As a result of the Hawthorne studies, it was concluded that (1) the level of production is set by social norms, not by physiological capacities; (2) often workers react not as individuals but as members of a group; (3) the rewards and sanctions of the group significantly affect the behavior of workers and limit the impact of economic incentive plans; and (4) leadership has an important role in setting and enforcing group norms, and there is a difference between formal and informal leadership.[58]

When workers react as members of an informal group, they become susceptible to the values of that group. Thus, the informal group can be a powerful force in supporting or opposing police programs. Illustratively, a number of police unions started as an unorganized, informal group of dissatisfied officers. Although many factors contribute to the enduring problem of police corruption, such as disillusionment and temptation, an informal group that supports taking payoffs makes it more difficult to identify and prosecute "bad cops." In 1972, the **Knapp Commission,** investigating corruption in the New York City Police Department, distinguished between "meat-eaters" (those who overtly pursued opportunities to profit personally from their police power) and "grass-eaters" (those who simply accepted the payoffs that the happenstances of police work brought their way).[59] The behavior of the grass-eaters can be interpreted within the framework of the power that informal groups have. The Knapp Commission was told that one strong force that encouraged grass-eaters to accept relatively petty graft was their feeling of loyalty to their fellow officers. By accepting payoff money, an officer could prove that he was "one of the boys" and could be trusted.

The foregoing discussion should not be interpreted to mean that informal groups always, or even frequently, engage in troublesome or unethical behavior but rather is an illustration of the potency that such groups have. Astute police administrators are always alert for opportunities to tap the energy of informal groups to support departmental goals and programs.

As might be expected, the collision between the human relations school, fathered by Mayo's Hawthorne studies, and traditional organizational theory sent theorists and researchers in the various disciplines off into new and different directions. From among these, at least three major themes are identifiable: (1) inquiries into what

Quick Facts

Parsons Biography

Parsons was born in Colorado Springs, Colorado, and received his doctorate in economics and sociology from the University of Heidelberg, Germany. He is one of the most distinguished contributors to the field of sociology. A Harvard faculty member (1927-1973), he advocated for a "grand theory" which would integrate all social science knowledge into one umbrella theoretical framework. He received substantial criticism for maintaining that Western civilization is far more advanced than other societies.

Source: Wikipedia, The Free Encyclopedia.

motivates workers, including the work of Maslow and Herzberg, which will be discussed shortly; (2) leadership, the subject of Chapter 7, Leadership; and (3) work on organizations as behavioral systems, covered later in this chapter. As a concluding note, the term "human relations" has been used in law enforcement with two entirely different meanings. Particularly from the mid 1960s to the early 1970s, the term was used as a label for training that was basically race relations; when used in describing the major content areas of more recent police management seminars, its use denotes a block of instruction relating to individual and group relationships in the tradition of the Hawthorne studies.

Parsons: Functionalism and Social Systems

Talcott Parsons's (1902–1979) functional approach to sociology became a dominant part of the sociological landscape and of the human relations school in the 1950s.[60] Functionalism studied the roles of institutions and social behavior in society and the way these are related to other social features. In "Suggestions for a Sociological Approach to the Theory of Organization," Parsons defines an organization as a social system oriented to the attainment of a specific goal contributing to the function of a larger, superordinate system—generally, society. An organization produces an identifiable product that can be utilized as part of society. In policing, this can be interpreted as enforcing the law and maintaining order.

As one can observe, Parsons presents one of the first systemic approaches to understanding how organizations interrelate with each other and society. Parsons developed an approach for the analysis of formal organizations using four categories.[61]

The Value System The **value system** in an organization defines and legitimizes the goals of that organization. Further, this system provides a functional definition of purpose and guides the activities of individual participants. Because the organization is a subsystem of society, the value system is a "subvalue" of society's comprehensive values. As a result, the value system of the organization reflects acceptance of the general values of society as a whole. According to Parsons, the most essential feature of the value system of an organization is "valuative legitimation" within the larger system. Placing this in the context of policing, the larger society must formally and informally provide justification and legitimacy to the police. This is a key component of the community policing philosophy: police must work in coordination with the larger society or community, building trust and relationships.

Adaptive Mechanism This concept focuses on an organization's methods for resource procurement. Fluid resources, such as employees, equipment and capital, and the coordination of these resources to facilitate goal attainment, are a product of the organization's relationship with society. Society can assist the organization, such as the police, through investment, support from taxation, and voluntary participation if the goals of the organization are regarded as integral to society at large. In our society, we place a high level of emphasis on safety and security, particularly since the events of September 11, 2001; hence, we have focused considerably on redefining the role of police agencies and the restructuring of resources to accomplish the police mission.

Operative Code An **operative code** explains how the goals of the organization are achieved through the internal mechanisms of the mobilization of resources. This involves decision making in the areas of policy, allocation, and coordination. Policy decisions, according to Parsons, directly commit the organization as a whole and stand in direct relation to the organization's primary functions. Hence, police organizations often deploy their resources through uniformed patrol officers dispersed over a specific geographical area in a direct attempt to reduce crime, arrest criminals, maintain order, and respond to community calls for service. Allocative decisions involve the delegation of authority and involve two aspects: the allocation of responsibility within the organization through the use of personnel and the allocation of resources within the organization so that the necessary tools (e.g., police vehicles and fuel, communication and radio systems, and vehicle maintenance) are available to achieve the organization's goals. According to Parsons, coordinating these decisions is critical to the integration of the organization as a system and is concerned mostly with the efficiency of the organization. These decisions maximize the performance of subunits and personnel in relation to the attainment of organizational goals.

Integrative Mechanisms These mechanisms are composed of institutional patterns that link the structure of the organization with the structure of society as a whole. According to Parsons, when the affairs of an organization are conducted, the norms of society as a whole must be upheld in order for the organization to maintain its place within normal societal constructs. **Integrative mechanisms** include the obligations of those within the organization, the limits on and ways in which any actor in the organization may bind others by his or her decisions or be bound by the decisions of others, and the universally defined norms and rules within both society and subsystems of that society that provide meaning to the job.

Parsons believed that the central phenomenon of organization is the mobilization of power for the attainment of goals. Value systems legitimize organizational goals, but goal achievement can be effective only through power. Power is generated within and external to the organization, and each layer of society gives to and takes power from other subsystems. According to Parsons, the generation of power depends on four fundamental conditions:

1. The institutionalization of a value system that legitimizes both the goal of the organization and the principal patterns by which it functions in the attainment of the goal
2. The regulation of the organization's procurement and decision-making processes through adherence to universalistic rules and to the institutions of authority and contract
3. The command of the more detailed and day-to-day support of the persons whose cooperation is needed
4. The command of necessary facilities, of which the primary category in our society is financial[62]

Maslow: The Needs Hierarchy

Abraham Maslow (1908–1970) was a psychologist who developed the **needs hierarchy** to explain individual motivation. The model appeared first in a 1943 article[63] and later received extended coverage in Maslow's *Motivation and Personality* (1954).

Figure 5.6 depicts the needs hierarchy. In Maslow's scheme, there are five categories of human needs:

1. Physiological, or basic, needs, such as food, shelter, and water
2. Safety needs, including the desires to be physically safe, to have a savings account for financial security, and to be safe in one's job, knowing that you will not be arbitrarily fired
3. Belongingness and love needs, such as the acceptance of one's work group in the police department and the affection of one's spouse, children, and parents

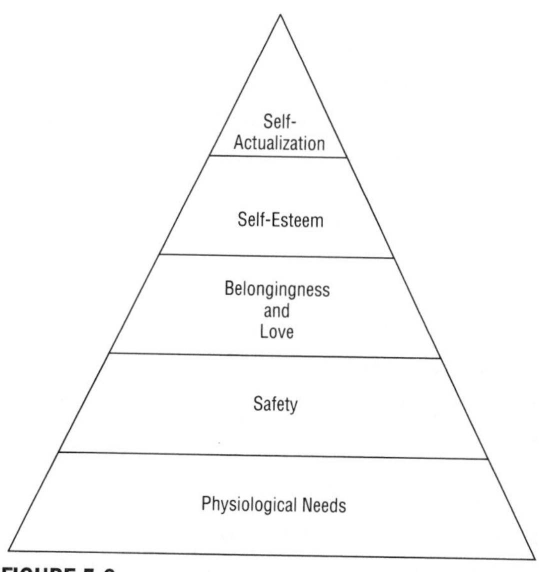

FIGURE 5.6

Maslow's needs hierarchy.

Quick Facts

Maslow Biography

Maslow was one of seven children born to Russian immigrants. In 1934, he received his Ph.D. in psychology from the University of Wisconsin, despite his parents' hopes that he would become a lawyer. He taught at Brooklyn College and Brandeis University. Best known for his hierarchy of needs motivational model, he died of a heart attack at the relatively young age of 62 following years of poor health.

Source: Wikipedia, The Free Encyclopedia.

4. Esteem needs, including the desire for a stable, fairly based, and positive evaluation of oneself as evidenced by compliments, commendations, promotions, and other cues
5. Self-actualization needs, such as the want to test one's self-potential and gain a sense of fulfillment[64]

The needs hierarchy is arranged, like the rungs on a ladder, from the lower-order to the higher-order needs. A person does not move from one level to the next-higher one until the majority of the needs at the level one are met. Once those needs are met, they cease to motivate a person, and the needs at the next level of the hierarchy predominate. For example, one does not attempt to self-actualize until one has feelings of self-confidence, worth, strength, capability, adequacy, and mastery;[65] these feelings are generated only with the meeting of the esteem needs. Conversely, if people's esteem needs are unmet, they feel inferior, helpless, discouraged, and unworthwhile and are unable to move to the self-actualization level and test themselves.

It is important to understanding the needs hierarchy that the character of something does not necessarily determine what need is met but rather to what use it is put; money can be used to buy food and satisfy a basic need, or it can be put in a savings account to satisfy safety needs. Also, any process up the hierarchy can be reversed; a police officer who is fired or is given a lengthy suspension may be thrust into a financial situation in which the physiological needs will predominate. Police agencies that are managed professionally attempt to make appropriate use of theoretical constructs. For example, the fourth level of Maslow's needs hierarchy is self-esteem, which includes the need for recognition as evidenced by compliments and commendations. Faced with a significant automobile theft problem in their state, Ohio State Highway Patrol officials wanted to develop a strategy that would have an impact on the problem. One of the programs they developed was the Blue Max award[66] (see Figure 5.7). In the Blue Max program, each time a state trooper arrested a suspect in a stolen car, he or she received a lightning bolt decal to place on the side of his or her patrol car. When troopers made their fifth apprehension in a year, they were given their own car for the rest of the year with a special license that read "ACE." At the end of the year, the trooper who had made the most apprehensions received the coveted Blue Max award and was given a car reserved only for his or her use during the next year. In the first 10 months in which the Blue Max program was operated, arrests of car thieves was up 49 percent, as compared to the entire prior 12 months. The Blue Max program demonstrates the utility of Maslow's theory and how organizational goals and individual goals can be compatible.

Quick Facts

Herzberg Biography

During Frederick Herzberg's army service in WWII, he became a firsthand witness to the horrors of the Dachau Concentration Camp. After the war, he returned to his studies at the City College of New York and later the University of Pittsburgh. A psychologist, he is best known for his work in motivation and job enrichment, which can briefly be described as structuring the jobs (e.g., by adding new and challenging tasks or changing how the work is processed) of employees, so that they are more satisfying. His article "One More Time, How Do You Motivate Workers?" is still the most requested reprint from the *Harvard Business Review.* Herzberg reports that his war experience was one of the key factors which triggered his interest in motivation.

Source: Wikipedia, The Free Encyclopedia.

FIGURE 5.7

The Blue Max medal and its presentation at an awards ceremony.
(Courtesy of the Ohio State Highway Patrol)

Herzberg: Motivation-Hygiene Theory

Because of their focus, the needs hierarchy, functionalism, and the motivation–hygiene theory are not organizational theories in the larger sense; they are included here because they are part of a stream of connected thinking. Motivation–hygiene theory developed from research conducted by **Frederick Herzberg** (1923–2000), Bernard Mausner, and Barbara Snyderman on job attitudes at 11 work sites in the Pittsburgh area and reported on in *The Motivation to Work* (1959). The major statement of the theory, which evolved out of this earlier research, is found in Herzberg's *Work and the Nature of Man* (1966).

Herzberg saw two sets of variables operating in the work setting: (1) hygiene factors, which he later came to call maintenance factors, and (2) motivators. Table 5.1 identifies Herzberg's hygiene factors and motivators. The hygiene factors relate to the work environment; the motivators relate to the work itself. Herzberg borrowed the term "hygiene" from the health-care field and used it to refer to factors that, if not treated properly, could lead to a deterioration in performance, creating an "unhealthy" organization. Hygiene factors that are not treated properly are a source of dissatisfaction. However, even if all of them are provided, a police department does not have motivated officers, just ones who are not dissatisfied. Hygiene factors and motivators operate independently of each other; the police manager can motivate subordinates if they are somewhat dissatisfied with their salaries. However, the greater the level of dissatisfaction, the more difficult it becomes to employ the motivators successfully.

TABLE 5.1 Herzberg's Motivation–Hygiene Theory

HYGIENE FACTORS	MOTIVATORS
Supervisory practices	Achievement
Policies and administration	Recognition for accomplishments
Working conditions	Challenging work
Interpersonal relationships with subordinates, peers, and superiors	Increased responsibility
Status	Advancement possibilities
Effect of the job on personal life	Opportunity for personal growth and development
Job security	
Money	

SOURCE: Frederick Herzberg, *Work and the Nature of Man* (Cleveland: World, 1966), pp. 95–96.

Note that police managers have more control over motivators than they do over basic hygiene factors; certain policies, such as automatically placing an officer involved in a shooting incident on suspension, may be mandated by the city administrator; the chief of police has little control over the status given the officer's job by society; and a chief cannot appropriate the money for higher salaries or improved fringe benefits.

In their leadership roles, police managers can try to influence, but they do not control, such matters. It is over those hygiene factors that police managers do exercise control that they can do a considerable amount of good in reducing dissatisfaction and facilitating the use of the motivators, or they can cause considerable unhappiness:

> *The commander in charge of the uniformed division of a 100-officer department suddenly announced that officers were going to be placed on permanent shifts. Surprised and angered by this move, the officers and their wives mobilized to oppose the plan, and after a mass meeting with the commander, the plan was abandoned. The legacy of this incident was a period of barely subdued hostility, distrust, and low morale in the police department.*

The nature of police work is challenging, and some motivational effect is thus naturally occurring. Police managers can build on this by varying assignments appropriately. Measures that employ various other motivators include an established and active commendation system, the creation of field training officer and master patrol

In The News

Police Suicides

Police officers commit suicide at a rate of 17 for every 100,000 officers; in contrast, the rate for this country's general population is substantially less, at a rate of 10.6 for every 100,000 people. According to experts at a recent seminar, the police rate may be as much as 20 percent higher than reported because investigators may classify some number of them as accidents to protect the name and benefits of the deceased officer's family.

The experts note that officers see a lot of suffering and misery, which can accumulate; the ghosts never go away. Three major factors rank as important in police suicides: "untreated depression, relationship problems and easy access to firearms" according to Dell Hackett, president of the Law Enforcement Wellness Association.

Source: Roxana Hegeman, "Researcher: Police Suicide Rate 'Epidemic,'" The Associated Press State and Local Wire, June 14, 2006.

Quick Facts

Lewin Biography

A German-born psychologist and one of the founders of the field of social psychology, Kurt Zadek Lewin was a Jewish Marxist who fled from Germany to America following Hitler's rise to power in 1933. Lewin served in the German army during WWI and was wounded in action. Following WWII, Lewin worked extensively in psychologically rehabilitating former occupants of camps for people displaced by the war.

Source: Wikipedia, The Free Encyclopedia.

[illegible] designations, an annual police awards banquet, an active staff development [illegible] system with various specialization tracks.

[illegible] hierarchy and Herzberg's motivation–hygiene theory can be in- [illegible] ical, safety, and love and belongingness needs of Maslow corre- [illegible] giene factors; the top two levels of the needs hierarchy—esteem [illegible] correlate with Herzberg's motivators.

[illegible] ns Theory

[illegible] tions in the tradition of the Hawthorne studies lacked vitality. Its successor, [illegible] es its ancestry to that 1927–1932 period, was **behavioral systems theory.** The theorists associated with this school saw organizations as being composed of interrelated behaviors and were concerned with making organizations more democratic and participative. Behavioral systems theory is basically a post-1950 development; many of the people involved in this movement are also described in other ways. For example, Argyris, Likert, Bennis, Maslow, Herzberg, and McGregor are often referred to as organizational humanists and are tied to organizational development (OD), a concept treated later in this section. OD is also treated in greater detail in the last chapter of this book, "Organizational Change and the Future."

Lewin: Group Dynamics

Kurt Lewin (1890–1947) was a psychologist who fled from Germany in the early 1930s.[67] His interests were diverse and included leadership; **force-field analysis,** a technique sometimes used in decision making; change; and group dynamics. Lewin's force-field analysis is illustrated in Figure 5.8. In force-field analysis, driving forces push for a new condition or state, and restraining forces resist the change, or perpetuate things as they are. In using force-field analysis, if there are exactly opposing driving and restraining forces, the arrows of these opposing forces meet at the zero, or balance, line. In some instances, there might not be an exactly opposite force, in which case an arrow is simply drawn, as in Figure 5.8, to the balance line. After all entries are made and the situation is summarized, the relative power of the driving and restraining forces must be subjectively evaluated. In this regard, the balance line should be regarded as a spring that will be moved in one direction, suggesting the action that needs to be taken or the decision that needs to be made.

Lewin is also regarded as the father of the behavioral systems school; he founded the Research Center for Group Dynamics at the Massachusetts Institute of Technology.[68] In the same year as Lewin died, one of his followers, Leland Bradford, established a human relations effort at Bethel, Maine.[69] This undertaking was later to be called the National Training Laboratories for Group Development, which earlier focused on stranger T-group, or sensitivity, training, a method whereby behavior is changed by strangers in a group sharing their honest opinions of each other. The popularity of T-groups was

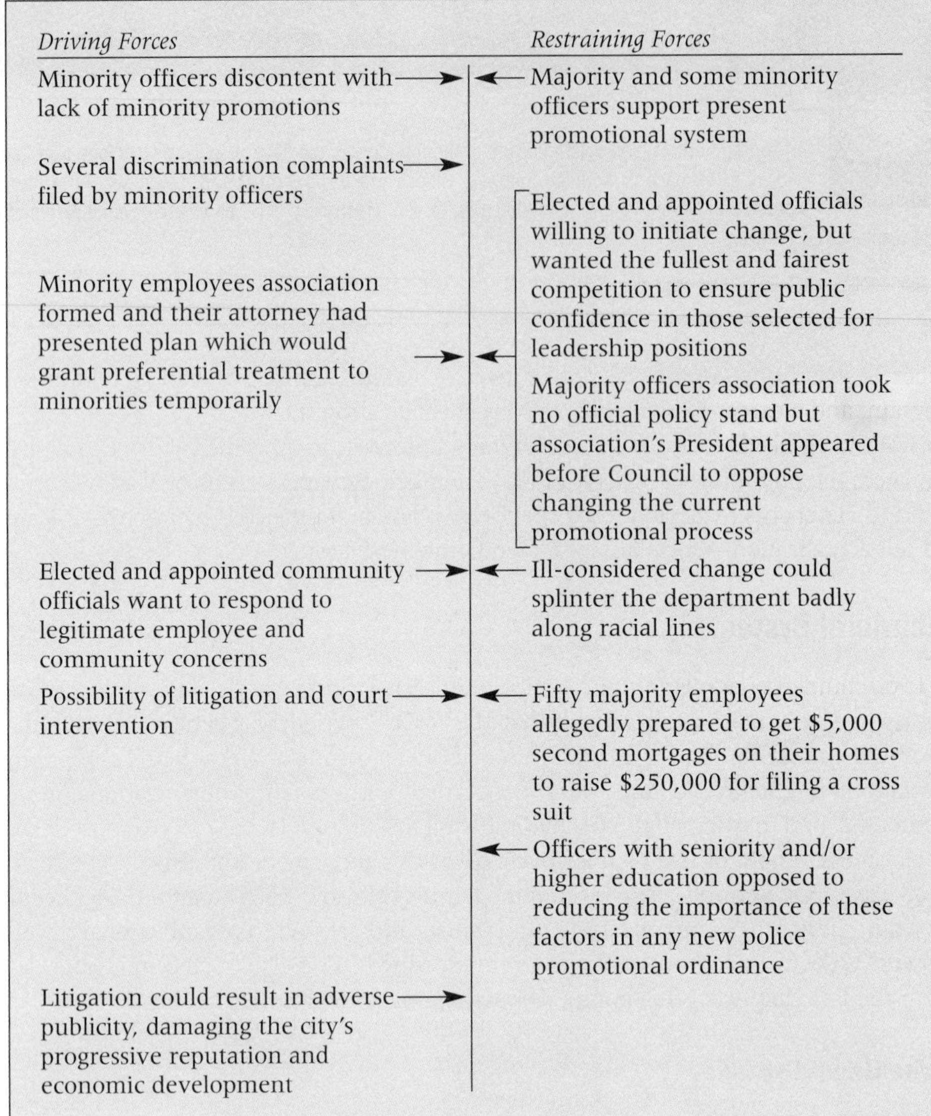

Driving Forces
Restraining Forces
Minority officers discontent with lack of minority promotions
Majority and some minority officers support present promotional system
Several discrimination complaints filed by minority officers
Elected and appointed officials willing to initiate change, but wanted the fullest and fairest competition to ensure public confidence in those selected for leadership positions
Minority employees association formed and their attorney had presented plan which would grant preferential treatment to minorities temporarily
Majority officers association took no official policy stand but association's President appeared before Council to oppose changing the current promotional process
Elected and appointed community officials want to respond to legitimate employee and community concerns
Ill-considered change could splinter the department badly along racial lines
Possibility of litigation and court intervention
Fifty majority employees allegedly prepared to get $5,000 second mortgages on their homes to raise $250,000 for filing a cross suit
Officers with seniority and/or higher education opposed to reducing the importance of these factors in any new police promotional ordinance
Litigation could result in adverse publicity, damaging the city's progressive reputation and economic development

FIGURE 5.8

The use of force-field analysis regarding the decision to adopt a new police promotional ordinance.

greatest during the 1950s; its present use is diminished in large measure because some organizations that tried it were troubled by its occasional volatility and the fact that not all changes were positive:

> *A division manager at one big company was described by a source familiar with his case as "a ferocious guy—brilliant but a thoroughgoing autocrat—whom everyone agreed was just what the division needed, because it was a tough, competitive business." Deciding to smooth over his rough edges, the company sent him to sensitivity training, where he found out exactly what people thought of him. "So he stopped being a beast," says the source, "and his effectiveness fell apart." The reason he'd been so good was that he didn't realize what a beast he was. Eventually, they put in a new manager.*[70]

Homans: External and Internal Systems

As a contemporary of Lewin's, **George Homans** (1910–1989) did work in the tradition of group dynamics. In *The Human Group* (1950), he advanced the idea that

Quick Facts

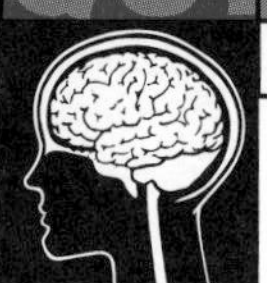

Homans Biography

Homans entered Harvard in 1923 and by 1939 was a faculty member there, teaching both sociology and medieval history. Born in Boston in 1910, he died in Cambridge, Massachusetts, 79 years later. In 1964, he was elected president of the American Sociological Association. From the 1950s until the 1970s, he was one of America's key figures in his field.

Source: Wikipedia, The Free Encyclopedia.

groups have both an internal and an external system.[71] The internal system comprises factors that arise within the group itself, such as the feelings that members of a group develop about each other during the life of the group. In contrast, the external system consists of variables in the larger environment in which the group exists, such as the administrative policies and supervisory practices to which the group is subject. Homans saw these two systems as being in a state of interaction and influencing each other.

For example, the decision of a chief of police to suspend an officer for three days without pay because of an accident while involved in a high-speed chase might result in a group of officers who saw the suspension as being unfair agreeing among themselves not to write any traffic citations during that time. This interaction brings the formal organization of the external system into conflict with the informal organization of the internal system. The formal sanction of the external system is countered with the informal sanction of reducing the city's revenue by the internal system.

Both Lewin and Homans had ties to the human relations school. Homans, for instance, drew on the switchboard wiring room study to illustrate his concept of internal and external systems. Analytically, his work falls into the behavioral systems category and foreshadowed the dynamic interaction theme of **open systems theory.**

Argyris: Immaturity–Maturity Theory and the Mix Model

Chris Argyris (1923–) is a critic of the mechanistic model of organization and a leading proponent of more open and participative organizations. In *Personality and Organization: The Conflict between System and the Individual* (1957), he states a theory of immaturity versus maturity. Argyris believes that, as one moves from infancy toward adulthood in years of age, the healthy individual also advances from immaturity to maturity. The elements of the personality that are changed during this process are summarized in Table 5.2. Simultaneously, Argyris views formal organizations as having certain properties that do not facilitate the growth into a mature state:

1. Specialization reduces the use of initiative by requiring individuals to use only a few of their skills doing unchallenging tasks.

Quick Facts

Argyris Biography

A native of Newark, New Jersey, and a Harvard faculty member, Argyris had an interest in how organizations learn, meaning how they identify and correct errors. Thus, a "learning organization" is one that consciously structures and reforms itself and its processes to maximize learning. This reduces errors and enhances quality, leading to a competitive edge.

TABLE 5.2 Argyris's Immaturity–Maturity Changes

INFANCY–IMMATURITY →	ADULTHOOD–MATURITY
Passive →	Self-initiative
Dependent →	Relatively independent
Behaving in a few ways →	Capable of behaving many ways
Erratic, shallow, quickly changed interests →	Deeper interests
Short time perspective →	Much longer time perspective
Subordinate position in the family →	Aspirations of equality or superordinate position relative to peers
Lack of self-awareness →	Self-awareness and self-control

SOURCE: Immaturity-maturity changes, page 50 from *Personality and Organization: The Conflict between System and the Individual* by Chris Argyris. Copyright 1957 by Harper & Row, Publishers, Inc. Copyright renewed 1985 by Chris Argyris. Reprinted by permission of HarperCollins Publishers.

2. The chain of command leaves people with little control over their work environment and makes them dependent upon and passive toward superiors.
3. The unity-of-direction principle means that the objectives of the work unit are controlled by the leader. If the goals do not consider the employees, then ideal conditions for psychological failure are set.
4. The narrow span of control principle will tend to increase the subordinate's feelings of dependence, submissiveness, and passivity.[72]

The needs of a healthy, mature individual and the properties of formal organizations therefore come into conflict; the individual's ensuing response may take any of several forms:

1. The employee may leave the organization, only to find that other organizations are similar to the one left.
2. To achieve the highest level of control over one's self permitted by the organization, the person may climb as far as possible up the organizational hierarchy.
3. The worker may defend his or her self-concept by the use of defensive mechanisms, such as daydreaming, rationalizing lower accomplishments, developing psychosomatic illnesses, or becoming aggressive and hostile, attacking and blaming what is frustrating personally.
4. The individual may decide to stay in spite of the conflict and adapt by lowering his or her work standards and becoming apathetic and disinterested.
5. Informal groups may be created to oppose the former organization.
6. The employee may do nothing and remain frustrated, creating even more tension.[73]

In 1964, Argyris published *Integrating the Individual and the Organization.* The book's purpose was to present his thinking about how organizations could deal with the problem he had identified in *Personality and Organization: The Conflict between System and the Individual.* Argyris doubted that it was possible to have a relationship between the individual and the organization that allowed the simultaneous maximizing of the values of both.[74] He did believe it was possible to reduce the unintended, non-productive side consequences of formal organizations and to free more of the energies of

Quick Facts

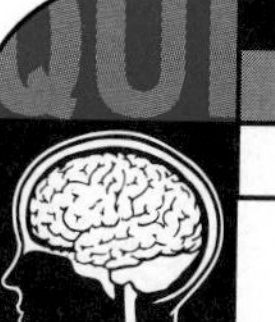

McGregor Biography

A management professor at the Massachusetts Institute of Technology's Sloan School of Management, McGregor was propelled to fame initially by his book *The Human Side of Enterprise* (1960). He is perhaps best known for his theory X and theory Y. He received his Ph.D. in psychology in 1935 from Harvard.

the individual for productive purposes; Argyris's mix model was the way in which this was to be done.[75] It is basically an attempt to "mix," or accommodate, the interests of the individual and the organization. The mix model favors neither people nor the organization. For example, Argyris saw the organization as having legitimate needs that were not people centered. He also believed that organizations could not always provide challenging work. The fact, however, that some work was not challenging was viewed by Argyris as an asset to the individual and the organization; the unchallenging work provided some recovery time for the individual and allowed the organization's routine tasks to get done.[76]

McGregor: Theory X and Theory Y

Douglas McGregor (1904–1964) believed that

> *every managerial act rests on assumptions, generalizations, and hypotheses—that is to say, on theory. Our assumptions are frequently implicit, sometimes quite unconscious, often conflicting; nevertheless, they determine our predictions that if we do A, B will occur. Theory and practice are inseparable.*[77]

In common practice, managerial acts, without explicit examination of theoretical assumptions, lead at times to remarkable inconsistencies in managerial behavior:

> *A manager, for example, states that he delegates to his subordinates. When asked, he expresses assumptions such as, "People need to learn to take responsibility," or, "Those closer to the situation can make the best decision." However, he has arranged to obtain a constant flow of detailed information about the behavior of his subordinates, and he uses this information to police their behavior and to "second-guess" their decisions. He says, "I am held responsible, so I need to know what is going on." He sees no inconsistency in his behavior, nor does he recognize some other assumptions which are implicit: "People can't be trusted," or, "They can't really make as good decisions as I can."*
>
> *With one hand, and in accord with certain assumptions, he delegates; with the other, and in line with other assumptions, he takes actions which have the effect of nullifying his delegation. Not only does he fail to recognize the inconsistencies involved, but if faced with them he is likely to deny them.*[78]

In *The Human Side of Enterprise* (1960), McGregor stated two different sets of assumptions that managers make about people:

Theory X

1. The average human has an inherent dislike of work and will avoid it if possible.
2. Most people must be coerced, controlled, directed, and threatened with punishment to get them to put forth adequate effort toward the achievement of organizational objectives.
3. The average human prefers to be directed, wishes to avoid responsibility, has relatively little ambition, and wants security above all.

Theory Y

1. The expenditure of physical and mental effort in work is as natural as play or rest.
2. External control and the threat of punishment are not the only means for bringing about effort toward organizational objectives. People will exercise self-direction and self-control in the service of objectives to which they are committed.
3. Commitment to objectives is a function of the rewards associated with their achievement.
4. The average human learns, under proper conditions, not only to accept but also to seek responsibility.
5. The capacity to exercise a relatively high degree of imagination, ingenuity, and creativity in the solution of organizational problems is widely, not narrowly, distributed in the population.
6. Under the conditions of modern organizational life, the intellectual potentialities of the average human are only partially utilized.[79]

American police departments have historically been dominated by theory X assumptions. Even police departments with progressive national images may be experienced as tightly controlling environments by the people who actually work in them:

> *The person leading a training session with about thirty-five managers of a West Coast police department observed that we often react to organizations as though they were living, breathing things. The managers agreed with this and noted the use of such phrases as "the department promoted me this year" and "the department hired me in 2000." They also understood that in fact someone, not the police department, had made those decisions. The managers were then divided into five groups and asked to make a list of what they thought the police department would say about them if it could talk. When the groups reported back, they identified a total of forty-two statements, some of which were duplicates of each other. These managers, all of whom were college graduates and many of whom held advanced degrees, indicated the police department would say such things as "They are idiots"; "They don't have any sense"; "Watch them or they'll screw up royally." All of the statements reported had a theory X character to them.*

Theory X assumptions are readily recognized as being those that underpin traditional organizational theory. For example, we can relate a narrow span of control to theory X's first two propositions. In contrast, theory Y is formed by a set of views that are supportive of Argyris's mix model; they postulate that the interests of the individual and the organization need not be conflictual but can be integrated for mutual benefit. The principal task of management in a theory X police department is control, whereas in a theory Y department it is supporting subordinates by giving them the resources to do their jobs and creating an environment where they can be self-controlling, mature, contributing, and self-actualizing.

The use of quality circles (QCs) or employee participation groups (EPGs) was one practice consistent with theory Y that was used in police departments. Widely used in Japanese industries and such American corporations as 3M, Union Carbide, Chrysler, and Lockheed, these procedures have been credited with achieving numerous productivity and product improvements while enjoying the support of both management and labor.[80]

Quality circles were small groups of people, roughly between 5 and 10, with 7 being regarded as ideal, who perform the same type of work, such as uniformed patrol, training, or robbery investigation. This group, or QC, voluntarily agreed to meet at least once a week during regular duty hours for an hour to identify, discuss,

QUICK FACTS QUICK FACTS QUICK

Quick Facts

Likert Biography

Likert was born in Cheyenne, Wyoming, in 1903 to an engineer for the Union Pacific Railroad. While working as a railroad intern, he saw the national railroad strike of 1922 firsthand, which ultimately led him to study organizations. In his 1932 Columbia University sociology dissertation, he developed a five-point scale still known as a Likert Scale. He is also remembered for his work on management styles and the linkpin theory. A founder of the University of Michigan's Institute for Social Research, he was its director from its inception in 1946 until his retirement in 1970, when he formed his own consulting firm, Rensis Likert Associates.

Source: Wikipedia, The Free Encyclopedia.

analyze, and solve specified work-related problems that the group members had identified as being important.

The fatal flaw in the use of QCs in policing and other organizations was that it made people at the bottom of the hierarchy assume too much responsibility for quality. As such, it was an isolated philosophy. Today, it is well understood that a successful quality movement requires that it be an organization-wide commitment and that it be a fundamental tenet of the organization, as opposed to an isolated practice. For the most part, QCs disappeared from American policing as community took hold in the 1980s.

Likert: Systems 1, 2, 3, and 4 and the Linkpin

The work of **Rensis Likert** (1903–1981) is compatible with McGregor's theory X and theory Y in that fundamentally it contrasts traditional and democratic or participative management. In *New Patterns of Management* (1961), Likert identified four different management systems, or climates: (1) exploitive authoritative, (2) benevolent authoritative, (3) consultative, and (4) participative group. In a subsequent publication, *The Human Organization* (1967), Likert extended and refined his notions of management systems, dropping the earlier designations and calling them system 1, system 2, system 3, and system 4, respectively. A partial description of these systems is given in Table 5.3.

Basically, Likert's system 1 reflects the content of McGregor's theory X, whereas system 4 incorporates the assumption of theory Y; system 2 and system 3 form part of a continuum in contrast to the simple opposites of McGregor's theory X and theory Y. Likert argues that system 2 management concepts predominate in the literature and that these conceptual tools do not fit a system 4 management style, which he believes most people prefer.[81]

Assuming some linkage between what Likert saw as predominating in the literature and actual practice, one would expect to find most people reporting their organization to be a system 2 environment. In a study of 18 different-size local police departments in 15 states throughout the country, Swanson and Talarico[82] asked 629 uniformed police officers assigned to field duties what type of management climate their department had. Some 16.6 percent of the officers reported a system 1, 42.9 percent a system 2, 35.9 percent a system 3, and only 4.6 percent a system 4. These data, then, provide some support for Likert's assertion.

Likert also contributes to the management literature by contrasting between the man-to-man and linkpin patterns of organization, depicted in Figure 5.9.[83] The man-to-man pattern is found in traditional organizations; the type of interaction characteristically is superior to subordinate, most often on an individual basis, and relies heavily

TABLE 5.3 Likert's Organizational and Performance Characteristics of Different Management Systems

ORGANIZATIONAL VARIABLE	SYSTEM 1	SYSTEM 2	SYSTEM 3	SYSTEM 4
Leadership Processes Used				
Extent to which superiors have confidence and trust in subordinates	Have no confidence and trust in subordinates	Have condescending confidence and trust, such as master has to servant	Substantial but not complete confidence and trust; still wishes to keep control of decisions	Complete confidence and trust in all matters
Extent to which superiors behave so that subordinates feel free to discuss important things about their jobs with their immediate superior	Subordinates do not feel at all free to discuss things about the job with their superior	Subordinates do not feel very free to discuss things about the job with their superior	Subordinates feel rather free to discuss things about the job with their superior	Subordinates feel completely free to discuss things about the job with their superior
Extent to which immediate superior in solving job problems generally tries to get subordinates' ideas and opinions and make constructive use of them	Seldom gets ideas and opinions of subordinates in solving job problems	Sometimes gets ideas and opinions of subordinates in solving job problems	Usually gets ideas and opinions and usually tries to make constructive use of them	Always gets ideas and opinions and always tries to make constructive use of them

SOURCE: *The Human Organization* by Rensis Likert. Copyright ©1967 McGraw-Hill Book Company. Used with permission of McGraw-Hill Book Company.

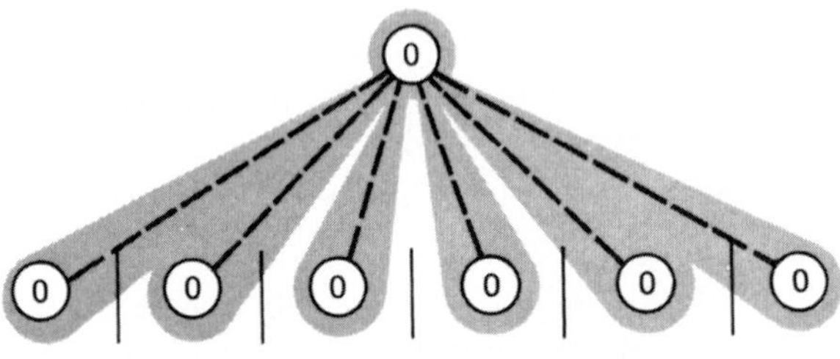

The Man-to-Man Pattern

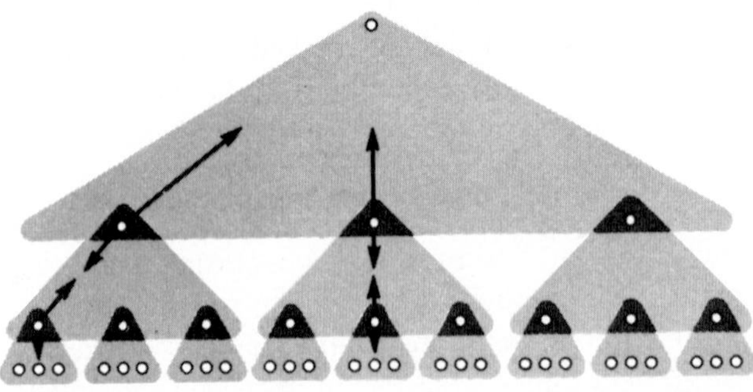

The Linkpin Pattern

FIGURE 5.9

Likert's man-to-man and linkpin patterns.

(*Source: The Human Organization* by Rensis Likert. Copyright © 1967 McGraw-Hill Book Company. Used with the permission of McGraw-Hill Book Company.)

In The News

Establishing Trust in the Police Department

In this news article, we lack sufficient information to know, in terms of Likert's management systems, what level of trust existed between the department and the former chief. But we see how important re-establishing it is to the new chief of police.

Venice, Florida, is a safe place to live, but earlier in 2006 it was not a good place to be a police officer. According to a consulting report, promotions weren't fair, policies weren't followed, communication was lacking, and therefore morale was low.

The new chief, the city's first woman in that position, started with one-on-one meetings with each of the department's 50 or so officers. She immediately saw the lack of trust the rank and file (the numerous low-ranking officers) had in the administration. In her view, this was a big thing on which to work. When people think they are not told the truth or their question are ignored, that's huge and it's her responsibility to re-establish that trust.

It's one thing to listen and another to act on what you hear. Chief Julie Williams didn't say "yes" to everything, saying "no" to take home cars, but saying yes to some things–such as implementing the 12-hour shift system officers wanted, rewriting the policies and procedures manual, and increasing training.

It appears the department is moving in a good direction. If Chief Williams did everything the rank and file wanted, they might regard her as a "pushover," and that would create difficulties in the future for her. If she had done too little, she would have been regarded as unresponsive and her one-on-one meetings labeled as wasted time. Moreover, some suggestions (take home cars) would have required a large financial commitment by the city council and the chief appears to have had other priorities, such as her commitment to increased training and applying for CALEA accreditation. Listening implies that one is willing to act on the good ideas one is able to implement. Inaction communicates that a leader thinks all of the ideas are bad or listening was a short-term, disingenuous strategy to defuse a situation; both of these are trust killers.

The principle here is that once you listen, you are almost bound to do something or else you quickly lose credibility.

on the use of positional authority. The linkpin pattern is found in the democratically and group-oriented system 4. In it, a police manager is simultaneously a member of one group—say, the chief's command staff—and the leader of another group—say, the operations bureau. The pattern of interaction is as a member of one group and as the leader of another, with the emphasis on open, honest communications in an atmosphere of mutual confidence and trust. In a loose sense, the traditional organization's managers perform a linkpin function, although it is man to man and is based on superior–subordinate interaction. However, in Likert's terms the linkpin function relies more on influence than on authority and connects groups rather than individuals.

Bennis: Organizational Development

An organizational humanist, **Warren Bennis's** (1925–) criticisms of bureaucracy have been noted. Much of his work has been in the area of organizational development, which is

> *the name given to the emerging applied behavioral science discipline that seeks to improve organizations through planned, systematic, long-range efforts focused on the organization's culture and its human and social processes.*[84]

Organizational development has two separate but entwined, stems: the laboratory training stem and the survey research feedback stem.[85] The laboratory approach involves unstructured experiences by a group from the same organization, the successor to stranger-to-stranger T-groups, whose popularity had waned by the late 1950s. Laboratory training grew out of the work of Lewin and his Research Center for Group Dynamics.[86] The survey research feedback stem makes attitude surveys within an organization and feeds them back to organizational members in workshop sessions to create awareness and to promote positive change.[87] The survey research stem also grew out of Lewin's Research Center for Group Dynamics, from which the senior staff—which had included McGregor—moved to the University of Michigan following

Lewin's death in 1947. There they joined with the university's Survey Research Center to form the Institute of Social Research, where some of Likert's work was done.

In a sense, organizational development began as a result of people rejecting stranger-to-stranger T-groups.[88] The laboratory stem began working with groups from the same organization, and the survey research feedback stem began using measurements. Fairly quickly, the focus spread from groups in the same organization to entire organizations. To illustrate the earlier point that many of the behavioral systems theorists are tied to organizational development, note that McGregor employed such an approach with Union Carbide in 1957 and that Argyris used it with the U.S. Department of State in 1967.

Organizational development as we know it today is an early 1960s movement. In his classic *Changing Organizations* (1966), Bennis describes it as having the following objectives:

1. Improvement in the interpersonal competence of managers
2. Change in value, so that human factors and feelings come to be considered legitimate
3. Increased understanding between and within groups to reduce tensions
4. Development of more effective team management, meaning an increased capacity for groups to work together
5. Development of better methods of resolving conflict, meaning less use of authority and suppression of it and more open and rational methods
6. Development of open, organic management systems characterized by trust, mutual confidence, wide sharing of responsibility, and resolution of conflict by bargaining or problem solving[89]

To produce the types of climates that Argyris, McGregor, Likert, and Bennis favor is hard work, and despite good intentions by the organization at the outset, there is always the prospect of failure:

> *The director of public safety in a major city wanted to implement a management by objectives (MBO) system. After discussions with the consultant who later directed the effort, it was agreed that this would be a long-term intervention. This effort focused on MBO as a rational management tool that had to be accompanied by behavioral shifts to be successful. The approach involved a survey research feedback component, training in MBO, and technical assistance in implementing it. After one year, the work had produced a good deal of paperwork, no small amount of confusion, and more than a little anger.*
>
> *The intervention failed because (1) the organization had not been prepared properly for change; (2) the project was seen as the director's "baby" and there was never widespread support for it; (3) many managers were threatened, denouncing it as "fad" or as an attempt by top management to find a way to evaluate them unfavorably; (4) not all managers were trained due to cost and scheduling difficulties; (5) success in part depended upon people in the organization taking responsibility for training lower-level managers and supervisors, a feat they did not accomplish; (6) the consultant's reservations about the likelihood of success given the specifics of the situation were never given sufficient weight by him or by others at the times they were voiced; (7) the time lines for the project were too ambitious; and (8) the resources dedicated to change were not sufficient.*

Organizations as Open Systems

Systems theory concepts have been discussed since the 1920s, but they came into general use only as recently as 1960. A system is a grouping of separate but interrelated components working together toward the achievement of a common objective. General systems theory (GST), on which the biologist Ludwig von Bertalanffy and the sociologist Talcott Parsons have written, is a broad conceptual framework for explaining relationships in the "real world" without any consideration of the specifics of a given situation.

Organizations may be characterized as closed or open systems. In actuality, there are no entirely closed or open organizations; these are terms used only to describe the extent to which an organization approximates one or the other.

The closed system view of an organization assumes complete rationality, optimizing performances, predictability, internal efficiency, and certainty.[90] Because all behavior is believed to be functional and all outcomes are believed to be predictable and certain, the closed organization can ignore changes in the larger environment, such as political, technological, and economic.[91] Thus, the closed system organization sees little need for interaction with its environment. The police chief who denies that she needs an automated management information system (MIS) prohibits subordinates from talking with politicians, prefers the "tried and true" over recent innovations, and refuses to justify budget requests carefully in a tight economic environment is reflecting a closed system view. Traditional organizational theory and the closed system fall into the same stream of thinking and are compatible.

The police department as an open system is depicted in Figure 5.10. Open systems are described by Katz and Kahn as having the following characteristics:

1. Open systems seek and continuously import sources of energy, including money, recruits, and information as inputs.
2. Once imported, the energy is transformed by the subsystems constituting the throughput function. For example, recruits are trained.
3. Although some energy is used by the subsystems in the throughput function, such as the efforts associated with training recruits, open systems export the bulk of the energy transformed into the environment as products, services (such as the trained recruits who are now assigned to patrol and respond to calls), and other forms.
4. There is a cyclical relationship among the inputs, the throughput, and the outputs as the services exported into the environment furnish the source of energy to repeat the cycle. Outputs both satisfy needs and create new demands for outputs.
5. All forms of organization move toward disorganization or death; this entropic process is a universal law of nature. To survive, open systems reverse the

In The News

Police as an Open System

The 2007 budget which Memphis Police Director Larry Godwin submitted was for $185.2 million, including 22 new recruits to help staff the new Hickory Hill Precinct. However, the city council, which appropriates the funds, was so concerned about the rising crime rate that it voted to add 50 new recruits, who will be trained to perform their police duties.

Support for the additional officers was not unanimous on the city council; Councilman Jack Simmons argued that you have to let criminals know that Memphis is "the wrong place to take up your career." Councilwoman Carol Chumney voted against the increase, maintaining that 22 officers could be assigned from "desk duty jobs," to which Godwin responded that he just didn't have 22 officers sitting around in clerical slots.

Source: Jacinthia Jones, "50 More Cops in City's 2007 Budget," *The Commercial Appeal* (Memphis, Tennessee), June 1, 2006, with restatement.

process by acquiring negative entropy. The cyclical character of open systems allows them to develop negative entropy by having energy flow continuously through them. Additionally, because open systems can import more energy than is expended, they have a storage capacity that allows them to survive brief interruptions of inputs. This may occur as one budget year ends and it is a short while until the city council enacts the new budget. Typically, the police department will have sufficient gasoline and other supplies to remain operational.

6. Open systems receive informational feedback as inputs from the larger environment in which they operate. As suggested by Figure 5.10, an open system has multiple points at which inputs occur. These inputs take place through both formal and informal exchanges. Police departments have a formally structured feedback loop to make them more responsive to control, and through it flows such things as technical evaluations of their programs and directions from the city council and the city manager. Open systems cannot absorb all informational and other inputs; excesses of inputs would overwhelm them. Therefore, open systems have a selective mechanism called "coding," which filters out some potential inputs and attunes them to important signals from the environment. A simple illustration of this principle is that, from among the dozens of daily telephone callers asking to talk to the chief of police, only a few actually get to do so. Switchboard operators, secretaries, and aides are taught to refer most callers to the appropriate department, handle the calls themselves, or connect them with someone empowered to deal with such matters, yet the telephone calls of the city manager and certain other people invariably find their way through these filters.
7. The continuous cycle of inputs, transformations, outputs, and feedback produces a steady state in an open system. A steady state is not a motionless or true equilibrium but a dynamic and continuous adjusting to external forces and of internal processes to ensure the survival of the system.
8. Over time, open systems develop specialized subsystems, as shown in Figure 5.10, to facilitate the importation and processing of energy and to enhance their survival.
9. As specialization proceeds, its fragmenting effect is countered by processes that bring the system together for unified functioning, the purpose of the managerial subsystem depicted in Figure 5.10.
10. Open systems can reach the same final state even though they started from different sets of initial conditions and proceeded down different paths; this is the principle of equifinality.[92]

The subsystems identified in Figure 5.10 have been discussed in various ways; more specifically, these overlapping subsystems have the following functions:

1. The managerial subsystem plays a central role in establishing goals, planning, organizing, coordinating, and controlling activities and in relating the police department to its environment.
2. Organizational goals and values represent an important subsystem; while the police department takes many of its values from the broader environment, such as the content of statutory law and appellate court decisions, it also influences society. An example illustrates the interplay between the police department's subsystems and the larger environment. Conditioned by the conservative nature of the

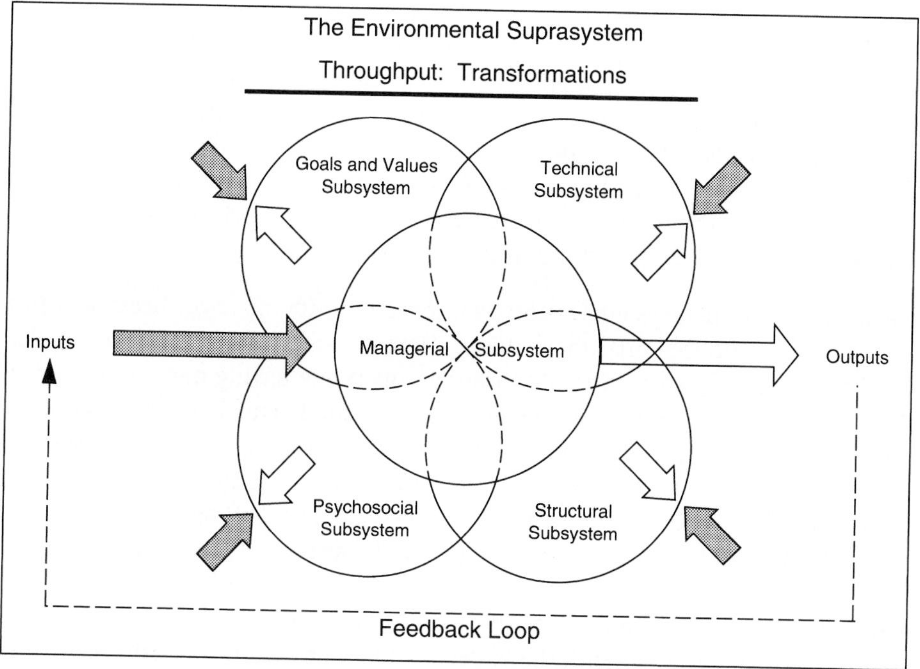

FIGURE 5.10

The police department as an open system.

(*Source: Contingency Views of Organization and Management* by Fremont E. Kast and James E. Rosenzweig. © 1973, Science Research Associates, Inc. Reprinted by permission of the publisher with modification.)

In The News

Police "Edit" Report on Football Star

The news article which follows is an example of how the managerial subsystem controls and coordinates activities and relates the organization to its environment.

Dallas football star T. O. Owens was taken to a Dallas hospital after his publicist, Kim Etheredge, called 911. Owens, who spent the night in the hospital, later called the incident an "allergic reaction to pain medication."

The original police report made reference to an attempted suicide. Etheredge disputed that she had told the police Owens was depressed or that she had taken something out of his mouth. Owens said he doesn't know what he told the police.

The police chief said the incident was being classified as an accidental overdose, as opposed to an attempted suicide. Subsequently, the police released what was described as a "heavily edited version" of the report and declined to discuss it because of privacy concerns.

The president of the Dallas Police Association, Glenn White, demanded that Owens and Etheredge apologize for challenging portions of the police report relating to the incident. The officers were called to do a job and "now they are being put under a microscope becaue of some fancy little football person."

Source: Matt Curry, "Police Group Upset with Statement by T. O.'s Publicist," The Associated Press State and Local Wire, September 28, 2006.

organization in which they operate, which is reflected in the police department's goals and values subsystem, the top leadership of the managerial subsystem—in relating the police department to its environment—may take positions against abortions and the legalization of marijuana and for gun control and mandatory sentences.

3. The technical subsystem is the means required for the performance of tasks, including the knowledge, equipment, processes, and facilities used to transform inputs into outputs.
4. Individual behaviors, motivations, status and role hierarchies, group dynamics, and influence systems are all elements of the psychosocial subsystem.

5. The structural subsystem is concerned with the ways in which tasks are divided and how they are coordinated. In a formal sense, structure can be set forth by organizational charts, job descriptions, policies, and rules and regulations. Structure is therefore also concerned with patterns of authority, communication, and work flow. Also, the structural subsystem provides for a formalization of relationships between the technical and the psychosocial systems. However, many interactions that occur between the technical and psychosocial subsystems bypass the formal, occurring informally.[93]

Knowledge of open systems theory is important to the manager because it provides a view of the police department that is more consistent with reality; the police department is not a closed system but rather an open one having many dynamic interactions with the larger society in which it is embedded. This interactive nature of policing is part of the core of the community police movement; thus, open systems theory and community policing are compatible orientations. Figure 5.11 demonstrates one aspect of the dynamic interactions a police department has with its larger environment: the relationship between the police department and external bodies in the fiscal management process.

Stressing the interrelatedness of the various subsystems and the interrelatedness of the police department with the larger world, open systems theory has the potential to foster increased cooperation. Also, the emphasis of open systems theory on

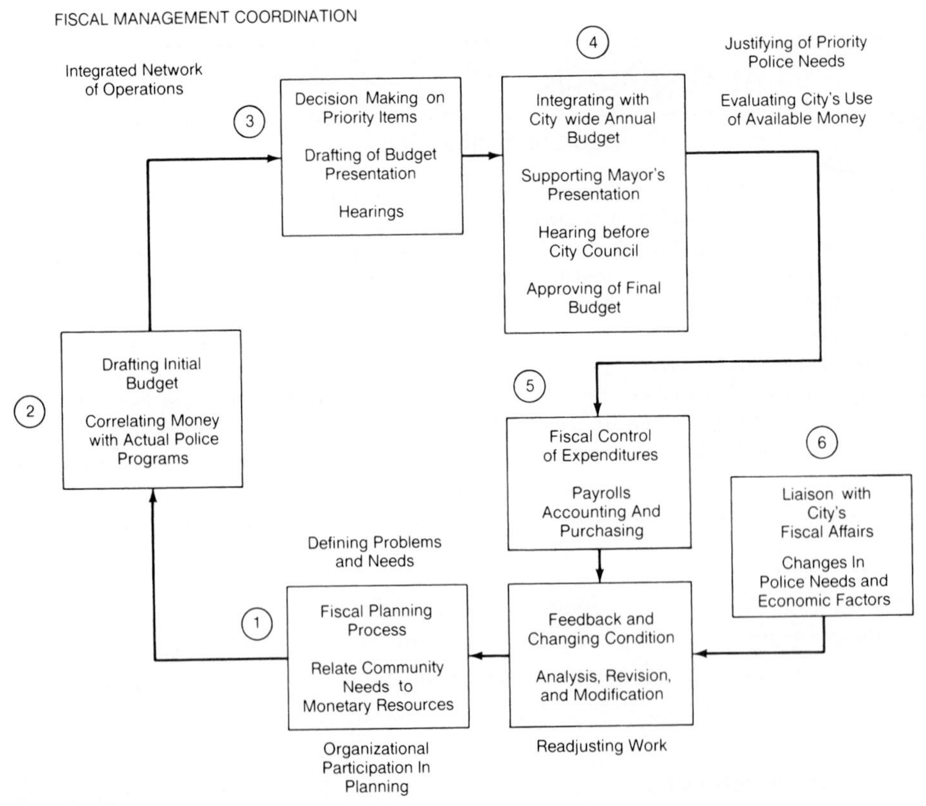

FIGURE 5.11

External relationships in the Houston Police Department's fiscal management process.

(*Source:* Kent John Chabotar, *Measuring the Costs of Police Services* [Washington, D.C.: U.S. Department of Justice, National Institute of Justice, 1982], p. 114)

achieving objectives reinforces the need for purposeful behavior and may lead to greater effectiveness in achieving goals.

Newer Paradigms of Administration

Within the 15 years, a new body of literature on administration that draws on the physical and biological sciences has begun to emerge. The two most important elements of this literature are chaos theory and quantum theory.[94] "Unfortunately, there is not one sentence, one paragraph, or even one book that can tell us what these new sciences are. They are a very loosely coupled set of ideas and findings"[95] that reflect some fundamental shifts in thinking about organizations. Because of the emerging nature of these theories, the purpose here is to provide a basic overview inasmuch as they are likely to be an increasingly prominent theme in the literature on administration. Both chaos theory and quantum theory have their roots in systems theory. Among early influential books applying these theories to organizations are Becker's *Quantum Politics,*[96] Wheatley's *Leadership and the New Science,*[97] Kiel's *Managing Chaos and Complexity in Government,* [98] and Zohar and Marshall's *The Quantum Society.*[99] Unlike other theorists and theories discussed in this chapter—such as Taylor and scientific management—chaos theory and quantum theory applied to administration do not have a single founder. Thus, the selection of theorists to associate with these theories, appearing in Table 5.4, is to a degree arbitrary.

The newer paradigms may not necessarily be helpful to police managers concerned with the problem of efficient service delivery. The essence of these paradigms is a broader look at administration in which chaos and complexity are not problems to be solved as much as they are important aspects of organizational life by which the living system (e.g., a police department) adapts to its environment, renews and maintains itself, and ultimately changes itself through self-organization.[100]

Thus, the newer paradigms do not simply offer innovative ways to manage police departments better; they question "the basic logic of most management philosophy,"[101] thereby asking different questions. For example, open systems theory holds that all organizations move toward disorganization or death, the entropic process discussed earlier in this chapter. The newer paradigms raise several questions. What if the complexity of police departments and their ambiguity about their mission and methods are not sources of entropy but instead important sources of the life-sustaining energy through which police departments organize themselves to adapt to these phenomena? Can police managers really separate themselves from the chaos they are trying to control when there is an event such as a natural disaster? Or do their very actions to control such events contribute to increased complexity by giving organizational systems new inputs to which they must react—for example, mobilizing all available on-duty personnel, recalling officers who are off duty, establishing a command post, evacuating citizens to safe areas, limiting access to devastated areas to prevent looting while granting entrance to insurance claims adjusters, operating a system for the collection and care of pets and other animals, providing a news media liaison officer, and coordinating with area hospitals and the Federal Emergency Management Agency?[102]

Chaos theory argues that, when events such as natural disasters happen and gaining control of events is a slippery affair, new structures and processes emerge—such as task forces and ad-hoc cooperation by individuals and groups—which are based on a recognition of their mutual interdependence. Helpful small actions taken everywhere—self-organization—produce the "butterfly effect." The butterfly effect ripples through the community, energizing people to use their talents and resources to help.

TABLE 5.4 The Interrelationships of the Three Major Streams of Theories

THEORISTS	TRADITIONAL THEORIES	BRIDGING THEORIES	OPEN SYSTEMS THEORIES
Taylor	Scientific management		
Weber	Bureaucratic model		
Fayol, Mooney and Reiley, Gulick, and Urwick	Administrative theory		
Mayo			Hawthorne studies and human relations
Parsons			Functionalism and social systems
Maslow	Bottom three levels of needs hierarchy		Top two levels of needs hierarchy
Herzberg	Hygiene factors		Motivators
Lewin			Group dynamics
Homans			Internal–external systems
Argyris	Immaturity		Maturity
McGregor	Theory X		Theory Y
Likert	System 1	System 2, System 3	System 4
Bennis			Organizational development
Bertalanffy, Parsons, and Katz and Kahn			Systems theory
Kiel, Wheatley, Becker, and Zohar and Marshall			New paradigms
Barnard		Cooperative system	
Simon and March		Administrative man	
Burns and Stalker, Woodward, Sherman and Lawrence, and Lorsch		Organizational contingency theory	
Vroom		Expectancy theory	
Fiedler		Situational leadership	
Katzell and Ouchi		Theory Z	

Chaos Theory

Chaos theory is illustrated by the following scenario. A city manager asked a consultant to do a management study of the police department. The "presenting symptoms" of the police department, as expressed by the city manager, were that the police department was in shambles, morale was low, and turnover was high. He therefore thought it was time to replace the chief of police. However, the consultant knew that the chief and the department had strong reputations and were working toward reaccreditation by the

Commission on Accreditation of Law Enforcement Agencies (CALEA). Thus, the consultant suggested that, before he commit to a study of the police department, he come and spend a few days assessing what—if any—intervention was needed.

During his investigation, the consultant learned that, six months previously, the chief had instituted community-oriented policing (COP), which had been strongly endorsed by departmental members. However, some opposition to COP now existed in part because it required more reports—the archenemy of street officers. Shortly after the implementation of COP, the city manager ordered that 360-degree performance evaluations be used and that a continuous quality improvement program be implemented. This new method of written evaluation—from subordinates, coequals, and superiors—frightened and angered members of the police department because it upset the established nature of things. Both COP and the continuous quality improvement program required many meetings, taking officers away from what they saw as "real police work." Roughly one year prior to this, the city's human resources director began recruiting only college graduates for the department. In the 36-officer police department, there was limited opportunity to advance, which frustrated the college graduates, who began casting about for better opportunities. Furthermore, the city's salary administration plan—implemented a year before the drive to recruit only college graduates—offered very little in the way of financial advancement, which made veteran officers discontent and exacerbated the frustration of recent hires into the police department. At the same time, competing departments in the same area increased their salaries and benefits, had much more attractive retirement plans, and offered greater potential for advancement into specialized units and supervisory assignments due to their greater size.

All police administrators know about organizational chaos. It is when too much happens too fast that things seem out of control and that collapse of the department seems not only possible but even imminent,[103] yet somehow out of this chaos order emerges as the department creates new structures and procedures to adjust to the new realities thrust on it. Chaos theory, which has its roots in systems theory, is therefore described as the study of complex and dynamic organizations that reveals patterns of order in what is seemingly chaotic behavior.[104] Chaos theorists argue that the language of systems theory—with its emphasis on maintaining the department's equilibrium—is "wildly incomplete."[105] What chaos theory teaches us is not to distrust chaos and stressfully uncertain times in an organization but that it is in such times that real change is possible as new structures and procedures emerge from the very chaos administrators are trying to control.[106]

In The News

Police Family Moves after Katrina

Hurricane Katrina, which may have resulted in 1,600 deaths, produced heretofore unknown levels of chaos. One of the people at the center of this disaster was New Orleans Police Officer James Gourlie, who recalls that he was going to a murder every week. At the height of the chaos, only he and 5 other officers–out of 200–from his district kept working when looters and snipers were flourishing. Some officers committed suicide. While Gourlie stopped short of saying there was anarchy in the streets, he does feel that authorities downplayed the situation. People needed the basics, water, shelter . . . we couldn't help them because we didn't have it . . . putting your life on the line is hard when there is no real leadership.

Gourlie now works for a 16-officer department in a town of 16,000 people in rural northeast Oregon. "I had to think of my family . . . I miss the action . . . but this is more peaceful . . . there hasn't been a murder in two or three years." In this tranquil setting, Gourlie and his wife await the birth of their first child.

Source: Mike Steere, "Scenes Haunt Cop Who Stayed to Help," *The Press* (Christchurch, New Zealand), August 23, 2006.

The consultant made his report to the city manager in the context of chaos theory and organizational change (the subject of Chapter 15, Organizational Change and the Future). He told him that he found no basis for removing the chief and that the department was simply suffering from "a normal case of chaos," which could be resolved by some new strategies and the passage of time. The department had been overwhelmed by large-scale changes being implemented so rapidly that none of them had yet taken root in the department, and each of the changes required more paperwork, yet out of the chaos of the ill-structured changes, progress was being made as new committees produced important reports resolving operational and administrative problems and as individual officers made butterfly effect contributions, such as developing new work schedules and reporting forms. Also pointed out at this meeting was the fact that some conditions that contributed to the low morale and turnover were projects mandated by the city manager.

The consultant asked the city manager to recall conditions in the department before the chief was selected from outside the police department. The manager said that there had been a burglary scandal in the police department and that several officers had gone to jail, causing merchants to distrust the department. He went on to note that CALEA accreditation had restored confidence in the police department. Moreover, at the time, he didn't think the police department "could pull reaccreditation off due to the massive amount of work which had to be done."

The consultant made several recommendations to the city manager, including getting a police administrator with substantial experience in COP to be a "guru" to their chief; reducing the pace of change; re-evaluating the city's pay, benefits, retirement plan, and recruiting policy; establishing a new career ladder as an alternative to movement up through the rank structure; increasing communications both ways between the chief and the city manager; using organizational awards and cash bonuses to reinforce the change process; and structuring the content of promotional examinations to reflect the new types of knowledge needed in the department. After considering the consultant's report, the city manager decided to retain the chief on the belief that some problems had been created for the chief and that "he is also the guy who made accreditation work when I thought it didn't have a prayer."

Quantum Theory

Like chaos theory, **quantum theory** has its roots in different scientific disciplines, such as physics and biology.[107] Because quantum theory deviates sharply from the traditional scientific method, explaining it is difficult and it can seem mystical and superstitious.[108]

Many management and policy problems involve significant proportions of "indeterministic elements," which means there are many things that we cannot know or understand in a given situation.[109] Police administrators cannot let such factors paralyze them; they live in a world in which they must resolve management and policy problems. In order to resolve them, they have to "fill in the blanks" by making assumptions and creating a "reality" that gives them a context in which to respond. Gone is the expectation of objective reality, certainty, and simple cause-and-effect explanations; taking its place are subjectivity, uncertainty, and the recognition that "reality" is different to different people because they construct our own realities.[110] Therefore, there are alternative explanations to the ones police administrators construct. Quantum theory also sees public institutions as energy fields in which the focus is on not what is but what could be.[111] Quantum theory's proposition that there are many things we do not know is consistent with Simon's concept of "bounded rationality"—the idea that, because we cannot know everything, our rationality is limited. Bounded rationality is discussed in Chapter 18, Planning and Decision Making.

Traditional police administrators argue that performance evaluations are meant to give officers objective feedback about their work behavior. Moreover, they assert that, if we link these evaluations to pay increases and promotions, they become a powerful motivational tool for shaping the behavior of officers.[112] Quantum police administrators see these views of traditional administrators as "pure hogwash" for several reasons. For one, they believe that current performance evaluation systems are a hopelessly inadequate method of accurately portraying the complex behaviors of officers over a period of six months or a year. In addition, it is impossible for administrators to know all examples of success and failure by the officers they rate.

Quantum administrators also believe that the traditionalists' view that pay increases and promotions motivate the behavior of officers is too simplistic because the actual causes of behavior are more complex and are likely to include factors such as the officers' values and role concepts, their peer groups, their levels of ambition, and the fact that any reality constructed about an officer's performance may or may not be consistent with the officer's own reality and that the same event can be considered both bad and good. Assume, for example, that a detective solved only 3 cases in the past six months out of an assigned load of 27 cases. Such a statistic is hardly impressive. But what if all 27 cases were unsolved criminal homicides that had not been investigated any further in the past three years because all possible leads had been exhausted? What if an officer is drinking off duty in a bar and sees a burglary suspect who specializes in stealing fine jewelry from penthouses? This burglar has committed many recent "jobs," and the news media have been highly critical of the police department's inability to catch him. Assume that the burglar "makes" the off-duty officer and bolts for the door before the officer can call for help. The officer arrests the burglar, but only after a vicious fight. The suspect files suit against the department, claiming the officer used excessive force. The news media wonder why "one intoxicated cop can arrest a burglar that an entire sober department couldn't even find" and criticize the officer for not having his off-duty gun with him, which would have prevented the needless violence. Is this a good or bad job? On whose reality do you base your conclusions?

The quantum police administrator also says that, in the very process of measuring things, such as an officer's performance, we change the officer's behavior and that it may or may not be for the better. To illustrate, Sergeant Abbruzzese has a hangover today, having gotten drunk yesterday after she went home and found her husband had left her for his accountant and had emptied their savings and checking accounts. Today, she completes Officer Dunagan's performance evaluation. Because of her immediate personal circumstances, she constructs a reality that is more critical than the reality that Officer Dunagan has of his own performance. Officer Dunagan subsequently leaves the department, feeling that he has no future there.

Critique of Open Systems Theory

Mayo's human relations school has been challenged on a number of grounds:

1. It rests on questionable research methods, a point raised earlier.[113]
2. The viewpoint that conflict between management and the worker can be overcome by the "harmony" of human relations attributes too much potency to human relations and ignores the potential that properly handled conflict has for being a source of creativity and innovation.
3. The single-mindedness with which advocates insisted on the importance of human relations was evangelistic.

4. Entirely too much emphasis was placed on the informal side of organization to the neglect of the formal.
5. The attention focused on the individual and the group was at the expense of consideration of the organization as a whole.[114]

Human relations is also criticized as having a pro-management bias from several perspectives. First, it saw unions as promoting conflict between management and labor, a condition antithetical to the values of human relations. Second, by focusing on workers, the Hawthorne studies provided management with more sophisticated means of manipulating employees. Finally, the end of human relations is indistinguishable from that of scientific management in that both aim for a more efficient organization:

> *Scientific management assumed the most efficient organization would also be the most satisfying one, since it would maximize both productivity and workers' pay . . . the Human Relations approach was that the most personally satisfying organization would be the most efficient.*[115]

Although the Hawthorne studies never showed a clear-cut relationship between satisfaction and job performance,[116] the human relations position that satisfied people are more productive has become a widely held and cherished belief. It is a logically appealing and commonsense position whose endless repetition has accorded it the status of "fact." However popular this "fact," the unqualified assertion that satisfied people are more productive is at odds with the research findings; there is no consistent relationship between job satisfaction and productivity.[117]

This does not mean that police managers should be unconcerned about any possible consequences of job satisfaction and dissatisfaction. Quite to the contrary, there are profoundly important organizational and humane reasons that they should be very concerned. On the positive side, job satisfaction generally leads to lower turnover, less absenteeism, fewer cases of tardiness, and fewer grievances; it was the best overall predictor of the length of life in an impressive long-term study.[118] Conversely, job dissatisfaction has been found to be related to various mental and physical illnesses.[119] As a final note, some work on job satisfaction and productivity reverses the usual causal relationships, suggesting that satisfaction is an outgrowth of production.[120]

Maslow used a portion of his *Motivation and Personality* to attack the scientific method, claiming that its rigors limited the conclusions one could reach.[121] In turn, the scientific method has found it difficult to state the concepts of the needs hierarchy in ways that they can be measured and the theory tested. Bennis[122] was baffled to discover that little had been done to test the needs hierarchy. Despite the lack of research and the fact that the few existing studies do not support Maslow, there remains an almost metaphysical attraction to the needs hierarchy,[123] a condition made even more perplexing by noting that Maslow's work on motivation came from a clinical study of neurotic people.[124]

In contrast to the lack of research on the needs hierarchy, there has been considerable research on Herzberg's motivation–hygiene theory; after reviewing this evidence, Gibson and Teasley conclude,

> *It would be fair to summarize these efforts as mixed as regards the validation of the Herzberg concepts. The range of findings run from general support . . . to a vigorous condemnation of Herzberg's methodology.*[125]

Behavioral systems theories have also been found wanting on a variety of grounds:

1. Insufficient attention has been paid to the organization as a whole, and too much emphasis has been placed on the individual and groups.

2. Some theories, such as Argyris's immaturity–maturity theory, McGregor's theory X and theory Y, and Likert's systems 1, 2, 3, and 4, depend as much on setting the bureaucratic model up as a "straw man" to be knocked down as easily as they do their own virtues.
3. However attractive the arguments for organizational humanism, the data supporting them are not powerful and are sometimes suspect. For example, in commenting on McGregor's theory X and theory Y, Maslow notes that

   > *a good deal of evidence upon which he bases his conclusions comes from my research and my papers on motivations, self-actualization, etc. But I of all people would know just how shaky this foundation is as a final foundation. My work on motivations came from the clinic, from a study of neurotic people . . . I am quite willing to concede this . . . because I'm a little worried about this stuff which I consider tentative being swallowed whole by all sorts of enthusiastic people.*[126]

   Concerns have also been expressed regarding what actually is being measured. For example, Johannesson[127] claims that studies of job satisfaction and organizational climate are tapping the same dimension; critics of Johannesson term his conclusion "premature and judgmental,"[128] while others argue that job satisfaction is the direct result of organizational climate.[129] Moreover, some data suggest conclusions that differ from some of the logical positions taken by behavioral systems theorists. Argyris's argument that the narrow span of control makes people passive and dependent is a case in point. From a study of 156 public personnel agencies, Blau[130] concluded that a narrow span of control provided opportunities for more mutuality in problem solving. Although not stated directly, this also suggests the possibility that wide spans of control may produce less collaboration, because the manager has less time to share with each subordinate, and a more directive relationship.[131]
4. In one way or another, humanistic theories depend on open and honest communication among organizational members in an environment of trust and mutual respect. A compellingly attractive theme, it gives insufficient weight to the consequences that can and do flow when authenticity meets power. Along these lines, Samuel Goldwyn is reputed to have said to his staff one day, "I want you all to tell me what's wrong with our operation even if it means losing your job."[132] The authenticity–power dilemma is not insurmountable, but it is a tall mountain whose scaling depends in large measure on personally secure and non-defensive people dedicated to improving the organization and how it is experienced by its inhabitants.
5. In large measure, the impetus to humanize organizations has been from the academic community; its belief that employees want more rewards than money from doing the work itself does not take into account the fact that some workers have a utilitarian involvement with the job. It simply provides the money necessary to live, and they save their energies and obtain their rewards from their families and other non–job related sources, such as hobbies. Also, workers may not see attempts to broaden their jobs in the same light as theorists.[133] Six American automobile workers spent four weeks in a Swedish Saab plant working to assemble engines as a team rather than on an assembly-line basis. Five of the six American workers reacted negatively to this experience. One of them expressed his dissatisfaction in the following way: "If I've got to bust my ass to be meaningful, forget it; I'd rather be monotonous."[134] Although neither controlling nor entirely persuasive, findings such as these at least provide another framework for thinking about theories of organization.

Despite the fact that open systems theory has enjoyed some popularity since 1960, its use has not penetrated into police departments to any discernible degree. Disarmingly straightforward as a concept, its application requires the investment of resources beyond the reach of most police departments, particularly when considered in relationship to needs perceived as more directly relevant to their mission.

Chaos theory and quantum theory do not offer a great deal of immediate assistance to police administrators looking for solutions to specific problems. Instead, they provide new lenses through which to look at administration. This allows police leaders to ask different questions. For example, a quantum belief is that a police department is an energy field and that we should focus not only on what exists now but also on what the possibilities are for the future. This could change the question from "How do we improve our Detective Division?" to "Assume there isn't a Detective Division and we are not going to create one. Under those conditions, what is the best use of the energy formerly vested in it?" Such questions have the potential to create exciting new possibilities for police departments in terms of organizational structure, the delivery of police services, and the roles of officers in departments. Because the application of the newer paradigms to administration is in its formative stages, it will be some time before we know whether they will have a significant impact or simply become part of the landscape of thinking about organizations.

Critical Thinking Question

1. The subject of opens systems theory constitutes the majority of this chapter because so many people have written about it. Within open systems theory, which two theories "rang true" to you? Why?

BRIDGING THEORIES

As noted earlier in this chapter, **bridging theories** are those that display a certain degree of empathy for both the traditional and the open systems perspectives. Trying to place a range of theories under the traditional or open systems streams of thinking is not unlike the experience of trying to fit a square peg in a round hole. This difficulty is created by the simple reality that the work of some theorists produces thinking that does not focus solely or even largely on a single dimension. Additionally vexing is the fact that over time the importance that theorists and others attach to their work may change. Perhaps equally perplexing to those newly introduced to organizational theory is the array of classification schemes for presenting work in this area—which also may change over time. For example, at one time organic models of organization were differentiated from general systems models, although in 1967 Buckley noted that the modern concepts of systems are now taking over the duty of the overworked and perhaps retiring concept of the organic organization.[135] All this is by way of noting that ultimately classification becomes a matter of judgment. For present purposes, it is sufficient to understand that the designation "bridging theories" is intended to encompass a range of theories that can be conceived of as falling into the middle ground between traditional and open systems theory.

Under the broad heading of bridging theories, two subheadings of theories will be considered: general bridging theories and contingency theories. Note that, as the various theories are covered, mention is made of other ways in which these theories have been categorized.

General Bridging Theories

In this section, the work of Chester Barnard (1886–1961), James March (1928–), and Herbert Simon (1916–2001) is treated. Barnard's thinking has also been identified by others as part of the human relations, social systems, and open systems schools; March and Simon's efforts are sometimes categorized as being part of a decision theory school.

Chester Barnard's principal career was as an executive with American Telephone & Telegraph, although he had other work experiences as well. During World War II, he was president of United Service Organizations, and from 1952 to 1953 he was the Rockefeller Foundation's president. In 1938, he wrote *The Functions of the Executive,* which reflected his experiences and thinking. Among his major contributions are the following ideas:

1. Emphasis is on the importance of decision-making processes and a person's limited power of choice as opposed to the traditionalist's "rational man."
2. An organization is a "system of consciously coordinated activities or forces of two or more persons," and it is important to examine the external forces to which adjustments must be made.
3. Individuals can overcome the limits on individual performance through cooperative group action.
4. The existence of such a cooperative system depends on both its effectiveness in meeting the goal and its efficiency.
5. Efficiency, in turn, depends on organizational equilibrium, which is the balance between the inducements offered by the organization and the contributions offered by the individual.
6. The informal organization aids communication, creates cohesiveness, and enhances individual feelings of self-respect.
7. Authority rests on a person's acceptance of the given orders; orders that are neither clearly acceptable nor clearly unacceptable lie within a person's zone of indifference.
8. Complex organizations are themselves composed of small units.
9. The traditional view of organizations is rejected as having boundaries and comprising a definite number of members. Included in this concept of organizations are investors, suppliers, customers, and others whose actions contribute to the productivity of the firm.
10. Executives operate as interconnecting centers in a communication system that seeks to secure the coordination essential to cooperative effort. Executive work is the specialized work of maintaining the organization and its operation. The executive is analogous to the brain and the nervous system in relation to the rest of the body.[136]

These ideas of Barnard reveal an appreciation for both traditional and open systems theories. On the one hand, Barnard was concerned with formal structure, goals, effectiveness, and efficiency; on the other hand, he viewed organizations as cooperative systems, having an informal side and many relationships with the larger world. Effectively, then, his thinking bridges the traditional and open systems streams of thinking.

Simon's *Administrative Behavior* has been mentioned with respect to its "proverbs" attack on the principles of organization, but it also made other noteworthy contributions. Simon believed that the "anatomy of an organization" was how the decision-making function was distributed; indeed, the central theme of *Administrative Behavior* is that organizations are decision-making entities.[137] Simon was, therefore, simultaneously interested in both structure and behavior. In *Organizations* (1958), March and Simon built on some of the ideas reflected in the earlier *Administrative*

Behavior. Organizations presented March and Simon's "administrative man," who was a modification of the rational economic actor behaving in his own self-interest postulated by traditional organizational theory. Administrative man reflects the tension between the traditional theory's normative values of rationality, effectiveness, and efficiency and the open system's views of human behavior and the complexity of organizations. The administrative man is characterized as follows:

1. He lacks complete knowledge of the alternatives available to him in making decisions.
2. He does not know the consequences of each possible alternative.
3. He uses a simple decision-making model that reflects the main features of decision situations but not the complexity of them.
4. He makes decisions characterized as "satisficing," which are short of optimizing but satisfy and suffice in that they are "good enough to get by."[138]

Contingency Theory

In the late 1950s and early 1960s, a series of studies was carried out in England and in this country that were to lead ultimately to the development of what is presently referred to as contingency, or situational, theory. This approach holds—with respect to organizing, managing, leading, motivating, and other variables—that there is no one best way to go about it. **Contingency theory** does not, however, also assume that all approaches to a situation are equally appropriate. It is a bridging theory in that it favors neither traditional nor open systems theory; rather, it is the specifics of a situation that suggest which approach should be used.

Ouchi's Theory Z

The concept of **theory Z**[139] was first popularized by William Ouchi's 1981 book *Theory Z: How American Management Can Meet the Japanese Challenge*[140] and is often referred to as the "Japanese" management style. It offers an approach that is inclusive of aspects of Japanese culture in which workers are loyal, participative, and capable of performing a variety of different tasks. Theory Z places a premium on the attitudes and responsibilities of workers and emphasizes that the responsibility for success or failure is shared among employees and management. Employees have considerable input in organizational decision making and are crucial to the process. Most employees do not specialize in one area but work at several different tasks, learning more about the company as they develop.

Theory Z assumes that workers want to participate in a working environment where cooperation and cohesion among all levels of personnel are highly valued. Theory Z workers traditionally are seen as having an innate moral obligation to work hard for their company as a result of family, culture, and social tradition. As a result, theory Z organizations support their employees in all aspects of their lives, regarding an employee's outside life equally as important as their working life. This breeds a high degree of loyalty in workers, who feel valued in their place of employment. Theory Z managers have a high degree of confidence in their workers as a result of the ability of these workers to perform a variety of tasks and are therefore able to let workers make many of the organizational decisions. Generalization allows employees to increase their knowledge of the company as a whole through the rotation of job tasks and by continuous training. This type of system slows the promotion process down because

Quick Facts

Ouchi Biography

William G. Ouchi (1943-) is a professor in UCLA's Anderson School of Management, where he was first appointed in 1979. His theory Z book was a *New York Times* bestseller, has been published in 14 foreign editions, and is the seventh most widely held title of the 12 million titles held in 4,000 libraries in this country. His most recent book, *Making Schools Work: A Revolutionary Plan to Get Your Children the Education They Need* is based on a study of 223 schools in six cities across the nation. Among his conclusions is that schools that perform consistently better have the most decentralized management systems, so that principals and not more remote administrators in a central office control school budgets and personnel.

Source: UCLA Anderson School of Management website. www.Anderson.ucla.edu

workers receive longer periods of training before they are ready to move up through the ranks. However, this also allows employees within an organization to learn all the intricacies of its operation. The purpose of prolonged in-depth training is to create a highly developed workforce who will know a great deal about the organization by the time they are promoted to a higher level, thereby producing a better manager. Further, the emphasis on training creates loyal employees who look at cross-training as grooming for a lifetime career. Accordingly, the increased knowledge empowers employees, relegating management to more of a "coaching" role, in which their main function is to support employees rather than act as traditional, rule-based supervisors.

Critique of Bridging Theories

Bridging theories, in a sense, simultaneously confirm and disconfirm both traditional and open systems theories. In so doing, they place traditional and open systems theories into a perspective of being useful, given appropriate qualifications. Barnard's and March and Simon's statements provide helpful orientations that are, however, somewhat limited by the absence of understandable guidelines as to their applications. Contingency theories of organizations rest on relatively limited research, often involving small samples of specific types of organizations. This, added to the fact that some of the important research has been done abroad in a similar but different culture, does not provide powerful data from which to generalize. Nonetheless, contingency theories of organizations provide an alternative and promising way in which to think about organizations as monolithic types—either closed or open.

Critical Thinking Question

1. "Administrative man" is characterized in four different ways. Do you think that is how work is for administrators? Why?

SYNTHESIS AND PROGNOSIS

Table 5.4 summarized the three major streams of thought: (1) traditional theories, (2) open systems, and (3) bridging theories. Note that Table 5.4 also illustrated the interrelationships among the theories. For example, McGregor's theory Y and Likert's system 4 are consistent with each other. There is not, however, an absolute correlation among all theories found under the same major heading; whereas Argyris's state of maturity is compatible with both theory Y and system 4, it falls only within the same stream of thought as the Hawthorne studies. Thus, the use of Table 5.4 depends in some measure on knowledge gained in the preceding pages. Throughout this chapter, reference has also been made at various points to material covered that was not a theory of organization. To repeat, the purpose of including it was to connect systems of thought as they were developed. Therefore, Table 5.4 included macrotheories of organization along with some microlevel statements. Table 5.4 provided a comprehensive and easily understood overview of the theories covered and illustrated their interconnectedness.

For the vast majority of all organizations in the world, including the police, the bureaucratic model is going to remain overwhelmingly the dominant type of structure. This does not mean that police administrators should ignore or fail to try to reduce dysfunctional aspects of bureaucracy; rather, reform efforts will generally take the form of improvements in how the bureaucratic model operates and is experienced by both employees and clients as opposed to abandoning it altogether. As discussed more fully in Chapter 6, Organizational Design, the police have experimented with structures that are alternatives to the bureaucratic model.

Attempts to modify bureaucracy may succeed temporarily in large police departments, if only because such efforts produce a Hawthorne effect. However, in large-scale organizations over time, the latent power of bureaucracy will assert itself—because it remains a superior form of organization for which there is no viable long-term alternative—and efforts such as team policing will largely fall away. The long-term implementation of true alternative models to the bureaucratic model may be possible only in smaller police departments of less than 100 officers. This smaller scale facilitates interpersonal and group processes, such as communication, which can help maintain and institutionalize alternatives to the bureaucratic model. This is not a call to abandon efforts or experimentation with alternative organizational structures in policing; it is a call for realism and reason. The human systems approach is flawed by its small-group orientation in what is largely a large-scale organizational world. The data supporting the humanists, who make up a good part of the behavioral systems theorists, are suspect on the basis of the often deductive posturing of this approach. What is left is that police managers must accept the bureaucratic form as a fact and embrace elements of the open systems perspective largely on faith. Bridging theories, particularly contingency, represent a potentially rich source of satisfying the organizational imperatives of efficiency and effectiveness and of accommodating the needs of sworn officers and civilian employees.

Critical Thinking Question

1. Do you agree or disagree with the assertion that the bureaucratic model is going to remain as the dominant form for most organizations? Why? What alternatives are there realistically for the majority of organizations?

CHAPTER REVIEW

1. State why organizations exist.
   The basic rationale for the existence of organizations is that they do those things that people are unwilling or unable to do for themselves.
2. Identify and give examples of the four types of organizations that result from asking *cui bono*.

These are (1) mutual benefit (e.g., police unions); (2) business concerns (the owners of Microsoft stock); (3) service organizations (community mental health centers); and (4) commonweal organizations (the military, police departments).

3. What is the key issue for the police as a commonweal organization?
   The issue is how to respond to (1) external pressure (the public expects the police to be responsive to democratic control, but the police must also be bureaucratically governed within and efficient and (2) internal pressures (police officers do not want to be treated like cogs in a machine and want some voice in how the department operates). Stated more succinctly, how do police administrators meet both society's and officers' needs?
4. Define traditional organizational theory.
   It is a body of thought that developed over centuries and crystallized between 1900 and 1940.
5. Discuss scientific management.
   Its father was F. W. Taylor; its essence was to find the one best way to perform tasks.
6. Describe how the exception principle operates.
   Developed by F. W. Taylor, the exception principle requires that routine decisions are to be made at the lowest level of the organization, where they can be made effectively, while unusual or "exceptions" are referred to higher authority for resolution.
7. Identify Henry Gantt's most important contribution.
   In 1917, he developed a chart which was revolutionary for its time because it identified time and not quantity as the most important variable in planning.
8. The bureaucratic form of organization is most closely associated with whom for what reasons?
   No name is more closely linked to bureaucracy than Max Weber. While he did not invent it, he described its features and spawned the formal study of it. While Weber saw bureaucracy as the most efficient form of organization, he was also concerned that its very efficiency was a threat to individual freedom by its impersonal and oppressive routines and he was critical of the petty bureaucrats it tended to create.
9. Discuss administrative theory.
   Administrative, or management, theory sought to identify generic or universal methods of administration which could be used in all organizations. It has a "how-to" orientation and is sometimes called "the principles" approach. Its benchmark was the 1937 publication of Gulick and Urick's edited Papers on the Science of Administration. *At the risk of oversimplification, the principles approach both operationalizes and reinforces features of the bureaucratic model (e.g., control). Henri Fayol was another key contributor to this school of thought with his 1916 book* General and Industrial Management; *it was also a "principles approach" (e.g., the scalar principle, unity of command, unity of direction) reinforcing the bureaucratic model.*
10. Critique traditional organizational theory.
    Criticisms of traditional organization have largely come from organizational humanists who fundamentally see it as being overcontrolling and keeping people in immature/dependent states. Scientific management has been dismissed because of its "man as machine" orientation. Herbert Simon argues that the principles are like proverbs, occurring in pairs which are both plausible and contradictory. Others have defended bureaucracy, noting that most criticisms are dogmatic, qualitative arguments which lack "empirical trimmings." Perror maintains that all of this preoccupation with "humanizing" organization keeps us from assessing bureaucracy's true nature and impact on society, and Goodsell asks, "How can any single human creation be so universally terrible in so many ways?" The bureaucratic model is not going away in our lifetime simply because there it

offers a high degree of control and is efficient despite its shortcomings. What needs to be done is to embrace the bureaucratic model, while implementing processes which eradicate or minimize its less desirable features.

11. Define the human relations school.
The human relations school, founded by the work of Elton May, arose in reaction to the mechanistic orientation of traditional organizational theory, which seemed to ignore the human element in organizations. It has three major divisions, or stems: (1) human relations, (2) behavioral systems theory, and (3) open systems theory.

12. Explain the Hawthorne effect.
It arose out of Elton Mayo's studies of the Western Electric Company's plant in Hawthorne, near Chicago. He changed working conditions (e.g., increased the lighting and gave or took away "perks"). To his surprise, even when things changed unfavorably, productivity increased, leading to the observation (the Hawthorne effect) that people being studied change. The study also (1) identified the role of the informal work group as being a very powerful determinant of how much people produced and limited the effect of financial incentive programs and (2) there is a difference between formal and informal leadership.

13. Describe Maslow's needs hierarchy.
A motivational theory initially developed in 1943, it received further development in Maslow's Motivation and Personality *(1954). The model has five levels ranging from its base (physiological needs) to its apex, or top (self-actualization). It is typically depicted as a pyramid. Its popularity seems to rest on its simplicity.*

14. Identify and define hygiene and motivation factors.
These factors are associated with Herzberg's Work and the Nature of Man *(1966), which grew out of earlier research. It is a motivational theory. Hygiene factors, which were later called maintenance factors (e.g., supervisory factors and working conditions), do not motivate people; instead, if properly provided for, they keep job dissatisfaction and avoid a deterioration of job performance, keeping the organization "healthy." The greater the amount of dissatisfaction, the harder it is for the motivators to be effective. Motivators (e.g., achievement, increased responsibility, and advancement possibilities) do just what the label suggests; they motivate people.*

15. Discuss the relationship between the human relations school (in the Hawthorne studies tradition) and behavioral systems theory.
By 1960, the human relations school in the Hawthorne tradition was losing its appeal. A post-1950 movement and the successor to the human relations school in the Hawthorne tradition was behavioral systems theory. Behavioral systems theory saw organizations as being formed by interrelated parts; the work of behavioral systems theory was to make organizations more democratic and participative.

16. State why the work of Kurt Lewin is notable.
Lewin is perhaps best known for being the father of behavioral systems theory. He had wide interests in leadership and group dynamics. He also developed an important tool, force-field analysis, which is still in use today.

17. Explain what Homans meant when he used the terms "internal systems" and "external systems."
Much of Homans's work was in the field of group dynamics. He advanced the idea that groups have internal systems (e.g., the feelings which group members have about each other) and external systems (e.g., the policies and procedures that apply to all group members).

18. Describe the immaturity–maturity and the mix model.
These concepts were developed by Argyris; he believed organizations tend to make people passive and dependent (because they have certain properties, such as a narrow span of

control, which subjects subordinates to close supervision), interfering with their growth from an immature to a mature state (characterized by self-initiative and deeper interests). To resolve this problem, he developed the mix model, the intent of which was to accommodate the interests of the organization and employees without favoring either interest.

19. Define theory X and theory Y.
Organizations tend to make assumptions about the nature of the people in them; these assumptions can reflect less favorably (theory X, e.g., the average person has an inherent dislike for work and will avoid it if possible) or more favorably (the capacity for people to be imaginative and creative is widely, not narrowly, spread throughout the organization). Douglas McGregor developed theory X–theory Y, identifying a number of theory X and theory Y statements.

20. What is the relationship between Likert's four types of management systems and McGregor's theory X–theory Y?
These two sets of theories are entirely compatible. Likert's system 1 management is consistent with McGregor's theory X statements and Likert's system 4 parallels McGregor's theory Y statements. Likert's system 2 and then system 3 management systems represent a movement away from theory X (system 1) and toward theory Y (system 4).

21. Explain the concept of organizational development.
Organizational development is a concept with close ties to the organizational humanist Warren Bennis, who was critical of the bureaucratic model. Basically, organizational development is a process which relies on behavioral science knowledge to improve the performance of organizations, making them more democratic and participative. Organizational development has two separate but related branches: (1) laboratory training, where organizational members come together in small groups to work on actual problems and receive feedback about how other members of the group perceived it was like working with them and (2) survey research, which conducts surveys and then "plays back" the data to employees in workshop sessions to create new awareness and to promote change. In both models, the creation of awareness is intended to be the basis for personal change and organizational improvement.

22. Discuss open systems theory.
Open systems theory can be thought about broadly or narrowly. In the broad context, it is a way of thinking about organizations which has three major divisions: (1) the human relations school, (2) behavioral systems theory, and (3) open systems theory (using the term narrowly). In the more narrow context, open systems theory is a specific way of describing how an organization functions. It comprises of five subsystems: (1) managerial, (2) technical, (3) structural, (4) psychosocial, and (5) goals and values. All organizations move toward their disorganization or death (the entropic process). To survive, they must combat entropy by acquiring negative entropy, meaning they must be able to import energy (e.g., annual budgets, new members, etc.) and usefully process the energy. Over time, organizations develop subsystems to help them import, store, and process energy. This produces a steady (but not motionless) state, which is constantly adjusting to inputs from the organization's larger environment.

23. Discuss how chaos theory and quantum theory may help police administrators understand their environment.
Roughly over the past decade, there has been a growth in the literature which seeks to draw on models from the physical and biological sciences and to modify and apply them to administration; chaos and quantum theory are part of this development.
Chaos theory notes that sometimes things seem or are out of control; recent examples include the September 11, 2001, attacks on this country by radical Muslim terrorists and Hurricane Katrina, whose impact simply overwhelmed existing systems and resources.

Chaos theory postulates that, under such overwhelming conditions, new and often spontaneous systems spring up (e.g., off-duty medical personnel rushing to hospitals and the Twin Towers to help or people with boats organizing themselves to help people stranded on roofs by flooding) which are based on the recognition that ultimately we are mutually dependent on each other. These small, helpful actions, repeated numerous times by "people pitching in," have a "butterfly effect," which ripples across the community, helping to bring things back under control. The key task for a police administrator is to quickly identify and support people involved in the butterfly effect, which—in support of formal systems—help bring things back under control.

Social science quantum theory acknowledges that there are some things in certain situations we do not know about and may never know about and, if we did, we might not understand them. Even after the passage of time, the "whys" or "hows" of some situations may remain invisible to us. Still, things have to get done; we can't allow ourselves to "get locked down" or paralyzed. Thus, we try to fill in the "gaps" by making what seems to us to be reasonable assumptions. When we do so, we create our own realities and gone is any objective reality. Quantum theory encourages administrators to go forward in some situations with the best data or reality they can forge. It is axiomatic that premature decisions (when you don't have all of the data you need to effectively make them) can create difficulties. Quantum theory responds to that by saying occasionally the situation is so dire, the need so great, that delaying a decision until you get perfect data will have catastrophic consequences and sometimes you simply have to go ahead based on your best present understanding of the reality of the situation.

24. Critique open systems theory.

Mayo's human relations school rests on research whose methods are questionable; the research places too much emphasis on the informal group and attention on individuals and groups was at the expense of the organization. Ironically, the human relations school is also criticized as having a pro-management bias—it sees unions as promoting conflict between workers and management at the expense of workplace harmony. The human relations school also rests on the implicit notion that "contended cows give more milk" or that there is a relationship between job satisfaction and productivity. However, there is no consistent relationship between job satisfaction and productivity.

The work of some open systems theorists rests on shaky ground: Maslow's needs hierarchy is based on a small study of clinically neurotic people and research on Herzberg's motivation–hygiene model produces results which range from general support to vigorous condemnation. Argyris's and McGregor's models essentially set up "straw men" arguments (bureaucracy is "bad"), which are knocked down by the qualitative humanistic statements. While humanists claim a narrow span of control promotes overly close supervision, there is some research evidence of just the opposite: it promotes closer collaboration in problem solving.

Humanist models depend on open and honest communication, yet such views are in conflict with the reality that, when authenticity (honesty) meets power, there are often some adverse consequences.

25. Define bridging theories.

These are theories or models which do not fit neatly into either traditional organizational theory or open systems theory, displaying instead elements associated with both of these schools.

KEY TERMS

Adaptive mechanism: a concept which focuses on an organization's methods for obtaining the resources it needs to function.

Administrative theory: a theory sought to identify generic or universal methods and principles of management which applied to all organizations, it is also referred to as the principles approach to management and has a "how to" orientation.

Chris Argyris: advanced the immaturity–maturity and mix models; he believed organizations had certain properties (e.g., narrow span of control, which made people passive and submissive) which got in the way of people moving from immaturity to maturity (characterized by such factors as self-initiative and deeper interests); Argyris believed that you could not simultaneously maximize the needs of the organization and those of its employees; the mix model was a way of trying to make some accommodation for both types of interests.

Behavioral systems theory: one of the major divisions of the open systems model, basically a post-1950 movement; by 1960, human relations in the tradition of the Hawthorne studies lacked vitality; behavioral systems theory was its successor and saw organizations as comprised of interrelated behaviors; its major concern was making organizations more democratic and participative.

Warren Bennis: an organizational humanist interested in organizational development; organizational development is the process by which knowledge of the behavioral sciences is used to move organizations toward greater effectiveness and improved quality of life for employees.

Bridging organizational theory: models which neither fit neatly into the traditional or open systems streams of thinking about organizations, reflecting some affinity for both camps.

Bureaucratic model: a form of formal organization which had, according to Max Weber, a series of characteristics, such as the principle of hierarchy, division of labor, a system of rational rules, and the appointment of employees on the basis of qualifications.

Chain of command: initially called the scalar principle; the lowest-ranking person in an organization reports to his or her immediate supervisor; this process is repeated all the way to the "big boss" of the organization.

Chaos theory: a theory that has its roots in open systems theory; when things appear out of control (and may actually be so), regaining control is often difficult, yet, in such events as Hurricane Katrina, new structures and processes often spontaneously emerge which are based on the recognition that we are mutually dependent on one another; these small, helpful actions have a ripple effect (the butterfly effect) as they move through the community, helping to bring things under control; essentially, even in apparently chaotic situations there are underlying orderly things happening; from an administrative perspective, there is a need to quickly identify and support those things so as to more readily end the chaotic conditions.

Charismatic authority: authority which stems from some outstanding quality in a person, such as because he or she is a hero and is of exemplary character or of exceptional sanctity or piety.

Contingency theory: a bridging theory which says there is no one best way to organize, lead, or motivate people and that it all depends on a number of factors which have to be specified (e.g., the nature of the work and its complexity and the capabilities of employees).

Cui bono: Who benefits? Blau and Scott used this question to identify four types of organizations: mutual benefit, business, service, and commonweal.

Division of labor: tasks are grouped and performed by qualified employees who have received special training, the net result of which is specialization within the organization (e.g., patrol, traffic, detective, and crime scene units).

Dysfunction of bureaucracy: associated with Merton, it notes that the structure, rigidity, and overbearing formality of the bureaucratic model can make it dysfunctional and unresponsive to its members and the clients it is supposed to serve; this criticism echoes those which Weber made: petty, self-serving, security-seeking bureaucrats can come to cling to oppressive routines for getting the work done and therefore lack creativity and spontaneity when handling problems.

Exception principle: routine matters should be handled at the lowest possible level, where the decisions can be made effectively; unusual or exceptional matters should be referred to higher levels of management for handling (i.e., sent up the chain of command).

Force-field analysis: a basic but powerful visual analysis tool, developed by Lewin, which identifies the driving and restraining forces in a situation.

Functional supervision: certain tasks or functions can be handled by a single supervisor or manager even if it involves people and resources from other units who report to other supervisors or managers on other matters on a day-to-day basis.

Gantt chart: a chart named after Charles Gantt, who developed it in 1917; it was radical then in that it asserted that *time, not quantity,* was the key factor in planning.

Hawthorne studies: a five-year series of studies at the Western Electric Company's Chicago plant; they were led by Elton Mayo; his associate, Fritz Roethlisberger; and to some extent the plant manager, William Dickson. Among the findings of these studies was the "Hawthorne effect" (people being studied change) and human relations or social norms among workers was as important as financial incentives and working conditions in determining on-the-job behavior; the identification of the informal group in determining productivity and work habits was a stunning revelation.

Frederick Herzberg: developed the theory of motivation–hygiene; hygiene factors (e.g., supervisory practices, status, working conditions) couldn't motivate workers, but if fulfilled, they could prevent dissatisfaction from setting in; motivators included such variables as achievement, recognition, challenging work.

George Homans: a contemporary of Lewin's; he advanced the idea that groups have internal systems (e.g., how members of the group feel about each other) and external systems (the administrative policies and practices to which the group is subject).

Integrative mechanisms: the mechanisms which are the institutional or organizational patterns of linking them to the larger society as a whole (e.g., mobilizing political and other support, so that the organization can attain its goals).

Human relations school: one of the three major divisions of open systems theory; the human relations school was founded by Elton Mayo's Hawthorne studies and developed in reaction to the wooden, mechanistic orientation of the bureaucratic model.

Knapp Commission: a commission that studied corruption in the New York City Police Department (NYPD) in 1972; among its findings were there were "grass-eaters" (officers who took whatever bribes happened to come their way) and "meat-eaters" (officers who aggressively sought out opportunities to get bribes).

Kurt Lewin: the father of the behavioral systems school; he had a major interest in group dynamics and sensitivity training.

Rensis Likert: developed the 5-point Likert Scale, which is still being used; he was interested in organizational climates and identified four systems of climate from Exploitive to participative; he contrasted man-to-man (traditional organizations) and linkpin (democratic, open organizations).

Abraham Maslow: developed the needs hierarchy theory of motivation.

Elton Mayo: father of the human relations school of management.

Douglas McGregor: articulated theory X and theory Y; organizations make assumptions about the nature of people; McGregor lists both theory X (negative assumptions) and theory Y (positive) assumptions.

Needs hierarchy: a five-level motivational model, initially developed in 1943 by Abraham Maslow, which is usually depicted as a pyramid; the highest level of the hierarchy is self actualization, or the need to test one's own potential and gain a sense of self-fulfullment.

Open systems theory: in the broadest sense, a line of thinking about organizations with three major divisions (human relations, behavioral systems, and open systems) which is a counterpoint to the bureaucratic model; open systems are described as flexible and organic, adapting to the world with which they interact; in the narrow sense, a model of organizations which is based on how they import and transform energy to achieve their goals and receive feedback about how well they are doing; in this view, the organization comprises five subsystems: managerial, goals and values, technical, structural, and psychosocial.

Operative code: a code that explains how an organization's goals are achieved through internal mechanisms (e.g., policymaking, delegation of authority, and decision making) which allocate resources.

Talcott Parsons: among other contributions, he worked for a "grand, overarching," or umbrella, theory which would integrate the social sciences.

Principle of hierarchy: each lower office or unit is under the supervision of a higher authority, which leads all the way to the top of the organization.

Quality circles: a widespread form of employee participation groups in which participants who volunteered met and developed recommendations to improve quality; as community-oriented policing spread in this country beginning in the early 1980s, policing Quality Circles (QCs) disappeared because implicit in Community Oriented Policing (COP) was the notion of quality.

Quantum theory: the theory that there are, in many situations, "indeterministic (unknowable) elements," things which we cannot know (they are "invisible") or sometimes cannot even understand; to resolve these "gaps" in our understanding, we develop assumptions which seem reasonable and base our decision making on these assumptions; in this context and in such situations, the expectation of an "objective reality" and simple cause-and-effect relationships are gone; in their place is uncertainty and the "reality" which each person (often differently) constructs.

Rate buster: someone who produces more than the amount he or she was expected to, thereby raising management's expectations for other workers (and perhaps resulting in management raising everyone's rate, meaning workers would be working harder and producing more for the same amount of pay).

Rational–legal authority: Weber identified this as a formal grant of authority from an organization to one of its members (e.g., promoting officers to sergeants); as sergeants, they have the backing of the police department for their decisions and actions, as long as such are consistent with departmental guidelines, are lawful, and so on.

Scientific management: a theory based on finding the one best way to do a job; it involved a careful study of job to eliminate wasted effort and to promote efficiency; flourished in the late 19th century and early 20th century and led to time and motion studies and the field of operations research.

F. W. Taylor: the father of scientific management.

Theory X: a series of negative assumptions which organizations make about the nature of people.

Theory Y: a series of positive statements which organizations make about the nature of people.

Theory Z: a theory popularized by William Ouchi; it is sometimes referred to as the "Japanese style" of management and its tenets reflect that country's culture (e.g., workers and management are both responsible for the success of the company).

Traditional authority: authority that rests on long-held beliefs, such as people accepting the rule of kings.

Traditional organizational theory: a body of knowledge which developed over several centuries and crystallized between 1900 and 1940; organizations based on traditional organizational theory are often described as bureaucratic, mechanistic, and stable to the point of tending to be change-resistant.

Unity of command: an employee should receive orders from only one supervisor for a particular task.

Value system: in an organization, the value system defines and legitimatizes its goals; it gives definition to the organization's purpose and guides the purposes and activities of its members.

Max Weber: often credited with developing the bureaucratic organizational model, he was, instead, the towering intellect who systematically recorded its characteristics and promoted study of it.

Work flow analysis: identifying all of the steps involved in completing any type of work; the end result of it is to identify blockages and wasted effort to promote efficiency.

NOTES

1. Amitai Etzioni, *Modern Organizations* (Englewood Cliffs, N.J.: Prentice Hall, 1964), p. 1.
2. Ibid., with some additions.
3. Ibid.
4. Talcott Parsons, *Structure and Process in Modern Societies* (Glencoe, Ill.: Free Press, 1960), p. 17.
5. Edgar H. Schein, *Organizational Psychology* (Englewood Cliffs, N.J.: Prentice Hall, 1965), p. 9.
6. Peter W. Blau and W. Richard Scott, *Formal Organizations* (Scranton, Pa.: Chandler, 1962), p. 43, with some changes.
7. The treatment of the central issues of the four types of formal organizations is taken from Blau and Scott, *Formal Organizations*, pp. 43, 55, with some changes.
8. Daniel A. Wren, *The Evolution of Management Thought* (New York: Ronald Press, 1972), p. 112.
9. Ibid., p. 114.
10. Ibid., pp. 114–15.
11. See the testimony of F. W. Taylor before the Special Committee of the House of Representatives Hearings to Investigate Taylor and Other Systems of Shop Management, January 25, 1912, p. 1387.
12. Wren, *Evolution of Management Thought*, p. 115.
13. Frederick W. Taylor, *Principles of Scientific Management* (New York: Harper & Row, 1911), pp. 44–47, with minor restatement.
14. See Frederick W. Taylor, *Shop Management* (New York: Harper and Brothers, 1911), for a discussion of this concept.
15. Ibid., p. 126.
16. Wren, *Evolution of Management Thought*, p. 132. Not only did Bethlehem Steel abandon the system, but it also fired Taylor.
17. Ibid., p. 131.
18. L. P. Alford, *Henry Lawrence Gantt* (Easton-Hive Management Series: No. 6, 1972; facsimile reprint of a 1934 edition by Harper and Brothers), pp. 207, 209.
19. Sudhir Kakar, *Frederick Taylor: A Study in Personality and Innovation* (Cambridge, Mass.: MIT Press, 1973), p. 2.
20. Fremont E. Kast and James E. Rosenzweig, *Contingency Views of Organization and Management* (Chicago: Science Research Associates, 1973), p. 7.

21. Michael Crozier, *The Bureaucratic Phenomenon* (Chicago: University of Chicago Press, 1964), p. 3.
22. Max Weber, *The Theory of Social and Economic Organization,* trans. A. M. Henderson and Talcott Parsons (New York: Free Press, 1947), p. 337.
23. Ibid.
24. Ibid., pp. 330–32, with limited restatement for clarity.
25. Ibid., p. 328.
26. On this point, see Nicos P. Mouzelis, *Organization and Bureaucracy* (Chicago: Aldine, 1967), pp. 20–21 and footnote 29 of that work.
27. H. H. Gerth and C. Wright Mills, *From Max Weber: Essays in Sociology* (New York: Oxford University Press, 1946), p. 50.
28. Wren, *Evolution of Management Thought,* p. 230.
29. Henri Fayol, *General and Industrial Management,* trans. Constance Storrs (London: Sir Isaac Pitman, 1949), p. vi.
30. Ibid., pp. 19–41.
31. Ibid., p. 34.
32. The 1939 edition was coauthored, but the 1947 edition appeared under Mooney's name.
33. Luther Gulick, "Notes on the Theory of Organization," in *Papers on the Science of Administration,* ed. Luther Gulick and L. Urwick (New York: August M. Kelley, a 1969 reprint of the 1937 edition), p. 13.
34. L. Urwick, "Organization as a Technical Problem," in Gulick and Urwick, *Papers on the Science of Administration,* p. 52.
35. Taylor, *Shop Management,* p. 184.
36. Warren Bennis, "Organizational Developments and the Fate of Bureaucracy," *Industrial Management Review* 7, no. 2 (spring 1966): 41–55.
37. This section on the dysfunction of bureaucracy is adapted from Merton's original work. See Robert K. Merton, *Social Theory and Social Structure* (Glencoe, Ill.: Free Press, 1957), pp. 195–206.
38. Ibid.
39. Ibid., p. 200.
40. Herbert A. Simon, *Administrative Behavior* (New York: Free Press, 1945), p. 20. For additional criticism of the principles approach, see Dwight Waldo, *The Administrative State* (New York: Ronald Press, 1948).
41. J. Hage, "An Axiomatic Theory of Organizations," *Administrative Science Quarterly* 10 (1965–1966): 305, table 4.
42. Charles Perrow, *Complex Organizations* (Glenview, Ill.: Scott, Foresman, 1972), pp. 6–7.
43. Charles T. Goodsell, *The Case for Bureaucracy,* 2nd ed. (Chatham, N.J.: Chatham House, 1985), p. 11.
44. Ibid., pp. 11–12.
45. Alvin W. Gouldner, "Metaphysical Pathos and the Theory of Bureaucracy," *American Political Science Review* 49 (June 1955): 501, as quoted by Goodsell, *The Case for Bureaucracy,* p. 12.
46. Goodsell, *The Case for Bureaucracy,* pp. 12–13.
47. Ibid., p. 29.
48. As early as 1924, researchers from the National Academy of Sciences had experiments under way; for present purposes, the work at the Hawthorne plant is described following the arrival of Mayo.
49. The definitive report of this research is by F. J. Roethlisberger and William J. Dickson, *Management and the Worker* (Cambridge, Mass.: Harvard University Press, 1939). Roethlisberger came from Harvard with Mayo, while Dickson was a company administrator.
50. The designation of this study as the bank wiring study is also found in the literature; banks were telephone switchboards.
51. There were actually two relay assembly test room studies, one following the other. The second involved a change in the wage incentive and confirmed the importance of the social group.
52. Roethlisberger and Dickson, *Management and the Worker,* pp. 58–59, 180–83.
53. Bertram M. Gross, *The Managing of Organizations,* Vol. 1 (New York: Free Press, 1964), p. 163.
54. Roethlisberger and Dickson, *Management and the Worker,* p. 522.
55. On this point, see ibid., pp. 179–86, 448–58.
56. During the last two weeks of the switchboard wiring room study, there was a new supervisor, "Group Chief 2," who acted much more formally than did "Group Chief 1"; "GC-2" was regarded as a "company man." See ibid., pp. 452–53.
57. Ibid., pp. 21, 397.
58. Etzioni, *Modern Organizations,* pp. 34–37.
59. Whitman Knapp, chairman, Commission to Investigate Allegations of Police Corruption and the City's Anti-Corruption Procedures, *Commission Report* (New York, 1972), pp. 4, 65; see also Herman Goldstein, *Police Corruption* (Washington, D.C.: Police Foundation, 1975).
60. See Talcott Parsons, "Suggestions for a Sociological Approach to the Theory of Organizations," *Administrative Science Quarterly* 1 (1956): 63–85, 225–39.

61. Ibid.
62. Ibid.
63. A. H. Maslow, "A Theory of Human Motivation," *Psychological Review* 50 (July 1943): 370–96.
64. These five elements are identified in A. H. Maslow, *Motivation and Personality* (New York: Harper and Brothers, 1954), pp. 80–92. Maslow later added a sixth category, "metamotivation," but it has never received substantial interest. See "A Theory of Metamotivation," *Humanitas* 4 (1969): 301–43.
65. Ibid., p. 91.
66. Robert M. Chiaramonte, "The Blue Max Award," *Police Chief* 11, no. 4 (1973): 24–25.
67. Wren, *Evolution of Management Thought,* p. 324. Lewin lived in this country for the 15 years preceding his death in 1947.
68. Ibid., p. 325.
69. Ibid.
70. This case is reported in Paul Hersey and Kenneth H. Blanchard, *Management of Organizational Behavior,* 3rd ed. (Englewood Cliffs, N.J.: Prentice Hall, 1977), p. 139, with credit to "The Truth Hurts," *Wall Street Journal,* no date. One of the key critics of T-groups has been George Odiorne.
71. George C. Homans, *The Human Group* (New York: Harcourt Brace, 1950), pp. 81–130.
72. Chris Argyris, *Personality and Organization: The Conflict between System and the Individual* (New York: Harper and Brothers, 1957), pp. 58–66.
73. Ibid., pp. 76–122.
74. Chris Argyris, *Integrating the Individual and the Organization* (New York: John Wiley & Sons, 1964), p. 3.
75. For extended treatment of this subject, see ibid., pp. 146–91.
76. Ibid., p. 147.
77. Douglas McGregor, *The Human Side of Enterprise* (New York: McGraw-Hill, 1960), p. 6. See also Louis A. Allen, "M for Management: Theory Y Updated," *Personnel Journal* 52, no. 12 (1973): 1061–67.
78. Ibid., p. 7.
79. Ibid., pp. 33–57.
80. The information on QCs is drawn from W. Troy McClain, "Focus on 'Quality Circles': In Quest of Improved Police Productivity," *Police Chief* 52, no. 9 (1985): 50–54; and Joyce L. Roll and David L. Roll, "The Potential for Application of Quality Circles in the American Public Sector," *Public Productivity Review* 7 (June 1983): 122–42.
81. Rensis Likert, *The Human Organization* (New York: McGraw-Hill, 1967), p. 109.
82. Charles R. Swanson and Susette Talarico, "Politics and Law Enforcement: Implications of Police Perspectives" (paper presented at the 1979 meeting of the Academy of Criminal Justice Sciences), the appendix, table 6.
83. Likert, *The Human Organization,* pp. 50–51.
84. Wendell L. French and Cecil H. Bell, Jr., *Organizational Development* (Englewood Cliffs, N.J.: Prentice Hall, 1973), p. xiv.
85. Ibid., p. 21.
86. Ibid., pp. 21–25.
87. Ibid., pp. 25–26.
88. Ibid., p. 24.
89. Warren G. Bennis, *Changing Organizations* (New York: McGraw-Hill, 1966), p. 118.
90. Stephen P. Robbins, *The Administrative Process* (Englewood Cliffs, N.J.: Prentice Hall, 1976), p. 259.
91. Ibid.
92. Daniel Katz and Robert Kahn, *The Social Psychology of Organization,* 2nd ed. (New York: John Wiley & Sons, 1978), pp. 23–30, with some change.
93. Kast and Rosenzweig, *Contingency Views,* pp. 13–15, with changes and additions.
94. E. Sam Overman, "The New Science of Administration," *Public Administration Review* 56, no. 5 (September/October 1996): 487. Some of this author's ideas have been written into a police context by the authors.
95. Ibid.
96. Theodore L. Becker, *Quantum Politics: Applying Quantum Theory to Political Phenomena* (New York: Praeger, 1991).
97. Margaret J. Wheatley, *Leadership and the New Science* (San Francisco: Berrett-Koehler, 1992).
98. L. Douglas Kiel, *Managing Chaos and Complexity in Government* (San Francisco: Jossey-Bass, 1994).
99. Danah Zohar and Ian Marshall, *The Quantum Society* (New York: William Morrow, 1994).
100. Linda F. Dennard, "The New Paradigm in Science and Administration," *Public Administration Review* 56, no. 5 (September/October 1996): 495.
101. Ibid.
102. Ibid., 496. While Dennard writes generically about these questions, the authors have written her cogent ideas into a police context.
103. Overman, "The New Science of Administration," 487.
104. Ibid.
105. Ibid.
106. Ibid., 488.
107. Ibid., 487.
108. Ibid., 489.

109. Ibid.
110. Ibid., 490.
111. Ibid., 489.
112. This example of a performance evaluation is drawn, with restatement, from ibid., 489–90.
113. The Hawthorne studies have continued to excite the imagination. See, for instance, H. W. Parsons, "What Caused the Hawthorne Effect?" *Administration and Society* 10 (November 1978): 259–83, and Henry Lansberger, *Hawthorne Revisited* (Ithaca, N.Y.: Cornell University Press, 1958).
114. These points are drawn, with change, from William H. Knowles, "Human Relations in Industry: Research and Concepts," *California Management Review* 2, no. 2 (fall 1958): 87–105.
115. Etzioni, *Modern Organizations,* p. 39.
116. Edward E. Lawler, *Motivation in Work Organizations* (Monterey, Calif.: Brooks/Cole, 1973), p. 62.
117. Edwin A. Locke, "The Nature and Cause of Job Satisfaction," in *Handbook of Industrial and Organizational Psychology,* ed. Marvin D. Dunnette (Chicago: Rand McNally, 1976), p. 1332.
118. In this regard, see A. H. Brayfield and W. H. Crockett, "Employee Attitudes and Employee Performance," *Psychological Bulletin* 52 (September 1955): 394–424; V. H. Vroom, *Motivation and Work* (New York: John Wiley & Sons, 1964); John P. Wanous, "A Causal-Correlation Analysis of the Job Satisfaction and Performance Relationship," *Journal of Applied Psychology* 59 (April 1974): 139–44; Niger Nicholson, Toby Wall, and Joe Lischerson, "The Predictability of Absence and Propensity to Leave from Employees' Job Satisfaction and Attitudes toward Influence in Decision Making," *Human Relations* 30 (June 1977): 449–514; Philip H. Mirvis and Edward E. Lawler III, "Measuring the Financial Impact of Employee Attitudes," *Journal of Applied Psychology* 62 (February 1977): 1–8; Charles L. Hulin, "Effects of Changes in Job Satisfaction Levels on Employee Turnover," *Journal of Applied Psychology* 52 (April 1968): 122–26: A. H. Marrow, D. G. Bowers, and S. E. Seashore, *Management by Participation* (New York: Harper & Row, 1967); L. W. Porter and R. M. Steers, "Organizational Work and Personal Factors Related to Employee Turnover and Absenteeism," *Psychological Bulletin* 80 (August 1973): 151–76; Frederick Herzberg et al., *Job Attitudes: Review of Research and Opinion* (Pittsburgh: Psychological Service of Pittsburgh, 1957); and E. Palmore, "Predicting Longevity: A Follow-Up Controlling for Age," *Gerontologist* 9 (1969): 247–50.
119. See A. W. Kornhauser, *Mental Health of the Industrial Worker: A Detroit Study* (New York: John Wiley & Sons, 1965), and R. J. Burke, "Occupational and Life Strains, Satisfaction, and Mental Health," *Journal of Business Administration* 1 (1969–1970): 35–41.
120. For example, Lyman Porter and Edward Lawler, *Managerial Attitude and Performance* (Homewood, Ill.: Dorsey Press, 1967), John E. Sheridan and John W. Slocum, Jr., "The Direction of the Causal Relationship between Job Satisfaction and Work Performance," *Organizational Behavior and Human Performance* 14 (October 1975): 159–72.
121. Frank K. Gibson and Clyde E. Teasely, "The Humanistic Model of Organizational Motivation: A Review of Research Support," *Public Administration Review* 33, no. 1 (1973): 91. Several of the points made in the treatment of Maslow are drawn from this excellent analysis.
122. Bennis, *Changing Organizations,* p. 196.
123. Walter Nord, "Beyond the Teaching Machine: The Neglected Area of Operant Conditioning in the Theory and Practice of Management," *Organizational Behavior and Human Performance* 4 (November 1969): 375–401; see also Lyman Porter, "Job Attitudes in Management," *Journal of Applied Psychology* 46 (December 1962): 375–84; and Douglas Hall and Khalil Nougaim, "An Examination of Maslow's Need Hierarchy in an Organizational Setting," *Organizational Behavior and Human Performance* 3 (February 1968): 12–35.
124. Maslow, *Motivation and Personality,* pp. 79–80.
125. Gibson and Teasley, "The Humanistic Model," p. 92.
126. Abraham Maslow, *Eupsychian Management: A Journal* (Homewood, Ill.: Dorsey Press, 1965), pp. 55–56.
127. R. E. Johannesson, "Some Problems in the Measurement of Organizational Climate," *Organizational Behavior and Human Performance* 10 (August 1973): 118–44.
128. W. R. Lafollette and H. P. Sims, Jr., "Is Satisfaction Redundant with Organizational Climate?" *Organizational Behavior and Human Performance* 13 (April 1975): 276.
129. J. M. Ivancevich and H. L. Lyon, *Organizational Climate, Job Satisfaction, Role Clarity and Selected Emotional Reaction Variables in a Hospital Milieu* (Lexington: University Press of Kentucky, 1972).
130. Peter Blau, "The Hierarchy of Authority in Organizations," *American Journal of Sociology* 73 (January 1968): 457.

131. Perrow, *Complex Organizations,* p. 38.
132. Bennis, *Changing Organizations,* p. 77.
133. Jobs can be manipulated in three ways: (1) jobs can be broadened by incorporating different tasks from the same skill level, referred to as "job enlargement"; (2) jobs can be made larger by giving some of the supervisor's tasks to the subordinate, called "job enrichment"; and (3) job enlargement and job enrichment may be employed simultaneously, also called "job enrichment."
134. "Doubting Sweden's Way," *Time,* March 10, 1975, p. 44.
135. Walter Buckley, *Sociology and Modern Systems Theory* (Englewood Cliffs, N.J.: Prentice Hall, 1967), p. 43.
136. This concise summary of Barnard's contributions is drawn from Gary Dessler, *Organization and Management* (Upper Saddle River, N.J.: Prentice Hall, 1988), pp. 44–45.
137. Simon, *Administrative Behavior,* p. 220.
138. James G. March and Herbert A. Simon, *Organizations* (New York: John Wiley & Sons, 1958), pp. 136–71.
139. Various names have been associated with theory Z. Writing in 1962, Harold J. Leavitt called for the use of "differentiating" approaches to structure and management, based on traditional and "newer" concepts, but did not use the term "theory Z"; see "Management According to Task: Organizational Differentiation," *Management International* 1 (1962): 13–22. On September 4, 1961, Raymond A. Katzell gave the presidential address to the Division of Industrial Psychology, American Psychological Association, and, after referring to McGregor's theory X and theory Y, called for the use of theory alpha and omega, which combined the best features of McGregor's opposites; see *American Psychologist* 17 (February 1962): 102–8. Later, Lyndall F. Urwick specifically discussed what Leavitt generally, and Katzell more specifically, had addressed; see "Theory Z," *S.A.M. Advanced Management Journal* 35, no. 1 (1970): 14–21. However, it was William Ouchi's work in 1981 that propelled theory Z as a modern contingency theory perspective. See William Ouchi, *Theory Z: How American Management Can Meet the Japanese Challenge* (Cambridge, Mass.: Perseus, 1981).
140. Ouchi, *Theory Z.*

CHAPTER 6

We trained hard . . . but it seemed that every time we were beginning to form up into teams we would be reorganized. . . . I was to learn later in life that we tend to meet any new situation by reorganizing and a wonderful method it can be for creating the illusion of progress while providing confusion, inefficiency and demoralization.

—Petronius, 210 B.C.

OUTLINE

Introduction

Organizing: An Overview

Specialization in Police Agencies

The Principle of Hierarchy

Span of Control vs. Span of Management

Organizational Structure and Design

Types of Organizational Design

Some Unique Organizational Features of Sheriff's Offices

Organizational Structure and Community Policing

Line and Staff Relationships in Police Agencies

The Informal Organization

Expanding the Law Enforcement Personnel Pool

Chapter Review

Key Terms

Notes

OBJECTIVES

1. Discuss the advantages and disadvantages of specialization within an organization.
2. Explain the principle of hierarchy as it relates to organizational design.
3. Describe the concept of span of management.
4. Distinguish between vertical and horizontal differentiation.
5. Discuss the differences between tall organizational structures and flat organizational structures.
6. List and describe four types of structural design.
7. Identify major organizational differences between sheriff's offices and municipal police departments.
8. Discuss how community policing and problem-oriented policing can impact organizational design.
9. Identify the basic causes for tension between line and staff and suggest strategies to be used as solutions.
10. Describe the characteristics of an informal organization.
11. List and describe four ways that law enforcement agencies can supplement their personnel pool.

ORGANIZATIONAL DESIGN

INTRODUCTION

In Chapter 5, Organizational Theory, we discussed the major theoretical concepts associated with organizations and the ways in which they function. In this chapter, we will see how many of these theories are applied in police organizations. We will first discuss the advantages and disadvantages of specialization, then discuss and differentiate between the concepts of span of control and span of management and the types of factors that affect them. We will also address police organizational structures and designs and focus on new spatial levels of differentiation—namely, vertical, which is based on levels of authority, and horizontal, which is based on activity. We will also discuss the four basic types of structural designs typically found in police organizations: line, line and staff, functional, and matrix.

The movement in the past 20 years toward community policing and the problem-oriented policing model has changed the traditional perspective on organizational structures. We will discuss the ways in which this has occurred. The rapid increase in the growth of many police departments and the corresponding growth in their need for support staff have created some conflicts. We will address the reasons for this conflict and suggest solutions. We will also discuss the informal organization. Although it does not appear on any organizational chart, if not attended to, it can have a very negative effect on the formal organization. Last, we will discuss the various uses of citizen volunteers who can be of considerable assistance to law enforcement agencies by supplementing their sometimes limited personnel pool.

ORGANIZING: AN OVERVIEW

Police administrators modify or design the structure of their organization in order to fulfill the mission that has been assigned to the police. An organizational chart reflects the formal structure of task and authority relationships determined to be most suited to accomplishing the police mission. The process of determining this formal structure of task and authority relationships is termed **organizing.** The major concerns in organizing are (1) identifying what jobs need to be done, such as conducting the initial investigation, performing the latent or follow-up investigation, and providing for the custody of physical evidence seized at the scene of a crime; (2) determining how to group the jobs, such as those responsible for patrol, investigation, and the operation of the property room; (3) forming grades of authority, such as officer, detective, corporal, sergeant, lieutenant, and captain; and (4) equalizing responsibility and authority, illustrated by the example that, if a sergeant has the responsibility to supervise seven detectives, that sergeant must have sufficient authority to discharge that responsibility properly or he or she cannot be held accountable for any results.[1]

SPECIALIZATION IN POLICE AGENCIES

Central to this process of organizing is determining the nature and extent of specialization. Some 2,300 years ago, Plato observed that "each thing becomes . . . easier when one man, exempt from other tasks, does one thing."[2] **Specialization,** or the division of labor, is also one of the basic features of traditional organizational theory.[3] As discussed more fully later in this chapter, specialization produces different groups of functional responsibilities, and the jobs allocated to meet those different responsibilities are staffed with people who are believed to be especially qualified to perform those jobs. Thus, specialization is crucial to effectiveness and efficiency in large organizations. However, specialization makes the organizational environment more complex by complicating communication, by increasing the number of units from which cooperation must be obtained, and by creating conflict among differing interests and loyalties. Also, specialization creates greater need for coordination and therefore additional hierarchy and can lead to the creation of narrow jobs that confine the incumbents and stifle their willingness or capacity to work energetically in support of the police department's goals. Police departments are not insensitive to the problems of specialization and attempt through various schemes to avoid the alienation of employees. Personnel can be rotated to different jobs, they can be given additional responsibilities that challenge them, they can be involved in organizational problem solving (such as through the use of quality circles previously discussed in Chapter 5, Organizational Theory), and the police department can try different forms of organizational structures. Thus, although specialization is an essential feature of large-scale organizations, any benefits derived from it have their actual or potential costs.

One of the first police executives to explore systematically the relationship between specialization and the organizational structure was O. W. Wilson.[4] He noted that most small departments do not need to be concerned with widely developed specialization because their patrol officer is a jack-of-all-trades. Conversely, in large departments particular tasks (such as traffic enforcement and criminal investigation) are assigned to special units and/or individuals within the organization. Specialization presents a number of advantages for large departments:

Placement of responsibility—The responsibility for the performance of a given task can be placed on specific units or individuals. For instance, a traffic division is responsible for the investigation of all traffic accidents, and a patrol division is responsible for all requests for general police assistance.

Development of expertise—A narrow field of interest, attention, or skill can be the subject of a specialized unit. For instance, many police agencies have highly skilled special weapons and tactics (SWAT) teams that train regularly to respond to critical incidents, such as terrorist activities, hostage situations, or high-risk search warrants. Advanced training in this area yields increased officer safety and a high degree of expertise. Specialization is also helpful during the investigation of narrowly defined, technical crimes, such as computer fraud, (see Figures 6.1 and 6.2) and bombings (see Figure 6.3).

Promotion of group esprit de corps—Any group of specially trained individuals sharing similar job tasks and to some degree dependent on each other for success tends to form a highly cohesive unit with high morale.

Increased efficiency and effectiveness—Specialized units show a higher degree of proficiency in job task responsibility. For instance, a white-collar fraud unit will ordinarily be more successful in investigating complex computer fraud than a general detective division.[5]

Specialization appears to be a sure path to operational effectiveness. It allows each employee to acquire expertise in one area, so as to maximize his or her contribution to the overall department. However, as noted earlier, specialization has also been associated with increased friction and conflict within police departments. As units such as traffic, detective, and SWAT teams develop, an increase in job factionalism and competition also develops. The result may be a decrease in a department's overall job performance as individuals within each group show loyalty primarily or only to their unit. This traditional problem may be observed in the relationship between patrol officers and detectives. Patrol officers are sometimes reluctant to give information to detectives because

FIGURE 6.1

Computer manipulation crimes involve changing data or creating electronic records in a system for the purpose of advancing another crime, typically fraud or embezzlement. For example, electronic payroll records may be altered so that an employee is paid for more hours than he or she actually worked. Internet scams, such as the sale of merchandise that is never delivered, are another common type of fraud.

they feel detectives will take credit for their work. Specialization also increases the number of administrative and command relationships, complicating the overall organizational structure. Additionally, each unit requires a competent leader. In some instances, this competent leader must also be a qualified specialist. A thorny problem here is when the specialist does not qualify for the rank usually needed to head a major unit. An example of such a problem is observed in the staffing of an air patrol unit in which the commanding officer may be a lieutenant or sergeant because that individual is the highest-ranking officer with a pilot's license. In this case, the level of expertise (high) does not coincide with the level of rank (lower), which may cause difficulties when trying to deal with other commanding officers of units who hold the rank of captain or major.

Finally, specialization may hamper the development of a well-rounded police program. As specialization increases, the resources available for general uniformed patrol invariably decrease, often causing a lopsided structure wherein the need for general police services are second to the staffing of specialized programs and units.[6]

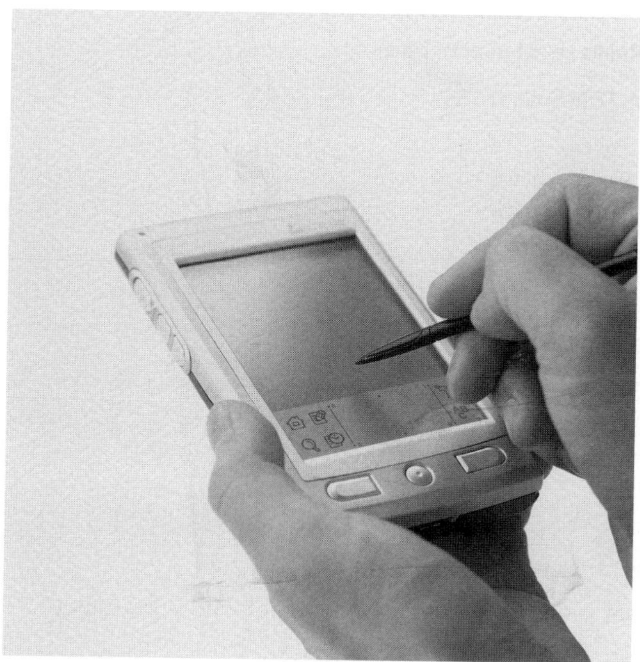

FIGURE 6.2

Wireless access to the World Wide Web has provided unlimited opportunities for computer manipulation and data alteration crimes, challenging even the most sophisticated computer security software.

(© TongRo Image Stock/Alamy)

FIGURE 6.3

An officer in a bomb suit prepares to respond to a bomb threat call. In searching a bomb threat site, searchers look for items that are foreign or out of place.

(Richard Drew/AP Wide World Photos)

TABLE 6.1 Traditional Police Ranks vs. Alternative Titles

TRADITIONAL RANKS	ALTERNATIVE TITLES
Chief of police	Director
Deputy chief	Assistant director
Colonel	Division director
Major	Inspector
Captain	Commander
Lieutenant	Manager
Sergeant	Supervisor
Detective	Investigator
Corporal	Senior officer/master patrol officer
Officer	Public safety officer/agent

Critical Thinking Questions

1. What are some examples of specialization in a municipal police department?
2. What are the advantages and disadvantages of specialization?
3. How might the extent of specialization be related to the size of a department?

THE PRINCIPLE OF HIERARCHY

The **principle of hierarchy** requirement that each lower level of organization be supervised by a higher level results not only in the use of multiple spans of control but also in different grades of authority that increase at each successively higher level of the organization. This authority flows downward in the organization as a formal grant of power from the chief of police to those selected for leadership positions. These different grades of authority produce the chain of command.[7] Although there are many similarities from one department to another, the American police service does not have a uniform terminology for grades of authority and job titles.[8] In recent years, some police departments have moved away from using traditional military-style ranks and have adopted, instead, alternative titles as summarized in Table 6.1. However, in many departments there remains a distinction between rank and title.[9] In these, *rank* denotes one's place in terms of grade of authority or the rank hierarchy, whereas *title* indicates an assignment. Where this distinction is made, a person holding the title of division director, for example, may be a captain, major, or colonel in terms of the rank hierarchy.

SPAN OF CONTROL VS. SPAN OF MANAGEMENT

The term **span of management** instead of "span of control" is used to describe the number of personnel a supervisor can personally manage effectively. The term "span of management" is broader than "span of control" and encompasses factors relating to an individual's capacity to oversee the activities of others directly, such as police manager's ability, experience, and level of energy.

"Span of management" more suitably describes the process of the number of personnel a supervisor can manage than does the term "span of control." Control is only one aspect of the management process. The term "span of management" encompasses more of the factors relating to the problem of an individual's capacity to oversee the activities of others.

How wide a span of management is depends on many factors. Some state that the ideal number of subordinates reporting to a supervisor is 4, while some have found up to 30 are manageable. The practices vary widely.

The groupings help to determine the span in actual practice. Grouping exists because the chief executive cannot directly manage an unlimited number of employees. Grouping—or compartmentalization—may be due to the following:

- The type of work to be performed
- The ability of personnel to be trained and put training into practice
- The quality of the supervisors and the managers in the organization

Without grouping, everyone would report directly to the chief administrator. Except in very small law enforcement agencies, this method is cumbersome and unworkable. Balance is needed. To establish layers of organization is expensive. More managers, staff, and money are needed. Coordination becomes a big factor, and communication and control of planning becomes complicated.[10]

While many law enforcement agencies prefer lower spans of management, with multiple layers of hierarchy, the growing trend is a move to flatter organizational structures with higher spans of management. This type of structure provides for much better communication within the organization, increased fiscal and personnel responsibility, greater organizational flexibility, and increased delegation by supervisors. Employees also favor flatter structures with higher spans of management because they receive less detailed and micromanaged supervision, and more responsibility and they feel more trusted by their supervisors. In these types of structures, employees have an environment in which to grow and create and hence become more fulfilled in their work.[11]

Graicunas Theory[12]

French management consultant V. A. Graicunas analyzed subordinate–superior relationships and developed a mathematical formula based on the geometric increase in complexities of managing as the number of subordinates increases. Although the formula may not be applicable to a given case, it focuses attention on the central problem of span of management perhaps better than any other device.

Graicunas's theory identifies three types of subordinate–superior relationships: (1) direct single relationships, (2) direct group relationships, and (3) cross relationships. The direct single relationships, easily understood and recognized, relate the superior directly and individually with his or her immediate subordinates. Thus, if A has three subordinates—B, C, and D—then there are three direct single relationships.

The direct group relationships exist between the superior and each possible combination of subordinates. Thus, a superior might consult with one of his or her subordinates with a second in attendance, with all of his or her subordinates, or with the various combinations of them. If A has three subordinates, these relationships include the following:

B with C

B with D

C with B

C with D

D with B

D with C

B with C and D

C with B and D

D with C and B

The rapid rise in the number of relationships with the increase in the number of subordinates is startling. Mathematically, an executive with four subordinates, by adding a fifth, increases the possible relationships for which he or she is responsible by 127 percent (from 44 to 100), in return for a 25 percent increase in subordinate working capacity. Clearly, an executive must think at least twice before increasing the number of subordinates, even though this mathematical truism does not prove he or she should not do so.

Other Important Factors Affecting Span of Management

- Harmony of subordinates
- Nature of task
- Preparation and ability of supervisor
- Amount of authority delegated
- Ease and simplicity of instructions
- Availability of special equipment[13]

Critical Thinking Question

1. What are some of the factors affecting span of management? Describe how each factor can affect the width of a span of management.

ORGANIZATIONAL STRUCTURE AND DESIGN

Tansik and Elliot suggest that, when we consider the formal structure (or pattern of relationships) of an organization, we typically focus on two areas:

1. The formal relationship and duties of personnel in the organization, which include the organizational chart and job descriptions
2. The set of formal rules, policies, procedures, and controls that guide the behavior of organizational members within the framework of the formal relationships and duties.[14]

Organizational design focuses on two spatial levels of differentiation—vertical and horizontal—depicted in Figure 6.4. **Vertical differentiation** is based on levels of authority, or positions holding formal power within the organization; Table 6.2 reflects one range of vertical differentiation found in police agencies. Persons with vertical authority have the power to assign work and to exercise control to ensure job performance.[15] In Figure 6.4, the deputy chief has a span of management of three, all of whom are captains and all to whom he or she can give assignments and control.

Horizontal differentiation, on the other hand, is usually based on activity. However, in some cases, horizontal differentiation is based on specific projects or even geographical distribution. For instance, many state police departments are responsible for large geographical areas. Their organizational structure often reflects horizontal differentiation based on location rather than function. Some of the more common

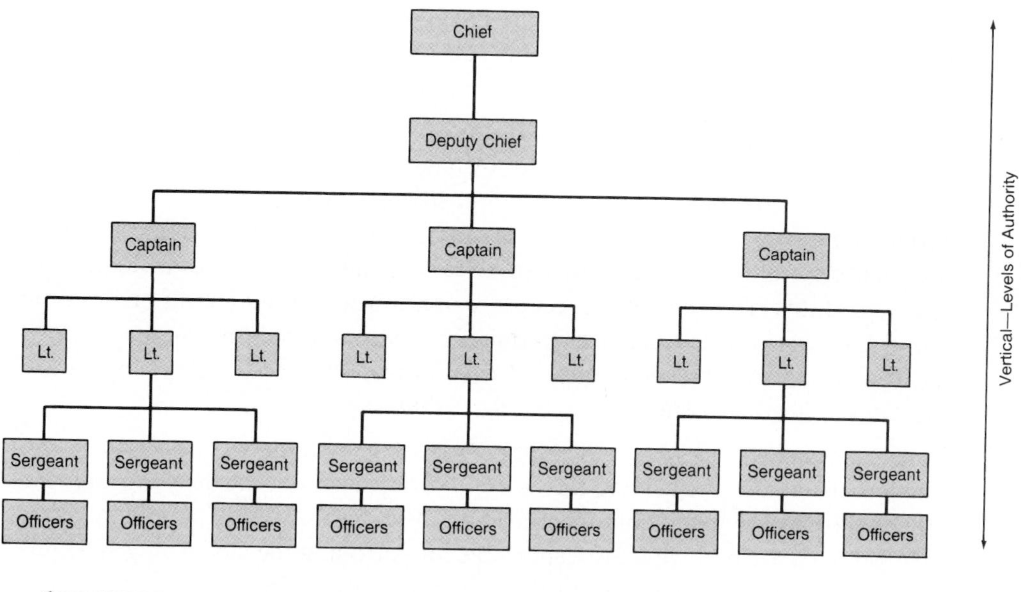

FIGURE 6.4

Organizational chart showing vertical and horizontal levels of differentiation. In some departments, especially large ones, a number of other ranks may be present within the chart.

TABLE 6.2 Line, Auxiliary/Support, and Administrative Staff Functions

	STAFF	
LINE	**AUXILIARY/SUPPORT**	**ADMINISTRATIVE**
• Uniformed patrol • Investigations • Vice and narcotics • Traffic enforcement • Juvenile service	Crime laboratory Detention and jail Records Identification Communications Property maintenance, transportation, and vehicle maintenance	Personnel Training Planning and research Fiscal/budgeting Legal services Media relations

ways in which activities of personnel are grouped within an organization (on a horizontal dimension) are as follows:

Grouping by clientele—The simplest method of grouping within a police department is by clientele. Personnel are assigned by the type of client served, such as juvenile division, senior citizen crime detail, mayor's security unit, and gang squad. Each group focuses on the needs of a special clientele, which may be either temporary or permanent. In this manner, officers become familiar with the specific enforcement problems and patterns associated with different client populations.

Grouping by style of service—A police department usually has a patrol bureau and a detective bureau. The grouping of uniformed patrol officers on the one hand and of plainclothes investigators on the other illustrates how the former are grouped by the nature of their services (conspicuous, preventive patrol, and preliminary investigations) and how the latter are grouped also by this same principle (follow-up investigations). This form of grouping also takes advantage of specialization of knowledge and skill and permits the pinpointing of responsibility for results.

Grouping by geography—Where activities are widespread over any given area, it may be beneficial to provide local command. Instances of this type of operation are large city precincts or district-type operations and state police posts that are located throughout a state. An example of this appears in Figure 6.5. Even in the headquarters building, activities that are related usually share the same floor. Instances of this arrangement are records, communications, and crime analysis in close proximity to each other. This permits supervisors to become familiar with operating problems of related units and to coordinate the various efforts by more direct and immediate control.

Grouping by time—This grouping occurs when the need to perform a certain function or service goes beyond the normal work period of a single eight-hour shift. Other shifts are needed to continue the effort. The division of the patrol force into three platoons, each of which is responsible for patrolling the city during an eight-hour period, is an example of this differentiation process. This form of grouping tends to create problems of coordination and unity of direction because top administrators work normal day hours, whereas many of their officers perform their functions on the evening and midnight shifts. The need to delegate authority becomes critical under these circumstances.

Grouping by process—This involves the placing of all personnel who use a given type of equipment in one function. Examples include stenographic pools, crime laboratory personnel placed in a section to handle certain types of scientific equipment, and automotive maintenance units. This type of grouping lends itself to expertise involving a single process and makes the most efficient use of costly equipment.[16]

Top-Down vs. Bottom-Up Approaches

The level of complexity within a police organization is largely determined by the amount of horizontal and vertical differentiation that exists.[17] Size is often, but not necessarily, related to complexity. Some organizations, even relatively small police departments, can be highly differentiated and quite complex in organizational design.

According to Hodge and Anthony,[18] the differentiation process can occur in two basic ways in police agencies. First, the bottom-up, or synthesis, approach focuses on combining tasks into larger and larger sets of tasks. For instance, a police officer's tasks may involve primarily routine patrol but would dramatically increase in complexity when the officer was assigned preliminary investigative duties. Tasks become more complex and therefore require additional and varied levels of supervision and accountability. The bottom-up approach is shown in Figure 6.5A. Second, the top-down, or analysis, approach looks at the overall work of the organization at the top and splits this into increasingly more specialized tasks as one moves from the top to the bottom of the organization. The top-down approach considers the overall police mission—to protect and to serve the public. At the top level of a police agency, this can be defined into various administrative tasks, such as budgeting, political maneuvering, and leadership, whereas at the street level, such a mission is carried out through activities such as patrol and arrest. This type of approach is shown in Figure 6.5B.

Both approaches are commonly found in police organizations. The top-down analysis is often used in growing organizations because it is easy to visualize the set of

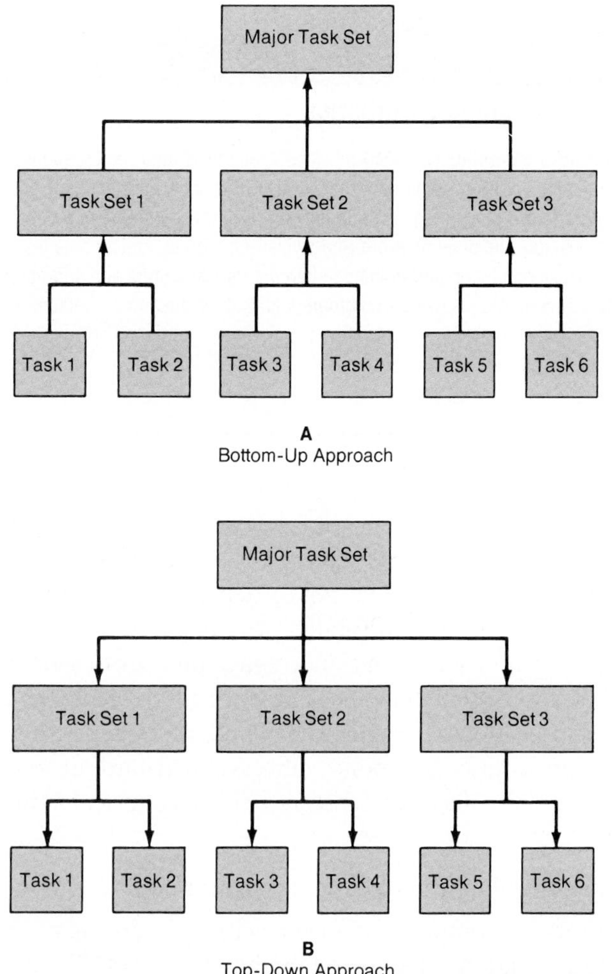

FIGURE 6.5

The bottom-up and top-down approaches to building structure around differentiation.

(*Source: Organization Theory: A Strategic Approach,* 6/E by Hodge/Anthony/Gales. Reprinted by permission of Pearson Education Inc., Upper Saddle River, NJ.)

tasks to be accomplished and then to break these sets down into specific tasks and subtasks. The bottom-up approach is often used during periods of retrenchment where organizational growth has declined because combining tasks such as those found in patrol and detective bureaus can consolidate jobs or even units.

Some organizations have narrow spans of management with tall structures and many levels, whereas others reduce the number of levels by widening the span of management at each level. Many narrower spans of control make a police department "taller." Shown in Figure 6.6A, the California Highway Patrol (CHP) appears to have five levels. These levels are commissioner, deputy commissioner, assistant commissioner, field division chief, and area office commander. From a more functional perspective, each area office also has a chain of command consisting of four layers—captain, lieutenant, sergeant, and officer. Thus, when the rank layers in the area offices are considered, the CHP is a tall organization with a number of different levels of authority. Seven to nine levels of rank are fairly typical of large police organizations. Figure 6.6B displays each CHP area office by geographical grouping, as described earlier in this chapter.

Quick Facts

Valuable Statistics

Law Enforcement Management and Administrative Statistics (LEMAS) provides a wealth of information about law enforcement administration. Conducted every three to four years, LEMAS collects data from over 3,000 state and local law enforcement agencies, including all those that employ 100 or more sworn officers and a nationally representative sample of smaller agencies. Data obtained includes agency responsibilities, operating expenditures, job functions of sworn and civilian employees, officer salaries and special pay, demographic characteristics of officers, weapons and armor policies, education and training requirements, computers and information systems, vehicles, special units, and community policing activities. LEMAS documents, as well as summaries and other documents related to the survey, are available on the Bureau of Justice Statistics website.

Source: U.S. Department of Justice, Bureau of Justice Statistics.

The complexity of a police department is increased by the proliferation of levels because they can negatively affect communication up and down the chain of command. For example, during urban riots, police departments found that an initially small incident grew rapidly beyond the ability of a small group of officers to control it. The process of getting approval from senior police officials to send additional officers took so long that, by the time the officers arrived at the scene, the once small incident had grown into an uncontrollable riot. Thus, most departments shifted the authority to deploy large numbers of police officers downward, in some cases all the way to the individual police officer at the scene. This example illustrates several important principles:

1. Narrow spans of control make police departments taller.
2. Taller organizations are complex and may react slowly during crisis situations, as effective communication is hampered by the number of different levels present within the chain of command.
3. Successful tall departments must develop policies and procedures that overcome problems created by increased complexity.

Many police agencies, such as the Phoenix, Arizona, Police Department, have redesigned their organizations to reflect larger spans of control or management and hence flatter organizational structures. Figure 6.7 represents only three major organizational levels—chief, division, and bureau. Although this structure is flatter than that of the CHP, traditional grades of authority, such as commander, lieutenant, sergeant, and officer ranks, continue to exist in the Phoenix Police Department. With higher educational standards for entry-level police officers and efforts toward professionalism, police organizational structures may reflect additional changes of this nature. Ultimately, however, the capacity to flatten out police organizational structures depends to no small degree on reducing the number of traditional ranks, a movement sure to be met with resistance because it means less opportunity for upward mobility.

McFarland[19] points out that flat structures associated with wider spans of control offer numerous advantages over the more traditional tall structures. First, they shorten lines of communication between the bottom and top levels. Communication in both directions is more likely to be faster and more timely. Second, the route of communication is more simple, direct, and clear than it is in tall organizations. Third, distortion in communication is minimized by a reduced number of people being involved. Fourth, and probably most important, flat structures are generally associated

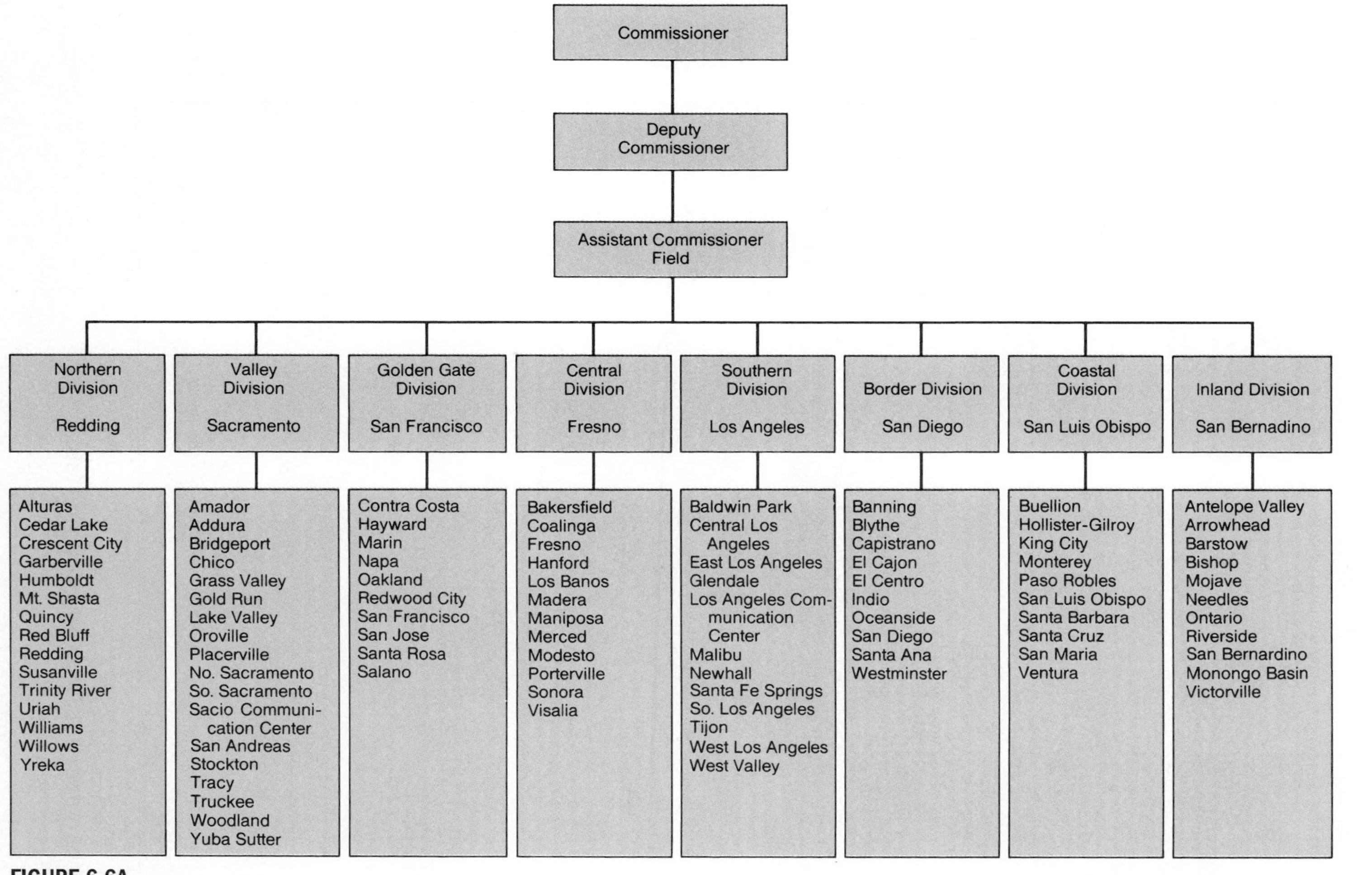

FIGURE 6.6A

Organizational chart for the California Highway Patrol (Field) with modification, showing five levels of control.

(Courtesy of the California Highway Patrol, Sacramento, California)

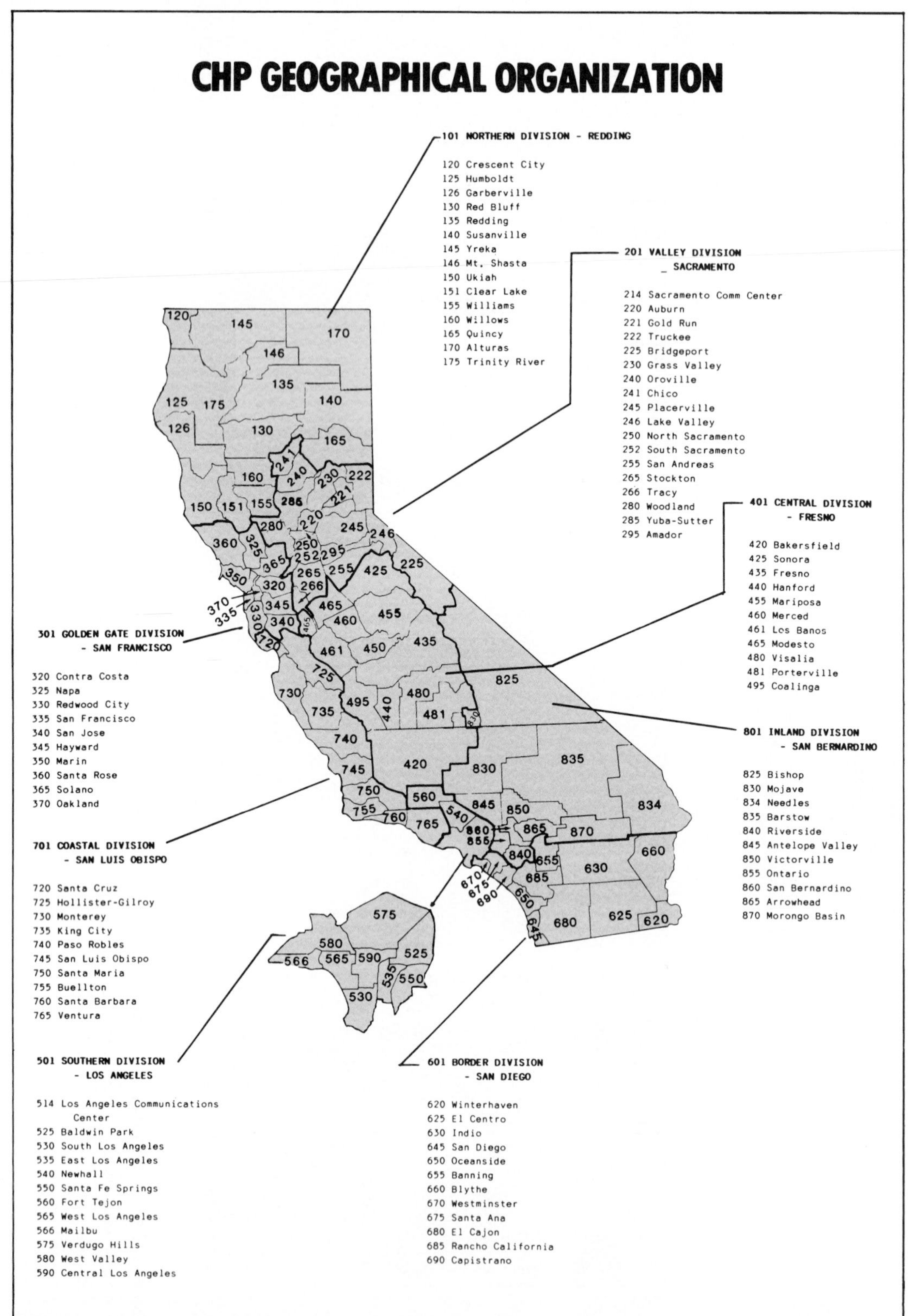

FIGURE 6.6B

Geographical organization of area offices for the California Highway Patrol.

(Courtesy of the California Highway Patrol, Sacramento, California)

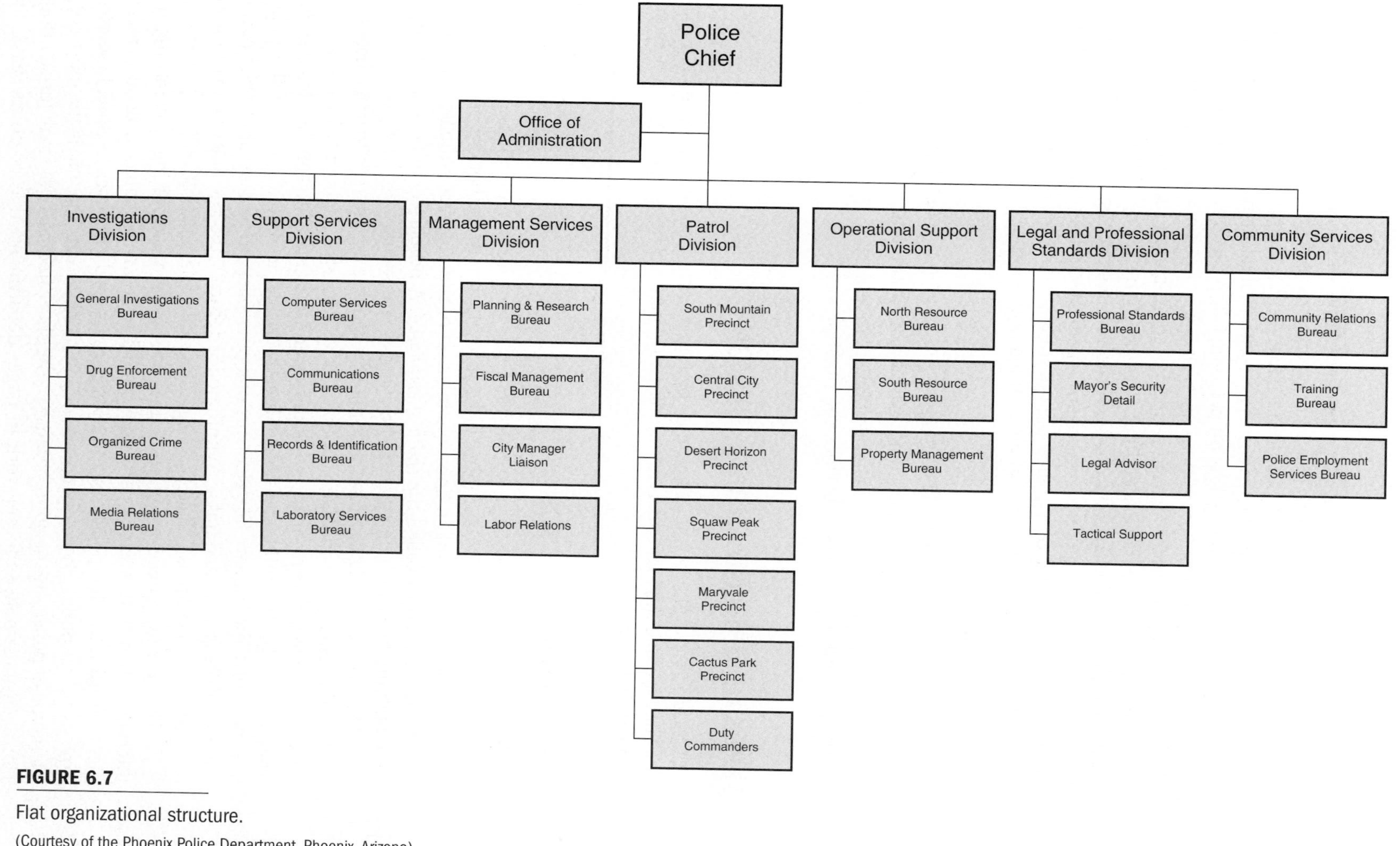

FIGURE 6.7

Flat organizational structure.

(Courtesy of the Phoenix Police Department, Phoenix, Arizona)

with employees with higher morale and job satisfaction as compared to employees in tall, structured organizations.

Flat structures do, however, place demanding pressures on supervisors, require high-caliber managers, and work best in organizations in which employees are held strictly accountable for measurable and objective results. Considering the role of the police and the continuing problems associated with evaluating police services, such a structure may cause inordinate stress on personnel. Top executives can attempt to direct the development of police agencies in such a way as to maintain structural balance. Some amount of hierarchy is needed for coordination, but the extremely tall police organization is neither needed nor particularly functional. In balance, no major city has successfully flattened out both the numbers of organizational layers or units and the traditional rank structure to any significant and continuing degree. Thus, any substantial flattening of a police organization is likely to be an experiment in organizational design rather than an institutionalized reform.

Critical Thinking Questions

1. Why might an organization need to group by geography rather than by function?
2. What determines the level of complexity within an organization?
3. Why must departments characterized by tall organization structures develop policies and procedures to balance their complexity?

TYPES OF ORGANIZATIONAL DESIGN

Four basic structural types of design may be found within organizations, such as police. They are line, line and staff, functional, and matrix. These types exist separately or in combination.

Line Structure

The **line structure** is the oldest, simplest, and clearest form of organizational design. As illustrated in Figure 6.8, authority flows from the top to the bottom of the organization in a clear and unbroken line, creating a set of superior–subordinate relations in a hierarchy commonly called the *chain of command.* A primary emphasis is placed on accountability by close adherence to the chain of command.

The term "line" originated with the military and was used to refer to units that were to be used to engage the enemy in combat. "Line" also refers to those elements of a police organization that perform the work the agency was created to handle. Stated somewhat differently, line units contribute directly to the accomplishment of the police mission. Thus, the primary line elements of a police department are uniformed patrol, criminal investigation, and traffic. Within police agencies, the line function may also be referred to as "operations," "field services," or a similar designation.

The pure line police organization does not have any supporting elements that are internal or part of it, such as personnel, media relations, training, or fiscal management. Instead, the line police organization uses its total resources to provide services directly to the public. Typically found only in small towns, the line is the most common type of police organization because of the sheer frequency of small jurisdictions. However, most police officers work in larger departments that retain the basic line elements but to which are added various types of support units. These larger police departments are often referred to as the *line and staff form of organization.*

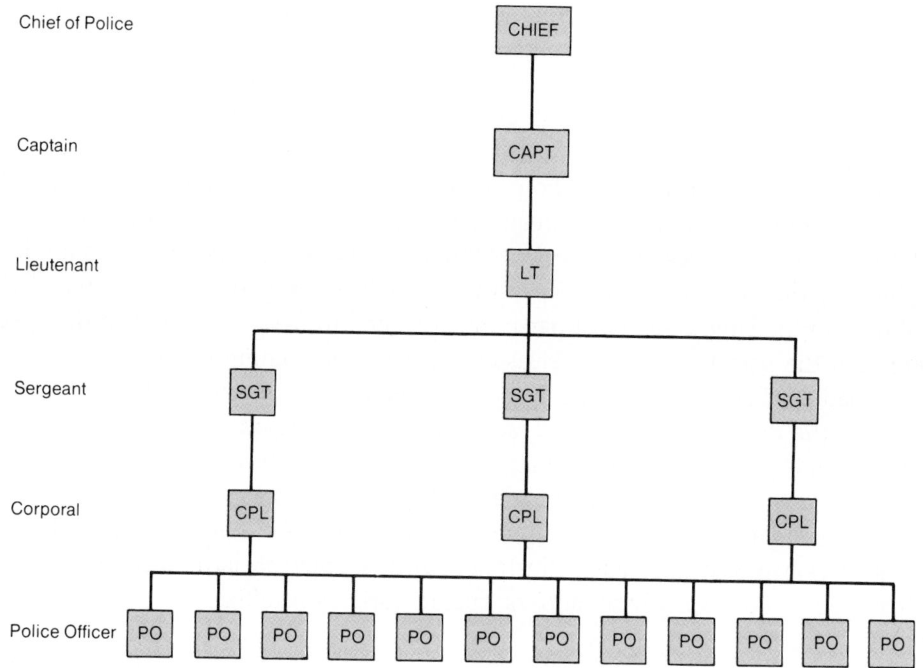

FIGURE 6.8

Line organizational structure in a small police department.
(Courtesy of the Tigard Police Department, Tigard, Oregon)

Line and Staff Structure

As more demands for services are placed on police departments, there is a need to add internal support functions, so that the line functions can continue to provide direct services to the public. The addition of support functions to the line elements produces a distinct organizational form: the **line and staff structure.** The addition of a staff component to the line structure offers a number of advantages because such units are helpful in the following:

1. Providing expert advice to line units in special knowledge areas as demonstrated by the opinions of legal advisers
2. Relieving line managers from performing tasks they least prefer to do or are least qualified to do, such as training and scientific analysis of physical evidence
3. Achieving departmentwide conformity in activities that affect the entire organization, such as disciplinary procedures
4. Reducing or eliminating special problems, such as corruption, because of the greater expertise they bring to bear on the issue and the greater amount of time they have to devote to the problem[20]

Staff functions are sometimes further broken down into two types: auxiliary or support and administrative staff services. Under this arrangement, auxiliary or support units, such as communications and crime laboratory services, are charged with the responsibility of giving immediate assistance to the operations of line elements. In contrast, administrative staff units, such as personnel and training, provide services that are of less immediate assistance and are supportive of the entire police department. Table 6.2 (shown earlier in this chapter) identifies typical line, auxiliary/support, and administrative staff functions. Depending on factors such as the history of the police department and the chief's preferences, there is some variation as to how functions are categorized. Less frequently, legislative enactments may establish the organizational structure, which is another source of variation in how functions are categorized.

Figure 6.9 shows a line and staff structure. In it the field services bureau (composed of the patrol districts) is the primary line function of the organization and is highlighted intentionally (by the Boston, Massachusetts, Police Department) to show that purpose. The investigative services bureau is also a line function but is not highlighted by the organization in contrast to the field services bureau. This may be attributed to the large number of personnel assigned to field services or to the special attention the patrol function receives considering the community policing concepts described in Chapter 2, Policing Today. Interestingly, the Boston Police Department refers to the Bureau of Field Services as the "heart" of its organization. Illustratively, the bureau is positioned and emphasized in the center of the organizational structure. The administrative services bureau and upper-echelon offices represent staff functions within the organization. Note in Figure 6.9 that two types of staff report directly to the chief of police: the generalist, illustrated by the chief of staff, and the specialist, illustrated by the legal adviser and internal investigations office.

Functional Structure

The **functional structure** is one means by which the line authority structure of an organization can be modified. Hodge and Johnson[21] state that functional structure "is a line and staff structure that has been modified by the delegation of management authority to personnel outside their normal spans of control." Figure 6.10 shows a police department in which the intelligence unit is responsible to three captains whose main responsibility is for other organizational units.

The obvious advantage of this type of structure is in the maximum use of specialized units. Successful police work requires the coordination of various subunits or specialized resources to attain a desired objective. All too often, a coordinated effort organizationwide is prevented by competing goals, energies, and loyalties to internal subunits. A classic example can be found between patrol and investigative bureaus. Examples of police subunits organized on the basis of purpose of function are investigative bureaus, homicide, robbery, burglary or vice control squads, traffic enforcement details, and so forth. Each of these units is responsible for some function or purpose of the police mission, such as detection, apprehension and prosecution of robbery suspects, prevention of traffic accidents and apprehension of violators, and suppression of vice activity. Organization by purpose facilitates the accomplishment of certain assigned objectives by bringing trained specialists and specialized resources together under a single manager who can be held accountable for the attainment of a desired state of affairs. The unit can be judged by what it accomplishes, not by its methodology. This type of organization is effective for gaining energies and loyalties of assigned officers because their purpose is clearly understood.

Difficulties arise when purposes overlap or conflict. A patrol unit and a specialized investigative unit may be jointly charged with responsibility for the same task. For example, a local patrol precinct and a specialized robbery squad may share responsibility for reduction of the robbery rate in a certain high-crime area. Each of the units reports to a separate commander, both of whom are at least informally evaluated by how effectively robberies in that area are reduced. Each of the commanders may have his or her own ideas how this might be accomplished and each wishes to receive credit for improving the crime situation. This type of core responsibility for the same results

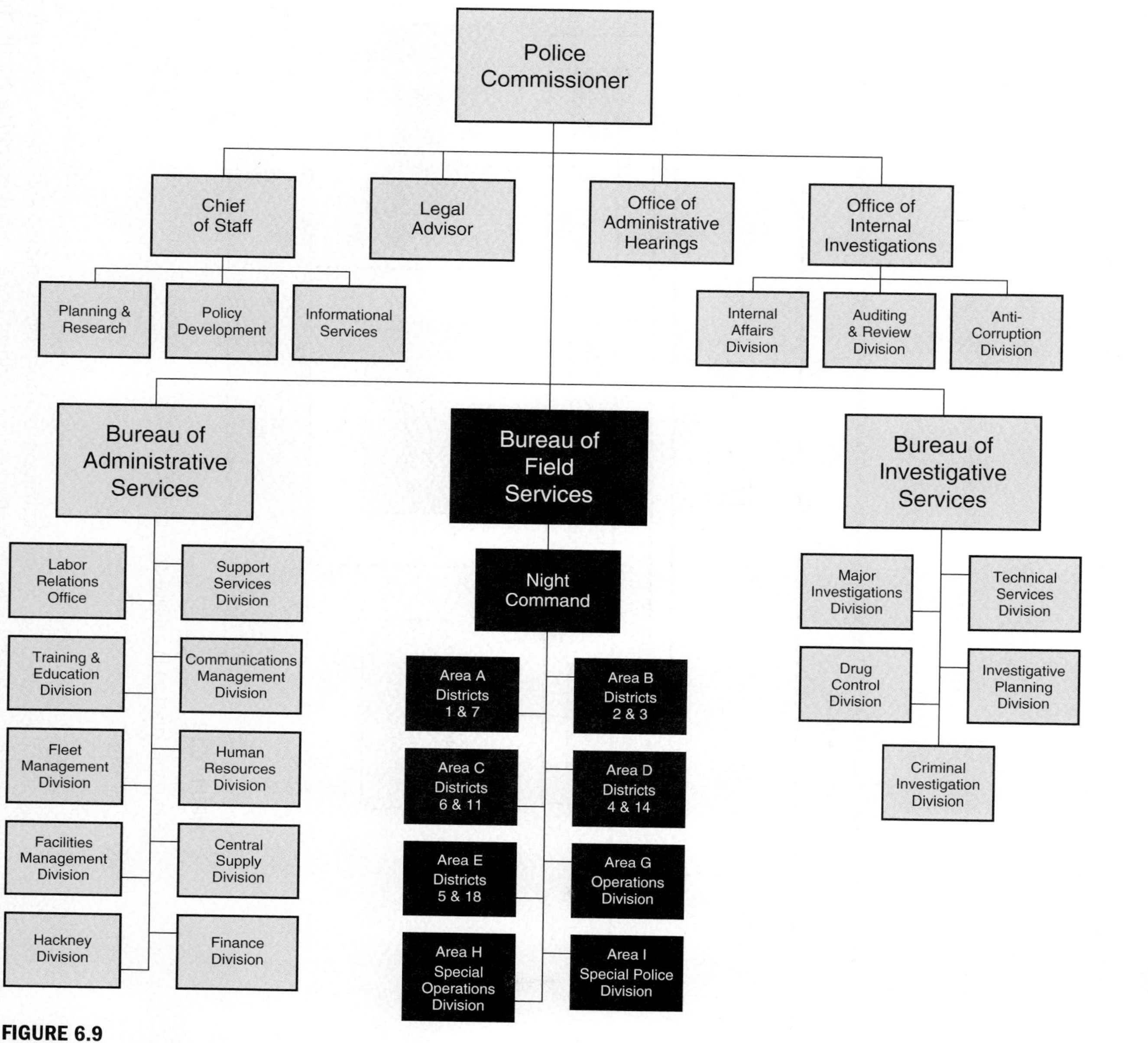

FIGURE 6.9

Line and staff structure in a police department. Note that line functions are grouped in the middle of the structure and highlighted as "Bureau of Field Services."
(Courtesy of the Boston, Massachusetts, Police Department)

Quick Facts

Factors Influencing Organizational Design

Organizational structure within police agenices varies widely across the country. While researchers have found it difficult to isolate all the factors that shape police organizations, 14 factors have been shown to influence organizational design in at least three separate studies:

1. Organizational size
2. City governance
3. Region
4. Concentration
5. Crime patterns
6. Organizational age
7. Political culture
8. Population size
9. Population heterogeneity
10. Poverty/income
11. Urbanization or ruralization
12. Span of management
13. Time
14. Vertical differentiation

Source: Edward Maguire and Craig D. Ucheda, "Measurement and Explanation in the Comparative Study of American Police," in *Measurement and Analysis of Crime and Justice,* Criminal Justice 2000, Volume 4, (2000).

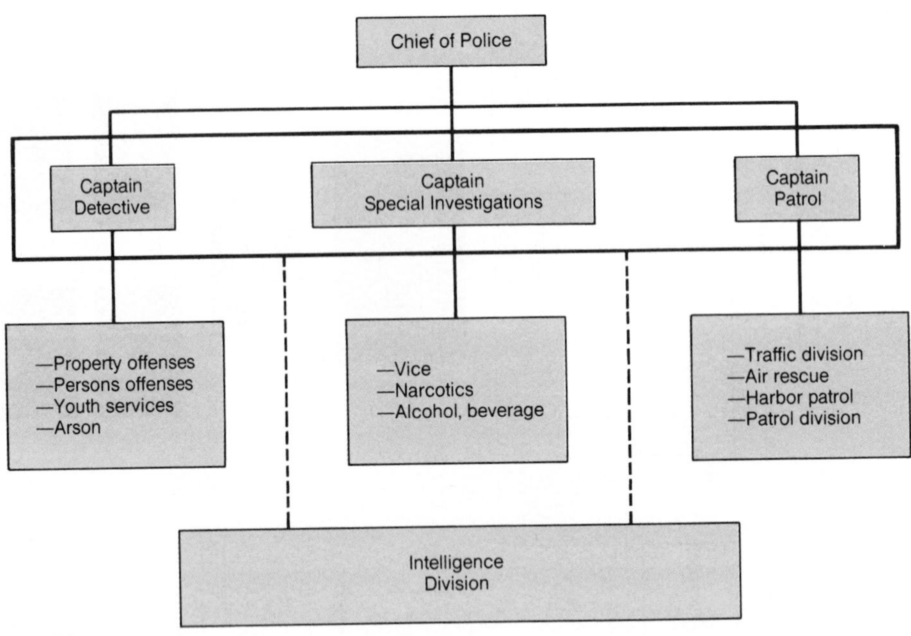

FIGURE 6.10

Functional structure in a police organization.

negates the advantage of specialization by purpose. It may result in the two units working at cross-purposes, refusing to share critical leads, and duplicating efforts. In this case, competition becomes dysfunctional, and cooperation and communications between the patrol and investigative units are impaired.[22]

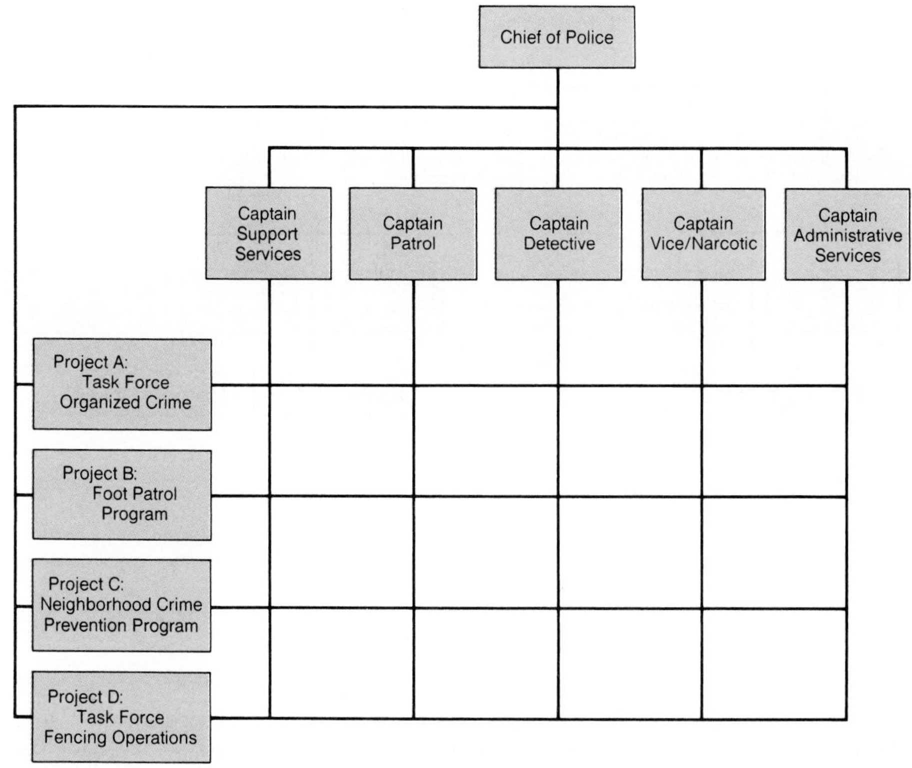

FIGURE 6.11

Matrix structure in a police organization.

Some of these problems can be eliminated by police organizations using functional design. By forcing specific units to be responsible to a variety of other unit commanders, critical information is assured of reaching other line officers. Sharing is promoted, while competing loyalties are diminished.

The major disadvantage of the functional design is that it increases organizational complexity. In Figure 6.11, members of the intelligence division receive instructions from several superiors. This can result in conflicting directions, and thus extensive functionalized structures are seldom found in police agencies. Law enforcement executives should explore the use of the functional design but be ever cautious of the confusion that could result if the process is not properly monitored and controlled.

Matrix Structure

One interesting form of organizational design is variously referred to as **matrix (or grid) structure.** In some cases, the style has been inclusively part of "project" or "product" management. The essence of matrix structure is in the assignment of members of functional areas (e.g., patrol, detective, and support services) to specific projects (e.g., task forces and crime-specific programs). The most typical situation in which the matrix approach is used is when a community has had a series of sensationalized crimes and the local police department announces it has formed a task force to apprehend the violator. One notable example of this occurred in Atlanta, Georgia, where a task force comprising over 300 federal, state, and local law enforcement officers searched for

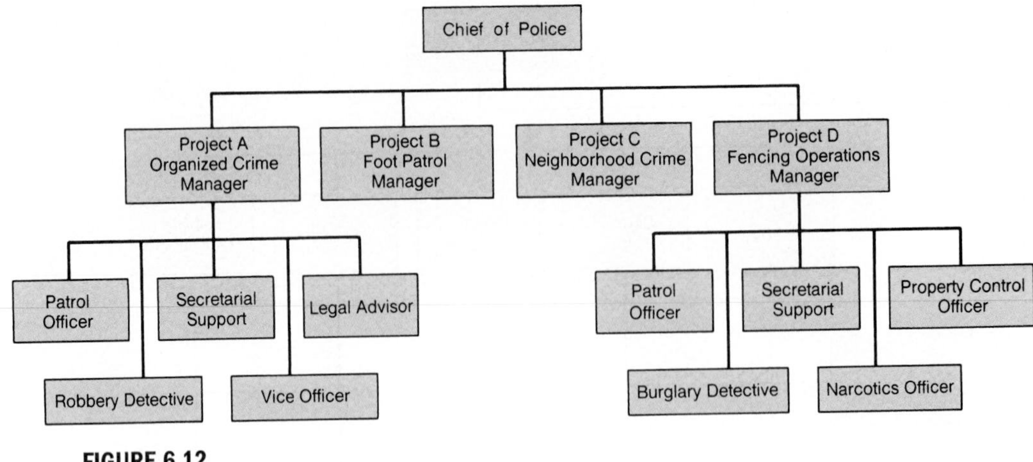

FIGURE 6.12

The detailed organization of projects.

the murderer of young males in that city. As a result of that combined effort, Wayne Williams was arrested and convicted. The advantage of this type of organizational design is in the formation of specific groups of individuals, combining varied talents and levels of expertise in order to fulfill a designated mission or goal. Quite often, the matrix structure is used for relatively short periods of time when specific programs are conducted. After the assignment is completed, individuals return to their respective units.

Figure 6.11 displays the matrix design applied to a police organization. This chart reflects the basic line and staff elements found in most police agencies. However, four specific projects have been initiated that require the use of personnel from five different units, which further requires each project to organize along the lines suggested by Figure 6.12.

Although the matrix structure greatly increases organizational complexity, it has been successful only in the short-term delivery of police services.

Critical Thinking Questions

1. Can you think of any examples of a police organization that utilizes the line structure? Where would this type of structure most likely be found and why?
2. What are the advantages of organization by function?
3. Describe a scenario where the matrix structure would be best suited.

SOME UNIQUE ORGANIZATIONAL FEATURES OF SHERIFF'S OFFICES

A detailed discussion of "politics and the county sheriff" was addressed in Chapter 4, Politics and Police Administration. However, in addition to some of the unique political features discussed therein, there are also some organizational differences that typically exist between municipal police departments and sheriff's offices. For example, most police departments do not have a single commanding officer positioned between the police chief and all of the operating and administrative bureaus. However, this

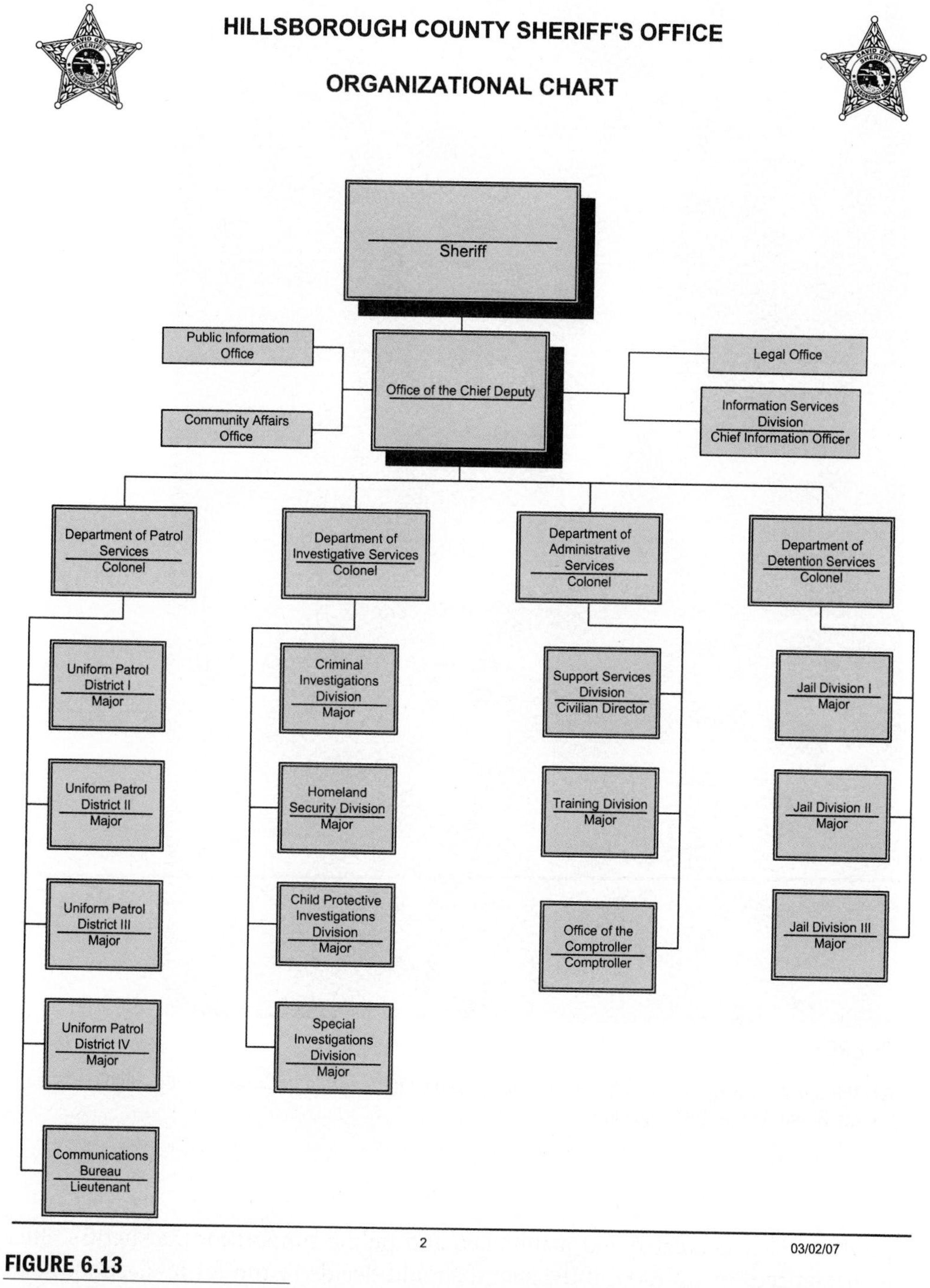

HILLSBOROUGH COUNTY SHERIFF'S OFFICE

ORGANIZATIONAL CHART

Sheriff

Public Information Office

Community Affairs Office

Office of the Chief Deputy

Legal Office

Information Services Division
Chief Information Officer

Department of Patrol Services
Colonel

- Uniform Patrol District I — Major
- Uniform Patrol District II — Major
- Uniform Patrol District III — Major
- Uniform Patrol District IV — Major
- Communications Bureau — Lieutenant

Department of Investigative Services
Colonel

- Criminal Investigations Division — Major
- Homeland Security Division — Major
- Child Protective Investigations Division — Major
- Special Investigations Division — Major

Department of Administrative Services
Colonel

- Support Services Division — Civilian Director
- Training Division — Major
- Office of the Comptroller — Comptroller

Department of Detention Services
Colonel

- Jail Division I — Major
- Jail Division II — Major
- Jail Division III — Major

2 03/02/07

FIGURE 6.13

Hillsborough County Sheriff's Office (organizational chart showing the office of the chief deputy in charge of the entire organization).

(Courtesy of the Hillsborough County Sheriff's Office, Tampa, Florida)

is not true of sheriff's offices. Most sheriff's offices have a chief deputy/undersheriff and, with the blessing of the sheriff, this person typically assumes complete operational command over the entire organization (see Figure 6.13). The position exists because, although the elected sheriff is the chief law enforcement officer of the agency, the sheriff must devote sufficient time during his or her term of office to address the political needs of the sheriff's office within the community in order to assure that a

FIGURE 6.14

Women are increasingly being elected as sheriff. Shown here is Sheriff Susan Benton, Highlands County Sheriff Office, Sebring, Florida.

positive image is created and maintained and public support for the sheriff's office is maximized. In addition, if the sheriff should decide to run for re-election, he or she must devote considerable time and effort to this endeavor.

In many respects, the role of the chief deputy/undersheriff is very similar to that of the police chief in a municipal police department, in that the person occupying this position assumes direct operating command over the entire organization. However, it is also important to note that, because sheriff's offices typically are responsible for supervising the operation of county jails, the chief deputy/undersheriff should also ideally have a good background in jail administration. This is so because jails consume a substantial portion of the agency's resources for both personnel and operating expenses. Interestingly, the position of sheriff, like that of police chief, has traditionally been held by men. However, there are some notable exceptions. Women are increasingly being elected as sheriff (see Figure 6.14).

Critical Thinking Question

1. Why would a sheriff delegate much of his or her authority to a chief deputy undersheriff?

ORGANIZATIONAL STRUCTURE AND COMMUNITY POLICING

Within the past two decades, several studies have questioned the effectiveness of traditional police methods that focus on incident-driven, reactive approaches. As a result, community policing methods have been offered that attempt to develop new, progressive strategies aimed at preventing crime and encouraging broad-based, problem-solving techniques. However, there are many variations of the community policing model that have been tried, and some approaches being tried in several cities around the country that are not without their skeptics.

Decentralizaton vs. Centralization

These new styles of policing under the banner of community policing have called for radical changes in the police mission. As Trojanowicz points out,

> *Community policing requires department-wide philosophical commitment to involve average citizens as partners in the process of reducing and controlling the contemporary problems of crime, drugs, fear of crime, and neighborhood decay, and in efforts to improve the overall quality of life in the community.*[23]

This approach includes developing changes in executive philosophy and community perception of the police, as well as organizational restructuring with an emphasis on decentralization of police services.[24]

The impact of community policing on organizational structure is most apparent in agencies that have recently adopted **decentralization** strategies. The purpose behind such strategies is that police departments can more effectively serve their communities through an organizational design focusing on individual areas and neighborhoods rather than the entire city. Further, decentralization in organizational structure is seen as being much more flexible and having a fluid design in which to provide essential public and human services.[25]

Decentralization in police departments has been conducted primarily in the patrol division. A survey by the Bill Blackwood Law Enforcement Management Institute of Texas, found that a number of methodologies have been used in the decentralization process.[26] These include the use of substations, storefronts, and mobile storefronts.

Some departments have found limited advantages in decentralization. Whereas it may be advantageous to decentralize the patrol function, it may not prove feasible to decentralize other police activities, such as administrative services and investigation/detective bureaus.[27] High operational costs, personnel overlap, role confusion, and general inefficiency have been cited as reasons to avoid the decentralization process in some departments.[28]

Community Policing Units vs. Departmental Philosophy

Electing to compartmentalize the activities of the community policing concept, some departments have opted to provide such services solely through one unit or bureau. For instance, the Anaheim Police Department in Anaheim, California, has a single bureau devoted to community policing (see Figure 6.15). Through this unit, the Community Policing Team develops strategies that employ a total community effort

Focus on Policy

Implementing Community Policing: The Administrative Problem

Community policing represents a fundamental shift in the way that police departments are organized in the United States. As a result, police departments across the country have had to restructure, reformulate, and reposition. The innovations required by a shift to a community policing model have been met with many challenges, perhaps the most daunting of which are presented by the resistance of middle management.

The resistance of middle management to the changes community policing presents derives from a major question about the roles of middle managers in the new model. Middle managers in police agencies, generally lieutenants and captains, have historically been charged with demanding results from their officers and ensuring that those within their span of management follow all procedures properly in order to fulfill greater responsibilities to detectives and prosecuting attorneys. This is a position in direct conflict with the principles of community policing, which requires that police respond differently to calls, establish new priorities, become innovative, and think creatively when dealing with the public. Accountability becomes more nebulous as rules are less rigid.

In order to lessen middle managers' confusion and increase their receptivity to changes that favor community policing, top management officials must employ a number of administrative tactics: transitioning goals to favor creativity over control; ensuring that middle management is involved in the process of planning innovations; encouraging leadership by middle management; clearly articulating and providing support for the new direction of the department; and encouraging middle managers develop the skills that will help them coach and inspire their charges. Only when top managers thoroughly, clearly, and properly direct their departments using these tactics will middle managers embrace and champion the organizational changes that community policing requires.

Source: George L. Kelling and William J. Bratton, "Implementing Community Policing: The Administrative Problem," *Perspectives on Policing*, June 1993.

involving the police department, city and county government, schools, churches, and businesses. These alliances form neighborhood partnerships. The mission of the Community Policing Bureau is to develop, promote, and implement community-based partnerships aimed at addressing various criminal and social problems confronting the city of Anaheim.[29] It is important to note that functions associated with community policing are relatively confined to the Community Policing Bureau.

In contrast, some departments (e.g., those in Portland, Oregon; Madison, Wisconsin; Dallas, Texas; and Minneapolis, Minnesota) have opted to implement the community policing concept holistically; that is, community policing is reflected in all aspects of the organization, and hence the organizational structure does not reflect a single unit devoted to community policing but rather an inferred assumption that the community policing philosophy is pervasive throughout the organization. In these cases, the organizational chart is reflective of the philosophical changes imbued in community policing. In the early 1990s, under the leadership of then-Chief Lee Brown, the Houston Police Department acted as a model for community policing departments (see Figure 6.16). Reflective of these philosophical changes, the organizational chart of the department provides a new and dynamic look. Note that the focus of the department is on service delivery and support rather than the traditional modes of assignment. The police department is viewed more as a community organization than as a control agency. As such, the organization is operated similarly to a service corporation that is fully responsible to an executive board comprising police and community leaders. In this manner, community policing makes individual police officers accountable directly to the people of Houston. The chief of police acts more as a chairman of the board or a chief executive officer for a major corporation than as a traditional police manager.

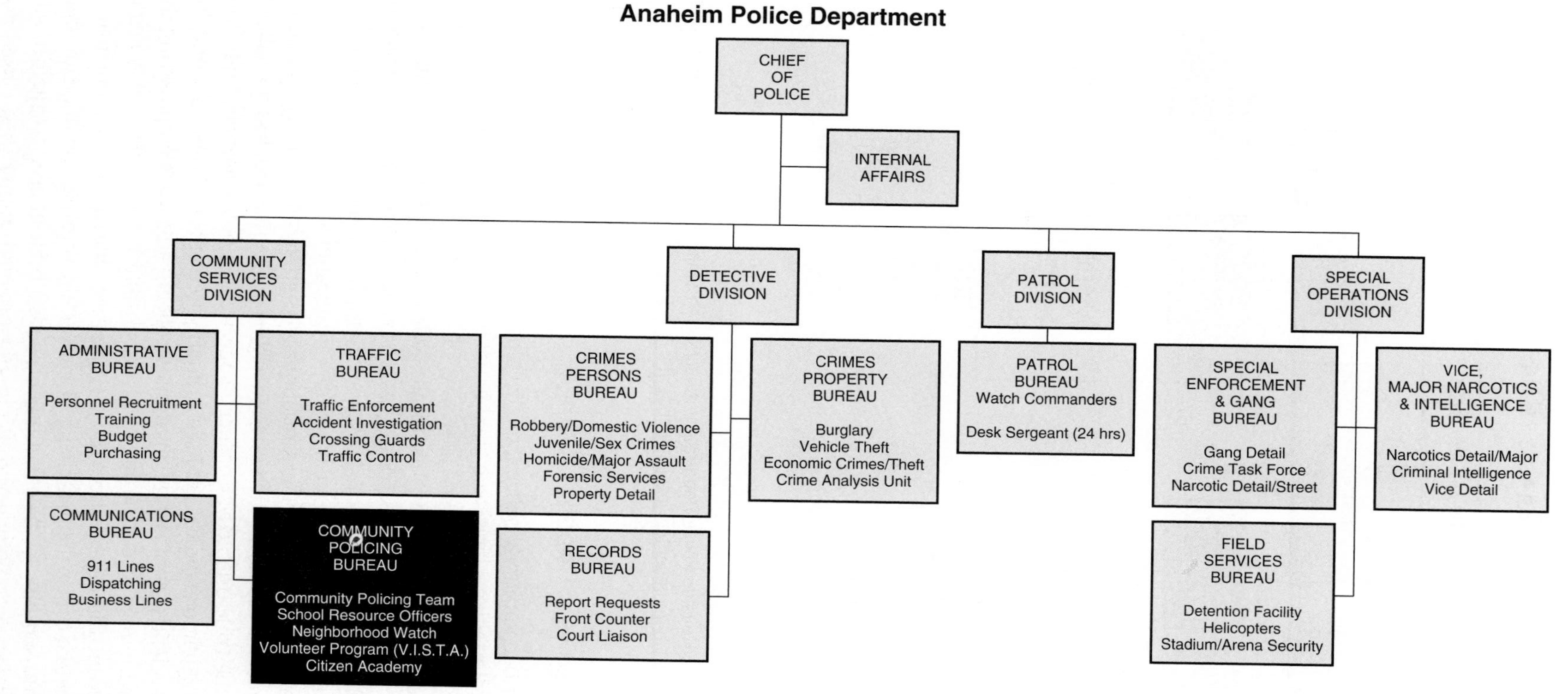

FIGURE 6.15

Organization chart showing one unit devoted to community policing.

(Reproduced under the California Public Records Act)

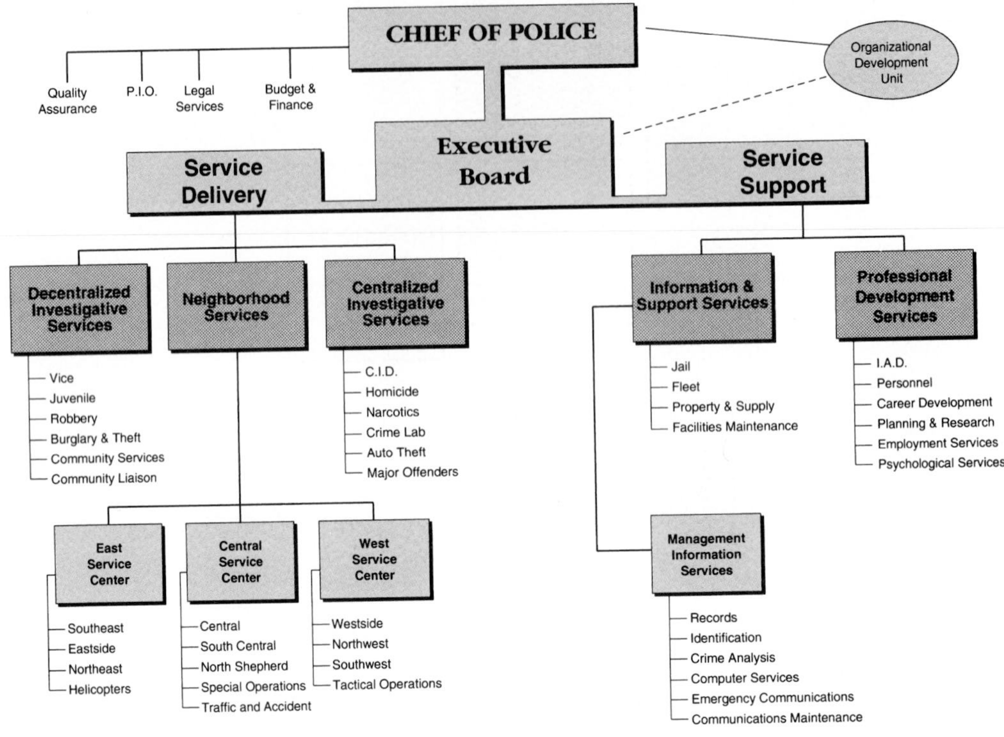

FIGURE 6.16

Organizational chart of the Houston Police Department reflecting an emphasis on service delivery and support through a community-represented "executive board."

(Courtesy of the Houston, Texas, Police Department)

Traditional Design vs. Structural Change

Although a number of community policing methods have been adopted across the country, several structural problems have been cited in the literature.[30] For instance, community policing revokes the paramilitary structure of the past 100 years. Traditional structures of police organizations have historically followed the principles of hierarchy that aim to control subordinates. These principles tend to stifle innovation and creativity, promote alienation and loss of individual self-worth, emphasize mediocrity, and diminish the ability of managers to lead (see Chapter 5, Organizational Theory). Community policing requires a shorter and flatter organizational design. Services are decentralized and community-based. Necessarily, such a design will be less formalized, less specialized, and less bureaucratic (rule-oriented). Cordner[31] suggests that police agencies shift from written rules and regulations (which are used primarily to control officers) to a straightforward, situation-oriented approach. Community policing advocates empowering the individual officer with more discretion and more responsibility than traditional policing; hence, direction from the organization must emphasize shared values, participatory decision making, and a collegial atmosphere. Moreover, the organization of community policing is open and sensitive to the environment, with a built-in need to interact with members of the wider community and to be "results-oriented" rather than closed and internally defined. The differences in organizational structure between traditional policing and community policing are outlined in Table 6.3.

TABLE 6.3 Differences in Organizational Structure

TRADITIONAL POLICING	COMMUNITY POLICING
1. *Bureaucratic*: rigid, formalized—paper-based, rule-oriented—"by the book policing," standardized	1. *Nonbureaucratic*: corporate flexible—rules to fit situation—paper where necessary, collegial atmosphere
2. *Centralized:* centralization of all management, support, operational, and authority functions	2. *Decentralization:* of authority and management function to meet operational requirements—organization driven by front end—and community-based demand
3. *Hierarchical:* pyramid with multiple rank levels	3. *Flattened management (rank) structure:* additional rank at operational level
4. *Specialization:* of varied police functions to increase efficiency (C.I.D. functions, crime prevention, etc.)	4. *Generalization:* specialization limited—support generalist officer—patrol-based
5. *Closed organization orientation:* distinct from environment, resistant to environmental influence, internally defined agenda, means over ends	5. *Open organization model:* interact with environment, open to change, sensitive to environment, results-oriented

SOURCE: Adapted from C. Murphy, *Contemporary Models of Urban Policing: Shaping the Future* (Ontario: Ministry of the Solicitor General, 1991), p. 2.

Some argue that community policing calls for too radical a change in organizational design—that such changes may be impossible under existing union and civil service constraints. Further, in Chapter 1, Historical Development we discussed Michael's "iron law of oligarchy," which indicates that modern, large-scale organizations tend toward specialization and centralization.[32] However, these organizational traits appear to be in conflict with more progressive community policing structures (see Table 6.3). Large police departments require a certain amount of specialization to handle diverse tasks efficiently, such as examining various types of physical evidence or handling unique situations, and the amount of hierarchy required to coordinate the various specialized parts produces a tendency toward centralization. This structural conflict causes significant role confusion and ambiguity among officers who are assigned traditional law enforcement duties as well as more contemporary police tasks. As a result of such difficulties, the continued implementation of community policing should provide a dynamic arena for police organizational structure in the future.

Critical Thinking Questions

1. What kind of changes in traditional police departmental philosophy might community policing require?
2. Why might traditional police organizational design pose a structural barrier to effective community policing programs?
3. What are the pros and cons of decentralizing the patrol division as a strategy for implementing community policing?

LINE AND STAFF RELATIONSHIPS IN POLICE AGENCIES

The rapid growth in size of many police agencies has been accompanied by a corresponding rapid growth in specialization and a need for the expansion of staff services to provide support for operating units. This expansion and division of responsibility, which occurs in all police departments except those that are a pure line form of organization, is sometimes fraught with difficulty and dissension. If left uncorrected, these conditions will have a serious negative effect on both the quality and the quantity of service a police agency is able to deliver to its citizens. The following represent some of the major causes of conflict between line and staff.

The Line Point of View

One of the basic causes of organizational difficulties, as line operations view them, is that staff personnel attempt to assume authority over line elements instead of supporting and advising them.[33] Line commanders feel that the chief looks to them for accountability of the operation; therefore, staff personnel should not try to control their operation because they are not ultimately responsible for handling line problems. Another commonly heard complaint is that staff personnel sometimes fail to give sound advice because their ideas are not fully thought out, not tested, or "too academic." This attitude is easy for line commanders to develop because of the belief that staff personnel are not responsible for the ultimate results of their product and therefore propose new ideas too quickly.

Communications problems sometimes emerge between the staff specialist and line commanders. Staff personnel on occasion fail to explain new plans or procedures and do not give line commanders sufficient time to propose changes. For example, a major staff project was installed in a patrol operation after only a very brief period of time had passed from its announcement until the starting date. Some attempts were made to prepare the personnel for the project by the use of general orders and memos, but this was left to line supervisors to do, and they did not have enough information to fully explain the new program. This resulted in confusion. Individual officers were unsure of what they were to do, so they did little. It took several weeks to recognize the problem and several more weeks to explain, train, and guide the personnel to operate under the new plan. After a three-month delay, the plan began to show results. However, the crime picture for this period was the worst in four years. The chief placed the blame at his precinct commanders' doors. They, in turn, blamed staff for poor preparation and lack of coordination.

Line commanders frequently claim that staff personnel take credit for successful operations and point the finger of blame at the line commander when programs fail. In one department, a new report-writing program was installed under staff auspices. This program was designed to improve the statistical data that the staff group would use in preparing the various departmental reports and to help the patrol commander to evaluate patrol personnel. During the first year of the program, several flaws showed up that prompted staff to write a report that stated the patrol supervisors were not checking the reports carefully, and as a result erroneous information was appearing that made evaluation impossible. A retraining program was instituted, and the defects were ironed out. The personnel assigned to do the training then wrote a report taking full credit for the improvement. The commander of the patrol division took a rather dim view of this self-congratulatory report because he, along with some of his subordinates, worked very closely with the training section in formulating the retraining program.

Operational commanders sometimes express the concern that staff personnel do not see the "big picture" because they have only limited objectives that reflect their own non-operational specialties. For example, the personnel unit of one police department developed a test for the rank of lieutenant. Most of the sergeants who took the examination did poorly. Many became frustrated and angry because they had built up fine work records and believed that the examination procedure failed to measure their potential ability for the rank of lieutenant accurately. The members of the personnel unit who developed the examination procedure were not sympathetic and suggested that the department just did not have the caliber of personnel who could pass a valid examination. The line commanders claimed that the personnel unit did not know enough about the department's needs, and if they would put more effort into helping instead of "figuring out reasons why we're no good, then we'd be better off."

The Staff Point of View

Staff personnel contend that line commanders do not know how to use staff. Instead of using their analytic skills, staff personnel feel that line commanders simply want to use them as writers. As an example, in one medium-size department, the robbery caseload was increasing at an alarming rate. When staff were approached to work on the problem, the chief of detectives told them how he saw the problem, asked them to prepare an order for his signature setting out the changes as he saw them, and refused any staff personnel the opportunity to contact the operating field units to determine what the problems were as they saw them.

Many staff personnel also feel that line officers are shortsighted and resist new ideas. As an example, a department had expanded and numerous personnel were promoted, but some of the personnel promoted to administrative and executive positions could not function effectively because they had not been properly trained to assume their new roles and responsibilities. The results were inefficiency and personal conflict. The planning and research officer had much earlier wanted to install a training program for career development for the ranks of lieutenant and above, so that there would be a trained group to choose from when needed. The planning and research officer blamed the line commanders for being shortsighted and not cooperating earlier to develop career development programs.

Solutions

The problems of line and staff relationships can be corrected. What is needed is a thorough indoctrination and training program and clear definitions as to the tasks of each.

The line is principally responsible for successful operations of the department, and therefore line employees must be responsible for operational decisions affecting them. Staff, on the other hand, exist to assist the line in reaching objectives by providing advice and information when requested to do so. This does not, however, prohibit staff from volunteering advice they believe is needed.

The use of staff assistance is usually at the option of line commanders, but they must recognize that the chief can decide to use staff services to review any operation and that this decision is binding. As an example, the chief may order a planning and research officer to determine if patrol officers are being properly used. The patrol commander is responsible for making effective use of advice received under such circumstances. If the patrol commander disagrees with staff findings, then an opportunity for reply and review by a higher authority should be available.

Staff exist to help line elements accomplish the objectives of the department. To do this effectively, staff must know what the line elements are doing. Illustratively, the personnel officer who does not know what tasks police officers must perform cannot effectively prepare selection standards for the hiring of personnel. Both staff and line must exert effort to ensure that staff stay in contact with what is going on in line units.

Line personnel are concerned primarily with day-to-day operating objectives within the framework of departmental goals. Staff can perform a valuable task for them by thinking ahead toward future problems and operations before they arise. The possibility of a plane crash is a subject that staff, in cooperation with line commanders, can anticipate. Thus, staff can accomplish time-consuming planning and the development of orders and procedures well before they are needed.

Line commanders should know what the various staff functions are and what they can contribute to the improvement of the line units. In some departments, this can be done at meetings by allowing the staff heads to explain what they can do for the line commanders. At the same time, line commanders can make known their expectations about staff support. Such discussions lead to closer coordination and to improved personal relationships that are essential for effectiveness. Staff's ideas will be more readily accepted if they demonstrate an understanding of line operations.

Staff activity deals primarily with change. However, people tend to resist change and ideas that threaten the status quo. Change by itself indicates the possibility that the old way is no longer acceptable. Staff should anticipate and dispel resistance to change by doing the following:

1. Determining to what extent the change proposed will affect the personal relationships of the people involved. Is the change a major one that will affect the social patterns established in the formal and informal organizations discussed later in this chapter? Can the change be broken down into a series of small moves that will have less negative impact than a single, large change?
2. Involving those most affected by the change in the early planning stages. When major changes are involved that will modify the relationships between line commanders and the people who work for them, opposition from commanders can be minimized if they participate from the early planning stages. Although it may not be possible for everyone to participate, the use of representative groups of employees is often effective in helping to facilitate change.
3. Communicating throughout the entire planning stage. The personnel who will be affected by the change will accept it better if (a) they believe it will benefit them personally—that it will make their work easier, faster, or safer (the change should be tied in as closely as possible with the individual's personal goals and interests—job, family, future); (b) the personnel have an opportunity to offer suggestions, ideas, and comments concerning the change as it affects them—provided these suggestions are sincerely wanted and are given serious consideration; and (c) they are kept informed of the results of the change (see Chapter 15, Organizational Change and the Future, for a more detailed discussion).

To achieve organizational objectives, a line commander should know how to use staff assistance. The specialized skills of staff people can be used to help achieve these goals more efficiently and economically. By involving staff in the problems of the line, staff personnel can become more effective by learning the line commanders' way of thinking. Line commanders must be able to identify their problems precisely before seeking assistance. They must not vaguely define a problem and then expect the staff unit to do all the work. It is also important for staff to keep other staff informed of decisions that will affect them. As an example, a department was given permission to hire and train 250 new officers, which was double the normal recruit class. The training unit was not advised of this until a week before the class was to start. Subsequently, many problems developed that could have been avoided.

Critical Thinking Questions

1. What are the essential differences between line and staff in police departments?
2. What solutions might be employed to lessen conflict between line and staff?

THE INFORMAL ORGANIZATION

The **informal organization** does not appear on organizational charts, but it does exist in every organization because people are not simply objects in boxes connected by lines. These people have needs, attitudes, and emotions that rules and regulations are not designed to accommodate. The informal organization is built on friendships and common desires. It, too, may have goals which may or may not coincide with the formal organization's goals. The informal organization has its own communications and behavior patterns, as well as a system of rewards and punishments to assure conformity.[34]

The task of management and supervision is to recognize the existence of the informal organization and to utilize it for the good of the formal organization. Too often, the informal organization is looked upon with disfavor for fear that it will infringe upon the formal organization's authority. As a result, cliques form and develop their own goals and objectives. This usually results in inefficiency, social conflict, and a general breakdown of morale within the formal organization.

It must be remembered that the tools used by management (the process of directing and controlling people and things so the organizational objectives can be accomplished)[35] and supervision (the act of overseeing people)[36] will be most effective and result in cooperation when people feel that they are an integral part of the organization. The task of administration is to make each employee aware of what the formal organizational goals are and how each employee plays an important part in achieving those goals through his or her efforts.

Through the feedback process, the informal organization can be an excellent source of measurement to determine if goals are being met. The feedback process involves both supervisors and managers listening to their employees and asking them questions in regard to operations and procedures. This information is then inserted into the formal organization's communication system to help the chief administrator evaluate how well operational plans are working. Once recognized, it can be an effective means to greater employee participation in both decision making and goal achievement.

The informal organization has several important characteristics:

Naturalness—The informal organization is natural and spontaneous; it does not ordinarily take on the characteristics of a social group as a result of an order or edict from higher authority. Rather, the informal group evolves and develops in response to conditions and needs.

Interactions (or group dynamics)—Group members interact with each other because they want to; they have a natural, spontaneous desire to do so.

Empathy—Members of a social group have a high degree of attraction and sympathy for each other. They like to be with each other. Their social inhibitions are at a minimum and they feel a lack of the type of restraint which results from expected disapproval of one's associates. While some members of a social group are attracted to each other more than others, the general level of mutual attraction is high.

Social distance—Members of a social group do not feel too much social distance. That is, they do not feel that there are status or other types of barriers between themselves and other members. Social distance is the reason that uninhibited interaction often fails to take place in management meetings attended by personnel from several rank levels.

Democratic orientation—The social group has a strongly democratic orientation. The very essence of social group action is the attraction which members have for each other, supplemented by uninhibited communication and self-expression. Naturalness and freedom characterize effective social groups.

Leadership—Leaders tend to emerge naturally from the group. This does not mean, however, that social groups cannot exist where leaders have been designated from the outside. Much depends on the characteristics and behavior of the leader. When an aggregation of people begins to become a social group, some people initiate interaction more than others and they are usually attractive to a large number of people. These are the natural leaders, but they may not necessarily also be designated as hierarchical leaders.

Group pressures—One aspect of the social group is the pressure exerted to get the members to conform to group standards in thought and action. The phenomenon can be used either to thwart the goals of management or to facilitate their achievement.

Cohesiveness and unity—In order to endure, a social group must have a certain amount of cohesiveness. Members must have sufficient desire to belong, to keep the group together and in continued existence. In short, there must be enough attractiveness in group goals and associations to ensure their observance as a means of maintaining the group.[37]

Critical Thinking Question

1. Why is it essential for management and supervision to utilize and integrate informal organizations within their departments?

EXPANDING THE LAW ENFORCEMENT PERSONNEL POOL

Citizen Police Academies

Agencies have expanded their personnel pool through the use of citizen police academies, citizen patrols, reserves, and volunteers within the department, frequently retired individuals, including retired police officers. Another trend is the civilianization of certain law enforcement functions.[38]

Several police departments seeking to facilitate the implementation of community policing have started citizen police academies (CPAs). Since the organization of the first recorded U.S. citizen police academy in Orlando, Florida, in 1985, many communities have developed their own academies, each with its own unique focus. According to Ellis,[39] CPAs allow residents to unite with their police departments to fight to keep what is theirs: the community.

Weinblatt[40] asserts that civilian academies permit law enforcement to take community policing to the "next level." One police captain maintains,[41] "The citizens involved essentially become ambassadors for our cause to the community and offer positive support for what we do." Maffe and Burke state,

Police "academies" for citizens are the latest hot item for law enforcement.

Citizen police academies enable the residents of a community to become more familiar with the day-to-day operations of their police departments. Participants gain a better understanding of the procedures, responsibilities, guidelines, demands of personnel and the policies and laws that guide decision making. . . . The benefits of a citizen police academy are significant and foremost is the power of proactive policing within the community. The only exposure most citizens have with a police officer is usually when a motor vehicle violation has occurred and a traffic citation is issued. This is usually viewed as a negative experience.

Proactive law enforcement, such as a police citizen academy, places officers in a positive light. Understanding and cooperating with citizens is vital for effective police-community relations. Pro-activity is the critical foundation of understanding, and a citizen police academy bridges the gap between the citizens and the police.[42]

Kanable[43] notes, "Although the concept of what the citizen police academy is all about is consistent across the nation, the curricula are as different as the departments putting them together." For example, the 12-week academy sponsored by the Fond du lac County, Wisconsin, Sheriff's Department teaches students about patrol, community services, domestics, drugs, arson, emergency communication, the canine unit, the dive team, the boat patrol, the SWAT team, crime scene processing, surveillance, investigation/interrogations, corrections, civil process, and the criminal justice system as a whole.[44] Many academies also offer ride-along programs.

The success of CPAs is without question. Kanable claims, "If citizen police academies were graded, there's no doubt they'd receive an A+ from law enforcement officers throughout the nation.[45]

Citizens on Patrol

In other jurisdictions, community policing strategies include citizen patrols. One such citizen patrol, operating in Fort Worth, Texas, encouraged community residents to patrol their own neighborhoods and be directly responsible for reducing crime. The program currently has over 2,000 patrollers, representing more than 87 neighborhoods in the city.

The St. Petersburg, Florida, Police Department has implemented a citizen patrol program, and Woodyard reports,

The main objective is to look for, and report, suspicious and unusual activity whether in the form of persons and/or vehicles. Under no circumstances do volunteers approach suspicious persons or vehicles, or stop a vehicle.

Complaints [that] volunteers are able to investigate [include] abandoned vehicles, assist patrol officer when requested, found property, area check, information, bicycle theft with no suspect, traffic hazards, disabled vehicle, accidents (Blue Form), contact messages (nondeath) and 911 hang-ups (children).[46]

In Delray Beach, Florida, a city with a population of 50,000, the police department's largest volunteer project is the Citizens Observer Patrol (COP), whose three primary goals are the following:

- Effectively reduce crime and disorder in selected communities
- Establish a working relationship between the Delray Beach police and its citizenry
- Empower people and have them take ownership of their communities to reduce crime

Overman notes, "Currently, the Delray Beach Citizens Observer Patrol has 850 members in 21 sectors. Crime has markedly diminished in every area. Some sectors report a 75 percent decrease in burglary, auto theft and vandalism."[47]

Reserves

Reserve officers, sometimes called part-timers, auxiliaries, specials, or supernumeraries, are valuable assets to police departments in the effort to expand law enforcement resources. Reserve officer programs vary considerably from department to department. Weinblatt notes,

> *Arroyo Grande [California], like many agencies in the western United States, trains and deploys reservists along the lines of the full-time officers. Standards and expectations remain equally high for both groups. At the other end of the spectrum, some agencies, such as many in the New York City metropolitan region, have gravitated towards a separation, which entails reserves patrolling along or with another reservist.*[48]

In some jurisdictions, reserve officers have powers of arrest and wear the same uniform as law enforcement officers, except for the badge, which says "reserve." They may even purchase their own firearm and ballistics vest and drive their personally owned vehicles during operations.

Some jurisdictions recruit reserves from those retiring from their full-time ranks. Weinblatt observes,

> *A lot of time and money is invested in veteran officers who could continue sharing that knowledge as a reserve officer when they retire.*
>
> *In an age requiring more sophisticated personnel, agencies are increasingly looking to benefit from the wealth of police experience residing in their communities. Retaining full-time expertise in the guise of a reserve officer is a cost-effective way of meeting law enforcement challenges.*[49]

Many reserve units function in specialized roles. For example, Weinblatt notes, numerous departments across the country are using reserves to perform search-and-rescue operations because of the prohibitively high costs of full-time, paid search-and-rescue personnel:

> *The Los Angeles County Sheriff's Department has 110 non-compensated reserve deputies and in excess of 40 civilians. Reserve Chief Jack said his group donated 13,000 hours last year in training and 7,600 hours in actual time in 350 search and rescue operations [see Figure 6.17).*
>
> *San Diego County also has its share of specialty units. Their array of 11 units include tactical search (man tracking), mounted unit, motorized unit (personally owned four wheel drives to move personnel in and out of areas), aero squadron (privately owned fixed wind aircraft), and medical unit.*[50]

In summarizing his opinion of the reserve program, the Union County, North Carolina, sheriff states, "They help us . . . to help the citizens. We've gotten tenfold over what we've put into this." He also asserts that volunteers involved in search-and-rescue operations are really an extension of community policing. "Through this partnership with the citizens, we have extended our reach into the community."[51]

Concerns exist regarding the use of reserves—in particular, labor and liability concerns. Weinblatt[52] notes, "The driving force behind some agency's reluctance to deploy

FIGURE 6.17

The Los Angeles County Sheriff's Department Volunteer Program is one of the largest in the country. Volunteers perform such functions as alarm incident aid, business alert/watch, crime analysis, disaster preparedness, graffiti watch, jail aid, pawn slip/pawn search, station tour, and victim/witness assistance. Sheriff Leroy D. Baca (second from left) is shown here with members of his agency's volunteer patrol.

(Courtesy of Sheriff Leroy D. Baca, Natalie Salazar Macias, Director, Community Law Enforcement Partnership Program; Kathy Vukovich, Asst. Director, Community/Law Enforcement Partnership Program)

reserves on an equal footing is based on resistance from employees and their labor organizations." To allay this concern, some departments have a contract with full-time officers stating that reserves are used only if a regular officer turns down the overtime or wants to take "comp" time off. To address liability issues, most agencies require reserves to complete rigorous training courses. Some, in fact, require reserves to go through the full basic academy, not accepting the reserve academy training as adequate.

As Bair,[53] a reserve officer, says, "Reserve officers really want to be the best that they can be, but we can only be as good as the training that we are given."

Volunteers

The three groups of law enforcement personnel just discussed—citizen police academy participants, citizen patrols, and reservists—consist primarily, if not solely in many jurisdictions, of volunteers. And, as discussed, their numbers are increasing. According to Jensen,[54] "Many a law enforcement agency has discovered one of the best ways to cope with shrinking budgets and the high cost of technology is looking to the community for volunteer help." Sharp adds,

> *Volunteers have been used by law enforcement agencies for different jobs for many years. They have done so because they have proved their worth.*
>
> *A growing number of police agencies are viewing volunteers as integral parts of their community policing programs. Not only do volunteers perform a variety of tasks that might otherwise occupy the time of sworn officers, but they can also save the department money.*[55]

In The News

Today's News

Basketball Star Sworn in as Reserve Officer

Shaquille O'Neal, the man recognized worldwide as a basketball hero, was sworn in as a reserve officer for the Miami Beach, Florida Police Department on December 8, 2005. The 7′1″ Miami Heat player was previously a reserve officer in Los Angeles and completed extensive training before being sworn in. O'Neal has aspirations of working as a police officer full-time after retirement, and he currently assists Miami Beach in a variety of investigations in the special victims detective unit.

Source: "Shaq Joins Crime-Fighting Team," *Miami Herald,* December 9, 2005. Shaquille O'Neal being sworn in as a reserve officer for the Miami Beach, Florida Police Department.
(AP Photo/Miami Beach Police Dept.)

Indeed, as Paynter[56] reports, volunteers in Phoenix, Arizona, donated more than 29,000 hours to the police department in 1998, saving the agency over $500,000. Paynter[57] notes, "Volunteers can be an untapped resource that can help law enforcement save money and add services. . . . Jobs volunteers can do for law enforcement run the gamut from traditional clerical work and data entry to things like assisting stranded motorists." A jurisdiction in New Jersey that found it needed extra help to investigate animal cruelty cases formed a volunteer division in conjunction with the Society for the Prevention of Cruelty to Animals (SPCA). Weinblatt states,

> *New Jersey has some 11 independent SPCA enforcement units that have volunteer investigative personnel carrying out the animal protection mandate. . . .*
>
> *In addition to reacting to reported investigative situations, the uniformed and armed volunteer officers have an active bike patrol that patrols the many sprawling mall parking lots . . . [looking] for jurisdictionally relevant violations such as dogs locked in hot cars during the summer.*[58]

QUICK FACTS QUICK FACTS QUICK

Quick Facts

Police Volunteers

Police volunteers can support law enforcement in a variety of ways. Examples of the types of assignments in which volunteers often lend a hand to law enforcement include reading parking meters, participating in graffiti abatement programs, writing handicap parking violations, compiling statistical data, providing support for traffic and crowd control, participating in search-and-rescue programs, serving on neighborhood watch committees, and participating in law enforcement or public safety training exercises.

Source: Volunteers in Police Service (VIPS): www.policevolunteers.org.

In Henderson County, North Carolina, approximately 60 people are part of the Volunteers in Partnership with the Sheriff, or VIP, a group that donates about 1,000 free hours to the department each month, performing functions such as answering telephones, greeting the public, doing report follow-ups, conducting research and development for new programs, assisting the Civil Process Division in serving subpoenas, manning the metal detector at the county courthouse, leading courthouse tours, providing security at the county library, fingerprinting, helping with traffic control, and assisting DARE officers.[59]

As with the concern over using reserves, some paid, full-time officers are hesitant to embrace volunteers. To overcome staff resistance to volunteer programs, Jensen advises "talking up" the program beforehand: "Stress that no volunteer is there to take work away from an employee, but only to make it easier on the paid staff." Paynter adds,

> *Increasing services and saving money by using volunteers can be a boon to the financially strapped law enforcement agency. But volunteers win too by helping their community. "My main goal is to put an officer out on the street where they can do their job best," [one volunteer] says. "My main motivation is to free up sworn personnel and put them somewhere doing a job only they can perform."*
>
> *And keeping officers on the streets, where they belong, is what a volunteer program is all about.*[60]

One innovative program uses volunteers to assist in a private/public sector partnership–state safety team. Weinblatt describes the team established by the North Carolina Transportation Association, which has counterparts nationwide. The association had 50 designated safety officers, of which 19 are active on road safety patrol. Other activities include public and law enforcement training endeavors geared toward drug interdiction, commercial vehicle inspection, and accident investigation.[61]

Another notable agency, the Anne Arundel County, Maryland, Police Department, has been selected as a national model on how police departments can use citizen volunteers.

Critical Thinking Questions

1. What are the advantages of using volunteers to expand the law enforcement personnel pool?
2. Describe an incident in which the use of reserve officers would be beneficial to a police department.

In The News

Maryland Police Volunteer Program Is Touted

A police volunteer program in Anne Arundel County, Maryland, was touted as a model for the Volunteers in Police Service Program (VIPS), an initiative launched by the Bush administration in 2002. The VIPS program at Anne Arundel Police Department, created in 1990, requires that volunteers give 16 hours a month to the department and perform activities such as traffic control and neighborhood canvassing. The national VIPS initiative for which Anne Arundel serves as a model was created as part the USA Freedom Corps, which supports programs that share the goal of helping communities prevent, prepare for, and respond to crime, natural disasters, and other emergencies.

Reserve officers are valuable assets to police departments in their effort to expand law enforcement services. These reserve officers in a training class are members of the Anne Arundel County, Maryland, Police Department. Some of the services they provide include assisting motorists with disabled vehicles, assisting with traffic control accidents, securing crime scenes, picking up and delivering legal papers, and protecting crime scenes.
Source: "Maryland Police Volunteer Program Is Touted," *Law Enforcement News*, February 28, 2002, p. 5. (*Courtesy of Anne Arundel County Police Department, Maryland*)

CHAPTER REVIEW

1. Summarize the advantages and disadvantages of specialization within an organization.
   Specialization can enhance operational effectiveness by placing responsibility for the performance of a given task on specific units, allowing for the development of expertise within a unit, promoting a group esprit de corps, and increasing overall proficiency in job task responsibility. However, specialization may also increase conflict and friction between units, complicate the overall organizational structure, and take resources from general services.
2. Describe the concept of span of management.
   Span of management is the number of personnel a supervisor can effectively manage; it is affected by groupings of subordinates, the nature of the task that the supervisor is responsible for, how well subordinates work together, the preparation and ability of the supervisor, the amount of authority delegated, the ease and simplicity of instructions, and the availability of specialized equipment.
3. Distinguish between vertical and horizontal differentiation.
   Vertical differentiation is based on levels of authority, or positions holding power within an organization. Horizontal differentiation is based on activity and features the grouping of activities by clientele, geography, style of service, time, or process.

4. Discuss the differences between tall organizational structures and flat organizational structures.

   Tall organizational structures have many different layers, which make them more complex and can impair effective communication. Flat organizations have fewer layers as a result of broadening the span of management, and they tend not to suffer from as many communication breakdowns as do taller departments.

5. List and explain four types of structural design.

   In line structure, the simplest form of organization design, authority flows from the top to the bottom of the organization, creating a clear, unbroken chain of command. Line and staff structure adds internal support to the line, such as auxiliary units and administrative functions. Functional structure gives management authority to personnel outside their normal spans of management, making specific units responsible to a variety of other unit commanders. Matrix structure assigns members of functional areas to specific projects, often in an attempt to address a specific, short-term mission.

6. Identify major organizational differences between sheriff's offices and municipal police departments.

   Most police departments do not have a single person positioned between the police chief and all of the operating and administrative bureaus, while sheriff's offices often have a chief deputy or undersheriff assuming full operational control over the entire organization with the blessing of the sheriff. Another major difference is that the undersheriff or chief deputy is typically responsible for supervisory operation of the county jail.

7. Discuss how community policing and problem-oriented policing can impact organizational design.

   Community policing requires that police services be decentralized and community-based, making an organizational design that is less formalized, less specialized, and less bureaucratic necessary.

8. Identify the basic causes of tension between line and staff.

   Causes of conflict include line operations sometimes feel that staff attempt to assume authority over line elements; there are often communication problems between line and staff; line commanders frequently claim that staff personnel take credit for success and blame line for failures; line often feels that staff cannot see the big organizational picture; staff feel that line does not properly utilize them; and staff resents line for being resistant to change.

9. Describe the characteristics of the informal organization.

   The characteristics of an informal organization include naturalness, interaction, empathy, lack of social distance, democratic orientation, leadership, group pressure, and cohesiveness and unity among the group.

10. List and describe four ways that law enforcement agencies can supplement their personnel pool.

    Law enforcement agencies can supplement their personnel pool by the use of citizen police academies, which familiarize citizens with police operations and increase citizen cooperation with police. Citizen patrols encourage community members to patrol the streets and report suspicious and unusual activity. Reserve officers often work side by side with police officers, especially in specialized roles, such as search and rescue. Finally, volunteers may help police departments in a variety of roles, from clerical duties to extra security or traffic control.

KEY TERMS

Decentralization: the process of distributing the administrative functions or powers of an organization among all levels of the structure.

Functional structure: a modified line and staff structure that brings together trained specialists and specialized resources under a single manager to accomplish a core responsibility.

Horizontal differentiation: an organizational design that is structured based on activity rather than rank.

Informal organization: an unofficial structure within an organization, often based on personal relationships, that has its own goals, communications, and behavior patterns.

Line and staff structure: an organizational structure that retains basic elements from line structure but adds auxiliary and administrative support units.

Line structure: a form of organizational design in which authority flows from the top to the bottom of the organization in a clear and unbroken line.

Matrix (or grid) structure: an organizational design that assigns members of functional areas to specific projects, such as a task force.

Organizing: the process of determining the formal structure of task and authority relationships best suited to accomplish a mission.

Principle of hierarchy: a requirement that each lower level of organization be supervised by a higher level.

Span of management: the number of personnel a supervisor can personally manage effectively.

Specialization: a division of labor wherein jobs allocated to meet different responsibilities are filled with those specially qualified to perform them.

Vertical differentiation: an organizational design based on levels of authority within an organization.

NOTES

1. S. P. Robbins, *The Administration Process* (Englewood Cliffs, N.J.: Prentice Hall, 1976), pp. 17–18.
2. *The Republic of Plato,* trans. A. Bloom (New York: Basic Books, 1968), p. 47.
3. For example, see Luther Gulick and L. Urwick, eds., *Papers on the Science of Administration* (New York: August M. Kelley, a 1969 reprint of the 1937 edition).
4. O. W. Wilson and R. C. McLaren, *Police Administration,* 3rd ed. (New York: McGraw-Hill, 1972), p. 79.
5. Ibid., p. 81.
6. Ibid., p. 83.
7. N. C. Kassoff, *Organizational Concepts* (Washington, D.C.: International Association of Chiefs of Police, 1967), p. 22.
8. Wilson and McLaren, *Police Administration,* p. 56.
9. Ibid.
10. Kassof, *Organizational Concepts,* pp. 16–18.
11. Troy Lane, "Span of Control for Law Enforcement Agencies," *National Academy Associate Magazine,* 8, no. 2 (March/April): 19–31.
12. V. A. Graicunas, "Relationships in Organization," *Bulletin of the Management Institute* (Geneva: International Labor Office, 1933), in *Papers on the Science of Administration* (New York: Institute of Public Administration, 1937) pp. 181–87. As discussed in H. Koontz and C. O'Donnell, *Principles of Management* (New York: McGraw-Hill, 1965), p. 212.
13. Kassoff, *Organizational Concepts,* p. 27.
14. D. A. Tansik and J. F. Elliot, *Managing Police Organizations* (Monterey, Calif.: Duxbury Press, 1981), p. 81.
15. Ibid.
16. B. J. Hodge and W. P. Anthony, *Organizational Theory: An Environmental Approach* (Boston: Allyn and Bacon, 1979), p. 240.
17. Richard Hall, *Organizations: Structure and Process* (Englewood Cliffs, N.J.: Prentice Hall, 1972), p. 143.
18. This section is a synopsis of the "Nature and Process of Differentiation" found in Hodge and Anthony, *Organizational Theory,* p. 249.
19. Darlton E. McFarland, *Management: Foundations and Practices,* 5th ed. (New York: Macmillan, 1979), p. 316.
20. Ibid., p. 309.
21. B. J. Hodge and H. J. Johnson, *Management and Organizational Behavior* (New York: John Wiley & Sons, 1970), p. 163.
22. Joseph J. Staft, "The Effects of Organizational Design on Communications between Patrol and Investigation Functions," in U.S. Department of Justice,

National Institute of Justice, Research Utilization Program, *Improving Police Management* (Washington, D.C.: University Research Corporation, 1982), p. 243.
23. Robert C. Trojanowicz, "Community Policing Is Not Police Community Relations," *FBI Law Enforcement Bulletin* 59 (October 1990): 8.
24. Ibid., pp. 8–10.
25. Richard Kitaeff, "The Great Debate: Centralized vs. Decentralized Marketing Research Function," *Marketing Research: A Magazine of Management and Applications* 6 (winter 1993): 59.
26. Bill Blackwood Law Enforcement Management Institute of Texas, "Decentralization in Texas Police Departments," *TELEMASP Bulletin* 2 (August 1995): 1–11.
27. Las Vegas Metropolitan Police Department (Las Vegas, Nev.), "Staff Study Decentralization of the Burglary Function," 1989.
28. Ibid., p. 12.
29. Anaheim Police Department (Anaheim, Calif.), "Community Policing Team Annual Report," 1994.
30. Several critiques of experimental police methods have been noted in the literature. See Robert W. Taylor and Dennis J. Kenney, "The Problems with Problem Oriented Policing" (paper presented at the Academy of Criminal Justice Sciences Annual Meeting, Nashville, Tennessee, March 1991); Kenneth W. Findley and Robert W. Taylor, "Re-Thinking Neighborhood Policing," *Journal of Contemporary Criminal Justice* 6 (May 1990): 70–78; Jerome Skolnick and D. Bayley, *Community Policing: Issues and Practices around the World* (Washington, D.C.: National Institute of Justice, 1988); Jack Greene and Ralph Taylor, "Community Based Policing and Foot Patrol: Issues of Theory and Evaluation, in *Community Policing: Rhetoric or Reality?* ed. Jack Greene and Stephen Mastrofski (New York: Praeger, 1988), pp. 216–19; Stephen Mastrofski, "Police Agency Accreditation: The Prospects of Reform," *American Journal of Police* (May 15, 1986): 45–81.
31. Gary W. Cordner, "Written Rules and Regulations: Are They Necessary?" *FBI Law Enforcement Bulletin* 58 (July 1989): 17–21.
32. See Robert Michaels, *Political Parties* (New York: Dover, 1959).
33. Kassoff, *Organizational Concepts,* pp. 31–38.
34. Ibid., pp. 22–26.
35. Nathan F. Ianone and Marvin D. Ianone, *Supervision of Police Personnel,* 6th ed. (Upper Saddle River, N.J.: Prentice Hall, 2001), p. 1.
36. Ibid.
37. John M. Pfiffner and Frank P. Sherwood, *Administrative Organization* (Englewood Cliffs, N.J.: Prentice Hall, 1965), pp. 43–44.
38. Wayne Bennett and Karen M. Hess, *Management and Supervision in Law Enforcement* (Belmont, Calif.: Wadsworth, 2001), pp. 486–90.
39. Tom Ellis, "The Citizen's Police Academy," *Law Enforcement Technology* 45, no. 10 (October 1997): 56–60.
40. Richard B. Weinblatt, "Academies Put Civilians in the Shotgun Seat," *Law and Order* 45, no. 9 (September 1997): 86–88.
41. Ibid., p. 86.
42. Steven R. Maffe and Tod W. Burke, "Citizen Police Academies," *Law and Order* 47, no. 10 (October 1999): 77–80.
43. Rebecca Kanable, "An Apple for the Officer: Citizen Police Academies Keep Officers in Touch with the Community," *Law Enforcement Technology* 26, no. 10 (October 1999): 56–58.
44. Ibid.
45. To learn more about citizen police academies, contact the national Citizen Police Academy Association at 630–801–6583.
46. Adele Woodyard, "Volunteers on Patrol," *Law and Order* 45, no. 10 (October 1997): 179–81.
47. Richard G. Overman, "Citizens and Police Form Solid Alliance," *Community Policing Exchange,* phase IV, no. 15 (July/August 1997): 3.
48. Richard B. Weinblatt, "Deploying Reserves: Solo or Partnering Patrol Options," *Law and Order* 47, no. 7 (July 1999): 25–26.
49. Richard B. Weinblatt, "Holding onto a Knowledgeable Resource: Recruiting Reserves from Full-Time Ranks," *Law and Order* 47, no. 6 (June 1999): 127–30.
50. Richard B. Weinblatt, "Discovering a Valuable Asset: Reserve Search and Rescue Units," *Law and Order* 47, no. 5 (May 1999): 18–20.
51. Ibid., p. 18.
52. Ibid., p. 20.
53. John M. Bair, "Just a Reserve? The Contributions Can Be Many," *Police* 24, no. 3, (2000).
54. Marilyn Jensen, "Volunteers Can Make a Difference." *Law and Order* 46, no. 9 (September 1998): 102–5.
55. Arthur G. Sharp, "The Value of Volunteers," *Law and Order* 47, no. 10 (October 1999): 204–10.
56. Ronnie L. Paynter, "Helping Hands," *Law Enforcement Technology* 26, no. 3 (March 1999): 30–34.

57. Ibid., p. 30.
58. Weinblatt, "Academies Put Civilians in the Shotgun Seat," p. 21.
59. Bob Noble, "Volunteers Find Numerous Ways to Help Police Serve Their Community," *Sheriff Times*, (spring 1997): 2.
60. Paynter, "Helping Hands," p. 34.
61. Richard B. Weinblatt, "Volunteers Assist in Private/Public Sector Partnership," *Law and Order* 48, no. 1 (January 2000): 19.

Leadership is not a spectator sport.

— Kouzes and Posner

CHAPTER 7

OUTLINE

Introduction

Leadership and Performance

The Nature of Leadership, Authority, and Power

The Power Motivation of Police Managers

The Leadership Skill Mix

Theories of Leadership

Styles of Leadership

The Leader and Conflict

Leadership and Organizational Control

Chapter Review

Key Terms

Notes

OBJECTIVES

1. Define leadership.
2. Contrast the two ways at looking at "great men" theories of leadership.
3. Identify and briefly discuss the three broad responsibilities all police leaders have.
4. Describe how authority and power are separate, but entwined, concepts.
5. Discuss the power motivation of managers.
6. State the components of the skill mix and how they operate.
7. Describe how the traits approach to leadership would select leaders.
8. Define the authoritarian, democratic, and laissez-faire leadership styles.
9. Outline the authoritarian–democratic leadership continuum.
10. Identify and briefly describe Downs's four types of leader behavior in bureaucratic organizations.
11. Contrast station house and street sergeants.
12. Identify the five major management styles from the Managerial Grid.
13. Define situational leadership.
14. Describe transactional and transformational leaders.
15. Conclude whether conflict is "good" or "bad."

LEADERSHIP

INTRODUCTION

During the 1970s and much of the 1980s, police departments placed considerable emphasis on rational management systems (such as sophisticated decision-making techniques) and the use of technology (e.g., computers). In an environment characterized by scarce resources for programs and a public demanding more and better services, chiefs of police tried to find new ways to improve productivity. This resulted in police chiefs thinking of themselves as managers, as opposed to leaders. While rational management systems and technology remain important arrows in the quivers of police chiefs, the role of leadership in making police departments function at a high level re-emerged as a vital concern by the very late 1980s as the community-oriented policing and quality movements began to take hold. Today, officials hiring police chiefs want to know what the candidates' visions are for the future of the agency, how they will stimulate employee participation, what efforts they will make to ensure that quality is driven by customer concerns, how they will empower employees, and other related issues. These officials are less concerned about finding someone who can simply control a police department and more focused on identifying someone who can envision a better future and take the concrete steps to bring it about.

Another factor that fosters concern with leadership in police organizations is that employees, who bring their own values, needs, and expectations into a police department, don't want to know just what to do; they want to know *why*. When these officers see better ways of doing things, they are not easily satisfied by answers such as "that's the way it has always been done." Today's employees do not want to be treated like mushrooms—kept in the dark and dumped on. They will work hard to achieve the police department's goals, but they also want the legitimacy of their own needs—such as being treated with dignity and respect and recognized for contributions. Finally, although some police chiefs still believe in "treating them rough and telling them nothing," they are rapidly following the path of dinosaurs because city managers are not willing to put up with high turnover rates, numerous grievances, and lawsuits.

In The News

New Chief Was Officer

Phillip Morse is the new chief of Washington D.C.'s Capitol Police, emerging from a pool of approximately 60 candidates. At 43, Morse is the youngest chief of the 178-year-old Capitol Police. One supporter noted that Chief Morse has a young force and therefore has some advantages in that he is not that far removed age-wise from being a member of Generation X.

Other factors figuring in the selection of Morse include his breadth of experience, strong leadership qualities, his education, the support of rank-and-file members, his desire to make the department one of the finest in the nation, and his understanding of "the Hill and its committees" (Congress). Morse, a 21-year veteran of the department, moved up through the ranks; as an insider, he can hit the ground running and not have to figure a lot of things out, something an outsider would have to do.

Source: John McArdle, "Hill Officials Back Morse's Promotion," Copyright 2006 Roll Call, Inc., October 31, 2006.

LEADERSHIP AND PERFORMANCE

The police leader is responsible for three equally important but essentially different broad responsibilities:

1. Fulfilling the mission of the police department
2. Making work productive and helping subordinates to achieve
3. Producing impacts[1]

A number of factors impinge on how well these responsibilities are met, such as the chief's leadership style, community preferences, available resources, and the selection process for a chief. Police leaders chosen by a competitive process or who are perceived by subordinates in the department as competent are viewed consistently as having greater expertise and, consequently, have more influence and power.[2] There are, additionally, "habits of minds" that police leaders who meet their three key responsibilities effectively must practice:

1. They know where their time goes and manage it actively. They identify and eliminate things that need not be done at all. They delegate to others things that can be done as well or better by someone else. And they avoid wasting their own time and that of others.[3]
2. They focus on outward contribution. They gear their efforts to results rather than to work. They start out with the question "What results are expected of me?" rather than with the work to be done, let alone with its techniques and tools.
3. They build on strengths—their own strengths; the strengths of their superiors, colleagues, and subordinates; and the strengths in the situation—that is, on what they can do. They do not build on weakness. They do not start out with the things they cannot do.
4. They concentrate first on the few major areas where superior performance will produce outstanding results. They force themselves to set priorities and stay with their priority decision. They know they have no choice but to do first things first—and second things not at all. The alternative is to get nothing done.
5. They make effective decisions. They know that this is, above all, a matter of system—of the right steps in the right sequence. They know that an effective

In The News

Leaders as "Difference Makers"

Leadership doesn't just mean you occupy a position; reduced to its simplest, it means that the incumbents are "difference makers." The example which follows reveals how leaders can focus on one or more programs to make a positive impact.

The Baldwinsville, New York, Police Department (BPD) won seven awards in 7 years from the American Automobile Association's Community Traffic Safety Program. In the first 2 years, it won Silver Awards, Gold Awards the next 4, and this year the highest level, the Platinum Award. The awards are given to communities that achieve outstanding success in local traffic safety issues, showing a consistent trend of improvement over 5 years or by submitting data which show that its traffic safety record is "substantially better" than statewide data for communities of a comparable size. Providing for the safe movement of people and vehicles is one of the historical strengths of the BPD; the Village of Baldwinsville has not had a pedestrian fatality in the past 25 years.

Source: Tom Leo, "Baldwinsville Police Receive Platinum Award for Safety," *The Post-Standard* (Syracuse, New York), December 14, 2006, with additions and restatement and www.baldwinsville.org, January 26, 2007.

In The News

Chief Admits Felonies

The Delhi, Louisiana, Police Chief admitted setting his own office on fire, resulting in his being sentenced to 15 years for "simple arson and two other felonies." The chief originally claimed that the 2005 fire probably resulted from his painting his office using candles for lighting.

However, Louisiana State Troopers conducting the investigation reached a different conclusion. They found that thousands of dollars and drugs had vanished from the evidence room and that there were e-mail and text messages revealing that the chief actually intended to commit suicide and burn his office down in the process.

Source: "Police Chief Gets Plea Bargain Max for Torching His Office," The Associated Press State and Local Wire, September 21, 2006.

decision is always a judgment based on "dissenting opinions" rather than on "consensus on the facts." And they know that to make many decisions fast means to make the wrong decisions. What is needed are few but fundamental decisions. What is needed is the right strategy rather than razzle-dazzle tactics.

If, as has been suggested, **leadership** is an intangible, the effects generated by its presence or absence and its character are not. Consider the following examples:

- Police officers, operating a dirty patrol vehicle, approached a motorist they had stopped for a traffic violation. The officers had a conversation with the person that was correct on the surface but that had an underlying tone of arrogance.
- A sergeant, already 35 minutes late getting off duty, was en route to the station when a burglary-in-progress call was given to another unit; he volunteered to help and subsequently was shot to death by two burglars.
- The chief of police of a medium-size city chronically complained to anyone who would listen that his commanders "aren't worth anything" and that he was "carrying the whole department on his back."
- A visitor to a city approached an officer walking a beat and asked where the nearest car rental agency could be found; he replied, "What the hell do I look like, an information booth?" and walked away. The next day, she asked an officer standing on a street corner where the First National Bank Building was. The officer took the woman's arm, escorted her across the street, and said, "Lady, you see that big building on the corner where we were just standing? Well, if it had fallen, we'd have both been killed by it."
- Based on limited new information, the commander of an investigations bureau reopened the case file on a convicted "no-good" who had already served 14 months for the offense in question. Subsequently, new evidence and a confession resulted in his release and the conviction of another person.

There are many definitions of leadership, each reflecting certain perspectives. For example, leadership may be defined as the characteristics exhibited by an individual or as a function of a position within the police department's hierarchical structure, such as captain. However, a generally accepted definition is that *leadership* is the process of influencing organizational members to use their energies willingly and appropriately to facilitate the achievement of the police department's goals.

Critical Thinking Question

1. Leaders manage their time effectively. What activities fill up your time? What criteria would you use to trim activities from your daily schedule? What would you do with the time saved?

THE NATURE OF LEADERSHIP, AUTHORITY, AND POWER

The definition of leadership in the previous section deserves some analysis. In Chapter 5, Organizational Theory, the basic **rationale for the existence of organizations** was that they do those things that people are unwilling or unable to do alone. It therefore follows that police departments, as is true for other organizations, are goal directed. The behavior of its members should be purposeful and in consonance with the department's goals. By "using their energies appropriately," it is meant that morally and legally accepted means are employed in the discharge of duties. The terms "influencing" and "willingly" are related to the concepts of **authority** and **power.**

Although these are often treated synonymously, authority and power are allied but separate concepts. Authority is a grant made by the formal organization to a position, the incumbent of which wields it in fulfilling his or her responsibilities. The fact that a formal grant of authority has been made does not mean that the person receiving it also is automatically able to influence others to perform at all, let alone willingly:

> *Officer James P. Murphy was among 50 officers to be promoted by the New York City Police Commissioner. Instead of accepting a handshake and his gold detective's shield, Officer Murphy removed the gold badge, placed it on the dais, and walked out of the ceremony. Officer Murphy took this action to protest the department's investigation of allegations that his unit—the Brooklyn Narcotics Tactical Team—had mistreated prisoners and lied about evidence to shore up shaky arrests. Officer Murphy was not believed to be a target of this investigation. A ranking police official with 40 years of service said he had never seen anything like Murphy's actions before.*[4]

This incident illustrates that, while the commissioner had the authority to promote Officer Murphy, he did not have the power to make him accept it. Some power to affect an officer's performance is inherent in positions of formal authority. But to a significant degree power, as suggested by Barnard, is a grant made by the led to the leader. The leader whose subordinates refuse to follow is not totally without power, for subordinates may be given verbal or written reprimands or suspensions, be forced or expelled from the organization, or be fined, imprisoned, or executed, depending on the specifics involved.[5] The use of this type of power must be considered carefully; failure to invoke it may contribute to a breakdown in discipline and organizational performance; the clumsy employment of it may contribute to morale problems, may divert energy from achieving goals, and may have other negative side effects, including calling into question the abilities of the involved leader:

> *A uniformed officer riding alone informed the radio dispatcher that he was stopping a possibly drunken motorist. His sergeant, who had only been promoted and assigned to the squad two weeks previously, heard the transmission and told the dispatcher that he would back up the officer. When the sergeant, a nine-year veteran of the force, but who had not served in any "street" assignment for the past six years, arrived, a Marine corporal was about to get into a taxi cab. When questioned by the sergeant, the officer who had stopped the Marine as a possible drunk driver related that the corporal had been drinking, but that it was a marginal case and after talking with him, the corporal agreed to park his car and had called the taxi cab from a nearby pay phone.*

In The News

Who Should Make Promotional Decisions?

Many police chiefs say that one of the most difficult recurring decisions they make is who to promote because there are more deserving candidates than there are promotional opportunities. From the candidates' perspective, they want to know what the rules are in advance and that they will be followed. If this is not the case, rumors will inevitably surface that the process was manipulated to the advantage of one person or group at the expense of others. In one state patrol agency, the test provider took eight months to get the scores back, retrieved them, and then distributed different scores based on additional analysis of the test results. Predictably, this situation resulted in a contentious period in the department and the use of a different test provider in the next round of promotional testing. In the news article summary which follows, an even more fundamental promotional issue is raised for you to consider, who should make promotional decisions?

During 2006 in Braintree, Massachusetts, a lively debate was underway: should the Police Chief be given full authority to make all promotions or should the Board of Selectmen (city council) continue to have final say? Some selectmen are of the opinion that they should continue to have final say because they are elected because they have good judgement and five voices (the Board of Selectmen) are better than one (the Police Chief). Advocates for change maintain that political interference would be eliminated and decisions would be made by a professional. Where do you come down on this issue?

Source: Sandy Coleman, "Town Mulls Leaving Hiring to Police Chief," *The Boston Globe*, April 16, 2006.

The sergeant talked to the Marine and concluded that he had drunk sufficiently to be charged with driving under the influence and directed the officer to arrest him. The officer declined and the sergeant angrily said, "I think you don't want to arrest him because you're an ex-Marine. . . . Arrest him, that's a direct order." The officer refused again, the sergeant got into his car and left, and the Marine departed in the taxi cab.

Later when the sergeant filed charges for refusal to obey the direct order of a superior, the officer was suspended without pay for two days. The other squad members felt the sergeant was not "streetwise" and had acted in a petty manner. Over time, it became apparent to the sergeant's superiors that he had lost the respect and confidence of the squad and could not regain it. The sergeant was then transferred to a minor staff position where he had responsibility for several functions but actually supervised no one.

Leadership also arises, as demonstrated by the Hawthorne studies, out of the informal side of an organization. Members of a work group give one or more of their members power by virtue of their willingness to follow him or her. This power may be given on the basis suggested by Weber's charismatic leader; thus, officers may look more to a seasoned and colorful officer in their squad or one who has been decorated several times for heroism than to their sergeant, who represents Weber's rational—legal type of authority. A variant of this situation is a problem more than occasionally in some departments as younger college-educated officers move up in rank rapidly, passing less-educated veteran officers. Dismissing them as "test takers," the more experienced officers sometimes use the informal group to vie for leadership with the formally appointed leaders. If, however, informal leaders support the police department's goals, they can be a significant additive and even help compensate for mediocre formal leadership.

Critical Thinking Question

1. Assume that you are promoted to Sergeant and assigned to lead a squad of eight officers in Patrol Division. You are the formal leader. However, one of your officers is a strong informal leader, with numerous years of experience and departmental decorations. She isn't actively opposing your leadership, but the others in the squad seem to be taking their cues to your leadership by how she reacts to your directions. What are your options and how do you handle this situation?

THE POWER MOTIVATION OF POLICE MANAGERS

Power is an indispensable dimension of police departments. As we have seen, power is both a grant made from the led to the leader and an extension of the formal authority granted to a particular position, such as sergeant. Power, however, is not always used for the same purpose; the term "**power motivation**" refers to the reasons, intentions, and objectives that underlie a police manager's use of power.[6]

Leadership requires that a person have an appreciation of the importance of influencing the outcome of events and the desire to play a key role in that process. This need for impact must be greater than either the need for personal achievement or the need to be liked by others. A police leader's desire for impact may take either of two forms; it may be oriented primarily toward the achievement of personal gain and aggrandizement (a personalized power motivation) or toward the need to influence others' behavior for the common good of the police department (a socialized power motivation). Additionally, police leaders have some desire to be accepted and liked, which is termed the "affiliation need." Affiliation needs and aspirations are not power needs because they reflect a greater preoccupation with being accepted and liked than with having an impact on events.

Table 7.1 summarizes the differences between managers who use personalized power and those who use social power. Hall and Hawker have developed an instrument

TABLE 7.1 Personalized vs. Social Power

POLICE MANAGERS WITH PERSONALIZED POWER TEND TO BE	POLICE MANAGERS WITH SOCIALIZED POWER TEND TO BE
■ Impulsive and erratic in their use of power	■ Inhibited and self-controlled in their use of power
■ Rude and overbearing	■ Respectful of others' rights
■ Exploitative of others	■ Concerned with fairness
■ Oriented toward strength	■ Oriented toward justice
■ Committed to the value of efficiency	■ Committed to the value of working per se
■ Proud	■ Egalitarian
■ Self-reliant; individualists	■ Organization-minded; joiners
■ Excited by the certitudes of power	■ Ambivalent about power
■ Competitive	■ Collaborative
■ Concerned with exceptionally high goals	■ Concerned with realistic goals
■ Defensive—protective of own sense of importance	■ Non-defensive—willing to seek help
■ Inspirational leaders	■ Builders of systems and people
■ Difficult to replace—leaves behind a group of officers who were dependent on the leader; does little to develop officers.	■ Replaceable by other managers—leave a system intact and self-sustaining
■ Sources of direction, expertise, and control	■ Sources of strength for others

SOURCE: From Jay Hall and James Hawker, "Interpreting Your Scores from the Power Management Inventory," The Power Management Inventory can be used with a variety of occupations.

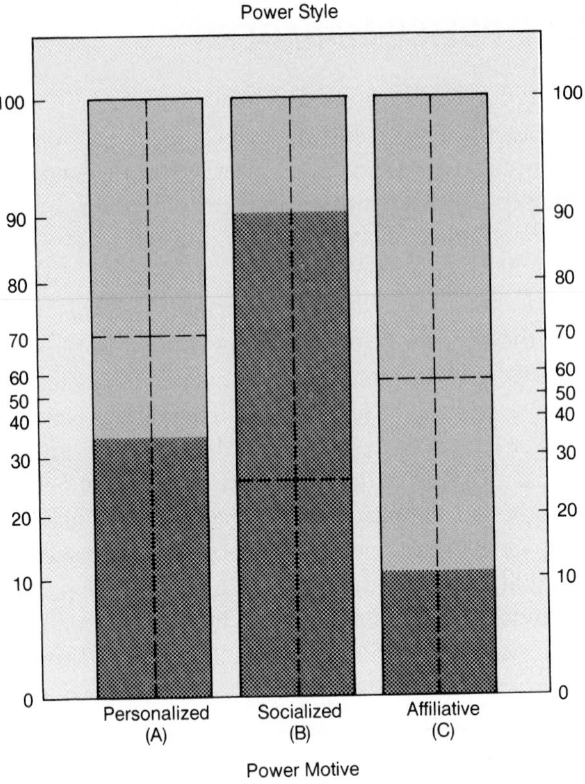

FIGURE 7.1

The Mean Power Management Inventory scores for 43 police managers from one medium-size department are indicated by the horizontal dotted lines and are contrasted from the ideal scores that are depicted by the shaded areas.

(*Source:* Jay Hall and James Hawker, "Interpreting Your Scores from the Power Management Inventory," © Teleometrics International, The Woodlands, Texas: special permission for reproduction of the figure is granted by the authors and the publisher, all rights reserved.)

for measuring personalized power, socialized power, and affiliative needs. In Figure 7.1, the shaded portions of the personalized, socialized, and affiliative columns represent what Hall and Hawker regard, based on research by McClelland and Burnham, as the theoretically ideal profile for managerial success; note that the ideal profile contains a mix of power motivations and affiliative needs. Affiliative needs serve as a check on power motivations, helping keep them in proper proportions. In the application of Figure 7.1, differences of more than 25 percentile points are required to denote a genuine preference for one approach in comparison to another. The dotted horizontal lines across the personalized, socialized, and affiliative columns reflect the scores of 43 police managers from one medium-size police agency and are intended as an illustration rather than as a generalization about police managers. Among the observations that can be made about the profile of those 43 police managers as a group are (1) the preference for the use of personalized power as opposed to socialized power and (2) a desire to be liked (affiliative needs), which closely approximates their preference for personalized power. This suggests that as a group these police managers are somewhat ambiguous about how to use power. They want to be seen as strong and self-reliant but also want to be liked. Their scores also reflect the absence of a clearly unified approach to the use of power and the lack of a crystallized philosophy of management; as a result, they are probably seen as somewhat inconsistent by their subordinates.

Critical Thinking Question

1. Why should a police leader's desire to have a positive impact on a situation always have priority over any desire to be personally liked?

THE LEADERSHIP SKILL MIX

As depicted in Figure 7.2, a police department can be divided into three levels with various mixes of three broad categories of skills associated with them.[7] The ranks indicated at each of the three levels of the organization identified in the figure are illustrative only and will vary depending on departmental size and other factors. Additionally, in the discussion of these skills that follows, it is possible to include only a few of the many examples available.

Human Relations Skills

Human relations skills involve the capacity to interrelate positively with other people and are used at all levels of a police department. Examples include motivation, conflict resolution, and interpersonal communication skills. The single, most important human relations skill is communication; without it, nothing can be set in motion, and programs under way cannot be guided.

As one progresses up the rank hierarchy of a police department, typically one becomes responsible for more people but has fewer people reporting directly to him or her. The human relations skills of a police department's top managers remain important,

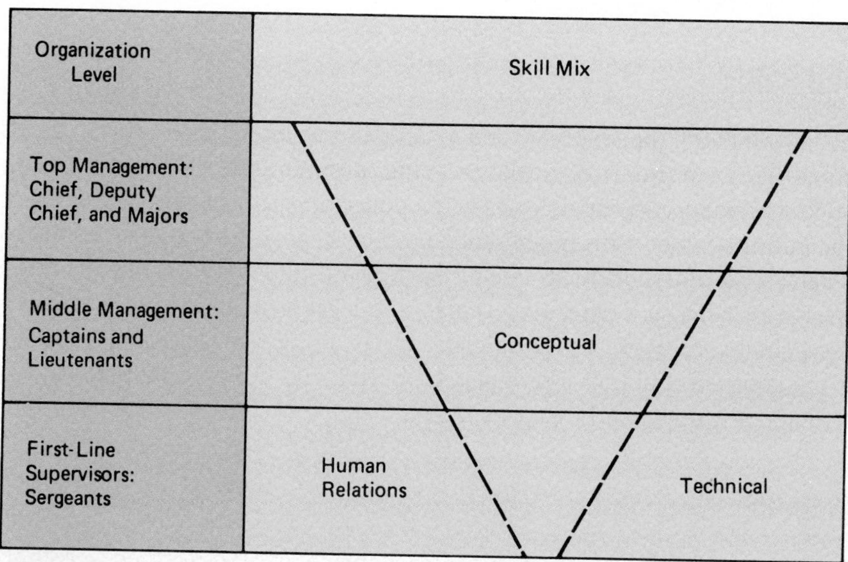

FIGURE 7.2

The leadership skill mix in a police department.

In The News

Lack of Human Relations TRIPS Chief

The City of Lamar, Colorado, placed its police chief and his second in command on administrative leave while a consultant conducted an audit of the department. The 32-page report revealed that opinions about leadership varied. Lower-level command staff were seen in positive terms, while the high command staff lacked communication skills and were known for "yelling and throwing things." Still, the chief was seen as backing officers, unless they were wrong and he got pay raises for officers.

The city administrator, Jeff Anderson, based in part on the report as well as other things, subsequently fired the chief and his second in command to make a change in the management and style of the Lamar Police Department. The attorney for the two men, Marc Colin, said the report contained "anonymous comments which have neither been investigated nor substantiated."

Source: Anthony A. Mestas, "Audit Reveals Problems with the Lamar Police Force," *The Pueblo* (Colorado) *Chieftain*, October 19, 2006.

however, as they are used to win political support for the agency's programs and to obtain the resources necessary to operate them. In particular, the chief's human relations skills are critical, as this person is the key representative of the department to the larger environment. The way in which he or she "comes across" is to a certain degree the way in which some significant others—such as the city manager and members of city council—will regard the police department. The question of the fairness of that fact aside, the practical implication is that the chief must be aware of and fulfill the symbolic leadership role.

Within the department, top management must communicate its goals and policies downward and be willing to receive feedback about them. As mid-level managers, lieutenants and captains play an important linking function, passing downward in implementable forms the communications they receive from top management and passing upward certain communications received from first-line supervisors. Because sergeants ordinarily supervise directly the greatest number of people, they use human relations with great frequency, often focusing on such issues as resolving interpersonal problems, communicating the department's vision, stimulating employee participation in problem solving, and maintaining a customer focus.

Conceptual Skills

Conceptual skills include the ability to understand and to interrelate various parcels of information that seem unrelated or the meaning or importance of which is uncertain. Although this skill is used at all levels of the police department, the standards for handling the information become less certain and the level of abstraction necessary to handle the parcels becomes greater as one moves upward. Illustrative is the difference between a sergeant helping a detective evaluate the legal significance of certain evidence and the chief sorting out and interrelating facts, opinions, and rumors about a productive but controversial police program supported and opposed by political figures, public interest groups, and the news media.

Technical Skills

Technical skills vary by level within a police department. Uniformed sergeants assigned to field duties must be able to help develop and maintain the skills of subordinates in such areas as the identification, collection, and preservation of physical evidence. As one progresses upward toward middle and top management, the range of technical skills narrows, and conceptual skills come to predominate. In that upward progression, the character of the technical skills also changes from being operations-oriented to management-oriented and gradually includes new elements, such as budgeting, planning, and the kind of decision making that increasingly requires the use of conceptual skills. To elaborate further, one may not be able to tell by the generic label whether a particular skill is, for example, technical or conceptual. A general understanding of the many aspects of financial management (see Chapter 12, Financial Management) is a conceptual skill, but the actual preparation of the budget is a technical skill required of middle-management or first-line supervisors, depending on the size and practices of a specific police department.

Critical Thinking Question

1. As a person advances from being a Sergeant to being a Chief, Deputy Chief, or Major the skills they need change. Why does this happen? Would there be any differences in these changes if you were a Chief of a 20-officer department or 1,500-officer-agency? If so, what?

THEORIES OF LEADERSHIP

Theories of leadership attempt to explain the factors associated with the emergence of leadership or the nature of leadership.[8] Included are (1) "**great man**" and genetic **theories,** (2) the **traits approach,** (3) behavioral explanations, and (4) situational theories.

"Great man" theories were advanced by Thomas Carlyle and George Wilhelm Friedrich Hegel.[9] Carlyle believed that leaders were unusually endowed individuals who made history. Reversing the direction of causality, Hegel argued that it was the events that produced the "great man." The "born leader" concept is associated with Francis Galton, who espoused that leaders were the product of genetics.[10]

It has also been maintained that leaders possess certain personality traits; for example, Field Marshal Montgomery[11] believed that, although leaders were made, not born, they had certain characteristics, such as an infectious optimism, confidence, intellect, and the ability to be a good judge of character. Goode determined that the following traits were important for successful leadership:

1. The leader is somewhat more intelligent than the average of his followers. However, he is not so superior that he cannot be readily understood by those who work with him.
2. The leader is a well-rounded individual from the standpoint of interests and aptitudes. He tends toward interests, aptitudes, and knowledge with respect to a wide variety of fields.
3. The leader has an unusual facility with language. He speaks and writes simply, persuasively, and understandably.
4. The leader is mentally and emotionally mature. He has come of age mentally, emotionally, and physically.
5. The leader has a powerful inner drive or motivation that impels him to strive for accomplishment.

6. The leader is fully aware of the importance of cooperative effort in getting things done and therefore understands and practices very effectively the so-called social skills.
7. The leader relies on his administrative skills to a much greater extent than he does on any of the technical skills that may be associated directly with his work.[12]

Parenthetically, by administrative skills, Goode seems to mean what has been described previously as conceptual skills. Stogdill analyzed over 200 studies and following the second review described a leader as being

> *characterized by a strong drive for responsibility and task completion, vigor and persistence in pursuit of goals, venturesomeness and originality in problem solving, drive to exercise initiative in social situations, self-confidence, and a sense of personal identity, willingness to accept consequences of decision and action, readiness to absorb interpersonal stress, willingness to tolerate frustration and delay, ability to influence other persons' behavior, and capacity to structure social interaction systems to the purpose at hand.*[13]

From an organizational standpoint, the traits approach has great appeal: find out which people have these characteristics and promote them, and successful leadership will follow. However, C. A. Gibb[14] has concluded that the numerous studies of traits do not reveal any consistent patterns, and Walter Palmer's[15] research does not provide support for the hypothesis that managerial effectiveness is a product of the personality characteristics of the individual.

Other theories of leadership focus on the behavior of managers as they operate. Whereas trait theories attempt to explain leadership on the basis of what the leader is, behavioral theories try to do the same thing by concentrating on what the leader does.[16] This is referred to as *style of leadership,* meaning the continuing patterns of behavior as perceived and experienced by others that they use to characterize the leader. Several of these approaches are discussed in the section that follows. Although not exclusively, many of the styles reflect elements of scientific management's task-centered and human relations' people-centered orientations.

Situational leadership theories postulate that effective leadership is a product of the fit between the traits or skills required in a leader as determined by the situation in which he or she is to exercise leadership.[17] Illustrative are Frederick Fiedler's contingency model,[18] Robert House's path–goal theory,[19] Robert Tannenbaum and Warren Schmidt's authoritarian–democratic leadership continuum, and Paul Hersey and Kenneth Blanchard's situational leadership theory. The last two are covered in detail in the next section because of their interrelatedness with leadership styles.

STYLES OF LEADERSHIP

General interest in the topic of leadership and the various theories of it have generated both commentary and research on different schemes for classifying styles of leadership. The purpose of this section is to provide a sense of some ways in which this subject has been treated and to discuss certain contributions in this area.

Lewin, Lippitt, and White: Authoritarian, Democratic, and Laissez-Faire

Although these three styles of leadership had been identified in earlier works, the 1939 publication of **Lewin, Lippitt, and White's**[20] classical study of boys' clubs has closely identified these approaches with them.

TABLE 7.2 The Authoritarian, Democratic, and Laissez-Faire Leadership Styles

AUTHORITARIAN/AUTOCRAT	DEMOCRATIC	LAISSEZ-FAIRE
1. All determination of policy was by the leader.	1. All policies were a matter of group discussion and decision, encouraged and assisted by the leader.	1. Complete freedom for group or individual decisions existed, with a minimum of leader participation.
2. Techniques and activity steps were dictated by the leader, one at a time, so that future steps were always uncertain to a large degree.	2. Activity perspective was gained during discussion period. General steps to the group goal were sketched, and when technical advice was needed, the leader suggested two or more alternative procedures from which a choice could be made.	2. Various materials were supplied by the leader, who made it clear that he or she would supply information when asked. The leader took no other part in work discussion.
3. The leader usually dictated the particular work task and work companion of each member.	3. The members were free to work with whomever they chose, and the division of tasks was left up to the group.	3. Total non-participation by the leader.
4. The leader tended to be "personal" in his or her praise and criticism of the work of each member and remained aloof from active group participation except when demonstrating.	4. The leader was "objective" or "fact-minded" in his or her praise and criticism and tried to be a regular group member in spirit without doing too much of the work.	4. Spontaneous comments on member activities were infrequent unless questioned, and no attempt was made to appraise or regulate the course of events.

SOURCE: From figure 1, p. 32, in *Autocracy and Democracy* by Ralph K. White and Ronald Lippitt. Copyright © 1960 by Ralph K. White and Ronald Lippitt. Reprinted by permission of Harper & Row, Publishers, Inc.; an earlier version of this appears in Kurt Lewin, Ronald Lippitt, and Ralph K. White, "Patterns of Aggressive Behavior in Experimentally Created Social Climates," *Journal of Social Psychology* 10 (1939): p. 273.

The contrasting approaches to Lewin, Lippitt, and White's styles are detailed in Table 7.2. Briefly, they may be characterized as follows: (1) the **authoritarian leader** makes all decisions without consulting subordinates and closely controls work performance, (2) the **democratic leader** is group-oriented and promotes the active participation of subordinates in planning and executing tasks, and (3) the **laissez-faire leader** takes a "hands-off," passive approach in dealing with subordinates.

White and Lippitt concluded that, although the quantity of work was somewhat greater under the autocratic leader, autocracy could generate hostility and aggression. The democratically controlled groups were about as efficient as the autocratically controlled ones, but the continuation of work in the former did not depend on the presence of the leader. Under the laissez-faire leader, less work was produced, the work quality was poorer, and the work was less organized and less satisfying to members of the group.[21]

Tannenbaum and Schmidt: The Authoritarian–Democratic Leadership Continuum

In 1958, Tannenbaum and Schmidt[22] published the leadership continuum, depicted in Figure 7.3. They believed that the successful leader could choose to be more or less directive, depending on certain factors:

1. Forces in the manager, such as his or her value system, confidence in subordinates, leadership inclinations, and need for security in uncertain situations
2. Forces in subordinates, including their needs for independence, readiness to assume greater responsibility, interests, knowledge, and experience
3. Forces in the organization, illustrated by prevailing views and practices, the ability of the group to work together effectively, the nature of the problem, and the pressures of time[23]

In The News

Chief Seen as Authoritarian

Houston police union leaders and Chief Hurtt are not getting along. The union president, Hans Matriciuc, charges that the chief runs the department like a dictator, having systematically returned it to an autocratic style of management, which has put public safety at risk. Hurtt maintains that he has an open door policy and welcomes feedback but maintains that the "buck stops with me."

Several factors seem to be driving the tension, including an increase of 200,000 residents during recent years, including Katrina refugees, which coincided with significant cuts in the number of officers and a surge in violent crime.

While the police department has announced sweeping crime-fighting efforts in recent days, including saturating five high-risk apartment complexes with 100 officers per day, Matriciuc says it is "too little, too late" and union members are being surveyed to see how they feel about Hurtt's leadership.

Matriciuc reports that officers are overworked; with 200 to 250 officers expected to retire each year, even if the academy graduates 350 officers a year, it only produces a net annual increase of 100 officers, which would take 10 to 15 years to get to the staffing level the department needs, according to him.

Source: Mike Glenn, "Union: Hurt Policies Imperil Public Safety," *The Houston Chronicle*, June 22, 2006.

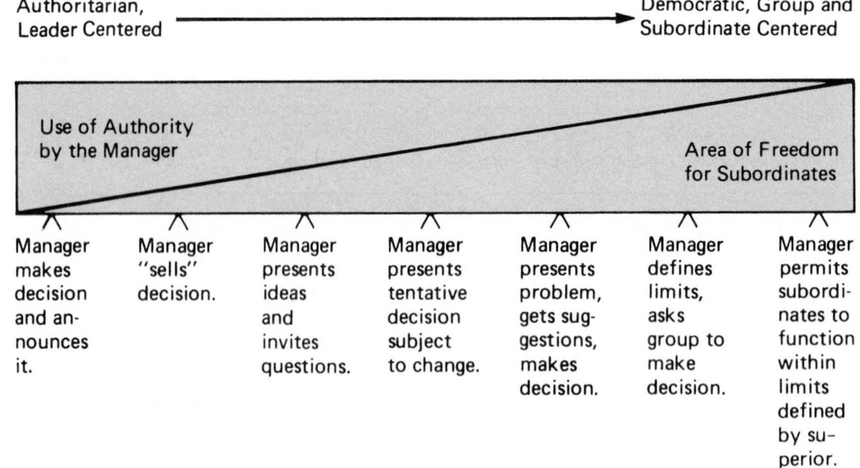

FIGURE 7.3

The authoritarian-democratic continuum.

(Reprinted by permission of *Harvard Business Review*. Exhibit from "How to Choose a Leadership Pattern" by Robert Tannenbaum and Warren H. Schmidt [May-June 1973]. Copyright © 1973 by the Harvard Business School Publishing Corporation; all rights reserved.)

Although their work is often simply presented as styles of leadership, by considering the previously noted three factors and noting that these forces working together might suggest one leadership style instead of another, Tannenbaum and Schmidt's findings reflect a situational approach to leadership.

Downs: Leadership Styles in Bureaucratic Structures

Anthony Downs[24] described four types of leader behavior in bureaucratic structures: (1) climbers, (2) conservers, (3) zealots, and (4) advocates.

Climbers are strongly motivated by power and prestige needs to invent new functions to be performed by their unit, particularly functions not performed elsewhere. If climbers can expand their functions only by moving into areas already controlled by others, they are likely to choose ones in which they expect low resistance. To protect their "turf," climbers tend to economize only when the resultant savings can be used to finance an expansion of their functions.[25]

The bias of conservers is toward maintaining things as they are. The longer a person is in the same job and the older one becomes, the lower one assesses any chances for advancement and the stronger one becomes attached to job security, all of which are associated with the tendency to become a conserver. Climbers may become conservers when they assess their probability for advancement and expansion to be low. Desiring to make their organizational lives comfortable, conservers dislike and resist change.[26]

The peculiarities of the behavior of zealots stem from two sources: their narrow interest and the missionary-like energy, which they focus almost solely on their special interest. As a consequence, zealots do not attend to all their duties and often antagonize other administrators by their lack of impartiality and their willingness to trample over all obstacles to further their special interest. Zealots rarely succeed to high-level positions because of their narrowness and are consequently poor administrators. An exception is when their interest comes into favor and they are catapulted into high office.[27]

Unlike zealots, advocates promote everything under their jurisdiction. To those outside their units, they appear highly partisan, but within their units they are impartial and fair, developing well-rounded programs. Loyal to their organizations, advocates favor innovation. They are also simultaneously more radical and more conservative than climbers. They are more radical in that they are willing to promote programs and views that may antagonize politicians, superiors, and other powerful groups, such as the news media, if doing so helps their departments. They are more conservative because they are willing to oppose changes from which they might benefit but which would not be in the overall interest of their agencies.[28]

Van Maanen: Station House Sergeants and Street Sergeants

In a study of a 1,000-officer police department, Van Maanen[29] identified two contrasting types of police sergeants: "station house" and "street." **Station house sergeants** had been out of the "bag" (uniform) before their promotions to sergeant and preferred to work inside in an office environment once they won their stripes; this preference was clearly indicated by the nickname of "Edwards, the Olympic torch who never goes out" given to one such sergeant. Station house sergeants immersed themselves in the management culture of the police department, keeping busy with paperwork, planning, record keeping, press relations, and fine points of law. Their strong orientation to conformity also gave rise to nicknames as suggested by the use of "by the book Brubaker" to refer to one station house sergeant.

In contrast, **street sergeants** were serving in the field when they received their promotions. Consequently, they had a distaste for office procedures and had a strong action orientation, as suggested by such nicknames as "Shooter McGee" and "Walker the Stalker." Moreover, their concern was not with conformity but with "not letting the assholes take over the city."

In addition to the distinct differences already noted, station house and street sergeants were thought of differently by those whom they supervised: station house sergeants "stood behind their officers," while street sergeants "stood beside their officers." Each of these two different styles of working as a sergeant also has its drawbacks and strengths. Station house sergeants might not be readily available to officers working in the field but could always be located when a signature was needed and were able to secure more favors for their subordinates than street sergeants were. Although immediately available in the field when needed, street sergeants occasionally interfered with the autonomy of their subordinates by responding to a call for service assigned to a subordinate and handling it or otherwise, at least in the eyes of the subordinate officer, "interfering."

A consideration of Van Maanen's work leads to some generalizations about the future careers of station house versus street sergeants. The station house sergeant is learning routines, procedures, and skills that will improve future promotional opportunities. Their promotional opportunities are further enhanced by contacts with senior police commanders who can give them important assignments and who can, if favorably impressed, influence future promotions. In contrast, street sergeants may gain some favorable publicity and awards for their exploits, but they are also more likely to have citizen complaints filed against them, more likely to be investigated by internal affairs, and more likely to be sued. Consequently, very aggressive street sergeants are regarded by their superiors as "good cops" but difficult people to supervise. In short, the action-oriented street sergeant who does not "mellow out" may not go beyond a middle manager's position in a line unit, such as patrol or investigation.

Blake and Mouton: The Managerial Grid

Developed by Robert Blake and Jane Mouton,[30] the **Managerial Grid** has received a great deal of attention since its appearance in 1962 in the *Journal of the American Society of Training Directors*. The grid is part of the survey research feedback stem of organizational development and draws on earlier work done at Ohio State University and the University of Michigan.[31]

Depicted in Figure 7.4, the grid has two dimensions: concern for production and concern for people. Each axis, or dimension, is numbered from 1, meaning low concern, to 9, indicating high concern. The way in which a person combines these two dimensions establishes a leadership style in terms of one of the five principal styles identified on the grid. The numbers associated with each of the styles reflect the level of concern for each of the two dimensions to the grid. For example, 9,1 indicates a maximum concern for production or the needs of the organization and a minimum orientation toward the needs of people in the organization.

Some of the leadership styles identified previously can be related readily to the grid. Authoritarian leaders are represented by the 9,1 style; laissez-faire leaders by the 1,1; and democratic leaders by the 5,5. Additionally, the 9,1 and 9,9 styles are consistent, respectively, with the streams of thought summarized in Chapter 5 under the headings of "Traditional Organizational Theory" and "Open Systems Theory."

The leadership style of an individual can be identified by using a questionnaire based on the work of Blake and Mouton. According to the grid, one moves from the "best" to the "worst" styles as one moves from 9,9 through 5,5; 9,1; 1,9; and 1,1. The most desirable combination of a primary and backup style is the 9,9 with a 5,5 backup.

A difficulty in using the grid questionnaire is that the data produced are no more accurate than the self-perceptions of the person completing the instrument. When working in an organizational development context, one way to overcome this is to have each manager complete the instrument and then have each of his or her subordinates fill out on how they experience the manager. Comparing these two sets of data provides useful information. Typically, more weight is given to the subordinate's combined data because it reflects now the leading is "coming across."

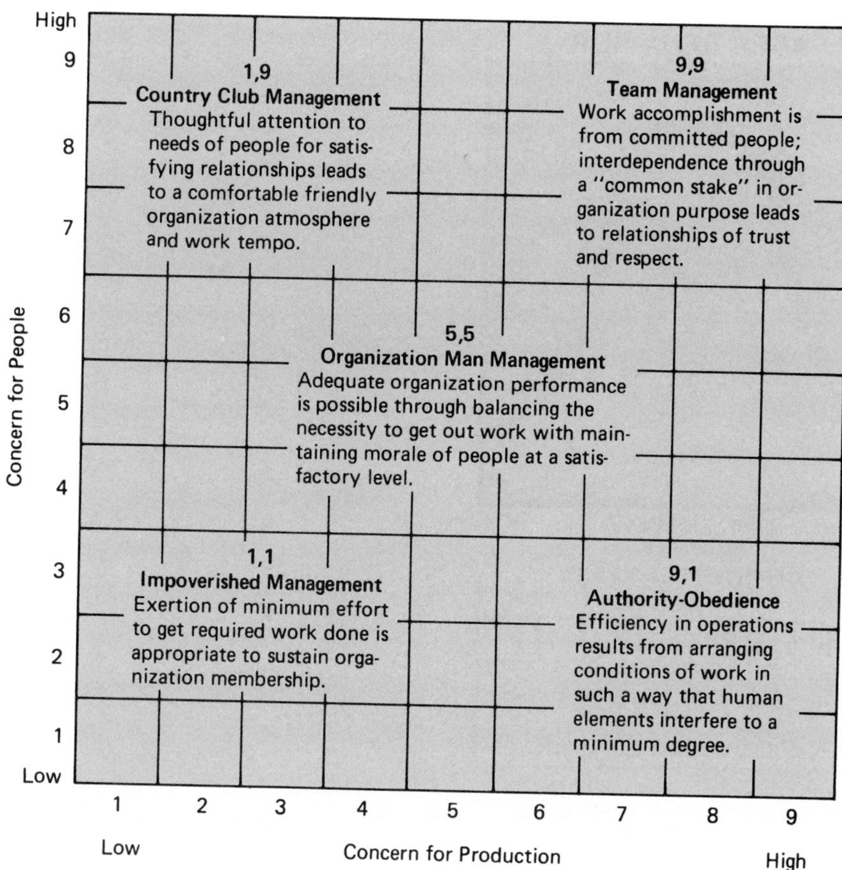

FIGURE 7.4

The managerial grid.

(*Source: The New Managerial Grid* by Robert Blake and Jane Syrgley Mouton. Houston: Copyright © Gulf Publishing Company. Reproduced by permission.)

In The News

Today's News

Chief Committed to Team Approach

Hartford's new police chief, Daryl Roberts, said he has no immediate plans to change the command structure and that without a team approach the department wouldn't be able to continue building relationships and making the community safer.

Roberts said that he couldn't be effective without cooperation from throughout the city, including the board of education, the city government, and the public. He elaborated by saying, "It's not about me; it's about us; I don't work alone."

Source: Tina A. Brown and Daniel Goren, "New City Chief Stresses Teamwork," *The Hartford* (Connecticut) *Courant*, July 1, 2006.

Hersey and Blanchard: Situational Leadership Theory

Hersey and Blanchard's[32] **situational leadership** model was influenced greatly by William Reddin's 3-D management style theory. Although many situational variables are important to leadership—such as the demands of time, the leader, the led, the superiors, the organization, and job demands—Hersey and Blanchard emphasize

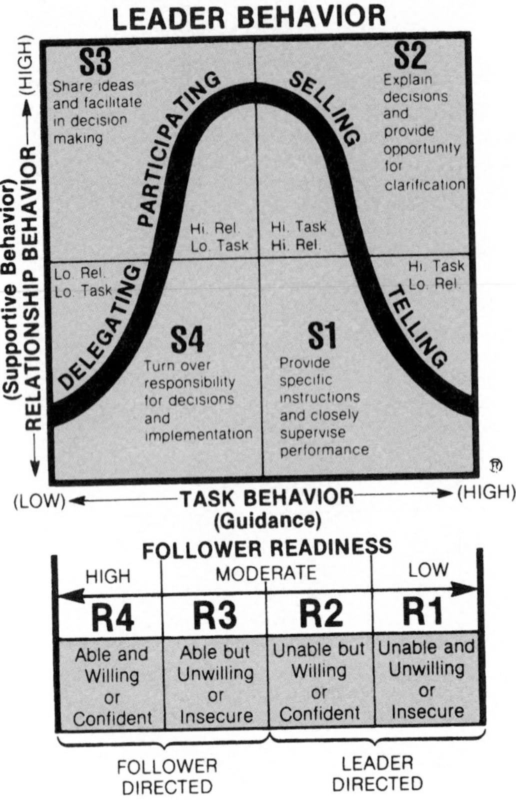

FIGURE 7.5

The situational leadership model.

(Situational Leadership® is a registered trademark of the Center for Leadership Studies, Escondido, CA. Used with permission.)

what they regard as the key variables: the behavior of the leader in relationship to the followers.[33] Although the examples of situational leadership suggest a hierarchical relationship, situational leadership theory should have application when trying to influence the behavior of a subordinate, boss, friend, or relative.[34]

Maturity is defined in situational leadership as the capacity to set high but attainable goals, the willingness to take responsibility, and the education and/or experience of the individual or the group.[35] Age may be a factor, but it is not related directly to maturity as used in situational leadership theory.[36] An individual or group is not mature or immature in a total sense but only in relation to the specific task to be performed.[37] This task-relevant maturity involves two factors: job maturity, or the ability and technical knowledge to do the task, and psychological maturity, or feelings of self-confidence and self-respect about oneself as an individual.[38]

Figure 7.5 depicts the situation leadership model; the various levels of follower maturity are defined as follows:

- *M1*: The followers are neither willing nor able to take responsibility for task accomplishment.
- *M2*: The followers are willing but not able to take responsibility for task accomplishment.

- *M3:* The followers are able but not willing to take responsibility for task accomplishment.
- *M4:* The followers are willing and able to take responsibility for task accomplishment.[39]

Task behavior is essentially the extent to which a leader engages in one-way communication with subordinates; relationship behavior is the extent to which a leader engages in two-way communication by providing socioemotional support, "psychological strokes," and facilitating behaviors.[40] The definition of the four basic styles associated with these two variables operates like the Managerial Grid and is described in the following terms:

- *S1:* High-task–low-relationship leader behavior is referred to as "telling" because this style is characterized by one-way communication in which the leader defines the roles of followers and tells them what, how, when, and where to do various tasks.
- *S2:* High-task–high-relationship behavior is referred to as "selling" because, with this style, most of the direction is still provided by the leader. He or she also attempts through two-way communication and socioemotional support to get the follower(s) psychologically to buy in to decisions that have to be made.
- *S3:* High-relationship–low-task behavior is called "participating" because, with this style, the leader and follower(s) now share in decision making through two-way communication and much facilitating behavior from the leader, since the followers have the ability and knowledge to do the task.
- *S4:* Low-relationship–low-task behavior is labeled "delegating" because the style involves letting followers "run their own show" through delegation and general supervision, since the followers are high in both task and psychological maturity.

The bell-shaped curve in the style-of-leader portion of Figure 7.5 means that, as the maturity level of leader's followers develops from immaturity to maturity, the appropriate style of leadership moves in a corresponding way.[41]

To illustrate, a police leader who had a subordinate whose maturity is in the M2 range would be most effective employing an S2 style of leadership. The probability of success of each style for the four maturity levels depends on how far the style is from the high-probability style along the bell-shaped curve; Hersey and Blanchard describe these probabilities as follows:

- *M1:* S1 and S2 2nd, S3 third, S4 low probability
- *M2:* S2 high S1 and S3 secondary, S4 low probability
- *M3:* S3 high S2 and S4 secondary, S1 low probability
- *M4:* S4 high S3 2nd S2 3rd, S1 low probability[42]

Although it is easier said than done, the effective use of Hersey and Blanchard's model depends on police leaders developing or having a diagnostic ability and the flexibility to adapt their leadership styles to given situations.[43]

Transactional and Transformational Leaders

In 1978, James **Burns** published a book that was simply titled *Leadership*. However modest the title, it was to become a very influential writing. In it, Burns identifies two types of leaders in the behavioral tradition: **transactional** and **transforming.**[44]

In The News

Today's News

Police Department Transformed

The Providence, Rhode Island, Police Department has been transformed in order to implement community policing and to reduce the number of layers in the agency, flattening out the structure by giving sergeants and lieutenants more authority. Now they can directly contact their counterparts in other divisions without going through an elaborate chain-of-command structure. The result is less protection of turf by units and more cooperation across the board.

Community policing involves decentralization of police work and close and continuing, collaboration with the community to solve problems rather than to simply react to calls for service. In order to accomplish this, another important transformation is to make sure that all departmental units use the same geographical districts as the uniformed community policing officers. This enables uniformed officers and detectives, for example, to have the same sense of commitment to an area when attending community meetings together.

Source: Gregory Smith, "Focus on Community Policing Puts More Cops in the Loop," *The Providence* (Rhode Island) *Journal*, May 30, 2006, with restatement.

Most leader–follower relations are transactional: the leaders approach the followers with the idea that they will exchange one thing for another, such as raises and favorable assignments for good performance or personal loyalty. Each party to the transaction, or "bargain," is aware of the resources of the other, and the purposes of both are entwined almost exclusively within the context of this relationship.[45] Transactional leaders emphasize values such as honesty, fairness, acceptance of responsibility, the honoring of commitments, and work done on time.[46] In contrast, transformational leadership occurs when leaders and followers interact in such a way that they are elevated and committed to—and sustained by—some great cause external to the relationship. Transformational leaders emphasize values such as justice, liberty, and equality. A classical example of transformational leadership is the pre-eminent role played by Martin Luther King, Jr., in the civil rights movement of the 1960s.

Burns's *Leadership* was written at a very broad level from a political science perspective; it was nearly another decade before his concepts began to be applied more narrowly to organizations. A 1984 article by Tichy and Ulrich[47] in the *Sloan Management Review* called for transforming leadership, as did two books the following year: *Leadership and Performance beyond Expectations* by Bass[48] and *Leaders* by Bennis and Nanus.[49] Despite the importance of these writings, a later book emerged as most influential in galvanizing widespread interest in the transforming leader. Published in 1987, *The Leadership Challenge: How to Get Extraordinary Things Done in Organizations* by James Kouzes and Barry Posner postulates that successful leaders have made 10 behavioral commitments. These commitments are organized under five major headings:

Challenge the Process

1. *Searching out challenging opportunities to change, grow, innovate, and improve*—Outstanding police leaders recognize that they must be change agents and innovators.[50] However, they also know that most innovations do not come from them.[51] Instead, these ideas often come from the officers who do the actual work and from the people who use the department's services.[52] "Leaders listen to the advice and counsel of others; they know that good ideas enter the mind through the ears, not the mouth."[53]
2. *Experimenting and taking risks and learning from the accompanying mistakes*—"Leaders experiment and take risks. Since risk taking involves mistakes and failure, leaders learn to accept the inevitable disappointments. They treat them as learning opportunities."[54]

Inspire a Shared Vision

3. *Envisioning an uplifting and ennobling future*—In the mold of Burns's transformational style, police leaders look forward to the future with visions and ideals of what can be.[55] "They have a sense of what is uniquely possible if all work together for a common purpose. They are positive about the future and they passionately believe that people can make a difference.[56]
4. *Enlisting others in a common vision by appealing to their values, interests, hopes, and dreams*—Visions seen only by the chief and his or her command staff are insufficient to create an organized movement, such as community policing.[57] Police leaders must get others to see and be excited by future possibilities.[58] One study found that, when senior executives were able to communicate their vision of the organization's future effectively, subordinate personnel reported significantly higher levels of the following:
   a. Job satisfaction
   b. Commitment
   c. Loyalty
   d. Esprit de corps
   e. Clarity about the organization's values
   f. Pride in the organization
   g. Encouragement to be productive
   h. Organizational productivity[59]

   Thus, police leaders breathe life into dreams, communicating their visions so clearly that others in the department understand and accept them as their own.[60] They show others how their own values and interests will be served by this long-term vision of the future.[61]

Enable Others to Act

5. *Fostering collaboration by promoting cooperative goals and building trust*— Police leaders know that having the trust of departmental members and the public is important. They develop collaborative and cooperative goals and cooperative relationships with others in the department, knowing that such relationships are the keys that unlock support for their programs.[62] Developing trust in

In The News

Consultant's Report Finds Low Police Job Satisfaction

Job satisfaction is an important but not static condition. Measuring job satisfaction is somewhat like taking a person's temperature; it is likely to vary from one time to another. In this article, a report on job satisfaction in the city of Columbia, Missouri, is discussed.

Although most of Columbia's 1,174 city employees are satisfied with their jobs, the results were less positive on some questions for personnel in the police and fire departments. Members of those departments were more likely to raise questions about their pay and whether people with the right skills were being recruited.

In the police department, 52 percent said they could not recommend the city as a good place to work and 62 percent said they were not encouraged to make suggestions about how to improve the workplace. This contrasts sharply with 74 percent of all respondents who said the city was a good place to work. Fire department employees–more than 50 percent–said that needed steps are not taken to deal with someone who will or cannot improve his or her performance.

The results are troubling to Police Chief Randy Boehm, but he felt like it was too early to say what steps needed to be implemented to correct problems.

Source: Matthew Leblanc, "Public Safety Workers Cite Job Troubles; Most City Employees Say They're Satisfied," *Columbia* (Missouri) *Daily Tribune*, June 6, 2006.

organizations can be a difficult task if the people with whom you work have had their trust abused. One way to build trust is to delegate, for this process is fundamentally a system of trust.[63] Ultimately, you have to be a risk taker when it comes to trust, trusting others first and having faith that they will respond in kind.[64]

6. *Strengthening people by sharing information and power and increasing their discretion and visibility*—In some circles, power is thought to be like a pie; there is only so much, and if I have more, then you have less. Kouzes and Posner[65] argue that this view is archaic and retards accomplishments in organizations. Their view is that, when people hoard power, others feel less powerful or powerless, leading the less potent to zealously guard their prerogatives and thereby become arbitrary, petty, and dictatorial.[66] According to Kouzes and Posner, it is not centralized power but mutual respect that sustains extraordinary group efforts; real leaders create an atmosphere of trust and human dignity and nurture self-esteem in others.[67] They make others feel strong and capable,[68] and they empower other officers by such strategies as the following:
   a. Giving them important work to do on important issues
   b. Giving them discretion and autonomy over their tasks and resources
   c. Giving them visibility and recognition for their efforts
   d. Building relationships for them by connecting them with powerful people and finding them sponsors and mentors[69]

Model the Way

7. *Setting the example for others by behaving in ways that are consistent with the leader's stated values*—Police officers are astute observers of behavior in organizations and are especially sensitive to differences between what their leaders say is important and how they behave. For instance, if patrol officers are told by their chief that the patrol division is the backbone of the department but they are the last ones every year to get new cars, then the patrol officers will dismiss the chief's statement as "hype." Leaders provide the standard by which other people in the organization calibrate their own choices and behaviors; in order to set an example, leaders must know their values and live by them.[70]

8. *Promoting small wins that reflect consistent progress and build commitment*—Some police chiefs fail because what they propose to do seems overwhelming and this frightens and paralyzes the very people whose support and enthusiasm are essential for success. A wiser strategy is to start with "small wins," doing things that are within the control of the department, that are doable, and that "get the ball rolling." These small wins form the basis for consistently winning, attract followers, and deter opposition: it's hard to argue with success. Moreover, each gain preserves past progress and makes it harder to return to the previously prevailing conditions.[71]

Encourage the Heart

9. *Recognize individual contributions to the success of every program*—Having high expectations for themselves and others is a must for police chiefs who wish to be successful; these expectations form the model to which others will adapt their behavior. Simply eliciting the behavior is insufficient. There must be a wide variety of ways police leaders can recognize and reward performance, such as praise, days off, cash awards, and formal award systems. For example, some departments grant officers an extra day off whenever they catch a burglar inside

of a building. For a performance reward system to be effective, three conditions must be met:

a. Personnel must know what is expected of them.
b. They must receive continuing feedback about their performance, so that errors can be corrected and solid practices reinforced.
c. Only people who meet or exceed standards of behavior should be rewarded; otherwise, all rewards are cheapened, and the system loses meaning.[72]

10. *Celebrate team accomplishments regularly*—The role of leaders in celebrations is often overlooked. Some police leaders conceive of their role in this area as limited to presiding over annual awards banquets and promotional ceremonies. However, this is a narrow view that is correct only when police department celebrations are limited to such occasions. As used here, "celebrate" simply means to gather people together to savor what they have accomplished and to recognize it jointly. For example, a unit or team who put together a successful grant application could be invited to the chief's home with their spouses for a cookout. Or investigators who have solved a particularly noteworthy case could, in addition to other recognitions, be the chief's guests at the monthly local chiefs meetings that are common throughout the country. There the chief could publicly introduce them and acknowledge their contributions. For Kouzes and Posner, such activities are both recognition tools and crucial ways of communicating important organizational values.

Transforming police leaders may act in a transactional style around particular issues without abandoning their transformational orientation. In fact, within the organizational setting it is essential that transformational leaders have transactional skills. Few transactional leaders, however, are able to convert to a transforming style because they lack that essential larger and ennobling vision of the future with which to excite potential followers.

The body of literature on transactional and transformational leadership is still evolving. Its most salient contribution is its emphasis on leadership as a primary force in elevating followers to higher levels of performance and purpose and carefully delineating the multiple roles of leaders as visionaries who articulate and teach organizational values.

Total Quality Leadership

Based on the pioneering work of Bell Laboratories's Walter Shewhart, Americans developed the concept of statistical quality control and applied it to production processes during the 1920s and 1930s.[73] After World War II, as the economy quickly expanded, the demand for products was so strong that quality control was less a priority for businesses, and they began issuing warranties to correct defective merchandise that consumers had purchased.[74] Also following World War II, the Japanese began applying statistical quality control methods and gradually expanded the notion of quality to be a broad philosophy of management involving everyone in the organization.[75]

Starting in the late 1970s and early 1980s, some American companies began using quality principles, largely because of strong competition from Japanese companies.[76] Roughly during this same period, public agencies began experimenting with some quality concepts, including a federal print shop that used a total quality leadership (TQL) forerunner, total performance management. In police departments, the earliest manifestation of the quality movement was the use of quality circles.

As community-oriented policing (COP; also referred to in some parts of the country as community-oriented policing and problem solving, or COPPS) gathered steam, its natural relationship to the quality movement was quickly recognized. In fact, retired Madison, Wisconsin, Police Chief David Couper recalls that his department's COP program really did not get implemented until personnel bought in to the notion that quality is important.[77] Many chiefs today take the position that, to be successful, a COP program inherently must have a quality orientation. This is because COP entails delivering police services that are customized to the needs of the neighborhoods being served and because an essential component of quality is a customer focus.

Critical Thinking Question

1. Assume that you have been selected to be the Chief of a 35-officer agency. You are an "outsider" with no ties to the department. Because several senior commanders were unsuccessful candidates for the job, you don't know if you can count on their support. The former Chief was very authoritarian; he was a "my way or the highway" leader. The police union was instrumental in the former Chief's ouster and is enjoying its new-found power. As a result of the former Chief's dysfunctional leadership style, job satisfaction and trust is low. The city manager and council are watching things closely. You have no natural or immediate allies as you begin your job. What options do you have as you go about rebuilding the department?

THE LEADER AND CONFLICT

Conflict is a condition in which at least two parties have a mutual difference of position, often involving scarce resources where there is a behavior or threat of behavior through the exercise of power to control the situation or gain at the expense of the other party.[78] Competition differs from conflict in that, in the former, each party is bound to abide by the same rules.[79]

Conflict is a pervasive and perhaps inevitable part of human existence; *it is not inherently "bad" or "good,"* and its consequences depend mainly on how it is managed.[80] Negative conflict is an energy-consuming and destructive phenomenon that divides individuals and groups within the police department, creates tension be-

In The News

Chief Sues Department

James Jackson, the Columbus, Ohio, Police Chief, is involved with his fifth legal battle with the city, claiming that he was defamed. If the appeal court declines to hear his case, it will mark the end of legal wrangling which began when the former mayor launched an investigation of the chief. At a cost of $3 million, the city has won all previous suits filed by the chief, sergeants, and commanders.

As a public figure, Chief Jackson has to prove that the city was malicious in its allegations. In a previous appeal, his attorneys argued that the city maliciously published statements from a felon that the chief had fathered an illegitimate child with a prostitute, knowing they were false. City officials said they put a disclaimer in the investigative report that the statements were likely to be false but felt they had to include the allegations.

Source: Jodi Andes, "Ohio Chief Presses Legal Fight with City," *The Columbus* (Ohio) *Dispatch*, November 14, 2006.

tween representatives of the police department and other agencies, and results in acrimonious and combative exchanges. However, positive conflict can do the following:

1. Stimulate interest
2. Prevent individual, group, and organizational stagnation
3. Be a source of creativity and change as alternative ways of viewing things are aired
4. Give individuals, groups, and organizations a distinctive identity by demarcating them from others
5. Create group and organizational solidarity
6. Be an enjoyable experience of testing and assessing the active use of one's full capabilities[81]

Although not unique to them, an unfortunate characteristic of many police departments is the view that conflict is destructive, so that its positive aspects and potential benefits are overlooked and lost. To tap the useful dimensions of conflict, the police leader must be able to differentiate between pathologically and productively oriented situations. Pathological symptoms in conflict include the following:

1. Unreliable and impoverished communication between the conflicting parties
2. The view that the solution of the conflict will result from the imposition of one view or position over the other
3. A downward spiral of suspicion and hostility that leads to oversensitivity to differences and the minimization of similarities[82]

Unresponded to, such symptoms are the prelude to hostile infighting, hardening of positions, and protracted opposition. In contrast, productively oriented conflict does the following:

1. Uses open and honest communication, which reduces the likelihood of misperceptions and misunderstandings, allows each party to benefit from the knowledge possessed by the other, and promotes a mutual and accurate definition of the issues
2. Encourages the recognition of the legitimacy of the other's interests and of the need to search for a solution that is responsive to the needs of each party
3. Fosters mutual respect and sensitivity to similarities and common interests, stimulating a comergence of positions[83]

The way in which police leaders will handle conflict is to some extent bound up in their leadership styles. Various methods for resolving conflict are summarized in Table 7.3. Each of the various methods identified may be appropriate or inappropriate at various times; to return to an earlier point, good diagnostic ability and flexibility are central attributes for leaders.

Critical Thinking Question

1. Although conflict can be positive, most often it is thought of as being negative. It often seems to leave us with "a bad taste in our mouths." Why is this?

LEADERSHIP AND ORGANIZATIONAL CONTROL

Because police leaders are responsible for the performance of their departments, they must be concerned with organizational control and organizational controls. **"Organizational control"** is synonymous with "organizational direction" and is normative,

TABLE 7.3 Leadership Style and Preference for Handling Conflict

MANAGERIAL GRID LEADERSHIP STYLE	PREFERENCE FOR HANDLING CONFLICT
1,1	Avoid it, withdraw when it occurs, ignore it, and do not take action. Conflict festers until it can no longer be ignored.
1,9	Gloss over differences, smooth things over, make appeals such as "Why can't we all just get along? We're all cops here." The immediate conflict is resolved, but smoldering differences may remain.
9,1	Handle it quickly and decisively. Use the power of the position to announce unilaterally how it will be handled. Both sides may resent the solution.
5,5	Get the parties to negotiate with each and endorse solution or compromise. May sometimes develop and impose a compromise. In negotiation, both sides get some of what they want.
9,9	Parties to the conflict are brought together to collaborate on a true group decision. In collaboration, the emphasis is on finding the best solution, regardless of what the initial positions were.

dealing with the future. In contrast, **organizational controls** consist of measurements of, information about, and analysis of what was and is.[84] Stated more simply, controls pertain to the means, and control pertains to an end.[85]

Of necessity, the issues of organizational control and controls permeate police departments. Despite the definitions given, practical distinctions between them require some thought. For example, planning, budget preparation, and the written directive system of a police department—consisting of policies, procedures, and rules and regulations—are all control devices in that they all deal with preferred future states, positions, and behaviors. However, when an officer violates a rule and disciplinary measures are invoked, the system of controls is in operation. During the execution of a budget, a mid-year review occurs in which performance over the first six months is summarized and analyzed and plans are made for the remaining six months. Thus, this mid-year review incorporates features of the system of organizational controls and control. Similarly, quarterly evaluations of police programs incorporate features of the system of controls and control, whereas the final program evaluation report is in the main part of the system of controls. Despite such variations, it is apparent that informed control is a function of the system of controls.

To give the police leader control, controls must satisfy the following specifications:

1. They must be specific and economical.
2. They must be meaningful, relating to significant events.
3. They must use the appropriate indicators.
4. They must be timely.
5. Their limitations must be understood.
6. They must be as simple as possible.
7. They must be directed to those who can take the necessary action.[86]

Perhaps paradoxically, the tighter a police leader attempts to control unilaterally, the less control he or she actually has. A simple illustration of this point is taking a handful of sand and squeezing it forcefully; a great deal trickles out and is lost. Alternatively, the same amount of sand cupped loosely in the hand remains in place. By involving others, by sharing power, the police leader secures the greatest amount of control because individual commitment—the best and most effective type of control—is secured.

Critical Thinking Question

1. How do effective police agencies achieve the needed level of organizational control without becoming mechanical bureaucracies that slavishly enforce procedures and rules?

CHAPTER REVIEW

1. Define leadership.
   It is the process of influencing organizational members to use their energies willingly and appropriately to facilitate the achievement of organizational goals.
2. Contrast the two ways at looking at "great men" theories of leadership.
   One line of thought is that great people are born with outstanding qualities and they make history; the other way of looking at it is that the events of history make people great.
3. Identify and briefly discuss the three broad responsibilities all police leaders have.
   These are (1) fulfilling the mission of the police department, (2) making work productive and helping subordinates to be achieving, and (3) producing impacts (making a difference in a positive sense).
4. Describe how authority and power are separate, but entwined, concepts.
   Authority is a formal grant from the organization to a position, the incumbent or holder of which wields it. With such a grant of authority, some power to compel a person to perform is inherent. But perhaps the more significant power is the informal type which is given from the led to leaders because the rank and file have confidence in them. The first type is granted to the leader; the second type must be earned.
5. Discuss the power motivation of managers.
   This concept has three components: (1) personalized power (producing an impact for personal and aggrandizement), (2) socialized power (producing an impact for the common good of the police department, and (3) affiliation needs (which have not to do with power but rather with the need to be accepted and liked).
6. State the components of the skill mix and how they operate.
   The skill mix has three components: (1) human relations, (2) conceptual, and (3) technical; at each of the different levels of an organization the mix of these skills and their content vary somewhat. For example, as a sergeant human relations and technical skills are more important than conceptual skills. However, at the top management level, conceptual skills are most important. At the sergeant level, technical skills include helping a subordinate decide what type of crime scene search pattern to use; at top management an example is budgeting skills.
7. Describe how the traits approach to leadership would select leaders.
   The traits approach believes that leaders have certain qualities (for example, intelligence, emotional maturity, powerful inner drive, or infectious optimism); in this view, the selection of leaders is simple once you identify the traits you find out who has them and select them as leaders.

8. Define the authoritarian, democratic, and laissez-faire leadership styles.
   Authoritarian leaders make all decisions without input from their followers and they closely control work; democratic leaders encourage the participation of subordinates in planning and performing tasks; and laissez-faire leaders take a passive, hands-off approach in dealing with subordinates.
9. Outline the authoritarian–democratic leadership continuum.
   This seven-point continuum has two polar opposites: authoritarian at the left end and democratic at the right end. Between these polar points, Tannenbaum and Schmidt identify five intervening styles of management as one progresses from authoritarian to democratic styles.
10. Identify and briefly describe Down's four types of leader behavior in bureaucratic organizations.
    These four types are (1) climbers, who are strongly motivated by power and prestige needs to invent new functions to be performed by their unit; (2) conservers, who seek to preserve the status quo, keeping things as they are; (3) zealots, who have a narrow interest and missionary-like zeal for it; and (4) advocates, who promote everything under their jurisdiction.
11. Contrast station house and street sergeants.
    Station house sergeants tend to have worked inside prior to getting their stripes and continue to work inside afterward. They go by the book. Street sergeants worked in the field prior to being promoted and prefer to stay there. They are action-oriented and are less concerned about conformity and more concerned about results.
12. Identify the five major management styles from the Managerial Grid.
    The five styles are 1, 9 (country club); 9, 1 (authority/obedience); 5, 5 (organizational man); 9, 9 (team management); and 1,1 (impoverished).
13. Define situational leadership.
    Leaders should adapt their leadership style to the maturity level of subordinates; as their maturity level increases, leaders can be less directive and controlling.
14. Describe transactional and transformational leaders.
    Most leader–follower relationships are transactional; that is, leaders exchange one thing (e.g., good evaluations or promotions) for certain follower behaviors (e.g., obedience or loyalty). Transactional leaders preach the value of honesty, fairness, acceptance of responsibilities, and the completion of assignments properly and on time. In contrast, transformational leaders interact with their followers in such a way that the followers are transformed by being elevated to, and sustained by, higher ideals, such as liberty, justice, and equality.
15. Conclude whether conflict is "good" or "bad."
    Conflict is not inherently bad or good. Its nature, or character, falls out from the way which it is handled. Handled improperly (e.g., bottled up), it can be a destructive force; handled properly (openly discussed to find the best possible resolution for the organization, as opposed to "who wins"), it can be a source of creativity and growth for the organization.

KEY TERMS

Authoritarian–democratic continuum: based on the work of Tannenbaum and Schmidt, this model shows the changes of behavior, along a continuum, as a manager shifts from one management style to another; the authoritarian and democratic styles represent the extreme ends of the model.

Authoritarian leader: a leader who makes all decisions without consulting subordinates and closely controls work.

Authority: a grant made by a formal organization to a position, the incumbents of which use it to fulfill their responsibilities.

Behavioral theories of leadership: theories that focus on what leaders do (their behaviors); these behaviors are also described as management, or leader, *styles*.

Burns: identified and defined transactional leaders (those who exchange one thing for another with their followers) and transformational leaders (those who emphasize justice, liberty, and equality and thereby transform and elevate their followers).

Conflict: a mutual difference of opinion between two parties, often involving scarce resources, in which one party is attempting to control the situation or gain at the expense of the other party.

Democratic leader: a leader who is group-oriented and includes subordinates in planning and executing tasks.

Downs: identified four leader styles in bureaucratic organizations: (1) climbers, (2) conservers, (3) zealots, and (4) advocates.

"Great man" theory: the theory in which one vein, associated with Carlyle, espouses that great people are born with unusual qualities, reduced to its simplest argument, Galton believed genetics explains who is a great leader; Hegel disagreed, claiming that it is the events of history which make people great.

Laissez-faire leader: a leader who takes a hands-off, or passive, approach in dealing with subordinates.

Leadership: the process of influencing organizational members to use their energies willingly and appropriately to facilitate the achievement of the police department's goals; leadership also arises, as shown by the Hawthorne studies, out of the informal organization when members of a group recognize charismatic leaders.

Lewin, Lippitt, and White: although earlier studies had identified the authoritarian, democratic, and laissez-faire leaders, their classical study has closely identified them with these styles.

Managerial Grid: developed by Blake and Mouton, this model interrelates two key organizational concerns: (1) concern for people, the vertical axis, and (2) concern for production, the horizontal axis. Along each of these axes, "1" represents low concern and "9" represents high concern. The interaction of these axes, (reading first from the horizontal axis) produces five styles of management or leadership: (1) 1 (low concern for production), 9 (high concern for people), or the country club management, (2) 9, 9, team management, (3) 5,5, organizational management, (4) 1,1, impoverished management, and (5) 9,1 authority–obedience management.

Organizational control: synonymous with organizational direction, concerned about dealing with what is normative, or "ought to be," in the future—for example, a policy or procedure requiring officers to halt a vehicle pursuit if it becomes too dangerous.

Organizational controls: the measures organizations put in place in order to achieve organizational control; it has a now (rather than a future) orientation to make sure that things don't get off track (e.g., disciplining officers who violate the policy).

Power: the ability to compel a performance or make people do certain things; there is some power inherent in the exercise of formal authority; Bernard believed that power was also a grant willingly made by the led to the leader.

Power motivation: the reasons, intention, and objectives that underlie a police manager's use of power; there are two types: (1) personalized power (primarily used toward personal gain aggrandizement) and (2) socialized power (influencing others for the good of the department); additionally, police leaders want to be liked and accepted; these are called affiliation needs and are not power needs because they are not oriented toward having an impact on the organization.

Rationale for organizations: the rationale that organizations exist to do the things which people will or cannot do for themselves.

Situational leadership: a theory advanced by Hersey and Blanchard, it focuses on the behavior of leaders in relation to the degree of maturity (as defined by Hersey and Blanchard) in their followers; the greater the level of maturity in followers, the less directive and controlling a leader needs to be.

Skill mix: a model based on three sets of skills needed by police leaders: (1) human relations (the capacity to interrelate positively with other people), (2) conceptual (understanding and relating parcels of information which often seem unrelated or whose importance is uncertain), and (3) technical (at the supervisory level, this may include helping subordinates recognize and properly handle physical evidence, while in top-level management it would shift to budgeting and other skills). The content and proportion of these skills in relationship to one another vary as one progresses from a first-line supervisor to top management.

Station house sergeants: identified by Van Maanen, they worked inside (as opposed to the field) before they were promoted and preferred to stay there after becoming a sergeant; they were the opposite of a street sergeant and go strictly by the book.

Street sergeants: identified by Van Maanen, they were the opposite of station house sergeants; they worked in the field prior to their promotion, preferred to stay there, and had a strong action orientation; they were more concerned with not letting than with conformity.

Traits approach: as relates to leadership, the traits approach believes that leaders possess certain qualities; when one has identified those traits, one finds out who has them and those people should be leaders; Gibb's research did not find any consistent patterns of traits which leaders have.

Transactional leaders: leaders who exchange one thing (e.g., good evaluations or promotions) for another (obedience or loyalty) with their followers; most leader styles have a transactional component.

Transformational leaders: leaders who relate to their followers on the basis of higher concepts, such as equality, liberty, and justice, and in the process transform and elevate them.

NOTES

1. Peter F. Drucker, *People and Performance: The Best of Peter Drucker on Management* (New York: Harper's College Press, 1977), p. 28.
2. Patrick A. Knight and Howard M. Weiss, "Effects of Selection Agent and Leader Origin on Leader Influence and Group Member Perceptions," *Organizational Behavior and Human Performance* 26 (August 1980): 17–21. See also Thomas Henderson, "The Relative Effects of Community Complexity and of Sheriffs upon the Professionalism of Sheriff Departments," *American Journal of Political Science* 19 (February 1975): 126.
3. Peter F. Drucker, *The Effective Executive* (New York: Harper & Row, 1966), pp. 23, 36–39. Points 2 to 5 were taken from this source at page 24. Also see Eugene Raudsepp, "Why Managers Don't Delegate," *Journal of Applied Management* 4–5 (1979): 25–27.
4. Jacques Steinberg, "Police Officer Rejects Promotion," *New York Times,* June 2, 1991.
5. The flip side of the coin is the question "Under what conditions do organizational members voluntarily elect to leave, stay and protest, or simply stay?" An important book addressing these issues is Albert O. Hirschman, *Exit, Voice, and Loyalty* (Cambridge, Mass.: Harvard University Press, 1970).
6. The description of power motivation styles is drawn, with restatement into a police context, from Jay Hall and James Hawker, "Interpreting Your Scores from the Power Management Inventory" (The Woodlands, Tex.: Teleometrics International, 1981).
7. Variants of this model appear in the literature; see, for example, Ronald G. Lynch, *The Police Manager,* 2nd ed. (Boston: Holbrook Press, 1978), figure 1.2, p. 11; Calvin J. Swank, "Police Management in the United States: A Candid Assessment," *Journal of Police Science and Administration* 4 (1976): 90–93: and Robert Katz, "Skills of an Effective Administrator," *Harvard Business Review* 33, no. 1 (1955): 33–42.
8. Ralph M. Stogdill, *Handbook of Leadership: A Survey of Theory and Research* (New York: Free Press, 1974), p. 17.
9. Thomas Carlyle, *Heroes, Hero-Worship and the Heroic in History* (New York: A. L. Burt, 1902), and G. W. F. Hegel, *The Philosophy of History* (Indianapolis: Bobbs-Merrill, 1952).
10. Francis Galton, *Hereditary Genius: An Inquiry into Its Laws and Consequences* (New York: D. Appleton, revised with an American preface, 1887).
11. Field Marshal Montgomery, *The Path to Leadership* (New York: Putnam, 1961), pp. 10–19. To some extent, Montgomery also holds with Carlyle in that the former asserted that the leader must be able to dominate and master the surrounding events.
12. Cecil E. Goode, "Significant Research on Leadership," *Personnel* 25, no. 5 (1951): 349.
13. Stogdill, *Handbook of Leadership,* p. 81, and "Personal Factors Associated with Leadership: A Survey of the Literature," *Journal of Psychology* 25–26 (January 1948): 35–71.
14. C. A. Gibb, "Leadership," in *Handbook of Sound Psychology,* vol. 2, ed. Gardner Lindzey (Reading, Mass.: Addison-Wesley, 1954).
15. Walter J. Palmer, "Managerial Effectiveness as a Function of Personality Traits of the

Manager," *Personnel Psychology* 27 (summer 1974): 283–95.

16. Gary Dessler, *Organization and Management: A Contingency Approach* (Englewood Cliffs, N.J.: Prentice Hall, 1976), p. 158.
17. Stogdill, "Personal Factors," pp. 35–71; Dessler, *Organization and Management*, p. 169.
18. F. E. Fiedler, *A Theory of Leadership Effectiveness* (New York: McGraw-Hill, 1967). Fiedler has worked on a contingency approach to leadership since the early 1950s.
19. Robert J. House, "A Path–Goal Theory of Leader Effectiveness," *Administrative Science Quarterly* 16 (September 1971): 321–38.
20. See K. Lewin, R. Lippitt, and R. White, "Patterns of Aggressive Behavior in Experimentally Created Social Climates," *Journal of Social Psychology* 10 (May 1939): 271–99; R. Lippitt and R. K. White, "The Social Climate of Children's Groups," in *Child Behavior and Development*, ed. R. G. Baker, K. S. Kounin, and H. F. Wright (New York: McGraw-Hill, 1943), pp. 485–508; Ralph White and Ronald Lippitt, "Leader Behavior and Member Reaction in Three Social Climates," in *Group Dynamics: Research and Theory*, 2nd ed., ed. Dorwin Cartwright and Alvin Zander (New York: Harper & Row, 1960), pp. 552–53; and Ronald Lippitt, "An Experimental Study of the Effect of Democratic and Authoritarian Group Atmospheres," *University of Iowa Studies in Child Welfare* 16 (January 1940): 43–195.
21. White and Lippitt, "Leader Behavior," pp. 539–45, 552–53.
22. Robert Tannenbaum and Warren H. Schmidt, "How to Choose a Leadership Pattern," *Harvard Business Review* 36, no. 2 (1958): 95–101.
23. Ibid., 98–101.
24. Anthony Downs, *Inside Bureaucracy* (Boston: Little, Brown, 1967).
25. Ibid., pp. 92–96.
26. Ibid., pp. 96–101.
27. Ibid., pp. 109–10.
28. Ibid., pp. 107–9.
29. John Van Maanen, "Making Rank: Becoming an American Police Sergeant," *Urban Life* 13, no. 2–3 (1984): 155–76. The distinction between station and street sergeants is drawn from Van Maanen's work with some restatement and extension of views. The speculation about future career patterns is the work of the present authors.
30. Robert R. Blake and Jane Srygley Mouton, "The Development Revolution in Management Practices," *Journal of the American Society of Training Directors* 16, no. 7 (1962): 29–52.
31. The Ohio State studies date from the mid 1940s and identified the dimensions of consideration and structure; the University of Michigan studies date from the late 1940s and identified employee- and production-centered supervisors.
32. Paul Hersey and Kenneth H. Blanchard, *Management of Organizational Behavior: Utilizing Human Resources*, 3rd ed. (Englewood Cliffs, N.J.: Prentice Hall, 1977), p. 105. See also William J. Reddin, *Managerial Effectiveness* (New York: McGraw-Hill, 1970).
33. Hersey and Blanchard, *Management of Organizational Behavior*, pp. 160–61.
34. Ibid., p. 161.
35. Ibid.
36. Ibid., p. 163.
37. Ibid., p. 161.
38. Ibid., p. 163.
39. Ibid., p. 162.
40. Ibid., p. 168.
41. Ibid., p. 165.
42. Ibid., p. 168.
43. Ibid., p. 159.
44. James McGregor Burns, *Leadership* (New York: Harper & Row, 1978). For an excellent overview on leadership, see Edwin P. Hollander and Lynn R. Offermann, "Power and Leadership in Organizations: Relationship in Transition," *American Psychologist* 45, no. 2 (1990): 179–89.
45. Ibid., pp. 4, 19–20.
46. Ibid., p. 426.
47. Noel Tichy and David O. Ulrich, "The Leadership Challenge: A Call for the Transformational Leader," *Sloan Management Review* 26, no. 1 (fall 1984): 59–68.
48. B. M. Bass, *Leadership and Performance beyond Expectations* (New York: Free Press, 1985).
49. Warren Bennis and Bert Nanus, *Leaders* (New York: Harper & Row, 1985).
50. James M. Kouzes and Barry Z. Posner, *The Leadership Challenge: How to Get Extraordinary Things Done in Organizations* (San Francisco: Jossey-Bass, 1987), p. 38. This book does not focus on the police; hence, the authors have taken the liberty of writing its important lessons into the police context.
51. Ibid., p. 29.
52. Ibid.
53. Ibid.
54. Ibid.
55. Ibid., p. 79.

56. Ibid.
57. Ibid.
58. Ibid.
59. Ibid., p. 108.
60. Ibid., p. 79.
61. Ibid.
62. Ibid., p. 131.
63. Ibid., p. 155.
64. Ibid., pp. 159–60.
65. Ibid., p. 162.
66. Ibid., pp. 162–63.
67. Ibid., p. 131.
68. Ibid.
69. Ibid., p. 175.
70. Ibid., p. 190.
71. Ibid., pp. 220–21.
72. Ibid., p. 245.
73. Stephen J. Harrison, "Quality Policing and the Challenges for Leadership," *Police Chief* 63, no. 1 (January 1996): 26.
74. Ibid.
75. Ibid.
76. Ibid.
77. David Couper and Sabine Lobitz, "Leadership for Change: A National Agenda," *Police Chief* 60, no. 12 (December 1993): 18.
78. Albert E. Roark and Linda Wilkinson, "Approaches to Conflict Management," *Group and Organizational Studies* 4 (December 1979): 441.
79. Ibid.
80. Ibid., p. 440; on this point, see also Kenneth Thomas, "Conflict and Conflict Management," in *Handbook of Industrial and Organizational Psychology,* ed. Marvin D. Dunnette (Chicago: Rand McNally, 1976), p. 889.
81. See Lewis A. Coser, *The Functions of Social Conflict* (Glencoe, Ill.: Free Press, 1956); G. Simmel, *Conflict* (New York: Free Press, 1955); and M. Deutsch, "Toward an Understanding of Conflict," *International Journal of Group Tensions* 1, no. 1 (1971): 48.
82. Morton Deutsch, *The Resolution of Conflict* (New Haven, Conn.: Yale University Press, 1973), p. 353.
83. Ibid., p. 363.
84. Peter F. Drucker, *Management: Tasks, Responsibilities, Practices* (New York: Harper & Row, 1973), p. 494.
85. Ibid.
86. Ibid., pp. 496–505.

The essence of ultimate decision remains impenetrable to the observer, often, indeed, to the decider himself. . . . There will always be the dark and tangled stretches in the decision-making process—mysterious even to those who may be most ultimately involved.

—John F. Kennedy

CHAPTER 8

PLANNING AND DECISION MAKING

OUTLINE

Introduction
Planning
Planning Approaches
Types of Plans
Effective Plans
Decision Making
Decision Making During Crisis Events
Group Decision Making
Ethics and Decision Making
Common Errors in Decision Making
Chapter Review
Key Terms
Notes

OBJECTIVES

1. Explain some advantages of planning within a police department.
2. Discuss the synoptic planning approach. Describe three methods of selecting a preferred course of action.
3. Discuss the differences among administrative, procedural, operational, and tactical plans.
4. Describe the characteristics of effective plans.
5. List the three major decision-making models.
6. Discuss Simon's concept of "bounded rationality."
7. Explain Lindblom's theory of incremental decision making.
8. Describe the decision-making process as presented by William Gore.
9. List some of the important recommendations, developed in this chapter, for handling future crisis events.
10. Discuss the advantages of group decision making.
11. List the steps decision makers should take when confronted with an ethical issue.
12. Explain the most common errors in decision making.

INTRODUCTION

Decision making is a complex process that includes not only procedures for reaching a sound decision on the basis of pertinent knowledge, beliefs, and judgments but also procedures for obtaining the required knowledge, ideas, and preconditions. Moreover, in the case of important decisions, these procedures may involve many minor decisions taken at various stages in the decision-making process. For example, a chief's decision to automate the records division by purchasing a computer and software usually follows a series of decisions. First, the chief decides that the present manual system is not adequate. Second, a decision is made to evaluate the number of systems available on the open market. This decision probably accompanied the decision to address the city council to request additional funding with which to purchase the necessary equipment. And finally, the chief resolves that records division personnel must be retrained to operate in an automated system. These minor decisions are only part of the overall process in arriving at a major decision. Thus, the decision to take a certain action, if sound, should be based on the judgment that this action probably will have more desirable results than any other action, and this judgment may be based on conclusions as to the probable consequences of alternative decisions.[1]

Decision making also involves the application of our knowledge, our experience, and our mental and moral skills and powers to determine what actions should be taken to deal with a variety of problem situations. Moreover, this decision-making process includes the application of logic for testing conclusions and the use of ethics for testing judgment.[2] For instance, an officer's decision to arrest a violent, drunk husband at a family disturbance is usually based on the officer's past knowledge that, if the current situation is left unattended, the probable result will be a criminal act involving assault, wife or child abuse, or even murder. Ethically, the officer is bound to deter crime and so will take the necessary course of action to prevent the physical harm of any family member.

Decision making is a responsibility that all police officers come to accept routinely. These decisions may be as ordinary as deciding whether to write a motorist a traffic citation or as complex as a split-second decision whether to shoot at someone. The quality and types of decisions made by police managers in their policy formulation and by the street-level officer in invoking arrest action are based, in part, on the personality characteristics of the individual making the decision, the recruiting and career development practices of the police department, and, equally important, the type of community being served. For example, one merely has to read the works of Wilson[3] and Skolnick[4] to conclude that enforcement decisions that appear to be quite adequate for one community may be totally unacceptable for another and that recruitment practices that would be acceptable to one community would draw objections from another. Thus, police administrators can follow no single model to make the best decisions all the time. However, certain principles, when understood and applied carefully, can result in good decisions much of the time. Although sometimes not understood as such, planning is basically part of the decision-making process.

PLANNING

Police administrators sometimes do not appreciate the importance of planning because of their pattern of career development. It is ironic that the pattern of career development for typical police managers carries with it seeds that sometimes blossom into a negative view of planning. Having spent substantial portions of their careers in line divisions, such as patrol and investigative services, police managers may see planning as "clerical" or "not real police work." Further, because many agencies have a "planning and research" unit, there is a natural tendency to believe that planning should occur only in that area by individuals assigned to that task. However, planning is an integral element of good management and good decision making.[5] Management needs to anticipate and shape events; it is weak if it merely responds to them.[6] The police manager whose time is consumed by dealing with crises is symptomatic of a department with no real planning or decision-making process. Police departments are sometimes said to be practicing "management by crisis"; in fact, it is "crisis by management."[7] That is, the lack of attention given by police managers to planning creates an environment in which crises occur with regularity. This is so because management by crisis produces a present-centered orientation in which considerations of the future are minimal. In contrast, planning can be expected to accomplish the following:

1. Improve the analysis of problems
2. Provide better information for decision making
3. Help to clarify goals, objectives, and priorities
4. Result in more effective allocation of resources

In The News

Today's News

Poor Planning Plagues New Orleans Police Department's Response to Hurricane Katrina

In the days after Hurricane Katrina made landfall in August of 2005, problems in communications and coordination, planning, and execution undermined the ability of the New Orleans Police Department (NOPD) to respond to victims of the storm. Many officers had to be rescued themselves, and the department lost nearly 7 percent of its officers in the days after the storm, because they either quit or were fired. The chief characterized the storm as one that was so incomprehensible that it was nearly impossible to have planned for. Communications broke down in such a way that the public, both within the ruined city of New Orleans and around the country, perceived that there was an atmosphere of absolute lawlessness. The breakdown of communication led to the perception among police officers that there was no chain of command, and protocols and procedures vanished as a result. Many officers concentrated on dealing with looters, which diverted valuable resources from more pressing issues, while many attempted search-and-rescue operations without proper equipment or adequate personnel. Due to the lack of command, many of these well-meaning search-and-rescue operations were duplicitous.

While the NOPD had a disaster plan on the books, many officers and administrators testified later that few were familiar with the plan and most had never participated in any sort of exercise to reinforce disaster training among the ranks of the force. The police infrastructure as a whole was not prepared, as vital communications centers, evidence storage, and police cruisers were all kept on lower floors, all of which flooded during the storm.

As a result of the catastrophic failure of the NOPD to maintain even the simplest of communications during the storm, the Disaster Response Center (DRC) has suggested that all police departments nationwide plan, drill, and train all officers on a disaster plan, as well as disaster contingency plans. Specifically, the DRC suggests that large departments, such as the NOPD, undergo planning for major organizational changes that must be made temporarily to deal with major disasters. These changes should include changing priorities in response to specific needs, delaying normal tasks, and shifting and making use of all organizational personnel, as well as absorbing additional, non-department personnel.

Furthermore, there should be five priorities in training police personnel for disaster management. The first priority is implementing the new organizational structure required for disaster response. Second, police departments should encourage individual decision making. Third, there should be a clear understanding of the chain of command, something that was clearly lacking in the case of Hurricane Katrina. Fourth, disaster response policies and training should establish centralized command posts. Finally, there should be unambiguous protocols that establish how police operations will be integrated with federal response, if necessary.

These protocols are currently being considered by the New Orleans Police Department, as it has committed to create new and better policies for disaster response. Hurricane Katrina may have been an unimaginable situation for police department planners, but with clear protocols regarding infrastructure, communications, and command, it is less likely that police departments, both in New Orleans and throughout the country, will be as overwhelmed by large-scale disaster in the future.

Source: Willoughby Anderson, "'This Isn't Representative of Our Department': Lessons from Hurricane Katrina for Police Disaster Response Planning," (Berkeley, CA: Boalt Hall School of Law, University of California at Berkeley, April 2006).

5. Improve inter- and intradepartmental cooperation and coordination
6. Improve the performance of programs
7. Give the police department a clear sense of direction
8. Provide the opportunity for greater public support
9. Increase the commitment of personnel

In short, competent planning is a sure sign of good police administration and the first step in accurate decision making.[8]

Definitions of Planning

There are no simple definitions of planning. The word **planning** became common terminology in the vocabulary of criminal justice with the introduction of the Omnibus Crime Control and Safe Streets Act of 1968. However, what appeared to be missing in that document was an examination of what planning actually involved or what it meant in the operation of criminal justice organizations. Hudzik and Cordner[9] have defined planning as "thinking about the future, thinking about what we want the future to be, and thinking about what we need to do now to achieve it." Stated more succinctly, planning involves linking present actions to future conditions. Mottley defines planning as

> *a management function concerned with visualizing future situations, making estimates concerning them, identifying the issues, needs and potential danger points, analyzing and evaluating the alternative ways and means for reaching desired goals according to a certain schedule, estimating the necessary funds and resources to do the work, and initiating action in time to prepare what may be needed to cope with changing conditions and contingent events.*[10]

There is also the assumption that planning is oriented toward action, which means that thinking is only a part of planning; the real purpose is determining what an organization should do and then doing it. And finally, planning is associated with empirical rationalism: planners gather and analyze data and then reach an objective conclusion.

Critical Thinking Question

1. Why are police departments prone to "management by crisis"? What are the problems created by this approach?

PLANNING APPROACHES

A variety of approaches are employed in the planning processes. Each is unique and can be understood as a method of operationalizing the word "planning." There are basically five major approaches to planning: (1) synoptic, (2) incremental, (3) transactive, (4) advocacy, and (5) radical.

Synoptic Planning

Synoptic planning, or the rational–comprehensive approach, is the dominant tradition in planning. It is also the point of departure for most other planning approaches, which in general are either modifications of synoptic planning or reactions against it. Figure 8.1 represents the typical synoptic model. It is based on "pure," or "objective,"

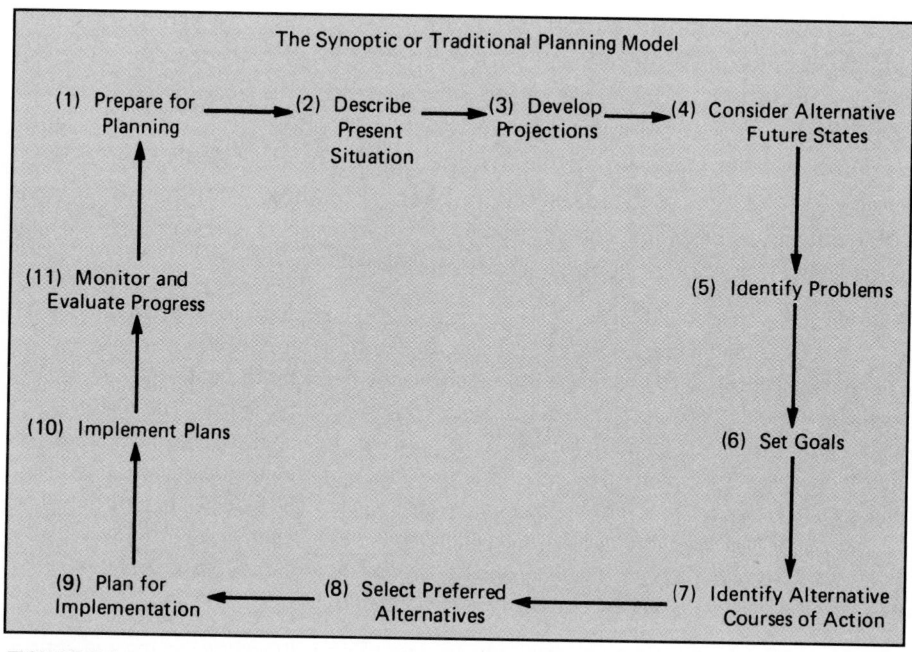

FIGURE 8.1

Synoptic planning, or the rational-comprehensive approach.

(From Robert Cushman, *Criminal Justice Planning for Local Governments* [Washington, D.C.: U.S. Government Printing Office, 1980], p. 26, with minor modification.)

rationality and attempts to ensure optimal achievement of desired goals from a given situation.[11] This model is especially appropriate for police agencies, as it is based on a problem-oriented approach to planning. It relies heavily on the problem identification and analysis phase of the planning process and can assist police administrators in formulating goals and priorities in terms that are focused on specific problems and solutions that often confront law enforcement. For instance, police administrators are more apt to appreciate a planning model centered around problem-oriented goals and priorities (such as the reduction of burglaries in a given residential area) than centered around more abstract notions (such as the reduction of crime and delinquency).[12] Then, too, police departments are designed for response, and it is easier to mobilize individual officers and gain cooperation between police units if concrete goals and objectives are set in reaction to a given problem.

Synoptic planning consists of 11 steps. Each step is designed to provide the police manager with a logical course of action.[13] The first step in synoptic planning is preparation for planning. It is during this step that the police chief organizes the planning effort with a central theme—what are we trying to accomplish and what type of information is required to understand the problem? Next, the present situation should be described. Weiss[14] states that a primary purpose of planning is in evaluation, or in comparing "what is" with "what should be." The third step in synoptic planning involves developing projections and considering alternative future states. Projections should be written with an attempt to link the current situation with the future, keeping in mind the desirable outcomes. It is important for the police executive to project the current situation into the future to determine possible, probable, and desirable future states while considering the social, legislative, and political trends existing in the community.

Identifying and analyzing problems is the next step in the synoptic model. Police managers should define the nature of the problem—that is, describe the magnitude, cause, duration, and expense of the issue at hand. This provides a clear, conceptual picture of the current conditions in which to develop the means for dealing with the problem. The fifth step of the synoptic model is to set goals. A goal is an achievable end state that can be measured and observed. Making choices about goals is one of the most important aspects of planning.[15] Hudzik and Cordner point out that several kinds of choices must be made concerning goals:

> *Several kinds of choices must be made. First, choices must be made about preferred states or goals. An important and sometimes ignored aspect of this choice involves the choice of the criteria for measuring goal attainment. This is often hard, much harder than setting the goal itself. For example, the goal of a juvenile treatment program may be to reduce recidivism among those treated. Yet, in measuring goal attainment several questions arise. First, what constitutes recidivism? Technical or status violation? Arrest for criminal violation? Conviction on a criminal violation, and only for those crimes against which the juvenile program may have been directed? Also, over how long a period will recidivism be monitored? A year? Two years? Five years? Ten years? It is not that those questions cannot be answered, but securing agreement on the appropriate criteria becomes a major difficulty.*[16]

The next step in synoptic planning includes identifying alternative courses of action. Alternatives are means by which goals and objectives can be attained. They may be policies, strategies, or specific actions aimed at eliminating a problem. Alternatives do not have to be substitutes for one another or perform the same function. For instance, improving officer-survival skills through training, modifying police vehicles, issuing bulletproof vests, using a computer-assisted dispatch program, and increasing first-line supervision may all be alternatives in promoting officer safety.

It is important that the activities (the means) that a police department engages in actually contribute to the achievement of goals (the ends). If the means are not connected to the ends, then a police agency could expend a great deal of resources in activities that keep personnel busy but do not contribute to fulfilling key objectives or responsibilities.

The seventh step in the synoptic planning process is selecting preferred alternatives. This process is often fraught with complexity and has been researched for decades by scholars in business management, public administration, systems science, and criminal justice in order to assist decision makers in this process. Three basic techniques to select alternatives are (1) strategic analysis, (2) cost-effectiveness analysis, and (3) must–wants analysis.

Strategic Analysis The first study addressing the selection of preferred courses of action originated at the U.S. Naval War College in 1936 and has been popular in police management circles.[17] Since that time, the model has been refined into a more systematic and objective treatment.[18] The process is shown in Figure 8.2. To visualize how the technique can be applied and selections made, it will be helpful to use an example currently confronting law enforcement managers—for example, the issue of automating a records division with particular reference to the improvement of officer-generated reports by use of laptop computers.

Given a set of possible alternatives or courses of action, the number of alternatives can be reduced in the following ways. First, make **suitability studies** of all alternatives. That is, each course of action is evaluated in accordance with general policies, rules, and laws. For example, in all jurisdictions it is illegal to maintain an automated records system that contains arrest and conviction data of juveniles to safeguard the juveniles' reputations. A manual records system is deemed more secure because access can be totally controlled.

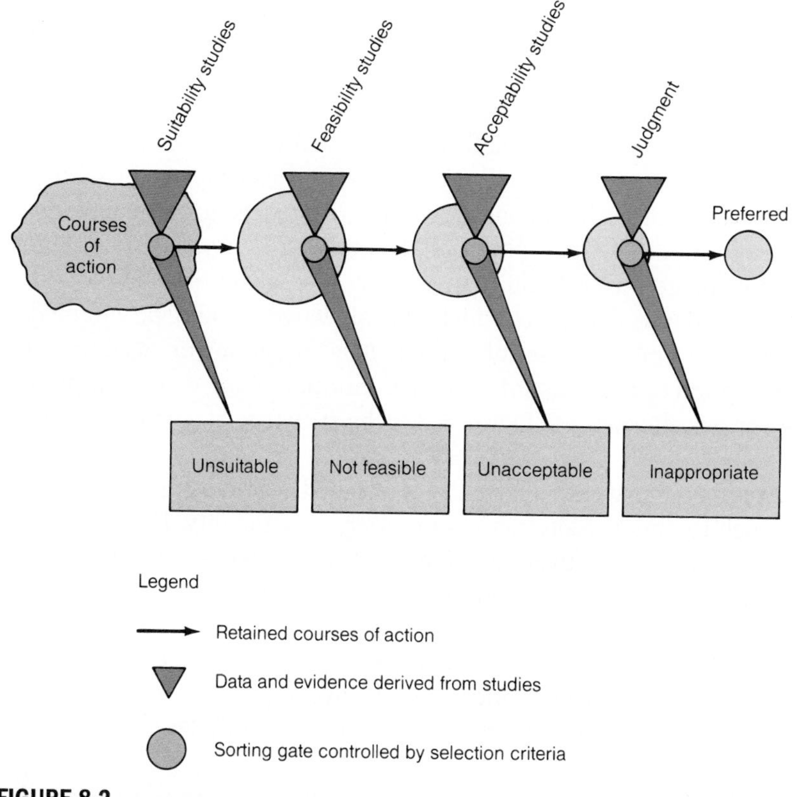

FIGURE 8.2

Strategic analysis: a process for deriving a preferred course of action.
(*Source:* C. M. Mottley, "Strategic Planning," *Management Highlights* 56 [September 1967, p. 271])

Second, subject the retained and suitable alternatives to **feasibility studies**. These include the appraisal of the effects of a number of factors weighed separately and together. Continuing with the example, the feasibility of an automated records system would be judged on the basis of meeting (1) the existing standards of operation (e.g., will an automated records system do everything the manual system can do?), (2) the conditions of the operational environment (e.g., is the police department facility large enough to accommodate a computer? Is it air-conditioned? Does it have proper electrical outlets?), (3) the restrictions imposed by the state of the art (e.g., is the desired software compatible with the existing computer system?), and (4) limitations on the resources available (e.g., is the cost for an automated records system beyond police funding approval? Can the records division personnel be retrained, and how much will that cost?).

Third, analyze the retained courses of actions (those judged to be suitable and feasible) in acceptability studies. Four principal factors are combined and enter into this evaluation: (1) the cost of each alternative, (2) the performance, (3) the effect of the alternative on the entire system, and (4) the time involved in implementation and setup. These factors are applied to each alternative to reveal critical limits and tradeoffs. Finally, a judgment is rendered that selects the preferred course of action.

Cost-Effectiveness Analysis This technique is sometimes called cost-benefit or cost-performance analysis. The purpose of this form of selection is that the alternative chosen should maximize the ratio of benefit to cost. The concept is based on economic rationalism: calculations are made "scientifically" through the collection of data and the use of models in an attempt to maximize benefits and minimize costs.

A model is a simplified representation of the real world that abstracts the cause-and-effect relationships essential to each course of action or alternative.[19] Using the example of automating a records division, each course of action would be analyzed in an attempt to compare the cost in dollars of each segment of the system (mainframe, software, laptop computers) with the benefits (increased officer safety, more efficient crime analysis, and subsequent apprehension that diminishes property loss and injury). In the analysis of choice, the role of the model (or models, for it may be inappropriate or absurd to attempt to incorporate all the aspects of a problem into a single formulation) is to estimate for each alternative (or course of action) the costs that would be incurred and the extent to which the objectives would be attained.[20] The model may be as complex as a set of mathematical equations or as simple as a purely verbal description of the situation in which intuition alone is used to predict the outcomes of various alternatives. Figure 8.3 is the structure of cost-effectiveness analysis.

It is important to note that each alternative is weighed against a criterion: the rule or standard by which to rank the alternatives in order of desirability. This provides a means to analyze cost against effectiveness.[21] Unlike strategic analysis, alternatives are not dismissed from the process but ranked in order of preference.

Must–Wants Analysis. This method of selecting a preferred course of action combines the strengths of both strategic and cost-effectiveness analyses. Must–wants analysis is concerned with both the subjective weights of suitability, feasibility, and acceptability and the objective weights of costs versus benefits.

In this method of selection, a must–wants chart is developed to assist the police administrator. This methodology is particularly well suited for comparing like brands or models of equipment (e.g., in the case of personal weapons, the strengths and weaknesses of 9-mm semiautomatic pistols versus .38-caliber revolvers, or for personal computers, the pros and cons of selecting among IBM, HP, or Dell personal computers). In this example, Figure 8.4 provides a chart for evaluating three popular police patrol vehicles—namely, the Chevrolet Impala, the GMC SU Yukon, and the Ford Crown Victoria.

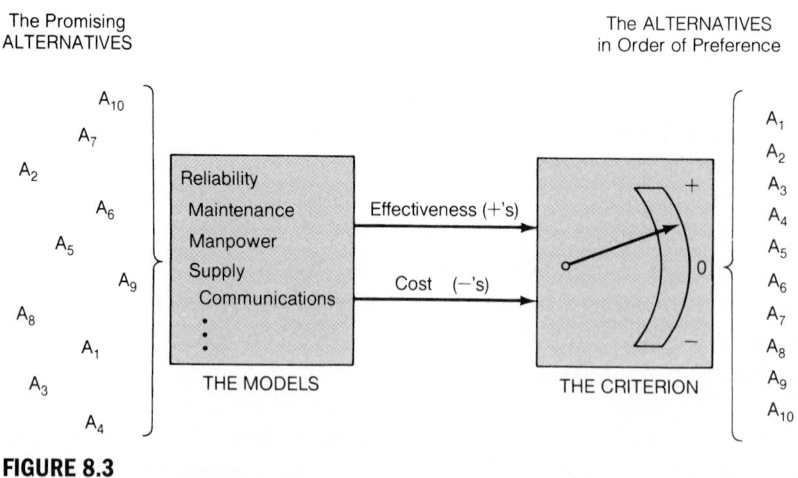

FIGURE 8.3

The structure of cost-effectiveness analysis.

(*Source:* E. S. Quade, "Systems Analysis Techniques for Planning-Programming-Budgeting," in *Planning, Programming, Budgeting: A Systems Approach to Management,* ed. F. J. Lyden and E. G. Miller [Chicago: Markham, 1972], p. 250)

Musts	*Alternative A: Chevrolet Impala*	*Alternative B: GMC SU Tahoe*	*Alternative C: Ford Crown Victoria*
Total purchase price not to exceed $28,000	$25,700	$27,800	$26,500
Dual airbags (driver & passenger side)	yes	yes	yes
Power-assisted, four wheel disc, antilock brake system	yes	yes	yes
Heavy-duty, automatic transmission	yes	yes	yes
Full-size, four-door sedan	yes	NO, NO GO	yes
Front & rear heavy-duty suspension	yes		yes
Goodyear police pursuit radial tires	yes		yes

Wants	*wt.*		*sc.*	*wt. × sc.*		*sc.*	*wt. × sc.*
Minimum total price	7	$23,700	8	56	$23,500	9	63
High engine displacement	4	350 cu. in.	7	28	281 cu. in.	5	20
High horsepower	7	260 @ 5000 rpm	8	56	250 @ 5000 rpm	7	49
Excellent acceleration (0 to 60 mph)	6	8.02 secs	8	48	9.1 secs	6	36
Good acceleration (0 to 100 mph)	3	21.47 secs	9	27	25.18 secs	6	18
Good top speed	4	139 mph	7	28	135 mph	6	24
Good quarter mile run from stop to finish (seconds/top speed)	5	16.14 sec/88 mph	7	35	16.89 sec/83.83 mph	7	35
Excellent braking—Stopping distance from 60 mph	7	133.1 feet	7	49	133.4 feet	7	49
Excellent turning capability	6	43 feet	7	42	39 feet	9	54
Large fuel capacity	4	23 gallons	7	28	20 gallons	5	20
Heavy frame and body	5	4,249 lbs.	8	40	3,974 lbs.	7	35
Excellent ergonomics:							
Front seating area	9	comfortable/roomy	9	81	slightly cramped	7	63
Interior headroom	8	39.2—very good	8	64	38.4—good	6	48
Rear seating area	5	easy entry & exit	8	40	tight and "bouncy"	7	35
Clarity of instrumentation	4	good	7	28	fair	6	24
Communications accessibility	4	good	8	32	good	8	32
High EPA mileage							
City	10	17 mpg-very good	8	80	17 mpg-very good	8	80
Highway	8	26 mpg-excellent	9	72	23 mpg-good	7	56
Combined	9	20 mpg-excellent	9	81	19 mpg-very good	8	72
Performance totals of wants objectives:				**915**			**813**

FIGURE 8.4

Must-wants chart for selecting a police patrol vehicle. The "results" in the illustration of must-wants analysis are hypothetical and should not be used as a basis of action.

(*Source: 2007 Model Year Patrol Vehicle Testing*, prepared by Michigan State Police [Washington, D.C.: National Institute of Justice, Office of Justice Programs, November 2006])

The must–wants chart is constructed in the following manner:

1. "Musts" are placed at the top of the page. These are conditions that are set by the police chief or selecting committee and that absolutely have to be met in order for an alternative (in this case, a specific police patrol vehicle) to continue to be a viable choice. The failure of any alternative to meet a must condition

immediately eliminates it from further consideration. In Figure 8.4, note that alternative B, the GMC Tahoe, did not conform to the must of being a full-size, four-door sedan. Because the 2007 sports utility Tahoe was available only in two-door SUV models, it was eliminated.

2. "Wants" are conditions, performances, characteristics, or features that are desirable but not absolutely necessary. They are listed below the musts, and corresponding data for each want are completed for each alternative that was not discarded at the previous step.
3. Weight (the column marked "wt." in Figure 8.4) reflects the subjective importance of the want as determined by the police chief or selection committee. Weight has a scale of 1 (lowest) to 10 (highest).
4. Score (the column marked "sc." in Figure 8.4) is the evaluation of the actual existence of wants by the chief or committee. A scale of 1 to 10 is also used in this column. The score is set by the evaluator to reflect an assessment of the subjective or actual existence of the want. In this example, the wants under "Excellent ergonomics" are subjective evaluations, while "EPA mileage—city, highway, combined" are objectively determined by an outside source. In general, the scoring of wants should be based on a limited number of factors because too many could distort the choice of an option.
5. The weight and score for each want are multiplied ("wt. × sc." in Figure 8.4) and summed. The sum of each "wt. × sc." column is called the performance total of wants objectives.
6. The second part of the must–wants chart, shown in Figure 8.5, is called the "possible adverse consequences worksheet." On this worksheet, statements concerning possible detriments or negative outcomes are listed for each alternative. The probability and seriousness of each comment are subjectively scored. The probability of an adverse consequence happening is scored on a scale from 1 (very unlikely) to 10 (certain to happen). Seriousness is scored on

Alternative A: Chevrolet Impala	*Probability*	*Seriousness*	*P×S*
Relatively large turning circle (difficult to perform u-turns)	8	7	56
100,000-mile bumper-to-bumper warranty is extra, $1,800	9	8	72
Chevrolet does not have a CNG option for fuel	6	5	30
Dealership is downtown, will be more difficult for precincts to access	9	8	72
TOTALS:			**230**

Alternative C: Ford Crown Victoria	*Probability*	*Seriousness*	*P×S*
Relatively small gas tank, will require more frequent refueling	5	3	15
Smaller vehicle with smaller inside and trunk volume	6	8	48
Department master mechanics are all GM trained, service & parts agreement with GM	8	6	48
Overall EPA mileage is lower in all categories, reducing cost savings	9	7	63
			174

FIGURE 8.5

Possible adverse consequences worksheet–police patrol vehicles.

	Alternative A *Chevrolet Impala*	*Alternative C* *Ford Crown Victoria*
Must-have objectives:	All met	All met
Wants performance total:	915	813
Possible adverse consequences total:	(230)	(174)
	685	**639**

FIGURE 8.6

The final step in must-wants analysis–selecting an alternative. The alternative with the highest point value should be chosen. The facts and figures presented are for illustrative purposes only and should not be the basis for action.

the same type of scale, with 1 representing "extremely unserious" and 10 denoting "very serious." The final scores are summed and used in the last choice, the selection step.

7. Some advocates of using the must–wants chart recommend that the totals of the possible adverse consequences worksheet be considered only advisory, whereas others recommend that the performance totals for each alternative be mathematically reduced by the value of the possible adverse consequences score. If the latter approach is used, the alternative with the highest total points should be chosen. In Figure 8.6, alternative A, the 2007 Chevrolet Impala, would be selected as the primary police patrol vehicle for the agency, with a total point score of 685.

Despite the "rational" and "objective" appearance of the must–wants analysis approach, there are a number of subjective scores, weights, and probabilities in the chart. The "bottom line" values in Figure 8.6 (685 and 639) were calculated on subjective measures. The real value in must–wants analysis is in the methodology. The chief must not become a captive of the device and follow the results mechanistically. He or she should use a must–wants chart to consider and weigh the intangibles that are not easily quantifiable between alternatives. The value of must–wants analysis is not in the end product but rather in the sharpening of differences or similarities between alternatives or courses of action.

As with must–wants charts, the other two approaches (strategic and cost-effectiveness analyses) are methods of selecting a preferred alternative or choosing a desired course of action. In the final analysis, the judgment of the police chief plays a key and indisputable role, one that cannot be taken lightly; the chief cannot afford to be ill informed about the alternative courses to be made.

The next two steps in synoptic planning include planning and carrying out implementation. Once a preferred course of action is selected, the police chief is required to execute plans that fulfill the goals or objectives of the process. Implementation often requires a great deal of tact and skill to alleviate complexities and anxieties related to change. It may be more important "how" an alternative is introduced into a police department than "what" it actually is.

The final step of the synoptic planning model is evaluation: were the objectives achieved? Were the problems resolved? The answer to these questions should be obtained through a system than monitors the implementation process.

Evaluation requires comparing what actually happened with what was planned for—and this may not be a simple undertaking.[22] Feedback must be obtained concerning the results of the planning cycle, the efficiency of the implementation process, and the effectiveness of new procedures, projects, or programs. This is an important step of synoptic planning—trying to figure out what, if anything, happened as a result of implementing a selected alternative. It is for this reason that baseline data are so critical (step 2—describe the present situation). Hudzik and Cordner[23] point out that evaluation completes the cycle of rational planning. The issue of identifying problems must be considered again. Does the original problem still exist, or was it solved? Is there a new problem?

Summation of the Synoptic Planning Approach

Considerable attention has been given to synoptic planning because it is the most widely used approach in police management. Most other approaches have been derived from the model just described. Synoptic planning basically comprises four activities: preparing to plan, making a choice between alternatives, implementing the plan, and evaluating the plan. Although the steps may be reduced or named differently, the 11-step synoptic approach is a refinement of this cyclical process. As shown, this process has proven to be very successful in many police departments and is especially well suited for implementing new technology within the organization (see Figure 8.7).

The following approaches are other methods commonly used in business forecasting of social planning. Although these approaches are not used as extensively in police management as the synoptic approach, they too deserve some attention.

Incremental Planning

Incremental planning levels a series of criticisms at synoptic planning, including its tendency toward centralization, its failure to appreciate the cognitive limits of police executives (decision makers), and unrealistic claims of rationality. Incrementalism concludes that long-range and comprehensive planning are not only too difficult but inherently bad. The problems are seen as too difficult when they are grouped together and easier to solve when they are taken one at a time and broken down into gradual adjustments over time. The incremental approach disfavors are exclusive use of planners who have no direct interest in the problems at hand and favors a sort of decentralized political bargaining that involves interested parties. The incrementalists feel that the real needs of people can best be met this way and the "tyranny of grand design" avoided.[24]

Transactive Planning

Transactive planning is not carried out with respect to an anonymous target community of "beneficiaries" but in face-to-face interaction with the people who are to be affected by the plan. Techniques include field surveys and interpersonal dialogue marked by a process of mutual learning. For example, in planning a crime prevention program in a particular neighborhood, the police might go to randomly selected houses to talk to residents about unreported crime, their concerns and fears, and the rise in residential burglary rates. The residents receive crime prevention techniques and a more secure feeling knowing that the police are concerned about their neighborhood. The police department also receives benefits: intelligence information is gathered about strange persons or cars in the area, a more aware citizenry is likely to detect and report crimes, and a more supportive public attitude concerning the police is developed.

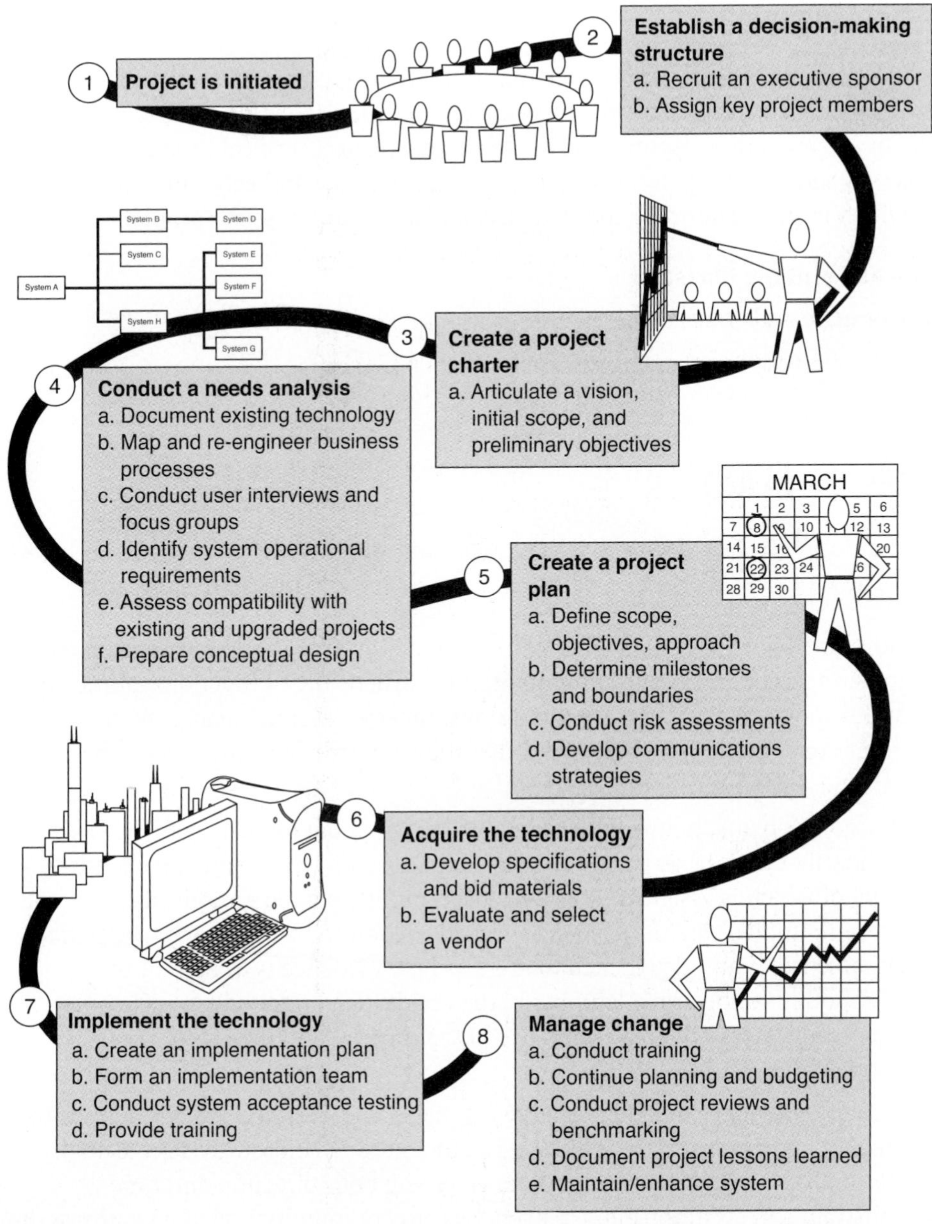

FIGURE 8.7

Law Enforcement Information Technology Projects: A Roadmap to Guide. The U.S. Department of Justice offers a guide to technology compiled by the Office of Community Policing. This excerpt is a visualization of initiating and implementing new information technology systems.

(*Source:* "Law Enforcement Tech Guide," www.cops.usdoj.gov)

Advocacy Planning

Advocacy planning grew up in the 1960s in the adversary procedures modeled by the legal profession. This approach is usually associated with defending the interests of the weak—the poor and politically impotent, for example—against the strong. Beneficial aspects of this approach include a greater sensitivity to the unintended and negative side effects of plans.

Radical Planning

Radical planning has an ambiguous tradition with two mainstreams that sometimes flow together. The first mainstream involves collective action to achieve concrete results in the immediate future. The second mainstream is critical of large-scale social processes and how they permeate the character of social and economic life at all levels, which in turn determine the structure and evolution of social problems.

Critical Thinking Questions

1. Compare and contrast five planning approaches.
2. Why are baseline data so critical in synoptic planning?

TYPES OF PLANS

From an applications perspective, the planning process yields an end product—a plan. These can be categorized by use and are delineated into four groups:[25]

1. Administrative or management plans include formulation of the department's mission statement, goals, and policies; the structuring of functions, authority, and responsibilities; the allocation of resources; personnel management; and other concerns whose character is that they are prevalent throughout the agency.
2. Procedural plans, in line with many but certainly not all management plans, are ordinarily included as part of a police department's written directive system, a copy of which is assigned to every officer and is updated periodically. Procedural plans are the guidelines for the action to be taken under specific circumstances and detail such matters as how evidence is to be sent or transported to the crime laboratory, the conditions under which male officers may search arrested females and the limits thereto, and how to stop and approach traffic violators.
3. Operational plans are often called work plans and describe specific actions to be taken by line units (patrol officers, precinct groups, and/or division teams). Work plans are usually short and terse, giving both direction and time constraints in accomplishing a given task. In community policing ventures, the work plan usually focuses on a defined community need in a specific neighborhood.
4. Tactical plans involve planning for emergencies of a specific nature at known locations. Some tactical plans are developed in anticipation of such emergencies as the taking of hostages at a prison or a jailbreak and are subject to modification or being discarded altogether in peculiar and totally unanticipated circumstances. Other tactical plans are developed for specific situations as they arise, such as how to relate to a demonstration in the park or a march on city hall. Although well-operated police agencies invest considerable effort in developing tactical plans that may seldom or never be used, their very existence stimulates confidence among field officers and lessens the likelihood of injury to officers, the public, and violators (see Figure 8.8).

Critical Thinking Question

1. What type of plan is strategic planning? Why?

Focus on Policy

Strategic Planning in Police Organizations

Police departments sometimes get caught up in planning for the here and now, an inherent condition for organizations required to react to critical incidents and to make tactical decisions on a routine basis. However, strategic planning can be an extremely useful tool for law enforcement agencies, outlining the mission, goals, and objectives of a police department for administrators, officers, and the community. A strategic plan is a product of a leadership process that lays out the blueprints for future decision making. Many police departments have policies requiring strategic plans or are bound by municipal requirements to draft or update one every few years.

Many strategic plans begin with a mission, value statement, vision statement, or combination of all three. The mission statement is a general, overarching declaration establishing the reason for the agency's existence. Police organizations should consider several factors in developing a mission statement, including their values and culture, their history, their present resources, and their intended direction. There is no strict rule for developing a mission statement, and a glimpse at strategic plans from departments across the nation yields a number of types of statements. Some are short and succinct, such as this one from Denver:

> *To deliver high quality public safety services so that all people may share a safe and healthy environment.*

Other mission statements, such as this one from Addison, Illinois, are more specific:

> *It is the mission of the Addison Police Department to safeguard life and property, promote and preserve civil order, create and maintain a sense of security in the community, eliminate the opportunity for the commission of crime, protect the constitutional rights of the citizens, diligently pursue and apprehend criminals, enforce all laws and ordinances uniformly, without the influence of personal feelings, prejudices, animosities or friendships, develop and maintain a reputation for integrity and professionalism within the community, and recognize and appreciate the value of ethnic diversity within the community.*

After an agency has developed a mission statement, it is important that it establishes a vision. The vision statement describes how the agency plans to carry out its mission, and it is the basis for all of the objectives and goals to be developed in the strategic plan. Vision statements should set high standards for excellence, reflect high ideals, be based on a sound philosophy, inspire commitment, be proactive and positive, be communicated clearly, and integrate the unique qualities and competencies of the organization.

The next step in the strategic planning process is the value statement. Value statements are an expression of how an organization should operate in relation to core moral or operational values. Moral values include integrity and respect, while operational values include efficiency, accountability, and customer service.

The next step in strategic planning is formulating long- and short-range goals and objectives that define how an agency will meet its mission. Objectives should be action-oriented, specific, time-limited, quantifiable, and realistic. Following that, police departments should describe a strategy to achieve each of these objectives.

Ideally, a strategic plan should aid a police department in communicating to its officers and the public it serves how the department's energy and resources should be focused in order to attain certain goals. Updating the strategic plan every few years allows departments to react to crime trends and to the concerns of officers, citizens, and city lawmakers. Truly successful strategic plans involve the participation of police administrators, crime analysts, lawmakers, line officers, and citizens in order to consider issues both inside and outside the agency's control and to craft a plan to meet the needs of the community as a whole, as well as the police agency itself.

Sources: Addison Police Department Strategic Plan 2006–2010; Randy Garner, "SWAT Tactics: Basics for Strategic Planning," *The FBI Law Enforcement Bulletin*, November 2005; "A Staircase to Strategic Planning," Community Policing Consortium. Available online at www.communitypolicing.org.

EFFECTIVE PLANS

Regardless of how plans are classified, the bottom line is that organizations with a formal and continuous planning process outperform those without one. This discrepancy in performance increases as the larger environment becomes more turbulent and the pace and magnitude of change increase.[26] This is the type of environment that police administrators have faced in recent years and is illustrated by Proposition 12 in California, which severely limited police expansion; fuel shortages and the attending swift rise in fuel prices; the unionization of police officers and job actions, such as strikes and demonstrations; the escalation of litigation by the public and police department employees; and times of fiscal restraint, producing cutbacks in the availability of resources.[27] Considering these and other circumstances, police administrators not only

Quick Facts

Tactical Planning for Major Sports Events

Many police administration students take for granted that police chiefs plan for crisis events or natural disasters. However, few people consider the tactical planning that goes into recreational events, such as parades or sports events. The 1990 riots in Detroit following the Pistons' National Basketball Association Championship victory, which killed seven and injured hundreds, led to a careful approach by major cities to celebrations following major championship games. During the 2005–2006 basketball season, the Dallas Mavericks were an early favorite for the championship. City of Dallas officials brought together representatives from all sectors of city government, including police, fire rescue, and transportation departments, in order to create a Public Safety Planning Committee. The committee was broken up into two entities, one in charge of strategic planning and one in charge of event operations. Together, the subcommittees determined a tentative schedule for any public celebrations, contingency plans for a final championship game held in Dallas or in the opposing city, routes for parades, police and fire rescue presence and locations, communications, and other public safety considerations. While the Mavericks eventually lost out to the Miami Heat, the plans drafted during that season remain as a template for the 2006 season and beyond.

Source: "Possible Major Sports Celebration Event Plan," City of Dallas, April 3, 2006.

must have a planning process and plans but also must be able to recognize the characteristics of effective plans:

1. The plans must be sufficiently specific, so that the behavior required is understood.
2. The benefits derived from the achievement of the goals associated with the plan must offset the efforts of developing and implementing the plan, and the level of achievement should not be so modest that it is easily reached.
3. Involvement in plan formulation must be as widespread as is reasonably possible.
4. Plans should contain a degree of flexibility to allow for the unforeseen.

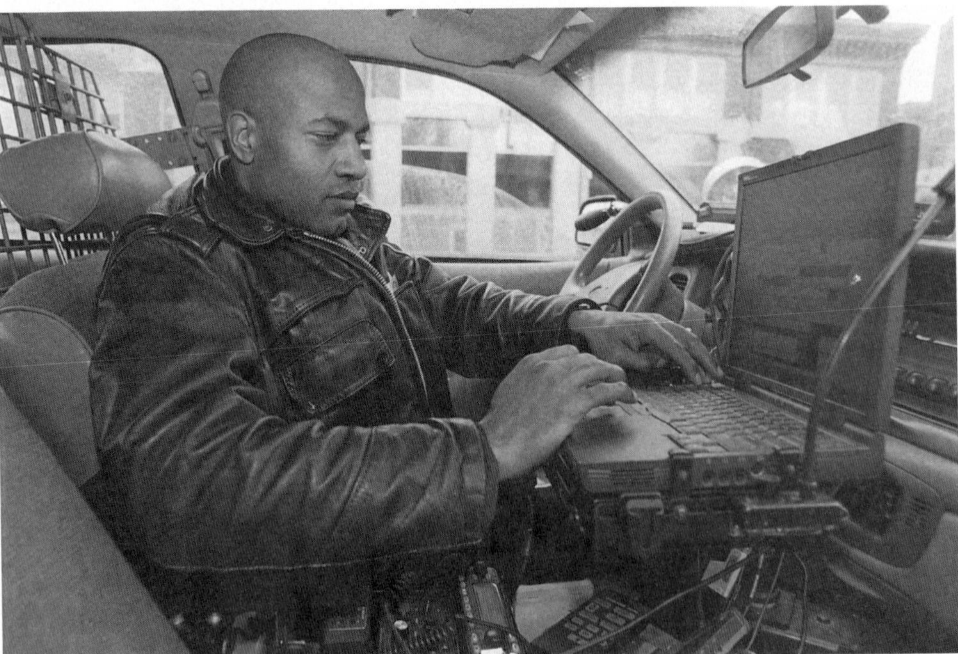

FIGURE 8.8

With the emergence of laptop computers in patrol cars, officers can access tactical plans immediately in response to a specific incident or crisis.

(Jim Commentucci/The Image Works)

5. There must be coordination in the development and implementation of plans with other units of government whenever there appears even only a minimal need for such action.
6. Plans must be coordinated in their development and implementation within the police department to ensure consistency.
7. As appropriate, the means for comparing the results planned for versus the results actually produced must be specified before implementation. For tactical plans, this often takes the form of an analysis, referred to as an after-action report.

Critical Thinking Question

1. Why is effective planning so critical for today's law enforcement agencies?

DECISION MAKING

As stated previously, planning is the first integral part of decision making. Planning is concerned primarily with coming to understand the present situation (problem) and widening the range of choices (alternatives or courses of action) available to the police chief (decision maker). Therefore, planning is aimed at providing information (a plan), whereas decision making is aimed at using this information to resolve problems or make choices.[28]

Decision-Making Models

The literature dealing with decision making in the police management field is not very extensive, and most of it is devoted to methods of applying the decision-making process. Whereas in theory it should be easy to divide decision-making processes into discrete, conceptual paradigms, in reality it is extremely difficult to separate one approach from another.

However, three models derived from decision-making theory appear to be basic in most of the literature. They are (1) the rational model, (2) the incremental model, and (3) the heuristic model.

The Rational Model

The traditional theory of management assumes that people are motivated predominantly by "economic incentives" and will, therefore, work harder given the opportunity to make more money. The "economic actor" concept also prevails in early decision-making theory. In Chapter 5, Organizational Theory, the scientific management approach developed by Taylor was presented. Within this concept, the economic person is presumed to act in a **rational** manner when faced with a decision-making situation. The assumptions for this rational behavior are (1) that a person has complete knowledge of all alternatives available to him or her, (2) that a person has the ability to order preferences according to his or her own hierarchy of values, and (3) that a person has the ability to choose the best alternative for him or her. Money is usually used as a measure of value for the decision maker. It is considered only natural that a person will want to work harder if that person can maximize the return of money by so doing. But these assumptions are difficult for a person to achieve in real life. Just by looking at the first assumption—that a person has knowledge of all available alternatives and their consequences in any given decision situation—we can see how impossible it would be to fulfill these requirements in most circumstances.

There is some evidence to suggest that administrative rationality differs from the "economic actor" concept of rationality because it takes into account an additional spectrum of facts relative to emotions, politics, power group dynamics, personality, and mental health. In other words, the data of social science are facts just as much as the carbon content of steel, but they are difficult and, in many cases, impossible to quantify with a high degree of accuracy.[29]

Police administrators bring to administrative decision making their own personal value system, which they inject into the substance of decision making while clothing their decision with a formal logic of the "good of the organization." They clothe the decision with the official mantle of the department's logic and respectability while their eyes remain fixed on more personal goals. But this does not lead to chaos because there is frequently a large element of commonality in personal value systems as related to organizational goals.[30] For example, the police executive who develops and directs a specialized unit to solve a series of murders will be accomplishing a law enforcement goal: to apprehend criminals. Although the executive's personal motives are to gain the public success of his or her unit, the personal objectives are in line with the organizational goals. Thus, conflict does not arise unless the personal values begin to compete with the department's mission.

In Chapter 5, Organizational Theory, the work of Gulick and Urwick was discussed as a description of administrative behavior focusing on the work of the chief executive. Part of their theory includes the act of making rational choices by following prescribed elements of work (PODSCORB). Their contribution set the stage for the rational model of decision making by suggesting that executives follow orderly and rational steps before making decisions. Subsequently, Simon[31] responded to these assumptions in his article "The Proverbs of Administration," in which he outlined several requirements for a scientifically based theory of administration. Simon's article was then included in his Administrative Behavior (1947).[32]

Simon explains that rational choices are made on a "principle of efficiency." His model of rationality contends that there are three essential steps in decision making: (1) list all the alternative strategies, (2) determine and calculate all the consequences of each strategy, and (3) evaluate all these consequences in a comparative fashion.[33] Whereas Simon is given credit for the development of this approach, its comprehensive expansion can be observed in the literature of several other theorists. Drucker's concept of the "Effective Executive," Iannone's "style" in Supervision of Police Personnel, and Sharkansky's decision-making model in Public Administration all exhibit an expansion of Simon's original work.[34] The rational model, often referred to as the rational–comprehensive model, sets forth a series of formalized steps toward "effective" decision making. These steps can be generally observed and listed as follows:

1. Identify and define the problem.
2. Ascertain all information regarding the problem.
3. List all possible alternatives and means to solving the problem.
4. Analyze the alternatives and assess the facts.
5. Select the appropriate alternatives and find the answer.

It is important to observe the elaboration on Simon's original method. The decision-making model assumes an ideal condition whereby the decision maker is aware of all available information related to the problem and has an unlimited amount of time in which to explore and narrow down proposed alternatives by a "rational" and comparative process. Unfortunately, actual practice rarely allows for the ideal.

Highly criticized for being too idealistic and irrelevant to the administrative functions of a police organization, the rational decision-making model has been subjected to harsh criticisms. Many of these criticisms have been noted as limitations by proponents of the method. For instance, Sharkansky[35] provided a detailed discussion of "roadblocks" to the fulfillment of the rational–comprehensive model in practical administration. He documented constraints of all available data and emphasized contingencies in the human ability to make decisions. Additionally, Simon elaborated on the concept of a "rational man." Noting that human beings are "bounded" by a triangle of limitations, he stated,

> *On one side, the individual is limited by those skills, habits, and reflexes which are no longer in the realm of the conscious . . . on a second side, the individual is limited by his values and those conceptions of purpose which influence him in making decisions . . . and on a third side, the individual is limited by the extent of his knowledge that is relevant to his job.*[36]

It is apparent that Simon understood not only the decision-making process but also the human factors associated in the term "rationality." A prerequisite to effective decision making is an acute awareness of the social, environmental, and organizational demands placed on the administrator. Simon[37] accurately stresses that one's ability to make rational decisions is bounded by the limitation of one's knowledge of the total organization. From this critical observation, Simon formulates a modified rational–comprehensive idea entitled "bounded rationality."[38] The emphasis, of course, is on human beings' inherent limitations to make decisions. Refer to Figure 8.9.

The Incremental Model

Another important approach concerning the modification of rational decision making is the "incremental" and "muddling through" theories explored by Lindblom.[39] Based on his study of government institutions in the United States, Lindblom states that the decision-making process is so fragmented and so complex, incorporating the interaction of various institutions, political entities, pressure groups, and individual biases, that rationality can have only a marginal effect. That is, the police administrator faces a set of limiting political factors (such as the mayor's wish to be re-elected) that prevent the decision-making process from being truly rational. For elected sheriffs, the political agendas may be so strong that purely rational decision making is inhibited.

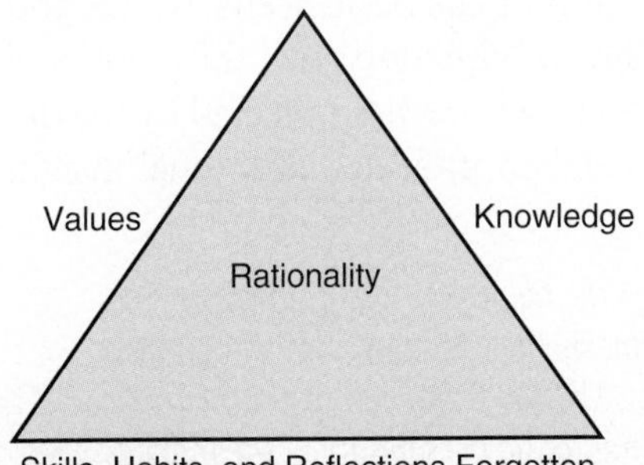

FIGURE 8.9

Simon's concept of bounded rationality.

Lindblom asserts that decision making is serial, that it is limited by time and resources as it gropes along a path where means and ends are not distinct, where goals and objectives are ambiguous, and where rationality serves no purpose. Contending that police managers and administrators "play things safe" and opt to move very slowly (incrementally) in decision making, Lindblom[40] proposes that managers "muddle through" problems rather than analytically choosing decisions. In Lindblom's view, decision making that occurs through a series of incremental steps provides the police administrator (and hence the public) with a number of safeguards against error:

> *In the first place, past sequences of policy (decision) steps have given him knowledge about the probable consequence of further similar steps. Second, he need not attempt big jumps toward his goals that would require predictions beyond his or anyone else's knowledge, because he never expects his policy (decision) to be a final resolution of a problem. His decision is only one step. . . . Third, he is in effect able to test his previous predictions as he moves on to each further step. Lastly, he often can remedy a past error fairly quickly—more quickly than if policy (decision) proceeded through more distinct steps widely spaced in time.*[41]

Lindblom's ideas have support—if not in theory, at least in practice—as many police managers find them to be "a description of reality."[42]

The Heuristic Model

In another opposing concept to rationality and logic, Gore[43] identifies the crucial element of humanism in decision making. He presents a **heuristic model** appropriately referred to as "the gut-level approach" when considering the police organization. The seasoned patrol officer frequently refers to an unknown quality or phenomenon known as "moxie" or the ability to be "streetwise." This unknown dimension is captured in Gore's decision-making method for police administrators. In an antithesis to the rational model, Gore identifies a process by which a decision is the product of the maker's personality. Gore views the heuristic process as "a groping toward agreements seldom arrived at through logic . . . the very essence of those factors validating a decision are internal to the personality of the individual instead of external to it."[44] Whereas the rational method is concrete, formalized by structure and calculations, the heuristic concept is nebulous, characterized by "gut feelings reaching backward into the memory and forward into the future."[45]

For Gore, decision making is basically an emotional, non-rational, highly personalized, and subjective process. Therefore, the facts validating a decision are internal to the personality of the individual instead of external to it. The key word in this statement is "validating"; it is intended to convey a sense of personal psychological approval or acceptance. The optimum situation is to select the decision alternative that creates the least anxiety about or disruption to the individual's basic needs, wants, and desires. In effect, every "objective" decision should be modified to meet the emotional needs of the various members of the police department who will be affected by the decision. The passage from which this statement was taken provides additional insight into Gore's heuristic decision-making scheme:[46]

> *Whereas the rational system of action evolves through the identification of causes and effects and the discovery of ways of implementing them, the heuristic process is a groping toward agreement seldom arrived at through logic. The very essence of the heuristic process is that factors validating a decision are internal to the personality of the individual instead of external to it. Whereas the rational system of action deals with the linkages between a collective and its objectives and between a collective and its environment, the heuristic process is orientated toward the relationship between that private core of*

values embedded in the center of the personality and its public counterpart, ideology. The dynamics of personality are not those of logic but rather those of emotion.[47]

In other words, although logic and reason may be the basic intellectual tools needed to analyze a given problem or to structure a series of solutions to a given situation, logic and reason may not prove to be completely effective in establishing intraorganizational agreement in connection with any given decision.[48]

Applauded for its contribution to the decision-making process, Gore's approach is also highly criticized as being too simplistic and non-scientific. Souryal[49] writes that "Gore's analysis is too unreliable. . . . It could complicate an existing situation, promote spontaneity, discredit the role of training and delay the advent of professionalism" in police organizations. This is an unfair assessment of the method. Gore views heuristic applications as adjuncts or alternatives to rational models. Further, some type of credibility must be assessed to that vague, unknown, and non-measurable entity we call experience, talent, or the "sixth sense." It was these elements that Simon had so much trouble with in calculating his "bound and limited" argument regarding the rational model. In any event, Gore's contributions remain as an opposite to decision making based solely on figures, formulas, and mathematical designs.

Alternative Decision-Making Models

Another attempt to outline various approaches to the decision-making process is Allison's[50] account of the 1962 Cuban Missile Crisis. He contends that the rational decision-making model, although most widely used, is seriously flawed. Allison presents two additional models (the organizational process model and the government politics model) to explain the decision making during crisis events that police and other government agencies often face. The organizational process model is based on the premise that few government decisions are exclusively the province of a single organization. In other words, police agencies are dependent on information and advice from other government units (such as the mayor's office, the FBI, and the district attorney's office) to make major decisions that affect public policy. The government politics model purports that major government policies are rarely made by a single rational actor, such as the chief of police. Rather, policy- and general decision making are the outcome of a process of bargaining among individuals and groups to support those interests. Implicit in both of the models is that the decision maker requires direction from his or her internal staff as well as support from other government agencies in the making of important decisions. This is especially true during crisis situations.[51]

Operational Modeling Other alternative models to decision making have evolved from the systems approach to management as described in Chapter 5, Organizational Theory. These techniques are vastly influenced by large, complex systems of variables. The application, collection, and analysis of data from decision making within the organization are called **operations research.**[52] In response to a need for a management science that addressed complex problems involving many variables, such as government planning, military spending, natural resource conservation, and national defense budgeting, operations research employs the use of mathematical inquiry, probability theory, and gaming theory to "calculate the probable consequences of alternative choices" in decision making.[53] As a result, techniques such as Program Evaluation and Review Technique (PERT) and Planning, Programming, and Budgeting Systems (PPBS) were developed for use in managerial planning, forecasting, and decision making.[54] By their very nature, these techniques must structure the system for analysis by quantifying system elements. This process of abstraction often simplifies the problem and takes it out of the real world. Hence, the solution of the problem may not be a good fit for the actual situation.

PERT is a managerial attempt to convert the disorganized resources of people, machines, and money into a useful and effective enterprise by which alternatives to problem solving can be assessed. This process is conducted by a cost-effectiveness analysis or an estimation for each alternative of the costs that would be incurred and the extent to which the objectives would be attained, which is similar to those discussed in the synoptic model.

Another model, the decision tree, is illustrated in Figure 8.10. In this model, the probabilities for various outcomes are calculated for each branch of the tree. In the example used in the figure, the first branch of the trunk has three possible outcomes: (1) arrest at the scene by a patrol officer, (2) no arrest at the scene, and (3) arrest at the scene by a detective. Note in the figure that the probabilities for those three events total 1.0, which is the mathematical value for certainty; all possible outcomes for that branch of the example are accounted for. The next-higher branch of the example decision tree deals with the various types of evidence obtained from investigation, and the final branches deal with the probability of arrest associated with the gathering of each type of evidence. Decision trees are very useful in analyzing situations and for reference when series of decisions that flow from one event are involved. For example, decision trees would be useful to the commander of a detective bureau in formulating policy and guidelines on when to continue or inactivate an investigation based on the

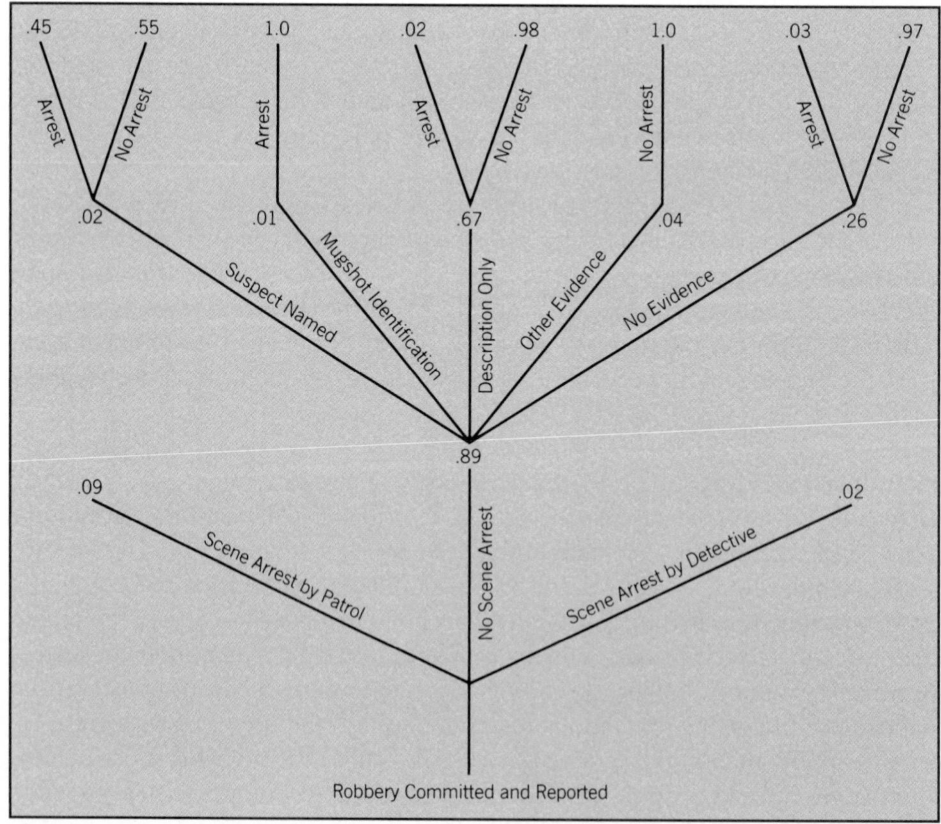

FIGURE 8.10

Decision tree of hypothetical probabilities of various outcomes in a robbery investigation.

types of evidence that were involved in order to make the best use of investigative resources. In this regard, decision trees can be seen as a tool of operations research. If an administrator is facing a decision for which there are no actual data, a decision tree can still be useful in analyzing the situation, and the "probabilities" can be the administrator's own subjective estimations based on past experience.

These approaches are highly sophisticated elaborations of the rational model using quantitative techniques. The weakness of the methods is in their practicality to real-world situations in which time and resources are not directly structured to gather intelligence about every problem and possible alternative. Further, these models assume that human biases will not enter the decision-making process. The most critical aspect of the approaches appears to be in their overriding insistence that decision making is not a human activity but the product of some scientific, computerized, and unimpressionable robot that digests quantitative information.

Wildavsky[55] has continually warned that the application of decision making to costs, benefits, resources, and budgets frequently results in the adoption of meaningless data and places unwarranted stimuli into the process.

Naturalistic Methods Recognition-primed decision making (RPD) is a model based on a more naturalistic view of decision making. While the previously discussed models focus on different courses of action, and the selection of one course of action over others, RPD distinguishes itself by focusing more on the assessment of the situation, its dynamics, and the experience of the decision maker. Much like incrementalism and heuristic models, RPD asserts that formal models of decision making are not possible in real-life situations, where decision makers are under time constraints and face poorly defined tasks, dynamic conditions, and ill-structured goals. RPD contains elements of the incremental and heuristic models and considers how a police official's experience affects his or her decisions. In RPD, police officials are primed to act in a situation and do not wait for a complete analysis of the facts before acting. Instead, elements of the situation are recognized as typical and action is taken based on previous experience. RPD relies heavily on the concept of satisficing, in which a solution is not so much optimal as it is sufficient, given the circumstances.[56] In other words, decision makers utilizing RPD identify an option that will suffice in a given situation based on past experiences with similar situations, then try to elaborate and improve on that option. Of course, the RPD model brings to mind questions about how decision makers react when they encounter situations that are absolutely not typical. In these cases, the RPD model states that the decision maker must identify anomalies in the situation and obtain as much information about the anomaly as possible in order to make a decision. The RPD model does not allow for much creativity or ingenuity in a situation, and it certainly allows for previous mistakes to be repeated. However, research indicates that RPD is the dominant form of decision making used in command and control organizations.[57]

Thin Slicing Malcolm Gladwell, in his 2005 book Blink, described a model of decision making called "thin-slicing." The **thin-slicing theory** states that, in situations where snap decisions are required, whether by a police administrator, a line officer, or anyone else in a decision-making capacity, instantaneous decisions may often be the best, particularly when paired with training and expertise.[58] Thin-slicing is clearly an offshoot of the heuristic model, as Gladwell maintains those decisions that are made in an instant can be equally good, or even better, than those made deliberately and with a lot of information. However, thin-slicing is more rational than traditional heuristic models. Unconscious decision making, which Gladwell describes as "a kind of giant computer that quickly and quietly processes a lot of the data we need in order to keep functioning as human beings,"[59] allows decision makers to thin-slice, a rational exercise in which we find patterns in situations and behavior based on very narrow slices of experience. According to Gladwell, our unconscious allows us to sift through situations that confront us, to the point that we throw out all irrelevant information and focus on the parts of the issue that are most relevant.

However, there is a dark side to rapid decision making, and Gladwell spends a good deal of time incorporating this into his theory. Often, unconscious attitudes and prejudices sneak into the decision-making process, leading thin-slicing astray. Under extreme pressure, researchers have found that decision makers tend to fall back on stereotypes and prejudices. The best way to counter this type of bias, according to Gladwell, is to train decision makers to slow down, even slightly, and find ways to mitigate the effects of stereotypes and biases by changing the environment where decisions might occur. This may at first glance seem paradoxical, and some might argue that Gladwell's concept of thin-slicing is at odds with itself because the theory asks that the decision maker go with his or her first reaction, but set rules ahead of time for the way that they might think. Gladwell acknowledges this but asserts that those with enough training and expertise are more able to extract the most meaningful amounts of information from the smallest, thinnest slice of an experience and are able to control the environment in which rapid cognition takes place.[60]

Critical Thinking Questions

1. What is the most likely model of decision making for police administrators? Which one are you most likely to use when making critical decisions?
2. How might training aid police administrators in decision making? What are the limitations of training in this area?

DECISION MAKING DURING CRISIS EVENTS

Police agencies, like all government organizations and private entities, are not immune to the necessity of effective decision making during **crisis events.** In this chapter, we have examined decision making in law enforcement from the traditional aspects of planning, organizational needs, theoretical models, and administrative roles. However, two major events, both over a decade old, remain banner incidents for the exploration of police decision making. The raid of the Branch Davidian Compound in Waco, Texas, in 1993 and the FBI siege of the Weaver family at Ruby Ridge, Idaho, in 1992 remain prime examples of the need for an examination of police executive decision making during crisis events. The purpose of this analysis is to bring applications of the various decision-making models to reality. It is not intended to be taken as a critical editorial but rather as an educational essay designed to identify the commonalities of the incidents and bring potential reason to action. It should not be taken lightly that each incident began with a sense of duty, good faith, honor, and courage yet ended in tragic losses of careers, agency reputations, and human life.

The Branch Davidians, Waco, Texas (1993)

During the early 1990s, a young, charismatic religious leader began to develop a group of followers known as the Branch Davidians. The group settled slightly northeast of

Waco, Texas, and began building a well-fortified compound in which to protect themselves from the outside world and the impending "Last Judgment Day." Their spiritual leader, David Koresh (commonly referred to by followers as "the Lamb of God"), was a high school dropout with a perceived mystical ability to teach from the apocalyptic Book of Revelation in the New Testament.

Police investigations of the Branch Davidians did not begin until late in 1992, when Alcohol, Tobacco and Firearms (ATF) agents were contacted by a postal driver who reported seeing hand grenades in a partially opened package delivered to the Waco compound. As a result of the investigation, an arrest warrant for Koresh was issued, along with a search warrant to seek out additional illegal weapons and explosives at the Waco compound.

In the early morning hours of February 28, 1993, tactical teams totaling approximately 75 men stormed the Waco compound. The agents were met with a fusillade of heavy gunfire. In the resulting exchange, 4 ATF agents and 6 Branch Davidians were killed. The incident prompted a 51-day standoff between federal agents and the Branch Davidians. Immediately following the initial confrontation between ATF and the compound occupants, the FBI assumed control of the operation. While negotiations during the ordeal were targeted initially at a peaceful resolution, the FBI began preparations to re-enter the compound by force, using armored vehicles to break through heavily fortified walls and distribute a debilitating dose of CS tear gas. The gas was supposed to be non-lethal, would not permanently harm adults or children, and would not cause fire during the delivery stage. As time lingered and negotiations lulled, Attorney General Janet Reno gave orders to commence with the assault. At 6:00 A.M. on April 19, 1993, several M-60 military tanks reconfigured with tear gas delivery booms began breaking through the compound walls (see Figure 8.11). Within hours of the operation, fire broke out. Fanned by 35-mile-per-hour winds, the fire raged, and the compound was rapidly incinerated. Seventy-two bodies were found among the remains, including several children.

Unfortunately, the flames of Waco have not been extinguished. In 1999, the Texas Rangers and lawyers for the Waco survivors revealed a blatant cover-up by the FBI. For six years, the FBI insisted that the Branch Davidians burned their own compound and denied to Congress that its agents fired any flammable tear gas canisters in the attack on April 19, 1993. Renewed investigations revealed that, not only did the FBI mislead Congress, but top decision makers may have overtly lied, finally admitting that the FBI did, indeed, fire at least two pyrotechnic M651 grenades at the Branch Davidian bunker. Even more troubling was the revelation that the U.S. military provided federal law enforcement agents with more than $1 million worth of support (supplying tanks, helicopters, aerial reconnaissance, munitions, and support personnel) during the standoff at Waco. At least 10 military advisers or observers attached to the U.S. Army's elite Delta Force were present at various times throughout the incident. The entire action came dangerously close to violating the Posse Comitatus Act, prohibiting the use of federal soldiers to act as police officers or in a law enforcement capacity within the borders of the United States. Further, Attorney General Reno admitted that her decision to allow the FBI to rush the Davidian compound was heavily based on tales of Koresh abusing children. Later, a Justice Department "clarification" said that there was no evidence of child abuse. According to Reno, the FBI convinced her that Koresh was a suicidal madman bent on destroying himself and others within the compound; however, she was never shown a letter by Koresh, dated just days before the attack, that promised that he would come out peacefully after completing his writing. The resulting publicity and trials caused serious questioning of the FBI's tactics, operations, and decision making.

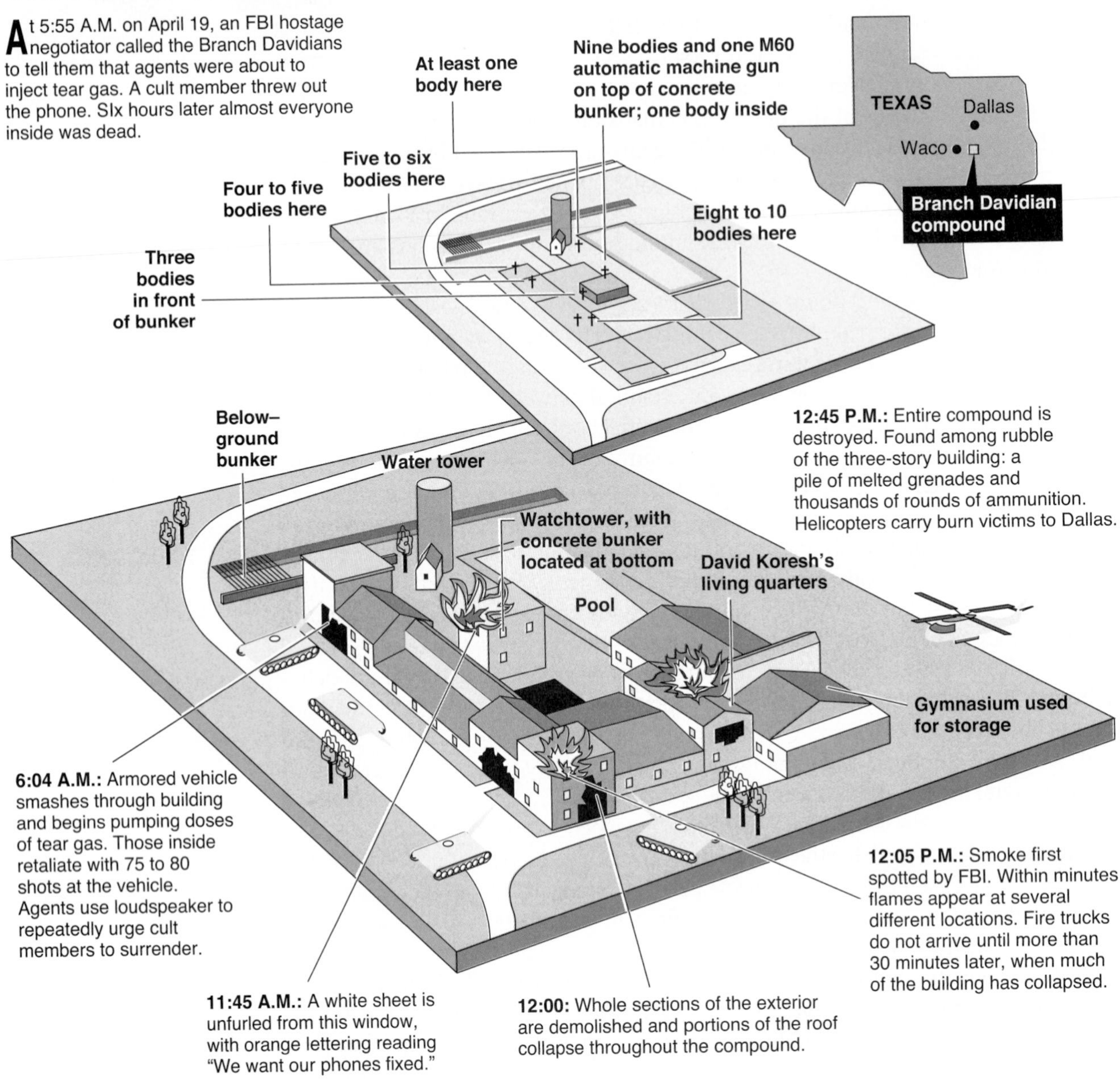
THE LAST ASSAULT
At 5:55 A.M. on April 19, an FBI hostage negotiator called the Branch Davidians to tell them that agents were about to inject tear gas. A cult member threw out the phone. SIx hours later almost everyone inside was dead.
At least one body here
Nine bodies and one M60 automatic machine gun on top of concrete bunker; one body inside
TEXAS
Dallas
Waco
Branch Davidian compound
Five to six bodies here
Four to five bodies here
Eight to 10 bodies here
Three bodies in front of bunker
Below–ground bunker
Water tower
12:45 P.M.: Entire compound is destroyed. Found among rubble of the three-story building: a pile of melted grenades and thousands of rounds of ammunition. Helicopters carry burn victims to Dallas.
Watchtower, with concrete bunker located at bottom
David Koresh's living quarters
Pool
Gymnasium used for storage
6:04 A.M.: Armored vehicle smashes through building and begins pumping doses of tear gas. Those inside retaliate with 75 to 80 shots at the vehicle. Agents use loudspeaker to repeatedly urge cult members to surrender.
12:05 P.M.: Smoke first spotted by FBI. Within minutes flames appear at several different locations. Fire trucks do not arrive until more than 30 minutes later, when much of the building has collapsed.
11:45 A.M.: A white sheet is unfurled from this window, with orange lettering reading "We want our phones fixed."
12:00: Whole sections of the exterior are demolished and portions of the roof collapse throughout the compound.

FIGURE 8.11

The siege of the Branch Davidians near Waco, Texas, resulted in a serious questioning of police (FBI) tactics, operations, and decision making.

(*Source: Newsweek*, May 3, 1993, illustration by Dixon Rohr. © 1993, Newsweek, Inc. All rights reserved. Reprinted by permission.)

The Weaver Family, Ruby Ridge, Idaho (1992)

In March 1992, federal prosecutors indicted Randy Weaver, a known white separatist, on a charge of selling two sawed-off shotguns to an undercover federal informant. The job of arresting Weaver, who had fled to his secluded and fortified retreat at Ruby Ridge, Idaho, was assigned to the U.S. Marshal Service. On August 12, 1992, marshals began their surveillance of the Weavers' cabin and surrounding terrain under the code name "Operation Northern Exposure."

Nine days later, on August 21, Randy Weaver; his 14-year-old son, Sam Weaver; and a family friend, Kevin Harris, followed their dog into the woods adjacent to the cabin. Deputy U.S. marshals surveilling the cabin were discovered, and gunfire was exchanged between the two groups. Sam Weaver and one U.S. marshal were fatally wounded. Confusion and speculation about who fired first and whose bullets killed the two victims continued to plague the investigation. In any event, information soon reached Washington, D.C., that federal agents were under attack at Ruby Ridge and that assistance was badly needed. The FBI deployed its Hostage Rescue Team (HRT) to the location, beginning an 11-day standoff between the FBI and the Weaver family.

Under normal circumstances, the HRT snipers followed specific rules of engagement that dictated the use of deadly force only under the threat of "grievous bodily harm." Although the reasoning behind changing this operational policy at Ruby Ridge and who was responsible for it are unclear, FBI snipers were told that they "could and should fire at any armed adult male" in the cabin. Hence, on August 22, one day after the initial confrontation and the deaths of Sam Weaver and a U.S. marshal, FBI snipers fired on cabin occupants to protect a surveillance helicopter. The resulting shots struck Kevin Harris and Vicki Weaver (Randy Weaver's wife), who was standing just inside the cabin, holding her infant child. Although Mrs. Weaver died of her wounds, FBI personnel did not learn of her death until Randy Weaver surrendered nine days later.

The actions of the FBI were debated in Congress, and a special Senate judiciary subcommittee was formed to investigate the incident. Both Randy Weaver and Kevin Harris were acquitted of murdering the U.S. marshal in the initial confrontation.

Analyses of Decisions During Crisis Events

At first glance, these incidents represent a series of individual decisions that seriously depart from the major theoretical models presented by Simon, Lindblom, and Gore. However, on closer inspection, each decision maker may have started out with firm plans to adhere to the step-by-step, purely rational model prescribed by Simon but was swayed by the emotionality and national attention of the event as it unfolded.

In The News

FBI's Ruby Ridge Order "In Error"

During Senate hearings to determine why an order was approved stating that FBI snipers "could and should" shoot at armed adult males during the Ruby Ridge conflict in 1992, a former Justice Department official testified that the order was "clearly in error." The resulting shooting during the 11-day Ruby Ridge siege killed Vicki Weaver as she stood behind a door. The FBI had been involved in a stand-off with her husband, white separatist Randy Weaver, since an initial shooting occurred while federal agents checked out Weaver's property as part of a sting on weapons charges. During the initial shooting, Weaver's 14-year-old son, Sam, was also killed.

Previous task forces had been unable to determine who was responsible for approving the "could and should" order. Former Deputy Attorney General George Terwilliger denied responsibility for the order, stating that the FBI had operational control. Documentation that might have shown whether an FBI official in Washington, D.C., or an agent on the scene approved the order was insufficient or missing. Former FBI Director William Sessions testified that he was vacationing at the time of the incident and let top aides handle the matter. The top aides insisted that they told snipers to shoot at armed adults but never issued the order in terms of "could and should." Senators involved in the hearing were perplexed at the "syndrome of plausible deniability" by key decision makers. Senator Dianne Feinstein of California remarked that all of the decision makers who would normally have a role in such incidents seemed to be saying, "'We had no part in it.'"

Source: "FBI's Ruby Ridge Order 'In Error.'" *Dallas Morning News*, September 23, 1995, p. 2A.

Similar to the incremental model, each event followed its own course, without direction or clear goal, disjointed and separated from a logical, straightforward path. Surely, decision makers relied on their "gut-level" feeling at the time.

The decision-making models developed by Simon, Gore, and Lindblom are not the only credible efforts to help students understand the decision-making process. Indeed, their models may be more appropriate for non-crisis, routine administrative ventures.

Irving Janis and Leon Mann have outlined a decision-making model, based on psychological conflict, that emphasizes the decision-making process under stress.[61] In contrast to the intellectual (rational) process presented by Simon, Janis, and Mann indicate that decision making involves "hot" emotional influences, similar to Gore's theory. The need to make a decision is inherently stressful. When a decision maker is faced with an emotionally consequential, no-win choice, how he or she copes with the problem depends on two major factors: hope and time. This process causes great stress, as the factors of hope and time are rarely within the control and purview of the decision maker. This can be uniquely observed in protracted, high-stress incidents involving the police, such as those observed in Waco and Ruby Ridge.

When the decision maker has control of time and has hope that conciliation is possible, that person's efforts are more likely to follow the desired pattern of the "vigilant decision maker."[62] The vigilant model closely resembles the rational–comprehensive model developed by Simon. The vigilant decision maker (1) thoroughly canvasses a wide range of alternatives; (2) surveys a full range of objectives to be fulfilled and the values implicated by choice; (3) carefully weighs the costs and risks of negative consequences as well as the positive consequences that could come from each alternative; (4) intensively searches for new information relevant to further evaluation of the alternatives; (5) correctly assimilates and takes account of new information or expert judgment to which he or she is exposed, even when the information or judgment does not support the course of action initially preferred; (6) re-examines the positive and negative consequences of all known alternatives, including those originally regarded as unacceptable, before making a final choice; and (7) makes detailed provisions for implementing or executing the chosen course of action, with special attention to contingency plans that might be required if various known risks materialize.[63]

While Janis is better known among students of politics, policy, and management for his earlier work on "groupthink,"[64] his development with Leon Mann of the concept of the vigilant decision maker has provided a practical model for measuring administrative responsibility. Most notable is the excellent essay by Jack H. Nagel in applying the decision-making theories of Janis and Mann to the 1985 MOVE incident in Philadelphia.[65] In his highly critical work, Nagel identifies several decision-making paradoxes that, unfortunately, are not uncommon in similar incidents (e.g., the SLA [Symbionese Liberation Army] shoot-out in Los Angeles in 1968, the AIM [American Indian Movement] siege of Wounded Knee in 1977, the FBI shootings at Ruby Ridge, and the ATF raid on Branch Davidians in Waco).

These paradoxes are identified and elaborated on by Taylor and Prichard.[66] All the incidents have commonality. They were all police precipitated—that is, each incident grew from the police advancing on the homes of well-armed, openly defiant, and hostile groups of individuals. Each incident grew from earlier encounters with the police, often highly charged, emotional encounters involving everything from civil and slander suits against the police for harassment to police–group shootings. In all the incidents, the police intelligence concerning the actual location of the assault and/or the number and armament of the suspects were in gross error. To complicate the issue, the primary decision maker was not at the scene. In both the Waco and Ruby Ridge incidents, critical decisions were made in Washington, D.C., several thousand miles away.

Then, too, the incidents were characterized by an overreliance on technology. Decision makers believed that tear gas would not ignite and burn but rather force hostages and suspects from their barricaded positions. The illusion of invulnerability also impacted each incident—who would believe that suspects would not surrender to a large, powerful, tactically trained, well-armed group of federal agents? This certainly was the case in the ATF raid on the Branch Davidians in Waco. The overreliance on intellectual rationality failed as police decision makers underestimated the power and control of a charismatic leader in a relatively small, religiously inspired group. Further, the belief that police Special Weapons and Tactics (SWAT) agents could act as an effective, highly specialized military unit performing a "surgical strike" on a bunker belonged more in the movies than in reality. Police officers and agents are simply not experienced, trained, or equipped to handle such encounters. Contrary to popular belief, highly trained police tactical units are rarely successful, since they must rely on meticulous timing, superlative intelligence, surprise, and the ability to use deadly force effectively. None of these conditions existed in the protracted events of Waco and Ruby Ridge.

Finally, in each incident, the decision maker lost hope for a peaceful outcome. When such a condition occurs, the decision maker enters the downward spiral of "defensive avoidance."[67] The pattern is characterized by procrastination and delay, followed by passing the buck and other ways of denying personal responsibility, followed by bolstering and gaining superficial support from others. The distorted view produced by bolstering results in a spreading of responsibility and an exaggerated value of the chosen course of action. More often than not, the chosen course is a "do something" reaction. As Janis and Mann state, the process of defensive avoidance "satisfies a powerful emotional need—to avoid anticipatory fear, shame, and guilt."[68] Delay followed by haste can result in wishful thinking, oversimplification of the problem, and the selection of the force option. Confusion, catastrophe, and denial soon follow.

Crisis Events in the Future

Several new directions for handling such crisis events in the future can be developed from the lessons of the past. These recommendations have been adopted as policy for the FBI Critical Incident Response Group, created in 1994 as a response to the Waco and Ruby Ridge encounters. Recommendations for protracted conflict can be summarized as follows:

1. Jack H. Nagel strongly argues that policies to deal with such events must be institutionalized.[69] That is, they must be concrete, written directives that reflect the overall philosophy of the department or agency. These policies must not be changed arbitrarily during a crisis event or for a specific operational strategy. Further, policies must identify key players and decision makers during such events. Who is the primary decision maker? Who is in charge of operational management? Who is in charge of coordination, communication, logistics, and so on? These are critical positions and must be identified in writing, well before an incident occurs.
2. Police agencies must adopt a philosophy that clearly articulates the importance of the safety and security of human life during such incidents. The force option through the use of SWAT team assault, selective sniper fire, and tear gas distribution must be last resorts. The primary philosophy must emphasize a patient, no-force negotiation strategy rather than a tactical solution for outcome. This is not a new concept. Frank Bolz and others have pressed for this type of departmental philosophy for the past 25 years.[70]

3. Police agencies must consider withdrawal as a strategy. Certainly, in most of these cases, the police could have arrested the primary leaders of these groups outside the confinement of a barricaded compound. The use of more modern surveillance equipment using forward-looking infrared (FLIR) and wall-penetrating radar technology could do much to increase the accuracy of intelligence and the development of an arrest plan before a barricaded standoff occurs.
4. Police executives must reconsider the role and use of SWAT teams. Their role must be limited to containment and use during routine search warrant executions. They should not be used as a skilled military group capable of executing high-risk operations requiring precision and exceptional teamwork. Police executives must fight the "testosterone syndrome" of SWAT team commanders who argue that their training and expertise prepare SWAT teams for such missions. They simply do not. The comparison between police SWAT teams and military strike force teams (such as the Navy SEALS or Army Delta Force) must be broken. The rules of engagement for each unit are unique, as are the desired goals and outcomes.
5. Training for protracted conflicts must include the top-level decision makers as well as operational commanders and chiefs. Attorney generals, governors, city managers, mayors, councilpersons, and top police executives must be trained in coping with such conditions. Significant attention must be paid to the development of a policy that emphasizes the no-force negotiation option. Further, decision makers should be trained to recognize the characteristics of "defensive avoidance" and **"groupthink"** before courses of action are taken.[71] Mock scenarios and role playing should accompany the training.
6. During crisis events, outside and neutral referees or observers should assist in the situation. These individuals should be well versed in the no-force negotiation option and should act as "coaches" for the negotiation team. These individuals should have no ownership or responsibility in the situation and should be paid a small fee for their time only. These are not high-level consultants but rather well-trained, neutral observers with whom operational managers and top-level decision makers can review potential tactics and strategies. Outside observers must be protected from any type of potential ensuing liability through the agency involved. Their main purpose is to act as a "reality check and review" for actions to be taken by the police.

Decision making during these types of protracted events, when the suspects appear to be anything but rational, is always a very difficult task. It is also a very human endeavor, and, as such, mistakes will inevitably occur. Remember that the purpose of studying these cases is not to criticize the agencies involved (hindsight is always 20–20) but rather to offer students and police executives alternatives to past experiences and tactics. No one decision-making model guarantees success. However, we owe it to the brave men and women who died in these past incidents to ensure that future decision makers always attempt to maximize the two most important factors in the negotiation strategy: hope and time. This can be accomplished by eliminating the force options of direct assault, selective sniper fire, and tear gas dispersal.

Up to this point, we have concentrated mainly on individual decision making. However, police administrators rarely act alone. They are surrounded by deputy chiefs, bureau commanders, and division captains who provide input into the working structure of a police department. Group actions in the decision-making process are critical to the success of a specific decision and therefore require exploration.

Critical Thinking Questions

1. Explain the psychological phenomenon defensive avoidance and groupthink. How do they impact decision making during crisis events?
2. What effects have the incidents at Ruby Ridge and at the Branch Davidian compound had on modern police decision making? Can you think of recent incidents in which the lessons learned from these incidents were applied?

GROUP DECISION MAKING

Research on group decision making reveals that this approach has both advantages and disadvantages over individual decision making. If the potential for group decision making can be exploited and its deficiencies avoided, it follows that group decision making can attain a level of proficiency that is not ordinarily achieved. The requirement for achieving this level of group performance seems to hinge on developing a style of leadership that maximizes the group's assets and minimizes its liabilities. Because members possess the essential ingredients for the solution, the deficiencies that appear in group decisions reside in the processes by which group decisions are made. These processes can determine whether the group functions effectively or ineffectively. With training, a leader can supply these functions and serve as the group's central nervous system, thus permitting the group to emerge as a highly efficient entity.[72]

Group Assets

The following advantages are found in group decision making.

Greater Total Knowledge and Information There is more information in a group than in any of its members; thus, problems that require the use of knowledge (both internal and external to the police agency) should give groups an advantage over individuals. If one member of the group (e.g., the police chief) knows much more than anyone else, the limited, unique knowledge of lesser-informed individuals can fill in some gaps in knowledge.

Greater Number of Approaches to a Decision Most police executives tend to get into ruts in their thinking, especially when similar obstacles stand in the way of achieving a goal and a solution must be found. Some chiefs are handicapped in that they tend to persist in their approach and thus fail to consider another approach that might solve the problem in a more efficient manner. Individuals in a group have the same failing, but the approach in which they are persisting may be different. For example, one police administrator may insist that the best way to cope with the increasing number of robberies of local convenience stores in a community is to place the businesses under surveillance by specially trained police officers who are equipped with sufficient firepower to either arrest or shoot the robbers if necessary. Another police administrator might insist that the best way to reduce the number of robberies is through the implementation of crime prevention programs designed to use procedures that would make the businesses in question either less attractive or less vulnerable to robberies (e.g., keep the amount of cash available to a minimum, remove large signs from the front of the store windows that block the view of passing patrol cars and other motorists). It is sometimes difficult to determine which approach or approaches would be most effective in achieving the desired goal. But undue persistence or allegiance to one method tends to reduce a decision group's willingness to be innovative.

Participation in Problem Solving Increases Acceptance Many problems require solutions that depend on the support of others to be effective. Insofar as group problem solving permits participation and influence, it follows that more individuals accept solutions when a group solves the problem than when one person solves it. When the chief solves a problem alone, he or she still has the task of persuading others. It follows, therefore, that, when groups solve such problems, a greater number of persons accept and feel responsible for making the solution work. A solution that is well accepted can be more effective than a better solution that lacks acceptance. For example, the decision to establish a crime prevention program in a ghetto neighborhood must have support from the level of chief to individual beat officer. Although other measures to reduce crime (such as increasing the number of patrol officers or stricter enforcement of juvenile gang activity) might have a more substantial impact, it is important to remember that most of the program participants must support the effort.

Better Comprehension of the Decision Decisions made by an individual but that are to be carried out by others must be communicated from the decision maker to the decision executors. Thus, individual problem solving often requires an additional state: that of relaying the decision reached. Failures in this communication process detract from the merit of the decision and can even cause its failure or create a problem of greater magnitude than the initial problem that was solved. Many police organizational problems can be traced to inadequate communication of decisions made by superiors and transmitted to officers who have the task of implementing the decision. The chances for communication failures are reduced greatly when the individuals who must work together in executing a decision have participated in making it. They not only understand the solution because they saw it develop but also are aware of the several other alternatives that were considered and the reasons they were discarded. The common assumption that decisions supplied by superiors are reached arbitrarily, therefore, disappears. A full knowledge of goals, obstacles, alternatives, and factual information tends to open new lines of communication, and this communication in turn is maximized when the total problem-solving process is shared (see Figure 8.12).

This maxim is especially important concerning law enforcement because officers assigned to regular beats often provide the administrator with additional information or new dimensions to the problem. Additionally, almost any new program aimed at reducing crime in a specific area (neighborhood crime prevention or neighborhood watches) must necessarily include the patrol officer for implementation and success.

Group Liabilities

Notwithstanding the benefits of group decision making, a number of liabilities are worth mentioning as a precautionary measure.

Social Pressure Social pressure is a major force for increasing conformity. The desire to be a good group member and to be accepted may become more important than whether the objective quality of a decision is the most sound. Problems requiring solutions based on facts, independent of personal feelings and wishes, can suffer in group decision-making situations.

FIGURE 8.12

A common group decision-making technique: the decision table.
(Michael Newman/PhotoEdit)

It has been shown that minority opinions in leaderless groups have little influence on the decisions made, even when these opinions are the correct ones. Reaching agreement in a group often is confused with finding the right answer, and it is for this reason that the dimensions of a decision's acceptance and its objective quality must be distinguished.

Individual Domination In most leaderless groups, a dominant individual emerges and captures a disproportionate amount of the influence in determining the final outcome. Such individuals can achieve this end through a greater degree of participation, persuasive ability, or stubborn persistence (wearing down the opposition). None of these factors is related to problem-solving ability, so that the best problem solver in the group may not have the influence to upgrade the quality of a solution (which the individual would have had if left to solve the problem alone). The mere fact of appointing a leader causes this person to dominate a discussion. Thus, regardless of the individual's problem-solving ability, a leader tends to exert a major influence on the outcome of a discussion. In police circles, the influence of the chief's opinion is undeniable. All too often, the chief dominates the group process so much that participation is squelched. The chief needs to be aware of his or her influence and make a cognitive effort to listen rather than dominate.

Conflicting Secondary Goals: Winning the Argument When groups are confronted with a problem, the initial goal is to obtain a solution. However, the appearance of several alternatives causes individuals to have preferences, and, once these emerge, the desire to support a particular position is created. Converting those with neutral viewpoints and refuting those with opposing viewpoints now enter the problem-solving process. More and more, the goal becomes having one's own solution chosen rather than finding the best solution. This new goal is unrelated to the quality of the solution and, therefore, can result in lowering the quality of the solution.

Groupthink The theory of groupthink was first introduced by Irving Janis in 1972.[73] Groupthink is an interesting psychological phenomenon that most often occurs in cohesive groups that are isolated from other political and decision-making bodies. This condition often occurs within police leadership circles, especially during crisis events. The political pressure and stress to make a decision, coupled with the presence of a strong leader, escalate the condition. Groupthink is most often characterized by a serious lack of methodical procedure that forces a misperception of the problem and a hurried search for answers. During groupthink, there is considerable focus on a shared rationalization that bolsters the least objectionable alternative as a decision, a suppression of unfavorable outcomes, and an illusion of unanimity and invulnerability. Indeed, Janis and Mann warn that the decision-making process may be so intense that more effort is expended on striving for concurrence than on finding an appropriate decision.[74] During such conditions, the leader should attempt to remain impartial, listening to ideas and alternatives. He or she must invite dissent and encourage individual advisers to express their reservations about suggested decisions. The leader should challenge the group's actions and play the devil's advocate, asking what might go wrong and what the possible adverse consequences might be to the proposed actions. Finally, outside experts or critical evaluators should be asked to review agreed-on actions or plans. The leader must accept criticism of his or her own judgments as well as those proposed by the group. Janis and Mann are quick to point out that groupthink occurs not only during crisis times but also during rather mundane policymaking meetings.[75] It is incumbent that the leader, as well as individual members of the group, be on guard for the signs and characteristics of groupthink. The best defense to such a condition is continual, open debate and discussion. This requires a highly democratic and participatory leadership style (refer to Chapter 7, Leadership). In addition, this practice needs to be reinforced by the development of a methodological procedure that encourages dissent and, of course, the acceptance of criticism by all parties involved.

Factors That Can Serve as Assets or Liabilities

Depending on the skill of the discussion leader, some elements of group decision making can be assets or liabilities.

Disagreement Discussion may lead to disagreement and hard feelings among members, or it may lead to a resolution of conflict and hence to an innovative solution. The first of these outcomes of disagreement is a liability, especially with regard to the acceptance of solutions; the second is an asset, particularly where innovation is desired. A chief can treat disagreement as undesirable and thereby reduce both the probability of hard feelings and innovative thought. The skillful police administrator creates a climate for disagreement without risking hard feelings because properly managed disagreement can be a source of creativity and innovation. The chief's perception of disagreement is a critical factor in using disagreements. Other factors are the chief's permissiveness, willingness to delay reaching a solution, techniques for processing information and opinions, and techniques for separating idea elicitation from idea evaluation.

Conflicting vs. Mutual Interests Disagreement in discussions can take many forms. Often, participants disagree with one another with regard to the solution, but when the issues are explored, it is discovered the solutions are in conflict because they are designed to solve different problems. Before there can be agreement on a solution, there must be agreement on the problem. Even before this, there should be agreement on the goal and on the various obstacles that prevent the goal from being reached. This is where the synoptic planning model can be an invaluable tool. Once distinctions are made among goals, obstacles, and solutions (which represent ways of overcoming obstacles), the opportunities for cooperative problem solving and reduced conflict are increased.

Often, there is also disagreement regarding whether the objective of a solution is to be of the highest quality or merely acceptable. Frequently, a stated problem reveals a group of related but separate problems, each requiring a separate solution, so that a search for a single overall solution is impossible. Communications are often inadequate because the discussion is not synchronized, and each person is engaged in discussing a different aspect of the problem. Organizing the discussion to explore systematically these different aspects of the problem increases the quality of solutions. The leadership function of guiding such discussions is quite distinct from the function of evaluating or contributing ideas.

When the discussion leader helps separate different aspects of the problem-solving process and delays the inclination of the group to come to a quick but not-well-thought-out solution, both the quality of the solution and the acceptance of it improve. When the leader hinders the isolation of these processes, there is a risk of deterioration in the group process. The leader's skill thus determines whether a discussion drifts toward conflicting interests or whether mutual interests are located. Cooperative problem solving can occur only after the mutual interests have been established, and it is interesting how often they can be found when a discussion leader makes this a primary task.

Risk Taking Groups are more willing than individuals to reach decisions that involve risk. Taking risks is a factor in the acceptance of change, but change may represent either a gain or a loss. The best protection against the latter outcome seems to be primarily a matter of the quality of a decision. In a group situation, this depends on the leader's skill in using the factors that represent group assets and avoiding those that make for liabilities.

Time Requirements In general, more time is required for a group to reach a decision than for an individual to reach one. Insofar as some problems require quick decisions, individual decisions are favored. In other situations, acceptance and quality are requirements, but excessive time without sufficient returns also presents a loss. On the other hand, discussion can resolve conflicts, whereas reaching consensus has limited value. The practice of hastening a meeting can prevent full discussion, but failure to move a discussion forward can lead to boredom and fatigue, and group members may agree to anything merely to put an end to the meeting. The effective use of discussion time (a delicate balance between permissiveness and control on the part of the leader), therefore, is needed to make the time factor an asset rather than a liability. Unskilled leaders either tend to be too concerned with reaching a solution and, therefore, terminate a discussion before the group's agreement is obtained or tend to be too concerned with getting input, allowing the discussion to digress and become repetitive.

Who Changes In reaching consensus or agreement, some members of a group must change. In group situations, who changes can be an asset or a liability. If persons with the most constructive views are induced to change, the end product suffers, whereas if persons with the least constructive points of view change, the end product is upgraded. A leader can upgrade the quality of a decision because the leadership position permits the individual to protect the person with the minority view and increase the individual's opportunity to influence the majority position. This protection is a constructive factor because a minority viewpoint influences only when facts favor it.

In many problem-solving discussions, the untrained leader plays a dominant role in influencing the outcome, and when the person is more resistant to changing personal views than are the other participants, the quality of the outcome tends to be lowered. This negative influence of leaders was demonstrated by experiments in which untrained leaders were asked to obtain a second solution to a problem after they had obtained their first one. It was found that the second solution tended to be superior to the first. Because the dominant individual had influenced the first solution and had won the point, it was not necessary for this person to dominate the subsequent discussion that led to the second solution. Acceptance of a solution also increases as the leader sees disagreement as producing ideas rather than as a source of difficulty or trouble. Leaders who see some of their participants as troublemakers obtain fewer innovative solutions and gain less acceptance of decisions than do leaders who see disagreeing members as persons with ideas.

Brainstorming

Brainstorming is a type of group decision making developed initially in advertising to help trigger creativity. The idea behind brainstorming is to establish a group environment in which individuals can present any idea that seems to apply even remotely to the subject being considered with the understanding that criticism will be withheld unless it can somehow improve on the original idea.[76] The practitioners of brainstorming have been able to determine some specific procedures that improve the effectiveness of brainstorming sessions. Whiting points out the following:

1. The sessions should last 40 minutes to an hour, although brief, 10- to 15-minute sessions may be effective if time is limited.
2. Generally, the problem to be discussed should not be revealed before the session.
3. The problem should be stated clearly and not too broadly.
4. A small conference table that allows people to communicate easily should be used.[77]

This approach can be useful in dealing with many public policy or administrative problems. When the major problem is one of discovering new ways of dealing with a situation, brainstorming may prove useful. One of the most difficult aspects of brainstorming, however, is creating a situation in which it can occur. Most of the "rules of the game" are based on an implicit level of trust between individuals, which sometimes does not exist in a politically volatile organization. This kind of trust must be developed for the procedure to be successful; thus, people tend to become freer and better able to use the process as they have repeated experiences with it.[78]

Critical Thinking Questions

1. Can you think of any situations in police administration that are better suited to group decision making than to individual decision making? What situations might be best handled by an individual decision maker?
2. Describe the things a group leader can do to minimize groupthink. Why is groupthink so important?

ETHICS AND DECISION MAKING

Making ethical decisions requires training and sensitivity to ethical issues. Ethical behavior is difficult to define, and while ethics aren't wholly based on feelings, religion, law, or science, individuals may take those things into account when defining their standards of behavior. In fact, simply put, **ethics** are standards of behavior that dictate how humans are supposed to act within the roles that they find themselves in, whether that role is as a parent, friend, police administrator, supervisor, police officer, or private citizen. Ethics differ among individuals, depending on their personal values, cultural influences, or what they feel is the level of personal behavior that they should aspire to. Police administrators must identify ethical issues in decision making and develop strategies to confront ethical dilemmas. However, this process does not differ from the decision-making process used by any other individual.[79]

There are various ways to deal with ethical issues. One strategy for administrators is the following, developed by the Santa Clara University Markkula Center for Applied Ethics.[80] The first step in this framework is to recognize an ethical issue. Decision makers should ask themselves if there something wrong personally, interpersonally, or socially and determine if the conflict, the situation, or the decision might be damaging to people or to the community. Then they should consider whether the issue goes beyond legal or institutional concerns and what it means to people who have dignity, rights, and hopes for a better life.

The next step in the framework is to get the facts, by determining what facts are relevant to the specific issue and what facts are unknown. Next, decision makers should decide what individuals and groups have an important stake in the outcome and should consider whether all stakeholders have been consulted or what they would say if they were consulted.

Decision makers should always evaluate alternative actions from various ethical perspectives when faced with an ethical dilemma. For instance, the utilitarian approach to ethics looks at which action is the one that will produce the greatest balance of benefits over harms. In this case, the decision maker asks which option will produce the most good and do the least harm. In approaching the decision using the rights approach, in which the ethical action is the one that respects the rights of all affected by the decision, one asks if everyone's rights and dignity will be respected, even if not everyone gets what he or she wants. The fairness approach, which defines an ethical action as one that treats people equally, or at least proportionately and fairly, requires that the decision maker ask which option is most fair to all stakeholders. The common good approach requires that an individual consider which option would help everyone involved participate more fully in society, and the virtue approach requires the decision maker to consider whether or not the action is one that embodies the habits and values of people at their best.

After decision makers carefully evaluate their options from one or more perspective, the framework requires that they make their decision based on which option they feel is the best or the right thing to do and then test it. After acting, it is important for decision makers to examine how it turned out for all concerned and to evaluate whether they would make the same decision if they had to do it all over again. Ethical decisions are not always the most cost-effective or popular ones, and they often cause some personal discomfort in the short term. However, by carefully evaluating the best course of action, a police administrator can avoid situations that may, over the long term, cause a great deal of personal stress, as well as remorse. Considering that ethical blunders in police administration tend to generate a great deal of negative publicity, taking the ethical route may also save police administrators from public shame or disgrace.

Critical Thinking Question

1. Describe an ethical issue that may confront a police administrator. Discuss how you would approach that issue using the framework discussed.

COMMON ERRORS IN DECISION MAKING

Analysis of the decision-making process indicates that certain types of errors occur at a higher frequency than others. Nigro and Nigro[81] have indicated that these errors are (1) cognitive nearsightedness, (2) the assumption that the future will repeat the past, (3) oversimplification, (4) overreliance on one's own experience, (5) preconceived notions, (6) unwillingness to experiment, and (7) reluctance to decide.[82]

Cognitive Nearsightedness

The human tendency is to make decisions that satisfy immediate needs and to brush aside doubts of their long-range wisdom. The hope is that the decision will prove a good one for the future also, but this actually is counting on being lucky. The odds for such good fortune to occur consistently across all decisions are poor.

Attempting to find a "quick fix" may create infinitely greater difficulties in the future. An example of this phenomenon is observed in barricaded hostage situations, in which the chief wants to assault the location immediately with a SWAT team. In crisis situations such as this, time has always proven to be an ally of the police.[83] Unfortunately, the complicated environment in which police officials function sometimes creates pressure to act on relatively narrow considerations of the moment. Also related to cognitive nearsightedness is the "narrow view," or the consideration of only one aspect of a problem while neglecting all other aspects of that problem, as occurred in the Branch Davidian and Ruby Ridge incidents.

Assumption That the Future Will Repeat Itself

In making decisions, police officials must try to forecast future conditions and events. Human behavior controls many events; in relatively stable periods of history, the assumption can safely be made that employees, client groups, and the public in general will behave much as they have in the past. The present period is, however, far from stable; many precedents have been shattered, and police officers, along with other public employees, can sometimes behave in surprising ways. Very rarely do dramatic changes occur without some warning signals. Early trends frequently can serve as valuable indicators of future behavior, but the police administrator must make the effort to be aware of these trends and develop strategies to cope with them.

Oversimplification

People tend to deal with the symptom of a problem rather than with its true cause because the cause may be too difficult to understand. It is also easier for those participating in the decision-making process to understand a simpler solution: it is more readily explained to others and therefore more likely to be adopted. Although a less involved solution may actually be the better one, the point is that the decision maker looking for an acceptable answer may take the first simple one, no matter how inferior it may be to other, somewhat more complicated alternatives.

Overreliance on One's Own Experience

In general, law enforcement practitioners place great weight on their own previous experience and personal judgment. Although an experienced police executive should be able to make better decisions than a completely inexperienced one, a person's own experience may still not be the best guide. Frequently, another police executive with just as much experience has a completely different solution and is just as certain that his or her solution to a problem is the most satisfactory one. In fact, past success in certain kinds of situations may be attributable to chance rather than to the particular action taken. Thus, there is frequently much to be gained by counseling with others whose own experience can add an important and uniquely different dimension to the decision-making process.

Preconceived Notions

In many cases, decisions allegedly based on facts actually reflect the preconceived ideas of the police executive. This appears to be dishonest, and it is dishonest if the facts are altered to justify the decision. However, in many cases, individuals are capable of seeing only the facts that support their biases. Administrative decisions might be better if they were based on social science findings, but such findings are often ignored if they contradict the ideas of the police chief.[84] In administrative policymaking, conclusions are often supported by a structure of logic that rests dangerously on a mixed foundation of facts and assumptions.[85] Decision makers may appear as if they are proceeding in an orderly way from consideration of the facts to conclusions derived logically from them, when, in fact, sometimes the conclusion comes first and then the facts are found to justify them.

Unwillingness to Experiment

The best way in which to determine the workability of a proposal is to test it first on a limited scale. However, pressure for immediate, large-scale action often convinces the police chief that there is no time to proceed cautiously with pilot projects, no matter how sound the case for a slow approach. Sometimes police executives are reluctant to request funding and other needed support for the small-scale implementation of new programs for fear that such caution may raise doubts about the soundness of the programs. In all fairness to the cautious police administrator, sometimes this assessment has merit.

Reluctance to Decide

Even when in possession of adequate facts, some chiefs try to avoid making a decision (see Figure 8.13). Barnard speaks of the natural reluctance of some people to decide:

> *The making of a decision, as everyone knows from personal experience, is a burdensome task. Offsetting the exhilaration that may result from a correct and successful decision is the depression that comes from failure or error of decision and in the frustration which ensues from uncertainty.*[86]

FIGURE 8.13

During future crisis situations, police executives will be forced to make decisions influencing a wide range of organizational, community, and political issues.

(Photo courtesy of the San Diego Police Department)

Critical Thinking Question

1. Why is overreliance on one's own experience a dangerous trap in decision making?
2. Discuss why you think even seasoned police administrators who have a grasp on all the facts of a matter might be reluctant to make a decision.

CHAPTER REVIEW

1. Explain some advantages of planning within a police department.
   The advantages of planning within a police department include an improved analysis of problems; better information for decision making; clarification of goals, objectives and priorities; more effective allocation of resources; improved inter- and intradepartmental cooperation and coordination; improved program performance; clear sense of direction; opportunities for greater public support; and increased commitment from personnel.
2. Discuss the synoptic planning approach. Describe three methods of selecting a preferred course of action.
   Synoptic planning is based on a rational, problem-oriented approach to planning and relies heavily on problem identification and analysis. The approach allows police administrators to develop goals and objectives that are focused on specific problems and solutions. Three methods of selecting a preferred course of action during synoptic planning are strategic analysis, cost-effectiveness analysis, and must–wants analysis. In strategic analysis, each alternative is studied for suitability. Those alternatives deemed suitable are then subjected to feasibility studies. Finally, the remaining alternatives are judged as to whether or not their cost, performance, effects, and time involved in implementation are acceptable. Cost-effectiveness analysis simply uses an economic model to

determine which alternative maximizes the ratio of benefit to cost. Finally, must–wants analysis is a method that measures both the subjective weights of suitability, feasibility, and acceptability and the objective weights of costs versus benefits.

3. Discuss the differences among administrative, procedural, operational, and tactical plans.
   Administrative plans are overall plans that outline a police agency's general mission, as well as its goals, policies, organization, and resources. Procedural plans provide guidelines for actions to be taken under specific circumstances and situations. Operational plans divide up which tasks are to be undertaken by which units. Tactical plans are specific plans for emergencies or special events.
4. Discuss the characteristics of effective plans.
   Characteristics of effective plans include specific language so that the behavior requested is understood by all; benefits that offset the efforts of developing and implementing the plan; widespread involvement in their formulation; flexibility to allow for the unforeseen; coordination with other units of government; consistent development and implementation; and a built-in method of postimplementation analysis.
5. List the three major decision making models.
   The three major decision making models are: 1) The Rational Model, 2) The Incremental Model, and 3) The Heuristic Model.
6. Discuss Simon's concept of "bounded rationality."
   Bounded rationality explains the theory that a person's ability to make rational decisions is bounded by limitations, including unconscious habits and reflexes, values, and the extent of that person's knowledge of the event.
7. Explain Lindblom's theory of incremental decision making.
   Lindblom's theory of incremental decision making asserts that decision making is a serial process, limited by time and resources. Lindblom believed that decision makers move slowly through the process of decision making, muddling through problems instead of analytically choosing decisions.
8. Describe the decision-making process as presented by William Gore.
   Gore views the decision-making process as a gut-level approach where a decision is a reflection of the personality of the person making it. Gore's view is non-rational, emotional, and highly subjective.
9. List some of the important recommendations, developed in this chapter, for handling future crisis events.
   Important recommendations include institutionalized policies for dealing with crises; departmental philosophies that clearly communicate the importance of safety and security of human life during conflicts; consideration of withdrawal as a strategy; limited roles and use of SWAT teams; inclusion of all levels of decisions makers, including those in local government, during training exercises; and the use of neutral observers and advisers during crisis events.
10. Discuss the advantages of group decision making.
    The advantages of group decision making are a greater total knowledge and information relevant to the decision; a greater number of approaches to a problem; the likelihood of greater acceptance of a decision when a group solves a problem as opposed to one person; and better comprehension and communication of the decision by all parties involved in implementation.
11. List the steps decision makers should take when confronted with an ethical issue.
    Ethical decisions should be made in a framework that emphasizes recognizing an ethical issue, determining the facts involved, deciding who the stakeholders are, evaluating

alternatives from various ethical perspectives, making a decision based on which option is best, and evaluating that decision.

12. Explain the most common errors in decision making.
The most common errors in decision making are cognitive nearsightedness, the assumption that the future will repeat the past, oversimplification, overreliance on one's own experience, preconceived notions, unwillingness to experiment, and a reluctance to decide.

KEY TERMS

Advocacy planning: a planning process that defends the interests of the weak.

Crisis events: events that contain elements of danger or extreme instability.

Ethics: rules and standards governing conduct.

Feasibility studies: the determination of whether an action is possible, given current standards of operation, conditions, and restrictions.

Groupthink: decision making by a group, characterized by a lack of both creativity and individual responsibility.

Heuristic model: a simplified, gut-level method of decision making that emphasizes internal personality attributes of the decision maker.

Incremental planning: an approach that breaks down problems individually and makes gradual adjustments to address them over time.

Operations research: the application, collection, and analysis of data from decision making within an organization.

Planning: a process that links present actions to future conditions.

Rational: based on logic or reason.

Suitability studies: the process that determines the appropriateness of an action in accordance with general policies, rules, and laws.

Synoptic planning: a process that comprises four activities: preparing to plan, making a choice between alternatives, implementing a plan, and evaluating the plan.

Transactive planning: a method of planning that is carried out face-to-face with those affected by the plan.

Thin-slicing theory: the concept that instantaneous or quick decisions made by well-trained and experienced administrators may often be better than those made more deliberately and with significantly more information and time.

NOTES

1. G. S. Fulcher, *Common Sense Decision-Making* (Evanston, Ill.: Northwestern University Press, 1965), p. 4.
2. Ibid., pp. 4–5.
3. J. Q. Wilson, *Varieties of Police Behavior* (Cambridge, Mass.: Harvard University Press, 1978). In this study, Wilson considers how the uniformed officers of eight communities deal with such offenses as assault, theft, drunkenness, vice, traffic violations, and disorderly conduct. He also analyzes the problems facing the police administrator both in deciding what patrol officers ought to do and then in getting the officer to do it, how patrol officers in various cities differ in performing their functions, and under what circumstances such differences are based on explicit community decisions.
4. J. H. Skolnick, *Justice without Trial* (New York: John Wiley & Sons, 1966). This book is based on the author's actual participation as a detective plus comparative community and case material. He discusses key issues, such as the organization of the police in America; the effects of police bureaucracy on criminal justice, narcotics, and vice investigation; the informer payoff and its consequences; and the relation between the police and black citizens. His findings are analyzed in light of organizational and legal controls over the police and their effect on the decision-making processes with law enforcement.
5. Israel Stollman, "The Values of the City Planner," in *The Practice of Local Government Planning*, ed. Frank S. So et al.

(Washington, D.C.: International City Management Association, 1979), p. 13.
6. Ibid.
7. Robert C. Cushman, *Criminal Justice Planning for Local Governments* (Washington, D.C.: U.S. Government Printing Office, 1980), p. 8; five of the elements identified are provided by Cushman, and the others have been added.
8. Ibid.
9. John Hudzik and Gary Cordner, *Planning in Criminal Justice Organizations and Systems* (New York: Macmillan, 1983), p. 1.
10. Charles M. Mottley, "Strategy in Planning," in *Planning, Programming, Budgeting: A System Approach to Management,* 2nd ed., ed. J. F. Lyden and E. S. Miller (Chicago: Markham, 1972), p. 127.
11. The term "pure," or "objective rationality," is taken from the alternative planning models identified by Tony Eddison, *Local Government: Management and Corporate Planning* (New York: Harper & Row, 1973), pp. 19–23.
12. Cushman, *Criminal Justice Planning,* p. 4.
13. The synoptic model is thoroughly discussed in Cushman, *Criminal Justice Planning.* Some of the following information relating to the model is paraphrased from that work.
14. Carol Weiss, *Evaluation Research: Methods of Assessing Program Effectiveness* (Englewood Cliffs, N.J.: Prentice Hall, 1972), p. 7.
15. P. Davidoff and T. A. Reiner, "A Choice Theory of Planning," *Journal of the American Institute of Planners* (May 1982): 103–15.
16. Hudzik and Cordner, *Planning in Criminal Justice,* p. 14.
17. U.S. Naval War College, *Sound Military Decisions* (Newport, R.I.: U.S. Naval War College, 1942).
18. The following discussion of strategic analysis is taken from Charles M. Mottley, "Strategic Planning," *Management Highlights,* Release 56, Office of Management Research, U.S. Department of the Interior, September 1967, pp. 103–19.
19. E. S. Quade, "System Analysis Techniques for Planning-Programming-Budgeting," in Lyden and Miller, ed., *Planning, Programming, Budgeting,* p. 249.
20. Ibid.
21. Ibid.
22. Hudzik and Cordner, *Planning in Criminal Justice,* p. 196.
23. Ibid.
24. The last portion of this paragraph is taken, with some restatement, from Stollman, "The Values of the City Planner," pp. 14–15.
25. A number of sources identify plans according to their use; see O. W. Wilson, *Police Planning,* 2nd ed. (Springfield, Ill.: Charles C Thomas, 1962), pp. 4–7, and Vernon L. Hoy, "Research and Planning," in *Local Government Police Management,* ed. Bernard L. Garmire (Washington, D.C.: International City Management Association, 1977), pp. 374–75.
26. Stanley S. Thune and Robert J. House, "Where Long-Range Planning Pays Off," *Business Horizons* 13 (August 1970): 81–90.
27. For information on managing organizational decline and cutback, see Elizabeth K. Kellar, ed., *Managing with Less* (Washington, D.C.: International City Management Association, 1979), and Jerome Miron, *Managing the Pressures of Inflation in Criminal Justice* (Washington, D.C.: U.S. Government Printing Office, 1979).
28. Hudzik and Cordner, *Planning in Criminal Justice,* p. 195.
29. J. M. Pfiffner, "Administrative Rationality," *Public Administration Review* 20, no. 3 (summer 1960): 126.
30. Ibid., p. 128.
31. Herbert A. Simon, "The Proverbs of Administration," *Public Administration Review* (winter 1946): 53–67.
32. Herbert A. Simon, *Administrative Behavior* (New York: Macmillan, 1961), p. 39.
33. Ibid., p. 40.
34. For a complete discussion of the rational–comprehensive model, see Peter F. Drucker, *The Effective Executive* (New York: Harper & Row, 1967); N. F. Iannone, *Supervision of Police Personnel* (Englewood Cliffs, N.J.: Prentice Hall, 1970); and Ira Sharkansky, *Public Administration* (Chicago: Markham, 1972).
35. See Sharkansky, *Public Administration,* p. 44, and Sam S. Souryal, *Police Administration and Management* (St. Paul, Minn.: West, 1977), p. 315.
36. Simon, *Administrative Behavior,* p. 40.
37. Ibid.
38. See Paul M. Whisenand and R. Fred Ferguson, *The Managing of Police Organizations,* 2nd ed. (Englewood Cliffs, N.J.: Prentice Hall, 1978), pp. 202–3, for a discussion of Simon's "bounded-rationality" concepts.
39. Charles F. Lindblom, *The Policy-Making Process* (Englewood Cliffs, N.J.: Prentice Hall, 1968).
40. Ibid., p. 209.
41. Charles F. Lindblom, "The Science of Muddling Through," *Public Administration Review* 19 (spring 1959): 86.

42. Jack Kuykendall and Peter Unsinger, *Community Police Administration* (Chicago: Nelson-Hall, 1975), p. 132.
43. William J. Gore, *Administration Decision-Making: A Heuristic Model* (New York: John Wiley & Sons, 1964).
44. Ibid., p. 12.
45. Souryal, *Police Administration,* p. 318.
46. L. G. Gawthrop, *Bureaucratic Behavior in the Executive Branch* (New York: Free Press, 1969), pp. 98–99.
47. Gore, *Administrative Decision-Making,* p. 12.
48. Gawthrop, *Bureaucratic Behavior,* p. 99.
49. Souryal, *Police Administration,* p. 319.
50. Graham T. Allison, *Essence of Decision: Exploring the Cuban Missile Crisis* (Boston: Little, Brown, 1971).
51. Some of this discussion was excerpted from an excellent review of Allison's book by Robert B. Denhardt, *Theories of Public Organization* (Monterey, Calif.: Brooks/Cole, 1984), pp. 81–85.
52. John Ott, "The Challenging Game of Operations Research," in *Emerging Concepts of Management,* ed. Max S. Wortmann and Fred Luthans (London: Macmillan, 1970), p. 287.
53. Ibid.
54. Peter P. Schoderbeck "PERT—Its Promises and Performances," in Wortmann and Luthans, *Emerging Concepts,* p. 291; E. S. Quade, "Systems Analysis Techniques for Planning-Programming-Budgeting," in *RAND Report* (Santa Monica, Calif.: RAND Corporation, 1966), p. 7.
55. Aaron Wildavsky, *Speaking Truth to Power: The Art and Craft of Police Analysis* (Boston: Little, Brown, 1979), p. 84.
56. C. Zsambock, and G. Klein, *Naturalistic Decision Making* (Mahweh, N.J.: Erlbaum, 1997), p. 286.
57. Ibid., p. 219.
58. Malcom Gladney, *Blink: The Power of Thinking without Thinking* (New York: Little, Brown, 2005), pp. 10–14.
59. Ibid., p. 11.
60. Ibid., p. 253.
61. Irving L. Janis and Leon Mann, *Decision Making: A Psychological Analysis of Conflict, Choice, and Commitment* (New York: Free Press, 1977).
62. Ibid., chap. 1.
63. Ibid., pp. 11–15.
64. Irving L. Janis, *Victims of Groupthink* (Boston: Houghton Mifflin, 1972).
65. John H. Nagel, "Psychological Obstacles to Administrative Responsibility: Lessons of the MOVE Disaster," *Journal of Policy Analysis and Management* 10, no. 1 (1991): 3.
66. Robert W. Taylor and Leigh A. Prichard, "Decision-Making in Crisis: Police Responses to Protracted Critical Incidents" (paper delivered at the Academy of Criminal Justice Sciences Annual Meeting, Las Vegas, Nev., March 13, 1996).
67. The concept of "defensive avoidance" was first developed by Janis and Mann in *Decision Making.* However, Nagel uniquely applied the concept to reality in his article "Psychological Obstacles to Administrative Responsibility."
68. Janis and Mann, *Decision Making,* p. 85.
69. Nagel, "Psychological Obstacles," p. 21.
70. The concept of a negotiated solution to crisis events has been developed over the past 25 years. See Frank A. Bolz and Edward Hershey, *Hostage Cop* (New York: Rawson, Wade, 1979); Ronald C. Crelinsten and Denis Szabo, *Hostage-Taking* (Lexington, Mass.: Lexington Books, 1979); Murray S. Miron and Arnold P. Goldstein, *Handbook for Hostage Negotiations: Tactical Procedures, Negotiating Techniques and Responses to Non-Negotiable Hostage Situations* (New York: Harper & Row, 1979); and Robert W. Taylor, "Hostage and Crisis Negotiation Procedures" in *Police Civil Liability,* ed. Leonard Territo (New York: Hanrow Press, 1984).
71. See Nagel, "Psychological Obstacles"; Janis and Mann, *Decision Making;* and Taylor and Prichard, "Decision-Making in Crisis."
72. N. R. F. Maier, "Assets and Liabilities in Group Problem Solving: The Need for Integrated Function," *Psychology Review* 74, no. 4 (1967): 239–48. Much of the information in this chapter dealing with the discussion of group decision making was obtained from this source.
73. See Irving L. Janis, *Victims of Groupthink* (Boston: Houghton Mifflin, 1972).
74. Janis and Mann, *Decision Making,* pp. 398–400.
75. Ibid.
76. W. Gortner, *Administration in the Public Sector* (New York: John Wiley & Sons, 1977), p. 124.
77. C. S. Whiting, "Operational Techniques of Creative Thinking," *Advanced Management Journal* 20 (1955): 24–30.
78. John Schafer, "Making Ethical Decisions: A Practical Mode," *FBI Law Enforcement Bulletin,* May 2002.
79. For more information about the framework for ethical decision making, visit www.scu.edu/ethics.
80. Markkula Center for Applied Ethics, Santa Clara University, "A Framework for Thinking Ethically." See http://www.scu.edu/ethics/practicing/decision/ framework.html (September 2, 2007)

81. Much of the information in this chapter dealing with the discussion of common errors in decision making was obtained from F. A. Nigro and L. G. Nigro, *Modern Public Administration* (New York: Harper & Row, 1977), pp. 226–32.
82. D. Katz and R. L. Kahn, *The Social Psychology of Organizations* (New York: John Wiley and Sons, 1966), p. 285.
83. Robert W. Taylor, "Hostage and Crisis Negotiation Procedures: Assessing Police Liability," *TRIAL Magazine* 19, no. 4 (1983): 64–71.
84. See, for example, A. Leighton, *Human Relations in a Changing World* (Princeton, N.J.: Princeton University Press, 1949), p. 152.
85. Ibid.
86. C. Barnard, *The Functions of the Executive* (Cambridge, Mass.: Harvard University Press, 1938), p. 189.

PART III

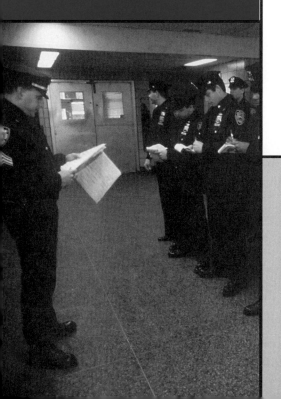

THE MANAGEMENT OF POLICE ORGANIZATIONS

THE FOLLOWING CHAPTERS ARE COVERED IN PART III:

9 Organizational Communication

10 Human Resource Management

11 Labor Relations

12 Financial Management

OVERVIEW

The internal dynamics of managing a police organization are often complex and fraught with political landmines. Most of these issues are a result of an informal subculture within the police organization that directly impacts general management, communication and labor relations within the department. In this section of the text we address the impact of these issues on organizational communication and human resource management within the police organization. We also consider the art of financial management; how to make every dollar count and make your department the most efficient organization possible.

The difference between the right word and the almost right word is the difference between lightning and lightning bug.

—Mark Twain

CHAPTER 9

ORGANIZATIONAL COMMUNICATION

OUTLINE

Introduction

The Communication Process

Communication Barriers

Organizational Systems of Communication

Interpersonal Communication

Group vs. Interpersonal Communication

Cross-Gender Communications

Communication with Other Cultures

Oral or Written Communication

Electronic Media (E-mail)

Chapter Review

Key Terms

Notes

OBJECTIVES

1. Discuss the elements that make up the communication process.
2. Describe sender-caused barriers, receiver-caused barriers, and other barriers in communications.
3. List and describe the four types of organizational communication.
4. Understand the elements of dynamic and persuasive oral and written communication.
5. Discuss the messages that people send which are not communicated verbally. What are the other means by which people communicate.
6. Describe the four phases in group interaction.
7. Understand the major differences between the ways female and male officers communicate, especially during conflict resolution.
8. Discuss the two main issues in communication between law enforcement and citizens from other cultures. And how law enforcement agencies can best address these challenges.
9. Describe the dominant form of communication used by police administrators.
10. Understand the advantages in oral communication to both the sender and the receiver.
11. List the advantages and disadvantages related to the use of e-mail in law enforcement agencies.
12. Describe how management should deal with the stress electronic communication can cause personnel.

INTRODUCTION

Effective communication is essential in all organizations in which people deal with one another. It is very difficult to imagine any kind of activity that does not depend on communication in one form or another. Today's police managers are aware that the efficiency of their personnel depends to a great extent on how well the efforts of individual members can be coordinated. Because coordination does not simply happen, managers must realize that communication is necessary if their subordinates are to obtain the understanding and cooperation required to achieve organizational and individual goals.

A major role of today's manager is that of communicator. Managers at all levels of the police organization spend an overwhelming amount of their time in the process and problems of communication.

Research in recent years has indicated that communication is the number one problem in management and that lack of communication is the employees' primary complaint about their immediate supervisors.[1] In this chapter, we will examine numerous facets of the communication process and discuss what it takes for a police administrator to maximize his or her effectiveness in both organizational and interpersonal communication. We will discuss the communication process and various steps in the communication process; including the sender, the message, the channel (medium), the receiver, feedback, the environment, and noise. We will also examine the numerous barriers to communication, including sender-caused barriers, receiver-caused barriers, and other barriers. To help the reader understand the pathways that communication takes in an organization, we will suggest ways to analyze a communication network. We will provide information about who talks to whom and will analyze a picture of human interaction and organization. We will also discuss the multidirectional flow of information (downward, upward, and horizontal) and provide suggestions to police administrators on how they can avoid creating barriers that disrupt the smooth flow of information throughout their organization. We will also discuss interpersonal communication and make suggestions on how the police manager can become a more effective communicator.

An important area of communication that is often overlooked by police managers relates to differences in communication between the genders. In order for police supervisors to be effective in communications, they must understand that men and women in our society often communicate quite differently and may solve problems in dramatically different ways. It is imperative these differences be understood, so that erroneous evaluations of female officers do not lead to unfair criticism by both peers and supervisors.

Because of the enormous cultural diversity existing in many parts of the United States today, it is essential that police officers understand as much as possible about the people they are serving. Our discussion of cross-cultural communications examines the ways that officers can respond to language differences along with other multicultural issues involved in the communication process. Further, we will examine specific scenarios that will lead to a better understanding of some of the difficulties associated with communicating with individuals from cultures that may be radically different from one's own. We also suggest ways of implementing cross-cultural training of police officers to help prevent some of the communication breakdowns that can occur.

Police administrators can choose from a number of ways to communicate. However, not surprisingly, there is still considerable confidence in the use of written words in the complex organizations that many police departments are. The very nature of police work makes this important because records need to be available for reference relating to both investigations and prosecutions. The use of the written word establishes a permanent record for ready reference. On the other hand, not all communications can or should be in writing. We will discuss the advantages and disadvantages of written, oral, and electronic communication. We will also discuss the instances in which police administrators may wish to use a combination of communication vehicles.

THE COMMUNICATION PROCESS

An explanation of communication begins with the basic problem that it cannot be examined as an isolated event. Communication is a process, so it must be understood as the totality of several independent and dynamic elements. An aggregate **communication** may be defined as the process by which senders and receivers interact in both professional and social contexts.

Steps in the Communication Process

To understand the steps in the communication process, assume that a midnight shift lieutenant informs a midnight shift patrol sergeant that there has been a dramatic increase in the number of burglaries in the sergeant's patrol sector during the past month and then suggests it may be the result of inattention on the part of the sergeant and the sergeant's subordinates. The following are the steps that are occurring in this communication process:

Sender. The sender (in this case, the lieutenant) is attempting to send a spoken message to the sergeant. The perceived authority and credibility of the sender are important factors in influencing how much attention the message will receive. Because of the authority and rank of the lieutenant, it is very likely the patrol sergeant will not ignore the message.

Message. The heart of the communication event is the message, a purpose or an idea to be conveyed. Many factors influence how a message is received. Among them are clarity, the alertness of the receiver, the complexity and length of the message, and how the information is organized. The patrol lieutenant's message will most likely get across if the lieutenant says directly, "I need to talk to you about last month's dramatic increase in burglaries in your patrol sector."

Channel (medium). Several communication channels, or media, are usually available for sending messages in organizations. Typically, messages are spoken (as in this case), written (increasingly electronically), or a combination. When a message is spoken, it is typically accompanied by nonverbal signs, such as a frown, smile, or hand gesture.

Receiver. A communication is complete only when another party receives the message and understands it properly. Perceptual distortions of various types act as filters that can prevent a message from being received as intended by the sender.

Feedback. Messages sent back from the receiver to the sender are referred to as **feedback.** Without feedback, it is difficult to know whether a message has been received and understood. The feedback step also includes the receiver's reactions. If the receiver—in this case, the patrol sergeant—takes appropriate action as intended by the lieutenant, then the message has been received satisfactorily. Effective

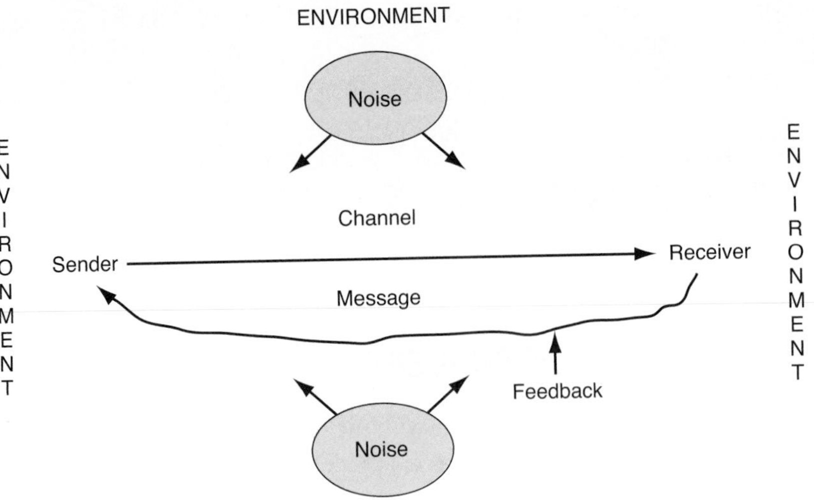

FIGURE 9.1

A basic model of the communication process.

(*Source:* Dubrin, Andrew J., *Human Relations: Interpersonal, Job-Oriented Skills*, 8th, © 2004. Reproduced by permission of Pearson Education, Inc., Upper Saddle River, New Jersey)

interpersonal communication involves an exchange of messages between two people. The two communicators take turns being receivers and senders.

Environment. A full understanding of communication requires knowledge of the environment in which messages are transmitted and received. The organizational culture (attitudes and atmosphere) is a key environmental factor that influences communication. It is easier to transmit controversial messages when trust and respect are high than when they are low.

Noise. Distractions, such as noise, have a pervasive influence on the components of the communication process. However, within this context, **noise** can also mean anything that disrupts communication, including the attitudes and emotions of the receiver, such as stress, fear, negative attitudes, and low motivation[2] (see Figure 9.1).

Critical Thinking Question

1. Why is feedback crucial to the communication process?

COMMUNICATION BARRIERS

Barriers to communication, or communication breakdowns, can occur at any place in the system. Barriers may be the result of improper techniques on the part of either the sender or the receiver.

The sender hinders communications when the following occur:

- The sender is not clear about what is to be accomplished with the message.
- The sender assumes incorrectly that the receiver has the knowledge necessary to understand the message and its intent and does not adapt the message to the intended receiver.
- The sender uses a communication medium not suited for the message. For example, some messages are better transmitted face-to-face, others in writing,

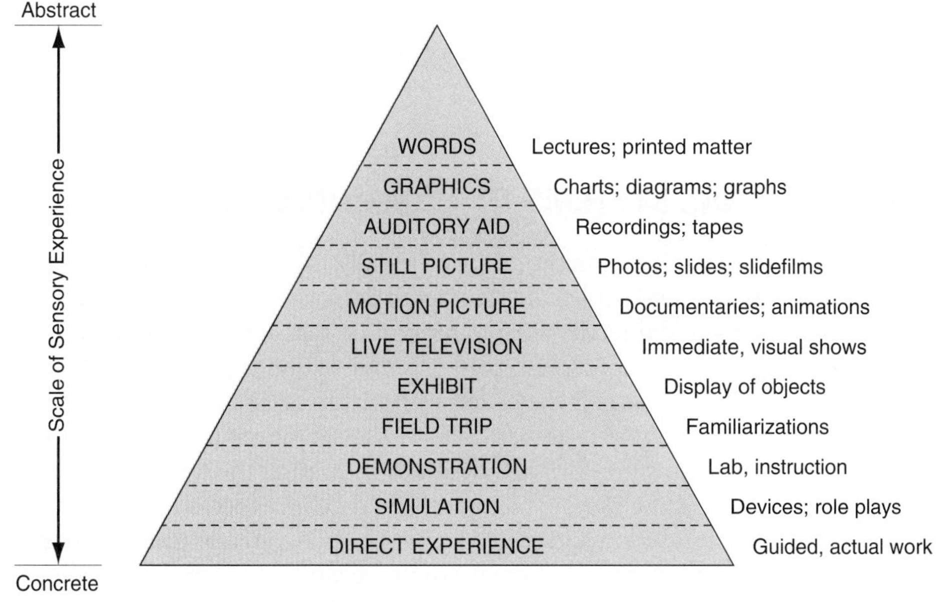

FIGURE 9.2

Scale of sensory perception.

while others most effectively transmitted with the use of visual aids. Still others are best taught with direct, hands-on experience. Figure 9.2 displays a scale of sensory perceptions which can be useful as a guide in determining which medium of communication is most effective for a particular message.

- The sender does not develop a mechanism for receiving feedback to determine if the message was understood correctly.
- The sender does not interpret feedback correctly or fails to clarify the message on the basis of feedback from the receiver.
- The sender uses language that causes the receiver to stop listening, reading, or receiving.
- The sender analyzes the audience improperly.
- The sender's background, experiences, and attitudes are different from those of the receiver, and the sender does not take this into account.

The receiver hinders communication when the following occur:

- The receiver is a poor listener, observer, or reader and therefore misinterprets the meaning of the message.
- The receiver jumps to conclusions.
- The receiver hears or sees only certain parts of the message.
- The receiver tends to reject messages that contradict beliefs and assumptions.
- The receiver has other concerns or emotional barriers, such as being mentally preoccupied.

Some other barriers to communication are as follows:

- Noise, temperature, and other physical distractions
- Distance or an inability to see or hear the message being sent
- Sender–receiver relationship, power structure, roles, and personality differences

Critical Thinking Question

1. How might an administrator ensure that communication barriers are minimized when delivering a message?

ORGANIZATIONAL SYSTEMS OF COMMUNICATION

Organizational systems of communication are usually created by setting up formal systems of responsibility and explicit delegations of duties, such as implicit statements of the nature, content, and direction of communication that are necessary for the performance of the group. Consequently, formal communication is required by the organization and follows the accepted pattern of hierarchical structure. Delegated authority and responsibility determine the path that communication should take, whether upward or downward. Messages that travel through the formal channels of any organization may follow routine patterns; they may be expected at a given time or presented in a standard form and receive a regularized degree of consideration.[3]

Most police managers prefer a formal system, regardless of how cumbersome it may be, because they can control it and because it tends to create a record for future reference. However, motivational factors of the individual and organizations affect the flow of communication. Employees typically communicate with those who help them achieve their aims and avoid communicating with those who do not assist or who may retard their accomplishing those goals. They direct their communications toward those who make them feel more secure and gratify their needs and away from those who threaten or make them feel anxious or generally provide unrewarding experiences. In addition, employees communicate in a manner that allows them to increase their status, belong to a more prestigious group, attain more power to influence decisions, or expand their control. The moving transaction identified as organizational communication can occur at several levels and can result in understanding, agreement, good feeling, and appropriate behavior; the converse may also be true.[4]

Downward Communication

Classical management theories place primary emphasis on control, chain of command, and downward flow of information. **Downward communication** is used by management for sending orders, directives, goals, policies, procedures, memorandums, and so forth to employees at lower levels of the organization. Five types of such communication within an organization can be identified:[5]

1. *Job instruction*—communication relating to the performance of a certain task
2. *Job rationale*—communication relating a certain task to organizational tasks
3. *Procedures and practices*—communication about organization policies, procedures, rules, and regulations
4. *Feedback*—communication appraisal of how an individual performs the assigned task
5. *Indoctrination*—communication designed to motivate the employee.[6]

Other reasons for communicating downward implicit in this listing are opportunities for management to spell out objectives, change attitudes and mold opinions, prevent misunderstandings from lack of information, and prepare employees for change.[7] A study conducted by the Opinion Research Corporation some years ago revealed that large amounts of information generated at the top of an organization did not filter down to the working levels. Studies of the flow of communications within complex organizations repeatedly demonstrate that each level of management can act as a barrier to downward communication.[8] In perhaps the best-controlled experimental research in downward communication, Dahle[9] proved the efficacy of using oral and written media together. His findings indicate the following order of effectiveness (from most effective to least effective):

1. Oral and written communication combined
2. Oral communication only
3. Written communication only
4. The bulletin board
5. The organizational grapevine

The research conducted thus far seems to indicate that most downward channels in organizations are only minimally effective. Findings indicate further that attempts at disseminating information downward in an organization should not depend exclusively on a single channel.

Upward Communication

Even though police administrators may appreciate the need for effective upward communication, they may not translate this need into action.[10] It becomes apparent at once that to swim upstream is a much harder task than to float downstream. But currents of resistance, inherent in the temperament and habits of supervisors and employees in the complexity and structure of modern police agencies, are persistent and strong. Let us examine some of these deterrents to **upward communication**.

Barriers Involving Police Organizations

The physical distance between superior and subordinate impedes upward communication in several ways. Communication becomes difficult and infrequent when superiors are isolated so as to be seldom seen or spoken to. In large police organizations, executives may be located in headquarters or operating centers that are not easily reached by subordinates. In other police agencies, executive offices may be placed remotely, or executives may hold themselves needlessly inaccessible.

Barriers Involving Superiors

The attitude of superiors and their listening behavior play a vital role in encouraging or discouraging communication upward. If, in listening to a subordinate, a supervisor seems anxious to end the interview, impatient with the subordinate, or annoyed or distressed by the subject being discussed, a major barrier to future communication may be created.

There is always the danger that a supervisor may assume the posture that "no news is good news" when, in fact, a lack of complaints or criticism may be a symptom that upward communication is operating at a dangerously low level.

Supervisors may also assume, often incorrectly, they know what subordinates think or feel and believe that listening to complaints from subordinates, especially complaints about departmental policies or even specific supervisors, is an indication of disloyalty. This attitude tends to discourage employees with justifiable complaints from approaching their superiors.

One of the strongest deterrents to upward communication is a failure of management to take action on undesirable conditions previously brought to their attention. The result is that subordinates lose faith both in the sincerity of management and in the value of communication.

Barriers Involving Subordinates

Communication may flow more freely downward than upward because a superior is free to call in a subordinate and talk about a problem at will. The subordinate does not have the same freedom to intrude on the superior's time and is discouraged from circumventing the chain of command and going over a superior's head or from asking for an appeal from decisions made by superiors. Thus, neither the system available nor the rewards offered to the subordinate for upward communication equal those for downward messages.

Horizontal Communication

When an organization's formal communication channels are not open, the informal horizontal channels are almost sure to thrive as a substitute.[11] If there is a disadvantage in **horizontal communication,** it is that it is much easier and more natural to achieve than vertical communication and, therefore, often replaces vertical channels rather than supplements them. Actually, the horizontal channels that replace weak or nonexistent vertical channels are usually of an informal nature. There are, of course, formal horizontal channels that are procedurally necessary and should be built into the system. Formal horizontal channels must be set up between various bureaus and divisions for the purposes of planning, interwork task coordination, and general system maintenance functions, such as problem solving, information sharing, and conflict resolution.

We can begin by acknowledging that horizontal communication is essential if the subsystems within a police organization are to function in an effective and coordinated manner. Horizontal communication among peers may also furnish the emotional and social bond that builds esprit de corps or a feeling of teamwork. Psychologically, people seem to need this type of communication, and police managers would do well to provide for this need and thus allow peers to solve some of their own work problems together.

Suppose, for example, that patrol sergeant A is having great difficulty communicating certain mutually beneficial information to detective sergeant B because the police department requires strict adherence to the chain of command in transmitting information. As indicated in Figure 9.3A, sergeant A would have to go up through the various hierarchical complexities of the patrol division and back down through the detective division to communicate with sergeant B. The time being wasted and the level-to-level message distortion occurring in the classically managed organization was recognized by Fayol[12] in 1916. Fayol proposed the creation of a horizontal bridge (see Figure 9.3B) that would allow more direct communications between individuals within an organization. The major limiting factor to the use of Fayol's bridge is a loss of network control and the subsequent weakening of authority and random scattering of messages throughout the system. Such random communication channels can lead to diagonal lines of communication, such as direct communication between sergeant A in the patrol division and sergeant B in the detective division. Diagonal lines of communication are not in and of themselves bad; however, they are very difficult to control from the management point of view.[13]

Despite the need for formal horizontal communication in an organization, there may be a tendency among peers not to formally communicate task-related information

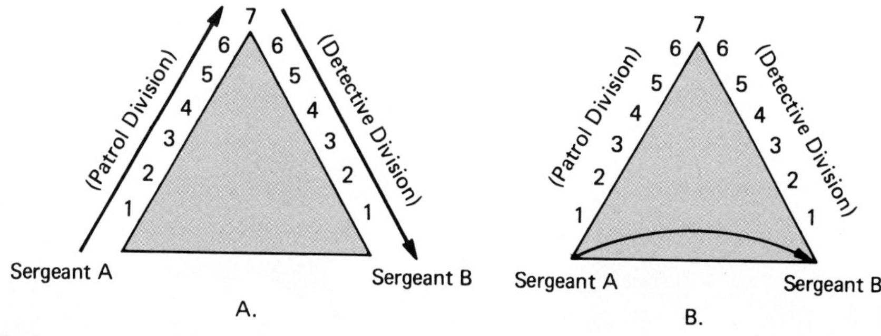

FIGURE 9.3

Horizontal lines of communication: (A) message path from sergeant A to sergeant B following the usual structured channels; (B) message path from sergeant A to sergeant B following Fayol's bridge.

horizontally. For instance, rivalry for recognition and promotion may cause competing subordinates to be reluctant to share information. Subordinates may also find it difficult to communicate with highly specialized people at the same level as themselves in other divisions.

In the main, then, formal horizontal communication channels are vital as a supplement to the vertical channels in an organization. Conversely, the informal horizontal channels, although socially necessary, can be detrimental to the vertical channels. Informal horizontal channels not only may carry false or distorted information but also may sometimes tend to replace the vertical channels.[14]

The Grapevine

The best-known system for transmitting informal communication is the **grapevine,** so called because it meanders back and forth like a grapevine across organizational lines. The grapevine's most effective characteristics are that it is fast, it can be highly selective and discriminating, it operates mostly at the place of work, and it supplements and relates to formal communication. These characteristics can be divided into desirable or undesirable attributes.

The grapevine can be considered desirable because it gives management insight into employees' attitudes, provides a safety valve for employees' emotions, and helps spread useful information. Dysfunctional traits include its tendencies to spread rumors and untruths, its lack of responsibility to any group or person, and its uncontrollability. Attributes of the grapevine—its speed and influence—may work either to the good or to the detriment of the organization. The actual operation of the grapevine can be visualized in four ways (see Figure 9.4):[15]

1. The single strand A tells B, who tells C, who tells D, and so on.
2. The gossip chain: A seeks and tells everyone, thus becoming the organizational Paul Revere.
3. The probability chain: A communicates randomly to D and F, then with the laws of probabilities, D and F tell others in the same manner.
4. Cluster chain: A tells three selected others; perhaps one of them tells two others and one of these tells one other person.

The grapevine is a permanent factor to be reckoned with in the daily activities of management, and no competent manager would try to abolish it. Rather, the astute manager should analyze it and consciously try to influence it.[16]

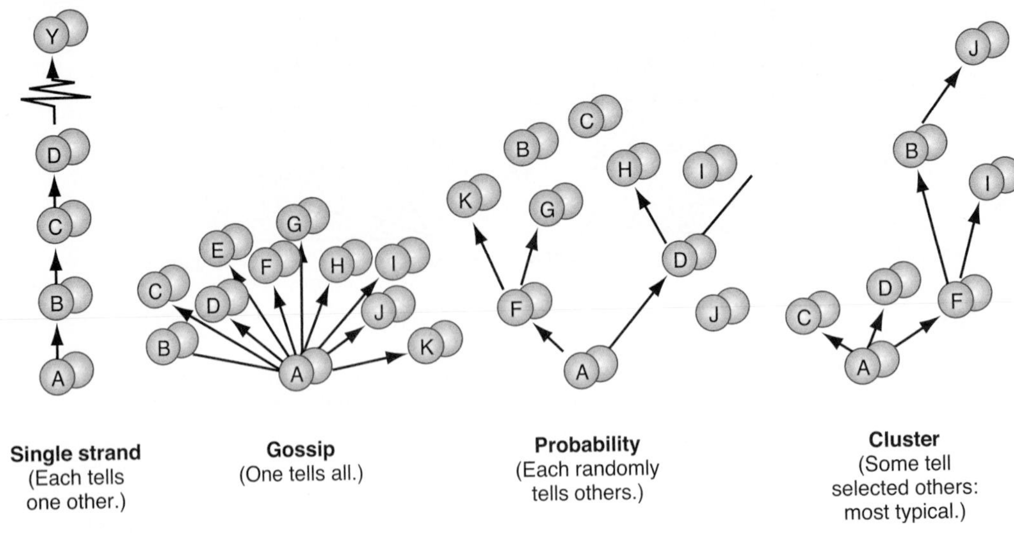

FIGURE 9.4

Grapevine patterns.

(*Source:* (John W. Newstrom and Keith Davis, *Organizational Behavior: Human Behavior at Work,* 9th ed., p. 445. © 1993 McGraw Hill Companies. Reproduced with permission from The McGraw Hill Companies.)

INTERPERSONAL COMMUNICATION

The information available about communicating persuasively and effectively is extensive.[17] However, in this section we will focus primarily on creating the high-impact communication that contributes to effective leadership. Both formal and informal leaders must be persuasive and dynamic communicators. Effective communication skills often help informal leaders be selected for formal leadership positions.

Suggestions for becoming effective communicators can be divided into the following two categories: (1) speaking and writing and (2) nonverbal communication. We will also discuss certain basic principles of persuasion.

Speaking and Writing

Many people are already familiar with the basics of effective spoken and written communication, yet the basics, such as writing and speaking clearly, maintaining eye contact, and not mumbling, are only starting points. Most effective leaders have extra energy in their communication style. The same excitement is reflected in both their speaking and their writing styles. Kouzes and Posner underscore the importance of colorful language in communicating a vision (one of the leader's most important functions) in these words:

> *Language is among the most powerful methods for expressing a vision. Successful leaders use metaphors and figures of speech; they give examples, tell stories, and relate anecdotes; they draw word pictures; and they offer quotations and recite slogans.*[18]

Group members and other constituents generally have more exposure to the spoken words of leaders, yet clearly the increased use of e-mail, printed memos, and the written word exerts considerable influence. The following are some suggestions for dynamic and persuasive oral and written communication.

Be Credible

Attempts at persuasion, including inspirational speaking and writing, begin with the credibility of the message sender. It has long been recognized that credibility is a powerful element in the persuasive process. If the speaker is perceived as highly credible, the attempt at persuasive communication is more likely to be successful.[19] The perception of credibility is influenced by many factors. Being trustworthy heavily influences being perceived as credible. A leader with a reputation for lying will have a difficult time convincing people of the merits of a new initiative. Being perceived as intelligent and knowledgeable is another major factor contributing to credibility.

Gear the Message to the Listener

An axiom of persuasive communication is that a speaker must adapt the message to the listener's interests and motivation. A review of the evidence concludes that the average intelligence and experience level of the group is a key contingency factor in designing a persuasive message. People with high intelligence tend to be more influenced by messages based on strong, logical arguments. Also, bright people are more likely to reject messages based on flawed logic.[20]

Persuade Group Members on the Benefits of Change

Sometimes a leader is constrained by the willingness of agency group members to conform to the leader's suggestions and initiatives for change. As a consequence, the leader must explain to agency members how they can benefit from what is being proposed.

For example, let us assume that the head of a law enforcement agency has decided to radically modify the agency's policy on high-speed pursuits (a topic discussed in much greater detail in Chapter 14, Legal Aspects of Police Administration). In the past, the agency has had a very liberal policy which allowed officers considerable latitude to pursue fleeing motorists irrespective of the violation, but the agency head is now seriously considering restricting the policy, so that officers will only be permitted to pursue known dangerous felons.

Selling agency members is quite often done more effectively when the persuader takes the time to build consensus rather than to change the policy through administrative fiat. Instead of trying simply to order a change without any discussion, it might be more effective to win over key personnel within a reasonable time frame. Persuasion guru (note the appeal to credibility) Jay Conger writes that successful persuasion often requires ongoing effort and suggests this pattern be followed:

- At the first meeting of key personnel, make every effort possible to ask them to consider the initiative carefully.
- At the second meeting, after they have had the opportunity to think about this modification, see if it is necessary to make adjustments in the policy.
- At the final meeting, it is imperative to have all the key members come to a consensus. If a consensus cannot be obtained but a final decision has been made to modify the policy, it is important that key personnel understand the importance of not undermining the policy. It should also be made very clear that such action will not be tolerated.[21]

Use Heavy-Impact and Emotion-Provoking Words

Certain words used in the proper context give power and force to speech. Used comfortably, naturally, and sincerely, these words project the image of a self-confident person with leadership ability or potential.

Closely related to heavy-impact language are emotion-provoking words. An expert persuasive tactic is to sprinkle one's speech with emotion-provoking—and therefore inspiring—words. Emotion-provoking words bring forth powerful images. For example, agency personnel must be made to understand that the existing policy on high-speed pursuits increases the likelihood of "death" and/or "injury" to them, as well as to "innocent" third parties, the fleeing motorist and in some cases "innocent" passengers in the fleeing vehicles. It will also result in "lawsuits" against the officer and the agency and in some rare cases may even result in their being "criminally charged," "convicted," and sent to "prison."

Back Up Conclusions with Data

A message either spoken or written will be more persuasive if it is supported with solid data. Published sources provide convincing data for arguments. Supporting data for many arguments can be found in professional journals, in government studies, in scholarly research, in books, on the Internet, on TV, and in newspapers. Extract from those various documents specific examples provided and statistics to support the previously discussed significant changes in the agency's high-speed pursuit policy. For example, the National Law Enforcement Officers Memorial Fund has reported a dramatic increase in the number of police officers killed in traffic accidents. From 1975 to 1984, 342 deaths occurred; from 1985 to 1994, 369 deaths occurred; and from 1995 to 2000, 477 deaths occurred.[22] These figures do not include the many thousands of police officers who have been seriously injured and disabled as a result of automobile accidents, many of which occurred during high-speed pursuits for what turned out to be in most cases minor traffic violations or misdemeanors.

Minimize Language Errors and Vocalized Pauses

Using colorful, powerful words enhances the perception of self-confidence. The use of words and phrases that dilute the impact of a speech, such as "like," "you know," "you know what I mean," and "uhhhhhhh," should be minimized. Such "junk words" (also known as parasitic words) and vocalized pauses convey the impression of low self-confidence—especially in a professional setting—and detract from a sharp communication image.

An effective way to decrease the use of these extraneous words is to tape record or video record one's own side of a conversation and then play it back. Many people are not aware that they use extraneous words until they hear recordings of their speech.

It is important always to write and speak with precision in order to convey the impression of being articulate and well informed, thus enhancing one's stature.

Write Crisp, Clear Memos and Reports, Including a Front-Loaded Message

According to Mercer, high achievers write more effective reports than do their less highly achieving counterparts. Mercer examined the business writing (memos, letters, and reports) of both high achievers and low achievers. He observed that the high achievers' writing was distinctive in that it had more active verbs than passive verbs, more subheadings and subtitles, and shorter paragraphs.[23]

Writing, in addition to speaking, is more persuasive when key ideas are placed at the beginning of a conversation, an e-mail message, a paragraph, or a sentence. Front-loaded messages are particularly important for leaders because people expect leaders to be forceful communicators.

Use a Power-Oriented Linguistic Style

A major part of being persuasive involves choosing the right **linguistic style,** which is a person's characteristic speaking pattern. According to communications specialist

Deborah Tannen, linguistic style involves such aspects as amount of directness, pacing and pausing, word choice, and the use of such communication devices as jokes, figures of speech, anecdotes, questions, and apologies.[24] Linguistic style is complex because it includes the culturally learned signals by which people communicate what they mean, along with how they interpret what others say and how they evaluate others. The complexity of linguistic style makes it difficult to offer specific prescriptions for using one that is power-oriented. However, there are several components of a linguistic style that will, in many situations, give power and authority to the message sender. Some of these, as observed by Tannen and other language specialists are the following:

- Downplay uncertainty. If you are not confident of your opinion or prediction, make a positive statement, anyway, such as saying, "I know this new restrictive high-speed pursuit policy will reduce deaths, injuries, and litigation."
- Keep an open mind and accept verbal opposition to ideas, especially at staff meetings, rather than becoming upset and defensive.
- Emphasize direct rather than indirect talk, such as by saying "I need your report by noon tomorrow" rather than "I'm wondering if your report will be available by noon tomorrow."
- Speak up without qualifying or giving other indices of uncertainty. It is better to give dates for the completion of a project rather than to say, "Soon," or "It shouldn't be a problem." Instead, make a statement like "I will have my portion of the strategic plan shortly before Thanksgiving. I need to collect input from my team and sift through the information."
- Know exactly what is needed. The chances of selling an idea increase to the extent that it is clarified in the mind of the presenter. The clearer and more committed the person is at the outset of the session, the stronger he or she will be as a persuader and the more powerful the language becomes.
- Strive to be bold when making statements. As a rule of thumb, be bold about ideas but tentative about people. If the head of the agency says something like "I believe that our new high-speed pursuit policy will significantly reduce injuries and deaths to our officers and citizens, as well as result in a reduction in liability to our agency," then it is an idea that is being attacked and not one's predecessor who may have been reluctant to implement a more conservative high-speed pursuit policy.[25]

Despite these suggestions for having a power-oriented linguistic style, Tannen cautions that there is no one best way to communicate. How one projects power and authority is often dependent on the people involved, the organizational culture, the relative rank of the speakers, and the other situational factors. The power-oriented linguistic style should be interpreted as a general guideline.

Nonverbal Communication

Effective leaders are masterful nonverbal as well as verbal communicators. **Nonverbal communication** is important because leadership involves emotion, which words alone cannot communicate convincingly. A major component of the emotional impact of a message is communicated nonverbally—perhaps up to 90 percent.[26] The classic study behind this observation has been misinterpreted to mean that 90 percent of communication is nonverbal. If this were true, facts, figures, and logic would make a minor contribution to communication, and acting skill would be much more important for getting across one's point of view. This, however, is not the case.

A self-confident leader not only speaks and writes with assurance but also projects confidence through body position, gestures, and manner of speech. Not everybody interprets the same body language and other nonverbal signals in the same way, but some aspects of nonverbal behavior project a self-confident, leadership image in many situations. For example:

- Using an erect posture when walking, standing, or sitting. Slouching and slumping are almost universally interpreted as an indicator of low self-confidence.
- Standing up straight during a confrontation. Cowering is interpreted as a sign of low self-confidence and poor leadership qualities.
- Speaking at a moderate pace, with a loud, confident tone. People lacking in self-confidence tend to speak too rapidly or very slowly.
- Smiling frequently in a relaxed, natural-appearing manner
- Maintaining eye contact with those around you
- Gesturing in a relaxed, non-mechanical way, including pointing toward others in a way that welcomes rather than accuses, such as using a gesture to indicate "You're right" or "It's your turn to comment"[27]

A general approach to using nonverbal behavior that projects confidence is to have a goal of appearing self-confident and powerful. This type of autosuggestion makes many of the behaviors seem automatic. For example, if you say to yourself, "I am going to display leadership qualities in this meeting," you will have taken an important step toward appearing confident.

External image also plays an important role in communicating messages to others. People have more respect and grant more privileges to those they perceive as being well dressed and neatly groomed. Appearance includes more than the choice of clothing. Self-confidence is projected by such items as the following:

- Freshly polished shoes
- Impeccable fingernails
- Clean jewelry in mint condition
- Well-maintained hair
- Good-looking teeth

A subtle mode of nonverbal communication is the use of time. Guarding time as a precious resource will help project an image of self-confidence and leadership. A statement such as "I can devote 15 minutes to your problem this Thursday at 4 P.M." connotes confidence and control. (However, under certain circumstances, too many of these statements might make a person appear unapproachable and inconsiderate.) Other ways of projecting power through the use of time include such behaviors as being prompt for meetings and starting and stopping meetings on time.

Critical Thinking Questions

1. Persuasion guru Jay Conger writes that successful persuasion often requires ongoing effort and suggests that a certain pattern be followed. What is this pattern?
2. There are several components of a linguistic style that would give power and authority to the message sender in many situations. What were some suggested by Deborah Tannen and other language specialists?
3. Why is nonverbal communication such an important component of the emotional impact of a message?

GROUP VS. INTERPERSONAL COMMUNICATION

For our purposes, interpersonal communication can be defined as the sharing of information between two persons. **Group communication** involves interaction among three or more individuals in a face-to-face situation. The three people have a common need that is satisfied by the exchange of information.[28]

Size of the Group

The term "group" has been defined as a number of persons gathered or classified together.[29] The definition of group communication does not set limits on the ultimate size of the group. However, practical considerations inherent in the definition do define a maximum number of people who would be able to interact effectively. Individuals attending a professional sporting event may have a commonality of interest, but they may not have an opportunity to become involved in a face-to-face situation where they can exchange information that satisfies a common need. If we compare the Super Bowl, with an attendance of 100,000 people, to a group of 5 fans planning a tailgate party before the game, it is easy to see that the size of the group can be a factor in determining the ability of individuals to communicate with each other.

Numerous scholars have examined the dynamics of group communications.[30] Various research has determined that the range between 3 and 20 is a natural size for purposes of defining group interactions.[31] Once the size of the group exceeds 20 people, the ability of individual members to influence each other diminishes. The nature of the gathering takes on more of the characteristics of a mass meeting or conference, in which one person may influence the group but the ability of individual members within the group to influence each other is limited. The size of the group has a direct bearing on the type of communication involved. Therefore, we will limit our discussion of communication to groups that do not exceed 20 individuals. Once the size of the group involved in the communication process has been determined, group interaction must be addressed.

Group Interaction

It is generally accepted by leading scholars that there are four phases in group interaction: (1) orientation, (2) conflict, (3) emergence, and (4) reinforcement.[32]

In the *orientation* phase, group members attempt to get to know each other and discover the problems that face the group. This may occur as strangers meet in a group for the first time, or it may happen with people who know each other and attend periodic meetings, such as roll call before the beginning of patrol shifts. In the latter situation, group members already know each other, and the orientation is aimed at common problems facing the group. These problems could range from new shift hours to planning a social gathering after the shift (see Figure 9.5).

The second phase, *conflict,* involves disagreement among the members of the group. This phase is characterized by an atmosphere of polarization and controversy. Using the previous two examples, patrol officers may be sharply divided concerning the benefits of the new shift hours or have strong feelings regarding the location of the social gathering.

During the *emergence* phase of group interaction, there is more emphasis on positive statements. This phase allows dissenting members to save face by moving toward

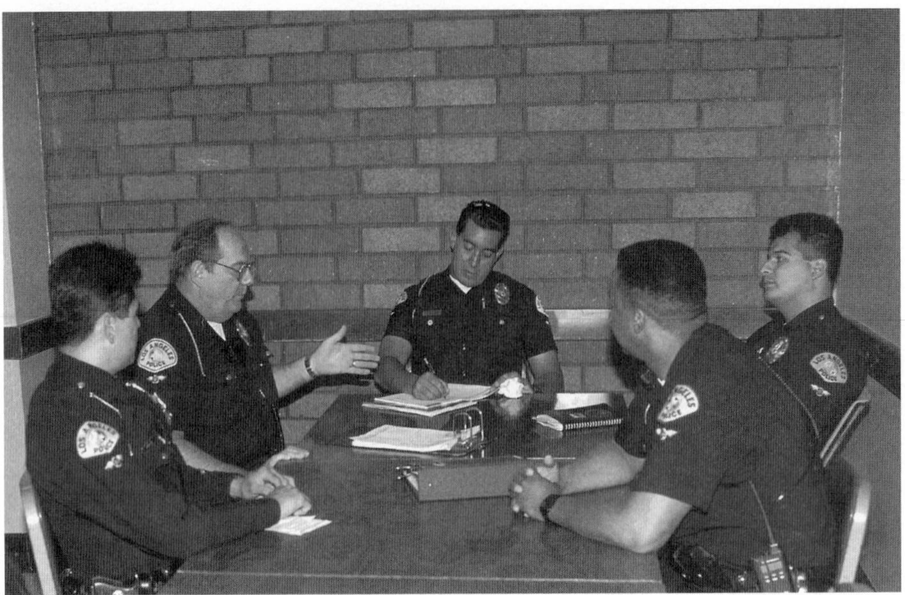

FIGURE 9.5

Group interaction is an important aspect of any organization, and law enforcement officers need to understand these group dynamics in order to carry out their duties. Here a group of traffic officers meet to discuss strategies for reducing traffic accidents.

(Michael Newman/PhotoEdit Inc.)

the majority's position. Officers who oppose the new shift hours may begin to find other benefits not previously discussed. Similarly, the location for the party may be a third alternative that is acceptable to all members.

The final phase is *reinforcement.* In this phase, group members comment on the positive aspects of the group and its problem-solving ability.

The preceding discussion focused on the dynamics that normally occur in a problem-solving group; however, this interaction is usually present in most groups.[33] A police officer may determine what phase a group is in by listening to the types of comments being made by members of the group, then use that information to express personal views in the most effective manner. Group interaction is an important aspect of any organization. Law enforcement officers need to understand these group dynamics in order to carry out their duties effectively. Once a group has been established, certain communication networks begin to emerge.

Critical Thinking Question

1. How is the size of a group a factor in determining the ability of individuals to communicate with each other?

CROSS-GENDER COMMUNICATIONS

Generally, an examination of the differences in the ways men and women communicate would be confined to scholarly books in the area of linguistics or perhaps to books in the popular market that examine male/female relationships. However, it is essential that police supervisors who must evaluate the actions of their subordinates understand that men and women in our society often communicate quite differently and may solve problems in dramatically different ways. A failure to understand these differences can result in erroneous evaluations of police officers' actions and even result

FIGURE 9.6

It is important for male officers and male superiors to understand that men and women in our society often communicate quite differently and may solve problems in dramatically different ways. In this photo, a male field training officer is interacting with a female officer.

(Bob Daemmrich/Bob Daemmrich Photography, Inc.)

in unfair criticism by fellow officers and superiors (see Figure 9.6). The following scenario used to illustrate this point was witnessed by one of the authors.

A young woman pulled up to the gas pumps at a filling station to fill up her car. While at the pumps, a young man pulled up behind her in his vehicle. She did not see him pull up. He walked up to her from behind, turned her around, and slapped her across the face. An off-duty police officer in plainclothes and in his personal car was filling up his car at an adjoining pump and witnessed the assault. He immediately identified himself as a police officer and advised the man he was under arrest. The officer requested the filling station attendant to call for a patrol unit. Prior to the arrival of the patrol unit, the assailant was placed in the front seat of the off-duty police officer's car unhandcuffed. Two uniformed officers arrived in separate police cars. One was a male, and the other was a female. The off-duty officer explained to the uniformed officers what he had witnessed and requested their assistance in filling out the necessary paperwork and transporting the assailant to the county jail. However, as the officers were conversing, the assailant, who was still agitated, was loudly expressing his anger at his female companion, who had apparently been out with another man the evening before. The female officer walked over to the assailant and in a very conciliatory way attempted to calm him down. The man was not threatening anyone, was not being aggressive, but was obviously still upset with the young woman he had assaulted. After a couple of minutes, the male officer became agitated with the prisoner "running his mouth." He walked over to the assailant and in very close physical proximity said very angrily, "If you don't shut your damn mouth, your ass is really going to be in trouble." At that point, the man proceeded to be quiet and was eventually handcuffed and transported to jail with no further difficulties. Now let us assume that this scenario was being witnessed by a traditionally trained male supervisor. He might believe that the female officer should have been less conciliatory and more assertive and that her failure to be more assertive could have been interpreted as a sign of weakness by the arrested man, thereby encouraging him to become more belligerent. The supervisor might have assessed the male officer's approach as being more effective because he did, in fact, get the individual to quiet down and there were no further difficulties. However, let us assume, on the other hand, as sometimes happens, that the individual being arrested was sufficiently agitated that, when the male officer spoke to him in this angry way, he in turn responded angrily and decided he would rather fight than go peaceably to jail. (Such scenarios are certainly not uncommon in police work.) If this had occurred, the outcome could have been quite different, and someone could have been injured.

The fact of the matter is that the female officer was behaving in a way that women in our society are generally taught to behave when attempting to resolve a conflict—namely, in a nonconfrontal, conciliatory, non-physical manner. In fact, this technique is recommended and employed in conflict resolution in many facets of police work.

Insights into the differences between the ways males and females communicate are important for police supervisors. If such insights are not present, the actions of female officers may be unfairly judged. Worse yet, if a female officer is criticized, she may believe that, in order to be accepted by her peers and her supervisor, she has to be overly aggressive, more confrontational, and more physical. This is not to suggest that assertiveness is not a positive quality for police officers to possess. However, like anything else, too much can lead to unfortunate consequences (see Figure 9.7).

Deborah Tannen, professor of linguistics at Georgetown University, wrote a book several years ago titled *You Just Don't Understand,* which examined differences in the ways

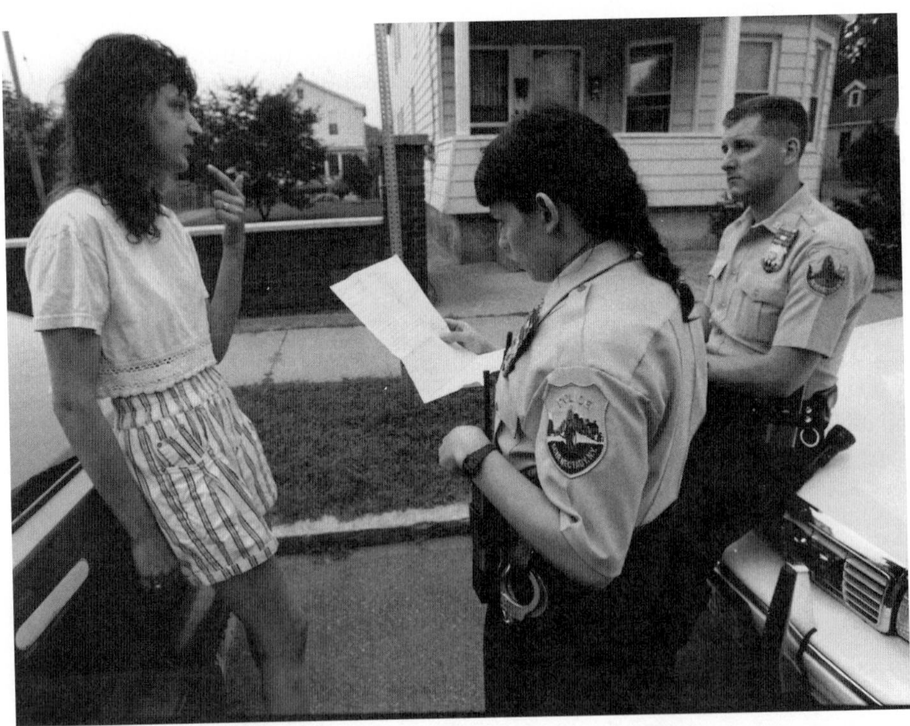

FIGURE 9.7

A male and a female officer are interviewing a victim of domestic violence. In such potentially violent situations, officers must be careful, especially in dealing with the assailant, that they do not unwittingly escalate a relatively tranquil situation into one of violence because of some thoughtless or provocative comment.

(© Viviane Moos/CORBIS)

men and women communicate.[34] The topic spawned a series of popular books focusing on communication differences between "the sexes," one even asserting that men and women were from different planets (*Men Are from Mars, Women Are from Venus*).[35] The issue of misunderstanding between men and women can lead to serious conflict not only in personal relationships but also in the workplace. The following material from Tannen's book illustrates the differences in cross-gender communication.[36]

Male/Female Conversation Is Cross-Culture Communication

If women speak and hear a language of connection and intimacy, while men speak and hear a language of status and independence, then communication between men and women can be like cross-culture communication, prey to a clash of conversational styles.

The claim that men and women grow up in different worlds may at first seem patently absurd. Brothers and sisters grow up in the same families, children to parents of both genders. Where, then, do women and men learn different ways of speaking and hearing?

Even if they grow up in the same neighborhood, on the same block, or in the same house, girls and boys grow up in different worlds of words. Others talk to them differently and expect and accept different ways of talking from them. Most important, children learn how to talk and how to have conversations not only from their parents but also from their peers. After all, if their parents have a foreign or regional accent, children do not emulate it; they learn to speak with the pronunciation of the region where they grow up. Anthropologists Daniel Maltz and Ruth Borker summarize research showing that boys and girls have very different ways of talking to their friends. Although they often play together, boys and girls spend most of their time playing in same-sex groups. And, although some of the activities they play at are similar, their favorite games are different, and their ways of using language in their games are separated by a world of difference.

Boys tend to play outside in large groups that are hierarchically structured. Their groups have a leader who tells others what to do and how to do it and resist doing what other boys propose. It is by giving orders and making them stick that high status is negotiated. Another way boys achieve status is to take center stage by telling stories and jokes and by sidetracking or challenging the stories and jokes of others. Boys' games have winners and losers and elaborate systems of rules that are frequently the subjects of arguments. Finally, boys are frequently heard to boast of their skill and argue about who is best at what.

Girls, on the other hand, play in small groups or in pairs; the center of a girl's social life is a best friend. Within the group, intimacy is key: differentiation is measured by relative closeness. In their most frequent games, such as jump rope and hopscotch, everyone gets a turn. Many of their activities (such as playing house) do not have winners or losers. Though some girls are certainly more skilled than others, girls are expected not to boast about it or show that they think they are better than the others. Girls do not give orders; they express their preferences as suggestions, and suggestions are likely to be accepted. Whereas boys say, "Gimme that!" and "Get outta here!" girls say, "Let's do this," and "How about doing that?" Anything else is put down as "bossy." They do not grab center stage—they do not want it—so they do not challenge each other directly. And much of the time, they simply sit together and talk. Girls are not accustomed to jockeying for status in an obvious way; they are more concerned that they be liked.

Styles in Conflict Resolution

Much of what has been written about women's and men's styles claims that males are competitive and prone to conflict, whereas females are cooperative and given to affiliation. But being in conflict also means being involved with each other. Although it is true that many women are more comfortable using language to express rapport, whereas many men are more comfortable using it for self-display, the situation is really more complicated than that because self-display, when part of a mutual struggle, is also a kind of bonding. And conflict may be valued as a way of creating involvement with others.

To most women, conflict is a threat to connection, to be avoided at all costs. Disputes are preferably settled without direct confrontation. But to many men, conflict is the necessary means by which status is negotiated, so it is to be accepted and may even be sought, embraced, and enjoyed.

Walter Ong, a scholar of cultural linguistics, shows in his book *Fighting for Life* that "adversativeness"—pitting one's needs, wants, or skills against those of others—is an essential part of being human, but "conspicuous or expressed adversativeness is a larger element in the lives of males than of females." He demonstrates that male behavior typically entails contest, which includes combat, struggle, conflict, competition, and contention. Pervasive in male behavior is ritual combat, typified by rough play and sports. Females, on the other hand, are more likely to use intermediaries or to fight for real rather than ritualized purposes.

Friendship among men often has a large element of friendly aggression, dotted with sexual innuendo and explicatives. Unfortunately, women often mistake these ritualized comments as the real thing. In the workplace, this type of "street language" can often result in serious charges of harassment and civil litigation, even though the offensive language was not directed at an individual. These are difficult situations from both male and female perspectives. In Chapter 14, Legal Aspects of Police Administration, we will further discuss the issue of a "hostile environment" as a form of sexual harassment.

Ong demonstrates the inextricable relationship between oral performance and "agonistic" relations. Oral disputation—from formal debate to the study of formal logic—is inherently adversative. With this in mind, we can see that the inclination of many men to expect discussions and arguments in daily conversation to adhere to rules of logic is a remnant of this tradition. Furthermore, oral performance is self-display and is part of a larger framework in which many men approach life as a contest.

Because their imaginations are not captured by ritualized combat, women are inclined to misinterpret and be puzzled by the adversativeness of many men's ways of speaking and miss the ritual nature of friendly aggression. At the same time, the enactment of community can be ritualized just as easily as the enactment of combat. The appearance of community among women may mask power struggles, and the appearance of sameness may mask profound differences in points of view. Men can be as confused by women's verbal rituals as women are by men's.

Critical Thinking Questions

1. Why is it important that law enforcement supervisors understand the differences in the way women and men communicate?
2. How is cross-gender communication comparable to cross-culture communication?

COMMUNICATION WITH OTHER CULTURES

Communication with other cultures is an area in law enforcement that is still evolving.[37] The United States is a melting pot (or, as some have characterized it, a salad) for other races and cultures. With the increase of Southeast Asian refugees and the increasing Hispanic population, the problem of communicating with persons who do not speak English as a primary language is critical within the law enforcement community.[38]

For example, Hispanics constitute the fastest-growing minority group in the United States. Population experts predict this group will outnumber African Americans by the end of the first quarter of the twenty-first century.

Development of "Survival Spanish for Police Officers" began in mid 1986 at Sam Houston State University in Texas in a cooperative effort between the police academy and a faculty member of the university's Spanish department. The cross-cultural training grew from a minor part of the language component when it became apparent that cultural barriers were just as important as the language barrier and had to be addressed in more detail.

Even with the awareness that minority populations continue to expand in the United States, the ability to communicate with them will continue to be a problem for most law enforcement agencies. Various departments are attempting to solve this problem in a number of ways. Some departments are hiring bilingual officers and offering additional compensation for their services, others maintain lists of qualified interpreters, and many others are including cultural awareness programs in their roll-call training (see Figure 9.8).

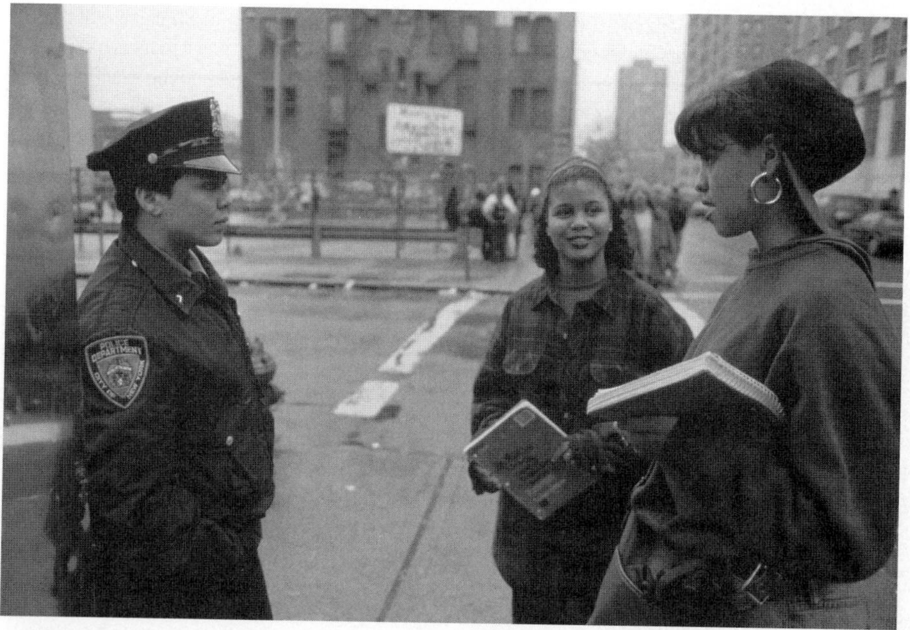

FIGURE 9.8

A Hispanic female and an African American female are discussing career opportunities in law enforcement with an African American female officer. Such officers not only can provide excellent role models for young minority females considering careers in law enforcement but, because of their own status and gender, have considerable credibility.

(© Robert Maass/CORBIS)

Methods of Responding in Language Differences

An officer who arrives at the scene of a crime and is confronted by a non-English-speaking citizen must attempt to gather information from that person. In some cases, this information must not only be gathered quickly but also be accurate. The citizen may be a victim of a crime or a witness who can provide a description of the suspect. One of the most obvious places to turn for assistance is family or neighbors who are bilingual. By using these individuals as on-the-scene interpreters, the officer can obtain the initial information quickly. The officer should ensure that not only the name of the witness but also the name and address of the translator are recorded. Follow-up investigations normally utilize the services of trained translators. In some cities, the courts, prosecutors, and police agencies maintain lists of interpreters to call on if the need arises. For example, in the main Los Angeles County Courthouse, interpreters are available for 78 languages.

However, there are inherent problems with using family or neighbors as interpreters. They may have difficulty with the English language, and some terms may be outside their knowledge or vocabulary. In addition, they may be biased and want to help the victim or witness, to the detriment of others. Because of these issues, departments should try to utilize bilingual officers. These are officers who are able to speak and write in both English and another language. In many cases, these officers not only

In The News

Bilingual Law Enforcement Officers Bridge Cultural Divides

Law enforcement officials in Tampa, Florida, face the challenges of dealing with a community where up to 18,000 households are characterized as having no resident over the age of 13 with a basic understanding of English. Up to 80 percent of those households are Spanish-speaking. Bilingual officers and sheriff's deputies in Hillsborough County are crucial to addressing language and cultural issues that come up during routine patrols and calls for service. As a result, both the police department and the sheriff's office have been working to recruit bilingual officers who speak Spanish, Russian, Vietnamese, Chinese, and other languages. Officers in the area report that being able to communicate properly with the people they encounter can often alleviate potentially violent situations, aid investigations, and leave citizens with a more positive impression of law enforcement.

Source: "The Power of Words: Tampa's Bilingual Law Enforcement Officers Bridge Cultural Divides," *Tampa Tribune,* October 21, 2004, 1.

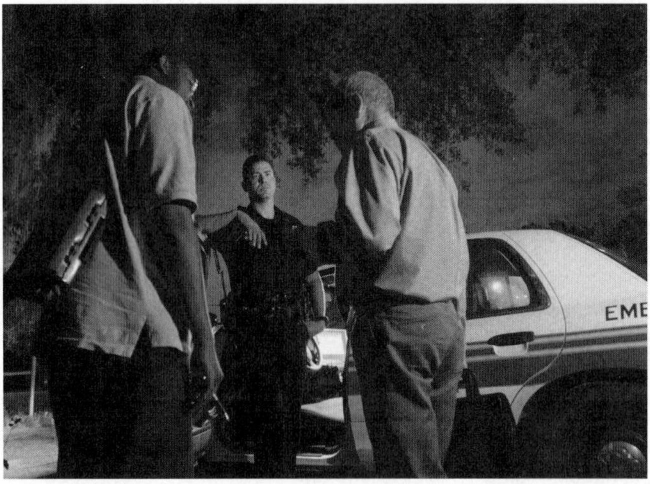

Officer Jeff Sanchez, center, is one of the Tampa Police Department's bilingual officers, who in combination with other officers are fluent in languages.
(Photo by Tampa [Florida] Tribune photographer Victor Junco)

speak a second language but are members of that ethnic group and are familiar with the history, traditions, and customs of the culture.

Many departments offer additional compensation to bilingual officers. Those officers respond to situations where their language skill is needed and provide an independent neutral interpretation without bias.

Many departments provide roll-call training that focuses on the cultures of minorities within their jurisdiction. This is another method by which officers may learn basic phrases of a different language. Some agencies will reimburse officers if they take and pass conversational language courses that enable them to interact with minority groups.

Other Multicultural Issues

The term **culture** can be applied to various population categories. However; it is normally associated with race and ethnicity. It is this diversity that both enriches and obstructs a law enforcement officer's involvement and interaction with other persons, groups, and cultures.

Officers should remember that most minorities have developed a sharp sense for detecting condescension, manipulation, and insincerity. There is no substitute for compassion as the foundation, and sincerity as its expression, in carrying out law enforcement services equally and fairly.

Although it is not possible to feel the same compassion for all victims, it is the responsibility of law enforcement officers to provide the same compassionate service to every victim. The plight of undocumented residents or illegal aliens, for example, involves complex issues of personal prejudice and international policies. Many of these persons suffer financial exploitation and other criminal victimization once they enter the United States. Officers must make an effort to understand their situation and not let personal opinions affect their interaction with these individuals when they are victimized.

The first contact minorities have with law enforcement officers will either confirm or dispel suspicion as to how they will be treated. Proper pronunciation of a person's surname is an excellent place to begin contact with him or her. Surnames have histories and meanings that allow for conversation beyond the introduction. In working with immigrant, refugee, or native populations, it is helpful to learn a few words of greeting from those cultures. This willingness to go beyond what is comfortable and usual conveys the officer's intent to communicate.

Listening is fundamental to human relationships. The principles and manner of listening, however, differ among cultures. Asians and Pacific Islanders, for example, deflect direct eye contact in conversation as a sign of patient listening and deference. These groups therefore consider staring to be impolite and confrontational. Many Western cultures, on the other hand, value direct eye contact as a sign of sympathy or respect. Looking elsewhere is seen as disinterest or evasiveness. Misunderstanding in the communication process can occur if some allowance is not made for these differences. Multicultural issues must be understood by all law enforcement officers. Understanding that "different" does not mean "criminal" will assist officers attempting to communicate in an environment that continues to become more and more diverse.

Consider this scenario. A Nigerian cab driver runs a red light. An officer pulls him over in the next block, stopping the patrol car at least three car lengths behind the cab. Before the police officer can exit the patrol car, the cabbie gets out of his vehicle and approaches the officer. Talking rapidly in a high-pitched voice and making wild gestures, the cab driver appears to be out of control, or so the officer believes.[39]

As the officer steps from his car, he yells for the cab driver to stop, but the cabbie continues to walk toward the officer. When he is about 2 feet away, the officer orders the cabbie to step back and keep his hands to his sides. But the cab driver continues to babble and advance toward the officer. He does not make eye contact and appears to be talking to the ground.

Finally, the officer commands the cab driver to place his hands on the patrol vehicle and spread his feet. What began as a routine stop for a traffic violation culminates in charges of disorderly conduct and resisting arrest.

This scene typifies many of the encounters that take place daily in the United States between law enforcement personnel and people of other cultures. A simple traffic violation escalates out of control and becomes more than a matter of communication and common sense. It represents two icebergs—different cultures—colliding with devastating results.

To understand the final outcome, we need to examine the breakdown in nonverbal communication. First, most Americans know to remain seated in their vehicles when stopped by the police. But the Nigerian exited his cab because he wanted to show respect and humility by not troubling the officer to leave his patrol car. The suspect used his own cultural rule of thumb (common sense), which conveyed a completely different message to the officer, who viewed it as a challenge to his authority.

The Nigerian then ignored the command to "step back." Most likely, this did not make any sense to him because, in his eyes, he was not even close to the officer. The social distance for conversation in Nigeria is much closer than in the United States. For Nigerians, it may be less than 15 inches, whereas 2 feet represents a comfortable conversation zone for Americans.

Another nonverbal communication behavior is eye contact. Anglo-Americans expect eye contact during conversation; the lack of it usually signifies deception, rudeness, defiance, or an attempt to end the conversation. In Nigeria, however, people often show respect and humility by averting their eyes. While the officer saw the cabbie defiantly "babbling to the ground," the Nigerian believed he was sending a message of respect and humility.

Most likely, the cab driver was not even aware of his exaggerated gestures, high-pitched tone of voice, or rapid speech. But the officer believed him to be "out of control," "unstable," and probably "dangerous." Had the cab driver been an Anglo-American, the officer's reading of the cabbie's nonverbal behavior would have been correct.

One of the primary results of a breakdown in communications is a sense of being out of control, yet in law enforcement, control and action are tantamount. Unfortunately, the need for control combined with the need to act often makes a situation worse. "Don't just stand there. Do something!" is a very Anglo-American admonition.

With the Nigerian cab driver, the officer took control using his cultural common sense when it might have been more useful to look at what was actually taking place. Of course, in ambiguous and stressful situations, people seldom take time to truly examine the motivating behaviors in terms of culture. Rather, they view what is happening in terms of their own experiences, which is ethnocentric—and usually wrong.

Law enforcement professionals need to develop cultural empathy. They need to put themselves in other people's cultural shoes to understand what motivates their behavior. By understanding internal cultures, they usually can explain why situations develop the way they do. And if they know their own internal cultures, they also know the reasons behind their reactions and realize why they may feel out of control.

Here's another scenario. During face-to-face negotiations with police at a local youth center, the leader of a gang of Mexican-American adolescents suddenly begins to make long, impassioned speeches, punctuated with gestures and threats. Other members of the group then join in by shouting words of encouragement and agreement.

A police negotiator tries to settle the group and get the negotiations back on track. This only leads to more shouting from the Chicano gang members. They then accuse the police of bad faith, deception, and an unwillingness to "really negotiate."

Believing that the negotiations are breaking down, the police negotiator begins to leave, but not before telling the leader, "We can't negotiate until you get your act together where we can deal with one spokesperson in a rational discussion about the issues and relevant facts."

At this point, a Spanish-speaking officer interrupts. He tells the police negotiator, "Negotiations aren't breaking down. They've just begun."

Among members of certain ethnic groups, inflammatory words or accelerated speech is often used for effect, not intent. Such words and gestures are a means of getting attention and communicating feelings.

For example, during an argument, it would not be uncommon for a Mexican American to shout to his friend, "I'm going to kill you if you do that again." In the Anglo culture, this clearly demonstrates a threat to do harm. But in the context of the Hispanic culture, this simply conveys anger. Therefore, the Spanish word *matar* (to kill) is often used to show feelings, not intent.

In the gang scenario, the angry words merely indicated sincere emotional involvement by the gang members, not threats. But to the police negotiator, it appeared as if the gang was angry, irrational, and out of control. In reality, the emotional outburst showed that the gang members wanted to begin the negotiation process. To them, until an exchange of sincere emotional words occurred, no negotiations could take place.

Each culture presents arguments differently. For example, Anglo-Americans tend to assume that there is a short distance between an emotional, verbal expression of disagreement and a full-blown conflict. African Americans think otherwise.[40,41] For African Americans, stating a position with feeling shows sincerity. However, white Americans might interpret this as an indication of uncontrollable anger or instability and, even worse, an impending confrontation. For most African Americans, threatening movements, not angry words, indicate the start of a fight. In fact, some would argue that fights do not begin when people are talking or arguing but rather when they stop talking.

Anglo-Americans expect an argument to be stated in a factual–inductive manner. For them, facts presented initially in a fairly unemotional way lead to a conclusion. The greater number of relevant facts at the onset, the more persuasive the argument.[42]

African Americans, on the other hand, tend to be more affective–intuitive. They begin with the emotional position, followed by a variety of facts somewhat poetically connected to support their conclusions. African Americans often view the mainstream presentation as insincere and impersonal, while white Americans see the black presentation as irrational and too personal. Many times, arguments are lost because of differences in style, not substance. Deciding who's right and who's wrong depends on the cultural style of communication and thinking used.

Differences in argumentative styles add tension to any disagreement. As the Chicano gang leader presented his affective–intuitive argument, other gang members joined in with comments of encouragement, agreement, and support. To the police negotiator, the gang members appeared to be united in a clique and on the verge of a confrontation.

Sometimes Anglo-Americans react by withdrawing into a superfactual–inductive mode in an effort to calm things down. Unfortunately, the emphasis on facts, logical presentation, and lack of emotion often comes off as cold, condescending, and patronizing, which further shows a disinterest in the views of others.

Law enforcement officers should remember that racial and cultural perceptions affect attitudes and motivate behavior. In close-knit ethnic communities, avoiding shame is very important. Then, too, loss of individual dignity and respect often comes with loss of economic means and wealth. In the community policing model described in Chapter 2, Policing Today police officers are being asked to confront a myriad of social and criminal problems (e.g., juvenile runaways, neighborhood disputes, vagrants, gangs, and homeless people). They often find themselves acting the role of mediator or facilitator between conflicting or competing groups. Their goal is to bring about compromise and share other potential resources in the community.

In complex urban societies, there is no assumption of indirect responsibility. If a matter must be resolved by intervention, then the police must appear neutral and service-oriented for the greater good. Resolution is determined by a decision of right or wrong based on the facts or merits of the case. Compromise and respect for individual dignity, racial pride, and cultural heritage must characterize the communication process of the police.

Because of naive assumptions, the criminal justice community seldom views cross-cultural awareness and training as vital, yet as society and the law enforcement workforce become more diverse, the ability to manage cultural diversity becomes essential. Those agencies that do not proactively develop cultural knowledge and skills fail to serve the needs of their communities. More important, however, they lose the opportunity to increase the effectiveness of their officers.

Unfortunately, cross-cultural training in law enforcement often occurs after an incident involving cross-cultural conflict. If provided, this training can be characterized as a quick fix, a once-in-a-lifetime happening, when in reality it should be an ongoing process of developing awareness, knowledge, and skills.

At the very least, officers should know what terms are the least offensive when referring to ethnic or racial groups in their communities. For example, most Asians prefer not to be called Orientals. It is more appropriate to refer to their nationality of origin, such as Korean American assuming the officer is positive about their nationality of origin.

Likewise, very few Spanish speakers would refer to themselves as Hispanics. Instead, the term "Chicano" is usually used by Mexican Americans, while the term "Latino" is preferred by those from Central America. Some would rather be identified by their nationality of origin, such as Guatemalan or Salvadoran.

Many American Indians resent the term "Native American" because it was invented by the U.S. government. They would prefer being called American Indian or being known by their tribal ancestry, such as Crow, Menominee, or Winnebago.

The terms "black American" and "African American" can usually be used interchangeably. However, "African American" is more commonly used among younger people.

Law enforcement executives need to weave cross-cultural awareness into all aspects of law enforcement training and realize it is not enough to bring in a "gender

Quick Facts

Cultural Diversity Training in Police Academies Is the Norm

Ninety-five percent of police training academies included cultural diversity as a core component of their curriculum in 2002, the last year for which data were available. A median of 14 hours of instruction in cultural diversity was reported.

Source: Matthew J. Hickman, "State and Local Law Enforcement Training Academies, 2002," Bureau of Justice Statistics, U.S. Department of Justice (2005).

expert" after someone files sexual harassment charges or a "race expert" after a racial incident occurs. Three-hour workshops on a specific topic do not solve problems. Cross-cultural issues are interrelated; they cannot be disconnected.

What can the law enforcement community do to ensure a more culturally aware workforce? To begin, law enforcement professionals must know their own culture. All personnel need to appreciate the impact of their individual cultures on their values and behaviors. Sometimes, the best way to gain this knowledge is by intensively interacting with those who are culturally different. However, law enforcement professionals must always bear in mind that culture, by definition, is a generalization. Cultural rules or patterns never apply to everyone in every situation.

The next step is to learn about the different cultures found within the agency and in the community. However, no one should rely on cultural-specific "guidebooks" or simplistic dos and don'ts lists. While such approaches to cultural awareness are tempting, they do not provide sufficient insight and are often counterproductive.

First, no guidebook can be absolutely accurate, and many cover important issues in abstract or generic terms. For example, several nations constitute Southeast Asia. Therefore, when promoting cultural awareness, law enforcement agencies should concentrate on the nationality that is predominant within their respective communities—that is, Vietnamese, Laotian, Cambodian, and so on. At the same time, these agencies should keep in mind that cultures are complex and changing. Managing cultural diversity also means being able to adjust to the transformations that may be occurring within the ethnic community.

Second, relying on a guidebook approach can be disastrous if it does not provide the answers needed to questions arising during a crisis situation. It is much more useful to have a broad framework from which to operate when analyzing and interpreting any situation. Such a framework should focus on internal, not just external, culture. Knowing values, beliefs, behaviors, and thought patterns can only assist law enforcement professionals when dealing with members of ethnic communities.

Law enforcement professionals should also understand the dynamics of cross-cultural communication, adjustment, and conflict. When communication breaks down, frustration sets in. When this happens, law enforcement reacts. This presents a potentially dangerous situation for officers because of the emphasis placed on always being in control. Understanding the process of cross-cultural interaction gives a sense of control and allows for the development of coping strategies.

Finally, law enforcement professionals should develop cross-cultural communicative, analytic, and interpretive skills. Awareness and knowledge are not enough. Knowing about the history and religion of a particular ethnic group does not necessarily allow a person to communicate effectively with someone from that group. The ability to communicate effectively can be learned only through experience, not by reading books or listening to lectures. At the same time, being able to analyze and interpret a conflict between people of different cultures can also be mastered only through experience.

Critical Thinking Questions

1. What are some of the difficulties associated with using family members or neighbors as interpreters when the police have to respond to a call for service?
2. Describe a scenario in which multi-cultural issues might complicate a police–citizen interaction. How would you address this issue as an administrator?

Focus on Policy

Hartford, Connecticut, Police Department Implements Cultural Sensitivity Training

Cultural sensitivity training was ordered for all Hartford, Connecticut, police supervisors following a complaint from an officer who claimed his lieutenant had issued him racially charged instructions during a roll call. The two-hour training block put together by the department and one of Hartford's community organizations had already been given to community service officers, their supervisors, and the incoming recruit class when Chief Patrick J. Harnett received a written complaint from Officer John Szewczyk, Jr., stating that his supervisor, Lieutenant Stephen Miele, had told him to go after people who do not belong downtown. Officers had been told to be more aggressive in an attempt to stanch an increase in downtown burglaries. When Szewczyk asked Miele exactly what he meant, the officer said he was told, "If they aren't white and they aren't wearing a suit I'd better have them in the back of my car and find something to arrest them for." An internal investigation found insufficient evidence to sustain the allegation of biased policing; however, Miele was demoted to sergeant for having retaliated against Szewczyk and another officer who sought an explanation of his orders.

In addition to diversity training, Harnett promised a revision of the agency's general orders clarifying language on racial profiling and officers' encounters with residents. It was necessary, he said, because biased policing was "an extremely important concern of the Hartford community." The program involves a facilitated discussion between members of the community and the department led by its Police Officer Standards and Training Commissions (POST) certified instructor in conflict management. Presented with a question, participants break up into smaller groups for discussion, then return with their thoughts to the larger groups. Agency representatives say they want police officers and community representatives to see each other through each others' eyes. The next step for the agency is to take the training departmentwide.

Source: "Hartford Takes Another Crack at Cultural Sensitivity Training," *Law Enforcement News*, fall 2004, pp. 1, 10.

ORAL OR WRITTEN COMMUNICATION

Suiting the Medium to the Recipient

Although a potentially great variety of media are available for issuing orders, the individual issuing the orders is generally forced to choose from among a few existing ones that have nothing more than tradition in their favor. When certain media have become established, all subsequent material is made to fit them. If, for example, an organization has a personnel policy manual, it may become the pattern to announce through a routine revision of the manual even those changes that are of immediate and crucial interest to the employees. A change in the design of an application form would not elicit widespread interest, but a new system for computing vacation allowances would interest everyone. Such differences in interest value are important factors in the proper selection of media, but the desired medium must be available in the first place.

Written Communication

There tends to be considerable confidence in the written word within complex organization, in part because it establishes a permanent record. Therefore, police administrators increasingly rely on written communication as their dominant medium for communication. The variety of duties that police officers perform, in addition to the officers' wide discretion in handling them, help account for the proliferation of written directives. The breadth of police duties and functions generates a tremendous number of tasks and situations that are potential topics of written guidelines. When compounded by the need for discretion, simple, straightforward directives are rarely possible. Instead, lengthy directives specifying numerous factors and offering preferred responses for different combinations of those factors are much more common.[43]

The tendency to promulgate rules, policies, and procedures to enhance direction and control has been exacerbated by three contemporary developments. One is the requirement for administrative due process in police discipline, encouraged by court rulings, police officer bill of rights legislation, and labor contracts. More and more, disciplinary action against police employees necessarily follows an orderly process and must demonstrate violations of specific written rules. Thus, police departments increasingly feel the need to have written rules prohibiting all kinds of inappropriate behavior they want to punish, along with written procedures outlining the disciplinary grievance processes.

Another development motivating police departments to establish written directives is civil liability. Lawsuits against local governments, police departments, and police managers for the wrongful acts of police officers have become more common in recent years. Written guidelines prohibiting certain acts provide a principal defensive avenue against civil litigation. In essence, police managers try to show that it was not their fault that officers erred. However, written policies and procedures are needed to make this avenue of defense available.

A third stimulus is the law enforcement agency accreditation movement. Although less than 10 percent of all police departments are presently accredited, many are either working toward accreditation or using the accreditation standards as a model for improvement. Agencies pursuing accreditation or simply looking to the program for guidance are clearly and strongly influenced by the possibility of enhancing their own policies and procedures.[44] For a more detailed discussion of the Commission on Accreditation for Law Enforcement Agencies, see Chapter 4, Politics and Police Administration.

The trend to rely on written communication as the principal medium for the transmittal of information also occurs quite frequently when dealing with individuals or groups outside the police department. Even in those cases for which the initial contact is made orally, a follow-up letter or memo is frequently filed in order to create a record of the communication. Such records are becoming routine partly as a result of the realization that they provide the greatest protection against the growing numbers of legal actions taken against police departments by citizens, activists, and interest groups.

Oral Communication

Oral communication offers some distinct advantages to both the sender and the receiver. The recipient of an oral order can probe for exactness wherever the meaning is not entirely clear, provided that the individual is not too unfamiliar with the subject matter. The recipient of the information may ask for a clarifying or confirming statement in writing, a sketch or a chart, or a demonstration of a manual operation. In this situation, both individuals can state their case as long as the elements of give-and-take are preserved.

The person issuing an order, on the other hand, has an opportunity for immediate feedback and can see whether the order has produced understanding or confusion. The person issuing the order can probably discern the recipient's attitude and determine whether it is one of acceptance or rejection, but the attitude of the person issuing the order will also be apparent to the recipient. It appears that an oral medium is highly suitable when it is believed that an instruction will be temporary. For example, a police sergeant instructing an officer to direct traffic at an intersection because of street construction will likely not put that instruction in writing if the problem is one of short duration. However, if the construction will be of long duration, a written order may be forthcoming, specifying that an officer will be assigned to direct traffic at that location until further notice. Further, the written order may also specify additional details, such as the times the officer is expected to be at the location. Therefore, the method is sometimes dictated by the duration of the problem.

ELECTRONIC MEDIA (E-MAIL)

The number of e-mail messages sent from businesses in North America has risen from 40 billion in 1995 to an estimated 2 trillion by 2008. In addition, an estimated 25 million workers throughout the United States are connected by e-mail networks.[45,46] According to one study, executives spend at least two hours a day using e-mail, and employees send an average of 20 e-mails and receive about 30 e-mails a day. Worldwide, about 4 trillion e-mails are sent each year.[47]

In law enforcement, communications systems among agencies have become equally dependent on technology. Over 29 percent of local police agencies, employing 73 percent of all officers in the United States, use in-field computers.[48]

Enhanced information systems, driven by increased personal computer support, have led to improved statistical analyses of law enforcement issues and performance, best exemplified by programs, such as the New York Police Department's Compstat (Computerized Analysis of Crime Statistics) program.[49]

For many police agencies, the technology boom is best characterized by the expansion of linkages of personal computers and the reliance on e-mail as one of the most common means of communication within the department. For many administrators, staff, and line personnel, the avalanche of e-mails has both positive and negative consequences. On the one hand, it offers a real-time, expeditious method of communication, especially over distance, and it can ensure that all of the recipients receive the same written message. On the other hand, in a number of agencies, it has replaced direct personal communication, it can become a crutch for managers and supervisors, and it often forces administrators to be tied to their desks, impacting hands-on leadership and the practice of "management by walking around."

This high-tech world is a significant stressor on law enforcement personnel, especially those in leadership and management positions. How can they best deal with it? How can they best prepare individuals and their agencies to handle the stress of high-tech communications? How can they best balance "high tech, high touch?"[50]

Personal Tactics

The stress caused by the volume and frequency of e-mails and the expected turnaround on responses necessitates the development of stress-mitigation practices and individual managers can take certain steps to ensure they efficiently handle the e-mails they receive and send.

Handling E-mail Overload

For many managers, communication via e-mail virtually ensures information overload (see Figure 9.9). Memoranda that administrative assistants historically have screened now go directly to managers, who become part of a myriad of mail lists, frequently without their request or permission in an effort by the sender to keep everyone informed.

However, similar to paper memoranda, not every piece of electronic communication demands a manager's personal attention. While requiring effort, managers should remove themselves from generic mailing lists that have little or no direct relevance to their current position; wean subordinates, and even bosses, from including

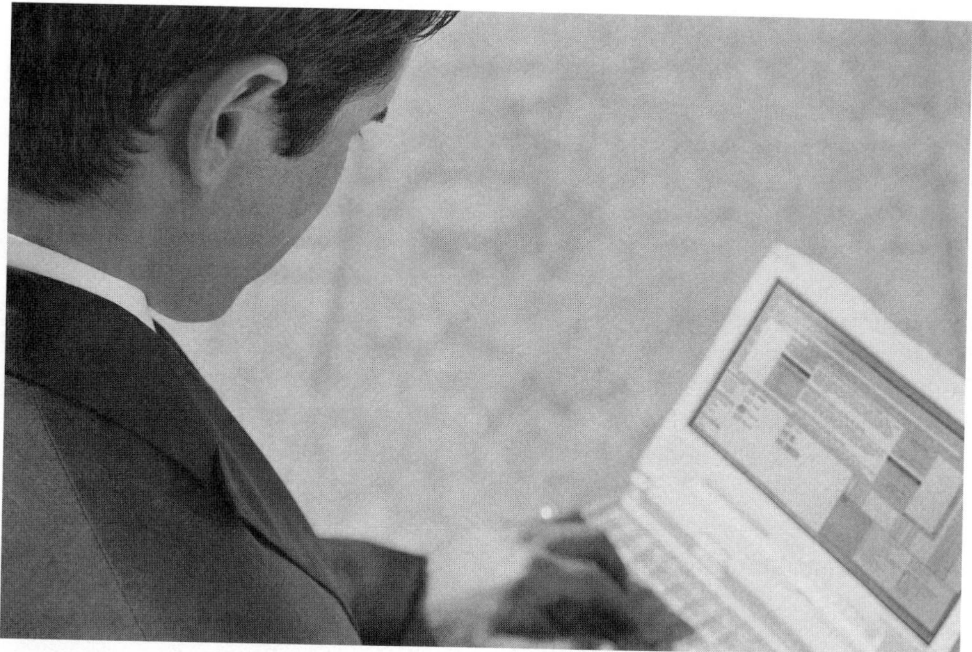

FIGURE 9.9

Enormous stress is caused by the volume and frequency of e-mails, and police managers must learn to handle this form of communication both efficiently and expeditiously.

(BananaStock/AGE Fotostock America, Inc.-Royalty-free)

non-affected personnel on mailing lists or as a "cc"; and, even on initial scanning, delete unimportant e-mails.

Overloading Others with E-mail

The admonition "screen your mail" applies not only to what people receive but also to what they send. The strength of e-mail correspondence lies in its immediacy and brevity. Short messages, especially when read on the screen, can better keep the attention of the reader and allow for the expeditious communication that e-mail offers. Further, before sending an e-mail, especially one with copies to multiple receivers, individuals should question whether it is something the recipients really need to spend time reading and whether the sender would want to receive it in a similar situation.

Treating E-mails with Etiquette

One of the strengths of electronic communication also is one of its most significant drawbacks—it allows people to respond immediately to a sender's message. For this reason, managers never should send an e-mail message or response when angry or upset. Once they hit the send icon, it is virtually impossible to retrieve that message.

The etiquette of social and business interaction applies even to electronic communications. *How* people say something in e-mail language, as in face-to-face communication, is just as important as *what* they say. While the computer affords a medium through which to vent emotions easily, executives and managers cannot afford to vent and send.

When individuals compose and send documents or messages without performing the same review appropriate for it in paper form, they risk leaving in typographical errors, grammatical mistakes, or information presented poorly or unclearly. Not only should managers reread electronic mail before sending it, but they should print it and read it aloud to reduce both errors and embarrassment.

Ensuring E-mail Efficiency

Time-management courses regularly encourage managers to streamline their process of handling written correspondence and, as a result, improve their efficiency. To this end, managers are encouraged to handle paper only once, write notes with assignments directly on the memorandum or document, and keep their inbox at a manageable level.

Some of the same advice can apply to electronic correspondence. To be most effective, managers in the electronic world should avoid handling an e-mail more than once. They should open it, respond to the sender or refer/forward it to a more appropriate respondent or staff member, or, if necessary, defer action, pending a more appropriate time or further information and let the original sender know immediately and electronically the action that they have taken. Managers also should avoid letting the electronic inbox build to a level higher than that accepted or tolerated for a paper inbox. Unless the electronic inbox is used as a "tickler system," it serves as a temporary holding device, not a permanent means of storage.

Avoiding Computer Stress at Home

The ease of accessing agency electronic systems via laptop computers, the volume of e-mails received at all hours by many managers, and the expectations of upper-level executives encourage managers to take their computers home on a regular basis. For many, it is far easier to work on electronic correspondence and projects at home than to face the electronic inbox every day.

However, from a stress-management perspective, while the practice of taking a laptop home may alleviate some short-term stressors, it actually can compound job stress when done on a regular basis. One of the most effective methods to alleviate stress is to assure a proper break from work issues and to get appropriate, and necessary, relaxation. Working in an office for 10 to 12 hours per day, as many managers do, and handling office work at home for an additional several hours fail to provide that necessary break. With a family at home, this type of behavior fosters even more stress.

Organizational Strategies

What can an organization do to control the stress caused by a rapidly changing electronic world? First, it is important to recognize that stress management often begins with, and is frequently caused by, management expectations and administrative practices. An agency's upper-level managers set the tone for both expected business practices and acceptable stress-management techniques. By their overt actions, e-mail habits, and, sometimes even more telling, their unvocalized but transparent attitudes, they iterate accepted uses of e-mail communication, established business protocols, and an unexpected level of reliance on and response to electronic communication within the organization.

These executives also define the ways in which employees may successfully deal with the stress of the electronic organization. In agencies that view e-mail as a highly advanced tool to get the job done but one clearly secondary to effective interpersonal skills and a balanced personal/professional life, the stress on employees may be less pronounced. In other agencies, employees throughout the organization are expected to have an office-connected computer at home because the highest-level executives may send messages at any time of the day or night.

Further, organizations should provide adequate training in computer use and etiquette for managers, as well as for line personnel. Managers often assume that employees, particularly younger persons, possess strong working knowledge of computers and programs, yet, while many colleges expect a certain level of computer literacy, many non-college-educated entry-level employees may lack the expected or desired minimum computer skills. Even higher-level managers who developed in their jobs prior to the consistent use of computers may lack more basic skills due to the commitments of their current jobs and demands as they rose in the organization.

Proper training, then, becomes the issue. As part of the new employees orientation process, managers should assess the recruits' computer skills. They should build agency training around the basic needs for each position. This approach avoids boring new employees with a regurgitation of lessons they already have learned and have demonstrated and ensures a minimum level of computer skills for all personnel.

Additionally, as employees advance into and through management ranks, an organization should identify and reward expected computer competencies. Agencies should ensure that ranking officers also have professionally adequate computer skills, just as they establish the minimum qualification level for personnel in other areas, such as firearms and fitness.

Finally, the organization should clearly define accepted e-mail practices and electronic etiquette. Employees should understand the rules for computer use within the agency and be held accountable for complying with those rules. A variety of websites offer helpful advice and practical guidelines for enhancing electronic communication.

Critical Thinking Questions

1. What are the advantages of combining both oral and written orders?
2. Describe how technology has led to increased stress on law enforcement personnel.
3. What 10 tips are helpful in successful e-mail correspondence?

Quick Facts

10 Tips for Successful E-mail Business Correspondence

- Maintain professionalism in e-mail correspondence, as in any other business correspondence; business etiquette does not change when a message is digitized.
- Respond to e-mail promptly, even if only to acknowledge initial receipt and that a more detailed response will follow.
- Check e-mail frequently, but do not allow it to interrupt other scheduled tasks.
- Read and reread e-mails for quality, tone, grammar, spelling, and punctuation before sending them. Do not rely solely on spell check to catch errors.
- Remember that e-mail is not private correspondence and easily can become public without intent or consent. It is a permanent record of written communication.
- Do not use business e-mail for jokes or frivolous messages.
- Deal with personal or sensitive issues in person, not through an impersonal electronic medium.
- Use business e-mail as a means to get information to a number of people in an expeditious fashion and to quickly involve others, but do not send e-mails to persons who do not need to receive it.
- Use caution when responding to e-mails. How something is said in e-mail language is just as important as what is said. No matter how emotional the issue or the contents of the e-mail received and the resultant need to verbalize emotions, do not vent and send.
- Treat an e-mail inbox similar to a paper one: review the document, act on it, and move on.

Source: James D. Sewell, "Handling the Stress of the Electronic World," *FBI Law Enforcement Bulletin,* August 2003, p. 14.

CHAPTER REVIEW

1. Discuss the elements that make up the communication process.
The first element in the communication process is the sender. The sender is the individual attempting to send a message to another. Next is the message. The message is the purpose or idea to be conveyed by the sender, and it is the heart of the communication event. The third element is the channel, also known as the medium. The channel is the form that the message takes, such as verbal, written, or a combination. The receiver is the next component of the communication process. This party must receive the message and understand it properly to complete the communication. The feedback is a message sent back from the receiver; it includes the reactions of the receiver. Understanding the environment is another important element of the communication process, as environmental factors can have a tremendous influence. The final element, noise, is anything that disrupts the communication process.
2. Describe sender-caused barriers, receiver-caused barriers, and other barriers in communications.
Sender-caused barriers include instances in which the sender is unclear about what is to be accomplished within the message; the sender assumes incorrectly that the receiver has the knowledge necessary to understand the message and its intent; the sender does not adapt the message to the receiver; the sender uses a communication medium not suited to the message; the sender does not develop a mechanism for receiving feedback to determine if the message was understood correctly; the sender does not interpret feedback correctly or fails to clarify the message on the basis of feedback from the receiver; the sender uses language that causes the receiver to stop listening, reading, or receiving; the sender analyzes the audience incorrectly; and the sender's background, experiences, and attitudes are different from those of the receiver and the sender does not take this into account. Receiver-caused barriers include the following: the receiver is a poor listener, observer, or reader and therefore misinterprets the meaning of message; the receiver jumps to conclusions; the receiver hears or sees only certain parts of the message; the receiver tends to reject messages that contradict beliefs and assumptions; and the receiver has other concerns or emotional barriers. Other barriers to communication are noise, temperature, and other physical distractions; distance or inability to see or hear the message being sent; and the relationship between the sender and receiver.
3. List and describe the four types of organizational communication.
The first type of organizational communication is downward communication. This type of message is used by management for sending orders, directives, goals, policies, and procedures. Next is upward communication, which involves subordinates initiating communication with administrators. Horizontal communication is communication among peers. Finally, the grapevine is a subset of organizational communication that transmits informal messages across agency lines; it is a fast, highly selective, discriminatory network that relates to formal communications.
4. What are some suggestions for dynamic and persuasive oral and written communication?
Establishing credibility by being trustworthy and by being perceived as intelligent and knowledgeable is a major way to ensure the success of persuasive communication. Also important is the ability to adapt messages to the listener's interests and motivation. Next, communicators should work to persuade group members on the benefits of change by building consensus. Heavy-impact and emotion-provoking words should also be utilized to give power and force to communication. Other suggestions include backing up spoken or written messages with solid data; minimizing language errors, junk words or parasitic

words (such as "like" and "you know"), and vocalized pauses; writing front-loaded messages that are clear and concise; and using power-oriented linguistic styles as a guideline for communication.

5. Perhaps up to 90 percent of the emotional impact of a message is communicated nonverbally. What are the other means by which people communicate?
   Nonverbal communication includes body position, eye contact, facial expressions, gestures, manner of speech, and external image.
6. It is generally accepted by scholars that there are four phases in group interaction. What are they?
   The four phases in group interaction are orientation, conflict, emergence, and reinforcement. The orientation phase occurs when group members get to know each other and assess the problems that face the group. The conflict phase involves disagreement among the members of the group. The emergence phase encapsulates the shift from an atmosphere of dissent to one in which positive statements are emphasized. This allows opposing members of the group to find common ground or compromise. Finally, reinforcement is the phase in which members comment on the group's problem-solving ability.
7. What are the major differences between the way that female and male officers communicate, especially during conflict resolution?
   Females in our society are generally taught to approach conflict resolution in a more nonconfrontational, conciliatory and nonphysical manner than males. As a result, female officers may use these techniques more frequently than male officers when attempting to solve problems in the field.
8. What are the two main issues in communication between law enforcement and citizens from other cultures? How do law enforcement agencies address these challenges?
   The two main issues are language differences and cultural differences. Law enforcement agencies can address these challenges by hiring bilingual officers, providing interpreters, and instituting cross-cultural awareness training.
9. What is the dominant form of communication used by police administrators? Why?
   Police administrators rely on written communication as their dominant medium for communication because it inherently establishes a permanent record that can outline complex policies and procedures; protect against civil liability; comply with accreditation guidelines; and create protection against legal actions by outside individuals or groups.
10. What are the advantages of oral communication to both the sender and the receiver?
    Oral communication allows for the receiver to ask immediately for clarification or confirmation from the sender. It also allows the sender to obtain immediate feedback.
11. What are the advantages and disadvantages of using e-mail in law enforcement agencies?
    E-mail is a fast, real-time method of communication that bridges any distance and ensures that all recipients get the same message. However, e-mail can be relied on too heavily, replacing important personal communication and tying administrators to their desks.
12. How should management deal with the stress that electronic communication can levy on personnel?
    Management should provide training in computer use and etiquette for all levels of the organization in order to ensure that employees possess the skills needed for electronic communication. Organizations should also identify and reward expected computer competencies. Finally, management should clearly define accepted e-mail practices and electronic etiquette, so that all employees understand the rules for computer use within the agency.

KEY TERMS

Communication: the process by which senders and receivers interact in both professional and social contexts.

Culture: the beliefs and behaviors characteristic to a particular ethnic, racial, or other population group.

Downward communication: communication used by management to send orders, directives, goals, policies, and so on to employees at lower levels of the organization.

Feedback: messages sent from the receiver to the sender in a communication.

Grapevine: a system for transmitting informal information that crosses organizational lines.

Group communication: interaction among three or more individuals in a face-to-face situation where all parties have a common need that is satisfied by the exchange of information.

Horizontal communication: communication among peers within an organization.

Linguistic style: a person's characteristic speaking pattern, including word choice, pacing, and use of communication devices, such as jokes, figures of speech, anecdotes, questions, and apologies.

Noise: a distraction that affects the components of the communication process.

Nonverbal communication: unspoken messages, such as body position, eye contact, gestures, manner of speech, external image, and the use of time.

Upward communication: communication used by lower-level employees to communicate with management.

NOTES

1. R. C. Husemen, *Interpersonal Communication: A Guide for Staff Development* (Athens: University of Georgia, Institute of Government, August 1974), p. 15.
2. A. J. DuBrin, *Human Relations: Interpersonal Job-Oriented Skills,* 8th ed. (Upper Saddle River, N.J.: Prentice Hall, 2004), pp. 42–46.
3. P. V. Lewis, *Organizational Communication: The Essence of Effective Management* (Columbus, Ohio: Grid, 1975), p. 36.
4. Ibid., pp. 36–37.
5. Ibid., pp. 37–38.
6. D. Katz and R. L. Kahn, *The Social Psychology of Organizations* (New York: John Wiley & Sons, 1966), p. 239, as cited in Lewis, *Organizational Communication,* p. 38.
7. Lewis, *Organizational Communication,* p. 38.
8. R. L. Smith, G. M. Richetto, and J. P. Zima, "Organizational Behavior: An Approach to Human Communication," in *Readings in Interpersonal and Organizational Communication,* 3rd ed., ed. R. C. Huseman, C. M. Logue, and D. L. Freshley (Boston: Holbrook Press, 1977), p. 11.
9. T. L. Dahle, "An Objective and Comparative Study of Five Methods of Transmitting Information to Business and Industrial Employees" (Ph.D. diss., Purdue University, 1954), as cited in Smith et al. "Organizational Behavior," p. 12.
10. E. Planty and W. Machaver, "Upward Communications: A Project in Executive Development," *Personnel* 28 (January 1952): 304–19.
11. R. K. Allen, *Organizational Management through Communication* (New York: Harper & Row, 1977), pp. 77–79.
12. H. Fayol, *General and Industrial Administration* (New York: Pitman, 1949), p. 34.
13. Allen, *Organizational Management,* p. 78.
14. Ibid., pp. 78–79.
15. K. Davis, "Management Communication and the Grapevine," *Harvard Business Review* (September–October 1953): 43–49, as cited by Lewis, *Organizational Communication,* p. 41.
16. Lewis, *Organizational Communication,* pp. 41–42.
17. Andrew J. Dubrin, *Leadership* (New York: Houghton Mifflin, 2004), pp. 364–71, 373, 374.
18. James M. Kouzes and Barry Z. Posner, *The Leadership Challenge: How to Get Extraordinary Things Done in Organizations* (San Francisco: Jossey-Bass, 1987), p. 118.
19. Roberta H. Krapels and Vanessa D. Arnold, "Speaker Credibility in Persuasive Work Situations," *Business Education Forum* (December 1997): 24–25.
20. Stephen P. Robbins and Phillip L. Hunsaker, *Training in Interpersonal Skills: Tips for Managing People at Work* (Upper Saddle River, N.J.: Prentice Hall, 1996), p. 115.

21. Refer to Jay A. Conger, *Winning 'Em Over: The New Model for Management in the Age of Persuasion* (New York: Simon & Schuster, 2001).
22. National Law Enforcement Memorial Fund, www.usatoday.com.
23. Michael W. Mercer, "How to Make a Fantastic Impression," *HR Magazine,* March 1993, p. 49.
24. Deborah Tannen, "The Power of Talk: Who Gets Heard and Why?" *Harvard Business Review* (September–October 1995): 138–48.
25. Ibid.; "How You Speak Shows Where You Rank," *Fortune,* February 2, 1998, p. 156; "Frame Your Persuasive Appeal," *Executive Strategies,* September 1998, p. 7; "Weed Out Wimpy Words: Speak Up without Backpedaling, Qualifying," *Working Smart,* March 2000, p. 2.
26. Albert Mehrabian and M. Wiener, "Decoding Inconsistent Communications," *Journal of Personality and Social Psychology* 6 (1947): 109–14.
27. Several of these suggestions are from *Body Language for Business Success* (New York: National Institute for Business Management, 1989), pp. 2–29 and "Attention All Monotonous Speakers," *Working Smart,* March 1998, p. 1.
28. Harvey Wallace, Cliff Roberson, and Craig Steckler, *Written and Interpersonal Communication Methods for Law Enforcement* (Upper Saddle River, N.J.: Prentice Hall, 2001), pp. 39, 40. Reprinted by permission of Pearson Education, Inc., Upper Saddle River, N.J.
29. *Webster's New World Dictionary* (New York: Warner Books, 1990), p. 262.
30. See Michael Burgoon, Judee K. Heston, and James McCroskey, *Small Group Communication: A Functional Approach* (New York: Holt, Rinehart & Winston, 1974), pp. 2–3, 12, 39.
31. See Robert Ardrey, *The Social Contract* (New York: Atheneum, 1970), p. 368, where the author theorizes that the range for a natural group is 11 or 12, and Marvin E. Shaw, *Group Dynamics* (New York: McGraw-Hill, 1971), which places the maximum number of persons at 20.
32. B. Aubrey Fisher, "Decision Emergence: Phase in Group Decision-Making," *Speech Monographs* 37 (1970): 53–66.
33. Field, "The Abilene Paradox," p. 89.
34. Deborah Tannen, *You Just Don't Understand* (New York: Ballantine, 1990). Copyright © 1990 by Deborah Tannen. Reprinted by permission of HarperCollins Publishers Inc.
35. John Gray, *Men Are from Mars, Women Are from Venus* (Westport, Conn.: Harper, 1993).
36. Tannen, *You Just Don't Understand,* pp. 42–44, 149–51.
37. Harvey Wallace, Cliff Roberson, and Craig Steckler, *Written and Interpersonal Communication Methods for Law Enforcement* (Upper Saddle River, N.J.: Prentice Hall, 2001), pp. 39, 40. (This discussion of communications with other cultures was adapted with permission from this source.)
38. Spanish is not the only language that officers will encounter. For a discussion of law enforcement agencies' experiences with Chinese, see C. Fredric Anderson and Henriettee Liu Levy, "A Guide to Chinese Names," *FBI Law Enforcement Bulletin,* March 1992, p. 10.
39. This section is adapted from Brian K. Ogawa, *Focus on the Future: A Prosecutor's Guide for Victim Assistance* (Washington, D.C.: National Victim Center, 1994).
40. G. Weaver, "Law Enforcement in a Culturally Diverse Society," *FBI Law Enforcement Bulletin,* September 1992, pp. 3–7. (This discussion of cross-cultural diversity in communication was taken with modification from this source.)
41. Thomas Kochman, *Black and White Styles in Conflict* (Chicago: University of Chicago Press, 1981).
42. Edmund Glenn, D. Witmeyer, and K. Stevenson, "Cultural Styles of Persuasion," *International Journal of Intercultural Communication* 1 (1977): 52–66.
43. G. W. Cordner, "Written Rules and Regulations: Are They Necessary?" *FBI Law Enforcement Bulletin* 58, no. 5 (1989): 18.
44. S. W. Mastrofski, "Police Agency Accreditation: The Prospects of Reform," *American Journal of Police* 5, no. 3 (1986): 45–81.
45. James D. Sewell, "Handling the Stress of the Electronic World," *FBI Law Enforcement Bulletin,* August 2003, pp. 11–16. (This discussion was adapted from this source.)
46. "Drowning in E-Mail," *St. Petersburg Times,* February 18, 2002, p. 11.
47. "Get a Handle on the Technology Overload," *St. Petersburg Times,* October 28, 2001, p. 1.
48. B. A. Reaves and A. L. Goldberg, *Local Police Departments 1997* (Washington, D.C.: U.S. Department of Justice, Office of Justice Programs, 2000), p. iv.
49. For more information on Compstat, see James Larsen, "STOP CRIME: Systematic Tracking Operation Program Community Reporting Incidents More Effectively," *FBI Law Enforcement Bulletin,* November 2002, pp. 6–8.
50. John Naisbitt, *Megatrends* (New York: Warner Books, 1982), p. 39.

There's only one corner of the world you can be certain of improving and that's your own self.

—Aldous Huxley

CHAPTER 10

HUMAN RESOURCE MANAGEMENT

OUTLINE

- Introduction
- Functions of the Human Resource Management Unit
- Police Personnel Selection and the Americans with Disabilities Act
- The Police Personnel Selection Process
- The Recruit Academy, Probationary Period, and Career Status
- Special Gender Issues
- College Education for Police Officers
- The Fair Labor Standards Act
- The Family Medical Leave Act
- Performance Evaluation
- Salary Administration
- Assessment Centers
- The Administration of Discipline
- The Internal Affairs Unit
- Retirement Counseling
- Chapter Review
- Key Terms
- Notes

OBJECTIVES

1. List the major functions of the human resource management unit.
2. Explain the significant provisions of the Americans with Disabilities Act.
3. Discuss the two schools of thought about physical ability testing.
4. Understand why law enforcement agencies use the polygraph in pre-employment screening.
5. Understand the difference between oral interviews and oral boards.
6. Discuss why police agencies use a multitude of psychological tests to determine candidate's adequacy for police officer selection.
7. Understand the function the field training officer serves in relation to new officers.
8. Discuss the problems that contribute to the attrition of women during police academy training.
9. Explain the advantages of a college education for police officers.
10. Understand what provisions of the Fair Labor Standards Act apply most direc to police officers.
11. Describe what rights the Family Medical Leave Act gives to police officers.
12. List the major purposes of performance evaluations.
13. Discuss what criteria must be met for a performance appraisal system to be acceptable by the courts.
14. Understand the objectives of pay plans.
15. Discuss what an assessment center is.
16. Discuss some of the factors that should be considered in applying discipline.
17. List five profiles of violence-prone officers.
18. Describe the three basic phases of the early warning system.
19. Understand the two philosophies guiding the assignment of persons to investigate personnel complaints.
20. Discuss when chemical testing is warranted during a personnel investigation.
21. Understand what types of issues are inherent in a law enforcement officer's life stage of retirement.

INTRODUCTION

Most authorities who examine the major issues involved in law enforcement come to the same inescapable conclusion—namely, that the ability of a police department to provide high-quality service to its citizens and to solve its major operating problems is significantly affected by the quality of its personnel and the ways in which they are managed.

As police departments have attempted to address external problems, such as rising crime rates, and internal problems, such as the effectiveness of their operating units, they have undertaken many studies, entertained numerous theories, launched various experiments, and invested heavily in new equipment. In most of these efforts, however, it has been apparent that eventual success depends on the critically important element of human resources. Sound personnel practices, therefore, are the single most vital consideration in the quest for effective law enforcement.[1]

In this chapter, we will start by discussing the human resource management unit as well as the basic responsibilities of the unit and the processes employed in selecting police officers. In conjunction with this process, we will also discuss the many aspects of the Americans with Disabilities Act and the most recent Supreme Court decisions that impact law enforcement, as well as other government agencies.

The police personnel selection process is certainly one of the more important aspects of human resource management, and in this chapter we will discuss the major aspects of the selection process, including guidelines provided by the Equal Employment Opportunity Commission, the entrance examination, reverse discrimination, physical ability testing, the polygraph, the character investigation, the oral board, and psychological testing.

In this chapter, we will also examine the role of the police academy and the role of the field training officer in the training of recruit officers. We will also discuss special gender issues and outline steps that can be taken to be certain the recruit basic training academy and field training officer programs are not intentionally or inadvertently creating biases that can result in a disproportionately large number of women being washed out.

The goal of providing higher education for police officers is traced from 1929 but focuses on the real impetus of the movement, which started in the 1960s, a decade of social disruption and violence. These include a police confrontation with students at universities and with anti–Vietnam War protestors.[2] Within this context, we will discuss the advantages of college education for police officers.

As a microcosm of the community, law enforcement agencies increasingly include among their personnel more women and ethnic and racial minorities. In this chapter, we will provide the police administrator with a self-assessment scale to assist in measuring his or her own agency's responsiveness to diversity. We will also make specific suggestions on ways to defuse racism and will discuss assignments based on diversity.

Two federal laws that have dramatically affected law enforcement and that will be discussed in this chapter are the Fair Labor Standards Act and the Family Medical Leave Act. These two laws have had a profound impact on law enforcement agencies.

One of the more controversial components of human resource management is the performance evaluation, which is often disliked and misunderstood by both the individuals doing the evaluation and those being evaluated. In this chapter, we will discuss the importance of the process and the benefits to be derived from doing it properly and some common rater errors.

We will also discuss one of the most important components of human research management—salary administration—as well as what a pay plan should accomplish.

The use of assessment centers for both the selection and the promotion of police officers has dramatically increased in recent years. In this chapter, we will discuss the training of assessors and why this tool can be such a valuable one in identifying highly qualified personnel while eliminating those who do not meet the high standards required of a specific position. We will provide a number of suggestions on the implementation of an assessment center as well as the role to be played by assessors.

We will also address the failures that administrators must consider when applying discipline to employees who sometimes abuse their authority or act in ways to bring discredit to their agencies. To assist police administrators in identifying certain high-risk employees, we will also discuss an early warning system that is a data-based management tool used to identify officers whose behavior is problematic. We will also suggest ways to intervene to correct those behaviors.[3]

Every police agency needs a functional internal affairs unit, or professional standards unit, or a person who can investigate allegations of misconduct or serious violations with agency policies. In this chapter, we will suggest ways in which the internal affairs unit can be organized to maximize its efficiency.

Finally, we will discuss retirement counseling for police officers and all the inherent problems associated with this career-ending event and will identify services a police agency can provide to assist with this transition.

FUNCTIONS OF THE HUMAN RESOURCE MANAGEMENT UNIT

In larger departments, a sound **human resource management unit** needs to be adequately staffed and financed and should report through the chain of command to the police chief. This unit must be specialized and have authority and responsibility to carry out its mission.[4] As a result of such factors as departmental philosophy, historical precedent, the chief executive's preference, intradepartmental power politics, and legislative requirements, broad statements about the functions of a human resource management unit are somewhat difficult to make.[5] However, the unit is generally responsible for the following:

1. Preparing policy statements and standard operating procedures relating to all areas of the administration of human resources, subject to the approval of the chief executive of the agency.
2. Advising the chief executive of the department and other line officials on personnel matters.
3. Maintaining a performance evaluation system.
4. Creating an integrated management information system (MIS) that includes all necessary personnel data, such as those pertaining to performance evaluation.
5. Maintaining an energetic and results-producing program to recruit qualified applicants.
6. Administering a carefully conceived process of selection—that is, administering a valid system for distinguishing those who are to be employed from those who may not be employed.
7. Establishing criteria for promotion to the various ranks, along with a method for determining the relative qualifications of officers eligible for such appointments.

8. Conducting a multi-faceted staff development program for personnel of all ranks from entry level through executive level.
9. Developing and administering position classification and assignment studies to form the basis for staff assignment and evaluation.
10. Developing a plan of adequate compensation, distributed fairly among rank assignments according to difficulty and responsibility of assignments and including provisions for differentials based on special assignments, shifts, or outstanding performance.
11. Representing the agency during negotiations with police employee groups and at other meetings with representatives of organized employees, such as at meetings pertaining to grievances and related matters.
12. Conducting exit interviews with resigning officers to identify and subsequently correct unsatisfactory working conditions.
13. Providing advice to managers and supervisors at all levels concerning human resource problems, with special attention to leadership and disciplinary problems, and administering reviews of disciplinary actions and appeals.
14. Conducting an ongoing personnel research program.
15. Representing the police department to the central human resource management office or civil service commission.[6]

Critical Thinking Question

1. What are some reasons that many police agencies do not properly maximize their human resources? How might these issues be mitigated?

POLICE PERSONNEL SELECTION AND THE AMERICANS WITH DISABILITIES ACT

Although there are no hard-and-fast rules about the exact sequence of steps to be followed in the police hiring process, the steps themselves traditionally have been arranged in order from least to most expensive (see Figure 10.1). However, the 1990 federal **Americans with Disabilities Act (ADA)** has changed the traditional sequencing.

The ADA was enacted by Congress to eliminate barriers to disabled persons in such areas as public transportation, telecommunications, public accommodations, access to government facilities and services, and employment (see Figure 10.2). The ADA makes it unlawful to discriminate against people with disabilities in all employment practices, including recruitment, hiring, promotion, training, layoffs, pay, firing, job assignments, transfers, leave, and benefits. The ADA is applicable to both private- and public-sector employers. In 1994, all employers with 15 or more employees were covered by its provisions. Although the federal Equal Employment Opportunity Commission (EEOC) has responsibility for the job discrimination provisions of the ADA, other federal agencies, such as the Department of Transportation and the Federal Communications Commission, oversee the parts of the ADA that fall within their areas of specialization.

The ADA covers both actual and regarded disabilities. Briefly, a **disability** is defined as a "physical or mental impairment that substantially limits a major life activity." A "regarded" disability case would be exemplified by a police administrator who, believing an employee had a disability, made an adverse employment decision on that basis; the administrator would then have violated that employee's rights under the ADA, even if no disability existed. For instance, assume that Chief Joe Garcia transferred

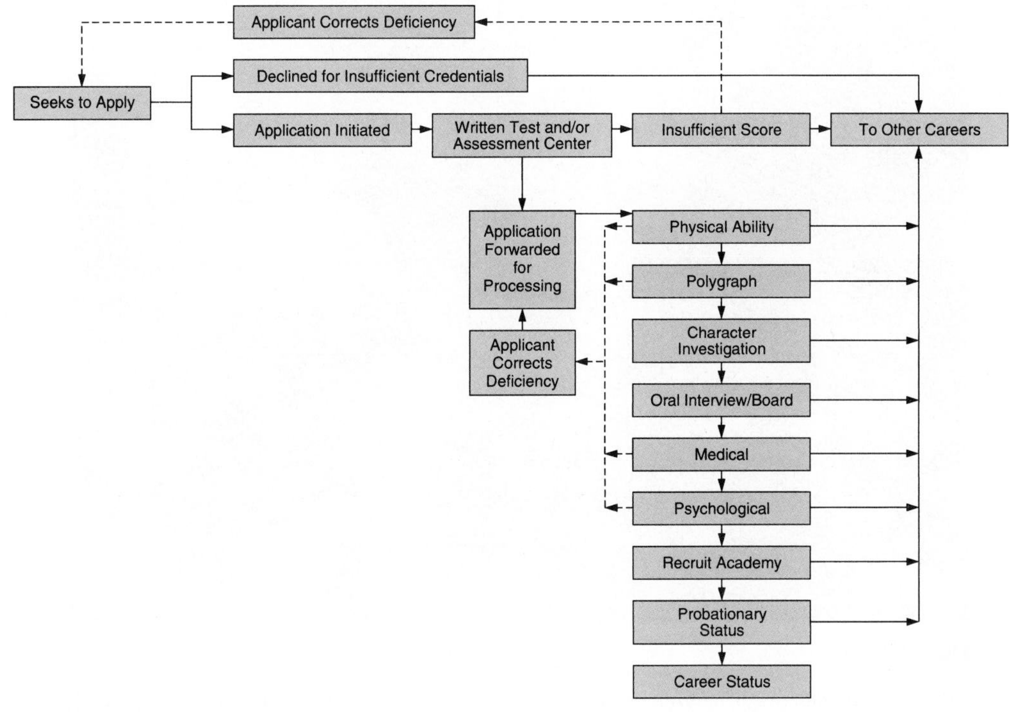

FIGURE 10.1

A model for processing police applicants.

(*Source:* L. Territo, C. R. Swanson Jr., and N. C. Chamelin, *The Police Personnel Selection Process* [Indianapolis: Bobbs-Merrill, 1977], p. 10. The original model has been modified to address changes brought about by the ADA.)

Officer Kathleen Tyler from the patrol division to a job assignment involving clerical duties in the records division because he erroneously believed she was infected with the AIDS virus and he wanted to reduce her contact with the public. If Officer Tyler learned of Chief Garcia's reasons for making the transfer, she could file a complaint under the ADA. Moreover, even if she actually tested positive for the AIDS virus, such a transfer for that reason would not be actionable unless she posed a significant health risk to others as determined by objective medical evidence and not through generalizations, fear, ignorance, or stereotyping. Also, if Officer Tyler had reached the point where she informed management of her disability or management reasonably determined that she could no longer perform field duties as a result of it, then reassignment to another, less demanding position may be required. Among the significant provisions of the ADA and the guidelines issued by the EEOC for its implementation are the following:

1. Discrimination in all employment practices is prohibited, including job application procedures, hiring, firing, advancement, compensation, training, and other terms and conditions of employment, such as recruitment, advertising, tenure, layoff, leave, and fringe benefits.[7] Job application sites must be accessible to those with disabilities. Although discrimination is prohibited, an employer is not required to give preference to a qualified applicant or worker with a disability over other applicants or workers.[8]
2. The ADA makes discrimination against individuals who have a relationship or an association with a person with a disability illegal.[9] For example, assume that

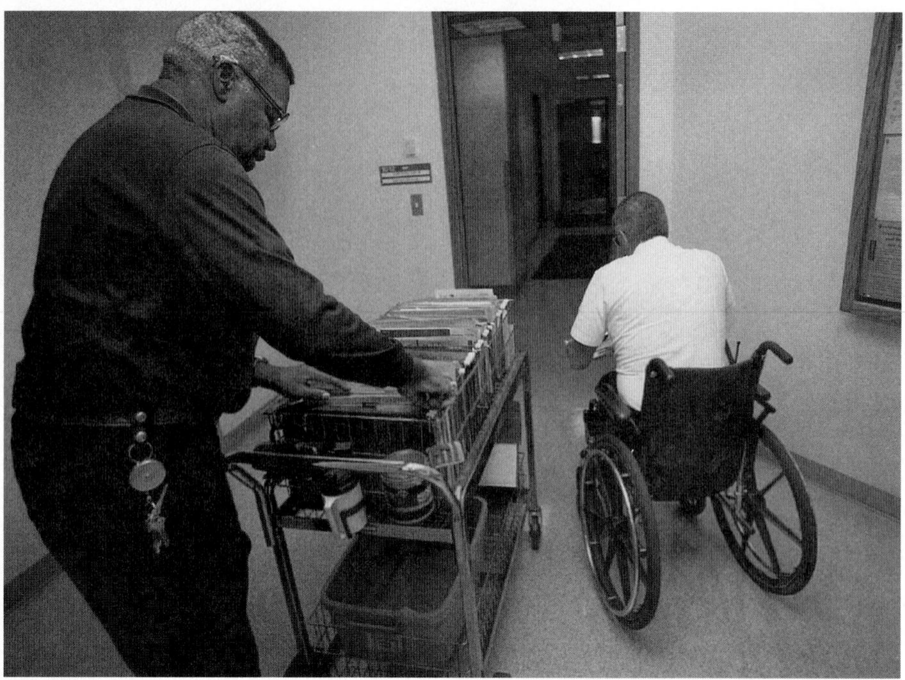

FIGURE 10.2

The Americans with Disabilities Act (ADA) was enacted by Congress with the intention of removing both physical and employment barriers for persons with disabilities. Here a police department civilian employee uses his wheelchair to get from one part of the police building to another.

(Sean Clayton/The Image Works)

Jane Johnson applies for a position in a police department for which she is qualified and that she has a disabled husband. It is illegal for the department to deny her employment solely on the basis of its unfounded assumption that she would take excessive leave to care for her spouse. Another illustration of a protected relationship or association is provided by a police officer who does volunteer work with dying AIDS patients. A chief of police who was uncomfortable with the officer's volunteer work and adversely affected any of the terms and conditions of the officer's employment would be in violation of the ADA. Similarly, police departments and other employers are prohibited from retaliating—for example, by transferring to undesirable precincts or hours of duty—against applicants or employees who assert their rights under the ADA.

3. The ADA expressly excludes certain conditions from protection,[10] including current illegal drug use, homosexuality, bisexuality, transvestitism, exhibitionism, voyeurism, gender identity disorder, sexual behavior disorder, compulsive gambling, kleptomania, pyromania, and psychoactive substance disorders resulting from current use of illegal drugs. However, former drug users who have successfully completed a rehabilitation program are covered by the ADA. Arguably, however, despite this provision, law enforcement employment could be denied to former drug users because such applicants' prior conduct raised material questions about their judgment, criminal associates, willingness to abide by the law, and character.[11]
4. As defined by the ADA, a person is disabled if that person has a physical or mental impairment that substantially limits one or more major life activities, has a record of such impairment, or is regarded or perceived as having such an

impairment, even if he or she does not actually have it. Generally, a person is disabled if the person has any physiological disorder, condition, disfigurement, anatomical loss, or mental or psychological disorder that makes the individual unable to perform such functions as caring for him- or herself, performing manual tasks, walking, seeing, hearing, speaking, breathing, learning, or working to the same extent as the average person.[12] A person is not "substantially limited" just because he or she is unable to perform a particular job for one employer or is unable to perform highly specialized professions requiring great skill or talent.[13] Protection against handicap discrimination does not include being able to work at the specific job of one's choice.[14]

5. A qualified individual with a disability is a person who meets legitimate skill, experience, education, or other requirements of an employment position that he or she is seeking and who can perform the "essential functions" of that position with or without reasonable accommodations.[15] Job descriptions are considered highly indicative of what the essential functions of a job are, and they should be drafted with considerably greater care than that used by some personnel and police departments in the past. The "essential functions" provision states that an applicant will not be considered to be unqualified simply because of an inability to perform minor, marginal, or incidental job functions.[16] If an individual is able to perform essential job functions except for limitations caused by a disability, police departments and other employers must consider whether the individual could perform these functions with a reasonable accommodation. A reasonable accommodation is any change or adjustment to a job or work environment that permits a qualified person with a disability to enjoy benefits and privileges of employment equal to those of employees without disabilities.[17] Reasonable accommodations may include the following:
   - Acquiring or modifying equipment and devices
   - Job restructuring
   - Part-time or modified work schedules
   - Reassignment to a vacant position
   - Adjusting or modifying examinations, such as physical ability tests, training materials, or policies
   - Providing readers and interpreters
   - Modifying the physical work environment[18]

Illustrations of this last point include installing elevators, widening doorways, relocating workstations, and making break rooms accessible or relocating the break room so that the employee with the disability has opportunity to interact with other police employees. Failure to provide reasonable accommodation to a known physical or mental limitation of a qualified individual is a violation of the ADA unless it creates an undue hardship on the employer's operations.[19] Undue hardship means that the accommodation would be unduly costly, extensive, substantial, or disruptive or would fundamentally alter the business of the employer.[20] Although some police departments may raise the "unduly costly" defense, the EEOC scrutinizes such claims carefully. Particularly when the accommodation needed for modified equipment, remodeled workspace, or the development of new policies and examinations is a small fraction of the overall budget, claiming undue hardship may be viewed by the EEOC as a pretext for discrimination against applicants and employees with disabilities. Among the remedies federal courts have invoked in other types of civil rights cases in which the defendants claimed an inability to pay is requiring jurisdictions to borrow money to finance the ordered remedies. The requirement to make a reasonable accommodation is generally triggered by a request from an individual with a disability.[21] Without this request, police agencies are not obligated to provide one.[22]

6. Police applicants and employees often have medical conditions that can be controlled through medication or auxiliary means. Examples are persons whose diabetes or high cholesterol is mitigated through appropriate medication. Even though their medical conditions may have no significant impact on their daily lives, such individuals are covered by the ADA.[23] The ADA does not cover employees whose impairments are temporary (e.g., a broken arm), do not substantially limit a major life activity, are of limited duration, and have no long-term effects.[24]
7. No medical inquiries can be made of an applicant, nor can any medical tests be required or conducted, before a job offer is made, although the offer can be made contingent on passing the medical test. Questioning applicants about their ability to perform job-related functions is permitted as long as the questions are not phrased in terms relating to a disability.[25] It is unlawful to ask applicants if they are disabled or the extent or severity of a disability.[26] It is permissible to ask an applicant to describe or demonstrate how, without reasonable accommodation, the applicant will perform job-related functions.[27]
8. Two other kinds of tests may also be given at this stage. Physical ability tests that demonstrate the ability to do actual or simulated job-related tasks, with or without reasonable accommodation, are permissible if given to all applicants.[28] Examples of such tests for police applicants are the trigger pull test, obstacle courses simulating police chases, and vision tests designed to determine if applicants can distinguish objects or read license plates. Employers may also require that applicants take physical fitness tests that measure their ability to do physical tasks, such as running and lifting, as long as all applicants must do so.[29] Neither test is considered a medical examination under the ADA unless applicants' physiological or psychological responses to the tests are measured.[30] It does not violate the ADA to require that applicants certify that they can safely perform these tests.[31] If such a certification is required, employers should describe the tests to the applicant and simply have his or her physician state whether the person can safely perform the tests. It is also important to understand that, if either physical agility or fitness tests screen out or tend to screen out disabled applicants, employers must be prepared to defend the tests as both job-related and consistent with business necessity.[32]
9. Applicants may also be given psychological tests that are not aimed at uncovering recognized mental disorders.[33] Psychological tests that measure such things as honesty, tastes, and habits are not considered medical examinations under the ADA.[34]
10. Polygraph examinations of applicants at the application/interview stage do not violate the ADA if no disability-related questions are asked during the exam.[35] However, to ensure accurate results, examiners generally must ask examinees prior to the exam if they are taking any medications that might affect the results. Such a question can violate the ADA because the answer is likely to elicit information regarding disabilities. Consequently, it may be wise to postpone the polygraph examination to the postconditional offer stage. Before administering any polygraph examinations, however, police administrators should consult with their legal advisers regarding their legality under state law and local labor contracts.

11. The ADA's statutory obligation to reasonably accommodate disabilities applies to the interview/application stage.[36] Employers must accommodate all applicants' known disabilities unless it would create an undue hardship on them. Employers may become aware of applicants' disabilities because it is obvious or because the applicants disclosed their disabilities in response to the employers' inquiry for the need to accommodate them during the application/interview process.

    Once the need for accommodation is demonstrated, the parties should decide what accommodations are appropriate. Typical accommodations at this stage include changing testing dates to accommodate doctor appointments, changing testing sites to those accessible by the disabled, and giving applicants with reading disabilities more time to complete written examinations. The forms of accommodation are as varied as the imaginations of employers and applicants.

    As can be seen from this discussion, the ADA limits the application/interview stage to employer inquiries and examinations designed to judge all the non–disability-related qualifications of applicants. But what if employers know at this stage that applicants are disabled? Must they ignore the disabilities entirely, even if they reasonably believe the disabilities will impact the applicants' ability to do the job?

    There are several ways employers can lawfully become aware of applicants' disabilities. The disability may be obvious, such as a lost limb or the use of a wheelchair. The applicant may have voluntarily disclosed the disability through a request for reasonable accommodation during the application/interview stage or in response to an employer's inquiries about his or her ability to perform job functions.

    The EEOC has stated that, when employers reasonably believe that applicants will need reasonable accommodation to perform job functions, they may discuss with applicants if accommodation will be needed and the form that accommodation may take.[37] After these discussions, employers may decide that they cannot accommodate the disability because the applicants cannot perform the essential functions of the job, or because the accommodation needed is unduly burdensome. If employers do not extend an offer to disabled applicants because of their disability, they must be prepared to defend their decisions against claims that they failed to hire the applicants because of the need to reasonably accommodate their disabilities.[38]

12. Once employers have judged applicants on the basis of their non–disability-related qualifications during the application/interview stage, found them qualified, and made bona fide job offers to them, the ADA permits employers to face the issue of disabilities. Employers may now inquire about disabilities, require medical examinations, and condition their employment offers on the results of these medical examinations.

    The EEOC considers job offers bona fide if they are made after employers have evaluated all the relevant non-medical information it reasonably could have gotten and analyzed it before making the offer.[39] Conditional offers do not have to be limited to current vacancies. Conditional offers are still bona fide if they are made in reasonable anticipation of future vacancies. The number of offers may even exceed the number of current and anticipated vacancies if employers can demonstrate that a percentage of offerees will likely be disqualified or will drop out of the pool.[40]

13. After making a conditional offer of employment, employers may ask applicants if they have disabilities and will need reasonable accommodation to perform the

job.[41] There is no restriction on the nature of the questions that may be asked. Consequently, employers may ask all the questions prohibited during the application/interview stage: questions regarding the existence of disabilities, workers' compensation histories, sick leave usage, or drug and alcohol addiction, as well as questions regarding general physical and mental health. The only conditions imposed on employers by the ADA are that all offerees be asked these questions and that information gathered in response to questions be kept confidential.[42]

If inquiries uncover disabilities, employers are bound by the basic requirements of the ADA. They reasonably must accommodate the disabilities unless the accommodation would pose an undue hardship.[43] If the conditional offer of employment is withdrawn because of the disabilities, employers must be prepared to show that the exclusionary criteria are not discriminatory based on disability or are job-related and consistent with business necessity,[44] that they could not reasonably accommodate the disability,[45] or that the offeree poses a direct threat to the health or safety of others.[46]

14. The ADA permits employers to require medical examinations after bona fide job offers have been made to applicants. The only conditions on these examinations are that all applicants be subject to the examinations and the results be kept confidential.

All the medical examinations barred at the application/interview stage are now permitted. There are no restrictions on the nature of these examinations, not even a requirement that they be job-related or matters of business necessity.[47]

As with postconditional offer disability-related inquiries, if medical examinations given at this stage reveal a disability and result in the offer being withdrawn, employers must be prepared to defend their decision and show that it does not discriminate against the disabled, because the disability could not be accommodated, because the criteria on which the decision was based are job-related and a matter of business necessity, or because the offeree poses a direct threat to health or safety.[48]

The Courts and the ADA

The federal Rehabilitation Act (RA) of 1973 (the forerunner to the ADA), state laws prohibiting employment discrimination on the basis of disabilities, and the ADA have formed the basis for a growing number of lawsuits against police departments on behalf of people with disabilities. The cases that follow illustrate some of the issues addressed through litigation.

In *Kuntz v. City of New Haven*,[49] plaintiff Walter Kuntz brought a suit under the RA. To establish a prima facie case of discrimination under the RA, Kuntz had to establish that (1) he was a handicapped person within the meaning of the act, (2) he was otherwise qualified for the position, (3) he was excluded or discharged from a position solely because of his handicap, and (4) the position was part of a program supported by federal funds. This last element did not require that Kuntz's individual position or the New Haven Police Department (NHPD) unit to which he was assigned be funded entirely with federal funds. This element of proof was satisfied by showing that both the City of New Haven and the NHPD received such funds. Sergeant Kuntz had suffered a heart attack four years previously and had undergone a triple bypass heart operation. Although he had passed the written and oral examinations for lieutenant, he was denied promotion twice solely because of his heart attack. The NHPD claimed that, because lieutenants can be assigned as assistant shift commanders or as shift commanders, they must be able to apprehend suspects and to engage in high-speed pursuits. However, in fact, supervisors in the NHPD were rarely involved in high levels of physical stress. Kuntz exercised regularly and had a very strong record of performance in the various positions he had held before and after his heart attack. He worked side by side with "full-duty" lieutenants and successfully performed the same assignments given to such personnel. The medical opinion was that his health was normal for a person his age. Moreover, the NHPD's adoption of community policing also provided the opportunity to assign Kuntz to one of many lieutenant positions that did not entail physical exertion. These factors were sufficient for Kuntz to overcome claims by the NHPD that his possible assignment to field duties would be dangerous to him, to other police officers, and to the public. The court held that the defendant had not shown that such risks were imminent and substantial, rising above the level of mere possibility. Kuntz was promoted to lieutenant and received back pay.

In Toledo, Ohio, police applicant Michael Bombrys was disqualified from further employment consideration because of health and safety concerns, as he was an insulin-dependent diabetic. Litigation was filed, claiming protection under the ADA, the RA, the Ohio Civil Rights Act, and the due process clause of the 14th Amendment. The city claimed that, because of his medical condition, Bombrys could become confused on duty, combative, or even unconscious. Bombrys requested an accommodation: that he be allowed to carry the means to treat himself, should it become necessary, pointing out that such an accommodation was not costly to the city, nor did it change the basic functions of a police officer. The court issued a restraining order requiring the city to allow the plaintiff to enter and complete the police academy while the litigation went on. In *Bombrys v. City of Toledo,*[50] the court held that the blanket exclusion of all insulin-dependent diabetics violated each of the protections cited in the plaintiff's suit. In so doing, the court noted that several cities do not categorically exclude diabetics from their police departments, and in these cities insulin-dependent diabetics were sent to a specialist, who evaluated their ability to perform on a case-by-case basis. When the case was decided, Bombrys had completed the academy. The court noted that, while Bombrys could not be summarily dismissed in a way that contravened the court's findings and the applicable law, the department was not prohibited from undertaking an investigation to determine if Bombrys was fit to perform the duties of a police officer. This was important in light of the fact that, while on duty, Bombrys suffered an insulin reaction and had to be taken to a hospital.

In *Champ v. Baltimore County,*[51] a disabled police officer, James Champ, could not use one of his arms because of an on-duty motorcycle accident. Over the next 16 years, the police department used Champ in different light-duty assignments. Subsequent to his accident, Champ was recertified by the Maryland Police Training Commission in the driving of emergency vehicles and the use of firearms. Because of budgetary constraints that prevented the hiring of new officers, the police department began channeling long-term light-duty officers into non–law enforcement positions. Then the light-duty officers were replaced by newly hired full-duty officers. Champ was placed on disability leave and subsequently filed suit under the ADA. The court found for the defendant in *Champ*. In so doing, it noted that the plaintiff could not perform the essential functions of a police officer (e.g., make a forcible arrest) and that there was no reasonable accommodation that would allow him to do so. Champ was also deemed to be a direct threat to the welfare and safety of others because of his inability to perform the essential functions, since even if he were assigned to an "inside" position he could still be subject to reassignment to field duties.

As the various components of the police selection process are described in subsequent sections of this chapter, some information about how the ADA and certain other legal provisions affect them will be presented. In all cases, individuals and agencies should consult their own attorneys in order to be fully informed before deciding on a policy or course of action in such matters.

Supreme Court Limits on State Workers' ADA Access

In a landmark decision handed down on February 21, 2001, the U.S. Supreme Court ruled that two Alabama state employees do not have the right to file suit against the state under the ADA. The decision effectively says that state employees who claim they faced discrimination on the job because of their disabilities may not sue their employers for damages in federal court.

The Court held that Congress does not have the consitutional authority to subject states to such lawsuits under the ADA. The 5–4 ruling was written by Chief Justice William Rehnquist, who was joined by Justices Sandra Day O'Connor, Antonin Scalia, Anthony Kennedy, and Clarence Thomas. The decision overturned a ruling by the U.S. Court of Appeals for the 11th Circuit, which in turn had overruled a federal district court.

The case, *Board of Trustees of the University of Alabama et al. v. Garrett et al.*, was based on the job discrimination claims of Patricia Garrett and Milton Ash. Garrett, a nurse at the University of Alabama hospital, was assigned a lower-paying job after returning from breast cancer treatment. Ash, a security officer with the Alabama Department of Youth Services, claimed that he was treated adversely on the job after demanding accommodations for his chronic asthma and other medical conditions. Both were seeking monetary damages under Title I of the ADA.

The Court held that the 11th Amendment protecting a state's sovereign rights gives that state immunity over a statute such as the ADA. The Court conceded that Congress may abrogate the state's immunity only when it clearly expresses such intent, when there is substantial evidence of state discrimination, and when the remedy created by Congress is congruent and proportional to the harm done by the state. However, the majority opinion stated that the ADA's legislative record failed to show a pattern of irrational employment discrimination by states against the disabled. While Congress made a general finding in the ADA that discrimination against the disabled continues to be "a serious and pervasive problem," the incidence falls far short of suggesting a pattern of constitutional discrimination that warrants federal intervention, according to the majority opinion.

In his dissenting opinion, Justice Stephen Breyer said that the Court majority was invading the lawmaking power of Congress. He called evidence of past discrimination against the disabled "powerful" and attached a 39-page list of examples of discriminatory acts by states that a congressional task force compiled during the drafting of the ADA. Breyer was joined in his dissent by Justices John Paul Stevens, David Souter, and Ruth Bader Ginsburg.

The practical implications of the ruling for millions of state workers across the country are unclear because other legal avenues remain. For example, state employees could ask federal courts to order states to cease alleged discrimination, the EEOC could enforce the ADA on behalf of state workers, or state employees could sue for damages in state court under state disability rights laws.

Although it does not affect private-sector employees and does not change the ADA's broader requirements of access to public places for the disabled, the decision is another step in the recent effort of the Supreme Court to limit the federal government's power over state government.

In The News

Departments Employ New Tactics in Recruiting Police

Aggressive and unprecedented recruiting efforts by police departments hoping to augment their ranks have become the norm in cities around the country. Large bonuses, such as Dallas's $10,000 sign-on enticement, increased starting salaries, and unusual perks (such as down payments on homes), have become increasingly common among departments that have faced stiff competition from higher-paying alternatives to police work. The Phoenix Police Department, for example, has employed a strategic recruiting campaign in the Southern California area, highlighting the city's lower cost of living through television and newspaper advertisements (see Figure 10.3). Similarly, the Honolulu Police Department, which has struggled to find applicants in Hawaii, has sent recruiters as far away as Portland, Oregon, in hopes of luring qualified candidates to the islands. Lexington, Kentucky, administrators boosted police salaries $8,000 recently and has offered a $7,400 down payment on new homes for qualified recruits. Recruiting experts say that intensified efforts by police departments are especially prevalent in rapidly growing areas of the country, as well as by police departments that have traditionally had a hard time competing with larger cities.

Source: Kevin Johnson, "Police Recruits in Heavy Demand," *USA Today*, November 11, 2005, p. 1.

Critical Thinking Questions

1. If a police officer candidate admits to former drug use, does the ADA prohibit a police agency from barring employment due to this fact? Why or why not?
2. When are employers allowed to require medical tests for job applicants?
3. If a police officer candidate is unable to complete physical ability testing due to a disability, does the ADA protect that employee from discrimination by the police agency? Why or why not?

THE POLICE PERSONNEL SELECTION PROCESS

The recruitment of a well-qualified applicant pool is the starting place for the hiring process. This recruitment process often incorporates several strategies, including police and personnel department representatives attending job fairs at churches, colleges, military bases, and other locations, as well as actively recruiting police officers from other police departments.

The Entrance Examination: The Written Test

In 1972, Congress amended Title VII of the Civil Rights Act of 1964, and the EEOC was charged with the responsibility for administering its provisions. Title VII made it illegal to discriminate impermissibly against any person on the basis of race, sex, color, religion, or national origin in employment decisions.

A major decision was made by the Supreme Court in 1971 in *Griggs v. Duke Power Company*. The Supreme Court established the test for employment discrimination, which has since led to a major overhaul of virtually all police entrance requirements. Griggs, a black employee with the Duke Power Company, had been denied a promotion to a supervisory position on the grounds that he did not possess a high school diploma, a credential the company required for such a position. Griggs's lawyers argued that he had been a highly satisfactory employee. They also demonstrated statistically that the high school diploma requirement discriminated against black employees because far fewer black than white employees possessed such diplomas. This was not enough to show that discrimination was unconstitutional because, as the Court reasoned, it was possible that the high school diploma requirement was

FIGURE 10.3

New York City police officers are sworn in at their graduation ceremony.
(Stuart Ramson/AP Wide World Photos)

job relevant in the sense that those who possessed such a credential made better supervisors than those who did not. The Duke Power Company was not able to show that this was so, and Griggs prevailed against the company.[52]

An example of a permissible discrimination is refusing to hire a man to model women's lingerie; in this situation, hiring only women would constitute a bona fide occupational requirement. "Employment decisions" is defined broadly and includes hiring, demotion, transfer, layoff, promotion, and firing decisions. Any procedure or requirement used in making these decisions is a test and comes under the scrutiny of the EEOC. Thus, application forms, interviews, oral boards, written tests, probationary ratings, assessment centers, performance evaluations, education, background investigations, physical fitness or ability tests, and other logically related matters are all subject to EEOC review for a determination as to whether there has been an unlawful act of discrimination.

Initially, the EEOC focused on entry-level requirements and testing because in many organizations there had been little progress in hiring minorities. In more recent years, the EEOC has directed greater attention to promotions and other personnel decisions as greater numbers of minorities have been hired and are affected by such decisions. A key concern of the EEOC is whether written tests and assessment center evaluations are job-related and predictive of future job performance. A survey of employment practices in police agencies revealed that 91.9 percent of the departments responding to a survey used a written or cognitive test to determine eligibility for hiring.[53] Such written tests are relatively inexpensive, are easy to administer, and can be quickly scored. Smaller jurisdictions may lease their examinations from firms specializing in such services, whereas larger cities and counties typically use those that have been developed by their own testing specialists, who often have been educated as industrial–organizational psychologists. Written entrance tests are usually given as an "assembled examination"—all of the candidates eligible to take it are brought together at the same time. In large cities, such as New York and Chicago, 25,000 or more applicants may take the written entrance examination simultaneously at public schools and other public properties designated as examination sites.[54]

TABLE 10.1 Hypothetical Group of Candidates for Employment as Police Officers

	WHITE	BLACK	TOTALS
Took test	400	100	500
Passed	120	10	130
Failed	280	90	370
Passing rate	30%[a]	10%[b]	26%

[a]120 (white passed) ÷ 400 (total white candidates) = 30% white selection rate.
[b]10 (black passed) ÷ 100 (total black candidates) = 10% black selection rate. Adverse impact calculation: 10% (black selection rate) ÷ 30% (white selection rate) = 33.3% or less than 80% (four-fifths).

The method by which a test can be shown to be associated with subsequent performance on the job is through a process of validation, the starting point for which is a job analysis. A job analysis reveals what the important tasks are for a position, such as police officer, as well as what specific knowledge and skills are needed to perform the job well.[55] Validation is a detailed undertaking whose thorough treatment is not possible here. However, some general statements are both proper and necessary. The question "Is this test valid?" seeks to determine whether it is appropriate (valid) to make a decision about a person's ability to perform a particular job on the basis of that person's score on a particular test.

A test that discriminates against a group of prospective or current employees and cannot be shown to be valid is impermissible discrimination under EEOC guidelines. However, if a police department or another employer can show that different test scores are associated with different levels of performance on the job, then even if the test discriminates against some identifiable group, including minorities, the courts are likely to find that it is a permissible discrimination, unless some other test would adequately meet the employer's needs and produce less of a discriminatory impact.[56]

Under EEOC guidelines, discrimination in testing occurs when a substantially different rate of selection in hiring, promotion, or other employment decision works to the disadvantage of members of a racial, gender, or ethnic group. This different rate of selection is termed "adverse impact" and is impermissible unless the test or another practice has been validated. As a rule of thumb, adverse impact occurs when the selection rate for any gender, racial, or ethnic group is less than four-fifths (80 percent) of the selection rate for the group with the highest selection rate.[57] Table 10.1 illustrates how the so-called four-fifths rule is applied; in that hypothetical case, adverse impact is demonstrated and will be judged to be impermissible if the test has not been properly validated.

The four-fifths rule does not allow up to 20 percent discrimination; it is not a legal definition but rather a means of keeping attention focused on the issue. Regardless of the amount of difference in selection rates, other unlawful discrimination may exist and may be demonstrated through appropriate means. To use an extreme example, assume that the president of the local minority employees' association is very militant and vocal about his or her opposition to the current chief of police's policies. Further assume that the president's daughter applies for a job with the police department. All other applicants taking the written test mark their answers in ink, but the daughter is required to use a pencil. Later, the daughter is told that she failed the test because she left half the answer sheet blank. An examination of that sheet reveals that half her answers were erased and that the majority of the erasures involved correct responses. In this situation, an impermissible discrimination would be shown even if there were no adverse impact on minorities overall.

Reverse Discrimination

Under EEOC guidelines, all discrimination is prohibited, and there is no recognized "reverse discrimination" theory. However, when the courts mandate preferential hiring and promotional opportunities for minorities to correct for past employment practices, problems arise. Majority individuals, who are typically white males, label the preferential treatment as "reverse discrimination" and at odds with the merit principle.

In a landmark case in 1978, *Regents of the University of California v. Bakke,* the Supreme Court dealt with this issue. The case presented a challenge to the special admissions program of the petitioner to the medical school at the University of California, Davis, which was designed to ensure the admission of a specified number of students from certain minority groups. The California Supreme Court held that the special admission program was unlawful and enjoined the petitioner from considering the race of any applicant and ordered Bakke's admission. The U.S. Supreme Court ruled that special admissions programs were unlawful and directed that Bakke be admitted. According to the decision, any consideration to a race admission process must be reversed.[58,59]

However, despite this ruling, many police departments have shown preferential treatment in the hiring and promoting of both minorities and women. One of the regrettable side effects of this effort to try to overcome years of blatant discrimination is the occasional tension created between majority officers who feel they have been passed over for promotion and those who receive the preferential treatment. Despite the clear necessity to correct for long-standing discrimination in the workplace, the use of such practices is difficult for many officers to support. They feel that the "rules of the game" have been unfairly changed—that such preferential treatment needlessly endangers the public if the less able are hired or selected to lead. Even when a clearly superior minority or female officer who would be promotable under any system is selected against them, their sense of anger may lead them to denigrate the minority and female officers' very real and substantial capabilities. Criticism of preferential consideration of minorities and females to correct long-standing abuses in hiring and promoting has come from various quarters, including the U.S. Commission on Civil Rights. Although such developments made civil rights leaders uneasy about the prospect of less support for their movement, two 1989 decisions by the Supreme Court both frightened and angered them, leading many to charge that the clock on civil rights was being turned backward. In *Wards Cove Packing v. Antonio,* the Court held that minorities could not be favored in hiring decisions and that the plaintiffs must disprove the claims of the employer—in this instance, an Alaskan salmon cannery—that the adverse impact on minority hiring was based on factually neutral considerations.[60] In *Martin v. Wilks,* the Court held that majority employees in the Birmingham, Alabama, Fire Department could challenge a consent decree because they had not been parties to the negotiations that had the effect of abrogating their rights.[61] Together these decisions made challenging employment decisions and practices more difficult for minorities while facilitating challenges from majority employees of consent decrees favorable to minorities. Thus, to no small extent, the Civil Rights Act of 1991 can be viewed as an attempt to strengthen the 1972 Title VII law administered by the EEOC, as well as an effort to limit the impact of or to negate court decisions unfavorable to civil rights interests. Although the 1972 Title VII law did not allow for the award of punitive damages, the Civil Rights Act of 1991—also administered by the EEOC—does so on the following bases: (1) for employers who have more than 14 and fewer than 101 employees in each of 20 calendar weeks in the current or preceding year (referred to as the base period), up to $50,000; (2) for employers who have more than 100 and fewer than 201 employees for the base period, a cap, or limit, of $100,000 in punitive damages; (3) for employers who have more than 200 and fewer than 501 employees during the base period, $200,000; and (4) in the case of employers who have 500 or more employees during the base period, a maximum punitive damage award of $300,000.[62] Unquestionably, this punitive damage provision is a significant development. Employers will abandon many questionable practices, employees will be more likely to litigate, and plaintiffs will be less likely to be satisfied with only the traditional EEOC remedies previously available to them, such as hiring or promotion, back pay, and orders to cease using the employment practices successfully challenged. However, under the Civil Rights Act of 1991, the punitive damage provision cannot be applied to a government, government agency, or political subdivision.

Physical Ability Testing

Entry-level physical ability tests are often outdated, are not job-related, and are testing for physical requirements not needed to perform the job of a modern law enforcement officer.[63] An important consideration for a law enforcement agency in reviewing its entry-level physical ability test is whether officers who are currently performing the job can satisfactorily pass the test. By establishing a standard of physical performance for entry-level candidates, agencies are saying that a particular level of performance is necessary to do the job of a law enforcement officer. However, if current law enforcement officers do not maintain that level of physical ability and they are still effective as officers, then the level of physical performance being tested for is obviously not required to perform the tasks of the job.

Types of Physical Tests

There are basically two schools of thought about physical ability testing: general fitness and job-task-based. Under the general fitness approach, candidates are given tests that measure their general physical fitness through activities such as running and sit-and-reach. The tests are usually gender and age formed. This means that the candidate's level of performance is measured by standards relative to gender and age. Fitness tests do not have an adverse impact on women and do not purport to be job-related. Instead, they provide some measure of assurance that candidates who pass are more likely to complete training successfully and less likely to experience on-the-job injuries. Under this approach, job-related physical abilities are taught and assessed after hire during academy training.

Task-based tests simulate duties performed by law enforcement officers and measure the candidate's ability to perform those tasks within established time parameters. Examples of these tests are a dummy drag, fence climbing, tire changing, and other similar activities. It may be problematic to demonstrate that these types of tests measure abilities that are required for the job. For example, some agility tests require that candidates push a police vehicle some specified distance, climb a 6-foot wall, lift and carry a dummy, or run obstacle courses that would be challenging for most athletes, much less for police officers successfully performing their jobs. These tests typically have an adverse impact on women and therefore must be documented to be job-related and consistent with business necessity in order to minimize adverse impact to the greatest extent possible.

A third type of physical testing has begun to be used by some agencies in recent years. This type of test contains events such as a 300-meter run, a vertical jump, sit-ups, push-ups, and a 1.5-mile run. Because this test is validated using a task-based physical test, it may have the same problems associated with those tests. In addition, with this type of test, there may be significant problems with the way the connection is drawn between the test events and the physical tasks actually required on the job. In evaluating such a test, an agency should consult with an expert in employment testing as well as an independent expert in testing statistics.

Legal Issues for Physical Testing

One of the biggest obstacles to women in physical testing is upper-body strength. Is upper-body strength a bona fide occupational requirement for law enforcement officers? The law does not absolutely require or prohibit testing applicants for upper-body strength, nor does the law require upper-body strength to be measured in a

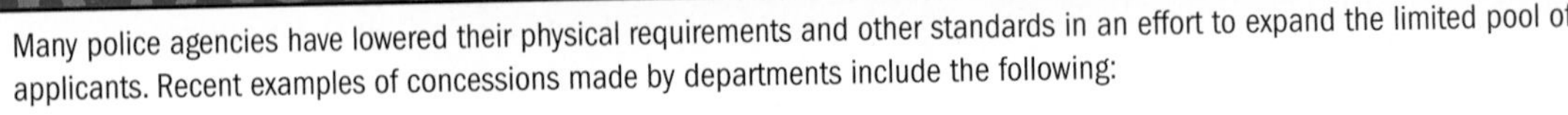

Quick Facts

Many police agencies have lowered their physical requirements and other standards in an effort to expand the limited pool of applicants. Recent examples of concessions made by departments include the following:

- Elimination of questions from written qualifying exams not directly related to the job
- Removal of difficult physical agility tests for recruits
- Shift from task-based physical testing to general physical fitness testing
- Elimination of age requirements
- Increased leniency on prior drug use, especially during a candidate's youth
- No height and weight requirements

Source: "Some Agencies Lower Standards," *American Police Beat,* October 2005, 30c.

Lowering fitness standards is one popular solution for recuitment
(Michael Newman/PhotoEdit Inc.)

particular way, if it is to be measured. However, because of inherent physiological differences between men and women, which are well established in scientific research, tests of upper-body strength typically have an adverse impact on women, meaning that men perform disproportionately better than women on such tests.

When an employment test has such an adverse impact, the law requires the employer who uses the test to demonstrate that the test is both "job-related to the position in question" and "consistent with business necessity." This almost always requires the employer to retain experts, such as industrial–organizational psychologists, statisticians, and exercise physiologists, to perform scientific studies. These studies must demonstrate both that the characteristic being tested is important to the job and that the cutoff score being used on the test is appropriate. With respect to the latter, these studies must establish that the cutoff score measures the minimum amount of the characteristic that is necessary for successful performance on the job. If the test is to be used on a rank-ordered basis, there must be substantial empirical evidence to demonstrate that higher scores on the test predict better performance on the job. Additionally, if there is another test that has less adverse impact but also serves the employer's interest in selecting qualified law enforcement officers, the law requires the employer to adopt this test. In the law, this is known as a *less discriminatory alternative test.* Employers should search for less discriminatory alternative tests early in the process of developing employment tests and should periodically renew and update this search, ideally before each recruitment and selection effort.

Preparation for Physical Testing

If a physical test is to be given, applicants should be provided information about the type of physical testing to be performed and opportunities to practice the test. This is best done through a training course given for a minimum of eight weeks immediately prior to the administration of the test. Some organizations work with local colleges and health clubs to ensure that these kinds of courses are offered. It has been demonstrated that such courses, if properly conducted, substantially improve female candidates' performance on the test. Physical tests should be used on a pass–fail basis and not be ranked by a score.

The Polygraph Test in Pre-employment Screening

The federal Employee Protection Act of 1988 prohibits the use of the polygraph in most private-sector preemployment screening, but all government bodies are exempt from this restriction.[64] However, a few state courts have prohibited even the police from using the **polygraph** in screening applicants.[65] Such state court decisions take precedent over the federal law. Nationally, 56.6 percent of police agencies reported using the polygraph in employment screening; municipal police departments are more likely (73.1 percent) than state police agencies (44.4 percent) to use it.[66] Typically, most departments (83 percent) conduct their own examinations rather than contract with a source outside the department.[67]

Law enforcement agencies using the polygraph in their pre-employment screening processes have indicated there have been many practical benefits derived from its use. First, they have found that, when it was widely publicized they were going to begin to use the polygraph to examine applicants, fewer undesirable applicants applied for positions with their agencies. This was supported by the decreased percentage of applicants who were being eliminated at the conclusion of the background investigation.

Second, although it was difficult to prove empirically, there was some indication that the polygraph reduced the rate of turnover. This was accomplished by determining whether an applicant was seriously interested in pursuing a law enforcement career or was merely trying to find temporary employment. It is unreasonable to expect a young person to make a career commitment at the time of the employment but clear-cut cases of using the agency as a "temporary meal ticket" should be dealt with accordingly. Third, by publically announcing that it uses the polygraph to screen all law enforcement applicants, the law enforcement agency is letting the community know that it is determined to hire only persons whose character and morals are above reproach. Fourth, it is psychologically beneficial to veterans of the law enforcement agency to know that rookie officers riding with them have been screened regarding their honesty, character, and morals.[68] (see Figure 10.4)

Quick Facts

Examples of Pre-employment Polygraph Questions

The following are some examples of questions polygraph examiners may ask police applicants. In most cases, the agency will specify acts which occurred after a certain age.*

Drug Use

- Did you ever sell any illegal drugs?
- Have you used any illegal drugs within the past number of months or years (to be specified by the agency)?
- Did you ever drive a vehicle under the influence of illegal drugs or alcohol?

Sexual Conduct

- Did you ever possess any child pornography?
- Did you ever expose yourself to a child?

Battery/Assault

- Did you ever deliberately strike someone?
- Did you ever start a fight with someone?
- Did you ever threaten someone with physical harm?

Robbery

- Did you ever take someone's property against his or her will?
- Did you ever carry a concealed weapon or firearm without a permit?
- Were you ever with someone when he or she committed a robbery?

Larceny

- Did you ever steal anything?
- Did you ever steal anything from an employer?
- Did you ever intentionally under-ring a sale at a place you have been employed?

Fraud/Forgery

- Did you ever intentionally write a check knowing you didn't have the money in the bank to cover it?
- Have you ever made a false report to a law enforcement authority?

Computer Crime

- Have you ever participated in theft of software?
- Did you ever attempt to access a website illegally?

For Law Enforcement Officers Past and Present

- Did you ever lie to your supervisor or any person in your agency about being sick so you didn't have to show up for work?
- Did you ever commit a policy violation and not get caught?
- Did you ever accept a bribe?

* These questions are not intended to be all inclusive.

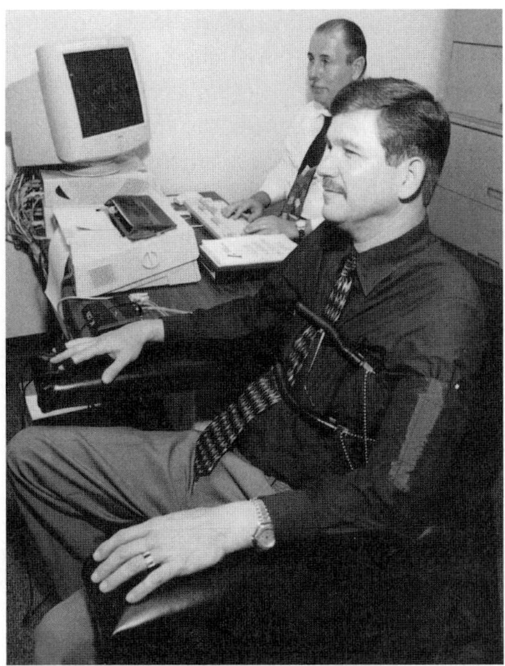

FIGURE 10.4

The polygraph examination is only one of the many phases of the pre-employment screening process. However, if properly utilized by a competent polygraphist, it can be one of the most critical and revealing tools.

(Courtesy of Sheriff Cal Henderson and Detective Herb Metzger, Hillsborough County, Tampa, Florida Sheriffs Office)

Polygraph tests do not violate the ADA as long as no medical questions are asked when they are used before making a conditional offer of employment. At that point, questions about current medication or whether the employee is currently under medical care are impermissible.

The Character Investigation

All police agencies conduct character or background investigations because, with the exception of observing the probationary officer's actual performance under varied field conditions, the single most important element of the process is the **character investigation.** The basic course of action in the character investigation is to review and verify all responses made by the applicant as to his or her education, military service, prior employment history, and related matters and to check the references listed and develop other references. The ADA mandates that any parts of the character investigation that are medical cannot be pursued until a conditional offer of employment has been made.

An editor once stated that the three basic rules for great journalists are "check your facts, check your facts, and check your facts." These three basic rules also apply to conducting the character investigation; making assumptions or failing to verify "facts" independently will result in an increase in negligent hirings. This creates, as is discussed in Chapter 14, Legal Aspects of Police Administration, a liability problem because people who should not have been employed are hired.

A case history illustrates this point. On his initial employment form, an applicant to a large city department reported that he had served a tour of duty in the Coast Guard. Among the documents he showed the department's personnel investigators were the original copy of an honorable discharge and DD 214 (Armed Forces of the United States Report of Transfer or Discharge). The investigators believed the discharge and DD 214 to be authentic. Still, they obtained an authorization for release of military records and medical information from the candidate. This release was then sent to the appropriate military records center. Meanwhile, the candidate's character investigation went on with respect to other factors. The candidate reported on his application form that, following his discharge from the Coast Guard, he and his wife spent five months traveling the country on money they had saved; thus, there was no employment history during that time. When the military record information arrived, it was learned that he had, in fact, been honorably discharged but in less than 30 days had reenlisted and 2 months into that tour of duty had become drunk, badly beat his wife, and had assaulted military authorities, who had been sent to his quarters on base to handle the domestic disturbance. Subsequently, he was dishonorably discharged from the service. When questioned about it, he readily admitted to these facts and added that he was hoping either that the police department would not check or that the record of the second enlistment would not yet be in his permanent personnel file if the department did check. Such incidents have made many agencies realize that character investigations are very specialized and very demanding and that a failure to conduct them properly will eventually produce results ranging from very serious to catastrophic.

Interviews and Oral Boards

An oral interview is a one-on-one interview between the applicant and an authority in the hiring process, such as the chief of police. In smaller jurisdictions, the interview may take the place of a written test or an assessment center. In other instances, although there may be a written test or an assessment center, the police chief may simply want a chance to see and talk with candidates before they are hired. In general, such interviews tend to be unstructured, free flowing, and either unscored or graded on a pass–fail basis. If legally challenged, unstructured interviews are difficult to defend because unskilled questioners may ask legally impermissible questions and because different candidates may be asked widely varying questions—a lack of standardization.

In contrast to interviews, **oral boards** usually involve a face-to-face contact between a three-or-more-member panel and the police applicant. Panel members may be police officials, representatives of the civil service or merit board, community members, or combinations of these people. A standard set of job-related questions is drawn up ahead of time, and panel members are trained in the use of the written evaluation form, which they incorporate into their consideration of each candidate.[69]

In addition to the standard questions that may be presented to the applicant, the following are some additional questions that can be used to help probe sensitive issues, such as use of force, community focus, ability to mediate disputes, and attitudes toward women:

- What types of people do you have the most trouble dealing with in tense situations? Why? (The response to this question may identify biases.)
- Have you ever been involved in a physical altercation? What led up to it? How did you feel about the outcome of it? (This question seeks information about the applicant's willingness or lack of willingness to resolve disputes through the use of physical force.)
- Imagine that you are a police officer and have been sent to a call about a neighborhood disturbance. When you arrive, you discover two men yelling at each other and pushing each other. They are fighting about who owns a power

tool. How would you handle this situation? (This question looks for mediation skills, not for knowledge of police procedures or the law.)

- Describe what you have done for your community without receiving pay for doing it. (This question reveals whether the person has a commitment to the community and to public service.)
- Have you ever known a victim of domestic violence? What types of things do you think it would be important to do for a victim of domestic violence? (This question may provide insight into whether the candidate understands any of the issues about domestic violence and the need to provide assistance to the victim. Is the candidate sympathetic?)
- Would it ever be appropriate for a man to use physical force against his wife or children? (This question further probes attitudes about domestic violence.)
- If you were a police officer, what do you think would be the biggest challenge in working with a partner of the opposite gender? (This questions examines possible gender bias.)[70]

Composition of the Oral Board

The oral interview panel should be gender and racially diverse and include members of the local community. Both sworn and civilian law enforcement employees may also be utilized as panelists. Raters should be thoroughly trained about the rules of the interview process. The training should include the following:

- An overview of discrimination law and the concept of adverse impact as they apply to the oral interview process
- A discussion of how bias can creep into ratings, even at a subconscious level, and the need for consistently applied and objective evaluation criteria
- A review of the job description for law enforcement officers and the knowledge, skills, and abilities the raters should be looking for
- The policing philosophy of the agency and the traits desired in a law enforcement officer
- A review of the questions to be asked and the reasons for each question (any follow-up questions permitted should be clearly delineated)
- The types of questions that should never be asked
- An explanation of the rating system and how to assign a score or rating
- Whether raters are allowed to discuss their ratings with other panel members
- The fact that their ratings will be reviewed and evaluated for reliability and possible bias[71]

Psychological Testing of Police Applicants

There are a variety of pre-employment **psychological testing** batteries (types) used throughout the nation in the screening of police candidates. Each test has varying degrees of validity and no test has been determined to be foolproof. For this reason, no one test should be relied upon but rather a multitude of tests must be utilized in order to assess the candidate's aptitude for police officer selection.[72]

"The International Association of Chiefs of Police strongly recommends, as do other psychology professionals associated with this field, that pre-employment psychological assessments should not be used as the sole determining factor for a 'hire/no hire' decision.[73] According to the 2005 COPPS questionnaire data tabulated by John Super in a poll of 478 agencies (federal, state, and local) offering a pre-employment psychological evaluation, the most popular tests (in order of their preference and percentage of use) were the following:[74]

Inwald Personality Inventory (IPI): (69 percent) Developed in the early 1980s, it is a 310-question "true–false" inventory designed specifically to aid law enforcement agencies in selecting new officers who satisfy specified "psychological fitness" requirements; documents combinations and patterns of historical life events which studies suggest correlate significantly with occupational failure in law enforcement, such as depression, anxiety, rigidity, antisocial tendencies, illness concerns, lack of assertiveness, and aggressiveness.[75]

California Psychological Inventory (CPI): (66 percent) First published in 1951, it is a self-administered paper-and-pencil personality test of items (60 minutes) devised for use with "normal" non-clinical populations; CPI allows the examiner to make statements about personality traits, strengths, and weaknesses that are within the normal limits; standard scales reflect traits such as dominance, sociability, self-acceptance, tolerance, flexibility, conformance, and responsibility.[76]

Minnesota Multiphasic Personality Inventory (MMPI) (Group Form): (51 percent) It was first developed in the 1930s and 1940s using hospital inpatients. The MMPI-2 (the revised MMPI) is a 567-item paper-and-pencil personality inventory that is sensitive to personal psychopathology. The MMPI/MMPI-2 are the instruments most frequently administered (60–90 minutes at an eighth-grade reading level); identifies individuals with mental dysfunctions who will be at a higher risk of performing poorly in training or on the job. Examples of identifiable traits are argumentativeness, hostility toward authority, adverse reactions to stress, irresponsibility, antisocial attitudes, impulsive behavior, and substance abuse tendencies.[77]

The Wonderlic Personnel Test (WPT): (49 percent) The WPT is a timed measure of cognitive aptitude that takes 12 minutes to complete. The WPT provides objective information that is generally used to match people with positions that suit their learning speed and aptitude. Extensive information is available regarding the reliability and validity of the Wonderlic. Its reliability has been measured in numerous studies.[78]

Personality Assessment Inventory (PAI): (42 percent) The 344 items constitute 22 non-overlapping full scales covering the constructs most relevant to a broad-based assessment of mental disorders: 5 validity scales, 11 clinical scales, 5 treatment scales, and 2 interpersonal scales. To facilitate interpretation and to cover the full range of complex clinical constructs, 10 full scales contain conceptually derived subscales. The test evaluates various clinical syndromes, such as anxiety, depression, mania, paranoia, and schizophrenia.[79]

In addition to the psychological tests, the psychologist should conduct a one-on-one interview with the police candidate.

Psychological tests deemed not to be medical tests by the ADA may be given prior to conditional offer to employ. For example, a test designed to test an applicant's honesty may not be considered medical. However, some tests, such as the Minnesota Multiphasic Personality Inventory, may be considered disability-related and therefore not allowable. For example, the following are some affirmative statements that appear in this psychological test in which the candidates must answer "true, false, or cannot say":

1. I am bothered by an upset stomach several times per week.
2. I have a cough most of the time.

In The News

The Implications of Not Administering Pre-employment Psychological Tests

In our highly litigious and politically charged society, law enforcement agencies must do everything reasonable to be certain they screen out psychologically unfit and high-risk applicants. Recent findings in the state of South Carolina indicated that a lack of psychological screening allowed troubled and violent officers to move from job to job, while small jurisdictions turned a blind eye. For example, a police officer from Charleston was hired by the Berkeley County Sheriff's Department in 2004 despite being charged with (and acquitted of) killing a man with his bare hands at the Charleston police headquarters. The same applicant was also sued for breaking a suspect's collarbone while with another police department. Another officer was a candidate for a police appointment in a small town after being fired from North Charleston for exposing himself to a small child.

Many officers resign during an internal investigation, halting further investigations into their actions and allowing official records to remain clean. Psychological testing may not have shown a specific trail of offenses but would have given these departments a clue as to the candidates' appropriateness for a public safety position. Such testing, along with thorough background checks, remains one of the most important tools available to police agencies in ensuring that their officers are of the highest integrity and that they pose no risk to the public they serve.

Source: "South Carolina Hit Hard by Lack of Psychological Screening." *Law Enforcement News*, June 2005, p. 9.

3. During the past year I have been well most of the time.
4. I have never had a fit or convulsion.
5. I have had attacks in which I could not control my movements or speech, but in which I knew what was going on around me.[80]

If an employer receives unsolicited medical information from a third party about the candidate's qualifications to perform the job and the candidate is otherwise qualified, then the information cannot be used.[81] However, if an applicant volunteers information about a disability that makes him or her unqualified for the job, then no offer has to be made.[82]

Critical Thinking Questions

1. What 1989 decisions by the Supreme Court frightened and angered civil rights leaders? Why?
2. Why are general physical fitness tests more accommodating to female police recruits than are job-task-based tests?
3. Describe the less discriminatory alternative test as it might relate to police agency recruitment.
4. Discuss how the administration of a polygraph test might reduce a police agency's rate of turnover.
5. Discuss the importance of the character investigation during the police hiring process.
6. What should the composition of the oral interview panel look like as it relates to the screening of police applicants?

THE RECRUIT ACADEMY, PROBATIONARY PERIOD, AND CAREER STATUS

Widespread use of the police academy to train police rookies for their new responsibilities is a common feature of American police departments. However, a survey of 383 cities by the Wickersham Commission in 1931 showed that only 20 percent of the municipalities provided police academy training.[83] At the time, the use of the police academy was limited almost exclusively to the larger cities. In many jurisdictions, new officers were simply equipped and told to go out and "handle things" or, at most, were assigned to work briefly with a veteran officer who "showed them the ropes."

Following World War II, there was increased recognition of the need to prepare newly hired personnel for police work, but, being a matter of local discretion, it remained largely undone. In 1959, California pioneered statewide legislation that statutorily established police minimum standards, including entry-level training or academy training. Today all states have legislation regulating entry-level police training.

It is important to note that, although state statutes require a minimum number of hours, many jurisdictions choose to exceed that amount considerably, depending upon their own needs and philosophies.

Field Training Officer

Police academy training is provided under a variety of arrangements. A state academy may offer the basic course, often referred to as *mandate training*; individual police agencies, usually the larger ones, operate their own academies; and regional academies provide training for police agencies in a multi-county area. Combinations of these arrangements exist in most states, and variations are possible. For example, for many years larger agencies that operated their own academies allowed smaller agencies to send recruits to their academies whenever they had unused seats. This practice initially was free under the "good neighbor" doctrine, but over time fiscal pressures have led to the use of fees. Police academy training is frequently followed by placing new officers in the care of a **field training officer (FTO).** The FTO carefully monitors the development of the rookie under actual job conditions; often, the rookie is rotated between shifts and FTOs to be further evaluated. FTO evaluations can be crucial in determining whether an officer stays with the department or is washed out. Figure 10.5 provides an example of the areas examined by the Seattle, Washington, Police Department. Some agencies have adopted officer retention boards to review all evidence on each probationary officer and to recommend to the agency head whether an officer should be granted career (or permanent) employee status or released.

Interestingly, at least one police department, the Albuquerque, New Mexico, Police Department, gives its recruits the opportunity to evaluate their FTOs. This is done in part to be certain the FTOs are fulfilling their professional obligations in a fair and impartial manner (see Figure 10.6).

Critical Thinking Question

1. Why is the selection of an FTO such a critical factor in rookie training? What factors should be considered when selecting an FTO for new officers?

SPECIAL GENDER ISSUES

Within the context of recruit academy training and FTO programs, there are certain potential problem areas that police executives must be aware of in order to avoid gender bias. For example, biased training academies and field training programs can result in large numbers of women recruits being washed out. The attrition rates for women in law enforcement academies are often double that of male recruits.[84] In a report prepared by the Los Angeles Police Department covering the years 1990–1999, women were twice as likely as men to wash out: 19 percent of the women who entered the police academy resigned or were terminated from the program, while only

SEATTLE POLICE DEPARTMENT

DAILY OBSERVATION REPORT FORM

PHASE II DOR #: ____________
DATE: ____________
UNIT: ____________
ROTATION: ____________

STUDENTS NAME: LAST, FIRST, M.I. SERIAL #

FTO'S NAME: LAST, FIRST, M.I. SERIAL #

RATING INSTRUCTIONS: Rate observed behavior with reference to the Standardized Evaluation Guidelines and numerically score on scale below. Comment on any behavior you wish, but specific comments are required on ratings of "3" or less, and "6" and above. Check the "N.O." box if not observed. If the student fails to respond to training, then reference FTG 1.43.6 "NRT".

	RATING SCALE	N.O.	N.R.T.	T.T.
Appearance				
1. General Appearance	1 2 3 4 5 6 7	☐	☐	☐
Attitude				
2. Acceptance of Feedback-FTO/Program	1 2 3 4 5 6 7	☐	☐	☐
3. Attitude toward Police Work	1 2 3 4 5 6 7	☐	☐	☐
Knowledge				
4. Knowledge of Department Policies and Procedures Reflected in Field Performance	1 2 3 4 5 6 7	☐	☐	☐
5. Knowledge of Revised Code of Washington Reflected in Field Performance	1 2 3 4 5 6 7	☐	☐	☐
6. Knowledge of Seattle Municipal Code Reflected in Field Performance	1 2 3 4 5 6 7	☐	☐	☐
7. Knowledge of Domestic Violence (DVPA) Laws and Procedures Reflected in Field Performance	1 2 3 4 5 6 7	☐	☐	☐
8. Knowledge of Basic Case Law Regarding Detention, Arrest, Search and Seizure	1 2 3 4 5 6 7	☐	☐	☐
Performance				
9. Driving Skill: Normal Conditions	1 2 3 4 5 6 7	☐	☐	☐
10. Driving Skill: Moderate and High Stress Conditions	1 2 3 4 5 6 7	☐	☐	☐
11. Orientation/Response Time to Calls	1 2 3 4 5 6 7	☐	☐	☐
12. Report Writing: Accuracy/Organization	1 2 3 4 5 6 7	☐	☐	☐
13. Report Writing: Grammar/Spelling/Neatness	1 2 3 4 5 6 7	☐	☐	☐
14. Report Writing: Appropriate Time/Appropriate Form Used	1 2 3 4 5 6 7	☐	☐	☐
15. Field Performance: Stress Conditions	1 2 3 4 5 6 7	☐	☐	☐
16. Investigation Skill	1 2 3 4 5 6 7	☐	☐	☐
17. Interview/Interrogation Skill	1 2 3 4 5 6 7	☐	☐	☐
18. Self-Initiated Field Activity	1 2 3 4 5 6 7	☐	☐	☐
19. Officer Safety: General	1 2 3 4 5 6 7	☐	☐	☐
20. Officer Safety: Suspects/Suspicious Persons/Prisoners	1 2 3 4 5 6 7	☐	☐	☐
21. Control of Incident/Persons: Verbal Skills	1 2 3 4 5 6 7	☐	☐	☐
22. Control of Incident/Persons: Physical Skills	1 2 3 4 5 6 7	☐	☐	☐
23. Problem Solving/Decision Making	1 2 3 4 5 6 7	☐	☐	☐
24. Radio: Appropriate Use of Codes/Procedures	1 2 3 4 5 6 7	☐	☐	☐
25. Radio: Listens/Comprehends/Transmissions	1 2 3 4 5 6 7	☐	☐	☐
26. Computer: Appropriate Use/Sends and Receives Messages/Accesses Information	1 2 3 4 5 6 7	☐	☐	☐
Relationships				
27. With Other Department Members/Supervisors	1 2 3 4 5 6 7	☐	☐	☐
28. With Citizens in General	1 2 3 4 5 6 7	☐	☐	☐
29. With Groups of Orientation Other than Own	1 2 3 4 5 6 7	☐	☐	☐
30. With Suspects, Complainants, Witnesses or Victims	1 2 3 4 5 6 7	☐	☐	☐

_______ Minutes of Remedial Training Time (Explain Training and Students Understanding.)

FIGURE 10.5

Seattle Police Department Daily Observation Report Form.

(Courtesy of the Seattle, Washington Police Department)

Albuquerque Police Department

FIELD TRAINING GUIDE AND EVALUATION PROGRAM

Field Training Officer Critique

Recruit: ______________________________

FTO: ______________________________ **Phase of Training I II III IV**

Note to Recruit Officer: Complete this form in privacy and after your phase of training with the FTO that you are evaluating. Please be honest in your evaluation. Submit this critique to Operations Support within five days following the end of this phase of training. Your evaluation will remain confidential.

Overall, how thorough was the FTO's knowledge of the material he/she was instructing?

In what area was the FTO the strongest?

Weakest? ______________________________

Overall, how was the FTO's ability as an instructor?

What could the FTO do to improve his ability as an instructor?

Did the FTO make an effort to cover areas you were weak in?

Did you feel you could talk freely with the FTO about problems you may have been having with him/her on the training program?

What specific problem did you experience with this FTO, if any?

FIGURE 10.6

Albuquerque Police Department Field Training Guide and Evaluation Program.

(Courtesy of the Albuquerque Police Department)

Did you feel you were evaluated fairly by this FTO?

____

____

____

How would you rate the FTO in the following areas:

	Poor		Average		Superior
Knowledge of department policy/procedures	1	2	3	4	5
Knowledge of criminal code/traffic code	1	2	3	4	5
Patrol procedures	1	2	3	4	5
Officer safety	1	2	3	4	5
General appearance	1	2	3	4	5
Attitude toward police work	1	2	3	4	5
Relationship with recruit officer	1	2	3	4	5
Relationships with other officers	1	2	3	4	5
Relationships with superior officers	1	2	3	4	5
How would you rate the FTO overall?	1	2	3	4	5

Comments on above ratings:

____

____

____

____

____

____

____

____

____

Recruit Officer Signature: ____________________ Date: __________

FIGURE 10.6 (CONTINUED)

9 percent of the men resigned or were terminated.[85] The following problems are contributing factors to this loss of women:

Military or boot camp style of training—Many law enforcement academies still use the boot camp style of training, which emphasizes tearing down individuals and rebuilding them to the military model. This military model, which places value on strict, unquestioning adherence to rules, is not only contrary to the skills desired in community policing officers but is also a culture foreign to most female recruits. Not only do female recruits generally have limited familiarity with this style of training, but experts in adult learning acknowledge that this type of training is not effective when trying to teach new skills to either male or female adult students. The emphasis is on training rather than teaching. Because of the small numbers of female recruits, live-in academies may also place additional burdens on women. A sense of isolation may develop and lead to increased dropout rates among them. In addition, live-in academies place a serious burden on parents with young children. Potential

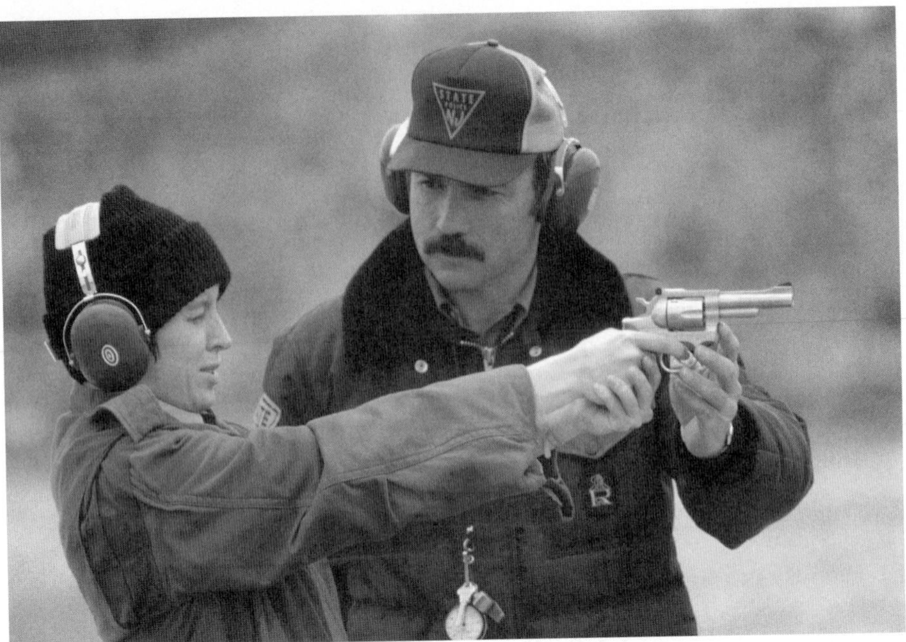

FIGURE 10.7

Many female recruits have never held or fired a gun before going to the police academy. It is important that a positive atmosphere be created that allows both male and female recruits to feel they will not be ridiculed because of their lack of experience or unfamiliarity with firearms.

(© Bob Krist/CORBIS)

child-care problems may be so severe that some excellent candidates may not even apply for police positions simply because of child-care issues.

Overemphasis on physical prowess—In many recruit academies, physical training still stresses a model in which size and force are overemphasized. Physical training, which emphasizes upper-body strength rather than self-defense skills and physical conditioning, negatively impacts women. In addition, with the new "less than lethal" technology available, the reliance on the use of physical force is less necessary and less desirable. The purpose of physical training should be to build skills and confidence, so the trainee is able to control physical confrontations when necessary.

Firearms training—Many female recruits have never held or fired a gun before going to the academy. Their unfamiliarity with guns may generate a sense of insecurity and uncertainty when learning to handle a firearm. They may be reluctant to express their concerns and be fearful of subjecting themselves to ridicule by other recruits if they do express concern. Additionally, the lack of familiarity with firearms may create an expectation of failure on the part of the trainer and the female recruit. Firearms training is sometimes done in a group, with little individualized training, thus increasing the potential for failure (see Figure 10.7).

Sexual harassment and discrimination—The boot camp training for recruits, the "tear them down, build them up" culture, uses hazing, shunning, and humiliation to build camaraderie. These techniques may become viewed as accepted uses of power. It is very easy for sexual harassment to join that acceptable list.[86]

Possible Solutions

The boot camp model of training should be replaced with training that is based on adult learning techniques. Studies have shown that adults respond best to training that is varied in presentation, such as video, lecture, and role playing, and that relates the training to their experience. Experts in adult learning should be consulted and should assist in developing training programs that are effective. The use of role playing should be emphasized to provide students with a safe environment to practice new skills.

In the case of live-in academies, extra effort should be taken to ensure that female recruits are not isolated. Agencies should avoid sending a lone woman recruit to a live-in academy because of the likelihood she will withdraw. A mentoring program would be helpful to assist women through this time. In addition, agencies should make attempts to ensure that parents are able to spend time with their families during the term of the live-in academy:

Training committee—The agency should establish a training committee to review and evaluate all academy course work, materials, and training components for relevance to the tasks that officers will be required to complete on the street. The committee should also review the material for gender and racial bias. Experts from the community, as well as female officers, minority officers, and command staff, should be included on the committee.

Curriculum—All officers should be trained in an atmosphere that recognizes and encourages innovation and individual strengths. Emphasis should be on problem solving, communications, conflict resolution skills, deescalation of violent situations, cooperation with the community, and the appropriate use of force.

Physical fitness and skills—The goal of physical training in the academy should be to increase students' confidence in their ability to perform their duties without injury. Physical fitness should be approached as a component of a healthy lifestyle. If recruits are given a solid foundation in developing a healthy lifestyle through exercise, stress reduction, and diet, they are more likely to stay fit and therefore less likely to be injured or disabled. Rather than emphasizing marching and other activities that have no relation to the job or the lives of the recruits, emphasis should be placed on physical activities that maintain fitness, so that they can continue these activities after they leave the academy.

Firearms training—Firearms instructors must be capable of training recruits who have no prior experience with firearms, as well as retraining those who may have been improperly trained. Each recruit, regardless of prior experience or skill level, should receive individual instruction to prevent stigmatizing those who lack prior experience. If an apparent need arises, instructors should help female recruits develop confidence to succeed in firearms training. If additional training is required, it should be accomplished while maintaining the recruit's sense of dignity and accomplishment. Firearms training, as with all training, should be done in a supportive atmosphere free of criticism and ridicule. As with physical training, using female firearms instructors provides a positive role model and shows all recruits that women are capable of firearms proficiency.

Sexual harassment, discrimination, and hostile work environment—Academy personnel should be held accountable for maintaining a harassment-free work environment. Any instructor found to have participated in, condoned, or even ignored any discrimination, harassment, or retaliation should be removed from the academy staff and appropriately disciplined. All academy staff should be trained in providing a hostile-free work environment, including the requirement to report inappropriate

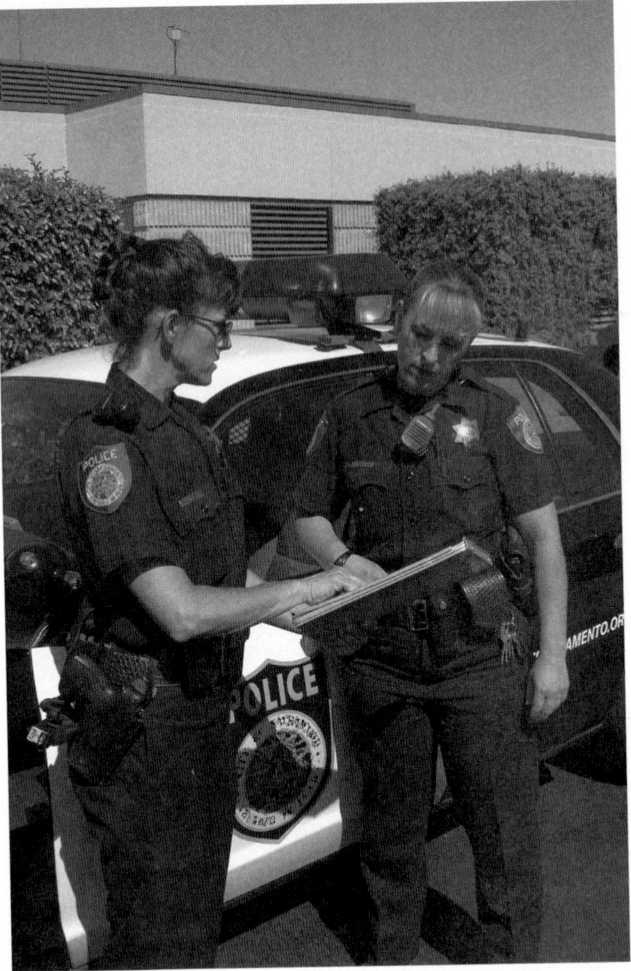

FIGURE 10.8

The role of a field training officer (FTO) should be that of teacher, guide, and mentor. It is important that FTOs be diverse in terms of gender, race, and ethnicity. This photo depicts a female FTO instructing a female police cadet on the proper way to complete a report form.

(Courtesy of the Sacramento Police Department)

actions of other staff members. (This topic is discussed in greater detail in Chapter 14, Legal Aspects of Police Administration.)

Selection of FTOs—Law enforcement agencies should regard the role of FTO as one of teacher, guide, and mentor. Great care should be taken to establish the job description of the FTO to include these traits, skills, and values. FTOs should never be selected on a strict seniority basis. Diversity among the FTO staff and their supervisors is important. All recruits should work with FTOs of both genders. The Commission on Accreditation for Law Enforcement Agencies (CALEA) states, "The selection process for FTOs is crucial to a successful program as many of the values, tactics, and attitudes of the FTOs are transmitted to inexperienced officers. Initial training as well as periodic in-service training should be provided to FTOs to prepare them for and keep them current with their assigned responsibilities.[87] An FTO should instruct all female recruits in the various avenues of reporting discrimination and harassment that the recruit may experience or observe. FTOs

Quick Facts

Females Rise to the Top of Police Organizations

In spite of the difficulties regarding special gender issues in police work, women are increasingly rising to the highest ranks in their police departments. Police chiefs in four of the nation's largest cities—Boston, San Francisco, Milwaukee, and Detroit—are women. Police Commissioner Kathleen O'Toole of Boston cites a shift in the policing paradigm, especially the move from paramilitary-style policy to a more community-based model, as the major factor in women's success in the field (see Figure 10.9). Women make up an average of 13 percent of all police officers and represent about 1 percent of police chiefs. However, while many doubt that the increasing number of highly ranked female officers signifies an overt feminization of policing in the United States, many administrators and researchers feel that it can only result in a gradual balancing of genders in our nation's police force.

Source: "Women Top Police Ranks in Several Cities." *New York Times,* May 27, 2004.

FIGURE 10.9

Boston, Massachusetts, Police Commissioner Kathleen O'Toole is an example of the many females rising to the top of their police organization.

(The Boston Globe/www.Merlin-Net.com)

should never encourage a recruit not to make such a report. FTOs should be required to report any harassment or discrimination they observe on the part of other FTOs. Both male and female recruits should be assigned to work with at least one female FTO (see Figure 10.8). This will expose them to a gender-diverse environment and reinforce the understanding that women are valued members of the organization, have expertise in policing, and are in positions of authority.

Critical Thinking Question

1. Describe some of the special issues encountered by female police recruits. Why do you think it is important for a police agency to address these issues?

COLLEGE EDUCATION FOR POLICE OFFICERS

Higher education for police officers can be traced to 1929, when the University of Southern California offered an advanced degree in public administration with a specialization in law enforcement. Michigan State University initiated its bachelor of science degree in police administration in 1935. Higher-education programs for the police grew slowly until the 1960s.[88]

During the 1960s, prominent groups, such as the International Association of Chiefs of Police and the International Association of Police Professors (now the Academy of Criminal Justice Sciences), began to issue public statements in support of higher education for law enforcement personnel.[89]

The President's Commission on Law Enforcement and Administration of Justice provided further impetus in its report *The Challenge of Crime in a Free Society.* The commission recommended that all police officers be required to have two years of college education at a minimum and that all future police personnel be required to possess a bachelor's degree.[90] As the commission explained,

> *Generally, law enforcement personnel have met their difficult responsibilities with commendable zeal, determination, and devotion to duty. However, the Commission surveys reflect that there is substantial variance in the quality of police personnel from top to bottom. . . .*
>
> *The Commission believes that substantially raising the quality of police personnel would inject into police work knowledge, expertise, initiative, and integrity that would contribute importantly to improved crime control.*
>
> *The word "quality" is used here in a comprehensive sense. One thing it means is a high standard of education for policemen. . . . A policeman today is poorly equipped for his job if he does not understand the legal issues involved in his everyday work, the nature of the social problems he constantly encounters and the psychology of those people whose attitudes toward the law differ from his. Such understanding is not easy to acquire without the kind of broad general knowledge that higher education imparts, and without such understanding a policeman's response to many of the situations he meets is likely to be impulsive or doctrinaire. Police candidates must be sought in college. . . .*
>
> *The 1960s was a decade of social disruption and violence. Police confrontations with students at universities and with anti–Vietnam war protesters were common events. The inability of the police to cope with the ghetto riots and their apparent helplessness to curtail the spiraling crime rate led both liberal and conservative politicians to believe that higher education was desirable. The National Advisory Commission on Civil Disorders and similar commissions of this period reflect these views.*[91]

The police were charged not only with being ineffective in controlling disorder but also with aggravating and precipitating violence through harassment of minority ghetto dwellers, student dissidents, and other citizens. The National Advisory Commission on Civil Disorders discovered that, in America's cities, aggressive police patrolling and harassment resulted from society's fear of crime. This practice created hostility and conflict between the police and minorities. Finally, President Johnson's Commission on Campus Unrest also advocated the belief that education for police might assist in decreasing police–citizen confrontations. That commission found that law enforcement agencies desperately need better-educated and better-trained police officers. There should be special monetary incentives for all who enter the police service with college degrees or who obtain degrees while in police service.[92]

The consensus was that to improve law enforcement, the quality of police personnel had to be upgraded through higher education. There is little doubt that law enforcement personnel had limited education. The median educational level of police officers in 1966 was 12.4 years. In December 1968, *Fortune* magazine estimated that fewer than 10 percent of American police officers had been to college; in October

1968, *Time* reported that Detroit police recruits were from the bottom 25 percent of their high school graduating classes.[93]

The 1960s focused on the need for criminal justice education. This need is determined by an analysis of the criminal justice system and by an assessment of the manpower requirements of the system's agencies.[94] Today, the need of the criminal justice field is for personnel with advanced degrees. New developments and techniques making criminal justice activities more sophisticated demand more sophisticated, well-prepared, well-schooled officers. Technology for policing has advanced by leaps and bounds to a point that a police officer in the 1960s would consider his or her role today to be science fiction.

Education is usually based on a solid foundation of liberal arts. A law enforcement practitioner (or a potential practitioner) must perceive policing as it relates to American society and the democratic process. Higher education exposes students to ideas, concepts, and problem-solving techniques. The educational process aims to develop individuals who know how to live within a group—individuals who understand conflicts in our society and who possess an understanding of the motivation, stress, and tension of other people in our society. An individual with this knowledge and understanding has the ability to apply past information to new situations.[95]

A college education will not transform an intellectually wanting person into an accomplished one. However, all things being equal, the college-educated individual is more qualified and better prepared than the high school graduate. The college-educated person has more experience with people and new situations. His or her responsibility and adaptability to new surroundings have been tested. In addition, he or she has been exposed to various cultural characteristics and ethical and racial backgrounds. This exposure should eliminate or reduce prejudice and bias. More important, a formal education should teach individuals to check their judgments regarding prejudices in favor of a more tranquil analysis.[96]

A basic concern of higher education in law enforcement is the need to study and improve the system. Academic study of policing is needed to identify problems and their solutions. Persons interested in research careers in criminal justice need a higher education.[97]

As the importance of high-quality personnel was finally recognized in the 1960s, the drive to upgrade personnel began. However, in the 1970s, the National Advisory Commission on Criminal Justice Standards and Goals stated,

> *Police agencies have lost ground in the race for qualified employees because they have not raised standards. College graduates look elsewhere for employment. Police work has often come to be regarded by the public as a second class occupation, open to anyone with no more than a minimum education, average intelligence, and good health.*[98]

The Commission on Criminal Justice Standards and Goals found it ironic that educational levels were not increased for the police because studies found that police officers with a college education generally performed significantly better than officers without a college education. According to the commission, upgrading the educational level of police officers should be a major challenge facing policing. Professions require a higher-educational degree, and if police officers hope to be recognized as a profession, they need to take notice of the professional criteria. The commission recommended that all police officers be required to possess a bachelor's degree by no later than 1982. Even into the year 2008, the police, as a universal standard, did not yet require an undergraduate degree. At a time when we have more college graduates than ever in our society, police still do not require a college education. However, it should be noted that a study sponsored by the Police Executive Research Forum (PERF) found that approximately 62 percent of policing agencies serving jurisdictions with populations of more than

50,000 people had some form of incentive program to encourage education. The same study found that only approximately 14 percent of these departments had a mandatory requirement of a college degree as a prerequisite for employment.[99]

In the past 40 years, police education has increased, but not to the point where all entry-level police officers are required to have an undergraduate degree as a requirement for employment. If police departments are to increase their professionalism and if they have any expectations of meeting the demands placed on them by their communities, they must improve the educational level of all police officers. The 14 percent of departments requiring a college degree must increase to 100 percent for all sworn police personnel. American society is becoming increasingly more complex, more sophisticated, better educated, multi-cultural, and multi-lingual; its police should do no less.

It is critical that police be familiar with the socioeconomic and cultural makeup of the community they serve. They must identify the cultural diversity among the people they protect. America's communities are heterogeneous, and a police officer with an adequate educational background should function better in the community than an officer unaware of various cultural differences among the numerous ethnic and racial groups. The police need to continue their pledge of professionalism, and professionalism implies standards and proficiency. A Police Executive Research Forum (PERF) study[100] hypothesized several advantages of college education for police officers:

- It develops a broader base of information for decision making.
- Course requirements and achievements inculcate responsibility in the individual and a greater appreciation for constitutional rights, values, and the democratic form of government.
- College education engenders the ability to flexibly handle difficult or ambiguous situations with greater creativity and innovation.
- Higher education develops a greater empathy for diverse populations and their unique life experiences.
- The college-educated officer is assumed to be less rigid in decision making and more readily accepts and adapts to organizational change.
- The college experience will help officers better communicate and respond to crime and service needs of a diverse public in a competent manner with civility and humanity.
- College-educated officers exhibit more "professional" demeanor and performance.
- The college experience tends to make officers less authoritarian and less cynical with respect to the milieu of policing.

Critical Thinking Question

1. What do you think the minimum educational standards for police officers should be at the entry level? Why?

THE FAIR LABOR STANDARDS ACT

The **Fair Labor Standards Act (FLSA)** is known as the "minimum wage law" and was passed following the stock market crash of 1929.[101] When initially passed, the FLSA applied only to the private sector, and federal, state, and local government employees were not covered by it. In 1985, the extension of FLSA coverage to government employees was held constitutional by the Supreme Court in *Garcia v. San Antonio Metropolitan Transit Authority.* The U.S. Department of Labor administers the FLSA.

In The News

Does Higher Education Mean a Lower Risk of Disciplinary Action?

Findings from a Florida study in 2002 indicated that police officers with just a high school diploma made up more than half of all law enforcement personnel in the state, yet they accounted for almost 75 percent of all disciplinary actions issued. The study, commissioned by the International Association of Chiefs of Police, also found that the severity of discipline imposed on the officers in question was disproportionately related to their educational levels. Those officers with only a high school diploma accounted for 76 percent of certification losses, while 11.6 percent of certification losses were attributed to those with bachelor's degrees and above. The information obtained from the study has been cited by researchers as proof that law enforcement agencies should adopt higher educational standards.

Source: "For Florida Police, Higher Education Means Lower Risk of Disciplinary Action," *Law Enforcement News*, October 31, 2002, pp. 1 and 10.

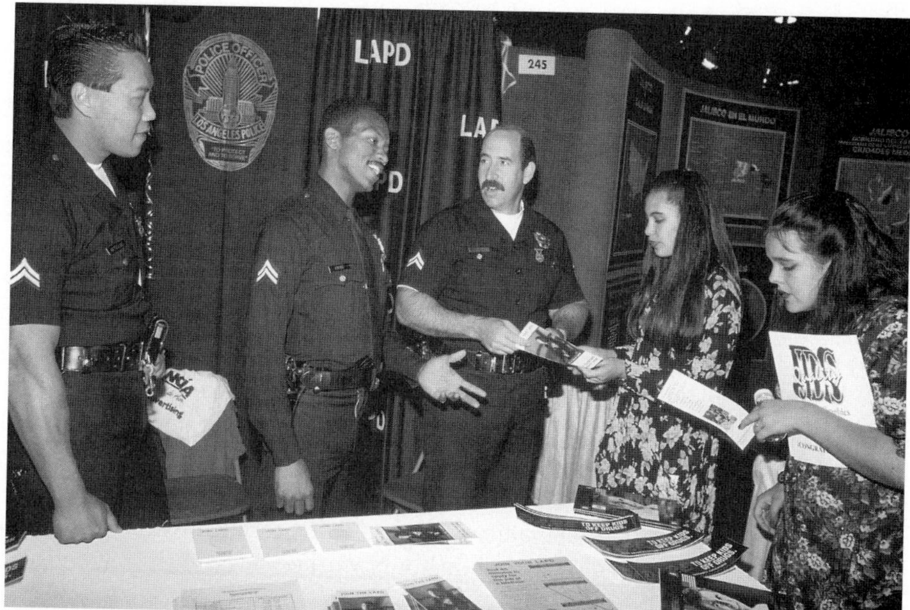

Recruiting on college campuses is one of the best ways to attract and recruit college graduates. Here police officers on a college campus discuss career opportunities with two interested college students.

(Michael Newman/PhotoEdit)

Quick Facts

Incentive Pay for a College Education

The Kansas City, Kansas, Police Department, like many other progressive agencies, has developed a program which both encourages and reimburses police officers who attend college. Officers are eligible for incentive pay of $37.50 for the completion of 12 credit hours or more, $75.00 for an associate's degree, $100 for a bachelor's degree, and $130 for a master's degree. The department also reimburses up to $50 per credit hour for an associate's degree, $75 for a bachelor's, and $100 for a master's for officers maintaining a *C* average or better.

Source: Kansas City, Kansas, Police Department.

As far as police officers are concerned, the most important aspect of FLSA is the requirement that, under specific circumstances, officers must be paid at an overtime rate or given compensatory time, which they can use like vacation days. Police officers commonly work a 28-day cycle, which means that, if they exceed 171 hours during any such period, they must be paid overtime at the rate of 1.5 times their regular rate of pay or given compensatory time at the rate of 1.5 hours off for each hour of overtime worked.[102]

Officers can accrue up to 240 hours of compensatory time. If they leave the agency, any unused "comp time" is paid at their current rate of pay and not the rate they were being paid at the time they earned it.[103] Regardless of when officers are paid for their overtime hours, the pay must include any special supplements, such as shift differential, hazardous duty, and educational incentive pay.[104] Unless there is a collective bargaining agreement or an agreement with a group representing the officers to the contrary, employers cannot require officers to accept comp time in place of overtime pay, nor do officers have a right to comp time instead of overtime pay.[105]

An important part of FLSA is determining what the "hours worked" by the employee are.[106] In general, "hours worked" means time spent in mental or physical exertion, performing tasks the employer wants done or permits the employee to do. Prior to *Garcia,* officers were required to attend a preshift briefing or roll call of 15 to 30 minutes for which they were not paid.[107] Under FLSA, that time now counts as hours worked. In general, meal breaks, which are free of duties and last at least 30 minutes, do not count as hours worked. However, if an officer is not free to leave his or her workstation while eating, then the meal time counts as hours worked, regardless of how long it lasts.[108] Time commuting to and from work is not part of the hours worked except in the case of an emergency call-out to a location substantially farther away than the workplace. Even then, only the time that exceeds the normal commute counts as hours worked.[109] The time spent by canine officers feeding and training dogs—including trips to the veterinarian—have consistently been held to be part of the hours worked by canine officers.[110] In most instances, officers who are "on call" in the evening or on weekends cannot count such time as part of their hours worked.[111] But if on-call officers are frequently recalled to duty, then their on-call time may be counted as part of their hours worked, even if they spend part of that time sleeping.[112]

Salaried employees—those whose pay is fixed regardless of how long they work—are exempt, or not covered by the FLSA.[113] However, if police supervisors and administrators are subject to short disciplinary suspensions without pay for violating the department's rules, then they are no longer exempt and are covered by the FLSA unless those suspensions are limited to major safety violations.[114] This synopsis of the FLSA reveals that it is yet another specialized aspect of personnel administration that requires constant attention as it continues to evolve.

Critical Thinking Question

1. What specific changes in police administration can be attributed to the FLSA?

THE FAMILY MEDICAL LEAVE ACT

The **Family Medical Leave Act (FMLA)** of 1993 gave eligible employees the right to family or medical leave and subsequently to be able to return to their jobs.[115] At his or her discretion, an employer can make the leave paid or unpaid. Almost all government employees are covered, including police officers. To be eligible for coverage, officers must have been employed by their department for 12 months and must have worked at least 1,250 hours during the 12 months before the FMLA leave request is made.

An eligible officer can take up to 12 weeks of leave during any 12-month period for one or more of the following causes:

1. *Birth of a child*—This includes a biological child, an adopted child, a foster child, a legal ward, a stepchild, or a child for whom the officer is acting in the role of a parent. If both spouses work for the same police department, then they are only entitled to a combined leave total of 12 weeks. At the police department's discretion, the leave may be taken intermittently, as opposed to being in a continuous block of time.
2. *Care for family members*—Within the meaning of "family members" are the officer's spouse, child, or parent with a "serious health problem." However, brothers, sisters, and in-laws are not specifically covered by the FMLA. In most instances, child-care leave is limited to children under 18 years of age. However, leave may be granted when a child older than 18 is incapable of self-care because of a physical or mental disability.

   The FMLA does not require that officers be granted leave to care for family members with routine illnesses, such as the flu or other short-term ailments, that are normally covered by the department's sick leave policy. A "serious health problem" is one that requires inpatient care in a hospital, hospice, or residential medical care facility or that requires "continuing treatment" by a health-care provider. "Continuing treatment" means that the family member has missed his or her normal activities, such as school or work, for more than three days and has been treated by or been under the supervision of a health-care provider at least twice. Examples of medical conditions in a family member that would qualify an officer for leave are heart attacks, strokes, cancer, substance abuse treatment, pneumonia, severe arthritis, prenatal care, and stress. Conversely, FMLA coverage is not extended to situations in which the family member has had outpatient cosmetic surgery, orthodontic care, acne treatment, or other similar conditions.
3. *Self-care*—Officers are allowed to take care leave for themselves under the same conditions as those for family members. If the need for medical leave is intermittent, then the officer must try to schedule the leave when it is least disruptive to departmental functioning. In response to self-care leave requests, the department may require certification by the health-care provider that the officer cannot perform the essential functions of his or her job and may transfer the officer to an equivalently paid position. On returning to duty, officers can be required to provide a medical fitness-for-duty report.

Police departments should have a carefully written policy on the FMLA. This policy should clearly identify what are the rights and responsibilities of officers and the department; how to apply for leave; whether FMLA leave is paid or unpaid; what benefits are continued or suspended during leave; how officers are restored to duty, including being reassigned to their former positions or equivalent positions; and how benefits that were discontinued during their leave are restored.

Critical Thinking Question

1. What types of things should be addressed in a police agency's written policies regarding the FMLA?

PERFORMANCE EVALUATION

Performance evaluation is often disliked by both the supervisors doing the evaluation and the officers being evaluated. Reaction occurs many times because the purposes of the performance evaluation are simply not understood.[116] The following items are part of performance evaluations:

Employee performance—Appraisals help motivate employees to maintain an acceptable level of performance. In this sense, "performance" refers to more than just measurable units of work. Law enforcement is too complex an undertaking to base appraisals solely on how a person fulfills assigned tasks. In addition to an evaluation of how an officer performs physically, the appraisal must address aspects that are difficult to quantify, such as attitudes and traits, but that are of utmost importance to the successful accomplishment of a mission.

Career development—Personnel evaluations, if administered properly, pinpoint strengths that can be developed and weaknesses that should be corrected, thereby furnishing administrators with a developmental and remedial device of considerable worth. Employees who consistently maintain a level of performance above the standards set by the department can, on the basis of their evaluations, be assigned to more responsible duties. Conversely, officers who are unable to meet reasonable standards can be given the guidance, supervision, and training necessary to save a career before it flounders.

Supervisory interests—Systematic evaluations encourage supervisors to take a personal interest in the officers under their command. Within this context, appraisals can have a humanizing effect on supervision by holding commanders responsible for the performance of subordinates. Ideally, the program will foster mutual understanding, esprit de corps, solidarity, and group cohesiveness.

Selection practices—When entry-level procedures are valid, most individuals selected for employment will make contributions to the department. If, however, many rookie officers in an agency are unable to perform adequately, something may be seriously wrong with the selection process. Personnel appraisal allows administrators to maintain a continuing check on entrance standards to determine if they are relevant or in need of modification.

Salary decisions—With the current managerial emphasis on rewards won on merit, personnel evaluations serve as a basis, often the only one, for pay increases. Officers with satisfactory appraisals will probably receive raises on time, whereas increases for those who fall below standards may be temporarily withheld.

Legal Standards

Cascio and Bernardin examined court cases centering around performance appraisals and found that the following criteria must be met for a performance appraisal system to be acceptable:

- Appraisals must focus on performance standards as identified by a job analysis.
- Performance standards must have been communicated to and understood by employees.
- Ratings should be based on specific, clearly defined dimensions, as opposed to undefined, global dimensions.
- The rated dimensions should be behaviorally anchored, and these ratings should be supported by objective, observable behaviors.
- Abstract dimensions, such as loyalty or honesty, should be avoided unless they can be defined in actual observable behavior.

- Rating scale anchor statements should be logical and brief.
- The appraisal systems and the ratings of the individual raters must be reliable and valid.
- Any system should contain an appeal mechanism for employees who disagree with their ratings.[117]

Common Rater Errors

The major problem with performance appraisals is that raters are sometimes subjective in their ratings. **Rater error** can result from such subjectivity. There are five types of such subjectivity problems: (1) the halo effect, in which the rater tends to judge subordinates on one factor that the rater deems important, and this one factor affects all the rating categories; (2) consistent error, in which some raters are too hard or easy on all their ratings, and ratings are skewed relative to other raters; (3) recency, in which a recent activity or event rather than performance from the total rating period is judged or has undue influence on the ratings; (4) biases, in which the rater is prejudiced against an individual or individuals because of personality, gender, race, or appearance; and (5) unclear standards, in which the rater is unclear about the rating dimensions' meaning, and the ratings become somewhat haphazard.

The most effective method to reduce rater error and build a reliable performance appraisal system is to train raters about the system and have management closely monitor the process. Rater training is extremely important because training helps raters better understand the activity that is being rated and the exact meaning of the dimensions and scales as they apply to the department. Specifically, raters should be trained on the activity and levels of productivity that are expected in each area. Such training tends to reduce rater error and is recognized by the courts as a way to increase reliability and validity of the performance appraisal system.

Management should monitor the performance appraisals process by cross-comparing the ratings of various raters and by comparing the ratings officers receive to their organizational measures of productivity. Raters should be required to explain ratings when an officer who is highly productive in terms of positive citizen contacts, arrests, convictions, citations issued, and low or no usage of sick time receives a lower rating than that of a less productive officer. When raters know that managers are reviewing ratings, they tend to be more consistent and reliable in their ratings.[118]

Critical Thinking Questions

1. How does rater error diminish the reliability of performance appraisals? How might that be countered?
2. What can be done to rectify or minimize these common rater errors?

SALARY ADMINISTRATION

Salary administration is one of the most critical components in the personnel administration function. The ability of a police agency to compete with business and industry in attracting the most highly qualified personnel is directly affected by the wages and other benefits offered. Thus, considerable administrative time and effort are expended in developing and updating **pay plans** and salary schedules to ensure that the police agency is in a sound competitive position in the labor market.[119]

Organization of a Pay Plan

When a pay plan is being developed, it must accomplish several objectives: (1) pay salaries that are equitable in relation to the complexity and responsibility of the work performed and maintain internal equity in the relation of pay and employees; (2) maintain a competitive position in the employment market and thereby attract and retain competent employees; (3) provide data needed in budgeting, payroll administration, and other phases of financial and personnel management; (4) stimulate personnel management and reward high-level performance; and (5) provide an orderly program of salary policy and control. (6) Be certain it is in compliance with federal and state labor laws involving pay for overtime.

Closely related to the development of the pay plan is the need for accurate information on existing employee benefits and trends regarding new benefits. Employee benefits can be classified into four basic categories: (1) income supplement (tax break) benefits, including the issuance of uniforms, clothing allowance, and paid medical and life insurance; (2) income supplement benefits, including overtime pay, standby pay, and shift pay differentials; (3) good life benefits, including paid vacations, holidays, and recreational facilities; and (4) protection benefits, including sick leave and other paid leave, retirement pensions, and workers' compensation.

There is considerable interest among police officers in a shorter workweek, early retirements, more paid holidays, longer vacations, payment for unused sick leave, and broader paid medical coverage for dental and eye care. Collective bargaining discussed in greater detail in chapter 11 Labor Relations and rising expectations of employees are likely to increase the demands for new and improved fringe benefits. Every effort should be made to use employee benefits as a tool for attracting and retaining the best employees. Cost information on employee benefits is needed not only to plan and implement a total compensation program but also to permit thorough explanations to employees and the public.

Police Salary Schedule

No standard salary structure can be applied universally in police departments simply because of the structural diversity and variations in classifications that exist among them. There are, however, some standards that experience suggests should be applied in designing the police salary schedule. For example, there must be enough ranges to permit salary differentiation among all the job classes in the classification plan and room enough in the total span of salaries to provide for significant differences in salary between successive ranks. The generally accepted rule of thumb is that pay grades should be at least 5 percent apart. Thus, if a law enforcement agency chooses to have various grades of patrol officers, a 5 percent differentiation should exist in addition to longevity considerations. Differentials between major ranks (i.e., sergeant, lieutenant, captain, and so on) should be at least 10 percent and preferably 15 percent.

ASSESSMENT CENTERS

An **assessment center** is both a process and a place. As a process, it is most often used as a means of evaluating the behavior of candidates for the purpose of determining whether they can perform a particular job, such as that of sergeant. As a place, the physical site might be continuously dedicated to conducting assessment centers, or it might be used for this purpose on an ad hoc basis. Candidates in an assessment center are also put through a series of situations that are also called simulations or exercises (discussed later in this chapter).

Historical Development of Assessment Centers

The first modern-day experiments with assessment centers were conducted by the Germans in World War I. Their objective was to select persons suited for intelligence assignments that required certain unique characteristics.[120] Simulation exercises were reactivated in World War II by German and British military psychologists to aid in the selection of military officers. In the United States, the Office of Strategic Services (OSS) used similar procedures for selecting intelligence agents. Candidates taking part in the OSS testing program participated in a wide range of paper-and-pencil tests, interviews, and simulations over a period of several days. The simulations were intended to reflect aspects of field intelligence work under wartime conditions, and some were therefore designed to be highly stressful.[121]

In the private sector, the use of assessment centers was pioneered by AT&T in 1956. For the most part, it was another 20 years before even a modest number of public agencies were using the concept.

Developmental Simulation Exercises

The first step in developing the simulation exercises used in an assessment center is to identify the behaviors that are important to successful job performance. For example, if the assessment center is being conducted to identify those who are qualified to advance from the rank of lieutenant to captain, then it is necessary to determine which behaviors (skills) are required to perform a captain's duties properly. Ideally, these skills would be identified as the result of a carefully conducted job analysis. Because of the technical skill, cost, and time required to perform a job analysis, many departments substitute a less rigorous job analysis consisting of a few interviews with job incumbents or a senior police commander's list of requisite skills. Care should be taken, however, with such substitutes because an improperly conducted or inadequate job analysis leaves a testing process open to legal challenge on the basis that it lacks validity.

Continuing with the example of a captain's assessment center, the skills identified as essential for effectiveness are termed *dimensions*. Illustrations of such dimensions include the following:

- Decisiveness
- Judgment
- Oral communication
- Stress tolerance
- Written communication
- Planning
- Flexibility

Once the dimensions are identified, simulation exercises that provide a context in which to evaluate the candidates' skill degrees must be developed. The common denominator in all exercises is that candidates competing for promotion assume the role that they would actually have to perform if selected for advancement (see Figure 10.10). Common types of exercise include the following:

1. The in-basket, in which candidates assume the role of a newly promoted captain who comes to the office and finds an accumulation of paperwork that must be dealt with. Included in the accumulated material may be such things as new regulations, requests for transfers, complaints against officers, letters from citizens, reports on shooting incidents, requests from officers to attend special

training schools or to have special days off, notification from the training bureau that certain officers must be at the pistol range on particular days for their annual qualification firing, and other, similar types of information. The length of time for in-basket exercises varies from 90 minutes to as much as 4 hours.

2. A leaderless group discussion (LGD), in which captain candidates are told that, as recent promotees to the rank of captain, they have been appointed by the chief to a committee to study a particular problem in their department and that they should come up with specific recommendations to solve it. Among the problems often given in this exercise are how to improve community relations, how to defend the department's budget against proposed reductions, and how to cut down on the number of on-duty traffic accidents by officers. Ideally, there are four or five candidates in an LGD exercise, which may last from 45 to 90 minutes. Over the past 10 years, a number of large corporations have stopped using LGDs because they do not resemble actual work situations: someone is always in charge. Some consultants have followed this practice. Despite these developments, many police departments continue to use LGDs, a matter they would probably be wise to reevaluate.
3. The written problem analysis, in which candidates are asked to analyze a problem in their department and to send a memo to the chief containing their rationale, alternatives considered, and recommended course of action. The problem may be an actual one in their agency or one that is specially written for the exercise. Depending on how complex the problem is, this exercise may last from 45 minutes to 2 hours.

Even when candidates have been given a detailed orientation to the assessment center process, they often become confused, thinking that they are being evaluated on

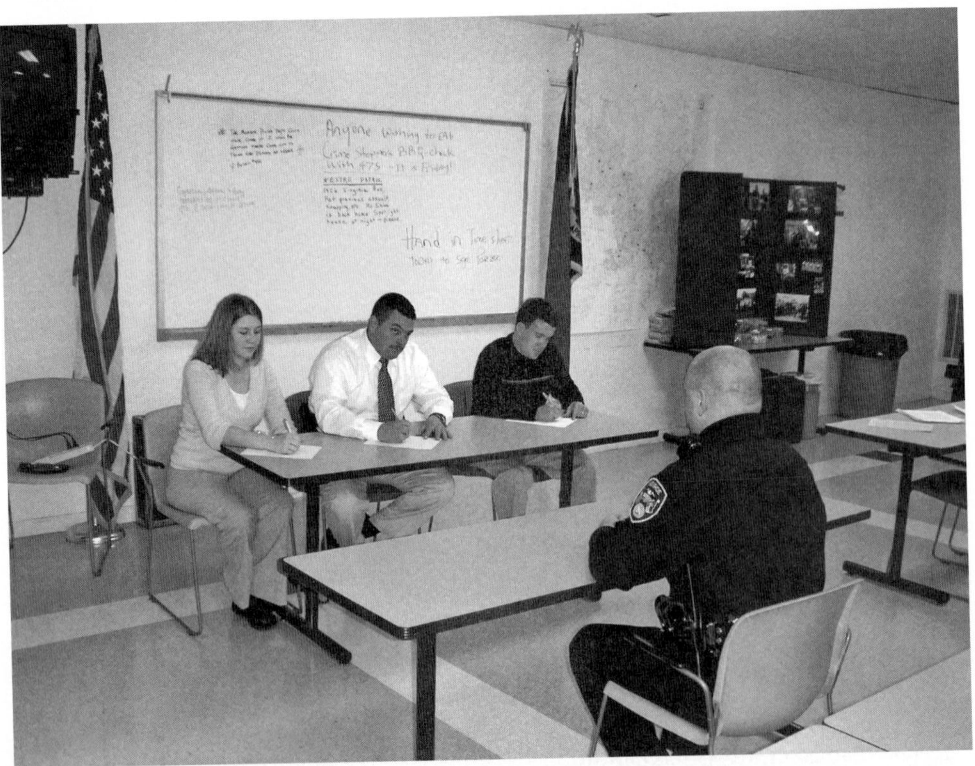

FIGURE 10.10

The role-playing portion of an assessment for a police promotion can include participants from both the law enforcement and civilian communities. Make sure that all participants are aware of the time commitment required.

(Source: Copyright © *Police*. Reprinted with permission from *Police Magazine*. All rights reserved.)

the basis of a particular exercise. Moreover, they may become very upset if they think they "blew" an exercise. However, candidates must be assessed on the basis of their cumulative performances on each dimension and not on a single exercise. Thus, candidates' final standings are based not solely on how they did on the in-basket or any other single exercise but rather on how well they performed on each dimension as it was repeatedly assessed over a number of exercises. Some candidates, thinking that they have failed an exercise, lose their confidence and fail to do well in those remaining. Their failure to manage themselves is regrettable from two perspectives: whatever troubled them about their performance on an exercise might not have been a dimension that was assessed on that exercise, and even if it had been assessed, they might have done so well in other exercises on that dimension that they were still competitive. It is part of the assessment center process for candidates to experience and manage their own feelings. However, candidates occasionally get very angry with assessment center directors who do not comfort or encourage them.

The Value of Assessment Center Testing

The true value of assessment center usage by a police agency cannot be measured only in terms of its evaluations and ranking of the potential of participants because there is also a residual training effect on the candidates as well. Not only does a properly administered and standardized police assessment process measure performance in actual work-related situations, but, through a proper feedback procedural mechanism, candidates' awareness of shortcomings can improve their future performance.

The biggest value of an assessment process is obviously to the police organization, inasmuch as the testing will validate the selection of the top performers in simulated work environments and will identify the performance potential of the candidates. This is essential to an organization's selection of the best people for the positions being appraised for.[122] Cohen articulated best the basic conception of the value of assessment center testing as "business, government and nonprofit organizations using the assessment center method to make better decisions in selecting and developing personnel needs."[123] He has listed the advantages and disadvantages of assessment centers as follows:

Advantages

- The exercise closely approximates real-life behavior because it focuses on relevant job-related simulations.
- Precision and depth are key characteristics of the assessment center method of observation.
- Studies show that center methods are valid and highly reliable.
- Centers provide valuable results for directly identifying and meeting training needs.
- Participants recognize that the assessment center provides an opportunity to demonstrate their skills and abilities.

Disadvantages

- Assessment centers can be very expensive, particularly if a consultant designed the center and trains the assessors.
- Centers also demand large investments of time. Organizations building internal centers may pay the high cost of many staff hours.
- Centers pose a major risk to participants. Information taken out of context or misused can have a long-lasting effect on a person's career.[124]

Advantages	Disadvantages
■ Participants know that the process is fair and relevant because each person performs situations similar to those they will confront when promoted or transferred.	

As can be readily discerned from the advantages and disadvantages identified, the value of an assessment center process is to both the law enforcement organization and the candidates.

In today's highly litigious society, a police organization can more effectively defend promotions, hirings, and transfers based on an objective, standardized assessment process. Its basic job relevancy and accuracy as a true measure of future job performance are documented through simulated activity. Organizational police management is beginning to realize that its most performance-skilled or productive workers will not always be the better persons to promote into a leadership position. The value of the assessment process is that it places these employees in a work-simulated situation to test their performance. Thus, it is most appropriate to say that an assessment center's value to a police organization resides in management's ability to ascertain the best candidates for the job based on validated relevant measures and that the value to the participants is realized through their experience, plus the feedback of better performance methods.[125]

Critical Thinking Question

1. For what types of situations might an assessment center be useful in the evaluation of a job candidate?

THE ADMINISTRATION OF DISCIPLINE

In almost all encounters with the public, police officers and non-sworn employees exercise their authority appropriately. At times, however, citizens raise legitimate questions about how this authority had been used. Unfortunately, there are also times when police personnel abuse this authority. Therefore, departments must establish a system of discipline that minimizes abuse of authority and promotes the department's reputation for professionalism.[126]

The most effective disciplinary system combines the reinforcement of the right set of values in all employees with behavioral standards that are consistently and fairly applied. Each employee must understand and be guided by the standards that have been established in the department's (and city's) general orders, rules, regulations, policies and procedures.

Employees should be expected to conduct themselves, both in interactions with one another and with the public, in a manner that conveys respect, honesty, integrity, and dedication to public service. In turn, employees should be treated fairly, honestly, and respectfully by everyone in the department, regardless of authority, rank, or position within the organization.

All employees make judgment errors from time to time when carrying out their responsibilities. Each error in judgment offers a learning opportunity for the employee and the department, although some errors come with greater consequences than others for the public, the department, and the employee.

Even so, the department has an obligation to make its expectations as clear as possible to employees. At the same time, it has an equal obligation to make clear the consequences for failing to meet those expectations. While meeting both obligations can be difficult, the latter is obviously more complex. Circumstances often contribute to errors in judgment and poor decisions that administrators must consider when determining the appropriate consequences for behavior found to be improper.

Employees often admit they would like the department to provide a list of prohibited behaviors, along with the penalties for engaging in those behaviors, yet experience has shown that employees directly involved in the disciplinary process, either as the subject of the process or in a review capacity, want to consider the results on one's actions in light of the circumstances that might have contributed to the violation. This consideration is critical to applying discipline fairly and consistently.

Determining Factors

A number of factors should be considered when applying discipline. Not all factors may be considered in every case, and some may not apply at all in particular situations. There may also be a tendency to isolate one factor and give it greater importance than another, yet these factors should be thought of as being interactive and having equal weight unless circumstances dictate otherwise:

Employee motivation—A police department exists to serve the public. Therefore, one factor to consider when examining an employee's conduct should be whether the employee was acting in good faith. An employee who violates policy in an effort to accomplish a legitimate police action should be given more positive consideration than one who was motivated by personal interest.

Degree of harm—The degree of harm resulting from employee error is another factor when deciding the consequences for errant behavior. Harm can be measured in terms of monetary costs to the department and community, such as repairs to a damaged vehicle, or in terms of personal injury claims for excessive force. Another way to measure harm is by the impact of employee error on public confidence. An employee who engages in criminal behavior, such as selling drugs, corrodes public trust in the police if discipline does not send a clear, unmistakable message that this behavior will not be tolerated.

Employee experience—Employee experience also has a bearing on the type and the extent of discipline. A relatively new employee or a more experienced officer in a new assignment should be given greater consideration for judgmental errors. Accordingly, errors by veteran employees may warrant more serious sanctions.

Employee's past record—To the extent allowed by law, policy, and contractual obligations, an employee's past record should be taken into consideration when determining disciplinary actions. An employee who continually makes errors should expect the penalties for this behavior to become progressively more punitive. Less stringent consequences should be administered to employees with records that show few or no errors. When determining disciplinary action, every consideration should be given to employees whose past records reflect hard work and dedication to the department and the community.

Intentional/unintentional errors—Supervisory personnel need to consider the circumstances surrounding the incident to determine whether the employee's error was intentional or unintentional. Obviously, the type of error will govern the extent and severity of the discipline.

The unintentional error occurs when an employee's action or decision turns out to be wrong even though at the time the employee believed it to be in compliance with policy and the most appropriate course to take based on information available.

Unintentional errors also include those momentary lapses of judgment or acts of carelessness that result in minimal harm (e.g., backing a police cruiser into a pole or failing to turn in a report in a timely fashion). Employees should be held accountable for these errors, but the consequences should be more corrective than punitive, unless the same or similar errors persist.

Employees make intentional errors when they take action or make a decision that they know or should know to be in conflict with law, policy, procedures, or rules at the time. Generally, intentional errors should carry greater consequences and be treated more seriously.

Within the framework of intentional errors, certain behaviors are entirely unacceptable, such as lying, theft, physical abuse of citizens, and equally serious breaches of trust placed in the police.[127] However, the type of police officer who generally causes the most grief and embarrassment to a police department is the one who is prone to violence.

Profile of Violence-Prone Officers

Several years ago, the National Institute of Justice conducted a survey of numerous police psychologists in an effort to develop a profile of officers who had been referred to them for the use of excessive force. Their answers did not support the conventional view that a few "bad apples" are responsible for most excessive-force complaints. Rather, their answers were used to construct five distinct profiles of different types of officers, only one of which resembled the "bad apple" characterization.

The data used to create the five profiles constitute human resource information that can be used to shape policy. Not only do the profiles offer an etiology of excessive force and provide insight into its complexity, but they also support the notion that excessive force is not just a problem of individuals but may also reflect organizational deficiencies. These profiles are presented in the ascending order of frequency, along with possible interventions:

Officers with personality disorders that place them at chronic risk—These officers have pervasive and enduring personality traits (in contrast to characteristics acquired on the job) that are manifested in antisocial, narcissistic, paranoid, or abusive tendencies. These conditions interfere with judgment and interactions with others, particularly when officers perceive challenges or threats to their authority. Such officers generally lack empathy for others. The number who fit this profile is the smallest of all the high-risk groups.

These characteristics tend to persist through life but may be intensified by police work and may not be apparent at pre-employment screening. Individuals who exhibit these personality patterns generally do not learn from experience, nor do they accept responsibility for their behavior. Thus, they are at greater risk for repeated citizen complaints.

Officers whose previous job-related experience places them at risk—Traumatic situations, such as justifiable police shootings, put some officers at risk for abuse of force but for reasons totally different from those of the first group. These officers are not unsocialized, egocentric, or violent. In fact, personality factors appear to have less to do with their vulnerability to excessive force than the emotional "baggage" they have accumulated from involvement in previous incidents. Typically, these officers verge on burnout and have become isolated from their squads. Because of their perceived need to conceal symptoms, some time lapses may occur before their problems come to the attention of others. When this happens, the triggering event is often a situation in which excessive force was used and the officer has lost control.

In contrast to the chronic at-risk group, officers in this group are amenable to critical-incident debriefing, but to be fully effective the interventions must be applied soon after involvement in the incident. Studies recommend training and psychological debriefings, with follow-up, to minimize the development of symptoms.

Officers who have problems at early stages in their police careers—The third group profiled consists of young and inexperienced officers, frequently characterized as "hotdogs," "badge happy," "macho," or generally immature. In contrast to other inexperienced officers, individuals in this group are characterized as highly impressionable and impulsive with low tolerance for frustration. They nonetheless bring positive attributes to their work and could outgrow these tendencies and learn with experience. Unfortunately, the positive qualities can deteriorate early in their careers if field training officers and first-line supervisors do not work to provide them with a full range of responses to patrol encounters.

These inexperienced officers were described as needing strong supervision and highly structured field training, preferably under a field training officer with considerable street experience. Because they are strongly influenced by the police culture, such new recruits are more apt to change their behavior if their mentors show them how to maintain a professional demeanor in their dealings with citizens.

Officers who develop inappropriate patrol styles—Individuals who fit this profile combine a dominant command presence with a heavy-handed policing style; they are particularly sensitive to challenge and provocation. They use force to show they are in charge as their beliefs about how police work is conducted become more rigid and this behavior becomes the norm.

In contrast to the chronic risk group, the behavior of officers in this group is acquired on the job and can be changed. The longer the patterns continue, however, the more difficult they are to change. As the officers become invested in police power and control, they see little reason to change. Officers in this group are often labeled "dinosaurs" in a changing police profession marked by greater accountability to citizens and by adoption of the community policing style of law enforcement.

If these officers do not receive strong supervision and training early in their careers or if they are detailed to a special unit with minimal supervision, their style may be reinforced. They may perceive that the organization sanctions their behavior. This group would be more responsive to peer program or situation-based interventions in contrast to traditional individual counseling. Making them part of the solution rather than part of the problem may be central to changing their behavior.

Officers with personal problems—The final risk profile is made up of officers who have experienced serious personal problems, such as separation, divorce, or even perceived loss of status, that have destabilized their ability to function effectively on the job. In general, officers with personal problems do not use excessive force, but those who do may have elected police work for all the wrong reasons. In contrast to their peers, they seem to have a more tenuous sense of self-worth and higher levels of anxiety that are well masked. Some may have functioned reasonably well until changes occurred in their personal situation. These changes undermine confidence and make it more difficult to deal with the fear, animosity, and emotionally charged patrol situations.

Before they resort to the use of excessive force, these officers usually exhibit behavior while on patrol that is erratic and that signals the possibility they may, indeed, lose control in a confrontation. This group, which is the most frequently seen by psychologists because of excessive-force problems, can be identified by supervisors who have been properly trained to observe and respond to the precursors of problem behavior. Their greater numbers should encourage departments to develop early warning systems to help supervisors detect "marker behaviors" signifying that problems are brewing. These officers benefit from individual counseling, but earlier referrals to psychologists can enhance the benefit and prevent their personal situations from spilling over into their jobs.[128]

Early Warning Systems

It has become a truism among police chiefs that 10 percent of their officers cause 90 percent of the problems.[129] Investigative journalists have documented departments in which as few as 2 percent of all officers are responsible for 50 percent of all citizen complaints.[130] The phenomenon of the "problem officer" was identified in the 1970s: Herman Goldstein noted that problem officers "are well known to their supervisors, to the top administrators, to their peers, and to the residents of the areas in which they work" but that "little is done to alter their conduct."[131] In 1981, the U.S. Commission on Civil Rights recommended that all police departments create an early warning system to identify problem officers—those "who are frequently the subject of complaints or who demonstrate identifiable patterns of inappropriate behavior."[132]

An **early warning system** is a data-based police management tool designed to identify officers whose behavior is problematic and provide a form of intervention to correct that performance. As an early response, a department intervenes before such an officer is in a situation that warrants formal disciplinary action. The system alerts the department to these individuals and warns the officers while providing counseling or training to help them change their problematic behavior.

How Does an Early Warning System Work?

Early warning systems have three basic phases: selection, intervention, and postintervention monitoring:

1. *Selecting officers for the program*—No standards have been established for identifying officers for early warning programs, but there is general agreement about the criteria that should influence their selection. Performance indicators that can help identify officers with problematic behavior include citizen complaints, firearm-discharge and use-of-force reports, civil litigation, resisting-arrest incidents, and high-speed pursuits and vehicular damage.[133] Although a few departments rely only on citizen complaints to select officers for intervention,

most use a combination of performance indicators. Among systems that factor in citizen complaints, most (67 percent) require three complaints in a given time frame (76 percent specify a 12-month period) to identify an officer.

2. *Intervening with the officer*—The primary goal of early warning systems is to change the behavior of individual officers who have been identified as having problematic performance records. The basic intervention strategy involves a combination of deterrence and education. The theory of simple deterrence assumes that officers who are subject to intervention will change their behavior in response to a perceived threat of punishment.[134] General deterrence assumes that officers not subject to the system will also change their behavior to avoid potential punishment. Early warning systems also operate on the assumption that training, as part of the intervention, can help officers improve their performance. In most systems (62 percent), the initial intervention generally consists of a review by the officer's immediate supervisor. Almost half the responding agencies (45 percent) involve other command officers in counseling the officer. Also, these systems frequently include a training class for groups of officers identified by the system (45 percent of survey respondents).
3. *Monitoring the officer's subsequent performance*—Nearly all (90 percent) of the agencies that have an early warning system in place report that they monitor an officer's performance after the initial intervention. Such monitoring is generally informal and conducted by the officer's immediate supervisor, but some departments have developed a formal process of observation, evaluation, and reporting. Almost half the agencies (47 percent) monitor the officer's performance for 36 months after the initial intervention. Half the agencies indicate that the follow-up period is not specified and that officers are monitored either continuously or on a case-by-case basis.

Characteristics of Officers Identified by Early Warning Systems

In studies conducted of the Miami–Dade County Police Department; the Minneapolis, Minnesota, Police Department; and the New Orleans, Louisiana, Police Department, it was learned that, demographically, potential problem officers identified by the early warning system do not differ significantly from control groups in terms of race or ethnicity. Males are somewhat overrepresented and females underrepresented. One disturbing finding was a slight tendency of early warning officers to be promoted at higher rates than control officers. This issue should be the subject of future research, which should attempt to identify more precisely whether some departments tend to reward through promotion the kind of active (and possibly aggressive) behavior that is likely to cause officers to be identified by an early warning system.[135]

When starting its early warning system, the Albuquerque, New Mexico, Police Department agreed that it wanted a system that would capture all the instances in which an officer used force (baton, hands, firearms, canine, or taser) in any of its internal investigations or citizen police complaints, was named in a lawsuit or notice of tort, or was involved in a chargeable motor vehicle collision. In the Albuquerque system, the threshold can be adjusted and an officer involved in a predetermined number of the previously mentioned incidents of a specific time is identified by the system. The information about the officer would include name, age, race, seniority, and cadet class. Information also included in a cross-reference is race, other complainants/citizen in order to identify possible profiling or discrimination concerns. The experience of the Albuquerque Police

Department was that any officer involved in a total combination of five or more of such incidents within the previous 12-month period would be flagged. A report is run monthly, and a printout of all incidents of the flagged officer(s) is generated. The report is then sent to the commander of the flagged officer for review, and the commander is then required to have a face-to-face meeting with the officer in reference to the report. Command staff were to examine the issues and see if there were any underlying causes for the high number of incidents involving the officer. Based on the interview, commanders then referred the officer for additional training to the behavioral science division or to other services. If the commander determined there was no inappropriate behavior or problems with the actions of the officer, the commander simply documented the meeting and the outcome in the officer's retention file. Within the first 18 months of operation, the system routinely flagged five officers each month, with over 90 percent being justified actions.

Additionally, the Albuquerque Police Department regularly conducted special audits of employees at the request of the city attorney's office or the city risk-management division in order to see what type of history the officer had. Conducting these special audits helps during the disposition process and lets the agency know what the officer has been involved in recently. Information is retained indefinitely, while the internal affairs files (the case files) are purged on the basis of incident. Letters of reprimand are purged after one year, while other disciplinary cases are purged after three years. The agency also keeps a one-page summary indefinitely of the case in the officer's file, should questions from the court need to be answered.[136]

The Impact of Early Warning Systems on Officers' Performance

Early warning systems appear to have a dramatic effect on reducing citizen complaints and other indicators of problematic police performance among those officers subject to intervention (see Figure 10.11). In Minneapolis, the average number of citizen complaints received by officers subject to early intervention dropped by 67 percent one year after the intervention. In New Orleans, that number dropped by 62 percent one year after intervention. In Miami–Dade, only 4 percent of the early warning cohort had zero use-of-force reports prior to intervention; following intervention, 50 percent had zero use-of-force reports.

Critical Thinking Questions

1. Which violence-prone officer profile should be most troubling to police administrators? Why?
2. What are some of the benefits of an early warning system?

THE INTERNAL AFFAIRS UNIT

Every police agency needs a functional **internal affairs unit (IAU)** or person charged with the responsibility for overseeing the acceptance, investigation, and adjudication of complaints about police performance (see Figure 10.12). The size of this unit depends on the workload.[137]

In most smaller agencies (25 or fewer employees), the internal affairs function is normally undertaken by the chief of police or assigned to the second in command. In smaller sheriff's departments, this duty is often handled by the chief deputy, usually on an as-needed basis. In all other police agencies, the internal affairs function should be designated as an IAU or another terminology, such as the current favorite, professional

FIGURE 10.11

Detective Toye Nash, a member of the development team that created the Phoenix, Arizona, Police Department Personnel Assessment Center, checks information in the data base of that agency's employee early warning system. Such systems appear to have a dramatic effect on reducing citizen complaints and other indicators of problematic police performance among those officers subject to intervention.

(Courtesy of the Phoenix, Arizona, Police Department)

standards unit. This unit or person can be assigned other ancillary duties, depending on the workload. Regardless of the designation or position in the agency, this function should be directly responsible to the chief of police or sheriff. Only in larger agencies should this function be assigned to a secondary layer within the organization, such as an assistant or deputy chief of police or a chief deputy/under sheriff.

Two primary philosophies guide the assignment of persons to investigate personnel complaints. Much of this is based on whether the agency views this function as principally one of investigation or one of supervision. Investigations can be conducted very well by a first-level officer or detective, just as they do in purely criminal matters. Internal affairs and personnel complaint investigations, however, are an essential element of agency control, discipline, and the supervisory function; thus, they should be conducted by a supervisor. This can be invaluable experience in the development of supervisors and future managers of the agency.

The agency that elects to assign these investigations to first-level officers should restrict the task strictly to the investigative function. Conclusions and recommendations should be a function for supervisory or command-level personnel. The investigation of allegations of misconduct against fellow officers can be a difficult task for the assigned officer. It is even more difficult to require first-level officers to do it. Usually they are in the same bargaining unit with the accused and may have to work directly with them in the future. Thus, investigating officers should not be held accountable for making conclusions, findings, or recommendations; their responsibility should be limited to fact-finding. Assignments to internal affairs should be limited in tenure. Two years would not be an unreasonable period of time. It should be considered as a career development opportunity to enhance the employee's understanding of discipline and supervisory techniques. Longer tours of duty can adversely affect an employee's outlook and inhibit his or her eventual return to other assignments in the agency. The regular rotation of personnel may assist in eliminating the "headhunter" reputation given to some IAU operations. Some agencies have been successful in encouraging members to undertake this assignment by offering them a reasonable guarantee of a selected assignment following their tour in internal affairs (see Figure 10.12).

Time Limits

An emerging issue is the imposition of rigid and inflexible time limits for filing a complaint, completing the investigation, and/or imposing discipline in a sustained case. Currently, there is no clear or common trend in law enforcement on this issue. One incentive for this movement is that such a policy would be beneficial for accused officers and employees in minimizing unnecessary delays in reaching closure on the allegation(s). On the other side, however, is the basic principle of administrative investigations that requires the agency to do everything reasonable to reach the truth of the matter. The ultimate issue appears to be whether a delay is unreasonable and unexplainable.

Some current examples of this practice follow. One large agency has a charter provision requiring that misconduct be discovered within one year of occurrence, or no discipline beyond a written reprimand may be given. One state mandates by statute that the complaint of misconduct be filed within 60 days of occurrence. Another large agency, by administrative ruling, must conclude the investigation and assess discipline

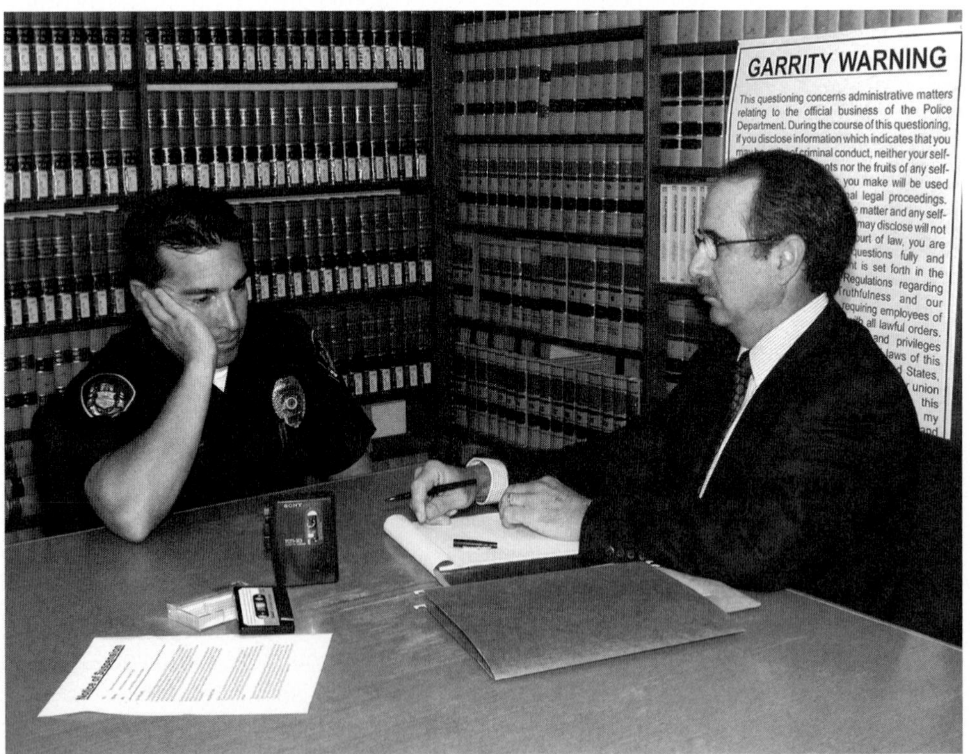

FIGURE 10.12

Internal affairs investigators tread the fine line of protecting the public from abusive police, individual officers from unfounded allegations, and their agencies from corruption.

within 120 days of the complaint, or no discipline can be imposed. Another agency, by mayoral decision, has forestalled any imposition of discipline unless the investigation is concluded and discipline administered within 45 days of the agency's notice of misconduct or the date when it should have been aware of possible employee misconduct.

Investigation by Line Supervisors

If field supervisors are to be used for some administrative investigations, the agency should ensure that they are adequately prepared for the task. This can be done through specific training and by use of a thorough exemplar for guidance.

Immediate supervisors of the accused officer can normally conduct a reasonable administrative investigation. Their closeness to the accused member or the probability of continued daily contact between the two should not be considered a hindrance to an effective investigation. Discipline is a function of supervision. Immediate supervisors should not be allowed to avoid direct involvement in this essential supervisory task.

Proactive Enforcement Operations

A Police Foundation study conducted several years ago reported that 11 percent of the police agencies surveyed indicated they conducted some form of proactive enforcement involving police misconduct. Some areas of misconduct that might be conducive to this type of administrative policing are the following:

- Involvement with narcotics
- Theft
- Unauthorized information release
- Perjury or false affidavits
- Sexual misconduct
  - Traffic stops of females
  - Voyeuristic activities
  - Repeated contacts with vulnerable persons (prostitutes, addicts, and runaways)
  - Citizen-initiated contacts for sex
- Excessive, unnecessary use of force

Agencies that are engaging in these forms of proactive enforcement may also refer to them as "integrity checks." Some are staged calls for officers' responses to burglaries or vehicle impoundments that contain some form of valuable property. The officer's conduct is checked to determine whether the property was properly inventoried and booked into evidence. Some agencies have used decoys when specific employee misconduct is suspected.

Some important considerations that should be evaluated before deciding to engage in any proactive administrative enforcement are the following:

- Resources and equipment
- Mutual aid provisions
- Ethical issues
- Agency environment

Investigations by Another Agency

Most police agencies, except very large ones, are not equipped or staffed for large-scale, intense, critical operations. Frequently in such cases, operative personnel are recruited from adjacent agencies, state and federal units, and/or community outreach sources.

However, an agency's reliance on an outside entity to conduct an investigation does not relieve it of its ultimate accountability. Outside agencies are sometimes reluctant to become involved in these administrative investigations. Some look at the task within the narrow framework of the possible criminal wrongdoing. This can seriously reduce the ability of an agency to use the investigation for the more intensive administrative analysis and subsequent determination of whether discipline may be warranted. It must be noted that the outside entity's investigation does not bring the administrative aspect to final closure. That investigation focuses primarily on criminal wrongdoing and will not normally make a satisfactory administrative finding in determining if any departmental policies or procedures have been violated.

In smaller agencies, investigations of the chief of police or other top administrators are often conducted by an outside unit. Some jurisdictions will designate the city manager or personnel director to conduct these investigations. Most, however, will look to another outside agency (usually state or federal) for this service.

Use of the Polygraph or Voice Stress Detection Equipment

The use of polygraphs and voice stress detection equipment in administrative investigations is controversial. Agency employees normally cannot be compelled to submit to such an examination. The results of this form of examination rarely can be used in disciplinary hearings or appeals, even if given voluntarily by an agency employee (see the discussion of Garrity v. New Jersey in Chapter 4, Legal Aspects of Police Administration for more details).

The polygraph and voice stress examination, however, can be useful when dealing with complainants and other civilian witnesses. This form of examination should be done only after the person has given a complete and formal statement. The final approval for requesting a person to submit to such an examination should be by the chief of police or his or her designee. The polygraph or voice stress should not be used as a means of intimidating or coercing a person. The investigator should explain that the results are simply a method of verifying the statement. This, of course, may be necessary when there is little physical evidence or disinterested witnesses are involved.

Refusal to submit to a requested polygraph or voice stress examination does not negate the validity of the person's statement or allegation. This refusal should be noted in the investigative report. Should a person submit to the examination and, in the examiner's opinion, show deception, the person must be reinterviewed and confronted with this inconsistency. It is becoming more difficult to admit the examiner's opinion in any formal hearing, whether criminal or administrative. However, this process can give the examiner and/or the investigator valuable information on which he or she can further develop the case. Skillful interviewing techniques both before and after the examination often can provide the investigation with more valuable information than the test itself.

The greatest value of these types of detection devices is to rule out issues, provide new direction for the investigation, and serve as one factor in the final adjudication of the complaint allegation.

Chemical Tests

Investigators conducting administrative investigations should attempt to maximize the use of chemical testing for the presence or absence of alcohol or drugs. Complainants and civilians should be requested to consent to such chemical tests, should there be objective symptoms or a reasonable suspicion that substance abuse is involved and has some relevance to the complaint. When a civilian dies from police actions, in a traffic accident involving a police vehicle or pursuit, or in an in-custody death, the medical examiner usually conducts a complete toxicological examination. The investigator should ensure that this will be done, and the results should be included in the investigative report, along with the autopsy report. When a civilian refuses to consent voluntarily to a chemical test, the investigator is required to follow the legal standards for obtaining a forced sample. This can be under the authority of the Vehicle Code or by warrant. If neither is successful, any observations should be fully noted in the investigative report.

Chemical testing of agency personnel is a vital element in an administrative investigation and in the maintenance of a professional police organization. A police agency cannot tolerate substance abuse by employees. Case law has continuously upheld the right of police agencies to require an employee to submit to a chemical test when done in a reasonable manner and under specific criteria. These should be delineated in the agency written policy. The following are the four times when such a test is warranted:

1. The employee exhibits objective symptoms of alcohol or other drug use or there is a reasonable suspicion that the employee is using drugs illegally.
2. The employee's actions have caused the death or serious injury of another person.
3. The test is consistent with the agency's policy on random drug screening.
4. The test is necessary to rule out an allegation that an employee is under the influence of alcohol or other drugs or is engaging in the use of illegal drugs.

The investigator should normally request the employee to consent to such a test, particularly when it is being used to rule out an allegation. If the employee refuses, the investigator and/or the employee's immediate supervisor should order the employee to submit to the test in cases involving category 1, 2, or 3. The employee cannot be ordered to submit to a chemical test simply to rule out an allegation (category 4) without some evidence of substance abuse or a reasonable suspicion. The best chemical test is the urine specimen. It is less intrusive and does not require the involvement of medical personnel, and it can detect drugs in the system for a longer period of time after use. A breath test is still applicable in cases involving symptoms of alcohol influence. A urine sample might be warranted if the breath results are lower than what the objective symptoms would lead a reasonable investigator to suspect. Investigators should be alert to the possible use and influence of anabolic steroids, particularly among police agency employees (see Chapter 13, Stress and Police Personnel, for a more detailed description). It should be noted that the employee does not have a right to choose the type of test to be used in an administrative investigation. Employees do have the right to have a test of their choice at their own expense. This cannot be allowed to interfere unnecessarily with the progress of the investigation.

Investigators should tape-record as much of the contact with employees as possible when they are suspected of involvement with or the use of illegal drugs. Normally, the employee should be ordered to the police facility if he or she is not there already. This is the most reasonable approach for several reasons. First, it is the most discreet. Second, it allows for closer supervisory control and validates the job relationship of the investigation. The investigator and any involved supervisor should view this activity as a contact to collect a piece of evidence rather than any form of interview or interrogation that would then necessitate additional formal procedures.

It is not unreasonable to allow the employee to have some form of representation present during this investigatory contact if the employee requests. However, should the delay be extended for more than an hour, the test or sample should be taken to avoid the drug being flushed through the system.

Photo and Physical Lineups

Both photo and physical lineups are reasonable investigatory tools to use. This is particularly important when multiple officers are involved in an incident that leads to an allegation of misconduct. The agency should maintain a file of photographs of all employees in uniform (with and without hat) and in civilian clothing. It should be the policy of the agency to update these photos every five years.

Both of these forms of lineups for identification must follow the criminal standards of care for objectivity. Whether using a photo display or physical lineup, the persons involved must be similar in appearance. Photo lineups are less intrusive and easier to conduct, but facial hair changes can cause problems.

Agency employees do not have a right to refuse to participate in a physical lineup. Likewise, they do not have a right to prohibit the use of their photograph in a photo lineup. As with any professional investigation, the photo lineup used should be preserved and become part of the investigative documents.

Financial Records

In some cases, such as corruption, bribery, or theft, the financial records of the employee may become an integral part of the investigation. This information normally should be obtained through warrant unless voluntarily provided by the employee.

Use of Covert Collection Techniques

Some allegations of misconduct may warrant the use of covert collection techniques. Investigators should adhere to the agency's policies and procedures when using any of these investigative techniques. Examples of these covert techniques are visual surveillance, decoy operations, controlled buys, and electronic/aural surveillance. If informants are to be used, the agency's guidelines on the identification, control, and use of informants must be followed.

Critical Thinking Question

1. If a police agency elects to assign first-level officers to internal affairs functions, what limitations should be put on their tasks? Why?

RETIREMENT COUNSELING

Inherent in the law enforcement officer's life stage of retirement are issues of finance, lifestyle, leisure time, identity, psychological needs, and marriage and family adaptation.[138] For some police officers, it also often involves retirement issues that are significantly different from those of the general population. Most police officers have spent their careers living decidedly separate from the community in which they serve. They live with a level of stress far surpassing that of most persons and experience the acute physiological and psychological ramifications of that stress. The realities of their

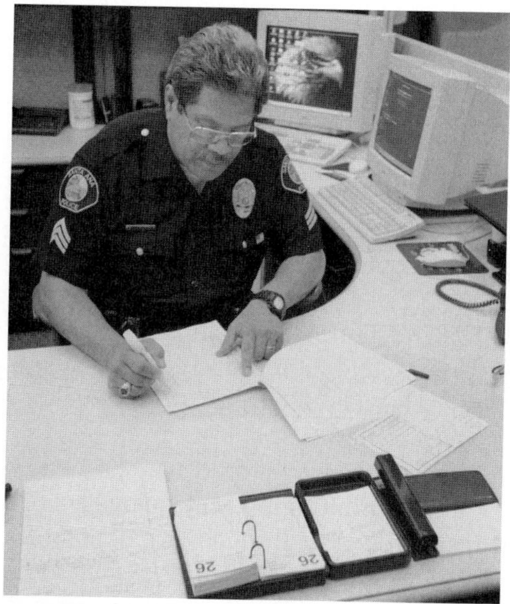

FIGURE 10.13

Retirement for law enforcement officers often raises issues of finance, lifestyle, leisure time, identity, psychological needs, and marriage and family adaptation. Increasingly, police agencies are providing retirement counseling for officers.

(Spencer Grant/PhotoEdit)

work often necessitate the development of a small, closed system of support, if any exists at all. Typically, their support system includes those with whom they work on a daily basis. Separation from the work environment includes the possibility of isolation and further withdrawal and most certainly brings new challenges to the officer's immediate family system as this unit becomes the predominant support system (see Figure 10.13).

Psychological Losses

Retirement from law enforcement does, in fact, symbolize loss of identity, of authority, and of family. According to Rehm[139] a key psychological factor in deciding to stay on the job past the time of retirement eligibility involves unfulfilled needs, as described by Maslow's Theory of Self-Actualization (discussed in Chapter 5, Organizational Theory). When reflecting on their careers, police officers may not be able to see any signs of lasting impact on the department or on the community to which they have dedicated their service. The legal system creates a revolving door that often places the same individuals (criminals) in prison time after time for brief periods. The result may be an officer's sense of powerlessness to impact that system. Staying long past the point of effectiveness may be an attempt to remedy that situation and to fulfill that psychological need. Sticking with the job without considering physical and psychological fitness for duty can result in shame, humiliation, poor morale, and heightened liability for the officer, for fellow officers, and for the department.

Officers who have relied primarily on police support networks struggle with loss of consortium when their everyday lives no longer include active police work. The absence of being at the center of what is happening in the community and being privy to specific confidential information often results in a sense of isolation, which may lead to the tendency to withdraw further.

Loss of structure provided by the profession for so many years is often a difficult phenomenon with which to cope. For many, this structure played a significant role in an internal sense of peace and control. It provided the officer with a sense of purpose and specific direction. Without it, the retired officer may experience an intense transition for a period of time, which can include a sense of hopelessness and chaos. As a result, the retired officer may resort to ineffective coping mechanisms to deal with the subsequent anxiety, fear, and loneliness.

For most police officers, their identity has been punctuated (and, for some, summarized) by their uniforms, their service weapons, and their badges. They may feel stripped naked on relinquishing these symbols. This may also be followed by feelings of fear, a perceived decrease in status, and a generalized sense of loss.

In postretirement counseling sessions, officers frequently report that "all I know how to do is to be a cop." Some believe they are unqualified for other employment opportunities after retirement. They frequently fail to recognize the repertoire of skills developed as a result of their careers. Police work requires the refinement of fluid skills rather than simply the development of more crystallized abilities. They have become master problem solvers as a vital part of their role. Conflict resolution has become second nature. Their communication skills far surpass those of the general community. They are self-starters requiring little supervision; they tend to be dependable, reliable, and ethical; they are uncharacteristically brave; and they generally consider the needs of others above themselves. These skills and qualities represent critical foundational pieces to a myriad of other jobs. Specific counseling regarding the transfer and marketability of skills and abilities can be invaluable in assisting officers with this transition.

Family Input and Adjustments

Most families of police officers have learned to function under unique circumstances. Shift work, rotating days off, off-duty jobs to augment income, overtime, court responsibilities, on-call status, community contact—all these sacrifices force police spouses to learn to function within a multiplicity of roles. The spouse of one retiring police officer recently reported, "I have spent the last 30 years running the household, raising the children, managing our finances, playing both father and mother, and now that he is home full-time, he insists on criticizing me and telling me what to do! I spent years waiting for him, learning how to live without him. Now, all of a sudden, he is my constant companion. He is driving me crazy! He doesn't know what to do with himself without his job to go to every day, and I don't know what to do with him here. I still love him very much, but I am afraid we can't adjust." For many, this marks the beginning of a new marriage with different agreements about roles and responsibilities and with the need for the development or discovery of common interests, goals, and ways of being together. For some, unfortunately, it marks the end of the marriage.

The average age of retirement for police officers often coincides with the time at which their children are leaving home. For officers whose focus has been more job- than family-related or whose shift work has not been conducive to family life, there may be unfinished business with those children. This may need to be resolved for the maintenance or establishment of a healthy future relationship.

Additionally, families must deal with other significant losses. Net income decreases by as much as 50 percent, and medical and dental coverage previously available may no longer be offered at the same level of coverage or cost. Vacation pay and sick time are no longer a part of everyday life. Annual raises to offset the cost of living have become things of the past.

The Need for Financial Planning

As reported by Rehm,[140] the U.S. Bureau of Labor estimates that retired individuals require an income equal to approximately 70 to 80 percent of their working income to maintain the same standard of living. For many, this means working at least part-time in addition to retirement investments. Unfortunately, many officers do not begin thinking about retirement early enough. Family demands render heavy investment in outside individual pension plans difficult, if not impossible. Optimally, retirement planning should begin at the outset of one's career, with regular review and adjustment as one's career progresses. If the officer can anticipate the date of retirement within three to five years, planning is significantly enhanced. In addition to financial options, such as deferred retirement option plans,[141] officers can also begin to consider postretirement employment options.

Career management should ideally be a consistent ongoing part of officers' entire work life. Annual or biannual meetings with supervisors as part of the evaluation process could include the planning of goals and directives for officers to maintain peak interest in their careers. The identification of strengths and exploration of placement options keep officers sharp and invested in their careers.

Some research suggests that job dissatisfaction can affect attitude.[142] There is some evidence that at least some officers work extra (non-police) jobs because they are not receiving adequate satisfaction from their police jobs.[143] Satisfaction with a career choice and the factors that determine that satisfaction or lack of it are valuable information during the initial screening and selection process. That information could also be useful in diagnosing behavioral problems and, more important, in preventing problems altogether throughout the course of an officer's career.

The results of a study conducted by Primm, Palmer, and Hastings[144] demonstrate a difference in the reported job satisfaction between officers who involve themselves in extracurricular activities and those who do not. These activities represent additional time and energy devoted to the career in an area of special expertise. Older officers with many years on the job may be successfully motivated and experience greater satisfaction if they become involved in these activities. While these interventions may increase the effective life span of the career, it is ironic that, the more satisfying the career, the more difficult it is to shape a satisfactory retirement.[145] Therefore, it seems imperative that there be a balance between ensuring a satisfying career and systematically preparing for retirement by encouraging officers to pursue outside interests as their time to retire approaches.

As officers age, planning meetings can include discussions of impending retirement. Ideally, this should begin three to five years prior to retirement. Planning is significantly impacted by the retirement system under which officers were hired. Since most officers are not likely to be ending their work years at the point of leaving the department (generally around age 50), officers could be counseled about possibilities such as returning to school for new training, continuing education in their field, exploring and planning self-employment options, and looking at new work sites as postretirement possibilities. Since most will have been outside the market for quite some time, seeking assistance with one's job-seeking skills, including résumé writing and interviewing techniques, would be helpful. Financially, officers should receive counseling regarding their specific status and needs. Planning for postretirement needs assists officers in determining the best time for retirement to ensure their financial stability.

Ideally, psychological intervention with police officers should begin at the beginning. In the postacademy, specific attention could be paid to discussion about the potential psychological impact of the job on both officers and their families. During the work life of officers, annual visits to the department psychologist would assist in identifying problems with job satisfaction and performance, psychological health and wellness, and potential family difficulties. Intervention at this stage often results in successful alleviation of the problems and adds significantly to the productive work and family life of officers. Ongoing psychological services made available to officers and dependents afford opportunities for stress reduction, addressing of duty-related difficulties, family conflict intervention, and alleviation of the symptomology associated with depression or anxiety. The early establishment of seeking and accepting psychological service as needed may likely result in an easier decision to seek assistance at the end of their careers.

In collaboration with field supervisors conducting annual job performance reviews and identifying those officers considering retirement, referral could be made for counseling with the police psychologist to explore reasons for retirement and potential postretirement issues. Additionally, spouses and family members need to be included in the counseling process to ensure a smooth transition and family stability. They, too, need to explore and address their feelings regarding this major life transition and to develop a working understanding of what to expect of their loved ones.

One method of beginning to address all these retirement issues is to have a series of seminars for all officers approaching retirement (see Figure 10.14). These seminars can cover issues such as community resources, retirement benefits, insurance, job-seeking techniques, the psychology of retirement, and financial management.[146] Additionally, a special seminar for family members can begin to prepare them for the transition and provide them an outlet for their concerns.

Finally, the department plays a huge role in the postretirement psychological adjustment of its officers. Retirement should be a time of celebration of a job well done. Far too often, officers simply slip away without acknowledgment until time has passed without their presence. A formal, public send-off with overt acknowledgment of the contributions made by retiring officers helps bring to a close their years of commitment and service. Presenting the officer's gun and badge as a gift symbolizes his or her contribution and sacrifice. A formal letter from the chief of police summarizing the officer's accomplishments and articulating the appreciation of the department and of the city provides tangible validation of a job well done.

Critical Thinking Question

1. Why do police officers have retirement needs that are significantly different from those of many civilians?

CHAPTER REVIEW

1. What are some of the major functions of the human resource management unit?
Some major functions of the human resource management unit include preparing policy statements and standard operating procedures for an agency; advising administrators and supervisors on personnel matters; maintaining a performance evaluation system; maintaining personnel data; recruiting and selecting employees; establishing criteria for the promotion of officers; conducting staff development programming; developing a pay plan; representing the agency during negotiations with employee groups; conducting exit interviews; and conducting ongoing personnel research.

ADMINISTRATIVE SPECIAL ORDER	DATE OF ISSUE 09 February 2007	EFFECTIVE DATE 13 February 2007	NO. 07-01
SUBJECT PRE-RETIREMENT PLANNING SEMINAR	DISTRIBUTION A*	RESCINDS Department Notice 01-06	

RELATED DIRECTIVES **Department Notice:** Mandatory Retirement.

I. PURPOSE

This notice informs members that the Department conducts an on-going series of Pre-Retirement Planning Seminars for sworn personnel approaching retirement age and their spouses or registered domestic partners.

II. GENERAL INFORMATION

A. The seminars are conducted four (4) times per year. The seminars are typically scheduled mid-week during the last half of the month in March, May, July, and October.

B. Each seminar addresses topics such as continuation of health benefits, credit union benefits, deferred compensation, financial planning, professional counseling service, pension benefits, social security benefits, and the legal aspects of retirement.

III. ELIGIBILITY REQUIREMENTS

A. To be eligible to register for a Pre-Retirement Planning Seminar, members must:

1. have at least fifteen (15) years of career service as a sworn member with the Chicago Police Department, **or**

2. reach sixty (60) years of age or older regardless of years of career service as sworn member with the Chicago Police Department.

B. To ensure that as many members as possible have the opportunity to attend a Pre-Retirement Planning Seminar, members will only be allowed to attend one seminar every four (4) calendar years.

IV. APPLICATION PROCEDURES

A. Registration for the Pre-Retirement Planning Seminar is now available on the Department's intranet. Department members who elect to register for the Pre-Retirement Planning Seminar and meet the requirements outlined in Item III of this directive will:

1. access the "Bureau Sites" page via the Department's intranet services home page,

2. select the "Employee Resource Services" link located under the Bureau of Administrative Services heading,

3. select the "Pre-Retirement Seminar Sign-Up" link,

4. enter his or her PC number and star number in the required form fields.

NOTE: A printable confirmation page will be displayed after the member has successfully registered.

B. A confirmation letter/form will be mailed to the applicant's unit of assignment/detail approximately four (4) weeks prior to the date of the seminar. Members must confirm their attendance for the seminar by completing and returning the confirmation letter/form to the Employee Resource Services Division no later than the date indicated on the letter/form.

FIGURE 10.14

Sample preretirement planning seminar outline. (Courtesy of the Chicago, Illinois, Police Department)

NOTE: Members must complete the confirmation letter/form and return it to the Employee Resource Services Division by the indicated date, including if the seminar date coincides with their regular day off (RDO) or a furlough day. Under no circumstances will a member be scheduled to attend the Pre-Retirement Planning Seminar if the confirmation letter/form is not received by the Employee Resource Services Division by the indicated date.

C. An Administrative Message Facsimile Network (AMFN) message indicating the members who are scheduled to attend the seminar will be sent to all units approximately two (2) days prior to the seminar.

V. **ADDITIONAL INFORMATION**

A. Attendance at a Pre-Retirement Planning Seminar is strictly voluntary.

B. Overtime will not be granted for members attending a Pre-Retirement Planning Seminar.

C. Members who attend a Pre-Retirement Planning Seminar may be carried code 047 when the seminar occurs on their normal working day.

NOTE: The member's unit of assignment has the final determination to assign the member's attendance code for the day the member attends the Pre-Retirement Planning Seminar.

D. Questions regarding the Pre-Retirement Planning Seminars can be directed to the Employee Resource Services Division at 312-745-5342 or PAX 0350.

Authenticated by:

MKH

Philip J. Cline
Superintendent of Police

07-002 MAV

*Read at roll call for four consecutive days.

*Post on bulletin board.

FIGURE 10.14 (CONTINUED)

2. What is the basic premise of the Americans with Disabilities Act?
The ADA makes it unlawful for private and public-sector employers to discriminate against people with actual or regarded disabilities in all employment practices, including application processes, recruitment, hiring, firing, advancement, pay, job assignments, transfers, training, leave, and benefits.
3. There are basically two schools of thought about physical ability testing. What are they?
The two schools of thought are the general fitness approach and the job task-based approach. Under the general approach, candidates are given tests that measure their general physical fitness through activities such as running and sit-ups. The candidates' levels of performance are measured by standards relative to age and gender. Task-based tests simulate duties required by law enforcement officers and measure the candidate's ability to perform those tasks within established time parameters.
4. Law enforcement agencies using the polygraph test in pre-employment screening have indicated there are very specific benefits derived from its use. What are these benefits?

The first benefit reported by law enforcement agencies is that polygraph tests result in fewer undesirable applicants applying to agencies, especially if it is well-publicized that a polygraph is part of the screening process. Second, there is some evidence that pre-employment polygraphs reduce agency turnover. Third, by using polygraph testing, an agency is representing to the public that it is determined to hire only those with strong moral character. Finally, veterans of law enforcement benefit psychologically from the knowledge that rookie officers have been screened regarding their honesty, character, and morals.

5. What is the difference between oral interviews and oral boards?
   An oral interview is a one-on-one meeting between an applicant and an authority in the hiring process. Such interviews tend to be unstructured and are difficult to defend against legal challenges. Oral boards involve face-to-face contact between a three-or-more member panel and an applicant. Standard questions are drawn up ahead of time, and panel members are trained in scoring the applicant during the interview.
6. Why should police agencies use a multitude of psychological tests to determine a candidate's adequacy for police officer selection?
   A combination of several psychological tests should be used because each test has varying degrees of validity, and no one test is foolproof.
7. What function does the field training officer (FTO) serve in relation to new officers?
   New officers are often placed under the supervision of a (FTO) following graduation from a police academy. The FTO monitors the development of the rookie officer under actual working conditions and provides feedback to the officer, as well as an evaluation of his or her suitability for police work. FTOs are often considered a teacher, guide, and mentor to new officers.
8. What problems contribute to the attrition of women during police academy training?
   High rates of attrition of women during academy training can be attributed to the military or boot camp style of training, an overemphasis on physical abilities, intimidation by firearms training, and sexual harassment and discrimination.
9. What are the advantages of a college education for police officers, as cited by the Police Executive Research Forum?
   The advantages of a college education for police officers include a broader base of information for decision making; a sense of responsibility honed by course requirements and achievements; a more creative approach to solving problems; a greater empathy for diverse populations and their needs; greater adaptability to change; better communication skills; higher levels of professionalism; a less cynical outlook on policing; and a less authoritarian style in dealing with the public.
10. What provision of the Fair Labor Standards Act applies most directly to police officers?
    The most important aspect of the Fair Labor Standards Act for police officers is the requirement that, under specific circumstances, officers must be paid at an overtime rate or given compensatory time.
11. What rights does the Family Medical Leave Act give police officers?
    The Family Medical Leave Act gives officers who have been employed for at least 1 year, and who have worked at least 1,250 hours during that year, the right to family or medical leave for up to 12 weeks. The time off may be paid or unpaid by the employer's discretion, but the officer must be able to return to work after the time off. Time off may be taken for the birth of a child, the care of a family member, or for self-care.
12. What are the major purposes of performance evaluations?
    The major purposes of performance evaluations are to motivate employees to maintain an acceptable level of performance, to assist in career development, to encourage supervisors to take a personal interest in employees under their command, to provide feedback on selection practices, and to serve as a basis for salary decisions.

13. What criteria must be met for a performance appraisal system to be acceptable by the courts?
    Appraisals must focus on standards identified by a job analysis to be legally acceptable. They must consist of standards that have been clearly communicated to and understood by employees and should be based on specifically defined dimensions. These dimensions should be anchored to objective and observable behaviors, and explanations of these behaviors should be logical and brief. The appraisal system and the ratings must be reliable and valid. Finally, an appeal mechanism should be available for employees who disagree with their ratings.
14. Pay plans must accomplish several objectives. What are they?
    When a pay plan is being developed, it must ensure that salaries are equitable in relation to the complexity and responsibility of the work performed; maintain a competitive position in the employment market to ensure recruitment and retention; provide data needed in financial and personnel management, such as budgeting and payroll; stimulate personnel management and reward good performance; provide an orderly system of salary policy and control; and ensure compliance with federal and state labor laws regarding overtime.
15. What is an assessment center?
    The term "assessment center" can describe both a process and a place. As a process, an assessment center uses a variety of simulated situations to evaluate the behavior and suitability of a job candidate. As a place, an assessment center is a physical site dedicated to conducting such evaluations.
16. What are some of the factors that should be considered in applying discipline?
    Some of the factors that should be considered during the administration of discipline against personnel include what motivated the employee to act in a way that requires discipline, the degree of harm resulting from the employee error, the experience of the employee, the employee's past record, and whether the incident was intentional or unintentional.
17. Five profiles of violence-prone officers were discussed in this chapter. Identify each.
    The five profiles of a violence-prone officer are officers with personality disorders that place them at chronic risk; officers whose previous job-related experience places them at risk; officers who have problems early in their police careers; officers who develop inappropriate patrol styles; and officers with personal problems.
18. What are the three basic phases of the early warning system?
    The three basic phases of the early warning system are identification of officers with problematic behavior, intervention, and monitoring of the officer's subsequent performance.
19. What are the two philosophies guiding the assignment of persons to investigate personnel complaints?
    The two philosophies guiding the selection of officers for the internal affairs unit are the investigative philosophy and the supervisory philosophy. In the investigative philosophy, internal affairs officers are charged with the investigation of personnel complaints but are entirely removed from the decision-making and punishment processes. The supervisory philosophy dictates that internal investigations are an inherent part of agency control, supervision, and discipline and should therefore be carried out by a supervisor.
20. When is drug testing warranted during a personnel investigation?
    Drug testing is warranted during a personnel investigation when objective symptoms of alcohol or other drug use are present or there is a reasonable suspicion that substance abuse is involved in a complaint against personnel.
21. What issues are inherent in a law enforcement officer's life stage of retirement?
    The issues inherent in a law enforcement officer's retirement include financial, lifestyle, leisure time, identity, psychological needs, and marriage and family adaptation.

KEY TERMS

Americans with Disabilities Act (ADA): a wide-ranging civil rights law enacted by Congress in 1990 that prohibits, under certain circumstances, discrimination based on disability.

Assessment centers: a means of evaluating the behavior of candidates for a job through a series of simulations or exercises, also the physical place where such exercises are conducted.

Character investigation: a review and verification of all information given by a job applicant regarding employment education, military service, history, and related matters.

Disability: a physical or mental impairment that substantially limits a major life activity.

Early warning system: a data-based police management tool designed to identify officers whose behaviors are problematic and need intervention.

Field training officer (FTO): an experienced field officer who acts as a teacher, a mentor, and an evaluator to rookie officers.

Fair Labor Standards Act (FLSA): the act, first passed in 1938 and extended to government employees in 1985, which established a minimum wage, guaranteed overtime compensation, and curtailed the employment of minors.

Family Medical Leave Act (FMLA): the labor law passed in 1993 that allowed workers to take leave due to illness or the birth of a child or to care for a sick family member; it guaranteed that workers could return to their jobs subsequently.

Human resource management unit: the department in an organization dealing with matters involving employees, such as hiring, training, performance evaluation, compensation, labor relations, and benefits.

Internal affairs unit (IAU): a unit or an individual within a law enforcement agency charged with the responsibility of overseeing the acceptance, investigation, and adjudication of complaints about officers within that agency.

Oral boards: face-to-face contact between a three-or-more-member panel and a job applicant, during which the trained panel members evaluate a candidate based on responses to standard job-related questions.

Polygraph: an instrument that simultaneously records changes in the physiological processes of a subject, including heartbeat, blood pressure, and respiration; often used as a lie detector.

Psychological testing: an assessment using standardized tests and other information, such as personal history, to measure and make inferences about an individual's personality.

Performance evaluation: an assessment by an employer that evaluates the performance of an employee and offers feedback and career development opportunities.

Pay plan: a schedule of salary ranges for specific job titles.

Rater error: an inherent problem in performance appraisals often attributed to non-standardized measurements and the subjectivity of the person doing the evaluation.

NOTES

1. O. G. Stahl and R. A. Staufenberger, eds., *Police Personnel Administration* (Washington, D.C.: Police Foundation, 1974), p. 111.
2. For a detailed analysis of these findings and recommendations, see President's Commission on Law Enforcement and the Administration of Justice, *Task Force Report on the Police* (Washington, D.C.: U.S. Government Printing Office, 1967), and *Report of the National Advisory Commission on Civil Disorder* (New York: New York Times, 1968).
3. The failure on the part of any law enforcement agency to identify high-risk police officers, especially those who have demonstrated a propensity for misconduct, will find that this issue is going to be raised in any litigation that results from the actions of such officers.
4. W. D. Heisel and P. V. Murphy, "Organization for Police Personnel Management," in *Police Personnel Administration,* ed. O. G. Stahl and R. A. Staufenberger (Washington, D.C.: Police Foundation, 1974), p. 1.
5. L. Tenito, C. R. Swanson, Jr., and N. C. Chamelin, *The Police Personnel Selection Process* (Indianapolis: Bobbs-Merrill, 1977), p. 3.
6. Heisel and Murphy, "Organization for Police Personnel Management," pp. 8–11.

7. U.S. Equal Employment Opportunity Commission, *The Americans with Disabilities Act: Your Responsibilities as an Employer* (Washington, D.C.: U.S. Government Printing Office, 1991), p. 2.
8. Ibid., p. 3.
9. U.S. Equal Employment Opportunity Commission and U.S. Department of Justice, *The Americans with Disabilities Act: Questions and Answers* (Washington, D.C.: U.S. Government Printing Office, July 1991), p. 7.
10. Jeffrey Higginbotham, "The Americans with Disabilities Act," *FBI Law Enforcement Bulletin* 60, no. 8 (1991): 26.
11. Ibid., 26–27.
12. Ibid., 26.
13. Ibid.
14. Ibid.
15. Ibid.
16. Ibid.
17. Ibid.
18. U.S. Equal Employment Opportunity Commission, *The Americans with Disabilities Act*, p. 4.
19. Ibid., p. 5.
20. Ibid.
21. U.S. Equal Employment Opportunity Commission and U.S. Department of Justice, *The Americans with Disabilities Act*, p. 4.
22. Ibid.
23. Ibid., p. 6.
24. Jody M. Litchford, "The Americans with Disabilities Act," *Police Chief* 58, no. 1 (1991): 11.
25. U.S. Equal Employment Opportunity Commission, *The Americans with Disabilities Act*, p. 10.
26. Ibid.
27. Ibid., p. 6.
28. J. D. Colbridge, "The Americans with Disabilities Act—a Practical Guide for Police Departments," *FBI Law Enforcement Bulletin* (January 2001): 25–27.
29. U.S. Equal Employment Opportunity Commission, "ABA Enforcement Guidance: Preemployment Disability-Related Questions and Medical Examination," October 10, 1995; 29 CFR 1630.14(a); 29 CFR, App., Pt. 1630.14(a). Employers should also consult their legal advisers on the impact of Title VII of the Civil Rights Act of 1964, as amended, on the use of physical agility and physical fitness tests as selection criteria.
30. See note 2.
31. See note 2.
32. See note 2.
33. 42 U.S.C. 12112(b)(6). In addition, employers must be prepared to meet challenges to these tests under Title VII of the Civil Rights Act of 1964 as well as other discrimination statutes. Recognized mental disorders are listed in the American Psychiatric Association's *Diagnostic and Statistical Manual of Mental Disorders.*
34. See note 2; *Barnes v. Cochran,* 944 F. Supp. 897 (S.D. Fla. 1996), affirmed 130 F. 3d 443 (11th Cir. 1997).
35. See note 2.
36. 442 U.S.C. 12112 (b)(S)(A).
37. See note 2.
38. 42 U.S.C. 1211 2(b)(5)(B).
39. See note 2.
40. See note 2.
41. See note 2; 29 CFR Pt. 1630, App. 1630, 14(b).
42. See note 2.
43. 42 U.S.C. 12112(b)(5)(A).
44. 42 U.S.C. 12112(b)(6); 42 U.S.C. 12113(a).
45. 42 U.S.C. 12112(b)(5)(A).
46. 42 U.S.C. 12113(b).
47. 42 U.S.C. 12112(d)(3). The only exceptions to the confidentiality requirement are that supervisors be informed about job-necessary restrictions because of the medical condition, that safety personnel be told if the condition may require emergency treatment, and that government compliance officials be given relevant information on request.
48. See note 2; 29 CFR Pt. 1630, App. 1630. 1 4(b).
49. *Kuntz v. City of New Haven et al.*, No. N-90-480(JGM), March 3, 1993.
50. *Bombrys v. City of Toledo,* No. 3:92CV7592, June 4, 1993.
51. *Champ v. Baltimore County et al.*, No. HAR 93-4031, April 19, 1995.
52. James J. Fyfe, Jack R. Greene, William F. Walsh, O. W. Wilson, and Roy Clinton McLaren, *Police Administration,* 5th ed. (New York: McGraw-Hill, 1997), p. 278.
53. Philip Ash, Karen Slora, and Cynthia F. Britton, "Police Agency Selection Practices," *Journal of Police Science and Administration* 17, no. 4 (1990): 262.
54. Ibid., 263.
55. U.S. Equal Employment Opportunity Commission, "Adoption of Questions and Answers to Clarify and Provide a Common Interpretation of the Uniform Guidelines on Employee Selection Procedures," *Federal Register,* March 2, 1979, p. 12007.
56. Ibid., p. 12003.
57. Ibid., p. 11998.
58. 438 U.S. 265 (1978).
59. For a more detailed discussion, see "Backgrounder on the Court Judgement of

the *University of California v. Bakke*" (http://USINFO.State.Gov/USA/Infousa/facts/DEMOCRAC/41.HTM).

60. 43 FEP Cases 130 (1989).
61. 57 Law Week 4616 (1989).
62. Civil Rights Act of 1991, Title 1, Section 1977A.
63. *Recruiting and Retaining Women: A Self-assessment Guide for Law Enforcement* (Los Angeles: National Center for Women and Policing, 2000), pp. 66–68.
64. Ash et al., "Police Agency Selection Practices," p. 265.
65. Ibid.
66. Ibid.
67. Ibid.
68. Leonard Territo, "Use of the Polygraph in the Pre-employment Screening Process," *Police Chief* (July 1974): 51–53.
69. Robert M. Guion, "Personnel Assessment, Selection, and Placement," in *Handbook of Industrial and Organizational Psychology*, vol. 2, eds. Marvin D. Dunnette and Leaetta M. Hough (Palo Alto, Calif.: Consulting Psychologists Press, 1991), p. 347.
70. *Recruiting and Retaining Women*, p. 71.
71. Ibid., p. 70.
72. Lt. Stephen Hartnett, Tampa, Florida, Police Department, interview with Tampa Police Contractual Psychologist, Vincent Skotko.
73. Daron D. Diecidue, *Development of Pre-employment Psychological "Screening-in" Testing for Police Dispatchers*. Retrieved November 10, 2005, from www.fdle.state.fl.us/FCJEI/HRissues.htm.
74. John Super, 2005 COPPS Questionnaire, 2005.
75. Ibid.
76. Ibid.
77. Ibid.
78. Daniel E. Martin, Lloyd R. Sloan, Peter J. Legree, and Ivy K. Yeung, *Self-Motivating, Unobtrusive Cognitive Aptitude Measures: New Survey Technology*, Proceedings of Hawaii International Conference on Social Science, 2003.
79. Lesley C. Morey, *Personality Assessment Inventory—Professional Manual* (Odessa, FL Psychological Assessment Resources, 2001).
80. *Minnesota Multiphasic Personality Inventory–2* (Minneapolis: University of Minnesota Press, 1989), questions 28, 36, 141, 143, and 182, as quoted in Paula N. Rubin, *Americans with Disabilities Act and Criminal Justice: New Employees* (Washington D.C: U.S. Department of Justice, National Institute of Justice, Research in Action, October 1994).
81. Ibid.
82. Ibid.
83. President's Commission on Law Enforcement and Administration of Justice, *Task Force Report on the Police*, p. 137.
84. *Recruiting and Retaining Women*, pp. 83–89.
85. Los Angeles Police Commission, "Police Academy and Probationary Officer Attrition," 2000.
86. Catherine A. MacKinnon, *Sexual Harassment of Working Women* (New Haven, Conn.: Yale University Press, 1979).
87. Commission on Accreditation for Law Enforcement Agencies, *The Standards Manual of Law Enforcement Agency Accreditation Program*, 4th ed. (Fairfax, Va.: 1999), pp. 33–44.
88. M. J. Palmiotto, "Should a College Degree Be Required for Today's Law Enforcement Officer?" in *Constitutional Issues in Policing*, ed. James D. Sewell (Boston: Allyn and Bacon, 1999), pp. 70–75. (This discussion was adapted with permission from this source.)
89. R. W. Kobetz, *Law Enforcement and Criminal Justice Education Directory, 1975–76*. (Gaithersburg, Md.: International Association of Chiefs of Police, 1997).
90. President's Commission on Law Enforcement and Administration of Justice, *The Challenge of Crime in a Free Society* (Washington, D.C.: U.S. Government Printing Office, 1967).
91. J. B. Jacobs and S. B. Magdovitz, "At LEEP's End? A Review of the Law Enforcement Education Program," *Journal of Police Science and Administration* 5, no. 1 (1977): 7.
92. National Advisory Commission on Criminal Justice Standards and Goals, *The Police* (Washington, D.C.: U.S. Government Printing Office, 1973).
93. Jacobs and Magdovitz, "At LEEP's End?"
94. J. J. Sienna, "Criminal Justice Higher Education—Its Growth and Directions," *Crime and Delinquency*, 20, no. 4 (1974): 389–97.
95. W. R. Anderson, "The Law Enforcement Education Act of 1967," *Congressional Record*, H.R. 188 (1967), January.
96. W. H. Hewitt, "The Objectives of Formal Police Education," *Police* 9, no. 2 (1964): 25–27.
97. Sienna, "Criminal Justice Higher Education."
98. National Advisory Commission on Criminal Justice Standards and Goals, *The Police*, p. 367.
99. Ibid.

100. D. L. Carter, A. D. Sapp, and D. W. Stephens, *The State of Police Education: Police Direction for the 21st Century* (Washington, D.C.: Police Executive Research Forum, 1986).
101. Will Aitchison, *The Rights of Police Officers,* 3rd ed. (Portland, Ore.: Labor Relations Information System, 1996), p. 361. (This source has been paraphrased in preparing this section.)
102. Ibid., p. 362.
103. Ibid., p. 375.
104. Ibid., p. 371.
105. Ibid., p. 374.
106. Ibid., p. 362.
107. Ibid., p. 363.
108. Ibid.
109. Ibid., p. 366.
110. Ibid., p. 365.
111. Ibid.
112. Ibid.
113. Ibid., p. 378.
114. Ibid.
115. J. Higginbotham, "The Family and Medical Leave Act of 1993," *FBI Law Enforcement Bulletin* (December 1993): 15–21.
116. W. Bopp and P. M. Whisenand, *Police Personnel Administration,* 2nd ed. (Boston: Allyn and Bacon, 1980).
117. W. F., Cascio and J. Bernadin, "Implications of Performance Appraisal Litigation for Personnel Decisions," *Personnel Psychology* 9 (1981): 211–26.
118. Larry K. Gaines, John L. Worrall, Mittie D. Southerland, and John Angell, *Police Administration,* 2nd ed. (New York: McGraw-Hill, 2003), pp. 384, 387.
119. J. N. Matzer, Jr., *Personnel Administration: A Guide for Small Local Governments* (Washington, D.C.: Civil Service Commission).
120. D. P. Slevin, "The Assessment Center: Breakthrough in Management Appraisal and Development," *Personnel Journal* 57 (April 1972): 256.
121. M. D. Dunnette and S. J. Motowidlo, *Police Selection and Career Assessment* (Washington, D.C.: U.S. Government Printing Office, 1976), p. 56.
122. M. McLaurin, "How to Run an Assessment Center," *Police* (March 2005): 22–23.
123. Ibid., p. 24.
124. Ibid.
125. Ibid., p. 26.
126. Darrel W. Stephens, "Discipline Philosophy," *FBI Law Enforcement Bulletin* 63, no. 3 (March 1994): 21.
127. Ibid., p. 22.
128. Ellen N. Scrivner, "Controlling Police Use of Excessive Force: The Role of the Police Psychologist," U.S. Department of Justice, Office of Justice Programs, *National Institute of Justice,* October 1994, pp. 2–4.
129. Samuel Walker, Geoffrey P. Alpert, and Dennis J. Kenney, "Early Warning Systems: Responding to the Problem Police Officers," U.S. Department of Justice, Officer Justice Programs, National Institute of Justice, July 2001, pp. 1–6. (This discussion was adapted from this source.)
130. "Kansas City Police Go After Their 'Bad Boys,'" *New York Times,* September 10, 1991, and "Waves of Abuse Laid to a Few Officers," *Boston Globe,* October 4, 1992.
131. Herman Goldstein, *Policing a Free Society* (Cambridge, Mass.: Ballinger, 1977), p.171.
132. *Who Is Guarding the Guardians?* (Washington, D.C.: U.S. Commission on Civil Rights, 1981), p. 81.
133. For discussions of recommended performance categories, see *International Association of Chief of Police, Building Integrity and Reducing Drug Corruption in Police Departments* (Washington, D.C.: U.S. Department of Justice, Bureau of Justice Assistance, 1989), p. 80, and Lou Reiter, *Law Enforcement Administrative Investigations: A Manual Guide,* 2nd ed. (Tallahassee, Fla.: Lou Reiter and Associates, 1998), p. 18-2.
134. Franklin Zimring and Gordon Hawkins, *Deterrence* (Chicago: University of Chicago Press, 1973).
135. Walker et al., "Early Warning Systems," p. 3.
136. Information provided by Deputy Chief Raymond D. Schultz, Albuquerque, New Mexico, Police Department, correspondence dated June 3, 2002.
137. L Reiter, *Law Enforcement Administrative Investigations: A Manual Guide,* 2nd ed. (Tallahassee, Fla.: Lou Reiter and Associates, 1998). (This discussion of the internal affairs units was adapted with permission from this source, pp. 3-6 through 3-11 and 6-9 through 6-12.)
138. Jeanette L. Palmer, "Police Retirement: Life after the Force," *American Criminal Justice Association Journal* 60–61, nos. 1–4 (spring/summer 1998, fall/winter 1999): 18–20.
139. B. Rehm, "Retirement: A New Chapter Not the End of the Story," *FBI Law Enforcement Bulletin* 65, no. 9 (1996): 6–12.
140. Ibid.
141. T. Carlton, "Police Pension and Retirement System," *FBI Law Enforcement Bulletin* 63, no. 4 (1994): 23.

142. V. H. Vroom, "Ego-Involvement, Job Satisfaction, and Job Performance," *Personnel Psychology* 15 (1962): 159–77.
143. M. G. Grant, "The Relationship of Moonlighting to Job Dissatisfaction in Police Officers," *Journal of Police Science and Administration* 5 (1977): 193–96.
144. M. Primm, D. Palmer, and P. Hastings, "An Examination of Career Satisfaction in Professional Police Officers: A Field Study," *American Criminal Justice Association L.A.E. Journal,* 58–59 (1997–1998): 42–45.
145. L. Harrison, "The More Satisfying the Career, the More Difficult It Is to Shape a Satisfactory Retirement," *Police Chief,* October 1981.
146. J. Violanti, "Police Retirement: The Impact of Change," *FBI Law Enforcement Bulletin* 59, no. 3 (1992): 12–15.

"You, a lowly policeman is going to tell me how to run my department! . . . Get out!" and you had to go; he hated me. . . .

—Rank-and-File Organization Leader John Cassese on an Early Meeting with New York City Police Commissioner Kennedy

11

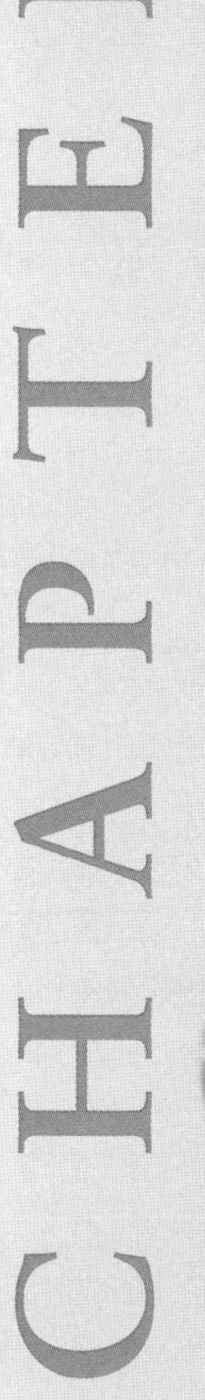

OUTLINE

Introduction

The Unionization of the Police and Its Impact

The General Structure of Laws Governing Collective Bargaining for Law Enforcement Officers

Establishing the Bargaining Relationship

Negotiations

Grievances

Job Actions

Chapter Review

Key Terms

Notes

OBJECTIVES

1. Identify and briefly discuss the seven major factors that led to unionization.
2. Discuss some ways that unions have impacted public policy decisions.
3. Understand the three simplified models of public employee collective bargaining laws.
4. Describe how a union begins an organizing drive.
5. Identify who generally serves on management and union teams during negotiations.
6. Understand the typical sequence of events involved in the grievance process.
7. List and describe the four major forms of job action.
8. Describe five things that police leaders do to limit the possibility of job actions by uniformed officers.

LABOR RELATIONS

INTRODUCTION

No single force in the past 50 years has had as much impact on the administration of police agencies as collective bargaining by officers. Police unions represent a major force that police managers must reckon with. In this chapter, we will first examine some of the historical as well as the contemporary reasons that police unions have grown so rapidly and become so powerful. We will also discuss the general structure of laws governing collective bargaining for law enforcement officers.

Since grievance issues are an inevitable part of the collective bargaining process, we will first examine what a grievance is and how such grievances can best be handled. The issue of job actions, such as votes of confidence, work slowdowns, work speedups, and work stoppages will also be discussed. Last, we will discuss the appropriate administrative reactions to job actions, along with anticipatory strategies.

THE UNIONIZATION OF THE POLICE AND ITS IMPACT

From 1959 through the 1970s, a number of events combined to foster public-sector collective bargaining. These significant forces were (1) the needs of labor organizations, (2) the reduction of legal barriers, (3) police frustration with the perceived lack of support for their "war on crime," (4) personnel practices in police agencies, (5) salaries and benefits, (6) an increase in violence directed at police, and (7) the success of police departments already unionized in making an impact through collective action.[1]

The Needs of Labor Organizations

The attention of labor organizations was devoted almost entirely to the private sector until the 1960s. However, as the opportunity to gain new members became increasingly constrained because of the extensive organization of industrial workers, unions cast about for new markets, and statistics such as these impressed them:

> *Public service is the most rapidly growing major sector of employment in the United States. In the last 40 years public employment has tripled, growing from 4.2 million to 13.1 million employees. Today nearly one out of five workers in the United States is on a government payroll.*[2]

Thus, as with any organization that achieves its primary objective, labor groups redefined their sphere of interest to include public employees. Concurrently, there were stirrings among public employees to use collective action to improve their lot.

The Reduction of Legal Barriers

Although workers in the private sector had been given the right to bargain collectively under the federal National Labor Relations Act of 1935, it was another quarter of a century before the first state enacted even modest bargaining rights for public employees. Beginning with the granting of public-sector collective bargaining rights in Wisconsin in 1959, many of the legal barriers that had been erected in the wake of the Boston police strike of 1919 began to tumble. Other states that also extended such rights to at least some classes of employees at an early date included California (1961) and Connecticut, Delaware, Massachusetts, Michigan, Oregon, Washington, and Wyoming, all in 1965. Many other states followed this lead, particularly from

1967 to 1974.[3] President John F. Kennedy granted limited collective bargaining rights to federal workers in 1962 by Executive Order 10988. The courts, too, were active in removing barriers; for example, in *Atkins v. City of Charlotte* (1969), the U.S. district court struck down a portion of a North Carolina statute prohibiting being or becoming a union member as an infringement on the First Amendment right to free association.[4] While *Atkins* involved firefighters, the federal courts reached similar conclusions involving Atlanta police officers in *Melton v. City of Atlanta* (1971)[5] and a Colorado deputy sheriff in *Lontine v. VanCleave* (1973).[6]

Police Frustration with Support for the War on Crime

Historically, the police have felt isolated in their effort to control crime. This stems from two factors: perceived public hostility and the impact of the due process revolution.

The police perceive a great deal more public hostility than actually exists. Illustrative of this is a survey of one big-city department, which found that over 70 percent of the officers had an acute sense of citizen hostility or contempt.[7] In contrast, a survey conducted by the National Opinion Research Center revealed that 77 percent of the respondents felt that the police were doing a "very good" or "pretty good" job of protecting people in their neighborhoods, and a Gallup poll showed that 70 percent of the public had a great deal of respect for the police.[8] These data notwithstanding, the police saw the public as hostile, and the most persuasive "evidence" of this emerged in the attempts to create civilian review boards, which carried several latent messages to police officers. First, it created anger with its implied allegation that the police could not, or would not, keep their own house in order. Second, it fostered the notion that politicians were ready to "throw the police to wolves" and thus were part of "them."

Particularly among street-level officers, the reaction of the police to the whirlwind of Supreme Court decisions, discussed in Chapter 4, Politics and Police Administration, was one of dismay at being "handcuffed" in attempts to control crime. It tended to alienate the police from the Supreme Court and to contribute to a general feeling that social institutions that should support the police effort in combatting crime were, instead, at odds with it.

Personnel Practices

Past practices become precedent, precedent becomes tradition, and tradition in turn becomes the mighty anchor of many organizations. By the late 1960s, the tendency to question the appropriateness of certain traditions was pervasive. Police rank-and-file members were no exception. This tendency was heightened by the increased educational achievement of police officers. Although management's general performance was often judged to be suspect, traditional personnel practices were the greatest concern, as these directly affected the individual officer.

Among the practices that were most distasteful to rank-and-file members were the requirement to attend, unpaid, a 30-minute roll call immediately before the 8-hour tour of duty; uncompensated court attendance during off-duty time; short-notice changes in shift assignments; having to return to the station from home for minor matters, such as signing reports without pay or compensatory time for such periods; favoritism in work assignments and selection for attendance at prestigious police training schools; and arbitrary disciplinary procedures. Gradually, the gap between officers and management widened. Officers began turning to employee organizations to rectify collectively the shortcomings of their circumstances. Subsequently, the solidarity of police officers was to prove of great benefit to employee organizations.

In addition to providing material for ferment through illegal, ill-conceived, abrasive, or insensitive general personnel practices, police managers often unwittingly contributed to the resolve and success of police unions by their treatment of leaders of police employee associations. In Atlanta, the chief of police transferred the president of the Fraternal Order of Police 51 times in 45 days for his outspokenness,[9] and in Boston, Dick MacEachern, founder and president of the then-fledgling Police Patrolmen's Association, was transferred repeatedly from precinct to precinct, and Mayor White subsequently refused to sign MacEachern's disability pension for the same reason.[10] Such actions provide free publicity, create a martyr (an essential for many social movements), put the leaders in contact with people they ordinarily would not meet, increase group cohesiveness, and provide compelling confirmation in the minds of rank-and-file members why they need and should join a union.

Salaries and Benefits

As did other government workers in the 1960s, police officers felt that their salaries, fringe benefits, and working conditions were not adequate. In 1961, mining production workers were averaging $111 a week in earnings, lithographers $114, tire and inner-tube producers $127, and telephone line construction workers $133,[11] whereas the pay of police officers averaged far less. Even by 1965, the salary range for patrol officer in the larger cities, those with more than 100,000 in population, was only between $5,763, and $6,919.[12] The rank-and-file members believed increasingly that, if what was fairly theirs would not be given willingly, they would fight for it. In New York City, the Patrolmen's Benevolent Association (PBA) was believed to have been instrumental, from 1958 to 1969, in increasing entry-level salaries from $5,800 to $11,000 per year; obtaining longevity pay, shift differential pay, and improved retirement benefits; and increasing the death benefit from $400 to $16,500.[13] In 1968, the Boston PBA, in negotiating its first contract—which required mediation—obtained increased benefits for its members—such as an annual increase of $1,010; time and a half for all overtime, including court appearances; and 12 paid holidays.[14] However, in recent years, police unions have been called upon not only to fight for pay raises for its members but also to oppose threatened pay cuts (see Figure 11.1).

When such objections are distilled and analyzed, what often remains is the fear that police unions will result ultimately in reduced executive prerogatives. There can be little serious question that such fears have a reasonable and factual basis. As coequal

In The News

Today's News

Battle Goes to the Wire and Boston Police Get a Raise

After working without a contract for two years, Boston police scored a victory over Mayor Thomas Menino in 2004 as their union campaigned for a pay raise. The Boston Police Patrolmen's Association (BPPA) fought for a 17 percent pay raise over four years for the city's police, while the mayor held out for an increase of just 11.5 percent. The BPPA mounted an aggressive campaign, enlisting union members to write to legislators and send letters to the editors of national publications. The union also manned informational picket lines throughout Boston and took out ads in *The Washington Post* and *The New York Times* to raise awareness nationwide.

The campaign by the BPPA coincided with the 2004 Democratic National Convention. Two weeks earlier, Senator John Kerry canceled a keynote address in Boston for the U.S. Conference of Mayors rather than cross a BPPA picket line; city officials were afraid the same would happen during the convention. The mayor entered into expedited **arbitration** shortly before convention delegates were set to arrive, and in a matter of hours the arbitrator handed down his decision. Boston police officers would receive a 14 percent salary increase over the next four years with no concessions in return. The BPPA credited its victory to the support of union members, the community, and police officers from around the country.

Source: "Battle Goes to the Wire, Boston Cops Get a Raise," *American Police Beat*, September 2004.

FIGURE 11.1

San Diego police officers stand in support of their union representative during a city council meeting recently in San Diego. San Francisco police officers are wondering how they will meet their financial commitments if they are forced to take a 6.5 percent pay cut to help the city out of its financial crisis. (Denis Porory/AP Wide World Photos)

to management at the bargaining table, police unions represent a new power center that has in many instances effectively diminished management's unilateral and sometimes ill-considered exercise of control. In some matters, administrators have simply made bad bargains, giving away prerogatives vital to the ability to manage properly. Far more difficult to assess are the consequences to the times that police executives have failed to act, or have acted differently, in anticipation of the union's stand.

Police unions have impacted public policy decisions in many ways. For example, in various cities they have thwarted the use of civilian review boards; advocated the election of "law and order" candidates; resisted the replacement of two-officer cars with one-officer cars; litigated to avoid layoffs; lobbied for increased budgets, especially for raises; caused the removal of chiefs and other high-ranking commanders; advocated the elimination of radar guns from patrol vehicles because of potential adverse health risks associated with their use; and opposed annexation and the firing of union members.

Police labor organizers often maintain that there is only one color that counts: the color of the uniform. Despite this low-pitched plea for solidarity among rank-and-file members, police employee associations and unions are believed by some observers to have contributed to racial tensions. The president-elect of the Boston Police Patrolmen's Association told a forum on crime and violence that "if black men want to go out and fornicate and don't want to take care of their nests . . . then we have a problem." The comment set off a firestorm of reaction from both African Americans and whites.[15] Other instances that have heightened racial tensions include the opposition of police unions to civilian review boards and the use of their support to help elect white candidates running against African Americans. Such incidents have created the feeling among African Americans that white-dominated employee organizations are insensitive to issues affecting minorities. Consequently, African Americans have tended to form their own organizations to address issues of importance to them.

When the objectives of the union and the police administrator are the same, the union can be a powerful ally. Even when they are not the same, the union may line up behind a chief and provide support if the cost to the union is not too great. In such instances, it may be simply a case of a display of police solidarity, the fact that the union likes a city manager or mayor even less than it likes the chief, the desire to improve the union's image by supporting something from which there is no apparent gain, or for some other reason. Also, when the union exercises its considerable political muscle, it can defeat important policy and program initiatives by the police chief, such as halting the use of one-officer cars as an alternative to two-officer units. It is here that the union confronts the police executive at a basic point: the control of the police department. One chief left a unionized department to take a similar position in another state that did not allow public-sector collective bargaining. Over a period of time, the city formerly employing him had given up control over many administrative matters as a substitute for demands made by the union for economic gains. As the chief himself put it, "I realized I had to get out because the union could do two things I couldn't; it could stop the department and it could start it." Although an extreme example, it does bring clearly into focus the issue of who controls the department for what purpose. Moreover, it squarely raises the issue of accountability: if police chiefs control increasingly less of their departments, to what extent can they be properly held accountable? Finally, presuming that a chief wants to administer for the common good, for the safety of the general public, but cannot do so, then for whose benefit is the department being operated?

Critical Thinking Questions

1. Discuss how the due process revolution contributed to police frustration. Can you think of current issues within policing that could contribute to a similar atmosphere?
2. How has the movement toward a more educated police force contributed to a more unionized police force?
3. Do you think that police unions have resulted in reduced executive prerogatives? Why or why not?

THE GENERAL STRUCTURE OF LAWS GOVERNING COLLECTIVE BARGAINING FOR LAW ENFORCEMENT OFFICERS

Without question, the broadest grant of rights to law enforcement officers exists in **collective bargaining** agreements. Under collective bargaining agreements, the wages and benefits of law enforcement officers are guaranteed for the duration of the agreement, and, most significantly, officers who dispute a decision of their employer concerning working conditions usually have the right to appeal that decision through a grievance procedure which culminates with a final and binding decision by a neutral third party.

Under the terms of the federal National Labor Relations Act, state governmental bodies and their political subdivisions, such as cities and counties, are excluded from the definition of "employer" and are not brought within the scope of federal labor laws. As a result, laws regulating collective bargaining for state, county, and city law enforcement officers have developed on a state-by-state basis and, occasionally, on a local basis.

Although public employee collective bargaining laws in each state are different, the general thrust of the laws can be summarized by three simplified models, the **binding arbitration model**, the **meet and confer model**, and the **bargaining not required model.**[16]

Binding Arbitration Model

In states following the binding arbitration model, public employees are granted the right to select exclusive representatives for the purposes of bargaining with their employers. In such states, the public employer and the labor organization are required to bargain in good faith until impasse, then to submit any unresolved disputes to a process known as "interest arbitration," in which a neutral third party selected by the parties makes a final and binding resolution of those issues.

In binding arbitration, the neutral third party decides what the terms and conditions of the new collective bargaining agreement will be, usually using standards established by state statute. For example, Michigan's collective bargaining law contains standard language governing the right of law enforcement labor organizations to binding arbitration, a right which is always accompanied by a ban on the right of law enforcement officers to strike:

> *It is the public policy of this state that in public police and fire departments, where the right of employees to strike is by law prohibited, it is requisite to the high morale of such employees and the efficient operation of such departments to afford an alternate, expeditious, effective and binding procedure for the resolution of disputes, and to that end the provisions of this act, providing for compulsory arbitration, shall be literally constructed.*[17]

There are three general types of binding arbitration laws, reflecting differences in the latitude given arbitrators to render decisions. Under the first type, known as an "issue-by-issue" law, an arbitrator has the obligation to render a decision on each issue independently and to craft an award on each issue that best accomplishes the purposes of the arbitration statute. Under the second type of law, known as "final offer, issue-by-issue," the arbitrator renders a decision on each issue independently, but must award the final offer made by one of the parties, and is not free to craft a compromise position which has not been specifically proposed by either party. The third type of law, known as "total package" arbitration, requires the arbitrator to select the most reasonable of the total packages submitted by each party, even if selected elements of that party's total package might not have been awarded by the arbitrator on an issue-by-issue basis. All states with binding arbitration require an arbitrator to analyze a set of criteria established by statute, usually including factors such as the wages and benefits paid in comparable jurisdictions, the cost of living, and an employer's ability to pay.[18]

Employers have challenged binding arbitration laws under a variety of theories, including arguments that binding arbitration is an unconstitutional delegation of legislative authority and that binding arbitration inappropriately interferes with a city or county's home rule status. Almost uniformly, such challenges have not been successful, with courts upholding binding arbitration as a rational means to bring about the resolution of bargaining disputes involving law enforcement officers.[19]

Meet and Confer Model

In states following the meet and confer model, law enforcement officers have the same rights to organize and select their collective bargaining representative as those in the binding arbitration model. However, in such states, employers are only obligated to "meet and confer" with the collective bargaining representative, with no method of impasse resolution typically specified in the bargaining law.

When negotiations end in impasse in a meet and confer setting, the employer is allowed unilaterally to implement its last best offer, or at least the portion of the offer that contains mandatory subjects of bargaining.[20] This leaves the officers in the position of accepting the employer's last offer of settlement, taking whatever form of job action is permissible under the laws of the state, or attempting political or other measures to resolve the collective bargaining dispute.

The bargaining obligations of an employer in a meet and confer state are (1) to meet the labor organization promptly on request, personally, and for a reasonable period of time and (2) to try to agree on matters within the scope of representation.[21] Good faith negotiations in a meet and confer setting have been characterized as a "subjective attitude," which requires a genuine effort to reach agreement, an effort which is "inconsistent with a predetermined position not to budge on particular issues."[22]

As is the case with states following the binding arbitration model, in meet and confer states both parties to the bargaining process are required to exchange information freely on matters pertaining to the bargaining relationship. The obligation to exchange information requires sharing information about bargaining issues, such as the comparable jurisdictions used by each party in negotiations,[23] the approach taken by each party in calculating changes in the cost of living, and how each evaluates the employer's ability to pay. The obligation to share bargaining information is also ongoing and requires an employer to provide information about the enforcement of its residency and drug testing requirements,[24] and justification of how it has made assignment decisions.[25] It even extends to sharing information about prior disciplinary cases, including the recommendations of line supervisors for discipline in a particular case.[26]

Bargaining Not Required Model

The third model for police-sector collective bargaining laws is found in states that do not statutorily require or, in some cases, allow collective bargaining for law enforcement officers. In some of these states, bargaining laws have been enacted by the state legislature, only to be declared unconstitutional later by the courts (Indiana, for example, has such a history). In the majority of such states, a statewide collective bargaining statute covering law enforcement officers has never been enacted. In some states where collective bargaining has not been granted on a statewide basis, certain cities and counties within the state have voluntarily chosen to bargain with their law enforcement officers.[27]

Table 11.1 summarizes the current status of collective bargaining laws governing law enforcement officers and lists which of the three general models are followed in each state.[28] As can be seen, the distribution of states with collective bargaining and those without such laws is quite geographically distinct. States without bargaining laws are centered in the South and the Southwest. States with bargaining laws are found in the Northeast, in the Midwest, and on the West Coast.

Unfair Labor Practices

States with collective bargaining almost always have statutes that list a number of labor practices deemed to be "unfair." The usual list of unfair labor practices includes the following:

- A refusal to bargain in good faith over subjects that are mandatory for bargaining[29]
- Interference, restraint, or coercion of employees because employees have exercised their collective bargaining rights

TABLE 11.1 Collective Bargaining Laws Governing Law Enforcement Officers

STATE	BINDING ARBITRATION MODEL	MEET AND CONFER MODEL	BARGAINING NOT REQUIRED MODEL
Alabama			X
Alaska	X		
Arkansas			X
California	X		
Colorado			X
Connecticut	X		
Delaware	X		
District of Columbia	X		
Florida		X	
Georgia			X
Hawaii	X		
Idaho			X
Illinois	X		
Indiana			X
Iowa	X		
Kansas	X		
Kentucky			X
Louisiana			X
Maine	X		
Maryland			X
Massachusetts		X	
Michigan	X		
Minnesota	X		
Mississippi			X
Missouri			X
Montana	X		
Nebraska			X
Nevada	X		
New Hampshire	X		
New Jersey	X		
New Mexico	X		
New York	X		

(continued)

TABLE 11.1 Continued

STATE	BINDING ARBITRATION MODEL	MEET AND CONFER MODEL	BARGAINING NOT REQUIRED MODEL
North Carolina			X
North Dakota			X
Ohio	X		
Oklahoma	X		
Oregon	X		
Pennsylvania	X		
Rhode Island	X		
South Carolina			X
South Dakota			X
Tennessee			X
Texas			X
Utah			X
Vermont	X		
Virginia			X
Washington	X		
West Virginia			X
Wisconsin	X		
Wyoming			X

SOURCE: Will Aitchison, *The Rights of Law Enforcement Officers*, 5th ed. (Portland, OR: Law Enforcement Relations Information System, 2004), p. 12.

- The "domination" of a labor organization by an employer
- The failure to furnish information relevant to the collective bargaining process
- Inappropriate "interference" by an employer with the internal activities of a labor organization
- Discrimination against employees who have exercised their collective bargaining rights[30]

The usual form of challenging any of these practices is through the filing of an "unfair labor practice" or "prohibited practice" complaint with the state agency responsible for administering the collective bargaining laws. Most states have a relatively quick statute of limitations—some as short as six weeks—for the filing of such complaints.[31]

Mandatory Subjects for Bargaining

Where a law enforcement employer is obligated to bargain collectively, the bargaining topics over which bargaining may be conducted are generally classified under one of three categories—mandatory, permissive, or illegal topics of bargaining.[32] Mandatory

In The News

Today's News

Bargaining Rights Rescinded

The International Union of Police Associations, which represented 1,400 state troopers and other law enforcement personnel in Indiana, dissolved its local branch in the state as a result of an executive order by Governor Mitch Daniels to end collective bargaining rights for state employees. Governor Daniels signed the executive order on January 11, 2005, the same day that Governor Matt Blunt of Missouri signed a similar executive order. The Indiana governor canceled union contracts covering nearly 25,000 employees, stating that the unions stood in the way of his efforts to overhaul the state government. Union officials across the country believe that this is a trend at both the national and state levels, citing the precedence of the U.S. Department of Homeland Security in slashing collective bargaining rights for 75,000 union member employees.

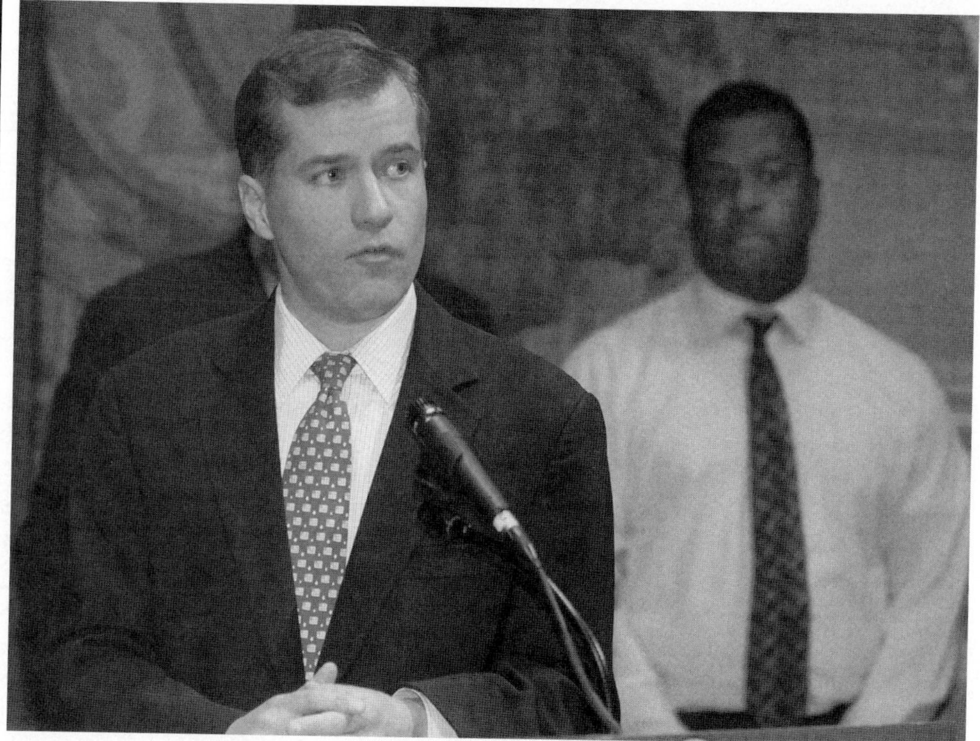

Incoming Missouri Governor Mike Blunt decided to eliminate collective bargaining on his first day of office. (Julie Smith, News Tribune/AP Wide World Photos)

Source: Joe Torres, "Bargaining Rights Eliminated" *American Police Beat*, March 2005, 34.

subjects of bargaining—usually those described as topics pertaining to wages, hours, and terms and conditions of employment—must be bargained if raised by either side.[33] Permissive subjects of bargaining—usually falling under the general heading of "management rights"—are those over which bargaining may occur but is not compelled.[34] Illegal subjects of bargaining are those over which the employer is forbidden by law from bargaining.[35] The distinction among the categories of bargaining subjects is particularly important when interest arbitration is the last step in the bargaining process, since only mandatory subjects of bargaining may generally be referred to interest arbitration.[36]

Where the obligation to bargain exists, it has importance not when negotiations for an actual contract are being conducted but also during the term of the contract and after the contract expires. The obligation to bargain is continual, a characteristic that may significantly limit an employer's flexibility in making certain decisions. If a matter is a mandatory subject for bargaining, an employer may not make changes in past practices affecting the matter without first negotiating with the labor organization representing its officers.[37] This restriction applies whenever a labor organization has been certified as the bargaining representative for employees. The continuing duty to bargain can even invalidate an employer's efforts to change its past practices through enacting a charter amendment.[38]

Two cases from Washington State provide a good example of this so-called continuing duty to bargain. In one case, the collective bargaining agreement covering a city police department had expired when the employer decided to change from a fixed-shift system, in which shifts were selected by seniority, to a system in which shifts rotated every few months. In the second case, the employer made changes in the method of allocating standby assignments. Even though a contract was in effect at the time of the changes, the contract did not address the method of standby assignment allocation. In both cases, the employers were held to have committed unfair labor practices by making the changes without first negotiating with their respective unions. The Washington State **Public Employment Relations Commission** held that, absent a clear waiver of the union's right to bargain, the continuing duty to bargain prohibited the implementation of any changes in such mandatorily negotiable hours of work issues.[39]

A labor organization can waive the right to bargain over changes in past practices in one of two ways: by "inaction" and by "contract." A waiver by inaction occurs when the labor organization has knowledge that the employer intends to make a change in past practice (or has actually made such a change) but does not timely demand to bargain over the change.[40] Even a six-week delay in demanding the right to bargain has been held to waive bargaining rights.[41] In order to have a labor organization's demand to bargain held untimely, the employer generally must establish that it provided actual and timely notice of its intended action.[42]

A waiver by contract exists when the labor organization has contractually given the right to the employer to make changes in mandatory subjects of bargaining. To be effective, "contract waivers" must be specific and clearly articulated. For example, a management rights clause that generally gives the employer the right to establish hours of work would likely not be specific enough to allow the employer the unilateral right to change work shifts, or to change from fixed to rotating shifts.

For bargaining rights to exist mid-contract, the labor organization must establish that the past practice the employer is intending to change has been consistent and long-standing.[43] The labor organization must also establish that there has been an actual change in past practices in order to demand bargaining during the term of the contract. For example, in one case, the police association in New York City was attempting to bargain over a department directive that banned "hog-tying" of suspects. The Court ruled that the directive was not negotiable because the labor association failed to prove the existence of a past practice which allowed hog-tying, resting its decision on testimony that hog-tying was not taught during training and on the word of the supervisor of the patrol force that, in 41 years of service, he had never seen hog-tying used in the department.[44] In addition, an employer's right to make changes in mandatory subjects of bargaining can also be limited by a collective bargaining agreement. Contractual clauses typically labeled "maintenance of benefits" or "existing conditions" forbid an employer from changing wages, hours, or working conditions. The contract covering Buffalo, New York, police officers contains an example of such a clause:

> *All conditions or provisions beneficial to employees now in effect which are not specifically provided for in this Agreement or which have not been replaced by provisions of this Agreement shall remain in effect for the duration of this Agreement, unless mutually agreed otherwise between the Employer and the Association.*[45]

Maintenance of benefits clauses enhance a labor organization's ability to prevent changes in past practices. When under the general continuing duty to bargain, a labor organization has the ability to demand only that an employer bargain to impasse over

QUICK FACTS QUICK FACTS QUICK

Quick Facts

Police National Representation

Police unions across the nation are effective entities within their local jurisdictions, but they may require a more organized presence to make a difference in state or national politics. The National Association of Police Organizations (NAPO) is one such organization, representing a coalition of over 2,000 police organizations and unions and nearly 250,000 active and retired officers. NAPO maintains a presence in Washington, D.C., in order to monitor legislative and administrative developments that affect law enforcement entities, and it often works directly with legislators and their staff to provide information and express organizational views on issues of concern. NAPO delegates take action annually to establish timely legislative goals and priorities, which are then relayed to NAPO's constituents to encourage grassroots action. Issues that NAPO has recently undertaken include support for the national AMBER alert system, support for a crime victims' rights amendment, a call for the repeal of a law prohibiting police officers convicted of misdemeanor domestic violence offenses from being able to continue to carry their firearms, support for federal collective bargaining legislation, and a call for the defeat of social security legislation that would require mandatory contributions by public safety officers. During election years, delegates also vote on endorsements of candidates for national and congressional office who have earned police support.

Source: National Association of Police Organizations.

changes in past practices that are mandatory negotiable, a maintenance of benefits clause allows a labor organization simply to refuse to agree to the change, even if the employer is willing to bargain over the issue. This distinction is particularly important in states where the bargaining process does not culminate with binding arbitration but, instead, allows an employer to unilaterally implement its last best offer on a bargaining issue.

When a topic is mandatory for bargaining, the employer must negotiate about the topic with the labor organization, not with individual union members. For example, since discipline is mandatorily negotiable, an employer would violate its bargaining obligation if it entered into a "last chance" agreement with a troubled employee unless the employee's labor organization also was a party to the agreement.[46] This ban on one-on-one contracts with individual union members is a strong one and has invalidated a wide variety of employer agreements with individual union members, including the payment of a signing bonus,[47] a contract with the newly hired officers that they will repay the costs of their training if they quit to go to work for another law enforcement employer,[48] and an agreement with a probationary employee to extend the probationary period.[49]

Critical Thinking Questions

1. Collective bargaining models tend to center in certain geographical areas of the United States, generally excluding the southern and southwestern states. What might explain this geographical distribution?
2. If a topic is mandatory for bargaining, why must an employer negotiate directly with the union, not with individual employees?

ESTABLISHING THE BARGAINING RELATIONSHIP

The Process

Assuming the existence of a legal provision for collective negotiations, the process of establishing a bargaining relationship is straightforward, although fraught with the opportunity for disputes. The mere fact that most members of a police department belong to a single organization does not mean that it automatically has the right to represent its members for the purposes of collective bargaining.[50] Those eligible to be

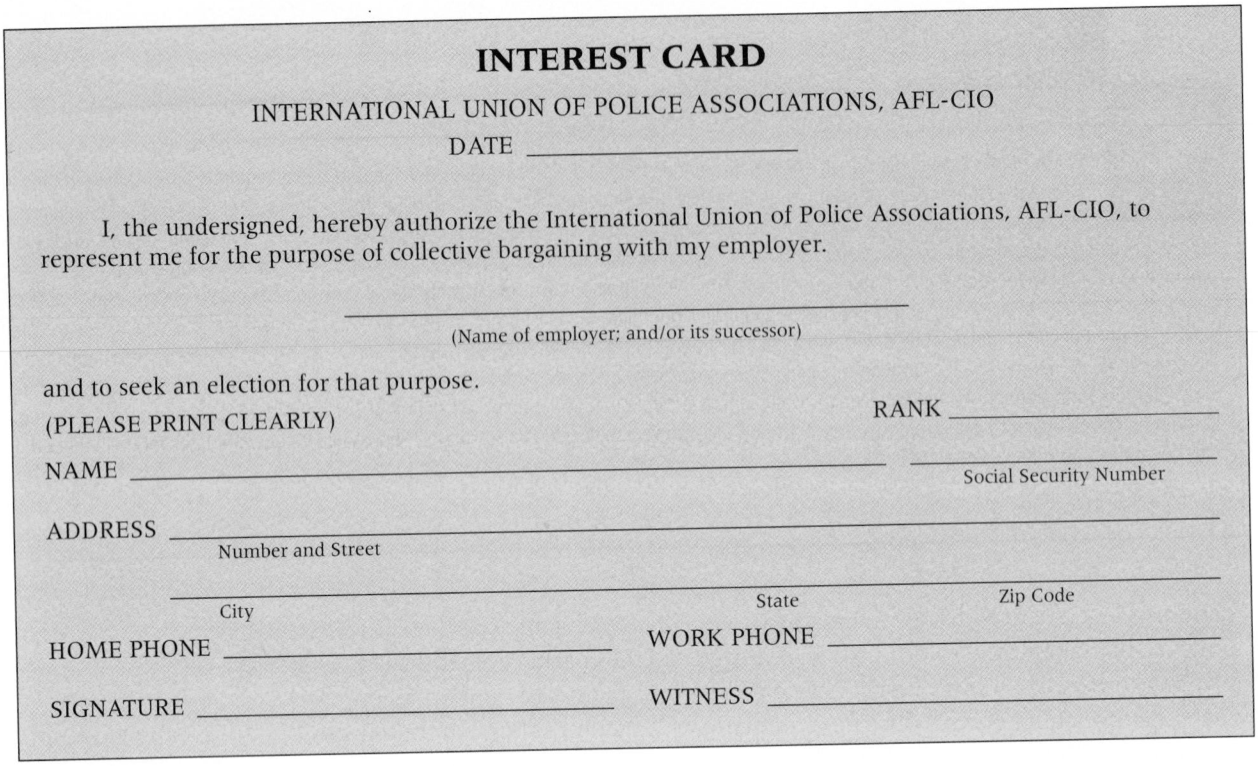

INTEREST CARD

INTERNATIONAL UNION OF POLICE ASSOCIATIONS, AFL-CIO

DATE ____________________

I, the undersigned, hereby authorize the International Union of Police Associations, AFL-CIO, to represent me for the purpose of collective bargaining with my employer.

____
(Name of employer; and/or its successor)

and to seek an election for that purpose.

(PLEASE PRINT CLEARLY) RANK ____________________

NAME ____ ____________________
Social Security Number

ADDRESS ____
Number and Street

____
City State Zip Code

HOME PHONE ____________________ WORK PHONE ____________________

SIGNATURE ____________________ WITNESS ____________________

FIGURE 11.2

A typical authorization card.

(Reprinted with permission from the International Union of Police Associations)

represented may, in fact, select an organization to which they already belong for this purpose, or they may select another one. This choice must be made, however, in ways that conform to the legislation providing for collective bargaining if the employee organization hopes to gain certification by the Public Employees Relations Commission (PERC).

The union begins an organizing drive, working to get 30 percent of the class or classes of employees it seeks to represent to sign authorization cards, of which Figure 11.2 is typical. Once this goal is reached, the union notifies the police department. An election is held, and the union must get 50 percent plus one officer to prevail. If management believes that the union has obtained a majority legitimately and that it is appropriate for the class or classes of officers to be grouped together as proposed by the union, it will recognize the union as the bargaining agent of the officers it has sought to represent. Once recognized by the employer, the union will petition the PERC or another body responsible for administering the legislation for certification. In such cases, the PERC does not check the authorization cards but only the appropriateness of the grouping of the officers. If the grouping is deemed appropriate by the PERC or a similar administrative body, then the employee organization is certified as the bargaining representative.

If the employee organization is not recognized by management, it can petition the PERC for an election; the petition must be accompanied by signed and dated representation cards from 30 percent of the group of employees the union seeks to represent. A secret vote is then held at the direction of the PERC, with the ballot including the union or unions that are contesting the right to represent the officers, along with the choice of no union. The union that receives a majority of the votes from among the officers who are eligible to be represented by the employee organization and who actually cast ballots is then certified. Alternately, a majority of those casting ballots may vote for no union. In the event that no majority is achieved, a runoff election is necessary.

The Opportunity for Conflict

In establishing the bargaining relationship, there is ample opportunity for disputes to develop. Management may undertake a campaign to convince officers they are better off without the union at the same time that the union is mounting its organizing drive. The employee organization may wish access to bulletin boards, meeting space, and mailing lists to publicize the advantages of unionizing to the officers, all of which management may not wish to provide. The decision as to what is an appropriate grouping of officers for the purposes of collective bargaining, technically referred to as "unit determination," is profoundly significant and one about which management and the union may have sharp differences.

Questions such as the following may arise. Are lieutenants part of management and therefore not eligible for representation by the union for purposes of collective bargaining? Should civilian radio dispatchers be part of the same bargaining unit as uniformed officers? Should detectives be in a bargaining unit by themselves? These decisions are important because they may affect the operation of the police department; may determine, to some degree, the dynamics of the employee organization; may impact the scope of bargaining; may affect the stability of the bargaining relationship; or even may be decisive in the outcome of a representation election.[51]

Both the union and management are pragmatic when it comes to defining the appropriate bargaining unit. In general, both may prefer a broad unit, the union, because the numbers will give it strength, while management resists the proliferation of bargaining units because each one that is recognized officially must be bargained with separately. Here, too, despite a similar orientation, disputes may arise. The union may know that it has the support of only one category of employees (e.g., detectives) and seeks to represent them as a single bargaining unit. Management may feel that particular union is too militant and, consequently, favors, as a part of a hidden agenda, the inclusion of detectives in a wider unit as a means of promoting the election of a more moderate union that is also seeking to represent employees. What constitutes an appropriate unit may be defined by state law. The most common method of unit determination, however, is for the PERC or a similar administrative body to make decisions on a case-by-case basis, applying certain criteria stipulated in the legislation.[52] Among the criteria often identified are the desires of the employees, the "community of interests" shared by the employees, the need to avoid creating too many bargaining units, the effects on efficiency of operations, and the history of labor relations in the police department.

Critical Thinking Question

1. What are some ways in which opportunities for conflict arise when establishing a bargaining relationship?

NEGOTIATIONS

Selection of the Management and Union Teams

Figure 11.3 depicts a typical configuration of the management and union bargaining teams. The union's chief negotiator will usually not be a member of the bargaining unit; rather, he or she will be a specialist brought in to represent it. This ensures a certain level of expertise, wider experience, an appropriate degree of objectivity, and an autonomy that comes from knowing that, once the bargaining is over, he or she will not be working daily for the people sitting across the table. It is not automatic that the union president will be a member of the bargaining team, although customarily a

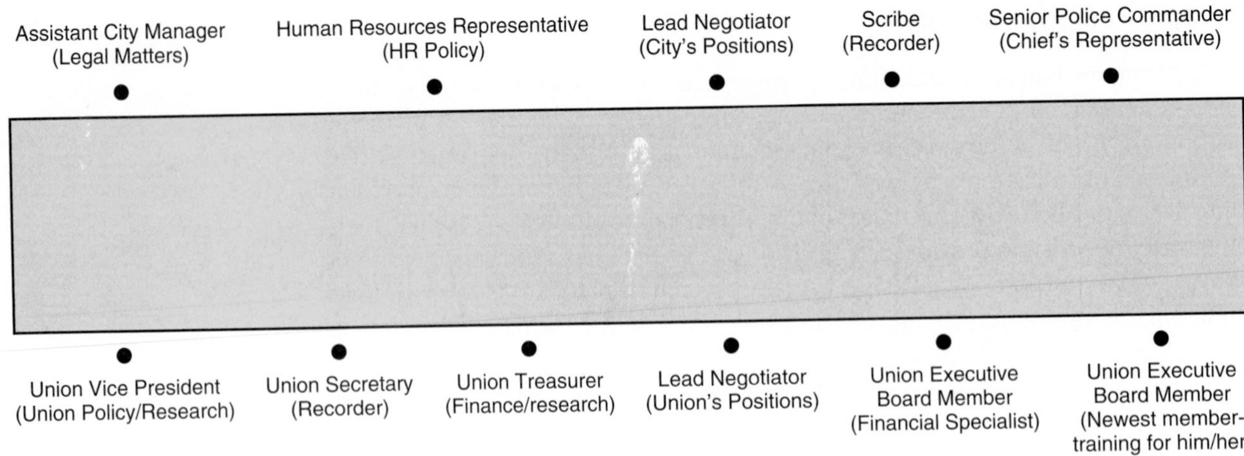

FIGURE 11.3

The management and union bargaining teams. Although the composition of management's and the union's bargaining teams varies somewhat from one jurisdiction to another and even within jurisdictions over time, the configuration shown here approximates the "typical" municipal situation. Occasionally, a member of the city council also sits in as an observer.

(Courtesy of Chuck Foy, past president of the Arizona Conference of Police and Sheriffs Local 7077 and past president of the Peoria [Arizona] Police Officers Association)

union officer is, and often it is the president. Accompanying the union's chief negotiator and president will be two or three team members who have conducted in-depth research on matters relating to the bargaining issues and who will have various types of data, facts, and documents—such as wage and benefit surveys, trends in the consumer price index, and copies of recent contracts for similarly sized jurisdictions—with them. Although there will be only several union research team members at the table, they will have had assistance in gathering their information from others in the union. Unless the union's chief negotiator is an attorney, there will seldom be an attorney sitting at the table with the union's team.

The chief negotiator for management may be the director of labor relations or the human resources director of the unit of government involved or may be a professional labor relations specialist. Some jurisdictions prefer the latter because, if there are acrimonious occurrences, once the bargaining is over the director of labor relations can step back into the picture and assume a relationship with the union that is unscarred by any incidents. The chief of police should not appear at the table personally, but a key member of the command staff who has his or her confidence should. The appearance of the chief at the table makes the task of leadership more difficult; to appear there on equal footing with the union's bargaining team on one day and then to step back atop the organizational hierarchy on the next requires greater adjustments by both the chief and the union members than the creation of any benefits associated with his/her presence are worth.

The way in which issues are presented, and the flexibility that both sides have will impact strongly on how the bargaining sessions will go. Perhaps equally important are the decisions made as to who will represent each side in what role at the table. It is not uncommon in evolving or newly established bargaining relationships to find that both parties put great effort into preparing for negotiations but select their representatives without the same thought. Zealots, those with "axes to grind," and firebrands are poor choices, as are those with a sarcastic, acrid, or abrasive personality. The purpose of bargaining is to produce a bilateral written agreement to which both parties will bind themselves during its lifetime. This is not only a profoundly important task but also one that is sufficiently difficult without including people on either side who have an agenda other than negotiating in good faith or whose personalities create yet another obstacle. For these reasons, management must exercise careful consideration in deciding who will represent the police department at the table and, if necessary, influence the selection of the city's other representatives.

Preparing for Negotiations

Management can ill afford to simply wait until the employee organization prepares its demands and presents them; effective action requires considerable effort on management's part before it receives the union's proposal. Management's negotiating team must be selected, agreement with the union obtained on the site where the negotiations will take place; the bargaining schedule established in conjunction with the union; and various types of data and information gathered, tabulated, and analyzed. Although final preparations for negotiating will begin several months before the first bargaining sessions, the preparation process is a continuous one; management should begin preparing for the next negotiations as soon as these are completed. The demands not obtained by the union in the past year may be brought up again in this year's bargaining sessions, and management should be prepared for this.

Various types of records should be kept and summaries made of such factors as the union membership; the types and outcomes of grievances; the costs of settling grievances; the numbers, kinds, and consequences of any contract violations by the employee organization; the subject matters brought before the union–management committee during the life of the expiring contract and the disposition of them; and the themes reflected in the union's newsletter. Additionally, just as the employee organization's bargaining team is doing, the management team must be familiarizing itself with changes in the consumer price index and the provisions of recent contracts in similarly situated jurisdictions and conducting its own wage and benefit survey or cooperating with the union on one.

From all these and other sources, it is essential that management do three things. First, it must develop fairly specific anticipations as to what the union will be seeking and the relative importance of each demand to the union. Second, it must develop its position with respect to the anticipated preliminary demands that it believes the union will present. Third, it must develop the objectives that it seeks to achieve during the forthcoming process of bilateral determination. If it is not already an institutionalized practice, arrangements should be made to have the union submit its demands in writing prior to the first scheduled round of negotiations. These demands may be submitted either in the form of a proposed contract or as a "shopping list," which simply lists the demands being made. The presentation of the demands in writing before the first bargaining session allows for a more productive use of the time allotted for the first negotiating session.

If management has done a good job, there will be relatively few surprises when the proposed contract is submitted. Surprises do not indicate that management's preparation was wasted; the knowledge gained through the process of anticipating the union's demands adds to the negotiating team's depth of understanding and overall confidence, key ingredients of bargaining table success. It is difficult to know precisely when management's bargaining team is prepared, but the employee organization will easily detect and capitalize on a lack of preparation.

The Negotiating Sessions

The publicity and attending atmosphere preceding the negotiating sessions focus considerable attention on them and may be barometers of or may influence the way in which they unfold. However, prebargaining publicity is also part of attempts to influence public opinion, to impress the public or rank-and-file members with the city's or union's resolve, and to create a façade behind which both sides may maneuver for advantage. Thus, one should not be too encouraged or discouraged about the content of such publicity; it should be considered and evaluated but not relied on solely as an informational source.

The number of bargaining sessions may run from one to several dozen, lasting from 30 minutes to 10 or more hours, although half-day sessions are more common, depending on how close or far apart the union and management are when they begin to meet face to face. Traditionally, any means of making verbatim transcripts, such as the use of a stenographer or tape recorder, have generally been excluded from the bargaining sessions, as it was believed that they tended to impede the progress of negotiations because people would begin speaking for the record.

In a related vein, the enactment of Florida's "sunshine law" opened up many previously closed government meetings to the general public, including bargaining sessions, and stirred up some controversy. Advocates of the legislation argued that it opened up government to the people and would make it both more responsive and responsible. With respect to its application to collective negotiations, critics of the law maintained that the real bargaining would be done secretly, that the scheduled public bargaining sessions would be merely a ritualistic acting out of what had been agreed on privately, and that real negotiating would be difficult because both sides would tend to "play to the audience." This last point is underscored by one negotiator's wry observation that bargaining under the sunshine law was like "a Roman circus with kibitzers."[53]

At the first meeting, friendly conversation may be passed across the table, or there may be merely strained greetings before the formal session begins. Much like the prenegotiations publicity, this may or may not reflect how the session will go. Friendly conversation may suggest that rapid and amicable bargaining will follow but instead no mutually acceptable positions will be reached because the friendly conversation has veiled only thinly the hostility or aggressiveness of one or both sides, which quickly comes to the fore. On the other hand, strained greetings may reflect the heavy responsibility that each party to the negotiations feels, and quick progress may follow.

In the initial session, the chief negotiator for each party will make an opening statement; management's representative will often go first, touching on general themes, such as the need for patience and the obligation to bargain in good faith. The union's negotiator generally will follow this up by voicing support for such sentiments and will outline what the union seeks to achieve under the terms of the new contract. Ground rules for the bargaining may then be reviewed, modified as mutually agreed on, or developed. The attention then will shift to the terms of the contract that the union is proposing, and the contract will be examined thoroughly in a "walk-through," during which time management will seek to learn what the union means by particular wording. This is a time-consuming process but of great importance because both parties need to have a common understanding of what it is they are attempting to commit each other to, or there will be frequent unresolved conflicts and many complex and expensive grievances filed during the lifetime of the contract. For purposes of illustration, the union may have proposed that "vehicles will be properly maintained to protect the health and safety of officers." Discussion of this proposal may reveal that their expectations are much more specific:

1. This is to apply to all vehicles, including marked, semimarked, and unmarked.
2. Each patrol vehicle, whether marked, semimarked, or unmarked, will be replaced at 60,000 miles.

3. All vehicles will be equipped with radial tires.
4. Plexiglas protectors will be installed between the front and rear seats.
5. Shotguns in locking mounts accessible from the front seat will be provided for in all marked and semimarked cars.
6. First-aid kits of a particular type will be placed in all vehicles.
7. Comprehensive blood body fluid pathogen protection kits will be provided.

Another illustration is reflected in Table 11.2; assuming that the union is seeking a two-year contract and wants a 20 percent raise during the lifetime of the contract, there are several ways that the cost of that raise might be spread. Management must find out what the union is bargaining for in very specific terms and then cost it out, so that the administration knows the budgetary implications of its commitments and counterproposals beforehand.[54] The walk-through may take several sessions to complete; during this time, little bargaining is being done, as management is basically attempting to obtain clarity about what the union's expectations are.

For bargaining purposes, the union will have categorized each clause in the proposed contract as being (1) "expendable," meaning that under certain circumstances it will be withdrawn as a symbol of good faith; (2) a "trade-off," indicating that it will be dropped as total or partial payment for obtaining some other benefit; (3) "negotiable," meaning that the benefit needs to be obtained in one form or another; and (4) "non-negotiable," meaning that the benefit is wanted exactly as proposed.[55] Management will study the information gained from the walk-through for several days, and then both parties will return to the table. Management then will respond to the union's proposal by indicating which clauses it has (1) "accepted," (2) "accepted with minor modification," (3) "rejected," and (4) wishes to make its own proposals and counterproposals to. Management cannot simply reject a clause out of hand; to do so would not constitute bargaining in good faith. Instead, it must give a reason for the rejection that is reasonable, such as an actual inability to pay.

Having been told formally of management's position on the contract proposed, the bargaining begins, concentrating on the items on which agreement can be reached immediately or fairly rapidly. Such an approach helps foster a spirit of mutualism that

TABLE 11.2 Alternative Ways to Costing Out a 20% Ralse over a Two-Year Contract

1. 10% increase each year of contract	
Year 1 cost: 10% of 980,000	= $ 98,000
Year 2 cost: 10% of year 1 wages, $1,078,000	= 107,800
plus continuation of year 1	= 98,000
	$303,800
2. 15% increase in year 1; 5% in year 2	
Year 1 cost: 15% of $980,000	= $147,000
Year 2 cost: 5% of year 1 payroll of $1,127,000	= 56,350
plus continuation of year 1	= 147,000
	$350,350
3. 20% in year 1; nothing in year 2	
Year 1 cost: 20% of $980,000	= $196,000
Year 2: no new increase but continuation of year 1 raise	= $196,000
	$392,000

Quick Facts

Boston Police Union Uses Political Muscle

Many labor unions include benefits for members, including life insurance, educational benefits, financial incentives (such as loan programs), and varying levels of health care or dental coverage. Union members often take these benefits for granted, but a highly unusual move by the Boston Police Patrolmen's Association (BPPA) in 2003 put union benefits in a new perspective for many members. During a battle between the union and the city's mayor in 2003 and 2004, the BPPA decided that all members of the union had to devote five to seven hours of their free time every other month to picketing the mayor. Those who did not comply would lose union benefits, such as dental coverage and life insurance. State and federal labor officials declined to intervene in the matter, saying that such benefits are internal union matters that are not regulated.

Source: Yvonne Abraham, "Police Union Can Suspend Benefits," *Boston Globe*, May 10, 2003.

can be useful in dealing with the issues about which there are substantial differences. As bargaining enters the final stages, the issues that must be dealt with usually become fewer but also more difficult in terms of securing agreement about them.

At such points, "side trips" may threaten to make the sessions unproductive. These side trips may involve wild accusations, old recriminations, character assassinations, or discussion of a specific clause in philosophical or intellectual terms as a means of not dealing with the concrete realities that may be threatening and anxiety provoking for one or both parties. At these times, a caucus or even a slightly longer space of time than ordinary until the next session may give enough time for tempers to calm or for more perspective to be gained. At other times, the police union may feel the need to "up the stakes" by engaging in picketing as a form of political pressure.

Ultimately, unless a total impasse is reached, agreement will be obtained on the terms of a new contract. The union's membership will vote on the contract as a whole. If approved by the membership, the contract then goes before the necessary government officials and bodies, such as the legislative unit that appropriates the funds, for its approval.

Critical Thinking Questions

1. Why must both sides in a negotiation carefully consider who will represent them in the bargaining process?
2. How should management prepare for union demands?

GRIEVANCES

Why Grievances Are Inevitable

There is a notion that, once the bargaining is completed and an agreement signed, the most difficult part of labor relations has been passed through and easy times are ahead. Such a notion is natural. Bargaining is high drama, with a great deal of attention focused on it by the news media and the community. The production of an agreement acceptable to both the union and management is, in fact, a significant achievement. Beyond it, however, is the day-to-day administration of the contract during its lifetime. Because the contract outlines the duties and rights of each party in its dealings with the other, it is ironically the basis not only for accord but also for conflict:

> *It would, of course, be ideal for all concerned, including the public, if in the negotiation of the agreement both parties were able to draft a comprehensive document capable of foreseeing and forestalling all potential disputes which might arise during its life.*

Unfortunately, such crystal-ball vision is usually lacking, particularly when the parties are pressured to obtain agreement in a period of negotiation tensions and time deadlines. It is not humanly possible in a new collective bargaining relationship to draft such a perfect document.

Therefore it is inevitable that questions will arise concerning the interpretation and application of the document drafted in the haste and pressure of contract negotiations. What is the meaning of a particular clause of the agreement? How does it apply, if at all, to a set of facts which occurred after the agreement was signed? These questions are not at all uncommon in any contractual relationship.[56]

The Definition of a Grievance

Whereas in common usage a **grievance** is a complaint or an expression of dissatisfaction by an employee with respect to some aspect of employment, what can be grieved formally is usually defined within the contract itself. Grievances may be limited to matters discussed specifically in the contract, that are primarily contract-related, or that pertain to the job, as is seen in these clauses from three different agreements:

1. A grievance is defined as a complaint arising out of the interpretation, application or compliances with the provisions of this agreement.
2. For the purpose of this agreement the term "grievance" shall mean the difference of dispute between any police officer and the Borough, or a superior officer in the chain of command, with respect to the interpretation, application, claim or breach, of violation of any of the provisions of this agreement, or with respect to any equipment furnished by the Borough.
3. A grievance, for our purposes, shall be defined as any controversy, complaint, misunderstanding, or dispute arising between an employee or employees and the City, or between the Brotherhood and the City.

The Grievance Procedure

The grievance procedure is a formal process that has been the subject of bilateral negotiations and is detailed in the contract. It involves seeking redress of the grievances through progressively higher levels of authority and most often culminates in binding arbitration by a tripartite panel or a single neutral. A typical sequence of steps includes the following:

Grievances shall be presented in the following manner and every effort shall be made by the parties to secure prompt disposition of grievances:

Step 1. *The member shall first present his/her grievance to his/her immediate supervisor within five (5) days of the occurrence which gave rise to the grievance. Such contact shall be on an informal and oral basis, and the supervisor shall respond orally to the grievance within five (5) working days.*

Step 2. *Any grievance which cannot be satisfactorily settled in Step 1 shall be reduced to writing by the member and shall next be taken up by his/her division commander. Said grievance shall be presented to the division commander within five (5) working days from receipt of the answer in Step 1. The division commander shall, within five (5) working days, render his/her decision on the grievance in writing.*

Step 3. *Any grievance not satisfactorily settled in Step 2 shall be forwarded, in writing, within five (5) working days, to the Chief of Police, who shall render his/her written decision on the grievance within five (5) working days.*

Step 4. *If the grievant is not satisfied with the response of the Chief of Police, he/she will forward his written grievance within five (5) working days to the City Manager, who will have ten (10) working days to reply, in writing.*

> ***Step 5.*** *If the grievance has not been settled to the satisfaction of the grievant in Step 4, the matter will be subject to arbitration. An arbiter will be selected, without undue delay, according to the rules of the American Arbitration Association. The arbiter will hold an arbitration hearing. When the hearing has ended, the arbiter will be asked to submit his/her award, in writing, within fifteen (15) days. His/her decision shall be final and binding on both parties.*[57]

Because the union must share equally the cost of arbitration with management, the decision to take a grievance to the last step is customarily the prerogative of the union rather than the individual officer who is grieved.

Enumerated in the agreement are not only the steps of the grievance procedure but also such matters as the manner of selecting the tripartite panel or the single neutral, along with their duties and powers. If the panel is used, management and the union each appoints one member, and those two appoint the third; where the two cannot agree on the neutral, the contract may provide for the referral of the choice of a chairperson to a designated agency,[58] such as the Federal Mediation and Conciliation Service, or a state agency. Where a single arbitrator is used, a variety of techniques are employed in selection, ranging from agreement on the person by the union and management on a case-by-case basis, to the appointment of a permanent arbitrator during the lifetime of the contract, to having an outside agency submit a list of qualified arbitrators from which management and the union take turns eliminating names until only one remains or they agree to accept any of some number remaining, such as three.

The arbitration hearing is quasi-judicial with more relaxed rules of evidence than are found in either criminal or civil proceedings. The burden of proof is on the grieving party, except in discipline cases, where it is always on the employer. The parties may be represented by legal counsel at the hearing, and the format will generally include obtaining agreement on what the issue is, an opening statement by each side (with the grieving party going first), examination and cross-examination of witnesses, and closing arguments in the reverse of the order in which the opening statements were made.

Arbitration Issues and Decision Making

Despite the many types of matters that can be and are grieved, the largest single category of cases, about 90 percent of the total, brought to an arbitration hearing are those involving discipline against an officer. Some arbitration decision making is not difficult because one side, perhaps the union, chooses to take a losing case to arbitration, because of its symbolic importance, and the need to appear supportive of union members. This rational can also be applied on the management as well in order to show support for managers.

If an employee is found to have done what he or she has been accused of, the arbitrator may then consider certain factors that might mitigate the severity of the penalty, including the officer's years of service to the department; the provocation, if any, that led to the alleged offense; the officer's disciplinary history, including the number, types, and recency of other violations; the consistency with which the applicable rule is enforced; and the penalties applied for similar offenses by other officers.[59]

One study of arbitrated police grievances reveals that the officer involved in the grievance was assigned to uniformed patrol 84 percent of the time, another police officer was involved in the incident slightly more than half the time (56 percent of the cases), the grieving officer's supervisor supported him or her 14 percent of the time, and in exactly three-quarters of the cases the involved officer had a clear disciplinary record.[60] Given that police unions must be selective in terms of the cases they take to arbitration, the results are not too surprising: the union won 77 percent of the grievances.

A key advantage of arbitration is the speed with which issues are heard and a decision is made, as compared with seeking resolution of the dispute in court. The deadline for issuance of the award may be established by statute; the parties; a government authority, such as the PERC; the arbitrator, if he or she is acting as an independent; or the body appointing the arbitrator.[61] The AAA requires arbitrators to render their decisions in writing within 30 days of (1) the conclusion of the hearing; (2) the receipt of the hearing transcript, if one has been made; or (3) the receipt of posthearing briefs.[62] In general, except in such instances as fraud or bias by the arbitrator, the hearing officer's decision, where binding arbitration is provided for, will not be reviewed by the courts.

Critical Thinking Question

1. Why do you think discipline charges against officers make up nearly 90 percent of matters brought to arbitration?

JOB ACTIONS

Job action is a label used to describe several types of activities in which employees may engage to express their dissatisfaction with a particular person, event, or condition or to attempt to influence the outcome of a matter pending before decision makers, such as a contract bargaining impasse. Job actions carry the signal "we are here, organized, and significant, and the legitimacy of our position must be recognized."

Through job actions, employees seek to create pressure that may cause the course of events to be shifted to a position more favorable or acceptable to them. Such pressure may come from a variety of quarters, including the city manager, elected officials, influential citizens, merchant associations, political party leaders, and neighborhood groups. Under such pressure, administrators may agree to something that they might not under more relaxed circumstances. When ill-advised agreements are made, they may be attributable at a general level to pressure but on a more specific plane to such factors as stress, miscalculations, the desire to appear responsive to a superior or constituency, or the mistaken belief that the implications of a hastily conceived and coerced agreement can be dealt with effectively later. Four types of job actions are recognizable: the vote of confidence, work slowdowns, work speedups, and work stoppages.

The Vote of Confidence

The vote of confidence, which typically produces a finding of no confidence, has been used somewhat sparingly in law enforcement. An extreme example of that infrequent use is the Massachusetts State Police, whose members, for the first time in their 129-year history, gave their commander a vote of no confidence in 1994.[63] Such a vote is how rank-and-file members signal their collective displeasure with the chief administrator of their agency. Although such votes have no legal standing, they may have a high impact because of the resulting publicity.

In mid 1996, the Houston Police Officers Association's board issued a vote of no confidence against then-Chief Sam Nuchia. Within six months, Nuchia was gone from the department. A year before, in Prince George County, Maryland, 300 members of the Fraternal Order of Police voted no confidence in the department's command hierarchy.[64] Five officers had been ordered to a warehouse to meet FBI agents investigating the alleged beating of a citizen. On arriving, the five officers were ordered to strip, which produced a fiery protest and the no-confidence vote.

Although the vote of no confidence may produce a change in leadership and policies, on rare occasions it creates the opposite effect. Years ago in Houston, the chief received a no-confidence vote. Members of the city council and the chamber of commerce quickly supported the chief, labeling the vote a sign that he was "clamping down" on police officers and making much needed changes in the department.[65]

Work Slowdowns

Although officers continue to work during a slowdown, they do so at a leisurely pace, causing productivity to fall. As productivity drops, the unit of government employing the officers comes under pressure to restore normal work production. This pressure may be from within the unit of government itself. For example, a department may urge officers to write more tickets, so that more revenue is not lost. Or citizens may complain to politicians and appointed leaders to "get this thing settled," so that the police will answer calls more rapidly and complete the reports citizens need for insurance purposes. In New York City, police officers protesting stalled contract negotiations staged a ticket-issuing slowdown that resulted in a loss of $2.3 million in just two months. This action also produced strong conflict within the rank and file among officers who did and did not support the slowdown. In order to counter New York City Police Department pressure to stop the ticket slowdown, the Patrolmen's Benevolent Association—which represents the city's 29,000 officers—picketed outside traffic courts, denouncing what it called the administration's traffic ticket quota policy.[66]

The adoption of new technologies in a police department, intended to speed up police responses, also offers the opportunity to create a work slowdown. One hundred fifty Alexandria, Virginia, police officers turned in their department-issued pagers to protest a pay scale that lagged behind neighboring jurisdictions. The pagers were used to call in off-duty officers in specialized units, such as homicide and hostage negotiations, when needed. Detective Eric Ratliff, president of Local 5, International Union of Police Associations, said "I won't sugar-coat it. The response time of specialized units . . . will be slower. What this does is take us back to the early '80s, before we had pagers, which is basically where our pay is."[67] In East Hartford, Connecticut, the police union contract approved by the city council included a provision to pay officers required to carry beepers an extra $1,500 annually, avoiding the wholesale return of pagers that Alexandria experienced.[68]

Work Speedups

As the term suggests, work speedups are an acceleration of activity, resulting in the overproduction of one or more types of police services. The purpose is to create public pressure on elected and appointed government leaders to achieve a union-desired goal. The purpose of a work speedup may be to protest a low pay increase proposed by the employer, to force the employer to make more or particular concessions at the bargaining table, or to pressure the employer to abandon a policy change that adversely affects union members. Examples of speedups include "ticket blizzards" and sudden strict enforcements of usually ignored minor violations, such as jaywalking, littering, or smoking in prohibited areas.

Work Stoppages

Work stoppages are the biggest hammer in any union's toolbox. The ultimate work stoppage is the strike, which is the withholding of *all* of labor's services (see Figure 11.4). This tactic is most often used by labor in an attempt to force management back to the

FIGURE 11.4

Police officers walk a picket line.
(AP/Wide World Photos)

bargaining table when negotiations have reached an impasse. However, strikes by public employees are now rare. In 1969, public employee strikes peaked at 412.[69] Today, there are fewer than 50 a year. The reasons for the sharp decline in strikes include the extension of collective bargaining rights to many public employees, state laws prohibiting strikes, the fines that may be levied against striking unions and employees, and the fact that striking employees may be fired. President Ronald Reagan's wholesale dismissal of the air traffic controllers remains a potent lesson for unionists. Additionally, the climate of the 1990s was not favorable to unionism. The growing conservatism in this country and the view that the unions are adept at getting what they want at "our expense" are also factors that make both private and public unions less likely to strike.[70] In states in which public-sector bargaining is not allowed, tough laws affecting strikers have made public employees think long and hard before striking. Even in those states, many public employers know what they have to do in order to reap the benefits of a well-trained and seasoned workforce, and they do so to prevent the labor unrest that would impede economic development. Companies are not likely to relocate to cities that cannot govern effectively. Without these relocations, a city's budget becomes increasingly tight because tax revenue is flat or falling; residents and business are hit with increased and new taxes, and they begin to leave to find more hospitable locations in which to live and work.

Short of a strike by all officers are briefer work stoppages, which may affect only specialized assignments or involve a large number of police officers, but not all of them, in epidemics of the **blue flu** (a job action in which officers organize mass absences on the pretext of sickness for the purpose of protest against their employer) that last only a few days. Work stoppages of this type are an important police labor tactic. While, like strikes, these briefer collective actions may be intended to force management back to the table, they are also used occasionally to punctuate the extreme displeasure of officers with a policy (e.g., one unreasonably restricting moonlighting by officers) or with particular actions by officials inside and outside the department (e.g., the decision of a district attorney to prosecute a police officer on what is seen as a public image–enhancing but "thin" case). These briefer job actions sometimes follow a vote of no confidence.

In The News

Today's News

Deputies' Union Fined for Blue Flu

The Association of Los Angeles County Deputy Sheriffs (ALADS) was fined over $100,000 by a judge in Santa Ana, California, for failing to stop members from participating in a blue flu job action. Ten bailiffs from a Beverly Hills courthouse participated in a sick-out to protest stalled contract negotiations during an attempt to secure pay raises and additional benefits for Los Angeles County deputies. The fine was levied specifically to stop the job action by the bailiffs, who defied a previous court order banning the sick-out. A county attorney said that the amount of the fine was unprecedented but was necessary to ensure that the deputies went back to work. ALADS representatives maintained that the bailiffs had acted without any type of authorization by the organization. A tentative contract was reached in 2005, allowing deputies a 3 percent pay raise, an additional 11 percent increase in retirement pay, and an allowance for additional pay negotiations in 2006.

Source: "Deputies' Union Fined for 'Blue-Flu'" *American Police Beat,* February 2004. "Tentative Agreement Reached for New Salary Contract," Association of Los Angeles County Sherriffs, February 11, 2005.

In Boston, three members of the department's sexual assault unit—a specialized unit—refused to be on call overnight for emergencies, protesting the fact that the officers were not well paid for such assignments.[71] Los Angeles officers staged their third blue flu when 45 percent of the daily workforce called in sick for two days in a row, just as the tourist season was beginning. This protest was made because officers had been working 21 months without a contract or pay raise and wanted to move the bargaining process forward.[72] In East St. Louis, police officers, angry that firefighters made more money, called in sick for one day—during which county and state police officers stepped in to patrol the streets. As a result, the city agreed to grant salary increases.[73] Ninety-five of 130 disgruntled Cook County, Illinois, deputies assigned to court security duties called in sick. Officials estimate that, in the juvenile court alone, some 700 cases had to be postponed. Other police departments which have experienced blue flu epidemics recently included New Orleans, Louisiana; Pontiac, Michigan; Sacramento County, California; and Santa Ana, California.

Police Unions: The Political Context

Although union job actions frequently center on economic factors, unions also take stances on other factors. In the 1990s, in Washington, D.C., Ron Robertson, president of the local Fraternal Order of Police, asked the federal government to take over the police department because the public and officers were in a "killing field."[74] Two days prior to Robertson's request, an officer working alone was shot four times and killed as he sat in his patrol car at a traffic light outside a nightclub. The city's inability to staff two officers to a car had been a continuing union concern.

While contract negotiations were ongoing between the state and State Police Association of Massachusetts (SPAM), the association opted at the last minute not to air an ad that blamed Governor Weld for the death of a state trooper gunned down by a convicted murderer who had been released early by the parole board. In the midst of the state–SPAM negotiations, Governor Weld reappointed one of the members of the parole board. This member had voted for the murderer's early release, prompting the preparation of the ad. Despite the fact that the ad was not aired, a controversy ensued. Weld aides asserted that the union's tactics were designed to make the governor capitulate to the union's demands, and one of the governor's political allies, a state senator, called the ad "the lowest." The union responded by stating that the state senator was "intruding into the collective bargaining process and acting beyond his realm."[75]

When Riverside County, California, deputies beat two suspected undocumented Mexican immigrants after a well-documented high-speed chase seen on the evening news, the AFL-CIO took strong exception. AFL-CIO Executive President Linda Chavez-Thompson said, "Our movement will not tolerate this kind of brutality, nor will we excuse officers because the situation [was] volatile. . . . This is not a question of immigration rights, but of basic civil and human rights."[76]

The Lautenberg Amendment to the federal "Brady Bill" gun control legislation retroactively denies anyone convicted of a domestic violence misdemeanor from having a gun. When applied to police officers and federal agents, this controversial law ends their careers. Women's rights groups have supported the law because it denies a firearm to "cops who batter." Police unions have been angered by the retroactive application of the law, claiming it is unfair to take away an officer's livelihood with no advance notice. The Grand Lodge of the Fraternal Order of Police filed a lawsuit challenging the constitutionality of the law, a move supported by a number of unions, including the Detroit Police Officers Association.

Police unions also use high-visibility, high-impact tactics to further their objectives. Fraternal Order of Police Lodge 89 in Prince George County, Maryland, spent $7,000 to erect billboards assailing what they saw as County Executive Wayne Curry's inaction on rising crime and an understaffed police department. Other police unions have used radio stations to broadcast 30- to 60-second messages designed to "bring heat" on politicians by mobilizing the public to their side. The Florida PBA (FPBA) has a "Van Plan" that delivers 100 uniformed police officers every day to the state legislature while legislators are in session to lobby for bills the FPBA supports. Some police unions also have in-state toll-free numbers that can be automatically connected to the offices of key legislators, so that members can lobby for their bills. When a sheriff spoke against the FPBA before a legislative committee, the FPBA campaigned against him in the next election; the incumbent was defeated, a strong showing of political muscle by the union.

In 1996, when Aurora, Illinois, Mayor David Pierce had a political fundraiser, 100 members of the police union picketed the affair to protest a lack of progress in stalled contract negotiations.[77] Conversely, in St. Louis, mayoral candidate Clarence Harmon was backed by three police groups, including the 1,250-member St. Louis Police Association. Not coincidentally, Harmon is the city's former police chief and had promised expanded community policing, a gun buyback program—which when previously implemented took 7,600 guns off the streets in a month, and other efforts, including the reduction of domestic violence. However, the city's Ethical Society of Police—a minority organization—was trying to decide which candidate to endorse. The society and Harmon had been at odds over affirmative action and promotions while he was chief.[78]

Unions have also found parades and other community events to be vehicles for highlighting their concerns. In New York City, 150 police officers protested the city's contract offer by picketing the parade and shouting, "Crime is down, and so is our pay." In Methuen, Massachusetts, a police union pay dispute threatened the cancellation of the city's annual Christmas parade.[79]

Critical Thinking Questions

1. Why is it so critical that both management and union representatives exercise restraint and good judgment in reacting to a job action?
2. In a post–job action environment, what steps must the union and administration take in order to ease the transition back to normal public service?
3. How might a police job action have an effect on local, state, or even national political climates?

Administrative Reaction to Job Actions

Anticipatory Strategies

There are no simple answers for what police administrators should do in the face of a job action. A short period of ignoring a work slowdown may see its natural dissipation, or it may become more widespread and escalate. Disciplinary action may effectively end a job action, or it may simply aggravate the situation further, causing the job action to intensify and become more protracted. In choosing a course of action, one must read the environment, assess the situation, review alternatives, decide on a course of action, implement it, monitor the impact, and make adjustments as necessary. In short, it is a decision-making process, albeit a delicate one.

The best way in which to handle job actions is for both management and the union to take the position that they have mutual responsibilities to avoid job actions. This may, however, not be uniformly possible; a union leadership that is seen to be too cooperative with management may, for example, be discredited by rank-and-file members, and a sick-out may occur. Negotiations that do not meet expectations, however unrealistic, of militant union members may produce a walkout. In general, the following can be expected to reduce the possibility of a job action:[80]

1. The appropriate city officials (both appointed and elected), union leaders, and management must be trained in the tenets and practices of collective bargaining, particularly as they relate to mutual trust and the obligation to bargain in good faith.
2. Formal and informal communications networks should be used freely within city government, the police agency, and the union for the transmission of messages between them. The timely sharing of accurate information is essential to good labor relations in that it reduces the opportunity for misinformation or non-information to create distance and build barriers.
3. On a periodic basis, key managers from the police department, along with the staff and its labor relations unit, should meet with union leaders and the representatives, including elected officials, of the city who are responsible for the implementation of its labor relations program. This strengthens existing communications networks, it allows new networks to open, and it is a continuing affirmation of the mutualism that is central to the process of collective bargaining.
4. Well before any job actions occur, management must develop and publicize the existence of a contingency plan that contemplates as many of the problems as reasonably can be foreseen with respect to each type of job action. For example, in planning for a strike, one must consider such things as how the rights and property of non-strikers will be protected.[81] What security measures are to be invoked for government buildings and property? What are the minimum levels of personnel and supplies required? What special communications arrangements are necessary? Does the city's insurance cover potential liabilities to employees and property? What legal options exist, and who has authority to invoke them under what circumstances? What coordination arrangements are needed with other police departments and government agencies? What effect will various strike policies have on labor relations after the strike? How will non-striking officers and the public react to various strike policies? May a striking employee injured on the picket line be placed on sick leave? Do striking employees accrue leave and retirement credit for the time they are out?

5. In attempting to determine the possibility of various job actions, must assess the philosophy, capabilities, strengths, weaknesses, and propensities of the union—its officers, negotiators, legal counsel, and members. That, along with an estimate of the financial resources of the union, will be useful in anticipating the actions in which it is likely to engage and toward which planning can be directed. Although the hallmark of good planning is that it provides for future states of affairs, management is most likely to underestimate the union's capabilities, and the planning bias should therefore be toward an overstatement of what is possible.

During the Job Action

Police managers must appreciate the long-range implications of any job action—a strike, for example. The striking officers are engaging, as is the employer, in a power struggle that has an economic impact on both parties. The union is not attempting to divest itself of its employer, and for both legal and practical reasons, the employer cannot unilaterally rid itself of its relationship with the union; at some point in the very near future, it is most likely that they will resume their former relationship.[82] Considering this, managers must be temperate in their private and public remarks regarding striking officers; emotionally laden statements and cynical characterizations regarding strikers may provide a degree of fleeting satisfaction, but at some cost to the rapidity with which antagonisms may be set aside and the organization restored to its normal functioning. The union leadership and the rank-and-file membership have the same obligation; in the face of either management or the union not fulfilling its obligation, it becomes even more important that the other side be restrained in its remarks, or the ensuing trail of recriminations and biting comments will lead only to hostility and a degeneration of goodwill, both of which will have negative effects on future relations.

Managers should strive to maintain a fair and balanced posture on the subject of the strike, and their dominant focus should be on ending it. In addition, the following points should be noted:

1. No reaction to a strike or another job action should be taken without first anticipating the consequences of a reaction from the union and the officers involved. For example, the decision to seek an injunction ordering the officers to terminate the action and return to work could result in the officers disobeying the order and forcing a confrontation with the court issuing the order. A public statement that all officers involved in the action will be fired places the chief in the difficult position after the conflict is terminated of either firing participating officers or losing face with his or her employees.
2. All management responses to a strike should be directed toward terminating it only, not toward an ulterior purpose, such as trying to "bust" the union. There have been job actions in which the employer's sole objective was to destroy the union, an objective that frequently results in aggravated hostility between the employer and the union, between the chief and the officers participating in the action, and among the officers themselves. The long-range effect of this approach is to injure the morale of the police department, affecting the quality of police services and ultimately the level of service to the public.[83]

The degree of support that non-striking employees, the media, the public, and elected and appointed officials will give management in the event of a strike is a product not only of the soundness of management's position but also of how effective management is in communicating. For a department whose workforce is depleted by a walkout, personnel are a scarce resource, and not to invest it in communications efforts is a natural temptation tinged heavily by the reality of other needs that must also be considered. To be borne in mind, however, is the perspective that the effective use of some personnel in communications efforts may shorten the strike.

It is essential during a strike that communications be rapid, accurate, consistent, and broadly based. Non-striking employees may be kept informed by the use of the daily bulletin, briefings, or other devices. Letters may be sent to the homes of striking officers, informing them of the applicable penalties for their actions, the status of negotiations, and management's present position with respect to these issues. Facsimile letters for this and other actions should already have been prepared as part of the development of the contingency plan.

Personal appearances by police managers before neighborhood groups, professional associations, civic clubs, and similar bodies can be useful in maintaining calmness in the community, in providing one means of informing the public of special precautionary measures that they can take to protect themselves, and in galvanizing public opinion for management's position. Care must be taken to ensure that in this effort the needs of lower-socioeconomic groups are not overlooked; they are not likely to be members of the Kiwanis or the local bar association, and special attention must be given to how they, too, will be informed and how their needs will be listened to.

In the Aftermath

At some point, either the strike will collapse or an agreement will be reached, or both sides will agree to return to the bargaining table on the return of personnel to the job. Often, a tense atmosphere will prevail for some time. Non-strikers will resent any threats made and any damage to their personal property. Those who walked out will view those who continued to work as not having helped maintain the solidarity necessary for effective job actions. Union members dissatisfied with what the strike did or did not produce may engage in the petty harassments of non-strikers, display thinly veiled contempt for management, or surreptitiously cause damage to city property. Management's posture during the strike can in part reduce the tensions inherent in the poststrike adjustment period, but it cannot eliminate the need for responsible action by the union or overcome the intransigence of a subversely militant union.

As soon as an agreement ending the strike is reached, a joint statement with the union should be released, announcing the settlement and highlighting its key features, and letters should be sent to the homes of all officers, urging them to put aside the matter and return to the business of public service with renewed commitment. All personnel in the department should take particular care not to discriminate between those who struck and those who did not.

Among the other items of business that must be handled after a strike relate to whether strikers are to be disciplined, although the union will typically insist on amnesty for all striking officers as a precondition to returning to the job; in addition it must be determined what disciplinary measures are to be taken against those who destroyed private or public property during the course of the strike; what measures are to be taken against those who undertook various actions against officers who did not walk out; and the securing of a union commitment not to act in any way against nonstrikers and to actively discourage such actions by union members.

There has been some experimentation with reconciliation meetings of parties to promote goodwill. Experience has demonstrated that, in most cases, the wounds are so fresh and the feelings so intense that it simply creates the opportunity for an incident; in one notable instance, a reconciliation party resulted in each of the groups remaining separated for two hours. Finally when each group reached the buffet table a fight broke out between the strikers and non-strikers.[84]

Critical Thinking Question

1. What are the ethical and personal dilemmas an officer might face as he or she participates in a job action?

CHAPTER REVIEW

1. Identify and briefly discuss the seven major factors that led to the unionization of police.
   The first major factor was the need of labor organizations to gain new members, as industrial workers were already extensively organized. Labor organizations discovered that the public sector was a ready market for collective action and began to encompass public employees in the 1960s. The next factor in unionization was the reduction of legal barriers to public employee unionization by state government, the federal government, and the judicial system. The third significant force that brought about police unionization was police frustration with a lack of support for the war on crime. The perceived public hostility and the effects of the due process revolution contributed to a general feeling that police should be more supported by social institutions, rather than hindered by them. Next, personnel practices began to be questioned by officers that were increasingly more educated. Officers were less likely to accept mandates that they perform police functions on unpaid time, and they were angered by managers' treatment of the leaders of police employee associations. This created an atmosphere of cohesiveness among rank-and-file members, leading directly to unionization. The fifth factor in unionization was that police officers felt that their salaries, benefits, and working conditions were inadequate. The sixth factor was an increase in violence against the police. Finally the seventh factor was a realization these union groups were successful at making an impact through collective action.
2. What are some ways that unions have impacted public policy decisions?
   Unions have wielded their influence over local elections by supporting candidates favorable to union viewpoints, lobbying for policies positively affecting union members and opposing those that negatively impact them, and causing the removal of local officials.
3. Although public employee collective bargaining laws vary by state, the general thrust of the laws can be summarized by three simplified models. What are these three models?
   The three models of employee collective bargaining laws are first the binding arbitration model, which grants public employees the right to select exclusive representatives for the purpose of bargaining with their employers, second the meet and confer model, in which law enforcement officers have the same rights as in binding arbitration but employers are obligated only to convene and discuss with bargaining representatives, and third the bargaining not required model, in which collective bargaining for law enforcement is not statutorily required by the state in which the police department is located.
4. Explain the process of a union organization drive.
   A union begins an organization drive by seeking to get at least 30 percent of the classes of employees it wishes to represent to sign authorization cards. The union notifies the law enforcement agency once this goal is reached. Then the union holds an election in which it seeks approval of 50 percent plus one officer. Management recognizes the union as the official bargaining delegate of the class of employees it sought to represent when the election is deemed to be legitimate, and the union must then petition the public employees relations commission of the state to ensure that the grouping of employees is

appropriate. If the commission approves, the union is certified to represent those employees. If management refuses to recognize that the union election was legitimate, the state commission may be petitioned to officiate another election among employees.

5. Who generally serves on union and management teams during negotiations?
   The union team generally consists of an outside negotiator, the union president or another high-ranking officer, and a few team members who have conducted in-depth research on the matters related to the negotiation. The management team is usually made up of a director of labor relations or professional labor relations specialist and a key member of the department command staff, though not the police chief.
6. What is the typical sequence of events involved in the grievance process?
   The first step in a grievance process is for the union member to present his or her grievance to a supervisor within a set number of days of the occurrence of the issue giving rise to the problem. If the situation cannot be settled by the supervisor, the union member takes the problem to a division commander within five days of the supervisor's response. The division commander also has a set number of days to give a written decision. If that decision fails to satisfy the union member, the grievance is then taken to the police chief. The police chief also has a fixed timeline to render a written decision, at which point the union member may take the issue to the city manager if it is not acceptably resolved. If the city manager cannot settle the grievance, the matter is then subject to arbitration.
7. List and describe the four major forms of job action.
   The first major form of job action is the vote of confidence. In this action, the union calls for a vote to determine the level of support for a department official. This generally results in a vote of no confidence, which may spur a removal from leadership or a change in policies. The second form of job action is the work slowdown. The slowdown is a conscious effort by union members to slow productivity significantly, so that government or private citizens begin to pressure the department to restore normal function. The third form of job action is the work speedup. In a speedup, productivity accelerates to the point that the public or a government entity is overwhelmed by the action and pressures the employer to make concessions. Examples of a work speedup include "ticket blizzards" and strict enforcement of minor violations. The fourth form of job action is the work stoppage. Work stoppages include the strike, which involves the withholding of all of labor's services, and brief work stoppages, which tend to last a few days and don't involve all union members at once.
8. Describe five things police leaders can do to limit the possibility of job actions by uniformed officers.
   The five things that police leaders can do to limit the possibility of job actions include first ensuring that appropriate city officials, union leaders, and management have completed training in the tenets and practices of collective bargaining; second make certain formal and informal networks are used freely within and between city government, police agencies, and unions; third meet regularly with union leaders and representatives to strengthen the communication and relationships key to collective bargaining; fourth develop and publicize a contingency plan that addresses as many of the issues as can reasonably be foreseen as related to job actions; and fifth assess the philosophy, capabilities, strengths, weaknesses, and propensities of the union and its officers, negotiators, legal counsel, and members to determine the likelihood of various job actions.

KEY TERMS

Arbitration: a process by which parties in a dispute submit their differences to an impartial third party established by statutory provision or mutual consent.

Bargaining not required model: the model for police-sector collective bargaining law in which collective bargaining is not statutorily required by the state.

Binding arbitration: a judgment made by a neutral third party to settle a dispute between labor and management, in which both parties agree in advance to abide by the result.

Blue flu: a job action in which officers organize mass absences on the pretext of sickness for the purpose of protest against their employers.

Collective bargaining: negotiation between an employer and a labor union, usually regarding issues such as wages, benefits, hours, and working conditions.

Grievance: an official expression of dissatisfaction brought by an employee or an employee organization as the initial step toward resolution through a formal procedure.

Job action: any organized protest or pressure used by employees or employee groups to accomplish a goal or to influence decisions by their employers.

Meet and confer model: in this model of collective bargaining, employers are only obligated to meet and confer with representatives, with no method of resolution specified.

Public Employment Relations Commission: an administrative body, often on a state level, responsible for administering legislation related to union bargaining.

NOTES

1. These themes are identified and treated in detail in Hervey A. Juris and Peter Feuille, *Police Unionism* (Lexington, Mass.: Lexington Books, 1973).
2. C. M. Rehmus, "Labor Relations in the Public Sector," Third World Congress, International Industrial Relations Association, in *Labor Relations Law in the Public Sector*, ed. Russell A. Smith, Harry T. Edwards, and R. Theodore Clark, Jr. (Indianapolis: Bobbs-Merrill, 1974), p. 7.
3. Public Service Research Council, *Public Sector Bargaining and Strikes* (Vienna, Va.: Public Service Research Council, 1976), pp. 6–9.
4. 296 F. Supp. 1068, 1969.
5. 324 F. Supp. 315, N.D. Ga., 1971.
6. 483 F. 2d 966, 10th Circuit, 1973.
7. President's Commission on Law Enforcement and Administration of Justice, *Task Force Report: The Police* (Washington, D.C.: U.S. Government Printing Office, 1967), p. 144.
8. Ibid., p. 145.
9. Charles A. Salerno, "Overview of Police Labor Relations," in *Collective Bargaining in the Public Sector*, ed. Richard M. Ayres and Thomas L. Wheeler (Gaithersburg, Md.: International Association of Chiefs of Police, 1977), p. 14.
10. Rory Judd Albert, *A Time for Reform: A Case Study of the Interaction between the Commissioner of the Boston Police Department and the Boston Police Patrolmen's Association* (Cambridge, Mass.: MIT Press, 1975), p. 47.
11. From various tables, U.S. Department of Labor, *Employment and Earnings* 8, no. 4 (October 1961).
12. Bureau of the Census, *Statistical Abstract of the United States, 1975* (Washington, D.C.: U.S. Government Printing Office, 1975), p. 162.
13. John H. Burpo, *The Police Labor Movement* (Springfield, Ill.: Charles C Thomas, 1971), p. 34.
14. Albert, *A Time for Reform*, p. 29. Several studies have reported that market forces other than unions explain better the rise in public employees' salaries than does union activity.
15. Joe Sciacca, "Cop Union Chief's Comment Draws Fire," *Boston Herald*, December 12, 1990.
16. Will Aitchison, *The Rights of Law Enforcement Officers*, 5th ed. (Portland Ore: Labor Relations Information Systems, 2004), pp. 8–11, 18–21. (This discussion and accompanying references were adapted from this source with permission.)
17. See §423.231 et seq., Michigan Comp. Laws Annotated (West, 1994).
18. *Hillsdale PBA v. Borough of Hillsdale*, 644 A. 2d 564 (N.J. 1994).
19. *Municipality of Anchorage v. Anchorage Police Department Employee's Association*, 839 P.2d

1080 (Alaska 1992); *City and County of San Francisco*, 43 Cal. Rptr.2d 421 (Cal.App. 1995); *City of Detroit v. Detroit Police Officers' Association*, 294 N.W.2d 68 (Mich. 1980); *City of Richfield v. Local 1215, Intern. Ass'n of Fire Fighters*, 276 N.W.2d 42 (Minn. 1979); *Medford Firefighters' Association v. City of Medford*, 595 P.2d 1268 (Or.App. 1979). But see *County of Riverside v. Superior Court*, 30 Cal.4th 278 (Cal. 2003) (binding arbitration violates unique provision of California state constitution); *Salt Lake City v. Inter. Assn. of Fire Fighters*, 563 P.2d 768 (Utah 1977) (overturns binding arbitration as unconstitutional delegation of legislative authority).

20. *City of Cocoa*, 15 NPER FL-23235 (Fla. PERC 1993) (employer may not unilaterally implement management rights clause).
21. *Los Angeles County Civil Service Commission v. Superior Court*, 588 P.2d 249 (Cal. 1978).
22. *Placentia Fire Fighters v. City of Placentia*, 129 Cal.Rptr 126 (Cal.App. 1976).
23. *City of Bellevue and IAFF, Local 1604*, 831 P.2d 738 (Wash. 1992).
24. *City of Detroit*, NPER MI-25066 (Mich. ERC 1994).
25. *State of California*, 18 NPER CA-26117 (Cal. PERB ALJ 1995).
26. *Washington State Patrol Troopers Association v. State of Washington*, Decision 4710 (Wash. PERC ALJ 1994).
27. This "local option" has been adopted by such cities as Phoenix, Arizona; Boise, Idaho; Denver, Colorado; and San Antonio, Texas. In states following the meet and confer model, there usually exists a local option to allow interest arbitration as the last step in the bargaining process. For example, even though for years California followed the meet and confer model, cities in California such as Oakland and San Jose had local laws providing for interest arbitration.
28. This table is taken from *Interest Arbitration*, 2nd ed. (Portland, Ore: Labor Relations Information System, 1988).
29. E.g., *Village of Dixmoor*, 16 PERI ¶2038 (Ill. SLRB Gen. Counsel 2000).
30. E.g., *California Correctional Peace Officers Association v. State California*, 25 PERC ¶32,015 (Cal. PERB ALJ 2000).
31. *Borough v. Pennsylvania Labor Relations Board*, 794 A.2d 402 (Pa.Cmwlth. 2002).
32. A good early discussion of bargaining topics can be found in Clark, *The Scope of the Duty to Bargain in Public Employment, in Labor Relations Law in the Public Sector* 81 (A. Knapp ed. 1977).
33. *Portland Firefighters Association v. City of Portland*, 751 P.2d 770 (Or. 1988).
34. If an employer chooses to agree to include a permissive subject of bargaining in a collective bargaining agreement, and finds the provision to its distaste, it may simply refuse to include the provision in a subsequent agreement. *Paterson Police Local v. City of Paterson*, 432 A.2d 847 (N.J. 1981).
35. *City of Portland*, 8 PECBR 8115 (Or. 1985).
36. *City of Buffalo*, 13 NPER NY-13036 (N.Y. PERB 1990).
37. *County of Perry*, 19 NPER IL-124 (Ill. LRB 2003).
38. *Plains Township Police Bargaining Unit v. Plains Township*, 33 PPER ¶33,019 (Pa. LRB ALJ 2001).
39. *City of Bremerton*, PEB ¶45,352 (Wash.) (CCH, 1987).
40. *City of Iowa City*, 17 NPER IA-26005 (Iowa PERB ALJ 1995) delay of 90 days in filing unfair labor practice charge); *County of Nassau*, 35 NYPER ¶4583 (NY PERB ALJ 2002); *City of Reading*, 17 NPER PA-26132 (Pa. LRB ALJ 1995)); *City of Philadelphia*, 13 NPER PA-22042 (Pa. LRB Hearing Examiner 1991) (six-week delay between filing of unfair labor practice charge and violation of duty to bargain did not render the charge untimely).
41. *Throop Borough*, 16 NPER PA-25012 (Pa. LRB ALJ 1993).
42. *Law Enforcement Labor Services, Inc. v. City of Luverne*, 463 N.W.2d 546 (Minn.App. 1990).
43. *Peekskill Police Association*, 35 NYPER ¶3016 (N.Y. PERB 2002).
44. *Caruso v. Board of Collective Bargaining of the City of New York*, 555 N.Y.S.2d 133 (A.D. 1990).
45. Quoted in *Model Law Enforcement Contract, 1993 Edition* (Portland, Ore.: Labor Relations Information System, 1993).
46. *Washington State Patrol*, 3 (8) Public Safety Labor News 7 (Wash. PERC 1995).
47. *City of Grosse Pointe Park*, 14 MPER ¶32051 (Mich. ERC 2001)
48. *City of Mt. Vernon*, 23 GERR 667 (New York)(BNA 1986).
49. *Howard County*, 1 (9) Public Safety Labor News 5 (Fishgold, 1993).
50. William J. Bopp, *Police Personnel Administration* (Boston: Holbrook HSS, 1974), p. 345.
51. See Richard S. Rubin et al., "Public Sector Unit Determination Administrative Procedures and Case Law," Midwest Center for Public Sector Labor Relations, Indiana University Department of Labor Contract J-9-P-6–0215, May 31, 1978.

52. In this regard, see Stephen L. Hayford, William A. Durkee, and Charles W. Hickman, "Bargaining Unit Determination Procedures in the Public Sector: A Comparative Evaluation," *Employee Relations Law Journal*, 5, no. 1 (summer 1979): 86.
53. Donald Slesnick, "What Is the Effect of a Sunshine Law on Collective Bargaining: A Union View," *Journal of Law and Education* 5 (October 1976): 489.
54. On costing out contracts, see Marvin Friedman, *The Use of Economic Data in Collective Bargaining* (Washington, D.C.: U.S. Government Printing Office, 1978).
55. Charles W. Maddox, *Collective Bargaining in Law Enforcement* (Springfield, Ill.: Charles C Thomas, 1975), p. 54.
56. Arnold Zack, *Understanding Grievance Arbitration in the Public Sector* (Washington, D.C.: U.S. Government Printing Office, 1974), p. 1.
57. Maddox, *Collective Bargaining*, p. 109.
58. Zack, *Understanding Grievance Arbitration*, p. 4.
59. Maurice S. Trotta, *Arbitration of Labor–Management Disputes* (New York: Amacon, 1974), p. 237, with changes.
60. See Helen Lavan and Cameron Carley, "Analysis of Arbitrated Employee Grievance Cases in Police Departments," *Journal of Collective Negotiations in the Public Sector* 14, no. 3 (1985): 250–51.
61. Zack, *Understanding Grievance Arbitration*, p. 32.
62. Ibid.
63. Indira A. R. Lakshmanan, "State Police Fault Colonel," *Boston Globe*, February 1, 1994, p. 24.
64. Terry M. Neal, "300 PG Officers Vote No-Confidence in Commanders," *Washington Post*, August 16, 1995, p. D3.
65. David Marc Kleinman, "Zinging It to the Chief," *Police Magazine* 2, no. 3 (1979): 39.
66. Michael Cooper, "Police Picket Traffic Courts, as Pact Protests Go On," *New York Times*, January 27, 1997, p. B3.
67. Peter Finn, "Police Officers Send Pointed Message: More Than 150 Pagers Turned in to Protest Alexandria Pay Scale," *Washington Post*, January 24, 1997, p. B6.
68. Stephanie Reitz, "Council Approves Police Contract in East Hartford," *Hartford Courant*, March 19, 1997, p. B1.
69. Jack Rabin, Thomas Vocino, W. Bartley Hildreth, and Gerald J. Miller, eds., *Handbook of Public Sector Labor Relations* (New York: Marcel Dekker, 1994), p. 6.
70. On these and related points, see Robert P. Engvall, "Public Sector Unionization in 1995 or It Appears the Lion King Has Eaten Robin Hood," *Journal of Collective Negotiations in the Public Sector* 24, no. 3 (1995): 255–69.
71. Indira A. R. Lakshmanan, "3 Allegedly Protest On-Call Police Duty," *Boston Globe*, July 10, 1995.
72. Daniel B. Wood, "Police Strike Hits L.A. as Tourist Season Opens," *Christian Science Monitor*, June 3, 1994, p. 2.
73. Kim Bell, " 'Blue Flu' Strikes in St. Louis," *St. Louis Post-Dispatch*, May 30, 1993, p. D1.
74. *Detroit Free Press*, February 8, 1997.
75. Don Aucoin, *Boston Globe*, September 27, 1997.
76. http://204.127.237.106/newsonline/96apr22/beatings.html.
77. Hal Dardick, "Cop Union at Odds with Mayor," *Chicago Tribune*, May 21, 1996.
78. Lorraine Lee, "3 Police Groups Back Harmon," *St. Louis Post-Dispatch*, January 29, 1997.
79. Caroline Louise Cole, "Pay Dispute Could Stop City's Parade," *Boston Globe*, December 1, 1996.
80. On September 29, 1976, Richard M. Ayres presented a paper, "Police Strikes: Are We Treating the Symptom Rather Than the Problem?" at the 83rd International Association of Chiefs of Police meeting, Miami Beach, Florida. Although it is not quoted here, some of his themes may be identifiable, and his contribution in that regard is acknowledged.
81. This list of questions with modifications and additions is drawn from Charles C. Mulcahy, "Meeting the County Employees Strike," in *Collective Bargaining in the Public Sector*, pp. 426–30. See also Carmen D. Saso, *Coping with Public Employee Strikes* (Chicago: Public Personnel Association, 1970).
82. Harold W. Davey, *Contemporary Collective Bargaining* (Englewood Cliffs, N.J.: Prentice Hall, 1972), p. 195.
83. John H. Burpo, *Labor Relations Guidelines for the Police Executive* (Chicago: Traffic Institute, Northwestern University, 1976), p. 14, with modifications and additions.
84. Lee T. Paterson and John Liebert, *Management Strike Handbook* (Chicago: International Personnel Management Association, 1974), p. 42.

Not least among the qualifications of administrators is their ability as a tactician and gladiator in the budget process.

—Frederick C. Mosher

CHAPTER 12

FINANCIAL MANAGEMENT

OUTLINE

Introduction

Politics and Financial Management

Federal, State, and Local Financial Management

Key Budget Terms

The Budget Cycle

Budget Formats

Supplementing the Police Budget: Tactics and Strategies

Chapter Review

Key Terms

Notes

OBJECTIVES

1. Explain why budgeting is important.
2. Define fiscal year, operating budget, and capital budget.
3. Define the budget cycle step and briefly describe the major steps within it.
4. Discuss the line item budget.
5. Explain what a program budget is.
6. Describe a performance budget.
7. Discuss hybrid budgets.
8. Identify the major ways in which a police budget may be supplemented.

INTRODUCTION

Taxation, a finance issue, was at the heart of the American Revolution. Today, newspaper articles about finance, including those dealing with police departments, are found on an almost daily basis. As discussed in the open systems theory section of Chapter 5, Organizational Theory, funds flowing into police departments are inputs which are processed and used to achieve goals. Budgeting is the nerve center of government; it is the decision-making system by which governmental resources are allocated to achieve goals.[1]

To a significant extent, the measure of police administrators is taken by how well they prepare, present, and execute their department's budget.

Occasionally, unforeseen circumstances arise which create demands for services far greater than those provided for in the budget. Illustrations of these include Hurricane Katrina (see Figure 12.1), which ravaged the Gulf Coast; severe flooding and mud slides in Hawaii and Oregon; significant wildfires in Colorado, Virginia, New Mexico, Texas, and Oklahoma; major winter storms in Minnesota and North Dakota; and tornados in Illinois, Missouri, Arkansas, and Tennessee.

Natural disasters are not the only potential "budget busters" for police departments, and examples of them are major increases in gasoline prices, prolonged searches for missing persons, protests and demonstrations (e.g., for immigrant right, see Figure 12.2), riots following a city winning a sports championship, complex investigations seeking to apprehend an active serial rapist or killer, terrorist attacks, protracted union strikes, and industrial disasters. In very small departments, the budget may be "busted" by lesser events, such as having to replace a copier machine or buying a new patrol car because of an accident.

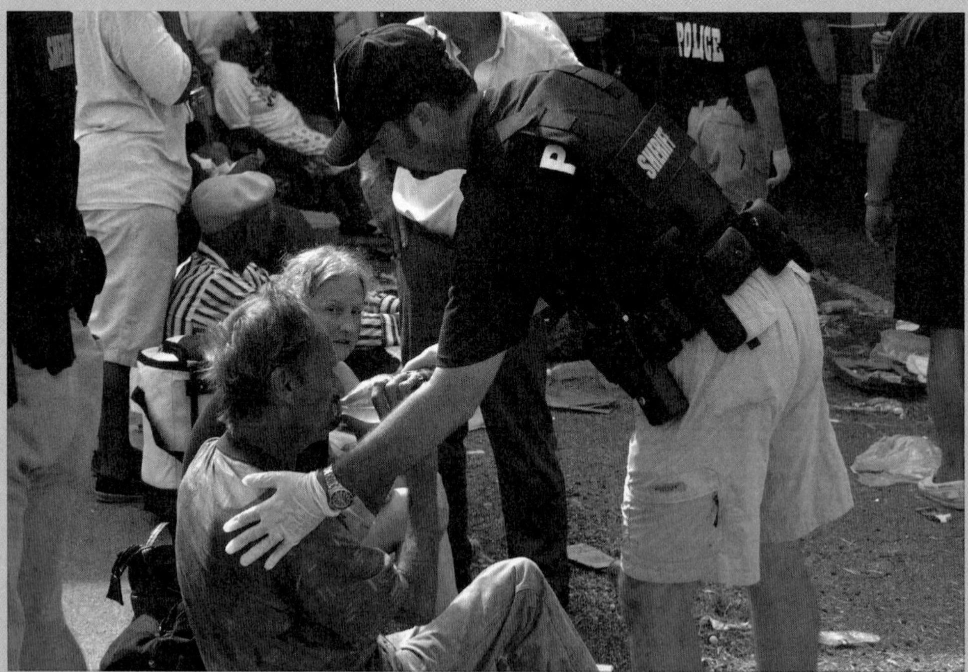

FIGURE 12.1

New Orleans, Louisiana, August 31, 2005. A sheriff's deputy helps an elderly man, too weak to lift his bottle of water, take a drink. Many elderly people were affected by Hurricane Katrina, which struck the area on August 29. New Orleans is being evacuated following hurricane Katrina and rising flood waters.

(Photo by Win Henderson/Federal Emergency Management Agency [FEMA])

FIGURE 12.2

Policing demonstrations is expensive. A sign made by Cipriano Murillo is shown. Murillo says he has been in the United States 20 years and would defend it with his life.

(Photo courtesy of The Hutchinson [Kansas] news)

Quick Facts

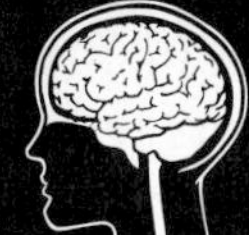

Budget Definition

"Budget" comes from the French *bougette,* meaning a leather bag. Originally, it referred to the bag in which the chancellor of the exchequer carried budget documents to the English Parliament. Later, it came to mean the documents themselves.

Source: A. E. Buck, *The Budgets in Governments Today* (New York: Macmillan, 1945), p. 5.

A police executive is not going to be criticized about the budget when unforeseeable natural or industrial disasters and terrorist attacks occur. However, when mistakes are made on basic matters, budget appropriators are typically unsympathetic. To his considerable embarrassment, one sheriff forgot to request any funds in his budget for ammunition, and a state police commissioner failed to request $4 million to train the new troopers the state legislature had authorized hiring. As a lesson to the commissioner, the state legislature then froze hiring of troopers for one year.

POLITICS AND FINANCIAL MANAGEMENT

Anything done by government involves the expenditure of public funds.[2] Even the expenditure of grant money from a private foundation requires the use of public funds to audit it.

Budgeting is inherently a political process because elected members of city councils, county commissions, state legislatures, and the Congress express their preferences when they vote on appropriations. These decisions are shaped by the appropriators' personal views and those of their constituents, the news media, police and other unions, polls, special interest groups, lobbyists, and other sources.

Critical Thinking Question

1. Why is it that the budget process for some departments of city or county government attracts more attention and is more political than for other departments?

FEDERAL, STATE, AND LOCAL FINANCIAL MANAGEMENT

One of the most controversial ways in which the federal government effects state and local finance is through the passage of mandates which require the implementation of the provisions of new laws for whose implementation the Congress has not provided any funding or has provided insufficient funds. This creates an estimated cost of $30 billion dollars annually. Examples of such "unfunded mandates" include the Americans with Disabilities Act, the Clear Air Act, and the Homeland Security Act. The net effect of unfunded mandates is to reduce money otherwise available for other programs or to force the adoption of new taxes or increases in existing taxes. At the state level, unfunded mandates account for an estimated two to eight percent of funds appropriated for the annual budget. Although the 1995 federal Unfunded Mandate Reform Act prohibits unfunded mandates, the problem persists because of important exclusions in it. Less controversial is the return of some tax money to units of state and local government through grant programs, such as those available from the Office of Community Oriented Policing Services (COPS in the Department of Justice, as well as grants from the Department of Homeland Security).

Cities and counties are under the authority of their respective state governments, which have considerable authority over them, including their financial management. Local governments cannot be created, cannot levy taxes and cannot deliver services without the approval of the state. Following the economic crash of 1929, thousands of local governments went under because they could not meet their financial obligations. As a result, many states passed laws which regulate local finance in such areas as revenue sources, tax collection, level of permissible indebtedness, and budgeting. A system of financial reports was also added which the states monitor carefully.

Quick Facts

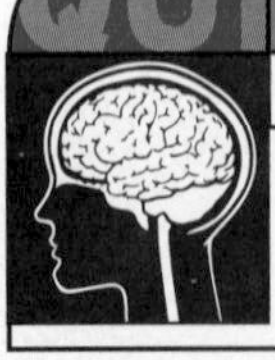

An Audit

A financial audit is an independent verification of financial activities; records are reviewed to determine their legality, accuracy, and compliance with policies, procedures, and laws, such as those guiding the procurement of police equipment.

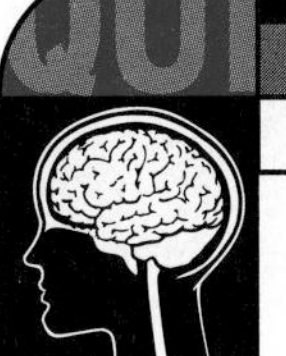

Quick Facts

The Ruin from the Crash of 1929

By 1933, 6,000 banks and 100,000 businesses had failed. Annual per capita earnings dropped by 50 percent. Foreclosures resulted in 600,000 homes being lost and 750,000 farmers being forced from their land. Suicide rates went up and the number of marriages went down.

In addition to whatever requirements the state or federal government establish, local financial management is guided by a maze of other guidelines, which include the city or county charter, ordinances, executive orders, regulations, and customary practices. Also, the form of local government shapes who the dominant figures are. In a strong mayor system, the mayor is the key player, while in the weak mayor form the council is the predominant force. In a mayor–city manager system, the manager holds great power. These generalizations are affected by other factors, such as how much influence a long-serving finance director has accrued and the degree to which a council is more or less proactive in the budget process.

Critical Thinking Question

1. Which forces are most important in shaping the budget in the area where you live?

KEY BUDGET TERMS

Every year, the most important statement any government makes is the enactment of its budget because it reveals in financial terms what its priorities are. There are different ways to think about a budget. For example, it is a plan expressed in dollars, it is the use of financial resources to meet human needs, and it is a contract between those who appropriate the money and those who execute the budget.[3]

A budget year is called a fiscal year (FY), and it may coincide with the calendar year. Often, FYs run from July 1 of one year until June 30 of the next year.

A budget which begins on July 1, 2008, and ends on June 30, 2009, is called a FY '09 budget. Budgets can also be defined as operating and capital. An operating budget usually covers a 12-month period and is for such things as salaries, fringe benefits, office supplies, and telephone service. A capital budget, or capital improvement budget (CIP), is for large-scale expenditures which may be "one-time" in nature and take place over several years, such as for acquiring land and building a new police station. The city/county's finance/financial services department (F/FSD) provides guidelines covering what types of expenditures should be in the operating versus the capital

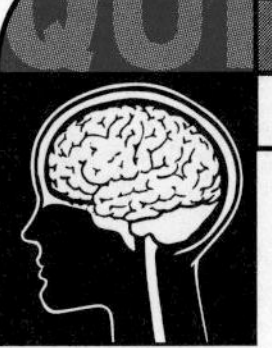

Quick Facts

Biennium Budget

Some local units of government have changed their fiscal year to October 1 of one year until September 30 of the next year to coincide with the federal budget year.

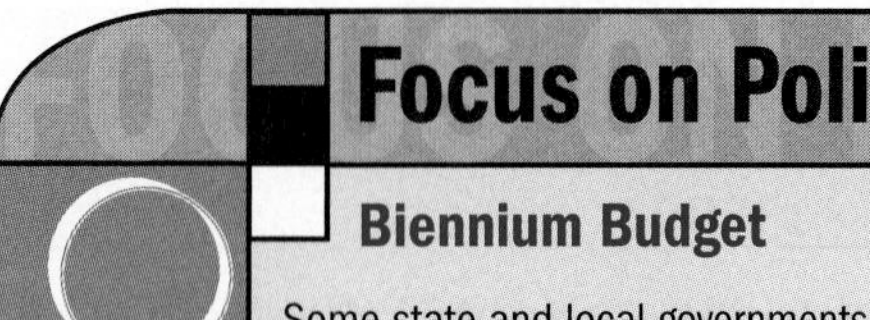

Focus on Policy

Biennium Budget

Some state and local governments, such as Kentucky, and Indiana, and Sandy, Oregon; and Auburn, Alabama, use a two-year budget called a biennium.

budget and these guidelines vary from one jurisdiction to another. For example, in one city any equipment which costs $500 or less per unit (e.g., one shotgun) is in the operating budget, while in another municipality if the unit cost is $250 or more and it has a useful life of more than one year it is in the capital budget. Operating and capital budgets are normally considered separately by the legislative bodies that appropriate the funds.

Critical Thinking Question

1. For annual and biennium budgets, give an advantage and disadvantage of each.

THE BUDGET CYCLE

At its heart, the budget cycle is a stream of four sequential steps, which are repeated at about the same time every year in a jurisdiction: (1) budget preparation and submission by all of a city or county's departments, which includes getting input from stakeholders, such as citizens, other departments, and advisory boards; (2) budget review and approval by the legislative body, which may involve controversies; (3) budget execution, doing the things for which public funds have been appropriated; and (4) the audit.[4] Many of these activities are going on simultaneously because the fiscal year and the budget cycle overlap. For example, while a state law enforcement, sheriff's, or police department is executing this year's budget, last year's budget is being audited and the next year's budget is being prepared.

Well before a police department starts preparing its budget, the F/FSD has been at work preparing the revenue forecast for the city and other data, including the budget preparation manual. These manuals focus on the technical aspects of putting the budget together and include definitions, forms, and the budget calendar (see Figure 12.3). The city or county manager then sends the budget manual to the department heads with specific guidelines on services to be emphasized and specific fiscal guidance as to the

Focus on Policy

Stakeholders

A stakeholder originally was one who held something of value while its ownership was being determined, as in holding the bets on a future event. Presently, the term refers to people who do not perform work but may be or are affected by it or have an interest in it.

Source: Wikipedia, The Free Encyclopedia.

ACTION	RESPONSIBILITY	DEADLINES
Budget kickoff: Budget manual and city manager's transmittal letter (the "budget call") distributed to all departments, often done in a meeting with additional comments	City manager	October 1
Department heads issue their budget message to immediately subordinate unit commanders, e.g., deputy chiefs or majors in–charge of bureaus or divisions	Police chief	October 15
City holds budget preparation workshops; police representatives–may be mix of civilians and sworn personnel–involved in preparing police budget attend	F/FSD holds workshop	October 22, 23
Recommended budgets for all police bureaus or divisions developed with justification and submitted to police budget office	Bureau/division commanders	February 1
Recommended bureau or division budgets reviewed with the respective commanders	Police budget office with bureau or division commanders; chief may participate	February 15-19
Bureau or division budgets consolidated into overall department budget	Police budget office	March 1
Overall police budget reviewed by chief	Chief, bureau or division commanders, police budget office	March 2-16
Police department budget approved for submission to city manager or F/FSD	Chief	March 17
City manager meets separately with department heads to review their budget requests	City manager, police chief, other department heads	April 1-16
Department budgets revised per city manager's guidance	Chief, police budget office	April 19-May 7
City manager forwards recommended budget to city council	City manager	May 12
City council as a whole or through its finance/ways and means committee reviews departmental budgets	City council	May 13-27
City manager and departments present their respective budgets separately to city council and respond to question	City manager, department heads, city council	June 3-10
City council holds public hearings on city budget[b]	City council	June 17-24
City council approves budget and it becomes effective	City council	July 1

FIGURE 12.3

Basic municipal operating budget preparation calendar for FY '11[a].

[a] Budget calendars vary widely in local government. This figure omits the handling of capital improvement projects (CIPs) and advanced financial topics, such as the submission of departmental earnings estimates and setting the tax millage rate.

[b] The number of public hearings required may be set in the city/county charter, by local ordinace, or by state law.

amount the budget may increase or must decrease, the availability to raise money for existing employees, limits on new positions and programs and other fiscal data. Often, the budget message from the city or county manager, the budget preparation manual, and past budgets are available online, along with the software needed to prepare the budget. Budget workshops may be held by the F/FSD to explain the process and to promote a uniformity of approach across all departments.

In The News

Council Members Blast Mayor's Budget

Two San Diego city council members ripped Mayor Sanders's public safety budget, saying there wasn't enough money in it to stem the tide of officers leaving for jobs in other cities. The mayor's budget would provide no police raises for the second year in a row. Some residents feel that the mayor and his staff were not taking the crisis of a shrinking police force seriously and that action needed to be taken before it was too late. San Diego is losing an average of 192 officers annually. The mayor maintains that raises are not in the picture because the city is facing a $1.4 billion pension fund deficit.

Source: Tony Manolatos, "New Light Shed on Staffing Shortages," *San Diego Union-Tribune*, May 5, 2006.

Before sending out the budget preparation manual, city and county managers usually meet with their mayor and council or commission informally or formally to get their views on budget priorities to avoid major conflict later in the budget process. Many jurisdictions conduct strategic planning and budget workshops at various points in the budget process to get city council or county commission input early in the process, especially with respect to goals and target budget figures. These measures do not guarantee there will be no conflict later, but they do reduce some potential for it.

Step One: Budget Preparation in the Police Department

In small police departments, roughly 10 or fewer officers, the chief's role in budget preparation is not very great. Most frequently, a strong mayor or city manager will have several conversations with the chief and formulate the budget him- or herself. In larger departments with seven or eight layers of hierarchy, the budget process is more formal. A chief's budget is shaped by the guidance given by a city or county manager and, in that context, is a top-down process. However, to know what the actual needs are, the lowest-ranking supervisors in the department, usually sergeants, may be involved in identifying needs and, in that regard, the budget is a bottom-up process. The budget is built by combining the budget requests from smaller units to form the budgets of bureaus or divisions. The single most important element in a police budget is people and their support costs; roughly 80 percent

In The News

Personnel Cost Dominant Budget

In the Ocean City, Maryland, Police Department, personnel and support cost is about 80 percent, while in Asbury Park, New Jersey, it reaches 94.5 percent.

Source: Jacob Cook, "OCPD's $17M Budget Leads to Questions," *The Maryland Coast Dispatch*, May 12, P 2006. Bob Cullinane, "War on Crime Suffers from Too Few Troops," Asbury Park Press, January 25, 2005.

Focus on Policy

Budget Cutting Strategies

Well-recognized attempts to cut the police budget are eliminating all overtime pay and forbidding the use of compensatory time. Both of these strategies impinge on the flexible delivery of police services.

or more of the overall budget is for personnel and personnel support costs, such as salaries, medical insurance, life insurance, and pension benefits, as well as overtime and training.

In a tight budget year, some chiefs cut back on training dollars and equipment, such as cars. This may make the budget work, but both choices are poor strategies. Any chief who submitted a budget without dollars in it for preventive maintenance of the police fleet would be criticized, yet training is the preventive maintenance on people; it keeps personnel fresh and at the cutting edge, prevents litigation or can be a defense to it, and is a principle means of importing new ideas and techniques into the police department. As to delaying the purchase of major equipment, such as cars, officers operating vehicles with 100,000 and more miles are using cars which are dangerously worn out, no matter how well they have been maintained.

When the chief meets with bureau or division commanders to review their budget requests, it is an opportunity to reward the "faithful" and to informally discipline those who are seen as "not toeing the party line" and are therefore "disloyal." In lean budget years, however, it is harder to reward the faithful by funding new programs and easier to harm a wayward subordinate's interests.

Chiefs are also concerned with budget strategy and making the best case for funding. If solid justifications cannot be made for programs, they should not be included in the request lest it set budget analysts in the F/FSD on a quest to find more programs to cut. As a matter of strategy, chiefs may include some "fat" in the budget, so that they can withstand a certain degree of reductions. The fat is not wasteful spending; it represents new positions or programs the department would like to have and would make good use of but whose loss would not endanger the delivery of important services.

In transmitting the budget to the city manager, the chief's cover letter will highlight accomplishments from the current budget and will call attention to the importance of new initiatives and the ills likely to arise if the request is cut. No matter what is happening in terms of the amount of crime, chiefs have an explanation which favors a budget increase. If crime is up, more personnel and programs are needed to reduce it; if things are going well, new funding will help keep crime in check.

Step Two: Budget Review and Approval

At some point, the city manager will meet with the police chief to review the department's request. Prior to that meeting, the F/FSD will have reviewed the budget and had discussions about it with the city manager. How the meeting with the city manager goes depends on many factors, including the chief's reputation as a fiscal

In The News

Chief's Budget Justification

The Bluffton Police Chief justified a $1 million budget increase by pointing to the town's rapidly growing population, already being understaffed to cover the city's 53-square miles, the need for a modern police facility and new community policing, traffic enforcement, marine patrol, and court liaison programs.

Source: Erinn McGuire, "Police Chief Asks for $1 Million Budget Increase," *Bluffton (S.C.) Today*, May 9, 2006.

In The News

Geese Police Restored in Budget

The Eatontown, New Jersey, city finance staff cut the budget $12,000 by eliminating the "Geese Police," a dog which chased the geese from Wampum Memorial Park. The city council's president expressed anger at the cut. One council member said the program was very effective, it maximized the use of the park, and the budget should be amended to fund the Geese Police.

Source: Sherry Conohan, Atlanticville (Long Branch, New Jersey), March 5, 2004.

In The News

Council Increases Taxes

For years, the City of Los Angeles had subsidized trash collection; increasing those fees was considered a political hands-off item. However, under Mayor Antonio Villaraigosa's leadership, the city council did the unthinkable and increased trash collection fees to fund a major police department expansion.

Source: Steve Hymon, "Council OKs Mayor's Plan to Add to Police Force by Hiking Trash Fee," *Los Angeles Times*, May 19, 2006.

manager, the priorities and direction given by the city council, and the confidence the public has in the chief and the police department. Even recent events can affect the outcome. For example, the chief may have a street crime unit whose tactics include using decoys who are victimized by predatory criminals. If in the past week three criminals have been killed attempting to rob decoys, the newspapers and public sentiment may run toward disbanding this "killer" unit. Ultimately, the city manager and chief come to an understanding about the department's request. That understanding is reflected in the budget the city manager recommends to council.

At the police department's budget hearing before the city council, the chief must tread a narrow path. If he or she attempts to have cuts made by the city manager restored, he or she risks alienating the city manager. Conversely, if the cuts have gone too deep, the chief as a matter of public safety may feel obliged to appeal for the funds to be restored. Safer than initiating the appeal on his or her own, the experienced chief may plant key questions with friendly members of council, so that the discussion can be had without his or her openly spearheading the discussion. City managers know this game and can tolerate it, versus having a chief openly defy the city manager. Generally, even council members who favor increasing the police budget may be reluctant to do so if it means voting for a tax increase.

Following several years of severe major budget cuts, one chief wrote a "budget impact" statement, explaining in detail to the city council that the effect of mandated cuts would be the loss of 110 positions and several programs.[5] This statement became a means of building budget support and mediating criticisms of slow service by the police department. One immediate result was that, through public donations, the mounted patrol continued to operate, albeit at about half its previous number of officers.

When making their budget "pitch" to the city council, chiefs should be able to anticipate questions. For example, one year Ford recalled 150,000 Crown Victorias because of potential fire hazards involving the dashboards. Any chief with "Crown Vics" should know a council member is going to ask, "Are any of the cars in your fleet

In The News

More Officers and More Overtime

The Worcester, Maryland, Police Department's budget request did not sit well with some council members reviewing it. The chief had requested an additional 13 officers and an increase to nearly $90,000 for overtime. One council member stated he was not happy with the budget, noting that, if they were hiring more officers, overtime should go down, not up and the police never stay within their overtime budget.

Source: Brian Gilliland, "Tempers Flare over Police Budget." *Worcester (Maryland) County Times,* May 11, 2006.

Focus on Policy

Budget Deadlines

The deadline for approval of a budget may be provided for in the city charter, local ordinance, or state law. In the State of Washington, cities 300,000 or greater in population must have adopted a balanced budget by December 2 for the fiscal year beginning January 1. A number of states have laws which establish administrative regulations over classes of cities; these classes are often based on population.

involved in the recall?" If the U.S. Department of Justice has just released a study on racial profiling, the chief is going to have to field the question "Are we involved in racial profiling?" In the final analysis, no matter how good a presentation chiefs make, some years they simply have to be political realists and gracefully take their budgetary "lumps."

In Table 12.1 is the budget approval process for the Sun Prairie, Wisconsin, Police Department. The Township of Sun Prairie has neither a mayor nor a city manager; one of the elected members of the town board, the equivalent of a city council, is elected as the chairperson of the town board and is responsible for budget preparation. Much of the day-to-day running of the township is handled by the chairperson and the city clerk. In Table 12.1, the columns "2003 Actual" and "2004 Actual" are included as historical data for the appropriators. There are two columns for 2005: (1) "2005 Approved" represents the amount authorized by the town board and (2) the 2005 budget was being executed as the 2006 budget was being prepared. Thus, "2005 Projected" represents that based on several months of experience, the Township has revised its estimate of actual cost for 2005. The "2006 Requested" column is what the chief of police requested, while "2006 Proposed" is what the chairperson recommended. Careful examination of the "2006 Approved" column shows that the town board adopted the chairperson's proposed budget without change. Table 12.2 is the 2006 approved staffing and costs for police department personnel. It shows that 72.6 people are employed at a cost of $5,014,723, which is 90 percent of the total police budget. After the budget is approved, its execution phase begins when the current FY ends.

Step Three: Budget Execution

This section deals with three key aspects of **budget execution:** (1) its objectives, (2) adjustments to the budget, and (3) budget controls.

TABLE 12.1 Sun Prairie, Wisconsin, Police Department Budget Approval Process, FY '06

	2003 ACTUAL	2004 ACTUAL	2005 APPROVED	2005 PROJECTED	2006 REQUESTED	2006 PROPOSED	2006 APPROVED
211 POLICE ADMINISTRATION							
Wage/fringe	1,123,512	1,238,184	1,229,716	1,230,808	1,279,377	1,271,562	1,271,562
Operating	52,083	135,082	136,420	178,420	192,468	181,468	181,468
Capital items	-	570	-	470	30,000	20,000	20,000
Department total	**1,175,595**	**1,373,836**	**1,349,044**	**1,409,698**	**1,501,845**	**1,473,030**	**1,473,030**
212 POLICE PATROL							
Wage/fringe	2,224,305	2,442,244	2,447,055	2,488,908	2,755,573	2,549,523	2,549,523
Operating	125,271	155,929	133,780	140,281	172,790	160,790	160,790
Capital items	434	25,852	6,325	97,065	75,445	23,445	23,445
Department total	**2,350,010**	**2,624,025**	**2,354,157**	**2,726,254**	**3,003,808**	**2,733,758**	**2,733,758**
213 CRIMINAL INVESTIGATION							
Wage/fringe	345,700	322,303	438,424	494,830	530,824	525,686	525,686
Operating	26,716	26,262	26,630	30,150	27,150	26,730	26,730
Capital items	998	-	-	-	27,500	-	-
Department total	**373,414**	**348,565**	**487,885**	**524,980**	**585,474**	**552,416**	**552,416**
214 DISPATCH							
Wage/fringe	509,734	557,483	629,980	555,617	666,250	664,292	664,292
Operating	13,323	13,956	17,450	19,700	30,700	29,600	29,600
Capital items	995	1,783	3,200	3,200	3,600	-	-
Department total	**524,052**	**573,222**	**603,797**	**578,517**	**700,550**	**693,892**	**693,892**
219 DARE/LIFE SKILLS							
Wage/fringe	-	-	-	-	-	-	-
Operating	4,000	4,000	4,000	4,000	-	-	-
Capital items	-	-	-	-	-	-	-
Department total	**4,000**	**4,000**	**4,000**	**4,000**	-	-	-
220 BIKE SAFETY							
Wage/fringe	-	-	-	-	-	-	-
Operating	1,200	1,200	1,200	1,200	1,200	1,200	1,200
Capital items	-	-	-	-	-	-	-
Department total	**1,200**	**1,200**	**1,200**	**1,200**	**1,200**	**1,200**	**1,200**

223 DRUG CONTROL GRANT							
Wage/fringe	5,252	3,437	-	12,800	-	-	-
Operating	-	-	-	-	-	-	-
Capital items	-	-	-	-	-	-	-
Department total	**5,252**	**3,437**	**-**	**12,800**	**-**	**-**	**-**
224 VILLAGE SQUARE							
Wage/fringe	-	-	-	-	-	-	-
Operating	-	-	-	-	-	-	-
Capital items	-	-	-	-	-	-	-
Department total	-	-	-	-	-	-	-
225 NEIGHBORHOOD POLICING							
Wage/fringe	2,801	4,283	3,660	3,660	3,660	3,660	3,660
Operating	18,689	8,442	9,000	9,000	9,000	9,000	9,000
Capital items	-	-	-	-	-	-	-
Department total	**21,490**	**12,725**	**12,660**	**12,660**	**12,660**	**12,660**	**12,660**
216 SCHOOL PATROL							
Wage/fringe	55,165	57,756	-	37,101	-	-	-
Operating	1,295	769	77,962	49,099	78,500	78,500	78,500
Capital items	-	-	-	-	-	-	-
Department total	**56,460**	**58,525**	**77,962**	**86,200**	**78,500**	**78,500**	**78,500**
POLICE DEPARTMENT TOTAL							
Wage/fringe	4,266,469	4,625,690	4,748,835	4,823,724	5,235,684	5,014,723	5,014,723
Operating	242,577	345,640	406,442	431,850	511,808	487,288	487,288
Capital items	2,427	28,205	9,525	100,735	136,545	43,445	43,445
POLICE TOTAL	**4,511,473**	**4,999,535**	**5,164,802**	**5,356,309**	**5,884,037**	**5,545,456**	**5,545,456**

SUMMARY OF INITIATIVE REQUESTS AND RECOMMENDATIONS:

	Description	Requested	Proposed	Approved
Initiatives:	Police officer	71,267	35,633	35,633
	Traffic safety officer	71,267	35,634	35,634
	Strategic planning	10,000	-	-
	Electronic control devices	14,000	14,000	14,000
	Evidence dryer	12,500	-	-
	Scheduling software	34,800	20,000	20,000

TABLE 12.1 CONTINUED

	2003 ACTUAL	2004 ACTUAL	2005 APPROVED	2005 PROJECTED	2006 REQUESTED	2006 PROPOSED	2006 APPROVED
Sliding shelves for evidence room					15,000	-	-
Replacement emergency medical dispatch license					3,600	-	-
2 Middle School Officers (school district grant)					182,535	-	-
Replacement Laser					3,495	3,495	3,495
Replacement Lightbar					2,350	2,350	2,350
Replacement Shotgun					600	600	600
TOTAL					421,414	111,712	111,712

SOURCE: Sun Prairie, Wisconsin, Police Department.

TABLE 12.2 Sun Prairie, Wisconsin, Police Department 2006 Approved Staffing and Costs

	STAFFING			PERSONNEL COSTS		
POSITION TITLE	CURRENT FTE	APPROVED FTE	CHANGE	CURRENT	APPROVED	CHANGE
Police chief	1.0	1.0	-	136,087	136,087	-
Assistant chief	1.0	1.0	-	102,639	102,639	-
Lieutenant	4.0	4.0	-	398,873	398,873	-
Shift sergeant	4.0	4.0	-	383,873	383,873	-
Detective sergeant	1.0	1.0	-	97,824	97,824	-
Detective	3.0	3.0	-	230,294	230,294	-
Detective trainee	1.0	1.0		73,595	73,595	
Police officer	29.0	30.0	1.0	1,928,803	1,993,570	64,767
Administrative director	1.0	1.0	-	86,945	86,945	-
Dispatch director	1.0	1.0			78,961	78,961
Records supervisor	1.0	1.0	-	66,483	66,483	-
Police assistant	1.0	1.0	-	76,704	76,704	-
Dispatch supervisor	1.0	1.0	-	64,449	64,449	-
Dispatcher	10.0	10.0	-	485,896	485,896	-
Community service officer	2.0	2.0	-	107,205	107,205	-
Evidence technician	1.0	1.0	-	54,666	54,666	-
Court officer	1.0	1.0	-	55,731	55,731	-
Court clerk	1.0	1.0	-	49,250	49,250	-
Administrative assistant	1.0	1.0	-	67,161	67,161	-
Confidential secretary	0.6	0.6	-	27,307	27,307	-
Secretary	6.0	6.0	-	246,104	246,104	-
Holiday/misc./premium pay				79,657	79,657	-
Overtime				103,774	103,774	-
Boards and commissions				1,500	1,500	-
Estimated turnover/ vacancy rate				(53,825)	(53,825)	-
Total	71.6	72.6	1.0	4,949,956	5,014,723	64,767

SOURCE: Sun Prairie, Wisconsin, Police Department.

Budget Execution Objectives

Budget execution is the action phase of budgeting, the phase in which plans contained in the budget are put into operation.[6] It has four objectives:

1. Ensure that the appropriated funds are spent to achieve the agreed upon goals
2. Make sure that no commitments are made or funds expended except for the purpose the appropriators agreed upon—for example, not filling personnel

vacancies and buying land on which to build a future police headquarters would be a serious breach by a chief

3. Conserve funds wherever reasonably possible
4. Periodically provide accounting and other information which demonstrates that the chief has been a good steward of the funds entrusted to him or her[7]

Budget Execution Adjustments

It is said that people plan and fate laughs; like other types of plans, budgets must be monitored and adjusted as needed. Common methods of adjusting the budget include (1) reallocating funds from one category to another, subject to any approval which is needed; (2) seeking a budget amendment to provide supplemental funds some months into the execution phase when it is clear that anticipated demands for police services are outstripping resources; (3) freezing expenditures when the city's or county's revenue collection may be slower than anticipated; and (4) cutting the budget when directed to do so by the city's or county's F/FSD; most often, this is due to significant shortfalls in revenue collection.[8]

Budget Execution Controls

Even if the budget is not changed during its execution, the means of controlling expenditures are crucial to avoid overspending, misspending, or other abuses. Means of control may be established by state law, city/county charters and ordinances, the F/FSD, or chiefs. There are two broad means of control in operation during the budget execution/expenditure state: external control and internal control.

External Control External control is the control exercised on a department's budget from outside the department. Each city's or county's F/FSD is the primary external control agent for police agencies. Its key function is to make sure that the funds are spent for the purposes agreed upon and set forth in the approved budget and according to the applicable regulations regarding accounting, procurement, and other fiscal guidelines, including an audit at the end of the budget year. Audits are discussed later in this chapter.

One universal method of external control is the allotment system. The F/FSD breaks each department's budget into portions, called allotments, which are amounts of money made available to the departments for specific periods of time, such as for a month or a three-month period, called a quarterly allotment. Allotments allow the F/FSD to time the availability of funding in the police department to the actual need for their expenditure. Therefore, allotments may vary in their amount from one month or quarter to another. This allows governments to invest funds not immediately needed. Freezing expenditures and cutting the budget are also external budget control measures.

In The News

Police Captain Reassigned

A Boston captain responsible for policing a high-crime district spent $132,415 on officer overtime in the first week of October, which was more than half of his overtime budget for the last quarter of the year. Finding the captain's explanation of the overspending "unacceptable," the police superintendent reassigned him to other duties.

Source: "Boston Police Remove Captain Who Overspent on Overtime," *Portsmith Herald,* October 9, 2005.

Internal Control Internal control encompasses both accounting controls and administrative/management policies and practices intended to safeguard access to, and use of, organizational assets, to verify financial transactions (such as cash payments from the informant fund), to encourage operational efficiency, and to foster adherence to fiscal policies. All together, the fundamental purpose of internal controls is to prevent mistakes before they happen and to rectify them when they occur. Internal controls are crucial not only in the budget context but for the operation of the police agency as well. Operational controls include policies on the use of force and high-speed pursuits and professional standards/internal affairs units.

The single most important aspect of internal controls is separating the responsibility for various functions, which promotes the benefits of specialization and limits the ability of a few people to misuse or corrupt the system. Thus, for example, in an F/FSD the purchasing/procurement office obtains competitive bids for equipment, but a different office, accounts payable, actually writes the checks, the receiving unit verifies the delivery of the equipment, and a separate inventory control system accounts for the placement and use of the equipment. In the law enforcement context, serious complaints against officers are investigative not by their parent unit but by the office of professional standards/internal affairs.

Examples of internal controls include breaking the overall budget for the police department into smaller, more easily managed amounts based on units or activities, often referred to as cost centers (see Figure 12.4). Expenditures must be authorized in advance by appropriate documentation and authorizations.

In smaller jurisdictions and particularly where there has been fraud or abuse in agencies, the F/FSD may conduct a pre-audit of transactions before purchases can be made. Periodically monitoring financial reports, such as Table 12.3, play a significant role in keeping financial management on track.

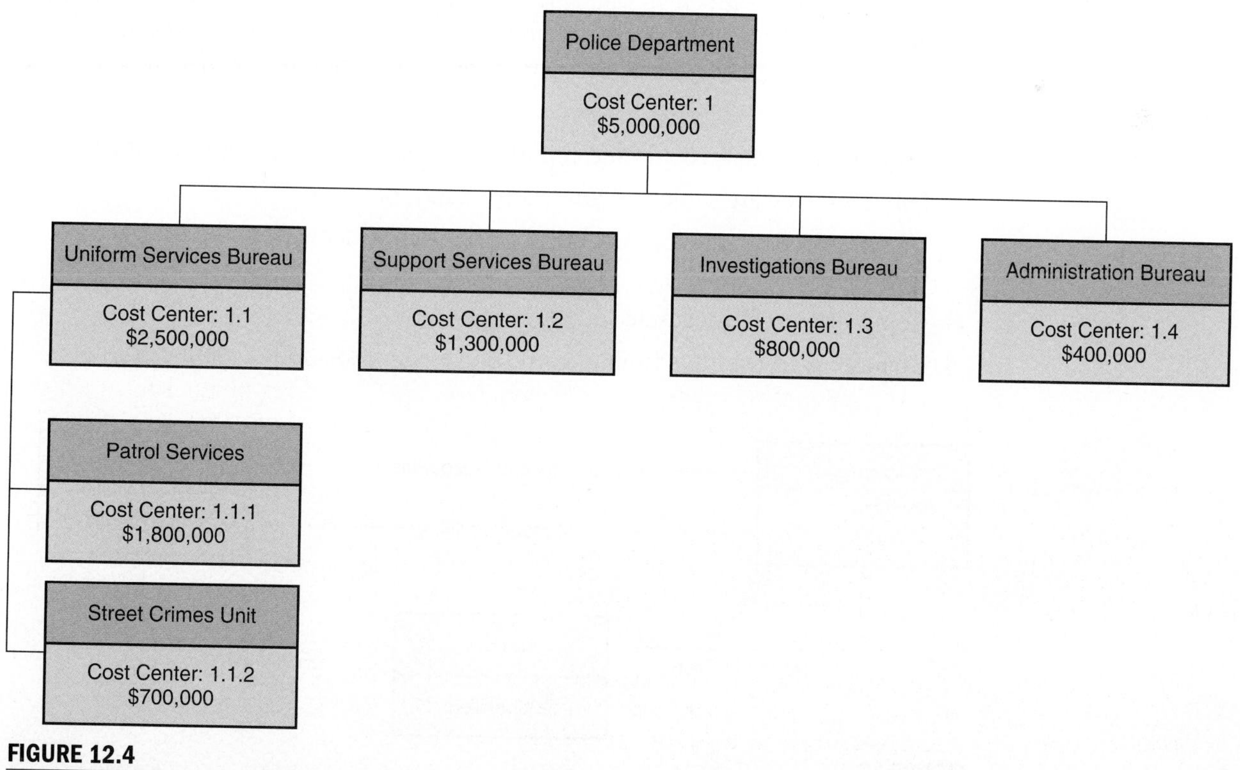

FIGURE 12.4

Major cost centers in a police department.

TABLE 12.3 A Portion of a Police Department's Budget Status Report, December 31, 2006

LINE ITEM	APPROVED	TO DATE EXPENDED	ENCUMBERED	BALANCE	% EXPENDED
Salaries	$1,710,788.00	$848,161.05	$0.00	$862,626.95	**49.58%**
Training	$15,000.00	$5,374.47	$6,098.00	$9,625.53	**35.83%**
Professional services	$6,000.00	$2,000.00	$0.00	$4,000.00	**33.33%**
Travel	$8,500.00	$3,500.57	$1,500.25	$4,999.43	**41.18%**
Dues and subscriptions	$3,100.00	$1,800.00	$0.00	$1,300.00	**58.06%**
Utilities	$35,000.00	$17,213.81	$0.00	$17,786.19	**49.18%**
Office supplies	$22,000.00	$7,688.93	$634.39	$14,311.07	**34.95%**
Printing	$8,300.00	$4,187.23	$0.00	$4,112.77	**50.45%**
Uniforms	$38,000.00	$18,725.13	$0.00	$19,274.87	**49.28%**
	$1,846,688.00	**$908,651.19**	**$8,232.64**	**$938,036.81**	**49.20%**

Step Four: The Audit

Stated simply, an **audit** is a check on something. The essence of all audits is that the checking is done by an independent party who has no stake in the outcome of the audit (see Figure 12.5). While a unit of government will audit itself on an ongoing basis, the annual audit of a budget is often conducted by an outside firm specializing in governmental accounting. In most states, this audit is submitted to the Office of State Auditor, where it is reviewed and any needed follow-up action taken. Auditors systematically collect and examine financial records, conduct interviews, and otherwise rely on competent evidence to determine such things as whether the following occurred:

1. Required financial records and reports were made in a timely and complete form
2. Public funds were subject to any waste, fraud, or abuse
3. Unauthorized charges to the budget or reimbursements from the budget were made
4. Computations are accurate
5. Unauthorized transfers from one budget category to another were made

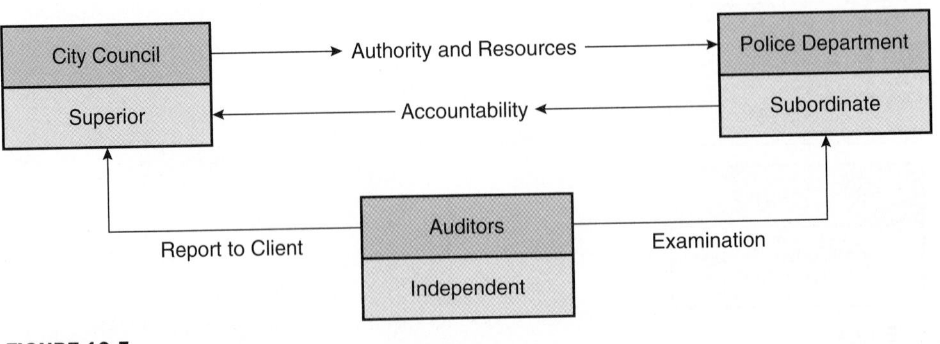

FIGURE 12.5

The audit process and roles.

6. Bidding requirements were followed
7. Expenditures were at or less than the approved budget

Before an audit report is submitted, it is discussed with the chief of police and any errors of fact, representation, or conclusion are corrected. In any remaining areas which the chief disputes, he or she may write a letter of exception, setting forth the reasons that it is believed that the audit report is wrong or manifestly unfair. After the city council reviews the audit report, the chief may be directed to appear before the council to answer questions, or the council may simply task the city manager or finance director to make sure the police department takes any needed corrective action. None of us enjoys criticisms because they identify weaknesses, yet a wise manager knows that correcting deficiencies is a pathway to enhanced performance and makes the needed changes without rancor.

Critical Thinking Question

1. Assume that you are assigned to conduct a program audit of a grant to a municipal police department whose purpose is to reduce driving while intoxicated violations. What documents would you want to review and what kinds of data would you think is important?

BUDGET FORMATS

At the turn of the twentieth century, there was nothing resembling the budget cycle previously described in this chapter; budgeting was a chaotic process because there was no central point where budget requests from departments were reviewed or revised. Moreover, committees, rather than a legislative body as a whole, often had the authority to appropriate funds for departments, lump sum budgets were requested by the departments without any supporting details, there was no uniform system of accounts because each department used its own method, and either audits were not done or in some cases decades went by between them.[9] The power center in budgeting was the legislative body and its respective committees. Thus, when President Taft submitted an executive budget, one developed by the executive branch of government, Congress received it coldly and practically ignored it.[10]

Despite such developments, strong reform forces, whose objectives were to promote efficiency in government, curtail waste, and eliminate fraud were at work. In 1899, the Model Municipal Corporation Act, which proposed an executive budget under the mayor, received significant national attention. The scientific management movement, discussed in Chapter 5, Organizational Theory, was seen in some circles as a tool for improving government; the 1907 publication of *Making a Municipal Budget* provided new vistas on public finance, as did the National Municipal League's model 1916 city charter. Additionally, the good government and city manager movements of the second decade of the twentieth century both influenced and were influenced by these events. Between roughly 1915 and 1925,[11] standard budget cycles and formats gained considerable use in local government and appeared in the federal government with the passage of the 1921 Budget and Accounting Act. These events are important because they (1) explain why substantial emphasis was placed on the control orientation in the early stages of budget reform and (2) underscore that budget control remains at the heart of budget execution, regardless of the type of budget format used. The sections which follow address five types of budget format: (1) line item, (2) program, (3) performance, (4) zero-based, and (5) hybrid.

The Line Item Budget

The line item, or object of expenditure, is the oldest and simplest budget format; it remains widely used today, although it is most closely associated with the period from 1915 to just after World War II. The line item is the basic system on which all other budget formats ultimately rest because of its excellence as a control device. It gets its name from its nature: every amount requested, recommended, appropriated, and expended is associated with a particular item or class of items (see Table 12.4). This budget format fosters control in a number of ways:

1. Control is comprehensive because no item escapes scrutiny.
2. Control can be exercised at multiple points—for example, the police department can check to make sure it has the funds available for an item and the F/FSD can conduct a pre-audit to make sure this is accurate.
3. Control is exact; an attempt by a police department to spend beyond the amount authorized in any given line of the budget is immediately apparent.[12]

Critical Thinking Question

1. Assuming that all personnel are full-time, estimate the number of employees you think the budget shown in Table 12.4 provides.

A line item budget offers five straightforward advantages:

(1) it is easy to construct; (2) because incremental changes in the appropriations are made annually on the basis of the history of expenditures, the likelihood of the police department having a budget that is grossly inadequate is reduced; (3) it is easy to understand; and (4) it is easy to administer. On balance, there are also some clear disadvantages to this budget format: (1) the emphasis on control results in an orientation toward the input to the detriment of managing toward results; (2) long-range planning is neglected; (3) any correlations between the input and results occur at only a very gross level, such as numbers of arrests made; and (4) it has limited utility with respect to evaluating performance. A line item budget format tends to favor the continuation of the police department's status quo—a disadvantage to the reform chief but an advantage to one who has less energy and drive.

The structure of a line item budget involves the use of standardly defined categories that are used throughout city government. In police departments large enough for functional specialization, there is an overall budget, and the budget is broken down into smaller line item budgets for the various organizational entities, such as patrol, investigation, and crime prevention. These smaller budgets further facilitate control and serve as the basis of allocations within the police department. Workload indicators for past years and the forthcoming budget year may also be included as part of a line item budget, although such are not present in a classical, or "pure" line item budget format. Typically such things as numbers of (1) arrests by various categories, (2) calls for service, (3) traffic and parking citations, (4) accident investigations, and (5) criminal investigations, along with other indicators, such as miles patrolled, are included.

The Program Budget

The term "program budget" has been used in various ways over the past 100 years and therefore has meant different things at different times.[13] In its earliest use, "program budget" essentially meant a line item budget which gave program results; thus, at that time the term meant something closer to what we today call a performance budget. The term "program budget" is used in so many ways and has so many variations that one noted authority was driven to remark that no one knows hot to do program budgeting. A key difficulty is the elasticity of the word "program." One jurisdiction

TABLE 12.4 A FY '06 Line Item Budget

ACCOUNTING CODE	DESCRIPTION	APPROVED
5040-10-160	Dues/membership	$250
5045-10-160	Education and training	$2,500
5060-10-160	Gas, oil, and vehicle repair	$20,000
5070-10-160	Repair and maintenance	$1,500
5075-10-160	Utilities	$1,800
5080-10-160	Legal services	$1,500
5087-10-160	Advertising	$-
5090-10-160	Misc. expense	$-
5091-10-160	Parking ticket expense	$2,000
5095-10-160	Office supplies	$2,600
5097-10-160	Operating supplies	$6,900
5100-10-160	Outside services	$250
5110-10-160	Printing and duplication	$4,000
5115-10-100	Telephone	$4,000
5125-10-160	Travel and meetings	$-
5600-10-160	Salaries and wages	$160,609
5605-10-160	Payroll taxes	$12,769
5610-10-160	Employee benefits	$14,439
5612-10-160	Volunteer bonus	$-
5615-10-160	Worker's comp. insurance—CIRSA	$3,273
5618-10-160	Uniform expense	$500
5620-10-160	Uniform allowance	$-
5625-10-160	Physical exams	$100
6205-10-160	Ordinance, firearms supplies	$750
6210-10-160	Hazardous waste authority	$250
6215-10-160	Animal control	$700
6218-10-160	LEA services	$58,000
7000-10-160	Equipment purchase	$4,000
7005-10-160	Vehicle purchase/lease	$1,500
Total		**$304,190**

SOURCE: Morrison, Colorado, Police Department.

will use it to denote all activities in each respective department, such as "police program or fire program," while other jurisdictions will use it to describe a single activity or closely related group of activities, such as criminal investigation. For this reason, program budgeting is sometimes also described as "activity budgeting."[14]

Table 12.5 is the criminal investigations portion of the Palatine, Illinois, Police Department's program budget and it has the following characteristics: (1) a program structure accompanied by a definition, (2) program objectives, (3) staffing data, and (4) a line item budget for control. Other information which may be found in a program budget format includes the statutory or other authority for providing the program, the sources which fund the program and their respective amounts, and some workload measures.

Critical Thinking Questions

1. The budget nearly doubles from the 2005 to the 2006 budget. What happened? What are some possible reasons for this to happen?

   Competent program budgets are more time-consuming to put together, they require carefully crafted program definitions if they are to be useful, and the workload measures must be meaningful. In balance, well-executed program budgets provide useful information and retain all of the control advantages of the line item budget.

The Performance Budget

As a generalization, the workload measures used in line item and program budgets have historically, and to a large extent continues to be, process rather than efficiency-oriented. For example, common process workload measures in these two types of budgets are numbers of miles patrolled, calls answered, and criminal investigations handled. Such measures do not answer such questions as "What is different now as a result of those miles being patrolled?" They do not tell us if citizens feel more or less secure in their homes and neighborhoods, nor do such measures tell us how much it costs to produce each unit of work, such as the average cost for answering calls for service. The performance budget is an efficiency-oriented tool designed to relate the amount of various types of work done to the amount of money spent to produce work. As a minimum, the performance budget characteristically has the following:

1. A program structure
2. A cost structure/budget for each program
3. A line item component for fiscal control
4. A detailed system of results-oriented (output) workload and unit cost (efficiency) measures

There are numerous examples of police budgets which are described as a "performance budget;" however, most of them fall short of fully satisfying the fourth characteristic listed. Table 12.6 is a portion of a police "performance budget" and it incorporates the following deficiencies:

1. Arguably, some of the "output" measures are "process" measures; for example, "hours dedicated to OWI enforcement" is a process and, while those data are important, the output should be the "number of OWI citations issued." An output measure tells what happened as the result of a particular effort.
2. An efficiency measure tells how much it costs to produce a unit of work. For example, what it costs for every call patrol officers answer, what it costs to conduct a felony investigation, or what it costs to process a crime scene. Some police departments using performance budgets attempt to provide cost data at only the level of what the jurisdiction's per capita cost for receiving police

TABLE 12.5 2007 Criminal Investigations Program Budget

Program Description

The Criminal Investigations Program exists to forward the overall department objectives by concentrating on vigorous, intelligent, legally sound, and thorough follow-up investigations of criminal offenses leading to case clearances by arrest and prosecution of persons who commit criminal acts.

Program Objectives

1. To measurably increase the development of investigative leads resulting in the arrest or identification of suspects through the use of criminal intelligence and well-cultivated informants.
2. To maintain a clearance rate of 20% for reported burglaries.
3. To continue to develop the Management of Criminal Investigations (MCI) program (i.e., case screening, managing continuing investigations, assessment of solvability factors, etc.).
4. To continue to interface known offenders, M.O. files and other pertinent data into the Record's Management System.
5. To address gang activity in the village through a combination of criminal intelligence, criminal investigations, tactical operations and multi-jurisdictional operations.
6. To maximize the quality of criminal cases preparation and court testimony.

	2005 ACTUAL	2006 BUDGET	2007 BUDGET	2008 BUDGET
PERSONNEL SUMMARY				
Full-time	25	25	25	25
Part-time	0	0	0	0

FUND	DESCRIPTION	2005 ACTUAL	2006 BUDGET	2007 BUDGET	2008 BUDGET
100	Salaries & Wages	$892,574	$1,767,920	$1,783,875	$1,873,070
100	Pensions & Benefits	389,630	720,645	792,130	880,210
Total Personnel Services		**1,282,204**	**2,488,565**	**2,576,005**	**2,753,280**
100	Printing & Duplicating	-	-	-	-
100	Telephone	7,106	7,665	8,690	8,860
100	Training	26,919	22,390	19,510	19,920
100	Materials	186	2,300	100	100
100	Equipment Rentals	10,472	8,940	8,425	8,600
100	Sm Tools/Equip (<$1,000)	-	-	4,000	-
100	Other Supplies & Services	1,898	4,500	4,750	4,840
100	Contractual Services	1,950	3,150	2,050	2,100
100	Motor Vehicle Maintenance	91,670	189,165	202,410	212,530
Total Commodities/Contractual		**140,201**	**237,110**	**249,935**	**256,950**
Total Criminal Investigations		**$1,422,405**	**$2,725,675**	**$2,825,940**	**$3,010,230**

TABLE 12.6 A Hypothetical Police Performance Budget

PERFORMANCE INDICATORS	2005/06 ACTUAL	2006/07 PROJECTED	2006/07 BUDGET	2007/08 BUDGET
OUTPUT				
OWI arrests	419	370	400	475
Hours dedicated to OWI enforcement	2,175	2,700	2,200	3,000
Underage alcohol enforcement	110	65	100	70
Number of liquor compliance inspections	542	600	635	680
Number of liquor law violations (LCC violations)	8	11	10	13
Number of alcohol abuse presentations	114	100	120	125
Number of directed/selective traffic enforcement details/assignments	130	110	120	140
Number of hazardous traffic citations issued	10,213	11,800	12,100	12,300
In-service professional development training classes attended	11	14	18	25
Number of crime prevention presentations	194	250	300	325
Number of electronic citizen/business communications	25	60	120	300
Number of cases assigned to investigators	978	1,120	1,200	1,280
Number of Group A crime arrests	1,071	1,050	1,100	1,080
EFFICIENCY				
Number of traffic crashes	3,322	3,400	3,500	3,600
Percent of traffic crashes involving alcohol	2.3%	2.0%	2.0%	1.7%
% of alcohol compliance inspections resulting in violations	1.6%	1.8%	2.0%	2.2%
Officers involved in professional/career development program	7	8	11	14
% of assigned cases resulting in warrant issuance	42%	36%	35%	40%
Group A crime clearance rate	29.0%	30.0%	30.0%	30.0%
Number of Group A crimes occurring	3,415	3,200	3,300	3,200

services is; however, such data fall substantially short of providing "unit cost measures" vis a vis the delivery of a full range of police services. The single most common failure in a performance budget is the failure to include unit cost measures expressed as the dollars needed to produce various types of work.

There is no universally agreed-upon date for the origin of performance budgets; this is probably because their use evolved over time. As an alternative to the line item budget format, the 1912 Taft Commission on Economy and Efficiency called for a budget with cost data for the type of work being done. There was a very limited amount of experimentation with unit cost data in budgets over the next 40 years. From roughly 1960 to 1990, San Diego, Phoenix, Cincinnati, Los Angeles, Rochester, and some other units of local government tried their hands at performance budgeting. With the

TABLE 12.7 A Portion of a Performance Budget Showing Detailed Cost Measures

Task: Receiving, storing, controlling, and disposing of physical evidence and property collected and seized
Standard Collection Procedures:
Data Collected: Number of cases assigned for evidence storage
Source of Data: Property/Evidence log maintained in Property/Evidence Bureau
Person responsible for collection: CSI Corporal

	UNITS	PERSONNEL COST	HOURS	TOTAL COST	UNIT/HOUR	UNIT COST
2004–05 Actual	5,455.00	115,377	3,554.50	122,793	1.535	22.51
2005–06 Budgeted	5,200.00	141,395	4,441.01	164,690	1.171	31.67
2005–06 Year to date	5,589.00	117,708	3,678.00	129,620	1.520	23.19
2006–07 Proposed	5,200.00	145,277	4,384.60	169,133	1.186	32.53

Unit of work: Number of cases assigned for evidence storage.

SOURCE: Concord, California, Police Department, FY '07 Budget.

significant revenue problems facing units of government from roughly 1990 onward, those who appropriated funds wanted to know how much it cost to produce various types of services. This provided an impetus toward the use of performance budget, which is done at various levels of sophistication across the country. Table 12.7 shows an example of a detailed unit cost measure for receiving, storing, controlling, and disposing of property and evidence logged into a department's property/evidence room.

The advantages of a properly executed performance budget include (1) focusing on output, or what a police department produces; (2) knowing what it costs to produce various types of police services, such as conducting community policing meetings with citizens; (3) having another means by which to evaluate the performance of police leaders; (4) emphasizing output, or results, as opposed to processes (e.g., number of miles patrolled annually); (5) emphasizing efficiency; and (6) increasing useful information for decision making.

Concurrently, there are disadvantages: (1) it is expensive to develop and implement performance budgeting, particularly from an accounting perspective; (2) appropriate workload and unit cost measures must be selected, which can be time-consuming and controversial; (3) there is a tendency to select measures which currently exist or are easy to collect, rather than important ones; and (4) unless comparisons over several fiscal years are made for the same measures, the data do not lend themselves to long-range planning.

The Zero-Based Budget (ZBB)

During the 1960s, the federal government used the Planning, Programming Budgeting System (PPBS), the dominant feature of which became planning. The intention of PPBS was to transform budgeting from an "annual ritual" to a "formulation of future goals and policies." It was cumbersome and unpopular with the federal agencies using it; PPBS made almost no headway in state and local government and by the very early 1970s no one was using it.

One component of PPBS was the concept of the "zero budget," which was popularly understood that an agency started each new budget year with no dollars and had to rejustify the entire next budget request. While, in fact, this approach was used by some units of government, such users were naive and did not fully understand ZBB. While the theory behind ZBB was to foster a fresh look at each new operating budget, such an approach wasted enormous amounts of energy rejustifying obvious needs, such as patrol officers, cars to respond to emergency calls, and salary increases called for under the collective bargaining agreement with the police union. Following Peter Phyrr's pioneering use of ZBB at Texas Instruments, former Georgia Governor Jimmy Carter championed its use in state government during the early 1970s and, as president, announced its use for the federal government in 1977.

Another difficulty with literally starting at zero for a budget is that many federal, state, and local programs are mandated and must be continued from year to year; in the federal government, as much as 80 percent of the annual budget is already committed to so-called entitlement programs, such as social security, so budgeting actually occurs with only about 20 percent of the funds available. As a result, many units of government using ZBB tell their departments to prepare an operating budget based on 80 percent of their past year's funding.

The core of ZBB is the use of "decision packages (DPs)," or "service levels (SLs)." A DP is a focused description of a service or program, typically including its cost and often including the associated performance measures, which details the effect of (1) reducing or eliminating a particular service or program, (2) continuing an existing service or program, (3) expanding an existing service or program, or (4) adding a new service or program. A police department submitting a ZBB ranks its decision packages from highest to lowest priority, and the appropriating authority determines how far down the list it would go to draw the line between funded and unfunded services and programs. The appropriators may also elect to do some limited reprioritizing of the DPs but tend to rely on the ranking of the agency submitting them. Table 12.8 is an example of some DPs used by a police agency; ZBB systems typically take the form of performance budgets, but they differ in that the former use decision packages to justify increases in funding.

The use of ZBB offers certain advantages: (1) police chiefs and other department heads must carefully scrutinize what they do, how they do it, the resources required, and the results of the effort; (2) it increases the accountability of leaders for what they do with the resources they are given; (3) there is better information for decision making; and (4) creativity is stimulated as departments find alternative ways to accomplish results at reduced costs. Conversely, the disadvantages are (1) there is a potential for conflict with the appropriators over what the priorities should be for a department, (2) there is increased paperwork and record keeping, (3) having to develop annual ranking of priorities helps keep a department nimble in responding to direction from elected and appointed officials; the downside is that departments may end up chasing new priorities and abandoning old ones without impacting them, creating a sense of organizational instability; and (4) departments may implicitly develop a mind-set that "If they don't funding our decision packages, we really can't accomplish much," leading to a slide in productivity.

The Hybrid Budget

Budget formats can be described with a great deal more purity than actually exists in real-world applications. The reason for this is that each jurisdiction uses a system that makes sense to it; history, unique local ordinances, the preferences of those who appropriate funds, and other variables all contribute to the reality that most budget formats used are a hybrid system that incorporates features from several others. For example, in the classical, or pure, formatted line item budget there are no workload data, yet in practice it is not uncommon for such information to be present.

Table 12.8 Example of Decision Packages Used in the FY '08 Budget for the Portland (Oregon) Police Bureau

	DECISION PACKAGE	REQUESTED FTE	RECOM-MENDED	GENERAL FUND DISCRETIONARY ONGOING	GENERAL FUND DISCRETIONARY ONE-TIME	REQUESTED TOTAL AMOUNT	RECOM-MENDED TOTAL
POL_01	One-time Recruitment Ad Campaign (CS)	0		$0	$50,000	$50,000	50,000
POL_02	Civilianize Background Investigators (CS)	15	15	$928,800	$0	$928,800	928,800
POL_03	Public Service Announcement Campaign (CS)	0		$0	$50,000	$50,000	50,000
POL_04	Project Manager for Regional Training Center (CS)	1	0	$82,968	$0	$82,968	-
POL_06	Restore Nine Investigator Positions	6	0	$498,360	$0	$498,360	-
POL_07	Field Reporting Application Support (CS)	2	2	$159,228	$0	$159,228	159,228
POL_08	Support for Handheld Devices (CS)	1	0	$76,200	$0	$76,200	-
POL_09	Ruggedized Laptop Purchase (CS)	0		$0	$962,500	$962,500	-
POL_10	TRIM User Licenses for Electronic Field Reporting (CS)	0		$19,300	$127,000	$146,300	127,000
POL_11	Schedule & Staff Management System (CS)	0		$12,000	$130,000	$142,000	-
POL_12	Handhelds for Precincts (CS)	0		$0	$75,000	$75,000	-
POL_14	Eight Desk Clerks/Precinct to Midnight (CS)	8	0	$368,832	$0	$368,832	368,832
POL_15	Program Coordinator for CIT (CS)	1	1	$79,476	$0	$79,476	79,476
POL_16	Emergency Mgmt Coordinator Contract (CS)	0		$42,640	$0	$42,640	-
POL_17	OT Maintain Current Service Level	0		$1,000,000	$0	$1,000,000	-
POL_18	Fund DVRT Sergeant Position	1	0	$92,892	$0	$92,892	-
POL_19	Elder Crime Investigators (CS)	4	0	$347,532	$0	$347,532	-
POL_20	Elders in Action Program	0		$40,000	$0	$40,000	-
POL_21	Domestic Violence Advocates	0		$200,000	$0	$200,000	100,000
POL_22	Service Level from City Attorney (CS)	0		$212,914	$0	$212,914	212,914
POL_23	Civilianize IAD Investigators (CS)	4	4	$247,680	$0	$247,680	247,680
POL_24	HR Support for Recruitment (CS)	0		$268,540	$0	$268,540	95,364
POL_26	Community Partnerships (CS)	0		$200,000	$0	$200,000	-
	Total	**43.00**	**22.00**	**$ 4,877,362**	**$ 1,394,500**	**$ 6,271,862**	**$ 2,419,294**

Citywide Initiatives: CB (Children and Youth Bill of Rights), CS (Community Safety), SE (Sustainable Industries/Clean Energy), SF (Schools/Families/Housing) and SS (Safe Streets)

Recommended Requests

1. *POL_01 One-time Recruitment Ad Campaign $50,000 / 0 FTE*

This request is for $50,000 of General Fund one-time resources to support a recruitment and advertising campaign to attract new recruits.

FPD Recommendation - $50,000

It is likely that Portland Police will continue to face fierce competition from other regional law enforcement agencies in attracting new employees. In addition, FPD realizes that enhanced outreach for recruitment is a crucial strategy for meeting the bureau's diversity goals. FPD recommends that Police maintain their recruiting outreach efforts.

2. *POL_02 Civilianize Background Investigators $928,800 / 15 FTE*

This request is to convert 15 limited term civilian background investigators to permanent status in order to achieve two bureau goals. The first goal is part of a larger strategy change that the bureau is engaging in which involves redeploying certain sworn positions to patrol and backfilling them with civilian positions. The second goal communicated to FPD is to increase hiring capacity for an expected surge in retirements.

SOURCE: Portland Police Bureau. Note that at the end of each of the 26 decisions packages in the table there are entries such as "(CS)." At the bottom of the table these entries are identified as city wide initiatives, which are comprehensive goals established by Portland's city council to ensure that all expenditures of appropriated funds contribute to important goals they have articulated. In the "Recommended Requests" section of this table, "FPD" appears; this is the city's Financial Planning Division. From these entries we know this is the budget recommended by the City Manager's Office to council and that the staff or the FPD analyzed the budget submitted by the Police Bureau to arrive at its recommendations.

Critical Thinking Question

1. Refer to Table 12.7. Can you determine how the "unit hour" and "unit cost" figures were established?

SUPPLEMENTING THE POLICE BUDGET: TACTICS AND STRATEGIES

There are a number of strategies for supplementing a budget, including federal and private foundation grants, donation and fundraising programs, forfeiture laws, and user fees and police taxes.

Federal and Private Foundation Grants

Although a number of federal agencies, such as the Department of Homeland Security and the National Highway Traffic Safety Administration, provide grant funds for law enforcement agencies, perhaps none has been more visible than the Community Oriented Policing Services (COPS) grants awarded by the U.S. Department of Justice. The program was created as part of the Violent Crime Control and Law Enforcement Act of 1994, with $9 billion earmarked for the hiring of additional officers who would provide community-oriented policing services; the grants covered 75 percent of each newly hired officer, for a period of three years. Other elements of the COPS program included grants to purchase technology and to pay civilian salaries in order to redeploy veteran officers from administrative duties to community policing; additionally, funds were available for innovative programs addressing special problems, such as domestic and gang violence.

Evaluations of the impact of the COPS program have been mixed in terms of reducing crime; most evidence seems to point to no or limited impact on crime for the hiring of additional officers, although the evidence is somewhat more positive with respect to the innovative program grants. The online portal to federal funding is Grants.Gov, which provides an automated data base to help locate and apply for grants.

A number of departments have created non-profit foundations to raise funds; typically, this has been done in the larger cities to provide unique opportunities for growth, support, and change. The New York City Police Foundation helps support NYCPD detectives who are posted throughout the world to forge relationships and gather information on threats to New York City; additionally, following the 9/11 attacks, the New York City Police Foundation provided over $1.5 million in short-term assistance to family members of the 23 NYCPD officers who died at ground zero. In general, police foundations' resources are not used to take the place

In The News

Tribal COP Grants

During 2006, 103 tribal law enforcement agencies were awarded grants totaling some $12 million. Since 1999, tribal agencies have received $211 million in COPS grants to strengthen their departments.

Source: COPS.uscbj.gov.

of what should be done with regularly appropriated funds, although this happens occasionally.

Predictably, private foundations have differing endowments, interests, and resources and make awards only within their areas of focus. Their spheres of interest are not only defined by topic but also sometimes by geography. To illustrate, the Stark Foundation limits its awards to applicants from southeast Texas. In 2004, the Orange County Sheriff's Office received $104,500 to purchase computer software. Even more sharply focused geographically is the Harrison County, Indiana, Community Foundation, which awarded the Milltown Police Department a grant to purchase two automated external defibrillators (AEDs) to place in the city's patrol cars to provide emergency help for those experiencing cardiac arrest. For both federal and private foundations, the key is knowing what the department's needs are and matching those needs with a funding source; in doing so, careful examination must be made of what, if any, obligation the department has for continuing to employ people and maintain equipment after the grant funds expire.

Donation and Fundraising Programs

Police donation and fundraising programs or efforts differ from foundations' in that they are informal organizations focused on a single need and have a short-term life of perhaps several months. In 2006, a couple gave up their dream vacation to Hawaii to purchase five ballistic vests for Delaware State Police K-9s; in other areas of the country, public donations have helped police acquire protective gloves, mountain bikes, and crime scene equipment. The public is also generous in donating to ad hoc funds established to help specific officers injured or killed in the line of duty; typically, these funds are used not only for medical costs but also for other special needs established by the officers' families on a case-by-case basis. There are also a number of ongoing organizations which accomplish the same goals through donations and annual fundraising activities, such as the Injured Police Officers Funds, established in 1982 to serve Las Vegas area officers. A number of special donation funds were established in the wake of Hurricane Katrina, including the Louisiana State Trooper Relief Fund and the International Union of Police Associations (IUPA) Law Enforcement Disaster Relief Fund. Both organizations are focused on assisting law enforcement officers affected by Hurricane Katrina. In addition to mobilizing donations for "their own," the

In The News

Today's News

Fund Established for Injured Officer

Donna Boswell, a U.S. Capitol Police Officer, remembers the rear-end collision that left her with a broken neck and no feeling in her fingers, hands, toes, or legs. Seeing a truck behind her closing in too quickly, she tapped her brakes to alert the driver to slow moving traffic in front of him. However, it was to no avail and her vehicle was pinned between the truck and the car immediately in front of her. Witnesses say the driver of the truck never hit his breaks before the impact.

Her insurance company will pay the hospital bills and for 60 days of rehabilitation. Then, she and her family are on their own. Doctors have not been "overly optimistic" about the possibility of her having a full recovery. Fellow officers have rallied to her and her family by establishing a Boswell Family Donation Fund; contributions to the fund can be made by contacting several people, including Sgts. Rhonda Jackson and Kim Bolinger at (202) 225-0400.

Source: Jackie Kucinich, "Capitol Police Officer Recalls Her Injuries From Crash," *The Hill*, April 3, 2007.

law enforcement community is always quick to help others. In Los Lunas, New Mexico, the department collects toys for needy families; the Philadelphia Police Department annually has its "Operation Thanksgiving" to provide turkeys to no- and low-income households; and the Paxton, Illinois, Fraternal Order of Police has contributed money to help fund after-school programs.

Forfeiture Laws

Federal and state **forfeiture laws** serve two purposes: (1) criminals are prevented from profiting from their illegal acts and (2) the seized assets can be used by law enforcement agencies to fund important initiatives. There are many state statutes regarding forfeitures, but they generally cover money and property obtained from four types of crime: (1) narcotics; (2) transportation of contraband goods; (3) organized crime, racketeering, and unlawful gambling; and (4) targeted crimes (e.g., in a few states, those convicted of serious driving under the influence may also forfeit their cars). Forfeiture proceedings begin with law enforcement officers making a request to the prosecutor to do so or retaining an attorney for that purpose. Care is taken to protect the rights of others who were not involved in the crime or who have an innocent financial interest in the forfeited property, such as the lien holder of a yacht. Five patterns exist as to how seized assets may be used:

1. All money goes to the city's, county's, or state's general fund, where it can be appropriated for any lawful purposes.
2. The police may keep all property, such as cars and planes for surveillance, but if the property is later sold, the proceeds go to the general fund.
3. The police may keep or sell the property, but if it is sold any excess beyond a "ceiling," such as $50,000, goes to the general fund.
4. All property and cash may be kept by the police.
5. All seized assets must go to education, which eliminates the criticism that police seize assets for their own benefit.

Multi-jurisdictional task force operations have been common for a long time; to a significant degree, such operations have been brought about by mobile criminals and the need to share investigative expertise and resources. In such operations, an occasional bone of contention is how forfeited assets can be split up equitably among the cooperating agencies.

User Fees and Police Taxes

User fees are common in policing (see Table 12.9) and are intended to help defray the cost of delivering police services. The new development in this area goes well beyond charging for the services identified in Table 12.9; some departments are attempting to pass on the cost of more substantial services. In 2006, Toledo, Ohio, proposed an ordinance which would charge the at-fault driver the cost of investigating a motor vehicle accident. In Greenville, Ohio, the insurance company of an at-fault driver is charged $375 in any accident involving property damage. In Santa Monica, California, the user fee is $1,500 for a police response to an accident involving driving under the influence which results in an accident or injury. By local ordinance, St. Paul,

TABLE 12.9 User Fees Charged by the Fond Du Lac Wisconsin Police Department

MAILING FEES ON ALL REQUESTS	ACTUAL
Fax	1.00 Per Page
Black and White Copies	.25 Per Page
Color Copies (Includes Digital Photographs)	.90 Per Page
Color Copies on Photo Quality Paper	1.05 Per Page
Photographs	
8 × 10 black & white	2.85
5 × 7 black & white	1.50
8 × 10 color	2.85
5 × 7 color	1.50
3 × 5 color (4 × 6)	.20
Polaroid	1.00
CD/DVD	.70*
Video Tape Created on Site	.55*
Duplicated Elsewhere	ACTUAL
Audio Tape	.90*
Guard Permits	40.00
Funeral Escorts	20.00
False Alarms	
3rd & 4th Response in Calendar Year	50.00
5th Response in Calendar Year	75.00
Each Response After 5	100.00
K-9 searches	75.00/Hour Plus .44 ½/ Mile
Building & Equipment Moves	
Less than 2 Hours	150.00/Hour
Additional Hours	75.00/Hour
Security Duty	50.15/Hour
Archery Permits	25.00
Fingerprints (Thursdays from Noon – 3 P.M.)	20.00
Mug Shots	5.00
Storage of Abandoned/Confiscated Vehicles	
Outside	18.00/Day
Inside	25.00/Day
CVSA (Voice Stress)	150.00
Process Service	12.00 Plus .44 ½/Mile
Vehicle Lock-Outs	50.00

NOTE: Requests which exceed a total cost of $5.00 may require prepayment per Wis. Stat. §19.35(3)(f)
*Reproduction cost may be added per Wis. Stat. §19.35(3)(b)

Minnesota, charges for "excessive consumption" of police services at "nuisance" locations which require repeated response by police units.

The most common type of police tax is for the delivery of enhanced or additional police services in special districts, including gated communities, marinas, malls, entertainment zones, and downtown business associations. Some civic leaders have argued that the existence of such districts is inequitable because the less prosperous areas cannot afford extra protection; in balance, however, such arguments are not long-lasting, nor do they carry any significant weight.

Critical Thinking Question

1. As a newly appointed police chief, you direct your planning and research unit to come up with a proposal to create a police foundation. From whom or what types of businesses would you solicit or not solicit funds?

CHAPTER REVIEW

1. Explain why budgeting is important.
   It is the decision-making process by which governmental resources are allocated to achieve goals. The budget is the most important statement a government makes because the budget reveals what its true priorities are.
2. Define a fiscal year, an operating budget, and a capital budget.
   A fiscal year (FY) is the 12-month period which the budget covers. It may or may not be a calendar year. For example, a budget which starts October 1, 2009, and ends September 30, 2010, is called the FY '10 budget. Almost all governmental budgets in this country start on January 1, July 1, or October 1.
   An operating budget is used for annual operating expenses, such as salaries and fringe benefits, office supplies, contractual services, and kindred recurring costs.
   A capital budget is also called a capital improvement budget (CIP); typically, it is used for large-scale, one-time purchases, such as the acquisition of land or construction of a new police building on it. Finance departments provide guidelines as to what is or isn't a capital item and these vary from one jurisdiction to another. Thus, in one city an item costing as little as $250 may appear as part of the capital budget.
3. Define the budget cycle step and briefly describe the major steps within it.
   The budget cycle is a stream of four sequential steps, which are repeated at about the same time every year in a jurisdiction. These steps are budget preparation, budget review and approval, budget execution, and the audit.
4. Discuss the line item budget.
   The line item budget is the oldest and simplest budget format; each object or class of objects for which funds have been appropriated has its own separate line. This facilitates control of the budget. All other budget formats ultimately rest on a line item component for control.
5. Explain what a program budget is.
   "Program budget" is a term which has meant different things at different times; the difficulty resides in the definition of "program," which one jurisdiction might use to describe all field services (e.g., patrol), while in another it might refer just to the school resource officer "program." The essential meaning of "program" is the description of a single activity or closely related set of activities.

6. Describe a performance budget.
This is an efficiency-oriented budget format that relates the amount of various types of work to be done to the amount of money necessary to produce it. The performance budget has four key characteristics.
7. Provide an overview of a zero-based budget.
When using a zero-based budget (ZBB) in its most literal sense, each department starts with zero dollars for the next year and must justify its entire budget each year. In practical application, most departments are directed to assume that they will have 80 percent of this year's budget for next year and to prepare decision, or service level, packages for all additional changes. The essence of ZBB are these decision packages (DPs), which reflect one of four conditions, such as starting a new program. The police department submits as part of its proposed budget both its 80 percent "continuation budget" and its ranked-by-priority DPs. The appropriators can then choose to fund none or some of the ranked DPs. In most budget system, the appropriators are not bound by the priority assigned by the police department but typically accord such rankings significant weight.
8. Identify the major ways in which a police budget may be supplemented.
The four ways are federal and private foundation grants, donation and fundraising programs, forfeiture laws, and user fees and a police tax.

KEY TERMS

Audit: essentially, "checking," the independent verification by an objective party; finances are audited to determine their accuracy, timeliness of recording, and adherence to established policies; programs are audited to determine how well they are functioning and to the degree to which they are accomplishing what they should be.

Budget: the allocation of resources to achieve goals.

Budget execution: the action phase of budgeting in which plans are put into operation.

Budget execution controls: the types of controls intended to control expenditures to avoid overspending, misspending, or other abuses; broadly, there are two types of budget execution controls: external and internal.

Forfeiture laws: state and federal laws by which the assets of convicted criminals may be legally seized; such seizures prevent criminals from profiting from their illegal acts, and in many cases all, or a portion of the assets may be used by police agencies to support other law enforcement purposes.

Hybrid budget: a budget that has features that reflect elements of more than one budget format; this is because local governments adopt budget formats that seem to meet their needs best.

Police tax: the most common type of police tax is the special service district, which essentially means that enhanced police services are provided to a gated community, mall, marina, or nightclub district or other entity at an additional cost to residents or businesses.

Stakeholder: an individual or a group that does not actually perform work but has an interest in how well it is done (e.g., citizens, other departments, and advisory boards).

User fees: a means of defraying the cost of delivering police services by charging some recipients a portion of the cost for doing so; historically, such charges have been for such things as copying police reports or providing police escorts for private purposes which also benefit the public.

NOTES

1. Donald Axelrod, *Budgeting for Modern Government* (New York: St. Martin's Press, 1995), p. 1.
2. Roland N. McKean, *Public Spending* (New York: McGraw-Hill, 1968), p. 1.
3. Aaron Wildavsky, *The Politics of the Budgetary Process*, 2nd ed. (Boston: Little, Brown, 1974), pp. 1–4.
4. For detailed information on budget practices, see Government Finance Officers

Association (GFOA), *Recommended Budget Practices* (Chicago: GFOA, 2000).

5. Police Chief Bruce G. Roberts, letter to the city of Ft. Lauderdale Commission, April 1, 2004.
6. Robert D. Lee and Ronald Johnson, *Public Budgeting Systems* (Gaithersburg, Md.: Aspen, 1998), p. 265.
7. Lee And Johnson, pp. 265–302.
8. These ideas are taken from David Nice, *Public Budgeting* (Belmont, Calif.: Wadsworth, 2002), pp. 104–10.
9. Allen Schick, *Budget Innovation in the States* (Washington, D.C.: Brookings Institution, 1971), pp. 14–15.
10. A. E. Buck, *The Budget in Governments of Today* (New York: Macmillan, 1945), p. 5.
11. In 1913, Ohio became the first state to adopt the executive budget.
12. Schick, *Budget Innovation in the States,* p. 23. Schick lists 10 ways in which the line item budget fosters control, but these 3 sum them up adequately.
13. During the 1960s and 1970s, some governments in this country, including the federal, used the Planning, Programming, Budgeting System (PPBS) format, which is very different from program budgeting as explained in this text. Despite the vast amounts of literature on PPBS, it made very little headway in state and local governments. Its most important contribution may have been that it fostered an interest in improving budgeting systems.
14. A different but related concept is activity-based budgeting (ABB), which is alternatively described as a variant of performance budgeting and zero-based budgeting. As this chapter focuses on the major budgeting formats, we merely note it in passing. See Jon M. Shane, "Activity Based Budgeting," FBI Law Enforcement Bulletin, 74, no. 6 (June 2005): 11–25. ABB incorporates a very high level of cost measures.

PART IV

ORGANIZATIONAL ISSUES

THE FOLLOWING CHAPTERS ARE COVERED IN PART IV:

13 Stress and Police Personnel

14 Legal Aspects of Police Administration

15 Organizational Change and the Future

OVERVIEW

In this final section, we address three of the most important issues confronting the police organization: the impact of stress on the individual officer, legal aspects of police administration, and understanding organizational change in the future. These issues clearly separate police organizations from other types of entities. While other organizations may well have to cope with everyday worker stress, liability arising out of errors and omissions, and changing business patterns, few are composed of a workforce that faces critical decisions involving another person's individual liberty (arrest), the potential use of deadly force, and the ensuing liability that may arise from these actions on a *daily* basis.

Jonathan Kim/The Stock Connection

If, under stress, a man goes all to pieces, he will probably be told to pull himself together. It would be more effective to help him identify the pieces and to understand why they have come apart.

— R. Ruddock

13

CHAPTER

STRESS AND POLICE PERSONNEL

OUTLINE

Introduction

What Is Stress?

Stress and Personality Type

Stress in Law Enforcement

Alcoholism and Police Officers

Drug Use by Police Officers

Police Suicide

Sources of Work Satisfaction as a Stress Reducer

Suicide by Cop

Critical Incident Stress

Stress and the Female Police Officer

Police Domestic Violence

Responding to Stress

Employee Assistance Programs

Chapter Review

Key Terms

Notes

OBJECTIVES

1. Discuss the concept of stress, as described by Selye and Basowitz.
2. Describe the three stages of physiological response to stress as described by Selye.
3. List the major characteristics of a type A personality.
4. Understand why police officers are more prone to stress than individuals in many other occupations.
5. Discuss the ways alcohol-related problems manifest themselves in police officers.
6. Describe some of the issues that police administrators must deal with in terms of drug use by police.
7. Discuss the four general principles defined by the courts in relation to random drug testing.
8. Describe some of the psychological effects of steroid use.
9. List the most common factors related to police suicide.
10. Discuss some of the typical warning signs that indicate an officer may be contemplating suicide.
11. Understand the supervisor's responsibilities regarding suicidal officers.
12. Identify the sources of work satisfaction as being stress reducers.
13. Discuss indicators of a potential suicide by cop.
14. Understand what is a critical incident.
15. Describe each phase of a critical incident, and the ways participants tend to respond.
16. Understand additional stresses the first women in law enforcement experienced that were not experienced by their male counterparts.
17. Describe what the most significant stressors on female officers were in Pinellas County, Florida, and how those differed from the stressors on their male coworkers.
18. Discuss some things police departments can do to curtail incidents of domestic violence among its officers.
19. Understand what steps a police supervisor must take if he or she notices a pattern of controlling or abusive behavior in an officer.
20. Describe the range of services that can be made available to police officers who are involved in domestic violence incidents.
21. List some examples of so-called stress inoculation activities.
22. Understand some of the benefits to employees of an employee assistance program.

INTRODUCTION

Historically, U.S. business and industry have been slow to identify and provide for the needs of workers. Largely because of the labor union movement, the U.S. worker has achieved a variety of benefits, ranging from increased wages to comprehensive medical care and retirement programs. The inclusion of mental health compensation as a significant management issue has evolved through a combination of union pressures and simple economics. A healthy, well-adjusted worker means increased efficiency and higher production for the corporation. As a consequence, job-related stress "has moved from the nether world of 'emotional problems' and 'personality conflicts' to the corporate balance sheet. . . . Stress is now seen as not only troublesome but expensive."[1]

Government and public service sectors generally lag behind industry and business in employee benefit innovations, and the mental health issue is no exception. However, the private sector's concern with the wide-ranging effects of job-related stress on workers is also shared by those in law enforcement. There is an abundance of literature on stress factors in policing that is available to the law enforcement executive for use in developing programs designed to reduce stress among police personnel.[2] In this chapter, we first discuss what stress is from a biological and psychological standpoint as well as the relationship between stress and different personality types. We also focus on specific stressors that are unique to law enforcement. Further, we address the factors that cause police officers to have alcoholism rates that may be as high as 25 percent. In reality, alcohol was at one time the only drug-related problem that police administrators had to deal with. This is no longer true. It is estimated that as many as 10 percent of American police officers may have a drug problem. In this chapter, we discuss this issue and the ways in which police administrators respond to it.

We also examine the phenomenon of police suicide and why it occurs and the responsibilities of management and supervision in suicide prevention. Another topic we discuss is suicide by cop (SbC), which describes an individual who wishes to die and uses the police to effect that goal. Further, we discuss the profile of an individual who engages in the practice, the indicators of potential SbC, and the ways in which these events affect the psychological well-being of the officers involved.

Police officers and other people who provide emergency care are often exposed to high levels of stress in both natural and human-made disasters. In this chapter, we discuss critical incident stress, the emergency response to critical incidents such as post-traumatic stress disorder, and the importance of the critical incident debriefing.

There is considerable evidence to suggest that women in law enforcement may experience stressors that are unique to them specifically because they are women in what is still a predominantly male-dominated profession. In this chapter, we examine some of the unique stressors they face and how such stressors have changed over the years.

It is an unfortunate fact of life that police officers are sometimes personally involved in domestic violence. In this chapter, we discuss the things that police administrators can and must do to deal with this problem.

Finally, we discuss the kinds of things that can be done by both police officers and their departments to deal with job-related stress.

WHAT IS STRESS?

Despite the volumes of research published on stress, the phenomenon remains poorly defined. Hans Selye, the researcher and theorist who pioneered the physiological

TABLE 13.1 Changes to the Body at the Alarm Stage

Heart rate increase	Blood flow increases to heart, lungs, and large muscles
Blood pressure increase	Perspiration, especially to palms
Large muscle groups tense	Digestive secretions slow
Adrenaline rush	Dry mouth due to saliva decrease
Increase blood sugar	Bowel activity decreases
Hypervigilance	Extremities become cool
Pupils dilate	Sphincters tighten
Increased hearing acuity	More white blood cells enter the bloodstream
Increased blood clotting	Cholesterol remains in the blood longer
Increased metabolism	Dilation of the lung passages and increased respiration

SOURCE: Wayne Anderson, David Swenson, and Daniel Clay, *Stress Management for Law Enforcement Officers*, 1st edition, © 1995, p. 37. Adapted by permission of Pearson Education, Inc., Upper Saddle River, NJ.

investigation of stress, defines **stress** in the broadest possible terms as anything that places an adjustive demand on the organism. Identified as "the body's nonspecific response to any demand placed on it," stress may be either positive (eustress) or negative (distress; see Table 13.1).[3] According to this distinction, many stressful events do not threaten people but provide them with pleasurable challenges. The excitement of the gambler, the thrill of the athlete engaged in a highly competitive sport, the deliberate risk taking of the daredevil stunt man—these are examples of stress without distress. For many people, this kind of stress provides the spice of life.

Basowitz and his associates define stress as stimuli that are likely to produce disturbances in most people. The authors postulate a continuum of stimuli that differ in meaning and in their anxiety-producing consequences. At one end are such stimuli, or cues, often highly symbolic, that have meaning only to a single person or to limited numbers of persons and that to the observer may appear as innocuous or trivial. At the other end are such stimuli, here called stress, that by their explicit threat to vital functioning and their intensity are likely to overload the capacity of most organisms' coping mechanisms.[4]

The authors also distinguish between pathological, neurotic, or harmful anxiety and the normal, adaptive, or healthy form of anxiety. In the first instance, anxiety is defined as a conscious and painful state of apprehension unrelated to an external threat. This kind of anxiety may render an individual incapable of distinguishing danger from safety or relevant information and cues from irrelevant ones. Ultimately, one's psychological and physiological functioning can become so reduced that death occurs. As the authors state, anxiety in this severe form is generally derived from "internal psychological problems and therefore is chronically present, leading to more serious, long-lasting somatic and psychological changes."[5] In the second instance, anxiety is defined as a state of increased alertness that permits maximum psychological and physiological performance. A state of fear, according to this formulation, is a simple form of anxiety characterized by the life-threatening or harmful nature of the stimuli. Unlike the more severe, harmful forms, simple forms of anxiety are temporal and beneficial to the individual. Of course, distinctions among the various levels of anxiety are difficult to make. For example, a person may react to a minimally threatening stimulus as though his or her life were in imminent danger. The fear response may have been appropriate and the overreaction inappropriate (perhaps indicative of psychological disturbance). Anxiety, then, can be defined as the individual's ability to cope with or respond to threatening situations.

Biological Stress and the General Adaptation Syndrome

Selye has formulated what he calls the **general adaptation syndrome (GAS)** to describe on the biological level how stress can incapacitate an individual. The GAS encompasses three stages of physiological reaction to a wide variety of stressors: environmental agents or activities powerful enough in their impact to elicit a reaction from the body. These three stages are alarm, resistance, and exhaustion.

The **alarm stage,** sometimes referred to as an emergency reaction, is exemplified on the animal level by the so-called fight-or-flight syndrome. When an animal encounters a threatening situation, its body signals a defense alert. The animal's cerebral cortex flashes an alarm to the hypothalamus, a small structure in the midbrain that connects the brain with body functions. A powerful hormone called ACTH is released into the bloodstream by the hypothalamus and is carried by the bloodstream to the adrenal gland, a part of the endocrine, or ductless gland, system. There, ACTH triggers the release of adrenaline, which produces a galvanizing, or energizing, effect on the body functions. The heart pounds, the pulse races, breathing quickens, the muscles tense, and digestion is inhibited. The adjustive function of this reaction pattern is readily apparent—namely, preparing the organism biologically to fight or to run away. When the threat is removed or diminished, the physiological functions involved in this alarm, or emergency reaction, subside, and the organism regains its internal equilibrium.

If the stress continues, however, the organism reaches the **resistance stage** of the GAS. During this stage, bodily resources are mobilized to deal with the specific stressors, and adaptation is optimal. Although the stressful stimulus may persist, the symptoms that characterized the alarm stage disappear. In short, the individual seems to have handled the stress successfully.

Under conditions of prolonged stress, the body reaches a point where it is no longer capable of maintaining resistance. This condition characterizes the **exhaustion stage.** Hormonal defenses break down, and many emotional reactions that appeared during the alarm stage may reappear, often in intensified form. Further exposure to stress leads to exhaustion and eventually to death. Even before this extreme stage has been reached, however, excessive hormonal secretions may result in severe physiological pathology of the type that Selye calls "diseases of adaptation"—for example, ulcers, high blood pressure, and coronary susceptibility.[6]

Psychological Stress

While life-threatening situations have understandably received considerable attention from researchers and theorists, there are many other circumstances in which the stress involved threatens something that the individual deems valuable: self-esteem, authority, and security, for example. The human being's highly developed brain, accumulated knowledge, and ability to perceive and communicate through the medium of symbols lead him or her to find unpleasant or pleasant connotations in an incredible number of situations and events. Human beings react not only to tangible, physical stresses but also to symbolic or imagined threats or pleasures.[7] The effects of the stimulus can vary widely, depending on a person's culture, personal and family background, experiences, and mood and circumstances at the time. The objective nature of an event is not nearly as significant as what the event means to a particular individual at any given time. People can influence the nature of stress through their ability to control and anticipate events in the environment. As anticipation can simplify stress, the lack of it does so even more. The unanticipated event often has the greatest impact on an individual and leaves the most persistent aftereffects.[8]

Reactions to Stress

Most people adjust their behavior to daily stress according to their adaptive range. At the high end of the range, when a person encounters an extremely demanding situation, his or her first reaction is usually anxiety, a varying mixture of alertness, anticipation, curiosity, and fear. At the low end of the range, when confronted with a stressful situation, an individual experiences a condition of overload. The ability to improvise deteriorates, and behavior is likely to regress to simpler, more primitive responses. Regardless of personality type, people under high stress show less ability to tolerate ambiguity and to sort out the trivial from the important. Some authorities report that people become apathetic and inactive when stress is either minimal or absent.

As stress increases slightly, the person becomes attentive and more active. When stress increases further, the individual becomes either interested and curious or wary and cautious. Greater stress, then, results in emotional states of unpleasant anxiety or pleasant expectation. When stress becomes extreme, anxiety may increase until it threatens to overwhelm the individual. At this point, panic, accompanied by paralysis, flight, or attack, may occur. Under high levels of emotion, an individual becomes less discriminating and tends to make either disorganized or stereotyped responses, to lose perceptual judgment, and to idealize and overgeneralize.[9] As one police psychologist puts it, "People under stress make mistakes." In policing where job-related stress is involved, the kind of mistakes that are likely to occur can result in potentially irreparable, even fatal, consequences.[10]

Critical Thinking Questions

1. How do Basowitz and his associates differentiate types of anxiety?
2. Describe how anticipation of an event can affect stress levels.
3. How do most people react to stress?

STRESS AND PERSONALITY TYPE

Friedman and Rosenmann identified certain distinctive personality types and the relationship among these personality types, stress, and coronary heart disease.[11]

Type A Personality

- Under constant stress, much of which is self-generated
- Continuous pressure to accomplish
- Hostile and demanding
- Always in a hurry; sense of time urgency
- Continuing impatience
- Intense and ambitious

- Believes time should be used "constructively"
- Has difficulty relaxing and feels guilty when not working
- Compelled to challenge, not understand, another type A personality
- Qualities underlying type A characteristics include the following:
  - Constant state of being "on guard"
  - Hypermasculinity
  - Constantly working against time
  - Ignorance of one's own psychological needs
- The physiological implications are as follows:
  - Seven times as likely to develop heart disease
  - Higher cholesterol and triglyceride (blood fat) levels (sudden stress increases triglyceride; prolonged stress increases cholesterol)
  - Clotting elements have greater tendency to form within coronary arteries
  - Excess accumulation of insulin in blood

Type B Personality

- Less competitive and less rushed
- More easygoing
- More able to separate work from play
- Relatively free of a sense of time urgency
- Ambitions kept in perspective
- Generally philosophical about life

Workaholic

- This phrase was coined in 1968
- Similar to type A
- Has an addiction to work
- When absent from the job, may experience withdrawal symptoms similar to other addictions
- Is agitated and depressed when not working
- May account for up to 5 percent of working world
- Typical workaholics
  - Readily buck the system; often bucked by the bureaucracy
  - Display well-organized hostility toward the system's imperfections
  - Obsessed with perfection in their work
  - Haunted by deep-seated fear of failure; will "play to win" at all games
  - Prefer labor to leisure
  - Constantly juggle two or more tasks
- Many are overachievers and "get things done"
- Takes its toll and may result in:
  - Gastrointestinal problems
  - Cardiovascular disease
  - Divorce

Critical Thinking Question

1. How might a law enforcement officer with a type A personality or workaholic personality approach his or her job, compared with one who has a type B personality?

STRESS IN LAW ENFORCEMENT

Police work is highly stressful—it is one of the few occupations in which an employee is asked continually to face physical dangers and to put his or her life on the line at any time. The police officer is exposed to violence, cruelty, and aggression and is often required to make extremely critical decisions in high-pressure situations.

Stress has many ramifications and can produce many varied psychophysiological disturbances that, if sufficiently intense and chronic, can lead to demonstrable organic diseases of varying severity. It may also lead to physiological disorders and emotional instability, which can manifest themselves in alcoholism, a broken marriage, and, in the extreme, suicide. Studies show that three-fourths of the heart attacks suffered by police officers are from job-related stress. As a result, courts have ruled that a police officer who suffers a heart attack while off duty is entitled to workers' compensation.[12] In California, a court held that the suicide of a probationary sergeant was directly related to his job stress. This ruling established the eligibility for certain benefits to the surviving family members. Thus, even a superficial review of the human, organizational, and legal impacts of stress-related health problems should sensitize every administrator to the prevention, treatment, and solution of these problems.

Police Stressors

Violanti and Aron distributed a 60-item Police Stress Survey (PSS) to a random sample of 110 officers in a large New York State police department.[13] Ninety-three percent of those sampled ($N=103$) completed the PSS and returned it. Table 13.2 displays the results of this survey. The single most potent stressor was killing someone in the line of duty. The empathy police officers have for victims is revealed by the fact that the fourth most potent stressor was handling child abuse cases, which ranked ahead of other well-known stressors, such as engaging in high-speed chases, using force, responding to felony-in-progress calls, and making death notices.

The stressors in Table 13.2 can be factored into two components: those that are organizational/administrative and those that are inherent in the nature of police work. Within these stressors, there were some variations. Sergeants in charge of substations reported the most organizational/administrative stress, while detectives reported the least. For officers in the 31- to 35-year-old range, the single most powerful stressor was shift work. However, for officers over 46 years of age, the mean values of all stressors dropped. This is probably due in part to the accommodations that such officers have learned to make as well as the nature of the jobs that people more senior in their

Quick Facts

Job Stress and Ailments

Since the 1970s, many studies have looked at the relationship between job stress and a variety of ailments. Mood and sleep disturbances, upset stomach, headaches, and relationship problems with family and friends are examples of stress-related problems that are quick to develop and are commonly seen in these studies. These early signs in job stress are usually easy to recognize. However, the effects of job stress on chronic diseases are more difficult to see because chronic diseases take a long time to develop and can be influenced by many factors other than stress. Nonetheless, evidence is rapidly accumulating to suggest that stress plays an important role in several types of chronic health problems, especially cardiovascular disease, musculoskeletal disorders, and psychological disorders.

Source: National Institute for Occupational Safety and Health.

TABLE 13.2 Police Stressors Ranked by Mean Scores

STRESSOR	MEAN SCORE	STRESSOR	MEAN SCORE
Killing someone in line of duty	79.38	Excessive paperwork	43.15
Fellow officer killed	76.67	Court leniency	42.65
Physical attack	70.97	Disagreeable regulations	42.27
Battered child	69.24	Ineffective judicial system	42.00
High-speed chases	63.73	Family demands	41.84
Shift work	61.21	Politics in the department	40.64
Use of force	60.96	Inadequate supervision	40.11
Inadequate dept. support	60.93	Public criticism	39.52
Incompatible partner	60.36	Assigned new duties	39.22
Accident in patrol car	59.89	Ineffective corrections	39.08
Insufficient personnel	58.53	Inadequate salary	38.45
Aggressive crowds	56.70	Rapid change from boredom to high stress	38.06
Felony in progress	55.27	Making arrests alone	37.23
Excessive discipline	53.27	Personal insult from citizens	36.67
Plea bargaining	52.84	Negative public image	36.17
Death notifications	52.59	Increased responsibility	33.03
Inadequate support (super.)	52.43	Exposure to pain and suffering	33.01
Inadequate equipment	52.36	Exposure to death	32.06
Family disputes	51.97	Second job	31.51
Negative press coverage	51.80	Lack of participation in decisions	31.10
Court on their day off	51.06	Public apathy	29.50
Job conflict with rules	50.64	Promotion competition	29.46
Fellow officers not doing their job	49.02	Promotion or commendation	28.79
Lack of recognition	48.10	Non-police tasks	27.94
Physical injury on the job	47.10	Demands for high morality	26.14
Making quick decisions	45.82	Politics outside the dept.	25.48
Restrictive court decisions	44.82	Strained non-police relations	23.60
Getting along with supervisors	44.48	Boredom	23.25
Disagreeable duties	43.90	Minor physical injuries	23.23
Mistreatment in court	43.50	Racial conflicts	22.53

SOURCE: Reprinted from the *Journal of Criminal Justice* 23, no. 3, John M. Violanti and Fred Aron, "Police Stressors: Variations in Perceptions among Police Personnel," p. 347, Copyright © 1995, with permission from Elsevier.

careers hold. For African Americans, the highest-ranking stressor was inadequate support by the police department.

Critical Thinking Question

1. Discuss how the following stressors can affect a police officer, both on and off the job: fellow officer killed, contact with a battered child, shift work, patrol car accident, excessive paperwork, negative public image, and promotion competition.

ALCOHOLISM AND POLICE OFFICERS

Alcoholism in government and industry is not only widespread but also extremely costly—a fact established most convincingly by many independent researchers. Some 6.5 million employed workers in the United States today are alcoholics. Loss of productivity because of the disease of alcoholism has been computed at $10 billion.

Alcohol problems among police officers manifest themselves in a number of ways. Some of these are a higher than normal absentee rate before and immediately following the officer's regular day off, complaints of insubordination by supervisors, complaints by citizens of misconduct in the form of verbal and physical abuse, intoxication during regular working hours, involvement in traffic accidents while under the influence of alcohol on and off duty, and reduced overall performance.

It has been suggested further that policing is especially conducive to alcoholism. Because police officers frequently work in an environment in which social drinking is commonplace, it is relatively easy for them to become social drinkers. The nature of police work and the environment in which it is performed provides the stress stimulus.

Traditionally, police departments adhered to the "character flaw" theory of alcoholism. This outdated philosophy called for the denunciation and dismissal of the officer with an alcohol problem. Today, police departments attempt to rehabilitate officers, and typically they are separated from the service only after such attempts have failed. Police departments now have a broad mix of employee assistance programs to assist officers with their drinking problems, including self-assessment checklists (see Table 13.3), peer counseling, in-house psychologists and those on retainers, and support groups.

Departmental Programs

There is no single best way for a department to assist its officers with a drinking problem, but some agencies have enjoyed a fair degree of success for their efforts. For example, the Denver Police Department has used its closed-circuit television system to teach officers who are problem drinkers and encourage them to join the in-house program. A major portion of the in-house program was designed to persuade the problem drinker, after having been exposed to a sufficient amount of the educational component, to enter the Mercy Hospital Care Unit and achieve the status of a recovering alcoholic.[14]

It is the responsibility of the individual police agency and its administrators to act on the fact that alcoholism is a disease and to create a relaxed atmosphere and an in-house program for the dissemination of information relative to this problem. As indicated earlier, the objective of such a program is ultimately to persuade individual officers to enter a care unit for treatment. The combination of unsatisfactory performance, excessive costs, and the almost certain progressive deterioration of the

TABLE 13.3 Alcohol Self-Assessment Checklist

Each of the following conditions or behaviors has been found to be associated with alcohol abuse or problem drinking. Check the ones that apply to you. This exercise will sensitize you to what to look for when evaluating a person for alcohol abuse potential.

_________ 1. Drinking alone regularly.

_________ 2. Needing a drink to get over a hangover.

_________ 3. Needing a drink at a certain time each day.

_________ 4. Finding it harder and harder to get along with others.

_________ 5. Memory loss while or after drinking.

_________ 6. Driving skill deteriorating.

_________ 7. Drinking to relieve stress, fear, shyness, insecurity.

_________ 8. More and more family and friends worrying about drinking habits.

_________ 9. Becoming moody, jealous, or irritable after drinking.

_________ 10. "Binges" of heavy drinking.

_________ 11. Heavy weekend drinking.

_________ 12. Able to drink more and more with less and less effect.

None of these represents a certain indicator of alcohol abuse or problem drinking. They are all signs that problems may be developing or already exist.

SOURCE: Theodore H. Blau, *Psychological Services for Law Enforcement,* p. 198. © 1994 by Theodore H. Blau. Reprinted by permission of John Wiley & Sons, Inc.

individual officer to the point of unemployability, if the illness goes unchecked, creates a situation that conscientious chiefs of police or sheriffs should neither tolerate nor ignore. If drinking affects an officer's health, job, or family, immediate action is essential—the officer is probably an alcoholic.

Reports by the Denver Police Department indicate that the organization has benefited in the following specific ways since the implementation of its alcohol abuse program:

- Retention of the majority of the officers who had suffered from alcoholism
- Solution of a set of complex and difficult personnel problems
- Realistic and practical extension of the police agency's program into the entire city government structure
- Improved public and community attitudes by this degree of concern for the officer and the officer's family and by eliminating the dangerous and antisocial behavior of the officer in the community
- Full cooperation with rehabilitation efforts from the police associations and unions that may represent officers
- The preventive influence on moderate drinkers against the development of dangerous drinking habits that may lead to alcoholism; in addition, an existing in-house program will motivate some officers to undertake remedial action on their own outside the scope of the police agency program.[15]

Critical Thinking Questions

1. Why is policing seen by some as especially conducive to alcoholism?
2. What are some of the specific benefits reported by the Denver Police Department since it implemented its alcohol abuse program?

DRUG USE BY POLICE OFFICERS

Drug abuse by police officers has garnered a great deal of attention.[16] A national study of 2,200 police officers found that 10 percent had serious drug problems.[17] As a result of this condition, police administrators have had to grapple with such issues as the following:

- What positions will the employee unions or other employee organizations take if drug testing is proposed?
- Who should be tested for drugs? Entry-level officers? Regular officers on a random basis? All officers before they are promoted? Personnel assigned to high-profile units, such as bomb disposal and special tactics and response?
- When does a supervisor have "reasonable suspicion" of a subordinate's drug use?
- Who should collect urine or other specimens and under what conditions?
- What criteria or standards should be used when selecting a laboratory to conduct the police department's drug testing program?
- What disciplinary action is appropriate when officers are found to have abused drugs?
- What duty does an employer have to rehabilitate employees who become disabled as a result of drug abuse?[18]

In recent years, issues concerning the testing of sworn officers for drugs have been debated and litigated. In the early days of such litigation, court rulings were sometimes wildly contradictory, with most courts striking down such requirements, typically on the basis that it was an unwarranted intrusion into officers' constitutional right to privacy.[19] Nevertheless, three major principles have emerged from the many random drug cases decided by the courts. The first is that drug testing—both on the basis of reasonable suspicion and when conducted on a random basis—does not violate the federal Constitution. The second is that, although drug testing may not violate federal constitutional rights, it may not be permissible under the constitutions of some states. The third principle is that, in states that have granted collective bargaining rights to police officers (see Chapter 11, Labor Relations), drug testing cannot be unilaterally implemented by the employer. Instead, it must be submitted to the collective bargaining process.

The selection of officers for drug testing must be truly random and part of a clearly articulated drug testing policy. The courts will not support the police department's operation of a non-random drug testing program except when there is reasonable suspicion to test for the presence of drugs.[20]

Anabolic Steroids

When police administrators consider the use of illegal drugs by their personnel, they typically think of the traditional illegal drugs, such as marijuana, cocaine, heroin, amphetamines, and barbiturates. However, drugs that are abused more than many people realize are **anabolic steroids.**

Background

The use of anabolic steroids by athletes began in the late 1940s.[21,22] It is estimated that 80 to 99 percent of male body builders[23] and perhaps as many as 96 percent of professional football players have used these drugs, as have many other athletes.[24] Sixty-eight percent of interviewed track-and-field athletes had used steroids in preparation for the 1972 Olympics in Munich.[25] Since then, the International Olympic Committee has banned all anabolic drugs, and the top six performers in each Olympic event are now tested for non-therapeutic drugs of all types. Despite such developments, steroid use is widespread. The Mayo Clinic has estimated that more than 1 million Americans are regular steroid users.[26]

The law enforcement community is not exempt from this form of drug abuse. For example, the U.S. Bureau of Customs investigated the smuggling of anabolic steroids into this country. Their investigation led them to certain health clubs in North Carolina, where it was determined that state patrol officers were illegally using anabolic steroids. The North Carolina State Patrol joined the investigation, and subsequently three troopers were terminated. In Miami Beach, Florida, a physical training sergeant noticed that one of his female charges was "bulking up" too fast. She also displayed street behavior that led a department supervisor to recommend that she be assigned to non-street duties. It was subsequently established that she had been using anabolic steroids. In addition to using steroids themselves, officers in New York have been convicted of selling anabolic steroids.

Adverse Health Impact

There are recognized medical uses of anabolic steroids. Among the conditions for which anabolic steroids may be therapeutically appropriate are deficient endocrine functioning of the testes, osteoporosis, carcinoma of the breast, growth retardation, and severe anemia.[27]

The use of anabolic steroids, as summarized in Table 13.4, is associated with a number of potential outcomes that are adverse to an individual's health. These risks are even greater when anabolic steroids are taken under the direction of a self-appointed "roid guru" or when self-dosing because the typical usage under these and related circumstances is 10 to 100 times greater than typical medical dosages.[28] Further complicating the non-therapeutic use of steroids is self-treatment with preparations not legally available in the United States and veterinary preparations, such as Boldenone (Equipose), for which it is difficult to estimate dosage equivalency,[29] virtually ensuring that dosages well beyond those recognized as medically appropriate will be taken.

Unknown or less well known to anabolic steroid abusers than the previously noted risks are certain affective and psychotic symptoms. Charlier[30] maintains that "aggressive behavior is almost universal among anabolic steroid users." There are documented case histories of severe depression, visual and auditory hallucinations, sleep disorders, thoughts of suicide, outbursts of anger, anorexia, psychomotor retardation, and irritability. In a survey of health club athletes who used steroids, 90 percent reported steroid-induced aggressive or violent behavior.[31] Pope and Katz conducted a study of 39 male and two female anabolic steroid abusers whose psychiatric histories were generally unremarkable, yet five subjects had psychotic symptoms, and others had manic episodes or periods of major depressions:

> *One 23-year-old man bought a $17,000 automobile. . . . When he stopped taking anabolic steroids he realized he could not afford the payments and sold the car. A year later, while taking steroids again, he impulsively bought a $20,000 sports car. . . . Another subject*

TABLE 13.4 Adverse Effects of Anabolic Steroids

MEN	WOMEN	BOTH SEXES
■ Breast enlargement ■ Testicular atrophy with consequent sterility or decreased sperm count ■ Impotence ■ Enlarged prostate	■ Breast diminution ■ Clitoral enlargement ■ Facial hair growth ■ Deepened voice ■ Menstrual irregularities ■ Excessive body hair ■ Baldness	■ Increased aggression, known as "roid rage" ■ Increased risk of heart disease, stroke, or obstructed blood vessels ■ Acne ■ Liver tumors, jaundice, and peliosis hepatitis, (blood-filled cysts) ■ Pre-teens and teenagers: accelerated bone maturation, leading to permanently short stature

SOURCE: C. Swanson, L. Gaines, and B. Gore, "Use of Anabolic Steroids," *FBI Law Enforcement Bulletin* 60, no. 8 (1991): 19–23.

bought an old car and drove it into a tree at 40 miles per hour while a friend videotaped him. . . . A third subject believed his mind was influencing the pictures on television and promised a friend he would show God to him.[32]

Although not physically addicting, steroids can cause a psychological dependence and can be divided into three stages namely the initial stage of exploration, a continuing stage of regular usage, and cessation from use. People are attracted to steroid use for a variety of reasons, all of which center on developing a more domineering physique. Initial users are generally "turned on" to the drugs by other abusers or seek them out at health clubs or gyms, where such drugs are commonly abused. The continuation stage occurs after initial use, when subjects have experienced some success with the drug. Thereafter, subjects become obsessed with their larger physiques, increased strength, or sexual appeal. Exercise becomes easier whenever steroids are used, and pain and a lack of strength appear when the drugs are discontinued. This process may continue until subjects are confronted with difficulties that result from their drug dependency. Cessation of usage will come only when the subjects become disinterested or are confronted with their problems.

Anabolic Steroids: The Legal Environment

The Drug Enforcement Administration (DEA) has the major responsibility for enforcing the federal Controlled Substances Act (CSA), which is intended to minimize the quantity of drugs available for illegal use. The CSA places a substance into one of five schedules on the basis of such factors as potential for abuse and whether there is a recognized medical use of the substance. Most over-the-counter (OTC) and prescription drugs do not fall within one of the CSA schedules, and the responsibility for enforcement efforts relating to them rests with the Food and Drug Administration (FDA) and state agencies. The FDA determines whether a substance falls within the OTC or prescription category; each state then has the legal power to determine who can legally prescribe and dispense OTC and prescription substances. The federal Anti-Drug Act of 1988—also referred to as the Omnibus Drug Abuse Initiative—created a special category of anabolic steroids within the prescription class, and all violations involving the sale or possession with intent to distribute anabolic steroids are now felonies.

Even before the passage of the Anti-Drug Act, it was illegal to possess anabolic steroids without a prescription in all 50 states. Thus, all officers in this country using anabolic steroids without a prescription are committing an illegal act.

Awareness of the nature and impact of illegal anabolic steroid use is seen in litigation. "Anabolic steroid–induced rage" has been used as a defense in sexual assault cases; in one instance, the judge accepted this argument as a mitigating factor when sentencing a defendant in a sexual assault. Liability is one of the most critical issues regarding steroid usage. It is only a matter of time before it will be alleged in a state tort or federal civil rights lawsuit that "but for the failure of the police department to conduct a proper background and drug screening, the anabolic steroid–induced violent assault on my client would never have occurred" (negligent selection) or that "but for the failure of the police department to properly train its supervisors on how to identify the manifestations of anabolic steroid abuse, the physical trauma to Mrs. Johnson would not be an issue before this court today" (failure to train and failure to supervise). Although there are almost limitless liability scenarios, there is only one inescapable conclusion: if administrators do not confront this issue quickly, harm will be done to citizens, officers, families, and public treasuries.

Administrative Concerns and Anabolic Steroids

Regarding administrative attitudes toward steroid use, people in the internal affairs, public information, and command positions as well as staff psychologists of 30 police departments across the country were interviewed. With few exceptions, the response was "That's not a problem in this department, and we've never had a problem with it," yet replies of that nature are deceiving. For example, a departmental representative who had stated in the morning that steroid abuse was not a problem called back in the afternoon, saying, "I've been thinking. . . . One of our retired officers runs a gym frequented by our officers and some of them have gotten very muscular awfully quick." Police officials readily recognize cocaine or marijuana abuse as a police personnel problem, but for the most part they still are not aware of the seriousness of steroid abuse. If this situation is not corrected soon, departments will be confronted with increasing numbers of steroid-related problems. Some agencies have decided to deal with this problem by randomly testing their officers for anabolic steroid use.

Critical Thinking Questions

1. Do you believe that random drug testing is necessary among police officers? Why or why not?
2. Why might police officers be prone to psychological dependence on anabolic steroids?
3. Why do many police departments underestimate the problem of anabolic steroid use?

POLICE SUICIDE

Considerable difficulty exists in studying police suicide.[33] Researchers often find that either information on officer suicide is not collected or departments are reluctant to allow access to such data.[34]

In The News

Code of Silence Prevents Open Discussions Regarding Officer Suicide

Police suicide has been a chronic problem among law enforcement officers for years. The causes of police suicide vary widely and can involve job stressors specific to police officers and problems that occur within any American family. However, statistics gathered by the Fraternal Order of Police show that police officers commit suicide at nearly twice the rate of non-officers.

Despite the growing acknowledgment of the problem among psychologists and police researchers, police themselves have a difficult time discussing the issue. Most departments do not keep official records of suicide among their ranks, afraid of liability if the death is linked to job stress and of tarnishing their image with the public. Furthermore, many officers perceive that, if they admit that they have thought about suicide or are feeling depressed, supervisors and other officers will view them as weak, and their ability to move through the ranks will be compromised. As a result, experts believe that only a fraction of the officers who really need help will seek it.

Source: Gary Fields and Charisse Jones, "Code of Silence Doesn't Help," *USA Today,* June 1, 1999.

In addition, police suicides may be misclassified routinely as either accidents or undetermined deaths. Because police officers traditionally subscribe to a myth of indestructibility, they view suicide as particularly disgraceful to the victim officer and to the profession.[35] The police represent a highly cohesive subculture whose members tend to "take care of their own." The desire to shield victim officers, their families, and their departments from the stigma of suicide may lead investigators to overlook certain evidence intentionally during the classification process. One study of the Chicago Police Department estimated that as many as 67 percent of police suicides in that city had been misclassified as accidental or natural deaths.[36]

Failure to correct for such biases could lead to false conclusions regarding the causes and frequency of police suicides. Therefore, accurate research must go beyond official rates; the preliminary results of an ongoing study of police suicides over a 40-year period indicate that nearly 30 percent of police suicides may have been misclassified.[37]

Why Police Officers Commit Suicide

One of the most comprehensive studies ever undertaken to examine police suicide was conducted by the New York Police Department. The study revealed that, while New York City police officers are more likely than the general public to commit suicide, they respond positively to training programs that offer them avenues of help.[38]

The study's recommendations included the further development of confidential counseling resources within the New York Police Department; additional training in handling depression, problematic interpersonal skills, and recognizing the effects of alcohol and drugs; and police academy training in officer "life-saving"—how and when to seek help for oneself or a fellow officer when necessary.

"Police officers are trained from day one not to show weakness, and officers believe discussion of problems or feelings is evidence of weakness," said Andre Ivanoff, an associate professor at the School of Social Work at Columbia University. "Training in the future must incorporate the idea that it's okay to ask for help and talk about negative feelings."

After viewing a film and participating in an in-service training session on police suicide, officers surveyed by questionnaire expressed a greater willingness to seek help for themselves and for fellow officers. Ivanoff conducted the research and trained officers who led the discussion groups.

The Police Suicide Project was a cooperative venture of the New York Police Department, the New York City Police Foundation, and Columbia University. The suicide rate among department officers is about 29 per 100,000 annually and is considerably higher than among the general U.S. population, which was 11.7 per 100,000 in 1992.

Responses to the survey indicate that police view interpersonal problems, depression, and the use of alcohol and other drugs as the primary reasons for suicide, not the generalized stress of police work, popularly cited in mental health journals. Of 57 police suicides reported by the department between 1985 and mid 1994, relationship problems and depression were the leading factors in cases in which a contributing factor was identified.

The method most used by officers committing suicide is the service weapon, according to police department statistics. Among the 57 reported police suicides, all but 4 were committed with the officer's gun. Ivanoff and other experts believe that police suicides are underreported, often classified as accidents, in part to spare an officer's family from embarrassment.

In 1992, the year of Ivanoff's study, the number of suicides plummeted from an average of between seven and eight per year to just one. She notes that this drop cannot be attributed solely to the training because in 1993 the number of suicides rose again to eight until September 6, 1994.

The goals of the Police Suicide Project were to increase knowledge about both the myths surrounding suicide and the actual risk factors linked to suicide, such as depression; to impart positive attitudes about getting help for problems that seem beyond control; and to publicize the department's counseling programs. "The project met and surpassed its initial objectives," Ivanoff said. "Attitudes toward getting help, specifically toward the use of helping resources for oneself and for others, improved dramatically."

In 1988, the police department asked the New York City Police Foundation, a non-profit organization that works to strengthen the department's performance, to help sponsor a film with the aim of reducing suicide. The foundation raised $140,000, hired filmmaker Jonathan David, and created an advisory board of police officials and mental health experts to oversee the project's implementation. The 39-minute film, *By Their Own Hand*, examines the lives of three police officers who attempted suicide, one successfully. The film was shown as part of two ongoing training programs conducted twice yearly by the police department. Those programs are Borough-Based Training (for patrol officers) and Centralized Management Training (for sergeants and lieutenants).

Officers participating in the program were asked to fill out a pretraining questionnaire; 5,197 did so for the sample. Immediately after the film and discussion, another questionnaire was administered; 6,149 officers filled that out. Six months after the training sessions, another questionnaire elicited 18,716 responses.

Responses to the surveys did not vary greatly by ethnicty, gender, age, or marital status, Ivanoff said, although more highly educated officers in general exhibited a greater willingness to seek help for problems.

In posttraining and follow-up questionnaires, police officers indicated they were significantly more likely to turn to all types of counseling resources, both inside the department and without, when faced by seemingly insurmountable problems. Six months after the training, more than half the officers indicated they were more aware of minor problems faced by fellow officers. Just half were aware of serious problems, and more than a quarter said they knew another officer who was in crisis or suicidal. Forty percent acknowledged that they were more aware of problems in their own lives.

A non-intrusive measure of the training program's effectiveness was a measured increase in utilization of the department's personal resources, including psychological services, counseling services, early intervention, and the help line. Statistics were collected for a full year prior to the project, through the course of the evaluation, and for one full year following the evaluation, from January 1990 through December 1993. Referrals rose from an average of about 75 a month to nearly double that once the pretraining questionnaire was administered in February 1991.

It is not clear why the Police Suicide Project was effective, Ivanoff said, or which component of the training was most responsible for the observed changes. Many law enforcement organizations mention suicide only in broader stress-management programs. "The dramatic nature of the film presentation and its specific focus on suicide appears to have been advantageous," Ivanoff said.

Ivanoff listed her name and telephone number on the questionnaire and received dozens of telephone calls in the course of the study. "Some called to argue with my approach to studying this issue, but the majority called because they needed help dealing with problems," she said.

Studies of other police departments have revealed that suicides are more common among older officers and are related to alcoholism, physical illness, or impending retirement.[39] Other clues have been cited to help explain the high rate of self-inflicted death among police officers: the regular availability of firearms, continuous-duty exposure to death and injury, social strain resulting from shift work, inconsistencies within the criminal justice system, and the perception among police officers that they labor under a negative public image. In addition, research confirms a higher propensity for suicide among males, who dominate the police profession.[40]

A study of the Detroit Police Department found that the vast majority of police officers who took their lives were white, young, male, high school educated, and married. Alcohol abuse was fairly common among the sample (42 percent), as was a formal diagnosis of psychosis (33 percent). However, marital difficulties appeared to be the most prevalent problem among the Detroit sample.[41]

Examination of 27 cases of police suicide in Quebec found that half the officers had a history of psychiatric and/or medical problems and that many had severe alcohol problems. Most officers in the sample experienced difficulties at work, and in every case a notable drop in work performance had been observed in the six months prior to the suicide.[42]

Among the occupational factors surrounding police suicide, frustration is often cited as particularly important. Almost unfailingly, officers enter policing with high ideals and a noble desire to help others. Over time, this sense of idealism may transform into hard-core cynicism.

The roots of frustration emanate from the central irony of American policing: society charges police officers with the task of regulating a public that does not want to be regulated. For individual officers, the resulting frustration is exacerbated by a largely unsympathetic press, a lack of community support, and a criminal justice system that values equity over expediency. A sense of social isolation often ensues, compelling officers to group together in a defensive stance. When an officer feels that the frustration is no longer tolerable or that no coping alternative is available, suicide may become an attractive option.

It also is possible that feelings of helplessness are brought about by the nature of the job.[43] A sense of helplessness is a disturbing realization for anyone but especially for police officers who are conditioned to view themselves as superheroes capable of anything. Suicide is one way of dealing with helplessness and emotional pain. The finality of the ultimate solution may be an attempt to restore feelings of strength, courage, and mastery over the environment.[44]

FIGURE 13.1

Sylvia Banuelos, whose husband, Ernesto, killed himself, holds his service badge at the grave site. Ernesto Banuelos was an Orange County, California, sheriff's deputy. Behind her are her children, Matthew (left), Adam, Andrew, and Justin.

(Photo by Bob Riha, Jr., *USA Today*)

Access to Firearms

Another factor that distinguishes police officers from the general population has been implicated in the high number of police suicides. That is, most law enforcement officers carry or have access to firearms (see Figure 13.1). An ongoing study of police suicides in the United States reveals that 95 percent involved the use of the officer's service weapon.[45]

Another study compared suicides in New York City and London. While the police suicide rate in New York City was twice that of the general population, the police suicide rate in London, where officers do not carry firearms, was similar to that of the city's civilian population.

The police firearm holds special significance for officers. It is a very potent symbol of the power of life and death. Society entrusts law enforcement officers with the authority to use their weapons and to take the life of another person in certain situations. In police suicides, officers in effect are claiming the right to take their own lives. After all, the weapon has been issued as a means to stop misery and to protect others from harm. Despondent officers may view suicide in such a way.

Alcohol Abuse

Alcohol abuse, discussed earlier in this chapter, has also been implicated as a significant contributing factor in police suicides. Administrators should be aware that alcoholism may lead to other work problems, such as high absenteeism, traffic accidents, or intoxication on duty. Given the established correlation between alcoholism and suicide, these symptoms should not be ignored. They should be considered indications of a larger problem.

Fear of Separation from the Police Subculture

As officers near the end of their law enforcement careers, another potential threat appears: separation. To individual officers, retirement may mean separation from the camaraderie and protection of police peers. During their years of service, officers may have clustered with other officers because of a general isolation from society and its prejudices toward the police. On retirement, these officers must enter the very society that they perceive as alien and hostile.

While the benefits of retirement may be viewed positively by the majority of officers, separation from the police subculture can be a frightful and devastating prospect for others. Fear, coupled with increasing age (a definite suicide risk factor), loss of friends, loss of status as a police officer, and loss of self-definition, leaves some retiring officers vulnerable to suicide. One study found a 10-fold increase in risk of suicide among police retirees.[46]

Recognizing the Warning Signs

Identifying at-risk officers is the first step toward helping them.[47] Is there any common pattern to be found in police suicidal behavior? In truth, any member of a department can become depressed and commit suicide under certain circumstances. However, a long trail of evidence typically leads to the final act. Many suicidal people have mixed feelings about dying and actually hope to be rescued. About 75 percent give some kind of notice of their intentions.[48] If recognized and taken seriously, these early warning signs make prevention and intervention possible.

Typically, multiple problems plague suicidal police officers, so supervisors should look for a cluster of warning signs. These might include a recent loss, sadness, frustration, disappointment, grief, alienation, depression, loneliness, physical pain, mental anguish, and mental illness.

The strongest behavioral warning is a suicide attempt. Generally, the more recent the attempt, the higher the risk factor for the officer. Police training officers need to incorporate education about suicide warning signs as a regular part of the department's mental health program.

When officers who have consistently been good performers begin to fail to perform at the optimal level for an extended period of time, the problem might be related to a major depressive episode. Clinicians agree that depression can be so serious that it sometimes results in a homicide typically of a spouse or significant other followed by suicide. (This topic will be discussed in greater detail later in this chapter.)

Supervisory Responsibility in Suicide Prevention

It is quite clear that police managers and supervisors can play a very important role in suicide prevention. For example, supervisors should schedule interviews with officers who appear depressed, sad, hopeless, or discouraged. During this interview, the supervisor should check the officer's body language, look for sad facial expressions, and be alert to a flat mood. The officer might complain of feeling down, not having any feelings at all, or being anxious. Complaints about bodily aches and pains might be reported to cover the officer's true feelings.[49]

The twin feelings of hopelessness and helplessness indicate a high risk of suicide. Officers who think and speak in these terms feel that their lives are devoid of hope, or they see themselves as unable to meaningfully alter their situations. When they reach this point, they often take action. The finality of suicide might be seen as a technique to restore feelings of former strength, courage, and mastery over the environment.[50] Supervisors should listen carefully for expressions of these feelings.

Suicidal officers might have negative influences in their personal lives as well. Supervisors should look for histories that include suicidal behavior, mental illness, chronic depression, multiple divorces, and alcoholism. Losses in an officer's life, drug abuse patterns, and stress overload also contribute to the problem. Older officers might experience physical problems or face impending retirement and feel that they will become socially isolated.[51] Such physical and social losses can generate the destructive feelings of hopelessness and helplessness.

Most people have mixed emotions about committing suicide, and suicidal feelings tend to be episodic, coming and going in cycles. Troubled officers want to be rescued but do not want to ask for assistance or know what specific help to request. This state of confusion actually works to a supervisor's advantage because suicidal officers want a strong authority figure to direct their emotional traffic and make sense of the confusion. Therefore, supervisors should quickly assure suicidal officers that support and assistance are available.

It is important for supervisors to ask specifically whether officers are having thoughts of hurting themselves. Many may find it difficult to ask such a basic question, but it must be done. Officers who indicate they are having suicidal thoughts must not be left alone. All threats must be taken seriously. Other people might not have heard their pleas for help. Supervisors should plan their intervention so that it leads to a professional referral. The specific methods of intervention must be thought out as carefully as possible in order to avoid violence directed inward or outward at other employees. Without careful plans in place, officers confronted by supervisors might react unpredictably. Because their thought processes are confused, they might strike out at coworkers, supervisors, or family members, resulting in a homicide followed by suicide. Even if that does not occur, the danger of suicide exists at the point of intervention.

Supervisors should refer officers to a certified mental health professional, even setting appointments and making arrangements for the officers to be there. The department's responsibility does not end there, however. Supervisors should monitor the situation to ensure that officers are evaluated and receive continued support and counseling.

Critical Thinking Questions

1. Why is suicide among police a difficult phenomenon to measure?
2. Discuss how access to a firearm may be one of the most potent factors in police suicide.
3. How might a supervisor use his or her position of authority to help a suicidal officer?

SOURCES OF WORK SATISFACTION AS A STRESS REDUCER

Thus far, we have focused on the aspects of police work that are negative and stress-inducing. However, it is very easy to find numerous police officers who would readily admit that there are many aspects of the job that are truly rewarding, believe it is the greatest job in the world, and leaves them with a tremendous sense of satisfaction. A number of years ago, a comprehensive study was conducted by Herzberg, Mausner, and Snyderman in part to determine the sources of work satisfaction for police officers.[52] The following sources were provided to them by police officers who responded to their research questions.

Providing Assistance to Citizens

The contributions that appear most valued by officers are those calls involving citizens who are manifestly helpless. One such category is that of elderly people, who may be demonstrably fearful, lonely, or confused:

> Example 1: An elderly man passed away, and naturally his elderly wife didn't exactly know what do to, right? So after the ambulance crew and the fire department left, we . . . sat down at the table and found out if her husband had any wishes as to which particular funeral home he wanted to handle his funeral services. Once we found out which one it was we called the funeral director, and then started helping her out by calling her relatives. Some of her family who had arrived by then thanked us for helping her out because she didn't know what to do or who or call. That made me feel good at least because I was able to help this woman who didn't know up from down in this kind of stressful situation. Any decent person would do something like that, but we get paid for doing that.[53]

Most of the officers proudly recalled giving assistance to children. These included situations of child neglect and circumstances in which services were arranged or brokered by the officers. In some instances, the officers reported they had followed up to make sure that the problem was solved:

> Example 2: About 4 years ago my partner and I responded to a call where there were accusations being made that a young kid had been kept in his room against his will for approximately 2 years. He was being let out briefly, maybe once or twice a month, to attend school, just to show up. So we went there, and we investigated. . . . It was obvious that he had been kept in there for an extended period of time. We found out that the windows were all boarded up. There were buckets in there [where] he could defecate and urinate, and we investigated that along with the state. After doing some research we were able to find out this kid had some mental problems and was also quite aggressive. His mother had come to this country a couple years ago and wasn't aware of the types of services that were available to her in the United States, such as child counseling and so forth. We were able to get help for the family, for the kids, and now today when I see this kid he always recognizes me. I see the difference in him and I am very much aware of how he could have been. The mother also expressed her appreciation for everything we were able to do for her. We stayed on it for about a good 4 or 5 months, and finally the outcome was that they got a better house and they got turned on to state agencies. Counseling was made available, the mother got employed and the kid got put into a special school system along with the other kids. It was gratifying to know they benefited from our help.[54]

Exercising Interpersonal Skills

Although policing is often equated with the use of legal power or force, officers appear to take great pride in their ability to resolve delicate situations through exercises of verbal ingenuity. In both human services and crime-related incidents, the deployment of interpersonal relations skills was clearly valued:

> Example 3: We were able to talk a guy out of his house who had a gun. We took the gun away from him when he exited the house and fortunately nobody got hurt. I felt good about this because we could have killed the guy, but we chose not to. I had several situations like that with people with weapons. If you want to take this as an opportunity to shoot people you can but I didn't and because I didn't I felt good. I'm glad we didn't do that. You know we walk into a lot of potentially violent situations but sometimes through discussion you can convince people to come out of the houses or put knives down and not hurt their spouse or kids. It's a good feeling to know when you have diffused a tense situation and were able to help people.[55]

Getting Feedback

A source of feedback to officers is any change or positive result that citizens attribute to their influence or to actions they have taken:

> Example 4: An older woman, I think she was 82, had her car stolen. She was getting her hair done someplace in the middle of the city. She comes out and finds her car is gone. She was very upset. She was so sweet, so we put her in the back of the patrol car and said, we were going to give her a ride home. "Oh, you would do that for me?" and we said, sure. We took the report, drove her home, and you wouldn't believe it, the best part is that two hours later we found her car and were able to return it to her. She was so grateful she wanted to make us cookies and coffee. "Oh please, you're so sweet," and when we found her car it was a good feeling to know we were able to help someone like that. It is just nice to get a thank you once in awhile, unfortunately, too often we don't get much respect for the job we do.[56]

Receiving Peer-Group Support

The officers cited two sources of satisfaction that had to do with peer support. One focused on the solidarity and loyalty of the police force, the other on relationships with partners and other work associates. The following example highlights rewards having to do with belongingness, solidarity, and support:

> Example 5: What really gives me a sense of satisfaction is the people I work with. The camaraderie that they have; it is a really tight-knit group. These are probably some of the closest friends I have ever had in my life, even in such a short period of time. You have a common bond. You all deal with the same situations, occasionally dangerous situations, and you kind of have an understanding of what the other one goes through. I found the degree of loyalty and friendship on the job that I didn't know existed when I was young. I found no matter what kind of background I had or what color I was, there was a sense of loyalty because we were all in the same profession.[57]

Critical Thinking Question

1. How does an officer's satisfaction with his or her work affect overall stress level?

SUICIDE BY COP

On hearing the term **suicide by cop (SbC),** the average person would probably think of police officers who take their own lives. However, to law enforcement officers, this refers to an individual who wishes to die and uses the police to effect that goal. Even when such shootings are clearly justified, they are often quite stressful for the officers involved. As indicated earlier in this chapter, shooting someone in the line of duty is the highest-rated police stressor (see Table 13.2). The following cases serve as an example of this phenomenon from both the officers' perspective and the offenders' perspective.

Case Studies

In a study conducted by Pinizzotto, Davis, and Miller, 12 offenders reported making an attempt to commit suicide prior to their assaulting or attempting to assault a law enforcement officer.[58] In the study, 21 offenders indicated they had contemplated suicide, and 10 offenders advised that they actually had attempted suicide prior to the incident. Six offenders reported that they had attempted to force a law enforcement officer to kill them at some point during the incident. A thorough review of the facts and circumstances surrounding two of these alleged attempted suicide by cop cases follows wherein the offender survived. This examination should provide a better understanding of these acts as seen through the eyes of the offender, as well as the officer. Each discloses specific behaviors exhibited by the offender and the interpretation of them by the officer.

Case #1: The Officer's Perspective

Two officers were dispatched to an apartment building in response to a woman yelling for help. On arriving at the location, they observed a female standing on the front steps. She waved them inside and then entered the apartment, leaving the door open behind her. As the officers approached the doorway, they could hear a male yelling and then saw him standing in the kitchen area. As the male observed the officers enter the apartment, he produced a large butcher knife. He held the blade of the knife firmly against his stomach with both hands and appeared highly intoxicated, agitated, and angry. The officers drew their service weapons and ordered the man to put down the knife. The offender responded by stating, "[Expletive] you, kill me!" He turned toward the kitchen counter, put the handle of the knife against it with the blade touching his stomach, and grabbed the counter with both hands as if to thrust himself fully onto the knife. The officers attempted to talk with the offender, who responded by turning around and slicing himself severely on his forearm, bleeding profusely. The officers repeatedly asked him to drop the knife. One officer aimed his service weapon at the offender while the other pointed a chemical mace container at him. Still armed with the knife, the offender advanced closer to the officers. This caused the officers to retreat to a position where they attempted to use the kitchen door frame as cover.

As this was occurring, a backup unit arrived on the scene. The offender repeatedly told officers to shoot him while continually ignoring commands to drop the knife. From a distance of approximately 12 feet, he raised the knife in a threatening manner and charged the officers. One officer fired two .45-caliber rounds from his service weapon. Both struck the offender in the chest but seemed not to have any effect, except to make him angrier. The officer then fired two more rounds, at which point his service weapon jammed. One of these rounds struck the offender in the hand, passing through it and lodging in his groin. The second round hit him in the chest. The offender continued to charge both officers as they retreated down the hallway and out of the front door. As the offender arrived at the front door, he received another .45-caliber gunshot wound to the groin, fired by the second officer. He dropped the knife and backed up against the wall inside the doorway but remained on his feet. The officers entered the premises, removed the knife, took the offender into custody, and called for an ambulance. The offender was transported to the hospital and survived the incident. The officer who fired the initial four rounds stated, "It was my life or his, and it became his. I was upset that his guy put us in a position where I had to do something like this. I was upset with the fact that this guy kept pushing the issue and had made the decision himself, where I didn't have a decision."

Case # 1: The Offender's Perspective

In the morning, the offender had a serious argument with his wife, one that would only escalate if he remained in the apartment. The previous day, he had had a disagreement with several friends, which resulted in a fistfight. He stated that "the argument with my wife increased the pressure on me." He left the apartment and went to several bars. He drank liquor for approximately seven hours and got extremely intoxicated. A relative helped him home, where he and his wife continued to argue.

While standing in the kitchen, he observed two police officers enter the apartment. The mere presence of the officers further enraged him. When asked if he wanted officers to end his life for him, the offender said, "Quickly, I figured when they seen the knife that would have been enough. It would have been all over. But it didn't end up that way." When asked about specific thoughts during the confrontation with the officers, the offender stated, "I never thought about suicide. Never in my wildest years. I'd take a beating before I'd commit suicide. But, at the time and at that point, the pressure was so great; the common reality wasn't there anymore. It was gone. I didn't care. I didn't care about nothing that was standing before me. I just wanted out." After advancing on the police officers, he was shot five times. Three bullets struck him in the chest and one in the groin, and one passed through his hand and struck him in the groin. The offender stated that the first several rounds that struck him "felt like bee stings" and only tended to enrage him. But by the time he reached the front of the building, he had become incapacitated. While being transported to the hospital, the offender told emergency medical technicians, "Let me die; don't try to save me." He pled guilty to several counts of assault on a police officer while armed and was sentenced to a short prison term.

Investigation of this incident demonstrated that the elements of an attempted suicide by cop were present. Therefore, the case would merit the appropriate classification as an attempted suicide by cop.

Case # 2: The Officer's Perspective

The officer learned that an offender wanted on a misdemeanor warrant for writing bad checks was at the storage lot of a private towing company. The officer responded to the location, properly identified the offender, and placed him under arrest. As the officer attempted to handcuff the offender, a struggle ensued. The offender gained possession of the officer's weapon and immediately fired one round, which struck the officer in the chest. The officer attempted to flee the area, but the offender fired four more times, wounding him in the thigh, arm, leg, and back. The officer fell to the ground.

The offender ran to the front of the premises, where he previously had parked a motor vehicle occupied by his girlfriend and her small child. As the offender neared the vehicle, a second officer, with his service weapon drawn, came around the corner of the building. The officer repeatedly told the offender to drop his gun. The offender responded by placing it in his mouth. Shortly thereafter, the offender removed the gun from his mouth and pointed it at the officer, who continued to repeat his earlier commands. On hearing numerous sirens converging on the crime scene, the offender dropped the handgun and was arrested without further incident. The first officer was transported to the hospital and eventually recovered from his wounds.

Case #2: The Offender's Perspective

The offender went to the storage lot to retrieve his motor vehicle, when he was approached by the officer. He felt relieved when the officer advised him that his arrest concerned a misdemeanor because he believed that authorities in another jurisdiction wanted him for a felony parole violation. He willingly went along with the officer because he assumed that he could post bond for the lesser offense. He stated that he had no intention of harming the officer, but when he asked the officer to let him go to the front of the premises and tell his girlfriend where he would be taken, the officer refused. This made him angry because he had been under a lot of pressure. He recently had lost his job and had fallen behind on his bills. As a result, he had moved out of his apartment and in with a friend. He had incurred a lot of debt, and his car had been repossessed. Further, he had violated probation by leaving the jurisdiction where he had been convicted. He left the area believing that his parole was going to be revoked for failing to make restitution as ordered by the court. His financial problems had created a "snowball effect," and he felt he was in a "no-win" situation. He said that the arresting officer seemed "not to care about me," which caused him to become very angry.

After taking the officer's weapon and shooting him five times, the offender attempted to flee. He intended to escape the shooting scene but encountered the second officer, who pointed a handgun in his direction and began yelling commands. The offender ignored the officer's command to drop the weapon, describing the confrontation as a "standoff" and stating that he felt the officer would shoot him if he complied. At that point, the offender knew that he could not escape the scene. He was very confused and later said, "I knew the officer out back was going to die. I thought I have nothing to live for now. I don't want to spend the rest of my life in jail or the death penalty. I've thrown everything away that I've tried so hard to build, and I put the gun in my mouth. And, I was going to commit suicide at that point." The offender realized that his girlfriend's small child could see him. The child and her mother were both crying and asking him not to commit suicide. The offender stated that he could not bring himself to do it with a small child looking on. The offender removed the gun from his mouth and pointed it at the police officer, who still was telling him to drop the weapon. The offender said, "I was convinced that as soon as I went to do that, I would be shot. But, to this day, he didn't shoot me, and I don't know why." The offender started walking backward when he heard numerous sirens closing in on the scene. He stated that he felt escape would be impossible, so he laid his handgun on the ground and surrendered.

Evidence of ambivalence often occurs in both completed and attempted suicides. "Hesitation cuts," surface wounds, and the ingestion of insufficient volumes of medication or poison all commonly occur. In this case, both the offender's decision to commit suicide by cop and his desire to live took place within in an extremely brief period of time, each triggered by the circumstances of a quickly unfolding series of events.

This represented a complex case. The offender initially considered only fleeing from the first officer. However, when escape became impossible, he wanted to end his life. Without statements from both the offender and his girlfriend, investigators could not have determined or even recognized that this would constitute a properly classified attempted suicide by cop incident (see Figure 13.2).

FIGURE 13.2

A man, armed with what would subsequently be learned were unloaded guns, confronted Chicago police officers. When the man refused to drop his guns and threatened to kill the officers, he was shot and killed.

(AP/Wide World Photos)

Indicators of an SbC

The indicators of a potential SbC include the following:

- As the subject of a self-initiated hostage or a barricade situation, he refuses to negotiate with authorities.
- He has just killed a significant other in his life, especially if the victim was a child or the subject's mother.
- He demands that he be killed by the police.
- He sets a deadline for the authorities to kill him.
- He has recently learned that he has a life-threatening illness or disease.
- He indicates an elaborate plan for his own death, one that has taken both prior thought and preparation.
- He says he will only "surrender" (in person) to the officer in charge, such as the chief or the sheriff.
- He indicates he wants to "go out in a big way."
- He presents no demands that include his escape or freedom.
- He comes from a low socioeconomic background.
- He provides the authorities with a "verbal will."
- He appears to be looking for a manly or macho way to die.
- He has recently given away money or personal possessions.
- He has a criminal record indicating past assaultive behavior.
- He has recently experienced one or more traumatic events in his life that affect him, his family, or his career.
- He expresses feelings of hopelessness and helplessness.

Although this list is not all-inclusive, the presence of one or more of these indicators will help identify a person who is depressed and/or suicidal. A combination of these indicators should be considered evidence of a possible SbC, especially if this individual confronts the authorities in a way that could bring about his own death.

Police Officers as Victims

Harvey Schlossberg, retired director of psychological services for the New York Police Department, indicates that an SbC shooting is often tantamount to a "psychological assault" on the officer involved in the shooting. When an officer determines that the suspect's weapon is inoperative or that the suspect is otherwise responsible for a confrontation to bring about his or her death at the hands of the authorities, the officer may question his own reaction to this confrontation.

Society may be quick to identify the dead SbC suspect as the victim in this incident, when the real victim is the officer forced into the situation by a suicidal person. We must be equally quick to provide the individual and departmental support needed by the victim officer in such circumstances. The officer must be made to understand that his or her actions were ethically correct and professionally justified.[59]

Critical Thinking Question

1. Discuss the effects that a suicide by cop might have on the officers involved.

CRITICAL INCIDENT STRESS

A **critical incident** is any crisis situation that causes emergency personnel, family members, or bystanders to respond with immediate or delayed stress-altered physical, mental, emotional, psychological, or social coping mechanisms and that may result from witnessing human suffering beyond the normal range. A critical incident can be a recognized disaster, such as an airplane crash or a hotel fire; an act of nature, such as an earthquake or a tornado; or any other event involving death, injury, destruction, and disruption.[60] There have been a number of such incidents in recent years, such as the 1992 bombing of the Alfred P. Murrah Federal Building in Oklahoma City, Oklahoma, and the terrorist attacks of September 11, 2001. In all these events, bodies were crushed and dismembered, many were cremated, and many more victims were critically injured. In the destruction of the World Trade Center, many of the victims were also police officers and firefighters. The global community was stunned. Sympathy and support poured out for the victims—living and dead.

In 2005 the worst natural disaster that ever hit the United States, Hurricane Katrina, devastated the city of New Orleans. Its officers found themselves in the position not only of being first responders but also of being the victims of the hurricane. This created tremendous pressures and stressors on the officers. There is little question these will have long-term, devastating psychological effects on some of the officers, based in part on their personal losses as well as the human tragedies they witnessed. (see Figure 13.3)

The people who generally provide emergency care are emergency medical technicians and paramedics, firefighters, and police officers. They often incorporate the paradoxical personality traits of resilient survivors. These traits include a commitment to important values, a sense of personal control, a capability for and understanding of personal limitations, a perception of crisis as challenge, and courage and caution. First responders may be trained or untrained bystanders who try to the best of their ability to help at the scene.

In The News

Officers Tell of Pain and Pressure Related to Hurricane Katrina

Police officers in New Orleans were under unprecedented strain during the aftermath of Hurricane Katrina in 2005. Officers with the New Orleans Police Department were exposed to multiple layers of emotional and physical trauma as they fought to rescue citizens from rooftops, wade through fetid water to help others, and keep the peace among a population that was tired, angry, and desperate.

Many officers abandoned the force due to the immediate stress that their jobs brought on, in combination with losing their own homes and family members. Those who stayed were concerned about whether they could be paid for their work during the hurricane or if they would lose their jobs if the city shut down for repairs. Although officers were offered counseling and given vacations, many felt that the emotional effects of the disaster would linger indefinitely. Two officers were reported to have committed suicide in the wake of the storm.

Source: Joseph B. Treater and John Desantis, "With Some Now at the Breaking Point, Officers Tell of Pain and Pressure," *New York Times,* September 6, 2005.

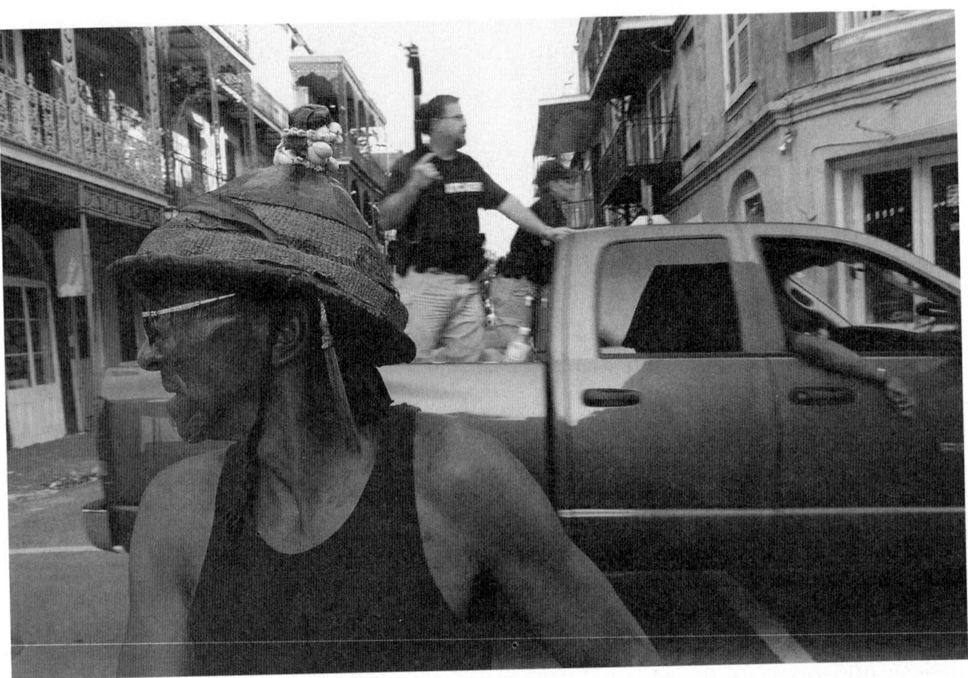

FIGURE 13.3

New Orleans Police officers in a pick-up truck patrol the French Quarter after Hurricane Katrina devastated the city—at the forefront a citizen looks on in disbelief. The officers were also traumatized by the loss of their homes and family members.

(© Marko Georgiev/The New York Times)

Posttraumatic Stress Disorder

People involved in a critical incident may be at risk to develop **posttraumatic stress disorder** and pathological grief reactions (see Table 13.5). The reactions to critical incidents involve the general system stress response with predictable symptomatology and more individualistic response patterns. As discussed earlier,[61] the alarm reaction to a situation of high emotional stress invokes mobilization of the body's resources to cope with the agent of stress. If adaptation or effective resistance is not possible, the unresolved distress reaction may manifest itself physically and psychologically

TABLE 13.5 Symptoms of Posttraumatic Stress Disorder

PHYSICAL REACTIONS	EMOTIONAL REACTIONS	COGNITIVE REACTIONS
■ Headaches	■ Anxiety	■ Debilitating flashbacks
■ Muscle aches	■ Fear	■ Repeated visions of the incident
■ Sleep disorders	■ Guilt	■ Nightmares
■ Changed appetite	■ Sadness	■ Slowed thinking
■ Decreased interest in sexual activity	■ Anger	■ Difficulty making decisions and solving problems
■ Impotence	■ Irritability	■ Disorientation
	■ Feelings of being lost and unappreciated	■ Lack of concentration
	■ Withdrawal	■ Memory lapses

SOURCE: Arthur W. Kureczka, "Critical Incident Stress," *FBI Law Enforcement Bulletin* 65, no. 2/3 (February-March 1996): 15.

FIGURE 13.4

A police officer weeps as he enters a church to attend the funeral service for a fellow officer who was killed in the line of duty.
(Randi Anglin/The Image Works)

(see Figure 13.4). Some physical reactions include gastrointestinal, respiratory, or cardiovascular distress or chronic fatigue. Some psychological reactions include anxiety, irritability, depression and moodiness, numbing of affect, involuntary flashbacks, and recurrent dreams. One researcher has concluded[62] that the predominant styles of response to perceived stress are direct action, rationalization with stressor avoidance, and passive acceptance. People who prefer direct coping act to alter the sources of stress; they provide emergency interventions as appropriate for their skills, participate in disaster debriefing or seek psychological counseling, and actively reconstruct their personal, family, and social lives. People who use indirect coping may try to alter the perceived significance of the stressor event.

Some dysfunctional strategies that reduce short-term severity contribute to the intensity of long-term crisis reactions. These include chemical coping, markedly increased environmental and interpersonal vigilance, a flight into activity, increased personal cynicism or interpersonal hostility, and sexual hyperactivity or incapacity. A variety of traditional psychological defense mechanisms, such as denial, regression, reaction formation, intellectualization, and rationalization, may be used. Personality factors that may make an individual more susceptible to posttraumatic stress disorder symptomatology include higher levels of anxiety, chronic or reactive apathy or depression, overt interpersonal hostility or repressed anger, and an experiential history of learned helplessness. A higher level of anxiety may occur as a reaction to trauma events perceived as central stressors, events that embody the loss of self-esteem, symbolically suggest the loss of a significant other, or have components that make horror personal.

Emotional Response to Critical Incidents

Critical incident participants respond with predictable, systematic stress reactions during each phase of the event. Although wide individual variation in behavior may occur in a critical incident, victims often respond during the initial impact phase with disorientation, shock, confusion, apathy, and emotional liability. Emergency responders attempt to assess the scene and the extent of the disaster, prepare and deliver search-and-rescue operations, provide needed intervention, and prevent escalation in physical and human terms. In the recoil phase, victims attempt to cooperate with emergency personnel and may express altruism and gratitude to the extent of minimizing their own injuries.[63] Survivors may harbor feelings of resentment toward those spared serious loss or toward caregivers. Many suffer feelings of self-blame with accompanying depression. They may transfer feelings of anger, originating from the emergency situation, into hostility toward significant others. For some individuals, these feelings will be expressed as suicidal or homicidal attempts.

In the postdisaster phase, civilian and emergency responders may manifest survivor euphoria and survivor guilt. They may deal with the crisis by participation in physical and psychological reconstruction efforts or may show posttraumatic stress disorder symptomatology. Commonly observed postdisaster stress disorder syndrome includes recurrent thoughts, dreams, or classically conditioned emotional trauma responses. Participants may manifest emotional numbness or marked agitation, initial apathy, depression with accompanying sadness, negative cognitions, learned helplessness responses, low self-esteem, and even suicide. The survivor may show hypervigilance, feelings of imminent danger, and conscious or unconscious re-enactment behaviors. A variety of other symptoms may be present, depending on the individual's characteristic coping style.

Critical Incident Debriefing

It is advisable that, after a disaster, a formal debriefing for involved emergency personnel be arranged within 24 to 48 hours. Debriefings may be restricted to emergency personnel but can also include people such as bystanders, family members, classmates of victims, coworkers and supervisory personnel, and those directly involved in or affected by the incident. Some differences in procedures and concerns

Quick Facts

Available Critical Stress-Management Training Programs

Critical stress management training programs are offered to police departments around the country by several non-profit agencies, such as the International Critical Incident Stress Foundation (ICISF), as well as some for-profit organizations. These programs emphasize the process of educating, preventing or mitigating the effects from exposure to an abnormal or highly unusual event. A comprehensive program includes preventive, educational, and informational programs for emergency service workers and police, including topics such as the following:

- On-scene support
- Advice to command
- Demobilization services
- Formal debriefings
- Resource referral services
- Family/loved one support services
- Support to emergency management
- Support to employee assistance programs
- Community awareness

Source: International Critical Incident Stress Foundation.

will be mandated by the constituency and the specific nature of the event. Separate debriefings are advisable for identifiably coherent groups, such as care providers and the families of deceased victims.

The appropriate use of critical incident stress debriefing procedures, crisis intervention techniques, and grief therapy, coupled with referral to traditional therapies when necessary, can aid in resolving issues related to critical incident crisis care.

Critical Thinking Questions

1. What might police agencies do to prepare for the effects of critical incident stress on officers?
2. Describe how posttraumatic stress might affect a police officer.
3. Why should police agencies utilize critical incident debriefing?

STRESS AND THE FEMALE POLICE OFFICER

Most of the early research on police officer stress focused on male officers. This is not surprising when one considers that law enforcement positions were filled almost exclusively with men up until the 1970s. The literature that does exist on female officers' stress tends to compare the performance of male and female officers or to measure male attitudes toward females.[64] Starting in the mid to late 1970s, the gender gap in police positions started to close. For example, women make up 14.3 percent of sworn law enforcement positions among municipal, county, and state law enforcement agencies with 100 or more sworn officers.[65] However, despite this modest progress, it has been suggested that female officers still face not only the same stressors as their male counterparts but also some others that are unique to them. We know that in the past this has been true. For example, not too many years ago, it was common for police administrators to dismiss the notion that women could adequately perform functions normally falling within the exclusive domain of male officers, such as patrol work, non-family-related crime investigations, SWAT teams, and motorcycle riding. Legislative, administrative, and judicial action has long since resolved the question of whether women should be permitted to perform these functions, and women have put to rest the questions about their ability to handle these tasks. There is ample empirical evidence to support the proposition that carefully selected and carefully trained females can be as effective as police officers as carefully selected and carefully trained males. This, however, is not meant to suggest that women have been universally and enthusiastically accepted by their male counterparts.[66] For example, in the past the first assignment for police women, like their male counterparts, was in the operating units, which traditionally were comprised exclusively of men. These women faced certain psychological pressures that would not be encountered by men or, for that matter, by women who would follow in their footsteps months or even years later. The first female officers performed their duties in an atmosphere of disbelief on the part of their supervisors and peers in their ability to deal physically and emotionally with the rigors of street work, particularly patrol functions. It must be remembered that peer acceptance is one of the greatest pressures operating within the police organization.[67] The desire to be identified as a "good officer" is a strong motivating force, and a failure to achieve that goal in one's eyes and in the eyes of one's peers can have a devastating and demoralizing effect.

For the rookie female officer, attaining the approval of her peers can be an even more frustrating task than it is for her male counterparts. As is true for her male counterparts, she must overcome her doubts about her own ability to perform her duties effectively, but unlike her male counterpart, she must also overcome the prejudice stemming from societal influences depicting the female as the "weaker sex" in every respect.[68] Also, unlike her male counterpart, she will very likely receive little support from her family, friends, and perhaps even her husband or other close male companions. Thus, she experiences additional stresses when she chooses a career in law enforcement that would not be imposed on men.

Studies of Male and Female Officers

As previously suggested, the majority of early studies on police stress used only male subjects because women filled a very small number of law enforcement positions. The early research involving women in law enforcement that does exist consists generally of comparative studies of performance between males and females or measures of males' attitudes toward females.

A 1973 study by Bloch and Anderson[69] in Washington, D.C., found that men and women performed in generally the same manner when on patrol. The women handled the same types of calls and had similar results in handling violent citizens. Citizens showed the same level of respect for both male and female officers. The women were found to have a less aggressive style of policing and were better able to defuse potentially violent situations. The male patrol officers and superior officers, however, expressed negative attitudes toward women. The male officers believed that they were better able to handle violent situations and rated the women as less competent, stating that they preferred not to work with the women.

Another study, done in St. Louis County, Missouri, in 1975 by Sherman, arrived at a similar conclusion.[70] The women were found to be equally effective as their male counterparts in handling calls with violent citizens. The study, along with the department's performance evaluations, showed that the performance of the women was no different from that of the men. The men, however, had some of the same negative attitudes toward the women as in the Washington, D.C., study. Neither of these studies addressed the question of stress in the female officer. One could infer that the attitudes of the male officers would be reflected in their interaction with female officers, and those experiences in turn would cause additional stress for female officers. However, the studies did not address this question.

A study done by Schwartz and Schwartz in 1981 found that the major stress in female officers was lack of support within the organization.[71] They found that women were subjected to harsher treatment than men and received little support from management and supervisors. There were also no assistance programs made available specifically for women.

In 1982, Glaser and Saxe found six psychological stressors that affect women officers: (1) doubts about competence and self-worth in doing a traditionally male job; (2) lack of support from men both on and off the job; (3) the need to develop greater assertiveness and authority in voice and stature; (4) inappropriate expectations regarding physical training, odd hours, and a quasi-military environment; (5) an inability to work 15-hour days and still maintain a household; and (6) a necessity to develop new defense mechanisms for stress that were more appropriate to law enforcement.[72]

In a 1983 study, Wexler and Logan found that women officers experienced the same stressors as their male counterparts, along with stressors unique to them. Wexler and Logan developed a category of four female-related stressors: negative attitudes of male officers, group blame, responses of other men, and lack of role models.[73] In this study, 80 percent of the women surveyed reported experiencing stress from negative attitudes of male officers. These negative attitudes included both official and individual harassment. The official harassment included having no separate locker rooms and being physically locked out of the police station. Types of individual harassment included questions about the women's sexual orientation, refusal to talk to the women, and blatant anti-women comments.[74]

A study done by Norvell, Hill, and Murrin found that higher stress levels in women officers resulted from dissatisfaction with their coworkers.[75] Overall, however, the women did not have higher stress levels or lower job satisfaction than the male officers. The males seemed to have more stress, more daily hassles, and greater emotional exhaustion than the females, and they had greater job dissatisfaction than the females.

Daum and Johns conducted a study specifically targeted at women officers. Their study showed that women did not feel they received enough acceptance and credit for the job they were doing. The women surveyed felt ostracized from the males and felt they were being evaluated according to "male" criteria. Most did not, however, regret the decision to enter law enforcement.[76]

Female Law Enforcement Officer Stress Today

To assess more accurately whether the stresses facing women entering law enforcement today are still greater and somewhat different from those exerted on their male counterparts, two Florida law enforcement agencies were studied. The agencies were the Largo Police Department, which is a medium-size municipal agency in Pinellas County, Florida, and the Pinellas County Sheriff's Office, which is a large, urban county agency serving the Clearwater/St.Petersburg area.

All the female patrol officers and patrol sergeants in each agency were surveyed, along with a proportionate, matched sample of male officers. The males were matched to the females by age, years of service, and rank. Fifty-six subjects participated.

Researchers suspected prior to conducting the study that the findings would show that females continue to experience stresses unique to them. However, the results showed this not to be the case. As a matter of fact, the findings of this survey indicated that male and female patrol personnel in these two agencies experienced similar levels of stress. In addition, the female officers of these two agencies no longer experienced unique, gender-related stressors. It seems that, over the years, as both law enforcement and the community at large have become accustomed to the idea of women in law enforcement, that female officers, at least with these two agencies, experienced less stress than their earlier counterparts. As law enforcement has become accepted as an appropriate career for woman, they no longer have the personal stressors associated with negative attitudes from family and on many eases high raiking female or from men they are dating. In addition, young female officers now have significant and in many cases high ranking female role models within their agencies. Women officers now feel the same stress associated with the job as their male counterparts. It would also seem that, as both males and females take more equal roles in family raising, the stress that female officers once experienced when handling dual roles has lessened.

The highest levels of stress experienced by male and female officers seemed to be involved with critical incidents, such as the violent death of an officer in the line of duty (94.4 percent), the suicide of an officer who was a close friend (94.4 percent), the taking of a life (87.2 percent) or shooting of someone (83.6 percent) in the line of duty, and dismissal (83.8 percent). Going through a divorce or separation (74.1 percent) also ranked high, along with responding to a scene involving the death of a child (73.8 percent). Interestingly, these findings followed the same pattern found by Sewell.[77] In Sewell's study, officers rated the following as the five most stressful events they could experience: violent death of a partner in the line of duty, dismissal, the taking of a life in the line of duty, the shooting of someone in the line of duty, and the suicide of an officer who is a close friend.

These findings underscore the need for department heads to be sure that all personnel involved in any critical incident be given immediate mandatory critical incident stress debriefing and be allowed to continue in counseling for as long as it takes the officer to recover from the incident. Officers who are dealing with a divorce or separation or who are recovering from the death of a close friend should also have counseling available to them to help with the recovery process.

Critical Thinking Question

1. In the early 1980s, studies found that female officers identified a number of stressors not experienced by their male counterparts. Why do you think recent studies have found no significant difference in the stressors affecting male and female officers?

POLICE DOMESTIC VIOLENCE

Given the stressful nature of police work, it is not surprising that officers sometimes have difficulty keeping what happened to them at work separate from their home lives. "Leave it at the office" is a common admonition to officers. While the intent of this message is clear, it is often hard to do so consistently.[78]

It is not known how many acts of **domestic violence** police officers commit in their own homes. The reasons for the non-reporting of such incidents include victims with low esteem who think they "got what they deserved," threats from their attackers of more severe physical harm if the victims do call the police, and the belief that fellow officers will not take action against "one of their own."

Early Warning and Intervention

Of critical concern to departments is how to screen and select new officers to minimize the risk of hiring officers who may engage in domestic violence.[79] To understand the connection among the various forms of family violence, it is essential to investigate whether a recruit has a history or likelihood of engaging in child abuse, domestic violence, or elder abuse. The process of investigating recruits must be handled in two stages: pre-employment screening and investigation and postconditional offer of employment.

Pre-employment Screening and Investigation

All candidates should be asked about any history of perpetrating child abuse, domestic violence, or elder abuse and past arrests or convictions for such crimes. They should be asked whether they have ever been the subject of a civil protective order. If the candidate answers positively to any of these questions or the department uncovers any information in the background check that indicates a history of violence, the candidate should be screened out of the hiring process.

During the background investigation, a check should be made for restraining orders issued in any jurisdiction where the candidate has lived.

Postconditional Offer of Employment

If the candidate's background investigation does not indicate a history of child abuse, domestic violence, or elder abuse, the department should proceed with a psychological examination, which should include indicators of violent or abusive tendencies. This portion of the screening process should be conducted by an experienced clinical psychologist or psychiatrist.

Zero Tolerance Policy

Departments must make it clear to all officers that the department has a zero tolerance policy on domestic violence, and the department should share this information with

In The News

Tacoma Police Department Develops Domestic Violence Program in the Face of Tragedy

The Tacoma, Washington, Police Department was forced to examine its policies pertaining to domestic violence among officers when its chief of police, David Brame, killed his wife and then himself during a dispute in 2003. The new policy is divided into five sections, including response to domestic violence calls involving officers, prevention of abuse, investigations, examination of applicants to the police department, and assistance for victims. The program differs from other police domestic violence programs in that it focuses attention on the victim and ensures that he or she is put in touch with authorities other than the police department. According to the department, this is important because police responding to the call may know the officer perpetrating the violence and should not be privy to information regarding the location of the victim.

Tacoma's program also requires that the supervisors of all officers, including the police chief, be notified immediately of any domestic violence incidents and initiate both criminal and administrative investigations of the officers. However, the program is not considered a zero tolerance policy. Although the International Association of Police Chiefs recommend a zero tolerance program, Tacoma officials believe that zero tolerance puts the victim at risk by exacerbating stress on the offender, sending the officer back to commit further acts of violence.

Tacoma's policy also focuses extensively on weeding out potential abusers during the hiring process, as well as on providing education on the effects of police work on relationships. Although Tacoma officials believe that the new policy provides a full spectrum of domestic violence responsiveness, some critics argue that domestic violence is merely a symptom of other problems, such as depression and posttraumatic stress disorder, and should be treated as such to maximize prevention.

Source: "Tacoma Unveils New Focus on DV by Officers," *Law Enforcement News*, April 2004, 10 and 14.

family members of the officer. Departments should look to develop a line of communication directly with the domestic partners of recruits and officers. For example, a department can hold a family orientation day prior to graduation. Family members should be provided with instructions on whom to contact within the department if any problems arise. The dual purpose of establishing such contact is to underscore the department's zero tolerance policy, even with the police chief, and to provide victims with an avenue for direct communication with a department employee who is trained in handling such calls.

Department Responsibilities

An individual or a family member of an officer may recognize early indicators of potential violence, such as issues of power and control. The power and control may take the forms of restricting contact with family and friends, requiring the partner to turn over his or her paycheck, and limiting activities outside the home. Victims may communicate their concerns "informally" at first, such as with calls to an officer's supervisor. These informal contacts must be treated with care, since this is a critical opportunity for a department to provide intervention using early intervention and prevention strategies. The model policy calls for a formal system of documenting, sharing, and responding to information from concerned partners and family members.

Departments need to provide officers and their families with non-punitive avenues of support and assistance before an incident of domestic violence occurs. Departments must establish procedures for making confidential referrals to internal or external counseling services with expertise in domestic violence. These referrals can be made on the request of an officer or family members or in response to observed warning signs.

Officers will not be entitled to confidentiality anytime they or family members disclose to any member of the department that an officer has engaged in domestic violence. Confidentiality should be extended to partners or family members who report an officer as a matter of safety. A report of such criminal conduct must be treated as an admission or a report of a crime and investigated, both criminally and administratively.

Departments must understand that other officers may become involved in domestic violence situations by engaging in inappropriate activities that interfere with cases against fellow officers who are engaged in such acts as stalking, intimidation, harassment, or surveillance of victims, witnesses, and/or family members of victims or witnesses. If this occurs, these officers must be investigated and sanctioned and/or charged criminally where appropriate.

Supervisory Responsibilities

Typically, an abusive person engages in certain patterns of behavior. These may include repeated actions of increasing control directed at his or her partner preceding an incident of physical or criminal violence.

The early indicators of potential violence are not limited to home life; the department may detect warning signs in an officer's behavior prior to a domestic violence incident. Supervisors must receive specific training on warning signs and potential indicators of violent or controlling tendencies. Warning signs that may indicate a likelihood of violent behavior include increased use of force in arrest situations, drug/alcohol problems, frequent tardiness or absences, verbal disputes, physical altercations, and other aggressive behavior.

When supervisors become aware of a pattern of controlling or abusive behavior exhibited by officers, the supervisors have a responsibility to document the information and notify their immediate ranking supervisor, who will then inform the chief in accordance with the department's chain of command. After making proper notification, supervisors should inform officers that the behaviors have been documented. A recommendation can be made to officers that they participate voluntarily in a counseling or support program to address the identified issue or behavior.

In cases in which behavior violates departmental policy, a department can seize the opportunity to mandate participation in a batterer intervention program in addition to any appropriate sanctions.

Early prevention and intervention strategies employed by a department at this phase of the continuum have tremendous potential not only to reduce future violence but also to save victims' lives and officers' careers. The services that can be made available includes the following:

- Employee assistance program referral (discussed in greater detail later in this chapter)
- Internal professional counseling (police psychologist)
- External professional counseling (contract/referral)
- Advocacy support from local agencies
- Peer support program (with clear reporting and confidentiality guidelines)

The department will need to ensure that the quality and expertise of these resources are sound. Collaboration with local domestic violence victim advocacy organizations is recommended.

Police Officer Responsibilities

As part of a department's zero tolerance policy, all officers need to understand their responsibility to report definitive knowledge they have concerning domestic violence on the part of an officer. Departments must be prepared to investigate and possibly sanction and/or charge criminally any officer who fails to report such knowledge or to cooperate with an investigation.

In addition, all officers need to know they will be investigated and sanctioned and/or charged criminally if they engage in activities such as stalking, surveillance, intimidation, or harassment of victims or witnesses in an attempt to interfere with investigations of other officers accused of domestic violence.

In the event that an officer is the subject of a criminal investigation and/or a protective or restraining order, the officer is responsible for informing his or her supervisor and providing copies of the order and timely notice of court dates regardless of the jurisdiction.

Incident Response Protocols

A department's response to 911 calls involving police officer domestic violence immediately sets the tone for how a situation will be handled throughout the remainder of the continuum. Further, the unique dynamics between the offending and responding officers (e.g., collegiality and rank differential) often make on-scene decisions extremely difficult.

A department must take the following actions, all of which are critical steps in responding to allegations of domestic abuse by police officers:

Communications officer/dispatcher documentation—When a call or report of domestic violence involves a police officer, the dispatcher should have a standing directive to document the call and immediately notify both the on-duty patrol supervisor and the chief of police. This directive ensures that key command personnel receive the information and prevents the call from being handled informally.

Patrol response—Any officer arriving at the scene of a domestic violence call or incident involving a police officer must immediately request the presence of a supervisor at the scene, regardless of the involved officer's jurisdiction.

On-scene supervisor response—The on-scene supervisor has responsibilities for the following:

- Securing the scene and collecting evidence
- Ensuring an arrest is made where probable cause exists
- Removing weapons in the event of an arrest
- Considering victim safety
- Notifying the police chief or sheriff if the incident occurs outside the officer's jurisdiction

The on-duty supervisor must respond to the call and assume all on-scene decision making. Leaving the decision making to officers of lesser or equal rank to the suspect officer puts the responding officer in a difficult situation. The presence of a ranking officer on the scene resolves this problem. The policy recommends that, in police officer domestic violence cases, no fewer than two officers, with at least one of senior rank to the accused officer, be present. This is also the case when serving arrest warrants and civil protective orders.

Crime scene documentation—Recanting or reluctant witnesses and victims are not uncommon when domestic violence occurs. Police on the scene of a 911 call must take specific actions to document all evidence, including color photographs/videotape of injuries, overturned/damaged furniture, interviews of neighbors and family members, and threats from the officer. Documentation of this evidence will be essential to the successful prosecution of the case with or without the victim's presence in court.

Arrest decisions—Policies on arrest for domestic violence incidents vary among state, county, and local jurisdictions. In all cases, responding officers should base arrest decisions on probable cause. When a crime has been committed, an arrest will be made, as in all other cases. The on-scene supervisor is responsible for ensuring an arrest is made if probable cause exists or for submitting written documentation to explain why an arrest was not made. All officers need sufficient training to enable them to determine which party is the primary (i.e., dominant) aggressor in domestic violence situations. Every effort should be made to determine who is the primary aggressor to avoid the unwarranted arrest of victims.

Weapon removal—If an arrest is made, the on-scene supervisor will relieve the accused officer of his or her service weapon. Some police officers may have several weapons at their home. Where multiple weapons are present, removing only the service weapon of the officer leaves the victim entirely vulnerable to further violence. While federal, state, and local laws vary on how and when such weapons can be removed, police have broad powers to remove weapons in certain circumstances, particularly if an arrest is being made. Where application of the law is questionable, the on-scene supervisor should suggest that the officer in question voluntarily relinquish all firearms. The supervisor can also simply ask victims if they want to remove any weapons from the home for safekeeping by the department. When no arrest has been made, the on-scene supervisor should consider removing the accused officer's weapon as a safety consideration.

After weapons are removed, decisions need to be made about how long they will or can be held. Where court orders of protection are in place, these orders may also affect decisions on gun removal or seizure.

When the accused officer is the chief, director, or superintendent of the department, a specific protocol must be in place to document and report the incident to the individual who has direct oversight for the chief, director, or superintendent.

When police respond to a domestic violence incident involving an officer from another jurisdiction, all responding officers, investigators, and supervisors will follow the same procedures to be followed if responding to a domestic violence complaint involving an officer from their own department. The on-scene supervisor will notify the chief of police from the accused officer's department verbally as soon as possible and in writing within 24 hours of the call.

Departments may be faced with domestic violence situations where the victim is a police officer. If this occurs, standard domestic violence response and investigation procedures should be followed. The department should take steps to protect the privacy of the officer and make referrals to confidential counseling services. The department should not allow the reported incident to impact negatively on the assignments and evaluation of the victimized officer.

If both the victim and the offender in a domestic violence situation are police officers, the protocols established by the department should remain substantially the same. Safety of the victim should be the paramount concern. In the event that an order of protection has been issued, a department will need to make careful decisions concerning work assignments for accused officers pending administrative and criminal investigations. Gun removal in this situation becomes extremely complex. In the development of the policy, individual departments should seek legal guidance to ensure that the rights of all concerned are protected.

Department follow-up—The department or supervisor should require a debriefing of all officers involved in a response to the scene of a police officer domestic violence case and may include communications officers. At the debriefing, the department's confidentiality guidelines should be reviewed. In addition, a command-level critical incident management review of every domestic violence case involving an officer should be conducted.

The department must take responsibility for conducting an assessment to determine the potential for further violence on the part of the accused officer. A specifically trained member of the command staff should review a checklist of risk factors with the accused officer. In addition, the evaluation should be supplemented by interviews with the victim, witnesses, and family members. Information gained from the assessment should be used to determine appropriate sanctions, safeguards, and referrals. The command officer assigned as the victim's principal contact should discuss the risk factors with the victim as part of safety planning.

Critical Thinking Questions

1. Do you think that police work attracts men with a propensity for violence toward women? Why or why not?
2. What barriers are there to identifying domestic violence among police officers?

RESPONDING TO STRESS

Some police officers think that stress is just "a fairy tale—something that those who can't hack it can blame for their problems." Thus, the first step is for officers to recognize that unchecked stress can cause them to be sick more frequently, to engage in self-destructive behaviors (such as substance abuse), to live life less fully, to lose their families, and simply to be more uncomfortable every day than they need to be. The second step for officers is to monitor their own bodies and actions for stress, even though this capacity for self-awareness and introspection is difficult for some people to develop. Simply put, officers need to be in touch with what they are feeling, to think about what they have said and done, and to ask, "Why?" The final step is to eliminate or reduce stress, the so-called **stress inoculation activities:**

- Exercising rigorously for 20 to 30 minutes at least three times per week
- Maintaining a proper diet, including minimizing the intake of foods high in salt and cholesterol
- Getting adequate rest—not drinking caffeine within five hours of going to bed and trying to get eight hours of sleep
- Developing leisure interests and hobbies, such as hiking, tying fishing flies, rock climbing, gardening, collecting stamps, writing poetry and fiction, learning a foreign language, and photography—in other words; learning new things that excite and refresh the mind
- Meditating and praying
- Avoiding maladaptive responses to stress, such as smoking and drinking
- Establishing support groups
- Developing a network of friends, including people outside the department
- Monitoring yourself; refer yourself for help before you have to be referred; you will avoid some problems, reduce others before they become entrenched, and get more out of the helping process
- Using relaxation techniques, such as biofeedback, yoga, progressive muscle relaxation, tai chi, imagery, and breathing exercises
- Making sure your career and other expectations are consistent with your actual situation[80]

Critical Thinking Question

1. What might a police agency do to encourage officers to engage in stress inoculation activities?

EMPLOYEE ASSISTANCE PROGRAMS

Although their evolution has been slow in development, a variety of employee assistance services are currently available within police departments.[81] The growth of **employee assistance programs (EAPs)** in the law enforcement field can be traced back to the early 1950s.[82] Many programs, such as those initiated in Boston, New York, and Chicago, were created to deal primarily with alcohol abuse.

In the 1970s, agencies such as the Los Angeles Sheriff's Office, the Chicago Police Department, (see Figure 13.5) and the San Francisco Police Department expanded their programs to include problems not related to alcohol. In 1980, mental health professionals began providing personal and job-related counseling services to FBI personnel. Mental health professionals were also used to assist FBI managers with a variety of employee-related matters. By 1986, many of the largest police departments in the United States had formed "stress units" or other sections to provide help for officers having personal or occupational difficulties. In the early 1990s, the U.S. Customs Service provided stress-management training for both its supervisory and its non-supervisory personnel throughout the country.[83] The majority of law enforcement agencies with 100 or more officers now have written policies regarding providing counseling assistance services for their officers.[84]

Benefits of Employee Assistance Programs

As the leaders and developers of an employee assistance program plan, implement, evaluate, and refine their program, it is critical not only to involve labor and management but also to facilitate cooperative and trusting relationships among all those involved. Identifiable, mutual, and cooperative tasks and activities are beneficial not only to labor and management but also to the EAP itself. The following are some noteworthy benefits deserving of special attention.

Increased probability of success—The active, mutual, and cooperative involvement of both labor and management with an employee assistance program increases the program's probability for success. This is important to the program.

Increased referrals—A well-run and effective employee assistance program will serve approximately 8 to 10 percent of the total number of individuals who have access to it (e.g., employees and their immediate family members). Achieving a rate such as this without full labor and management cooperation and involvement is very unlikely. An EAP must be postured to respond to the needs of its constituency group.

Joint training sessions—The training sessions typically conducted by EAP staff members are attended by representatives from both labor and management. This provides serendipitous opportunities for cooperative interaction on behalf of labor and management representatives, as well as on behalf of the EAP staff. For example, the EAP professional enjoys the opportunity to work with both supervisors from management and employee representatives in a non-crisis, non-problem-oriented situation; to train mixed intervention teams focusing on employee concerns; to educate and market the program; and above all to assist critical supervisory personnel on knowing how to assist troubled workers in recognizing they have a problem and recommending where to go for assistance. This is essential if seriously troubled employees are to be identified and helped.

Benefits to the Employee

In the ultimate sense, the vast majority of the previously discussed benefits of mutual cooperation and trust on behalf of labor and management will directly and indirectly result in benefits to employees. Of the numerous identifiable benefits to employees, the following five appear to be worthy of special attention:

A meaningful employee benefit—First of all, it is important to remember that the mere existence of a good EAP is a meaningful employee benefit. Moreover, those who are supported jointly by labor and management tend to be more efficient, more effective, and helpful to a larger proportion of the employees and their families who have access to them. EAPs with joint labor–management support also tend to facilitate the existence of other positive qualities within the agency (e.g., high morale), and with the existence of joint labor–management support, the longevity and continuance of the EAP assuredly is on more solid ground.

Help in response to one's "cry for help"—In most instances, it takes caring, trained, and cooperating individuals to recognize and helpfully respond to a hurting employee's cry for help. For example, many authorities in the field of alcoholism believe that people troubled with alcohol or other drugs suffer from a catch-22 situation. Part of them wants to hide their problem and not be found out, but another part wants to be identified and helped. When labor and management cooperatively and in trusting ways work together with an effective EAP, the latter alternative is more likely to be the effected outcome.

Stigma reduction—When labor and management jointly communicate and demonstrate that to be troubled is to be human, a much more trusting environment exists, and employees tend to feel more comfortable asking for and accepting help. It is not easy for employees and/or families to admit they need help. The cultural stigma that suggests people should be able to solve their own problems without help from others, especially among law enforcement personnel, can be a very powerful influence and may make people reluctant to seek assistance. However, when supervisors or peers recommend that employees seek assistance from the EAP, an altogether different atmosphere exists, and assistance is then more likely to be sought.

Feeling cared for as a person—No one advocates coddling, especially in the workplace. At the same time, however, employees do not like to feel as if they are "a dispensable tool" or "just a badge number." When employees have feelings like these, morale tends to go down, job satisfaction dwindles, and productivity often suffers. Nonetheless, in environments where labor, management, and the EAP cooperatively, trustingly, and mutually work together, employees are more apt to feel that others care about them as people. This attitude, in turn, tends to enhance morale, job satisfaction, and productivity.

Affordable access to help—One of the primary reasons that employees seek help early from an EAP is that they can afford to. Effective EAPs are well financed, at least to the extent that feared economic hardship is not an up-front deterrent to seeking help. Affordability, in terms of the perceptions of troubled employees, also means they can seek help without immediate fears that it might cost them their jobs (or benefits, opportunities for promotion, and so on). In an ideal EAP environment, troubled employees do not consider whether they can afford to seek help; they consider why they cannot afford not to seek help. It is hoped that their considerations produce the conclusion that seeking help is the best course.

The following is an example of a case handled by an EAP in one agency. A self-referred couple arrived to see the employee assistance program counselor. They requested to go into the session together. The husband was 30 years old, and the wife was 27. They had dated for four years before getting married and at the time had been married for seven and a half years and had one child, an 18-month-old son.

The husband was a college graduate, and his wife, who had a two-year junior college degree, was working as a medical secretary. When they sat down to talk with the counselor, both were very nervous and uncomfortable. Nonetheless, after an atmosphere of trust and acceptance was established and the purpose of the assessment sessions was explained, toward the end of the first session the husband volunteered that he had had an affair. He stated he felt relieved after he was "found out" (after about three months) but still felt guilty and responsible—not only for his wife's pain and hurt but for the feelings of the other woman as well. The wife explained she, indeed, did feel hurt and betrayed, and she felt very indignant in view of the fact that the other woman was a friend and coworker in the same medical complex where she was working.

Two days later, each of them went in for individual, one-hour sessions. She revealed that, before her husband's affair, she had been feeling down, caught in the trap of work and child care, and possibly not as attentive to herself as she had been previously. He expressed feelings of inadequacy as a provider. He believed he should have been further along in his career and generally felt quite frustrated. He also indicated he had not shared these feelings with his wife (seeing them as his problem).

At that juncture, it appeared clear to the counselor that, in the absence of other possible coexisting and/or confounding problems, they needed to see a marriage counselor to help them learn to communicate with each other more meaningfully and share with each other their feelings of inadequacy and being trapped. It is important to note that, in view of their having pulled apart from each other and his three-month affair, the counselor might have drawn a premature and inaccurate assessment that they were having "sexual boredom problems." Had this been the case, inappropriate treatment could have been recommended, and this would have been very unfortunate. Nonetheless, an accurate assessment was gleaned, an appropriate referral was made, and the couple's readiness for help was established by the counselor.

Through follow-up (with appropriate signed releases for follow-up information), the EAP counselor learned that the couple had seen a marriage therapist, had improved their interpersonal communication, and had regained the meaningfulness of their relationship that they both desired. Moreover, the husband was allowing himself to feel more adequate, and he was becoming more assertive as to his own needs. The wife became aware that she had not been taking care of herself and had not been assertive to her own needs. She joined an inexpensive spa and began feeling "less down and more attractive." She started communicating her needs and feelings to her husband; in the process, she received more attention from him and, importantly, was feeling more adequate.

This is somewhat of a typical marital situation that an EAP counselor may encounter. When clients with severe psychiatric problems, mental health concerns, and serious physical problems go to an EAP, the importance of thorough and accurate diagnosis; the use of appropriate medical and paramedical professionals, facilities, and centers in the community; and the facilitation of readiness for help can be even more demanding of the professional assessment and counseling skills of the case manager.[85,86]

Critical Thinking Question

1. Why are EAP programs a good investment for an employer?

CHICAGO POLICE DEPARTMENT'S

Professional Counseling Service

Employee Assistance Program

FOR FURTHER INFORMATION
CALL 747-5492 or
747-1371 (24 hours)

CONFIDENTIALITY

Officers and/or their family members may wonder if counseling sessions or contacts with our program are completely confidential, or will they become part of some department record which can be used against them in the future. The answer is **NO.**

All contacts with the Professional Counseling Service/Employee Assistance Program are held in the strictest confidence based on state and federal guidelines, related to client confidentiality and client privilege. (Rule 501 of the Federal Rules of Evidence, 13 June, 1996.)

Unlike facilities which rely on insurance payments, we are not required to record session notes or retain records for any purpose.

WHY SEEK COUNSELING?

Do you feel tense all the time? Is there someone you love who drinks too much? Are you experiencing marital problems?

You are not alone

Job pressures . . . finances...death of a loved one . . . marital difficulties . . . gambling . . . your son or daughter experimenting with drugs. There are countless factors which add stress to your life and may lead to these difficult situations in different ways.

Many people attempt to escape from their problems by turning to alcohol. Others begin to lose their temper and punch walls . . . or someone they love. Still others withdraw, feel it just is not worth it anymore, and sink into a deeper depression.

These responses don't relieve the problems—they create other, more serious ones.

Professional Counseling Service
407 South Dearborn–Suite 800
Chicago, IL 60605

But remember, you are not alone.

There is help.

THE PROFESSIONAL COUNSELING SERVICE

EMPLOYEE ASSISTANCE PROGRAM

The Chicago Police Department recognizes the unique demands placed upon its members, their families, and the connection between personal and professional life.

Thus, the Professional Counseling Service–Employee Assistance Program was established to provide all Department members and their families who desire assistance a *confidential* means to find solutions to a variety of problems.

The Professional Counseling Service–Employee Assistance Program is here to assist you.

SERVICES PROVIDED

The Professional Counseling Services–Employee Assistance Program offers a variety of assessment and counseling services including:

- INDIVIDUAL
- MARITAL
- FAMILY
- COUPLES
- REFERRAL FOR FINANCIAL COUNSELING
- STRESS MANAGEMENT TRAINING
- REFERRALS FOR DEATH AND BEREAVEMENT GROUPS
- FAMILY VIOLENCE ISSUES (Physical, Emotional and Verbal Violence)
- COUNSELING, ASSESSMENT AND REFERRAL FOR "TROUBLED TEENS"
- TRAUMATIC INCIDENT DEBRIEFING PROGRAM

FIGURE 13.5

Chicago Police Department's information brochure for its employee assistance program.

(Courtesy of Superintendent Terry G. Hillard and Sergeant Robert J. Delaney, Chicago Police Department)

ALCOHOL ASSISTANCE UNIT

Alcoholism is a devastating, progressive, fatal illness which can take a tremendous toll on the individual and their family members. The Alcohol Assistance Unit was established to provide a viable alternative, and linkage with treatment programs to effectively confront this disease and other addictions.

Trained sworn personnel are available to assist in every aspect of recovery.

The unit affords Department members and their families who have alcohol problems with a *confidential* objective and nonjudgmental resource to which they can go voluntarily for advice and assistance.

The Department recognizes alcoholism as an illness which negatively affects the major areas of a person's life such as health, family situations and work.

If any part of your life is negatively affected by alcohol or drugs, take advantage of this service.

Do it for yourself and those you love!

TRAUMATIC INCIDENT DEBRIEFING PROGRAM

The first thing that needs to be said about "trauma debriefing" is that *it is not counseling*. Officers do not need counseling for doing their job.

Trauma is a response to events which occur during an officer's tour of duty, which is shocking and disturbing. It does not mean that the officer's judgment is being called into question or that he/she is "falling apart."

What it does mean is that the officer should be paying special attention to how they are being affected by the impact of vulnerability to Post-Traumatic Stress Disorder, to which our officers may be prone to experience.

This service is also offered to members of an officer's family should they choose to participate. As with other services, there is

NO CHARGE.

WHO IS ELIGIBLE?

This free confidential service is available to all active Chicago Police Department members and their family members as well as retired sworn personnel.

Contacts with our office may be made anonymously for those seeking information about the program or any services but not yet ready to reveal their identity.

It is important to remember that if someone you care about has a problem, you also have a problem and should seek assistance for yourself.

FIGURE 13.5 (CONTINUED)

CHAPTER REVIEW

1. Discuss the concept of stress, as described by Selye and Basowitz.
   Selye describes stress as the body's non-specific response to any demand placed on it. Basowitz describes it as stimuli that are likely to produce disturbances in most people.
2. Describe the three stages of the general adaptation syndrome, as described by Selye.
   The first stage is the alarm stage. In this stage, the body perceives a threat, and releases hormones that produce an energizing effect on the body. The next stage, resistance, mobilizes the body's resources in order to deal with specific stressors and to adapt to the incident at hand. Finally, in the exhaustion stage, the body's ability to maintain resistance breaks down.
3. What are the major characteristics of a type A personality?
   The major characteristics of a type A personality are constant stress, a demanding nature, impatience, intensity, and difficulty relaxing.
4. Why are police officers more prone to stress than individuals in many other occupations?
   Police work is one of the few occupations in which an employee is continually asked to face physical danger and to put his or her life on the line. Also, police officers are constantly exposed to violence, cruelty, death, and aggression and are often required to make critical decisions in life-or-death situations.
5. Alcohol-related problems manifest themselves in police officers in a number of ways. What are they?

Some of the ways in which alcohol problems manifest themselves in police officers include high absentee rates immediately following days off, complaints of insubordination by supervisors, complaints by citizens of misconduct in the form of verbal and physical abuse, intoxication during working hours, involvement in traffic accidents while under the influence of alcohol, and reduced overall performance.

6. Describe some of the issues that police administrators must deal with in terms of drug use by police officers within their agencies.
Some of the issues police administrators must deal with in terms of drug use among police officers are within their agencies include defining departmental drug testing policies, anticipating employee and union reactions to these policies, determining appropriate disciplinary reactions to officers found to be using drugs, and determining the employer's responsibility in the rehabilitation of officers disabled due to drug use.

7. What are the three general principles defined by the courts in relation to random drug testing?
The first principle defined by the courts in relation to drug testing is that testing based on reasonable suspicion and when conducted randomly does not violate the federal Constitution. The second principle is that, although testing may not violate the federal Constitution, it may not be permissible in some states. The third principle is that, in states that have granted collective bargaining rights to police officers, drug testing must be submitted to the collective bargaining process before being implemented by the employer.

8. What are some of the psychological effects of steroid use?
Some of the psychological effects of steroid use include aggressive behavior, severe depression, visual and auditory hallucinations, sleep disorder, suicidal ideation, outbursts of anger, anorexia, psychomotor retardation, and irritability.

9. What are the most common factors related to police suicide?
One of the major factors related to police suicide is a sense of frustration and helplessness engendered by a gap between an officer's desire to help people and the reality that the public is often reticent to this. Other factors include ready access to firearms, domestic problems. alcohol abuse, and fear of separation from the close-knit police subculture, especially among police retirees.

10. What are some of the typical warning signs that an officer may be contemplating suicide?
Some of the warning signs are: recent loss; sadness; frustration; expressions of disappointment, loneliness, or grief: alienation; depression; complaints of physical pain or mental anguish; history of mental illness; and previous suicide attempts.

11. What are a supervisor's responsibilities regarding suicidal officers?
Supervisors should schedule interviews with officers who appear to be experiencing depression or who exhibit signs of sadness, hopelessness, or discouragement. During the interview, supervisors should closely observe body language and be aware of other behaviors that suggest an officer is suicidal. Supervisors should also look at an officer's personal history for events or influences that might exacerbate suicidal behavior. They should reassure a suicidal officer that help is available and reinforce their expectation that the officer should respond to their directions. Supervisors should ask specifically if the officer is suicidal and should be prepared to deal with the response in a manner that minimizes the chance of the officer following through on his or her threat or harming another. Finally, supervisors should refer the officer to a certified mental health professional and follow up to ensure that he or she is evaluated and receives continued help.

12. What sources of work satisfaction are stress reducers?
The first source of work satisfaction identified as being a stress reducer is providing assistance to citizens who are unable to help themselves. Another source of stress reduction

occurs when officers are able to resolve complex situations with their interpersonal skills. Officers also attribute positive feedback from citizens to work satisfaction. Peer-group support, as a result of police solidarity or from individual relationships with partners and other coworkers, is the final source of work satisfaction identified as being a stress reducer.

13. What are indicators of a potential suicide by cop?
The indicators of a potential suicide by cop include the refusal of a person who initiates a hostage or barricade situation to negotiate with authorities; a person who has just killed a significant other in his life, particularly a child or the subject's mother; a demand from the person that the police kill him; a deadline from the person for the police to kill him; a recent diagnosis of a life-threatening illness; indication that an elaborate plan for death has been prepared; statements that he will only surrender in person to the officer in charge; none of the demands made include a provision of escape for the individual; he comes from a socioeconomically disadvantaged background; he provides authorities with a "verbal will"; the individual states that he wants to "go out in a big way"; the person appears to be looking for a macho way to die; the person has recently given away money or personal possessions; the individual involved has a prior record of assaultive behavior; he has recently experienced a traumatic event in his life; and he expresses feelings of hopelessness and helplessness.

14. What is a critical incident?
A critical incident is any crisis situation that causes emergency personnel, family members, or bystanders to respond with immediate or delayed stress-altered physical, mental, emotional, or psychological coping mechanisms and that may result from witnessing human suffering beyond the normal range. Critical incidents can be any disasters, such as airplane crashes, hurricanes, and incidents such as those that occurred on September 11, 2001.

15. During each phase of a critical incident, participants tend to respond with predictable systemic stress reactions. Describe these.
The first phase of a critical incident, the initial impact phase, is often met with disorientation, shock, confusion, apathy, and emotional liability. During the second phase, known as the recoil phase, victims attempt to cooperate with emergency personnel and may express altruism and gratitude to the extent that they minimize their own injuries. Survivors may also harbor resentment to those spared the effects of the incident and may transfer feelings of anger toward significant others. Depression and self-blame is common during recoil. All of these feelings may eventually be expressed as suicidal or homicidal attempts. In the final phase of a critical incident, the postdisaster phase, posttraumatic stress becomes a factor. Participants may manifest emotional numbness, marked agitation, recurrent thoughts and dreams, apathy, depression with accompanying sadness, low self-esteem, learned helplessness responses, and even suicide.

16. What additional stresses did the first women in law enforcement experience that were not experienced by their male counterparts?
The first women in law enforcement often worked with very little peer acceptance and commonly dealt with a lack of organizational support and lack of support from family and friends. These women also had to overcome significant societal prejudice against female officers, as well as a lack of role models in policing at the time.

17. According to recent studies, what were the most significant stressors on female officers in Pinellas County, Florida? How did those differ from the stressors on their male coworkers?
The most significant stressors on the female officers were those involved with critical stress incidents, such as the death of a fellow officer in the line of duty, suicide of a fellow officer, the taking of a life or shooting of someone in the line of duty, or a scene involving the death of a child. These stressors did not differ from those reported by their male counterparts.

18. What are some things police departments can do to curtail incidents of domestic violence among its officers?
This can be best accomplished by the careful screening and selection of police officers including psychological testing. In addition the police department must have a zero tolerance for domestic violence as well as employing intervention strategies such as counseling. Officers must also be required to report all incidents of domestic violence on the part of other officers that come to their attention. The police department must also set up protocols to deal with 911 calls related to police officer domestic violence.
19. If a police supervisor notices a pattern of controlling or abusive behavior in an officer, what steps should be taken?
Supervisors should document the information and notify their immediate ranking supervisor. Supervisors should then inform the officer involved that the behaviors have been documented and should make a recommendation that the officer participate voluntarily in a counseling program to address the identified issues.
20. What range of services can be made available to police officers who are involved in domestic violence incidents?
Some services that are often available include employee assistance program referrals, internal professional counseling, external counseling referrals, advocacy support from local agencies, and peer support programs with clear reporting and confidentiality agreements.
21. What are some examples of so-called stress inoculation activities?
Examples of stress inoculation activities include rigorous exercise, proper diets, adequate rest, leisure activities and hobbies, meditation or prayer, avoidance of smoking and drinking, support groups, a network of friends, self-monitoring, relaxation techniques, and realistic expectations related to work and other situations.
22. What are some of the benefits of an employee assistance program (EAP) to employees?
An EAP can engender higher morale among employees, since many see the EAP as a truly meaningful benefit. Also, EAPs provide caring, trained, and cooperating individuals to recognize and respond to an employee's cry for help. EAPs help reduce the stigma of asking for and accepting help, and they allow employees to feel cared for as a person. Finally, EAPs offer affordable help to those who otherwise might not be able to access it.

KEY TERMS

Alarm stage: the component of general adaptation syndrome that puts the body on a "fight-or-flight" alert by releasing hormones that produce an energizing effect on the body.

Anabolic steroids: a group of synthetic hormones usually derived from testosterone, which promote the storage of protein and the growth of muscle tissue.

Critical incident: a crisis situation, often involving human suffering beyond the normal range, that causes emergency personnel, family members, or bystanders to experience a strong physical, mental, or emotional reaction that interferes with usual coping skills.

Domestic violence: acts of violence by one family or household member against another.

Employee assistance programs (EAPs): programs made available by employers to help employees having personal or occupational difficulties.

Exhaustion stage: the point in general adaptation syndrome when resistance can no longer be maintained, and the body's defenses against stress begin to break down.

General adaptation syndrome (GAS): the biological and physiological reactions, caused by stress, that may eventually incapacitate an individual.

Posttraumatic stress disorder: a psychological reaction that occurs after experiencing a highly stressful event outside the range of normal human experience; it is usually characterized by physical reactions (such as sleep disorders), emotional disorders (such as anxiety), and cognitive reactions (such as debilitating flashbacks).

Resistance stage: the second step in general adaptation syndrome, exemplified by specific responses to continued stress by the body in order to optimize adaptation.

Stress: a body's non-specific response to any demand placed on it.

Stress inoculation activities: activities that help eliminate or reduce stress.

Suicide by cop (SbC): an individual who wishes to die uses the police to effect that goal.

Type A personality: the personality type characterized by an intense and ambitious mindset, which puts the person under constant stress and physiological strain.

Type B personality: the personality type characterized by a more easygoing state of mind than that of the type A personality.

Workaholic: the personality type similar to type A; the person develops a compulsive need to work.

NOTES

1. K. Slogobin, "Stress," *New York Times Magazine*, November 20, 1977, pp. 48–55.
2. For a comprehensive treatment of literature on police stress, see L. Territo and James D. Sewell, eds 2nd ed., *Stress Management in Law Enforcement* (Durham, N.C.: Carolina Academic Press, 2007).
3. H. Selye, *Stress without Distress* (Philadelphia: Lippincott, 1974), p. 60.
4. H. Basowitz, *Anxiety and Stress* (New York: McGraw-Hill, 1955), p. 7.
5. Ibid., p. 4.
6. Selye, *Stress without Distress*, pp. 35–39.
7. J. C. Coleman, "Life Stress and Maladaptive Behavior," *American Journal of Occupational Therapy* 27, no. 3 (1973): 170.
8. O. Tanner, *Stress* (New York: Time-Life Books, 1978).
9. For a comprehensive treatment of defensive behavior patterns, see J. M. Sawrey and C. A. Tilford, *Dynamics of Mental Health: The Psychology of Adjustment* (Boston: Allyn and Bacon, 1963), pp. 40–67.
10. J. G. Stratton, "Police Stress: An Overview," *Police Chief* 45, no. 4 (April 1978): 58.
11. Meyer Friedman and Ray Rosenmann, "Type A Behavior Pattern and Its Association with Coronary Heart Disease," *Annals of Clinical Research* 3, no. 6 (1971): 300.
12. "Compensation for Police Heart Attacks Allowed," *Crime Control Digest* 9, no. 10 (1975): 3.
13. John M. Violanti and Fred Aron, "Police Stressors: Variations in Perceptions among Police Personnel," *Journal of Criminal Justice* 23, no. 3 (1995): 287–94.
14. L. Dishlacoff, "The Drinking Cop," *Police Chief* 43, no. 1 (1976): 32–39.
15. Ibid., 39.
16. On this point, see Mary Niederberger, "Random Drug Test for Police Opposed," *Pittsburgh Press*, April 6, 1989; Rob Zeiger,

"14 Fired Officers Returned to Duty," *Detroit News*, July 22, 1988; Shelly Murphy, "Court Upholds Drug Tests for Hub Cops," *Boston Herald*, May 13, 1989; Marilyn Robinson, "Drug Use Cuts Police Recruits by Nearly 50%," *Denver Post*, July 15, 1983; and David Schwab, "Supreme Court Backs Drug Tests for South Jersey Police Officers," *Newark Star-Ledger*, April 4, 1989.

17. J. J. Hurrell and R. Kliesmet, *Stress among Police Officers* (Cincinnati: National Institute of Occupational Safety and Health, 1984), p. 12.
18. *Newlun v. State Department of Retirement Systems*, 770 P. 2d 1071 (Wash. App. 1989). Relatedly, *McElrath v. Kemp*, 27 Govt. Emp. Rel. Rep. (BNA) 605 (D.D.C. 1989), deals with an alcoholic employee who had relapses after being treated and was terminated but was reinstated later.
19. Will Aitchison, *The Rights of Police Officers*, 3rd ed. (Portland, Ore.: Labor Relations Information System, 1996), pp. 228–33, is the source of the information in this paragraph, with restatement by the authors.
20. *Delaraba v. Nassau County Police*, 632 N. E. 2d 1251 (N.Y. 1994).
21. C. Swanson, L. Gaines, and B. Gore, "Use of Anabolic Steroids," *FBI Law Enforcement Bulletin* 60, no. 8 (1991): 19–23. This discussion of anabolic steroids was adapted from this source.
22. R. F. Doerge, ed., *Wilson and Grisvold's Textbook of Organic Medicinal and Pharmaceutical Chemistry* (Philadelphia: Lippincott, 1982), pp. 679–84.
23. Schuckitt, "Weight Lifter's Folly: The Abuse of Anabolic Steroids," *Drug Abuse and Alcoholism Newsletter* 17, no. 8 (1988); and Hecht, "Anabolic Steroids: Pumping Trouble," *FDA Consumer*, (September 1981): pp. 12–15.
24. Couzens, "A Serious Drug Problem," *Newsday*, November 26, 1988.
25. Doerge, *Wilson and Grisvold's Textbook*.
26. Couzens, "A Serious Drug Problem."
27. A. G. Gilman et al., *Goodman and Gilman's The Pharmacological Basis of Therapeutics* (New York: Macmillan, 1985), pp. 1440–58.
28. Harrison G. Pope and David L. Katz, "Affective and Psychotic Symptoms Associated with Anabolic Steroid Use," *American Journal of Psychiatry* 145, no. 4 (1988): 488.
29. Ibid.
30. Charlier, "For Teens, Steroids May Be Bigger Issues Than Cocaine Use," *Wall Street Journal*, October 4, 1988.
31. Pope and Katz, "Affective and Psychotic Symptoms," pp. 187–90.
32. Ibid., pp. 487 and 489.
33. J. M. Violanti, "The Mystery within: Understanding Police Suicide," *FBI Bulletin*, (February 1995): pp. 19–23.
34. J. H. Burge, "Suicide and Occupation: A Review," *Journal of Vocational Behavior* 21 (1982): 206–22.
35. J. Skolnick, *Police in America* (Boston: Educational Associates, 1975), p. 21.
36. J. M. Violanti, "Police Suicide on the Rise," *New York Trooper*, January 1984, pp. 18–19.
37. M. Wagner and R. Brzeczek, "Alcohol and Suicide: A Fatal Connection," *FBI Law Enforcement Bulletin*, (March 1983): pp. 7–15.
38. Andre Ivanoff, "Police Suicide Study Recommends Additional Training, Counseling," *Columbia University Record* 20, no. 2 (September 16, 1994), www.columbia.edu/cu/record/record2002.14.html.
39. J. Schwartz and C. Schwartz, "The Personal Problems of the Police Officer: A Plea for Action," in *Job Stress and the Police Officer*, ed. W. Kroes and J. Hurrell (Washington, D.C.: U.S. Government Printing Office, 1976), pp. 130–41.
40. S. Labovitz and R. Hagehorn, "An Analysis of Suicide Rates among Occupational Categories," *Sociological Inquiry* 41 (1971): 67–72; see also Z. Nelson and W. E. Smith, "The Law Enforcement Profession: An Incidence of High Suicide," *Omega* 1 (1970): 293–99.
41. B. I. Danto, "Police Suicide," *Police Stress* 1 (1978): 32–35.
42. G. Aussant, "Police Suicide," *Rural Canadian Mounted Police Gazette* 46 (1984): 14–21.
43. M. Heiman, "Suicide among Police," *American Journal of Psychiatry* 134 (1977): 1286–90.
44. P. Bonafacio, *The Psychological Effects of Police Work* (New York: Plenum, 1991); see also S. Allen, "Suicide and Indirect Self-destructive Behavior among Police," in *Psychological Services for Law Enforcement*, ed. J. Reese and H. Goldstein (Washington, D.C.: U.S. Government Printing Office, 1986).
45. P. Friedman, "Suicide among Police: A Study of 93 Suicides among New York City Policemen 1934–40," in *Essays of Self Destruction*, ed. E. S. Schneidman (New York: Science House, 1968).
46. C. W. Gaska, "The Rate of Suicide, Potential for Suicide, and Recommendations for Prevention among Retired Police Officers" (doctoral diss., Wayne State University, 1980).

47. T. E. Baker and J. P. Baker "Preventing Police Suicide," *FBI Law Enforcement Bulletin*, October 1996, pp. 24–26.
48. See, for example, J. M. Violanti, J. E. Vena, and J. R. Marshall, "Disease Risk and Mortality among Police Officers: New Evidence and Contributing Factors," *Journal of Police Science and Administration* 14 (1986): 17–23; and K. O. Hill and M. Clawson, "The Health Hazards of Street Level Bureaucracy Mortality among the Police," *Journal of Police Science* 16 (1988): 243–48.
49. Thomas E. Baker and Jane P. Baker, *Preventing Police Suicide,* (October 1996): www.fbi.gov/publications/leb/1996/oct966.txt.
50. P. Bonafacio, *The Psychological Effects of Police Work* (New York: Plenum, 1991).
51. J. Schwartz and C. Schwartz, *The Personal Problems of the Police Officer: A Plea for Action* (Washington, D.C.: U.S. Government Printing Office, 1991), pp. 130–41.
52. F. Herzberg, B. Mausner, and B. B. Snyderman, *The Motivation to Work* (New Brunswick, N. J.: Transaction, 1993) as cited in H. Toch, *Stress in Policing* (Washington, D.C.: American Psychological Association, 2004), pp. 26–46.
53. Ibid.
54. Ibid.
55. Ibid.
56. Ibid.
57. Ibid.
58. A. J. Pinizzotto, E. F. Davis, and C. E. Miller III, "Suicide by Cop: Defining a Devastating Dilemma," *FBI Law Enforcement Bulletin,* February 2005, p. 14. (This discussion was adapted from this source.)
59. Clinton R. Vanzandt, "Suicide by Cop," *Police Chief*, (July 1993): pp. 29, 30.
60. Gail Walker, "Crisis Care in Critical Incident Debriefing," *Death Studies* 14 (1990): 121–33.
61. H. Selye, *The Stress of Life* (New York: McGraw-Hill, 1976).
62. S. W. Lilfeld, Jr., "Coping Styles," *Journal of Human Stress* 6 (June 1980): 2–10.
63. A. C. Hargreaves, "Coping with Disaster," *American Journal of Nursing* 80, no. 4 (1980): 683.
64. Meredith A. Bowman, "Female Specific Police Stress: A Study of the Stressors Experienced by Female Police Officers" (master's thesis, University of South Florida, 1999). Much of the information regarding female stress resulted from research completed for this master's thesis.
65. U.S. Department of Justice Bureau of Justice Statistics, Law Enforcement Management and Administrative Statistics, 2000: Data for Individual State and Local Agencies with 100 or More Officers, www.ojp.usdoj.gov/bjs/abstract/lemas00.htm.
66. C. R. Swanson, L. Territo, and R. W. Taylor, *Police Administration* (New York: Macmillan, 1988), pp. 215–16.
67. Brenda Washington, "Stress Reduction Techniques for the Female Officer," in *Job Stress and the Police Officer*, ed. W. H. Kroes and J. J. Hurrel, Jr. (Washington, D.C.: U.S. Government Printing Office, December 1975), p. 36.
68. Ibid.
69. Bloch and Anderson, as cited in J. Balkin, "Why Policemen Don't Like Policewomen," *Journal of Police Science and Administration* 16 (1988): 29–38.
70. Sherman, as cited in ibid.
71. J. Schwartz and C. Schwartz, as cited in P. W. Lunneborg, *Women Police Officers: Current Career Profile* (Springfield, Ill.: Charles C Thomas, 1989).
72. Glaser and Saxe, as cited in ibid.
73. J. G. Wexler and D. D. Logan, "Sources of Stress among Women Police Officers," *Journal of Police Science and Administration* 11 (1983): 46–53.
74. Ibid.
75. N. K. Norvell, H. A. Hills, and M. R. Murrin, "Understanding Female and Male Law Enforcement Officers," *Psychology of Women Quarterly* 17 (1993): 289–301.
76. J. M. Daum and C. M. Johns, "Police Work from a Woman's Perspective," *Police Chief* 19 (1994): 339–48.
77. James D. Sewell, "Law Enforcement Critical Life Events Scale," *Journal of Police Science and Administration* 11 (1983): 113–14.
78. L. D. Lott, "Deadly Secrets: Violence in the Police Family," *FBI Law Enforcement Bulletin*, November 1995, pp. 12–15. This discussion was adapted from this article.
79. André Ivanoff, "Police Suicide Study Recommends Additional Training, Counseling," *Columbia University Record* 20, no. 2, (September 16, 1994): www.columbia.edu/cu/record/record2002.14.html.
80. Many of these factors are identified in Robert W. Shearer, "Police Officer Stress: New Approaches for Effective Coping," *Journal of California Law Enforcement* 25, no. 4 (1991): 97–104.
81. Max Bromley and William Blount, "Criminal Justice Practitioners," in *Employee Assistance Programs*, ed. William R. Hutchison, Jr., and William G. Emener (Springfield, Ill.: Charles C Thomas, 1997), p. 400.

82. J. T. Reese, *The History of Police Psychological Service* (Washington, D.C.: U.S. Department of Justice, 1987).
83. C. Milofsky, E. Astrov, and M. Martin, "Stress Management Strategy for U.S. Customs Workers," *EAP Digest* 14, no. 6 (1994): 46–48.
84. Bromley and Blount, "Criminal Justice Practitioners," p. 401.
85. Fred Dickman and William G. Emener, "Union Involvement: A Key Ingredient to Successful Employee Assistance Programs," in *Employee Assistance Programs*, ed. William S. Hutchison and William G. Emener (Springfield, Ill.: Charles C Thomas, 1997), pp. 100–104.
86. William G. Emener and Fred Dickman, "Case Management, Caseload Management, and Case Recording and Documentation: Professional EAP Service," in Hutchison and Emener, *Employee Assistance Programs*, pp. 121–22.

Law is order, and good law is good order.

—Aristotle

CHAPTER 14

OUTLINE

Introduction

Liability for Police Conduct

Who Can Be Sued?

Scope of Liability Trends in Tort Liability for Police Supervisors and Administrators

Administrative Discipline: Due Process for Police Officers

Constitutional Rights of Police Officers

Other Grounds for Disciplinary Action

Misuse of Firearms and Deadly Force

Police Liability and High-Speed Pursuit

Liability and Emotionally Disturbed Persons

Testing in the Work Environment

Terms and Conditions of Employment

Sexual Harassment

Chapter Review

Key Terms

Notes

OBJECTIVES

1. Explain the three general categories of torts. How do they differ?
2. What does "acting under the color of state law" mean? How does this statement relate to Section 1983 actions?
3. What is a *Bivens* action?
4. List and describe the negligence theories applicable to police supervision and management.
5. What are procedural and substantive due process?
6. What types of limitations does due process place on disciplinary rules?
7. When might rules infringing on the free speech of officers be upheld?
8. Under what circumstances can an officer use deadly force?
9. What four elements must be proven in order to sue the police for negligence in a high-speed pursuit?
10. What are a department's responsibilities in reducing liability in high-speed pursuits?
11. What do most training programs regarding emotionally disturbed persons focus on?
12. What is the balancing test as referred to in alcohol and drug testing in the workplace?
13. What two things must a department prove in order to prove that an age-based mandatory retirement rule is valid?
14. What policy recommendations have been made in order to reduce the potential for sexual harassment allegations and lawsuits against police departments?

LEGAL ASPECTS OF POLICE ADMINISTRATION

INTRODUCTION

One of the primary characteristics of our nation's law is its dynamic nature. Rules of law are promulgated in three basic ways: by legislation, by regulation, and by court decision. Statutes and ordinances are laws passed by legislative bodies, such as the U.S. Congress, state legislatures, county commissions, and city councils. These lawmaking bodies often produce legislation that establishes only a general outline of the intended solution to a particular problem. The legislation authorizes a particular government agency to fill in the details through rules and regulations. Such rules and regulations have the full force of the law.

When the solution to a legal dispute does not appear to be specifically provided by an existing statute, rule, or regulation, a judge may rely on precedent. When a judge makes a decision based on precedent, he or she bases a legal solution on similar decisions already made in that or other courts. Case decisions can be reversed or modified by a higher-level court or by passage of new legislation. Sometimes judges must develop their own tests or rules to resolve an issue fairly through creative interpretation of a statute or constitutional provision. This is known as judge-made law.

Clearly, the fluid nature of our lawmaking system renders it impossible to offer a definitive statement of the law that will remain true forever or perhaps even for very long. The task of stating rules of law is complicated further by the vast number of legislative bodies and courts in this country. Statutes and judge-made law may vary considerably from state to state and from one court to another. However, interpretations of the U.S. Constitution and federal law by the U.S. Supreme Court are given special attention in this chapter because they are binding on all other courts, whether local, state, or federal.

The reader should view the material that follows as instructive background rather than as an authoritative basis for action. Police administrators should always seek qualified legal counsel whenever they face a problem or a situation that appears to have legal ramifications. A primary objective of this chapter is to make police administrators more capable of quickly determining when they face such a problem or situation.

Jack Call and Donald D. Slesnick were the coauthors of this chapter in the first edition, Slesnick and Janet E. Ferris were the coauthors in the second edition, and the authors of *Police Administration* have assumed responsibility for it in this edition, with Robert W. Taylor and Jennifer Davis having revised and updated much of the material.

LIABILITY FOR POLICE CONDUCT

One of the most troubling legal problems facing police officers and police departments in recent years has been the expanded impact of civil and criminal **liability** for alleged police misconduct. It is commonplace to hear police spokespersons complain that law enforcement officers are widely hampered by the specter of being undeservedly sued for alleged improper performance of duty. Although one may argue that the magnitude of police misconduct **litigation** may be overstated, the amount of litigation appears to be increasing and is apparently accompanied by a movement toward larger monetary damage awards.

Basic Types of Police Tort Actions[1]

Law can be divided into two parts: criminal law and civil law. Police officers and other criminal justice practitioners are generally more familiar with criminal law because they deal with it on a daily basis. Each "piece" of the law addresses a specific type of action. For instance, criminal law focuses on crimes, whereas civil law applies to torts.

Barrineau defines a crime as a public injury, an offense against the state, punishable by fine and/or imprisonment. It is the violation of a duty one owes the entire community; the remedy for a breach of such duty is punishment (fine or imprisonment) imposed by the state. Crimes are exemplified in the FBI Crime Index (murder, assault, robbery, rape, burglary, larceny, auto theft, and arson), wherein each crime is composed of specific elements and has an affixed penalty.

On the other hand, a **tort** is a private injury inflicted on one person by another person for which the injured party may sue in a civil action. Such action may bring about liability that leads to an award of money damages. Tort actions encompass most personal injury litigation. The injured party initiates the lawsuit and is called the **plaintiff.** The sued person is called the **defendant** and is often referred to as the *tort feasor.*[2]

One example of a tort action brought against police officers is an allegation of criminal behavior, such as assault and battery (police brutality). More commonly, they are civil actions brought about by claims of false arrest, false imprisonment, invasion of privacy (through illegal search and seizure), negligence, defamation, or malicious prosecution.[3] Most of the suits against police officers fall into three general categories: negligence torts, intentional torts, and constitutional torts.[4]

Negligence Torts

Our society imposes a duty on individuals to conduct their affairs in a manner that does not subject others to an unreasonable risk of harm. This responsibility also applies to criminal justice practitioners. If a police officer's conduct creates a situation recognizable as dangerous by a reasonable person in like circumstances, the officer will be held accountable to those injured as a result of his or her conduct.

In **negligence** suits, defendants are not liable unless they foresaw or should have anticipated that their acts or omissions would result in injury to another. The key in negligence suits is the standard of the reasonably prudent person, also referred to as **reasonableness.** Was the care provided at the same standard that a reasonably prudent person would observe under a given set of circumstances?[5] Examples of negligence involving police officers often arise from pursuit driving incidents in which the officers violate common traffic laws, such as speeding, running a stop sign, or failing to control their vehicles, resulting in the injury or death of another person.

Intentional Torts

An intentional tort is the voluntary commission of an act that to a substantial certainty will injure another person. It does not have to be negligently done to be actionable. Intentional torts are therefore *voluntary* and *deliberate* acts, such as assault, false arrest, false imprisonment, and malicious prosecution.

Constitutional Torts

The duty to recognize and uphold the constitutional rights, privileges, and immunities of others is imposed on police officers and other criminal justice practitioners by statute, and violation of these guarantees may result in a specific type of civil suit. Most of these suits are brought under Title 42, U.S. Code, Section 1983, in federal court.

In our system of government, there are court systems at both federal and state levels. However, federal courts are intended to be courts of somewhat limited jurisdiction and generally do not hear cases involving private, as opposed to public, controversies unless a question of federal law is involved or the individuals involved in the lawsuit are residents of different states. Even then, the suit may be decided in a state court if both parties to the controversy agree to have the dispute settled there. As a result, most tort suits have been brought in state courts.

Title 42, U.S. Code, Section 1983

A major trend in the area of police misconduct litigation is the increase in the number and proportion of these suits that are being brought in federal court. The most common legal vehicle by which federal courts can acquire jurisdiction of these suits is commonly referred to as a **1983 action.** This name derives from the fact that these suits are brought under the provisions of Section 1983 of Title 42 of the U.S. Code. This law, passed by Congress in the aftermath of the Civil War and commonly referred to as the Civil Rights Act of 1871, was designed to secure the civil rights of the recently emancipated slaves. It prohibits depriving any person of life, liberty, or property without due process of law. Specifically, Section 1983 states,

> *Every person who, under color of any statute, ordinance, regulation, custom, or usage of any State or Territory, subjects, or causes to be subjected, any citizen of the United States or any other person within the jurisdiction thereof to the deprivation of any rights, privileges, or immunities secured by the Constitution and laws, shall be liable to the party injured in an action at law, suit in equity, or other proper proceeding for redress.*[6]

After 90 years of relative inactivity, Section 1983 was resuscitated by the U.S. Supreme Court in the landmark case *Monroe v. Pape* (1961).[7] In this case, the Court concluded that, when a police officer is alleged to have acted improperly (for example, in conducting an illegal search), that officer can be sued in federal court by alleging that he or she deprived the searched person of his or her constitutional right under the Fourth Amendment to be free from unreasonable searches and seizures. A critical element of Section 1983 is that the violation must have occurred while the officer was acting "under color of State law"—that is, while the officer was on duty and acting within the scope of employment as a sworn police officer. Unless there is direct personal participation by police supervisory personnel, they are not generally liable for Section 1983 damages, even if there are broad allegations of failure to properly train and supervise police officers who are liable in the Section 1983 lawsuit.[8]

Bivens Action

Section 1983 is the primary civil rights statute involved in litigation against municipal and state police officers. However, the statute rarely applies to federal agents (such as officials of the FBI, Secret Service, and Drug Enforcement Administration) because its terms require that the plaintiff be acting under "color of State law." Federal officials can be sued under one of two complaints. The first is a *Bivens action* for a violation of constitutional rights. The *Bivens* action applies only to the individual, not to the government. The second is a tort action against the United States under the Federal Tort Claim Act (FTCA).[9] Both actions can be combined into one lawsuit.

Essentially, a *Bivens* action is a judicially created counterpart to a Section 1983 tort action. The Supreme Court has permitted suits against federal officials (not, however, against the United States) for violations of constitutional rights that would otherwise be the subject of a Section 1983 action against a state or local officer. Its name is derived from the landmark case *Bivens v. Six Unknown Federal Narcotics Agents* (1971), wherein the Supreme Court held that a cause of action for violation of the Fourth Amendment (search and seizure clause) can be inferred from the Constitution itself.[10] Hence, federal courts have jurisdiction to hear federal question cases involving suits against federal employees in their individual capacities.[11]

In summary, there are three basic types of tort actions that may be brought against police for misconduct: traditional state law torts, Section 1983 torts, and *Bivens* torts. It is important to understand these classifications because the type of tort action brought will determine who can be sued, what kind of behavior will result in liability, and which immunities might be available to the defendants.

Critical Thinking Questions

1. Why do you think Title 42, U.S. Code, Section 1983 was initially enacted? What political movements during the 1960s may have been instrumental in this decision?
2. Can a police officer be sued for committing a crime? Why or why not? What conditions must be present for tortious liability to extend to the officer?

WHO CAN BE SUED?

At common law, police officers were held personally liable for damage caused by their own actions that exceeded the boundaries of permissible behavior. This rule applied even if the officer was ignorant of the boundary established by the law. As unjust as many of such results may seem, the rule establishes one of the traditional risks of policing.

A more difficult question concerns whether the supervisors of the officer and/or the government unit by which he or she is employed can be sued for that individual's misbehavior. Generally, an effort to impose liability on supervisors for the tortious conduct of their employees is based on the common-law doctrine of *respondent superior*. That doctrine, also called **vicarious liability**, developed along with the growth of industrial society and reflected a conscious effort to allocate risk to those who could afford to pay for the complaint of damages.[12]

Although American courts have expanded the extent to which employers can be sued for the torts of their employees, they have traditionally been reluctant to extend the doctrine of vicarious liability to police supervisors and administrators.[13] There appear to be two primary reasons for this reluctance.

The first is that police department supervisors and administrators have limited discretion in hiring decisions.[14] The second reason is that police officers are public officials whose duties are established by the government authority that created their jobs rather than by their supervisors or police administrators.[15] Therefore, police supervisors do not possess as much ability to control the behavior of their employees as their counterparts in private industry.

The court decisions that have refused to extend vicarious liability to police supervisors or administrators do not go so far as to insulate them from liability for acts of their subordinates in all cases. If the supervisor authorized the misbehavior, was present at the time of the misbehavior and did nothing to stop it, or otherwise cooperated in the misconduct, he or she can be held partially liable for the officer's tortious behavior.[16] However, these situations are not classic examples of vicarious liability; rather, they are instances in which it can be said that the supervisor's own conduct is, in part, a cause of the injury giving rise to the lawsuit.[17]

Nevertheless, the growing area of negligence as a Section 1983 cause of action has caused concern within police supervisory ranks. The courts have supported several negligence theories applicable to police supervision and management. The following is a discussion of important negligence cases and subsequent legal development in this area.[18]

Negligent Hiring

The law enforcement administrator and the local government entity have a duty to "weed out" those obviously unfit for police duty. Further, the courts have held that an employer must exercise a reasonable standard of care in selecting persons who, because of the nature of their employment (such as policing), could present a threat of injury to members of the public.[19] Further, in 1997 the Supreme Court held that law enforcement and government entities could be held liable under Section 1983 if the plaintiff's injury was an obvious and direct consequence of a bad hiring decision on the part of an agency. In this case, an officer was hired by a local police department *after* it was discovered that the officer had lied on his original application and had been convicted of a felony, barring him from police service under state regulatory agencies.[20]

Negligent Assignment, Retention, and Entrustment

Police administrators who know or should have known of individual acts or patterns of physical abuse, malicious or threatening conduct, or similar threats against the public by officers under their supervision must take immediate action. If an internal investigation sustains an allegation of such serious conduct by an officer, appropriate action by a police chief could be suspension—followed by assignment to a position with little or no public contact—or termination. A police chief failing to take decisive action when required could be held liable for future injuries caused by the officer. In addition, entrustment of the "emblements of office" (e.g., a badge, a gun, or a nightstick) subjects a municipality and appropriate administrators of a municipal agency to liability whenever injury results from the known misuse of such emblements. In other words, administrators and supervisors have a duty to supervise errant officers properly.[21]

Negligent Direction and Supervision

The administrator and/or supervisor have the duty to develop and implement appropriate policies and procedures. Therefore, a written manual of policies and procedures is an absolute must. This manual must provide clear instruction and direction regarding the position of police officer, be widely disseminated, and be accompanied with training so that all officers understand the significance of the manual.[22] Further, the courts have held that supervisors must "take corrective steps" where evidence indicates that official policy is being abridged and/or the public is being placed at an "unreasonable risk" because of the actions of a police officer. Inaction on the part of the police supervisors and/or administrators is enough to establish negligence if there is a pattern or custom of police abuse and accession to that custom by police supervisors and/or administrators.[23] For example, the failure of a police sergeant to order the termination of a high-speed pursuit of a minor traffic violator through a congested downtown business area that results in serious personal injuries or deaths to members of the public is sure to bring litigation based on an allegation of failure to supervise (see Figure 14-1).

Negligent Training

The local unit of government and the administrator or supervisor of a police department have an affirmative duty to train their employees correctly and adequately. In a recent landmark case (*City of Canton v. Harris*), the Supreme Court limited the use of inadequate police training as a basis for Section 1983 actions. The Court held that inadequate police training may form the basis for a civil rights claim "where the failure to train amounts to deliberate indifference to the rights of persons with whom the police come in contact" and that such official indifference amounts to "policy or custom." Therefore, it is incumbent on the plaintiff to prove that the training program is inadequate as to the expected duties of an officer and that the deficiency of training is closely related to the ultimate injury.[24]

The two areas of negligence that have been the greatest sources of litigation under Section 1983 in recent years have been negligent supervision and negligent training. Incidents arising out of the use of deadly force have certainly raised significant questions regarding training and are covered later in this chapter.

A second difficult question with respect to who may be sued for damages caused by police misconduct concerns the liability of the police department and the government unit of which the department is a part.[25] To answer this question, it is necessary to briefly consider the concept of sovereign immunity.

Under common law in England, the government could not be sued because the government was the king, and in effect the king could do no wrong. Although this doctrine of sovereign immunity was initially adopted by the American judicial system, it has undergone extensive modification by court decisions and acts of legislative bodies.

FIGURE 14.1

As described in Chapter 2, community policing places additional responsibility on the supervisor to instruct and direct officers during routine incidents. Neighborhood disturbances are often characterized by high emotion and potentially violent confrontations, that may require the presence of a supervisor at the scene. The failure to provide such direction and/or supervision can result in a negligence tort action.

(Bob Dammrich Photography, Inc.)

The courts were the first to chip away at the doctrine as it related to tort action in state courts. Most of the courts taking this action did so on the basis that the doctrine had been created initially because the times seemed to demand it, and thus the courts should abrogate the doctrine because modern times no longer justified it. Kenneth Culp Davis,[26] a commentator on administrative law, reported that 18 courts "had abolished chunks of sovereign immunity" by 1970, 29 had done so by 1975, and 33 had done so by 1978.

Davis noted that the trend toward abrogation of sovereign immunity by judicial action was on the wane by 1976 and that the state legislatures had become the primary movers toward limiting or eliminating the doctrine. As a result of combined judicial and legislative action, by 1978 only two states still adhered fully to the traditional common-law approach that government was totally immune from liability for torts occurring in the exercise of government functions.[27]

Lawsuits brought in federal courts against state and local officials are analyzed somewhat differently. The courts first examine the claim asserted by the plaintiff in the case and then determine whether the relief requested can be imposed against the defendants named in the action. For government officials and government entities named as defendants, the plaintiff's ability to succeed will depend on which immunities are available to those defendants. These immunities will be applied to determine whether government defendants remain in the lawsuit and whether damages can be assessed against them.

In federal lawsuits against a state or state officials sued in their official capacities, the courts have concluded that the Eleventh Amendment to the Constitution precludes awards of monetary relief.[28] The courts have arrived at this result by deciding that the essence of the Eleventh Amendment is its protection of state treasuries against damage awards in federal court. The Supreme Court recently extended this principle to bar the recovery of attorneys' fees against state officials sued in their official capacity under 42 U.S.C. 1983.

The Eleventh Amendment does not, however, preclude courts from ordering state officials to do certain things in the future,[29] even if such orders will require the expenditure of substantial sums from the state treasury.[30] The rationale behind such orders is that federal courts can require that the actions of state officials comport with the federal Constitution. The Supreme Court decided in 1984 that the federal Constitution does not allow those courts to consider allegations that a state official violated state law; such claims must be addressed in state courts.

Individuals pursuing damage claims under Section 1983 against local government officials and state officials who are sued in their individual rather than official capacities will have to overcome the defense available to such parties of "qualified, good-faith immunity." Such official immunities are not creatures of Section 1983; they arose from traditional, common-law protections that were historically accorded to government officials. Basically, the good-faith immunity doctrine recognizes that public officials who exercise discretion in the performance of their duties should not be punished for actions undertaken in good faith. Imposing liability on public officials in such situations would inevitably deter their willingness to "execute . . . [their] office with the decisiveness and the judgment required by the public good."[31]

Over the years, the courts have struggled to develop a test for good faith. In 1975, the Supreme Court articulated such a test that considered both the official's state of mind when he or she committed the act in question (the subjective element) and whether the act violated clearly established legal rights (the objective element).[32]

However, seven years later, the Supreme Court decided that the subjective element of the text should be dropped, leaving only the standard of "objective reasonableness."[33]

Now a court must determine only whether the law at issue was "clearly established" at the time the challenged action occurred. Furthermore, if the plaintiff's allegations do not show a violation of clearly established law, a public official asserting good-faith immunity will be entitled to dismissal of the lawsuit before it proceeds further.[34]

The immunities available to state and local officials are generally designed to protect individuals from liability arising out of the performance of official acts. With the Eleventh Amendment providing similar protection to the states, the question of the immunity of a local government was raised. Initially, the Supreme Court concluded that Congress had not intended to apply 42 U.S.C. 1983 to municipalities, thereby giving municipalities what is called "absolute," or unqualified, immunity from suit.[35] On re-examination of this issue in the 1978 case *Monell v. Department of Social Services*,[36] the Court decided that Congress had intended for Section 1983 to apply to municipalities and other local government units. The Court further concluded that, although certain other immunities were not available to a municipality in a Section 1983 lawsuit, the municipality could not be held liable solely because it employed an individual who was responsible for Section 1983 violations. The Court made it clear that local government entities will be liable under Section 1983 only when that government's policies or official procedures can be shown to be responsible for the violation of federally protected rights.

Unfortunately, the *Monell* decision did not fully articulate the limits of municipal liability under Section 1983. The result has been considerable litigation to establish when a deprivation of federally protected rights actually results from enforcement of a municipal policy or procedure and at what point an official's actions can be fairly treated as establishing the offending policy.[37]

More recently, the Supreme Court has held that "single acts of police misconduct" do not, by themselves, show that a city policy was involved in the alleged tortious act.[38] Generally, a plaintiff must show a pattern of negligence or deliberate indifference by the agency.[39]

Critical Thinking Questions

1. Describe some situations that might be tortious for the police under the concepts of negligent hiring, negligent training, and negligent supervision?
2. What do you think the U.S. Supreme Court meant by using the term "deliberate indifference" on the part of the city or agency when proving a tortious claim?

SCOPE OF LIABILITY

In general, state tort actions against police officers provide a greater scope of liability than do the Section 1983 and *Biven* suits. That is, in tort actions under state law, a greater range of behavior is actionable.

The types of torts under state law that commonly are brought against police officers can be categorized as intentional or negligence torts. An intentional tort is one in which the defendant knowingly commits a voluntary act designed to bring about certain physical consequences. For example, the tort of assault is the purposeful infliction on another person of a fear of a harmful or offensive contact. If X points an unloaded pistol at Y, who does not know the pistol is unloaded, X has created in Y an apprehension that Y is about to experience a harmful contact from a bullet. X voluntarily lifts the pistol and points it at Y, fully expecting that it will cause Y to be apprehensive about being hit by a bullet. Thus, X is liable to Y for the intentional tort of assault.

Focus on Policy

Police Compliance Officers

Litigation is an expensive and time-consuming fact of life in police work. The very essence of police work, working with potentially violent individuals in unstable situations and attempting to lend a hand to citizens in need, is fraught with potential for lawsuits in the form of excessive use of force, negligence, harassment, or any number of other situations. The private sector has, for years, used a system of risk reduction in order to combat potential liabilities. In recent years, many public and government agencies have followed suit by instituting a centralized compliance office in their institution.

A centralized compliance office will often involve the appointment of an administrator as a chief compliance officer, or CCO. The CCO in a police department would ideally be responsible for monitoring such things as adherence to constitutional requirements relating to the use of force; arrests; the stopping of pedestrians and motorists; searches; seizures; electronic surveillance; infiltration and interrogations; violations of internal rules, regulations, policies, procedures, and standards of conduct; unauthorized release of criminal history and driver information; improper disclosure of personnel information; illegal or unethical access of restricted data or privileged information; inadequate investigation of citizen complaints of officer misconduct; de-policing, profiling, and other equal protection failures; adherence to injunctions and other judicial decrees; misuse of funds, equipment, or personnel; safety violations; and employee whistle-blowing.

An effective compliance system has six characteristics. The first is the commission of periodic inspections. Periodic inspections should employ the use of checklists and audit manuals in order to ensure uniformity. The second is the use of random audits. Such examinations encourage voluntary compliance and uncover errors and misconduct. Third, compliance programs should include personnel education and training, including course work on ethics. Fourth, inducements should also play a role in compliance, in the form of periodic employee competency ratings leading to promotion and assignment preferences. Fifth, fairness and objectivity are crucial to a good compliance system. According to the non-profit organization Americans for Effective Law Enforcement (AELA), "Employee associations need assurance that compliance inspections and random audits will be conducted on a non-selective basis, in a standardized manner, and that assessments will be free from bias and political or fraternal influence." Finally, compliance officers should not focus on improprieties alone; they should also recognize areas in which the department excels.

CCOs should report directly to the chief of police and should be completely accessible to all employees of the organization. CCOs must also have direct access to an agency's legal representatives in order to be effective.

Creating a central compliance office may seem a costly endeavor to many departments, especially when budgets are tight. However, CCOs have clear benefits to a police department. For example, a CCO can provide objective proof to a civil jury that management has established a system to reveal mistakes, to uncover misconduct, and to encourage professional behavior, thereby potentially lessening liability due to managerial negligence. By adopting such a solid internal control system, police administrators may be less subject to political pressure and criticism from special interest groups. Also, according to the AELA, "periodic reporting by the CCO enhances agency transparency and provides assurances of proper self-governance." Finally, agencies seeking accreditation will find that CCOs are an asset to the process, often able to work to ensure that accreditation standards are met and maintained.

In short, the establishment of a central compliance office within a police agency can be a great means of ensuring the integrity of that agency, as well as reducing liability against civil suits. The CCO is not yet commonplace in police departments, but as legal issues continue to consume time and energy that would best be directed toward providing police service to the public, it is certainly an idea worth a closer look.

Source: Wayne Schmidt, "Criminal Justice Compliance Officer: A New Title and Duties for Self-Governance Responsibilities within Law Enforcement and Corrections Agencies," *Law Enforcement Executive Forum*, May, 2004.

The tort of negligence involves conduct that presents an unreasonable risk of harm to others that, in turn, is the proximate cause of an actual injury. Whereas in an intentional tort the consequences following an act must be substantially certain to follow, in the tort of negligence the consequences need only be foreseeable. When X drives through a stop sign, even if unintentionally, and hits the side of Y's car, X's behavior presents an unreasonable risk of harm to others and is the proximate cause of the damage to Y's car. Although X would have been negligent for "running the stop sign" even without hitting the other car, he or she would not have committed the tort of negligence in that no injury was caused.

The Supreme Court has limited the scope of liability in reference to negligence as an element of deprivation of constitutional rights in Section 1983 and *Bivens* actions. In *Daniels v. Williams* (1986), the petitioner sought to recover damages as a result of injuries sustained in a fall caused by a pillow negligently left on the stairs of the city jail in Richmond, Virginia. The Court held that the petitioner's constitutional rights were "simply not implicated by a negligent act of an official causing *unintentional* loss or injury to life, liberty, or property."[40] This case has had a profound impact on limiting Section 1983 and *Bivens* actions to intentional torts; hence, the sheer volume of such cases has significantly decreased in past years. It is important to note, however, that the Supreme Court "has not changed the rule that an intentional abuse of power, which shocks the conscience or which infringes a specific constitutional guarantee such as those embodied in the Bill of Rights," still implicates serious liability.[41]

As noted earlier in this chapter, many lawsuits against police officers are based on the intentional torts of assault, battery, false imprisonment, and malicious prosecution.[42] Suits against police officers for intentional torts can be brought as state tort actions, Section 1983 suits, or *Bivens* suits. Although suits against police officers for negligence torts can be brought as state tort actions, the issue is not so clear-cut with regard to Section 1983 and *Bivens* suits.

Generally, damages assessed in civil litigation for negligence are ordinary (compensatory) damages that are paid by the employing government entity (or its liability insurance carrier) on behalf of the defendant officer. Therefore, as a general rule, the individual employee is not required to pay ordinary damages that result from a civil negligence suit. This is so because, normally when government employees are performing their duties within the scope of employment, they are deemed to be the agents or representatives of the employing agency and therefore not personally liable for their acts. However, where punitive damages are assessed for conduct that is grossly negligent, wanton, or reckless, individuals who have been responsible for such acts are personally liable and, generally speaking, these assessments are not absorbed by the employing government entity or by liability insurance. Thus, law enforcement employees who act in reckless, wanton, or grossly negligent manners will be subject to and personally liable for punitive damage awards. See Figure 14.2.

FIGURE 14.2

When police officers use wholesale "roundup" procedures on gang members without probable cause to arrest or search, they may run the risk of being sued under the Section 1983 tort claims of harassment, false imprisonment, and malicious prosecution.

(Bob Daemmrich/Bob Daemmrich Photography, Inc.)

In this constantly changing area of the law, the Supreme Court has established a rule that police are entitled to "qualified" immunity for acts made in good faith that can be characterized as "objectively reasonable." In *United States v. Leon*,[43] the Court focused on the objectively ascertainable question of whether a reasonably well-trained officer would have known that the act committed was illegal. Subsequently, following that logic the Court held that, if police personnel are not "objectively reasonable" in seeking an arrest warrant, they can be sued personally for many damages, despite the fact that a judge has approved the warrant. In fact, the Court stated that a judge's issuance of a warrant will not shield the officer from liability if a "well-trained officer in [his] position would have known that his affidavit failed to establish probable cause and that he should not have applied for the warrant."[44] However, the Court modified its position in a later case when an FBI agent conducted a warrantless search of a resident's home for a fugitive by holding that an alleged unlawful warrantless search of an innocent third party's home does not create an exception per se to the general rule of qualified immunity. The Court held that the relevant question is whether a reasonable officer would have believed the search lawful once the clearly established law and the information possessed by the agent were taken into consideration and, if the answer is yes, whether the agent is protected by qualified immunity from civil liability.[45] This standard was upheld in 2001.[46]

As with many areas of the law, lower courts have somewhat modified this landmark decision. In 1987, a U.S. district court found that qualified immunity protects all but the plainly incompetent or those who knowingly violate the law.[47] And in 1992, a federal court ruled that law enforcement officers are protected by immunity from "bad guesses in gray areas" but are liable for "transgressing obviously bright lines of law,"[48] essentially leading the way for protective immunity for officers honestly attempting to do their job. Still, whereas public officials exercising discretion (e.g., judges and prosecutors) have absolute immunity for their unreasonable acts, the only person in the system left to sue for damages for a wrongdoing will be the police officer, unless his or her acts can be attributed to the policy or procedural custom established by the employing government agency.

Critical Thinking Question

1. When can an officer be held personally liable for his or her actions? Do you think police officers should be given absolute immunity for their actions when working under color of law? Why or why not?

TRENDS IN TORT LIABILITY FOR POLICE SUPERVISORS AND ADMINISTRATORS

Although there has been a reluctance to hold police supervisors and administrators liable for the misbehavior of their subordinate officers, some courts have been increasingly willing to extend liability to these officials where the plaintiff has alleged negligent employment, improper training, or improper supervision.[49]

Under negligent employment, a police official may be held liable for his or her failure to conduct a thorough investigation of a prospective employee's suitability for police work if he or she hires an applicant with a demonstrated propensity "toward violence, untruthfulness, discrimination or other adverse characteristics."[50] Of course, under this theory, the injuries suffered by the plaintiff would have to have been the result of the negative trait that had been demonstrated by the individual before employment as an officer. If the negative trait is not demonstrated until after employment, a party injured by the officer may be able to sue a police official successfully for negligently retaining the officer or otherwise failing to take appropriate remedial action. In some circumstances, the official may not be able to dismiss an officer who has demonstrated unfitness, but the official still might be found liable if he or she negligently assigns the unfit officer to duties where the public is not protected adequately from the officer's particular unfitness. Finally, the official is potentially liable for negligently entrusting a revolver to an officer who has a history of alcohol or other drug abuse or the misuse of a weapon.

Suits alleging that police officials have improperly trained a police officer have been particularly successful where firearms were involved in inflicting the injury. Courts have stressed that the "law imposes a duty of extraordinary care in the handling and use of firearms"[51] and that "public policy requires that police officers be trained in the use of firearms on moving and silhouette targets and instructed when and how to use them."[52] Suits alleging lack of necessary training are also becoming increasingly successful in cases involving the use of physical force to overcome resistance, the administration of first aid, pursuit driving (see Figure 14.3) and false arrest.[53]

Another emerging theory of recovery against police officials is an allegation of failure to properly supervise or direct subordinate officers. This type of suit is typically brought where officials have failed to take action to rectify a recurring problem

FIGURE 14.3

Police officers responding to hostage and/or barricaded suspect situations often require specialized training in crisis negotiations and the use of firearms. In this case, a man was taken hostage at a local television station while the suspect shouted demands from the control room. After hours of skilled negotiations by local detectives, the hostage was released without harm, avoiding potential liability stemming from the incident.

(Photo courtesy of the Phoenix, Arizona, Police Department, 1991)

exhibited in the conduct of police operations by subordinates.[54] An interesting development in this area concerns the situation in which the police department issues a written directive that establishes a policy more stringent than the law requires. In several cases involving such a situation, the courts have held that the written directive establishes a standard of conduct to which police officers must conform or face the possibility of civil liability for their actions.[55]

The last area to which courts have given increased attention concerns cases in which it is alleged that the police officer failed to provide needed medical care to people with whom the officer came in contact.[56] Although the incidents giving rise to such allegations can occur in a variety of situations, they seem to occur with greatest frequency when the plaintiffs have been in custody or have been mistakenly thought to be intoxicated when they actually were suffering from a serious illness. These cases are based on four categories of recovery: (1) failure to recognize and provide treatment for injury, (2) failure to provide treatment on request, (3) failure to provide treatment on recognition of an injury, and (4) negligent medical treatment. Suits in the first three categories may allege either negligent conduct or intentional behavior. Court rulings suggest that police officers who ignore classic signs of illness, such as a heart attack, are depriving arrestees of their Fourteenth Amendment right to receive medical care as a pretrial detainee. To prove that an officer is subject to liability because he or she failed to provide medical treatment requires a showing that the officer acted with deliberate indifference to the serious medical needs of an arrestee.[57] Recent cases have affirmed that holding.[58] Some courts have held that police officers do not have a duty to care for injured persons with whom they come in contact,[59] although such a holding is not likely to occur when the injured person is in their custody.

Critical Thinking Questions

1. Describe situations where you think the Court "imposes a duty of extraordinary care" on the attending police officer. Why do you think the Court has placed such a high standard on these types of situations?
2. Do you think that training all police officers as emergency medical technicians would help eliminate their exposure to liability in this area? Why or why not?

ADMINISTRATIVE DISCIPLINE: DUE PROCESS FOR POLICE OFFICERS

The Fifth and Fourteenth Amendments to the Constitution state that "no person shall be . . . deprived of life, liberty, or property, without **due process** of law."

Liberty and Property Rights of Police Officers

There are two general types of situations in the disciplinary process in which an employee of a law enforcement agency can claim the right to be protected by the guarantees of due process.[60] The first type involves those situations in which the disciplinary action taken by the government employer threatens **liberty rights** of the officer. The second type involves a threat to **property rights**.

Liberty rights have been defined loosely as rights involving the protection and defense of one's good name, reputation, and position in the community. It has, at times, been extended further to include the right to preserve one's future career

In The News

Kansas City, Missouri, Police Blamed for Woman's Miscarriage

Two Kansas City, police officers were suspended on February 1, 2007, pending an investigation regarding a miscarriage suffered by a woman following her arrest in early 2006. Thirty-two-year-old Sofia Salva was arrested after police saw her put an illegal temporary tag on the back of her vehicle. On checking her identification, they discovered that she had several warrants. Salva pleaded with police officers to summon medical help as she was experiencing bleeding. She is shown on videotape telling officers that she was three months pregnant and needed to be taken to the hospital. The tape also shows the officers seemingly ignoring her requests and at one point the female officer is heard clearly saying, "How is that my problem?" after Salva reiterated her plea. She is now suing officers Melody Spencer and Kevin Schnell for wrongful death, personal injuries, and failure to provide medical assistance. She is seeking $25,000 in actual damages, as well as punitive damages.

Kanas City Police Chief James Crown stated that the officers' behavior was "inconsistent with the values and policies of this department and inconsistent with the training they received in the police academy." The suspension came just days after the release of police dashboard video showing the arrest.

Source: Christine Vendel, "Police Ignored Woman's Pleas," *Kansas City Star*, January 31, 2007. Photograph was taken from a still image of the police officer's dashboard camera. at www.kansascity.com/m/d/kansascity/news/local/16584384.htm

opportunities as well. Thus, when an officer's reputation, honor, or integrity is at stake because of government-imposed discipline, due process must be extended to the officer.[61]

It should be noted that the use of the "liberty rights" approach as a basis for requiring procedural due process has proven extremely difficult. The Supreme Court further restricted the use of this legal theory by holding that it can be utilized only when the employer is shown to have created and publicly disseminated a false and defamatory impression about the employee.[62]

The more substantial and meaningful type of due process guarantee is that pertaining to the protection of one's property. Although the general concept of property extends only to real estate and tangible possessions, the courts have developed the concept that a person's property also includes the many valuable intangible belongings acquired in the normal course of life, such as the expectation of continued employment. However, not all employees are entitled to its protection.

The courts have consistently held that an employee acquires a protected interest in a job only when it can be established that there exists a justifiable expectation that employment will continue without interruption except for dismissal or other discipline based on just or proper cause. This expectation of continued employment is sometimes called "tenure," or "permanent status."

In 1972, the Supreme Court issued two landmark decisions on tenure.[63] In one of these cases, the plaintiff was a state university professor who had been hired under a one-year contract and had been dismissed at the end of that year without notice or a hearing. The Court held that the professor was not entitled to notice or a hearing because, under the circumstances, the professor had no tenure because he had no justifiable expectation of continued employment after his contract expired. Therefore, he had no vested property interest protected by the Fourteenth Amendment. The other case also involved a state university professor employed on a one-year contract, but this professor had taught previously in the state college system for 10 years. Under these circumstances, the Court held, the professor had acquired de facto tenure (a justifiable expectation of continued employment) and therefore possessed a vested property interest protected by the Fourteenth Amendment.

Because property rights attach to a job when tenure has been established, the question of how and when tenure is established becomes crucial. Public employment has generally used certain generic terms, such as "annual contract," "continuing contract," and "tenure" in the field of education and "probationary" and "permanent" in civil service systems, to designate the job status of employees. However, court decisions indicate that it is the definition of these terms as established by the employer rather than the terms themselves that determines an employee's legal status. Thus, the key to the establishment of the rights of an employee is the specific wording of the ordinance, statute, rule, or regulation under which that person has been employed.[64]

Merely classifying jobholders as probationary or permanent does not resolve the property rights question. Whether or not a property right to the job exists is not a question of constitutional dimension; rather, the answer lies in a careful analysis of the applicable state and local laws that might create legitimate mutual expectations of continued employment.[65]

Federal courts have been inclined to read employment laws liberally so as to grant property rights whenever possible. For example, the Fifth Circuit Court of Appeals found that a city employment regulation that allowed termination "only for cause" created a constitutionally protected property interest.[66] A federal district court held that a Florida statute (Section 112.532), known as the "Law Enforcement Officers' and Correctional Officers' Bill of Rights," created a property interest in employment because of its disciplinary notice provisions.[67] That approach is consistent with those of other jurisdictions in which state statutes have been interpreted to give property interests in a job to local government employees.[68]

Once a liberty or property right has been established, certain due process guarantees attach to protect the employee. The question becomes, What process is due?

The question of due process for police officers falls into two categories: **procedural due process** and **substantive due process.** The former, as its name implies, refers to the legality of the procedures used to deprive police officers of status or wages, such as dismissal or suspension from their job. Substantive due process is a more difficult and elusive concept. Simply, substantive due process is the requirement that the basis for government disciplinary action be reasonable, relevant, and justifiable.

Procedural Due Process

Kenneth Culp Davis has identified 12 main elements of a due process hearing:

> *(1) timely and adequate notice, (2) a chance to make an oral statement or argument, (3) a chance to present witnesses and evidence, (4) confrontation of adverse witnesses, (5) cross-examination of adverse witnesses, (6) disclosure of all evidence relied upon, (7) a decision based on the record of evidence, (8) a right to retain an attorney, (9) a publicly-compensated attorney for an indigent, (10) a statement of findings of fact, (11) a statement of reasons or a reasoned opinion, (12) an impartial deciding officer.*[69]

The courts have not examined all the trial elements in the context of the police disciplinary process. However, some cases have held that police officers must be informed of the charges on which the action is based,[70] be given the right to call witnesses,[71] be confronted by the witnesses against them,[72] be permitted to cross-examine the witnesses against them,[73] be permitted to have counsel represent them,[74] have a decision rendered on the basis of the record developed at the hearing,[75] and have the decision made by an impartial hearing officer.[76]

A question that has proven particularly troublesome for the courts is whether due process requires that an evidentiary hearing be held before the disciplinary action being taken. In *Arnett v. Kennedy,* a badly divided Supreme Court held that a "hearing afforded

Quick Facts

Americans for Effective Law Enforcement (AELE)

The Americans for Effective Law Enforcement (AELE) is a non-profit agency founded in 1967, and today it is one of the most highly respected sources of legal advice and training for police officers. The AELE holds workshops on legal issues that affect police officers and administrators, such as the use of force, sudden and in-custody death, and discipline and internal investigations. Officers and administrators who attend special training courses are eligible to earn Certified Litigation Specialist credentials, which honor those who pursue litigation-related studies and increase their understanding of public agency litigation. The AELE is also a resource for officers and administrators facing legal action. The agency can offer legal advice or refer officers to local attorneys or expert witnesses. The AELE also offers monthly newsletters, including the *Law Enforcement Liability Reporter* and the *AELE Monthly Law Journal*, both available on its website at www.aele.org. The website also offers an extensive law library, organized by topics of interest to law enforcement officers.

by administrative appeal after the actual dismissal is a sufficient compliance with the requirements of the Due Process Clause."[77] In a concurring opinion, Justice Powell observed that the question of whether a hearing must be accorded before an employee's removal "depends on a balancing process in which the government's interest in expeditious removal of an unsatisfactory employee is weighed against the interest of the affected employee in continued public employment."[78] In *Mathews v. Eldridge,* the Supreme Court set forth the competing interests that must be weighed to determine what process is due: (1) the private interest that will be affected by the official action; (2) the risk of an erroneous deprivation of such interest through the procedures used and the probable value, if any, of additional or substitute procedural safeguards; and (3) the government's interest, including the function involved and the fiscal and administrative burdens that the additional or substitute procedural requirement would entail.[79]

In 1985, the Court further clarified the issue of pretermination due process in *Cleveland Board of Education v. Loudermill.*[80] The Court found that public employees possessing property interests in their employment have a right to "notice and an opportunity to respond" before termination. The Court cautioned that its decision was based on the employee's also having an opportunity for a full posttermination hearing. Therefore, assuming that a public employee will be able to challenge the termination in a full-blown evidentiary hearing after the fact, pretermination due process should include an initial check against mistaken decisions—essentially, a determination of whether there are reasonable grounds to believe that the charges against the employee are true and support the proposed action. The Court went on to describe an acceptable pretermination procedure as one that provides the employee with oral or written notice of the charges against him or her, an explanation of the employer's evidence, and an opportunity to present his or her side of the story. The Court reasoned that the government interest in the immediate termination of an unsatisfactory employee is outweighed by an employee's interest in retaining employment and the interest in avoiding the risk of an erroneous termination.[81] In 1997, the Court ruled that public employees do not have the right to a hearing before suspension without pay as long as the suspension is short, the effect on pay is insubstantial, and the employee is guaranteed a postsuspension hearing.[82]

Thus, it is clear that public employees who can legitimately claim liberty or property right protections of due process for their jobs are guaranteed an evidentiary hearing. Such a hearing should be conducted before disciplinary action is taken unless the predisciple protections just mentioned are provided, in which case the full-blown hearing could be postponed until afterward.

For administrators with a collective bargaining relationship with their employees, where minimal procedural safeguards are provided in contractual grievance–arbitration provisions, that avenue of relief may provide an acceptable substitute for constitutionally mandated procedural rights.[83]

Substantive Due Process

As mentioned earlier, due process requirements embrace substantive as well as procedural aspects. In the context of disciplinary action, substantive due process requires that the rules and regulations on which disciplinary action is predicated be clear, specific, and reasonably related to a valid public need.[84] In the police environment, these requirements present the greatest challenge to the commonly found departmental regulations against conduct unbecoming an officer or conduct that brings discredit on the department.

The requirement that a rule or regulation be reasonably related to a valid public need means that a police department may not intrude into the private matters of its officers in which it has no legitimate interest. Therefore, there must be a connection "between the prohibited conduct and the officer's fitness to perform the duties required by his position."[85] In addition, the conduct must be of such a nature as to adversely affect the morale and efficiency of the department or have a tendency to destroy public respect for and confidence in the department.[86] Thus, it has been held that a rule prohibiting unbecoming conduct or discrediting behavior cannot be applied to a police officer's remarks that were highly critical of several prominent local figures but were made to a private citizen in a private conversation in a patrol car and were broadcast accidentally over the officer's patrol car radio.[87]

The requirements for clarity and specificity are necessary to ensure (1) that the innocent are not trapped without fair warning, (2) that those who enforce the regulations have their discretion limited by explicit standards, and (3) that where basic First Amendment rights are affected by a regulation, the regulation does not operate unreasonably to inhibit the exercise of those rights.[88]

The courts' applications of these requirements to unbecoming conduct and discrediting behavior rules have taken two courses. The first course, exemplified by *Bence v. Breier,* has been to declare such regulations unconstitutional because of their vagueness. In its consideration of a Milwaukee Police Department rule that prohibited "conduct unbecoming a member and detrimental to the service," the court found that the rule lacked

> *inherent, objective content from which ascertainable standards defining the proscribed conduct could be fashioned. Like beauty, their content exists only in the eye of the beholder. The subjectivity implicit in the language of the rule permits police officials to enforce the rule with unfettered discretion, and it is precisely this potential for arbitrary enforcement which is abhorrent to the Due Process Clause.*[89]

The second course taken by the courts has been to uphold the constitutionality of the regulation because, as applied to the officer in the case at hand, it should have been clear to him that his behavior was meant to be proscribed by the regulation. Under this approach, the court is saying that there may or may not be some circumstances in which the rule is too vague or overbroad, but the rule is constitutional in the present case. Thus, it should be clear to any police officer that fleeing from the scene of an accident[90] or making improper advances toward a young woman during the course of an official investigation[91] constitutes conduct unbecoming an officer or conduct that discredits the police department.

Many police departments also have a regulation prohibiting neglect or dereliction of duty. Although on its face such a rule seems to possess some of the same potential vagueness and overbreadth shortcomings characteristic of the unbecoming conduct rules, it has fared better in the courts because the usual disciplinary action taken under neglect-of-duty rules nearly always seems to be for conduct for which police officers could reasonably expect disciplinary action. The courts have upheld administrative sanctions against officers under neglect-of-duty rules for sleeping on the job,[92] failing to prepare for planned demonstrations,[93] falsification of police records,[94] failure to make scheduled court appearances,[95] failure to investigate a reported auto accident,[96] and directing a subordinate to discontinue enforcement of a city ordinance.[97] The courts have refused to uphold disciplinary action against a police chief who did not keep eight-to-four office hours,[98] and against an officer who missed a training session on riot control because of marital problems.[99]

Damages and Remedies

In determining an employee's entitlement to damages and relief, the issue of whether the employer's disciplinary action was justified is important. For example, when an employee's termination was justified but procedural due process violations occurred, the employee can recover only nominal damages in the absence of proof of actual compensable injuries deriving from the due process violation. On proof of actual injury, an employee may recover compensatory damages, which would include damages for mental and emotional distress and damage to career or reputation.[100] However, injury caused by the lack of due process when the termination was justified is not compensable in the form of back pay.[101]

Critical Thinking Question

1. What are the differences between procedural and substantive due process? Discuss different examples of each.

CONSTITUTIONAL RIGHTS OF POLICE OFFICERS

Police officers have the same individual rights that all citizens within the United States are afforded under the U.S. Constitution. Even though they have been given significant training, held to a higher standard of conduct, and are subject to public and legal scrutiny, they still enjoy the same protections as anyone else in our society.

Free Speech

The First Amendment of the U.S. Constitution prohibits Congress from passing any law "abridging the freedom of speech." It has been held that the due process clause of the Fourteenth Amendment makes this prohibition applicable to the states, counties, and cities as well.[102]

Although freedom of speech is one of the most fundamental of all constitutional rights, the Supreme Court has indicated that "the State has interests as an employer in regulating the speech of its employees that differ significantly from those it possesses in connection with regulation of the speech of the citizenry in general."[103] Therefore, the state may place restrictions on the speech of its employees that it could not impose on the general citizenry. However, these restrictions must be reasonable.[104] Generally, disputes involving the infringement of public employee speech will be resolved by balancing the interests of the state as an employer against the employee's constitutional rights.[105]

There are two basic situations in which a police regulation or other action may be found to be an unreasonable infringement on the free speech interests of an officer. The first is when the action is overly broad. A Chicago Police Department rule prohibiting "any activity, conversation, deliberation, or discussion which is derogatory to the Department" was ruled overly broad because it prohibited all criticism of the department by police officers, even if the criticism occurred in private conversation.[106] The same fate befell a New Orleans Police Department regulation that prohibited statements by a police officer that "unjustly criticize or ridicule, or express hatred or contempt toward, or . . . which may be detrimental to, or cast suspicion on the reputation of, or otherwise defame, any person."[107]

The second situation in which a free speech limitation may be found unreasonable is in the way in which the government action is applied. The most common shortcoming of police departmental action in this area is a failure to demonstrate that the statements by the officer being disciplined adversely affected the operation of the department.[108] Thus, a Baltimore police regulation prohibiting public criticism of departmental action was held to have been applied unconstitutionally to a police officer who was president of the police union and who had stated in a television interview that the police commissioner was not leading the department effectively and that "the bottom is going to fall out of this city."[109] In this case, no significant disruption of the department was noted. However, when two officers of the Kinloch, Missouri, Police Department publicly complained of corruption within city government, the court held that the "officers conducted a campaign . . . with complete disregard of chain of command motivated by personal desires that created disharmony among the 12-member police force."[110] Because the allegations were totally unfounded and were not asserted correctly through channels instituted by state "whistle-blower" procedures, the dismissals were upheld.

A more recent basis for enforcing employees' First Amendment freedom of speech is that of public policy. The Court of Appeals for the Eighth Circuit held that discharging an employee who violated the police department's chain of command by reporting misconduct to an official outside of the city violated the employee's First Amendment rights. The court reasoned that the city's interest in maintaining discipline through the chain-of-command policy was outweighed by the public's vital interest in the integrity of its law enforcers and by the employee's right to speak out on such matters.[111] Generally, speech about corruption or criminal activity within the officer's law enforcement agency is very likely to be given protection under the First Amendment, especially when such speech is protected by a state "whistle-blower statute."[112] Central to a successful claim under a whistle-blower statute is that the employee show that discipline resulted from the employee's reporting of a violation of the law. Essentially, there must be an element of retaliation against the employee for publicly reporting illegal conduct.[113] The employee need only have a reasonable belief that illegal conduct has occurred and need not have absolute proof of the illegality.[114]

It appears that one's right to speak openly about the policies of a police department may well depend on four important factors: (1) the impact of the statements on the routine operations of the department, (2) the truth of the statements, (3) the manner in which the statements are made regarding existing policy orders involving chain-of-command and state whistle-blower regulations, and (4) the position occupied by the officer. For instance, statements made by dispatchers, clerks, and first-line officers in a large department that have relatively little impact may be given much more tolerance than supervisory or command personnel complaining of departmental policy because the degree of influence, validity, and credibility significantly increases with rank.

Other First Amendment Rights

A basic right of Americans in our democratic system of government is the right to engage in political activity. As with free speech, the government may impose reasonable restrictions on the political behavior of its employees that it could not impose on the citizenry at large. It is argued that, if the state could not impose some such restrictions, there would be a substantial danger that employees could be pressured by their superiors to support political candidates or causes that were contrary to their own beliefs under threat of loss of employment or other adverse action against them for failure to do so.[115]

At the federal level, various types of partisan political activity by federal employees are controlled by the Hatch Act. The constitutionality of that act has been upheld by the Supreme Court.[116] Many states have similar statutes, which are usually referred to as "little Hatch" acts, controlling political activity by state employees. The Oklahoma version of the Hatch Act, which was upheld by the Supreme Court,[117] prohibited state employees from soliciting political contributions, joining a partisan political club, serving on the committee of a political party, being a candidate for any paid political office, or taking part in the management of a political party or campaign. However, some states, such as Florida, specifically prohibit local governments from limiting the off-duty political activity of their employees.

Whereas the Supreme Court decisions might appear to have put to rest all controversy over the extent to which the government can limit political activity by its employees, that has not been the case. In two, more recent cases, lower courts have placed limits on the authority of the state in limiting the political activity of state employees.

In Pawtucket, Rhode Island, two firefighters ran for mayor and city councilmember, respectively, in a non-partisan election despite a city charter provision prohibiting all city employees from engaging in any political activity except voting and privately expressing their opinions. In granting the firefighters' requests for an injunction against the enforcement of this provision, the court ruled that the Supreme Court precedents did not apply to the Pawtucket charter provision because the statutes upheld in the prior decisions had prohibited only partisan political activity. However, the court of appeals vacated the injunction after applying a balancing test that weighed the government's interests against the employees' First Amendment rights, finding that the government has a substantial interest in regulating the conduct and speech of its employees that is significantly different than if it were regulating those of the general public.[118] In a very similar case in Boston, the court upheld the police departmental rule at issue there on the basis that whether the partisan–non-partisan distinction was crucial was a matter for legislative or administrative determination.[119]

In a Michigan case, the court declared unconstitutional two city charter provisions that prohibited contributions to or solicitations for any political purpose by city employees because they were overly broad.[120] That court specifically rejected the partisan–non-partisan distinction as crucial, focusing instead on the office involved and the relationship to that office of the employees whose political activity was at issue. For example, the court saw no danger to an important municipal interest in the activities of a city employee "who is raising funds to organize a petition drive seeking a rate change from the Public Service Commission."[121]

Thus, whereas the Supreme Court has tended to be supportive of government efforts to limit the political activities of government employees, it is clear that some lower courts intend to limit the Supreme Court decisions to the facts of those cases. Therefore, careful consideration should be given to the scope of political activity to be restricted by a police regulation, and trends in the local jurisdiction should be examined closely.

The cases just discussed dealt with political activity as opposed to mere political affiliation. Can police officers be relieved of their duties because of their political affiliations on the basis that those affiliations impede their ability to carry out the policies of superiors with different political affiliations? The Supreme Court addressed this question in a case arising out of the sheriff's department in Cook County, Illinois.[122] The newly elected sheriff, a Democrat, had discharged the chief deputy of the process division and a bailiff of the juvenile court, both of whom were non-merit system employees, because they were Republicans. The Court ruled that it was a violation of these employees' First Amendment rights to discharge them from non-policymaking positions because of their political party memberships.[123]

Non-political associations are also protected by the First Amendment. However, it is common for police departments to prohibit officers from associating with known felons or other persons of bad reputation on the basis that "such associations may expose an officer to irresistible temptations to yield in his obligation to impartially enforce the law, and . . . may give the appearance that the community's police officers are not themselves honest and impartial enforcers of the law." Sometimes the prohibition is imposed by means of a specific ordinance or regulation, whereas in other instances the prohibition is enforced by considering it conduct unbecoming an officer. Of course, if the latter approach is used, the ordinance or regulation will have to overcome the legal obstacles discussed earlier, relating to unbecoming conduct or discrediting behavior rules.

As with rules touching on the other First Amendment rights, rules prohibiting associations with criminals and other undesirables must not be overly broad in their reach. Thus, a Detroit Police Department regulation that prohibited knowing and intentional associations with convicted criminals or persons charged with crimes except in the course of an officer's official duties was declared unconstitutional because it proscribed some associations that could have no bearing on an officer's integrity or the public's confidence in an officer. The court cited as examples an association with a fellow church member who had been arrested on one occasion years ago and the befriending of a recently convicted person who wanted to become a productive citizen.[124]

The other common difficulty with this kind of rule is that it is sometimes applied to situations in which the association has not been demonstrated to have had a detrimental effect on the performance of the officer's duties or on the discipline and efficiency of the department. Thus, one court has held that a police officer who was a nudist but was fully qualified in all other respects to be a police officer could not be fired simply because he was a practicing nudist.[125] On the other hand, another court upheld the firing of a police officer who had had sexual intercourse at a party with a woman he knew to be a nude model at a local "adult theater of known disrepute."[126] The court viewed this behavior as being of such a disreputable nature that it had a detrimental effect on the discipline and efficiency of the department. In 2005, the Supreme Court determined that the Police Department could terminate an officer for selling a sexually explicit videotape of himself, in which he identified himself as a police officer. The Court ruled that, even though the activities of the officer took place outside the workplace, the department "demonstrated legitimate and substantial interests of its own that were compromised by the officer's speech" and the activities did not fall under free speech protections.[127]

In The News

Police Officers Lose the Battle to Show Their Tattoos

Mike Riggs, a police officer with the City of Fort Worth, lost his suit against the city, alleging that he was subjected to discriminatory treatment when the department forced him to wear long sleeves and long pants during his duties in the bike unit. Riggs was hospitalized for heat exhaustion in 2001, and he blamed his illness on having to wear the long clothing in the extreme Texas heat. Other officers in the unit were allowed to wear shorts and short-sleeved shirts on duty, but the department claimed that the tattoos were excessive to the point of unprofessionalism. Riggs's tattoos were not racist or obscene in any manner and included a Celtic tribal band, a Celtic design that included his wife's name, a mermaid, a family crest, the cartoon character Jessica Rabbit, and a 2-foot by 2-foot full-color rendering on his back of St. Michael spearing Satan.

However, the district court found that the police department had "legitimate, non-discriminatory reasons for requiring the only officer in the Fort Worth Police Department who has tattoos covering his arms and legs to wear a uniform that is not required of other police officers." Furthermore, the court stated that a police officer's uniform may not be a forum for expressing one's personal beliefs.

Connecticut police officers were also recently ordered to cover spider-web tattoos on their arms that are sometimes associated with racist groups and white supremacists. The officers insisted that they picked their tattoos merely because they liked the designs and not because they were linked with any type of ideology. Much like the Texas case, the district court and circuit court ruled against the officers, as the department had a legitimate interest in requiring that the tattoos be covered.

Fort Worth Police Officer Michael Todd Riggs was ordered to wear a long-sleeve shirt to cover his tattoos, even in the heat of summer.
*(Richard Michael Pruitt/*Dallas Morning News*)*

Sources: Riggs v. City of Fort Worth, 229 F.Supp.2d 572 (N.D. Tex. 2002); *Inturri v. City of Hartford*, #05-2114, 165 Fed. Appx. 66, 2006 U.S. App. Lexis 2538 (2d Cir., Jan 31, 2006); "Grooming and Appearance Rules for Public Safety Workers," *AELE Monthly Law Journal* (January 2007).

The First Amendment's protection of free speech has been viewed as protecting means of expression other than verbal utterances.[128] That issue as it relates to an on-duty police officer's personal appearance was addressed by the Supreme Court decision in *Kelley v. Johnson*,[129] which upheld the constitutionality of a regulation of the Suffolk County, New York, Police Department that established several grooming standards for its male officers. The Court in *Kelley* held that either a desire to make police officers readily recognizable to the public or a desire to maintain an esprit de corps was a sufficiently rational justification for the regulation. The issue of personal grooming and style continues to be a subject of hot debate in departments across the nation, particularly as officers move closer to their constituencies through community policing endeavors.

Searches and Seizures

The Fourth Amendment to the U.S. Constitution protects "the right of the people to be secure in their persons, houses, papers, and effects, against unreasonable searches and seizures." This guarantee protects against actions by states and the federal government.[130] Generally, the cases interpreting the Fourth Amendment require that, before a search or seizure can be effectuated, the police must have probable cause to believe that a crime has been committed and that evidence relevant to the crime will be found at the place to be searched. Because of the language in the Fourth Amendment about "persons, houses, papers, and effects," for years the case law analyzed what property was subject to the amendment's protection. However, in an extremely important case in 1967, the Supreme Court ruled that the amendment protected individuals' reasonable expectations of privacy and not just property interests.[131] Interestingly, twentieth-century technology brought forth a number of key Fourth Amendment issues regarding privacy, especially involving private communications and wiretaps. In a case involving a police officer suspected of gambling, the Supreme Court held that the use of a pen register did not require the same constitutional safeguards as those surrounding a wiretap. The pen register uses a "trap-and-trace" device that records phone numbers and the duration of each call but does not capture any type of communication between parties. The Court reasoned that no warrant or probable cause was needed, as the Fourth Amendment was applicable to captured communication only and that there was no reasonable expectation to privacy regarding the actual phone number.[132]

The Fourth Amendment usually applies to police officers when at home or off duty as it would to any other citizen. However, because of the nature of the employment, a police officer can be subjected to investigative procedures that would not be permitted when an ordinary citizen is involved. One such situation arises with respect to equipment and lockers provided by the department to its officers. In this situation, the officer has no expectation of privacy that merits protection.[133] The rights of prison authorities to search their employees was at issue in a 1985 Iowa case. There the court refused to find a consent form signed as a condition of hire to constitute a blanket waiver of all Fourth Amendment rights.[134]

Another situation involves the ordering of officers to appear at a lineup. Requiring someone to appear in a lineup is a seizure of his or her person and, therefore, would ordinarily require probable cause. However, a federal appeals court upheld a police commissioner's order to 62 officers to appear in a lineup for the purpose of identifying officers who had allegedly beaten several civilians. The court held that, in this situation, "the governmental interest in the particular intrusion (should be weighed) against the offense to personal dignity and integrity." Because of the nature of the police officer's employment relationship, "he does not have the full privacy and liberty from police officials that he would otherwise enjoy."[135]

To enforce the protections guaranteed by the Fourth Amendment's search-and-seizure requirements, the courts have fashioned the so-called exclusionary rule, which prohibits the use of evidence obtained in violation of the Fourth Amendment in criminal proceedings. However, in a series of cases, the Supreme Court has redefined the concept of "reasonableness" as it applies to the Fourth Amendment and the exclusionary rule. In *United States v. Leon* and the companion case of *Massachusetts v. Sheppard,* the Court held that the Fourth Amendment "requires officers to have reasonable knowledge of what the law prohibits" in a search.[136] In essence, *Leon* and *Sheppard* began to develop the concept of "totality of circumstances" confirmed in *Illinois v. Gates*—that is, that evidence cannot be suppressed when an officer is acting "under good faith" whether or not a warrant issued is good on the surface.[137] These cases have far-reaching implications in civil actions against police officers, in that officers enjoy the benefits of qualified immunity when they are acting in good faith and under the belief that probable cause does exist.[138] Indeed, the Court has held that only a clear absence of probable cause will defeat a claim of qualified immunity.[139]

Finally, the exclusionary rule and the previously mentioned cases have an important bearing on disciplinary hearings involving the police. In *Sheetz v. Mayor and City Council of Baltimore,* the court held that illegally seized drugs in the possession of an officer could be used in an administrative discharge proceeding against that officer.[140] The Court reasoned that only a bad-faith seizure would render the evidence inadmissible because the police are not motivated to seize illegally for the purpose of use in an administrative discharge proceeding; hence, the exclusionary rule was not applicable, and the officer's firing was upheld.

Right against Self-Incrimination

On two occasions, the Supreme Court has addressed questions concerning the Fifth Amendment rights of police officers who are the subjects of investigations. In *Garrity v. New Jersey,*[141] a police officer had been ordered by the attorney general to answer certain questions or be discharged. The officer testified, and the information gained as a result of his answers was later used to convict him of criminal charges.

The Fifth Amendment protects an individual from being compelled "in any criminal case to be a witness against himself."[142] The Supreme Court held that the information obtained from the police officer could not be used at his criminal trial because the Fifth Amendment forbids the use of coercion of this sort to extract an incriminating statement from a suspect.

In *Gardner v. Broderick,*[143] a police officer had declined to answer questions put to him by a grand jury investigating police misconduct on the grounds that his answers might tend to incriminate him. As a result, the officer was dismissed from his job. The Supreme Court ruled that the officer could not be fired for his refusal to waive his constitutional right to remain silent. However, the Court made it clear that it would have been proper for the grand jury to require the officer to answer or face discharge for his refusal, as long as the officer had been informed that his answers could not be used against him in a criminal case and the questions were related specifically, directly, and narrowly to the performance of his official duties. The Court felt that this approach was necessary to protect the important state interest in ensuring that the police officers were performing their duties faithfully.

In its ruling, the Supreme Court set forth a basic standard for disciplinary investigations of police officers. Referring to *Garrity,* the Court ruled that, although a police agency can conduct an administrative investigation of an officer, it cannot in the course of that investigation compel the officer to waive his or her privilege against self-incrimination. As it has been interpreted, *Garrity* requires that, before a police agency can question an officer regarding an issue that may involve disciplinary action against the officer for refusal to answer questions, the agency must do the following:

1. Order the officer to answer the questions
2. Ask questions that are specifically, directly, and narrowly related to the officer's duties
3. Advise the officer that the answers to the questions will not be used against the officer in criminal proceedings[144]

If the officer refuses to answer appropriate questions after being given these warnings and advisement, then he or she may be disciplined for insubordination.

As a result of these cases, it is proper to discharge police officers who refuse to answer questions that are related specifically and directly to the performance of their duties and who have been informed that any answers they do give cannot be used against them in a criminal proceeding.[145]

Historically, it was not uncommon for police departments to make use of polygraph examinations in the course of internal investigations. The legal question that has arisen most frequently is whether an officer may be required to submit to such a procedure under threat of discharge for refusal to do so. There is some diversity of legal authority on this question, but the majority of courts that have considered it have held that an officer can be required to take the examination.[146]

An Arizona court overturned a county merit system commission's finding that a polygraph examination could be ordered only as a last resort after all other investigative efforts had been exhausted and held that

> *a polygraph is always proper to verify statements made by law enforcement officers during the course of a departmental investigation as long as the officers are advised that the answers cannot be used against them in any criminal prosecution, that the questions will relate solely to the performance of official duties, and that refusal will result in dismissal.*[147]

On the other hand, a more recent decision of the Florida Supreme Court held that the dismissal of a police officer for refusing to submit to a polygraph test constituted "an unjust and unlawful job deprivation." Further, the court recognized that granting to public employers a carte blanche authority to force employees to submit to unlimited questioning during a polygraph test would conflict with the employees' constitutional right of privacy and would abrogate thier protection against self-incrimination.[148]

Further, the use of a polygraph test to screen job applicants for police jobs has fallen under severe criticism. In 1987, a federal judge declared the test to be both unconstitutional and unreliable and ordered the city of Philadelphia to reconsider the applications of individuals denied positions because of their failure to pass a polygraph test. Conversely, the court of appeals reversed the district court holding and stated that the use of polygraph tests for pre-employment screening did not violate either equal protection or substantive due process.[149]

As a result of these cases and the resulting ambiguity concerning polygraph testing and the Fifth Amendment, most jurisdictions have limited the use of the polygraph by statute and/or administrative regulation. Also, most agencies have developed extensive internal policies to limit the use of the polygraph and to expressly detail circumstances in which the test may be used to corroborate officer statements.

Critical Thinking Questions

1. Do you think police officers should be allowed to have long hair, beards, tattoos, and piercings visible to the public while in uniform? Discuss the legal precedents that allow a police department to set grooming standards.
2. What do you think are the differences between the Miranda warning and the Garrity warning? Do you think police officers should be given both when being investigated for a crime? Why or why not?

OTHER GROUNDS FOR DISCIPLINARY ACTION

While police officers enjoy the same constitutional rights as other citizens within the United States, they are clearly held to a different standard of conduct both on and off the job. In many cases, their actions do not arise to the level of a criminal complaint yet still become the grounds for disciplinary actions that may result in termination and loss of career.

Conduct Unbecoming an Officer

By far the largest number of police disciplinary cases arise under rules prohibiting conduct unbecoming an officer. These rules have traditionally been vague and overly broad in order to control officers both on and off duty.[150] Most "conduct unbecoming" regulations have been challenged for being unconstitutionally vague.[151] The basis of this claim rests in the concept of reasonableness as applied to the misconduct.[152] In a leading case, the California Supreme Court held that the permissible application of a "conduct unbecoming" regulation turns on whether the officer could reasonably anticipate that his or her conduct would be the subject of discipline:

> *We construe "conduct unbecoming" a city police officer to refer only to conduct which indicates a lack of fitness to perform the functions of a police officer. Thus construed, [the rule] provides a sufficiently specific standard against which the conduct of a police officer in a particular case can be judged. Police officers . . . will normally be able to determine what kind of conduct indicates unfitness to perform the functions of police officer.*[153]

A wide variety of conduct has been held to fall appropriately within the scope of a "conduct unbecoming" regulation. It is important to note that the regulation must reasonably warn the officer of what type of conduct would be considered unbecoming and that said conduct would tend to affect the officer's performance of his or her duties adversely or cause the department to fall into public disrepute.[154] Some of the activities that commonly fall within the scope of a "conduct unbecoming" regulation and that have been upheld by the courts include associating with crime figures or persons with a criminal record,[155] verbal abuse and swearing,[156] off-duty drinking and intoxication,[157] criminal conduct,[158] dishonesty,[159] fighting with coworkers,[160] insubordination,[161] and a number of improprieties involving sexual activity, including promiscuity and fraternizing (see Figure 14.4).

Sexual Conduct

The cases in this area tend to fall into two general categories: cases involving adultery and cases involving homosexuality. Most cases are in general agreement that adultery, even though committed while the police officer is off duty and in private, created a proper basis for disciplinary action.[162] The courts held that such behavior brings adverse criticism on the agency and tends to undermine public confidence in the department. However, one case involving an Internal Revenue Service agent suggests that, to uphold disciplinary action for adultery, the government would have to prove that the employing agency was actually discredited; the court further stated that the discreditation would not be presumed from the proof of adulterous conduct.[163]

More recently, the Supreme Court justices appeared to be divided on the issue of extramarital sexual activity in public employment. In 1984, the Court of Appeals for the Sixth Circuit held that a Michigan police officer could not be fired solely because he was living with a woman to whom he was not married (a felony under state law). In 1985, the Supreme Court denied review of that decision over the strong objection of three justices who felt the case "presented an important issue of constitutional law regarding the contours of the right of privacy afforded individuals for sexual matters."[164]

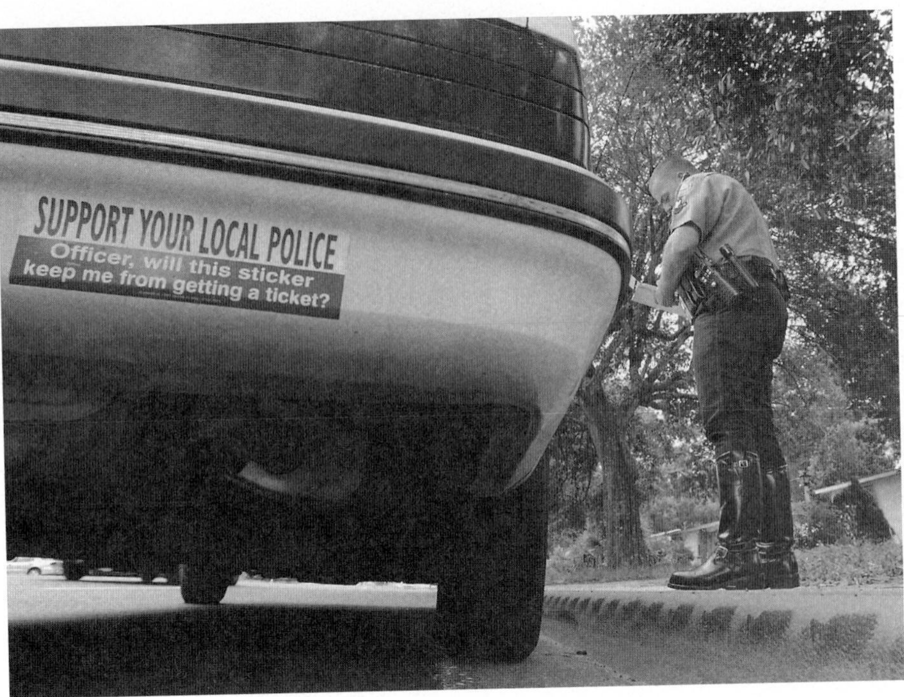

FIGURE 14.4

The routine traffic stop has been the setting for activities that commonly fall within the scope of conduct unbecoming an officer. Complaints often include verbal abuse, swearing, unprofessional conduct, and/or sexual harassment by police officers. Some agencies have placed hidden cameras and microphones in police vehicles, in part to defend themselves against such allegations.

(AP Wide World Photos)

In cases involving sexual improprieties that clearly affect an officer's on-the-job performance, the courts have had far less controversy. In a series of cases, the courts have consistently supported the disciplinary action attached to the department's "conduct unbecoming" regulation, including cases in which officers were cohabiting or in which the sexual activities were themselves illegal (e.g., public lewdness, child molestation, sexual activity with prostitutes, and homosexuality).[165] In fact, the courts have upheld internal regulations barring the employment of spouses, in part because of the concern for an officer's work performance.

The issue of homosexual activity as a basis for discharge was presented to the Supreme Court. Oklahoma had a law permitting discharge of schoolteachers for engaging in "public homosexual activity." The lower court held the law to be facially overly broad and therefore unconstitutionally restrictive. The Supreme Court affirmed the decision.[166] Another federal court held that the discharge of a bisexual guidance counselor did not deprive the plaintiff of her First or Fourteenth Amendment rights. The counselor's discussion of her sexual preferences with teachers and other personnel was not protected by the First Amendment. Her equal protection claim failed because she did not show that the heterosexual employees would have been treated differently for communicating their sexual preferences.[167]

In an equally important federal case involving 13 lesbian deputies terminated from the Broward County, Florida, Sheriff's Department, the Supreme Court held that homosexuals are not a suspect class accorded strict scrutiny under the equal protection clause and, therefore, the dismissal did not deprive the plaintiffs of any constitutional or equal protection right.[168] However, in 2003 the Supreme Court ruled that state sodomy laws are unconstitutional,[169] nullifying many police departments' argument that homosexuality is a criminal violation that is a viable basis for discharging a police officer. Amid recent debates regarding the civil rights of homosexuals, the legal and cultural climate is changing rapidly in this area.

Residency Requirements

A number of local governments have established requirements that all or certain classes of their employees live within the geographical limits of the jurisdiction. These residency requirements have been justified by the governments imposing them as desirable because they increase employees' rapport with and understanding of the community. When police officers were concerned, it has been asserted that the presence of off-duty police has a deterrent effect on crime and results in chance encounters that might lead to additional sources of information.

Before 1976, challenges to the legality of residency requirements for public employees dotted the legal landscape. In 1976, the Supreme Court in *McCarthy v. Philadelphia Civil Service Commission* ruled that Philadelphia's residency requirement for firefighters did not violate the Constitution.[170]

Since the *McCarthy* decision, the legal attacks on the residency requirements have subsided. The cases now seem to be concerned with determining what constitutes residency. The most obvious means of attempting to avoid the residency requirement (by establishing a second residence within the city) appears doomed to failure unless the police officer can demonstrate that he or she spends at least a substantial part of his or her time at the in-city residence.[171] A strong argument has been made that, in areas where housing is unavailable or prohibitively expensive, a residency requirement is unreasonable.[172] In upholding the application of such requirements, courts have focused on the issues of equal enforcement and the specificity of the local residency standard.[173]

Religious Belief or Practice

In part, Title VII of the Civil Rights Act of 1964 prohibits religious discrimination in employment. The act defines religion as including "all aspects of religious . . . practice, as well as belief, unless an employer . . . is unable to reasonably accommodate to an employee's . . . religious . . . practice without undue hardship on the conduct of the employer's business."[174] Title VII requires reasonable accommodation of religious beliefs, not accommodation in exactly the way the employee would like. Title VII also does not require accommodation that spares the employee any cost whatsoever.[175] For example, an Albuquerque firefighter who was a Seventh-Day Adventist refused to work the Friday night or Saturday day shifts because they fell on what he believed to be the Sabbath day. Although department policy would have permitted the firefighter to avoid working these shifts by taking leave with pay, taking leave without pay, or trading shifts with other firefighters, he refused to use these means and insisted that the department find other firefighters to trade shifts with him or simply excuse him from the shifts affected by his religious beliefs. The department refused to do either. Under these circumstances, the Court ruled that the department's accommodations to the firefighter had been reasonable and that no further accommodations could be made without undue hardship to the department. Therefore, the firefighter's discharge was upheld. However, as the Court itself emphasized, decisions in cases in this area depend on the particular facts and circumstances of each case.[176] Recently, the Courts have held that the termination of a fundamental Mormon police officer for practicing plural marriage (polygamy), in violation of state law, was not a violation of his right to freely exercise his religious beliefs.[177]

Moonlighting

Traditionally, the courts have supported the authority of police departments to place limits on the outside employment of their employees.[178] Police department restrictions on moonlighting range from a complete ban on outside employment to permission to engage in certain endeavors, such as investments, rental of property, teaching of law enforcement subjects, and employment designed to improve the police image. The rationale in support of moonlighting prohibitions is that "outside employment seriously interferes with keeping the [police and fire] departments fit and ready for action at all times."[179]

However, in a Louisiana case, firefighters offered unrefuted evidence that moonlighting had been a common practice before the city banned it; during the previous 16 years, no firefighters had ever needed sick leave as a result of injuries suffered while moonlighting, there had never been a problem locating off-duty firefighters to respond to an emergency, and moonlighting had never been shown to be a source of fatigue that was serious enough to impair a firefighter's alertness on the job. Under these circumstances, the court ruled that there was not a sufficient basis for the prohibition on moonlighting and invalidated the ordinance.[180]

It is important to note that, in several cases involving off-duty officers moonlighting (as private security guards or store detectives), the same legal standards imposed on sworn officers acting in the capacity of their jobs apply. The Court has held that off-duty officers act "under color of State law" and are subject to Section 1983 liability while working in a private security or "special patrolman" capacity.[181] Therefore, it follows that police agencies and departments may be liable under the same ramifications, opening up a new wave of future litigation involving police officer off-duty employment.

Critical Thinking Questions

1. Consider the following scenario. A male police officer poses nude for a national magazine in a photograph that clearly links him with the department he is employed by. Can the officer be fired without posing liability issues to the department? Why or why not?
2. Why do the requirements of substantive due process pose challenges to departmental regulations against conduct unbecoming an officer?
3. Discuss some of the grounds for disciplinary action often brought against a police officer.

MISUSE OF FIREARMS AND DEADLY FORCE

The past two decades have been witness to an enormous increase in the number of lawsuits filed against police departments for wrongful deaths. In the vast majority of these cases, the issue is not that an officer injured an innocent third party while shooting at a "bad guy" but rather that the "bad guy" should not have been shot in the first place.

Unfortunately, in the past, police officer training has too often focused on the issue of how to shoot and not when to shoot. Many times when a problem does arise relating to the use of deadly force, it is not that the officer failed to qualify at the police pistol range or that the weapon malfunctioned but that the officer made an error in judgment.

The police chief and his or her legal counsel must question whether this error in judgment was merely a human error resulting from the pressure of the moment or whether the police department failed to provide proper guidelines to the officer.

If proper guidelines were made available to the officer, did the police department incorporate these guidelines into its formal training program?

Let us examine what areas a use-of-deadly-force policy should cover and the formalized mechanisms by which officers can be trained to understand this policy.

Tennessee v. Garner (1985)

Until 1985, the courts nationwide had not established a standard of law regarding the use of deadly force. Likewise, law enforcement agencies had not developed a standard, written directive that would establish national guidelines. While most larger police agencies had established use-of-deadly-force policies, those policies certainly were not consistent in form or content.[182]

On March 27, 1985, all this started to change when the Supreme Court ruled unconstitutional a Tennessee law that permitted police officers to use deadly force to effect an arrest.[183] The Tennessee statute on the police use of deadly force provided that if, after a police officer has given notice of an intent to arrest a criminal suspect, the suspect flees or forcibly resists, "the officer may use all the necessary means to effect the arrest."[184] Acting under the authority of this statute, a Memphis police officer shot a juvenile, Garner, as he fled over a fence at night in the backyard of a house he was suspected of burglarizing. The officer ordered him to halt, but he failed to stop. The officer then fired a single shot and killed him. The officer used deadly force despite being "reasonably sure" that the suspect was unarmed and believing him to be 17 or 18 years old and of slight build. The father subsequently brought an action in federal district court, seeking damages under 42 U.S.C.S. 1983 for asserted violations of his son's constitutional rights. The district court held that the statute and the officer's actions were unconstitutional. The court of appeals reversed and the Supreme Court affirmed the court of appeals' decision.

The Supreme Court held that the Tennessee statute was unconstitutional insofar as it authorized the use of deadly force against, as in this case, an apparently unarmed, non-dangerous, fleeing suspect. Such force may not be used unless necessary to prevent the escape and the officer has probable cause to believe that the suspect poses a significant threat of death or serious physical injury to the officer or others. The Court's reasoning was as follows:

1. Apprehension by the use of deadly force is a seizure and subject to the Fourth Amendment's reasonableness requirement. To determine whether such a seizure is reasonable, the extent of the intrusion on the suspect's rights under that amendment must be balanced against the government interests in effective law enforcement. This balancing process demonstrates that, notwithstanding probable cause to seize a suspect, an officer may not always do so by killing him or her. The use of deadly force to prevent the escape of all felony suspects, whatever the circumstances, is constitutionally unreasonable.
2. The Fourth Amendment, for purposes of this case, should not be construed in light of the Common-Law rule allowing the use of whatever force is necessary to effect the arrest of a fleeing felon. Changes in the legal and technological context mean that the rule is distorted almost beyond recognition when literally applied to criminal situations today.

   Whereas felonies were formerly capital crimes, few felonies are now. Many crimes classified as misdemeanors or non-existent at Common Law are now felonies. Also, the Common-Law rule developed at a time when weapons were rudimentary. The varied rules adopted in the states indicate a long-term movement away from the Common-Law rule, particularly in the police departments

Quick Facts

The Use of Force

In a study of the use of force among six large police departments in the United States, the most common and consistent predictor of the use of force by police officers was the use of force against the officer. Other predictors included situations involving arrest for a felony offense, arrest for a violent offense, and an officer call for backup. Also, prior injury to the officer was a factor, as were the facts that the officer was male, the suspect was male, the officer was older, the suspect was younger, there were antagonistic actions toward the police by the suspect, and the arrest took place in a location known for criminal behavior. The characteristics associated with a decreased use of force included situations in which the victim and suspect were friends, in which the officer was dispatched to the scene, and in which the suspect was known to be compliant.

Source: Joel Garner and C. Maxwell, *Understanding the Use of Force by and against the Police in Six Jurisdictions* (Williamston, Mich.: Joint Center for Justice, 2002).

themselves; thus, that rule is a dubious indication of the constitutionality of the Tennessee statute. There is no indication that holding a police practice, such as that authorized by the Tennessee statute, will severely hamper effective law enforcement.

3. While burglary is a serious crime, the officer in this case could not reasonably have believed that the suspect—young, slight, and unarmed—posed any threat. Nor does the fact that an unarmed suspect has broken into a dwelling at night automatically mean he or she is dangerous.

Evaluation of Written Directives

As suggested earlier, when an alleged wrongful death case is being evaluated, the adequacy of the police department's policy must be considered. Generally speaking, an adequate policy addresses the following topics: defense of life and fleeing felons, juveniles, shooting at or from vehicles, warning shots, shooting to destroy animals, secondary guns, off-duty weapons, and registration of weapons (see Figure 14.5).

Defense of Life and Fleeing Felons

State laws and departmental policies still remain fairly diverse even after *Garner,* although with narrower bounds. No longer can these provisions leave officers virtually untethered, as in the extreme case of one small American town whose only gun guidance to its officers was the homily "Never take me out in anger; never put me away in disgrace."[185]

The range of firearms policies hereafter is likely to be from the "defense-of-life" regulations, which permit shooting only to defeat an imminent threat to an officer's or another person's life. At the other extreme, a minimal compliance with the *Garner* rule permits shooting at currently non-violent, fleeing suspects who the officer reasonably believes committed a felony involving the threat but not the use of violence. Both approaches are currently employed by many large police departments.

The defense-of-life approach significantly reduces the possibility of wrongful death allegations.

Juveniles

For the most part, police departments do not instruct their officers to make a distinction between adults and juveniles in using deadly force, unless it is readily apparent that the individual is a juvenile. This is not based on a callous disregard for youthful

FIGURE 14.5

Officers enter a suspected drug house during a search warrant execution. Police firearms regulations should provide direction during incidents in which the probability for the use of deadly force is high.

(The Baltimore Sun/AP/Wide World Photos)

offenders; rather, it is based on the pragmatic view that an armed juvenile can kill with the same finality as an armed adult. Further, it is often difficult, if not impossible, to tell if an offender is a juvenile or an adult.

Shooting at or from Vehicles

The trend in recent years has been to impose severe limitations on police officers shooting at or from vehicles except as the ultimate measure in self-defense or the defense of another when the suspect is using deadly force by means other than the vehicle.

Some of the reasons presented against shooting at or from vehicles are difficulty in hitting the target, ricochets striking innocent bystanders, population densities, difficulty in penetrating the automobile body and steel-belted tires, inability to put a stop to the vehicle's momentum even when the target suspect is hit, damage that might result from causing the vehicle to go out of control, difficulty in hitting a moving target, and striking of an innocent passenger in the fleeing vehicle.[186]

There is little question that, if a motorist is trying to run a police officer down and the officer has no reasonable means of escape, then the officer has every right to defend his or her life. What often happens, however, is that the officer starts shooting at a vehicle when he or she is no longer in danger. For example, if a vehicle attempts to run a police officer down and the officer is able to take evasive action and get out of harm's way, under the provisions of many police departments' policies, the officer is no longer permitted to shoot at the vehicle, since the officer is no longer in danger. Naturally, if the driver turns the vehicle around and goes back toward the officer, the officer once again has the right to protect his or her life.

Warning Shots

There seems to be a general consensus among administrators that department policies should prohibit warning shots, as they may strike an innocent person. Privately, however, officials may fear something else: that officers shooting at and missing a suspect may claim that they were merely firing a warning shot and attempt to avoid answering for their actions. In addition, police officials point out that warning shots rarely accomplish their purpose, especially if suspects know that officers will not or cannot shoot them.[187]

Shooting to Destroy Animals

Police departments generally allow their officers to kill an animal in self-defense, to prevent substantial harm to the officer or others, or when an animal is so badly injured that humanity requires its relief from further suffering. A seriously wounded or injured animal may be destroyed only after all attempts have been made to request assistance from the agencies (i.e., humane society, animal control, or game warden) responsible for disposal of animals. The destruction of vicious animals should be guided by the same rules set forth for self-defense or the defense and safety of others.[188]

Secondary Guns

Police officers in the United States are all conspicuously armed with a revolver or semiautomatic handgun. This fact is recognized and for the most part approved by our citizenry. A second fact not commonly known is that many police officers also carry a concealed secondary weapon. There are stated reasons for the practice: officers are concerned about being disarmed (with sound justification) during a confrontation, officers are less likely to be caught off guard when confrontation is not anticipated, and officers can less conspicuously be prepared to protect themselves during routine citizen stops. Regardless of the rationale, the practice is considered acceptable by knowledgeable police officials but treated by many police administrators as something understood but not formally admitted.

A major criticism of backup weapons is that they may be intended as "throwaways" in the event an officer shoots an unarmed suspect. In order to protect the officer from such allegations, it is generally recommended that there be a strict policy of registering all backup guns with the department.[189]

Off-Duty Weapons

The rationale for officers to be armed while off duty is based on the assumption that police officers within their own jurisdictions are on duty 24 hours a day and are therefore expected to act in their official capacity if the need to do so occurs. This, for the most part, was the policy of many police departments. Until recently, an officer who failed to comply with this regulation was subject to disciplinary action if a situation occurred that needed police action, such as responding to a robbery in progress, and the officer could not respond because he or she was unarmed.

Many police departments now make being armed while off duty optional but still compel their officers to register any weapons they choose to wear off duty with the department and to qualify regularly with the weapons. Most police departments also designate the type of ammunition the officers may carry in all weapons they use, regardless of whether they are used on duty or off duty.[190]

Registration of Weapons

Most police departments require their officers to use only department-approved weapons on and off duty and further require that the weapons be inspected, fired, and certified safe by the departments' armorers. Further, the firearms must be registered with the departments by make, model, serial number, and ballistics sample.[191]

Familiarization with the Department's Policy

It does a police department little good to have an adequate use-of-deadly-force policy if its officers are not familiar with all aspects of that policy. Following are some examples of formalized administrative means by which officers can become familiar with their agencies' policies:

1. *Recruit training*—Instructions dealing with the deadly-force policy should be incorporated into the unit of instruction dealing with firearms training. As suggested earlier, the judgmental aspects of using deadly force are as important as the hands-on skill development of police officers in firearms training. Such a unit of instruction should involve a discussion of the numerous situations that officers will typically encounter and what course of action would keep these officers in strict compliance with their departments' policies and minimize wrongful deaths.
2. *Field training officer*—The field training officer to whom a rookie officer is assigned immediately on graduation from the police academy is responsible for continuing the training process started by the police academy and for evaluating the suitability of the rookie for police work. Such programs frequently incorporate training features designed to reinforce topics covered in the formal classroom setting of the academy. This component of the training program should be examined to be certain it deals with the topic of police use of deadly force.
3. *Roll-call training*—A part of this training, which typically occurs just prior to the officers going on patrol, can be spent in reviewing newly developed departmental policies, procedures, and regulations, including those dealing with the use of deadly force.
4. *In-service training*—In-service training classes typically range from one to five days (see Figure 14.6). It is quite clear that the *Garner*[192] decision has resulted in many police departments rethinking and rewriting their use-of-deadly-force policies. The importance of the *Garner* decision will not be fully appreciated if a police department merely rewrites its policy and hands it out to its officers with no explanation. It is imperative that some explanation be provided, preferably by legal counsel, so that there is no misunderstanding about what this policy means. This familiarization and orientation can occur in conjunction with the firearms requalification training that officers have to go through regularly, or it can be treated within the context of an in-service training course.[193]

Critical Thinking Questions

1. Discuss how *Tennessee v. Garner* relates to the use of deadly force by police. Exactly how did this case impact police use of deadly force?
2. What elements should an adequate policy regarding the use of deadly force contain?
3. Why do many police departments compel their officers to register any weapons used off duty and to qualify regularly with these weapons?

FIGURE 14.6

Police use of deadly force requires extensive training in firearms techniques that can be validated and documented by qualified personnel.

(Kathy McLaughlin/The Image Works)

POLICE LIABILITY AND HIGH-SPEED PURSUIT

The legal theory underlying most pursuit-related lawsuits is that the police were negligent in conducting a pursuit.[194] A negligence action is based on proof of the following four elements: (1) the officer owed the injured party a duty not to engage in certain conduct, (2) the officer's actions violated that duty, (3) the officer's negligent conduct was the proximate cause of the accident, and (4) the suing party suffered actual and provable damages.[195] Negligence litigation focuses on the alleged failure of an officer to exercise reasonable care under the circumstances.

Duty Owed

Courts first determine the duty owed in a pursuit situation by examining the officer's conduct in light of relevant laws and department regulations. With the exception of some police departments that prohibit all pursuits, police officers have no duty to refrain from chasing a criminal suspect, even when the risk of harm to the public arising from the chase is foreseeable and the suspect is being chased for a misdemeanor.[196] In *Smith v. City of West Point,*[197] the court stated that police "are under no duty to allow motorized suspects a leisurely escape."[198] However, police do have a duty of care with respect to the manner in which they conduct a pursuit. This duty is derived from state statutes, court decisions defining reasonable care, and departmental pursuit policies.

Statutes in most jurisdictions confer a special status on police and other authorized emergency vehicles, exempting them from certain traffic regulations, such as speed limits, traffic signals, and a right of way.[199] Statutes exempting emergency vehicles from ordinary traffic regulations generally make the privilege conditional on

Focus on Policy

Excessive Use of Force

One of the most litigious areas against the police under 42 USC, Section 1983 are lawsuits alleging excessive use of force. Individuals have a clear constitutional right to be free from excessive use of force when they are being arrested. In *Graham v. Connor* (1989), the Supreme Court established a guideline to examine claims of excessive force during an arrest. The Court established that excessive force claims should be analyzed under the Fourth Amendment's Objective Reasonableness Standard. That is, was the force used in a given instance "reasonable" under the Fourth Amendment perspective of seizing a "free citizen" by the police? The Court emphasized that the overriding function of the Fourth Amendment is to protect an individual's personal privacy and dignity against unwarranted intrusion by the police. Thus, to be successful in stating a claim for excessive force under the Fourth Amendment, the claimant must show that the force was unreasonable by showing that the force resulted in an injury to the plaintiff, that the force was clearly in excess of the force needed to effect the arrest, and that such excessiveness was objectively unreasonable. The Fourth Amendment's objectively Reasonableness Standard is made on a case-by-case basis and in light of the facts and circumstances of each incident, not 20-20 hindsight. It is not a subjective standard relating to an officer's thoughts, which are irrelevant. The Court went on to discuss a number of important criteria in balancing whether the use of force was appropriate to the need of the state to apprehend or arrest an individual. For instance, what was the severity of the crime at issue, what was the relative threat to the officer or others, and was the subject fleeing from arrest or actively resisting arrest? In looking at the "totality of the circumstances" of an event, the Court concluded that the real issue in each case in whether the officer's actions were objectively reasonable in light of the facts and circumstances confronting him or her, at that moment, without regard to their underlying intent or motivation.

As a result, many agencies have developed policies that provide officers with a variety of force options based on the specific event or situation at hand. With a very strong emphasis on using the minimum amount of force necessary to effect an arrest, prevent an escape, or overcome resistance by an unruly subject, officers are trained to communicate and be flexible in their attempt to deescalate a use-of-force situation. Note the emphasis that the Los Angeles Police Department places on reporting incidents where officers use force other than verbalization in confronting a subject.

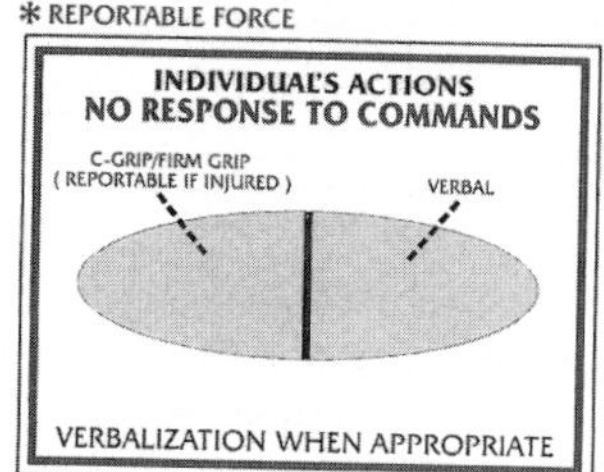

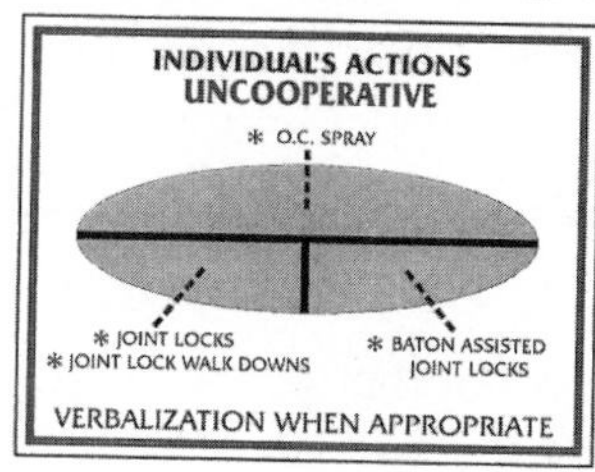

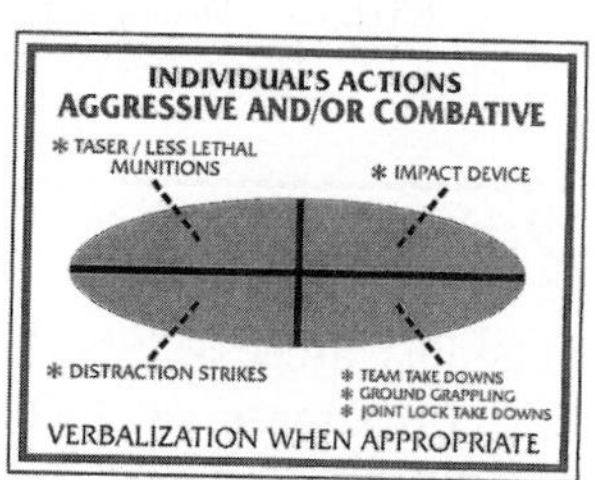

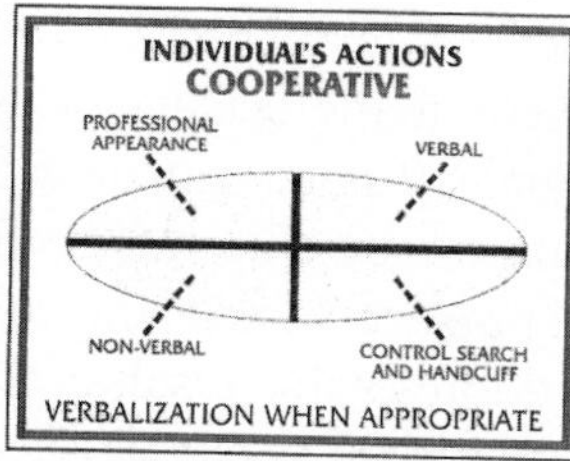

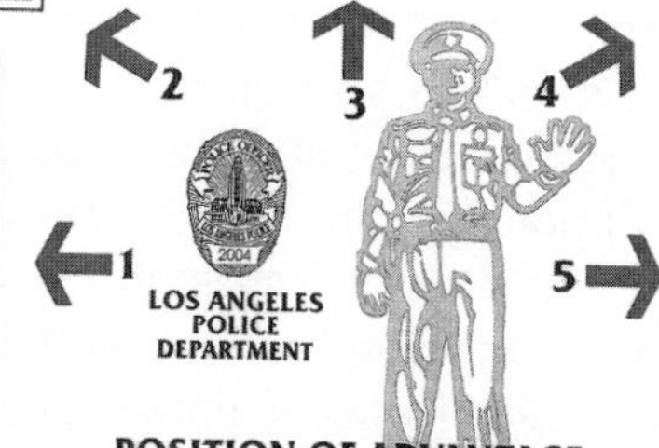

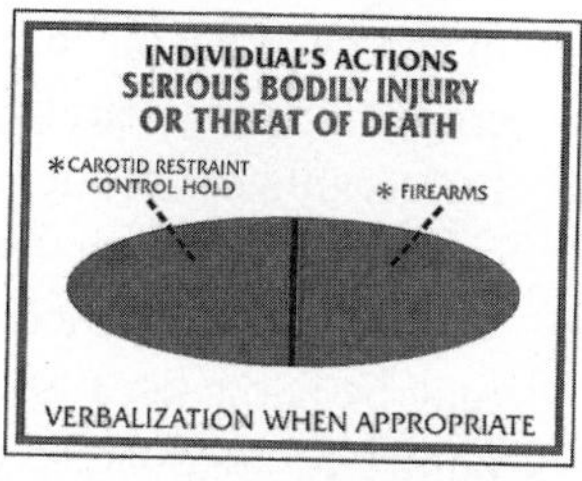

Source: *Graham v. Connor*, 109 s. Ct. 1865, 1872 (1989).

(1) the existence of an actual emergency, (2) the use of adequate warning devices, and (3) the continued exercise of due care for the safety of others. Whether a government unit or its officers may be held liable depends in large part on the construction of such statutes. As a general rule, police drivers are not liable for negligence as a matter of law solely because they disregard a traffic regulation during an authorized emergency run. However, these statutes provide no protection against liability for an officer's reckless driving. Drivers of emergency police vehicles have a statutory duty to drive with due regard for the safety of others.

Court decisions defining the reasonable care standard constitute a second source from which to derive a duty owed by police pursuit drivers. Most courts have translated the reasonable care standard into a duty to drive with the care that a reasonable, prudent officer would exercise in the discharge of official duties of a like nature.[200] "Reasonable care" is a relative term depending on the exigencies of the situation and the degree of care and vigilance reasonably dictated by the circumstances of the chase.

A third source from which to derive a duty owed by police pursuit drivers is department policy. A law enforcement organization's policies, procedures, and training material concerning high-speed pursuits are generally admissible as evidence in lawsuits against the department or its officers for the negligent operation of a pursuit vehicle.[201] For example, in order to ascertain the standard of care applicable to a particular pursuit situation, a court could admit into evidence a police department regulation defining the proper speeds at which police cars responding to emergency calls were supposed to enter intersections when proceeding against red traffic signals. Depending on the jurisdiction involved, departmental pursuit policies may be merely a guideline to assist juries in determining the reasonableness of pursuit conduct, or they may actually constitute a duty owed, the violation of which would be considered negligent.

Proximate Cause

Liability must be based on proof that police conduct in breaching a duty owed was the **proximate cause** of a pursuit-related accident. Proximate cause is difficult to establish in cases involving the intervening negligence of other drivers, such as a case in which a fleeing motorist collides with an innocent person. In such cases, some courts impose liability on the officer and the department if the accident was a foreseeable consequence of police negligence.[202] For example, if police pursue without activating their lights and siren and an innocent citizen enters an intersection without being warned of the pursuit and collides with the pursued vehicle, the police may be liable because the accident was the proximate and foreseeable result of their failure to adequately warn other drivers of the pursuit. In *Nelson v. City of Chester, Ill.*,[203] the court held that the city's breach of its duty to properly train its police officers in high-speed pursuit might be found to be the proximate cause of the pursued driver's death, notwithstanding the contributing negligence of the pursued driver.

Legal barriers to civil actions, such as immunity, have been removed in many jurisdictions by a combination of legislation and judicial decisions, even though the extent of immunity continues to vary.[204] Statutes in most states have limited sovereign immunity to discretionary as opposed to ministerial decisions. Accordingly, the decision to pursue is viewed as discretionary, rendering the public entity immune, but the manner of pursuit is a ministerial decision for which there is no general grant of immunity. *Rhodes v. Lamar*[205] used this bifurcated approach to hold that the decision to institute a pursuit is a discretionary decision for which a sheriff enjoyed sovereign immunity, but liability was not precluded if the pursuit was conducted in a manner that violated a reasonable duty of care. In *Fagan v. City of Vineland,* the court of appeals allowed the municipality to be sued directly under Section 1983 when the pursuit causing a constitutional tort was pursuant to municipal policy or custom. Furthermore, the court allowed the municipality to be held liable for lack of training its officers in high-speed pursuit even if none of the officers involved in the pursuit at issue violated the Constitution.[206]

Federal Civil Rights Act

Pursuit-related liability under the federal Civil Rights Act, 42 U.S.C. 1983, requires proof that an officer's conduct violated a constitutionally protected right.[207] In *Cannon v. Taylor,*[208] the court of appeals for the 11th Circuit concluded that "a person injured in an automobile accident caused by the negligent, or even grossly negligent, operation of a motor vehicle by a police officer acting in the line of duty has no Section 1983 cause of action for violation of a federal right."[209] The Supreme Court in *County of Sacramento v. Lewis* decided that a police officer does not violate the Fourteenth Amendment's guarantee of substantive due process "by causing death through deliberate or reckless indifference to life in a high speed automobile chase aimed at apprehending a suspected offender."[210] The only violation of substantive due process occurs when there is a purpose to cause harm unrelated to the arrest. Automobile negligence actions are grist for the state law mill, but they do not rise to the level of a constitutional deprivation.[211] The common thread running through the cases is that negligent conduct during a pursuit does not suffice to trigger jurisdiction under 1983. However, a municipality may be held liable under Section 1983 if there was no or inadequate high-speed pursuit training for its officers, even when the officers involved with a pursuit were not individually negligent.[212]

Certain techniques employed by police during a pursuit may raise constitutional issues cognizable under 1983. For example, in *Jamieson By and Through Jamieson v. Shaw*[213] the court held that the constitutionally permissible use-of-force standard set forth by the Supreme Court in *Tennessee v. Garner*[214] was violated when a passenger in a fleeing vehicle was hurt when the vehicle hit a so-called deadman roadblock after officers allegedly shined a bright light into the driver's eyes as the vehicle approached the roadblock. In *Bower v. County of Inyo,*[215] a high-speed pursuit of over 20 miles ended when the fleeing suspect was killed when his vehicle hit a tractor-trailer that police had placed across the road as a roadblock. The court of appeals held that police use of a roadblock could constitute a constitutional violation of substantive due process if it was designed as an intentional deathtrap where the approaching driver does not have a clear option to stop because the roadblock is concealed around a curve or inadequately illuminated. The Supreme Court went further in stating that the deceased driver was unreasonably "seized" when the roadblock was placed completely across the highway in a manner likely to kill the driver and that the police officers were liable under the Fourth Amendment and Section 1983 for the use of excessive force.[216]

Factors Determining Liability

Pursuit-related litigation usually involves an inquiry into whether the manner in which the pursuit was conducted was reasonable under the circumstances of that case. Each pursuit situation is different and requires a particularized assessment. Following is a brief discussion of certain factors that most frequently determine the extent of pursuit-related liability.

Purpose of Pursuit

This factor relates to the need or reason for a pursuit. Does the purpose of the pursuit warrant the risks involved? What is the nature and seriousness of the suspected offense? Is the fleeing motorist suspected of committing a serious crime or only a misdemeanor? Was the motorist already operating the vehicle in a reckless and life-threatening manner before the pursuit started, or had the motorist committed a minor, non-hazardous traffic violation prior to the pursuit but then started driving in a reckless and life-threatening manner after the pursuit was initiated? Is there a need for immediate apprehension, or has the suspect been identified so that apprehension at a later time is possible?

Driving Conditions

This factor involves a general assessment of equipment, the weather, roadway and traffic conditions, and the experience and personal ability of the drivers involved in the chase.

Use of Warning Devices

The use of adequate visual and audible warning devices, such as flashing lights and a siren, not only is a statutory mandate for most pursuit situations but also ensures to the greatest extent possible that other vehicles and pedestrians are alerted to approaching emergency vehicles and to the need to yield the right of way.

Excessive Speed

Whether a particular speed is excessive depends on the purpose of the pursuit, the driving conditions, and the personal ability of a police driver to control and effectively maneuver the vehicle. Speed when crossing an intersection against a light or sign is an especially critical consideration, since statistics suggest that most pursuit-related collisions occur at intersections.[217] Liability may be based on the failure to sufficiently decrease speed when approaching an intersection so that a complete stop can be made to avoid a collision.

Disobeying Traffic Laws

Pursuit vehicles are statutorily obligated to use due care for the safety of others when disobeying traffic laws, such as operating a vehicle on the wrong side of the road, passing on the right, going the wrong way on a one-way street, passing in a "no passing" zone, or proceeding against a traffic signal. These dangerous and high-risk driving situations should be avoided because police are generally held liable for any resulting accidents.[218]

Roadblocks

Special care is required when using roadblocks to ensure that innocent persons are not placed in a position of danger and that the fleeing motorist is afforded a reasonable opportunity to stop safely.[219] To reduce the risk of liability, it is recommended that roadblocks be used only when authorized by a supervisor and only as a last resort to apprehend a fleeing motorist who is wanted for a violent felony and who constitutes an immediate and serious threat. Although the Supreme Court stated that a roadblock could be a Fourth Amendment unreasonable seizure granting Section 1983 liability,[220] the Court of Appeals for the First Circuit qualified the definition of "seizure" to apply to roadblock accidents constituting a "misuse of power" as opposed to the "accidental effects of otherwise lawful governmental conduct."[221]

Termination of Pursuit

Every police department's pursuit policy has a provision dealing with termination of pursuit. When officers are expected to terminate varies considerably, depending on the agency's philosophy. Some agencies allow their officers very broad latitude, while others greatly restrict officers' actions. Policies generally fall into one of three models:[222]

1. *Judgmental*—Allowing officers to make all major decisions relating to initiation, tactics, and termination
2. *Restrictive*—Placing certain restrictions on officers' judgments and decisions
3. *Discouragement*—Severely cautioning or discouraging any pursuit, except in the most extreme situations

However, despite these variations in department policies, a noticeable trend has been emerging. Increasingly, police departments are permitting their officers to pursue only individuals who are known to have committed dangerous felonies—that is, murder, felonious assault, rape, robbery, kidnaping, and so on. This trend is occurring because it is becoming increasingly difficult to justify pursuits that result in injuries and the death of innocent third parties, as well as the injuries and death of police officers. Another reason for the dramatic shift in these policies has been because of the enormously high monetary judgments imposed by juries for injuries to innocent third parties.

Alpert[223] and Beckman[224] show that the vast majority of pursuits are for traffic violations and/or misdemeanors and not felonies. The issue of when the violator would eventually stop was addressed by Alpert.[225] He interviewed 146 inmates who had fled from the police and who were confined to jails in three cities: Omaha, Nebraska; Miami, Florida; and Columbia, South Carolina. Over 70 percent of the suspects said they would have slowed down "when I felt safe" whether the pursuit was on a freeway, on a highway, or in a town. The phrase "when I felt safe" was interpreted by the respondents as outdistancing the police by 2.2 blocks on surface streets, 2.3 miles on highways, and 2.5 miles on freeways. Fifty-three percent of the suspects responded that they were willing to run at all costs from the police in a pursuit, and 64 percent believed that they would not be caught; however, 71 percent said they were concerned with their own safety, and 62 percent stated they were concerned with the safety of others while engaged in a chase.[226]

Thus, law enforcement agencies that allow their officers broad discretion in pursuit can expect a greater number of arrests of violators who flee. However, they can also expect to have more uninvolved third parties injured or killed, as well as more police officers injured and a greater number of lawsuits. Conversely, those departments that have more restrictive policies can expect more conservative results. The final decision is ultimately left to the chief administrator of the agency.

Departmental Responsibility for Liability Reduction

To reduce the risks and liability associated with vehicular pursuits, law enforcement organizations must carefully evaluate their pursuit policies, training, supervision, and postincident evaluations. Liability reduction is accomplished through sound management controls and a reduction in the number of pursuit-related accidents.

Policy Development

The function of a well-written pursuit policy is to state the department's objectives, establish some ground rules for the exercise of discretion, and educate officers as to specific factors they should consider when conducting a vehicular pursuit. Where

Quick Facts

Police Pursuit Statistics, 2004

- Traffic violations are by far the most common initial event that results in police chases, followed by non-violent felony offenses, such as auto theft and burglary.
- Sixty percent of pursuits end in three minutes or less, and 67 percent cover three miles or less.
- Suspects end the pursuit in 35 percent of events. Police voluntarily end one in five pursuits.
- Ninety-five percent of pursuits occur on dry roads.
- Seventy-seven percent of pursuits occur in light traffic.
- Seventy-six percent of pursuits occur in urban areas.
- The vast majority of suspects involved in high-speed pursuits are not impaired by alcohol, other drugs, or mental illness.
- Ninety-nine percent of pursuits end with no injury to law enforcement or uninvolved citizens. Ninety-five percent of pursuits end with no injury to the suspect.
- Five percent of pursuits are terminated by police intervention, the most common being tire deflators.
- All statistics are from a data base created by the International Association of Chiefs of Police to capture 28 elements related to police pursuits.

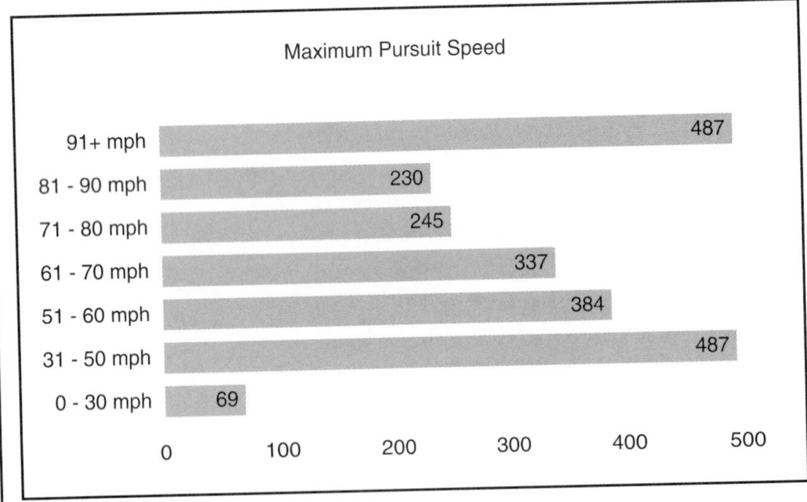

Source: International Association of Chiefs of Police (IACP), *Managing Police Pursuits: Findings from IACP's Police Pursuit Database* (Arlington, Va.: IACP, 2004).

feasible, a comprehensive policy statement should give content to terms such as "reasonable" and "reckless" and provide officers with more particularized guidance. A policy should be tailored to a department's operational needs, geographical peculiarities, and training capabilities. A written policy also provides a basis for holding officers accountable for their pursuit-related conduct.

Training

Lack of adequate training may contribute to many pursuit-related accidents. The natural tendency for many police drivers is to become emotionally involved and therefore lose some perspective during a pursuit. They are also required to drive different police vehicles with unique handling characteristics under various road and weather conditions. It is easy to lose control of a vehicle that is driven beyond its or the driver's capabilities, and law enforcement organizations can be held liable for failing to provide adequate driver training to prepare officers to handle vehicles safely in pursuit situations.[227] The extent and type of training required depend on a department's operational needs and objectives. A minimal level of cost-effective training can be accomplished by emphasizing defensive driving techniques and carefully instructing officers about departmental pursuit policies and relevant state regulations concerning the operation of emergency vehicles.

Supervision

Police departments are responsible for providing adequate supervision of officers involved in a pursuit. Experts who have studied the emotionalism and psychology associated with pursuits recommend that, as soon as possible after a pursuit has been initiated, a supervisor who is not in any of the pursuit vehicles be tasked with the responsibility of supervising the pursuit.[228] The supervisor who is not immediately involved is in a better position to oversee objectively the pursuit and decide whether it should continue and under what circumstances. The supervisor should track the location of the pursuit, designate the primary and secondary pursuit vehicles, and maintain tight controls on the desire of other officers to get involved or parallel the action. Effective communication between the pursuing vehicles and the supervisor is essential. The failure to transmit information concerning the location of a pursuit or the condition of the pursued driver may contribute to a subsequent accident.

Evaluation and Documentation

Law enforcement organizations should provide for an ongoing process of evaluation and documentation of pursuit-related incidents. All pursuits, including those successfully terminated without an accident, should be routinely critiqued to determine whether departmental policy was followed and the extent to which any policy modification, training enhancement, or other remedial action is warranted.

Critical Thinking Questions

1. List some of the important management controls that might be implemented to reduce liability related to high-speed chases.
2. If a particular jurisdiction has specific statutes related to high-speed pursuits, are officers completely protected from liability related to such events? Why or why not?
3. What are some of the factors that determine liability in a pursuit-related incident?

LIABILITY AND EMOTIONALLY DISTURBED PERSONS

Forty percent of persons suffering from serious mental illness will be arrested at least once during their lifetime. For this reason, it is imperative that progressive law enforcement agencies assume responsibility for evaluating potentially dangerous situations and recognizing those individuals suffering from various forms of mental illness. These individuals are commonly referred to as **emotionally disturbed persons (EDPs)**.[229]

Police responses to emotionally disturbed persons are determined to some degree by the manner in which the contact is initiated. The largest percentage of police officer contacts with EDPs are a result of on-the-street observations of bizarre, disruptive, or abnormal behavior. These encounters often end in an arrest of the subject for a relatively minor charge (e.g., disturbing the peace, disorderly conduct, vagrancy, or loitering), especially if alcohol use can be easily detected. See Figure 14.7. In other cases, the police receive complaints on an EDP as a result of a family disturbance or neighborhood problem. In either event, officers are often confronted by an individual with whom they have had prior contact (perhaps multiple prior contacts) and one that may unexplainably burst into a violent confrontation endangering everyone at the scene. As a result, many police departments are beginning to address this issue through basic and advanced training. For example, the Washington State Criminal Justice Commission has developed a unique curriculum focused on five key areas:

1. Recognizing abnormal behavior and mental illness (neuroses, psychoses, and psychopathic/sociopathic behavior)
2. Dealing with suicidal subjects (true versus parasuicidal behavior)
3. Developing crisis intervention skills (legal considerations in subject committal, tactical responses to handling the EDP, and responses to mental disturbance calls)
4. Developing awareness and knowledge of community services (interim facilities, hospital and emergency services, community care homes)
5. Recognizing and caring for Alzheimer's patients (physical cues and behavior)[230]

Other departments have also developed specialized in-service courses designed to provide more information to officers. The Monterey County Police Chief's Association has developed a Crisis Intervention Team (CIT) Academy in San Jose, California. The academy has distinguished itself through community collaboration and is well respected as a training model by the legislature and law enforcement community in California. The CIT Academy provides a 40-hour intensive training course that

FIGURE 14.7

A New York City police officer asks a homeless woman, who was sleeping on the floor at New York's Penn Station, to move along.
(AP/Wide World Photos)

includes role playing, interactive participation of people with mental illness (consumers), identification of various symptoms and signs of medication use by consumers, crisis negotiation skills and tactics, panel discussions and feedback, visits to interim-type housing facilities, suicide and crisis training, and a constant review of all countywide protocols and incident procedures.[231] The training focuses on developing the most useful tool available to officers on the street: the ability to communicate in a non-threatening manner.

The effective training of police officers in dealing with EDPs should result in two significant changes. First, there should be fewer incidents in which the use of force is necessary, thereby increasing officer safety. Second, effective training will provide a strong defense to litigation, should the department become entangled in litigation arising from the handling of an emotionally disturbed person.

Critical Thinking Questions

1. Why is it important for officers to be thoroughly trained on how to deal with emotionally disturbed persons?
2. What topics should be covered in training related to emotionally disturbed persons?

TESTING IN THE WORK ENVIRONMENT

Alcohol and Drug Testing

It is common for police departments to require that their officers not be under the influence of any intoxicating agent while on duty. Even in the absence of such specific regulation, disciplinary action has been upheld when it was taken against an officer who was suspected of being intoxicated while on duty by charging him or her with neglect of duty or violation of a state law.[232]

Regulations that prohibit being under the influence of an intoxicating or mind-altering substance have been upheld uniformly as reasonable because of the hazardous

In The News

Police Get New Rules on Excited Delirium

The Dallas Police Department implemented new plans in 2006 designed to prevent deaths caused by the condition known as excited delirium. Excited delirium is a medical condition caused by a severe chemical imbalance in the body resulting from mental illness or long-term drug use, particularly methamphetamines and cocaine. Symptoms include accelerated heart rate, profuse sweating, a significant increase in body temperature, and erratic and violent behavior. According to the new policy, officers are to call a supervisor and an ambulance immediately if excited delirium is suspected.

Dr. Vincent Di Maio, the chief medical examiner for Bexar County, Texas, says that 30 deaths in his county between 1997 and 2005 were attributed to excited delirium. Dallas has not compiled similar statistics, but at least three deaths in 2005 were attributed to the condition. Assistant Chief Daniel Garcia said that the policy was drawn from medical, safety, and liability concerns.

Excited delirium can result in death because the afflicted person seems to possess an almost "super-human" strength due to a surge in adrenaline. Officers often have to exert an extraordinary amount of force in order to restrain individuals in this state. The type of restraint used against afflicted individuals may cause positional asphyxiation. Electrical shocks from a Taser gun may also be a factor. As a result of the somewhat broad nature of the disease, as well as the safety challenges posed to involved officers, Dallas police have also instituted additional training measures meant to increase officer awareness of the condition, as well as defensive tactics to deal with it.

Source: Martin Martin-Hidalgo, "Police Get New Rules on Excited Delirium," *Dallas Morning News*, July 14, 2006.

nature of a police officer's work and the serious impact his or her behavior or misbehavior is sure to have on the property and safety of others. The necessity to require a clear head and rational action, unbefuddled by alcohol or drugs, is clear.[233] A Louisiana court upheld a regulation that prohibited an officer from consuming alcoholic beverages on or off duty to the extent that it caused the officer's behavior to become obnoxious, disruptive, or disorderly.[234]

Effective enforcement of regulations against an officer's being under the influence of drugs or alcohol will occasion situations when a police supervisor or administrator will order an officer to submit to one or more tests to determine the presence of the prohibited substance in the subject's body. It has been held that a firefighter could be ordered to submit to blood sampling when reasonable grounds existed for believing that he or she was intoxicated and that it was permissible to discharge the firefighter for his or her refusal to comply with the order.[235] More recently, the courts have also been asked to review police department policies that require officers to submit to urinalysis for the purpose of determining the presence of drugs or alcohol. In *United States v. Jacobsen*, the Supreme Court defined the concept of search and seizure:

> *A "search" occurs when an expectation of privacy that society is prepared to consider reasonable is infringed. A "seizure" of property occurs when there is some meaningful interference with an individual's possessory interests in that property.*[236]

According to the Supreme Court, removing urine from an individual's body is a search within the meaning of the Fourth Amendment. Consequently, when a government agency tests an employee's urine, due process must be applied, which involves providing probable evidence of illegal activity. In the case of public employer drug testing, the search is justified from the beginning, when "reasonable grounds exist for suspecting that the search will turn up evidence of work-related drug use."[237]

A reasonable search depends on a "balancing test" set forth by Justice Sandra Day O'Connor:

> *A determination of the standard of reasonableness applicable to a particular class of searches requires balancing the nature and quality of the intrusion on the individual's Fourth Amendment interests against the importance of the governmental interest alleged to justify the intrusion. In the case of searches conducted by a public employer, we must balance the invasion of the employee's legitimate expectations of privacy against the government's need for supervision, control, and the efficient operation of the work place.*[238]

The Supreme Court ruled on two cases in the late 1980s that would become landmarks for drug testing in the public sector. In *Skinner v. Railway Labor Executives' Association*, the Court upheld a mandatory drug testing program in cases in which the government had no reasonable suspicion about any particular public employee but had a substantial interest in maintaining public safety.[239] In a case even more important to police agencies, the Court considered in *National Treasury Employees Union v. Von Raub* whether the U.S. Customs drug testing program was constitutional. The customs service drug tested employees who sought a promotion to positions that required seizing or safekeeping illegal drugs, carrying firearms, or handling classified documents. The Court held that such employees have a diminished expectation of privacy and that drug testing is a minimal intrusion that is far outweighed by the government's interests.[240]

The prevailing view appears to be that totally random, unscheduled drug testing is unacceptable but that particular officers can be required to submit to urinalysis if there exists a "reasonable suspicion" that the officer has been using a prohibited substance.[241] The results of such compulsory tests are appropriate evidence for introduction in administrative discharge proceedings.[242] Decisions involving other government employees and similar kinds of personal intrusions (e.g., strip searches of prison guards) seem to support the view that random testing is unreasonable under the Fourth Amendment.[243] However, without a definitive decision from the Supreme Court on random drug testing, lower federal court decisions concerning public agency personnel appear to allow random drug testing without reasonable suspicion of individual drug abuse if (1) an employer knows that drugs are used in the workplace; (2) the testing will not totally disrupt the employee's privacy expectation; and (3) the jobs are "safety-sensitive" in nature.[244]

In an attempt to skirt the issue of mandatory or random testing, some departments have incorporated drug testing as a "usual and customary" part of a required medical examination. For instance, the Philadelphia Police Department requires a medical examination for all individuals attempting to secure employment under the following conditions: (1) when an officer is first hired, (2) when an officer is transferred to a "sensitive" position (i.e., vice and narcotics division, SWAT, and hostage negotiation teams), (3) when an officer is promoted to a higher rank, and (4) when an officer returns to duty after an extended period of time (e.g., long illness, disability, or suspension). Drug abuse is viewed as a medical malady and subject to disclosure similar to the findings of other tests that show spinal problems, poor vision, hearing loss, and the like. Hence, drug testing can be viewed as a routine part of the medical examination for pre-employment to a new position.

In Arlington, Texas, all police officers are required to take an annual medical examination and perform acceptable physical agility tests that "qualify" them for continued employment. The department links these tests to "insurability" through policies and regulations. Officers with physical disabilities (including alcohol and drug addiction) cannot be insured through the city of Arlington. An important note regarding both the Arlington and the Philadelphia police departments is the attitude expressed about officer drug abuse. Each department views the problem as a medical issue; therefore, extensive programs for counseling and rehabilitation have been established. Although these regulations have *not* been court tested, it appears reasonable that a comprehensive look at the issue of drugs in the workplace will support drug testing as a routine part of a medical examination.

Critical Thinking Question

1. How have many departments skirted the issue of mandatory and random drug testing?

TERMS AND CONDITIONS OF EMPLOYMENT

The nature of policing is different from most other employment environments primarily because it is one of the few services that is mandated 24 hours a day, 365 days a year. As a result, individual police officers often work the "graveyard shift" through the early morning hours when everyone else is sleeping; they also work on weekends and on holidays. Police officers are required to wear a uniform, to be physically fit, and to handle themselves appropriately in dangerous situations. Aside from causing added stress to an officer's personal life and family, these unusual circumstances often produce unique terms and conditions of employment.

Wage and Hour Regulations

The Fair Labor Standards Act (FLSA) was initially enacted by Congress in 1938 to establish minimum wages and to require overtime compensation in the private sector. In 1974, amendments to the act extended its coverage to state and local government employees and established special work period provisions for police and fire. However, in 1976 the Supreme Court ruled that the extension of the act into the realm of traditional local and state government functions was unconstitutional.[245] Almost a decade later, the Court surprisingly reversed itself, thus bringing all local police agencies under the coverage of the FLSA.[246] Shortly thereafter, Congress enacted the Fair Labor Standards Amendments of 1985 (effective April 15, 1986), which set forth special wage and hour provisions for government employees in an effort to reduce the monetary impact of the overtime requirements on state and local governments.

Generally, all rank-and-file law enforcement officers are covered under the FLSA. Exemptions include elected officials, their personal staffs, and those employees in policymaking positions. The law requires that overtime be paid to police personnel for all work in excess of 43 hours in a 7-day cycle or 171 hours in a 28-day period. Employers are allowed to establish or negotiate a work/pay period as they see fit within those boundaries. (The FLSA sets minimum standards that may be exceeded by offering greater benefits.) The appropriate wage for overtime hours is set at one and one-half times the employee's regular rate of pay. This may be given in money or compensatory time. Public safety officers may accrue a maximum of 480 hours of "comp" time, which, if not used as leave, must be paid off on separation from employment at the employee's final regular rate or at the average pay over the last three years, whichever is higher.

Of special interest to police agencies is that off-duty work and special details for a separate independent employer voluntarily undertaken by the employee are not used for calculating overtime payment obligations. Thus, specific hourly rates may still be negotiated for such work.

Age-Based Hiring and Retirement Policies

State and local governments have adopted a variety of personnel policies to ensure that police officers are in adequate mental and physical condition in order to perform the normal and the unexpected strenuous physical activities of the job satisfactorily and safely. Based on the assumption that increasing age slows responses, saps strength, and increases the likelihood of sudden incapacitation because of breakdowns of the nervous and/or cardiovascular systems, many police departments and state law enforcement agencies have established mandatory hiring and retirement ages.

During the 1970s, the courts allowed employers much latitude in enforcing retirement age requirements, finding such standards to be rationally related to a legitimate state interest in seeing that officers were physically prepared to protect the public's welfare.[247] In more recent decisions, however, the Supreme Court has significantly restricted the employer's ability to require that an employee be terminated on reaching a certain age.

The Age Discrimination in Employment Act (ADEA) is a federal law that prohibits discrimination on the basis of age against employees who are between the ages of 40 and 70, unless age is shown to be a "bona fide occupational qualification (BFOQ) reasonably necessary to the normal operation of the particular business."[248] The Supreme Court has held that the BFOQ exemption is meant to be an extremely narrow exception to the general prohibition of age discrimination contained in the ADEA.[249] For an employer to demonstrate successfully that its age-based mandatory retirement rule is valid, it must first prove the existence of a job qualification reasonably necessary to the essence of its operation. Second, the employer must show that it has reasonable cause, based on fact, for believing that substantially all persons in the prohibited age group would be unable to perform the job duties safely and efficiently or that it is impractical or impossible to accurately test and predict the capabilities of individuals in the excluded group.[250] The courts have also held that involuntary retirement policies must be designed so that they do not act as a means to address failure in accommodating individuals with disabilities. Retirement policies must take into consideration all employees in a fair and equitable manner.[251]

In a 1985 decision, the Supreme Court stated that stereotypical assumptions about the effects of aging on employee performance were inadequate to demonstrate a BFOQ. Instead, the Court held that employers are required to make a "particularized, factual showing" with respect to each element of the BFOQ defense.[252]

The federal courts have considered an ADEA challenge to a New York state law setting a maximum age of 29 for those applying for jobs as police officers. The court concluded that age 29 was not a BFOQ and ruled that the requirement was a violation of the law. The court noted that the employer has the same burden of proof to justify an age-based hiring standard as it does to justify an age-based retirement requirement.[253]

SEXUAL HARASSMENT

The increasing number of women joining law enforcement agencies poses a challenge to law enforcement managers and executives. As in many other professions, women joining the law enforcement ranks are sometimes stereotyped by those who believe that they are not capable of being good police officers. Moreover, the addition of women to a male-dominated profession, where notions of machismo may prevail, can create a situation in which women are singled out and made to feel unwelcome solely because of their gender, regardless of their work performance.[254]

The challenge to law enforcement managers and executives is to break down the inaccurate stereotypes attached to women and eliminate any notion of disparate treatment of employees based on gender. Although common sense and good management practice dictate these must be done, the law requires it.[255] Under Title VII of the 1964 Civil Rights Act, commonly referred to simply as Title VII, when an employer causes, condones, or fails to eliminate unfair treatment of women in the workplace, liability may be found.[256] See Figure 14.8.

Sexual Harassment: A Definition

It is somewhat difficult to provide a precise definition of conduct that constitutes **sexual harassment**; it is apparently more easily recognized than defined. Sexual harassment falls within the broader, prohibited practice of sex discrimination and may occur when an employee is subjected to unequal and unwelcome treatment based solely on the employee's sex.

Specific guidance on the types of conduct that would constitute sexual harassment is provided in the Equal Employment Opportunity Commission's (EEOC's) *Guidelines on Discrimination Because of Sex*.[257] These guidelines, although not carrying the force of law, "constitute a body of experience and informed judgment to which courts and litigants may properly resort for guidance."[258] The EEOC describes sexual harassment as follows:

> *Unwelcome sexual advances, requests for sexual favors, and other physical or verbal conduct of a sexual nature constitutes sexual harassment when submission to or rejection of this conduct explicitly or implicitly affects an individual's employment, unreasonably interferes with an individual's work performance, or creates an intimidating, hostile or offensive work environment.*

FIGURE 14.8

Employment discrimination on the basis of age, gender and/or race is prohibited by federal law.

(Dwayne E. Newton/PhotoEdit)

Sexual harassment can occur in a variety of circumstances, including but not limited to the following:

- *The victim as well as the harasser may be a woman or a man. The victim does not have to be of the opposite sex.*
- *The harasser can be the victim's supervisor, an agent of the employer, a supervisor in another area, a coworker, or a nonemployee.*
- *The victim does not have to be the person harassed but could be anyone affected by the offensive conduct.*
- *Unlawful sexual harassment may occur without economic injury or discharge of the victim.*
- *The harasser's conduct must be unwelcome.*[259]

In general, sexual harassment can take two forms. First, sexual harassment exists when an employee is requested or required to engage in or submit to a sexual act as a term or condition of a job benefit or assignment. Second, sexual harassment may arise when the comments, conduct, or actions of the employer, supervisors, or coworkers create an unwelcome and hostile work environment for an employee based on gender. Both denigrate the workplace and must be prevented.

Sexual and Racial Harassment: Theories of Liability

Because, by general definition, sexual harassment falls into two categories, it is not surprising that courts have imposed liability on employers and coworkers for participating in, condoning, or permitting sexual harassment at work under two parallel theories. These two theories on which liability may be found have been referred to as *quid pro quo liability* and *hostile environment liability.*[260]

Quid pro quo liability is established when a sexual act is the condition precedent before an individual is hired or promoted or becomes the recipient of any other job benefit. The converse is also true. Quid pro quo liability can be found where the refusal to engage in a sexual act is the reason for a refusal to hire, a firing, a denied promotion, or a withheld job benefit. Unlike the hostile working environment theory, the plaintiff in a quid pro quo case must show that the sexual demand was linked to a tangible, economic aspect of an employee's compensation, term, condition, or privilege of employment.[261]

The second legal theory on which sexual harassment can be predicated is the hostile working environment. Individuals who must work in an atmosphere made hostile or abusive by the unequal treatment of the sexes are denied the equal employment opportunities guaranteed to them by law and the Constitution.[262] As the Court of Appeals for the 11th Circuit said,

> *Sexual harassment which creates a hostile or offensive environment for members of one sex is every bit the arbitrary barrier to sexual equality at the workplace that racial harassment is to racial equality. Surely, a requirement that a man or woman run a gauntlet of sexual abuse in return for the privilege of being allowed to work and make a living can be as demeaning and disconcerting as the harshest of racial epithets.*[263]

The elements of a hostile environment case were most clearly spelled out in *Henson v. City of Dundee.*[264] To prevail in such a case, the court noted that a plaintiff must establish four elements:

1. As in all Title VII cases, the employee must belong to a protected group (either by sex, gender, or race).
2. The employee must show that he or she was subjected to unwelcome sexual or racial harassment.
3. The harassment was based on sex, gender, or race, and, but for the employee's sex, gender, or race, the employee would not have been subjected to the hostile or offensive environment.
4. The sexual harassment affected a term, condition, or privilege of employment.[265]

Accordingly, sexual harassment can be perpetrated by members of the same or opposite sex, no matter the sexual orientation of the harasser.[266] Further, a hostile or offensive work environment can exist in a variety of ways.[267] The pervasive use of derogatory or insulting terms relating to women or minorities generally and addressed to female or minority employees personally can be evidence of a hostile work environment,[268] as can the use or display of obscene language or sexually explicit pictures or cartoons in the workplace.[269]

To the extent that an officer is a willing participant in jokes of a sexual nature or sexual banter, the officer's claim of harassment will be much harder to establish (see further discussion on this issue later in the chapter).[270] This line of reasoning has led the Supreme Court to temper previous interpretations of Title VII discrimination cases relating to hostile and/or offensive work environments. For instance, in 1998 the Court ruled that Title VII is directed at *discrimination* based on sex, gender, and/or race, not merely conduct tinged with offensive sexual or racial connotation.[271] Hence, each case must be weighed with an understanding of the innocuous differences in the ways men and women routinely interact with members of the same and opposite sex, considering all the circumstances of the case.[272] The lower courts have affirmed this decision. In *Washington v. Board of Trustees,* the court denied a Title VII claim that calling an African-American woman an "oreo, a bitch, and an Uncle Tom" was sufficient to establish racial or sexual harassment.[273] And in *Russ v. Van Scoyok Associates, Inc.*, no sexual harassment claim was awarded where a supervisor told a female subordinate that he admired her breasts, that he wanted to have sex with her and perform oral sex on her, and that she could make more money working for Hooters than with her current employer.[274] To constitute harassment, there must be a pattern of racial or sexual comments; isolated comments usually do not rise to the level of unlawful harassment due to a hostile or offensive environment.[275] For instance, in one case a court ruled that a supervisor's reference to an employee as a "white token" and a "white faggot" did not create an inference of racial discrimination.[276]

Clearly, these cases signal a change in the Supreme Court's attitude in developing a Title VII claim based on a hostile or offensive environment. There must be clear evidence of *discrimination* based on sex, gender, and/or race. However, it is dangerous to presuppose the Court's relatively new attitude in this area, especially since a great number of racial and sexual harassment claims focus on the hostile or offensive environment issue. If a plaintiff can establish each of the elements outlined previously and that the elements directly caused discrimination against the individual, with membership in a protected group being a given, then a successful claim of sexual harassment can be developed, and liability may attach. Because these last three elements form the core of the sexual harassment claim, each is discussed in turn.

Unwelcome Sexual Harassment

In 1986, the Supreme Court had the occasion to address the issue of what constituted unwelcome sexual harassment. In *Meritor Savings Bank v. Vinson,*[277] a bank employee alleged that, following the completion of her probationary period as a teller trainee, her supervisor invited her to dinner and, during the course of the meal, suggested they go to a motel to have sexual relations. The employee first declined but eventually agreed because she feared she might lose her job by refusing. Thereafter, over the course of the next several years, the employee alleged that her superior made repeated demands of her for sexual favors. She alleged she had sexual intercourse 40 to 50 times with her superior, had been fondled repeatedly by him, had been followed into the women's restroom by him, and had even been forcibly raped on several occasions. In defending the suit, the defendant bank averred that, because the employee had voluntarily consented to sexual relations with her superior, the alleged harassment was not unwelcome and not actionable.

The Supreme Court disagreed. The Court stated that "the fact that sex-related conduct was 'voluntary,' in the sense that the complainant was not forced to participate against her will, is not a defense to a sexual harassment suit brought under Title VII."[278] Sexually harassing conduct is unwelcome if the "employee did not solicit it or invite it, and the employee regarded the conduct as undesirable or offensive."[279]

The determination of whether specific conduct, even if "voluntary," constitutes unwelcome sexual harassment is a fact-bound inquiry.[280] Each case brings different facts and parties, leading to potentially different results. However, the courts have provided some guidance as to the types of facts that are relevant in determining whether the conduct considered in a sexual harassment suit was unwelcome.

For example, in *Meritor Savings Bank v. Vinson,*[281] the Supreme Court noted,

> *While "voluntariness" in the sense of consent is not a defense to such a claim, it does not follow that a complainant's sexually provocative speech or dress is irrelevant as a matter of law in determining whether he or she found particular sexual advances unwelcome. To the contrary, such evidence is obviously relevant.*[282]

Thus, the Supreme Court ruled that, to some extent,[283] the employee's own conduct is at issue when he or she files suit alleging sexual harassment. The nature of relevant employee conduct extends to the employee's participation in office vulgarities and sexual references,[284] the employee's non-work conduct where a moral and religious character particularly sensitive to sexual jokes is claimed,[285] and proof that the employee actually initiated the sexual advance or innuendo.[286] Also relevant to the issue of "unwelcome" conduct is whether and when the employee complained. At least one court has ruled that a failure to report instances of alleged sexual harassment, where the opportunity and mechanism to do so existed, was proof that the conduct later complained of was not genuinely offensive or unwelcome.[287]

Whether the conduct is unwelcome is a "totality of circumstances" analysis. Conduct alleged to be sexual harassment must be judged by a variety of factors, including the nature of the conduct; the background, experience, and actions of the employee; the background, experience, and actions of coworkers and supervisors; the physical environment of the workplace; the lexicon of obscenity used there; and an objective analysis of how a reasonable person would react to and respond in a similar work environment.[288] However, rather than risk making an incorrect ad-hoc determination of whether conduct is or is not unwelcome in each instance of alleged sexual harassment, police managers should be prepared to take appropriate action when conduct directed against employees because of sex first appears to be offensive and unwelcome.

Harrassment Based on Gender

As stated earlier, the second major element of a Title VII claim of hostile environment sexual harassment requires that the harassment be directed against an employee based on the employee's gender.[289] Conduct that is offensive to both sexes is not sexual harassment because it does not discriminate against any protected group.[290] The essence of a disparate treatment claim under Title VII is that "an employee . . . is intentionally singled out for adverse treatment" on the basis of a prohibited criterion.[291]

The prohibited criterion here is, of course, an employee's gender. In quid pro quo cases, this requirement is self-evident. The request or demand for sexual favors is made because of the employee's gender and would not otherwise have been made. However, discrimination based on gender is not always as clear in a hostile environment case. "In proving a claim for a hostile work environment due to sexual harassment, . . . the plaintiff must show that but for the fact of her [or his] sex, [the employee] would not have been the object of harassment."[292]

The term "sexual harassment" usually brings to mind sexual advances or acts and comments and jokes relating to sexual activities. However, whereas sexual harassment includes all those types of conduct if they are unwelcome, the concept itself is broader. Any unwelcome conduct aimed at an employee that would not have occurred but for the employee's gender is sexual harassment. For example, in *Hall v. Gus Construction Co.*,[293] three female employees of a road construction firm filed suit alleging sexual harassment by fellow male employees. The conduct the women complained of included the use of sexual epithets and nicknames, repeated requests to engage in sexual activities, physical touching and fondling of the women, the exposure of the men's genitals, "mooning," the displaying of obscene pictures to the women, urination in the women's water bottles and gas tank of their work truck, refusal to perform necessary repairs on the work truck until a male user complained, and refusal to allow the women restroom breaks in a town near the construction site. The defendant construction company argued that some of the conduct—such as the urination in water bottles and gas tanks, the refusal to perform needed repairs on the truck, and the denial of restroom breaks—could not be considered sexual harassment because the conduct, although perhaps inappropriate, was not sexually oriented.

The court disagreed. It concluded that the "incidents of harassment and unequal treatment . . . would not have occurred but for the fact that [the employees] were women."[294] Intimidation and hostility toward women because they are women can obviously result from conduct other than explicit sexual advances. Additionally, there is no requirement that the incidents, sexually oriented or not, be related to or part of a series of events. Sexual harassment can be based on repeated, though unrelated, events.[295]

Police managers and executives should be aware that any type of unwelcome conduct that is directed at an employee because of that person's gender may constitute sexual harassment. The lesson, as before, is to be alert and stifle any conduct that threatens disparate treatment because of the employee's gender.

Harassment Affecting a Condition of Employment

Title VII prohibits discrimination based on sex with respect to "compensation, terms, conditions, or privilege of employment."[296] Although it can readily be seen how the quid pro quo theory of a sexual harassment claim is sex discrimination with regard to compensation, terms, conditions, or privileges of employment, how can a sexually hostile environment affect a condition of employment if no economic or tangible job detriment is suffered?[297]

The answer is simple. One of the conditions of any employment is the psychological well-being of the employees.[298] Where the psychological well-being of employees is adversely affected by an environment polluted with abusive and offensive harassment based solely on sex, Title VII provides a remedy. "The language of Title VII is not limited to 'economic' or 'tangible' discrimination. The phrase 'terms, conditions or privileges of employment' evinces a congressional intent 'to strike at the entire spectrum of disparate treatment of men and women' in employment."[299]

However, this is not to say that any conduct, no matter how slight, directed against an employee because of sex constitutes a hostile working environment. "For sexual harassment to be actionable, it must be sufficiently severe or pervasive to alter the conditions of the victim's employment and create an abusive working environment."[300] Isolated incidents[301] or genuinely trivial ones[302] will not give rise to sexual harassment liability. Not every sexual epithet or comment will affect the conditions of employment to a sufficient degree to create a hostile environment in violation of Title VII. Nonetheless, law enforcement management must realize that Title VII obligates it to provide a workplace where the psychological health of its employees is protected against sexual harassment.

Grounds for Sexual Harassment Claims

Generalizations about the kinds of conduct that translate into a legal finding of sexual harassment are difficult because each case is a fact-oriented determination involving many factors. However, an analysis of the cases indicates that at least three broad categories of conduct, if found, generally lead to a legal finding of sexual harassment.

First, invariably when allegations of quid pro quo sexual harassment are proved, liability follows.[303] That is not surprising. Demands for sex acts in exchange for job benefits are the most blatant of all forms of sexual harassment. In addition, whenever a job benefit is denied because of an employee's refusal to submit to the sexual demand, a tangible or economic loss is readily established. The primary difficulty in a quid pro quo case is in carrying the burden of proof and establishing that the alleged event(s) actually occurred. Because such incidents usually occur in private conversations, the cases often involve a one-on-one contest of testimony.[304] However, if the employee sufficiently proves the event(s) happened, courts readily conclude that sexual harassment existed.

Second, courts frequently conclude that sexual harassment exists where the alleged conduct was intentionally directed at an employee because of the employee's gender, was excessively beyond the bounds of job requirements, and actually detracted from the accomplishment of the job. When the conduct becomes so pervasive that the offending employee's attention is no longer focused on job responsibilities and significant time and effort is diverted from work assignments to engage in the harassing conduct, courts will generally conclude that sexual harassment exists.

This principle can be illustrated by examining two law enforcement–related cases. In *Vermett v. Hough,*[305] a female law enforcement officer alleged sexual harassment by her coworkers. One specific act alleged to have been offensive to her was a male officer placing a flashlight between her legs from behind. The court ruled that the conduct was nothing more than "horseplay"[306] and a stress-relief mechanism in a high-pressure job. The "horseplay" was viewed by the court to be more indicative of the female's acceptance as a coworker than sexual harassment. Moreover, horseplay was an occasional part of the police station behavior but not on an inordinate basis.

The second case, *Arnold v. City of Seminole,*[307] illustrates the other side of the coin—out-of-control office joking, leading to sexual harassment. In *Arnold,* a female officer chronicled a series of events and conduct to which she was subjected because she was female. Among the offensive conduct that created a hostile working environment were the following: (1) a lieutenant told her he did not believe in female police officers; (2) superior officers occasionally refused to acknowledge or speak to her; (3) obscene pictures were posted in public places within the police station with the female officer's name written on them; (4) epithets and derogatory comments were written next to the officer's name on posted work and leave schedules; (5) false misconduct claims were lodged against her; (6) work schedules were manipulated to prevent the female officer from being senior officer on duty, thus denying her command status; (7) she was singled out for public reprimands and not provided the required notice; (8) members of the female officer's family were arrested, threatened, and harassed; (9) other officers interfered with her office mail and squad car; (10) attempts to implicate the female officer in an illegal drug transaction were contemplated; and (11) the female officer was not provided equal access to station house locker facilities. Based on this amalgam of proof, which far exceeded any colorable claim of office camaraderie, the court ruled that the female officer had indeed been subjected to an openly hostile environment based solely on her gender.

A note of caution is in order. The line between innocent joking that contributes to esprit de corps and offensive sexual harassment can be a fine one. Police managers should be cognizant of such conduct and be prepared to take immediate and corrective action at the first moment it appears to be in danger of exceeding acceptable bounds.

The third category of sexual harassment generally arises from conduct or statements reflecting a belief that women employees are inferior by reason of their sex or that women have no rightful place in the workforce. For example, where a supervisory employee stated, among other things, that he had no respect for the opinions of another employee because she was a woman, sexual harassment was found.[308] Similarly, a supervisor who treated his male employees with respect but treated his women employees with obvious disdain, used the terms "babe" and "woman" in a derogatory fashion, and indicated his belief that women should not be working at all was found to have sexually harassed his female employees.[309]

Although the law alone cannot realistically dispossess people of their personal prejudices, it can require that they not exhibit them in the workplace. Police managers have the responsibility to see that they do not.

Liability for Sexual Harassment

One of the primary goals of Title VII is to eliminate sexual harassment from the workplace.[310] However, to the extent it does not, civil liability remedies are available against both employers and offending coworkers. Both are matters of concern for law enforcement managers.

The Supreme Court, in *Meritor Savings Bank v. Vinson,*[311] made it clear that an employer would not be held liable simply because sexual harassment occurred in the workplace. Rather, the Court ruled that employer liability would be guided by agency principles, although it declined "to issue a definitive rule on employer liability."[312]

In addition to *Meritor,* the Supreme Court found that, under Title VII, an employee who refuses the unwelcome and threatening sexual advances of a supervisor can recover against the employer without showing that the employer is otherwise at fault for the actions of the supervisor. The victim need not suffer any tangible job consequences to recover. This holding accommodates the agency principles of vicarious liability for harm.[313]

The lower courts have consistently applied agency principles to effect a remedy for sexual harassment. Three such principles can be identified. First, where a supervisory employee engages in quid pro quo sexual harassment—that is, the demand for sex in exchange for a job benefit—the employer is liable. As one court explained,

> *In such a case, the supervisor relies upon his apparent or actual authority to extort sexual consideration from an employee. . . . In that case the supervisor uses the means furnished to him to accomplish the prohibited purpose. . . . Because the supervisor is acting within at least the apparent scope of the authority entrusted to him by the employer when he makes employment decisions his conduct can fairly be imputed to the source of his authority.*[314]

Second, in cases where a plaintiff has successfully proved that sexual harassment by supervisory employees created a hostile working environment, courts will hold employers liable. The Fourth Circuit Court of Appeals noted this to be the rule:

> *Once the plaintiff in a sexual harassment case proves that harassment took place, the most difficult legal question typically will concern the responsibility of the employer for that harassment. Except in situations where a proprietor, partner or corporate officer participates personally in the harassing behavior, the plaintiff will have the additional responsibility of demonstrating the propriety of holding the employer liable under some theory of respondent superior.*[315]

Third, if the sexually hostile working environment is created at the hands of coworkers, employers will be liable only if they knew or reasonably should have known of the harassment and took no remedial action. It is the burden of the offended employee to "demonstrate that the employer had actual or constructive knowledge of the existence of a sexually hostile working environment and took no prompt and adequate remedial action."[316] Actual knowledge includes situations in which the unwelcome, offensive conduct is observed or discovered by a supervisory or management-level employee and supervisory employees are personally notified of the alleged sexual harassment.[317] Constructive knowledge arises when the sexually harassing conduct is so pervasive that knowledge is imputed to the employer.[318] Absence of actual notice to an employer does not necessarily insulate that employer from liability.[319]

These three principles suggest the manner in which sexual harassment liability can be prevented. Law enforcement managers and executives must not engage in any conduct that constitutes sexual harassment. In addition, when such conduct comes to their attention, corrective action must be taken. Further, management has an affirmative obligation to monitor the workplace to ensure that sexual harassment does not become a widespread practice.

Although the remedies available under Title VII are directly against the employer only and are limited by statute to primarily equitable relief,[320] not including compensatory damages,[321] other remedies may also be available to impose liability against employers or coworkers for sexual harassment claims. In addition to the relief available under Title VII, a plaintiff may seek monetary damages for a violation of federal civil and constitutional rights[322] as well as for state tort violations.[323] The important point to be noted is that liability may not be appropriate where no sexual harassment exists or where the employer takes swift remedial action.[324] The primary goal of law enforcement managers and executives should be to prevent the occurrence of any type of sexual harassment. If it does exist, sexual harassment must quickly be confronted and stopped. If this is done, no liability will attach.

Prevention of Workplace Harassment

Policy Development

One of the most important steps toward eradicating workplace harassment and thus minimizing the chances of liability for harassment is the development of an agency policy prohibiting harassment in the workplace. A written policy begins the process of establishing the agency's philosophy that workplace harassment is prohibited conduct that will not be condoned. It provides officers with notification of what acts are prohibited. In addition, it provides a shield for those officers who do not want to participate in harassing behavior but do so because of group pressure. Finally, a written policy informs all employees of their right not to be subjected to harassment and how to remedy the situation, should harassment occur.[325]

The development of a policy prohibiting harassment is an issue of importance to all law enforcement executives, whether or not they currently have such a policy in place. The *Meritor* case suggests that employer liability for maintaining a hostile work environment will be determined by weighing all the facts of the case, including whether the employer had a well-developed policy prohibiting workplace harassment.

It is crucial to note, however, that *Meritor* emphasizes that having a policy does not necessarily shield the employer from liability.[326] In fact, more recently the court held that an employer need not be at fault for the actions of a supervisor in order to be liable.[327] Law enforcement executives familiar with policy implementation and civil liability will appreciate that a bad policy is often as damning as no policy. Further, once a policy is established, it must be enforced. Even the best of policies provides no protection if it is not followed.

Several points should be considered when developing a quality policy that will meet the necessary legal standards. The policy must be clearly written, so that it is easily understood. There should be a statement within the policy that discriminatory harassment is illegal, is prohibited by the agency, and will be dealt with through disciplinary action. This statement should have a prominent position within the policy.

It is crucial that the policy clearly delineate specific types of conduct that are prohibited. The scope of workplace harassment is defined legally and is not assumed to be common knowledge. Many agencies choose to include in their policies a set of examples and/or definitions of harassment. This is an excellent practice because it notifies employees of the types of activity prohibited while continually reinforcing that knowledge.

On the other hand, many agencies provide a brief legal definition of workplace harassment and then rely on special training programs to provide more specific examples of discriminatory harassment. The rationale behind this approach is that, by stating a set of examples in the policy, it may be misconstrued as an exclusive list of prohibited conduct. The benefit of the model policy approach is that it allows officers to focus on specialized training and examine for themselves whether certain conduct could be construed as unwelcome harassment. Where this approach is adopted, it is imperative that the agency provide training on harassment for its officers, which is discussed in the next section.

Finally, the policy should state how an employee can register a complaint of harassment. Again, clarity in drafting is necessary, so that employees do not bypass agency remedies because of frustration. A complex, multi-step procedure or one that is too vague can lead to misunderstandings and thus frustrate both the employees' and the agency's attempts to eliminate harassment.

A copy of the policy should be distributed to every employee, regardless of rank. The policy will have little impact if access is limited to those employees with the initiative to seek it out. A rather popular and effective way to make sure the policy is read and continuously reinforced is by the use of posters. Many agencies place posters discussing workplace harassment in conspicuous places within their administrative complexes. The use of both posters and a policy on harassment signals employees that the agency is serious about prohibiting workplace harassment.

Training

The boundaries of what constitutes prohibited harassment can often be confusing. While a written policy provides a good framework for delineating prohibited acts, the law enforcement executive should also consider implementing training programs to combat harassment.

A good training program will help instill and reinforce the agency's philosophy against harassment. Special training programs that are carefully developed can be a valuable tool in fleshing out the policy description of what acts are prohibited. The training program should explain the agency's policy, philosophy, and applicable laws pertaining to workplace harassment. Such training should be used at the recruit level and on a regular basis with the entire agency.

A number of companies offer training programs using speakers and/or videos that focus on workplace harassment. The Equal Employment Opportunities Commission regional office may be able to suggest such a program. In addition, the International Association of Chiefs of Police has developed a training course devoted to workplace harassment and can develop a custom program for any law enforcement agency that so requests. The cost of any of these programs is a small price when compared to the costs of discrimination litigation.

Supervision

No law enforcement agency can fulfill its duty to maintain a workplace free of harassment without the assistance and support of its supervisors. Apathetic or hostile supervisors can quickly undermine an otherwise effective and meaningful policy against harassment through their actions or non-actions in implementing the policy.

By contrast, through their daily supervision of employees, supervisors can assist the agency in spotting, stopping, and preventing harassment.

Supervisors' responsibilities include watching for signs that harassment may be occurring in their unit. As agency liability may turn on the effectiveness or negligence of supervisors in monitoring the workplace, it is important that supervisors receive thorough training in identifying harassment.

Complaint Procedure

The development of an effective complaint procedure is the most important action that the agency can take to stop workplace harassment and minimize liability. The *Meritor* case emphasized the importance of maintaining an accessible and effective complaint procedure as a factor to be considered in determining employer liability for maintaining a hostile work environment.[328]

Employee Responsibilities

Employees are encouraged to assist victims of harassment by reporting any observed incidents or at least by encouraging the victim to complain. Victims of harassment often feel that everyone agrees with the harasser and that they are powerless. This feeling of isolation may keep victims from realizing that other employees may also be subject to the harassment and not reporting it. Support from coworkers can encourage the employees to file complaints.

Finally, law enforcement executives should encourage employees to document each incident of harassment, regardless of the severity. Harassment, especially sexual harassment, can often begin with acts so slight that the targeted employee may not know what is intended. As a result, the dates on which the alleged harassment occurred may be inexact. The documentation should include information such as the time, date, and location of the incident; the actions taken by the harasser and employer; the names and actions of any bystanders; and any physical or stress problems resulting from the incident.

Employers should encourage victims of harassment to make clear that the harassing conduct is offensive and unwanted. Employees should be encouraged to report incidents of harassment as soon as possible.

Critical Thinking Questions

1. Discuss how age-based hiring and retirement policies are of particular interest to police departments.
2. Why do you think sexual harassment presents such a unique challenge to law enforcement agencies?
3. Discuss the two legal theories on which sexual harassment claims may be predicated.
4. What are employee responsibilities related to sexual harassment?

CHAPTER REVIEW

1. Identify and explain the three general categories of torts.
   The three general categories of torts are negligence torts, intentional torts, and constitutional torts. In negligence torts, defendants will not be liable unless they foresaw or should have anticipated that their acts or omissions would result in injury to another.

Intentional torts involve acts that are committed voluntarily and deliberately and that will, to a substantial certainty, injure another person. Finally, constitutional torts allege than an officer failed to uphold the constitutional rights, privileges, and immunities of others.

2. Explain the statement "acting under the color of state law" as it relates to U.S. Code 42, Section 1983 actions.
   "Acting under the color of state law" means the officer was on duty and acting within the scope of employment as a sworn police officer. This is an essential element of a 1983 action, which gives federal courts the jurisdiction to hear police misconduct litigation related to constitutional torts.
3. Describe a *Bivens* action.
   A Bivens *action is a complaint against a federal official for a violation of an individual's constitutional rights. The* Bivens *action applies only to the federal official as an individual and not to the government as a whole.*
4. List and describe the negligence theories applicable to police supervision and management.
   The negligence theories applicable to police supervision and management include negligent employment, improper training, and improper supervision. Negligent employment may include liability against a police official for a failure to conduct a thorough investigation of a prospective employee's suitability for police work. Improper training negligence means that police officials failed to provide necessary training for officers. This can include firearms training or training in the use of physical force. Finally, failure to properly supervise or direct subordinate officers is applicable to police supervisors. This type of suit tends to be brought where officials have failed to take action to rectify a recurring problem exhibited in police operations by subordinates.
5. Describe procedural and substantive due process.
   Procedural due process is the legality of the procedures used to deprive police officers of status or wages, such as dismissal or suspension. Substantive due process is the requirement that the basis for government action against an officer is reasonable, relevant, and justifiable.
6. Explain the limitations due process places on disciplinary rules.
   Due process requires that disciplinary rules be clear, specific, and reasonably related to a valid job requirement.
7. Identify when department rules and polices might infringe on the free speech of officers.
   Rules that infringe on the free speech of officers can be upheld if the legitimate interest of the employer is found to be more important than the officer's free speech interest.
8. Describe the circumstances when an officer can use deadly force.
   Deadly force can be used if an officer must defeat an imminent threat to his or her or another person's life. Deadly force may also be used to prevent the escape of a felon if it is necessary to prevent the escape and the officer has probable cause to believe that the suspect poses a significant threat of death or serious physical injury to the officer or others.
9. Identify the four elements that must be proven in order to sue the police for negligence in a high-speed pursuit.
   The first element is that the officer owed the injured party a duty not to engage in certain conduct. Next, it must be shown that the officer's actions violated that duty. Third, the officer's negligent conduct was the proximate cause of the accident, and finally, the suing party suffered actual and provable damages.
10. Describe a police department's responsibility in reducing liability in high-speed pursuits.

The department's responsibilities in decreasing liability for high-speed chases include careful policy development, training of all officers in defensive driving techniques and departmental pursuit policies, adequate supervision of officers involved in a pursuit, and evaluation and documentation of all pursuit-related incidents.

11. Identify the desired outcomes of effective training of police officers in dealing with emotionally disturbed persons.
The first outcome should be fewer incidents in which the use of force is necessary against emotionally disturbed persons. The second outcome of effective training is that is provides a strong defense to litigation regarding entanglements with emotionally disturbed persons.
12. Describe the "balancing test" as referred to in alcohol and drug testing in the workplace.
The balancing test requires that police officials weigh the nature and quality of the intrusion into the police officer's Fourth Amendment interests against the importance of the governmental need for supervision, control, and the efficient operation of the workplace.
13. Identify the two most important elements to prove the validity of a mandatory age-based retirement rule.
A department must first prove the existence of a job qualification reasonably necessary to the essence of its operation. Second, the department must show that it has reasonable cause, based on fact, for believing that all persons in the age group prohibited would be unable to perform the job duties safely and efficiently or that it is improbable or impossible to accurately test and predict the capabilities of the individuals in the excluded group.
14. Describe policy recommendations designed to reduce the potential for sexual harassment allegations and subsequent lawsuit in the police work environment.
It is recommended that several points be considered when developing policies against sexual harassment. The first is that the policy be clearly written, so that it is easily understood. The second is that there should be a prominent statement within the policy that discriminatory harassment is illegal, is prohibited by the agency, and will be dealt with through disciplinary action. The policy should clearly delineate the types of behavior that are prohibited. The policy should also set forth procedures for how an employee may make a complaint of harassment. Finally, the policy should be distributed to every employee, regardless of rank.

KEY TERMS

1983 action: a tort action by which federal courts obtain jurisdiction of suits that involve the deprivation of any rights, privileges, or immunities secured by the Constitution by an individual acting under color of any statute, ordinance, regulation, custom, or usage of any state.

***Bivens* action:** a judicially created counterpart to a 1983 action that gives the federal courts jurisdiction over torts involving federal officials.

Defendant: the person or organization being sued, also called a tort feasor.

Due process: a guarantee of fairness in legal matters that requires that all legal procedures set by statute and court practice must be followed for every individual, so that there is no prejudicial or unequal treatment.

Emotionally disturbed persons (EDPs): individuals suffering from various forms of mental illness that may complicate interactions with police officers.

Liability: legal responsibility for a person's or an organization's acts or omissions.

Liberty rights: rights involving the protection and defense of one's good name, reputation, and position in the community.

Litigation: a lawsuit or another question to the court that resolves a legal matter or question.

Negligence: the failure to exercise the care toward another person which a reasonable person would do in the same circumstances; also includes taking action that a reasonable person would not take; negligence is accidental.

Plaintiff: the injured party that initiates a legal action.

Procedural due process: the legality of the procedures used—in this case, to deprive police officers of status or wages.

Property rights: rights involving the protection of one's property; in some cases, an individual's right to his or her job is considered a property right.

Proximate cause: an event that directly results in another event, particularly injury due to negligence or an intentional, wrongful act.

Reasonableness: a standard applied to many legal questions in which it must be determined if conduct or action was reasonable in the eyes of the court.

Sexual harassment: unwelcome sexual advances, requests for sexual favors, and other physical and verbal conduct of a sexual nature, particularly when submission to or rejection of this conduct affects an individual's employment or work performance or contributes to a hostile work environment.

Substantive due process: the requirement that the basis for government disciplinary action be reasonable, relevant, and justifiable.

Tort: a private injury inflicted on one person by another person, for which the injured party may sue in a civil action.

Vicarious liability: a legal doctrine also known as "respondent superior" imposing liability on supervisors and managers for the tortious conduct of their employees.

NOTES

1. Much of this section is taken, with some addition, from H. E. Barrineau III, *Civil Liability in Criminal Justice* (Cincinnati: Anderson, 1987), pp. 3–5.
2. Ibid., p. 3.
3. False arrest is the arrest of a person without probable cause. Generally, this means making an arrest when an ordinarily prudent person would not have concluded that a crime had been committed or that the person arrested had committed the crime. False imprisonment is the intentional illegal detention of a person. The detention that can give rise to a false imprisonment claim is any confinement to a specified area and not simply incarceration in a jail. Most false arrests result in false imprisonment as well, but there can be a false imprisonment after a valid arrest also, as when the police fail to release an arrested person after a proper bond has been posted, the police unreasonably delay the arraignment of an arrested person, or authorities fail to release a prisoner after they no longer have authority to hold him or her. "Brutality" is not a legal tort action as such. Rather, it must be alleged as a civil (as opposed to a criminal) assault and/or battery. Assault is some sort of menacing conduct that puts another person in reasonable fear that he or she is about to have a battery committed on him or her. Battery is the infliction of harmful or offensive contact on another person. Harmful or offensive contact is contact that would be considered harmful or offensive by a reasonable person of ordinary sensibilities. See Clarence E. Hagglund, "Liability of Police Officers and Their Employers," *Federation of Insurance Counsel Quarterly* 26 (summer 1976): 257, for a good discussion of assault and battery, false arrest, false imprisonment, and malicious prosecution as applied to police officers.
4. Although a fourth category (strict liability tort action) does exist in the wider body of law, such a general category is rare in police officer litigation. Therefore, for the purposes of this book, strict liability actions are not discussed. Under strict liability, one is held liable for one's act, regardless of intent or negligence. The mere occurrence of certain events will necessarily create legal liability. A good example of such cases is often found in airplane disasters in which the air transportation company is strictly liable for the passengers' health and well-being, regardless of other factors.
5. *Black's Law Dictionary,* 4th ed. (St. Paul, Minn.: West, 2004), p. 470.
6. Title 42, U.S. Code Section 1983.
7. See *Monroe v. Pape,* 365 U.S. 167, 81 S. Ct. 473 (1961). The plaintiff and his family sued 13 Chicago police officers and the city of Chicago, alleging that police officers

broke into their home without a search warrant, forced them out of bed at gunpoint, made them stand naked while the officers ransacked the house, and subjected the family to verbal and physical abuse. The court held that the definition of "under color of State law" for Section 1983 purposes was the same as that already established in the criminal context and concluded that, because Section 1983 provides for a civil action, the plaintiffs need not prove that the defendants acted with a "specific intent to deprive a person of a federal right" (365 U.S. at 187). The court also held that municipalities (such as the city of Chicago, in this case) were immune from liability under the statute, although the Supreme Court later overruled this part of *Monroe v. Pape,* holding that municipalities and other local governments are included among "persons" open to a Section 1983 lawsuit. See *Monell v. Dept. of Social Services of the City of New York,* 436 U.S. 658, 98 S. Ct. 2018 (1978). (Citations to case opinions give the volume number in which the opinion is located followed by the name of the reporter system, the page number, the court if other than the Supreme Court, and the year in which the opinion was rendered.)

8. The resuscitation of Section 1983 hinges on the misuse and abuse of power imbued to individuals acting as police officers. All municipal and county law enforcement officers take an oath to uphold and enforce the laws of a specific state in which their municipality resides. Therefore, municipal police officers are squarely within the confines of Section 1983. "Misuse of power," possessed by virtue of state law and made possible only because the wrongdoer is clothed with the authority of state law, is action taken "under the color of law." *United States v. Clasic,* 313 U.S. 299, at p. 326, 61 S. Ct., 1031, at p. 1043 (1941) as quoted in *Monroe v. Pape.* Thus, private citizens cannot be sued under Section 1983 unless they conspire with state officers. (See *Slavin v. Curry,* 574 F. 2d 1256 [5th Cir. 1978], as modified by 583 F. 2d 779 [5th Cir. 1978].) Furthermore, if a state officer has immunity to a Section 1983 lawsuit, private citizens who conspired with him or her do not have "derivative immunity" to the lawsuit. (See *Sparks v. Duval County Ranch Co., Inc.,* 604 F. 2d 976 [5th Cir. 1979], at p. 978.) In addition, see *Sanberg v. Daley,* 306 F. Supp. 227 (1969), at p. 279.
9. Most tort actions against the U.S. government must be brought under the FTCA. The FTCA is a partial waiver of sovereign immunity, with its own rule of liability and a substantial body of case law. Federal employees can be sued for violation of constitutional rights and for certain Common-Law torts. For more information, see Isidore Silver, *Police Civil Liability* (New York: Mathew Bender, 1987), section 1.04, from which this material is taken.
10. See *Bivens v. Six Unknown Federal Narcotics Agents,* 403 U.S. 388, 91 S. Ct. 1999 (1971). See also Silver, *Police Civil Liability,* section 8.02.
11. Silver, *Police Civil Liability,* Section 8.02.
12. See William L. Prosser, *Handbook of the Law of Torts,* 4th ed. (St. Paul, Minn.: West, 1971), p. 69, for a good discussion of the philosophical basis for and development of the doctrine of vicarious liability.
13. Wayne W. Schmidt "Recent Developments in Police Civil Liability," *Journal of Police Science and Administration* 4 (1976): 197, and the cases cited therein.
14. "[T]he Courts have very generally drawn a distinction between a sheriff and a chief of police, holding that the deputies of the former are selected exclusively by the chief of police, and are themselves officers and do not act for the chief of police in the performance of their official duties," *Parish v. Meyers,* 226, at p. 633 (Wash. 1924).
15. *Jordan v. Kelly,* 223 F. Supp. 731 (1963), at p. 738, followed in *Mack v. Lewis,* 298 F. Supp. 1351 (1969).
16. Ibid., p. 739.
17. Schmidt, "Recent Developments," p. 197.
18. Although this list does not include all types of negligence theories regarding 1983 action against police supervisors and managers, it does provide a starting point in understanding this issue. This part has been adapted from Barrineau, *Civil Liability,* pp. 59–60.
19. See *Peter v. Bellinger,* 159 N.E. 2d 528 (1959); *Thomas v. Johnson,* 295 F. Supp. 1025 (1968); *McKenna v. City of Memphis,* 544 F. Supp. 415 (1982), affirmed in 785 F. 2d 560 (1986); *McGuire v. Arizona Protection Agency,* 609 P. 2d 1080 (1908); *Di Cosal v. Kay,* 19 N.J. 159, 450 A. 2d 508 (1982); *Pontiac v. KMS Investments,* 331 N.W. 2d 907 (1983); and *Welsh Manufacturing Div. of Textron, Inc. v. Pinkertons, Inc.,* 474 A. 2d 426 (1984).
20. See *Board of the County Commissioner of Bryan County v. Brown,* 117 S. Ct. 1383 (1997).
21. See *Moon v. Winfield,* 383 F. Supp. 31 (1974); *Murray v. Murphy,* 441 F. Supp. 120 (1977); *Allen v. City of Los Angeles*

(No. C-9837), LA Sup. Ct. (1975); *Stengel v. Belcher*, 522 F. 2d 438 (6th Cir. 1975); *Dominguez v. Superior Court*, 101 Cal. App. 3d 6 (1980); *Stuessel v. City of Glendale*, 141 Cal. App. 3d 1047 (1983); and *Blake v. Moore*, 162 Cal. App. 3d 700 (1984).

22. See *Ford v. Breiser*, 383 F. Supp. 505 (1974); *Dewel v. Lawson*, 489 F. 2d 877 (10th Cir. 1974); *Bonsignore v. City of New York*, 521 F. Supp. 394 (1981), affirmed in 683 F. 2d 635 (1st Cir. 1982); *Webster v. City of Houston*, 689 F. 2d 1220 (5th Cir. 1982), reversed and remanded on the issue of damages in 739 F. 2d 993 (5th Cir. 1984); and *District of Columbia v. Parker*, 850 F. 2d 708 (D.C. Cir. 1988), cert. denied in 489 U.S. 1065, 109 S. Ct. 1339 (1989).
23. See *Marusa v. District of Columbia*, 484 F. 428 (1973); *Webster v. City of Houston*, supra note 22; and *Grandstagg v. City of Borger*, 767 F. 2d (5th Cir. 1985), cert. denied in 480 U.S. 917, 107 S. Ct. 1369 (1987).
24. *City of Canton v. Harris*, 389 U.S. 378, 103 L. Ed. 412, 109 S. Ct. 1197 (1989), at pp. 1204–5; *Merritt v. County of Los Angeles*, 875 F. 2d 765 (9th Cir. 1989); *Owens v. Haas*, 601 F. 2d 1242 (2nd Cir. 1979), cert. denied in 444 U.S. 980 (1980).
25. Prosser, *Handbook of the Law of Torts*, pp. 977–78.
26. Kenneth Culp Davis, *Administrative Law of the Seventies* (Rochester, N.Y.: Lawyers Cooperative, 1976), p. 551; p. 207, 1978 Supplement.
27. In most states in which abrogation of sovereign immunity has occurred, the abrogation has not been total. In some states, the abrogation is an unconditional waiver of the sovereign immunity, but the waiver extends only to certain activities, to cases in which the employee had a particular state of mind, to cases in which liability is not to exceed a designated monetary amount, or to cases that are limited to a particular level of government. In some states, the insured is responsible for the potential loss. Yet another approach taken by some states is not to allow government units to be sued but to require indemnification of public employees who have been sued successfully. (For an example, see *Florida Statutes*, Chapter 768.28.)
28. *Hans v. Louisiana*, 134 U.S. 1, 10 S. Ct. 504 (1890); *Edelman v. Jordan*, 415 U.S. 651, 94 S. Ct. 1347 (1974); and *Scheuer v. Rhodes*, 416 U.S. 232, 94 S. Ct. 1683 (1974).
29. *Alabama v. Pugh*, 438 U.S. 781, 98 S. Ct. 3057 (1978).
30. *Davis v. Sheuer*, 46 U.S. 183, 104 S. Ct. 3012 (1984).
31. *Scheuer v. Rhodes*, at p. 240.
32. *Wood v. Strickland*, 420 U.S. 308, 95 S. Ct. 992 (1975).
33. *Harlow v. Fitzgerald*, 457 U.S. 800, 102 S. Ct. 2727 (1982).
34. *Mitchell v. Forsyth*, 472 U.S. 511, 105 S. Ct. 2806 (1985).
35. *Monroe v. Pape*, supra note 7.
36. 436 U.S. 658, 98 S. Ct. 2018 (1978).
37. See, for example, *Rookard v. Health and Hospitals Corp.*, 710 F. 2d 41 (2d Cir. 1983).
38. *Oklahoma City v. Tuttle*, 471 U.S. 808, 105 S. Ct. 2427 (1985); but see *Pembauer v. Cincinnati*, 475 U.S. 469, 106 S. Ct. 1292 (1986).
39. M. S. Vaughn et al., "Assessing Legal Liabilities in Law Enforcement: Police Chief's Views," *Crime and Delinquency* 47, no. 1 (January 2001): 22.
40. *Daniels v. Williams*, 474 U.S. 327, 106 S. Ct. 662 (1986).
41. *New v. City of Minneapolis*, 792 F. 2d 724, at pp. 725–26 (8th Cir. 1986). See also *McClary v. O'Hare*, 786 F. 2d 83 (2nd Cir. 1986).
42. Hagglund, "Liability of Police Officers," p. 257.
43. *United States v. Leon*, 468 U.S. 897, 104 S. Ct. 3430 (1984).
44. *Malley v. Briggs*, 475 U.S. 335, 106 S. Ct. 1092 (1986).
45. *Anderson v. Creighton*, 483 U.S. 635, 107 S. Ct. 3034 (1987).
46. *Saucier v. Katz*, 533 U.S. 194, 121 S. Ct. 2151 (2001).
47. *Malley v. Briggs*, 475 U.S. 335, 341 (1986).
48. *Maciarello v. Summer*, 973 F. 2d 295, 298 (1992).
49. Schmidt, "Recent Developments."
50. Ibid., p. 198.
51. *Wimberly v. Patterson*, 183 A. 2d 691 (1962), at p. 699.
52. *Piatkowski v. State*, 251 N.Y.S. 2d 354 (1964), at p. 359.
53. Schmidt, "Recent Developments," p. 199.
54. *Fords v. Breier*, 383 F. Supp. 505 (E.D. Wis. 1974).
55. *Lucas v. Riley*, Superior Court, Los Angeles County, Cal. (1975); *Delong v. City of Denver*, 530 F. 2d 1308 (Colo. 1974); *Grudt v. City of Los Angeles*, 468 P. 2d 825 (Cal. 1970); *Dillenbeck v. City of Los Angeles*, 446 P. 2d 129 (Cal. 1968).
56. *AELE Law Enforcement Legal Defense Manual*, "Failure to Provide Medical Treatment," Issue 77-6 (1977).
57. *Watkins v. City of Battle Creek*, 273 F. 3d 682, 685–86 (6th Cir. 2001).

58. *Carter v. City of Detroit*, 480 F. 3d 305, 310, 311 (6th Cir. 2005).
59. *AELE Law Enforcement Legal Defense Manual*, "Failure to Provide Medical Treatment."
60. See, generally, Joan Bertin Lowy, "Constitutional Limitations on the Dismissal of Public Employees," *Brooklyn Law Review* 43 (summer 1976): 1; Victor G. Rosenblum, "Schoolchildren: Yes, Policemen: No—Some Thoughts about the Supreme Court's Priorities concerning the Right to a Hearing in Suspension and Removal Cases," *Northwestern University Law Review* 72 (1977): 146.
61. *Wisconsin v. Constantineau*, 400 U.S. 433, 91 S. Ct. 507 (1970); *Doe v. U.S. Department of Justice*, 753 F. 2d 1092 (D.C. Cir. 1985).
62. *Codd v. Velger*, 429 U.S. 624, 97 S. Ct. 882 (1977). See also *Paul v. Davis*, 424 U.S. 693, 96 S. Ct. 1155 (1976), which held that injury to reputation alone does not constitute a deprivation of liberty. See also *Swilley v. Alexander*, 629 F. 2d 1018 (5th Cir. 1980), where the court held that a letter of reprimand containing untrue charges that was placed in an employee's personnel file infringed on his liberty interest.
63. *Board of Regents v. Roth*, 408 U.S. 564, 92 S. Ct. 2701 (1972); *Perry v. Sinderman*, 408 U.S. 593, 92 S. Ct. 2694 (1972).
64. *Arnett v. Kennedy*, 416 U.S. 134, 94 S. Ct. 1633 (1974); *Bishop v. Wood*, 426 U.S. 341, 96 S. Ct. 2074 (1976). See Robert L. Rabin, "Job Security and Due Process: Monitoring Administrative Discretion through a Reasons Requirement," *University of Chicago Law Review* 44 (1976): 60–67, for a good discussion of these cases; see also *Bailey v. Kirk*, No. 82-1417 (10th Cir. 1985).
65. See Carl Goodman, "Public Employment and the Supreme Court's 1975–76 Term," *Public Personnel Management* 5 (September–October 1976): 287–89.
66. *Thurston v. Dekle*, 531 F. 2d 1264 (5th Cir. 1976), vacated on other grounds, 438 U.S. 901, 98 S. Ct. 3118 (1978).
67. *Allison v. City of Live Oak*, 450 F. Supp. 200 (M.D. Fla. 1978).
68. See, for example, *Confederation of Police Chicago v. Chicago*, 547 F. 2d 375 (7th Cir. 1977).
69. Davis, *Administrative Law*, p. 242.
70. *Memphis Light Gas & Water Division v. Craft*, 436 U.S. 1, 98 S. Ct. 1554 (1978).
71. *In re Dewar*, 548 P. 2nd 149 (Mont. 1976).
72. *Bush v. Beckman*, 131 N.Y.S. 2d 297 (1954); *Gibbs v. City of Manchester*, 61 A. 128 (N.H. 1905).
73. *Morrissey v. Brewer*, 408 U.S. 471, 92 S. Ct. 2593 (1972).
74. *Goldman v. Kelly*, 397 U.S. 254, 90 S. Ct. 1011 (1970). See also *Buck v. N.Y. City Bd. of Ed.*, 553 F. 2d 315 (2d Cir. 1977), cert. denied in 438 U.S., 98 S. Ct. 3122 (1978).
75. *Morrissey v. Brewer*, supra note 70.
76. *Marshall v. Jerrico, Inc.*, 446 U.S. 238, 100 S. Ct. 1610 (1980); *Hortonville J.S.D. No. 1 v. Hortonville Ed. Assn.*, 426 U.S. 482, 96 S. Ct. 2308 (1976); *Holley v. Seminole County School Dist.*, 755 F. 2d 1492 (11th Cir. 1985).
77. 94 S. Ct. 1633, 416 U.S. 134 (1974), at p. 157.
78. Ibid., at pp. 167–68.
79. 96 S. Ct. 893, 424 U.S. 319 (1975), at p. 335.
80. 105 S. Ct. 1487, 470 U.S. 532 (1985).
81. Ibid., at p. 1494.
82. See *Gilbert v. Homar*, 520 U.S. 924 (1997).
83. *Gorham v. City of Kansas City*, 590 P. 2d 1051 (Kan. S. Ct. 1979); *Winston v. U.S. Postal Service*, 585 F. 2d 198 (7th Cir. 1978).
84. *Bence v. Breier*, 501 F. 2d 1185 (7th Cir. 1974), cert. denied in 419 U.S. 1121, 95 S. Ct. 804 (1975).
85. *Perea v. Fales*, 114 Cal. Rptr. 808 (1974), at p. 810.
86. *Kramer v. City of Bethlehem*, 289 A. 2d 767 (1972).
87. *Rogenski v. Board of Fire and Police Commissioners of Moline*, 285 N.E. 2d 230 (1972). See also *Major v. Hampton*, 413 F. Supp. 66 (1976), in which the court held that an IRS rule against activities tending to discredit the agency was overbroad as applied to a married employee who had maintained an apartment for illicit sexual liaisons during off-duty hours.
88. *Grayned v. City of Rockford*, 92 S. Ct. 2294, 408 U.S. 104 (1972), at pp. 108–9.
89. *Bence v. Breier*, supra note 81, at p. 1190.
90. *Rinaldi v. Civil Service Commission*, 244 N.W. 2d 609 (Mich. 1976).
91. *Allen v. City of Greensboro, North Carolina*, 452 F. 2d 489 (4th Cir. 1971).
92. *Petraitis v. Board of Fire and Police Commissioners City of Palos Hills*, 335 N.E. 2d 126 (Ill. 1975); *Haywood v. Municipal Court*, 271 N.E. 2d 591 (Mass. 1971); *Lewis v. Board of Trustee*, 212 N.Y.S. 2d 677 (1961). Compare *Stanton v. Board of Fire and Police Commissioners of Village of Bridgeview*, 345 N.E. 2d 822 (Ill. 1976).
93. *DeSalvatore v. City of Oneonta*, 369 N.Y.S. 2d 820 (1975).
94. *Marino v. Los Angeles*, 110 Cal. Rptr. 45 (1973).
95. *Guido v. City of Marion*, 280 N.E. 2d 81 (Ind. 1972).

96. *Carroll v. Goldstein*, 217 A. 2d 676 (R.I. 1976).
97. *Firemen's and Policemen's Civil Service Commission v. Shaw*, 306 S.W. 2d 160 (Tex. 1957).
98. *Martin v. City of St. Martinville*, 321 So. 2d 532 (La. 1975).
99. *Arnold v. City of Aurora*, 498 P. 2d 970 (Colo. 1973).
100. *Carey v. Piphus*, 435 U.S. 247, 98 S. Ct. 1042 (1978).
101. *County of Monroe v. Dept. of Labor*, 690 F. 2d 1359 (11th Cir. 1982).
102. *Gitlow v. New York*, 268 U.S. 652, 45 S. Ct. 625 (1925).
103. *Pickering v. Board of Education*, 88 S. Ct. 1731, 391 U.S. 563 (1968), at p. 568.
104. *Keyishian v. Board of Regents*, 385 U.S. 589, 87 S. Ct. 675 (1967).
105. *Pickering v. Board of Education*, supra note 100.
106. *Muller v. Conlisk*, 429 F. 2d 901 (7th Cir. 1970).
107. *Flynn v. Giarusso*, 321 F. Supp. 1295 (E.D. La. 1971), at p. 1299. The regulation was revised and later ruled constitutional in *Magri v. Giarusso*, 379 F. Supp. 353 (E.D. La. 1974). See also *Gasparinetti v. Kerr*, 568 F. 2d 311 (3rd Cir. 1977), cert. denied in 436 U.S. 903, 98 S. Ct. 2232 (1978).
108. *In re Gioglio*, 248 A. 2d 570 (N.J. 1968); *Brukiewa v. Police Commissioner of Baltimore*, 263 A. 2d 210 (Md. 1970); *Kannisto v. City and County of San Francisco*, 541 F. 2d 841 (9th Cir. 1976), cert. denied in 430 U.S. 931 S. Ct. 1552 (1977). Compare *Magri v. Giarusso*, supra note 104; *Hosford v. California State Personnel Board*, 141 Cal. Rptr. 354 (1977); and *Simpson v. Weeks*, 570 F. 2d 240 (8th Cir. 1978).
109. *Brukiewa v. Police Commissioner of Baltimore*, supra note 105.
110. *Perry v. City of Kinloch*, 680 F. Supp. 1339 (1988).
111. *Brockell v. Norton*, 732 F. 2d 664 (8th Cir. 1984).
112. See *Perez v. Agostini*, 37 F. Supp. 2d 103 (D.P.R. 1999); *Dill v. City of Edmond, Oklahoma*, 155 F. 3d 1193 (10th Cir. 1998); *Cahill v. O'Donnell*, 7 F. Supp. 2d 341 (S.D.N.Y. 1998); *Hadad v. Croucher*, 970 F. Supp. 1227 (N.D. Ohio 1997); *Saunders v. Hunter*, 980 F. Supp. 1236 (M.D. Fla. 1997); *Forsyth v. City of Dallas, Texas*, 91 F. 3d 769 (5th Cir. 1996); and *Glass v. Dachel*, 2 F. 3d 733 (7th Cir. 1993).
113. Adapted from Will Aitchison, *The Rights of Law Enforcement Officers*, 4th ed. (Portland, Ore.: Labor Relations Information System, 2000), p. 298.
114. See *Lytle v. City of Haysville*, 138 F. 3d 857 (10th Cir. 1998), and *Frederick v. Department of Justice*, 73 F. 3d 349 (4th Cir. 1996).
115. *Broaderick v. Oklahoma*, 413 U.S. 601, 93 S. Ct. 2908 (1973), and *Reeder v. Kansas City Bd. of Police Comm.*, 733 F. 2d 543 (8th Cir. 1984).
116. *United Public Workers v. Mitchell*, 330 U.S. 75, 67 S. Ct. (1947): *U.S. Civil Service Commission v. National Association of Letter Carriers*, 413 U.S. 548, 93 S. Ct. 2880 (1973).
117. *Broaderick v. Oklahoma*, supra note 112.
118. *Magill v. Lynch*, 400 F. Supp. 84 (R.I. 1975), vacated in 560 F. 2d 22 (1st Cir. 1977), cert. denied in 434 U.S. 1063, 98 S. Ct. 1236 (1978).
119. *Boston Police Patrolmen's Association, Inc. v. City of Boston*, 326 N.E. 2d 314 (Mass. 1975).
120. *Phillips v. City of Flint*, 224 N.W. 2d 780 (Mich. 1975). But compare *Paulos v. Breier*, 507 F. 2d 1383 (7th Cir. 1974).
121. Ibid., at p. 784.
122. *Elrod v. Bruns*, 427 U.S. 347, 96 S. Ct. 2673 (1976). See also *Ramey v. Harber*, 431 F. Supp. 657 (1977), cert. denied in 442 U.S. 910, 99 S. Ct. 823 (1979), and *Branti v. Finkel*, 445 U.S. 507, 100 S. Ct. 1287 (1980).
123. *Connick v. Myers*, 461 U.S. 138 (1983); *Jones v. Dodson*, 727 F. 2d 1329 (4th Cir. 1984).
124. *Sponick v. City of Detroit Police Department*, 211 N.W. 2d 674 (Mich. 1973), at p. 681. But see *Wilson v. Taylor*, 733 F. 2d 1539 (11th Cir. 1984).
125. *Bruns v. Pomerleau*, 319 F. Supp. 58 (D. Md. 1970). See also *McMullen v. Carson*, 754 F. 2d 936 (11th Cir. 1985), where it was held that a Ku Klux Klansman could not be fired from his position as a records clerk in the sheriff's department simply because he was a Klansman. The court did uphold the dismissal because his active KKK participation threatened to cripple the agency's ability to perform its public duties effectively.
126. *Civil Service Commission of Tucson v. Livingston*, 525 P. 2d 949 (Ariz. 1974).
127. *City of San Diego v. John Roe*, 543 U.S. 77, 125 S. Ct. 521 (2005).
128. See, for example, *Tinker v. Des Moines School District*, 393 U.S. 503, 89 S. Ct. 733 (1969).
129. 425 U.S. 238, 96 S. Ct. 1440 (1976).
130. *Mapp v. Ohio*, 367 U.S. 643, 81 S. Ct. 1684 (1961).
131. *Katz v. United States*, 389 U.S. 347, 88 S. Ct. 507 (1967).

132. *Smith v. Maryland,* 442 U.S. 735, 99 S. Ct. 2577 (1979), and *Chan v. State,* 78 Md. App. 287, 552 (1989). The "expectation to privacy" clause was developed in *Katz v. United States,* supra note 12, a case that involved warrantless electronic surveillance of a public telephone booth. The Court said that "the Fourth Amendment protects people, not places. What a person knowingly exposes to the public, even in his own home or office, is not subject to Fourth Amendment protection. But what he seeks to preserve as private, even in an area accessible to the public, may be constitutionally protected. . . . There is a two-fold requirement, first that a person have exhibited an actual expectation of privacy, and second that the expectation by one's society is prepared to recognize it as reasonable/legitimate."
133. See *People v. Tidwell,* 266 N.E. 2d 787 (Ill. 1971).
134. *McDonnell v. Hunter,* 809 F. 2d 1302 (8th Cir. 1987).
135. *Biehunik v. Felicetta,* 441 F. 2d 228 (2nd Cir. 1971), cert. denied in 403 U.S. 932, 91 S. Ct. 2256 (1971).
136. *United States v. Leon,* 468 U.S. 897, 104 S. Ct. 3430 (1984), and *Massachusetts v. Sheppard,* 468 U.S. 981, 104 S. Ct. 3424 (1984).
137. *Illinois v. Gates,* 462 U.S. 213, 103 S. Ct. 2317 (1984).
138. The concept of the "good faith-reasonable belief" defense as either a qualified or an absolute immunity has significant case history. See Isadore Silver, *Police Civil Liability* (New York: Matthew Bender and Company, 1987), chapters 4 and 7.
139. See *Floyd v. Farrell,* 765 F. 2d 1 (1st Cir. 1985); *Malley v. Briggs,* 475 U.S. 335, 106 S. Ct. 1092 (1986); *Santiago v. Fenton,* 891 F. 2d 373 (1st Cir. 1989); and *Hoffman v. Reali,* 973 F. 2d 980 (1st Cir. 1992).
140. *Sheetz v. Mayor and City Council of Baltimore, Maryland,* 315 Md. 208 (1989).
141. 385 U.S. 493, 87 S. Ct. 6126 (1967).
142. The states are bound by this requirement as well. *Malloy v. Hogan,* 378 U.S. 1, 84 S. Ct. 489 (1964).
143. *Gardner v. Broderick,* 392 U.S. 273, 88 S. Ct. 1913 (1968).
144. These procedural rights in police disciplinary actions have often been referred to as the "Garrity Rights." They were developed through a series of cases; see *Lefkowitz v. Turley,* 414 U.S. 70, 94 S. Ct. 316 (1973), and *Confederation of Police v. Conlisk,* 489 F. 2d 891 (1973), cert. denied in 416 U.S. 956, 94 S. Ct. 1971 (1974). Further, as the rights appear here, see Aitchison, *The Rights of Law Enforcement Officers,* p. 118.
145. See *Gabrilowitz v. Newman,* 582 F. 2d 100 (1st Cir. 1978). Cases upholding the department's authority to order an officer to take a polygraph examination include *Eshelman v. Blubaum,* 560 P. 2d 1283 (Ariz. 1977); *Dolan v. Kelly,* N.Y.S. 2d 478 (1973); *Richardson v. City of Pasadena,* 500 S.W. 2d 175 (Tex. 1973); *Seattle Police Officer's Guild v. City of Seattle,* 494 P. 2d 485 (Wash. 1972); *Roux v. New Orleans Police Department,* 223 So. 2d 905 (La. 1969); *Coursey v. Board of Fire and Police Commissioners,* 234 N.E. 2d 339 (Ill. 1967); *Frazee v. Civil Service Board of City of Oakland,* 338 P. 2d 943 (Cal. 1959); and *Hester v. Milledgeville,* 777 F. 2d 1492 (11th Cir. 1985). Cases denying the department's authority include *Molino v. Board of Public Safety of City of Torrington,* 225 A. 2d 805 (Conn. 1966); *Stape v. Civil Service Commission of City of Philadelphia,* 172 A. 2d 161 (Pa. 1961); and *Farmer v. Fort Lauderdale,* 427 So. 2d 187 (Fla. 1983), cert. denied in 464 U.S. 816, 104 S. Ct. 74 (1983).
146. *Eshelman v. Blubaum,* supra note 141, at p. 1286.
147. *Farmer v. City of Fort Lauderdale,* supra note 141.
148. *Faust v. Police Civil Service Commission,* 347 A. 2d 765 (Pa. 1975); *Steward v. Leary,* 293 N.Y.S. 2d 573 (1968); *Brewer v. City of Ashland,* 86 S.W. 2d 669 (Ky. 1935); *Fabio v. Civil Service Commission of Philadelphia,* 373 A. 2d 751 (Pa. 1977).
149. *Anderson v. City of Philadelphia, Pennsylvania,* 668 F. Supp. 441 (1987), reversed by 845 F. 2d 1216 (3rd Cir. 1988).
150. See Aitchison, *The Rights of Law Enforcement Officers,* pp. 58–62.
151. See *Bigby v. City of Chicago,* 766 F. 2d 1053 (7th Cir. 1985), cert. denied in 474 U.S. 1056, 106 S. Ct. 793 (1986); *McCoy v. Board of Fire and Police Commissioners* (Chicago), 398 N.E. 2d 1020 (1979); *Davis v. Williams,* 588 F. 2d 69 (4th Cir. 1979); *Parker v. Levy,* 417 U.S. 733, 94 S. Ct. 2547 (1974); *Bence v. Brier,* 501 F. 2d 1184 (7th Cir. 1974), cert. denied in 419 U.S. 1121, 95 S. Ct. 1552 (1977); and *Gee v. California State Personnel Board,* 85 Cal. Rptr. 762 (1970).
152. Whether or not reasonable people would agree that the conduct was punishable so that an individual is free to steer a course between lawful and unlawful behaviors is the key to "reasonableness." See *Cranston v.*

City of Richmond, 710 P. 2d 845 (1986), and Said v. Lackey, 731 S.W. 2d 7 (1987).
153. Cranston v. City of Richmond, supra note 148.
154. See City of St. Petersburg v. Police Benevolent Association, 414 So. 2d 293 1982, and Brown v. Sexner, 405 N.E. 2d 1082 (1980).
155. Richter v. Civil Service Commission of Philadelphia, 387 A. 2d 131 (1978).
156. Miller v. City of York, 415 A. 2d 1280 (1980), and Kannisto v. City and County of San Francisco, 541 F. 2d 841 (1976), cert. denied in 430 U.S. 931, 97 S. Ct. 1552 (1977).
157. McIntosh v. Monroe Police Civil Board, 389 So. 2d 410 (1980); Barnett v. New Orleans Police Department, 413 So. 2d 520 (1982); Allman v. Police Board of Chicago, 489 N.E. 2d 929 (1986).
158. Philadelphia Civil Service Commission v. Wotjuski, 525 A. 2d 1255 (1987); Gandolfo v. Department of Police, 357 So. 568 (1978); McDonald v. Miller, 596 F. 2d 686 (1979).
159. Monroe v. Board of Public Safety, 423 N.Y.S. 2d 963 (1980).
160. Redo v. West Goshen Township, 401 A. 2d 394 (1979).
161. Brase v. Board of Police Commissioners, 487 N.E. 2d 91 (1985).
162. Major v. Hampton, 413 F. Supp. 66 (1976).
163. City of North Muskegon v. Briggs, 473 U.S. 909 (1985).
164. National Gay Task Force v. Bd. of Ed. of Oklahoma City, 729 F. 2d 1270 (10th Cir. 1984).
165. See Whisenhund v. Spradlin, 464 U.S. 964 (1983), and Kukla v. Village of Antioch, 647 F. Supp. 799 (1986), cohabitation of officers; Coryle v. City of Oil City, 405 A. 2d 1104 (1979), public lewdness; Childers v. Dallas Police Department, 513 F. Supp. 134 (1981); and Fout v. California State Personnel Board, child molesting; Fugate v. Phoenix Civil Service Board, 791 F. 2d 736 (9th Cir. 1986), sex with prostitutes; and Doe v. Commonwealth Attorney, 425 U.S. 901, 96 S. Ct. 1489 (1976), Smith v. Price, 616 F. 2d 1371 (5th Cir. 1980), and Bowers v. Hardwick, 478 U.S. 186, 106 S. Ct. 2841 (1986), sodomy as a state law prohibiting homosexuality.
166. Bd. of Ed. v. National Gay Task Force, 729 F. 2d 1270 (10th Cir. 1984), affirmed in 470 U.S. 903, 105 S. Ct. 1858 (1985).
167. Rowland v. Mad River Sch. Dist., 730 F. 2d (6th Cir. 1984), cert. denied in 470 U.S. 1009, 105 S. Ct. 1373 (1985).
168. Todd v. Navarro, 698 F. Supp. 871 (1988).
169. Lawrence v. Texas, 539 U.S. 558, 123 S. Ct. 2472 (2003).
170. McCarthy v. Philadelphia Civil Service Comm., 424 U.S. 645, 96 S. Ct. 1154 (1976).
171. Miller v. Police of City of Chicago, 349 N.E. 2d 544 (Ill. 1976); Williamson v. Village of Baskin, 339 So. 2d 474 (La. 1976); Nigro v. Board of Trustees of Alden, 395 N.Y.S. 2d 544 (1977).
172. State, County, and Municipal Employees Local 339 v. City of Highland Park, 108 N.W. 2d 544 (1977).
173. Hameetman v. City of Chicago, 776 F. 2d 636 (7th Cir. 1985).
174. 42 U.S.C. S2003(j).
175. Pinsker v. Joint Dist. No. 281, 554 F. Supp. 1049 (1983), affirmed in 735 F. 2d 388 (10th Cir. 1984).
176. United States v. City of Albuquerque, 12 EPD 11, 244 (10th Cir. 1976). See also Trans World Airlines v. Hardison, 432 U.S. 63, 97 S. Ct. 2264 (1977).
177. Potter v. Murray City, 760 F. 2d 1065 (10th Cir. 1985), cert. denied in 474 U.S. 849, 106 S. Ct. 145 (1986).
178. Cox v. McNamara, 493 P. 2d 54 (Ore. 1972); Brenkle v. Township of Shaler, 281 A. 2d 920 (Pa. 1972); Hopwood v. City of Paducab, 424 S.W. 2d 134 (Ky. 1968); Flood v. Kennedy, 239 N.Y.S. 2d 665 (1963). See also Trelfa v. Village of Centre Island, 389 N.Y.S. 2d 22 (1976). Rules prohibiting law enforcement officers from holding interest in businesses that manufacture, sell, or distribute alcoholic beverages have also been upheld. Bock v. Long, 279 N.E. 2d 464 (Ill. 1972); Johnson v. Trader, 52 So. 2d 333 (Fla. 1951).
179. Richard N. Williams, *Legal Aspects of Discipline by Police Administrators*, Traffic Institute Publication No. 2705 (Evanston, Ill.: Northwestern University, 1975), p. 4.
180. City of Crowley Firemen v. City of Crowley, 264 So. 2d 368 (La. 1972).
181. See Rojas v. Alexander's Department Store, Inc., 654 F. Supp. 856 (1986), and Reagan v. Hampton, 700 F. Supp. 850 (1988).
182. Kenneth James Matulia, "The Use of Deadly Force: A Need for Directives in Training," *The Police Chief*, May 1983, p. 30.
183. Kenneth James Matulia, "A Balance of Forces: Model Deadly Force and Policy Procedure," *International Association of Chiefs of Police*, (1985): 23, 24. See also Tennessee v. Garner, 471 U.S. 1, 105 S. Ct. 1694 (1985).
184. Tennessee v. Garner, supra note 17.
185. Tennessee v. Garner, supra note 179.
186. Matulia, "A Balance of Forces," p. 72.
187. Catherin H. Milton, Jeanne Wahl Halleck, James Lardnew, and Gray L. Albrecht, *Police Use of Deadly Force* (Washington, D.C.: Police Foundation, 1977), p. 52.

188. *Matulia,* "A Balance of Forces," p. 52.
189. Ibid., p. 77.
190. Ibid.
191. Ibid., p. 78.
192. 471 U.S. 1, 105 S. Ct. 1694 (1985).
193. Matulia, "A Balance of Forces," p. 78.
194. Daniel L. Schofield, "Legal Issues of Pursuit Driving," *FBI Law Enforcement Bulletin,* May 1988, pp. 23–30. This discussion was adapted from this source.
195. Richard G. Zivitz, "Police Civil Liability and the Law of High Speed Pursuit," *Marquette Law Review,* 70, no. 237 (1987): 237–79.
196. *Jackson v. Olson,* 712 P. 2d 128 (Or. App. 1985).
197. 457 Do. 2d 816 (Miss. 1985).
198. Ibid., at p. 818.
199. See generally Annotation, "Emergency Vehicle Accidents," *American Jurisprudence, Proof of Facts* (St. Paul, MN: West, 1985), p. 599.
200. See *Breck v. Cortez,* 490 N.E. 2d 88 (III. App. 1986).
201. See generally Annotation, "Municipal Corporation's Safety Rules or Regulations as Admissible in Evidence in Action by Private Party against Municipal Corporation or Its Officers or Employees for Negligent Operation of Vehicle," *American Law Review.*
202. See *Fiser v. City of Ann Arbor,* 339 N.W. 2d 413 (Mich. 1983).
203. 733 S.W. 2d 28 (Mo. App. 1987).
204. For a general discussion of immunity, see David Charlin, "High-Speed Pursuits: Police Officer and Municipal Liability for Accidents Involving the Pursued and an Innocent Third Party," *Seton Hall Law Review* 16, no. 101 (1986).
205. 490 So. 2d 1061 (Fla. App. 1986).
206. *Fagan v. City of Vineland,* 22 F. 3d 1283 (3rd Cir. 1994).
207. 42 U.S.C. 1983 provides in relevant part: "Every person who, under color of any statute, ordinance, regulation, custom, or usage, of any State of Territory, subjects or causes to be subjected, any citizen of the United States or other person within the jurisdiction thereof to the deprivation of any rights, privileges, or immunities secured by the Constitution and laws, shall be liable to the party injured in an action at law, suit in equity, or other proper proceedings for redress."
208. 782 F. 2d 947 (11th Cir. 1986).
209. Ibid., at p. 950.
210. See *Country of Sacramento v. Lewis,* 98 F. 3d 434 (1998).
211. Ibid.
212. See *Allen v. Cook,* 668 F. Supp. 1460 (W.D. Okla. 1987). See also *Fagan v. City of Vineland,* supra note 202.
213. 772 F. 2d 1205 (5th Cir. 1985).
214. 471 U.S. 1, 105 S. Ct. 1694 (1985). The Supreme Court held that the use of deadly force to apprehend an unarmed fleeing felon was an unreasonable seizure which violated the Fourth Amendment.
215. 817 F. 2d 540 (9th Cir. 1987). In *City of Miami v. Harris,* 490 So. 2d 69 (Fla. App. 1985), the court held that a city can be liable under 1983 for a pursuit policy that is adopted with a reckless disregard of whether such policy would cause loss of life without due process.
216. *Brower v. County of Inyo,* 489 U.S. 593, 109 S. Ct. 1378 (1989).
217. A discussion of empirical studies regarding pursuits is set forth in Geoffrey P. Alpert, "Questioning Police Pursuits in Urban Areas," in *Critical Issues in Policing: Contemporary Readings,* ed. R. G. Dunham and G. P. Alpert (Prospect Heights, Ill.: Waveland Press, 1989), pp. 216–29.
218. *Jackson v. Olson,* supra note 192.
219. See Annotation, "Municipal or State Liability for Injuries Resulting from Police Roadblocks or Commandeering of Private Vehicles," 19 *American Law Review* 4th 937.
220. *Brower v. County of Inyo,* supra note 212.
221. *Horta v. Sullivan,* 4 F. 3d 2 (1st Cir. 1993), at p. 10.
222. Edmund Fennessy, Thomas Hamilton, Kent Joscelyn, and John Merritt, *A Study of the Problem of Hot Pursuit by the Police* (Washington, D.C.: U.S. Department of Transportation, 1970).
223. Geoffrey P. Alpert, "Questioning Police Pursuit in Urban Areas," *Journal of Police Science and Administration* 15 (1987): 298–306.
224. Eric Beckman, "Identifying Issues in Police Pursuits: The First Research Findings," *The Police Chief* (July 1987): 57–63.
225. Geoffrey P. Alpert, *Police Pursuit Policies and Training* (Washington, D.C.: U.S. Department of Justice, Office of Justice Programs, National Institute of Justice, May 1997), pp. 1–8.
226. Ibid.
227. See, for example, *Nelson v. City of Chester, Ill.,* 733 S.W. 2d 28 (Mo. App. 1987); *Biscoe v. Arlington County,* 738 F. 2d 1352 (D.C. Cir. 1984).
228. Alpert, "Questioning Police Pursuits in Urban Areas," pp. 227–28.
229. International Association of Chiefs of Police, *Dealing with the Mentally Ill: Concepts and Issues* (Alexandra, Va.: IACP Law Enforcement Policy Center, December 1, 1997).
230. Washington Criminal Justice Training Commission (WCJTC), *Crisis Intervention*

Skills: Abnormal Behaviors, Mental Illness, and Suicide (Seattle: WCJTC. 2000).

231. Michael Klein, "Law Enforcement's Response to People with Mental Illness," *Law Enforcement Bulletin* (February 2002): 12–16.
232. *Reich v. Board of Fire and Police Commissioners*, 301 N.E. 2d 501 (Ill. 1973).
233. *Krolick v. Lowery*, 302 N.Y.S. 2d 109 (1969), at p. 115, and *Hester Milledgeville*, 598 F. Supp. 1456, at p. 457, n. 2 (M.D. Ga. 1984), modified in 777 F. 2d 1492 (11th Cir. 1985).
234. *McCracken v. Department of Police*, 337 So. 2d 595 (La. 1976).
235. *Krolick v. Lowery*, supra note 229.
236. 466 U.S. 109, 104 S. Ct. 1652 (1984), at p. 1656.
237. *National Federation of Federal Employees v. Weinberger*, 818 F. 2d 935 (1987). See also related cases: *National Treasury Employees Union v. Von Raab*, 816 F. 2d 170 (1987), and *Lovvorn v. City of Chattanooga, Tennessee*, 846 F. 2d 1539 (1988).
238. *O'Connor v. Ortega*, 480 U.S. 709, 107 S. Ct. 1492, (1987).
239. 489 U.S. 602, 109 S. Ct. 1402 (1989).
240. Supra note 195.
241. *City of Palm Bay v. Bauman*, 475 So. 2d 1322 (Fla. 5th DCA 1985).
242. *Walters v. Secretary of Defense*, 725 F. 2d 107 (D.C. Cir. 1983).
243. *Security of Law Enforcement Employees, District Counsel 82 v. Carly*, 737 F. 2d 187 (2d Cir. 1984); *Division 241 Amalgamated Transit Union v. Suscy*, 538 F. 2d 1264 (7th Cir. 1976) cert. denied in 429 U.S. 1029, 97 S. Ct. 653 (1976); *McDonnell v. Hunter*, 612 F. Supp. 1122 (S.D. Iowa 1984), affirmed in 746 F. 2d 785 (8th Cir. 1984).
244. For a comprehensive review of the cases in this area, see Gregory P. Orvis, "Drug Testing in the Criminal Justice Workplace," *American Journal of Criminal Justice* 18, no. 2 (spring 1994): 290–305.
245. *National League of Cities v. Usery*, 426 U.S. 833, 96 S. Ct. 2465 (1976).
246. *Garcia v. San Antonio Transit*, 469 U.S. 528, 105 S. Ct. 1005 (1985), overruled *National League of Cities*, supra note 241.
247. *Massachusetts Board of Retirements v. Murgia*, 427 U.S. 307, 96 S. Ct. 2562 (1976).
248. 29 U.S.C. 623(*f*).
249. *Western Airlines v. Criswell*, 472 U.S. 400, 105 S. Ct. 2743, at p. 2751 (1985), and *Dothard v. Rawlinson*, 433 U.S. 321, 329, 97 S. Ct. 2720 (1977).
250. *Usery v. Tamiami Trail Tours, Inc.*, 531 F. 2d 224 (5th Cir. 1976).
251. *Sheehan v. Marr*, U.S. Court of Appeals for the First Circuit, No. 98-1813, March 2000.
252. *Johnson v. Mayor and City Council of Baltimore*, 472 U.S. 5353, 105 S. Ct. 2717, at p. 2722 (1985).
253. *Hahn v. City of Buffalo*, 770 F. 2d 12 (2nd Cir. 1985).
254. Jeffrey Higgenbotham, "Sexual Harassment in the Police Station," *FBI Law Enforcement Bulletin* 57 (September 1988): 22–28. This discussion of sexual harassment was adapted from this article.
255. 42 U.S.C. S2000e-2(a)(I) makes it "an unlawful employment practice for an employer . . . to discriminate against any individual with respect to his compensation, terms, conditions, or privileges of employments, because of such individual's . . . sex."
256. See, for example, 41 U.S.C. S2000e-5 and 2000e-6.
257. 29 C.F.R. S1604.11 (1987).
258. *General Electric Co. v. Gilbert*, 97 S. Ct. 401, 429 U.S. 125 A, at pp. 141–42 (1975).
259. See U.S. Equal Employment Opportunity Commission, "Facts about Sexual Harassment," www.eeoc.gov/facts/fs-sex.html.
260. *Katz v. Dole*, 709 F. 2d 251 (4th Cir. 1983).
261. *Henson v. City of Dundee*, 681 F. 2d 897 (11th Cir. 1982). See also *Vernett v. Hough*, 627 F. Supp. 587 (W.D. Mich. 1986).
262. See U.S. Constitution, Amendment 14.
263. *Henson v. City of Dundee*, supra note 257, at p. 902.
264. Supra note 242.
265. Ibid.
266. See *Doe v. City of Belleville, Illinois*, 119 F. 3d 563 (7th Cir. 1997), and *Quinn v. Nassau County Police Department*, 53 F. Supp. 2d 347 (E.D.N.Y. 1999).
267. This section adapted from Aitchison, *The Rights of Law Enforcement Officers*, pp. 430–33.
268. *Ways v. City of Lincoln, Nebraska*, 871 F. 2d 750 (8th Cir. 1989) (racial epithets directed at an American Indian); *Daniels v. Fowler*, 57 FEP Cases 65 (N.D. Ga. 1991) (racial epithets directed at an African American).
269. See *Andrews v. City of Philadelphia*, 895 F. 2d 1469 (3rd Cir. 1992); *Carillo v. Ward*, 56 FEP Cases 1558 (S.S.N.Y. 1991); *Arnold v. City of Seminole, Oklahoma*, 614 F. Supp. 853 (E.D. Okla. 1985); and *Grievance of Deborah Butler*, No. 97-17 (Vt. LRB 1994), affirmed in 697 A. 2d 659 (Vt. 1997).
270. See *Staton v. Maries County*, 868 F. 2d 996 (8th Cir. 1989).
271. See *Oncale v. Sundowner Offshore Services*, 523 U.S. 75 (1998).
272. Ibid.

273. *Washington v. Board of Trustees*, 2001 WL 47006 (N.D. Ill. 2001).
274. *Russ v. Van Scoyok Associates, Inc.*,122 F. Supp. 2d 129 (D.D.C. 2000).
275. Ibid.; *Bennett v. New York City Department of Corrections*, 49 F.E.P. Case. 134 (S.D: N.Y. 1989).
276. *Young v. City of Houston*, 906 F. 2d 177 (5th Cir. 1990).
277. 106 S. Ct. 2399 (1986).
278. Ibid., at p. 2406.
279. Ibid.
280. *Moylan v. Maries County*, 792 F. 2d 746 (8th Cir. 1986), reheard as *Staton v. Maries County*, 868 F. 2d (8th Cir. 1989).
281. *Meritor Savings Bank v. Vinson*, 447 U.S. 57, 106 S. Ct. 2399, at p. 2406 (1986).
282. Ibid.
283. Ibid., at p. 2407.
284. The Supreme Court noted that a trial court must exercise its discretion to decide whether the relevance of the evidence is outweighed by the danger of unfair prejudice but may not establish a per se rule excluding such evidence. Ibid.
285. See *Loftin-Boggs v. City of Meridian*, 633 F. Supp. 1323 (S.D. Miss. 1986), affirmed in 824 F. 2d 921 (5th Cir. 1987), cert. denied in 484 U.S. 1063, 108 S. Ct. 1021 (1988).
286. *Laudenslager v. Covert*, 45 F.E.P. Cas. 907 (Mich. Ct. App. 1987).
287. *Highlander v. K.F.C. National Management Co.*, 805 F. 2d 644 (6th Cir. 1986).
288. See *Silverstein v. Metroplex Communications*, 678 F. Supp. 863 (S.D Fla. 1988); *Neville v. Taft Broadcasting Co.*, 42 F.E.P Cas. 1314 (W.D. N.Y. 1987). However, in *Meritor Savings Bank v. Vinson*, supra note 277, the Supreme Court refused to hold that the failure of an employee to use an employer's grievance procedure automatically insulated the employer from liability. That issue was "plainly relevant" but not conclusive. 106 S. Ct., at p. 2409.
289. *Rabidue v. Osceola Refining Co.*, 805 F. 2d 611 (6th Cir. 1986); see also 29 C.F.R. S1604.11(b) 260.
290. *Henson v. City of Dundee*, supra note 257. See also *Bohen v. City of East Chicago, Ind.*, 799 F. 2d 1180 (7th Cir. 1986) (conduct equally offensive to men and women is not a violation of equal protection).
291. *Henson v. City of Dundee*, supra note 259, at p. 903.
292. Ibid., at p. 904.
293. 842 F. 2d 1010 (8th Cir. 1988).
294. Ibid., at p. 1014.
295. *Vermett v. Hough*, 627 F. Supp. 587 (W.D. Mich. 1986).
296. 42 U.S.C. S2000e-2(a)(1).
297. See *Meritor Savings Bank v. Vinson*, supra note 277, at p. 2404. The existence of a tangible effect on a condition of employment is inconsequential. No economic or tangible job detriment need be suffered.
298. *Rogers v. EEOC*, 454 F. 2d 234 (5th Cir. 1971), cert. denied in 406 U.S. 957 (1972); *Meritor Savings Bank v. Vinson*, supra note 277, at p. 2405. See also *Broderick v. Ruder*, 685 F. Supp. 1269 (D.D.C. 5/13/88) (sexual activities in the workplace between other employees can affect the psychological well-being of an employee and create a hostile environment).
299. *Meritor Savings Bank v. Vinson*, supra note 277, at p. 2404 (citations omitted).
300. Ibid., at p. 2406.
301. See *Fontanez v. Aponte*, 660 F. Supp. 145 (D. Puerto Rico 1987); *Sapp v. City of Warner Robins*, 655 F. Supp. 1043 (M.D. Ga. 1987); *Strickland v. Sears, Roebuck & Co.*, 46 F.E.P. Cas. 1024 (E.D. Va. 1987); and *Petrosky v. Washington-Greene County Branch*, 45 F.E.P. Cas. 673 (W.D. Pa. 1987).
302. See *Moylan v. Maries County*, supra note 276, and *Katz v. Dole*, supra note 256.
303. See, for example, *Arnold v. City of Seminole*, 614 F. Supp. 853 (E.D. Okla. 354-18 1985). See also discussion at note 48 and accompanying text, *infra*.
304. See *Lake v. Baker*, 662 F. Supp. 392 (D.D.C. 1987).
305. 627 F. Supp. 587 (W.D. Mich.).
306. Ibid., at p. 599.
307. Supra note 299.
308. *Porta v. Rollins Environmental Services*, 654 F. Supp. 1275 (D.N.J. 1987), affirmed in 845 F. 2d 1014 (3rd Cir. 1988).
309. *DelGado v. Lehman*, 665 F. Supp. 460 (E.D. Va. 1987).
310. See *Arnold v. City of Seminole*, supra note 300, at p. 872. See also 29 C.F.R. S1604.11(*f*).
311. Supra note 12.
312. *Meritor Savings Bank v. Vinson*, supra note 277, at p. 2408.
313. *Burlington Industries, Inc. v. Ellerth*, 123 F. 3d 490 (1998).
314. *Henson v. City of Dundee*, supra note 257, at p. 910.
315. *Katz v. Dole*, supra note 256, at p. 255.
316. Ibid., at p. 255.
317. *Hall v. Gus Construction Co.*, 842 F. 2d 1010, at p. 1061 (8th Cir. 1988).
318. *Sapp v. City of Warner Robins*, 655 F. Supp. 1043, at p. 1050 (M.D. Ga. 1987). See also *Hall v. Gus Construction Co.*, supra note 286, at p. 1016.
319. See, e.g., *Arnold v. City of Seminole*, supra note 306; *Hall v. Gus Construction Co.*, supra

note 313; *Henson v. City of Dundee*, supra note 257; and *Lipsett v. Puerto Rico*, 864 F. 2d 884 (1st Cir. 1988). See also the five-post test established in *Chamberlim v. 101 Reality, Inc.*, 915 F. 2d 777 (1st Cir. 1990), at pp. 783–85.

320. *Meritor Savings Bank v. Vinson*, supra note 277, at p. 2408.
321. See 42 U.S.C. S2000e-5(g).
322. See, for example, *Arnold v. City of Seminole*, supra note 304, at p. 871.
323. See, for example, *Johnson v. Ballard*, 644 F. Supp. 333 (N.D. Ga. 1986); *Bohen v. City of East Chicago, Ind.*, supra note 286; *Brown v. Town of Allentown*, 648 F. Supp. 831 (D.N.H. 1986); and *Hunt v. Weatherbee*, 626 F. Supp. 1097 (D. Mass. 1986).
324. See, for example, *Brown v. Town of Allentown*, supra note 314; *Priest v. Rotary*, 634 F. Supp. 571 (N.D. Cal. 1986); and *Owens v. Tumage*, 46 F.E.P. Cas. 528 (D. N.J. 1988).
325. International Association of Chiefs of Police, *Harassment in the Workplace* (Arlington, Va.: IACP, 1990), pp. 6–7 and 9–10.
326. *Meritor Savings Bank v. Vinson*, supra note 277, at p. 72.
327. Supra note 313.
328. Supra note 326.

15 CHAPTER

Change is not made without inconvenience, even when moving from worse to better.

—Richard Hooker (1554–1600)

Trying to change the federal bureaucracy has the same effect as punching a curtain.

—President John F. Kennedy (1917–1963)

Nothing is more difficult . . . more uncertain of success . . . than introducing change.

—Niccolo Machiavelli (1469–1527)

OUTLINE

Introduction

Why Change Occurs

When Change Should Not Be Made

Two Organizational Change Models

Politics and Organizational Change

Police Futures Research

Chapter Review

Key Terms

Notes

OBJECTIVES

1. Distinguish between non-directed and directed change.
2. Identify eight recurring reasons that change occurs in law enforcement agencies.
3. State five reasons when change should not be initiated.
4. Define organizational development.
5. Explain why apathy is a worse response to change than resistance.
6. Identify and briefly explain three categories of change resistance.
7. Describe Lewin's three-step change model.
8. Identify the major steps in the traditional action research model.
9. Describe the purpose of police futures research.

ORGANIZATIONAL CHANGE AND THE FUTURE

INTRODUCTION

If, as some critics maintain, police agencies are rigid, mechanistic, closed-system bureaucracies, there is no need to address organizational change. However, the reality is that law enforcement is continuously involved in change, including adapting to the requirements of new laws and court decisions, adopting new policies and procedures, implementing new community policing programs, reacting to the guidance given by elected and appointed community leaders, and finding new ways to do more with less resources. Police leaders know how difficult, risky, and necessary change is. Broadly, change can be thought of as directed and non-directed (see Figure 15.1).[1]

Directed change is a carefully planned formal action designed to bring about a new condition, such as transitional training to ensure proficiency when a department moves from using one type of firearm to another. Characteristically, directed change affects the whole organization, it involves the most senior levels of management, its implementation is usually linked to accomplishing important goals, and progress is formally evaluated. In contrast and less dramatically, non-directed change occurs when informal adjustments are made at lower levels of the department, often by first-line supervisors, that creep into the organization over time. For example, while a department's policies may not require that homicide investigators attend autopsies, a detective supervisor may want this done routinely; this informal change in "policy" in one unit impacts how detectives use their time and reduces their flexibility in planning their daily schedule. **Non-directed change** may eventually rise to the level of becoming a directed, formal change or simply "rock along" informally. This chapter is about directed change.

VARIABLES	DIRECTED CHANGE	NON-DIRECTED CHANGE
Scope	Departmentwide/macro	Unit-by-unit/micro
Nature	Proactive/formal	Reactive/informal
Initiator	Top management	First-line supervisors
Goals	Linked to important goals	Little or no linkage to goals
Policy	Consistent	Mutates and is idiosyncratic within units; may be important adaptations which compensate for gaps in formal systems; as such, could eventually become part of formal policy
Feedback	Required, detailed, written	Little, informal, verbal
Planning	Systematic, comprehensive	Minimal, response to unique need within unit

FIGURE 15.1

Directed vs. non-directed change in police departments.

(*Source:* Patricia Felkins, B. J. Chakiris, and Kenneth N. Chakiris, *Change Management: A Model for Organizational Effectiveness* [New York: Quality Resources, 1993], from content at pp. 5–6, with changes and additions.)

WHY CHANGE OCCURS

While any number of factors may be the catalyst for change, there are several recurring themes, which lead to it in police agencies; among these are:

1. A single catastrophic event, often followed by civil liability litigation, leads to the chief of police being replaced. Illustratively, "Chief Jones" had come up through the ranks in his hometown 45-member police department of "Georgetown." A war hero as a young man, he was well liked by all segments of the community, largely because he had coached Little League baseball for years and knew many parents and was active in the local high school football boosters club, where he was well liked by the town's "movers and shakers." A town resident was raped and beaten; a second rape occurred within a few days, and this victim was cut multiple times with a knife. In both crimes the suspect was a local man with a teardrop-shaped tattoo, under one eye and an arrest warrant was issued for his arrest. There was considerable fear that, if not rapidly apprehended, the suspect might kill his next victim because of the increase in the level of violence between the first and second rapes.

   One evening, a detective received a call from a citizen, reporting that as he drove down a road he saw the rape suspect entering a home outside the city limits in the county. This and other information from the caller, who was unknown to the detective, was never critically evaluated. The speed limit in this area was 55 MPH; the house was set nearly 40 yards from the highway, and there were no street lights in the area; it was dark and the porch light was off. Moreover, if the suspect was entering the house, his back would have been to the highway and, even if it was not so momentarily, how did the citizen, who did not know the suspect, see a small tattoo of a teardrop at that distance in the dark?

   The detective rapidly went through the building, asking, "Who wants to go get this son of a bitch?" Without a search warrant for the home the suspect was alleged to be in and without requesting the assistance of the county sheriff's office, approximately eight officers went to the home, which was dark inside; broke into it; and shot and killed the 70-year-old homeowner, who fired two shots at shapes charging into his house.

   The state investigative agency's report on the shooting found that the department's policies and procedures were non-existent or inadequate, there was no raid plan or briefing, the "raid team" had never trained together, there was no attempt to verify the information the detective received before acting on

In The News

Today's News

Unusual, Police Are Plaintiffs

Although the more usual case is that the police are sued, occasionally they're the plaintiffs. The Quincy (Massachusetts) Police Department is one of about 65 law enforcement agencies nationally who will receive part of a large settlement from a company that sold what may have been defective bulletproof vests.

After the U.S. Department of Justice finished a two-year study, it determined that Zylon, a synthetic used in the vests, could be penetrated by bullets. Among the incidents leading to questions about the vests' safety were the death of a California officer and the serious wounding of a Pennsylvania officer, both of who were wearing Second Chance vests.

Zylon may wear down faster than anticipated. Under the settlement agreement, police departments get $730 for each vest they purchased or an $803 voucher to buy a new one.

Source: Jessica Van Sack, "Quincy to Get Settlement for Police Vests," *Patriot Ledger*, July 11, 2006.

it, and the suspect was not only not at the home but had never been there. The shooting took place two days before Christmas, leading citizens to ask, "Whose house are the police going to break into next and kill someone?" The city council concluded there was a massive failure of leadership and newspaper editorials called for the chief's dismissal. In the wake of these events, Georgetown hired a professional from outside the community to head the police department, and he came in with a mandate for sweeping reforms.

2. A new governor or mayor is elected or the balance of power shifts in the county commission city council, with the consequence that the current chief is replaced with one of their own choosing. The new chief may bring his or her own vision of how the agency should be organized and operated;[2] alternatively, the new chief is selected with the understanding that he or she has a mandate to implement certain changes.[3]
3. A key political figure suffers a major embarrassment and feels the law enforcement agency is to blame, resulting in the chief being forced out. For example, a governor who was a competent fixed-wing, multi-engine pilot with an instrument rating was being flown around his state in the state patrol helicopter. When the governor wanted to fly the helicopter, the aircraft commander, who was a sergeant, refused to allow him to do so, citing a lack of training and safety concerns. One version of this is that the governor gracefully accepted this, while the other version is that there was a "nasty confrontation" about it. Subsequently, this story was covered by the news media and the governor felt that, not only had the event been blown out of proportion but that "someone at the State Patrol had been talking out of school." When reportedly pressured by a member of the governor's staff, the state patrol director refused to discipline or transfer the pilot, resulting in additional bad publicity for the governor. Shortly thereafter, the state patrol's director quietly retired.
4. A chief of police retires, takes another position, or is fired. A consultant is hired to conduct an evaluation of the department[4] and the report is given to the new chief as a blueprint for change in the department. A few consultants seem to specialize in "headhunter" type of reports. City managers desiring to get rid of chiefs have been known to hire such consultants, as opposed to using ones who are more even-handed and balanced in writing their reports. At the risk of oversimplification, the headhunter type of report is filled with negative statements, while the more professional consultant notes both the department's strengths and its weaknesses. While the latter type of report may lead to the chief's dismissal, it is on the basis of a fundamentally fair summation of present conditions in the department.
5. A new sheriff is elected and implements the changes that were part of the platform on which he or she ran. In one county, the defeated sheriff had insisted on buying a helicopter; its purchase price and operating costs were considerable for that county. As a candidate, the new sheriff promised he would get rid of the helicopter and "get back to basics, putting officers where they were needed instead of using a pie in the sky strategy."

   The "Green County" Sheriff's Office (GCSO) was not doing particularly well or badly. Although in recent months the local newspaper had questioned the GCSO's policy on high-speed chases and had raised the question of whether the GCSO SWAT Team had used force somewhat quickly in a barricaded person situation, most observers felt the sheriff would be re-elected. Except for the fact that he then made two significant political errors, he might have survived these criticisms.

The sheriff decided to remove his legal advertising from the town's daily newspaper and run it in the town's small, weekly newspaper. Shortly thereafter, instead of continuing to buy the department's cars from the large dealer used for a number of years, the sheriff awarded the contract to a smaller, competing dealer. Later, the sheriff publicly said he was just trying to be fair in the distribution of the car contracts, although privately he conceded that perhaps he should have simply bought some cars from both dealers. The large dealership owner was a generous contributor to local politicians and had access to influence and power. The daily newspaper became more critical of the sheriff's office and subsequently supported his opponent, whose campaign centered on "returning to doing basic things well." In the background, the large dealership owner also worked against the incumbent, who was defeated in the next election.

What the defeated sheriff failed to appreciate is that, over time, expectations build up for how an organization operates and that to some degree it becomes "captured" by these expectations of other organizations. The large dealership owner expected he would routinely get the contract for the cars and the newspaper believed it could influence how the sheriff's office operated. When major expectations are abruptly not honored, serious conflict invariably follows. The sheriff also violated one of the most important tenets of elected office: don't get into a fight with newspapers—they buy their ink by the barrel.

6. The chief's conduct or style becomes an issue that leads to his or her dismissal. In one instance, a chief arrived at the department's ball when he already had been heavily drinking. As the evening wore on, he got progressively drunk and refused to allow his staff members to drive him home, electing to stay at the party, where he got into several major confrontations with members of his department and one of their spouses. His dismissal was predicated on a public debate: "he is supposed to be a model for others; if he cannot control himself, how can he lead others?"
7. Morale in the police department is low, too many things seem to be going wrong, the present administration is always reacting to problems for which it seems no thought has been given or preparation has been made, or citizen groups are vociferous in their criticisms of the department. In such situations, police unions or associations may also oppose the chief and have given him or her a vote of no confidence. In such environments, complaints against police officers may be on the upswing, the use of sick leave by officers is excessive, the turnover rate is high and the level of experience in the department is dangerously low, the agency has difficulty attracting quality candidates or cannot even fill vacancies with the minimally qualified, the use of force incidents are increasing, and the crime rate is climbing while clearance levels are dropping out of sight.
8. As we learned in Chapter 2, paradigms are ways or models of doing things and they often have an accompanying set of rules and procedures. Max Weber's bureaucratic model can be thought of as a paradigm; when new paradigms are developed, they may have significant potential for causing significant organizational change. It is possible that the three most important paradigm shifts in the last 30 years of policing have been: (1) individual identification by DNA, which has created demands for new skills, training, and procedures in investigation, especially in the areas of evidence identification, collection,

In The News

Conditions Require Police Reorganization

A new chief says his first task is a major reorganization, from top to bottom, of the police department. Resignations and retirements have left the department 16 officers down from full strength. As a result, the community police division and SWAT Team don't exist anymore. Some officers are working two or three double shifts weekly due to the personnel situation.

There have been scathing reports from outside agencies about the police department; a half-dozen civil rights violations were filed against the department. Although most of these suits have been settled, a major one is approaching trial. The widow of one officer, who was accidentally shot by another officer at the station, is considering legal action. A 2005 consultant's report recommended that the department concentrate on basic services instead of specialized units.

Source: Joe MacDonald and Tracy Jordan, "Easton Chief to Reorganize Unit," *The Morning Call* (Allentown, Pennsylvania), June 12, 2006.

preservation and processing, as well as quantum leaps in clearing decades old cold cases and exonerating those who were erroneously convicted; (2) the shift from the traditional policing model, responding to incidents **(R2I)** to the widespread adoption of the community policing model; and (3) the development of fusion centers in the wake of the multiple terrorist attacks on September 11, 2001, such as the San Diego Regional Threat Assessment Center, which is creating significant new roles for local law enforcement agencies. However important these new roles are, they have exacerbated already existing staffing shortages in state and local law enforcement agencies. Prior to the implementation of fusion centers, many police agencies had difficulties recruiting and retaining officers and were also experiencing staffing shortages from sworn members in Reserve or National Guard units being called up for extended active military service. Moreover, even with federal funding to assist with the creation of the fusion centers, a number of officers being reassigned to them are only being made available by stripping personnel from lower priority functions, for example, by reducing the number of investigators in non-violent crimes units.

Historically, there have also been smaller paradigm shifts. For example, in many jurisdictions up until the mid to late 1960s, two officers walked high-crime area beats together. However, a large number of agencies concluded that this was unnecessary when personal handheld Motorola radios became available; a lone officer could call for backup if it was needed and the other officer was freed for other duties.

WHEN CHANGE SHOULD NOT BE MADE

Because change is a perilous process, some thought should be given to whether it should be presently undertaken; among the conditions that indicate that a contemplated change should be delayed are:

1. Inside the department, the knowledge, skill, or other resources needed to carry out the change effectively do not exist.
2. An appropriately experienced external change agent is not presently available.
3. The effort of making the change is greater than any benefits to be derived; former Georgia Governor Zell Miller expressed this as "the juice isn't worth the squeezing." This principle can also be stated as "all motion isn't progress; some of it is just thrashing around."

4. Collateral damage, such abandonment by key supporters or significant union opposition, may lead chiefs to use their limited stack of "political chips" on another issue of greater concern to them and the community.
5. Too much change is already underway in the department and the nature of the change is not sufficiently important to make now versus its potential for personnel to feel confused about priorities or conclude that the organization is becoming unstable.

Critical Thinking Questions

1. Never answered in the helicopter incident was "who leaked the information to the news media?" Give two different explanations of who might have provided the information to the news media.
2. Implementing change is a difficult decision. What factors do you think are important in deciding, as a chief executive, when to institute change in your organization?

TWO ORGANIZATIONAL CHANGE MODELS

There is an old story about a boy who wanted his dog to have a short tail. But rather than hurt the dog by cutting the tail off all at once, the boy sliced an inch off at a time. This story illustrates what is described as "pain level" associated with gradual and radical change strategies in public organizations. One camp maintains that it is better to implement change swiftly (radical change) and get the upheavals which follow done and over with, versus implementing changes incrementally over time (gradual change) so that personnel have an opportunity to adjust to new realities and requirements. Proponents of radical change argue that when change is gradual, unanticipated events may derail the effort before it can be completed and that it gives opponents time to organize themselves to thwart further implementation. Figure 15.2, "Effect of Change Strategies on Police Department Members," is a general model of the likely impact on police members when authoritarian and participative strategies using wide input and involvement are used as the basis for gradual and radical organizational change. Regardless of whether change is gradual or radical, the chief cannot sit passively on the sidelines to see how it turns out; they must actively help lead the change; as noted in Chapter 6, leadership is not a spectator sport.

While some changes can be accomplished through the pronouncement of Chiefs, especially in very small departments, larger departments are more complex and therefore require greater planning, the use of more sophisticated techniques, and wide involvement to garner crucial input and support before moving forward to the implementation phase. This often involves the use of organizational development (OD). In Chapter 5, "Organizational Theory," the OD process was defined and described. To briefly recapitulate, OD is an applied behavioral science method of changing organizations through long-term efforts designed to improve the work culture and work processes.

In this section, two models of directed change are presented. The first one, **Lewin's Three-Step Model,** was selected because it is one of the oldest, simplest and yet, the most durable. The second model, the **Traditional Action Research Model,** represents a fairly typical change process. If the second one seems somewhat familiar, it may be due to the fact that planning was covered in an earlier chapter (see Chapter 8, Planning and Decision Making). The Traditional Action Research Model is simply a special type of planning. Both Lewin's Three-Step Model and the Traditional Action Research Model rely on the use of organizational development (OD).

Focus on Policy

The Chief as Change Agent

WILLIAM J. BRATTON, CHIEF OF POLICE, LOS ANGELES POLICE DEPARTMENT

One of the country's foremost chiefs of police is William J. Bratton. He is currently the 54th chief of the Los Angeles Police Department and was formerly commissioner of the New York Police Department. He is the only person to have occupied the highest executive position in each of the two largest cities in the United States.

Born in 1947, in Boston, Massachusetts, Bratton joined the Boston Police Department, and at age 32 was appointed as the youngest executive superintendent of the Boston Police, the department's second highest rank. In 1994, he was appointed the 38th commissioner of the New York City Police Department by then-Mayor Rudolph Giuliani, and in October 2002 he was appointed chief of the Los Angeles Police Department.

Bill Bratton represents the classic "change agent" in policing. As commissioner of the NYPD, he introduced the Compstat system of tracking crime and holding police executives accountable for strategies to reduce crime in specific areas. He went on to develop a real-time police intelligence computer system, which became the first fusion center in the United States at the local level and began the emergence of intelligence-led policing. Under his leadership, New York's crime rate plummeted during the 1990s, when he initiated "zero-tolerance" policing, and in Los Angeles he has been charged with changing the internal dynamics of the LAPD. Currently, under a Federal Consent Decree issued in November 2000, arising in part from the Rampart Precinct corruption scandal in the late 1990s and a series of excessive force, false arrest, and unreasonable search and seizure complaints, the LAPD faces significant internal policy changes from the past. To his credit, Chief Bratton has totally revamped the department's Internal Affairs Division and has reduced complaints relating to police brutality. At the same time, he has lowered violent crime rates in LA.

Like all change agents, Bratton's decisions have not been without criticism. He has relaxed the hiring standards for police in LA, allowing candidates with minor drug use in their past to join the department. He has also been criticized by the LAPD officer associations for being arrogant and non-caring, particularly relating to discipline associated with various police shooting incidents. He has also been referred to as an "absentee chief" because of his extensive schedule. In 2005, he was "out of town" for a full third of the year.

(Corbis Digital Stock)

CHANGE STRATEGY	GRADUAL CHANGE	RADIAL CHANGE
Top down/Authoritarian	Some resistance to compliance	Resistance to rebellion
Participative = Participative	Support	Limited resistance to substantial support

FIGURE 15.2

Effect of change strategies on police department members.

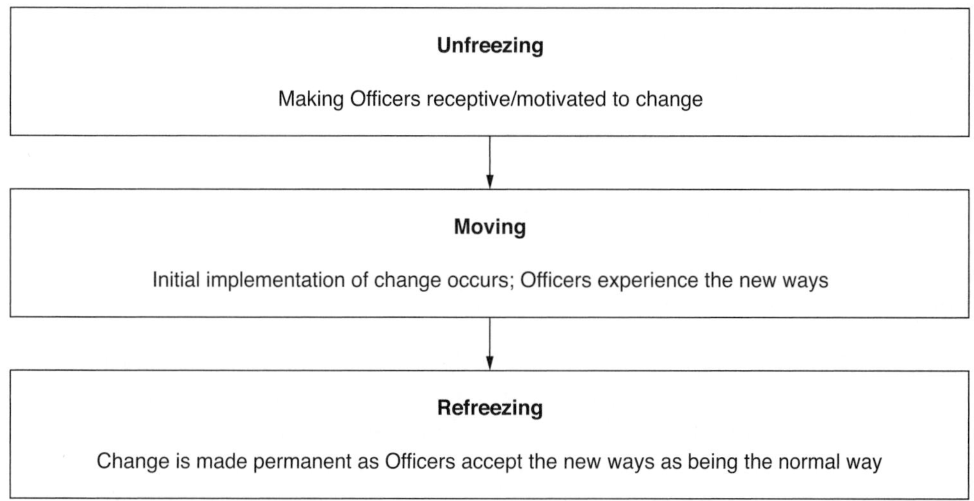
Unfreezing
Making Officers receptive/motivated to change
Moving
Initial implementation of change occurs; Officers experience the new ways
Refreezing
Change is made permanent as Officers accept the new ways as being the normal way

FIGURE 15.3

Kurt Lewin's three-step model.

Kurt Lewin's Three-Step Model

This 1951 model involves three sequential steps (see Figure 15.3):

1. *Unfreezing.* Officers, like all other people, get into their "comfort zones." Before change can occur, they have to be "unfrozen" from the perceptions and behaviors that are presently part of who they are and how they approach their jobs. Often, this is accomplished by creating a sense of urgency that the present way of doing things is deficient in some way and that a shift to some new procedures will produce better results more efficiently. This tactic is know as "disconfirmation" because to some degree it invalidates what is presently being done. The heart of unfreezing is making people be receptive to change.
2. *Moving.* This is a transitional phase in which officers actually experience the changes which were planned; there will be less resistance if officers, to the maximum extent possible, are included in the planning process and feel that they have some impact in shaping events. While there are top-down decisions chiefs make which constitute major change, such as to begin using Compstat, there is ample room to involve sworn and civilian personnel from across the agency on the details of implementation, such as the design of forms to capture data and what types of data are most useful for planning various types of

operations. The use of officers on task forces or committees cannot be symbolic or gratuitous; such motives will be "sniffed out" immediately and provoke an unpleasant set of dynamics for the chief to preside over.

3. *Refreezing.* The purpose of this phase is for officers to make permanent the changes they experienced in the previous phase, part of the normal way in which they see things, think about them, and behave. Some of the refreezing can be accomplished by appealing to the professionalism of officers—"When we get this thing fully up and running, everybody in the state will be looking at us, wondering how we got so far ahead of them." However, drawing upon the lessons learned from the shift from R2I to community policing, resistance tapered off and refreezing occurred faster when departmental awards were realigned with community policing goals, such as recognition for enrolling 25 businesses in a crime prevention program. Thus, as part of any large-scale change process, the use of awards to reinforce the desired behaviors should be carefully considered.

Traditional Action Research Model

There are many OD change models; however, most of them approximate the Traditional Action Research Model with the following five steps (see Figure 15.4):

1. *Recognizing the need for change.* Without this awareness, it is simply "business as usual" for police agencies. The change awareness may come from the need to implement the provisions of a Supreme Court decision or a consent decree entered into in partial settlement of a civil liability suit. The department's planning and research unit may have identified lapses in performance that need to be addressed or unusual opportunities on which to capitalize, such as the availability of federal grants to implement community policing programs or to upgrade crime scene investigation capabilities. Individual officers, supervisors, command staff members, or the union may make written recommendations in the form of memos or completed staff work which leads to change. Additionally, any of the situations discussed in the earlier section, Why Change Occurs, may take place, such as a new chief being hired with a mandate to make specific changes in the department's operating philosophy, organizational structure, programs and policies, and procedures.
2. *Assessing/diagnosing the situation.* There are two fundamental tasks in assessing the situation which must be executed flawlessly: (a) determining the opportunity or the problem; care must be taken to make sure that attention is given to the real problem and not a symptom of it and (b) determining the gap or difference between what is now happening and what department would like to have happen. In order to accomplish these twin objectives, data must be gathered. Sources of such data include 911, training, and other records; surveys of personnel and clients; and reviews of disciplinary records and litigation trends.
3. *Action planning.* The gap or difference between what is happening and what is desirable is the zone of impact, where meaningful change can occur if something significant is selected to work on. The chief must decide who will be in charge of the change process. Internal candidates for this responsibility know the organization, its capabilities, and its personnel but may lack the necessary skills to lead an effective intervention or may not have the time to devote to the change effort. External consultants don't have any "baggage" because people in

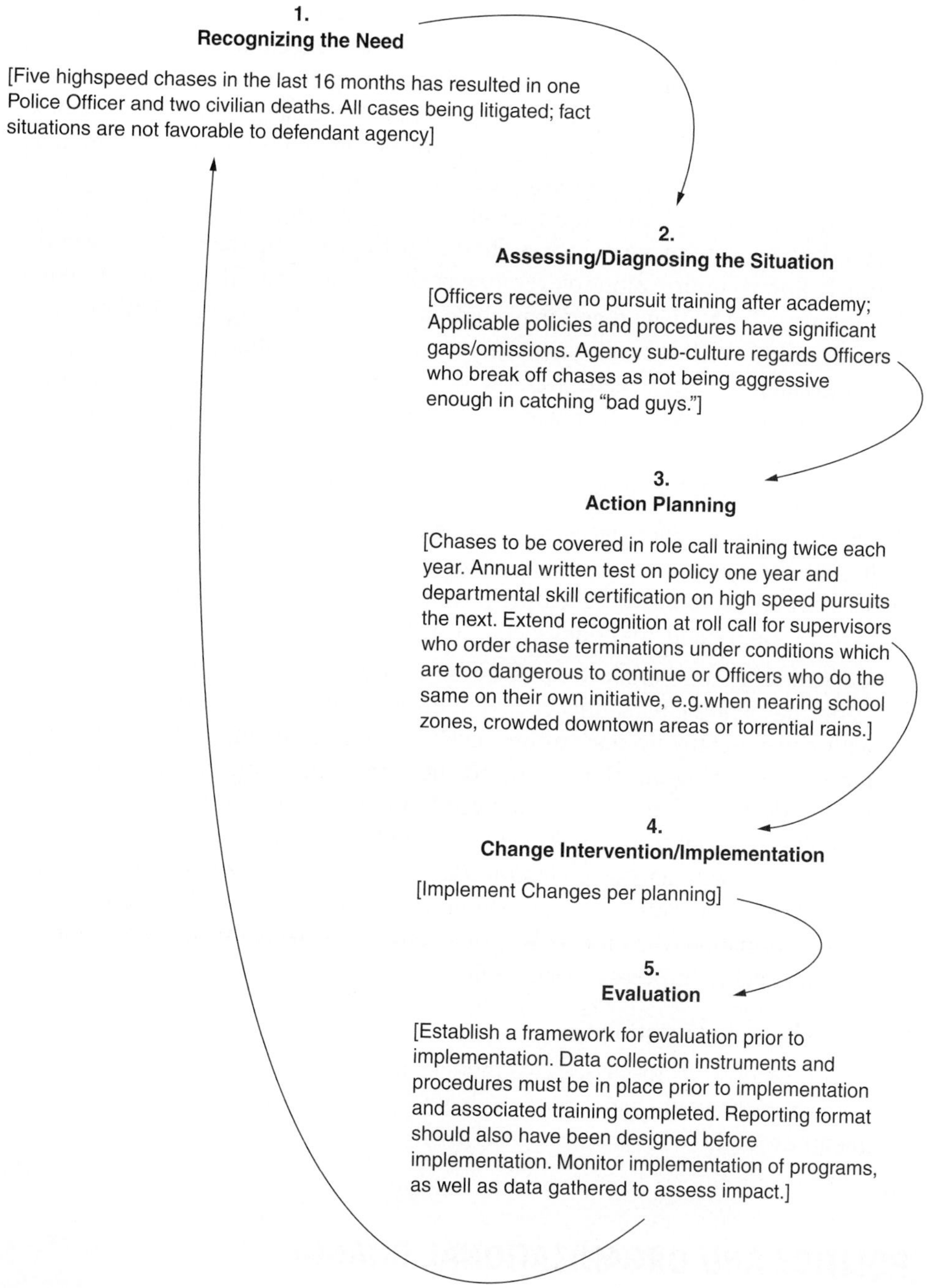

1.
Recognizing the Need

[Five highspeed chases in the last 16 months has resulted in one Police Officer and two civilian deaths. All cases being litigated; fact situations are not favorable to defendant agency]

2.
Assessing/Diagnosing the Situation

[Officers receive no pursuit training after academy; Applicable policies and procedures have significant gaps/omissions. Agency sub-culture regards Officers who break off chases as not being aggressive enough in catching "bad guys."]

3.
Action Planning

[Chases to be covered in role call training twice each year. Annual written test on policy one year and departmental skill certification on high speed pursuits the next. Extend recognition at roll call for supervisors who order chase terminations under conditions which are too dangerous to continue or Officers who do the same on their own initiative, e.g.when nearing school zones, crowded downtown areas or torrential rains.]

4.
Change Intervention/Implementation

[Implement Changes per planning]

5.
Evaluation

[Establish a framework for evaluation prior to implementation. Data collection instruments and procedures must be in place prior to implementation and associated training completed. Reporting format should also have been designed before implementation. Monitor implementation of programs, as well as data gathered to assess impact.]

FIGURE 15.4

Traditional action research model.

the department typically don't know them, but they lack the depth of knowledge about the department an insider would have. Although outsiders come with a certain amount of instant credibility, any missteps they make are often judged harshly with biting comments such as "If he's the expert and making big bucks, how come we've got such a mess on our hands?"

As mentioned earlier, it is crucial to involve people from throughout the department and to have a continuous stream of information flowing to all personnel through posting on the department's intranet, announcements at roll call, information posted on bulletin boards, and the dissemination of memos and newsletters. When officers don't know what is going on, the rumor mill works overtime, seldom to the benefit of the process or the changes being implemented.

In many instances, officers serve on one or more task forces or committees involved in the change. For example, officers may be appointed to a steering task force, which has overall responsibility for the change, or the information coordination committee, which is charged with providing the continuing and timely flow of information to everyone in the department. Many lower-ranking officers are field-oriented and may chafe at being in meetings, particularly if they become restless at the slow progress being made initially, cannot immediately see any benefit from the work of the committee, or have doubts about whether it can really make a difference.[5] Ultimately, a written plan identifying the process to be used and the results desired will be produced during the action planning phase, with responsibilities assigned for all activities.

4. *Change Intervention/Implementation*. This is when the action plans are implemented. It is not the end of the process but rather the end of the beginning. As the various activities are set in motion, their progress must be carefully monitored against the time lines and standards established during the previous phase.
5. *Evaluation*. This is best accomplished by a series of informative, scheduled reports and periodic personnel checking through observation and conversations with personnel involved at various levels of the department. The two most common needs during this time are (a) the need to further articulate or increase the level of detail in plans and (b) the need to initiate corrective action because the time lines initially set were too ambitious and cannot be met or the activities have somehow otherwise gotten off track (e.g., an equipment supplier cannot make delivery as previously agreed upon). As the decision makers receive evaluative information, the process loops back to step 1, recognizing the need for change, and the process repeats itself.

Critical Thinking Question

1. In this section, we discussed two models of directed change. Can you think of some non-directed change models that might be at work in many police departments around the country?

POLITICS AND ORGANIZATIONAL CHANGE

We know that politics is neither inherently "bad" nor "good"; instead, its character is derived from how it is used. The larger an organizational change, the more likely politics will inevitably come into play. In many instances, political figures want to champion important changes in police departments; by consistently voicing their support in front of the audiences they address, politicians can be a potent adjunct to the change process, helping underscore both its significance and the backing it has. This is critical in preparing the organization for change and in helping it to maintain its focus and drive, so that the changes can be successfully implemented.

Conversely, politicians can be a barrier to change when they want to make unneeded modifications to the scope of the change or attempt to micro-manage implementation details. However well intended, some politicians end up being an impediment when they attempt to become too involved with change. They must learn to trust the people charged with leading the police department and not attempt to substitute their judgment for that of the Chief's and the command staff and to hold them accountable for the results or lack thereof.

Personal politics are typically at work during large-scale organizational changes in law enforcement agencies. This is normal and should be expected. Senior police officials seek to have those they mentor promoted and assigned to desirable commands. Personnel on promotional rosters will seek to be among those selected to fill openings created by a reorganization of their department. The fact that people work to have themselves promoted during a reorganization should surprise no one. However, it is unsavory and kills morale when unqualified or marginally competent people with unbridled ambition successfully use politics to their personal advantage at the considerable expense of others or when the use of politics interferes with the timely and effective implementation of the changes. The case study which follows illustrates this point.

"Boss Town" had a strong mayor form of government and a police department with 500 sworn officers. For 18 months the department worked on a major reorganization; as part of the this effort, 63 new positions were created, into which people had to be promoted. The ranks involved ranged from corporal, a rank new to the department, to one deputy chief/lt. colonel position. It was widely known that the brain power behind the changes was "Major Thompson," perhaps the most highly able and respected of the senior commanders. Everyone in the department considered it a foregone conclusion that he would get the newly created deputy chief position. "Major Handshake" had come up through the ranks, but at every level exceptions to the regular promotional process were made so that he could be advanced. His most recent promotion was just 10 months previous, when he had been promoted to major. Because the department's probationary period for supervisory positions was 12 months, Major Handshake was still on probation for another 2 months and not eligible for the deputy chief position.

At this point, politics, in the worst sense, was relied upon by Major Handshake. The mayor's son served on the state road board and was up for reappointment by the governor. It was personally important to the mayor that his son be reappointed and it was an economic development asset to the region for the son to continue to serve, so that he could funnel additional funds to the area for improved road systems. Major Handshake's uncle was not only a member of the governor's cabinet but also close personal friends with him. The mayor received a call from the state capitol, expressing interest that Major Handshake be promoted to deputy chief. To ensure his son's reappointment, the mayor froze the implementation of the police reorganization for 60 days, at the end of which Major Handshake was off probation and promoted to deputy chief.

One cost of this delay was that the promotions, additional pay, and growth in seniority in grade for over 60 people were non-starters for two months. Another cost was that a group of 11 very highly regarded detectives and sergeants informally met to discuss what it meant when the most qualified and professional person in the department couldn't get the promotion he deserved. What did that mean or suggest in terms of their own futures? Four members of this group subsequently resigned and went on to distinguished careers elsewhere. Of the 3 that stayed, one ultimately became the chief, who privately lamented in later years the substantial loss of talent caused by the promotion of Major Handshake.

Resistance to Change

A common topic when planning and implementing change in law enforcement agencies is resistance to change. Intuitively, it would seem that, if things aren't going well in an agency, change, which is likely to improve operations and management, would

In The News

Change Successfully Blocked by Labeling It "Quota System"

Quotas in law enforcement have traditionally been resisted by officers who maintain that no one really knows how many good cases they will see during a day, week, or month. Moreover, the number and types of offenses vary by geographic area and demographic characteristics; for example, older people commit fewer crimes. Moreover, officers are quick to point out that quotas force them to make marginal cases in order to get good evaluations, decreasing public good will and support. In the news story which follows, we see officers resisting traffic ticket quotas.

The Ogden (Utah) City Council dropped a controversial police performance evaluation plan which included 18 factors, including a score for the number of traffic tickets given. This followed a period during which the wife of an officer who drove a van used to display signs critical of the traffic quota and Mayor Godfrey. Within hours, the officer was placed on administrative duty, although the police chief maintains this was due to other alleged actions by the officer. A two-day "blue-flu" was also used, with officers calling in "sick" during it. The city's administration has agreed to meet with officers to identify and discuss issues; the meetings will be led by a professional mediator to keep them on track.

Source: "Ogden Rescinds Ticket Quota for Police," The Associated Press and Local Wire, August 16, 2006.

be warmly received. However, in any present situation, people know and understand their roles and how things get done. There is no uncertainty. Change threatens the loss of stability and predictability and therefore resistance often occurs simply out of fear of the unknown, concern that change might inconvenience or demand too much of "me" or change "my" job in ways that "I" wouldn't like.

Thus, some resistance to change is rooted in self-interest as to what exactly the effect of change will mean personally. As difficult as resistance is, it is far better than having an apathetic response to change.[6] This is true because resistance means officers are at the first stages of engaging in the change process, while apathy denotes that they haven't even reached that threshold; they are not sufficiently engaged with the department and their jobs to care whether things remain the same or change.

There are three types of change resistance:

1. **Blind resistance,** or an automatic anti-change position. Officers in this category oppose the notion of change long before they know any of its details. At some level, they may experience being an aggrieved party; change is being "done to them" and they don't like it. Officers don't like feeling powerless and will resist change in order to avoid feeling helpless. Relatedly, some people are energized by opposing or fighting something; it helps give meaning and definition to who they are.
2. **Ideological opposition,** which may be rooted in a philosophical position that the shift is ill-conceived, such as the shift from traditional to community policing. Usually, ideological opponents of change craft specific arguments to support their opposition, such as "the timing is not right for a shift of this magnitude;" "it is unlikely that the change will actually work;" "more harm than good will result from attempting this change;" or "this change diverts attention and effort from the real work of policing, catching 'bad guys.'"
3. **Political resistance,** which is often rooted in the concern that, somehow as a result of the change, people feel they will lose something of value to them, such as influence, authority, power, or status. Recall that the team policing concept failed, in part, because the role and importance of middle managers were reduced and therefore incumbents of those positions came to oppose the concept, contributing substantially to its demise. Political resistance can usefully be thought of as "turf protection" responses.[7]

Quick Facts

Up to 80% of Changes Foil

Just how hard is organizational change? Research suggests that between 50 and 80 percent of the time, the major results that were anticipated are *not* produced. Smith interviewed 210 managers who reported a change failure rate of over 75 percent.

Source: M. E. Smith, "Implementing Organization Change: Correlates of Success and Failure," *Performance Improvement Quarterly*, 15, no. 1 (2002): 67-83.

Levels of Change

Not all change is momentous. However, the wider the scope of the change and the greater the number of people significantly impacted, the more difficult it is to implement, sustain, and institutionalize it. For example, assume that historically in a department the ranking patrol supervisor at the scene of a serious crime was in charge of the scene. A new policy is issued that, whenever detectives are dispatched to the scene of a serious crime, they are in command of all aspects of conducting the on-site investigation. Usually, this would affect the job of patrol sergeants and, although they would grouse at the loss of authority, the change would be implemented without any significant turbulence or opposition. In fact, some sergeants would simply say, "That's fine by me; it's one less thing I have to worry about." But when there is large-scale directed change, "more people are going to be ticked off and eating Rolaids." While some policy changes can be made without controversy, others will provoke opposition; an excellent example of this is when an agency goes to a very restrictive high-speed chase policy and rank-and-file officers feel that their "hands are being tied when it comes to catching bad guys."

When automobiles started becoming more commonplace, police chiefs assigned their best officers to traffic duty because they would be coming into contact with the wealthy and professionals who could afford the cars. In a sense, police professionalism had its first modest start in traffic units; officers assigned there considered themselves elite. Once in a while, that leftover manifestation of this fact still appears.

In 2006, a consultant finished a major organizational study of a police department with 200 sworn officers. One of his recommendations was that the Traffic Division (TD) be eliminated and the personnel combined with the Patrol Division to form a Uniform Division. In order to maintain a high level of ability to investigate serious personal injury and fatality accidents, each patrol division shift would be assigned several of the best qualified TD accident investigators, who would continue to specialize in the same jobs they formerly held. The rest of the TD officers would be assigned to patrol duties. The reason for the recommendation was that the Traffic Division, whose members considered themselves the elite of uniformed officers, had become increasingly dysfunctional over a period of years. Among the indicators of this was that no traffic unit worked past 10:00 P.M., meaning that they were not working during some of the prime hours for driving while intoxicated (DWI) enforcement. Moreover, compared with similarly sized cities, the TD officers generated fewer cases, despite having more personnel; used more sick leave than other officers in the department; and were often antagonistic to personnel in other divisions. The change was implemented, but not without great upheaval. Some TD officers and supervisors attempted to have the change killed before it was implemented by visiting politicians who began to voice various concerns pro and con about the change. Some experienced TD officers left to take jobs in police departments in several nearby, smaller municipalities. The chief, who had risen through the ranks internally and had only recently been appointed felt that the "change was long overdue, but messy." The mayor, who had appointed the chief, dismissed the controversy by noting that "you can't make an omelette without breaking a few eggs; we can't have a few malcontents trying to make policy." Slowly, things changed. DWI arrests went up because there were more officers working during the prime enforcement hours for them, response times to calls for service dropped slightly because there were more patrol officers on duty to answer calls, and the number of accidents declined marginally each month.

As the positive aspects of the change were "kicking in," a radical shift occurred that no one had foreseen. After some discussion and study, the city's voters approved merging their police department under the sheriff's office, which had a Traffic Unit. The benefits of the city police department having gone through a hard, large-scale organizational change were lost when the two agencies actually combined operations 18 months later. Under the sheriff, the former TD officers remembered who had supported the elimination of their division and made life difficult for them whenever they could, although slowly that behavior seemed to lessen over time. Thus, in large organizational change there can be some lingering unanticipated difficulty for years beyond when the change actually happens.

Critical Thinking Questions

1. Whether in professional organizations or in a personal matter, why do you think people are so resistant to change?
2. The largest and most expansive reorganization in the federal government in the last 50 years was the development of the Department of Homeland Security after the attacks on 9/11. The new Department of Homeland Security was touted to be more operationally effective and efficient than previous decentralized agencies in combating terrorism. However, what do you think were the *political* advantages of this massive change?

POLICE FUTURES RESEARCH

Historically, there has been great interest in forecasting the future, and there are a number of intriguing examples. Condorcet (1743–1794), a French philosopher, foresaw that all European colonies in the New World would become independent; social insurance would be provided for the aged, widowed, and orphans; education would become public and universal; women would receive equality with men; advances in medicine would eliminate infectious and hereditary diseases; and scientific knowledge would expand and improve technology.[8] Malthus (1766–1834) believed that unchecked human population growth would outstrip food supply, the result of which would be famine, disease, and poverty.[9] A Harvard sociologist, Sorokin (1889–1968), identified the basic characteristics and long-range trends of Western civilization, which he characterized as increasingly this-worldly, secular, materialistic, pragmatic, utilitarian, and hedonistic.[10] In 1967, Bell foretold of a "post-industrial society" to be created by a decline in "blue-collar" workers and a rise in "white-collar" employees.[11] What Condorcet, Malthus, Sorokin, and Bell share is having accurately forecast future events. Despite the existence of a body of literature that one way or another reflects concern about social, technological, and economic change, the police have traditionally remained remarkably uninterested in futures research.

There are a number of possible reasons for this disinterest: (1) a time horizon, for many law enforcement agencies, no longer than the next budget cycle; (2) a "hot stove" approach to managing, meaning that "we'll handle today's crisis now and worry about tomorrow when it gets here"; and (3) a lack of any perceived need to consider what conditions may be like in 10 to 20 years. In 1973, the California Commission on Peace Officer Standards and Training (POST) completed Project Star, a study of the impact of social trends on crime and criminal justice, the first major comprehensive futures study involving the police in this country.[12] After momentary excitement about Project Star, interest in law enforcement circles about futures research rapidly waned, although there was, in one form or another, intermittent interest among police scholars as evidenced by occasional publications.[13] Since roughly 1980, there has been growing interest among law enforcement executives in futures research. To no small degree, this interest has been fueled by the growing imperative to make sense out of a turbulent and sometimes chaotic environment and the highly visible work of Tafoya, who developed the nation's first graduate- and doctoral-level futures courses geared specifically to law enforcement. Echoing this development are several state agencies, such as California's POST, which now include a futures research component in their training curricula for law enforcement executives.

Establishing a Futures Research Unit/Capability

Futures research is a discipline devoted to addressing potential changes in our society.[14] The use of the plural futures reflects a basic premise of this type of research: the future is not predetermined or predictable and can be influenced by individual and organizational choices. Through the use of environmental scanning—analytically examining the right data with the appropriate forecasting methods—the futures research unit produces forecasts and policy options that allow law enforcement administrators to improve the odds of a preferable future from among the many existing alternatives.[15] One of the forecasting methods frequently used is the Delphi Technique. The Delphi was developed by the RAND Corporation in the mid-1950s and involves pooling the individual judgments of panel members selected on the basis of their expertise. Forecasts developed with a properly conducted Delphi Technique have had 85 percent or higher accuracy.[16] Unlike a prediction, which describes an event ahead of time and does not allow for error or probability, a forecast is a probabilistic statement of what may occur at some future time.

A futures research unit/capability (FRU/C) is not redundant if a law enforcement agency already has a planning unit because its missions are different and a great deal of planning, such as structuring a grievance procedure, is conducted without any real forecasting.[17] Moreover, futures research is also distinguishable from planning in that it assesses trends, countertrends, shifting values, and other indicators and attempts to provide an understanding of what they mean, where a department is going, and what should be done. In terms of organizational structure arrangements, the FRU/C can be placed within an existing planning component or made a separate unit altogether. The dynamics within individual agencies will dictate which approach to use.

To a substantial degree, any success the FRU/C has is indicative of access to and support from the agency's chief executive, reporting arrangements, and the quality of personnel selected for or by it. The FRU/C staff must be capable of using a variety of forecasting methodologies, be computer literate and statistically proficient because of the many types of data to be analyzed, and be self-starters who are imaginative, flexible, and inquisitive and who relish challenges.[18] To the greatest possible extent, FRU/C personnel should come from the ranks of the police department as opposed to being civilian experts, giving them one less issue with which to deal while on the road to gaining credibility.

As a minimum, all FRU/C members should have their own personal computers, have access to internal and external databases, and be provided with appropriate forecasting and database management software. Ideally, all computers would be networked to facilitate e-mail and the sharing of information.[19] Selecting the right leader for an FRU/C is a crucial decision. Essentially, the FRU/C is an organizationally sponsored center for creativity, and creative people can be difficult to manage. Tradition-bound leaders who require inflexible working hours, strict observance of rules and regulations, and reverence for their positions may find the situation unsatisfactory and possibly hamper performance. Moreover, creative individuals do not perform best in traditional, hierarchical organizational structures. Companies that manage creativity and innovation will work at fostering and nurturing these attributes.[20] The best choice for police departments may be to locate the FRU/C away from headquarters at sites where the FRU/C can develop its own work culture. In this way, the culture of the larger organization remains intact while a separate environment is designed that maximizes productivity and impact.

Although FRUs/C are still evolving, often within the umbrella of a planning or planning and research unit, there are already a number of law enforcement agencies with futures capabilities, including the police departments in Madison, Wisconsin; Seattle, Washington; Portland, Oregon; Alexandria, Virginia; Tulsa, Oklahoma; Santa Ana, California; and the San Diego County, California, Sheriff's Office. Indeed, many of these cities have representatives in the Society of Police Futurists International (PFI).[21] This is a relatively new organization, composed of law enforcement practitioners, educators, researchers, private security professionals, and technology experts from around the world. They are actively studying the future of crime, communities, and policing in an attempt to prevent the mistakes of the past. Futures research links the conditions, events, and trends of today with the potential problems of tomorrow. Armed with such information, new programs can be initiated in thoughtful anticipation rather than in crisis reaction to the rapidly changing environment of the future.

Critical Thinking Questions

1. What do you think will be the most pressing issues in the future confronting police and communities? Terrorism? Violent crime? Immigration? School shootings? Racial conflict? Gangs? Other problems?
2. What do you think will be the most pressing issues in the future confronting police organizations? Recruiting new officers? Selecting progressive leaders and chiefs? Implementing diversity within the organization? Other issues?

CHAPTER REVIEW

1. Distinguish between non-directed and directed change.
   Non-directed change is small, often spontaneous change which occurs at the lower levels of the department. It is not systematic and "creeps" into the department. In contrast,

directed change is a carefully planned formal action designed to bring about a new situation or condition. Figure 15.1 contains additional information about differences between these two types of change.

2. Identify eight recurring reasons change occurs in law enforcement agencies.

   These reasons are (a) there is a single catastrophic event, often filed by civil liability litigation; (b) a new governor or mayor is elected or the balance of power shifts in a city council, with the consequence that the current chief is replaced by one of their own choosing; (c) a key political figure suffers a major embarrassment and feels the law enforcement agency is to blame; (d) a chief of police retires or takes another position, and a new chief is hired; (e) a new sheriff is elected; (f) the chief's style or conduct becomes an issue, which leads to his or her dismissal; (g) departmental morale is low, too many things seem to be going wrong, the chief always seems to be reacting to problems to which he or she apparently has given no previous thoughts or for which no preparations have been made and citizens and unions may oppose the chief; and (h) there is a major paradigm shift.

3. State five reasons change should not be initiated.

   The five reasons are (a) internally the department lacks the knowledge, skills, or other resources to carry out the change; (b) an appropriately qualified external change agent is not presently available; (c) the change effort is greater than any benefits to be derived; (d) collateral damage may be a greater cost than the chief is willing to bear; and (e) too much change is already underway in the department.

4. Define organizational development.

   Organizational development is an applied behavioral science method of changing organizations through long-term efforts designed to improve the work culture and processes.

5. Explain why apathy is a worse response to change than resistance.

   If officers are apathetic, they aren't sufficiently engaged with their job to care one way or another; officers who resist change are engaged with their jobs; moreover, resistance is the first step toward eventually accepting a change.

6. Identify and briefly explain three categories of change resistance.

   These are (a) blind resistance, or a reflex anti-change attitude; (b) ideological opposition, which is rooted in a philosophical position that the shift is ill-conceived or for some other stated reason; ideological opponents often will craft specific supporting arguments to bolster their positions, such as "the timing is not right for a change this big"; and (c) political resistance, at the heart of which is the feeling that the person is going to lose something of value (such as authority, influence, status, or power) if the change is implemented.

7. Describe Lewin's Three-Step Model.

   It consists of three major sequential steps: (a) unfreezing, (b) moving, and (c) refreezing.

8. Identify the major steps in the Traditional Action Research Model.

   There are five major steps: (a) recognizing the need, (b) assessing/diagnosing the situation, (c) action planning, (d) change intervention/implementation, and (e) evaluation.

9. Describe the purpose of police futures research.

   Police futures research is devoted to understanding the linkages between today's events and conditions with potential future changes in our society that impact the police. The goal is to provide and suggest new programs that can be initiated in thoughtful anticipation rather than in crisis reaction to the rapidly changing environment of tomorrow.

KEY TERMS

Blind resistance: an automatic anti-change position.

Change agent: an individual or a group from within or outside the police department that stimulates, guides, facilitates, and stabilizes the change process.

Directed change: a carefully planned, formal action designed to bring about a new condition.

Ideological opposition: change resistance rooted in the philosophical position that the shift is ill-conceived; often accompanied by carefully crafted arguments, such as "the timing is not right for a change of this magnitude."

Interventions: actions conducted by change agents that include structuring learning experiences, diagnosing problems, helping to generate and implement solutions, and encouraging certain types of human interactions that facilitate the change process.

Lewin's Three-Step Model: a change model that has three sequential steps: (1) unfreezing, (2) moving, and (3) refreezing.

Non-directed change: informal adjustments made at the lower levels of a department, sometimes thought of as "creeping change." Non-directed change may eventually give rise to directed change or simply "rock along" informally.

Political resistance: change resistance caused by the concern that the individual will lose something of value (e.g., status, influence, authority or power) because of the change.

R2I: the traditional policing model, respond to incident.

Traditional Action Research Model: a five-step change model consisting of the following: (1) recognizing the need for change, (2) assessing/diagnosing the situation, (3) action planning, (4) the intervention, and (5) evaluation.

NOTES

1. The distinction between these two types of change is drawn, with restatement and added examples, from Patricia K. Felkins, B. Chakiris, and Kenneth N. Chakiris, *Change Management: A Model for Effective Organizational Performance* (New York: Quality Resources, 1993), pp. 5–6.
2. In Citrus Heights, California, the main reasons given for selecting a new chief were his "organizational skills and fresh approach to law enforcement." See David Richie, "Citrus Heights Names Top Cop," *Sacramento Bee*, November 30, 2005.
3. See Robert Rogers, "Rialto, Police Lay Blueprint for Future," *Inland Valley Bulletin*, April 17, 2006.
4. For example, see Ivan Moreno, "Littleton PD Morale Rated Low; Consultants Find Distrust, Fear Expensive Turnover." *Rocky Mountain Times*, September 13, 2006.
5. Hans Toch and J. Douglas Grant, *Police as Problem Solvers* (Washington, D.C.: American Psychological Association, 2005), p. 342.
6. On this point, see W. Warner Burke, "Implementing and Continuing the Change Effort," in *Practicing Organizational Development: A Guide for Consultants*, ed. William J. Rothwell and Roland Sullivan, Ch. 11 (San Francisco: John Wiley & Sons, 2005), p. 314.
7. These three points are taken with a number of additions from D. D. Warrick, "Launch: Assessment and Action Planning," in Rothwell and Sullivan, *Practicing Organizational Development: A Guide for Consultants*, Ch. 10, pp. 314–16.
8. California Commission on Peace Officer Standards and Training, *The Impact of Social Trends on Crime and Criminal Justice: Project Star* (Cincinnati: Anderson and Davis, 1976), p. 12. For additional information on Condorcet's forecasts, see Burnham P. Beckwith, *The Next 500 Years* (New York: Exposition Press, 1967), pp. 6–7.
9. Ibid., p. 12.
10. Ibid., pp. 12–13. See also Pitirim A. Sorokin, *Social and Cultural Dynamics* (Boston: Extending Horizon Books, 1957).
11. Ibid., p. 13. This idea is fully elaborated in Pitirim A. Sorokin, "Notes on the Post-Industrial Society," *The Public Interest* 6 (winter 1967, pt. 1): 25–35; 7 (spring 1967, pt. 2): 102–18.
12. POST, *The Impact of Social Trends.*
13. For example, see John E. Angell, "Organizing Police for the Future: An Update on the Democratic Model," *Criminal Justice Review*, (fall 1976): pp. 35–51, and Gerald Caiden, *Police Revitalization* (Lexington, Mass.: Lexington Books, 1977).

14. John Henry Campbell, "Futures Research: Here and Abroad," *Police Chief* 57; no. 1 (1990): 30.
15. Ibid.
16. William Tafoya, "Rioting in the Streets: Deja Vu?" in *Bias Crimes: The Law Enforcement Response*, ed. Nancy Taylor (Chicago: Office of International Criminal Justice, University of Illinois at Chicago, 1991), p. 7.
17. Campbell, "Futures Research," p. 30.
18. Ibid., p. 31.
19. Ibid.
20. Ibid., p. 33.
21. See www.policefuturists.org.

INDEX

3-D management style theory, 283
9/11 attacks
  Bush, George W., 108
  citizen involvement, 143
  critical incident stress, 555
  FBI, 116–117
  political violence, 82–85
  private security and, 25
  terrorism, 27, 28–29, 82–85
  U.S. response to, 30–32
1983 action, 584, 641

A

Abbas, Mahmoud, 93
Abbey, Edward, 99
Abraham, Yvonne, 476
Abu Nidal, 86, 88
Academy of Criminal Justice Sciences, 418
Accommodations, 391–392, 393–394
Accountability, 50–51, 154. *See also* Police accountability
Accreditation movement, 375
Acronyms, definition of, 172
Action planning, 662–664
Adaptive mechanism, 179–180, 215
Addison Police Department (Illinois), 313
Administration, 5–7
  anabolic steroids and, 542
  job actions and, 484–487
  newer paradigms of, 199–203
Administrative Behavior (Simon), 207–208, 316
Administrative discipline, 594–599
Administrative due process, 375
Administrative plans, 312
Administrative theory, 170–172, 215
"Administrative Theory of the State" (Fayol), 171
Administrators, tort liability and, 592–594
Adulthood, 188
Adversativeness, 366
Advocacy planning, 311, 340
Advocates, 280, 281
Afghanistan, 89
AFL-CIO, 483
After-action report, 315
Age-based hiring, 628–629
Age Discrimination in Employment Act (ADEA), 628, 629
Ahern, James F., 130–131
Ailments, stress-related, 535
Alabama Department of Youth Services, 396
Alarm stage, 531, 532, 577
Alaska Department of Public Safety, 60
al-Banna, Sabri, 88
Albuquerque Police Department (New Mexico), 410, 412–413, 435–436
Alcohol abuse, 546
Alcoholism, 537–539
Alcohol Self-Assessment Checklist, 538
Alcohol testing, 625–627
Alderman, 6, 34
al-Fatah, 86
Alfred P. Murrah Building. *See* Oklahoma City bombing
All-hazard, 78, 102
Allison, Graham T., 319
Alpert, G. P., 621
al-Qaeda, 27, 85, 86, 89–90, 91, 92, 102, 122
al-Zawarahi, Ayman, 89
America Online, 31, 60
American Airlines, 27
American Association of Retired Persons (AARP), 143, 144
American Indian Movement (AIM), 326
American Telephone & Telegraph, 207
Americans for Effective Law Enforcement (AELE), 590, 597
Americans with Disabilities Act (ADA), 386, 388–397, 405, 408, 451
Amish school shooting, 148–149
Anabolic steroids, 539–542, 577
Anaheim Police Department (California), 247–248, 249
Anderson, Jeff, 276
Anderson, Wayne, 531
Anderson, Willoughby, 301
Anderson School of Management, 209
Andes, Jodi, 290
Animal Liberation Front (ALF), 86, 99–100, 102
Animal rights groups, 99–100
Animals, shooting to destroy, 614
Anne Arundel County Police Department (Maryland), 261, 262
Anthony, W. P., 232
Anti-Defamation League, 14
Anti-Drug Act (1988), 541–542
Applications, accommodations for, 393
Arbitration, 478–479, 489
Argumentative styles, 371
Argyris, Chris, 185, 187–189, 194, 215
Aristotle, 581
Arizona v. Fulminante, 113–114
Arizona Vipers, 96
Arlington Police Department (Texas), 627
Arnett v. Kennedy, 596–597
Arnold v. City of Seminole, 635
Aron, Fred, 535, 536
Arreola, Philip, 134, 136
Arrests, 112–113, 566
Artificial intelligence (AI), 56–59, 65
Aryan Nation, 14, 27, 96
Asbury Park Police Department (New Jersey), 500
Ash, Milton, 396
Ashcroft, John, 69
Aspen Institute, 122
Assad, Haffez, 87
Assessment, 662, 663
Assessment centers, 426–430, 451
Assignment, negligent, 586
Association of Los Angeles County Deputy Sheriffs (ALADS), 482
Assumptions, faulty, 336
AT&T, 427
AT&T Worldnet, 31
Atkins v. City of Charlotte, 459
Atwater, Gail, 114
Atwater v. City of Lago Vista, 112, 114
Audience, 357
Audits, 496, 510–511, 525
Authoritarian leadership style, 278–279, 295

Authoritarian–democratic leadership continuum, 278, 279–280, 295
Authority, 169, 171, 271–272, 295
Authority–obedience management, 283

B

Baca, Lee, 110
Baca, Leroy D., 259
Bailey, Colorado, 148
Bair, John M., 259
Baird, Gabriel, 169
Balchen, Bernt, 174
Baldwinsville Police Department (New York), 269
Bali terrorist attack (2002), 92
Baltimore Police Department (Maryland), 58–59, 600
Banuelos, Ernesto, 546
Banuelos, Sylvia, 546
Bargaining not required model, 463, 464, 465–466, 489
Barnard, C., 206–207, 209, 271, 295, 337
Bashir, Abu Bakar, 91, 93
Basowitz, H., 531
Bass, B. M., 286
Bass, Virginia, 163
Bayley, David H., 39
Becker, Theodore L., 199
Beckman, Eric, 621
Behavioral leadership theories, 277, 295
Behavioral systems theory, 185–194, 204–205, 215
Beirut, Lebanon, bombing in, 27, 94
Bell, Sean, 116, 117
Bell Laboratories, 289
Belongingness needs, 181
Bence v. Breier, 598
Benefits, 426, 460–462
Bennis, Warren, 173, 175, 185, 193–194, 215, 286
Benton, Susan, 246
Berkeley County Sheriff's Department (South Carolina), 409
Bernardin, J., 424
Bertalanffy, Ludwig von, 195
Bethlehem Steel, 165
Biases, 425
Biennium budget, 498
Bilingual law enforcement officers, 368–369
Bill Blackwood Law Enforcement Management Institute of Texas, 247
Bill of Rights, 111
bin Laden, Osama, 27, 85, 87, 89, 90, 122
Binding arbitration, 463, 489
Biological stress, 532
Birmingham Fire Department (Alabama), 400
Birth, 423
Bivens action, 584–585, 591, 641
Bivens v. Six Unknown Federal Narcotics Agents (1971), 585
Black June, 86
Black September Organization, 86
Blake, Robert, 282–283, 295
Blanchard, Kenneth, 278, 283–284, 285, 295
Blau, Peter W., 162, 205
Blau, Theodore H., 538
Blind resistance, 666, 672
Blink (Gladwell), 321
Bloch, 560
Block, Robert, 95
Bloomberg, Michael, 25, 116, 117
Bloomington Police Department (Minnesota), 170
Blue flu, 481, 482, 489, 666
Bluffton Police Department (South Carolina), 501
Blunt, Matt, 467
Board of Trustees of the University of Alabama et al. v. Garrett et al., 396
Boehm, Randy, 287
Boldenone, 540
Bolinger, Kim, 521
Bolz, Frank, 327
Bombrys, Michael, 395
Bombrys v. City of Toledo, 395
Bona fide occupational qualification (BFOQ), 628, 629
Boot camp training style, 413–414
Booze boats, 12
Borough-Based Training, 544
Boston PBA, 460, 461, 476
Boston Police Department (Massachusetts), 240, 241, 508, 660
Boston police strike (1919), 458
Boswell, Donna, 521
Boswell Family Donation Fund, 521
Bottom-up approaches, 232–238
Boulder Police Department (Colorado), 132, 133–134
Bounded rationality, 202, 317
Bower v. County of Inyo, 619
Bradford, Leland, 185
Brady Bill, 108, 483
Brady Handgun Prevention Act (1994), 26
Brainmaker, 59
Brainstorming, 334
Braintree Police Department (Massachusetts), 272
Brame, David, 563
Brammer, Dana B., 137
Branch Davidians, 116, 122, 322–324, 326–327
Bratton, William, 39–40, 47, 119, 134, 248, 660
Breyer, Stephen, 396
Bridging theories, 200, 206–209, 215
British M-9, 86
Brooklyn Narcotics Tactical Team, 271
Broward County Sheriff's Department (Florida), 608
Brown, Lee P., 43, 248
Brown, Tina A., 283
Brown v. City of Oneonta, 119
Brueger, Michael, 121
Brutality, 114–118
Buck, A. E., 495
Buckley, Walter, 206
Budget, 494, 495
  definition, 525
  hybrid, 518, 525
  line item, 512, 513
  performance, 514, 516–517
  program, 512–514, 515
  zero-based, 517–518, 519
Budget adjustments, 503, 508
Budget and Accounting Act, 511
Budget cutting strategies, 500
Budget cycle, 498–511
Budget deadlines, 503
Budget execution, 503, 507–510, 525
Budget execution controls, 503, 508–510, 525
Budget formats, 511–520
Budgeting, 172, 496
Budget objectives, 503, 507–508
Budget preparation, 500–501
Budget review and approval, 501–503, 504–507
Budget supplementation, 520–524
Budget terms, 497–498
Bum blockades, 14
Bureaucracy, 173–176, 215, 251, 280–281
Bureaucratic model, 168–170, 215
Bureau of Alcohol, Tobacco, and Firearms (ATF), 26, 27, 80, 96, 109, 323
Bureau of Prisons, 26
Burgess, Christopher, 163
Burke, Tod W., 256–257
Burns, James, 285, 286, 287, 295
Bush, George W., 31, 79, 87, 108–109, 112
Business organizations, 162
Butler, Richard, 96
Butler, Smedley, 10
By Their Own Hand (film), 544

C

Caeti, Tory J., 98
Cali cartel, 95
California Commission on Police Officer Standards and Training (POST), 669
California Highway Patrol (CHP), 233, 234, 235, 236
California Psychological Inventory (CPI), 408
Call, Jack, 582
Cannon v. Taylor, 619
Capital budget, 497
Career development, 424
Career status, 409–410
Carlyle, Thomas, 277, 295
Carroll v. United States, 112, 113
Carte, Gene Edward, 8–9
Carter, David L., 72, 73, 122–123
Carter, Jimmy, 518
Cascio, W. F., 424
Case analysis and management system (CAMS), 53
Case for Bureaucracy, The (Goodsell), 176
Cassese, John, 457
Central Intelligence Agency (CIA), 30, 31, 80, 82, 84
Centralization, 171, 247, 251
Centralized Management Training, 544
Chabotar, Kent John, 198
Chain of command, 188, 215
Chakiris, B. J., 654
Chakiris, Kenneth N., 654
Challenge of Crime in a Free Society, The, 17, 20, 418
Challenges, 286
Chambers of Commerce, 144
Chamelin, N. C., 389
Champ, James, 395
Champ v. Baltimore County, 395
Change, resistance to, 665–666. *See also* Organizational change
Change agents, 660, 672
Change intervention/implementation, 663, 664
Changing Organizations (Bennis), 194
Chaos theory, 199, 200–202, 215
Character investigation, 405–406, 451
Charismatic authority, 169, 215
Charlier, 540
Chavez, Cesar, 18
Chavez-Thompson, Linda, 483
Chechen rebels, 95
Chemical tests, 440–442
Chertoff, Michael, 80, 85
Chicago Alternative Policing Strategy (CAPS), 42–47, 65, 135
Chicago Police Department
  artificial intelligence, 59
  CAPS, 42–47, 135
  Democratic National Convention (1968), 18, 19
  Deployment Operations Center (DOC), 77
  EAPs, 568–569, 572–573
  free speech issues, 600
  police chiefs, 134
  police suicides, 543
  preretirement planning seminar outline, 447–448
Chief compliance officer (CCO), 590
Child Abduction and Serial Murder Investigative Resources (CASMIRC), 26
Child birth, 423
Child labor, 6
Christian Identity Church, 14, 96
Christianity, 96, 122
Chumney, Carol, 195
Churches, 145
Churchill, Winston, 6
Citizen involvement, 142–145
Citizen Observer Patrol (COP), 257–258
Citizen police academies (CPAs), 256–257
Citizens, assisting, 549
Citizens on patrol, 257–258
City councils, 129–131
City managers, 128–129, 130
City of Canton v. Harris, 587
City resources, under CAPS, 45
Civil Action for Deprivation of Rights, 117–118
Civil liability, 375
Civil Rights Act (1964), 18, 397, 609, 629
Civil Rights Act (1983), 619
Civil Rights Act (1991), 400–401
Civil service, 10
Clark, Ryan, 149
Clay, Daniel, 531
Cleveland Board of Education v. Loudermill, 597
Cleveland Police Department (Ohio), 134, 169
Clientele, grouping by, 231
Clift, R. E., 137
Climbers, 280–281
Clinton, Hillary, 143
Clinton, William Jefferson, 108
Closed organizational model, 251
Closing the frontier, 4, 34
Clothing allowances, 426
Cluster grapevine pattern, 356
CODEFOR, 48, 65
Code of silence, 543
Cogan, Morris L., 7
Cognitive nearsightedness, 336
Cognitive science applications, of AI, 57, 58
Cohesiveness, 255
Cold War, 16
Coleman, Sandy, 272
Colin, Marc, 276
Collaboration, 287–288
Collective bargaining, 17
  definition, 489
  laws governing, 463–469
  pay plans, 426
  relationships, 469–471
College education, for police officers, 418–420, 421
Columbia Police Department (Missouri), 287
Columbia University, 543, 544
Columbine High School shooting (1999), 148, 149
Columbus Police Department (Ohio), 290
Combined DNA Index System (CODIS), 26, 27
Command, unity of, 171, 217
Commentary-Fourchambault Company, 171
Commission on Accreditation for Law Enforcement Agencies (CALEA), 23, 34, 124–125, 154, 201, 202, 416
Commission on Law Enforcement and Criminal Justice, 17
Commitment, 288
"Common Characteristics of Drug Couriers, The" (FDHSMV), 119
Commonweal organizations, 162
Communication barriers, 350–352
Communication process, 349–350
Communication
  CAPS, 45
  community policing and ILP, 73
  Compstat, 50
  cross-gender, 362–366
  culture and, 367–374
  definition, 382
  downward, 352–353
  electronic media (e-mail), 376–379
  grapevine, 355–356, 382
  group, 361–362
  horizontal, 354–355
  interpersonal, 356–360
  job actions and, 484
  nonverbal, 382
  oral, 375–376
  upward, 353–354
  written, 374–375
  See also Organizational communication

Communications officer
documentation, for domestic violence reports, 566
Communism, 17
Community events, 483
Community oriented policing (COP), 23, 24, 201, 202, 290
Community policing, 38–40, 70–72
Chicago, Illinois, 42–47
Compstat, 47–51
definition, 65
departmental philosophy versus, 247–250
ILP and, 73
information technology and, 62
Minneapolis, Minnesota, 48
Newport News, Virginia, 40–42
organizational design and, 247–251
review of, 63–65
traditional policing versus, 250–251
Community Policing Bureau (Anaheim Police Department), 248
Community Resources Against Street Hoodlums (CRASH), 116
Community resources, under CAPS, 45
Compartmentalization, 229
Compensatory time, 421–422
Competition, 290
Complex Organizations (Perrow), 176
Compstat, 47–51, 376
Bratton, William, 39–40, 47
crime analysis and, 53–55
definition, 65–66
ILP and, 73
impact of, 49
information technology and, 62
Minneapolis Police Department, 48
NYPD, 39–40, 47
Computer science applications, of AI, 57, 58
Computer stress, 378
Conceptual skills, 275, 276
Conclusions, data-backed, 358
Concord Police Department (California), 517
Conditional offers, 393–394
Condorcet, 668
Conduct unbecoming an officer, 607, 608
Conflict, 290–291, 295
Conflicting interests, in group decision making, 332–333
Conflict phase of group interaction, 361
Conflict resolution, 366
Conger, Jay, 357, 360
Coniston (Churchill), 6
Conservers, 280, 281
Consistent error, 425
Constitutional rights of police officers, 599–606
Constitutional torts, 583–584
Contingency model, 278
Contingency plans, 484
Contingency theory, 206, 208, 215
Contracts, for police chiefs, 135–136
Controlled Substances Act (CSA), 541
Conversation, male/female, 365–366
Cook, Jacob, 500
Cook County Sheriff's Department (Illinois), 602
Cooke, Morris, 166
Cooperative goals, 287–288
Coordinating, 172
Cordner, Gary W., 250, 302, 304, 310
Corruption, 6, 7, 110, 114–118, 178, 660
Cost-effectiveness analysis, 305–306, 309
Counterterrorism, 30. *See also* Terrorism
Country club management, 283
County of Sacramento v. Lewis, 619
County sheriff, 137–140
Couper, David, 290
Covenant, Sword, and Arm of the Lord, 96
Covert collection techniques, 442
Credibility, 357
Crime analysis, 45, 52–56, 66
Crime and the State Police (Parker and Vollmer), 137
Crime Bill (1994), 108
Crime control and prevention, under CAPS, 44, 45
Crime labs, new, 27
Crime scene documentation, in police domestic violence incidents, 566
Crime-specific analysis, 52
Criminal Justice System: Its Functions and Personnel (Felkenes), 137
Crisis events, 322–329, 340
Crisis Intervention Team (CIT) Academy (San Jose, California), 624–625
Critical incident, 577
Critical incident debriefing, 558–559
Critical incident stress, 555–559
Critical infrastructure and key resources (CI/KRs), 77–78, 102
Cross relationships, 229–230
Cross-cultural communication, 365, 367–374, 382
Cross-gender communication, 362–366
Crown, James, 595
Cuban DGI, 86
Cuban Missile Crisis (1962), 319
Cui bono, 162, 215
Cullinane, Bob, 500
Cultural diversity training, 372
Cultural sensitivity training, 374
Culture, 367–374, 382
Curriculum, 415
Curry, Matt, 197
Curry, Wayne, 483
Curtsinger, Curt, 133
Cushman, Robert, 303

D

Dahle, T. L., 353
Daley, Richard, Jr., 42
Daley, Richard, Sr., 9
Dallas Mavericks, 314
Dallas Police Association, 197
Dallas Police Department (Texas), 53–55, 57, 71, 625
Damages, 599
Daniels, Mitch, 466
Daniels v. Williams, 590–591
Data, 358
Data analysis, 73
David, Jonathan, 544
Davis, E. F., 551
Davis, Keith, 356
Davis, Kenneth Culp, 588, 596
Deadly force, 610–616, 617
Debriefing, 558–559
Decentralization, 38, 247, 251, 264
Decision making, 299–300, 315
arbitration and, 478–479
crisis events and, 322–329
errors in, 336–338
ethics and, 335–336
group, 329–334
heuristic model, 318–319
incremental model, 317–318
naturalistic methods, 321
operational modeling, 319–321
organizational change and, 658–659
rational model, 315–317
reluctance, 337–338
review, 338–340
thin-slicing theory, 321–322
Decision packages, 518
Decision tree, 320–321
Defendants, 583, 641
Defense of life, 612
Defensive avoidance, 327, 328
Degree of harm, 431
Delaney, Robert J., 572
Delaware State Police K-9s, 521
Delhi Police Department (Louisiana), 269
Deliberate acts, 583
Delphi Technique, 669
Delray Beach Citizen Observer Patrol, 257–258

Delta Force, 323
Democratic leadership style, 278–279, 295
Democratic National Convention (1968), 18, 19
Democratic National Convention (2004), 460
Democratic orientation, 255
Demonstrations, 495
Dental insurance, 426
Denver Police Department, 537, 538
Departmental philosophy, 247–250
Depression, 12, 14–15, 34
Desantis, John, 556
Deterrence, 435
Detroit Pistons, 314
Detroit Police Department, 545, 602
Detroit Police Officers Association, 483
Developmental simulation exercises, 427–429
DGI, 86
Diagnosis, 662, 663
Diallo, Amadou, 116, 121
Dickson, William, 177
Digital hate, 97–99
Dignity, 372
Di Maio, Vincent, 625
Directed change, 654, 672
Direct group relationships, 229–230
Directing, 172
Direction
  negligent, 586
  unity of, 171, 188
Directives, written, 612–615
Direct single relationships, 229–230
Disability, 388, 451
Disagreement, in group decision making, 332
Disaster Response Center (DRC), 301
Disciplinary action, 375, 606–610
Discipline, 171
  administration of, 430–436, 437
  administrative, 594–599
  education and, 421
  job actions and, 484
Discouragement pursuit policies, 621
Discretion, 288
Discrimination
  ADA and, 389–390, 396–397
  entrance examination, 399
  gender issues, 414, 415–416
  labor relations and, 466
  religious, 609
  sexual, 631, 632
  See also Reverse discrimination
Dispatcher documentation, for domestic violence reports, 566
Division of labor, 171, 215
DNA typing, 25, 26, 27
Documentation
  police domestic violence, 566
  pursuit policies, 623
Doig, J. W., 20
Domestic terrorism, 27, 86. *See also* Terrorism
Domestic violence, 562–567, 577
Donation programs, 521–522
Douglas, Dave, 163
Downs, Anthony, 280–281, 295
Downward communication, 352–353, 382
Driving conditions, in high-speed pursuits, 620
Driving forces, 186
Drucker, Petrer F., 316
Drug Enforcement Agency (DEA), 26, 541–542
Drug tests, 440–442, 625–627
Drug trafficking, 95, 119
Drug use, 539–542
Dubrin, Andrew J., 350
Due process, 375, 594–599, 641
Due Process Clause, 597, 598
Due process revolution, 110–111
Duke Power Company, 397–398
Durant, Chris, 163
Durgin, Leslie, 134
Dust bowl, 14–15
Duty owed, 616, 618
Dysfunction of bureaucracy, 215

E

Early retirement, 426
Early warning, for domestic violence, 563
Early warning systems, 434–436, 451
Earth First, 99
Earth Liberation Front (ELF), 86, 99, 100, 102
East Hartford police union (Connecticut), 480
Eck, John E., 41
Economic rationalism, 305–306
Ecoterrorists, 99–100
Education, 18–20, 418–420, 421, 435
"Effective Executive," 316
Effectiveness, 225
Effective plans, 313–315
Efficiency, 225
Eighteenth Amendment, 11, 34
Electronic media (e-mail), 376–379
Eleventh Amendment, 396, 588–589
Elliot, J. F., 230
Ellis, Tom, 256
E-mail, 376–379
E-mail overload, 376–377
Emergence phase of group interaction, 361–362
Emerson, Watlington, 166
Emotionally disturbed persons (EDPs), 623–625, 641
Emotional response, to critical incidents, 558
Emotion-provoking language, 357–358
Empathy, 255
Employee assistance programs (EAPs), 568–573, 577
Employee experience, 431
Employee motivation, 431
Employee performance, 424
Employee Protection Act, 403
Employee record, 431
Employment, sexual harassment and, 634
Employment discrimination, 389–390
Employment terms and conditions, 627–629
Entrance examination, 397–399
Entrustment, negligent 586
Environment, 350
Equal Employment Opportunities Commission (EEOC)
  workplace harassment prevention, 638
Equal Employment Opportunity Commission (EEOC), 386
  ADA and, 388, 389, 391, 393, 396
  entrance examinations, 398, 399
  reverse discrimination, 400, 401
  sexual harassment guidelines, 629–630
Equipose, 540
Equity, 171
Errors
  decision making, 336–338
  discipline and, 431–432
Escobedo v. Illinois, 111
Esprit de corps, 171, 225
Esteem needs, 181, 182
Etheredge, Kim, 197
Ethics
  decision making and, 335–336
  definition, 340
  police training and, 122–124
Ethnic Cleansing (computer game), 98
Ethnic profiling, 118–122
Etiquette, for e-mails, 377
Eureka Police Department (California), 163
Evaluation
  CAPS, 45–47
  performance, 423–425
  pursuit policies, 623
  synoptic planning, 309–310
  Traditional Action Research Model, 663, 664
  written directives, 612–615
Exceptional Case Study Project (ECSP), 26

Exception principle, 165, 215
Excited delirium, 625
Exclusionary rule, 111, 112
Executive Order 10988, 459
Exhaustion stage, 532, 577
Experience
  employee, 431
  overreliance on, 337
  violence-prone officers and, 432–433
Experiment, unwillingness to, 337
Expertise, development of, 225
Expert systems, 56–59
External budget controls, 508
External incidents, 132–135
External systems, 186–187
Eyal, 88
Eye care, 426
Eye contact, 369, 370

F

Fagan v. City of Vineland, 619
Fair Labor Standards Act (FLSA), 386, 420–422, 451, 627–628
Fair Labor Standards Amendments, 628
Family input and adjustments, after retirement, 444
Family Medical Leave Act (FMLA), 386, 422–423, 451
Family members, care for, 423
Farrell, Andy, 121
Fatah, 93
Fatah Revolutionary Council, 87
Fax machines, 59–61
Fayol, Henri, 171–172, 175, 354
FBI Crime Index, 583
Feasibility studies, 305, 340
Federal Bureau of Investigation (FBI), 14
  9/11 attacks, 30, 83–84, 116–117
  Brady Act, 26
  Branch Davidians, 323
  CODIS, 26
  crime labs, new, 27
  Critical Incident Response Group, 327
  decision-making errors, 323, 325, 326
  DHS and, 80, 82
  DNA typing, 25
  EAPs, 569
  ecoterrorism, 100
  expert systems, 59
  fax machines, 60
  IFCC, 26
  Intelligence Cycle, 75, 76
  JAG database, 26
  McVeigh, Timothy James, 95, 116
  NCIC, 26
  NIBIN, 26
  NIPC, 26
  Rowley, Coleen, 83
  terrorism, 25
  USA Patriot Act, 31
  vote of confidence and, 479
  Weaver family (Ruby Ridge, Idaho), 325
  website, 60
  WTC bombing (1993), 88–89
Federal Emergency Management Administration (FEMA), 80, 82, 109
Federal financial management, 496–497
Federal grants, 520–521
Federal Mediation and Conciliation Service, 478
Federal Tort Claim Act (FTCA), 584
Feedback, 309–310, 349–350, 352, 382, 550
Fees, user, 522–524, 525
Feinstein, Dianne, 325
Felkenes, George, 137
Felkins, Patricia, 654
Felons, fleeing, 612
Female police officers, 559–562
Fiedler, Frederick, 278
Field training officer (FTO), 410, 411–413, 416–417, 451, 615
Fields, Gary, 543
Fifth Amendment, 594
Fighting for Life (Ong), 366
Financial management, 493–495
  budget cycle, 498–511
  budget formats, 511–520
  budget supplementation, 520–524
  budget terms, 497–498
  federal, state, and local, 496–497
  politics and, 496
  review, 524–525
Financial planning, 445–446
Financial records, 442
Firearms
  access to, 546
  misuse of, 610–616, 617
  training, 414, 415
First Amendment, 146, 459, 599–603, 608
Flat organizational structure, 234, 237, 238, 251
Fleeing felons, 612
Florida Department of Highway Safety and Motor Vehicles, 119
Florida PBA, 483
Fogelson, Robert M., 126
Fond du lac County Sheriff's Department (Wisconsin), 257
Food and Drug Administration (FDA), 541
Force, misuse of, 610–616, 617
Force-field analysis, 185, 186, 215
Ford, Gerald, 134
Ford Foundation, 61
Forecasting, 336, 669–670
Forfeiture laws, 522, 525
Forrest, Nathan Bedford, 12
Fort Worth Police Department (Texas), 603
Fosdick, Raymond B., 10
Foundation grants, 520–521
Fourteenth Amendment, 111, 119, 594, 595, 608, 619
Fourth Amendment, 112, 114, 584, 604–605, 611, 617, 619, 620, 626, 627
Frankford Arsenal, 166
Fraternal Order of Police, 460, 479, 482, 483, 543
Fraternal Order of Police Lodge 89, 483
Free speech, 599–601
Friendship, 366
Fringe benefits, 426
Fritsch, Eric J., 98
Front-loaded messages, 358
Fry, Marquette, 17
Fuhrman, Mark, 115, 117
Functional structure, 240, 242–243, 264
Functional supervision, 165, 216
Functions of the Executive, The (Barnard), 207
Fundamentalist Christianity, 96
Fundraising programs, 521–522
Fusion centers, 75, 77–78, 102–103
Futures research, 668–670
Futures research unit/capability (FRU/C), 669–670

G

Gain, Charles, 136
Gaines, L., 540
Galton, Francis, 277, 295
Gantt, Henry L., 166
Gantt chart, 166, 216
Garcia, Daniel, 625
Garcia, Joe, 388–389
Garcia v. San Antonio Metropolitan Transit Authority, 420, 422
Gardner v. Broderick, 605
Garner, Joel, 612
Garrett, Patricia, 396
Garrity v. New Jersey, 605
Gates, Daryl, 132, 134
Gaza, 93
Geese Police, 502
Gender issues
  communication, 362–366
  human resource management, 410, 413–417

labor unions, 483
physical testing, 402–403
stress, 559–562
General adaptation syndrome (GAS), 532, 577
General and Industrial Management (Fayol), 171, 172
General bridging theories, 206–208
General fitness tests, 401
Generalization, 208, 251
General systems theory (GST), 195
Genetic theory of leadership, 277
Geographic information systems (GIS), 56, 57, 66
Geographic responsibility, under CAPS, 44–45
Geography, grouping by, 232
Gibb, C. A., 278, 296
Gibson, Frank K., 204
Gilbreth, Frank, 166
Gilbreth, Lillian, 166
Gilliland, Brian, 503
Ginsberg, Ruth Bader, 396
Giuliani, Rudolph, 143, 660
Gladwell, Malcolm, 321–322
Glaser, 561
Glenn, Mike, 280
Global Intelligence Working Group (GIWG), 72
Goals, 287–288, 313
Godwin, Larry, 195
Goldman, Ronald L., 115
Goldstein, Herman, 38, 41, 42, 61, 434
Goldwyn, Samuel, 205
Good life benefits, 426
Goode, Cecil E., 277–278
Goodsell, Charles, 176
Gore, B., 540
Gore, William J., 318–319, 325, 326
Goren, Daniel, 283
Gossip, 356
Gouldner, Alvin, 176
Gourlie, James, 201
Graciunas, V. A., 229–230
Graham v. Connor, 617
Graicunas, A. V., 172
Grand Lodge of the Fraternal Order of Police, 483
Grants, 520–521
Grapevine, 355–356, 382
Great Depression, 12, 14–15, 34
"Great man" theory, 277, 295
Grid structure, 243–244, 264
Grievances, 476–479, 489
Griggs v. Duke Power Company, 397–398
Group communication, 361–362
Group decision making, 329–334
Group dynamics, 185–186, 255
Grouping, 229
Grouping by clientele, 231
Grouping by geography, 232
Grouping by process, 232
Grouping by style of service, 231–232
Grouping by time, 232
Group interaction, 361–362
Group members, persuasion of, 357
Group pressures, 255
Group size, 361
Groupthink, 328, 332, 340
Guidelines on Discrimination Because of Sex (EEOC), 629–630
Guide to Modern Police Thinking, A (Clift), 137
Gulick, Luther, 170, 171, 172, 316
Guns. *See* Firearms

H

Hackett, Dell, 184
Hage, J., 175
Hall, Jay, 273–274
Hall v. Gus Construction Co., 633
Halo effect, 425
Hamas, 86, 93, 103
Hambali, 92
Hanssen, Robert, 117
Harakat al-Muqawama al-Islamiya, 93
Harden, Blaine, 100
Harding, Warren G., 6
Harm, degree of, 431
Harmon, Clarence, 483
Harnett, Patrick J., 374
Harnett, Susan M., 44, 46
Harris, Kevin, 325
Harrison County Community Foundation (Indiana), 521
Hartford Police Department (Connecticut), 283, 374
Harvard School of Business, 177
Harvard University, 61
Hatch Act, 601
Hate crimes, 97–99, 103
Havlik, Spense, 134
Hawker, James, 273–274
Hawthorne experiments, 177–179, 216
Health insurance, 426
Heavy-impact words, 357–358
Hegel, Georg Wilhelm Friedrich, 277, 295
Hegeman, Roxana, 184
Henderson County Sheriff's Department, 261
Henson v. City of Dundee, 631
Hersey, Paul, 278, 283–284, 285, 295
Herzberg, Frederick, 179, 182, 183, 184–185, 204, 216, 548–549
Heuristic model, 318–319, 340
Hezbollah, 86, 92, 93–94, 103
Hickman, Matthew J., 372
Hierarchy, 216, 228, 251, 264
Highlands County Sheriff's Office (Florida), 246
High-relationship–low-task leader behavior, 285
High-speed pursuits, 616–623
High-task–high-relationship leader behavior, 285
High-task–low-relationship leader behavior, 285
Hill, Terry, 57
Hillard, Terry G., 572
Hills, H. A., 561
Hillsborough County Sheriff's Office (Florida), 245, 368
Hilsher, Emily Jane, 149
Hippies, 18, 19
Hiring
age-based, 628–629
negligent, 586
Hitler, Adolph, 86–87
Hodge, B. J., 232
Holidays, 426
Homans, George, 186–187, 216
Homeland Security. *See* U.S. Department of Homeland Security
Homeland Security Act, 31
Honey, Tim, 134
Honolulu Police Department (Hawaii), 397
Hooker, Richard, 653
Hoover, Herbert, 14
Hoover, J. Edgar, 14
Hoovervilles, 14–15
Horizontal communication, 354–355, 382
Horizontal differentiation, 230–231, 264
Hostage Rescue Team (HRT), 325
Hostile environment liability, 630, 631
Hostile work environment, 415–416
House, Robert, 278
Houston Police Department (Texas), 134, 198, 248, 250, 280, 480
Houston Police Officers Association, 479
Hudzik, John, 302, 304, 310
Human Group, The (Homans), 186–187
Human Organization, The (Likert), 191, 192
Human relations school, 176–185, 203–204, 216
Human relations skills, 275–276
Human resource management, 385–387
Americans with Disabilities Act and, 388–397
assessment centers, 426–430

career status, 409–410
college education for police officers, 418–420, 421
discipline, administration of, 430–436, 437
Fair Labor Standards Act, 420–422
Family Medical Leave Act, 422–423
field training officer, 410, 411–413
functions of, 387–388
gender issues, 410, 413–417
internal affairs unit, 436–442
performance evaluation, 423–425
police personnel selection process, 397–409
probationary period, 409–410
recruit academy, 409–410
retirement counseling, 442–446, 447–448
review, 446, 448–450
salary administration, 425–426
Human resource management unit, 387–388, 451
Human Side of Enterprise, The (McGregor), 189–190
Hunter, Alex, 134
Hurley, James E., 137
Hurricane Katrina, 80, 82, 201, 301, 494, 521, 555, 556
Hussein, Saddam, 87
Huxley, Aldous, 385
Hybrid budget, 518, 525
Hygiene factors, 183, 184
Hymon, Steve, 502

I

i2 Corporation, 79
I2 Visual Notebook, 27
Ibn Wahhab, 89
Ideological opposition, 666, 672
Illegal bargaining topics, 466
Illinois v. Gates, 604
Immaturity, 188, 284–285, 433
Immigration and Naturalization Service (INS), 26, 109
Implementation
synoptic planning, 309
Traditional Action Research Model, 663, 664
Impoverished management, 283
In-basket exercise, 427–428
Incident response protocols, 565–567
Income supplements benefits, 426
Incremental model, 317–318
Incremental planning, 310, 340
Individual contributions, recognizing, 288–289
Individual domination, 331
Indoctrination, 352
Infancy, 188
Informal organization, 255–256, 264
Information
group decision making and, 329
sharing, 288
Information Collection for Automated Mapping (ICAM), 45
Information management, 73
Information technology, 51–52
artificial intelligence, 56–59
crime analysis, 52–56
expert systems, 56–59
fax machines, 59–61
geographic information systems, 56, 57
impact of, 61–62
Internet, 59–61
Websites, 59–61
Initiative, 171
Injured Police Officers Funds, 521
In-service training, 616
Institute for Intergovernmental Research, 122
Institute for Law Enforcement Administration (ILEA), 122
Institute of Social Research, 194
Insurance, 426
Integrating the Individual and the Organization (Argyris), 188
Integrative mechanisms, 180, 216
Intelligence, 72–73
definition, 73–74, 103
process and cycle, 74–75, 76
Intelligence agencies. *See specific agencies*
Intelligence analysis, 53
Intelligence Commanders Working Group, 72
Intelligence Cycle, 75, 76
Intelligence-led policing (ILP), 72–73, 75, 77–78, 103
Intentional torts, 583
Interactions, 255, 361–362
Interagency investigations, 440
Internal affairs unit (IAU), 436–442, 451
Internal budget controls, 509–510
Internal Revenue Service (IRS), 96
Internal systems, 186–187
International Association of Chiefs of Police (IACP), 23
accreditation, 124
college education, 418, 421
information technology, 60
police domestic violence, 563
profiling, 121
psychological testing, 407–408
pursuit statistics, 622
workplace harassment prevention, 638
International Association of Police Professors, 418
International Critical Incident Stress Foundation (ICISF), 559
International Olympic Committee, 540
International terrorism, 27, 86. *See also* Terrorism
International Union of Police Associations, 467, 521
Internet, 59–61, 66, 97–99
Internet Fraud Complaint Center (IFCC), 26
Internet Service Providers (ISPs), 31
Interpersonal communication, 356–360
Interpersonal skills, exercising, 549–550
Interpreters, 368
Interventions, 435, 563, 663, 664, 672
Interviews, 393, 406–407
Investigations, 439, 440, 563
Investigative technology, 23, 25, 26–27
Inwald Personality Inventory (IPI), 408
Iraq War (2003–), 89
Isamuddin, Riduan, 92
Islam, 121–122
Islamic Resistance Movement, 93
Israel, 86, 93–94
Israeli Mousad, 86

J

Jackson, Frank, 169
Jackson, James, 290
Jackson, Rhonda, 521
Jamieson By and Through Jamieson v. Shaw, 619
Janis, Irving, 326, 327
Jemaah Islamiyah (JI), 90–93, 103
Jensen, Marilyn, 259
Jewelry and Germ (JAG) database, 26
Jewish Defense League (JDL), 88
Jewish extremism, 88
Jihad, 89, 90, 103
Job actions, 479–487, 489
Job instruction, 352
Job offers, 393
Job rationale, 352
Job satisfaction, 287
Job stress, 535
Johannesson, R. E., 205
John Birch Society, 31
Johnson, Jane, 390
Johnson, Kevin, 397
Johnson, Lyndon B., 17, 418
Jones, Charisse, 543
Jones, Jacinthia, 195
Jordan, Tracy, 658
Josephson institute, 122

Journal of the American Society of Training Directors, 282
Judgmental pursuit policies, 621
Judiciary, 141–142, 154
Jungle, The (Lewis), 6
Justice Prisoner and Allen Transport System (JPATS), 26
Juveniles, 612–613

K

Kach, 88
Kahane Lives, 88
Kahane, Meir, 88
Kahl, Gordon, 96
Kahn, Robert, 195–196
Kanable, Rebecca, 257
Kansas City Police Department (Kansas), 421
Kansas City Police Department (Missouri), 595
Kansas City Preventive Patrol Experiment, 21, 34
Kast, Fremont E., 197
Katz, Daniel, 195–196
Katz, David L., 540
Kelley v. Johnson, 603
Kelling, George L., 14, 38, 248
Kennedy, Anthony, 396
Kennedy, John F., 18, 299, 459
Kennedy, Robert, 18
Kent, Sherman, 74
Kentucky State Police, 147
Kenya, U.S. embassy bombing in, 27
Kerner Commission, 18
Kerner, Otto, 18
Kerry, John, 460
Keyes, Emily, 148
KGB, 86
Khobar Towers bombing, 27
Kiel, L. Douglas, 199
King, Martin Luther, Jr., 18, 286
King, Rodney, 114, 121, 132
Kinloch Police Department (Missouri), free speech issues, 600
Kinney, J. A., 52
Knapp Commission, 178, 216
Knowledge, group decision making and, 329
Koby, Tom, 133, 134
Koran, 89
Korean War, 16–17
Koresh, David, 122, 323
Kouzes, James, 267, 286, 287, 289, 355
Kucinich, Jackie, 521
Ku Klux Klan (KKK), 12–13, 14, 86, 96
Kuntz v. City of New Haven, 394
Kurdish Workers Party (PKK), 86
Kureczka, Arthur W., 557

L

Labor organizations, needs of, 458. *See also* Labor unions
Labor relations, 457–458
- collective bargaining laws, 463–469
- collective bargaining relationship, 469–471
- grievances, 476–479
- job actions, 479–487
- negotiations, 471–476
- review, 487–488
- unionization, 458–463

Labor unions, 162, 280, 482–483. *See also* Labor organizations; Labor relations; *specific unions*
Lago Vista Police Department, 114
Laissez-faire leadership style, 278–279, 295
Lamar Police Department (Colorado), 276
Language, emotion-provoking, 357–358
Language differences, 368–369
Language errors, 358
Largo Police Department, 561
Law enforcement, 14, 34, 125–127. *See also* Policing
Law enforcement agency accreditation movement, 375
Law Enforcement Assistance Administration (LEAA), 19, 20–21, 127
Law Enforcement Disaster Relief Fund, 521
Law Enforcement Education Program (LEEP), 20
Law Enforcement Intelligence: A Guide for State, Local, and Tribal Law Enforcement Agencies (Carter), 72, 73
Law Enforcement Management and Administrative Statistics (LEMAS), 234
Law Enforcement Officers' and Correctional Officers' Bill of Rights (Florida), 596
Law Enforcement Wellness Association, 184
Lawsuits, 585–589
Leaderless group discussion (LGD), 428
Leaders (Bennis and Nanus), 286
Leadership, 255, 267–268
- conflict and, 290–291
- definition, 295
- job actions and, 484
- nature of, 271–272
- organizational control and, 291–293
- performance and, 269–271
- police managers, 273–275
- power motivation, 273–275
- review, 293–294
- skills, 275–277
- styles of, 278–290
- theories of, 277–278

Leadership (Burns), 285, 286
Leadership and Performance beyond Expectations (Bass), 286
Leadership and the New Science (Wheatley), 199
Leadership Challenge, The (Kouzes and Posner), 286
Leave, paid, 426
Leblanc, Matthew, 287
Lee, Robert E., 11
Legal issues, 581–582
- administrative discipline, 594–599
- constitutional rights of police officers, 599–606
- deadly force, 610–616
- disciplinary action, grounds for, 606–610
- emotionally disturbed persons and liability, 623–625
- employment terms and conditions, 627–629
- firearms, misuse of, 610–616
- high-speed pursuits and liability, 616–623
- lawsuits, 585–589
- liability for police conduct, 582–585
- review, 639–641
- scope of liability, 589–592
- sexual harassment, 629–639
- testing in work environment, 625–627
- tort liability, 592–594

Legal standards, 424–425
Leo, Tom, 269
Less discriminatory alternative test, 403
Levitt Towns, 16
Lewin, Kurt, 216
- Bennis, Warren, 193–194
- group dynamics, 185–186
- leadership styles, 278–279, 295
- three-step model, 659, 661–662, 672

Lexington Police Department (Kentucky), 397
Liability
- definition, 642
- emotionally disturbed persons and, 623–625
- high-speed pursuits and, 616–623
- police conduct, 582–585
- pursuit-related, 619
- scope of, 589–592

sexual and racial harassment, 630–632
sexual harassment, 636–637
tort, 592–594
vicarious, 585, 642
Liberty rights, 594–596, 642
Lieberman, Joe, 109
Liederbach, John, 98
Life insurance, 426
Likert, Rensis, 191–193, 194, 205, 209–210, 216
Lincoln Legion, 11
Lincoln–Lee Legion, 11, 12
Lindbergh, Charles, 14
Lindblom, Charles F., 317–318, 325, 326
Line and staff structure, 238, 239–240, 241, 251–255, 264
Line commanders, 252, 254
Line item budget, 512, 513
Line structure, 238–239, 251–255, 264
Lineups, 442
Linguistic style, 358–359, 382
Link analysis, 52
Linkpin pattern, 191, 192, 193
Lippitt, Ronald, 278–279, 295
Listeners, 357
Listening, 369
Litigation, 582, 642
Littleton, Colorado, 148
Local DNA Index System (LDIS), 26
Local financial management, 496–497
Local government, 125–127
Local political forces, 127–132
Logan, D. D., 561
Loper, D. Kall, 98
Los Angeles County Courthouse, 368
Los Angeles County Sheriff's Department, 138, 258, 259
Los Angeles Police Department (LAPD), 95
Bratton, William J., 660
brutality, 116, 118, 119
gender issues, 410–411
King, Rodney, 132
media and, 147
police accountability, 110
police chiefs, 132, 134
Los Angeles Sheriff's Department, 59, 568–569
Los Angeles trash collection taxes, 502
Los Lunas Police Department, 522
Louima, Abner, 115, 118, 120, 121
Louisiana State Troopers, 269
Louisiana State Trooper Relief Fund, 521
Love needs, 181
Lowe, Zach, 162
Low-relationship–low-task leader behavior, 285
Lyden, F. J., 306
Lynch, Charles, 13
Lynch, Kevin J., 59
Lynching, 13

M

M-9, 86
M-19, 95
MacDonald, Joe, 658
MacEachern, Dick, 460
Machiavelli, Niccolo, 653
Machine politics, 6–7
Macias, Natalie Salazar, 259
Madison Police Department (Wisconsin), 290
Maffe, Steven R., 256–257
Maguire, Edward, 242
Maintenance factors, 183
Major City Chief's Intelligence Commanders Working Group, 72
Making a Municipal Budget, 511
Making Schools Work (Ouchi), 209
Malthus, 668
Malvo, Lee Boyd, 145
Management plans, 312
Management teams, in negotiations, 471–472
Managerial accountability, 50–51
Managerial Grid, 282–283, 292, 295
Managing Chaos and Complexity in Government (Kiel), 199
Mandatory bargaining topics, 466–469
Mann, Leon, 326, 327
Manolatos, Tony, 500
Man-to-man pattern, 191, 192, 193
Mapp v. Ohio, 111, 112
Mara Salvatrucha (MS-13), 95
March, James, 206, 207–208, 209
Marin County Sheriff's Office (California), 60
Market crash (1929), 497
Marketing, of CAPS, 45
Markkula Center for Applied Ethics, 335
Marshall, Ian, 199
Marshals Service, 26
Martin v. Wilks, 400
Martin-Hidalgo, Martin, 625
Maryland Police Training Commission, 395
Maslow, Abraham, 179, 181–183, 185, 204, 216, 443
Massachusetts Institute of Technology (MIT), 185
Massachusetts State Police, 479
Massachusetts v. Sheppard, 604
Mathews v. Eldridge, 597
Matriciuc, Hans, 280
Matrix structure, 243–244, 264
Maturity, 188, 284–285
Mausner, B., 183, 548–549
Maxwell, C., 612
Mayo, Elton, 177–179, 216
Mayo Clinic, 540
Mayors, 128, 129
McArdle, John, 268
McCarthy, Joseph, 17
McCarthy v. Philadelphia Civil Service Commission, 609
McFarland, Darlton E., 234
McGreevey, Patrick, 119
McGregor, Douglas, 161, 216
behavioral systems theory, 185
Bennis, Warren, 193, 194
theory X and theory Y, 189–191, 205, 209–210
McGuire, Erin, 501
McVeigh, Timothy James, 95, 116
Medellin cartel, 95
Media, 145–148, 150
Medical conditions, 392
Medical examinations, 394
Medical insurance, 426
Meehan, Albert, 120
Meet and confer model, 463–464, 484
Melton v. City of Atlanta, 459
Memorial Institute for the Prevention of Terrorism (MIPT), 88, 91
Memos, 358
Memphis Police Department (Tennessee), 195
Menino, Thomas, 460
Meritor Savings Bank v. Vinson, 632–633, 636, 637, 639
Merton, Robert K., 8, 173–175
Messages
front-loaded, 358
tailoring, 357
Mestas, Anthony A., 276
Metapol website, 60
Metropolitan Operations and Analytical Intelligence Center (MOSAIC), 77
Metzger, Tom, 96
Miami Beach Police Department, 260
Miami–Dade County Police Department, 435, 436
Michaels, Robert, 251
Michigan Militia, 96
Michigan State University, 14
Mickolus, Edward, 85
Middle class, 16
Middle Easterners, profiling of, 121
Midvale Steel Company, 164
Miele, Stephen, 374
Military analogy model, 10–11, 34
Military-style training, 413–414
Militia groups, 14, 96
Miller, C. E., 551
Miller, E. G., 306

Miller, Zell, 658
Milltown Police Department (Indiana), 521
Milwaukee Police Department (Wisconsin), 134, 136, 598
Minneapolis Police Department (Minnesota), 48, 435, 436
Minnesota Bureau of Criminal Identification, 27
Minnesota Multiphasic Personality Inventory (MMPI), 408
Mintzberg, H., 132
Minutemen, 96
Miranda v. Arizona, 18, 111, 112, 113
Missing Persons Index (MPI), 27
Model Municipal Corporation Act, 511
Monell v. Department of Social Services, 589
Monkey Wrench Gang, The (Abbey), 99
Monroe v. Pape, 584
Monterey County Police Chief's Association, 624
Montgomery (Field Marshal), 277
Montgomery County Police Department (Alabama), 145–146
Mooney, James, 171, 172
Moonlighting, 610
Moose, Charles A., 145–146
Mormons, 609
Morrison, Duane Roger, 148
Morrison Police Department (Colorado), 513
Morse, Phillip, 268
Mosher, Frederick C., 493
Motivation
  employee, 431
  power, 273–275, 295
Motivation and Personality (Maslow), 181, 204
Motivation–hygiene theory, 184
Motivation to Work, The (Herzberg), 183
Motivators, 183, 184
Mottley, Charles M., 302
Mousad, 86
Mouton, Jane, 282–283, 295
MOVE incident (1985), 326
Moving, 661–662
MS-13, 95
Mueller, Robert, 83–84
Muhammad, John Allen, 145
Murillo, Cipriano, 495
Murphy, C., 251
Murphy, James P., 271
Murrin, M. R., 561
Muslim Brotherhood, 86, 93
Muslim movement. *See* Radical Muslim movement
Muslims, profiling of, 121
Must–wants analysis, 306–309
Mutual benefit association, 162
Mutual interests, in group decision making, 332–333

N

NAACP, 116
Nagel, Jack H., 326, 327
Nakamura, David, 134
Names, pronunciation of, 369
Nanus, Bert, 286
Nash, Toye, 437
Nasrallah, Hassan, 94
National Advisory Commission on Civil Disorders, 17–18, 418
National Advisory Commission on Criminal Justice Standards and Goals, 127, 419
National Alliance, 14, 86, 96, 99
National Association of Police Organizations (NAPO), 469
National Association of Triads, Inc. (NATI), 144
National Commission on Law Observance and Law Enforcement, 13–14
National Counterterrorism Center (NCTC), 31–32, 87
National Crime Center (NCIC), 26
National Criminal Intelligence Sharing Plan (NCISP), 74–75, 77
National Criminal Justice Reference Service (NCJRS), 23, 60
National DNA Index System (NDIS), 26
National Drug Pointer Index (NDPIX), 26
National Highway Traffic Safety Administration, 520
National Infrastructure Protection Center (NIPC), 26
National Instant Criminal Background Check System (NICS), 26
National Institute for Occupational Safety and Health, 535
National Institute of Justice, 26, 61, 432
National Institute of Law Enforcement and Criminal Justice, 21–22
National Institutes Against Hate, 97
National Integrated Ballistic Information Network (NIBIN), 26
National Labor Relations Act (NLRA), 460
National Law Enforcement Officers Memorial Fund, 358
National Law Enforcement Telecommunications System (NLETS), 26
National Municipal League, 7, 511
National Opinion Research Center, 459
National Organization of Black Law Enforcement Executives (NOBLE), 23, 34, 124
National police, 125–126
National Police Academy, 14
National Prohibition Act, 11–12, 34
National Rifle Association (NRA), 108
National Security Agency (NSA), 30
National Sheriff's Association (NSA), 23, 124, 144
National Threat Assessment Center (NTAC), 26
National Training Laboratories for Group Development, 185
National Treasury Employees Union v. Von Raub, 626
National White Collar Crime Center (NW3C), 26
Natural disasters, 494
Naturalistic methods, 321
Natural language applications, of AI, 57, 58
Naturalness, 255
Natural soldiering, 164
NBA Finals, tactical planning for, 314
NBC News, 150
Needs hierarchy, 181–183, 216
Negligence, 583, 642
Negligence torts, 583
Negligent assignment, retention, and entrustment, 586
Negligent direction and supervision, 586
Negligent hiring, 586
Negligent training, 587
Negotiating sessions, 473–476
Negotiations, 471–476, 484
Neighborhood orientation, under CAPS, 44
Nelson v. City of Chester, 618
Neo-Nazis, 86, 96
New Haven Police Department (Connecticut), 130–131, 394–395
New Orleans Police Department (Louisiana), 201, 301, 435, 436, 556, 600
New Patterns in Management (Likert), 191
New York Bureau of Municipal Research, 7
New York City Police Foundation, 520, 544–545
New York PBA, 460, 480
New York Police Department (NYPD), 16
  9/11 attacks, 29
  Bratton, William J., 660
  brutality, 115–116, 118
  Compstat, 39–40, 47, 375

corruption, 178
Knapp Commission, 178
leadership and, 271
New York City Police Foundation, 520
police chiefs, 134
police suicide, 543, 544–545
private security and, 25
work slowdowns, 480
Newport News Police Department (Virginia), 40–42, 43, 60, 123
Newport Police Department (Rhode Island), 174
News media, 145–148, 150
Newstrom, John W., 356
Nickel Mines, Pennsylvania, 148–149, 150
Noise, 350, 382
Non-directed change, 654, 672
Nonverbal communication, 359–360, 369–370, 382
Norquist, John O., 136
North Carolina State Patrol, 540
North Carolina Transportation Association, 261
Northwestern University, 14
Norvell, N. K., 561
"Notes on the Theory of Organization" (Gulick), 172
Nuchia, Sam, 479

O

Oakland Police Department (California), 136
Objective Reasonableness Standard, 617
Objectives, 313
Ocean City Police Department (Maryland), 500
O'Connor, Sandra Day, 113, 396, 626
Off-duty weapons, 614
Office of Community Oriented Policing Services (COPS), 496, 520
Office of Community Policing, 311
Office of Law Enforcement Assistance (OLEA), 20
Office of Strategic Services (OSS), 427
Ogden City Council (Utah), 666
Ogden Police Department (Utah), 165
Ohio Civil Rights Act, 395
Ohio State Highway Patrol, 182
Oklahoma City bombing, 27, 28, 84, 91, 95, 116, 443, 555
Omnibus Crime Control and Safe Streets Act, 20, 127, 302
Omnibus Drug Abuse Initiative, 542
O'Neal, Shaquille, 260
Ong, Walter, 366
On-scene supervisor response, 566
Onward Industry (Mooney and Reiley), 172
Open organizational model, 251
Open systems theory, 176, 187, 200
administration, newer paradigms of, 199–203
behavioral systems theory, 185–194
critique of, 203–206
definition, 216
human relations school, 176–185
organizations as open systems, 194–199
Operational commanders, 252–253
Operational modeling, 319–321
Operational plans, 312
Operation Enduring Freedom, 89
Operation Northern Exposure, 324
Operations research, 319, 340
Operation Thanksgiving, 522
Operative code, 180, 216
Optical insurance, 426
Oral boards, 406–407, 451
Oral communication, 375–376
Orange County Sheriff's Office, 521
Order, 171
Order, The, 96
Organizational change, 653–654
decision making and, 658–659
models, 659–664
politics and, 664–668
reasons for, 655–658
review, 670–671
under CAPS, 45–47
Organizational communication, 347–349
barriers, 350–352
cross-gender communication, 362–366
culture and, 367–374
electronic media (e-mail), 376–379
group communication, 361–362
interpersonal communication, 356–360
oral communication, 375–376
process, 349–350
review, 380–381
systems of, 352–356
written communication, 374–375
Organizational control, 291–293, 295
Organizational controls, 292, 295
Organizational design, 223–224
citizen police academies, 256–257
citizens on patrol, 257–258
community policing and, 247–251
functional structure, 240, 242–243
hierarchy, principle of, 228
informal organization, 255–256
line and staff structure, 239–240, 241, 251–255
line structure, 238–239, 251–255
matrix structure, 243–244
organizational structure and, 230–238
police agencies, 251–255
reserves, 258–259, 260
review, 262–263
sheriff's offices, 244–247
span of control vs. span of management, 228–230
specialization in police agencies, 224–228
staff structure, 251–255
types of, 238–244
volunteers, 259–262
Organizational development (OD), 185, 193–194
Organizational management, 283
Organizational stress management strategies, 378–379
Organizational structure. *See* Organizational design
Organizational theory, 161–163
bridging theories, 206–209
open systems theory, 176–206
review, 210–214
synthesis and prognosis, 209–210
traditional, 163–176
"Organization as a Technical Problem" (Urwick), 172
Organizations
as open systems, 194–199
rationale for, 271, 295
Organizations (Simon), 207–208
Organizing, 172, 224, 264
Orientation phase of group interaction, 361
O'Toole, Kathleen, 417
Ott, John E., 49
Ouchi, William, 208–209
Our Cities Awake (Cooke), 166
Overman, Richard G., 258
Oversimplification, 336–337
Overtime, 421, 426, 503, 508
Owens, Terrell, 197

P

Palestine, 86, 93–94
Palatine Police Department (Illinois), 513
Palestinian Authority, 93
Pan Am Flight 103, 27
Papers on the Science of Administration (Gulick and Urwick), 170, 171, 172
Parades, 483
Paradigm shift, 72, 103
Parker, A. E., 137
Parker, Mike, 138
Parsons, Talcott, 162, 179–180, 195, 216

Partnership Against Violence Network (PAVNET), 60
Path–goal theory, 278
Patriot Act. *See* USA Patriot Act
Patrol response, 566
Patrol styles, inappropriate, 433
Patrolmen's Benevolent Association (PBA), 115, 460, 480
Pauses, vocalized, 358
Paxton Fraternal Order of Police (Illinois), 522
Pay plans, 425–426, 451
Paynter, Ronnie L., 260, 261
Peel, Sir Robert, 38
Peer-group support, 550
Pegasus the Immortal, 19
Pendleton Act, 10–11, 34
Pentagon attacks (2001), 27, 29, 82. *See also* 9/11 attacks; Terrorism
People for the Ethical Treatment of Animals (PETA), 99
Pereira, Federico, 114
Performance, 269–271
Performance budget, 514, 516–517
Performance evaluation, 423–425, 451
Performance monitoring, 435
Permissive bargaining topics, 466
Perrow, Charles, 176
Personality and Organization (Argyris), 187, 188
Personality Assessment Inventory (PAI), 408
Personality disorders, 432
Personality types, 533–534
Personalized power, 273–274
Personal problems, police officers with, 433–434
Personnel practices, 459–460
Persuasion, 357
Petronius, 223
Philadelphia Police Department (Pennsylvania), 522, 627
Philosophy, departmental, 247–250
Phoenix Police Department (Arizona), 27, 234, 237, 397, 437, 593
Photo lineups, 442
Physical ability tests, 392, 401–403
Physical fitness and skills, 415
Physical fitness tests, 392
Physical lineups, 442
Physical prowess, overemphasis on, 414
Physiological needs, 181
Pierce, David, 483
Pierce, William L., 96
Pinellas County Sheriff's Office (Florida), 561
Pinizzotto, A. J., 551
Plaintiffs, 583, 642, 655
Planning, 172, 299–302
  advocacy, 311
  CAPS, 45–47
  definitions of, 302, 340
  incremental, 310
  Programming, and Budgeting Systems (PPBS), 319–320, 517
  radical, 312
  review, 338–340
  synoptic, 302–310, 311
  transactive, 310
Plans
  effective, 313–315
  types of, 312–313
Plato, 224
Platte County High School (Bailey, Colorado), 148
PODSCORB, 172, 316
Police accountability, 109–110
  brutality and scandal, 114–118
  CALEA, 124–125
  federal influence, 110
  racial and ethnic profiling, 118–122
  self-incrimination, 113–114
  traffic stops and arrests, 112–113
  training and police ethics, 122–124
  U.S. Supreme Court decisions, 110–112
Police administration, 107–109. *See also* Police accountability; Politics
Police Administration (Wilson), 9, 137
Police agencies
  organizational design and, 251–255
  specialization in, 224–228
Police auxiliary officers, 16
Police brutality, 114–118
Police chiefs
  external incidents and, 132–135
  politics and, 131–132
  tenure and contracts for, 135–136
  women, 417
Police compliance officers, 590
Police conduct, liability for, 582–585
Police departments
  firearms policy, 615–616
  high-speed pursuits and, 621–623
  police domestic violence and, 564
Police domestic violence, 562–567
Police ethics, 122–124
Police Executive Development Project, 136
Police Executive Research Forum (PERF), 23, 34, 60, 124, 419, 420
Police Foundation, 439
Police futures research, 668–670
Police in Trouble (Ahern), 130–131
Police managers, 273–275
Police officers
  alcoholism and, 537–539
  college education for, 418–420
  constitutional rights of, 599–606
  drug use by, 539–542
  due process for, 594–599
  early warning systems, 434–436
  liberty and property rights for, 594–596
  personnel practices, 459–460
  as plaintiffs, 655
  police domestic violence and, 565
  as victims, 555
  violence-prone, 432–434
  See also Stress
Police Officer Standards and Training Commissions (POSTs), 18–19, 127
Police organizations, communication barriers involving, 353
Police Patrolmen's Association, 460
Police personnel selection
  ADA and, 388–397
  process, 397–409
Police Planning (Wilson), 9
Police professionalization, 7–11
Police Records (Wilson), 9
Police salary schedule, 426
Police stressors, 535–537
Police Stress Survey (PSS), 535
Police subculture, 547
Police Suicide Project, 544–545
Police suicides, 184, 542–548
Police taxes, 522–524, 525
Police tort actions, 582–584
Police unions. *See* Labor unions
Policing
  artificial intelligence, 56–59
  crime analysis, 52–56
  expert systems, 56–59
  fax machines, 59–61
  geographic information systems, 56, 57
  information technologies and, 51–62
  intelligence-led, 72–73, 75, 77–78, 103
  Internet, 59–61
  traditional, 38, 39, 66
  Websites, 59–61
  See also Community policing; Team policing
Policing a Free Society (Goldstein), 38
Policing history, 3–5
  9/11 attacks, 30–32
  1960s, 17–20
  1970s, 20–23
  1980s and beyond, 23–30
  politics and administration, 5–7
  professionalization, 7–11
  prohibition to 1940, 11–15
  World War II and 1950s, 15–17

Political resistance, 666, 672
Political rights, 601
Political violence, 82–84. *See also* Terrorism
Politics, 107–109
- citizen involvement, 142–145
- county sheriff, 137–140
- definition, 34, 154
- financial management and, 496
- judiciary, 141–142
- local political forces, 127–132
- machine, 6–7
- news media, 145–148
- organizational change and, 664–668
- police accountability, 109–125
- police chiefs, 131–136
- policing history and, 5–7
- review, 152–154
- school violence, 148–152
- state and local government, 125–127
- state prosecutor, 140–141

Polygraph, 392, 403–405, 440, 451
Ponder, Michael, 120
Pope, Harrison G., 540
Popular Front for the Liberation of Palestine (PFLP), 85, 87
Portland Police Bureau, 519
Posner, Barry, 267, 286, 287, 289, 355
Posse Comitatus Act, 96, 323
Postconditional offer of employment, 563
Posttraumatic stress disorder (PTSD), 556–558, 577
Power, 271–272, 288, 295
Power motivation, 273–275, 295
Power-oriented linguistic style, 358–359
Practices, 352, 459–460
Pravda (Soviet newspaper), 166
Preconceived notions, 337
Pre-employment screening, 563
President's Commission on Campus Unrest, 418
President's Commission on Law Enforcement and Administration of Justice, 418
President's Commission on Law Enforcement and Criminal Justice, 17, 20
Prichard, Leigh A., 326
Principle of hierarchy, 216, 264
Principles of Organization, The (Mooney and Reiley), 172
Principles of Public Administration (Willoughby), 7
Private foundation grants, 520–521
Private security, 23, 24–25
Proactive enforcement operations, 439
Probability grapevine pattern, 356
Probationary period, 409–410
Problem analysis, 45, 428
Problem-Oriented Policing (Goldstein), 61
Problem solving, 45, 73, 330
Procedural due process, 596–598, 642
Procedural plans, 312
Procedures, 352
Process, 232, 287
Prodigy, 31
Profession, 7–8, 34
Professional, 7–8
Professionalization, 7–11, 18–20
Profiling, 118–122
Profiling, 154
Program budget, 512–514, 515
Program Evaluation and Review Technique (PERT), 319–320
Progress, 288
Prohibition, 11–15, 34
Prohibition Party, 11
Project Star, 669
Promotional decisions, 272
Pronunciation, 369
Property rights, 594–596, 642
Proposition 12 (California), 313
Prosecutor, 140–141, 154
Protection benefits, 426
"Proverbs of Administration" (Simon), 316
Providence Police Department (Rhode Island), 286
Provisional Irish Republican Army (PIRA), 95
Proximate cause, 618–619, 642
Psychological conflict, 325
Psychological losses, 443–444
Psychological stress, 532–533
Psychological testing, 392, 407–409, 451
Public Administration (Sharkansky), 316
Public Administration (White), 7
Public Employees Relations Committee (PERC), 470, 471, 479, 489
Public Employment Relations Commission, 468
Puerto Rico independence groups, 27
Pursuit-related liability, 619, 620
Pursuits, high-speed, 616–623

Q

Quade, E. S., 306
Quality circles (QCs), 190–191, 216
Quantum Politics (Becker), 199
Quantum Society, The (Zohar and Marshall), 199
Quantum theory, 199, 202–203, 216
Qubt, Sayyid Muhammad, 89, 91
Quid pro quo liability, 630–631
Quincy Police Department (Massachusetts), 655
Quotas, 165, 666

R

Race and Reason (TV program by WAR), 96
Racial harassment, 630–632
Racial profiling, 118–122, 154
Radelet, Louis A., 13–14, 122–123
Radical Islamic terrorism, 87–90
Radical Muslim movement, 29–30, 86
Radical planning, 312
Rahman, Sheik Abdul Omar, 86, 89
Ramsey, Charles, 135
Ramsey, JonBenet, 132, 133–134
RAND Corporation, 61, 669
RAND Criminal Investigation Study, 21–22, 34
Rate buster, 177, 217
Rater errors, 425, 451
Rational, definition of, 340
Rational model, 315–317
Rational–comprehensive approach. *See* Synoptic planning
Rationale for organizations, 271, 295
Rational–legal authority, 169, 217
Ratliff, Eric, 480
Reagan, Ronald, 112, 134, 481
Reasonableness, 583, 617, 642
ReBES (Residential Burglary Expert System), 58–59
Receivers, 349, 351
Recency, 425
Recognition-primed decision making (RPD), 321
Recreational facilities, 426
Recruit academy, 409–410
Recruit training, 615
Red Brigades, 95
Reddin, William, 283
Reformation period, 6–7, 34
Refreezing, 662
Regents of the University of California v. Bakke, 400
Registration, of weapons, 614–615
Rehabilitation Act (RA), 394
Rehm, B., 443
Rehnquist, William, 113, 396
Reid, Richard, 27
Reiley, Alan, 171, 172
Reinforcement phase of group interaction, 361, 362
Religious beliefs or practices, 609
Remedies, 599
Remuneration, 171
Reno, Janet, 108, 323
Reporting, 172

Reports, 358
Republic of Texas Militia, 96
Research, 20–23, 39
Research Center for Group Dynamics, 185, 193
Reserves, 258–259, 260
Residency requirements, 14, 34, 609
Resistance Radio (website), 98
Resistance stage, 532, 577
Respect, 372
Responding to incidents (R2I), 24, 658, 672
Responsibility, placement of, 225
Restraining forces, 186
Restrictive pursuit policies, 621
Retention, negligent, 586
Retirement, early, 426
Retirement benefits, 426
Retirement counseling, 442–446, 447–448
Retirement policies, 628–629
Reverse discrimination, 400–401
Rhodes v. Lamar, 618–619
Ridge, Tom, 79
Riggs v. City of Fort Worth, 603
Riggs, Mike, 603
Right-wing extremism, 95–99
Risk taking, 286, 333
Roadblocks, 620
Roberts, Carl Charles, IV, 148–149
Roberts, Daryl, 283
Robertson, Ron, 482
Robotic applications, of AI, 57, 58
Rockefeller Foundation, 207
Rodriguez, Matt L., 42
Roethlisberger, Fritz, 177
Rogers, Frank J., 59
Role conflicts and ambiguity, 18
Role-playing, 427–428
Roll-call training, 616
Rosenbergs, 17
Rosenzweig, James E., 197
Rowley, Coleen, 83
Ruby Ridge, Idaho, 324–325, 326
Ruddock, R., 529
Rural Crime Control (Smith), 137
Russ v. Van Scoyok Associates, Inc., 631
Russell, Howard, 11

S

Safe School Initiative (SSI), 26
Safety needs, 181
St. Louis Police Association, 483
St. Petersburg Police Department (Florida), 132–133, 257
St. Valentine's Day Massacre, 13
Salaries, 460–462
Salary administration, 425–426
Salary decisions, 424
Salary schedule, 426
Salva, Sofia, 595
Sam Houston State University, 367
Sanchez, Jeff, 368
Sanders (San Diego mayor), 500
San Diego city council, 500
San Diego County Sheriff's Department, 258
San Diego Police Department, 460
San Diego Regional Threat Assessment Center, 658
San Francisco Police Department, 568–569
Santa Clara University Markkula Center for Applied Ethics, 335
SARA (Scanning, Analysis, Response, Assessment), 40–41, 66
Saxe, 561
Scalar chain, 171
Scalia, Antonin, 396
Scandal, 114–118
Schlossberg, Harvey, 555
Schmidt, Warren, 278, 279–280
Schmidt, Wayne, 590
Schnell, Kevin, 595
School of Social Work at Columbia University, 543
School resource officers (SROs), 150, 152, 154
School violence, 148–152
Schwartz, C., 561
Schwartz, J., 561
Science Applications International Corporation (SAIC), 84
Scientific management, 164–168, 204, 217
Scientific Principles of Organization (Urwick), 172
Scope of liability, 589–592
Scott, W. Richard, 162
Screening, pre-employment, 563
Searches and seizures, 604–605, 626
Seattle Police Department (Washington), 410, 411
Secondary goals, in group decision making, 331
Secondary guns, 614
Section 1983. *See* Title 42, U.S. Code, Section 1983
Security. *See* Private security
Selection practices, 424
Self-actualization needs, 181, 443
Self-care, 423
Self-esteem needs, 181, 182
Self-incrimination, 113–114, 605–606
Selye, Hans, 530–531
Sendero Luminoso, 95
Senders, 349, 350–351
Senior citizen organizations, 143–144
Seniors and Law Enforcement Together (S.A.L.T.), 144
Sensory perception, scale of, 351
September 11 attacks. *See* 9/11 attacks
Sergeants, 281–282, 296
Service clubs, 144
Service labels, 518
Service organizations, 162
Service style, grouping by, 231–232
Sessions, William, 325
Seung-Hui, Cho, 149–150
Seventh-Day Adventists, 609
Sewell, James D., 379
Sexual conduct, 607–609
Sexual harassment, 414, 415–416, 629–639, 642
Sexual harassment claims, grounds for, 634–636
Shame, 371–372
Shame of the Cities, The (Steffens), 6
Shane, John M., 49
Shared vision, 287
Shariah, 89
Sharkansky, Ira, 316, 317
Sharp, Arthur G., 259
Sharpton, Al, 116
Sheetz v. Mayor and City Council of Baltimore, 605
Sheriff, 137–140
Sheriff's offices, 244–247
Sherman, 560–561
Shewhart, Walter, 289
Shift pay differentials, 426
Shooting, 613–614. *See also* Firearms
Sick leave, 426
Simmons, Jack, 195
Simon, Herbert, 175, 206, 207–208, 209, 316–317, 325, 326
Simon Wiesenthal Center, 97
Simpson, Nicole Brown, 115
Simpson, O. J., 114, 115
Simulation exercises, 427–429
Sinclair, Upton, 6, 165
Single strand grapevine pattern, 356
Situational leadership theories, 277, 278, 283–284, 295
Skill mix, 275–277, 295–296
Skinheads, 96
Skinner v. Railway Labor Executives' Association, 626
Skogan, Wesley G., 44, 46
Skolnick, J. H., 39, 141–142, 300
Slesnick, Donald D., 582
Sloan Management Review, 286
Smith, Bruce, 137
Smith, Chad, 57
Smith, Gregory, 286
Smith, M. E., 667
Smuggling, 12
Snyderman, B. B., 183, 548–549, 567
Social distance, 255
Social power, 273–274

Social pressure, 330–331
Social Theory and Social Structure (Merton), 173
Society for the Prevention of Cruelty to Animals (SPCA), 260
Sorokin, Pitirim A., 668
Souryal, Sam S., 319
Souter, David, 396
Southwestern Law Enforcement Institute, 122
Soviet-Afghan War (1979–1989), 89
Span of control, 188, 228–230
Span of management, 228–230, 264
Speakeasies, 12
Speaking, 356–359
Specialization, 187, 224–228, 251, 264
Spelman, William, 41
Spencer, Melody, 595
Sports events, tactical planning for, 314
Staffing, 172
Staff structure, 251–255
Stakeholders, 498, 525
Stalin, Joseph, 86–87
Stallo, Mark, 56
Stamford police union (Connecticut), 162
Standards, legal, 424–425
Standby pay, 426
Stark Foundation, 521
State and Local Anti-Terrorism Training Program (SLATT), 121–122
State employees, ADA limits for, 396
State financial management, 496–497
State government, 125–127
State militias, 96
State Planning Agencies (SPAs), 20–21, 127
State Police Association of Massachusetts (SPAM), 482
State Police, The (Smith), 137
State prosecutor, 140–141
State terrorism, 86–87
Station house sergeants, 281–282, 296
Steere, Mike, 201
Steffens, 6
Stephens, Darrel, 40, 133
Steroids, 539–542, 577
Stevens, John Paul, 396
Stewart, James K., 14
Stock market crash (1929), 497
Stogdill, Ralph M., 278
Stormfront (website), 98
Strategic analysis, 304–305, 309
Strategic crime analysis, 52
Strategic planning, 313
Strategy, under CAPS, 45–47
Street sergeants, 281–282, 296
Stress, 529–532
  alcoholism, 537–539
  biological, 532
  computer-related, 378
  critical incident, 555–559
  definition, 577
  drug use, 539–542
  employee assistance programs, 568–573
  female police officers and, 559–562
  personality type and, 533–534
  police domestic violence, 562–567
  police stressors, 535–537
  police suicide, 542–548
  psychological, 532–533
  reactions to, 533
  responding to, 568
  review, 573–576
  suicide by cop, 551–555
  work satisfaction and, 548–550
Stress inoculation activities, 568, 577
Strikes, 480–481
Strong mayor form of government, 128, 129
Structural change, 250–251. *See also* Organizational design
Structured response, 45
Study of the Office of Sheriff in the United States Southern Region, A (Brammer and Hurley), 137
Subordinates, communication barriers involving, 354
Substantive due process, 596, 598–599, 642
"Suggestions for a Sociological Approach to the Theory of Organization" (Parsons), 179
Suicide, 184, 542–548
Suicide by cop (SbC), 530, 551–555, 577
Suicide prevention, 547–548
Suitability studies, 304, 340
Sullivan, Cheryl, 96
Sungkar, Abdullah, 91
Sunni extremists, 27
Sun Prairie Police Department (Wisconsin), 503, 504–507
Super, John, 408
Superiors, communication barriers involving, 353–354
Supervision
  negligent, 586
  pursuit policies and, 623
  workplace harassment prevention, 638–639
Supervision of Police Personnel (Drucker), 316
Supervisors
  communication barriers involving, 353–354
  police domestic violence and, 564–565, 566
  police suicides and, 547–548
  tort liability and, 592–594
Supervisory interests, 424
Support system, 443
Survey Research Center, 194
"Survival Spanish for Police Officers," 367
Swanson, C., 540
Swanson, R., Jr., 389
SWAT teams, 327, 328
Swenson, David, 531
Symbionese Liberation Army (SLA), 326
Synoptic planning, 302–310, 311, 340
Syrian Secret Police, 86
Systematic soldiering, 164, 177
Systems, internal and external, 186–187
Szewczyk, John, Jr., 374

T

Tacoma Police Department (Washington), 563
Tactical crime analysis, 52
Tactical plans, 312, 314
Taft Commission on Economy and Efficiency, 516
Tammany Hall corruption, 6
Tampa Police Department (Florida), 368
Tannen, Deborah, 359, 360, 364–365
Tannenbaum, Robert, 278, 279–280
Tansik, D. A., 230
Tanzania, U.S. embassy bombing in, 27
Task-based physical tests, 401–402
Task behavior, 284, 285
Task Force Reports, 17
Taxation, 494, 502, 522–524, 525
Taylor, Blair, 119
Taylor, Frederick W., 164–168, 173, 217, 315
Taylor, Robert W., 98, 326
Team accomplishments, celebrating, 289
Team management, 283
Team policing, 21, 22–23, 34
Teapot Dome scandal, 6
Teasley, Clyde E., 204
Technical skills, 275, 276–277
Technology. *See* Investigative technology
Telephone toll analysis, 52
Tennessee v. Garner, 611–612, 616, 619
Tenure, 135–136, 154, 171
Territo, L., 389
Terrorism, 23, 25, 27–30
  animal rights groups, 99–100

Cali cartel, 95
crime, traditional, 95
definition, 84–87, 103
drug trafficking and, 95
ecoterrorists, 99–100
Hamas, 93
Hezbollah, 93–94
intelligence and, 72–73
Jemaah Islamiyah (JI), 90–93
Jewish extremism, 88
M-19, 95
Mara Salvatrucha, 95
Medellin cartel, 95
Memorial Institute for the Prevention of Terrorism, 91
political violence and, 82–84
private security, 25
Provisional Irish Republican Army (PIRA), 95
radical Islamic, 87–90
Red Brigades, 95
right-wing extremism, 95–99
Sendero Luminoso, 95
See also 9/11 attacks
Terrorist Threat Integration Center (TTIC), 31
Terwilliger, George, 325
Testing, in work environment, 625–627
Texas Instruments, 518
Texas Rangers, 323
T-groups, 185–186, 194
Theory X, 189, 190, 191, 205, 217
Theory Y, 190, 191, 205, 209–210, 217
Theory Z, 208–209, 217
Theory Z: How American Management Can Meet the Japanese Challenge (Ouchi), 208–209
Thin-slicing theory, 321–322, 340
Thomas, Clarence, 396
Thomasson, Todd, 57
Three-Step Model, 659, 661–662, 672
Tichy, Noel, 286
Ticket blizzards, 480
Ticket quotas, 165
Time limits, for complaints, 438–439
Time requirements, in group decision making, 333
Time, grouping by, 232
Title VII (Civil Rights Act)
entrance examination, 397
religious beliefs and practices, 609
reverse discrimination, 400
sexual harassment, 629, 631, 632, 633, 634, 636, 637
Title 42, U.S. Code, Section 1983, 583, 584–585, 586, 587, 588, 589, 591, 610
Toledo Police Department (Ohio), 395
Top-down approaches, 232–238
Torres, Joe, 467
Tort, 583, 642
Tort actions, 582–584
Tort feasor, 583
Tort liability, 592–594
Total quality leadership (TQL), 289–290
Trade Partnerships Against Terrorism (TPAT), 27
Traditional Action Research Model, 659, 662–664, 672
Traditional authority, 169, 217
Traditional organizational theory, 163–164, 200, 217
administrative theory, 170–172
bureaucratic model, 168–170
critique of, 172–176
scientific management, 164–168
Traditional policing, 38, 39, 66
Traditional policing design, 250–251
Traffic laws, in high-speed pursuits, 620
Traffic stops, 112–113
Training, 413–414
CAPS, 45
in-service, 616
negligent, 587
police ethics and, 122–124
pursuit policies and, 622–623
recruit, 615
roll-call, 616
workplace harassment prevention, 638
Training academies, 19–20
Training committees, 415
Training School for Public Service, 7
Traits approach, 277, 296
Transactional leaders, 285–289, 296
Transactive planning, 310, 340
Transformational leaders, 285–289, 296
Transnational terrorism, 86
Transportation Security Administration, 80
Treater, Joseph B., 556
Trench Coat Mafia, 148
Trojanowicz, Robert C., 247
Trust, 287–288
Tuch, Steven, 118, 120
Turbulent 1960s, 17–20, 34–35
Turek, Bart, 114
Turner Diaries, The (Pierce), 96
TWA flight 800, 84
Twain, Mark, 347
Twenty-First Amendment, 12, 34
Tyler, Kathleen, 389
Type A personality, 533–534, 577
Type B personality, 534, 577

U

Ucheda, Craig D., 242
UCLA Anderson School of Management, 209
Ulrich, David O., 286
Undue hardship, 391, 393
Unfair labor practices, 464, 466
Unfreezing, 661
Uniforms, 426
Union Carbide, 194
Union County Sheriff's Department (North Carolina), 258
Unionization, 458–463. *See also* Labor organizations; Labor relations; Labor unions
Union teams, in negotiations, 471–473
United Nations, 61
United Service Organizations, 207
U.S. Army, 323
U.S. Border Patrol, 109, 112–113
U.S. Bureau of Customs, 540
U.S. Coast Guard, 80, 109
U.S. Commission on Civil Rights, 400, 434
U.S. Customs Service, 80, 569
U.S. Department of Education, 26
U.S. Department of Homeland Security (DHS), 77, 79–82, 109, 496, 520
U.S. Department of Justice, 20, 84, 311, 496, 503, 520, 655
U.S. Department of Labor, 420
U.S. Department of State, 87, 194
U.S. Department of Transportation, 79–80
U.S. Department of Treasury, 79–80
U.S. Marshal Service, 324–325
U.S. Naval War College, 304
U.S. Secret Service, 26, 80, 109
U.S. Supreme Court cases, 110–112, 394–396. *See also specific cases*
United States v. Jacobsen, 626
United States v. Leon, 112, 592, 604
Unity, 255
Unity of command, 171, 217
University of Alabama, 396
University of California at Berkeley, 14
University of California at Davis, 400
University of Michigan, 7, 193–194
University of Southern California (USC), 418
Upward communication, 353–354, 382
Urwick, Lyndall, 170, 171, 316
USA Freedom Corps, 262
USA Patriot Act, 30–31
User fees, 522–524, 525

V

Vacations, 426
Validation, 399
Values, 288
Value statements, 313
Value system, 179, 217

Van Maanen, John, 281–282, 296
Vehicles, shooting at or from, 613
Vendel, Christine, 595
Venice Police Department (Florida), 193
Vermett v. Hough, 635
Vertical differentiation, 230, 231, 264
Vicarious liability, 585, 642
Victims, police officers as, 555
Victory gardens, 16
Vietnam War, 18
Villaraigosa, Antonio, 502
Violanti, John M., 535, 536
Violence-prone police officers, 432–434
Violent Crime Control and Law Enforcement Act, 108, 520
Virginia Tech University, 25, 52–53, 149–150
Virtual Case File (VCF), 84
Visibility, 288
Vision, shared, 287
Vision statements, 313
Visual investigative analysis (VIA), 52–53
Vocalized pauses, 358
Voice stress detection equipment, 440
Vollmer, August, 8–9, 35, 137
Volstead Act, 11–12, 34
Voluntary acts, 583
Volunteers, 259–262
Volunteers in Police Service (VIPS), 261, 262
Vote of confidence, 479–480
Vukovich, Kathy, 259

W

Waco, Texas, 116, 122, 322–324, 326–327
Wage regulations, 627–628
Wahhabism, 89, 93
Walsh, William F., 37
Wards Cove packing v. Antonio, 400
War in Iraq. *See* Iraq War
Warning devices, in high-speed pursuits, 620
Warning shots, 613–614
Warning signs, for suicide, 547
War on crime, 459
Warren, Earl, 110–111
Washington, D.C. Capitol Police, 268
Washington, D.C. Police Department, 135
Washington State Criminal Justice Commission, 624
Washington State Patrol, 27
Washington v. Board of Trustees, 631
Watson, Elizabeth, 134
Watts riots, 17
Weapon removal, in police domestic violence incidents, 566–567
Weapons. *See* Firearms
Weather Underground, 86
Weaver, Randy, 325
Weaver, Sam, 325
Weaver, Vicki, 325
Weaver family (Ruby Ridge, Idaho), 324–325, 326
Weber, Max, 168–170, 173, 217, 272, 657
Websites, 59–61
Weinblatt, Richard B., 256, 258–259, 260
Weitzer, Ronald, 118, 120
Weld (Massachusetts governor), 482
West Bank, 93
Western Electric Company, 177
Wexler, J. G., 561
Wheatley, Margaret J., 199
White, Glenn, 197
White, Ralph K., 278–279, 295
White Aryan Resistance (WAR), 96
Whren v. United States of America, 119
Wickersham Commission, 13–14, 128, 409
Wildavsky, Aaron, 321
Williams, John Allen, 145
Williams, Julie, 193
Williams, Wayne, 244
Williams, Willie, 132, 134
Willoughby, 7
Wilson, James Q., 38, 127, 300
Wilson, O. W., 9, 137, 225
Wilson, Woodrow, 6
Withdrawal, 327
Women. *See* Gender issues
Women's Christian Temperance Union (WCTU), 11
Wonderlic Personnel Test (WPT), 408
Worcester Police Department (Maryland), 503
Workaholic, 534, 577
Work and the Nature of Man (Herzberg), 183
Work environment
  hostile, 415–416
  testing in, 625–627
Workers' compensation, 426
Work flow analysis, 217
Work hour regulations, 627–628
Workplace harassment, prevention of, 637–639
Work plans, 312
Work satisfaction, 548–550
Work slowdowns, 480
Work speedups, 480
Work stoppages, 480–482
World Church of the Creator, 98, 99
World Trade Center attack. *See* 9/11 attacks
World Trade Center bombing (1993), 27, 84, 88–89
World War I, 427
World War II, 15–17, 35, 167, 427
Wounded Keen siege (1977), 326
Writing, 356–359
Written communication, 374–375
Written directives, evaluation of, 612–615
Written problem analysis, 428

Y

Yassin, Sheik Ahmed, 93
Yeltsin, Boris, 166
Yippies, 18, 19
You Just Don't Understand (Tannen), 364–365
Youth International Party (YIP), 19

Z

Zealots, 280, 281
Zero-based budget, 517–518, 519
Zero tolerance policy, 563–564
Zohar, Danah, 199

Scalpel

MEN WHO MADE SURGERY

By Agatha Young

LIGHT IN THE SKY

BLAZE OF GLORY

CLOWN OF THE GODS

SCALPEL

MEN WHO MADE SURGERY

Agatha Young

RANDOM HOUSE
NEW YORK

First Printing

 Published in New York by Random House, Inc., and simultaneously in Toronto, Canada, by Random House of Canada, Limited.

Library of Congress Catalog Card Number: 56-5214

Manufactured in the United States of America

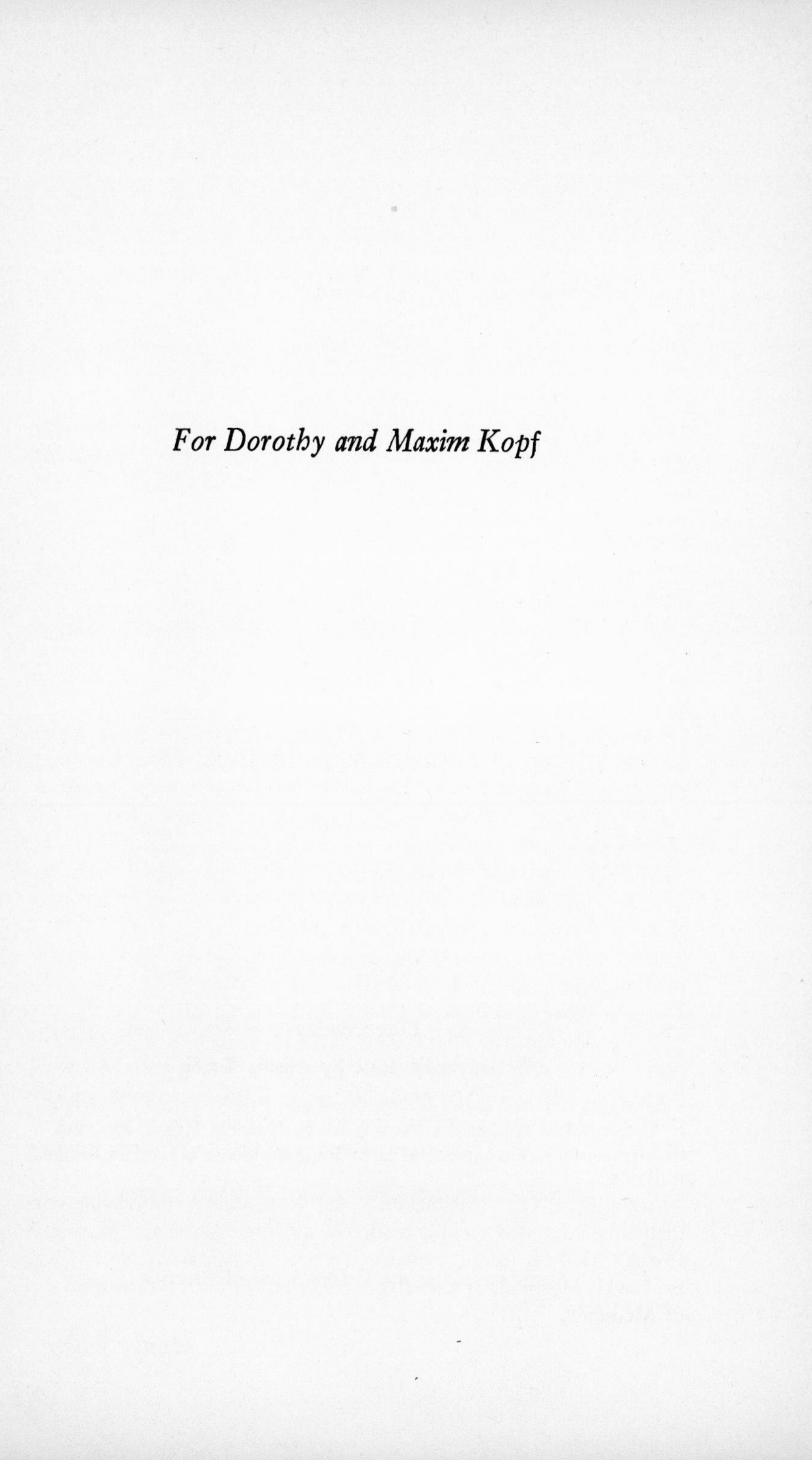

For Dorothy and Maxim Kopf

ACKNOWLEDGMENTS

Among the more pleasant aspects of book writing are the new friendships which develop during the course of the undertaking and the willingness of friends, both old and new, to help with advice and the gift of time. To these it is a pleasure to acknowledge indebtedness. I have, moreover, received help through innumerable letters, conversations and published works without which my work would have suffered immeasurably.

Special thanks go to Lola L. Szladits, Diana Forbes-Robertson, Dr. Leo M. Davidoff, Dr. Joseph F. Artusio, Dr. John H. Nichols and Dr. Bronson Ray. The late Dr. Robert H. Bishop gave me both help and encouragement.

I am grateful to the staff of the library of the New York Academy of Medicine, and especially to the librarians of the rare book room, for aid, favors and kindnesses too numerous to mention. Long experience with libraries here and abroad has shown me the worth of this one.

A library need not always be large to be valuable, and there are qualities apart from the number of books in the stacks which may greatly enhance its usefulness. A small library to which I owe a debt of gratitude, and one so rich in these qualities that it might well serve as a model, is the William Gwinn Mather Library at the Western Reserve School of Medicine.

Other fine libraries which made their facilities available were the libraries of the Royal College of Surgeons, the Royal College of Physicians and the Wellcome Historical Medical Museum, all in London. My thanks go to the library of the Yale University School of Medicine, to the University of Padua and to the Vatican Library in Rome.

Among the many institutions which have shown remarkable cordiality to a layman seeking their aid are the New York Hospital–Cornell Medical Center and Mount Sinai Hospital, in New York; St. Luke's Hospital, in Cleveland; and the Western Reserve School of Medicine.

Agatha Young

CONTENTS

Acknowledgments vi

PART I—THE CONTROL OF HEMORRHAGE

Andreas Vesalius 10
Ambroise Paré 32
William Harvey 57
John Hunter 79
Ephraim McDowell 112

PART II—THE CONTROL OF PAIN

The Anesthetists 134

PART III—THE CONTROL OF INFECTION

Joseph Lister 165
William Stewart Halsted 199
Harvey Cushing 224
The Revolution 268

PART IV—THE CONTROL OF SHOCK

Democritus's Well 287
Partial Bibliography 302
Index 305

ILLUSTRATIONS

	following page
Andreas Vesalius	24
A Skeleton from the *Fabrica*	
A Pre-Vesalian Skeleton	
Ambroise Paré, 1561	56
Battlefield Surgery, 1573	
An Operation in 1573	
William Harvey	72
Harvey's Notes on Circulation of Blood	
John Hunter	
The Lion House and the Fort on Top	
The Dissecting Room	
Skeleton of the Irish Giant	100
John Hunter's Copper Vat	
The First Ovariotomy	152
Crawford W. Long, M.D.	
William Thomas Green Morton	
Horace Wells	
Charles T. Jackson	
The First Public Demonstration of the Use of Ether	184
Robert Liston, Performing the First Operation Under Ether	
Lord Lister as President of the Royal Society	
One of Lister's Famous Urine Flasks	
William S. Halsted	232
Dr. Halsted, Operating in 1904	
Harvey Cushing	
Harvey Cushing, Operating	

THE CONTROL OF HEMORRHAGE

I.

There have been four great battles in the long history of surgery, four major conflicts spaced widely apart in time. They have been the struggles for the control of hemorrhage, the control of pain, the control of infection and the control of shock. Establishing each control was like demolishing a barricade; each destruction permitted surgery to advance until a new barricade blocked the path and a new battle was begun.

In each instance the main engagement was fought by one or two, or at most a very few, men who had the ability to see, as their colleagues for the most part did not, that further progress was impossible until the battle was won.

Advances in surgery have been made largely through the ability, the character and the obsessions of these few great men. They are the men who have made discoveries and developed new techniques, men who have had the vision and the daring to challenge the unknown. They are men of great achievement, but they are also tremendously interesting people, for they possess more than the common vitality, their characters are complex and sometimes startling, and they have led dedicated lives. It would not be true to say that these men have held the attainment of their goal to be of greater importance than their personal happiness, for not one of them thought of life in those terms, and all appear to have been capable of sacrificing without misgivings the happiness of others when it came in conflict with their own aims.

In point of time, surgery came before the surgeon—if the

kind of operating done with the blade of a flint knife can be called surgery. Men lived through a good many thousand years of hacking at each other's bodies with good intent and bad before anyone who might be called a surgeon appeared on the pages of history. And still more time went by before the mists blew away sufficiently to reveal one of these great men, not as a semi-mythical figure of legend but as a real human being with a personality and a biography based on fact.

Surgery before there were surgeons, back in the days of prehistoric man, was not limited, as might be assumed, to the repair of wounds received in accidents and battle. Ancient skulls have been found which were neatly trepanned, sometimes more than once, as early as ten thousand years ago. Trepanation, in fact, seems to have had a special fascination for primitive people, for evidences of it have been found in different cultures and widely separated geographical locations, the earliest just north of Paris (thus making Paris the first surgical center of the world).

In addition to trepanation, primitive man cut off fingers, and prints of these mutilated hands have survived as evidence. We do not know certainly why these operations were performed. Perhaps crushed fingers were amputated and depressed fractures of the skull treated by trepanation. There must have been another reason, for the number of trepanned skulls is startling. In one burial ground in France, where 120 skeletons were found, forty of the heads had been trepanned. That would seem to indicate that these operations were performed for reasons having to do with magic, gods and devils. Fingers may have been the price of appeasement, and insane people or people suffering with severe headaches may have had holes made in their skulls for the purpose of letting out the devil which was causing the malady.

Some primitive people today still practice operations for similar reasons. Sometimes the intent is not repair but mutilation—not surgery but ritual. They are performed, as they undoubtedly were in prehistoric times, by priests who are also witch doctors and medicine men, or the other way about. These merchants of the mystic cannot by any stretch of the imagination be called surgeons, and the mutilations they practice have only the remotest relation to surgery.

Surgeons emerged as a professional group, whose aim was not magic but true surgery, in Babylon, about 2000 B.C. As a professional class they were subject to regulations and penalties under the code of laws known as the Code of Hammurabi, which was inscribed on a stone discovered at the beginning of this century, and if they are a somewhat startlingly direct approach to the problem of regulating medical practice, these provisions of the Code were obviously written with good intent:

"If a physician operate on a man for a severe wound with a bronze lancet and cause the man's death; or open an abcess of a man with a bronze lancet and destroy the man's eye, they shall cut off his fingers."

"If a physician operate on a slave of a freeman with a bronze lancet and cause his death, he shall restore a slave of equal value."

There is a good deal more, and though the title used is "physician," it is obvious that the writer had in mind a clear distinction between surgery and medicine.

In Grecian times disease, or any condition which was thought to be disease, became the province of the healer-priests in temples which were, in effect, clinics. Surgery, which was still confined to the repair of wounds, fractures and dislocations, was carried on mainly by private practitioners, not connected with the temples, who were the equivalent of surgeons. Their surgery was of the crudest sort and not very successful, as the records show, for of the 147 kinds of wounds described in the *Iliad*, 114 were considered incurable.

The separation of surgical work from the treatment of disease came about quite naturally. The wounds the surgeon was called on to treat had nothing mysterious about them. Their cause was known. Disease, however, was quite another matter. The cause of disease was a mystery and was classified with other mysteries as supernatural. Disease was caused by gods and demons, and the physicians were the priests who interceded with them in behalf of the sick. The cause of disease being a mystery, it was thought to be, like all other mysterious phenomena, of supernatural origin. Therefore, since disease was caused by gods and devils, the physicians were priests who treated the disease by acting as intermediaries between the sick person and these supernatural beings in an attempt to make them desist from tormenting him.

After a time it slowly began to be realized that the causes of disease might be natural, not supernatural. This change of thinking did not come quickly, and traces of the old belief that unseen powers cause disease linger even today, but the dawn of the new concept was a great turning point in medical history, for as it grew physicians began to make a direct attack on disease itself. This revolutionary change in thinking was begun by the Greeks, but it was not carried to its logical conclusion before the leadership of Greek civilization came to an end. Early Christian thought never faced the issue squarely, and though it was generally conceded that disease might come from natural causes, it was thought to do so as a manifestation of divine intent. This was a dilemma of the sort with which the tortuous theological mind was eminently suited to deal. It was reasoned that, though disease appeared at the instigation of the divine will, it was not an act of impiety to treat the disease with medicine and other curative measures, since their success or failure was also a matter of divine discretion.

Crudely, the difference between this bifurcated concept and the more ancient one was this: In the old philosophy, when a man became sick after eating green apples, there was a demon in his belly and the apples had nothing to do with it, except possibly that he might have inadvertently eaten the demon who was inside the apple, much as he might accidentally eat a worm. The treatment by incantation and spells was aimed wholly at the demon. In the new philosophy it was conceded that it was the *apples* which made the man sick, though his sickness might be at the will of God. The cure was aimed at counteracting the effect of the apples and was successful if such was God's will.

Though the divorce between disease and religion was not total, it eventually brought the physician out of the cloister and into private practice and, much later in history, established him in the university. Nevertheless, most of the mystery about what caused particular diseases still remained. This was a matter of importance in the history of both medicine and surgery, for though the physician was a dealer in mysteries, the surgeon in the main was not.

That difference automatically made the physician a far more important person in a worldly sense than the surgeon, a disparity which grew more marked through the early centuries of the Christian Era. The physician, being a semi-philosopher, was almost forced to be an intellectual; the surgeon, on the other hand, could meet the standards of his day with little education or none at all. The physician's work was not menial or messy, but the surgeon's involved basins of blood and knives and saws and dirty bandages. Gentlemen's sons became physicians; barbers and lesser persons, including a high percentage of riffraff, took up surgery. But because both medicine and surgery were healing in their intent, the superior beings, the physicians, asserted their right to direct and supervise the work of the surgeons. They wrote about surgery in their book-lined studies. They did not dirty their hands with it.

In talking about the evolution of physician and surgeon we are a little ahead of our story. When the shadow of the Dark Ages fell on scientific thought, advancement in medicine and surgery alike ceased altogether in Western Europe. In most respects, in fact, medical work retrogressed, and it was a long time before medical science once again reached the level of Grecian times. Until the tenth century there were no centers in this part of the world where medicine was taught, except the school at Salerno, and even after the teaching of medicine was finally begun, there was no experimentation, no dissecting of the human body and only an occasional dissection of an animal for the purpose of demonstrating anatomical structure.

Students were taught mainly from the writings of one famous doctor of the past, a Greek named Galen, who had lived under Roman rule, born in 130 A.D. Galen was an opinionated man who wrote voluminously and he had an unshakable conviction of his own worth. "If anyone desires to become famous," he wrote, "all that is necessary is to accept what I have established." And again, "Never yet have I gone astray."

This consummate egoist, who was in point of fact a very mediocre physician, though a somewhat better surgeon, was accepted at face value in the universities and schools of Europe. His precepts were taught as absolute fact, and he dominated medical thought until well into the Renaissance. This didactic doctor had, however, been progressive enough to cut up a few pigs and apes and to write about the organs he found (without, unfortunately, making it clear that he was talking about animal, not human, anatomy), but for even this bit of original research he should not be given too much credit. Dissection of the human body was not permitted in Greece and Rome, but in his youth Galen had studied in Alexandria. There, before Galen's time, there had been a great medical center where anatomy was taught by dissection of the human body.

The glories of the Alexandria school had faded, but in Galen's day the great tradition still had some life, and it was probably there that he learned to study by making experiments. That Galen based his studies on experimentation was forgotten by the teaching physicians of Western Europe. Until the Renaissance, there was nothing in Western Europe which could be dignified by the name of scientific research and scant attempt was made to increase the bulk of medical knowledge. Medicine had become more a system of philosophy than a science, and the lordly physicians preferred scholarly disputation to the search for fact.

At the beginning of the sixteenth century, though medicine was still bigoted, cloistered and bound by tradition, a few signs of new life were beginning to appear. There were a number of schools where an ambitious lad could go to learn his Galen and perhaps some of the teachings of the Arabian physician Avicenna and the Persian Rhazes. A few books on anatomy were beginning to appear, though all followed the ancient teaching and all of them were bad by Renaissance standards. It had been possible for some time to get a degree in medicine as in other subjects, and in the fourteenth century holders of such a degree had begun to be called doctors. There was little if any improvement in surgery, however, for there was no real knowledge of anatomy. Surgery had been born in superstition; it grew in ignorance.

Before long the old forms of traditional philosophic scholarship had begun to be hard pressed by the vigorous intellectualism of the Renaissance. The old order and the new were fighting for supremacy, making the universities, the schools and the churches their battleground. And in the midst of the conflict there grew up one of the first giants of surgical history. His name was Andreas Vesalius and, true son of the Renaissance, he was vigorous in mind and body and as full of intellectual vitality as the age in which he lived. He was not a practicing surgeon, for his interest, his preoccupation, his driving obsession was the study of anatomy. Without a knowledge of anatomy there can be no true surgery, and the work of Vesalius laid the foundation on which the advance of surgery has been built.

Andreas Vesalius

1514–1564

"... a young man, by Hercules, most diligent in anatomy ..." —*Johann Günther*

André Wesel, better known as Andreas Vesalius, was born in Brussels in 1514. Louis XII was then king in France, Henry VIII in England. Columbus had died eight years earlier (without suspecting that he had discovered a new continent). Balboa had just discovered the Pacific Ocean, and Martin Luther was beginning the agitation which culminated in the Reformation.

Vesalius came of a family of writing doctors, and his parents understood his curious and unusual cast of mind, so that he grew up in a home environment of sympathy and understanding. When he was still quite young he had an insatiable curiosity about the mechanisms of bone and muscle under the skins of small living creatures. His was more than the normal small boy's interest in natural history. He dissected all the small animals he could lay hands on—toads, rats, dogs, anything which came his way—working with care and intense concentration. The work was delicate, and as he acquired skill his dissections became more and more precise and searching. His hands grew strong and flexible during the long hours the fascinated boy bent over his dissecting board. The mangled little corpses he so painstakingly dismembered had for him a strange sort of beauty, and their physical mechanisms absorbed him.

His family sent him to school in Louvain, and there was no better place in all Europe to acquire the preliminaries of an education. He attacked his studies with vigor and energy, for he was intelligent, quick and tough-minded. It was not his way to trouble about adapting himself to others. He left the adjusting to other people and pursued his own independent interests. He was short, but stocky and strong, with black hair and bold dark eyes. He thought well of his own abilities, and with reason. He was probably quick-tempered and irritable, and he had to dominate any situation in which he found himself. He liked facts in hard, classifiable nuggets, but he would rather discover them through his own efforts than collect them out of books. In this he was a modern and a rebel against the ideals of the older generation. Scholarship was for him a means, never an end. At Louvain he learned arithmetic, astronomy, dialectics, Latin and Greek. In later life he implied that he had also acquired a knowledge of Hebrew and Arabic. This may have been an overstatement, for boasting was not the social sin it is today.

At eighteen he was ready to leave Louvain, and he chose to go to Paris to study anatomy. There had never been any doubt in his mind about what his career was going to be, and he probably was attracted to Paris because there was a famous teacher there, Jacobus Sylvius, who occasionally performed an anatomy on a human body. That was an unusual thing in the year 1533. Two hundred years earlier, Pope Boniface VIII had issued an edict forbidding the cutting up of a dead human body, an edict not aimed at the teachers but at the knights of the Crusades who sometimes disjointed and boiled the bodies of their dead comrades in order to bring them home for burial. The misapplication of that edict to cover anatomical study, backed by the popular belief that the resurrection of the body could not take place if it had been dissected, made it virtually impossible for the universities to obtain anatomical specimens.

Few teachers seriously deplored the lack, however, since bodies were wanted only to demonstrate the teachings of Galen, not for original research. The one legal source of anatomical material in Vesalius' time was the supply of executed criminals, though even that had not been regularized. The bodies Professor Sylvius used were from this source. Professor Sylvius had no more thirst for new knowledge than other scholars of his generation, but he was one of the first to adopt the practice of throwing his anatomical demonstrations open to the public and pocketing the proceeds. Thus the accident of this man's greed gave Vesalius his opportunity.

So Vesalius turned his face toward Paris. If, as he neared Paris, he stopped on the road to look ahead toward the city where his ambitions centered, he saw a group of tightly packed, utterly fantastic structures rising from the plain, the whole mass belted in by a formidable wall. That compact pile, that jumble of strange shapes, was Paris. If he stood on high ground where he could see over the thick woods, he had a view of pleasant country dotted with small clearings where houses crowded close to the walls of some monastery, for Paris was just beginning to have environs and a few people were trading the security of the city for freedom from taxes and the police. The countryside was beautiful, but it was not safe for a traveler alone, especially toward nightfall. The wolves of Villon's day had been driven out, but the marauders, the lawless parasites of the abominable roads, still remained.

As Vesalius approached nearer to that great fagot-bundle of buildings, the effect of the weird architecture would grow stronger, for Paris was still a medieval city, the manifestation in stone of the tortuous fancies of the medieval mind. Thin spires and round turrets with witch-hat roofs pointed toward the heaven which so preoccupied the thought of the Middle Ages. From the turret tops thin, forked pennants streamed in the breeze. Every wall, every arch, every spire was a mass of ornament in stone—intricate, twisting patterns, gargoyles, attenuated saints. Some of it was half mad, some had a quality of nightmare terror, some was lyrical, some morbid, some inspired by coarse, lusty humor, and a great deal of it was beautiful. But above all it was fantastic. There could be no better exposition of the medieval mind than the one it had made of itself in stone.

The great wall around the city was thick and in good repair, with watchtowers evenly spaced along the top, for Paris was a fortress still. We do not know by which of the many gates Vesalius entered, but once inside the day would seem to darken suddenly, for the streets were narrow and the upper stories of the houses jutted over them, shutting out much of the sunlight. Most of the houses were ancient and made of blackened beams and yellowed plaster. They jostled each other crazily, lurching one against the other for support like drunkards. Each house had a name worked into the plaster of the wall, or painted on a sign which swung from a bracket over the street. The narrow windows of the houses had no glass, the floors were dirt or stone, strewn with rotting straw for warmth in winter if the owner was a poor man, or with sweet herbs if he was rich.

The narrow streets where the sunlight seldom penetrated

were ankle-deep in stinking mud. Housewives emptied slops into them from upper windows, and there were no gutters to drain off the liquid sewage. Pigs wallowed in the vile muck, dogs pawed in it for food. Carts and carriages splashed it high against the house walls. Wherever there was a depression of any size in the ground, the liquid filth collected in stagnant pools called *trous*, kept always full by sluggish streams which crawled through the city. The *trous*, malignant breeders of disease, could be smelled a long way off.

The streets had names, some poetic, some obscene, some topical: Rue Agnes-la-Bouchere Bordelle, Rue des Ecrivains, Chemin aux Vaches and Rue des Juifs. The large intersections were partly blocked by huge crosses. Massive chains were kept at the entrances to the main streets and on boats in the Seine ready to be hauled across as a barricade in case of enemy attack.

The whole city teemed and swarmed with lusty, violent, noisy life, but these citizens of Paris were no longer people with a wholly medieval cast of mind. Forces had been at work in them, stirring them, changing them—the yeast, the ferment of the Renaissance. Here and there through the city the new mentality showed itself in stone. The new buildings no longer climbed fantastically toward heaven but reposed with simplicity and dignity closer to earth and to reality. In these few buildings the influence of Italy was strongly marked.

Paris was in transition, but the traveler Vesalius belonged wholly to the new age, and his mind was unfogged by medieval mysticism. His modernism brought him into sharp and almost immediate conflict with the reactionary scholarship of his principal teacher. In the meeting between Sylvius and Vesalius two periods of history faced each other. They were opposite and opposed in the basic attitudes of their minds, the bigoted against the inquiring, tradition against freedom, theory against knowledge, intolerance against enlightenment, age against youth. Each to a great extent symbolized his generation, and each was a purposeful, strong-willed personality. Sylvius was at the peak of his career, and his position was one of eminence in his profession, but he had reached it only after a grinding struggle with poverty and frustration. He was the son of a poor weaver, one of fifteen children. He had been able, through the influence of a successful brother, to enter the college of Tournai, where he had studied with the intense avidity which all his life characterized his acquisition of anything, whether learning or property. He was fiercely ambitious, desperately determined. His main interest, like Vesalius' own, was anatomy, his aspiration a degree in medicine. Poverty prevented him from studying for his degree, and to raise the money he needed he held classes in anatomy. The powerful Faculté de Médecine at Paris forbade him to teach. He gained his degree at last from Montpellier, but not until he was fifty-three and soured, embittered and warped in outlook by his long struggle.

Armed with his degree, he returned to Paris to teach. The Faculté could no longer molest him, he was brilliant and he was a good showman. His teaching attracted students from all over Europe. In the bright light of success the warping of the long lean years stood out plainly. His bitterness released itself in arrogance, and his conceit and perhaps the consciousness of his lowly origin were expressed in a jealous guarding of his own prestige. Poverty had been his enemy for so long that he had become obsessed with the desire to hoard and save, and there were many rumors about his eccentric thrift. It was said that he half starved his servants and denied himself a fire in winter, and that he kept warm by throwing a ball against the walls of his room.

He knew Galen as few scholars even of that day knew him, and believed implicitly in all the master's cocksure dogmas. Sylvius taught Galen, not medicine. He had a will as strong as Vesalius' own, and he would not tolerate any questioning of his Galenic precepts. He carried this attitude to lengths only possible to one who had inherited the mentality of the Middle Ages.

No doubt Sylvius' method of teaching followed pretty closely the pattern of pedagogy common throughout Europe in those times, a pattern which was as standardized as a ritual. The professor in his long gown sat on a raised throne-like chair, which in itself would have appealed to Sylvius' sense of his own importance. Below him on a table lay the subject for dissection—dog, pig or human. The professor never touched the corpse. The actual dissecting was done by one or more barber-surgeons in short gowns with clumsy knives. The students gathered around, and if the anatomy had been opened to the paying public, they had to struggle with sensation-seekers for places from which they could see.

The anatomy was begun by a surgeon's laying open the body. The professor turned to the lesson he had chosen for the day in his book of Galen and read aloud. As he read, the surgeons pointed to the various organs to which the text referred, and if they did not always correspond to the written description in appearance, size or even location, nobody but Vesalius seems to have been seriously disturbed.

Sylvius was one of the last guardians of the medieval point of view, which did not regard facts as facts so much as philosophical concepts. Scholars such as he did not arrive at the reality of a fact by experimentation, but merely asserted what they believed to be true. And if, perchance, their assertion was challenged, they did not then have recourse to scientific methods of proof but defended their concept with a flood of rhetoric and scholarly argumentation. In Sylvius' case, facts existed so much more in the realm of the mind than in reality that he could, without hesitation or misgiving, deny the evidence of his own eyes as it lay on the dissecting table before him, if what he saw did not happen to correspond with the sacred word of Galen the Master. And so forceful was Sylvius in his teachings, so certain of the truth of what he taught, that he bemused even the clear, sharp mind of his most brilliant pupil. For some time after Vesalius had left the sphere of Sylvius' influence, he continued automatically, in his writings, to respect Galenic ideas.

Vesalius had come to Paris to learn the mysteries of the human body, and what he watched was no more informative than the work of a butcher, and scarcely as skillful. On the third such occasion he pushed the surgeons away from the corpse and, seizing a knife, proceeded to do the dissecting himself. He did a brilliant job of it, probably a better piece of dissecting than anyone there had ever seen. His subject may have been a dog, and he must have had Sylvius' consent. Nevertheless, it is quite possible that the enmity and jealous hatred which Sylvius later showed toward his ruthless young pupil began on this very day.

Since it is hard to imagine Vesalius as tactful under any circumstances, he probably made no secret of the scorn he felt for Sylvius' methods. There was another occasion on which Vesalius publicly humiliated the proud and arrogant professor. Sylvius said in class that he was not able to locate the valves of the arterial vessels beside the aorta, and Vesalius pointed them out to him. Sylvius was a vulnerable man, vulnerable in both his pride and his knowledge. His hatred of Vesalius had already begun to smolder, and no doubt every incident like this one added fuel.

Dissatisfied with the teaching he was receiving, it was altogether characteristic of Vesalius to take action. With him a strong emotion never failed to result in action, always vigorous though not always wise. He began dissecting dogs on his own account with a group of his fellow students, but this did not satisfy him long, for he had known the essentials of a dog's anatomy since he was a boy. No doubt he was already convinced that human anatomy could not be studied by the use of animals—a revolutionary concept for his time. Human bodies were essential to his work. There was support for his conviction in the writings of the great Galen himself. "I would ask you," Galen wrote, "to make yourself acquainted with human bones . . . I have often had the chance to do this where tombs or monuments have been broken up." Vesalius, however, was interested in more than bones, and since anatomical parts were not to be had by legal means, he became a thief in the night and went by stealth, sometimes with a companion and sometimes alone, to the execution grounds at Montfaçon.

On this grim hilltop, where there was a large pile of bones and where the stench was horrible, executed criminals were for the most part left to dangle in the chains in which they had been hung. According to the custom of the day, most of these corpses had been too much mutilated by the executioner to make fit subjects for a public anatomy, but a student eager to acquire knowledge by any means whatsoever could use dismembered arms and legs or heads or torsos.

Montfaçon was a lonely, deserted place except when the crowds surged out of Paris to see a public execution. It was a silent place except for the creaking of the gibbet chains, the occasional howl of the wild dogs, fierce as wolves, who ate what remained of the dead, or the raucous cry of the carrion birds, who tore at the flesh of the gibbeted skeletons. Vesalius' stocky young body would have joined those on the gibbets if he had been discovered. He hid such specimens as he could under his cloak and carried them back to Paris, where, if there was any flesh and muscle left on them, he dissected them carefully, cleaning and preserving the bones. And later he wrote, "Never would I have been able to accomplish my purpose in Paris if I had not taken the work into my own hands."

If supplies at the execution grounds ran out, he went at night to the cemetery of Saint Innocents. In those times, graves were dug without respect to the location of older graves. The wooden coffins soon rotted away and the grave digger's spade tossed bones to the surface with the earth. (This was the way Yorick's skull came to light.) When the new coffin was placed in the grave, the earth and bones together were shoveled back, none too painstakingly, and all Vesalius would have had to do was search the loosened dirt.

Luckily for them both, no doubt, Sylvius was not Vesalius' only teacher, for he seems to have studied also with Johann Günther, or Guinterius in the Latinized version of the name. Günther was a medical man, author and commentator. Vesalius and he were much in each other's company, and Günther mentions his friend frequently in his writings.

In 1536 Vesalius returned to Louvain to continue his studies. He had profited greatly by his stay in Paris. He was still little more than a boy, but he had hardened and toughened, and quite possibly coarsened a little. More important, he had measured his intelligence against that of some of the foremost men of his day, and as a result his youthful cocksureness had matured into confidence. He had learned the wisdom and also the adventurous excitement of thinking for himself and gaining knowledge through observation rather than by rote. He was ready to begin his life work. It must be admitted that he was also boastful, egocentric and a show-off, but it should be remembered that lusty individualism was characteristic of the Renaissance male. These qualities probably contributed to his success and certainly to his renown.

At Louvain, though he was still a student, he began to teach. He was a born teacher, and this gave him an opportunity to put into practice his own bold ideas. He taught by example, he trained his students to observe, and he did his dissecting with his own hands.

Outside the classroom he pursued his studies with the drive and precision which is the hallmark of distinguished work. He kept records. There can be little doubt that he was already gathering material for his great book on anatomy, *De Humani*

Corporis Fabrica, and it is characteristic of him that his conception of the book was of a scale and quality to set a new standard.

The shortage of dissecting material still plagued him as it had in Paris, and he resumed his scavenging among the criminal dead. One night he and a friend, having persuaded the porter to let them out of the locked precincts of the university, went to the execution grounds and for the first time Vesalius found a nearly whole skeleton. It hung high on a pole, held together by its own ligaments and out of reach of the wild dogs. The bones had been picked clean by the birds. In life, this man had been a notorious robber, and he had been condemned to die in a slow fire. To prolong his agony, he was hung high, and his flesh, made tender by slow roasting, had been easy for the birds to tear away. The skeleton lacked only a foot, a finger and a kneecap, all of which Vesalius was subsequently able to replace. He carried the skeleton piecemeal to the university, and there he mounted it with care and skill.

Vesalius had begun to have a reputation as a clever, dangerous free-thinker of medicine, and his work, which in Louvain began to show the thoroughness, the quality and the style which distinguished it from this time on, could no longer be ignored. The medical profession was forced to take him seriously, whether they liked him or not. It was in Louvain that he produced his first literary work, a free translation of the ninth book of the Persian physician Rhazes, which remained a medical classic for the next hundred years.

Louvain was somewhat more liberal toward the study of human anatomy than Paris had been, but more and more Vesalius chafed under restrictions of any sort. A true son of the Renaissance, he would be satisfied with nothing less than full freedom of thought and action. There was no real reason for him to remain in Louvain, especially as he appears always to have had sufficient funds to do more or less as he pleased. Perhaps Italy, where the light of the Renaissance burned brightest, had been tempting him for some time. In any event, he deserted the priest-dominated university at Louvain after a comparatively short stay.

He went first to Venice, and there he found a way of life totally different from any he had known. Venice was then about the same size as Paris and crowded with an international society of intellectuals and artists who had been attracted to Venice for reasons similar to Vesalius'. Titian was there, and Jan Stephan van Calcar, a pupil of Titian's and a Fleming like Vesalius. Calcar was a superb draftsman, one of the finest who ever lived. He had made anatomical drawings for members of the medical profession, and he knew the structure of the body from the artist's point of view as thoroughly as Vesalius knew it from that of the anatomist.

Ignatius Loyola and his followers were also in Venice, tending the sick at the Hospital for Incurables. Vesalius joined them for a time in the role of practicing doctor, adopting an attitude of humility and service quite out of keeping with his real character. He had no interest in the sick, however. He was a discoverer, not a healer, and this experiment was short-lived.

That same year, 1537, Vesalius received his degree and, shortly afterward, an appointment to teach at the University of Padua, some twenty miles from Venice, which was one of the great liberal universities of Europe. It is located in the heart of the ancient city, and its beautiful buildings still stand. The anatomy theatre where Vesalius lectured was replaced after his time, but much of the architecture remains today as it was over four hundred years ago. The halls are finely proportioned, and the smallness of their scale is a reminder that men in those days were shorter in stature than they are today.

Vesalius' teaching schedule was an arduous one, for during three-week periods he lectured twice a day. In the absence of preservatives, it was the corpse on the dissecting table which dictated the hours of work. In addition to his teaching, Vesalius held public anatomies from time to time. In a short while the brilliance of his teaching grew famous and pupils came to him from all over Europe. Some of these students might otherwise have gone to Sylvius, who smoldered with resentment in Paris because of the loss of this revenue.

In Padua, as in Louvain and Paris, Vesalius was hampered by the shortage of dissecting material. With characteristic directness he addressed himself to the judges of the criminal courts. He urged them in the name of science to have their sentences of execution carried out at times which would suit his teaching schedule and to order less mutilating forms of death. How far the judges were willing to cooperate we do not know, but we do know that Vesalius was forced to get much of his dissecting material by the shady means to which teachers of anatomy always had to resort until modern times. Males were easier to acquire than females, and Vesalius' more thorough knowledge of male anatomy is reflected in his writings. He was able to dissect only six females in all, and three of those were in public anatomies, which gave him little opportunity for observation and study.

Outwardly at least, and no doubt as a deliberate policy, he conformed in the main to the teachings of Galen. He even influenced his friend Calcar, who was working with him on anatomical drawings, to incorporate some Galenic inaccuracies. But as Vesalius' knowledge of anatomy increased, he realized more and more fully the extent of these errors and the harm they had caused and were continuing to cause. His mind had become acutely sensitive to Galenic fallibility.

The final enlightenment which was to emancipate him and the entire medical profession came to him with the suddenness and force of a revelation. The occasion was the mounting of two skeletons for a friend, Professor Albius, a kind of work in which he had considerable skill. One was the skeleton of a man, the other of a monkey, and when he had finished mounting them, Vesalius began to compare their bones. He was startled to discover that, though the structure of the monkey corresponded to Galenic anatomy, the human skeleton did not.

It was a momentous discovery and possibly the confirmation of suspicions which Vesalius had been harboring for some time. It cleared away the last of his uncertainties. Looking back on this period, Vesalius wrote: "I could not get over my own stupidity and overconfidence in Galen and other anatomists."

Immediately after this discovery, Vesalius proclaimed over two hundred errors in Galen. The result was that, as one of his biographers has expressed it, students at his lectures were like "excited mobs." There were "stormy objections, stormy applause." He was the most talked-of man in the medical profession.

His work was reaching its great climax. How long he had been preparing the manuscript of the *Fabrica*, and how long Calcar had been working on the illustrations, we do not know. A dust storm of scholarship has been raised around this issue. We need not enter it except so far as to say that no work of such magnitude can be produced quickly. In the late summer of 1542 the text and the drawings had been completed and the woodblocks cut for the printer.

On August 24, 1542, Vesalius wrote a letter to Oporinus, the famous printer of Basel, Switzerland, saying, "You will shortly receive . . . together with this letter, the plates engraved for my *De Humani Corporis Fabrica* and for its Epitome. I hope they will reach Basel intact; for I have carefully packed them . . . so that they may nowhere rub against one another or receive any other damage in transit . . ." The precious packages were packed on the backs of mules and sent on a journey of three weeks or more through war-ravaged country over the Alpine mountain roads, where, as the great Vesalian authority, Harvey Cushing, remarks, ". . . the misstep of a single donkey on the high passes, known to be in a state of great disrepair, might thwart all his labors of the preceding three years." Vesalius himself followed on to Basel to oversee the printing of his book and was received by the scholars there with honors.

In June of 1543 the *Fabrica* appeared. It is one of the great books of the world, and it marks the divide between the ancient and the modern in medical practice. After more than four hundred years it is still in print. The symbolism of the frontispiece serves notice to the reader that this book is a break with the ancient traditions. Vesalius himself is shown standing beside the dissecting table, on which a body lies. The high place, customarily occupied by the professor, is filled by a skeleton, a subtle suggestion not only that the old order is dead but that science has unseated the Galenic doctrines. Two surgeons, their traditional occupation taken away from them by Vesalius, sit at the foot of the dissecting table, idly comparing their knives, and the young man in the audience close to the skeleton's crooked elbow is believed by Cushing to be Calcar holding his sketchbook. The magnificent architecture of the setting is Calcar's idealized conception of an amphitheatre.

When Vesalius made the long return journey down from the mountains he was descending also from the peak of his career, for with the publication of the *Fabrica* his greatest work had been accomplished. The wave of excitement over his exposure of Galen's errors had died down, and the medical profession was not ready for his book. Here and there it was received with understanding, but in the main it was ineffectual against the stubborn forces of tradition. It made enemies for Vesalius all over Europe. Sylvius, because of his great reputation, was the most dangerous, and he attacked Vesalius and the *Fabrica* with a fury that was close to insanity. The virulence of the attack was such as to suggest that Sylvius was aware of the book's latent power to destroy the old order to which his own life had been dedicated.

There was trouble awaiting Vesalius even in Padua, where his assistant and former disciple, a man named Realdo Colombo, had been plotting to supplant him. In the months which followed his return, many of Vesalius' followers deserted him, and in many places where he had once been a prophet he was no longer listened to with respect. Vesalius had never be-

Andreas Vesalius

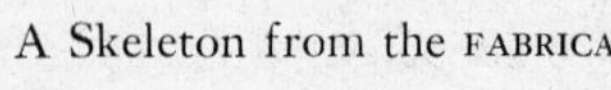

A Skeleton from the FABRICA

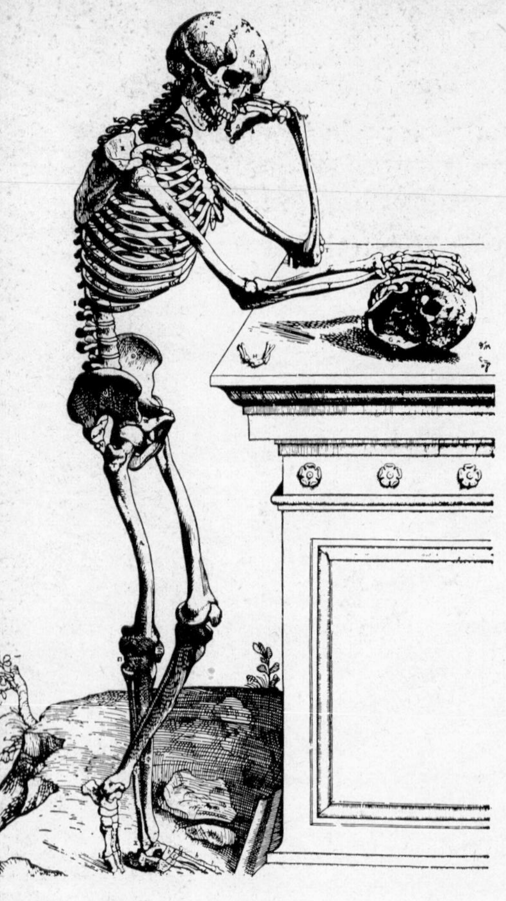

A Pre-Vesalian Skeleton

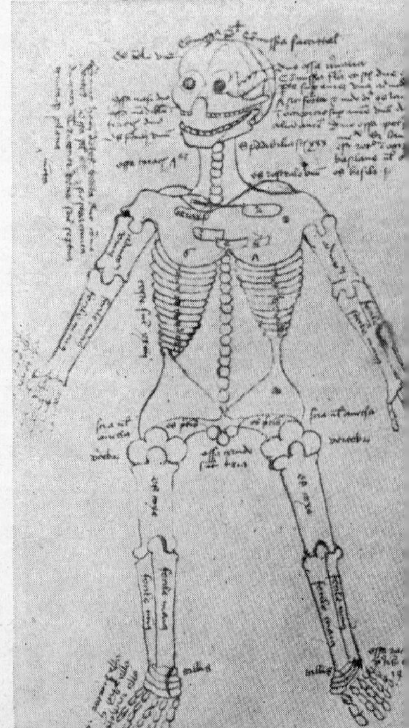

fore encountered criticism on a large scale. In his short life (he was only twenty-nine when the *Fabrica* was published) there had never been any serious obstacles in his path and his road to fame had been short and extraordinarily smooth. The opposition he now met on every side wounded and angered him, and the man who had so great an objectivity toward his science had none at all about himself of the product of his pen.

He fought back and succeeded in demolishing a few of the enemies close to him, including the ambitious Colombo, but against the more dangerous enemy, the opinion of the medical world, he was powerless. He wrote, he fulminated, he denounced, but he could not move that solid wall of opposition.

The pen was a poor weapon for a man of Vesalius' temperament, who was accustomed all his life to translate every emotion into action. He fumed under the discovery that no action would avail him anything against the intangible force of opinion, and in the end his need to release his pent-up rage through some physical deed became too strong. After a long night of what agony of spirit may be imagined, he gathered together his papers and his notes for a book on medicine and pathology that he had been preparing, and threw them into the fire.

The bonfire of his papers marked the end of his effective career. He resigned his teaching position and abandoned his research. The rest of the story can be quickly told. He secured for himself the position of court physician to the Emperor Charles V and followed that restless monarch around Europe, prescribing medicine and treating gunshot wounds. He was finished forever with the only life he had ever cared to live, except for a few short works that were like brief flares from a dying fire. He made his renunciation of his old way of life complete by taking a wife, though he had once said that he who would marry must not follow medicine, for there was not time for both.

In the portrait of Vesalius attributed to Titian, which dates from the later period of his life, we see a man drawn into himself behind a screen of reserve. There is suffering in the face, a barely perceptible trace of the old arrogance and the kind of weary patience which an impatient man acquires after he has lost the battle with life. It is difficult to recognize in that picture the same man who appears in an earlier portrait, shown in this book. Seen in the light of the earlier portrait, it is a tragic face.

Vesalius did not live to realize the importance of the book he had written. As time passed, however, the opposition died down somewhat, though Sylvius never ceased to shout that Vesalius was a "madman."

Sylvius died in Paris in 1555. By that time he had lost much of his reputation and his own pupils sometimes jeered openly at him, but he never lost the fierce determination with which he had fought his way upward to eminence. As he lay dying in delirium this old and feeble warrior thought that he must go to conduct a class which was waiting for him, and he rose, struggled into his boots and so died. His epitaph was a cruel, mocking verse scribbled on his tomb by his former students.

In Vesalius' last years our view of him grows dim. There is a story, though whether it is fact or legend we do not know, to the effect that he was hastily summoned to Paris to attend, in consultation with Ambroise Paré, the King of France, who had been injured in a hunting accident. There is another story which relates that he opened what he believed to be a dead body—some said of a young man, some said of a woman—only to find the heart still beating. This, so the story goes, aroused the power of the Inquisition against him and he was condemned to die; the Emperor pardoned him but required that he make a pilgrimage to the Holy Land.

In any event, he did go to the Holy Land, expecting on his return to end his retirement and teach once more at Padua. He never returned. He died on the island of Zante in the Ionian

Sea in 1564, when he was fifty years old. Perhaps he was shipwrecked there—we do not know. It is said that while he lay dying on the beach the people of Zante would not come near him, fearing he had the plague, but that a Venetian goldsmith found him and nursed him until he died.

Like all great men, Vesalius has had many detractors. They have pointed out that his was not the first illustrated book of anatomy and that it contains errors. They have named other teachers with knowledge as extensive as his. They have said, in short, that he was no better than many of his colleagues, but only more conspicuous. Even these detractors have not denied that his work focused attention on the technique of gaining knowledge through recorded observation.

II.

The practice of surgery was on a lower plane during the lifetime of Vesalius than it had been in the great days of Rome. Operations were largely confined to the repair of wounds, the removal of surface tumors, an occasional attempt to correct hernia and the removal of stones from the bladder. This last operation, which was perhaps the most successful, was performed by itinerant surgeons who had learned their trade by the apprentice system and who did no other kind of surgical work. There was much need for a good technique for amputating diseased and injured arms and legs, but amputations were avoided whenever possible, because of the difficulty of controlling hemorrhage. The suppuration of wounds was thought to be natural and desirable.

The great limitation to the advance of surgery, aside from the imperfect anatomical knowledge of the day, was the inability to control the loss of blood. The ligature was used infrequently, the vessels being tied after they were cut rather than before, and the ends of the ligature were left hanging out of the wound for easy removal. The ligature was not used in amputations. The main reason for this was that suppuration almost invariably took place around the knot, and when this happened the end of the tied vessel frequently rotted away and there was a fresh deluge of blood.

Because of the fear of this sort of secondary hemorrhage, cauterization by the application of hot metal or boiling oil was preferred to ligation. But this also frequently resulted in secondary hemorrhage, when the scar cracked and gave way. Nothing at all was known about the circulation of the blood, without which knowledge no hemostasis can be more than accidentally successful.

For all these reasons, Renaissance surgery, like that of the Middle Ages, was a blood bath. Blood poured from wounds, it flowed in torrents at operations. It stiffened the gown of the barber-surgeon, the extent of the staining and stiffening frequently being the only credentials he had to offer. Hospitals and surgeons' shops reeked of blood, and, alternating in stripes with white bandages painted on a pole, blood became the trademark of the barber-surgeon.

In the Middle Ages and the Renaissance, all barbers practiced some surgery, but there were in addition surgeons who had no other occupation. For the most part they were quacks, with no training for their work, who traveled from town to town, butchering their patients as they went. In England in 1462 the barbers and the better-class surgeons joined forces in the Barber-Surgeons Company in order to eradicate these quacks. The corporation was granted a charter by Edward IV and proceeded to create professional standards and requirements for membership which did a little, though not very much, to raise the standards of surgery in London.

In the years which followed, the fortunes of the barbers and the surgeons and their relationship to the physicians went through a series of complicated changes. In 1540 the barbers and surgeons were re-incorporated under a charter from Henry VIII.

The same complicated relationships between barbering, surgery and medicine existed in France in the sixteenth century. In the main, the physicians, who wore long robes and held degrees from some school of medicine, directed the work of the barber-surgeons but did not themselves practice surgery. The barber-surgeons wore short robes and held no degrees. The master surgeons wore long robes, had received some sort of medical education and were the holders of licenses issued by their governing body, the Collège de Saint Côme.

The hospitals of the time were run as institutions of charity by religious orders. They were places of horror. The wards were filled with great canopied beds placed as close together as possible, and patients were crowded into the darkness of these great cave-like structures, three, sometimes four, to a single bed. Sometimes these miserable humans were all laid out in one direction; sometimes with feet and heads alternating. Usually the sexes were not kept separate.

Surgical cases were put in with medical cases, with little regard to whether the disease might be contagious, except in the case of plague, which was universally recognized and feared. Plague patients were not wanted in hospitals; if they appeared, they were bundled off to special pesthouses and largely left to fend for themselves. There was no real comprehension of the connection between dirt and disease, and the sheets of these great beds, when indeed there were any, were thick with blood and pus and grime. Lice swarmed in the bedding, carrying disease from patient to patient, and it is not surprising that epidemics within these hospitals were not uncommon.

The hospital buildings were dirty, ill-lit, usually damp, sometimes cold in winter, sometimes steaming with the heat of sick bodies and chimneyless charcoal braziers. Sewage facilities usually consisted of a hole in the floor at one end of the ward, into which slops and refuse were dumped to drain into the river or to gather in the stagnant *trous*. The stench which rose into the wards from these sewage holes can scarcely be imagined.

Through the wards, all day and all night long, the tinkling of a bell could be heard as some priest and his acolyte passed along to perform the last rites for the dying. And during the day the screams of those who were undergoing operations echoed through the buildings. There were no operating rooms. Some dark corner, some place not needed for other purposes, was made to serve. Because operations were so frequently fatal, proceedings were begun by a priest, who administered the Last Sacrament. Perhaps the patient was made drunk or given some opiate, but such palliatives, if they can be called that, were usually reserved for well-to-do patients, who did not go to hospitals. The patient was tied securely to the table, the surgeon picked up his knife (there was no such thing as a truly sharp knife) and, with the victim's screams ringing in his ears, began the operation. And always there was the blood —the torrent, the deluge of blood.

The moral and cultural level of society at large was more to blame for the conditions which existed in these hospitals than the religious orders which ran them. In point of fact, appalling as these hospitals were, they represented a higher standard of behavior toward suffering and poverty than that held by the lay public generally. Humanity toward suffering and the responsibility of society toward the unfortunate, though the cornerstone of Christianity, were then concepts without conviction, precepts without practice.

The first of the great surgeons to regard humanity as a basic principle of his profession was Ambroise Paré. He was a simple, kindly man of good judgment in surgical matters, who strove to cure his patients with as little suffering as possible, to insure their comfort in so far as he was able, and to insist that they receive as good care as he could procure for them. In his concern for the welfare of his patients he made no distinction between the rich and the poor.

Ambroise Paré

1510–1590

"*Je le pensay, Dieu le guarit.*" —*Ambroise Paré*

Ambroise Paré was born in 1509 or 1510 in Bourg Hersent, which is now part of the city of Laval in the province of Maine. His parents were poor and he had little education, with the result that when in later life he took to writing (that charming, ingenuous writing which is pleasant to read even today) he was forced to use French instead of the humanistic Latin of scholarship. Though the pedants scorned his books in consequence, they could be read by those most in need of them, the humble barber-surgeons who had no Latin at their command. The little education which Paré received is supposed to have come from a kindly parish priest who gave him instruction in return for work in the garden. This is the first of many places in Paré's life story where history is vague, and there is another account to the effect that the priest was paid to teach the boy Latin but made him work in the garden instead of instructing him.

Sometime in his early youth Paré was apprenticed to a barber-surgeon. It probably took place in Paris, where a member of his family was practicing, but there is a picturesque story which relates that while watching a famous surgeon (who could not possibly have been in that place at that time) perform an operation (which he had not then learned to do), young Paré was so enthralled that he dedicated himself to surgery on the spot and went starry-eyed to Paris to begin his life work.

All we know with any certainty is that he did go to Paris, though a young man without money and without education had little prospect of ever becoming anything better than a lowly barber-surgeon. As such, he might in time aspire to owning his own shop, where he would shave customers, practice cupping and leeching, perform a limited range of minor operations on his own account and a few of a more complicated nature under the supervision of a gentleman of the long gown, and might occasionally be called on to act as prosector at a formal anatomy.

Arrived in Paris, Paré became a student and "companion surgeon" at the Hôtel Dieu, the big, dirty hospital close to the Cathedral of Notre Dame on the left bank of the Seine. The Hôtel Dieu, which was founded in 660 A.D., was washed on one side by the evil-smelling waters of the river, which made the building damp the whole year through. The wards were heated by iron stoves, though as one historian remarks, these were scarcely necessary because of the body heat—*la chaleur morbifique*—of the sick. The humid stench crept like a fog out of the curtained beds. Cries, groans, prayers and delirious shrieks filled the halls. As companion surgeon, young Paré must have spent most of his time in the ward to which the wounded and victims of accidents were brought. Some of the survivors of the operating table and women who had been badly injured in childbirth were put there also. Maternity work was in the hands of midwives, who had a ward of their own. It was a sort of cellar, its windows opening just above the stinking waters of the river, which flooded the place several times each winter. Paré would have been summoned down to this stink-hole only when some poor girl was dying in difficult labor, but only then and as a last resort when the midwives could do no more.

If, as Paré asserted during his later life, experience is the best school of surgery, then this big city hospital was the right place for him to begin. Every sort of case came here, and he studied them all, but he never let himself grow callous to suffering or lose sight of the fact that his patients were human beings.

Paré stayed at the Hôtel Dieu for three years, and when he was twenty-seven, he left to go to war as the personal surgeon of a Monsieur Montejon. In this capacity he had no rank or title. He was with the army, not in it. This arrangement was in no way unusual, for the army was still half feudal in that it was organized not so much under the central authority of the king as under individual noblemen who, with their followers, added themselves to the army as a unit.

Paré's duties were ill-defined. Primarily, he was expected to care for Montejon (and probably to shave him). Beyond that he was free to do what he felt inclined to undertake for the care of the wounded, but this was left to his own discretion. His patients paid him individually, if they could, and it was they, not he, who decided what his services were worth. Sometimes the men took up a collection of coins for him, or if currency happened to be scarce in the campaign, he was paid with wine, a horse or a piece of equipment.

There was no organized provision for caring for the wounded and no idea of salvaging the wounded in order to maintain the fighting strength of the army. If a soldier was so badly hurt that he could not keep up with the army, he was left behind. His government had finished with him. And yet there was no shortage of soldiers, for among a large part of the civilian population hard times were endemic, like the plague, and wars offered an opportunity to sack and plunder. War for the common soldier of the Renaissance was primarily a get-rich-quick project.

Such an army as the one Paré had joined lived off the country through which it passed, in theory buying food from the farmers but in practice stealing anything which could be carried along. A wide swath of ruin and destruction marked the passage of the troops through the fertile land, and the farmer (to whom these intricate campaigns came under the generic name of "the wars") would as soon be visited by the enemy as by the mob-army of his king and country. What these roistering soldiers could not eat on the spot they drove before them on the hoof to eat another day, and so we have the edifying spectacle of a drunken serpent-march of men accompanied by wenches, hangers-on, bellowing cows and squealing pigs, crawling across the countryside, leaving its filthy trail behind.

Young Paré cared little about the historical significance of this or subsequent campaigns. The soldiers, their woes and their ills, were his chief concern. He saw his first fighting at Passe de Suze, near Turin, and here on the heights a certain Captain Rat was shot in the ankle. Paré cared for him and made a careful record of the case, ending with the humble words which have become famous: "Je le pensay, Dieu le guarit" (I dressed him and God healed him). Again and again in his writings this gentle phrase appears.

The army won its battle at the pass and pressed on into Turin. "We thronged into the city," Paré wrote, "and passed over the dead bodies and some that were not yet dead, hearing them cry under the feet of our horses, which made a great pity in my heart . . . Being in the city, I entered a stable to lodge my horse and that of my man, where I found four dead soldiers and three who were propped against the wall, their faces wholly disfigured, and they neither heard, nor saw, nor spoke, and their clothes yet flaming from the gunpowder which had burned them. Beholding them with pity, there came an old soldier who asked me if there were any means of saving them. I told him no. At once he approached them and cut their throats gently and without anger. Seeing this great cruelty, I said to him that he was a bad man. He answered me that he prayed God that when he should be in such a case, he might find someone who would do the same for him. . . ."

A large proportion of the wounds which Paré was called on to treat were caused by gunshots. Firearms in those days were not powerful and they were fired more or less at point-blank range, so that the wounds involved powder burns. The general belief among medical men was that all such wounds were poisoned and the standard treatment of them was based on this mistaken idea. The lips of the wound were pulled as far apart as possible and wedged open. The wound was then filled to overflowing with scalding-hot oil of elder and treacle, or a similar mixture. Such treatment not only increased the severity of the wound but caused agonizing pain to the patient.

Paré followed it meticulously, conscientious doctor that he was, but the suffering that he was forced to inflict distressed him immeasurably. Then in one day of heavy fighting, when the casualties were many, he ran out of oil. In this emergency he did the best he could. He invented a concoction of egg yolk, oil of roses and turpentine which he applied cold to the wounds. He could do no more, but that night he could not sleep for worrying about these men, his patients, who were, he feared, doomed to die of poison because their wounds could not be treated with scalding oil. Early in the morning he got out of bed and hurried to them. To his astonishment he found them in excellent condition and feeling comparatively little pain. The flesh around their wounds appeared to be clean and healthy. The others, those whom he had treated in the orthodox way, were in far worse straits. Their pain was severe, they were feverish and the flesh around their wounds was red and swollen. He never again poured boiling oil into gunshot wounds.

He did not, however, have a great deal of faith in the makeshift salve of egg and rose oil, perhaps because it was uncomplicated and because he himself was the inventor. While he was near Turin, he heard of a doctor who used a supposedly miraculous salve for dressing wounds, and he determined to get its formula. But the doctor was equally determined not to part with his lucrative secret. "He made me," Paré wrote later, "court him for years before I could draw the recipe from him." Paré valued the salve highly and used it for many years.

The recipe, which shows that the good Paré, for all his common sense, was not free from the superstitions of his times, has been preserved. The salve was concocted as follows:

2 new-born puppies
1 pound earthworms
2 pounds oil of lilies
16 ounces Venice turpentine
1 ounce aqua vitae

Boil the puppies (alive) in the oil. Add the worms, which have been drowned in white wine. Boil and strain. Add the other ingredients.

When Paré returned to Paris, he went to see Jacobus Sylvius—that same Sylvius who was Vesalius' teacher and from whom Paré had received instruction during his stay at the Hôtel Dieu. Paré told Sylvius about his discovery that gunshot wounds were not poisoned and could be healed without being cauterized with burning oil. Sylvius was greatly interested and urged Paré to publish his findings. If this seems to be an uncharacteristically enlightened attitude on the part of Sylvius, that great defender of ancient traditions, it should be remembered that since there were no guns in Galen's time, there was no Galenic precedent for the treatment of gunshot wounds. It was one of the few times in Sylvius' life that he allowed his naturally fine intellect to work unhampered by his belief in Galen's infallibility.

From that time on Paré made every possible effort to put forward his case for the new type of treatment. He pleaded for it on humanitarian and medical grounds with all the earnestness of his nature, he wrote about it in his stilted, unformed style. But a man who could not write or speak in the language of scholarship was not able to make headway with the dignitaries of the all-powerful Faculté de Médecine and gunshot wounds continued to be treated with scalding oil long after Paré's death.

Paré remained a surgeon with the army for four or five years, and at the end of that time, weary of wars, he returned to Paris to settle down. In spite of his extensive experience he could not practice barber-surgery there, however, until he had passed the necessary examinations and received a license. He appears to have taken the examination twice, perhaps because he failed in the first attempt. His license was granted to him and, secure in the future, with war, as he believed, forever behind him, he married. History has preserved no more of this girl than her name, Jeanne Mazelin.

Paré practiced his trade (it could scarcely be called a profession). He amassed property, he worked at the writing of his book on the treatment of gunshot wounds and was happy. He was above all else a man of peace, this man who was to see more battle, murder and bloodshed than most of the men of his day. In 1545 his book appeared. It became in a few years the standard work in its field. Paré wrote, much as he must have talked, in a discursive, informal style, and the success of his first literary venture encouraged him to pursue his writing career. His handbook of anatomy, the first to be written in French, was published in 1549, and though it was not illustrated, it was a book of great value to the barber-surgeons.

In 1552, Paré was off to the wars again, on an expedition for King Henri II against Charles V, Emperor of the Holy Roman Empire. One day, when the army was preparing for a retreat, Paré came on a group of soldiers digging a grave. The grave was to be for one of their comrades, who had been badly wounded. Rather than let him fall into the hands of the enemy, or be abandoned to the ferocity of the peasants, who hated all soldiers because of the devastation they caused, his comrades were preparing to administer the *coup de grâce* and give him a decent burial.

Paré's kind heart was touched by the wounded man's plight. He used his authority to commandeer a cart and had a soft bed made in it for the soldier. Throughout the retreat Paré himself nursed the wounded man and even cooked for him. The wounds healed, and the man's comrades, greatly moved by this unusual display of humanity toward one of themselves, took up a collection for Paré.

While Paré was returning with the army from the same campaign he tried an experiment which he had been considering for some time and had discussed with the surgeons of the Collège de Saint Côme. It had to do with the large proportion of leg wounds, caused by firearms, which had to be dealt with by amputation. The standard practice in such cases was to stop bleeding by burning the stump with red-hot irons or by dipping it in a kettle of boiling oil. The pain caused by either kind of cautery was frightful, and often, after a few days, the scab would break loose, fresh hemorrhage would start and the burning would have to be done all over again.

For some time Paré had been turning over in his mind the

possibility of securing the blood vessels with catch forceps very like those in use today, and tying the vessels with a ligature. At the siege of Danvilliers he finally experimented with the new technique on the leg of a wounded officer. Paré was not by any means sure that his new method would succeed and he had irons heated and ready in case he should need them. The ligation of the blood vessels succeeded, and through that battlefield experiment surgery took a long forward stride.

Paré had read about the use of the ligature in Galen. Ligation had fallen into considerable disuse and Paré was the first man of his day to apply the principle to amputation. As soon as he was able, he made his discovery public and the controversy which he stirred up went on raging long after he was dead. Many years after his first experiment, when he had reached the top of his profession, he was still forced to defend what he had done, for, as he says himself, his opponents took the position that "To tie the vessel after amputation is a new remedy . . . therefore it should not be used."

This year 1552 was a crowded, eventful one for Paré. He had begun it as a comparatively obscure barber-surgeon; he emerged from it with considerable fame. When the forces of King Henri II were besieged in Metz, and there was fear that the soldiers were being poisoned because of the great mortality among the wounded, the King directed Paré to enter the city through the enemy lines and to make an investigation. The weather was bitterly cold, and as Paré neared Metz he dared travel only at night and with the utmost caution. From a height of ground he could see the city ringed by the campfires of the enemy. At midnight he crept through the enemy camp and was admitted to the besieged city. When morning came the war lords and the remnants of the besieged army received him as their deliverer.

Paré made his investigation and discovered that the troops were not being poisoned. The high mortality rate during war in those days was not caused by enemy action. Firearms were low-powered and of uncertain aim, and the bombardment of a besieged city seldom consisted of more than twenty or thirty cannon shots a day. Men died rather from the diseases which accompany overcrowding, bad water supplies, complete lack of sanitation, infections, exposure and insufficient food. Some of these factors were causing the high mortality in Metz.

The siege lasted for two months of hardship, not only for those inside the city but for the troops camped around its walls. The weather continued cold and the ground was covered with snow. Sometimes, when Paré stood on the city wall looking out over the camp of the enemy, he was stirred by the beauty of this land of suffering, and he wrote, "Each soldier had . . . a coverlet all strewn with stars, glittering and brilliant, brighter than fine gold, and every day they had white sheets and lodged at the sign of the Moon."

The following year Paré was trapped in the besieged city of Thérouanne, where there was much suffering and a shortage of water. The prostitutes, who by time-honored tradition were the laundresses of the armies, washed the surgical dressings, beating them with sticks to get them clean. With the scant supply of water and the total absence of soap, the bandages emerged from the washing dirty and stiff. Fire broke out in the city and the soldiers extinguished it with beer. The dead were heaped in a pile "like fagots" and the smell of them fouled the air. Paré worked hard among the wounded, dispensing his egg-yolk-and-oil-of-roses salve and doing what he could for their comfort.

In the end, the town was forced to surrender, and Paré disguised himself in the dirty clothes of a common soldier, hoping in that way to escape a long captivity. After he was taken prisoner, however, he could not resist the temptation to show off his surgical skill, and he abandoned his disguise. He tells the story in his memoirs with ingenuous boastfulness. After a captivity of some weeks he was given his freedom as a reward for curing one of the enemy notables of an ulcerous sore of long standing.

When Paré returned to Paris, he found himself a man of considerable fame. He was an author, a trusted surgeon of the King, and he had introduced a number of important innovations in surgical technique. Nevertheless, he still had only the official status of a barber-surgeon, and therefore he must still suffer the indignity of the short robe. In view of his accomplishments and the trust placed in him by the King, this state of affairs verged on the ridiculous. In 1554 the authorities of the Collège de Saint Côme consented to overlook the fact that he had little education and to permit him to take the examination for the rank of master surgeon. The examination was a form only and he was granted his degree. He was forty-five years old when he put on the long robe, and from this time on all his actions showed a maturity, a mellow dignity which marked him as the great man he had become.

In the capacity of surgeon to the King, Paré went frequently to court, but he found there little of the tranquility he so much enjoyed. Court life was riddled with intrigue, and the authority of the crown was disputed by the great nobles. France was a pitiful, war-ravaged land; the people were restive under their misery, and to the general deterioration of society, which affected every class from the court to the humblest peasant, was added the dangerous foment of religious controversy. The Protestant faith had been spreading through France like a brush fire, especially among the well-to-do middle class. The persecutions, which culminated in the horrors of the Saint Bartholomew massacre, had already begun, given impetus by many great nobles who saw in the confiscation of Huguenot property a means of relieving their own chronic financial difficulties.

The whole nation, including Paris and the court, lived in a constant state of dread and suspicion, in which it was all but impossible to avoid siding openly with one faction or the other. That Paré was able to maintain a position of neutrality is astonishing, but he did so with such circumspection that not only did he avoid the dangers of becoming a partisan, but also we do not know to this day with which side his sympathies really lay.

In 1559, King Henri II, husband of Catherine de' Medici, was accidentally struck in the head with a lance while out hunting and the point of the lance remained imbedded in his skull. Paré was summoned, and this is the occasion on which it is said that Vesalius was called from his retirement to act as consulting surgeon. The story is that the two famous doctors sent for the heads of two freshly executed criminals, which they dissected together in an effort to determine the proper treatment for the King. Their efforts failed, the King died, and Paré was appointed surgeon to Henri's son, now François II. François, husband of Mary Stuart, was sixteen years old when he came to the throne, and frail in both body and intellect. He died after reigning only eighteen months, leaving Mary to follow her own road to tragedy. When the boy king died, it was whispered that Paré had poured poison in his ear, and it was fortunate for Paré that the passionately violent Queen Mother never believed these whisperings.

From the start of François' illness, Paré had felt certain that it would end fatally, and at first he told no one about his views except Admiral Coligny. The Admiral was a Huguenot, but because of his distinguished service to France, Catherine de' Medici had welcomed him at the Catholic court with an outward show of friendship. He was a good and wise man, and he seems to have persuaded Paré that to keep the seriousness of the King's illness a secret in the court atmosphere of perfidy and intrigue would be a dangerous course to follow. During these days the Admiral and the distinguished surgeon, who had many traits in common, found themselves greatly drawn toward each other.

The boy king François was succeeded by his brother, Charles IX, a brutish young man given to violent rages and so unstable of will that his scheming mother, Catherine, could use him much as she pleased. There is little that is good to be said of Charles, though it is to his credit that he seems to have had for a time a real affection for Paré.

One day Charles showed Paré a small gray stone, called a bezoar stone, for which he had paid a great price. Bezoar stones, which were in reality gallstones taken from animals, were greatly valued at this period of history for the magic properties they were supposed to possess, and Charles believed his to be an antidote for poison, truly a worthwhile possession at a court dominated by Catherine de' Medici. Paré, though frequently credulous in such matters, was skeptical about the bezoar stone and proposed to the King that they test it on a criminal waiting for execution.

Their choice fell on a luckless cook who had stolen two silver plates from his master, for which crime he was shortly to be hanged. The cook was offered his liberty if he would take poison and then swallow the bezoar stone. The poor cook does not seem to have had much faith in the stone, but he agreed nevertheless, saying that he liked much better to die of poison in privacy than to be hanged in view of all the people. An apothecary mixed the poison, the cook swallowed it and then the stone; immediately he became violently ill. Paré himself tells the story of what followed. "Having these two good drugs in his stomach, he took to vomiting and purging, saying that he was burning inside, and calling for water to drink, which was not denied him. An hour later, having been told that the cook had taken this good drug, I prayed the provost to let me see him . . . I found the poor cook on all-fours, going like an animal, his tongue hanging out of his mouth, his eyes and face red, retching and in cold sweat, bleeding from his ears, nose and mouth. I made him drink oil, thinking to aid him and save his life, but it was no use because it was too late, and he died miserably, crying that it would have been better to have died on the gibbet."

The bezoar stone was carefully retrieved from the stomach of the dead cook and returned to the King, but when Charles heard what had happened, he threw it into the fire.

The years which followed were busy ones for Paré, and as tranquil as could be in the midst of religio-political unrest. He wrote constantly, his style improving with practice, and he went his way, avoiding the pitfalls of controversy, while around him tension mounted as France came closer and closer to her darkest hour. In 1562 a bloody civil war broke out between Catholics and Protestants, in which both sides perpetrated many cruelties. Once again Paré went with the army on the side of the Catholic forces of the King, while his friend, Admiral Coligny, became a leader of the Huguenots. Paré was at the sieges of Bourges and Rouen and he was present at the battle of Montcontour, where the Huguenots under Admiral Coligny were defeated.

Ten years went by, years of misery for the war-torn land. In 1572 the policy-makers of the court, thinking to restore peace to the country, hit on the scheme of marrying the King's sister Margaret to a leader of the Huguenots, that king without a country, Henri of Navarre.

The leaders of both factions assembled in Paris for the wedding. The Catholics made a show of friendliness which they did not feel, and the Huguenots, deceived and overconfident, displayed themselves with arrogance in the hostile streets of Paris. The wedding festivities were the thinnest of veneers over Catholic hate. Events had moved one step nearer to the blood bath of Sunday, August 24, 1572, the Feast of Saint Bartholomew.

Admiral Coligny, kind and good man, elder statesman and hero of France, was in many respects the symbol of the Huguenot movement and as such the focal point of Catherine's hate. He had been much at court prior to the wedding, feeling it his duty to remain near the emotionally immature King, who could sometimes be prevailed on to listen to wise counsel and who called the Admiral "my father." The moral atmosphere was distasteful to Coligny and the endless festivities of the wedding wearied him. He wrote to his wife—it was the last letter he ever wrote her—that he longed to leave Paris.

Catherine was insanely jealous of Coligny's influence over the King, and it was with her consent, and quite possibly at her insistence, that the Dukes of Anjou and Guise sent for a man named Maurevel, sometimes called the King's assassin (*le tueur du roi*). On Friday the twenty-second of August, when Coligny was returning after spending some time watching the King play tennis, he was fired on from a window of a house belonging to a follower of the Duc de Guise. Two bullets struck him, one wounding a finger and the other lodging in his arm. He was taken to his own house and Paré was sent for. Paré amputated the wounded finger and removed the bullet from Coligny's arm, but he was forced to cause the Admiral great pain, for his instruments were not in good condition. When the operation was over, Paré remained with his old friend and so by chance was present through the events which followed.

Several accounts of the subsequent events have come down to us, but they are written by witnesses whose testimony conflicts. Scholars have challenged the accuracy of all of them. It has been necessary to make from them a sequential story, and if the events did not happen precisely as recounted, the broad outlines of the narrative are nevertheless true in all their horror.

Paré remained with Coligny. A little distance away, at the Louvre, the Queen was in a state of terrible agitation because the plot to murder Coligny had failed. She had begun to fear that the lords of the Huguenot faction, when they heard about the attempted assassination, would be able to raise a force strong enough to avenge the Admiral. Throughout the next day, which was Saturday, she brought continual pressure on the King to support her plans, and in the end she persuaded that unpleasant young man to consent to a new attempt to murder the man whom he had called "my father."

Paré remained that night with the Admiral. At the palace the Queen had not gone to bed. The plan for the massacre was complete and waited only for her signal, which was to be given the following day. Hatred, anxiety and suspicion filled her, and at half-past one o'clock on the morning of Sunday the twenty-fourth she suddenly issued the command, hours before the expected time, to ring the tocsin signal from the bell tower of Saint Germain l'Auxerrois.

Paré and Coligny must have heard the tolling of the bell but they could not know its significance. Sometime afterward there were muffled sounds in the street below the Admiral's window. It was the stealthy assembling of a large force of men under the command of the leader of the Catholic faction, the Duc de Guise. Presently there was a great pounding on the door and shouts of "Open, in the King's name." The Admiral's men within the house, having no reason to suspect treachery from the King and thinking it some message from the Louvre, threw wide the door.

The assassins rushed in. The man who had opened the gate was killed on the spot. The others ran for the stairs to the upper story but they were overtaken and slain. In his room the Admiral heard the tumult and guessed instantly what was afoot. While the desperate fight was taking place on the stairs and in the passage, he had himself helped from his bed. He put on a long robe and sat himself in a chair to await with dignity the fate he knew he could no longer escape. Paré stayed by his side. An instant later the door burst open and one of the Admiral's own gentlemen, named Cornation, rushed into the room. Paré demanded to know the meaning of the tumult. Cornation turned to the Admiral and said, "Sir, it is God calling us to himself."

The Admiral told him with great calm that all his household should save themselves if they could. Cornation rushed out (somehow he managed to escape what followed), and Paré was left alone with the Admiral. He could not have been blamed if he too had taken flight. He was definitely suspected of being a Huguenot himself, and in what appeared to be a sudden reversal of the King's favor toward the Admiral, Paré must have believed himself to be in great danger.

The door was thrown open a second time and a man with a bloody sword in his hand rushed in. Others crowded in behind him. For a moment they hesitated, evidently astonished to find only two calm, unarmed men. Then a German named Behm went up to the Admiral and, putting the point of his sword at his breast, asked him if he was Coligny. The Admiral said he was but that, "You cannot shorten my life except by the permission of God." The next instant he had been pierced by the sword.

The stab did not kill him but it released the fury of the other assassins in the room. They all rushed at Coligny with swords and daggers in their hands and struck him until he fell to the floor. As he fell, the murderer Behm went to the window and shouted to Guise and the men who waited below that it was all over. Guise demanded proof. The Admiral's body, with life not yet extinct in spite of the ferocious attack of the assassins, was dragged to the window. Behm tried to raise it to throw it out, but with his remaining strength, Coligny braced himself with his feet against the wall. At that, Behm cried out in rage, drew his dagger and stabbed him. Seconds later the Admiral's mutilated and hardly recognizable body hit the paving stones of the courtyard below.

Paré was alone in the house with the assassins and the corpses of the Admiral's men, which littered the stairs and passages. Below, Guise kicked the Admiral's body and departed. The street remained full of fighting men and the riffraff citizens of Paris crowded to the scene. Someone cut off the Admiral's head and carried it away, right out of recorded history, so that no one has ever discovered what became of it. Paré was escorted in safety to the Louvre, or at least he got there somehow. The fighting men departed from the neighborhood, leaving the headless body where it lay.

Paré played no part in the horrors which followed. Children came to gaze at Coligny's bloody, headless body where it lay on the stones—the loathsome, depraved, evil children who were the product of sixteenth-century Paris. They played with the body, kicked it around and finally tied a rope around its feet and dragged it through the streets for hours. Tiring of this sport, they built a fire and tried to burn it. Sometime later it was thrown into the river, pulled out again and turned over to the hangman, who dragged it up the hill to Montfaçon and hung it by the feet from the gallows. Subsequently the King and all his court went to see it hanging there. By this time it had begun to decay, and the King remarked that, "The smell of a dead enemy is always sweet."

The massacre of Saint Bartholomew does not equal in size the massacres of our times, but in many ways it exceeded them in ferocious depravity. The tocsin released the long-pent-up feelings of insecurity and religious hate in the people of Paris. A madness swept through the city, a frenzy that had some of the characteristics of a mental contagion. For three days Paris was a city filled with homicidal maniacs.

The King himself did not escape the contagion. He was standing at a window when he saw a number of Huguenots running toward the palace to seek his protection. He called for his *arquebuse* and, leaning out the window, fired on them. From the hour that the tocsin had rung, this unbalanced monarch had been in a state of feverish excitement, and on the second day he collapsed.

After Paré returned to the Louvre, the King had insisted that he remain in the safety of the royal apartments. When the King broke down under the excitement of the bloody scenes, he sent for Paré and said to him, "I do not know what ails me . . . I burn with fever; all around me grin pale bloodstained faces. Ah, Ambroise, if they had but spared the weak and innocent." After that he grew wild and boisterous, indulging himself in buffoonery, but there is no convincing record to the effect that his remorse was anything but temporary.

The year following the massacre, Paré's wife Jeanne died, and three months afterward, at the age of sixty-two, he married Jacqueline Rousselet. In 1575, three years later, he published the first collection of his writings and by so doing roused the wrath of the powerful Faculté de Médecine in the person of a certain Dr. Gourmelen, a traditionalist of the old school, who had long resented, and had probably been consumed with jealousy of, this upstart Paré who knew no Latin and had yet risen to fame. Gourmelen invoked an old decree of the parliament which prohibited the publication of any medical book without the permission of the Faculté. The controversy became a *cause célèbre* in which all sorts of charges were brought against Paré, including plagiarism and corruption of morals. In the end, the parliament reaffirmed its edict, but by that time it was too late, for Paré's book had been published and was selling exceedingly well, as might have been expected after the publicity of a public trial.

Other editions followed, and Gourmelen continued to attack Paré until that mild man was finally stung to sarcasm and occasionally to a real burst of anger. On one such occasion Paré wrote, "Now will you dare say you will teach me to perform works of surgery, you who have never yet come out of your study? . . . the operations of surgery are learned by the eye and by the hand."

Paré's old age was an active one, and in spite of the continued enmity of the Faculté, he was an honored man. Some of his accomplishments belong in the category of technical advance. Such are the application of the ligature to amputation, his famous treatment of gunshot wounds, his revival of a method of turning a child in a difficult delivery and the improvement of the design of numerous surgical instruments. Even more important are the intangible contributions he made simply by being the sort of person he was. Through his work he brought about what might be called a renaissance of surgery; through his example he set a new standard of humanitarianism in dealing with the sick and the poor.

It is altogether fitting that the final glimpse we have of him is among these sick and poor. His last recorded appearance was at the siege of Paris in 1590, a siege which brought great hardship to the citizens. Food was so scarce that many were dying of starvation. One day Paré, while walking through the streets, found himself in the midst of a crowd of miserable wretches who were surrounding the Archbishop of Lyons, a leader of the Catholic party, begging him to give them bread. Paré interceded for them, saying, "Monseigneur, these poor people whom you see about you are dying of the cruel rage of hunger, and demanding pity of you. For God's sake, Monsieur, give it to them."

He said much more. It was almost a speech that he made, standing there in the midst of the throng. And there he fades from view. He died in the same year and was buried in the church of Saint André des Arts, the church where he married Jeanne, at the foot of the nave near the tower. He rested there for two hundred and ten years, until, in 1800, Saint André des Arts was demolished. No one thought to preserve his remains. They were transferred to the ossuary of the catacombs, where their identity was lost among thousands upon thousands of other human bones.

III.

At the beginning of the seventeenth century there were only a few men in Europe and England who were surgeons in the true sense of the word. The rest had little technique or knowledge of anatomy, and a large proportion of them were disreputable, untrained itinerant mountebanks. These latter performed their limited range of operations in temporary booths, or made them into public spectacles on the village green, to the accompaniment of clashing cymbals, which served the double purpose of attracting the crowd and drowning out the cries of the victims. This was the surgery that surgeons of the better class had banded together to eradicate, but their efforts had curtailed these malpractices only slightly.

Even the better type of surgeon was still ruled, for the most part, by tradition and superstition. There was no organized distribution of books, and there were no periodicals, so that the only way for surgeons and students to keep informed of recent advances was to travel to the various centers of medicine, a thing few were able to do. As a result, surgical practice at the beginning of the seventeenth century was still derived more directly from Galen and the ancients than from the teachings of such men as Vesalius and Paré. Most surgeons still believed the Galenic dogma that "no wound can heal unless an evil-smelling laudable pus appears." If the wound did not produce pus, but showed signs of healing "by first intention," cleanly and without suppuration, the surgeon became alarmed. He manipulated the wound and rubbed salve into it with the result that inevitably, and to his satisfaction, the yellow pus appeared.

Here and there a voice was crying out against the faith in "laudable pus." A few men realized that nature had power to heal and that the wound was best treated to which the least was done. These advanced thinkers were seldom heeded, and sometimes persecuted. The controversy about the desirability of pus continued for another two centuries and a half, until Lister demonstrated that pus and wound infections in general were caused by the action of bacteria.

The seventeenth-century surgeon still believed in magic, charms and spells, crediting devils and evil spirits for that which he could not understand. One school of surgical thought believed in leaving a wound untended and treating the weapon which had caused the wound. A weapon salve was concocted of such substances as earthworms, powdered loadstone, human mummy, animal brains and moss scraped from the skull of a man who had been hanged. The weapon was carefully anointed with this mixture and a dressing or bandage applied and changed every few days. Sometimes the salve was rubbed into the wound also, but usually the wound was merely covered and left alone—which was probably the most fortunate thing that could have happened to it.

Physicians were more prone to superstition than surgeons, perhaps for the old reason that the cause of a disease is obscure and the cause of a wound is not. The Renaissance physician, as the medical historian, Fielding Garrison, has said, "usually believed in astrology and went in for the lore of amulets . . . or the determination of the proper time for purging and blood letting by the conjunction of the planets," and these beliefs persisted well into the seventeenth century.

The reliance on spells and on the weird substances which filled the shelves of the apothecary shops recalls the witches' magic brew in *Macbeth*.

Witches' mummy, maw and gulf
Of the ravin'd salt-sea shark,
Root of hemlock digg'd i' the dark,
Liver of blaspheming Jew,
Gall of goat and slip of yew . . .

In spite of lingering superstition and ignorance, surgery was slowly making progress. Anatomical knowledge had improved, especially where Vesalius' *Fabrica* had been available to surgeons, and post mortem dissection as a means of determining the cause of death had become fairly common. Except in England, public anatomies were still held in the spirit of entertainment, and they were often followed by food, drink, music and theatricals.

With the improved knowledge of anatomy, a greater variety of operations became possible. The techniques of the tourniquet and of the ligature were improved, though nothing was known about the principles which underlay their use. Amputations were undertaken more frequently on the battlefield, but they were still avoided in civilian practice unless the patient was at the point of death, the civilian mortality rate being approximately eight in ten. The advances in surgery required a higher standard of manual dexterity and, because the more elaborate operations meant more prolonged suffering for the patient, more and more emphasis was placed on speed.

The new field of plastic surgery was developed toward the end of the sixteenth century by Tagliacozzi, who was persecuted for his labors. Little came of Tagliacozzi's work, for even so enlightened a surgeon as Paré believed that it was impious to alter the face which God had created or man had marred.

The first Caesarian section had been performed in 1500 by a sow-gelder on his wife, who not only survived but bore other children and lived to the age of seventy-seven. Subsequently Caesarian section was performed by surgeons with enough success to attract the attention of religious authorities, who thereafter usually sanctioned the operation only after the mother had died. As a result, Caesarian section, which had begun with promise, fell into disuse—a pattern which is all too familiar in surgical history.

Inquiring minds of the Renaissance had concentrated largely on anatomical studies, but the anatomy of the sixteenth century was dead anatomy. In the cadaver on the dissecting table the heart did not reveal its beat, the blood was still, the machinery of every part of the body had lost its motion. Toward the beginning of the seventeenth century, however, scientific men became less interested in the structure of the body and more in how it functioned.

As a leading subject of research, physiology superseded anatomy. Formerly, the little that was known about what occurred in the living body had been arrived at largely by guesswork, but toward the end of the Renaissance, questions which formerly had been the subject of philosophical academic debate were settled by experiment. Scientists invented precision instruments for measuring and weighing the body and its parts, and for recording temperature. They left off debating and retired to their laboratories to use these new instruments in their search for knowledge. The night of the medical philosopher had ended, and the long day of the solitary research worker had begun.

One of the questions which increasingly preoccupied the scientists was the behavior in life of the heart and of the blood. At the beginning of the seventeenth century there were several theories, the most prevalent being that the blood moved back and forth in the veins and arteries like a tide. Noting that some blood was bright red and spurted from the body, and some was dark and sluggish in its flow, the assumption was that there were two kinds of blood. Many believed that one of them contained a mysterious something, which they called "vital spirits," while the other possessed an equally vague property, known as "natural spirits."

This semi-anatomical, semi-mystical concept was finally destroyed by the discovery of the circulation of the blood. It has been called the most important medical discovery ever made, and though it was the culmination of a long evolution of thought, the final truth was brought to light by one man, working alone. His name, as all the world knows, was William Harvey.

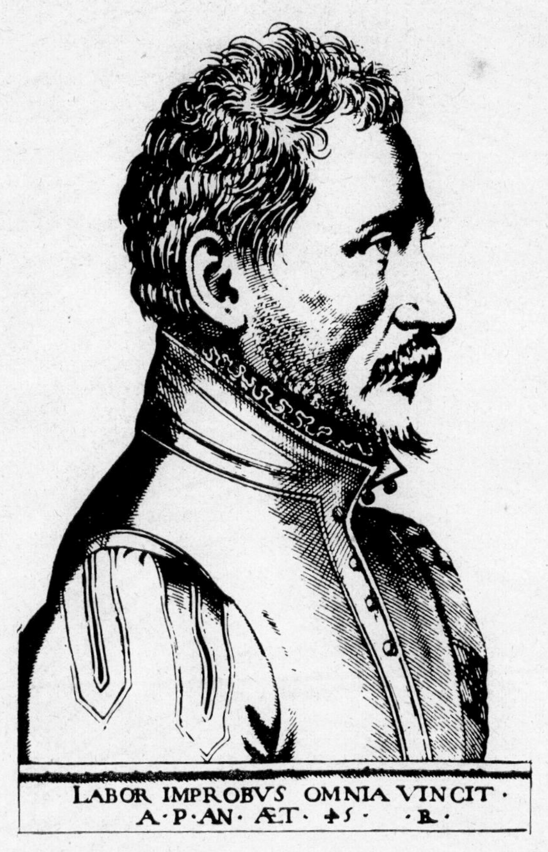
LABOR IMPROBVS OMNIA VINCIT ·
A·P·AN· ÆT· 45 · ·R·

Ambroise Paré, 1561

Battlefield Surgery. *From* Chirurgiae, *by Joannes Andreas a Cruce.*

An Operation in 1573. *From* Chirurgiae, *by Joannes Andreas a Cruce.*

The dog in the foreground appears in many surgical prints of the period and may have had some symbolic significance. Possibly he represented science.

William Harvey

1578–1657

"For toil the Gods sell everything." —*William Harvey*

William Harvey was born in Kent during the reign of Queen Elizabeth. Paré had died twelve years before and Shakespeare was fourteen years old. Harvey was the oldest of a family of seven sons and two daughters. His father was a merchant who had sufficient means to own a large house and to educate his sons well. When young William was a boy of ten, the Spanish Armada was defeated, and in that same year, 1588, he was sent to King's School at Canterbury. Boys' schools, in those days, were rough places. The students lived in cell-like rooms with no glass in the windows, discipline was harsh, the work hard.

It was a life designed for the survival of the fittest, but young Harvey had all the physical stamina that was necessary.

From King's School he went to Caius College, Cambridge. He seems to have been a determined lad who knew exactly what he wanted, and to have gone about the business of preparing himself with none of the vacillation and uncertainty shown by many youths toward their future careers. The choice of Caius probably indicates that he had already made up his mind to be a doctor, for the majority of students who went there planned to make medicine their profession. Dr. Caius, the founder, was an anatomist of distinction and the college had been granted the right to dissect two cadavers a year, though whether this privilege was used while Harvey was there we do not know.

Harvey's choice of a life work was medicine rather than surgery, but the discovery of the circulation of the blood affected the course of both so profoundly that it cannot be said to belong to one more than to the other. In point of fact, he was well versed in both surgery and medicine, but it was with the intention of becoming a physician that, when he left Caius College, he went in 1598 to the University of Padua. Harvey found there, as Vesalius had before him, an atmosphere of liberalism and culture. There was less religious intolerance at Padua than elsewhere, and as a result the university attracted students from all over Europe, including many of Protestant faith. The scholastic standards were high, but the student life was rough-and-tumble.

The students governed themselves and elected their own professors, a not unusual arrangement in those days. Most of them had come there to learn, not to fritter away their time, and they made their professors feel their attitude. The spirit of Vesalius was still dominant there, still molding and influencing generations of medical students, and largely for this reason Harvey acquired an interest in anatomy that colored the work of his later life.

The academic year at Padua opened on October eighteenth. That day is sacred to Saint Luke, patron saint of medicine, who was himself a physician. There were ceremonies at Padua, and it is not hard to imagine the English youth more or less lost in the crowd of other students, all strangers from far places, all unknown and untried. Harvey was shorter than the average, and slight in build. His eyes were black and their expression was alert, guarded, watchful. His hair was black, his complexion dark "like the wainscot," his long-fingered hands were thin and sensitive. He did not make friends on impulse but only after measuring them against his own critical standards. He lived under a good deal of nervous tension and he disciplined himself severely, but he was exceedingly quick to lose his temper. He carried a dagger, like most young men of those times, and when his temper flared he whipped it out, though there is no record of his quarrelsomeness ever having involved him in serious trouble.

Though across the distance of more than three hundred years, it would be absurd to state categorically that Harvey's short stature was responsible for the traits of his character, nevertheless, defensiveness, independence, quick resentment and wariness are traits which not infrequently appear in those who in some way physically vary from the average. So many of Harvey's actions can be explained in this way that it is easy to believe his attitude toward the world was his protective armor.

As a young man in Padua, Harvey's personality must have been an odd contrast of raw spots and dignity, of bad temper and intellectual flights, with friendliness for the few and aloofness toward many. But if he was unequal to others physically, he was superior mentally and he soon stood out from the other students at Padua. He was elected to one of the student councils and he made a friend on the faculty. This new friend was Dr. Fabricius, who held the same position in the university that once had been filled by Vesalius. Dr. Fabricius was in his middle years and famous, but he recognized the quality of Harvey's mind, and the older man and the young student spent much time in each other's company. Fabricius had discovered the valves in the veins and showed them to Harvey, which may well have been the beginning of Harvey's interest in the functioning of the circulation.

The theatre where Fabricius conducted his anatomies had been built after Vesalius' time. It is still standing, and recently I went there to visit the scenes where Harvey had worked. I was conducted through the halls and passages of the old university to an enclosed stair which curved around the outside of the theatre. The impression was of a hidden way to a secret room, which may well have been the intention, in spite of the blaze of publicity which the dissections at Padua received.

Narrow doors opened from the stairs at various levels, and, stooping through one of them, I found myself standing on one of the six tiers from which the students watched the dissections. The tiers rise steeply, and I could look almost directly down on the dissecting table. Behind the painted railings each tier was only wide enough for standing, and there was no room to pass another person. In the theatre, as in the ancient study halls, one is startled by the smallness of scale. The effect is almost of a theatre in miniature.

There was no daylight in the theatre in those days, and no way to ventilate a room which held a dead body and some two hundred men. Light came from a chandelier and from candles held by students. The center of the dissecting table lowered into a vault-like room under the theatre, where the cadavers were stored, and it must have been an awesome thing to see a body rising slowly into the light of the sparkling candles.

The theatre is no longer used, but something more than wood and plaster has survived the passing of the centuries. There lingers still in this deserted room a sense of vitality and a feeling of the force behind the search for knowledge which took place here. The greatness of the seventeenth century still dominates the solitude.

Harvey remained at Padua until he was twenty-four years old and returned to England with the degree of Doctor of Physic. In that same year he received a similar degree from Cambridge. As he commenced his career, a new historical era was beginning in England. Queen Elizabeth was dead and James I ruled—a king with a shrewd mind, weak legs and a tongue which lolled out of his mouth like a dog's. Harvey's practice grew rapidly, and in 1604, when he was twenty-six years old, he married Elizabeth, daughter of Dr. Lancelot Brown, who was physician to the King. We know of Mrs. Harvey only that she was tall, dark like her husband, somewhat severe in appearance, and that she was fond of a parrot. Having married Harvey, who recorded that one human touch about her fondness for her pet, she fades out of history, and we never hear of her again, not even to learn how or when she died.

The young London practitioner gravitated naturally toward the intellectuals in his profession and, as he had done in Padua, soon rose to the top of the group. He became a Fellow of the Royal College of Physicians, and he was appointed chief physician to Saint Bartholomew's Hospital. The ceremony at Saint Bartholomew's in which he took office was held just before Saint Luke's Day in 1609. He was the first physician-in-chief to be allowed to live outside the precincts of the hospital, and his duties were not heavy. He was expected to meet the patients one day a week, to prescribe for them, to advise the surgeons and to see patients at his house whenever the hospital staff thought that advisable. The remainder of his time he was free to devote to his own practice.

His fellowship and the hospital appointment were conventional steps toward solid establishment in a medical career. To outward appearances he was a successful practitioner, and no one suspected that he would ever become anything more. No one knew that he was carrying on research into the action of the heart and blood, for he worked on his experiments alone, in secrecy, and we do not know when these researches were begun. He dedicated himself to them, with the result that he was never more than a mediocre physician. In his spare time he went off by himself to collect his material in the fields and along the shores, and he shut himself in his study for hours at a stretch.

In the course of his experiments he dissected many different kinds of animals and sea creatures. He watched the beat of their living hearts and discovered that the motion which takes place during a heartbeat is complicated and so swift that he could not see what it was that happened. He tried to follow the motion again and again, in all sorts of creatures, over a long period of time, until he was "almost tempted to think . . . that the motion of the heart was only to be comprehended by God."

Gradually, he came to realize two important things. First, the function of the heart in every animal he examined was the same. Second, the structure of the heart was not the same, for in the lower forms of life, though the heart served exactly the same purpose, the anatomy of the heart was simpler and there were fewer stages, or phases, in a single beat. He began to study these lower forms of life—toads, snakes, shrimps, fish—and he found that in the cold-blooded creatures the heart moved more slowly and he could watch its rise and fall. He began to compare the species, one with another, the lower with the higher, and by doing that, though he did not realize it himself, he made a contribution of inestimable value. He had become the founder of comparative anatomy. Every medical student today studies comparative anatomy. It is basic to the work of pathologists, biologists, microbe hunters and those newest arrivals in the field, the men who are trying to discover the secrets of the viruses.

Having watched the heart drive the blood in the simplest of living creatures, Harvey was able to understand what took place in the more complicated forms. The rapidity of the heart's movement and its more intricate architecture no longer confused him. In the end he knew what no man before him had ever known: that the heart is a muscle with a jerky movement, at one instant in swift, complicated action, at the next in complete rest. He knew that the heart drives the blood through the arteries—and that they contain nothing but blood and certainly no mystic spirits. He knew that the blood returns via the veins to the heart and that the whole cycle is repeated indefinitely. What he did not know, and never did discover, was how the blood reached the veins from the small arteries. The discovery of the capillaries through which the transfer is made had to wait for the invention of the microscope. That was the only point in the whole complicated cycle of the circulation which Harvey did not have clear, and he bridged that gap by reasoning.

Harvey did not make his great discovery suddenly, but gradually, laboriously, through patience, intelligence and perseverance. The price in toil was enormous, but no single mind in medicine has ever advanced knowledge by so much. He continued to keep his own counsel about his work. London saw only "little Mister Doctor Harvey" making his rounds on a horse with expensive trappings and a man servant attending him. Little Mister Doctor Harvey had grown a trifle testy, and he was impatient with people who wasted his time. Much of the time he was preoccupied, but he was able to come out of his meditations and be, as a contemporary remarked, "very communicative" and "willing to instruct any who were modest and respectful to him."

In 1615, the year before Shakespeare died, Harvey was chosen to give a course of surgical lectures which had been founded some years earlier by Lord Lumley. The appointment was only given to men of the first rank, it was for life, and it entailed giving lectures on surgery twice a week the year around. Harvey prepared for these lectures with characteristic thoroughness, and some of the notes he made for them have miraculously survived. They contain the first written mention of the theory of the circulation of the blood. They are kept now in the British Museum, where generations of scholars have studied them, revered them and struggled with their illegibility. They were written, obviously, for no eye but his own, on folded pieces of paper in a hand that can only be described as villainous. It is a desperately hurrying, execrable script, next to impossible to decipher, but strangely alive, for it reveals plainly the busy, anxious man who was feeling acutely the swiftness of time's passing. The words of these notes are a strange jargon, part Latin, with which he was thoroughly familiar, part English. There are many abbreviations and small symbols. Before the important passage which notes the circulation of the blood, he put "W. H.," his own initials, to indicate, no doubt, that the material which followed was his and his alone. The momentous passage reads:

> *W. H. Constat per fabricam cordis sanguinem*
> *per pulmones in Aortam perpetuo*
> *transferri, as two clacks of a*
> *water bellows to rays water*
> *constat per ligaturam transitium sanguinis. . . .*

And there it is. Though it is impossible not to smile at the mixture of tongues, these are some of the most important words ever written. What he has said is, "It is proved by the structure of the heart that the blood is continually transferred through the lungs into the aorta [the large vessel which distributes arterial blood through its branches to every part of the body], as by two clacks of a water bellows to raise water. It is proved by the ligature that there is a perpetual flow of blood. . . ." (The remainder of the passage is complicated and fairly untranslatable.)

We do not know how this first announcement was received. Twelve years later, after a great deal more work designed to meet the critical objections he expected from the anatomists, he published a book which he called *Exercitatio Anatomica de Motu Cordis et Sanguinis in Animalibus*, or, more conveniently, *De Motu Cordis, The Motion of the Heart*. It was printed at Frankfort-on-the-Main, which was then the center of the book trade, and unfortunately it was a very poor job of bookmaking. The paper is bad in most of the existing copies and it has begun to turn brown and crumble. There are many printing errors, which have led authorities to believe that Harvey did not see proofs before the book was printed, though perhaps, the good doctor's handwriting being what it was, the printer should not be made to carry all the blame.

His book stirred up a controversy, and it has been said that during Harvey's lifetime not one man over forty accepted his theory. Harvey backed away from the controversy, refusing as consistently as he could to be drawn into it. Part of the reason why the book had a delayed effect was that it did not bring about any sudden changes in the practice of surgery or medicine; Harvey's theory was not a new technique, but an explanation. It supplied the reason for many things the doctors did with good results without knowing why. Harvey's work eliminated confusion, put research on the right track and so opened the way for a long series of dependent discoveries the end of which is not yet. Before Harvey's theory could have a direct effect on techniques, it needed to be assimilated and elaborated. This took time—more time than there was remaining to Harvey himself.

Nevertheless, he lived to see the truth of his discoveries widely acknowledged. It was the death blow to superstition, and from this time on we hear no more about those "spirits," vital and natural, inhabiting the blood. Harvey had solved the last great anatomical mystery and brought to an end the semi-mystic, semi-theological attitude toward medical science.

Harvey was in his prime when *De Motu Cordis* was published. His face at this period resembled Shakespeare's, but in his expression there were signs of strain, sensitivity and preoccupation. The wariness of his youth had become intensified into an attitude of defensiveness against the world. Though he had become famous, he had few friends and he allowed himself few pleasures. He liked to drink coffee and to read Virgil. He liked to walk by himself in the fields and to sit in the dark and think. He took an interest in the state of the nation, and he must have found a great deal in the events of those days to trouble him, for he was a temperate man living in intemperate times.

He had not the slightest inclination to involve himself in the life of the court, though he went there often, for in 1618, the year in which Sir Walter Raleigh was executed, he had been appointed physician extraordinary to James I. James died in 1630, and Harvey went to the Continent, at the request of King Charles I, to accompany the Duke of Lennox. The trip, which was a long one, took Harvey into war-devastated country. "I can only complain," he wrote, "that by the way we could scarce see a dog, crow, kite or raven, or any other bird, or anything to anatomize, only some few miserable people, the relics of the wars and the plague where famine had made anatomies before we came. . . . It is time to leave fighting when there is nothing to eat, nothing to be kept, and nothing to be gotten."

Because the plague was raging in Italy, the party did not go there—which was a disappointment to Harvey, who had not visited Italy since his student days. They went back to England in 1632 (the year in which Galileo was forced to adjure his beliefs before a papal tribunal), and that year Harvey was appointed physician to the little King Charles. The undersized monarch and the short, peppery little doctor became as nearly friends as two men in such different stations can be. The King, who was probably the shorter of the two, was fascinated by scientific matters, and Harvey sometimes broke his customary silence to tell the King about the work he was doing. Harvey brought curious objects to show the King. Once it was an egg with two shells, and once Harvey let Charles see an animal's tiny heart while it was still palpitating. They took real pleasure in being together, and comfort also, for each of these two men, for different reasons, found life hard. Their companionship was an escape for both of them, and for the little King there was not to be much more peace left on this earth.

The King appears to have been the only enduring companion that Harvey ever had in his laboratory work. On one occasion the King gave Harvey permission to anatomize some of the deer in the royal park and came to watch the dissecting. And once, having heard of a young nobleman who had a large permanent cavity in his side through which might be seen what was thought to be his lung, the King sent Harvey to investigate. Remembering all this later, Harvey wrote, "What did I find? A young man, well grown, of good complection and apparently possessed of an excellent constitution, so that I thought the whole story must be a fable . . . he immediately laid open his left side for my inspection, by removing a plate which he wore there against accidental blows. I found a large open space in his chest into which I could readily introduce three of my fingers and my thumb . . ." When Harvey did this, he felt a fleshy protuberance inside the young man's chest which seemed alternately to swell and shrink under his fingers. The opening, Harvey thought, was the result of an old ulcer now healed over. He examined the young man with the greatest care and finally concluded that the fleshy object ". . . was no portion of the lung . . . but the apex of the heart covered over with a layer of fungus flesh . . ."

To Harvey it seemed a wonderful thing—as indeed it was—that it was possible to touch a living heart and feel the ventricles contract under his hand. He took the young man to the King and they examined him together, noting that the heart in the diastole was "retracted and withdrawn," but in the systole it "emerged and protruded"—a vivid description of the heart's motion. The little doctor and the little King, absorbed in these wonders, studied the relation of each heart-beat to the pulse in the wrist and observed that ". . . the heart struck the walls of the chest and became prominent at the time it bounded upward and underwent contraction on itself." Interesting and rewarding hours these must have been for both King and doctor.

Through the Earl of Arundel, Harvey discovered another scientific curiosity. The Earl had found an old man, Thomas Parr, living in the country. Parr was said to be a hundred and fifty-two years old. He had first married, so the story went, at eighty and had two children. At a hundred and five he had an illegitimate child and for his sin did penance at Alderbury Church. At a hundred and twenty-two he married again, but his powers must have been failing, for this time he had only one child. Arundel brought old Parr to London, but there he died. Harvey performed the autopsy and, finding no visible cause of death, concluded that it must have been brought about by bad city air and high living. (There is, of course, not one scrap of evidence, except village gossip, that Parr was the age he claimed to be.)

The Earl was sent on an ambassadorial visit to Vienna, and Harvey, who had received the surprising commission to pick up some fine art for the King in Italy, went along. On the trip Harvey was as preoccupied, busy and energetic as ever, and the Earl seems to have regarded himself as the little doctor's protector. Harvey needed a protector, for he was beginning to have an absent-minded disregard for what went on around him. He was forever wandering off alone into the country to collect his eternal specimens and make his scientific observations. This was dangerous, for these were lawless times. When Harvey disappeared, the Earl worried, and when Harvey, in his abstraction, got himself lost, the Earl grew angry. Arundel seems to have regarded Harvey with an affectionate exasperation and Harvey the Earl with tolerant indifference, though sometimes the Earl's fussing exasperated him. Harvey went off on a side trip of his own and Arundel, worrying again, wrote to a friend in Florence, "I do hope I shall see the little perpetual movement called Dr. Harvey here before my going."

After a time Harvey left the diplomatic mission and set off on horseback for Venice, intending no doubt to visit Padua also. He got only as far as Treviso when he was seized by the local authorities and put into quarantine because of their fear that he might have brought the plague with him from one of the towns he had passed through. Harvey, whose temper had grown exceedingly short with advancing years—he was now fifty-eight years old—was indignant when the authorities refused to look at his *fede*, or certificate of health, which he had taken the trouble to have signed at various points along the way. He was told he must stay in the *lazaretto*, or pesthouse. He indignantly refused. Nevertheless, they sent him there. He refused to stay in the quarters he was given in the pesthouse and, burning with indignation, camped in the field outside. He was very uncomfortable and very cross. He wrote again and again to Lord Fielding in Venice, in that abominable, hurrying script of his, apologizing for this "scribbling on the grass" and begging to be got out of the place. He, a man of reason, could not comprehend why the authorities were not susceptible to reason—a common failing among the reasonable. The authorities refused to release him but they offered to give him better quarters. He was so angry at the injustice of his imprisonment that he refused to move into them. The whole affair, he declared, was as "unseasonable as phisick when a man is ded."

It was on this same trip that he undertook to meet one of the chief critics of his circulation theory, a man named Caspar Hofmann, who had been at Padua when Harvey was there. Hofmann had accused Harvey of belittling nature by claiming that the same blood was used over and over again, spoiling good blood and rejuvenating it merely to give her something to do. The story is that Harvey, who usually avoided controversy whenever he possibly could, agreed to hold an anatomy to demonstrate to Hofmann and other scientists the truth of his theory. He succeeded in convincing everyone but Hofmann, who continued to raise objections, until Harvey, utterly exasperated, threw down his dissecting knife and hurried angrily out of the theatre.

On his return to London, Harvey found that relations between the King and Parliament, which had not been good before he left, had grown seriously bad. In 1642 civil war broke out. During some of the proceedings in Parliament, Harvey's name had been brought up. It was little more than a mention, but the searchlight of publicity had picked him out, and though it rested on him only briefly, it was enough to draw attention to his royalist connections. While he was out of London with the King, an anti-royalist mob broke into his house and stole or smashed his possessions. In the course of the plundering his papers and scientific notes were destroyed. They represented years of toil, and he was deeply grieved.

From 1642 until 1648, with England torn apart by the two factions of King and Parliament, Harvey managed to lead, if not a peaceful life (which was a thing no man in England could be sure of doing in those days), at least one which was comparatively free from adventure. He was present at the Battle of Edgehill, however, where the two princes, ten and twelve years old, were turned over to him to look after. While the battle was being fought around him, Harvey retired to a ditch, where all three sat on the ground while Harvey read a book. The ditch was not well-chosen, and before they had been there long, a cannon ball struck the ground close to them and they were forced to retreat in haste. After that we hear of him helping with the wounded for a time, but he had no taste for battlefield surgery.

After Edgehill, the King retired to Oxford and turned that quiet university town into a military base and the seat of his refugee government. London was in the hands of the Parliamentarians, and Harvey, who was marked as a royalist, was forced to abandon his practice and follow Charles to Oxford. There was no more pleasant dabbling in science for the two little men, for Charles, at the head of his rapidly vanishing army, was fighting to save his kingdom.

To Oxford came trooping a throng of royalist refugees, nobles, officers, courtiers and women from every social class. There was not enough room in the town for half their number. Ladies of fashion slept in garrets on lumpy beds; cow sheds took the overflow. Food grew more and more difficult to buy. Harvey retired to the precincts of the university, but he could not wholly escape the tumult of the town. The aches and pains of age had begun to plague him, but the scholastic atmosphere of the university suited him and he resumed the research which had been interrupted by war.

He found a friend at Trinity College, a man named Bathurst, who also had a scientific turn of mind. They kept a hen in Bathurst's room to supply eggs for the research in generation which they had undertaken together, and each day opened one of the eggs to examine the stage of development of the embryonic chick.

Before the end of his first year at Oxford, the university conferred on Harvey the degree of Doctor of Physic, and in 1645 he was elected warden of Merton College, a post which he had some difficulty in filling, for Merton was impoverished and most of the students had left because of the war. Royalist refugees had moved into the deserted quarters and even into the house assigned to the warden.

Meanwhile, the King came and went, clattering into Oxford with his retinue to spend some anxious days in conferences, and departing again to fight. His army had begun to melt like wax in the sun. The enemy came slowly closer to Oxford, until the teeming city was virtually in a state of siege and the shortage of food grew acute. The end came when the King escaped from the city. With the King's departure the siege was lifted and the royalists began to flow like a tide out of Oxford. Harvey went with them and, feeling that victory had quenched the animosity of the Parliamentarians toward himself, returned to London.

He was sixty-eight years old and subject to frequent attacks of gout, which were a torture to him. His wife was dead, his practice gone, his friends defeated in the war, his personal possessions scattered or destroyed. He made no attempt to rebuild his life, and from that time on he lived with one or another of his brothers outside of London. In retirement his life was tranquil, but he was not a happy man, for no one who loved peace, tolerance and justice could be happy in those troubled years.

Charles's position went from bad to worse. Finally he was taken into custody, brought to trial and condemned to death. Cromwell was one of the signers of the order for execution. He wrote his name with a flourish, then indulged his high spirits in some horseplay with one of the other signers, each of them trying to dab the other with ink from their pens.

On the thirtieth of January, 1649, Charles was brought to Whitehall to be executed. He was led out on a high scaffold, but the people crowding the street below could see little more of him than his head over the black-draped railing. He made a short speech, then he knelt down and the railing hid the rest from view.

Harvey, filled with the weary sadness of old age, continued to live in retirement. He did not regret that his active days were finished. About a year after the King's death Harvey confided to a friend, Dr. Ent, that ". . . this life of obscurity, this vacation from public business, which causes tedium and disgust to so many, has proved a sovereign remedy to me." The two men talked of many things, Harvey speaking always with his "wonderful fluency and facility." He showed Dr. Ent

William Harvey. *Attributed to Van Dyck*

Harvey's All-But-Illegible Notes on the Circulation of the Blood

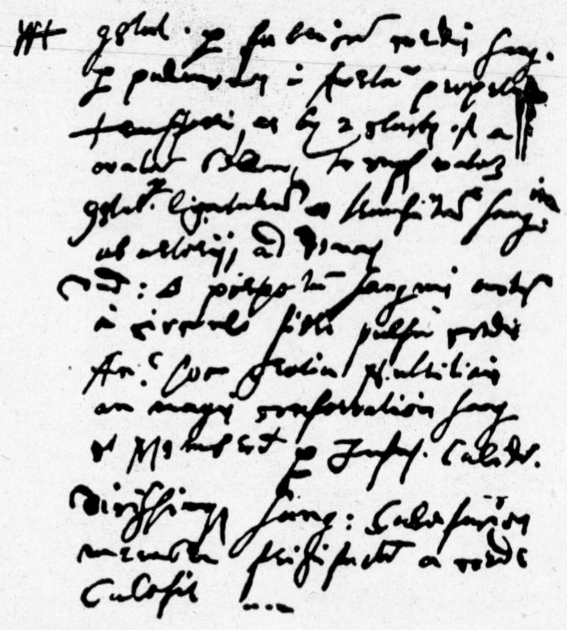

".WH Constat per fabricam cordis sanguinem per pulmones in aortam perpetuo transferri—as by two clacks of a water bellow to rays water.

"Constat per ligaturam transitum sanguinis ab arteriis ad venas.

"Unde △ [demonstratur] perpetuus sanguinis motus in circulo fieri pulsu cordis.

"An? hoc gratia nutritionis, an magis conservationis sanguinis et membrorum per infus. calidi, vicissimque sang. califaciens membra frigifactus, a corde calefit."[1]

"W-1. By the structure of the heart it appears that the blood is continually transfused through the lungs to the aorta—as by the two clacks of the water ram for raising water." (Sieveking)

John Hunter. *After Sir Joshua Reynolds*

The Lion House and the Fort on Top. *From the Collection of The Royal College of Surgeons, London.*

The Dissecting Room, *by Rowlandson*

The figure standing higher than the others is William Hunter. John Hunter is on his right-hand side.

the work he had been doing, a finished book which he had called "Exercises on the Generation of Animals." Apparently it was enough for Harvey that he had completed the studies and written the book, for he had no intention of publishing it or of involving himself in controversies once again. "Much better," he told Dr. Ent, "is it oftentimes to grow wise at home and in private, than by publishing what you have amassed with infinite labor, to stir up tempests that may rob you of peace and quiet for the rest of your days." Ent did not agree, and after a great deal of argument he persuaded Harvey to turn the book over to him for publication. He went away with the precious manuscript under his arm feeling, he says, "like another Jason laden with the golden fleece."

This book, which was published in 1654, was Harvey's last. Three years later he was elected president of the College of Physicians. This final honor he declined in a speech which contained a note of sadness and had the grace which distinguished his every meeting with the world. In 1656 he resigned from the Lumleian lectureship, his last tie with his old life. With this renouncement he passed into the final stage of his long life. He relinquished even his studies. His work was done. He spent much of his time reading, and he meditated a great deal, on the warm leads of the roof when the days were cool, in a dim cave in the earth when the weather was warm. He liked to wander in the open fields, combing his long white hair as he walked. At table he had his own private salt cellar, which he kept filled with sugar. His always precarious temper turned into the uncertain testiness of age, and he grew set in his ways, insisting on sitting down to meals exactly on time whether the company had gathered or not.

He made a will, a simple document full of homely concern for his favorite brother, to whom he left the bulk of his estate, the rest going to his two remaining friends and to his beloved College of Physicians.

Touching my books and household stuff, pictures and apparell of which I have not already disposed I give to the Colledge of Physicians my best Persia long Carpet and my blue sattin Cushion one paire of brasse Andirons with fireshovell and tongues of brasse for the ornament of the meeting roome I have erected for that purpose.

Item I give my velvet gowne to my lo friend Mr Doctor Scarborough desiring him and my lo friend Mr Doctor Ent to looke over those scattered remnant of my poore Librarie and what bookes papers or rare collections they shall see fit to present to the Colledge and the rest to be Sold and with the money buy better And for their paines I give to Mr Doctor Ent all the presses and shelves he please to make use of and five pounds to buy him a ring to keepe or weare in remembrance of me And to Doctor Scarborough All my little silver instruments of surgerie.

Harvey died in 1657 at his brother Eliab's house. He was in his eightieth year, weakened by gout but with unclouded mind. His body was encased in lead, a custom followed by the Harvey family, and laid in a chapel which Eliab had built at Hampstead. There it remained, while for 226 years rain from the glassless window beat on the slowly corroding lead. There, in 1883, it was found and moved to a tomb in Hampstead Church in a final ceremony held, appropriately enough, on Saint Luke's Day.

IV.

Throughout the history of surgery there has been a constant pendulum swing between theory and practice. For a long period of time, practice may lead, and during this phase surgeons may use techniques which they have found to be successful without understanding the reason why they succeed. This may continue for some time until discoveries are made which explain the principles underlying the successful practices, with the result that surgeons not only know what to do but why their techniques succeed. In other words, theory has caught up with practice, making further technical advance possible. Progress may be made in either phase, but the degree of progress is limited unless one keeps approximate pace with the other.

With Harvey's discovery of the circulation of the blood, the pendulum swung from practice to theory. Paré had reintroduced the ligature; Harvey explained the principles involved in its use, and thereafter when a surgeon tied off a blood vessel he did it in awareness of the relation that the vessel bore to the whole cycle-flow of blood. The use of the ligature and of the tourniquet improved after Harvey's discovery, though the change came slowly, and technicians have never ceased to make improvements on the various forms of hemostasis. The deluge of blood which flowed at every operation gradually began to diminish, and the death rate from uncontrolled bleeding went slowly down. With Harvey's discovery of the circulation of the blood, the first of the four great barriers across the path of surgical progress had been cleared away.

Scientists continued to examine the world and the human body with the new precision instruments and to make discoveries which changed radically their views of man and the universe. They looked through the telescope at the stars, learned that the earth was only one of many worlds and saw man and God in new perspective. They peered into their thirty-two-power microscopes and discovered another unsuspected world in miniature.

Malpighi (1628–1694), an unassuming, cheerful, warm-hearted Italian doctor, used his microscope on the circulatory system and in 1661 discovered the missing link in Harvey's theory, the capillary openings between the small arteries and the veins. Athanasius Kircher (1602–1680), a German Jesuit working in Italy, was the first to study disease with a microscope, and he discovered, to his astonishment, quantities of little "worms" in putrefying matter and in the blood of plague victims, though in the latter he was probably seeing corpuscles and not microorganisms. Leeuwenhoek (1632–1723), a Dutchman who owned 247 microscopes and 419 lenses, turned his glass on everything from cheese to semen and discovered a teeming world of microbes, which he delightedly called his "little animals." He saw them gathered in chains and clumps, he saw the red corpuscles and discovered spermatozoa, and wrote excitedly about his finds.

London had been a more healthful city since the great fire of 1666 had consumed the rabbit-warren dwellings left from the Middle Ages. More light and air was allowed to come into the new houses, but the connection between dirt and disease was not yet understood, and in the new parts of the city sanitary conditions were only slightly improved. Sewage was still all too apt to find its way into sources of drinking water, and when it rained, the gutters turned into miniature rivers:

Filth of all hues and odors seemed to tell
What streets they sailed from, by their sight and smell.

Sweepings from butchers' stalls, dung, guts and blood,
Drowned puppies, stinking sprats, all drenched in mud,
Dead cats and turnip-tops came tumbling down the flood.

The atrophied social conscience of London, which had produced the social decline of the seventeenth century, was slowly reawakening, however. Hospitals, which had been at a low ebb, began to reorganize and expand. Saint Bartholomew's and Saint Thomas' attracted the better surgeons, of whom there were an increasing number in late-seventeenth-century London, and these men in turn attracted younger men who came to the hospitals as students and members of the staffs.

Such groups as these were the nuclei of the great medical schools of the future. Harvey Graham (Isaac Harvey Flack) makes the comment that the theatres of these hospitals had as many patients passing through them in a day as the Barber-Surgeons Hall had bodies for dissection in a year. The hospital teaching and the work of the excellent private schools of anatomy, which were opening all over England, soon put a stop to the old system of education by which a student apprenticed himself for a time to the Barber-Surgeons Company.

One of the immediate effects of these changes was a further increase in the number of good surgeons, those reliable hard-working men whose names seldom appear on the pages of history. Then, as now, surgeons may be separated into three groups, the great, the good and the mediocre or worse. This book is concerned primarily with the great, of whom in the sixteenth and seventeenth and early eighteenth centuries there was only about one in a generation. And then, as now, the group immediately below the great (the group of "good" surgeons) was responsible for putting the discoveries of the great into practice, and for maintaining surgical standards. In the late seventeenth and early eighteenth centuries, the "good" surgeons were becoming increasingly dissatisfied with their association with the barbers, a dissatisfaction augmented when the Barber-Surgeons Company, for financial reasons, formed an alliance with the wig-makers. The good surgeons were beginning, with reason, to regard themselves as gentlemen, and the social stigma of being associated with razors and wigs was exceedingly distasteful to them. The mediocre element in the Barber-Surgeons Company had, moreover, opposed the hospital system of education and other forms of progress sponsored by the leading men. Tension grew until, in 1745, the break finally came, and the surgeons were free to control their own professional destiny.

With the beginning of the eighteenth century the interest in anatomy, which had been superseded by the discoveries in the realm of physiology during the preceding century, underwent an important revival. All that had previously been learned of "dead" anatomy was reexamined in the light of physiology, with the aid of precision instruments and the technique of injecting the circulatory system of the cadaver with a colored substance—a by-product of Harvey's discovery—which made the veins and arteries easier to study. Much anatomical work was carried on in the private schools of anatomy, and toward the middle of the century the work began to focus on pathological anatomy, the study of special conditions produced in the body by disease. This trend was given tremendous impetus by the work of one man, a picturesque surgeon named John Hunter, the first of the great surgical pathologists.

John Hunter

1728–1793

"Jesse Foot accuses me of not understanding the dead language but I could teach him that on the dead body which he never knew in any language, living or dead." —*John Hunter*

John Hunter was born in the southeast of Scotland, on a farm called Long Calderwood, seven miles from Glasgow. This is a country of wind-swept moors, where the waters of the brooks run amber brown from the seepings of the peat, a country where the winter chill lingers long into the damp spring. The soil of the farm was poor, the yield scant and the family lived in close touch with poverty, but John's father was a "bonnet laird" who brought his children up properly and educated the boys, though to do it he had to sell off pieces of his land from time to time.

John, the youngest, was born in a bare little room over the kitchen, just under the thatched roof of the stone house. The year was 1728, the month was February, but the church records and the family Bible do not agree about the date, which may have been the thirteenth or the fourteenth or possibly the ninth. He was the youngest of ten children, but three of them died in childhood and four in the prime of life. Tuberculosis was all through that countryside in those days, and dreary little processions were forever leaving these damp stone homes to carry some member of the family off to the crowded churchyard. Merely to survive from one hard year to the next used up a great deal of vitality, and anyone who succeeded in rising above such conditions and making a name for himself had to have a most unusual amount of mental and physical stamina.

John was a short, stocky child, with a thatch of reddish hair and light gray-blue eyes. His mother spoiled him because he was her youngest and the last baby she could have. His father was well on in years, and while John was growing up he was too ill to discipline this boy as he had the others. As a result, "Jackie" grew into a stubborn, willful, disobedient boy, a great trial to everyone and probably to himself. When he couldn't get what he wanted he would cry for it, even when he was quite a big lad, and keep right on crying for hours, if need be, until he got his way. It proved he had persistence, if nothing else, but his parents understandably saw no good in it. And as John grew older, they were distressed to find that he was interested in little but the birds and small animals which he found under the hedges and in the fields. Later, John remembered this time with amusement and wrote, "I pestered people with questions about what nobody knew or cared anything about," a sentence which he might have constructed with more craftsmanship if he had taken more interest in his schoolbooks. It never occurred to anyone that his absorption with nature could turn into anything useful.

His parents sent their problem child to a grammar school in the nearby town of Kilbride, and if they didn't expect much good to come of it, they proved to be entirely right. John hated school. He was shorter than the other boys of his age, but in spite of that, or more likely because of it, he was quarrelsome, intractable and independent. He refused to study his lessons and no one could force him to do it. The only mark that Kilbride left on him was a hatred of book-learning which lasted all the rest of his life.

The two earnest, upright people who had brought John into the world were, of course, bitterly disappointed, the more so because the two older brothers, William and James (whom they called "Wullie" and "Jamie"), were showing signs of becoming everything their parents could desire. William, who was ten years older than John, had been studying for the ministry in Glasgow, but he had given it up for reasons of conscience and was now assistant to a country doctor named Cullen. William was able, industrious and well-bred—in short, everything which John was not. Cullen said of him in later years, "His whole conduct was more strictly and steadily correct than that of any other young person I have ever known." Such rectitude as that can be pretty trying to a boy when it is constantly held up to him as a model. John grew up with this example of the perfect William forever before his eyes, and it is easy to believe that this was the main cause of his rebellious behavior.

The other brother, James, who was in Glasgow studying to be a lawyer, was, if possible, even more brilliant and promising than William, though at this distance he fails to give the same impression of infallible righteousness. It was William who was the elder and who would some day be head of the family. The dignity and authority of that position were already beginning to show in his manner, and the red-headed scamp, John, was thoroughly tired of his virtues.

John's father's health was failing more and more. He could no longer work the farm, which was the family's only source of income, and often he "was kept awake in the night from thinking upon the difficulties of his situation." He died in the winter of 1741, when John was thirteen years old, and John's mother took him out of school, which had proved a waste of time and money anyway, to help her do what she could to keep the farm going. He couldn't have been much use to her, for his mind was still on those animals and birds' nests he was forever discovering, and a plow is a heavy implement for a thirteen-year-old boy.

William, in the meantime, had gone to London with glowing recommendations from the good Cullen. There he formed a sort of partnership with a Dr. Douglas and became engaged to his daughter, Martha Jane. He studied surgery at Saint George's Hospital, where he again impressed everyone with his ability and character, and the future looked so bright that on the strength of it James went to join his brother in London, where he too began to study medicine. The black sheep stayed at home on the farm.

He stayed there until he was seventeen, a youth without an aptitude for any useful occupation. He did have a certain manual dexterity, however, and it may have been this ability to use his hands which gave his mother the idea of sending him on a visit to his brother-in-law, who was a cabinetmaker in Glasgow. His name was Buchanan. He was charming, lazy, and he loved music and good company. John's older sister, Janet, had married him much against the wishes of her family. Buchanan was neglecting his woodworking shop for his friends in the tavern, and Janet and Mrs. Hunter seem to have had the fatuous hope that, if Buchanan had John to help in the shop, he might pay some attention to business. Nothing like that happened, of course. John had been there only a few months when Buchanan went bankrupt for good, and the shop was taken away from him. John went home again and shortly afterward Janet died. Buchanan took to earning a precarious living as a clerk and a music teacher—after which he fades gently from view.

So there was John, back on his mother's hands, and the problem of what to do with him still unsolved. There followed an avalanche of trouble. First, William's benefactor, Dr. Douglas, died, then William's fiancée, Martha Jane, followed him to the grave, and William was so stricken with grief that what little lightheartedness he had once possessed vanished forever. Then James, the "Jamie" whom William loved as the image of himself, began to show alarming symptoms of disease. He grew rapidly worse until there could be no doubt that he had in his turn contracted tuberculosis. He gave up his work and went home to the damp stone house at Long Calderwood, which was probably the worst possible place for him, and there he died.

John was now twenty, with nothing to look forward to but a lifetime on the gloomy farm, a prospect which filled him with restless discontent. In London, William was working doggedly on toward the success which everyone had predicted for him. Finally John reached the point where he could stand the life at Long Calderwood no longer, and he wrote to William asking to be allowed to join him in London, saying, in a frenzy of despair, that he would go off to join the army if William refused. William not only had a strong sense of duty toward the family of which he was now the head, but he had reached the point in his work where he needed an assistant, and so he replied with his customary graciousness, saying that he would be pleased to have John come. In the fall of 1748, John set out on horseback for the great adventure. A friend went with him and quite possibly both lads rode the same horse. His mother never saw him again. The trip to London took two weeks, and John, every inch the country bumpkin, with no money to speak of, arrived to find to his astonishment that brother William had become a polished London gentleman.

William was then establishing his own private school of anatomy, and he put John to work at once dissecting an arm to be used in a lecture he was about to give. John was familiar enough with the sight of death from his own family experience, and he may have done considerable dissecting of the wild life he came across in his ramblings at Long Calderwood. He dissected the arm so well that William was pleased with him and soon gave him another arm to work on, one in which the blood vessels had been injected with colored wax in order to make them easier to see. This was a technique which William had learned on a trip to Europe. He was the first to introduce it into England, and it revolutionized the teaching of anatomy. John's task was to expose these brightly colored veins and the muscles by cutting away the flesh and fat. It was delicate, fussy work and he performed it well, for he had at last found an occupation which he liked.

The two brothers got along together smoothly enough, considering the difference in their temperaments. John threw himself into the fascinating work of the dissecting room as though he were trying to make up for all the starved years. William was astonished and pleased, for it was evident that John was no longer going to be a family problem, though William made up his mind that John must be given at least a little education and some of the polish which he himself had been at such pains to acquire. He was sincerely proud of young Jackie, and if he let himself become a trifle patronizing, John was too grateful for all William had done and too much absorbed in his work to harbor the old resentment.

William's school was for many years the best in London, and the only one where each student was supplied with a body to dissect, an ideal arrangement which is not possible today, when commonly four students, alternating places, work on one cadaver. There was no legal way in which William could procure bodies. The laws permitted the dissecting of executed criminals and suicides, but such of these as there were—and the supply was totally inadequate—were allocated to the universities and the medical corporations, but none to the private schools. The laws were old and needed revising, for at the same time that they failed to produce an adequate supply of cadavers, they also stipulated that before a student could be given a degree he must be able to show that he had dissected a certain number of bodies. It was this contradiction that gave rise to the private anatomy schools, which bought their bodies from the black market and had, therefore, a supply limited only by their means and the enterprise of the grave robbers.

Right down to the present time, procuring enough bodies for study has been a constant problem. In this country, even after the passage of the anatomy laws by the state legislatures in the nineteenth century, medical schools often simply passed the problem on to the student, requiring him to show up in class with a body to work on, exactly as they required him to supply his own textbooks. In England, a great change had taken place in body-snatching since Vesalius stole out of Paris at night to rob the gallows of Montfaçon. It was big business, illegal, of course, but well organized, with middlemen—popularly known as "resurrectionists" or "sack-em-up men"—who held a monopoly of the field, fought gang wars, resisted the intrusion of newcomers and conducted blackmail operations in the classic style of our prohibition era.

The resurrectionist had a price scale which fluctuated with the market. A good corpse, unmutilated, fresh, of a person who had not died of the dreaded smallpox, cost at this time in the neighborhood of two guineas, or a little over ten dollars. In time the price rose to eight guineas, or forty-one dollars, and once, at least, in the next century, it went to twice that amount. The resurrectionists worked only in winter, and then only in the dark of the moon, but even so a skillful man could dispose of approximately three hundred to three hundred and fifty bodies a year. At two guineas each, that amounted to three thousand dollars or more for a season's work, which was a princely income in those days. Toward the beginning of the new century the schools were forced to pay the resurrectionists a retainer fee, which was nothing more or less than blackmail, in addition to the price of the bodies, and eventually also a "finishing fee" at the time when warm spring weather forced the closing of the schools.

The business developed a slang of its own. A body was a "thing," a "crib" was a burying ground, and a "hole" a grave. "Go out to look," meant going out to watch for and follow funerals to see where the body was being taken. The funeral itself was called a "black." A "large" was an adult body and a "small" was one under three feet long.

There was also a profitable by-product of the industry in the sale of "canines," which is to say, the two canine teeth and the four front teeth between them. These are single-rooted teeth, easy to extract, and they were in great demand for the making of dentures, the back ones which didn't show commonly being made of wood. In a day when teeth were pulled out instead of being filled, an enormous quantity of "canines" was needed to keep up with the demand, and a good set brought eleven shillings, or about $1.75. Cemeteries, however, were not the only source of supply for teeth, and the resurrectionists had a certain amount of competition from men who roamed the field of a recent battle, collecting teeth from the dead. This happened, for example, after Waterloo.

If the local supply of bodies gave out, the organized network of grave robbers shipped them, either fresh or pickled in brine, from some place where the yield of the cemeteries was currently greater. The industry had its hangers-on, the barmaids who informed the resurrectionists of recent deaths in the neighborhood, the prostitutes who, dressed in black, went to the cemeteries to note the location of a new grave and to discover, while kneeling beside it in fake tears, whether the wilting floral tributes concealed the trip-wires of a spring gun. If some doctor whom one of these resurrectionists considered his exclusive customer bought bodies from a rival, the resurrectionist would hire an accomplice, who was usually a woman, to stand in the street outside the doctor's establishment, weeping and wailing and lamenting to the quickly gathering crowd that someone dear to her was being cut up into little pieces on the dissecting table inside. The crowd seldom failed to storm the place, wreck it or burn it to the ground. Good and bad motives may become inextricably mixed when legislation does not keep pace with the changing demands of an expanding society.

It was John who was charged with purchasing bodies from the resurrectionists and he who received them when they were delivered to the school secretly by night. John, the young dissecting room assistant, was still an uncouth lad, in spite of William's efforts to civilize him. He was vigorous, quick-tempered and rapidly changing his country coarseness for the special brand of city coarseness which was current in this tough, rowdy period of London's history. He made friends with the resurrectionists and other roistering characters, he loved to go to the taverns or to sit in the pit of some theatre and join in the heckling of the actors. Coarse behavior has been a traditional refuge of the medical student, who, right down through the ages, up to and including our times, has reacted to the shocks of the dissecting room in this way. John was, no doubt, doing just that. Also, his old resentment against William was building up again and no doubt he thoroughly enjoyed behaving in a way of which William was sure to disapprove. If William were going to make himself into the perfect gentleman, then a gentleman was the last thing in the world John wanted to be.

John, who had never worked seriously at anything before,

worked now literally from daylight until dark, preparing specimens, preserving them in spirits and carrying out dissections on his own account. It was the worst possible work for a boy with a tendency toward weak lungs. The dissecting was done in a room without any windows, to keep curious outsiders from seeing what went on. There were no preservatives used in those days, and though, for precisely this reason, the work was done only in winter, the stench in the closed room must often have been almost overpowering. Moreover, handling these rotting bodies was a risky business and the dissector had to take great care, for even a slight scratch was likely to become infected and many a medical student in those days died from what was called "corpse poisoning."

Contrast that reeking room with the premises of a modern department of anatomy. The dissecting room today is as aseptic as a hospital—more so, perhaps. The light is excellent, walls and fixtures gleaming white, all the paraphernalia neat and clean. There is usually a chapel nearby. Only the part of the cadaver being worked on is uncovered. It is no scene of horror, but one so permeated with the spirit of science that the layman scarcely experiences any shock. There is a smell, it is true, but a faint one—the odor of disinfectant, not of death.

Through William's influence, which in one way or another controlled everything he did, John was permitted to work at Chelsea Hospital in the summer, when the school was closed. There he was under the eye of an exceedingly able surgeon named Cheselden. There he learned the rudiments of surgery as he watched the great man at work. When the winter of 1750 came around, John began to help a little with the teaching in William's school, but he was exceedingly shy of standing up in front of a group of students, a difficulty which stayed with him all the rest of his life. Then Cheselden died and John became a student at Saint Bartholomew's. It wasn't much of a surgical education by our standards, and the best part of it was the eternal dissecting, to which he gave up every spare minute in the winter season. He was learning fast, displaying an aptitude which nobody had suspected he possessed.

It soon became evident that John would some day be an eminent man in his field, and it must be said for William that he never showed the slightest jealousy of his young protégé or made any attempt to stand in the way of his advancement. There was certainly no reason for jealousy, for William himself was advancing fast into a lucrative and fashionable practice outside of the school. Moreover, he was making plans to abandon surgery in favor of what was then regarded as the more dignified profession of medicine, a complicated step in those days, which involved making an official renunciation of the one before being permitted to practice the other.

But if William was not jealous of John's ability, neither was he satisfied with his young brother's lack of refinement and education, and no doubt he was convinced that this deficiency would prevent John from making the fullest use of his talents —a sound piece of reasoning if there ever was one, the only flaw in it being that it didn't turn out to be true. So once more William did the right thing for John, who already owed him everything. He sent him to study at Oxford. By doing this he was not only committing himself to a considerable outlay of money but also depriving himself of the best assistant he could ever hope to find. It was a really generous gesture, but somehow it is not possible to feel any warmth for this living example of all the virtues. It is the uncouth John—who had never done a conspicuously disinterested deed in his life, who seemed to have no ambition and little sense of duty—that never fails to inspire both liking and sympathy.

At this period of its history, Oxford was leisurely to the point of torpidity, which tried exceedingly the patience of a lad who was accustomed to packing as much into twenty-four hours as John. And the young gentlemen of the college must have seemed fairly insipid to him, compared to his companions among the resurrectionists and roisterers of London. Book-learning he liked no better than he had at the grammar school in Kilbride, and at the end of two months, he left. In after years he was proud—a trifle belligerently so—of having taken his departure, for he wrote, "They [by whom he meant William, of course] wanted to make an old woman of me; or that I should stuff Latin and Greek . . . these schemes I cracked like so many vermin as they came before me."

So back he went happily to the old life among the spirit jars, human fragments and foul air of William's school. Thanks to William's influence, he was taken in as a student at Saint George's Hospital. A staff appointment came in due course, and he maintained his association with Saint George's for the next quarter-century.

All this time both William and John were making anatomical discoveries which William presented to the medical world. William was always meticulous in giving credit to John whenever he merited it, even going so far as to acknowledge that in certain subjects he was no more than John's interpreter. It was kind of William, but the truth is that at this time John was not equal to writing and presenting a paper on his own account. He had an almost psychopathic dread of the lecture platform, and he wrote so badly that to the end of his days his friends found it necessary to edit his grammar and correct his spelling. John should, of course, have been grateful to William for placing his work before the public, and he may have thought he was, but the first time William failed to give the credit John believed was due him, he was far more angry than the occasion justified.

In 1759, when he was thirty-one years old, he was taken sick with a severe case of pneumonia from which he did not recover very well. Then the dreaded symptoms of the family scourge began to show in him, and though the fresh-air cure for tuberculosis was not known in those days, it was clear to everyone that he must get away from the hard work and the unwholesome surroundings of the anatomy school. A sea voyage was recommended, which would have been beyond the brothers' means had not the happy solution occurred to them of sending John as an army surgeon to the war on the Continent between the Austrians and the Prussians—later known as the Seven Years War (1756–1763)—in which England was allied with the Prussians. So William used his endless influence once more, this time with Robin Adair, Inspector General of Hospitals. Robin Adair was an able surgeon, but he is remembered now chiefly by the familiar song which was written about him:

What made the assembly shine?
Robin Adair!
What made the ball so fine?
Robin was there!
What, when the play was o'er
What made my heart so sore?
O, it was parting with
Robin Adair.
[*Second Stanza*]

Robin Adair gave John the appointment and John sailed with the fleet for Belle Isle in the spring of 1761. This was the first time since he had gone to London that John had been away from William's watchfulness for any considerable length of time, and though he was subject to army discipline, he must have rejoiced in his freedom. With distance between them, he seems to have grown suddenly much fonder of his guardian brother, or conceivably the knowledge that William's influence at home could help him to promotion had something to do with it, but whatever the reason, his letters to William were almost affectionate.

About a paper which William had recently presented, John wrote, "I think my name will live now that it is joined with yours." And again, "I am very much obliged to you for the trouble that you have been at in enquiring after my future steps that I am to take; and shall beg your assistance, in letting me know any news that may concern me, with your opinion of it. . . ." John meant by this that he would like any information William might hear in high quarters about where the army was likely to send him next, for he had already made the soldier's discovery that it is well to have a friend to speak for him at home. As might be expected, John found the men he had to work with a "damn'd disagreeable set" and declared that the two heads of the army hospital where he worked were as "unfit for their employment as the devil was to reign in Heaven." It was the age-old army gripe.

The first action he saw was an amphibious attack on Belle Isle in flat-bottomed boats. It was repulsed not long after it hit the beach, but a second attempt established a beachhead and drove inland. It was some time, however, before all the pockets of resistance on the heights were overcome. John had plenty of work with the wounded, and then he was ordered off to Portugal, which was an ally of England against Spain. Here he worried about promotion and wrote that if he received a certain appointment which he hoped for, "I shall be a Dr. as well as the best of you."

In Portugal he found out for the first time since he had left Long Calderwood what it was like not to have enough to do, and his boyhood curiosity about nature came back in full force. On Belle Isle he had somehow found time to study hibernating animals, and here in Portugal he stretched himself out on his stomach by a fish pond in a nobleman's garden, watching the fish while a friend fired a gun, to see if they showed evidence of hearing. He wrote papers on both these subjects, but the great piece of work which resulted from his army service, his famous *Treatise on the Blood, Inflammation and Gunshot Wounds*, was not published until thirty years later, a time lag which today, with the rapid changes in weapons, would have made his observations out of date.

When the peace was signed, John returned to London and,

taking advantage of the fact that he was still on half-pay from the army, set himself up as a private practitioner of surgery.

He was now thirty-five, and for the first time in his life he was free of surveillance of any kind. He chose not to go back to William and the school, though thirty-five was rather old in those days to be setting up in practice for himself. The restrictions under which he had lived in the past had not been really severe, but they had irked him nevertheless and kept him from maturing, and now that he was on his own there followed the most extraordinary outburst of personality. It was a regular explosion. He threw all his astonishing energy into arranging his life exactly as he wanted it, displaying in the process traits and tastes which no one had ever suspected he possessed. No one ever enjoyed himself more. As soon as he was sufficiently established in town he bought himself two acres of ground at Earl's Court, and though his financial situation most certainly did not warrant it, he built himself a house there—not to live in, for he could not leave his tiny practice, but to go to whenever he could get away for a day or two.

All his imagination went into the designing of that house, and the result was startling even in a day when façades of country houses not infrequently leaned toward the fanciful. Over the door there was carved a crocodile with gaping mouth, and scattered around the lawns were statues of lions rampant and lions couchant. There were two cairns of sea shells and a huge mound of earth over a den where live lions were kept. The den was at the back and to the right of the house, so placed that he could watch the lions from his sitting-room window, and from the top there was a fine view of Westminster Abbey. Hunter crowned the earth mound with a miniature fort in which he mounted a small gun, and whenever he was feeling more than usually exuberant, he would rush out of the house, scramble up the mound and fire the gun. That seemed to relieve some of his emotional pressures.

The truly bizarre feature of the place, however, was the

menagerie, animals both domestic and wild. In addition to the lions, there were buffaloes and shawl goats, dogs, chickens—any sort of beast he could beg or buy, the more exotic the better. He kept an ostrich in the cow house, and he built a pond where he tried to harry Scotch river mussels into growing pearls. He even had a pair of leopards which he kept in the lions' den while he was temporarily out of lions. Once the leopards escaped, and the little surgeon seized one around the middle as it was about to climb a fence, and hauled it down. The leopards, who were probably too astonished by this whirlwind attack to turn on him, were shut up again, and when Hunter realized what he had done he collapsed in a state which was just short of a faint.

Hunter acquired these animal specimens of his—they can scarcely be called pets—in any condition whatever. Their state of decrepitude made no difference to him. He got some of them from the keeper of the menagerie at the Tower, some he bought from traveling shows. Anyone who had a beast he wanted to get rid of could send it to Hunter, and once the Queen herself donated three elephants. One of them was cumbersomely dead, but that made not the slightest difference to John Hunter, for the ultimate destination of all these creatures was the dissecting table. Once he begged a friend who was going on a voyage to send him a whale, and when segments of one actually arrived he was delighted.

Sometimes he preserved the skeletons of his dead animals, boiling the flesh off the bones in a huge copper vat, into which, it must be said, not merely bones from animals found their way. Certain parts of his specimens that interested him especially—and almost every part of every beast interested him—he dried or preserved in jars filled with spirits. Before long he had accumulated a great many queer and outlandish items, which became the start of his great collection, known today as the Hunterian Museum. He worked and worked, the hours of the day were never long enough, and the smell of his great boilings must have filled the whole neighborhood, not to mention the lesser but still pungent odors which filled the house. He was learning a great deal. He was already a fine anatomist and now he was building up, little by little, a vast store of knowledge in comparative anatomy and pathology as well. No one had ever known so much about these subjects before, and it was quite a while before anyone did again.

Looking back at Hunter at Earl's Court—short, tubby, energetic, firing his toy cannon, lugging some huge carcass or cooking up some noisome brew—it is impossible to keep a wholly straight face, even though we know how invaluable his work was rapidly becoming. Most of his contemporaries didn't even try. He was laughed at everywhere and only saved from being considered a hopeless eccentric by the wonderful skill he showed when he operated and by the unexpected pieces of useful knowledge he was able to produce about disease. Almost no one came to see his collection, though he himself used it as another sort of scholar might use a library, turning out an incredible quantity of scientific papers on a wide range of subjects.

Earl's Court during the latter part of its history, after Hunter's death, was used as an insane asylum. In 1886 the property was sold at auction. At that time the lions' mound was still standing and some of the trees still showed traces of Hunter's experiments with grafting. Subsequently, the house was torn down.

Hunter thoroughly enjoyed his reputation for eccentricity, and sometimes he went out of his way to foster it, as on the occasion when he drove a buffalo in harness through the streets of London. Perhaps in this sort of behavior he was still showing his rebellion against brother William, who had been growing more distinguished and conservative and fashionable all the time. They had been seeing less and less of each other as it grew increasingly difficult for them to meet without disagreeing. Eventually there was a complete estrangement, but by the time that happened, dislike of everything William stood for had grown to be second nature to John. William had become a symbol.

William's poise and the perfection of his deportment may also have been responsible for John's shyness, by making him perpetually aware of his own deficiencies. Eccentricity is a strange sort of armor for a shy person to put on, but that is often what it amounts to. He never really overcame his self-consciousness, even before his own students. The thought of beginning a course of lectures so tormented him that he usually fortified himself for the ordeal by taking a good stiff dose of laudanum.

A revolt against convention in general, no matter what inspired it, was probably the best thing that could have happened to John, for he discarded medical conventions along with the others. The effect of that was an extraordinarily clear-sighted approach to the problems of his profession. With the inquisitiveness of the born research worker, caring not a fig what dogmas he outraged, he opened doors which had never been opened before and left them open for those who followed him.

John was well liked, even loved, by his friends of both sexes, who referred to him as "that dear man." He was good company, full of life and always boiling over with ideas. He was one of those people who inspire very positive feelings in others, either of liking or dislike. As he grew older, his circle of friends increased and his enemies grew more heated. His practice was not large—he was earning scarcely a thousand pounds a year—but he had become a very able surgeon and his operating technique was so good that others were forced to improve their own. In 1767 he was elected a Fellow of the Royal Society, an honor which he relished the more because it was given to him before it was given to brother William.

His collection had grown very large, and he was taking time away from sleep in order to work on it. He had to employ a number of people to help him look after it, and it all cost him a great deal more money than he could afford. He had come to look on private practice chiefly as a means of earning more to spend, but he never seemed to catch up with what he considered to be his needs. When he was short of cash he borrowed, and no rarity was too expensive for him.

In middle life, quite suddenly and with his customary violence, he fell in love with a talented, well-educated girl named Anne Home. He could not marry her at once, however, for there was that eternal problem of money. Then, before he solved it, in the course of some laboratory experiments with what he thought was only gonorrhoea pus, he accidentally gave himself syphilis, and marriage for the time was out of the question. He had inoculated himself with the gonorrhoea pus, and the spirochetes of syphilis, which were also present, took a firm hold on him. He watched the progress of his disease with great interest, but he had to treat himself with mercury off and on for the next three years. Later, he wrote a treatise on venereal disease, and the characteristic sore which commonly develops at the place of entrance of the infection is to this day known as the Hunter chancre.

By 1771 he felt himself to be in condition to marry, and he wrote to his brother William, with whom he had not yet had his final quarrel:

Dear Brother: Tomorrow morning at eight o'clock and at St. Jame's Church, I enter into the Holy State of Matrimony. As that is a ceremony which you are not particularly fond of, I will not make a point of having your company there. I propose going out of Town for a few days; when I come to Town I shall call upon you. Married or not married, ever yours, John Hunter.

The "few days" were spent at Earl's Court, of all places, in the company of its beasts and smells and pale, diseased organs floating in their spirit jars.

John was now forty-three and Anne was twenty-nine. She had good looks, great dignity and a liking for social life, for which she had a rather special gift. She enjoyed giving parties, and many distinguished people came to them, but sometimes when John arrived at home to find the house full of guests, he was annoyed, for he had begun to curtail his own sociability in order to lengthen his working hours. Anne wrote poetry—not silly rhymes, like other young ladies of her day, but serious verses of real merit. The words of the song, "My Mother Bids Me Bind My Hair," are hers, and also the words of Haydn's *Creation.*

On the surface, the match between this irascible little surgeon and this worldly, charming lady-poet seems a strange one, especially as some of the qualities which he admired in her were very much the same as those he had resented in brother William, but he loved his "Anny" and she loved him, though he was not exactly a romantic figure. He was bald, with a bushy fringe of hair over his ears. His waistline had long since disappeared, he was not very neat about his dress and there must have been a faint aroma of the collection always with him. Her house was constantly full of a miscellany of students—who lived there—surgeons and other scientific folk whose shop talk would not have been to the taste of every young lady. On the other hand, John was undeniably a most stimulating person, and in those hours when they were together—which were growing fewer as he worked harder and harder—she found him an excellent companion.

Two years after his marriage he had his first attack of angina pectoris, and three years later he had a much more severe one. The average man would regard such an experience as a warning and take steps to curtail his activities, but on Hunter it had the opposite effect. At this time he may not have known the exact nature of his disease, but, great pathologist that he was, he could not have failed to realize its seriousness. Nevertheless, he merely conceded a brief vacation at Bath, and from that time on he increased his work load and shortened his hours of rest. As though the intimation of mortality had brought home to him how much there still remained to accomplish, he threw himself into his work in a manner approaching frenzy. And from this time on the attacks of angina recurred with increasing frequency.

His collection had always been conceived on a grand scale. Now he made ambitious plans for enlarging it. He fairly bombarded his friends with letters asking them to send him specimens. His most regular correspondent was his friend and pupil, Edward Jenner, that same Jenner who is famous for discovering the smallpox vaccine. "Have you made," Hunter wrote, "any experiments with hedgehogs, and can you send me some this spring? for all those you sent me died and I am hedgehogless."

The hedgehogs came and he demanded more. "Frogs," he wrote, "live an amazing time after they are dead," and no doubt Jenner knew what he meant by that. He asked for young blackbirds in spirits and for nests and fossils. Previously, he had written, "I want a nest with eggs in it; also one with a young cuckoo. I hear you saying, there is no end to your wants." And again, "Have you any eaves where bats go at night?" Sometimes he forgot what he had already written, for he was very tired these days, and his acknowledgments of forgetfulness had a pathetic sound. He was driving himself by the strength of his will alone.

In 1783 he added the prize specimen of them all. He had heard about an Irish giant, named Byrne or O'Brien, who was appearing in a London freak show. That was an evil day for O'Brien, for the moment Hunter laid eyes on the giant he made up his mind that he must some day have the skeleton of that giant for his collection. There are various versions about what happened then, but apparently Hunter put the matter to him plainly, explaining to O'Brien that giants did not, as a rule, live very long, and that, since so huge a carcass was a medical curiosity of the first order, he ought to be willing to let his remains be dissected in the interests of science. O'Brien was, quite understandably, horrified. He wanted neither to die young nor to be stretched on a dissecting table afterward. The bumptious little surgeon threw him into panic, and he fled.

Hunter, of course, pursued. There followed a grim game of hide-and-seek, the giant frantically moving from one lodging to another and Hunter always tracking him down again. Tracking a man who stands seven feet seven inches is not, after all, very difficult. Hunter turned the sleuthing over to a servant named Howison and, biding his time, went back to work.

For O'Brien the shadowing began to have the aspect of a nightmare; wherever he went, there too would be this man Howison, silently watching and waiting. It was all the worse because, in accordance with Hunter's prophecy, the giant had begun to feel not so very well. He took to his bed, certain that death was near, and he made every arrangement he could think of to prevent his dead body from falling into Hunter's hands, directing that as soon as possible after he had breathed his last, his body was to be put into a lead coffin, taken on a ship to the middle of the Irish Channel and there sunk. Until these arrangements could be carried out, his body was to be watched ceaselessly, night and day, by men hired for the purpose.

So at the age of twenty-two the giant died—happy, we hope, in the belief that he had outsmarted Hunter. At this point Hunter relieved Howison and took over himself. He waylaid one of the watchers, bought him drinks in a tavern and offered to pay him and his companions fifty pounds if they would deliver the body to him. It must have taken a great many drinks and a great deal of conferring, for in the end the offer was raised to, it is said, five hundred pounds, or about twenty-five hundred dollars. Hunter, who was perpetually

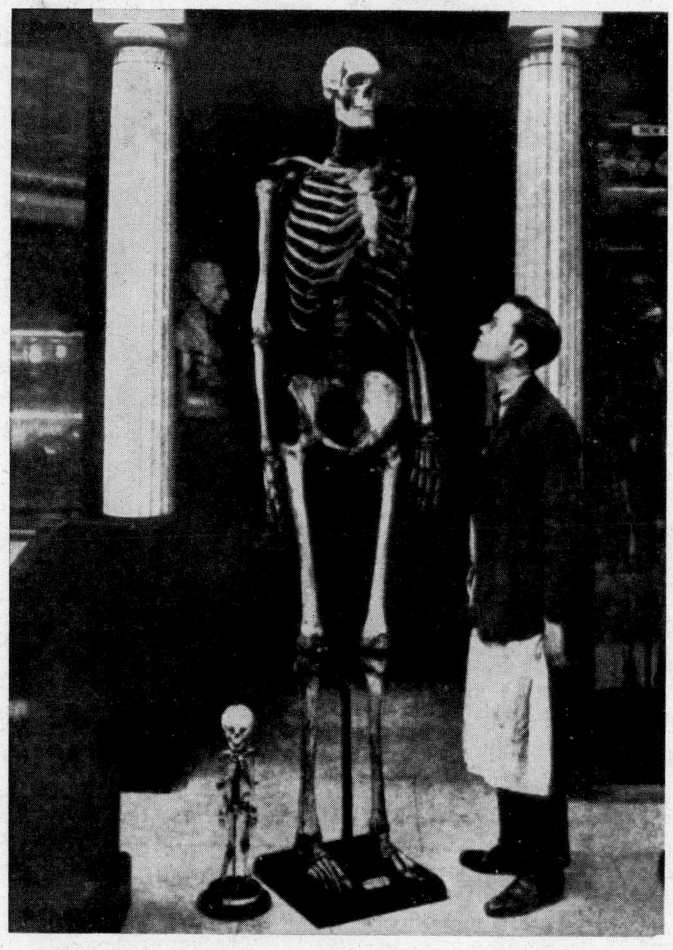

Skeleton of the Irish Giant in the Hunterian Museum, Royal College of Surgeons, London.

Shown with a member of the College staff and the skeleton of a dwarf.

The Copper Vat Where Hunter Boiled the Bones of the Irish Giant.
From the Collection of The Royal College of Surgeons, London.

short of funds, didn't have that much money, so he borrowed it. Then, in the silent watches of the night, the great, unwieldly corpse of the poor giant was crammed into a hackney coach and driven around awhile to shake off possible pursuers, for Hunter was by no means the only anatomist in London who wanted that extraordinary body—in fact, the competition was lively. In a dark, secluded spot, Hunter was waiting in his own carriage. The body was hastily transferred and Hunter set off with his prize in great haste for Earl's Court.

The whole business was, of course, illegal and potentially much more risky than ordinary body-snatching, and at this stage Hunter was in some fear of being discovered. He didn't, therefore, dissect the giant in the usual way, but cut him up, instead, into convenient-sized pieces and boiled off the flesh in the huge copper vat. It is not the orthodox way to prepare a skeleton, but Hunter was in no position to be a perfectionist, and the boiling method did nothing worse to the bones than turn them brown. So O'Brien, reconstructed after the boiling, became a specimen and joined the collection along with one of his stockings and a boot. He is still playing that role, for he stands today in a showcase at the Royal College of Surgeons. The staff there speaks of him with affection; he is, in effect, their mascot. During the Second World War the Royal College was struck by a bomb and two-thirds of the specimens which Hunter collected were destroyed. I remarked that I was glad the giant had survived. "Oh, we wouldn't take a chance on *him* in the blitz," I was told. "We evacuated *him*."

The diagnosis of the giant's deformity was made by the brain surgeon Harvey Cushing in 1909. Cushing received permission to saw off the top of O'Brien's skull and found, as he had expected, evidences in the bone formation of a sizable pituitary tumor which had created gland disturbances, causing O'Brien's extraordinary size. This skeleton is probably the most famous in the world; certainly no other has so much personality.

The copper kettle in which Hunter boiled the Irish giant's bones was still in place when Earl's Court was sold in 1886, and it brought thirty-six shillings at the auction. It was built into the wall of a cellar which was entered through a tunnel or "burrow" from the house. Conceivably, the kettle was hidden away to keep the anatomical specimens out of Mrs. Hunter's sight. The imagination creates a picture of the little man (he was only five feet two) struggling to drag some fearsome object, a huge piece of elephant destined for boiling, perhaps, along this dark earth burrow.

It was in 1783, the same year in which Hunter discovered the giant, that William died. John was called in consultation, but only as another doctor might have been. William died as he had lived, a model of decorum with an appropriate dying speech. That year, also, John built the house of his dreams. It was a very costly undertaking but it was all part, no doubt, of his defiance of death. The place actually consisted of two houses, which he remodeled and joined together with a third building. The work was so extensive that two years passed before it was completed. Thereafter, he and Anne lived in a kind of institute, for there were a lecture hall, a museum and countless offices. The collection, which had grown to such proportions that it occupied most of their house in town as well as Earl's Court, was transferred to the new quarters, an operation that occupied a number of people for the whole summer. There was a special place of honor for the Irish giant and for a Camela Perda which had been given to him but which was so tall that he had to cut off its legs. He had a special glass roof built over a yard to protect the skull of a whale. He even had his private printing press.

There is a tradition to the effect that this fantastic establishment was the model Stevenson used for Dr. Jekyll's house, and it is hard to think where he could have found a better one. John and Anne lived here in a sort of mad grandeur, in the midst of the creeping smells and the noise of the press, with a butler and two coachmen and a lady's maid. Anne's sedan chair had its place in the hall. They kept the Earl's Court place as a sort of retreat, and the combined establishments required a staff of fifty people, more or less, to keep them running.

John at this time was making more money than he ever had in his life, but he was spending most of it. The attacks of angina had finally made him realize, however, that he had made no proper provision for his wife and children in case of his death. The new house was held only on a long lease and he considered the collection his main asset. With the help of two assistants he had been trying to put it into order and to make a catalogue, but it was a monumental task.

When Hunter took the lease on the new house he was fifty-five years old and his prospects for the future were, because of his health, uncertain, to say the least. He was ill often now, and he rose from each new threat to fight an incredible offensive action against the onset of death. It was as though his ambitions had grown steadily as his health deteriorated. He simply would not accept defeat. He had come a long way in his profession, but he was not satisfied and he struggled on against greater and greater difficulties, his temper short, his will indomitable, working still with an unswerving intensity. His hair was white, his light eyes faded, but he had lived to see himself, if not appreciated as a scientist, at least regarded as the most eminent surgeon in London. He was, as his biographer, Stephen Paget, says, "anatomist, biologist, naturalist, physician, surgeon and pathologist, all at once and all in the highest . . . Contrast him with Ambroise Paré, a surgeon in some ways like him, shrewd, observant, ahead of his age; the achievements of Paré, side by side with those of Hunter, are like child's play in comparison with the serious affairs of men; Paré advanced the art of surgery, but Hunter taught the science of it."

In 1787, Hunter was prevailed on to sit for his portrait to Sir Joshua Reynolds. The sittings did not go well, for Hunter was bored and fidgety and Reynolds was dissatisfied with his work. Then one day Hunter lapsed into a deep abstraction, forgetting, no doubt, where he was and that he was not alone. Seeing him that way, with the light of his thoughts in his face, Reynolds quietly turned the canvas upside down and began to draw a new head. The final result was one of Reynolds' finest portraits.

The painting now hangs in the great hall of the Royal College of Surgeons. I spent a long time there standing in front of it, for though I have in my possession a number of reproductions both in color and in black and white, the original made plain a great deal about Hunter's character which I had not perceived in the copies. In the original, the eccentric and the ludicrous in Hunter's personality recede, and it is plain that though these aspects of him have attracted a great deal of attention, they were not as dominant as might be assumed.

The man in the original is, before everything else, an idealist, a visionary, a poet of science. Here is the face of a man who, for all his contacts with the world, lived his real life alone among the wondrous mysteries he alone saw in his stinking specimens, in his lice-filled birds' nests and dried pieces of organs with which he filled his shelves. In his own day his eccentricity made it easy to laugh at and belittle him, and to assume that his collection was nothing more than a noisome hobby gone out of control. Few realized, as Reynolds did, that it was the outward expression of a tremendous yearning to discover the mysteries of creation. In the original portrait his thoughts are far away and his face is lit by happiness, and it seems clear that this happiness—so unexpected and so deeply moving—was one of his strongest and most enduring characteristics. That profound spiritual happiness must have been with him always, his refuge from the world and the source of his strength. He must have seen the world through its perspective, and it would seem to be the reason why his worldly values differed so greatly from those of other men. Reynolds' painting and Anne's love are the only clear records of this quality in Hunter, but when his life and his work are seen in the light of this understanding, Hunter emerges as a man who was not only great in the achievements of the mind but great in spirit.

Hunter's illness progressed to the point where any fit of anger brought on an attack. "My life," he said, "is at the mercy of the first rascal who chooses to annoy me." No day passed without pain, and still he refused to give in. Those close to him must have watched with dread the uneven struggle, as little by little his mortal disease gained the upper hand. His assistants, who were devoted to him, took over as much of his work as they were able, but in spite of his handicap he remained the driving force behind each of his many enterprises. Then the pain began to attack him even at night, while he was sleeping, and all about him knew that the end could not be far off.

He was engaged, at this time, in a wrangle over money at Saint George's Hospital, in which his position was not, it must be admitted, altogether creditable. It was so unlike him that it is impossible to believe he would have taken part in it except for his belated fear that his family would be in financial difficulties after his death. At a meeting at the hospital two days before Saint Luke's Day, October 18, 1793, one of his colleagues flatly contradicted a statement Hunter had just made. The old quick anger flared up again, but before he could reply he was gripped by a fierce pain. He turned away from the group of doctors with whom he had been talking and went into the next room. There he collapsed into the arms of someone standing near him. An instant later he was dead.

He had indeed left his family in a difficult financial position, for it developed that there were numerous debts and almost no money, even for current expenses. For years he had been spending everything he earned as fast as it came in, and

Anne could not afford the fee required to have him buried in Westminster Abbey. His body was placed in the vaults of Saint Martin's-in-the-Fields. Anne and the two living children received some money from the Crown, but not enough to support them for long, and Anne became a companion to two young ladies of fashion, for which she was, fortunately, well paid.

The great collection proved disappointingly difficult to sell, but finally, six years after Hunter's death, the government bought it for fifteen thousand pounds, about seventy-five thousand dollars, and it was given into the care of the Royal College of Surgeons.

Most of Hunter's unpublished papers, notes, records and lectures, of which there were vast quantities, were turned over to Anne's brother, Everard Home, who was supposed to have undertaken to make a catalogue. The catalogue was never made, and in 1823 he burned almost all of them. He never properly explained his reasons for doing such a thing, and eleven years later there was a parliamentary inquiry on the subject, at which one of Hunter's devoted assistants, in giving evidence about their loss, broke down and wept.

In 1859, Hunter's remains were moved, with ceremony, to Westminster Abbey. His grave there is next to that of Ben Jonson, who had been buried, according to his own wishes, standing up. In the course of Hunter's interment, Jonson's skull came to light and was handed around and examined with interest.

Hunter was an eccentric in the great English tradition, but men had ceased to laugh at him. He was never a gentleman in the narrow sense of the word, but he made surgery a gentleman's profession by setting a new high standard of professional knowledge. And he who had no education himself so raised his calling as to make a scientific education henceforward a prerequisite. He had been born in a day when barbers and surgeons belonged to the same organization, and he once said with characteristic vigor, that a surgeon was "a savage with a knife." Unfortunately, it was fairly true that when he was beginning his own practice, surgery was both coarse and brutal, but by the example of his own dexterity and the refinements of his operating technique he created new standards which those who followed him were forced to strive for.

He opened the whole field of pathological surgery and left behind him such a legacy of knowledge that a historian, writing fifteen years after his death, said, "When we make a discovery in pathology we only learn what we have overlooked in his writings or forgotten in his lectures." In addition to all this he gave to the profession an extraordinary number of students who were well grounded in his unique scientific methods and fired with his own zeal. If the extent to which a man influences other people is a measure of his greatness, then John Hunter belongs in the first rank, for through these students, not to mention the educative value of his much-ridiculed collection, he remained an active force in surgery long after he had died.

V.

Surgery in Colonial America was in a backward state of development even in the larger cities. The first medical diploma was granted by Yale in 1723 to Daniel Turner, not for medical work but in return for a gift of books. Yale had no department of medicine at the time and there were no schools of medicine anywhere until shortly before the Revolutionary War. Some few medical students went abroad to study, but the greater number learned by being apprenticed to older doctors. There were almost no laws regulating the practice of medicine or surgery, and no requirements or standards with which these apprentices were forced to comply.

The apprentice system was not wholly bad, however. The apprentice learned both surgery and medicine, since there was no opportunity to specialize even in the towns, and in the rural districts a knowledge of both was essential. As a result, the division between surgery and medicine which had come about in Europe never took root in this country, and when the time for specialization arrived, having made an equal start, each developed on an equal basis.

As compared to the teaching in European schools, which was almost wholly confined to theory, the apprentice system was practical and related to the needs of the community. From the first, the student learned at the bedside and from experience. This was, however, the only respect in which the apprentice system was to be preferred to the foreign university system, and the best doctors in these early days were the fortunate few whose education had comprised a little of both. So disproportionately large was the group of apprentice-trained doctors that at the beginning of the Revolutionary War, of an estimated 3,500 physicians in the country only 400 had received medical degrees. After the Revolution the number of degree-holding doctors rose rapidly, and today there are more than 200,000 physicians in the United States.

Leadership in surgery, as in medicine, has shifted its geographical location from country to country and from city to city. In the middle of the eighteenth century, London was in the ascendancy and Edinburgh's star was rising. In this country, Philadelphia, which was the leading city at that time, was in the ascendancy in surgery and medicine alike. Three great men were largely responsible for the quality of the work which was done there, and for giving impetus to medical education and the care of the sick. They were John Morgan, William Shippen and Benjamin Rush. The first two studied with the Hunters in London, and all three received their degrees from Edinburgh. Morgan established a medical school at Philadelphia. Rush, who was a delegate to the Continental Congress and a signer of the Declaration of Independence, was famous for his work in combating yellow fever, which in those days was epidemic in Philadelphia. William Shippen gave the first systematic course of anatomy lectures in this country.

After the Revolution, fewer students went to England, many preferring Paris, which was fast becoming the leading center of surgery. Opportunities for a sound medical education were slow in developing in this country. The medical school at the College of Philadelphia was founded in 1765, that of King's College (later Columbia) three years later. Harvard had no medical school until 1781 and Yale none until 1810. Various medical schools with no university or hospital connections began to appear after the Revolution, though the weed-growth of these small institutions did not begin until after the turn of the century. They remained the curse of American medicine until the Flexner report, published by the Carnegie Foundation in 1910, exposed their scandalously low standards and resulted in their elimination.

In the eighteenth century there was no legislative control of these small schools, and some of them turned out "physicians" in as little as sixteen weeks. In the best of them the period of study was two years, though the second year was little more than a repetition of the first, and the teaching material usually consisted of no more than a chest full of bones and a few well-worn books. Most students never saw a dissection. Massachusetts was the first state to provide for anatomical material; a law passed in 1784 permitted the bodies of persons killed in duels or executed for fighting duels to be used for dissection.

Like the medical schools, the hospitals made a slow start, most of them evolving gradually from their beginnings as almshouses, as they had in Europe at a much earlier period. Pennsylvania Hospital, which had been an almshouse for a good many years and commenced its hospital work in 1751, was the first important institution for the care of the sick. Twenty years later New York Hospital was founded as the Society of the Hospital in the City of New York in America, and Bellevue Hospital had its confused beginnings in the latter part of the century.

The first chair of medicine in America was founded at the University of Mexico in 1580, forty years before the landing of the Pilgrims and not quite two hundred years before our first medical school opened its doors. Mexican hospitals were in existence in the early part of the sixteenth century, when Paré was a medical student at the Hôtel Dieu in Paris.

In the eighteenth century and most of the nineteenth, the great men of surgery and medicine in the United States served only the large cities. Throughout the country, the bulk of the medical work was done by men who were country doctors in every sense of the word. Few of them had ever seen the inside of a medical school, and what anatomy they knew had been learned beside improvised operating tables. They were doctors on horseback, serving their pioneer communities with rough-and-ready surgery. Few of them lived within reach of a hospital, but they used their own houses as nursing homes for patients who could not be cared for by their families or the neighbors. These pioneer practitioners had little opportunity to keep in touch with new developments in surgery and medicine. For the most part, they went through life on the store of knowledge they had accumulated in their apprentice days, plus whatever they might have accumulated afterward in the hard school of experience.

Though these country doctors were valuable men to the isolated communities they served, and though they were for the most part hard-working and self-sacrificing, their names do not appear even in the footnotes of history. There was, however, one outstanding exception among them. His name was Ephraim McDowell. He was a doctor-surgeon in Kentucky, and, unlike his colleagues, he had been given the benefit of a foreign education. He is famous because of one operation, but that single bold venture was the beginning of a new field of surgery.

Ephraim McDowell

1771–1830

"When doctors differ, who decides . . ."
—*The Kasidah of Haji Abdu*

Ephraim McDowell was an undistinguished first-year medical student at the University of Edinburgh in 1793. He was a tall, broad-shouldered young man of twenty-two, who moved with the easy strength of an athlete. He had an open, friendly face, a genial manner and a self-reliance which came of being raised in tough, new country where boys matured early, where the price of survival was sometimes the ability to make quick judgments and to stand steadfast behind them. He must have presented a considerable contrast, both in character and in appearance, to the city-bred part of the student body, but he was well liked and he became as much a part of the university life as these differences would permit.

McDowell had come from Danville, Kentucky, where his family had settled when he was thirteen years old. He was born in Rockbridge County, Virginia, in 1771. Danville was still a backwoods community of less than a thousand (some say of less than half that number). There were panthers and an occasional Indian in the woods around Danville, and except for the Wilderness Road—over which many immigrants traveled to the West because it was safer than the Ohio River route—the trails through the forest were seldom passable except on horseback. The elder McDowell was a judge, not particularly well-to-do, and he never seems to have had ambitions for Ephraim beyond the career of a country doctor, nor did Ephraim himself ever think in any larger terms. Young McDowell might have been contented with the customary apprenticeship, or he might have gone to the medical school in Philadelphia, which was well established by this time. That they decided upon a costly foreign education as a preparation for so humble a career would be amazing were it not that there seems always to have been in the McDowell blood a love of intellectual adventuring.

So young McDowell appeared in Edinburgh's ancient halls of scholarship in his rough American clothes, with the rustic atmosphere about him of the town which not so many years before had been a fighting frontier. In order to realize the full benefit from his stay, he supplemented his work at the university by attending lectures given by John Bell, an iconoclastic young surgeon who was teaching with considerably more *éclat* and disregard for tradition than the regular professors. A good many of the students supplemented their university work in this way, but in spite of McDowell's apparent zeal, he was no scholar, nor did he burn with a desire for knowledge. He wanted no more than to make himself into as good a practical, all-around doctor as he could while his money held out, and then to return to the backwoods and put what he had learned into practice. He had never had any formal education beyond the equivalent of a grade school, and certain aspects of the work at the university must have been hard for him. He was not at home with the written word, and never in later life learned to express himself easily with a pen in his hand.

McDowell was not wholly ignorant of doctoring when he came to Scotland, for he had been "reading" medicine in the office of Dr. Alexander Humphreys in Staunton, Virginia. All that really meant was that he had been Humphreys' apprentice, with a chance to watch him in action and to listen to such instruction as the doctor had the time or the inclination to supply. Humphreys probably had other student-assistants at the time McDowell was with him, and he may have been an unusually conscientious teacher, for a confused story has come down about a slight brush with the law over the remains of a Negro which the doctor was using for an anatomical dissection.

At Edinburgh, McDowell learned run-of-the-mine surgery having to do with tumor removal, wound treatment, amputations and other more or less routine surgical procedures of the day. He also learned something about the new field of blood-vessel surgery, to which John Hunter had made important contributions.

McDowell and his fellow students were most solemnly warned that the abdomen was forbidden territory for the surgeon's knife, since the mortality rate of experimental cases (mostly for Caesarian section) had been close to a hundred percent.

The caution was no doubt applied not only to Caesarian section but was also intended to forestall any inclination to tamper with ovarian cysts—a fairly common type of cyst which, unchecked, grows to enormous size and kills by slow and painful stages. All through medical history, warnings such as these have been loudest at precisely the time when the bolder surgeons have reached the point where they are almost ready to defy the taboos of tradition and do what the conservatives warn should not be attempted. Surgeons had already begun to speculate about these ovarian cysts. Some years earlier John Hunter had written in his forthright style, "I cannot see any reason why, when the disease can be ascertained in an early stage, we should not make an opening into the abdomen and extract the cyst itself. Why should not a woman suffer spaying without danger as well as other animals?" Other surgeons had begun to be of the same mind, but it seems unlikely that McDowell heard any serious discussion of the subject.

McDowell did not stay long enough in Edinburgh to earn a degree. Probably the money ran out, for there is in existence a worried letter from the elder McDowell in which he doubts his ability to meet the combined requirements of this foreign education and the expense of setting his son up in practice afterward. Young McDowell returned to Danville in 1795 and very shortly money ceased to be a problem, for the young doctor, because of the prestige of his foreign education, found himself sought after by the whole countryside.

His practice covered a radius of a hundred miles around Danville. Sometimes he would be away attending distant cases for as much as a week at a time, traveling always on horseback through the wilderness. These rides were not in theory dangerous, but neither were they altogether safe; though the hostile Indians had been driven farther West, there were still some dubious characters about, both red-skinned and white. There were also the panthers and a man had to be fearless, alert and hardy to match such a life. McDowell was all of these things.

Most of the operations he performed were emergencies, done in some remote log cabin, a plank on two barrels for an operating table and only neighbors or a terrified family to help him. Dealing daily with life and death in this grim fashion sobered him and firmed his character. The genial medical student had matured into a dignified doctor who felt the weight of his responsibility keenly and whose manner was stern and purposeful. Over the years, useless eulogy has obscured McDowell's personality, but through it we see a tall, broad-shouldered figure, unsmiling, iron-willed, reliable. He was a strict disciplinarian toward the slaves which he accumulated in his growing prosperity, and the slaves of his neighbors in Danville were so afraid of him that they would not venture into the streets after dark when it was known that the doctor was in town.

He built himself a house, four-square and solid, bought land and was respected as the best doctor west of Philadelphia. When he was thirty-one years old, he married the governor's daughter, Sarah Shelby, and they raised a family of six children. He became strongly religious in a bleak, God-fearing manner. Every detail of his life was carefully regulated to conform to his religious views, and he never swore or permitted others to swear in his presence.

Though his religion was stern, it was of the Southern rather than of the Puritan stamp. He did not believe, as the New Englanders did, that Sundays should be kept holy by refraining from activity of any sort; whenever he could he chose that day to operate, feeling that the prayers of the congregation would bring him help. He seldom kept any records of his cases, and he avoided writing of any sort, but as part of his preparation for an operation he would carefully write out a prayer, which he kept in his pocket while the operation was in progress, perhaps believing a written prayer would prove more durable than a spoken one. He felt the strain and the responsibility of an operation greatly, and he perspired prodigiously all the time he had his instruments in his hand.

One December day in 1809 he was called to visit a woman named Jane Todd Crawford, who lived with her husband and her five children in a clearing in the woods at a place picturesquely called the Blue Spring Branch of the Caney Fork, some distance out of Danville. Jane's house was a log cabin, the cracks between the logs filled in with white plaster, giving it an odd, striped effect. She and her husband made a meager living raising tobacco and wheat. Jane was pregnant, or so it was believed, for when McDowell was sent for she had been having continuous labor pains for some time. She had had two doctors attending her when McDowell was summoned, but every effort had failed to deliver her of her child.

McDowell examined her and found that her supposed pregnancy was in reality an ovarian tumor, which had grown to such an enormous size that it would inevitably cause her death in a short time. He told Jane precisely what her situation was, explaining to her carefully, so that she could not fail to understand, that her condition was, unfortunately, fairly common, but that no doctor dared perform an operation which involved opening the abdomen. Then he told her that if such an operation were to be performed, the chance that it would be successful was very small indeed, but if she had the courage, and was willing to take the terrible risk, he would attempt to operate. He called the operation an "experiment," nothing more, and she knew that it could not be performed swiftly, that there would be no way of relieving the pain she would have to endure and that she was more than likely to die while the "experiment" was in progress. But Jane was brave. She accepted.

They were both brave people, for that matter, for the doctor must have been fully aware that if Jane died as a result of the operation, he would have exposed himself to criticism of the severest kind from other members of his profession, he would be lucky if his practice survived and would be considered by many of his friends no better than a murderer. He knew the rough-and-ready retribution in his part of the country, and he must at one time or another have seen the violence of a lynching mob.

Why did he do it? Was it that he felt himself bound as a

doctor to take a chance, however slim, when the alternative was certain death? No other doctor alive would have agreed with that interpretation of his professional obligation. Was it pity for the poor woman? He knew that in all probability he would only shorten the time left to her. Was it confidence in himself, the feeling that a man of strong character and determined outlook sometimes has, that he can conquer the forces of nature? Or was this, perhaps, an opportunity for which he had been waiting for some time, and had he already made up his mind, before ever he met Jane Crawford, that he would attempt this untried operation as soon as a likely opportunity presented itself? There is no way of knowing the answer.

To Jane he made only one stipulation, that she must come to Danville to have the operation performed, for he felt that he should only undertake it under the most favorable conditions which could be devised, and her log cabin, crowded with children, was not a suitable place. The sixty-mile journey was something of a risk in itself, since there was danger that the jolting would tear the tumor loose and bring on a fatal hemorrhage. Jane made her preparations and set out for Danville on horseback, with the great tumor propped on the horn of her sidesaddle. Four days later she arrived, badly bruised by the saddle horn, but though the pain she suffered on the journey must have been considerable, she was calm and ready for her ordeal.

McDowell did not operate immediately, but waited to give Jane time to rest. He waited, in fact, until Christmas Day, no doubt choosing this day of days for the most critical operation of his career for the same reason that made him prefer to operate on Sundays. By this time everyone in the community knew what was about to be attempted. Feelings ran high. Many of the townspeople believed that what their stern, masterful doctor was about to do was little short of murder. There is a story (though no written testimony) that on Christmas a crowd gathered outside McDowell's house, a crowd which had every intention of lynching him, should Jane die on the operating table.

McDowell was not a man to be deterred by a mob, even a mob in a hanging mood. Preparations for the operation went forward. A part of them consisted of the usual written prayer. It was long, and toward the end of it he made an almost passionate appeal. "Direct me, Oh! God," he wrote, "in performing this operation for I am but an instrument in Thy hands . . . Oh! spare this afflicted woman."

He called in his nephew, James McDowell, and a colleague, Dr. Alban Smith, to help him. He gathered together a few pans from the kitchen, laid out a few instruments, had a wooden table set in the middle of the floor and called for warm water. That was all. He was ready. An illustration made by the careful artist, George Knapp, shows a comfortable room with a fire burning on the hearth and a bed in an alcove. Jane was brought in. She was a short woman, made shapeless by the pendulous tumor which hung down almost to her knees, and she was fully dressed. McDowell helped her onto the table and stretched her out on her back. Then he took off those garments which covered the site of the operation, leaving on her dress. He dipped a pen in ink and slowly traced out on Jane's skin the line the incision would follow. Jane began to repeat a psalm.

McDowell picked up a knife and handed it to his nephew James, who made the first cut through the skin. Then McDowell took the knife back and completed the nine-inch-long incision into the abdominal cavity. The instant this stupendous wound gaped apart the tumor came into view and in the same instant a mass of Jane's intestines spilled out to lie exposed on the table by her side. Jane was still reciting psalms.

The tumor was too big to take out in one piece, but it could be moved a little, and McDowell shifted it to one side and tied a ligature around its stem. Describing all this later, McDowell wrote, "We then cut into the tumor and took out fifteen pounds of a dirty, gelatinous-looking substance. After that we extracted the sack, which weighed seven and one half pounds." Halfway through the operation he thought about those intestines lying exposed in a room which was warm only in the vicinity of the fireplace, and he took time out to bathe them in tepid water to warm them and keep them moist. When the tumor had been completely cut away, he tucked the intestines back in place and turned Jane on her side to drain out the accumulated blood. Then he fastened the edges of the wound together, leaving the ends of the ligature hanging out of the wound to be pulled away later, when healing had progressed. The whole operation had been done in twenty-five minutes.

He had performed the first ovariotomy with success. Five days later he found Jane up and making her bed, and he gave her a scolding. In less than a month she was ready to return to her home. Through her twenty-five minutes of agony Jane had won herself thirty-two years of life. She died at the grand old age of seventy-nine.

There has never been so notable a case of cooperation between patient and doctor, and together, through her courage and his daring, they had achieved far more than either of them ever guessed, for this operation was the real beginning of general abdominal surgery. McDowell had performed one of the great feats of surgical history, and though he did not know it, he had made his name immortal.

The advance into the new field of surgery came slowly, however. McDowell did not rush to publish his success, but waited for seven years until he could support it with the records of two more cases. When his report finally did appear it was brief, labored and obscure, the work of a busy man, a man who was not accustomed to recording his cases and who chafed under the necessity of putting words on paper.

The aftermath of his long-delayed report followed the dreary pattern of most pioneer attempts in the field of surgery.

He was either severely censured or ignored. Two years after his first report he issued a second, covering two more cases, but this additional evidence met with much the same fate as the first. A copy of one of the reports was sent to Dr. Physick in Philadelphia. Dr. Physick, a professor of surgery there, was a younger member of the group that had made Philadelphia the center of medical work in America. Like Morgan and Shippen, he had been a pupil of John Hunter and received his medical degree from Edinburgh. Though of the original great trio of Philadelphia doctors, Benjamin Rush was still alive, Physick was at this time the best-known doctor in the country. Dr. Physick's favorable comment on McDowell's report could have done a great deal to further the cause of ovariotomy, perhaps hastened its general acceptance by a number of years. Unfortunately, he ignored it altogether.

Dr. Johnson, editor of the London *Medico-Chirurgical Review,* which was widely read in the United States, went on record with vehemence. "In spite of all that has been written in respect to this cruel operation," he wrote, "we entirely disbelieve that it has ever been performed with success, nor do we think it ever will," which was no more than a wordy way of calling the good doctor a liar. Johnson later made a retraction, however, saying ". . . we ask pardon of God and Dr. Ephraim McDowell of Danville." Then he ruined his own effort by adding, "It was the mode of narration which excited our skepticism, and we must confess it is not yet removed."

More heavy artillery of the medical world was brought up to annihilate the doctor from Kentucky, but by this time he was fighting back vigorously with his pen and with a lack of scholarly ornament in his style which would be enough in itself to startle the university men abroad.

"I thought," he wrote, "my statement was sufficiently explicit to warrant any surgeon's performing the operation when necessary without hazarding the odium of making an experiment, and I think my description of the mode of operating, and of the anatomy of the parts concerned, clear enough to enable any good anatomist, possessing the judgment requisite for a surgeon, to operate with safety. I hope no operator of any other description may ever attempt it. It is my most ardent wish that this operation may remain to the mechanical surgeon forever incomprehensible. Such have been the *bane* of the science; intruding themselves into the ranks of the profession, with no other qualification but boldness in undertaking, ignorance of their responsibility, and indifference to the lives of their patients." There was a good deal more in the same vein. Anger had made the doctor almost eloquent.

McDowell did not live to see his operation widely accepted or any of the advance into other branches of abdominal surgery. He never had a taste of glory or fame—which, it is safe to guess, he would not have liked very much. He went on with his practice, doling out pills sparingly, for he had little faith in them, and operating whenever he had to, under the old primitive conditions. One of his patients was a skinny, unhealthy lad named Polk, who later became President of the United States, but no one else of any great distinction came to him for treatment. He was simply carrying on as he always had, taking no more part than he had to in the controversy which went on and on about his operation on Jane. The opposition to ovariotomy in this country was tremendous, and no one dared for a long time to repeat what he had done. Here and there, however, he had a few supporters, and in 1825 the University of Maryland gave him a degree, so he became a documented Doctor of Medicine at last. By 1830 he had performed his famous operation thirteen times, with a record of eight cures, four deaths and one failure because of extensive adhesions which prevented the removal of the tumor. It was a remarkable achievement.

One June day, McDowell wandered out into his vegetable garden to pick some strawberries. They were unusually large and sweet that year, and he liked to eat them off the vine when they were warm with the sun. He ate a good many, standing there between the rows, resting himself. Then he went back into the house, but almost immediately he began to feel ill. Shortly, he was very sick indeed, and one of his colleagues was called in, who diagnosed the trouble as "inflammation of the stomach," a term which in those days covered every known malady that organ is heir to. McDowell himself thought that he might have swallowed a poisonous bug along with one of the berries. There is little doubt, however, that the real cause of the trouble was a gangrenous appendix—about which, in those days, nothing at all was known. He could not be saved and so, ironically, this great pioneer in abdominal surgery died of an abdominal malady.

THE CONTROL OF PAIN

VI.

Guillaume Dupuytren, one of the most cold-blooded surgeons who ever lived, once acknowledged that "pain kills like hemorrhage." He had put into words a concept which had grown slowly as surgical techniques became more complicated and penetrating, lengthening the time the patient lay on the operating table and prolonging his agony. In the early days, when surgery was superficial and uncomplicated, it was not clear that suffering would ever become so prolonged or so intense that surgery would be unable to make any further advance until the pain was conquered. The need to cause suffering was deplored for humanitarian rather than for technical reasons.

These considerations were enough, however, to prompt the less callous men to seek ways of relieving pain. The search for palliatives is probably as old as surgery itself. The interest in plants and herbs in early Christian times and in the Middle Ages, which was the period of the great herbals, led doctors to seek them in growing things, in opium, hemp, lettuce and a root called mandragora, which were all used to deaden pain. Of mandragora a fifth century botanist wrote, ". . . if anyone is to have a limb mutilated, burnt or sawn, he may drink half an ounce with wine, and while he sleeps the member may be cut off without any pain or sense." Another recipe called for a "sleeping sponge," which was a sea sponge soaked in a brew of herbs and "applied to the nostrils of him who is to be operated on, until he has fallen asleep and so let the surgery be performed." He was then to be awakened by the application of another sponge, soaked in vinegar and held under his nose.

A modern experimenter tried these drugs in their ancient form on some laboratory animals and found that they did not "even make a guinea pig nod." Most of them were poisons of varying degrees of virulence, and as there was no way of standardizing a dose or of discovering how strong a dose might be, the patients to whom they were given not infrequently died. As a result, though doctors for the most part followed tradition and wrote glowing accounts of their effects, they did not always use them in their practice.

Each age has experimented with pain-killers which have a relation to the dominant medico-surgical interests of the time. Though herbs and the sleeping sponge were still used to some extent, the sixteenth century, the age of anatomy, experimented with such purely anatomical methods for relieving pain as pressure on the carotid artery or other arteries and nerves. The method was in reality a revival of an ancient technique which had long been forgotten. Paré, credulous as he was concerning some of his weird salves, used pressure rather than drugs, a method which also had its dangers and often produced as much pain as it was intended to prevent.

The seventeenth century, the age of physiology, experimented with such modern-sounding physiological techniques as refrigeration anesthesia and intravenous injection of opium. The refrigerating agent was snow, recommended in a book by Marco Aurelio Severino called *The Medical Use of Snow*. These techniques were, however, too far in advance of the scientific knowledge of the day to take a firm hold and their interest lies mainly in the field of medical curiosities.

By the middle of the century the public had learned to fear the action of the ancient drugs, however they might be administered, and the French passed a law forbidding their use. The churches, both Catholic and Protestant, took part in what should have been a purely medical question, and turned what had been merely the patient's somewhat serious dilemma into a moral issue by declaring that suffering should not be relieved since it was the will of God. Pain became a duty, and in foisting it on the sick and suffering, state and church between them succeeded in creating a number of medical martyrs. Because childbearing seemed to these moralists the most "natural" of all painful ills, the interdiction was enforced most sternly against women, and among those who died to expiate the sin of attempting to ease their pain there stands out the pathetic Scottish woman who was burned alive for begging the midwife to relieve a suffering she could no longer bear.

By the beginning of the eighteenth century, doctors and lay public alike had become thoroughly disillusioned about painkillers in any form. With the field of drugs tried and found useless, the situation of the sufferer was hopeless, for nothing offered any promise whatsoever. Some surgeons before an operation got their patients as drunk as possible. Some did not bother with even this precaution, since the subject invariably sobered up the instant the knife laid open his flesh.

Toward the end of this century the wonders of electricity became a major preoccupation of the physicists and attracted the interest of the general public. Stephen Gray demonstrated that electrical attraction could be passed from one human body to another, Galvani showed that weak electrical currents could cause muscles to contract and medical men saw in these mysterious currents the possibility of miraculous cures. The time was ripe for someone to utilize the invisible powers which affect our bodies for the relief of pain, and there appeared on the medical horizon as odd a character as ever caused the pages of history to flutter. His name was Franz Anton Mesmer and he held out hope in a new form to the ill and suffering.

Mesmer claimed to heal by a power which he alone possessed, and which he called "animal magnetism." He asserted that by making certain signs and passes with his hands he could use this animal magnetism to draw out pain and disease, and though many doctors and scientists denounced him, his theories swept across Europe like a contagion. Following his star of prosperity, Mesmer left Vienna, where he had been practicing his strange mixture of magic and medicine, and in 1778 he presented himself to the fashionable world of Paris. There the public flocked to him, especially the neurotic men and women of the tottering aristocracy. Marie Antoinette made an idol and a pet of him; Lafayette wrote to Washington that he was bringing to America something more valuable than soldiers and cannon, "the secret of Mesmer"; and the learned societies, including the Académie des Sciences (of which Benjamin Franklin was a member), denounced him as a fraud.

When the patients crowded to Mesmer's rooms in such numbers that he could no longer handle them, he made the convenient discovery that he had the power to "magnetize" any object he chose and that thereafter the object would have power to draw out pain. On the basis of this brilliant idea he increased the profits of his practice enormously, for it was no longer necessary to see all his patients personally and he was able to sell the "magnetized" objects for enormous sums. He "magnetized" mirrors for the neurotic ladies and musical instruments for the men. His wealth became so great that he even indulged in charity and "magnetized" trees, which would then give off his powers entirely free, and a common sight in Paris was a group of people solemnly seated under one of them. Once a physician asked him why he told his patients to bathe in river water rather than in water drawn from springs, and he replied, "Dear Doctor, water which is exposed to the rays of the sun is superior to all other water because it is magnetized. I myself magnetized the sun some years ago."

The emotional hysteria about this one man was as symptomatic as anything could be of the unstable balance of France. Underneath the alarums and excursions of fashionable Paris about their petty aches and pains, the Revolution was brewing. Suddenly the pot boiled over. One after another of Mesmer's fashionable neurotics mounted the steps of the guillotine, and Mesmer fled to Vienna, leaving all his possessions behind him. The crest of his popularity had passed, and before he died, in 1815, he had been completely forgotten.

Mesmer was a faith healer, a superficial mind joined to a colossal ego, who never realized that his discoveries had any real significance. His work lay on the borderline of hypnotism, but he never took the short step which would have led him to the discovery of the somnambulistic trance. That remained for one of his followers, Count de Puységur. The Count had "magnetized" a lime tree in his park, to which the peasants came to be cured of their ills. One day a shepherd named Victor was tied to the tree to receive the cure and the Count was moving his hands in front of Victor's face, as Mesmer had taught him to do, when suddenly he discovered that the shepherd was fast asleep. Startled, the Count ordered Victor to untie himself from the tree and, without waking, Victor obeyed. Thus accidentally Count Puységur discovered hypnotism.

His was not an entirely new discovery, for hypnotism was not a wholly unknown phenomenon, but it had never become a part of medical practice. After some experimenting the Count made his discovery public, and following closely on the furor over magnetism, it attracted wide attention. A number of operations, including one for the removal of a breast, were performed in the early years of the nineteenth century while the patients lay in a hypnotic state.

An Edinburgh medical student named Esdaih, who became interested in hypnotism, removed himself to India in search of a sympathetic atmosphere in which to practice. He found it for a time, and in a period of six years performed several thousand operations on hypnotized patients, some three hundred of them being in the category of major surgery.

The hypnotists, who still, for the most part, called their technique mesmerism, were never a large group and they made the mistake, common among reformers, of allying themselves to other causes, such as phrenology, housing reform and later —astonishingly enough—ether anesthesia. They soon reversed their position on ether, but they were always looked on as radicals.

It is sometimes possible to perform certain operations painlessly, while the patient is in a hypnotic sleep, but hypnotism is slow, the effects at best unreliable, and some patients cannot be hypnotized at all. It is useless for emergency operations. Before many more years had passed it ceased to be regarded seriously.

Prior to the early nineteenth century few operations lasted more than five minutes. Some surgeons could incise a bladder and remove a stone in less than sixty seconds. James Syme could whisk a leg off at the hip joint in one minute, William Ferguson used to warn the spectators not to blink or they would miss the operation altogether, and there was a popular joke about the lightning operator who could "with one sweep of his knife cut off the limb of his patient, three fingers of his assistant and the coattail of a spectator." The surgeon who was quickest was always the most popular, but there were an increasing number of operations, such as McDowell's ovariotomy, in which speed was neither practicable nor wise. Surgery had passed the point where pain could be combated by speed alone, and with each technical advance that prolonged the torture of the operation, more and more patients died of shock, of terror, of agony—died screaming from the pain which literally tore their bodies to pieces.

Some surgeons grew callous to the shrieks and prayers and cries for mercy which filled their operating rooms, proceeding with a cold disregard for suffering and occasionally with a wholly unnecessary brutality. Some surgeons suffered tortures because of the necessity to torture others, and there is little doubt that the dread of inflicting pain kept out of the profession a certain type of sensitive intellectual and attracted a number of those who were psychologically unsound. Abernethy, successor to John Hunter, was so distressed by the need to cause pain that he vomited whenever he left the amphitheatre. Cheselden could not sleep the night before he had to operate. Charles Darwin abandoned his intentions of becoming a doctor after watching the horrors of two operations, one of them on a child. "The two cases fairly haunted me," he wrote, "for many a long year." And Dupuytren, the cold-blooded, opened a door from all this tragedy on a glimpse of the ludicrous. When he was about to operate on a woman, he made a remark to her which was so deliberately insulting that she fainted, whereupon he proceeded to operate—a solution to the problem of anesthesia which surely would not occur to any but a Frenchman.

Long before the middle of the nineteenth century the situation had become intolerable for patients and doctors alike. Mortality following operations was, conservatively stated, in the neighborhood of two in three, a considerable proportion of the deaths being attributable more or less directly to the effects of pain. Of those who survived the ordeal in the operating room, many had permanently undermined constitutions and psychic scars which would never be eradicated. Although some surgeons still repeated the dogma that pain is the inescapable will of the Almighty, surgery could in fact make no further important advance until some solution could be found to the problem of pain. Surgery had come face to face with the second great barrier to progress.

The Anesthetists

"*And then awake as from a pleasant sleep.*"

—*William Shakespeare*

Though the struggle to conquer pain had once more come to a standstill, important developments were meanwhile taking place in the laboratories of men who were experimenting in the field of chemistry. In the closing years of the eighteenth century a young and handsome research worker named Humphry Davy heard of a gas called nitrous oxide which had been discovered by Joseph Priestley in 1772. Davy knew that nitrous oxide was believed to be an agent of contagion, causing diseases which ranged from cancer to leprosy. Nevertheless, he decided to experiment with it, using himself as the subject. He found that nitrous oxide had no bad effects, that it had a sweetish taste, a pleasant odor, and that it produced in him a desire to laugh. He continued to experiment on animals and on some of his acquaintances. Occasionally one of them, while breathing the gas, would slip into unconsciousness, but the sleep-producing properties of the gas did not interest Davy so much as the state which preceded loss of consciousness, in which pain appeared to be deadened. In the year 1800 Davy wrote a book about his work in which the following sentence appeared:

"*As nitrous oxide . . . appears capable of destroying physical pain, it may probably be used with advantage during surgical operations in which no great effusion of blood takes place.*"

Not one surgeon in England or America paid the slightest attention to what he had written.

The same year in which Davy's book appeared there was born in the English village of Lady Halton a boy named Henry Hill Hickman. He grew up to be a country surgeon and began to conduct a series of experiments in the effects of inhaling the fumes of carbon dioxide. He found that with it he could put animals to sleep and that they would remain unconscious while he performed operations on them. He was convinced that his discovery would be of great benefit to surgery, and he appealed to a Fellow of the Royal Society (by a strange caprice of fate, Humphry Davy was now its president), but the society failed to give Hickman its support.

Davy had abandoned and all but forgotten his researches in inhalation anesthesia. But that he should have been in a position to block the recognition of a rival in the field is the first knot in the tangled skein of personalities, antagonisms, jealousies, ambitions, coincidences, hates and simple stupidity which is the story of anesthesia. Sir Humphry Davy had changed greatly from the eager, brilliant young man of twenty-one who had tried his brave experiments on himself.

Success and his own cleverness had gone to his head and he had become haughty, opinionated and disinclined to pay attention to any work but his own, and the village Milton was beneath his notice. A word from Davy would have made Hickman famous. Davy merely ignored him. Hickman went to France, where he made a futile attempt to have his work recognized, and died at the age of thirty without anyone's realizing that he had demonstrated what Davy had merely suggested—namely, that operations can be performed while the subject remains unconscious from the effects of inhaling a gas.

There the matter rested as far as any surgeon was concerned. When nitrous oxide was dragged out of obscurity, it was not by the medical profession but by show business. Quasi-scientific "demonstrations" and "lectures" were becoming popular in the United States at the beginning of the eighteen thirties, and a lad of eighteen named Samuel Colt saw in them a means of raising money to promote the revolver which later made him famous. Colt advertised himself as "Doctor Coult of New York, London and Calcutta" (he came from Hartford) and in 1832 set out with a homemade apparatus for inhaling nitrous oxide, about whose properties he knew nothing whatsoever. He staged his demonstrations on street corners and village greens, using for his subjects anyone who could be persuaded to inhale the gas, and the entertainment consisted of their strange antics while partly under its influence. All went well for some time and he was occasionally making as much as ten dollars a day when he had an experience which startled and sobered him. The account of what followed is by Dr. Victor Robinson (in *Victory over Pain*).

"He had hired six Indians to appear in a gas-inspired comedy . . . The inventor of the revolver administered the gas to his six Indians—who promptly fell asleep with not so much as a preliminary whoop or a drunken giggle. Sam knew very well that his customers had not paid their admission to see Indians taking a nap. He saved the day by administering gas to a blacksmith who obliged by furiously chasing Sam about the stage. He finally careened into the Indians who woke to find themselves on the floor."

The audience thought they had seen a prearranged performance, and a good one, but young Colt had the sense to realize how close he had come to disaster, and he gave up his nitrous oxide demonstrations altogether.

By the eighteen forties young people all over America had made the delightful discovery that it was possible to get very drunk indeed by inhaling not only nitrous oxide but the fumes of ether as well. Inhalation "frolics" became a peculiarly American craze. Young people sniffed, grew light in the head and reeled around, bumping into the furniture and each other without feeling any hurt, laughing, cavorting, going through what seemed to them the most preposterously hilarious antics, and then, when they took a few whiffs too many, falling suddenly into a deep sleep. And still, astonishing as it may seem, no one saw the significance of this insensible sleep.

In Georgia, in the town of Jefferson, there lived a handsome young doctor, very popular with the ladies, named Crawford Williamson Long. When the young people of the town wanted ether for their parties, he supplied it to them and joined in the parties himself. He enjoyed it all thoroughly, though sometimes afterward he would find that he had bruised himself quite severely, though he had no recollection of having felt any pain. He knew that others had been as insensible to hurt as he.

Long had a patient, James M. Venable, who had two small tumors on the back of his neck, which Dr. Long had told him a number of times should be removed. Venable, afraid of the pain he would feel, put the operation off until one day the doctor said to him that since he himself had never felt pain while inhaling ether, probably Venable could have his tumors cut out without pain if he would inhale some of it. Venable, who had been on ether frolics himself, agreed to try the experiment on one of the tumors. Long gave him some ether on a towel, waited until Venable had inhaled some of it, and went to work on the tumor. When he had finished, Venable refused to believe that Long had done anything at all until he was shown the tumor as proof.

The date was March 30, 1842. The first operation had been performed under ether without pain. What did Dr. Long do about his great discovery? Nothing at all. He made no announcement of any sort, either in the interest of his own glory or to aid suffering mankind. Years later, when he was trying to have himself recognized as the discoverer of ether, he sought to excuse his failure to make his discovery public on the grounds that he was waiting to see if any other doctor had made the same discovery.

Opposition to a forward step in medicine sometimes comes from the sufferers whom it is intended to benefit. This was the case when Dr. Long continued to use ether in his practice, for presently rumor spread through the town that ether was a poison and that Long was deliberately risking human lives. A deputation of townspeople called on him to demand that he discontinue the use of ether, and as he was already alarmed by the way in which his practice was falling off, he agreed readily. Later, when other doctors in the state were using ether and public opinion had largely changed, Long's courage revived and he began to use it once again.

Two years after Long had deadened the pain in Venable's neck, a successful young dentist in Hartford, Connecticut, named Horace Wells, read in his newspaper an advertisement of one of the itinerant science shows. It interested him and he decided to go. A man from the audience named Cooley, who had volunteered to inhale nitrous oxide, went berserk under its influence and leaped around the stage flailing his arms and bumping into wooden benches. Then the effects of the gas suddenly wore off and Cooley collapsed into the seat he had left to go on stage, which, by a coincidence that would strain credulity if this story were fiction, happened to be next to the seat occupied by the dentist Wells.

Then it developed that Cooley had severely abraded the skin of his knees, much to his own astonishment, for, as he told Wells, he had not the slightest recollection of any pain.

As the audience was leaving, Wells asked the proprietor of the show, Gardner Quincy Colton, why a tooth could not be pulled under the gas. Colton said he did not know, that the idea had never occurred to him. Wells asked him for some of the nitrous oxide and the next morning Colton took a bag of it to the dentist's office. There Colton administered the gas while a colleague pulled one of Wells's teeth. When it was over, Wells said, "It is the greatest discovery ever made! I didn't feel so much as the prick of a pin!" He was sure that with the use of the gas to pull teeth he could make a fortune.

His excitement at his discovery and at the prospect of riches knew no bounds. He did a little more experimenting with the gas—but not enough, for he was in a hurry for fame—then went to Boston, where he had once tried unsuccessfully to practice, and looked up his partner of those lean days. This man was a young dentist, of more cautious temperament than the precipitate Wells, whose ample name was William Thomas Green Morton. He persuaded Wells that they should do nothing until they had gone to see an acquaintance of his, a doctor-chemist named Charles Thomas Jackson. (Jackson was descended from a Puritan woman with the prophetic name of Remember Morton.) He was an able worker, but he was by nature bitter, selfish, egocentric and sly. As Wells and Morton unfolded their tale, Jackson may have begun to suspect the possibilities of nitrous oxide in dentistry, but he told the two dentists flatly that the idea of using it for painless extraction was not sound and urged them to abandon it at once.

This Wells was not willing to do. He had been successful with about half the cases in which he had used gas, and in his ignorance he thought he had experimented enough. He saw himself a rich and famous Boston practitioner, and he could wait no longer to make the golden dream come true. In 1845 he arranged to give a demonstration of his miraculous discovery before a group of medical students and physicians at the Massachusetts General Hospital. One of the students volunteered to be the victim and Wells gave him gas, but something went wrong. Either Wells waited too short a time for the gas to take effect, or he gave too little gas, or the patient, though anesthetized, could still groan. At the last moment, just as he drew the tooth, the patient yowled with pain. There was an uproar in the lecture hall, and Wells, dropping his forceps, fled.

After this fiasco Wells returned to Hartford. He continued to administer nitrous oxide to his own patients there, apparently with success, but he brooded over his failure at the Massachusetts General Hospital until his health began to fail.

Wells's friend Morton was made of sterner stuff. The *dramatis personae* of "Anesthesia" were mediocrities to the last man, Morton included, but Morton had an obsessive persistence lacking in his friend Wells. Morton had attended lectures at the Harvard Medical School for two years, he had gone so far as to keep a skeleton in the bedroom where he and his young bride slept, and his interest in the conquest of pain was such that he could not leave the subject alone. He had, however, no real grounding in the principles of experimentation, and his judgment was not always of the best.

Morton went to see Jackson once more, to discuss the possibility of other kinds of pain-killers. In the course of the conversation Morton asked Jackson if he thought that ether, which was known to cause numbness when applied to the skin, could be used to deaden the pain of a tooth extraction. Jackson thought that quite probably it could be so used, and gave Morton a small bottle of ether with which to experiment. All that Morton knew about ether at this time he seems to have learned from Jackson, a fact which, along with every word of this and subsequent conversations, became of the utmost importance later on. Morton used some of the ether on the tender tooth of a lady patient and found that it did in fact allay pain to a certain extent, but that it was so volatile that the effect quickly wore off.

Morton and Jackson had been having a tiff—the first gust of the coming storm—and for a while Morton pursued his search for a pain-killer without Jackson's aid or knowledge. It was in this span of time that Morton had the idea that ether fumes, if inhaled more steadily and under different conditions from those at the ether frolics, might be the analgesic for which he was searching. This hope fixed itself firmly in his mind, but he had no idea how to proceed. He read all the literature he could find on the subject of ether, which was little enough and not very helpful. He talked to a number of people who might be expected to know something about ether, and was thoroughly confused by their reports. In view of the quarrel he did not want to go back and talk over his problem with Jackson.

Finally, after much uncertainty, he decided to take his wife and Nig, their spaniel, to a country place he owned near Wellesley. He described the expedition as a vacation, but, unknown to his wife, he had a large supply of ether in his luggage, and when they arrived he went off to his improvised laboratory with the dog at his heels. Nig then joined the heroes of science. Protesting violently, he sniffed the ether which Morton held under his nose and then slept so soundly that he frightened Morton, who dreaded what his wife Elizabeth might say. When Nig finally awoke, he reeled around the room as though he were drunk and had to be kept out of Elizabeth's sight for some little time.

The family goldfish were Morton's next subjects, and when Elizabeth came unexpectedly into the room and saw the fish out of water, apparently dead, she burst into tears. Morton threw them back into their bowl (they were quite unhurt) and told her what he was doing—which would have been much wiser to do in the first place, even though Elizabeth, who was only eighteen years old and emotional by nature, knew nothing about science and could not understand her husband's need to experiment. Her only concern was to make her husband promise never, never, never to experiment on poor darling Nig.

So Morton left the pets alone, went fishing in the brook and gathered caterpillars from the trees. Poor Elizabeth's house was filled with everything he could lay hands on which crawled or swam or flew—all of them being sent off from time to time into that mysterious, uncanny, death-like sleep. The "vacation" went on and on. Morton would have tried his ether on Nig again, but Nig had learned wisdom and refused to come within arms' reach. Then one day Elizabeth found Morton himself stretched out on the floor, to all appearances dead, and she had an attack of hysterics.

They went back to Boston after that, and Morton continued his experiments, this time on human subjects. He failed again and again to get the results he wanted, and he was advised to consult Jackson once more. Jackson had previously attracted a great deal of attention to himself by laying claim to the invention of the telegraph, a claim which Morse had the greatest difficulty in proving false. (This "scientific octopus," as Victor Robinson called him, also tried to appropriate Beaumont's discoveries of the stomach's functions and laid claim to Schönbein's discovery of gun cotton.) Disturbed by Jackson's attempt to pirate Morse's invention and reluctant because of their own quarrel, Morton hesitated to consult Jackson again or let him know what he was doing. He had, however, reached an impasse in his work and in the end he went once more to consult the dangerous Jackson.

Morton tried to conceal from Jackson the real purpose of his visit by starting to talk about nitrous oxide, but Jackson told him in so many words to use ether vapor instead. He also added the information that the fumes of chloric ether (which Morton had been using) were unreliable and only the vapor of sulphuric ether would give the proper result. That was the information Morton wanted.

A dentist named Hayden had been looking after Morton's much neglected practice, and now Morton, after trying the sulphuric ether on himself with great success, told Hayden the whole story. Eagerly, they decided to try it on a patient right away. There is one characteristic of ether, however, which neither of them knew. It is highly explosive and very easily set off. Evening came and the two dentists lit their oil lamp and waited for a patient. The one who walked innocently through their door and into history was a musician named Eben Frost, who was suffering from the pain of a tooth which needed pulling.

It is not hard to imagine with what delight Frost was greeted by the two excited dentists. Dr. Morton took out his handkerchief, soaked it in ether and held it to Frost's nose. Hayden approached with the lamp. He held it closer and closer so Morton could see to work. By rights, they should all have been blown into Kingdom Come, but nothing happened. Frost came out of his painless sleep to see his tooth lying on the floor and he, who had joined the cast of characters so casually, was there to stay. Frost became Morton's disciple, his showpiece, Exhibit A, and a happy man.

Morton was fully satisfied with the effects of his sulphuric ether. There remained only to patent his discovery, make a fortune and live happily ever after. Frost had that historic bicuspid of his pulled on the thirtieth of September, 1846. Before the end of October a patent application had been filed.

Morton, however, soon began to enlarge his horizons. He thought not merely of becoming a rich dentist, an ambition he was rapidly realizing. He began to think that ether could be used for surgical operations and thus make him the benefactor of all mankind. His first step was to design an inhaler;

his next, to call on a surgeon. He could not have selected a better, for this open-minded man was Dr. John Collins Warren, senior surgeon of the Massachusetts General Hospital. Dr. Warren agreed to let Morton use his ether vapor on a patient who was to undergo an operation.

The patient Dr. Warren chose was a young man named Gilbert Abbott, who had a tumor on his neck. Morton was notified, but the inhaler which he was having especially made for the occasion was not finished. In the little time that remained he and the instrument-maker worked frantically. On the morning of the operation the theatre of the Massachusetts General Hospital was ready—the tiers of seats rising toward the ceiling were filled with doctors and students, for news of the experiment which was about to take place had traveled fast.

Everything was ready, the operating table was covered with sheets, pails and basins stood nearby, but the mysterious dentist had not arrived. The spectators were talking together in low voices when the door opened. The talking stopped instantly. The patient, a pale, consumptive young man, whose large tumor was near the hinge of his jaw, was shown in and taken to the operating table, where he stretched himself out. He was dressed in trousers and a shirt open at the neck to expose the bulging tumor. Then Dr. Warren appeared and all the eyes in the theatre shifted to him.

Dr. Warren stood beside the operating table and addressed the audience, explaining to them what was about to take place. When he finished his talk there was silence. Warren and everyone else looked at the clock. It was now a quarter past the hour set for the operation and Morton had not appeared. Warren looked impatient, Abbott lay still on the operating table and the spectators began to talk, then to laugh and to comment loudly on the man who had not dared to face them.

Dr. Warren spoke again. "Since Dr. Morton has not appeared I presume he is otherwise engaged." He picked up his knife and bent over Abbott. At that instant the door burst open and Morton, out of breath, rushed in, followed by Eben Frost. Morton explained the instrument-maker had kept him waiting, but that he had the new inhaler with him and he was ready to begin.

Dr. Warren heard him out. Then he said a trifle sarcastically, "Well, sir, your patient is ready."

Morton went directly to the operating table and said to Abbott, "Are you afraid?" He pointed to Eben. "There is a man who has breathed it and can testify to its success."

But Abbott was not afraid, and in a profound, tense silence which filled the theatre he followed Morton's instructions carefully. The glass tube of the instrument was put into his mouth. He inhaled deeply and evenly. Then he began to breathe faster and irregularly. His face grew flushed, his arms and legs moved spasmodically. Then he lay quiet. The spectators were leaning forward to see, clutching the railings in front of them. Morton, from his place at the head of the operating table, looked toward Dr. Warren.

"Doctor, *your* patient is ready."

In the profound, attentive silence Dr. Warren stepped forward, picked up his knife and went swiftly to work. Abbott did not move. The tumor was laid bare, rapidly cut away and the wound sutured. Toward the end, Abbott moved his legs a little and uttered incoherent sounds, but afterward he said he felt no pain.

When it was all over, Warren turned to the spectators. He was clearly deeply moved.

"Gentlemen," he said, "this is no humbug!"

He said a great deal more, but the gist of it all was in those words. It was no humbug. The cause for which men had worked and prayed was won. But it was not the end of the story, for no one, neither Dr. Warren nor any of the spectators in that theatre, knew what the glass inhaler contained.

Two months after Morton administered ether to Gilbert Abbott at the Massachusetts General Hospital, it was used at a major operation for the first time in England. The surgeon was Robert Liston, the operation an amputation. When the patient regained consciousness and realized that the operation was over and he had felt no pain, he dropped back on the operating table weeping. Liston turned to the spectators and said, "This Yankee dodge, gentlemen, beats mesmerism hollow."

A year later James Young Simpson, the Scottish surgeon, experimented with ether in obstetrics, and not being satisfied with the results, he turned to chloroform, the anesthetic properties of which had been demonstrated by a French physiologist named Flourens. The Calvinist clergy of Scotland at once denounced him for attempting to relieve the sufferings of women in labor, smiting him with the text from Genesis 3:16, "In sorrow shalt thou bring forth children."

Simpson promptly pointed out that in Genesis there was also the account of "the first surgical operation ever performed on man," hurling back at the clergy the text, "the Lord God caused a deep sleep to fall upon Adam; and he slept; and he took out one of his ribs, and closed up the flesh instead thereof." Simpson's agility with biblical quotations had less to do with the final acceptance of anesthesia in childbirth, however, than the fact that Queen Victoria consented to use chloroform some years later at the birth of her eighth child.

Before the discovery of inhalation anesthesia, two patients out of every three undergoing operations died; after the discovery, only one in three died.

Following his operation on Gilbert Abbott, Dr. Warren had but one idea, which was to keep all his surgical cases from suffering pain. He sent at once to the instrument-maker to order an inhaler for the hospital, but there he was told that the instrument could not be made for him because Morton had applied for a patent. Warren sent for Morton. Warren had no objection to paying Morton for his sleep-producing mystery, and said so, but at this point the Massachusetts Medical Society intervened. It stated flatly that to reserve the secret of an invention of such benefit to mankind solely for private profit was not ethical, and that until Morton made some arrangement more acceptable to the medical profession, the society would not countenance its use. The inexperienced Morton, who knew nothing about medical ethics and wanted only to make the money he felt he had earned, found himself in a world grown suddenly strange.

Warren could not very well disregard the stand the Medical Society had taken, and he wrote to Morton. To his eternal glory, Morton wrote to Warren that same day:

"*Dear Sir: As it may sometimes be desirable that surgical operations should be performed at Massachusetts General Hospital under the influence of the preparation employed by me for producing temporary insensibility to pain, you will allow me, through you, to offer to the hospital the free use of it for all the hospital operations.*"

In his efforts to make himself rich by commercializing his invention, Morton went heavily into debt. But it soon developed that the patent had slight validity and afforded him no substantial protection. From then on, his principal activity was a struggle with Wells and Jackson to establish that he, and not either of them, was the real discoverer of the anesthetic use of ether.

It is exceedingly difficult to arrive at the truth in the tangle of events which followed. Some writers on anesthesia appear to have resorted to distortion and overstatement in order to heighten the drama of a tale which is so inherently dramatic that any coloring of the facts makes the story ring false. The accounts written by reliable historians are all too brief, and the recollections of the principal characters, if not actual fabrications, are frequently tinged by bias, inaccuracy and *arrière pensée*. In such case, he who would tell the tale honestly is frequently forced to choose between conflicting statements, and if he is not to complicate his story by telling everybody's side of it, then he must proceed on judgment alone. It is unlikely that all the facts in the controversy will ever come to light, and those who feel inclined to make judgments of their own will find a fertile field.

In 1847 Wells went to Paris to buy pictures for resale, and while he was there, he announced himself to be the true discoverer of the gift to mankind which Oliver Wendell Holmes had christened "anesthesia." He was claiming by this time that he had used not only nitrous oxide but ether also. He was accepted everywhere, and for a time he had a taste of fame. He returned home to find ether anesthesia had made great progress but that nitrous oxide was fast being forgotten.

After this brief Paris interlude Wells wasted the rest of his life in acrimonious attempts to force a doubting world to acknowledge his claim. Selling pictures now seemed a paltry occupation to a person who had come to regard himself as one of the great. Then he had an idea. Chloroform was by this time much used in Europe but it was almost unknown in the United States. Wells, with his usual too great assurance, decided he could still make himself famous by persuading American surgeons of its superiority over ether, a question about which he himself knew nothing.

Accordingly, he bought a large supply. He had no intention of repeating his former mistake and presenting his pain-killer without sufficient previous experimenting. In this new venture his judgment did not fail him—it was as bad as ever. He chloroformed himself again and again until he was satisfied that the vapor really worked; then he set out to convince surgeons that they should use it instead of ether. He met with very scant success, but in the process of experimenting on himself, an unexpected thing had happened. He had become an addict.

From here on the story of Wells is like a melodrama of the day. He lived in New York, leaving his family in Hartford to shift for themselves. He kept himself in a constant state of drunken stupor. His money gave out, his health began to break. He wandered the streets, shabby, hungry, telling his troubles to anyone who would listen to him. Then one day a chance acquaintance, a man he hardly knew, told him a long tale about a prostitute who had ruined a suit of his clothes out of spite. Wells was deeply stirred by the tale. He brooded and worked himself into a state of unnatural excitement by inhaling his chloroform until that tale of injustice to his chance acquaintance seemed to him the most hideous of crimes. He bought some vitriol and went in search of the prostitute.

When he found her in the company of another girl, he threw the vitriol on both of them. He was arrested, tried and convicted. In prison, he seems to have come to himself enough to realize what he had done and the disgrace he had brought on his family. He asked for writing materials and wrote two letters, one to the public, the other to his wife. At the end of the first he wrote, "My dear, dear wife and child, how they will suffer. I cannot proceed. My brain is on fire." In the second, "Oh my dear wife and child, whom I leave destitute of means of support—I would still live and work for you, but I cannot. . . . May God forgive me."

He had smuggled into the prison a razor and a bottle of chloroform. After the guard had made his last rounds for the night, Wells took them from the place where he had hidden them.

He was found the next morning, the twenty-fourth of January, 1848, with his femoral artery cut, a handkerchief tied over his mouth and nose, and the empty bottle of chloroform on the floor. The hapless dentist from Hartford had succeeded at something at last.

Wells's story does not end here. Shortly after his funeral his wife received the news that the Medical Society of Paris had voted that "Horace Wells, of Hartford, Connecticut, United States of America, is due all the honor of having first discovered and successfully applied the use of vapors or gases whereby surgical operations could be performed without pain."

These events left the field to Jackson and Morton. Jackson continued his campaign to discredit Morton and to take the whole credit himself for the discovery of anesthesia. Setting about it with the skill of a born intriguer and the animosity of a true bigot, he claimed that Morton had done no more than carry out instructions for using ether that he, Jackson, had originated. He made it appear that Morton had done nothing on his own initiative, that he had no standing in the medical profession, and that his only desire had been profit.

By this time most of the medical and scientific societies of Europe were ready to enter the controversy and anxious to bestow credit where credit was due. The simple, honest Morton did his best to defend himself against the unscrupulous Jackson. The battle for recognition went now this way, now that, and the longer it lasted the more determined each man was to become the victor.

The French Institute, which had been trying for some time to decide which of the two deserved the credit, found the controversy too complicated and acknowledged them both. An award of five thousand francs was voted, 2,500 of it going to Jackson for his observation and experiments in regard to the anesthetic *effects* of inhaling ether, and an equal amount to Morton for introducing the *method* of etherization into surgical practice. Morton, however, refused to share an honor to which he felt himself alone to be entitled. The institute solved this dilemma by having his 2,500 gold francs melted and made into a medal, and this Morton was willing to accept. At one point Oliver Wendell Holmes gave his opinion that the credit should go "to e(i)ther."

The war with Mexico had begun in the spring of 1846. Morton offered ether inhalers to the army at the cost to him, but he asked that, since he was now fully protected by a patent, the government pay him a license royalty as other users were doing. The government refused. Worried about his financial plight, Morton had a nervous breakdown. He retreated to the house in Wellesley with the long-suffering Elizabeth, but before he had been there a sufficient time to recover, the house was seized by his creditors.

At this point the trustees of the Massachusetts General Hospital heard about Morton's plight and called on him, bearing a silver box on which was engraved "For William Thomas Green Morton, who has become poor in a cause which has made the world his debtor." Inside the box were one thousand dollars.

Morton's luck seemed suddenly to have changed, for unexpectedly Congress proposed to make him a grant of a hundred thousand dollars as the true originator of anesthesia. But Jackson appeared on the scene and laid claim to the money. The grant was delayed while Congress investigated. Such an investigation could result only in the discrediting of Jackson, but he would not give up. When it became clear that he would not receive the money, he used the whole of his malicious cunning to destroy Morton's chances for receiving the award.

He went to see Wells's widow and told her that he would push her claim before Congress to have her husband recognized as the true discoverer of anesthesia and the hundred thousand dollars paid to her. Then, having heard about the claims of Crawford Long, he went rushing off to Georgia to interview Long. Perhaps Long showed him the entry in his ledger about the operation on Venable as proof that he and not Wells or Morton or Jackson himself had been the first to use anesthesia. The delay in Congress which Jackson's maneuvers had brought about gave time for other claimants to appear and present their cases. By this time the issue was thoroughly confused and in the end Congress took no action at all.

After this terrible blow, Morton, who had been in Washington, went back to the house at Wellesley, which he had managed to rescue from his creditors, and in this quiet backwater he supported himself by farming. Though he was not a happy man in his seclusion, he was at least at peace. But fate was not to let this semblance of contentment endure. News reached him that Congress proposed to buy his patent, and he went to Washington once again. More than a year passed and Congress took no action.

Morton had borrowed to finance his stay in the capital. His creditors pressed him, the sheriff arrived, his household goods and farm implements were sold at auction. His house was saved for him by his friends, but his means of making a living were gone. One disaster followed another, most of them precipitated by the whispering campaign of slander carried on by Jackson. In those dark days only the trustees and staff of the Massachusetts General Hospital remained faithful to Morton's cause, but there was little practical help that they could give.

When the Civil War broke out, Morton left his seclusion to administer ether to the wounded. After the war he returned to Wellesley and to poverty, broken in health and deeply depressed by the continuing struggle against Jackson for the recognition which had come to be his only ambition.

In July of 1868, when Morton was forty-eight years old, he left his home and went to New York to reply to an article which had appeared in one of the monthly magazines, advocating Jackson's claim to be the discoverer of anesthesia. Elizabeth Morton has told the story of what followed.

"It was some time since anything of the sort had appeared, for medical journals the world over had admitted Dr. Morton's right to the discovery, and this article agitated him to an extent I had never seen before. The weather was very hot, and on July 11 he telegraphed me that he was ill and wished me to come to him. I went at once, and found he was suffering with rheumatism in one leg. Under the treatment of the dis-

The First Ovariotomy

Ephraim McDowell stands at the right of the operating table

Crawford W. Long, M.D., Discoverer of Anesthesia.

Demonstrated on James M. Venables by the use of sulphuric ether at Jefferson, Jackson County, Georgia, March 30, 1843.

William Thomas Green Morton

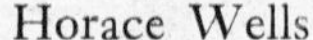

Horace Wells

Charles T. Jackson

tinguished Dr. Sayre, my husband improved, and on Wednesday after dinner, he proposed that we should drive to Washington Heights and spend the night there at the hotel, as a change from the hot city. We started about eight o'clock in the evening, Dr. Morton himself driving.

"After a little he complained of feeling sleepy, but refused to give me the reins or to turn back. Just as we were leaving the park, without a word he sprang from the carriage, and for a few moments stood on the ground, apparently in great distress. Seeing a crowd gathered about, I took from his pocket his watch, purse, also his two decorations and the gold medal. Quickly he lost consciousness, and I was obliged to call upon a policeman and a passing druggist, Dr. Swann, who assisted me. We laid my husband upon the grass, but he was past hope of recovery. We sent at once for a double carriage but it was an hour before one came. Then two policemen lifted him tenderly upon the seat, I being unable to do anything from the condition I was in: horror of the situation had stunned me, finding myself alone with a dying husband, surrounded by strangers, in an open park at eleven o'clock at night.

"We were driven at once to St. Luke's Hospital, where my husband was taken in on a stretcher, and immediately the chief surgeon and house physicians gathered about him. At a glance the chief surgeon recognized him, and said to me: 'this is Dr. Morton?'

"I simply replied 'Yes.'

"After a moment's silence he turned to the group of house pupils, and said: 'Young gentlemen, you see lying before you a man who has done more for humanity and for the relief of suffering than any man who has ever lived.'

"In the bitterness of the moment, I put my hand in my pocket, and taking out the three medals, laid them beside my husband, saying, 'Yes, and here is all the recompense he has ever received for it.' "

Time passed and the controversy receded a little in men's

minds. Then Gardner Quincy Colton, the itinerant showman who long before had supplied Wells with a bag of nitrous oxide, came wandering back onto the stage of these strange events. He was still an itinerant showman and he still had faith in his gas as an analgesic for dentistry, though nitrous oxide had been superseded by ether. Occasionally Colton mentioned the use dentists might make of nitrous oxide in the lecture he delivered during his show, and eventually he interested Dr. J. H. Smith, of New Haven. Colton and Smith began to work together with such success that in a period of three weeks and two days they extracted a little over three thousand teeth. Eventually, Colton established the Colton Dental Association in New York and was able to operate it with great success.

Colton seems to have been the exact opposite of Jackson, for he was an honest man with no desire to take any credit to himself that he did not deserve. In 1886 he published a pamphlet account of the part he had played with Wells in the first use of nitrous oxide in dentistry, stating categorically that the idea of using the gas in dentistry came from Wells and not from himself.

After Morton's death, Jackson continued his fight for recognition with as much virulence as ever. One authority, who has, perhaps, more sense of story than of accuracy, tells how one day when Jackson was out walking he suddenly found himself face to face with a monument to Morton erected by the citizens of Boston. Jackson, so the story goes, started to scream, then to rave; a crowd gathered, and he was dragged off to an insane asylum.

Jackson's insanity had almost surely been developing for a long time. In 1873, five years after Morton's death, he was admitted to the McLean Asylum, a department of the Massachusetts General Hospital. He spent the following seven years within those walls and died there on August 28, 1880, at the age of seventy-five.

Neither Wells, Jackson nor Morton can truly be said to

have discovered the principle of anesthesia. Jackson may actually have suggested the use of sulphuric ether to Morton as a pain-killer, and as to that the controversy continues to this day. A discovery, however, is not valuable until it is available, and of all the *dramatis personae* involved in this strange tale, two men and two only took steps to make anesthetic agents available to the medical profession and to the public. They were Horace Wells and William Thomas Green Morton.

In this century the anesthetist has developed from a scared medical student with a folded newspaper for an ether cone in one hand, and an unmeasured quantity of ether in the other, into a highly trained specialist in command of an intricate technique. He administers his anesthetic in controlled quantities, frequently in mixtures, through various points of entry to the body. He can hold the patient without risk at any level of consciousness he desires, a technique that is helpful in studying mental states as well as in surgery. He can collapse a lung when required and reinflate it at the proper time. He controls a formidable array of dials, flasks, mechanisms and gadgets, and he is able to inform the surgeon at any moment about the state of the patient's blood pressure, respiration, oxygen content of the blood and degree of shock. He can lower the patient's body temperature under anesthesia to a point at which the cold itself is anesthetic. He is a scientific newcomer, but no branch of the healing art has developed more spectacularly than his.

THE CONTROL OF INFECTION

VII.

The history of surgery is like a great river, fed as it rolls along by tributary waters which join and swell the stream. We turned back to follow from its source one of these tributaries, the River Lethe, the river of sleep, and now we have come again to the main river.

In the early part of the nineteenth century, patients who survived the operating room were dying afterward in great numbers from infection. The wound made by surgery which did not become infected was exceedingly rare. Pus was still "laudable," and its presence was thought to indicate that the wound was draining properly. In addition to the suppurating wounds, there were blood poisoning diseases which affected the whole body: pyemia, erysipelas and a frightful disease known as "hospital gangrene," which has since vanished. No hospital was free from such cases, and frequently one or another of these "septic diseases" would rise to epidemic numbers. Some surgeons thought they were caused by overcrowding, and some that the infection lurked in the walls of old hospital buildings, but the majority believed that the evil was caused by oxygen in the air coming in contact with the raw surfaces of the wound.

The pattern was all too familiar. One day the patient's fever, which was as much a part of his post-operative condition as the pus filling his wound, would shoot suddenly higher and the area around the wound would be red, swollen and dreadfully painful. That was the danger signal. John Bell, a prominent surgeon of the day, described what characteristically followed in the case of a leg wound—and it is a sight which few surgeons see today. "The great wound begins to open very wide, the whole limb swells to an enormous degree [and] . . . you are aware that great suppurations are forming within. . . . Often it happens that all your cares are unavailing. Every time you make examination of the limb you make discoveries of more extensive destruction, you find the whole limb swelling more and more, you find the matter running profusely from the openings . . . with intolerable foetor. . . . And in the end . . . the hollow eyes . . . the long, bony fingers . . . the quick, short breathing and the small, piping voice declare the last stages. . . ."

This was blood poisoning. Today we know it is caused by microbes, and we recognize a number of different varieties of septic diseases. Then, only the three main types were known. Of these, hospital gangrene was the most dreaded, for it caused unimaginable suffering and a lingering death. A gray slough would appear on the surface of the wound. Under it, the infection would slowly eat its way into the healthy body, attacking first the soft part which divides and protects the muscles, literally eating it away until the living muscles resembled a dissection. Next the muscles would be attacked and disjointed, the great blood vessels eroded. "Thus," Bell writes, "a lad by the name of Handling, who had at first but a slight wound in the thigh, had the cellular membrane in the course of a few days so destroyed that you could put your clenched fist into the hip and lay the hand sidewise betwixt any two muscles of the thigh." This horrible disease was a commonplace of any large hospital, and anyone brought to a surgical ward with an injury, however small, or anyone who had been operated on might catch it. If one case appeared in a ward, the whole ward was likely to become infected, and there were few recoveries.

Hospitals in England and on the Continent had been greatly

expanded in the previous seventy-five years, but in spite of this they were always full, and in times of epidemic they fell far short of the needs. The old days of the huge beds were gone forever, but, though each patient—children excepted—had a bed to himself, with clean linen on it, the beds were pushed close together and sometimes there were patients on shake-downs in the aisles and corridors. Fresh air, especially fresh night air, was carefully kept away from the sick until after Miss Nightingale came back from the Crimean War and started her whirlwind campaign of reform. These great new hospitals were cold. The huge room at Saint Thomas' Hospital, where Miss Nightingale met her nurses—and which survived until it was struck by a bomb in World War II—was heated only by a coal fire, and that, I can testify with feeling, had no mitigating effect on the atmosphere ten feet away. In many a ward in England today there can still be seen a double row of patients, with blankets up to their chins, their breath turning into little columns of white vapor.

The hospitals were well run according to the standards of the day. They were clean, and if they were not so clean as we think a hospital should be, the reason was that no one had yet made a cause-and-effect association between dirt and disease. The operating was no longer done in a filthy corner and the operating theatres in the better hospitals were large and reasonably well lighted.

Although they were a fine expression of this charitable age, these hospitals were responsible for the alarming increase in septic diseases because they brought patients with infected wounds into close contact with the uninfected, and it was easy for doctors with unwashed hands to transfer infection from bed to bed. Surgical cases in these great humane institutions had actually a worse chance of leaving the hospital alive than in those days when Paré walked the wards of the Hôtel Dieu in the sixteenth century. Patients who had their operations in their homes had a far greater chance of survival, no matter what the state of dirt and squalor in the home might be. The more honest surgeons said plainly that a man with an open wound was better off in a slum than in the finest hospital in England, though they did not understand why this was true.

Here and there a surgeon, suspecting that overcrowding might be in some way responsible, would try to abolish the state of congestion in his wards. Others advocated destruction of the great hospitals, many of which had only recently been built, in favor of a group of small, temporary buildings, which could be torn down whenever the septic diseases began to increase alarmingly, and in Germany a start in this direction was made. By far the greater number of surgeons, however, believed that nothing could be done and took no action whatsoever. No one guessed that the surgeons themselves transplanted the evil from wound to wound on their unwashed hands and instruments. None suspected that the deaths in the wards were associated with those microscopic creatures, Leeuwenhoek's "little animals," which some of them had seen swimming under their microscopes. Not suspecting that, they could not know that a microbe strain, transplanted from host to host, may grow more and more virulent.

The public called the various forms of blood poisoning "hospital diseases," and it was no secret that they were never epidemic outside of hospitals. The fear which hospital diseases aroused was sufficient to deter those who could afford home operations from going to hospitals long after they had become safer than any home.

The ravages of the hospital diseases are reflected in the mortality rate following amputations during those years. Approximately a fourth of all operations were amputations. Fractures which involved a break in the skin contributed to the number of amputations, since the danger of infection was slightly less if the limb was cut off than if the fracture was set. In the United States, deaths following amputations ranged between approximately twenty-four and twenty-six percent, an unusually fine record for the period. In Paris the mortality rate was nearly sixty percent, and in Edinburgh, which had become the center of surgical work, thirty-five percent of all patients with amputated limbs died of one or another of the hospital diseases.

These figures are estimates only, and they do not take into account such factors as contributing causes of death. They are, nevertheless, reliable to the extent that they show the trend, and if not taken too literally, they are useful. A general warning should be sounded, however, not only about these data but about those which appear in subsequent chapters. The gathering of medical statistics is complicated by many factors, and unless a great deal is known about the background of the data, they should be thought of always as estimates and generalizations rather than as statements of precise fact.

In the early part of the nineteenth century the practice of surgery had come to require a large background of factual knowledge. For this reason more doctors specialized in the field of surgery. And for the same reason the surgical career was attracting in greater numbers men of intelligence and education. The whole level of the profession had risen. In the fourteenth century Guy de Chauliac wrote that a surgeon must be learned, expert, ingenious and willing to be of service. Five centuries later the basic requirements were still the same, but the need for them had become intensified and the surgeon was compelled to possess those qualities to a more marked degree. The result was that what may, with some admitted inaccuracy, be called the surgical type emerged with its characteristics more pronounced. Men who possessed the requisite characteristics rose to the top of the profession; those who lacked them tended to disappear.

The nineteenth century added some special requirements of its own, which tended further to intensify the surgical type and to attract men to the practice of surgery whose sum of personality traits differed from those of men in other professions. The need for highly developed manual dexterity and for extreme speed created by the more complicated surgical techniques was one of these newer requisites.

Another demand on the surgeon was being created by the increasing number of operating amphitheatres and the growing numbers of spectators who came to see exhibitions of virtuosity. Each year more and more students crowded into the amphitheatres; more and more distinguished visitors arrived. The surgeon who could not operate before these spectators and remain calm and untroubled, he who could not perform with the brilliance which any sort of audience expects of any performer, lost out in the competition against men whose surgical skill was joined with an instinct for the dramatic.

The surgeon had become a showman and surgery a show. And inevitably some of the more spectacular surgeons, or those who could perform spectacular operations without flinching in the limelight, attracted attention outside the confines of the medical profession. Romance had come to surround the surgeon and his work. Some who became popular heroes, and on whom shone the fierce light of publicity, had no claim to their fame but their showmanship. Some were truly great surgeons. In the main the public choice was sound, and the surgeons who captured public imagination were men of merit.

These conditions produced the titans of surgery—Liston, Gross, Halsted, and in our times Crile, the Mayos and Harvey Cushing—for they attracted the bold, the confident, the talented, the self-assured. But they worked hardship on certain men who preferred the solitude of their laboratories to the crowded amphitheatre, and such men, unless their solitary experiments were of great importance, never won public acclaim. Joseph Lister was one of those retiring men who never made a satisfactory adjustment, who was shy and stammering when he faced his students and whose contribution to surgery grew out of research. Yet few men have stood in such a blaze of publicity as he, for no surgeon except William Harvey ever so changed the course of surgery.

Joseph Lister

1827–1912

"Who dreamed that living air poisoned our surgery coating
All our sheeny weapons with germs of invisible death,
Till he saw the sterile steel work with immunity, and save
Quickly as its warring scimitars of victory had slain."
—Robert Bridges

If there is such a thing as an ideal environment for scientific genius, Joseph Lister was born into it. His father, Joseph Jackson Lister, was a scientist whose discoveries contributed to the improvement of the microscope at a period of time when that instrument, in the hands of such men as Pasteur and Koch, was about to revolutionize the practice of both medicine and surgery, and through his father, young Lister was in touch with the scientific attitude of mind from his earliest days. His mother, before her marriage to Joseph Jackson, had been a supervisor in a school maintained by the Society of Friends, and young Lister learned much from her. Both parents were Quakers who lived by the Quaker principles of simplicity and goodness, and they trained their children in these virtues. The Listers were prosperous and able to give young Joseph a good education, though not many schools or colleges welcomed the Friends.

Joseph's early education was at the Quaker schools of Hitchin and Tottenham, where he showed himself to be a conscientious student, not quick but unfailingly thorough. He worried about his work, and when he was still quite young he had to be taken out of school for a time to rest. Little is known about this interlude, which seems to have been in the nature of a breakdown, though a large correspondence relating to it has been preserved by the library of the Wellcome Historical Medical Museum in London. These letters would repay research, for if we knew more about that shadowy and evidently emotional time in Lister's boyhood, much about him that is not clear would be easier to understand. Possibly these letters would shed some light on the reason why, all his life long, he was plagued by a stammer, and why, in later years, he had so much difficulty organizing his lectures that, after days of preparation, he would still be working on them as the carriage drove him to the lecture hall. If we knew more about this boyhood crisis, we might come closer to understanding why he found it almost impossible to be prompt when he had to face an audience or what it was that caused the shyness of which he was never wholly cured.

The college which was selected for Lister was the nonsectarian University College of London, one of the few institutions where Friends were welcomed, and there he received his B.A. degree in 1847. He remained at the university to study medicine, and as a first-year student he had the good fortune to be present when Liston performed the first major operation to be done in England under ether. The university medical school was associated with a hospital where the students were trained. The operating theatre, which was of modest dimensions, contained one small cupboard where all the instruments were kept, a sturdy wooden table, a single gas jet and a solitary wash basin. Here the students assembled every Wednesday to watch the three senior surgeons operate, performing in the order of seniority. With the introduction of anesthesia, surgeons did not at once abandon their technique of high-speed operating, and one afternoon was usually a long enough time in which to perform all the operations of the week except those of emergency. "There was," one of Lister's biographers wrote, "a plentiful display of manual dexterity; but, looked at as a whole, it was rough and ready surgery."

While Lister was attached to University Hospital a virulent epidemic of hospital gangrene broke out in the wards. The wounds, many of which were surgical incisions that had begun to heal, would show around their edges the dreaded gray substance which would creep rapidly into sound flesh, literally eating away the tissues as it spread. It was Lister's duty to give the anesthetic before the surgeon scraped away the gray matter from these gangrenous wounds and to cauterize them with acid pernitrate of mercury. Cauterization was the only known treatment; sometimes the patient was cured by it and sometimes the gray slough would reappear. Most surgeons regarded hospital gangrene and the other septic diseases as inescapable scourges, without troubling to do more than speculate about their cause. Young Lister, however, examined the results of the cautery treatment and reasoned that if some patients recovered and some did not, though all had been exposed to the oxygen in the air which most doctors vaguely assumed to be the cause of the trouble, then oxygen could not be responsible.

Having made this simple deduction, there was little that

Lister knew to do about it. He put some of the gray matter under his microscope and studied it, but he could not see any microorganisms because he knew nothing about staining them with dye to make them visible. He had no idea what it was he was looking for, but he did see some curious objects which he took to be some sort of fungus and thought might be the cause of the disease. He made notes and drew painstaking sketches of what he saw, but he had no idea how to test his theories, and so for the time he set his studies aside. He remained convinced, however, that oxygen was not the cause of hospital gangrene.

Lister finished his studies at University College in 1852 and was made a Fellow of the Royal College of Surgeons in the same year. He had planned to go to the Continent to observe surgical techniques, and then to settle down to practice in London, but one of his professors persuaded him that he would be wise to go to Edinburgh to finish his studies under the famous surgeon James Syme, professor of surgery at the university there. Syme was perhaps the best surgeon of his day, with a reputation for conservative surgery and a painstaking technique rare in a man trained in the cut-fast-and-get-it-over days before the introduction of anesthesia. Like those of so many of the great surgeons who suffered daily the strain of causing their patients agony, Lister's temper was quick, and he had a lifetime of quarrels with his colleagues, including James Young Simpson. As a young man he had quarreled with his hospital. He and that other medical maverick, Robert Liston, set up a small school where they taught anatomy, but he quarreled with the resurrectionists, so he and his friend Liston did their own grave-robbing. Then he quarreled with Liston and they parted, Liston going to London to practice.

Young Lister was warned that Syme, who was nicknamed "the formidable" by his students, was difficult to get along with, but when he and Syme met they took an instant liking to each other. Lister had planned to stay in Edinburgh only a month, but at the end of it Syme asked him to remain and assist him at the operations he performed. It was a splendid opportunity for a young surgeon, and Lister accepted

The older man and the young one became friends. Lister went often to Syme's home, a comfortable house named Millbank, where he met Syme's daughter Agnes, a serious, intellectual young lady, not beautiful or even pretty, but whose outlook on life was not very different from that of the young Quaker ladies Lister had known. Slowly, with a sort of quiet dignity, these two fell in love. Lister was a tall and well-built young man, handsome in an unpretentious, honest-looking way. He still wore the black, oddly cut coat of the Friends and he had grown a little bush of side whiskers on each cheek. Agnes wore her dark hair parted and brushed down close to her head in the uncompromising fashion of the day; her eyes were dark, their expression reserved. They were a model young couple, replete with rectitude and industry.

Before their sedate courtship reached its gentle climax, the position of assistant surgeon at the Edinburgh Infirmary became vacant, and after characteristically careful consideration, Lister decided to apply for the appointment, though it would mean relinquishing all idea of the London practice and living at a distance from his beloved father. On the other hand, Lister was anxious to continue his association with Syme, and with Syme's daughter. He wrote to his father explaining his professional reasons for not wanting to leave Edinburgh, but evidently he was not yet clear in his mind about his feelings for Agnes; though the letter, with its graceful "thees" and "thous," was twenty pages long, he did not once mention her name.

The appointment was granted him, but before beginning his duties he went to Paris for a month, no doubt as much for the purpose of doing some soul-searching about Agnes as with the idea of observing surgical techniques in the hospitals there. The decision was a difficult one, for Agnes had been brought up in the Church of England, and to marry her Lister would have to break his ties with the Society of Friends. He returned with his doubts about Agnes cleared away, and in due course, without hurry, he made her a formal declaration of his love, though not until he had asked permission of her father. They were married at Millbank in 1856, and when Lister listened to the clergyman's admonition that marriage is not to be entered into lightly and inadvisedly but soberly, discreetly and in the fear of God, he could have the satisfaction of knowing that he was complying to the full. If Lister had a vice, it was excess of virtue.

For a honeymoon, the young Listers set out on a grand tour of the medical centers of the Continent. Agnes proved to be a good companion, unperturbed by the petty inconveniences of travel, and always ready to be interested in those things which interested him. The only remarkable thing about this tour, aside from the fact that it was not the sort of honeymoon to appeal to most young people, was that, while Lister was in Vienna, no one told him about the great discovery which had been made there in the prevention of puerperal fever, a blood poisoning disease of childbirth.

A doctor named Ignaz Semmelweis, attached to one of the maternity wards of a great hospital in Vienna, had been seriously concerned because of the high mortality rate in his ward from this disease. In another maternity ward in the same hospital the rate was consistently lower, but Semmelweis could see no difference between the two wards, except that in his ward the patients were cared for by doctors and students and in the other by midwives only, except in cases of seriously difficult labor. He could see nothing in that difference to cause the fever. Then one day a friend of his received an accidental cut while dissecting the body of one of the victims. The cut was a trifling one, but in a few days the man died of an illness with symptoms like those of the infected mothers.

Semmelweis realized that it was morbific material from the dead woman which had infected the cut. The students and doctors were in the habit of going straight from the dissecting room to the ward, where, without washing their hands, they examined the women. In a flash of understanding Semmelweis saw that this was the way the infection was being carried. It is quite possible that he had never heard of microbes, and if he had, he would not have associated them with disease, but he no longer doubted that it was the particles of morbific material clinging to the hands of the doctors and students when they left the dissecting room which were infecting the women in his ward, and that this explained why the mothers in the care of midwives, who never went near a dissecting room, were safe unless a doctor was called in.

The rest of Semmelweis' story is a tragic struggle to make the world realize that the one simple act of hand-washing could save thousands of lives each year. He proved this point by reducing the deaths in his own ward almost to zero, but in spite of this solid evidence he was ridiculed by most of his colleagues and by the world at large. His anger and depression became abnormal. In the end his mind gave way, and he died in an insane asylum from the blood poisoning from which he had saved so many women.

Semmelweis' discovery was purely empirical. He knew he had discovered a truth but he did not know why it was true. Nevertheless, had his theories been mentioned to Lister, even by one of Semmelweis' many adversaries, it may be supposed that Lister would have understood their significance and applied Semmelweis' discovery to the wider practice of surgery.

The Listers returned to Edinburgh in the fall and he took up his duties at the Infirmary. In respect to hospital diseases, the Edinburgh Infirmary had a better record than most hospitals, thanks largely to Syme's insistence on cleanliness in his wards and his preference for dry gauze dressings instead of the customary dressings which had been soaked in unsterilized water. But even in an institution as advanced as the Infirmary, conditions were far from sanitary, as we understand the meaning of the word. It is possible to piece together a picture of those conditions from the old records, especially as they applied to the care of compound fractures, for which no satisfactory treatment had been discovered. A compound fracture is one in which the skin has been broken, with sometimes a splintered end of bone protruding from the wound. They occur most frequently in the leg, and because they are the result of an accident, there is usually dirt in the wound.

Surgeons of Lister's day had noticed that, while ordinary fractures never developed blood poisoning, a patient with a compound fracture had only a slight chance of escaping one or another of the hospital diseases. Knowing this, surgeons made no attempt to treat the fracture. Instead, the leg was cut off as soon as possible after the patient reached the hospital, before blood poisoning could start. Even this drastic treatment did not prevent blood poisoning in about thirty-five percent of the cases, for the stump, exposed to the unsanitary conditions of the operation and the polluted air of the ward, was only a little less likely to develop an uncontrollable infection than the untreated fracture.

The patient, arriving at the hospital, would be carried first to the ward to wait for the surgeon to examine his injury. There, if he was in any condition to notice his surroundings, and had never been in a surgical ward before, the thing which would strike him first and fill him with horror would be the smell. A foul, sickish-sweet odor of decay hung in the air, a stench that no amount of fresh air could dissipate, so powerful that it could be smelled in the street outside. This horrible stench came from the wounds, for all of them which had been in the wards more than a few days were filled with decaying matter which oozed into the dressings. It was known as the "surgical stink," and it was so strong in some overcrowded hospitals that it fouled the air outside and could be smelled a block away.

Presently the house surgeon would arrive to make the examination, dressed as he always was for hospital duty, in a black frock coat and striped trousers. Both coat and trousers were usually stiff with dried blood and pus, but the profession of surgery, having become one of dignity, required this formal dress. The house surgeon would examine the fracture case without washing his hands, even though he might have been called away from an autopsy to make the examination. In fact, there was no place in the ward for him to do so unusual a thing as washing, even if he had wanted to. He would wash afterward, if at all. That was standard practice in all hospitals, though Semmelweis' desperate exhortations had here and there planted the vague idea that an exception should be made in the case of women in childbed. At Saint Thomas' Hospital in London, for example, there was a sign which read, "Gentlemen who are dissecting or doing post-mortem work should wash their hands in chlorinated soda before going to their cases." That notice was science's farthest outpost, no soda and no basins being provided.

The inevitable verdict of amputation having been given, the patient would be lifted into a contraption like an undertaker's basket, an agonizing ordeal, and borne off through stone corridors, up steps and down, until the procession arrived at the operating theatre. This might be a large room with some students lounging in the tiers of seats to watch the operation. The floors of these theatres were invariably of wood, stained brown in the vicinity of the operating table with the blood of countless patients, and sprinkled over with sawdust to absorb some of the fresh deluge. A fainter replica of the ward smell was here also, rising from the decaying blood in the saturated floor, from the surgeon's coat, from the students' clothes, even from the operating table itself, which usually was of the ordinary wood found in kitchens. The table in Edinburgh was one of those, and near it—close enough to allow a good view but far enough to be out of reach of spurting blood—was a half-circle of upholstered chairs reserved for distinguished visiting surgeons.

The patient was transferred from basket to table, and the surgeon's assistant, who was seldom a trained anesthetist, administered the anesthetic, which might be chloroform or ether. There was an element of risk at this stage, for deaths from chloroform were by no means uncommon (Lister preferred chloroform to ether, supervised its administration himself, and never lost a patient from this cause).

Meanwhile, if the broken leg was exceedingly dirty, the site of the incision was washed off with soap and water. Since an amputation was a bloody business in those days, the surgeon usually took off his coat, but some surgeons kept a special frock coat for operating, which had become too blood-soaked to appear even in the dissecting room. It hung on a peg in the operating room with an assortment of threaded suture needles thrust through the lapel.

The surgeon usually had one or more assistants, but no nurses were present, and when, in the course of the operation, he had to use both hands to tie one of the ligatures, which he took from a bunch hanging over his vest button, he held his knife in his teeth. After the leg had been amputated, the flap of skin was stitched in place—but loosely, to allow the escape of the inevitable pus—and the ends of the ligatures were left to dangle out—to form, it was hoped, a channel for drainage. Instead of providing drainage, these ligatures became saturated with blood and pus, making the finest sort of breeding ground for microbes.

When the operation was over, the patient was carried back into the pestilential air of the ward. Then, and not until then, the surgeon washed his hands—or perhaps, if another operation was to follow immediately, he only wiped them off. Meanwhile, in the ward, the patient was awaking to pain, and to the nausea which is the aftermath of chloroform. He would be made as comfortable as possible, for this was a new era of charity, and though he might be a pauper, he would have the best care his community could supply.

For some days after his operation the patient would probably fare well enough. The doctor on his rounds might find a little pus on the dressing, there would be a little fever, pain and restlessness, but these signs were normal, an indication that, according to the standards of the hospital wards, all was going well. If the fever seemed slight, no one would bother to check it, for frequent temperature recordings were not made. Then one day the patient might be seized with a fit of shivering. This was the precise moment when the microbes had broken out of the confines of his wound and were literally flooding his system. He himself would not be alarmed at so slight a chill, but the doctors knew what it foreboded, and afterward they would watch him anxiously. Presently he would have another attack of the shivers and then a sudden burning temperature. Pyemia—and his chance of ever seeing the outside world again was small indeed. "It doubtless happens," wrote a surgeon of the day, "that patients occasionally recover from this disease . . . but such a result may be looked on as a happy exception to the commonly fatal termination."

If the patient did not contract pyemia, his body might be filled with strange, microscopic germs that looked like strings of beads—though no one who took care of him knew they were there—the microbe of erysipelas. His doctors would recognize the symptoms of the disease, once called Saint Anthony's fire, and the patient would be hurried away to an isolation ward, for everyone believed then that erysipelas was highly contagious. If the patient was lucky and escaped not only pyemia and erysipelas but also hospital gangrene, he might have no more than a local infection which would exude pus and heal after a long time with a broad, angry-looking scar, but infection of some sort he could not escape, for it was universal. Today the number of deaths from pyemia and erysipelas is infinitesimal, hospital gangrene has disappeared, and wound infections after operations commonly run as low as five or six percent.

If the patient of those days who had undergone amputation did not contract any of the hospital diseases, then his wound would merely stink and ooze for a little while, as all the other wounds in every bed in the ward were also stinking and oozing. But one day, when he was moving a little in a vain effort to make himself more comfortable, there might be a sudden gush of blood, a bright red torrent. This was a "secondary hemorrhage," an all too common thing, but it must be stopped quickly, for his life blood was flowing away. The doctor would come running, and he would know without having to examine the stump that the wound had suppurated around one of the unsanitary silk ligatures and caused the wall of an artery to give way. The damage was difficult and excruciatingly painful to repair, and sometimes—frequently, in fact—there would have to be another amputation higher up and the whole frightful business gone through all over again.

Incredible as it seems, people recovered from these amputations more frequently than they died. Recovered, that is, in the technical sense, and had a wooden leg strapped onto the stump. There would be a huge broad scar to show, and a constitution more or less impaired forever.

In Edinburgh it was the custom for young medical men to hire a hall in which to deliver lectures and do their best to attract students to come to them. When the lecturer was a medical man of standing, the university granted credits for his lecture courses. Lister set himself up as one of these extramural teachers, but he was not a brilliant, or even an interesting, teacher at the start of his career, and his students were few. He found no pleasure in lecturing, and sometimes when he was required to address a gathering of his colleagues, he was filled with downright dread.

Before one of these speeches he invariably sat up all night feverishly dictating to the patient Agnes. In these early days he never trusted himself to speak from notes but put the entire speech on paper. He had the utmost difficulty in organizing his material. Writing for him was a process of discarding, consulting notes, substituting and rewriting. His thoughts were lucid, but when it came to expressing them on paper he was no more facile with a pen than in his stammering speech. Some shy men, when they communicate in writing, are not conscious of the barrier between themselves and other men. For Lister the barrier was always present, and though every event of his life has been subjected again and again to the closest scrutiny, the barrier is indestructible, and much of the real man remains hidden behind it.

Lister seldom finished writing a speech on time. Sometimes he continued to scribble in the carriage on his way to the lecture hall and he appeared on many a platform still clutching his unedited notes. He sometimes arrived so late that his audience had almost given him up. His father wrote long, worried letters to Lister about this fault and Lister replied with promises to reform, but the inability to be prompt at these ordeals grew from too deep a root.

Lister's private patients, like his students, were at this time few in number. In addition to his work outside the university he held the post of assistant surgeon at the Infirmary, but these varied duties did not completely fill his time. He used his leisure for research. He had never become reconciled to the prevalence of the hospital diseases and he began once more to speculate about the causes of suppuration and putrefaction in wounds. He was more than ever convinced that the trouble could not be traced to the action of oxygen in the air on the raw surfaces of the wound, and he had begun to suspect that the agent which caused the poisoning and rotting of living flesh was not external but something which worked from within the wound. He noticed that frequently the infection seemed to start in a clot of blood buried in the wound or around the base of the ligature. The clot of blood would putrefy, the decay would affect surrounding healthy tissue and the dire sequence of blood poisoning would have begun.

With the putrefying blood clots in mind, Lister experimented with the coagulation of blood and published a paper which removed some generally held misconceptions on the subject and brought him considerable credit.

Though the knowledge he gained from this research did not throw any direct light on the causes of infection, it was part of the foundation which made his later discovery possible. He had observed that the dread post-operative symptoms of the septic diseases always began with inflammation in the wound. This led him to study the stages of inflammation, using as his subject the foot of a frog. He had come a long way by this time from the medical student who could think of nothing to do but gaze helplessly at the slough of hospital gangrene through a microscope. His fine mind grasped the nature of the problem, he planned his research and pursued it logically from step to step. The experiments were delicate, fussy. Frogs cannot stand the heat of a hand, and he had to use forceps to tie the threads which held the tiny toes apart. He was convinced that vivisection was necessary to the welfare of mankind, but he was a tender-hearted man who, in hot weather, put tins of water on his roof for the thirsty sparrows, and he saw to it that the frogs felt no pain.

He sent off long letters to his father, describing these experiments of his in great detail. "I dare say," he wrote, "thee may wish I could tell thee of having done with that animal for good and all." The long hours of work were rewarding, for in the end he was able to add to his conviction that the cause of infection was not oxygen the certain knowledge that inflammation damages the vitality of tissues, making them less able to resist the agent which attacks them. He did not yet know what that agent was, but he could show that it was this weakening of the tissues which gave it a foothold.

Lister was thirty-three years old. He had been at Edinburgh seven years, during which he had matured, married, become a young man of considerable distinction among medical scientists and though he himself didn't know it, he had laid the solid foundation for his great life work. It was then that he was appointed professor of surgery at the University of Glasgow. His students made him a farewell gift of a silver flagon, and his associates gave him a dinner at which he was obliged to make his first nonprofessional speech. He worried about the speech a good deal, and on the appointed night he was, as usual, almost late. He got through the speech well enough, however, and he and Agnes set out with some misgivings for their new home.

In Glasgow, Lister had his lecture hall refurbished at his own expense in the shining varnish, chocolate browns and yellow creams which were esteemed so highly in those days. Agnes was proud of it. They both worried about how the first lecture would go, for they were still young people, not very sure of themselves in this strange city away from the counsel of the great Syme. The attendance turned out to be better than they had hoped, and the students were so impressed both with the young professor from Edinburgh and the shiny varnish that they paid him the rare compliment of taking off their hats. Once he was in the swing of it, Lister lectured easily and well, and he quoted to all these strange young men that phrase so often used by the gentle Paré, "I dressed him and God healed him."

The one serious disadvantage of the Glasgow appointment was that it did not carry with it a hospital position. An official connection with a hospital was essential to Lister. He applied for an appointment to the Glasgow Infirmary, but the granting of the appointment was in the hands of the government, and governments moved as slowly then as they do now. A year passed before his request was finally granted.

The Infirmary was big, ugly, parsimoniously managed and unclean. Hospital diseases raged inside its gray stone walls. Lister insisted that some of the beds be removed from his wards and that a certain standard of cleanliness be maintained, but here he found himself in conflict with the managing authorities, who did not believe dirt and overcrowding had anything to do with the bad record of the Infirmary and objected to the cost of remedying these conditions. Lister prevailed to a certain extent, and hospital diseases in his wards decreased a little, though even after this improvement he continued to lose about half the patients who came to him. He spent many hours thinking about this problem while he walked in a small neighborhood park which he called his "academia for peripatetic study."

Then one day in 1865 the professor of chemistry at the university, a man named Thomas Anderson, who knew of Lister's preoccupation with the problems of hospital diseases and putrefaction in wounds, gave Lister a paper which he thought would interest him. It was as though this man Anderson, with the paper in his hand, had stepped into the spotlight of immortality for an instant and then retired into the shadows. The paper, which was in a bound volume of publications of the Académie des Sciences, pointed out that putrefaction was caused by the action of microorganisms. It was Pasteur's famous paper which he called *Recherches sur la putréfaction.*

Louis Pasteur was the first to present conclusive proof that microorganisms cause putrefaction and that these minute creatures are to be found on particles of dust floating in the air. Lister instantly saw the applicability of the little French chemist's theory to his own problem of the putrefaction of living tissues in a wound. It was a mighty moment, though the full implication of Pasteur's work in its bearing on the hospital diseases did not at once occur to Lister. He spent much time brooding under the trees of the little park, and in the end he had the concept firmly in mind that the air of his wards swarmed with these invisible, living enemies and that they were harmless until they lighted on a substance which afforded them a spawning ground. The tissues of a wound, already weakened, as he had shown in his experiments, by inflammation, were as unable to resist the decay as though the flesh were already dead. As in dead tissues, the microbes caused these living, weakened tissues to putrefy.

Gradually Lister fitted together in his mind the essential parts of the picture and understood at last that the problem was one of sepsis, that the reason why septic disease raged in hospitals, but only in surgical wards, was that the air in these wards contained a lethal concentration of microbes. He believed that the chief source of infection was from the air, but he realized that these microbes might also be carried on surgical instruments, on the sponge which was used to dress wound after wound without being cleaned, and on the surgeon's hands. The problem, as he understood it at the beginning, was to free the wound of all microbe life and then seal it with an antiseptic dressing through which infection could not enter until the surfaces of the wound had healed. Not all of this mighty concept was evolved at the same time, nor was it the product of pure reason. He learned many things from experience. He discovered that no wound is too small for microbes to enter and do their deadly work, and no wound is safe from them so long as any unhealed part remains. Though we have now progressed from the technique he called antiseptic to one we know as aseptic, he had laid the foundation of modern surgery.

Lister began a search for an antiseptic chemical with which to wage a war on the tiny creatures he could not see but which he believed in with the mixture of faith and reason that is characteristic of the scientific mind. Various antiseptic chemicals had been used before—the word was not new—but as they had been used inconsistently and without knowledge of the germ theory, they were in the main ineffectual. Lister had heard that the town of Carlisle had been in serious difficulties because of the stench of its decaying sewage and that the seepage had poisoned cattle in nearby pastures. The municipal authorities had ended the trouble by treating the sewage with

German creosote, which was an impure form of carbolic acid. He went to his friend, the chemist Thomas Anderson, who had given him Pasteur's paper, and asked for some carbolic acid.

The carbolic acid we know today is an almost clear, faintly oily liquid. The chemical Anderson gave to Lister was as thick as molasses, dark with tar and all sorts of impurities, and it could not be mixed with water to reduce its strength. Lister carried the smelly stuff away with him and bided his time, waiting for the ideal case on which to try the experiment that was now clear in his mind. In March, 1865, he thought the great opportunity to subject his theory to a rigid test had arrived. It was the case of a worn-out factory worker who had a severe compound fracture of the leg, a patient who, it may be supposed, was too frail to survive the ordeal of amputation. Lister smeared his carbolic acid thickly on the wound, but it was without avail, for the man had no strength to withstand the shock of his accident and he died too soon for the treatment to show any conclusive results.

Lister waited for two more months, until an eleven-year-old boy who had been run over by an empty cart was brought into the hospital. Both bones in his leg had been broken, and there was a small open wound. Lister had the wound dressed with a piece of lint saturated in carbolic acid, then the bones were set, the leg splinted and a new carbolic acid dressing applied. This dressing was left in place until the fourth day, the day on which suppuration usually began. The boy had been complaining of pain, and so it was in fear of what he might find that Lister lifted the dressing. It was precisely the sort of wound which, in the ordinary course, would have become infected, but instead of the old familiar sight of oozing pus, Lister found the wound covered with a scab, no suppuration evident and no smell of decay. All was well, and the pain of which the boy had complained was no more than discomfort from some tender places in the skin around the wound, caused by the burning of the undiluted carbolic acid. From then on the wound progressed from stage to stage of normal healing. The treatment was a success.

At the end of eighteen months, Lister had used the carbolic acid treatment on thirteen cases of compound fracture, with results which could be tabulated as follows:

Deaths	*2*
Hospital gangrene	*2*
(*amputation & recovery*	*1*)
(*recovery without amputation*	*1*)
Recovery without complications	*9*

These were not enough cases to prove conclusively that carbolic acid was the weapon which Lister sought to fight hospital diseases, but they represented a mortality of only fifteen percent as against the usual record of more than twice that figure. Moreover, seven of these cases were severe injuries with extensive skin lacerations—precisely the sort of injury which past experience had shown to be almost certainly fatal unless the patient could be saved by amputation of the limb. But scant as the evidence was from the point of view of the modern scientists, who piles up hundreds of cases before he is willing to hazard a judgment, these few were enough to convince Lister that he was at least on the right track.

From the treatment of accident wounds Lister soon extended the carbolic acid technique to the treatment of abscesses, and then he turned his attention to the far more complicated problem of eliminating the risk from operations. In treating wounds, Lister had learned many things. One of the first was that undiluted carbolic acid was too strong and caused damage to the tissues of the wound. It is astonishing that his patients escaped carbolic poisoning, but they did, probably because the raw carbolic acid made the wound bleed a little and the blood, mixing with the acid, diluted it. From this mixture an antiseptic scab formed, under which the wound could heal in safety.

In time Lister learned to weaken the carbolic acid by mixing it with plaster of Paris, boiled linseed oil or some other substance, and eventually he secured a purer form of carbolic acid which could be mixed with water to reduce its strength. He learned to make various sorts of antiseptic dressings with carbolic acid as the base, though he was not satisfied with any of them, and in later years, when he was still inventing dressings, he used to say that he would not retire from practice until he had evolved one which seemed to him perfect.

He discovered too that it was not safe to entrust a patient to someone to whom he himself had not taught the principles of the antiseptic treatment, or to someone who believed in them less implicitly than himself. The principles of the germ theory seemed especially difficult for the older men to grasp. Since they had never been accustomed to taking minute pains with dressings, it was hard for them to understand the necessity for doing so now. Moreover, there was always the temptation to lift up this newfangled dressing to see how the wound was doing and so to admit the germs it was intended to exclude. Surgeons here and there began trying Lister's methods without understanding them, and when they failed, it was only natural to blame the treatment, not themselves.

Lister had not shouted his discovery to the world, but, feeling that it was of too great potential benefit to mankind to keep hidden for long, he published the results of his treatments of compound fractures and abscesses in the *Lancet*. In this article he used a moving phrase, one which, oddly enough, has been little quoted. It was, "the element of incurability has been eliminated." It is a modest phrase, but it meant that people in numbers too great to estimate have lived out their lives because Lister had eliminated "the element of incurability."

The first reaction to this announcement of the antiseptic method was decidedly mixed. One prominent surgeon, who failed entirely to see the point and attacked him with unnecessary violence, pointed out that Lister was not the first to use

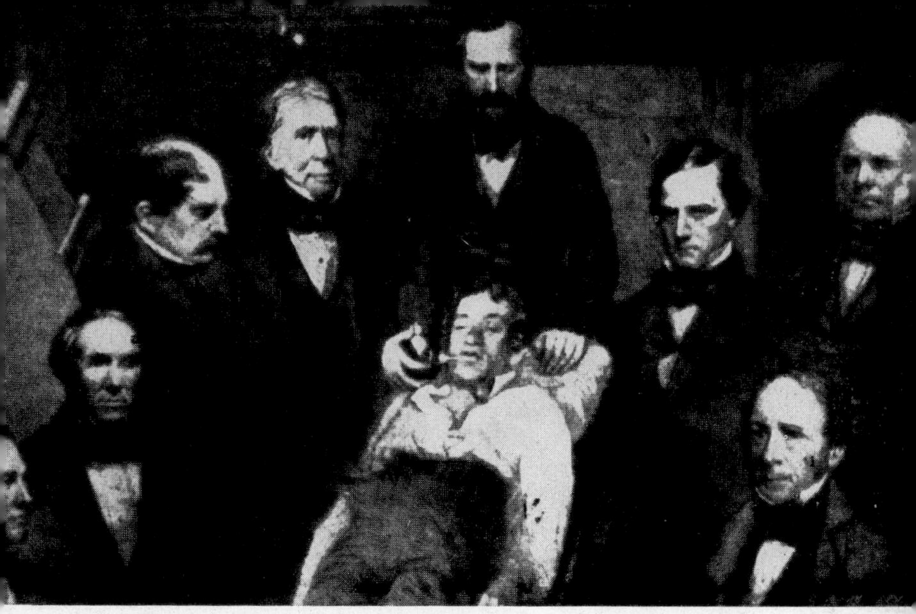

The First Public Demonstration of the Use of Ether.

Robert Liston.

Performing the first operation under ether anesthesia in Britain at University Hospital, London, in December, 1846. Joseph Lister appears in profile at the extreme upper left.

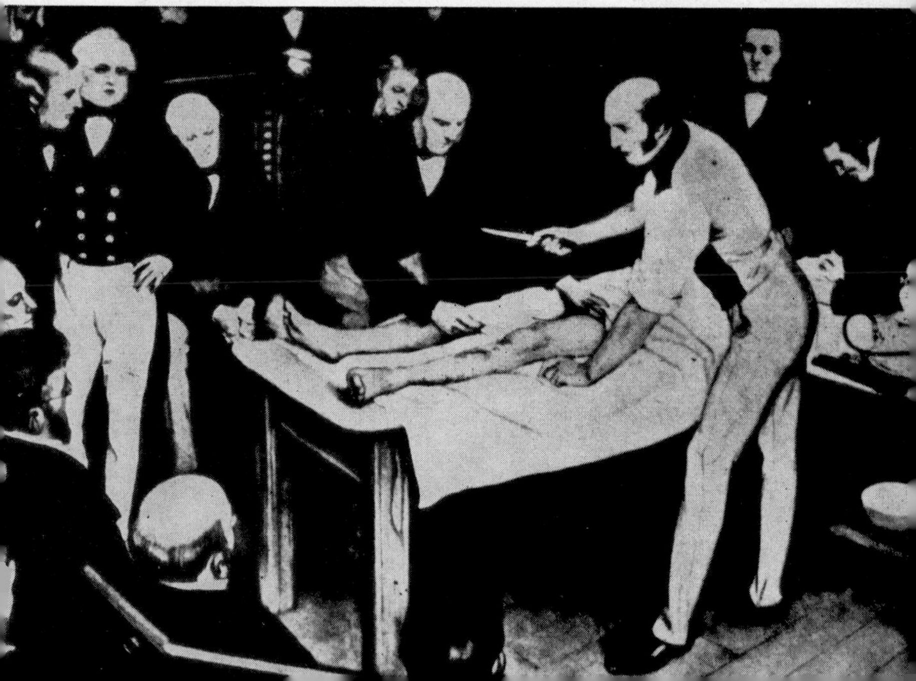

Lord Lister as President of the Royal Society. *Copyright, Wellcome Historical Medical Museum.*

One of the Famous Urine Flasks Used by Lister to Demonstrate Bacterial Infection. *Copyright, Wellcome Historical Medical Museum.*

carbolic acid in the dressing of wounds, a thing Lister never claimed. This surgeon and others like him could not realize that Lister's was a wholly new approach to surgery, a revolutionary technique of thorough antisepsis, beginning in the operating room and continuing through every stage of the healing process.

But there were others who understood that something great had happened at Glasgow, and many of them came for instruction. They came from England, from the Continent and from America, a steady pilgrimage. And they went away convinced, to put what they had learned into practice. Before long, the germ theory and the carbolic acid treatment were known in many hospitals all over the world, and in these enlightened places hospital diseases showed a sharp decline.

Only London lagged behind. Various prominent doctors there had tried the technique and, through faults of their own, had failed and afterwards become the implacable foes of progress. But even among those who did not subscribe to Lister's theories, the impression slowly got around that dirt and overcrowding were dangerous. The old order began to change, and with improved sanitary conditions in hospitals the appalling death rate began to sink. Soap, water and open windows could do no more than reduce it a little, however, and the great change in London and in other scattered, backward places had to wait until control of the hospitals had passed into the hands of the younger generation who believed in the antiseptic technique.

A long time passed before the transformation took place. Meanwhile, after publishing his first results, Lister continued his work, only taking part in the controversy he had precipitated when that seemed to him necessary. Like Harvey, he had no taste for dispute. With the new freedom which the antiseptic technique gave him, he began to extend the field of surgery, performing operations which formerly had been considered too dangerous to attempt.

He had a laboratory in his home, and here he spent many long night hours making original experiments and repeating those which Pasteur had made. One of the latter, which he made primarily to demonstrate to his classes that the air swarms with microbes which cause decomposition, became famous with a whole generation of his students, for it had about it the irresistibly comic touch which crops up occasionally in the most dedicated, solemn and serviceable doings of the great. He filled four laboratory flasks with urine, which is a putrescible fluid. He then heated the necks of the flasks until the glass was pliable, and drew three of them out into long tubes, which he bent at various angles. The fourth he left straight and cut off short. Then he boiled all four flasks to kill any microbes in the urine. After that, he let them all stand uncorked. The bent necks of the three flasks prevented any dust, and consequently any microbes, from entering. Days later the urine in these three flasks was as uncontaminated as it had been in the beginning, and it stayed that way for weeks, for months, for years. The urine in the flask with the short, unbent neck, however, putrefied and grew a rich crop of mold. It was a graphic demonstration of the truth of the microbe theory. These veteran flasks became a most valued aid to him in his teaching, and from this time on, the tall, handsome figure of the eminent professor was often seen riding in his ultra-conservative carriage on his way to a lecture, dressed in his fine, conservative clothes, nursing his precious flasks of urine tenderly on his lap.

Lister had never been satisfied, since the beginning of his antiseptic technique, with any of the ligatures in common use. Silk and whipcord ligatures always caused suppuration, and sometimes the end of the ligatured vessel would rot away, blood would suddenly spurt out and the patient might bleed to death before help could reach him. In any event, these ligatures had eventually to be removed, and so they were left dangling out of the wound until they had rotted through and could be pulled away. Ligatures of silver wire caused less suppuration, but they often brought on severe neuralgic pains and had to be cut out. Lister experimented with soaking silk ligatures in carbolic acid to destroy their septic effect. Not only was the carbolic irritating to the wound but it also seemed to be impossible to make it penetrate all the fibers of the silk, and he finally came to the conclusion that he must find an altogether different kind of material.

He had noticed that living tissues tend to assimilate or "eat up" any organic material left in the wound ("organize" was the word Lister used). The wound simply took into itself such substances as the edges of the scar and even pieces of dead bone. The silk ligatures, being themselves organic, should have been assimilated in the same way and Lister had noticed that there was in fact a tendency in that direction. He realized that what he needed was a ligature of organic material which the tissues of the wound could "organize" more readily than silk, and which could easily be made antiseptic and left in the wound permanently.

At the end of a long series of experiments he came to the conclusion that catgut was a material most likely to be "organized" by the wound. Catgut ligatures, which are in reality made from the intestines of sheep, were not Lister's invention. They had been tried and discarded many times in the past, for no satisfactory method of treating them to make them uniformly strong and pliable had been devised.

In addition to giving it these qualities, Lister was faced with the problem of so sterilizing the catgut that it would not cause infection. He found that the greatest degree of sterility could be achieved with melted wax which contained carbolic acid. By repeated trials and failures he discovered that aging increased the strength of his catgut, and one day this was confirmed when Lister heard a fiddler, who had come to the Infirmary to amuse the patients, complain that his strings would not work well because the weather was damp and they had not been seasoned by age.

In 1868, during the last Christmas holiday Lister spent at

his old home in Essex, he and his nephew, Richman Godlee, who later became his biographer, experimented with a seasoned, sterile catgut ligature on a chloroformed calf. The operation was performed in a private museum filled with objects Lister and his father had collected, among them an alabaster Buddha who presided over the scene from the mantel shelf. A month later, the calf was sacrificed and the parts involving the ligature sent to Lister for dissection. He found that the ligature had not only served its purpose well but had been absorbed and replaced by living tissue.

Lister was still experimenting with methods of seasoning catgut as late as 1908, and the general acceptance of catgut ligatures was slow. Though as late as the end of the seventies, long thread ligatures continued to dangle from amputated stumps exactly as they had in Paré's day, eventually the absorbable ligature which could be left in the wound completely changed the former method of controlling hemorrhage. Today, ligatures of various materials are used, and the sterilization of them has become a complicated process, but the principle which Lister devised as an adjunct to his antiseptic technique has not been superseded.

In 1869, when the Listers had been living in Glasgow nine years, Agnes' father, Mr. Syme, was stricken with a paralytic stroke which forced him to retire from his active work at the university and the Infirmary. Lister was elected to fill the place which Syme was forced to vacate, and he and the faithful Agnes returned to Edinburgh. And those famous urine flasks come back into the story, for the Listers, not daring to trust them to the packers, carried them in their arms on the train to Edinburgh, greatly to the delight of their fellow travelers.

The Listers were glad to move. Edinburgh was a pleasanter place in which to live than the slum-filled, industrial city of Glasgow, and the managers of the university were more enlightened. But their return was overshadowed not only by Syme's ill health but by the death of Lister's beloved father.

Mr. Syme lingered only a little while and then he too died. With them the older generation which had advised and encouraged Lister was gone, and he himself had moved up into the ranks of the seniors.

Lister was now generally regarded as the leading surgeon in Scotland, and Scotland had for some time been leading the world in surgery. The fame of his antiseptic treatment was spreading all over the world. Some of the older men of the profession who in the past had formed Lister's chief opposition were beginning to die off, and almost in direct ratio to the taking over of the new generation, the antiseptic principle was gaining ground.

Eventually, Lister came to overemphasize the dangers of infection from the air. He conceived of the atmosphere as teeming with swarms of deadly microbes, and in this he was partly right, for the air in the old-fashioned wards filled with patients with putrefying wounds must indeed at times have contained lethal concentrations of germs. Even in a modern operating room, microorganisms rain on the operating field at a rate which has been estimated to reach sometimes as high as sixty thousand in an hour, though not all of these are virulent. What Lister did not know, and so failed to take into account, was that a living body has a power of its own to combat microbe infection, unless the concentration of microbes is unusually strong or unless the infection is carried deep into the wound by the instruments or the surgeon's hands. For this reason the rain of microbes in a modern operating room is harmless if other precautions are taken. The power to resist infection varies greatly in individuals, and it is not surprising that Lister did not grasp it, for in some respects it remains a mystery to this day.

Lister believed that the danger of infection from the atmosphere was especially great in the operating room, where the wound must necessarily remain uncovered for a time. He recognized that there would be other periods of danger following the operation whenever it was necessary to remove or change a dressing on an open wound. He became more and more convinced that the microbes must be destroyed down to the last invisible microcosm, while they were still in the air and before they could alight on the raw surfaces of a wound.

This line of thought led him in 1870 to invent an extraordinary contraption that sent out a mistlike spray of carbolic acid. He used this spray during operations and whenever it was necessary to expose wounds to the air. The spray, of which there were eventually several models, was handled by an assistant, while Lister and his dressers worked through and under it in a state of most acute discomfort. The carbolic mist wet their coatsleeves to the elbow and chapped their skin, so that, as someone pointed out, it was possible to tell whether or not a surgeon was a disciple of Lister merely by looking at his hands.

The spray became famous and was used by many surgeons all over the world for a number of years. It had its enemies also, though none so articulate as the German who denounced it in a paper with the ringing title, *Fort Mit Dem Spray!* Lister eventually abandoned the spray, but not until 1887, when he had come to understand that germs on hands and instruments are a greater menace than those which ride the dust motes in the air.

Lister was happy in Edinburgh, and so was Agnes. His classes had grown large with his fame, and he had a voice in the policies of the university and the Infirmary. His private practice was all that he could desire. This state of things might have continued for the rest of his life, had the opportunity not come to move to London as professor of clinical surgery at King's College. His friends warned him against it, telling him that he would have fewer students, fewer hospital beds under his control and a far less enlightened management, but these considerations were outweighed in Lister's mind by the fact that London still lagged behind the rest of the world in the acceptance of the antiseptic theory. He felt that if he himself were there, his influence would prevail, and so, to the great regret of his students and his colleagues in Edinburgh, he accepted the appointment.

In 1877 he and Agnes moved once more, carrying by way of hand baggage on the four-hundred-mile trip those venerable urine flasks. And here three of those flasks disappear from history. No one is quite sure what became of them, though it is thought that they may have perished in a fire. The fourth has achieved honorable retirement as a cherished exhibit in the Wellcome Museum in London. They had done their duty, for they had helped to convince hundreds of students that the germ theory was valid, in the days before a new science with its own teachers and research workers had been founded on the teeming microorganisms.

Lister's friends had not misrepresented conditions at King's College. The students were ill-mannered, listless and inattentive, and at the first lecture they failed to show him even the courtesy of taking off their hats. Their attendance was so irregular that Lister's assistants, who had come with him from Edinburgh, went themselves to the lectures in order that their beloved chief need not appear to be lecturing to an almost empty hall. In the wards, conditions were even worse. John Stewart, who was one of those loyal assistants, has this to say about them:

"To us, coming from the Royal Infirmary [in Edinburgh] with its simple, kindly, common sense routine, in which the patients' welfare and comfort were the first consideration, this cold, machine-like system was intolerable. . . . One afternoon as Lister was about to leave the hospital, Dr. Duffin asked him to see a boy in his ward. . . . Lister soon satisfied himself that it was a case of osteomyelitis of the femur and advised immediate operation. While some of us proceeded to get things ready in the operating theatre, I went with others to have the patient removed. . . . When we arrived at the lad's bedside the sister in charge told us we could not be allowed to remove him. Why? Because no patient could be removed without a permit from the Secretary! I pointed out the fact that the Secretary had now left the Hospital and would not be back until 10 A.M. next day, that Dr. Duffin himself and Mr. Lister were now in the theatre waiting for the patient and had decided that immediate operation was the proper treatment. All to no avail. I lost patience and proceeded to wrap the unconscious boy in his bed-clothes in order to place him on the stretcher. But the sister and the nurses adopted so resolute, and, I may say, so menacing an attitude that all of my dressers fled—except Addison, who held the ward door open while I walked out with the patient in my arms, the nurse actually pulling at the bed-clothes in an attempt to *rescue* the patient. I carried him to the operating theatre, and he was then our property."

In time, surgeons began to send Lister cases which they themselves despaired of, in order that, as a last resort, Lister might try his methods on them. These were difficult cases, but he succeeded so well with them that he began to make converts, and little by little his days grew less troubled. He had come now into the afternoon of his life. Honors were heaped on him from the Continent and from the United States. He and Agnes had gone to Philadelphia to attend a medical meeting in 1876, and the newspaper reporters made him a celebrity, American style.

From this time on Lister's life outside the college was a crowded one. He wrote, lectured and, with Agnes, traveled widely. (On one of his travels he was at last told about the work of Semmelweis, but Semmelweis was long since dead.) Lister took an active part in the fight against the anti-vivisection bill, and he found himself in opposition to the Queen herself. The bill was passed—a triumph of ignorant sentimentality—and its provisions were in some respects so stringent that Lister and other scientists were forced thereafter to do much of their experimental work outside of England. In 1883, Lister was knighted. This period of his life was busy and constructive, and he took a lively interest in the growing flood of scientific discoveries.

When he was sixty-five years old, he retired from his professorship at King's College, and in the year following from King's Hospital also. That was the year in which Agnes died while they were on a vacation together in Italy, and from this blow Lister's spirits never fully recovered.

Now that he had retired from teaching, he took more interest in the affairs of various professional organizations, and in 1895 he was elected president of the Royal Society. Two years later, the year of Queen Victoria's second Jubilee, he was raised to the peerage. The other honors which he received make a long list, for he was that rare thing among men of science, a man who is considered great in his own lifetime. In 1903, Lister's health, which had always been excellent, began to fail, and in 1904 he had a serious illness. Just what it was the doctors never determined, though Lister himself believed he had suffered a slight paralytic stroke. His eightieth birthday was celebrated all over the world, but he himself kept to his house and listened to the footsteps of the procession of people coming to his door. When the day had passed, he wrote to his brother, "What a change of opinion has taken place during the years in which I have been doing nothing!"

Lister lived until 1912 and died on February 10, honored, famous and alone. A great funeral was held in Westminster Abbey, but by his own order he was buried beside Agnes in the cemetery of West Hampstead. And there he lies, the man of whom the poet Henley, who had long before been one of his patients, wrote:

> ". . . *A modern Hercules,*
> *Wrestling with Custom, Prejudice, Disease,*
> *As his great prototype with Hell and Death.*"

VIII.

In 1873, Sir John Erichsen said, in the course of an address at the University Hospital in London, ". . . there must be portions of the human frame which will ever remain sacred" from the surgeon's knife. Subsequently he defined those sacred portions as the abdomen, the chest and the brain. No worse prophet of the coming years could possibly have been found. Because of the discovery of anesthesia and antisepsis, it is safe to invade not only those fields but another which was so remote from the thinking of Erichsen's day that he did not include it on his list. This is the heart.

The first effect of anesthesia and antisepsis was to increase the number of operations. In Lister's old hospital, the Glasgow Infirmary, before antiseptic surgery had taken firm root less than four hundred operations were performed in a year. Twenty-five years later more than two thousand were performed in a similar span of time, and the same sort of thing was happening all over Europe and America. A patient with a serious malady no longer had to choose between almost certain death from what ailed him and almost certain death from one of the forms of hospital disease, and certain kinds of operations which formerly had been more dangerous to have than to forgo could for the first time be performed safely. Under the safeguard of the antiseptic technique, new operations were devised for many conditions formerly thought to be inoperable.

One of the early results of the Lister method was a swift

drop in amputations, that operation which once had been the surgeon's chief stock in trade and by which his skill was judged. Limbs with compound fractures were mended instead of being summarily sawn off; the progressive cutting and cauterizing to keep ahead of spreading hospital gangrene had ceased to be necessary. The word hospital was no longer a synonym for death, although the dread of hospitals remained for a long time. The well-to-do still had their operations in their homes, but what had once been a safety measure had by this time become a matter of social prestige, for the hospital was still associated in the mind of the public with the need to accept charity. Even after it became generally known that hospitals were safer than homes—in fact, well into the present century—the home operation remained a hallmark of social standing.

The preparations for home surgery were formidable, and many surgeons sent written instructions for the family to follow. Carpets and straw matting were to be removed. Ceilings and walls were to be swept with a broom. All wood surfaces had to be washed in a carbolic solution. The result of all this activity probably was that more dislodged dust filled the air than would have been there after an ordinary cleaning.

Lister had become a popular hero for whom institutes, antiseptics and children were named, but there were several reasons, other than stupidity on the part of a good many surgeons, why Lister's teachings were slow to spread. In practice, the antiseptic method was cumbersome. It required constant vigilance and it could not be entrusted to untrained people. With the number of operations steadily increasing, hospital staffs were finding the elaborate ritual of antisepsis more and more burdensome. In 1885, Neuber introduced boiling as a means of simplifying the process and his results were so good that surgeons generally began to follow his example, for it was easier to convert the reluctant to an easy technique than to an elaborate one. In 1886, Ernst von Bergmann introduced the steam sterilizer, which required only the supervision of a nurse and converted sterilization into a mass-production process. Even these new methods did not spread as fast as might have been expected. Many large hospitals delayed installing steam sterilization, and as late as the last years of the century, the interns in one institution had to put their instruments into the hospital oven to be sterilized while the bread was baking.

At the same time the methods for preventing infection were changing, the concept itself was evolving from *anti*-sepsis to *a*-sepsis. The distinction is that the antiseptic technique aims at destroying bacteria in the wound, and the aseptic technique aims at destroying them before they reach the wound. Lister's carbolic-soaked dressings belong to the old practice; the sterilization of instruments and paraphernalia, the surgeon's mask and gloves belong to the new. The distinction is a subtle one, and the two techniques are not mutually exclusive. The antiseptic technique has not been wholly abandoned. The medical historian, Ralph Major, has summed it up by saying that "Lister achieved aseptic surgery by the application of antiseptic methods."

The aseptic principle was gradually applied to one detail after another, until the scene in the operating room, which had been approximately the same for a hundred years, was completely changed. The surgeon abandoned his blood-spattered Prince Albert coat for a white gown. Women nurses who had received regular training appeared in the operating room and took charge of the instruments, so that the surgeon or his assistant no longer had to grope for them. The instruments multiplied from a few knives and clamps—perhaps as few as ten in all—and some special-purpose instruments to a hundred or more, and they had metal, instead of stained wooden, handles. The nurse became responsible for the ligatures, which formerly were hung over the surgeon's vest button or held in the intern's mouth. The nurse still wore a long-sleeved dress, for it was some time before she was included in aseptic reform, but she was required to rinse her hands as the doctors did in carbolic solution.

The patient began to disappear under sterile white sheets which became more and more enveloping until only his face and the site of the operation remained visible. The old blood-absorbing table was discarded for one which could be adjusted in various ways. The single gas jet was replaced by groups, which hissed and smelled but gave off a fairly adequate light.

The anesthetist was always a man, and usually a medical student who knew next to nothing about what he was doing. He wore street clothes long after the surgeon had donned the white gown, and he was far from suspecting that there was anything more complicated to the administration of ether or chloroform than putting the patient under as fast as possible, with a dose that it was hoped would last through the operation. It was asphyxiation, not anesthetization, and it not infrequently carried the patient close to the portals of death. The ether or chloroform was poured on any handy object and held over the patient's nose, though occasionally someone with a complicated patented machine would replace the student with his rag and bottle. He was usually an inventor who had no more training, though possibly more experience, than the student, and some of his machines were weird contraptions involving cranks, lengths of hose and frighteningly formidable face pieces.

Bacteriology, which had received that name in 1884, had become a thriving science, and it had made doctors as aware of the millions of microorganisms which filled the air and swarmed over every object as long ago they had been alert to invisible demons and evil spirits. Surgeons attacked these invading armies of germs not only in the operating room but inside the patient as well. As preparation for the operation the patient was regularly subjected to terrific purgings which kept him perched on the bedpan for three days before he was wheeled off to the operating room, weakened, terrified, but thoroughly "cleaned out." When he emerged from the protracted bloody procedures which took place there, still half strangled by the anesthetic, it was small wonder that he was in a state of shock. Every operative patient was expected to show symptoms of shock. Surgeons were becoming increasingly interested in these symptoms and concerned because many patients died in shock when the operation should not have had a fatal outcome.

Old practices die hard, and one which survived long after there was need for it was the custom of lightning operating. A good deal, in fact most, of the surgery of this period was both slap-dash and bloody, and a great many surgeons, even exceedingly prominent ones, were wedded to the heroics of their art. The patient lost a great deal more blood than the state of the technique of hemostasis warranted, and the gentle handling of tissues, toward which Lister's studies of the dangers of inflammation had pointed, was not considered important. If the patient survived without infection, technique had won its victory, for the conception of conservative surgery had not yet taken root.

The surgeon who was to create the school of conservative surgery was a lonely, unhappy man—not gifted with manual dexterity—and through part of his life a drug addict. His name was William Stewart Halsted. The surgeon must have two main abilities. The first is the manual skill to perform the mechanics of the operation, the second is the quality of good judgment to plan the technique of the operation, to meet emergencies and to make the right choice at every stage of the procedure. The hand and the mind. Halsted's manual skill was not brilliant, but few have equaled his ability to form correct judgments, both in the diagnosis and under the strain of the operation itself. The sum of them created a new standard in surgery.

William Stewart Halsted

1852–1922

"The fire that on my bosom preys
Is lone as some volcanic isle." —*Lord Byron*

William Halsted's parents were well-to-do, with a house on Fifth Avenue, where William was born, and another at Irvington, New York, where the family spent the summer months. Here young William dissected frogs and small garden animals, like Vesalius and Hunter and many another embryo surgeon before him. He was taught by a governess until he was ten years old, then he went to the Phillips Academy at Andover and from there to Yale.

He was no student, and the only part of his school career which he valued in the slightest was sports, in which he did very well. He was well proportioned, and good-looking in a bold sort of way which suggested that he estimated his own worth pretty highly. He was popular when he wanted to be, but he had a knack for saying witty, sarcastic things about those he didn't like that made him enemies and kept him from being elected to a senior society. Nevertheless, he became captain of the football team in 1873. Clothes interested him a good deal, but no more than is usual with many young men in college. He was not at all averse to being the center of attention, and one day as a joke he appeared on the campus in a well-tailored suit of bed ticking.

This is not, perhaps, a prepossessing picture, but in a few years the canvas was painted over by the events which began the real story of William Halsted.

In his last year at Yale he bought—for what reason no one knows—a copy of Gray's *Anatomy*. Surprisingly enough, this most unstudious young man found he had at last discovered something besides sports which interested him. He read Gray carefully, and dropped in at the medical school now and again to watch a clinic there. By the time he left Yale, when he was twenty-two, he had made up his mind to be a doctor.

The medical school he chose was the College of Physicians and Surgeons at Columbia University. He had not been there very long before he discovered that he had a mind, and he used it. Two years later, in 1876, he suddenly decided to take the examinations for an internship at Bellevue Hospital, though he was not really eligible since he had not yet received his medical degree. He had set his heart on having the appointment, but nevertheless he was filled with astonishment when he was notified that he had passed and would be accepted. The ex-playboy could not sleep all that night for happiness.

Bellevue at this time was the storm center of the antiseptic controversy. Two surgeons, and two only, Doctors Smith and

Sabine, subscribed to the Lister creed. The rest waited for a day when there was no north wind to blow erysipelas through the narrow windows, took their dirty butchers' aprons off the peg, or donned old frock coats, and proceeded to operate without bothering to do anything more than wipe off the scalpel. Lister had recently visited the United States, but in their view his teachings were nonsense.

The anesthetic was given by a nervous intern using a folded newspaper for an ether cone. It was administered as fast as the patient could be made to take it. There were struggles, and often it needed two doctors and a nurse to hold the patient on the table.

There was one spot in this grim plague house reserved for the amputees, of which there was still a plentiful supply. Their stumps had a way of bursting open suddenly, a day or two or three after the operation, and pouring out blood in a frightful hemorrhage. Since they could not be watched every minute all day and all night, they were gathered together and arranged in a semicircle, their exposed stumps pointing toward an intern who sat on a stool in the center, ready for the moment when the flood broke loose.

When Halsted arrived at Bellevue, he was already convinced of the virtues of the antiseptic technique. He worked hard in both the medical and surgical wards, and when he took his examination for the M. D. degree in 1877, he passed in the honors group. He was invited to compete for a prize of one hundred dollars, which he won, and he followed this up by taking an examination for house doctor at New York Hospital. This too he passed. He moved into quarters there, and began operating with some brilliance. Whenever he found a tumor, he put it in a jar and sent it to William Welch, who was conducting the first laboratory course in pathology in America. Welch's laboratory, which was ill equipped, ill lighted and makeshift in every respect, was in the old morgue on the East River. Here Halsted began to get an understanding of how the pathologist and his laboratory can help the surgeon—a revolutionary, and indeed an almost unique, idea in those times. Welch and Halsted became friends, and what Halsted learned in the dreary old morgue building was eventually to have a far-reaching effect on American surgery.

Halsted did not consider his medical education complete, however, and as he was not hampered by lack of money, he went to study for two years in Austria and Germany, which at that time were the medical Meccas of the world. One of his teachers gave him private lessons in the dissection of the brain. These took place at six o'clock in the morning in the professor's "unsavory" bedroom. Halsted invariably had to wake the teacher up and get him out of bed, and he found this so distasteful that he gave up the lessons.

In this period, the late eighteen seventies, developments in surgery were coming so fast that textbooks were out of date almost before they were printed. Bacteriology was a new and very live science. The antiseptic technique was far more widely practiced in Germany and Austria than in the United States. At the end of the two years Halsted returned to New York with his head full of new ideas.

He was immediately made an associate surgeon at Roosevelt Hospital, where he startled the authorities by the number of hemostats he used to control bleeding. While he was abroad, Halsted had seen as many as two hundred and fifty used in a single major operation, but until he started buying instruments for Roosevelt Hospital, no hospital in New York had ever owned more than six. All operations in those days were bloody affairs, and no one had fully grasped the idea that they need not be, or that the control of bleeding would reduce the shock which was the inevitable aftermath of major surgery.

About the same time Halsted started a private practice, which he limited to surgery, and he was appointed demonstrator of anatomy at the College of Physicians and Surgeons. Halsted had a special fondness for anatomical work. He would appear in the dissecting room in shirt sleeves and a shiny tall hat, his arms full of assorted parts, which he would proceed to distribute to the students. Then he would go from table to table, inspecting each student's work, his blue eyes bright and piercing, his long-fingered hands swift and accurate. He had matured a great deal while he was in Europe. The bold good looks of his youth were gone. He was growing bald, which made his prominent ears look bigger, he was near-sighted, and he wore the little tuft of beard which belongs to the story-book doctor. But his vitality and interest were infectious. He was a good teacher.

The next year, when he was twenty-eight, he was appointed attending physician to both Presbyterian and Bellevue hospitals, surgeon-in-chief to the Immigrant Hospital on Ward's Island, attending surgeon at Charity Hospital on Blackwell's Island and substitute attending surgeon to the Chambers Street Hospital. His days were so full that his visits to Ward's and Blackwell's Islands had to be made at night, and some of the spare time which he managed occasionally to have he spent sitting around Welch's grubby laboratory in the ancient morgue.

Nor was this all, for he also conducted what was called a "quiz," a course of private lessons, for which each student paid a hundred dollars. These quiz courses, run by faculty members of the College of Physicians and Surgeons, were a common practice in medical schools, a sort of apprenticeship which was expected of all medical students—where some of them learned a good deal more medicine than they did at the school lectures. Halsted enjoyed his quiz thoroughly.

His energy and endurance were amazing, and in addition to a daily schedule of these appalling proportions, he found time for original research. The development of local anesthesia had come to interest him greatly, and he told the authorities at Bellevue that he proposed to use it in an operation for cancer of the breast, which was another of his special interests. The

Bellevue commissioners refused to allow such an experiment to be made within their building. Halsted offered to build and pay for a separate structure in which to operate, but this too was refused. The authorities did, however, settle for a tent on the lawn, a rather ridiculous compromise. Halsted erected the tent, which cost him ten thousand dollars, and had hot and cold running water and an inlaid maple floor, for when this somewhat dramatic young surgeon undertook a project, nothing but the best seemed to him adequate. The tent was not used long, however, for events shortly overtook him which changed the course of his life.

Halsted was living in these days with a friend, Thomas McBride, in a house on Twenty-fifth Street. The house was an excellent one, the furniture very fine, the food was good and there was always plenty for an unexpected guest. The two bachelors gave supper parties and musicales. Halsted's tastes in music and décor were good, and he had considerable knowledge about antiques, rugs in particular, though he must have absorbed it by a process of osmosis, for there was no time in the strenuous life he led to read about such things.

Strange as it seemed to those who knew him only after he had passed through the great crisis which divided his life into two parts, the Halsted of these days was a friendly, social person, joyous and full of life. He had the reputation of being a bold surgeon, not afraid of an original approach to an operating problem, and his willingness to try new techniques had produced a number of favorable results. He was, perhaps, a trifle spectacular in the operating room, and he was always very rapid, which was still the fashion of the day, though the advent of anesthesia had taken away the necessity for speed.

In 1884 the announcement had been made in Germany that cocaine could be used to anesthetize the eye. Halsted was greatly interested, and he and two associates at once began a series of experiments to discover whether cocaine could not be used to anesthetize other parts of the body as well. They experimented on themselves and on each other. They had no idea that cocaine was habit-forming, though it is in fact the most pernicious of all the habit-forming drugs. They worked hard, and under the influence of the cocaine they all felt wonderfully exhilarated. They sniffed the powdered cocaine, and their heads grew clearer and clearer. They could work for hours without fatigue, they needed no sleep; they were discovering not only the principles of nerve-block anesthesia but the way to the fuller intellectual life. They were supermen. Sometimes they gave a friend who happened into the laboratory some of the drug to sniff, and they did not stint themselves, for the more cocaine they took into their systems the more brilliant their work appeared to them to be. Not one of them knew that they were in what is sometimes called the "honeymoon stage" of drug addiction.

Halsted published a paper on cocaine anesthesia in 1885, but it was not a very good piece of work and failed to attract much attention, for by this time the drug which had stimulated them at first had begun to slow them down. They tried to give it up and found that they could not. When they stopped taking it, their legs grew unsteady, they became dizzy and nauseated, and they had severe pains in their stomachs. The craving for the drug grew and grew until it was beyond the power of any of them to resist. Even under the influence of a dose they were not able to work. They all began in their several ways a struggle to set themselves free, but the most insidious characteristic of drug addiction is that it undermines the victim's will.

Those who are under the influence of the drug do not, in fact, have the least desire to resist. Cocaine, like many another habit-forming drug, transports the addict onto another plane, where the ego, with all its complex relationships to life, is no longer the center of the universe. Ambition and love become concepts without meaning, and as self sinks into oblivion, the everyday world of reality, losing both meaning and virtue, fades away. The traveler sees no reason for return.

Addicts vary in their reaction to any drug, but it frequently happens that the world which displaces that of ordinary human values, the only world which now has any meaning for the addict, is one in which perceptions have replaced the ego (or so it appears to those outside these mysteries). The addict perceives a cosmic meaning and a strange beauty in material objects which in his former state he had scarcely so much as noticed. He perceives life in what in his previous state had merely been the materials of life. Aldous Huxley, under the influence of mescalin, lost himself in wonder at the flame-like blue of the shadows of a garden arbor, at the glow in the heart of a rose, at the bamboo legs of a chair which seemed to give to him a "new direct insight into the very Nature of Things."

The cocaine addict is a god, but a god with a magnifying glass, for cocaine often has the peculiar property of narrowing down the mind's vision and at the same time enhancing the importance of the smallest aspect of material things. The proportions of the universe are turned topsy-turvy and there ensues an intense, an all-absorbing, preoccupation with detail.

Halsted and his two associates all entered this strange world. The associates never left it again and, in the end, died hopeless addicts. Halsted, urged by his friends, went into a mental hospital in Providence, where he remained for a year.

It was a year of silence and darkness, and of torture as the drug was slowly withdrawn from him. What he suffered there is unimaginable, and it affected every part of his character, for when he came out into the world once more he was a completely changed man. Once he had been gay; he had become gloomy. Once he had been gregarious; he emerged so painfully shy that contacts with other people made him suffer acutely. Once he had been showy, rapid and didactic in everything he did; he had become slow, meticulous, fussy, careful. He had been cheerful, bustling, full of healthful vigor. He had become remote, punctilious and frail. And though he fully reentered the world of reality, he brought with him his preoccupation with detail and minutiae. It was to have a far-reaching effect on his work.

When he left the hospital in Providence he went timidly back into the city, but he avoided all his former friends except Welch. He tried to work, but he who had been so prodigious a worker could not focus his mind, and the series of lectures which he wrote at this time were never delivered. His friends pitied him, but they did not know how to help him, and they suspected that there were times when the temptation to take his drug was too much for him. They were right, for in these months he was slowly losing ground, slipping back little by little into the habits of the drug addict.

Welch was now associated with Johns Hopkins in Baltimore, though neither the medical school nor the hospital had yet been opened. He knew exactly what was happening to his friend and did what was probably the only thing which could have saved him. He arranged to take Halsted into his own laboratory, where Halsted could be as secluded as he liked and where he could work without accounting to anyone but Welch himself. Moreover, Welch took Halsted into his own home to live, so there need be no solitary hours of temptation. Friendship could do no more, but Welch was trying an almost impossible thing, for only about ten in a hundred cocaine addicts ever return to a normal life.

Shortly after going to work at Johns Hopkins, Halsted decided to help along his own cure and restore his none too robust health by going on a trip to South America, taking with him less than the amount of cocaine he had been using in a similar length of time. The experiment did not work, for his supply of cocaine gave out on the return journey and there followed a horrible, degrading incident. Half-crazy for lack of his drug, he broke into the captain's cabin and stole the cocaine he found there. Miraculously, he was not arrested, and the story was not known until he was dead.

While he was working at the laboratory at Johns Hopkins he had to return to the Providence hospital at least once, but this time he went on his own decision and without the intervention of his friends. When he came back he was much better, though whether he ever entirely conquered his addiction is a question which will never be settled. Perhaps this last trip to Providence really did complete his cure, or perhaps, like De Quincey, he continued to be a mild drug addict all the rest of his life. It would hardly seem to matter. What was important, however, was that he was working—really working—once more. No one at Johns Hopkins knew about his trouble but Welch, and so there were none of those suspicions and doubts in the minds of other people which are so formidable a hurdle for those who try to shake off an addiction and reconstruct a useful life. Halsted was making studies of the action of the thyroid gland, of the presence of bacteria in wounds treated by the Lister method, of the structure of blood clots, of methods of closing operative wounds and a number of other subjects, all of which were in time to have a far-reaching effect on surgical techniques. His experiments were done on anesthetized dogs, on which he operated with the painstaking attention to detail that had become deeply imbedded in his character, and for which he cared as though they had been human beings.

Halsted was still on guard, shy—indeed, he never recovered from that—but now sometimes he worked with other people, and while the work was absorbing him he would forget his shyness. His mind was clear and sharp, and though he missed a good many days because of ill health, he was a richly productive man once more. Outside the laboratory he still kept to himself and saw almost no one but his friend Welch. He had become exceedingly fastidious about his dress. No tailoring was good enough to suit him, no linen fine or soft enough.

There was no one else who took such pains with his appearance in that sprawling, untidy Southern town, where in those days the streets were paved with cobblestones, the sidewalks made of loose-laid brick, and where the gutters overflowed every Saturday night with soapy bath water. In such a place his shiny silk hat, his flawless cravats, his English-made shoes were a marvel.

He had never had this sort of extreme preoccupation with the niceties of dress before that year, but one of the peculiarities of cocaine is that it makes its addicts feel unclean—which not infrequently produces a persistent desire to change into other clothes which they believe to be cleaner, newer or better pressed. It is only a guess that Halsted's unusual interest in dress had its roots in the hallucinations of drug addiction, but whatever it may have been that prompted him, his closets began to fill up with expensive suits, some of which he wore only a few times.

The quality of the local laundry work distressed him exceedingly, and after a time he began to send his shirts to Paris to be washed. He saw nothing strange in this, for in his own view he was merely being fastidious. Whenever he discovered other refinements of living he adopted them at once—for a time he even went so far as to use a quill pen. A great part of his day was taken up with the observance of his private ritual.

He never fully entered the world of normal social give-and-take again, but his skill and ability in his work had greatly impressed the authorities at Johns Hopkins, and in 1889 he was appointed associate professor of surgery of the new medical school. The hospital opened in the same year, and by 1892 Halsted was both chief surgeon and professor of surgery. The famous "Great Four" of Johns Hopkins was complete: Welch, whom the students affectionately called "Popsy," Halsted, called "The Professor," Howard Kelly and William Osler. These great men immediately put the school in the first rank, and many students were attracted there who later became famous doctors, among them Walter Reed and Harvey Cushing.

In the operating room, Halsted's devotion to detail showed the marked change that his cocaine addiction had brought about. The bold, slashing manner of former days was gone forever. With the scalpel in his hand his motions became deliberate almost beyond the endurance of those who were in the operating room with him. He was fanatical about stopping to tie off or clamp all points of bleeding, and though this cautious progress ate up time, his operations were as nearly bloodless as it was possible for them to be. He avoided catgut because certain problems of infection had not yet been wholly conquered. He handled tissues with painstaking gentleness, and he closed the wound with precision, matching layer on layer of muscle, fascia and skin, until it seemed as though he were actually searching for some small detail on which to concentrate his attention.

Such operative procedures were unheard of. It was a new approach to surgery. His operations were interminable—the removal of a breast, for example, which ordinarily took an hour or an hour and a half, Halsted protracted into four hours. But instead of harming the patient, the long ordeal produced exactly the reverse effect. When Harvey Cushing went to work under Halsted he was already a surgeon of some experience, but when the first of his patients was operated on by Halsted, Cushing was appalled at the length of time he remained in the operating room. During the long wait, Cushing, more and more concerned, prepared all the usual emergency measures for resuscitation, but when the patient emerged at last, Cushing discovered to his astonishment that they were not needed. He was to learn that they were never needed, for Halsted's patients scarcely ever went into shock.

Since his student days Halsted had been committed to the antiseptic methods of Lister. It has been said of him that he was a better surgeon than operator, and that is true, for he excelled, not so much in manual dexterity as in his whole approach to a surgical problem. More and more he supported his operating work with laboratory research, for he was far more scientific-minded than any other surgeon of his day, and no surgeon since John Hunter had ever made pathology so intimately his concern. Under his guidance the laboratory and the operating room became almost a unit, and the tie with which Halsted bound them together has never since been loosened.

Halsted trained many brilliant students, though in the period after his drug addiction he was not a good teacher in the accepted sense. Standing at a bedside in a ward, he would sometimes talk on and on about some minor point which interested him to a bored group of young men who often had not the slightest idea what he was talking about. Either he had no realization of this or he simply did not care. In contrast to the jovial Osler, who was often seen with an arm familiarly about a student's shoulders, Halsted was distant and reserved. For the most part he was courteous, though on occasion he could be bitingly sarcastic. His pedagogical methods violated every canon of good teaching, but somehow he made what he taught stick in the students' minds, and he so convinced them of the rightness of his ideas that thereafter hardly any of these young men ever discarded an important Halstedian precept.

Surrounded by the multitudinous activities of the hospital, Halsted remained a lonely man, but not, one feels certain, out of choice so much as through an inability to bridge the gap between himself and other people. When he saw someone he knew coming toward him down a hospital corridor he would turn back rather than go through what was for him the ordeal of a friendly greeting. Welch remained on intimate terms with him, but few others saw behind the façade of his formality. And then one day this tragic man found another soul who was isolated from the world, with traits not very different from his own. She was a tall, reserved, dark-eyed girl named Caroline

Hampton, daughter of an old Southern family which had been impoverished by the war. She had been raised in the aristocratic tradition of the South, but rather than stagnate on a plantation where there was little money for anything beyond the family necessities, she went to New York where she trained as a nurse. She left New York for Baltimore when Johns Hopkins Hospital was opened and became the head nurse in Halsted's operating room. Her reserved, ladylike manner and her romantic background appealed greatly to Halsted's own selective, aristocratic tastes. A strangely formal romance, an undemonstrative regard, a love without warmth, grew up between them.

Halsted first noticed her as a personality when she consulted him about a trouble she was having with her hands, caused by the strong antiseptic solution which they all used for disinfecting. This was a solution of mercuric chloride, which is highly irritating, but as no one else suffered from it to the same extent as she, Halsted saw in it a proof of her gentle blood—a sort of surgical version of the princess and the pea.

Nothing he could devise seemed to help her, and then one day he had the idea of having rubber gloves made for her. He had plaster casts of her hands prepared, and he himself took them to the Goodyear Rubber Company in New York. The year was 1890 or 1891—there seems to be some confusion about which it really was. Those first gloves were thick and clumsy, but they served their purpose, and they had the additional advantage that they could be boiled. Then a young intern who had charge of placing instruments in carbolic acid took to wearing rubber gloves. The Professor himself did not take to them until 1896, when he sent bronze casts of his hands to the Goodyear Company and ordered gloves that were thin, pliable and close-fitting. The aseptic advantage of gloves was so apparent that their use soon spread.

The white gown had begun to replace the surgeon's dirty frock coat for operating room attire about the time Johns

Hopkins Hospital was opened, and Halsted was among the first to wear it. He himself introduced the skull cap—love produced the rubber gloves. The surgeon's costume was completed by the innovation of the surgeon's gauze mask, which was first used by Dr. William Hunter at Charing Cross Hospital in 1920.

Caroline Hampton and Dr. Halsted were married and lived together a life of aristocratic chill. Their contacts with the outside world were few and formal, for she was no more adept than the Professor at meeting people on terms of friendliness. He occasionally dined at the club with Welch and one or two others, when he relaxed a little and gave his caustic wit free rein, but she remained aloof from almost everyone. On rare occasions they gave a dinner—not the sort of pleasant little party for which Baltimore was famous, but grim, stately affairs which involved the whole household in days of preparation and invariably put Mrs. Halsted in bed afterward with a severe attack of migraine headache. Both these people—the great surgeon and the cold, plain aristocratic woman—were merely trying, of course, to conceal their burning, unhappy awareness of their social inadequacy. Poor people. These appalling functions on which they worked so hard never made them anything but miserable.

After one of these state dinners Harvey Cushing wrote to his mother, giving her as much of the menu as he could recall. The meal started with caviar and went on to bouillon, roast oysters and terrapin stew. The Professor had made the stew himself, with turtles he had carefully chosen from a stock of live ones he kept in the cellar. The stew was followed by an asparagus course, then quail in blocks of jelly and pâté de foie gras, omelet soufflé, ice, cheese and finally fruit. There were many kinds of wine and the coffee was made in the library by the Professor from freshly roasted beans which had been carefully selected.

The party drank the coffee while gathered around an open

fire made from a special kind of rare wood and laid earlier in the day by the Professor, who would trust no one else to do it. Conversation was hard to keep going; the Halsteds, who had no small talk, were temperamentally incapable of unbending and the guests were fully aware of the painful effort the feast had involved. When at last the party dragged to its end, both hosts and guests were filled with a dismal sense of failure.

After Halsted's death a great deal of eulogy was written about him, and some of it painted his home life as full of charm and coziness. In reality it was never anything but grim, and when there was no need to put up a front for company it was scarcely so much as comfortable. One day Cushing took the girl he later married to call on the Halsteds, and afterward he wrote to his mother: "The Chief and his wife are certainly queer people. A great magnificent cold stone house full of rare old furniture, clocks, pictures and what not in topsy-turvy condition, cold as a stone and most unlivable. The dog room upstairs and the Chief's library alone have fires in them. Such independent people. Mrs. H met us or received us in the 'dog room' in a large dirty butcher's apron. Such a blunt outspoken plain creature you never saw. They are so peculiar, eccentric, so unlike other people yet so interesting, doubtless because of their oddities, that one is inclined to shelve his thoughts about them along side of those of people from fiction—Dickens perhaps. She was a daughter of Gen'l Wade Hampton, perhaps you know. . . ."

Mrs. Halsted's true life was in their country place, High Hampton, in North Carolina, where she spent her time with her dogs and horses or, dressed in any old clothes which happened to be handy, working in the fields helping to plant and harvest the crops. She went to High Hampton early in the spring, but the Professor did not join her there until later in the season, after his annual trip abroad. While he was in Europe he spent most of his time visiting clinics and informing himself on new developments in the field of surgery. The rest of it he spent alone, shut up in some small hotel in Paris or Folkestone or Brighton. What he did there no one knew. After his death, when every part of his life was scrutinized by scholars in an attempt to explain this man who will never be wholly explicable, some of them thought that he was indulging himself in his addiction to cocaine. Perhaps Welch, who was in a better position to know than anyone else, thought he had been entirely cured.

Halsted never ceased trying to conquer his shyness sufficiently to make friendly contacts with his associates, but he was overly polite, overly anxious to please, with the result that he embarrassed those whom he was most anxious to win. Occasionally the Halsteds had house guests at High Hampton, and then Halsted would rise early, pick a bunch of dahlias—for which the place was famous—and arrange them in the sitting room of the guest house before his guests were out of bed. In the Baltimore house, which was only partly heated by a furnace, he would insist on carrying firewood up three flights of stairs and laying the fire himself.

The Halsteds had a number of servants, but the Professor cooked his own breakfast on a gas stove in his bathroom. When a guest was staying in the house, however, he always went downstairs to see that the food was properly cooked, and if the eggs did not suit him, back to the kitchen they went, time after time if he was not satisfied. He even did this for his assistant, Dr. Heuer, a young man accustomed to boarding-house fare.

On one occasion when this same Dr. Heuer was staying in the Halsted house he ran out of ink for his fountain pen and went to the Professor's study to ask for some. Halsted took out of his desk a box which had in it a dozen new fountain pens and gave it to Heuer, telling him that it was most difficult to find a really good pen and to take these back to his room and try them until he found one which suited him exactly. There were, Heuer saw, two more boxes in the drawer, each holding a dozen pens. All the pens had been filled with ink.

Such overkindnesses as these only ended in embarrassment on both sides. Halsted's loneliness and isolation were pitiable, but he never learned the simple knack of getting on with people. He mellowed a little with time. He gave up the shiny silk hat, which made him so conspicuous a figure on the streets of Baltimore, in favor of an immaculate black derby, and he actually found a little laundry there which could wash and iron his shirts to his satisfaction. He learned to live with himself a little more comfortably, as most of us do as we grow older, but he was never a happy man.

His appearances at the hospital had always been erratic, and the reason given was ill health, but his real difficulty was with nervous exhaustion, which overtook him frequently, an inability to pull himself together to face the ordeal of another day. He left a great deal of his work to his assistants, often spending his time on one or two cases which interested him. He seldom operated more than three times a week, though that is not an unusual practice, and he would not permit the scheduling of more than one operation in a day. He never built up a large private practice, and if a paying patient offended his fastidious taste, as one lady did who presented herself for examination with a dirty umbilicus, he lost all interest in the case.

Occasionally he operated in private homes, arriving with a retinue and a great quantity of equipment. For these excursions he charged an enormous fee. In the medical profession he was recognized as a great surgeon, but his was not the type of personality to attract honors, and the list of those he received is short. He was so reticent about his experiences with cocaine that he never referred to the work he had done with nerve-block anesthesia; and Harvey Cushing actually rediscovered the principle and published a paper on it while he was in Halsted's service without suspecting the existence of Halsted's work.

There is no climax to the story. His work continued at the same steady, productive pace from the time he finally mastered his drug addiction until his death of pneumonia in September, 1922, following an operation for gallstones. He had made contributions to the technique of surgery which are too numerous to list, the most important being concerned with wound healing and repair, but his greatest service was in his approach to the larger problem of surgery. The very traits of character which the sniffing of cocaine had implanted in him had made him, strangely enough, the outstanding surgeon of his day. This drug addict, this man whose mind was so preoccupied with the painfully minute, the trivial, that he selected the beans for his coffee one by one, was among the few men of whom it can be said that he founded a school—the school of safe, conservative surgery.

IX.

As the beginning of the present century approached, the speed-up of scientific discovery bearing on surgery had become exceedingly noticeable. Two of the greatest discoveries, anesthesia and antisepsis, had come one on the heels of the other, and lesser developments were changing the practice of surgery almost year by year. The work of the pathologist, the bacteriologist and the roentgenologist were all coming to the support of the surgeon. The surgeon was fast ceasing to be a lone worker.

In former days there had been perhaps two or three good surgeons in any of the largest cities at any one time. In the last decade of the nineteenth century their numbers had increased, and men whose work was of the highest order were to be found in most of the cities of smaller size. The names of these men do not appear in history, though their knowledge was great and their skill considerable, and their combined efforts raised the standards of their profession to a new level. These unknown men numbered many thousands, and were any one of them transplanted into any era of the past, with all subsequent knowledge subtracted, the remaining qualities of heart and mental outlook would have made him famous. They were selfless men. Their surgical feats, which were sometimes prodigious, were as often as not accomplished in some home kitchen, and they never appeared in the limelight of the big amphitheatres. Their fees were small, their charity patients numerous. Their reward for a lifetime of hard and constant work was love, not glory. They sedulously attended medical meetings and read medical periodicals. It was they who put into everyday practice the discoveries of the great pioneers.

One of these men was a New England doctor named Oliver Cotton Smith, and his story is included here because his was typical of those dedicated lives to which the country owes so great a debt. He was born in Hartford, Connecticut, shortly before the Civil War. He went to a public school and to high school, but not to college, for a college education was not considered necessary for a doctor, and few could afford to postpone their careers for that length of time. Smith chose to go to the Long Island Medical School, which was one of the hundred and fifty-odd medical schools scattered around the country, most of which were private institutions, in business with the single aim of making money for their owners. Their courses were usually not more than two, or at best three, years long. Their professors, who were never full-time teachers, were usually men who had not succeeded very well in private practice and were glad to earn additional money from the schools. Two thirds of these schools had no university or hospital connections, and they were flooding the country with poorly trained doctors. The majority of the country's hundred thousand physicians received a part or all of their education in one of them.

Some anatomy was taught in the first year, but most schools required the students to supply their own cadavers, and the adventures in some of the midnight raids on cemeteries were full of macabre incidents and grisly humor. The student had scant practice in even the simplest surgery, and the theory he acquired consisted of little more than a fairly good idea of where not to cut.

Long Island Medical School was considerably above this dismal average, but nevertheless, the greater part of what Oliver Smith knew—and at the end of his life it added up to a great deal—he learned through the years of practice. Internships were not required in those days, and the summer after graduating, Smith signed up as doctor on a ship bound for South America. He returned with a strong desire to continue his education. The account of what followed is from a letter written to the author by his son.

"My father's postgraduate training was provided by Dr. Waterman of Westfield, Massachusetts, a Civil War surgeon. He lived in his house, and, as was the custom in those days, fell in love with the doctor's daughter, Clarabel. I suspect that country doctors looked for a son-in-law as well as an assistant. It is likely that my father's later interest in surgery came from his future father-in-law's tales of Civil War hospitals and camps. When he returned to Hartford he rented a small house near the railroad station, married Clarabel, and settled down to practice medicine. When his wife died, leaving twin children four years old, he did not remarry, perhaps because he knew that he would have no time for domestic life.

"My father is an example of the small city doctor who started in to practice in the 1880's when little was known of antisepsis, modern drugs, or surgery. The best of them were still explorers and inventors who shortened their lives by endless, underpaid labor; early breakfast, driving in a buggy to the office, seeing patients, calling on an apparently endless list of sick people, incurable old folk, women waiting for childbirth, trying to get the seriously ill into crowded hospitals, looking after youngsters afflicted with now almost forgotten diseases. His daily life was an endless round of calls. Then a brief time for dinner, or often none at all, another visit to the office; then perhaps a call to a critically ill patient in his own or the Hartford Hospital. I slept in the room next to my father's, with the door open. Every time the phone rang I woke to hear him groan and then stumble out of bed. One night he got up shortly before dawn to attend an old lady's dying dog.

"The bulk of his practice came from Hartford and from older doctors in the hospital. When he began to practice surgery and the first automobiles arrived, he used his open touring car to take a nurse, an assistant and a folding operating table into the countryside to operate in farm houses and villages. I had the privilege of going along with him on these night excursions in my high school years, often to hold a kerosene lamp over the patient. He realized that small Connecticut cities like Winsted and Torrington needed their own hospitals and was instrumental in seeing that money was raised for them.

"My father employed a nurse in his office and later an assisting physician, also, surprisingly for those early days, a psychiatrist, Dr. Paul Waterman, his brother-in-law. Later several faithful nurses were dependent on him, either in his office or his private hospital. More than one of them remained with him during his life. He never discussed money or his fees in our home; he was the least venal man I have known. Nor did he keep account of time, and vacations were almost unknown. One summer in my junior year in high school he went abroad with my sister and myself to attend a surgical conference in Vienna.

"I presume he worked twelve hours a day or more. Except at breakfast, or more rarely at the dinner table, my sister and I saw too little of him, so that there was a deep affection for him but a complete absence of family life. I thought of him as a hero.

"My father's fees were reasonable, I am sure, but I recall that once I was told he received one thousand dollars from a wealthy surgical patient. His acquaintance and correspondence with the Mayos gave him the latest surgical methods. He invented several surgical instruments and, though he performed every kind of operation, his specialty was the surgical treatment of goiter. I have watched him perform this terrifying operation surrounded by young surgeons. Occasionally he wrote for medical journals and addressed meetings of state and local societies. He was both a practitioner and a teacher of young doctors and would-be surgeons. He kept records and furnished his office and private hospital with up-to-date equipment, and I am sure, paid for it himself.

"When he was making a sizeable income for those days, he moved with his children and our Irish nurse and housekeeper to a larger house on the verge of West Hartford. He sent my sister to an excellent boarding school and me to Yale, where I was reasonably frugal; but if I asked for money, I received it immediately. He was admired by rich and poor, from the governor of the state to a neighboring gardener's family. He had, in one sense, no social life; there was no time for it, or for church services.

"He never retired. He was taken from his last operation straight to his bed where he soon died of cancer. The summer before his death I sailed abroad with him. The night before we landed he told me he had not long to live, and I must not worry or speak about it to anyone."

Oliver Smith died at the age of fifty-seven, and in this also his life was similar to the lives of other dedicated men who wear themselves out before their usefulness is ended. His death was caused by the second great killer of men in the medical profession, the first being heart disease. He was a surgeon with a specialty rather than a specialist, but had he specialized, his statistical chances for a longer life would have been greater, for there is good evidence that specialists live longer than those whose practice is more general.

Oliver Smith's son is a famous editor and publisher. Many doctors' sons have carried on their fathers' work, and there are many families in America in which a medical career has become almost a tradition. The Cushing family is one of these. Harvey Cushing was the fourth doctor in the direct line. All were distinguished men, but Harvey Cushing became perhaps better known than any surgeon in the history of medicine. A librarian at the Academy of Medicine in New York once told me that in Budapest during the twenties the names of only three Americans were known to her and to most people of education. They were Washington, Lincoln and Harvey Cushing. Cushing not only created a new field of surgery but brought it, through his own work, to a high degree of technical perfection.

Harvey Cushing

1869–1939

"O Lord, we thank Thee for the Oxygen Gas; we thank Thee for the Hydrogen Gas; and for all the gases. We thank Thee for the Cerebrum; we thank Thee for the Cerebellum; and for the Medulla Oblongata. Amen!"

—President Wheelock of Dartmouth, 1798

Recollecting anecdotes about Harvey Cushing has almost reached the proportions of an industry, so let me hasten to join the multitude. I too "remember Cushing." It is not a recollection which is important to anyone but myself and it was a very brief encounter, lasting perhaps not more than two minutes and a half, but the effect on me endured for a long time. He was a man who always had a strong effect on others, usually favorable, though there were those who disliked him with a good deal of violence. It was one or the other. No one ever felt neutral about him.

I was only eight or nine years old when this encounter happened to me. Cushing was on one of his periodic visits to Cleveland, the city in which he was born. He came often to our house when he was in town, but in those days children did not mix with their elders and I did not know what went on outside the nursery walls. Then one day, for what reason I do not know, I was summoned. The governess hurriedly crammed me into a starched white dress, tied a "Roman" sash around my waist, pulled up my black ribbed stockings and gave my long corkscrew curls a quick brush-up over the wandlike curling stick.

At the drawing-room door she gave me a shove from behind which precipitated me well into the middle of the roomful of people. I don't think I hesitated for one moment in deciding which was the honored guest. I never gave it any thought at all, for he had a magnetic quality which drew all eyes in his direction. I can see him to this day, standing in front of our archaic William Morris mantel, his thin, well-proportioned body seeming to curve inward toward his own backbone. (He was short for a man, and it is probably true that his shortness had some bearing on his extraordinary character, much as was the case with William Harvey.) His hands were in his pockets, pushing his coat forward, like a pair of misplaced wings—a characteristic attitude—and he was smiling. The smile had charm, but I discounted that instinctively because of his eyes. I can't now tell what color they were, for it was their intensity, their searching quality, their through-and-throughness, which I both saw and felt. They were like a probe.

I was terrified, but training told me exactly what I should do. I advanced toward him like an automaton, without taking my eyes from that compelling gaze of his. I came to a stand directly in front of him, seized my white skirts on either side, dancing-school style, hit the toe of my strapped shoe smartly on the ground and bobbed a curtsy.

If he said anything at all to me, which I have no doubt he did, I don't remember what it was. I had suddenly discovered that I was the focal point of his attention, and it was this which made the incident unforgettable. He seemed to be seeing through me and into me, but there was more to it than that. The look was in some mysterious way a challenging one, as though he were asking me to show him what manner of person I was—what mettle, if any, I might possess.

This came in part, no doubt, from his habit of clinical observation. He was really interested, and not, I instinctively felt, through warmth of friendliness toward a child, but because he had an intellectual interest in human beings, in their potentialities and in their complications. His regard had none of the aloof superiority of an adult toward a child, and by implication it gave me an individuality. It aroused something in me which I suppose was ego. It took me out of the classification "child," and I found myself standing all alone in a world which was not bounded by the nursery walls. It frightened me, but it stimulated me immeasurably. I don't suppose that after that I was ever so wholly a child again.

Years passed before I discovered that Cushing not infrequently brought out in other people a response of which they themselves did not know they were capable. A doctor who was once one of his pupils said to me, "I felt more fully alive, more at the top of my powers, when listening to him lecture or while working with him at the hospital than at any other time." It has been said that one aspect of greatness is the power to influence others. Cushing most assuredly had that power.

This extraordinary person, Harvey Cushing, was born in Cleveland in 1869. The house in which he lived was on Prospect Avenue, a few doors from my father's house, and though at the time my memory begins Cushing had long been living in the East, I don't suppose the home of his childhood had changed very much in those years. The house was spacious, with an old woodbine climbing up the pillars of the front porch. There was a birch tree in the front, and an iron picket fence with a wide gate across the drive on which Cushing's nephew "Pat"—the Dr. Harvey Cushing of the present generation—and other children of the neighborhood delighted to swing. The inside of the house was formal, rather dark and very orderly, the brass well polished and all the letters from Harvey Cushing, the youngest of the ten Cushing children, carefully preserved and neatly docketed. At the back of the house was a barn, which was called the carriage house even after it housed an automobile. There were a garden, a croquet lawn and shrubbery which I remember as a vast, exciting jungle and which I was surprised to discover, when I myself had grown up, consisted of only a few privet bushes and a lilac or two.

Cushing's father, Dr. Henry Kirke Cushing, was a stern, upright, God-fearing Victorian who was nevertheless affectionately known as "Dr. Kirke." He kept a watchful eye on all his children, rebuking young Harvey for his fits of temper with the nickname "Pepper Pot." Harvey was a normal boy, with perhaps more energy than most, keenly interested in all a normal boy's activities, but more especially in various aspects of natural history and in his collection of butterflies, nests and birds' eggs. He got along well enough in his studies, though he couldn't conquer the intricacies of spelling either then or in later life.

He went to Yale in 1887, where he rented a room with his cousin, Perry Harvey. His letters home were filled with complaints about the calcimined walls of their room, which came off on his clothes, and the dust which no sweeping would eliminate from the straw matting which covered the floor. "We have a terrible time," he wrote, "with the dust which rises off this matting. Everything is just covered with it. My last bottle of ink got so full of it I had to buy another which is rapidly being spoiled. I have to stand on a chair when I put on my pants in the morning for if they touch the floor they get covered with matting dust." Rugs were forthcoming from home, which was what he wanted, and a lambrequin for the mantel. He made a sketch of the lambrequin to show his mother how it looked in place. His pen-and-ink drawings were clever and he had so great a facility that at one time he seriously considered being an artist.

Dr. Kirke gave his son no regular allowance, nor would he forward any money until the last had been meticulously accounted for. The good man could never understand why the incidentals of a college education should cost so much. As a result, young Cushing was painfully aware of financial problems throughout his college life.

"Dear Father," he wrote during that first year, "I was very sorry to have received such a letter from you as I did last week . . . I don't know as you have any reason to think that I have not been studying, and do not intend to study faithfully, I am sure you know I always did at home and I don't see why you should suspect I do not here. As for repenting that you sent me here I am very sorry if I have been the cause but if you are afraid I won't study here I don't see why you should suppose I would elsewhere. I went up to N. Y. to spend Thanksgiving . . . but did not go expressly to see a football game although we did go to see the game, and I am sure from the accounts of one of the boys who stayed here that the excitement in New Haven was as great as in New York, if not more so, with bonfires and so forth. I believe you went to college once, and although one has to grind the greater part of the time, there are times when one doesn't. I don't know whether I will make the first division or not as there are a great many remarkably bright men in our class but I have studied hard for it. I hope I haven't said too much but I was surprised and disappointed very much . . ."

Cushing was, in fact, a good student, though not one to whom learning came easily. He made up for this lack by studying more conscientiously, showing an anxiety to take pains and to perfect his work which later became so conspicuous a characteristic. He managed to add to his heavy load of studies a good deal of participation in sports—greatly to his father's distress.

Parental letters showered him like a not-too-gentle rain. His mother wrote, "Here is a little private word for my darling boy. May I say it without offense? You know you have a propensity to scold. Watch against it, my dear; remember your mother's anxious love . . . 'A word to the wise is sufficient.' . . ." The Pepper Pot had most likely been boiling over. And from his father: "Please buy a dictionary and consult it as you write. In almost every letter I note misspelt words . . ." Later, when Cushing had broken the news of his election to a sophomore society, his father, who disapproved of such societies as frivolous, wrote, "I trust you will critically examine your Society relations and calmly judge if you do not think the price asked for its blandishments [an initiation fee of thirty-five dollars] is not large for its worth."

Cushing regarded his relations with his stern father with anxious concern, but he persisted in doing pretty much what he wanted to do, which was to accomplish as much as possible and to enjoy himself while doing it. Now and then he made the busy doctor out in Cleveland downright angry, as on the occasion when Cushing went to Cambridge with the baseball team. "It looks to me," Dr. Kirke wrote, "as if in the glamor and excitement of College sentiments and surroundings, you have reasoned yourself into feeling that if you only kept in the first division, it was none of my business what else you did. . . ." This letter did not end the heated comments on the theme of college sports.

In his junior year Cushing was tapped for Scroll and Key, and we find him anxiously extolling and explaining the senior societies to a doubting Dr. Kirke. In his senior year he began to be concerned about his future. He considered taking up architecture, then chemistry, and then, after a visit to the wards of New York Hospital, his mind turned toward medicine. After that, he never wavered.

He was graduated in June, 1891, and the affection he had for Yale was an active force all the rest of his life. In the autumn Cushing entered the Harvard Medical School, and his concern about lodgings, which were always a worry to him, commenced all over again. He joined forces with another Scroll and Key man and together they found a room on Beacon Hill and bought some oddments of furniture and a large map of Boston. In the dissecting class Cushing was lucky enough to draw a table near a window—lighting in those days not being what it is now. His first problem in dissecting, like John Hunter's, was an arm. He did it with such skill that presently both students and teachers came to watch. After that he was a conspicuous figure as long as he remained in the school.

He worked hard, but he managed to find time for girls, especially for one Cleveland girl named Katharine Crowell, who was visiting friends in Boston. When Kate left, it was Cushing who put her on the train, and took so long saying good-by that he was very nearly carried off. Cushing continued to have money problems, but Dr. Kirke seemed to realize that his son was growing into a man and no longer demanded an accounting of every cent. Cushing's letters home were full of that light humor which was his most charming attribute, and he still made the clever little pen-and-ink sketches.

In his second year Cushing began to work in the wards in the Massachusetts General Hospital, and the contact with suffering seems to have intensified the seriousness which was the bedrock of his nature. And as though his medical studies were not enough, he undertook at various times extra work in the outpatient department of the hospital, showing that ability to add extra work to what the average person would consider a full-time occupation, which seems to be a universal characteristic of successful men.

From time to time he visited New Haven, to "renew," as he put it, his "youth," and his old college did, in fact, have a special power to rest and calm him. He needed relaxation, for he was taking his work very hard and sometimes he was filled with despair at his own imagined inadequacies. There was one incident in particular which so distressed him that he considered giving up medicine altogether. It occurred while he was substituting for one of his classmates at the Massachusetts General Hospital. A woman was to be operated on for strangulated hernia, and Cushing, who had given anesthetics a few times before, was to administer the ether. He was nervous, and well he might be, for he had been given only the most casual instructions. It was, however, not in the least unusual for an untrained student to give the anesthetic. This was before the day when a trained anesthetist presided over a formidable array of dials, charts and complicated equipment. Cushing had no equipment at all, and the dangers of ether had not yet been fully realized. No readings were taken of the patient's blood pressure, and no continuous records were made of pulse or respiration. The ether was still given in one big dose—enough, it was hoped, to last throughout the operation.

On this particular morning the surgeon in charge, a Dr. Porter, was in a hurry, so Cushing put the patient under as fast as he could. No sooner had the operation begun, however, when without warning the patient died. Cushing was shocked and horrified. There was no doubt in his mind that he alone was responsible, and he spent the rest of the day tramping the streets of Boston in an agony of remorse.

He did a good deal of growing up in those hours of anguish. That evening, exhausted and closer to despair than he had ever been in his life, he went to see Dr. Porter at his house and told him that he intended to give up the study of medicine, since he was not fit to be a doctor. To Cushing's astonishment Dr. Porter explained that the patient would not have lived anyway, and that Cushing was not to blame. Moreover, he said, deaths from ether were fairly common; Cushing was not for a moment to consider abandoning his studies.

Though Cushing remained at the medical school, he continued to brood over what had happened. He discussed it with a friend, Amory Codman, and together they hit on the idea of a continuous recording of pulse and respiration during operations. They sought some advice from one of the doctors, and in the end they worked out charts which were put into use in the hospital. Now, for the first time, the surgeon could tell at any moment what his patient's condition was. The use of charts spread to other hospitals, and reduced considerably the number of deaths from ether anesthesia.

Kate Crowell came to Boston again, and Cushing recorded in his diary, "Beautiful day—dog-tooth violets." And again, "She's a fine girl but it's best methinks for me not to see too much of her." The summer of his second year he went home for a rest, which turned into a busman's holiday, for he involved himself in work at two of the hospitals there. Kate was in Cleveland that summer, and Cushing said to himself sternly in his diary, "making a fool of myself about her."

In April of his last school year, when he was twenty-six years old, Cushing began his internship at the Massachusetts General Hospital, and in the same month he watched the first brain operation he had ever seen. It was a case of a compound fracture of the skull, and it interested Cushing so keenly that he followed the patient's progress for some time afterward. This patient survived, but the mortality rate for skull fractures in those days was somewhere around eighty-seven percent. In the notes he kept of the operation Cushing wrote of the "fearful" hemorrhage from the dural sinuses, and he seems to have

William S. Halsted, *by Hermann Becker*

Dr. Halsted, Operating in 1904

Rubber gloves are being worn but not masks. Note large ether cone.

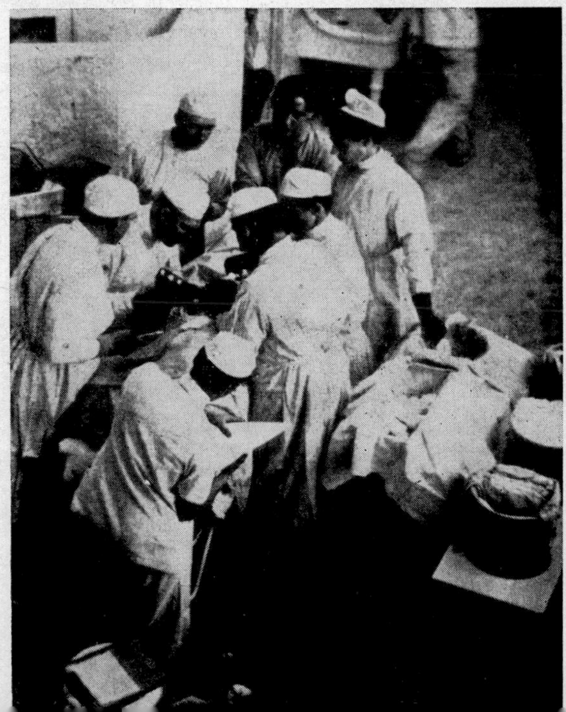

Harvey Cushing

Harvey Cushing, Operating

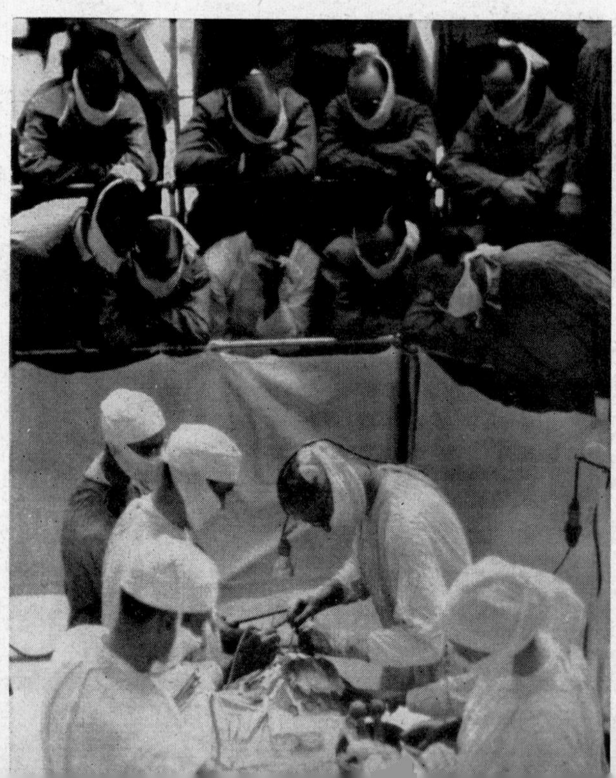

realized then and there that the great barrier to brain surgery was the inability to control the excessive loss of blood.

His school days were over, and he had to move from the room which he had occupied since his second year. He wrote, "This little old top floor room with its retreating frontal bone I have become most attached to . . . All my belongings are boxed up . . . I've always found it as hard to give up a room as an old shoe. They are alike in certain ways."

At the hospital, under the strain of the hard work, the long hours and the unfamiliar responsibility his irritability began to appear. He was kindness itself to the patients, but toward the other interns and the nurses he kept an attitude of tense reserve which occasionally broke into flashes of anger as damaging as the cut of a knife. He was showing himself to be sensitive, nervous, ambitious, energetic and highly intelligent.

About this time he first heard of William Roentgen's discovery of the X-ray. It would, he wrote his father, "revolutionize medical diagnosis." When an X-ray machine was installed at the hospital—to which he contributed out of his small funds—he spent as much time as he could experimenting with it.

As Cushing's term of duty at the Massachusetts General Hospital drew to a close, he became more and more intrigued with the idea of trying to get an appointment at Johns Hopkins Hospital, that gloomy pile on the dusty hill in Baltimore, where the "Great Four," Welch, Osler, Kelly and Halsted, were even then making medical history. Johns Hopkins specialized in graduate medicine, and the entrance requirements were so high that Osler often said he was lucky to be a professor, for he never could have qualified as a student.

Cushing could not have made a better choice, but such an appointment was not easy to come by. He opened negotiations with Halsted, chief of surgery, and after several months, during which Cushing alternately hoped and despaired, he was made assistant to the great man. But when he had to move out of his lodgings and accustom himself to new quarters in Baltimore, the unfamiliarity of his new surroundings upset him. It was not so much that he loved the place which had become his home, for he was the least domestic of men, as that he resented having to give time and thought to problems such as these. He didn't much care where he kept his books or his shirt studs, so long as they were always where he could find them without having to think about it—a simple matter of efficiency. He even resented the strangeness of the city, and he wrote home complaining of everything from the Southern custom of serving sausage with griddle cakes to the monotony of the rows of brick houses, "as alike as streptococci." But the unfamiliarity of the hospital, which touched him far more closely, did not bother him in the least.

Halsted was then struggling with bad health and the need for psychological readjustment, the aftermath of his drug addiction, and Cushing, who knew nothing about this, found him moody, taciturn and hard to get along with. William Osler, the great Canadian physician, was a very different sort of person, and there grew up between him and the young surgeon a liking which was to develop into the warmest friendship in Cushing's life. Osler was a cheerful humanist who believed medicine should be taught at the bedside. He was constantly seen in the wards, surrounded by his students, smiling as he taught his kindly wisdom.

Cushing worked early and late, but he found time to write regularly to Kate. They were not even yet formally engaged, though there had been an "understanding" between them for the past four years, and Kate must sometimes have wondered whether it would ever come to anything more. In those days an engagement was a state just one degree less binding than marriage, with an elaborate ritual of its own. Cushing was not ready to bind himself so definitely. His letters were half teasing, half serious and guardedly affectionate, nothing more. Kate went to Baltimore to visit friends, and the two young people had a very good time, but no amount of moonlight and propinquity could make Cushing commit himself until he was ready. Kate went back to Cleveland to wait some more.

Time passed, and life at Johns Hopkins gradually turned Cushing into a wiry, indefatigable young surgeon who could outwork everyone around him. He was sensitive, high-strung and a prey to all sorts of tensions, but he knew how to discipline himself, and in the operating room he was absolutely reliable. He could perform surgical work of the most delicate sort for hours at a stretch without ever relaxing his minute attention to detail, and time and again he gave proof that he had those special qualities of good judgment and strength in emergencies which are so essential to a surgeon. Both Halsted and Osler were watching him with interest, for he not only gave promise, he fulfilled it.

Halsted's bad health often prevented him from doing his work at the hospital, and his frequent absences drew from Cushing, who didn't know their cause, some sarcastic comments. Halsted wrote him, "Dear Cushing, *You* may have the operating room tomorrow for I should like to watch the cases which interest me for a day or two longer. P.S. I send you over some papers for the one-armed boy in D." Cushing scribbled on the margin, "Characteristic note of the Professor—not operated for a week. One-armed boy left hospital a week ago."

But though this apparent neglect of duty filled Cushing with scorn, he didn't fail to see the advantages in it for himself. To Kate he wrote, "Here I am, a youth, doing surgical work that not one of my school confreres will hope to do for years. It frightens me sometimes. The Chief rarely operates. Today I did all his private cases . . ." The next paragraph began, "I think it's all due to you . . ."

Kate (he called her his "Puss Cat") came to Baltimore again

and they were very happy. This time her presence stirred him into taking the first real forward step in seven years. When Kate went back to Cleveland he wrote to Mrs. Crowell (since Kate's father was dead), formally asking permission to marry her daughter. After he had mailed the letter he was seized with an agony of worry for fear—of all things in the world—he had been too precipitate!

A charming reply came from Mrs. Crowell and he calmed down. To Kate he wrote, "I never felt my strength before—never so confident of my ability to surmount obstacles." But now it appeared that all he had wanted was to feel sure he could have his Puss Cat when he was ready. With that point settled he became the elusive lover once more. Their engagement was not announced. Time passed—swiftly for the busy young surgeon, slowly for the girl who wanted so much to marry him. But Kate could wait, his career could not, and there is no denying that marriage at this point would have put a crimp in that career. Two years after their engagement the Puss Cat was still waiting. Then Cushing went abroad to study.

The Puss Cat didn't like it. She showed her claws a little, and from across the sea Cushing had to do a good deal of explaining. "My dear child," he wrote, "your letter troubles me a wee bit. When your flag is not flying I always feel that I must chase home and marry you instanter. It's wicked of me to have made you wait . . ." As a love letter, that one must have been fairly exasperating. He made excuses for himself. "I want you to move in," he told her, "with the house furnished and the carpets down and a warm fire burning for you." In other words, Kate was to be the ornament of his success, not the helpmate of his struggling years. This trip to Europe lasted fourteen months.

During his stay abroad Cushing worked with many prominent men, and when he returned in August, 1901, Kate must have seen quite a change in him, for he had gained immeasurably not only in knowledge and experience but in self-confidence as well. Technically, his appointment at Johns Hopkins had terminated, but he was anxious to remain and specialize in surgery of the nervous system and the brain. It was a bold thought, for if he carried it out he would be the first man ever to specialize exclusively in neurological surgery. Trephining (trepanation) is an ancient operation, but the first operation in the United States for the removal of a brain tumor had been performed by Dr. W. W. Keen only fifteen years before. (That historic tumor is still floating peacefully in a jar of alcohol at the Jefferson Medical College in Philadelphia.) Cushing looked into the whole question and discovered that in a ten-year period thousands of cases of brain tumor had been admitted to Johns Hopkins Hospital but only thirty-two of them had been correctly diagnosed while the patient was still alive. Of these thirty-two, only two had been operated on and both had died. And this was the field that the young surgeon proposed to make his life work!

Halsted suggested that Cushing take up orthopedics instead. Cushing repudiated orthopedics with considerable heat. He was sure that surgery of the brain would be attempted more often if doctors in general practice could be taught to recognize easily those symptoms which point to tumor of the brain, and he took it for granted that in time operating techniques could be worked out so that these operations on the brain would not be, as they were then, universally fatal. He was thirty-two years old. He was proposing to educate himself and the medical profession at the same time. He knew that there would be many deaths—a kind of responsibility that was not lightened very much by the knowledge that these patients were already doomed. There has never been a more intrepid young man in the whole history of medicine.

How much Cushing discussed these views with Halsted is not known. The two were often antagonistic. Halsted delayed Cushing's appointment, and Cushing, who felt that his European studies would make him an exceptionally valuable staff doctor, grew morose, bad-tempered and depressed. In the end, however, it was agreed that he was to remain at Johns Hopkins and that his duties were to include the neurological part of the surgical clinic. He cheered up at once and set about establishing himself, along with two friends, in lodgings next door to the Oslers' house. It was a happy choice of location, for it contributed greatly toward the intimacy which was growing up between the great doctor and the brilliant young neurological surgeon. Cushing and his friends took turns marketing and polishing their brass name plates, which adorned the front door. They had a gay time, for Cushing, when he felt inclined, could be the most delightful and witty of companions.

For some time past, Cushing's ambition had been to rise to the top of his profession by the most direct route. He had a precise and very high estimate of his own abilities, and he attacked his work with the driving energy and the burning personal pride which is the natural accompaniment of so much certainty. More and more he had grown to hate any obstacle, however small, which impeded him. He drove himself and he drove others. Impatient irritability was too often his attitude toward anyone who failed to understand and execute his orders as he thought they should be carried out. He was in a position of great responsibility now, and he often felt the strain of it. His anger was quick to flare up, and his tongue was often exceedingly sharp.

The days when he was to operate were days of tension for all concerned. When he entered the operating room the bustle of preparation ceased instantly, to be replaced by a tight silence in which those present moved with a machine-like exactness. There were no smiles or friendly greetings. Even while he was scrubbing up he permitted no talking, and during the operation those around him had to maintain absolute silence. In this strained, alert atmosphere, he would work on and on, never hurried, never neglecting any minor detail—one hour, two, three. If someone snapped this tension by a wrong move, Cushing's anger would blaze out and he would say things which sometimes made the victims harbor resentment toward him for the rest of their lives.

An associate in surgery is expected to be part of a team, not a prima donna, and this attitude of his gave rise to a good deal of unfriendly talk. Some of it got to Osler's ears, and he wrote Cushing a letter.

"*Dear Cushing: I arranged with Dr. Hurd—he did not understand that they were your private patients. He must have you put on the Hospital staff in some way officially.*

"*You will not mind a reference to one point. The statement is current that you do not get on well with your surgical subordinates & colleagues. I heard of it last year & it was referred to by a strong admirer of yours in New York. The statement also is made that you have criticized before the students—the modes of dressings, operations &c of members of the staff. This, I need scarcely say would be absolutely fatal to your success here. The arrangement of the Hospital staff is so peculiar that loyalty to each other, even in the minutest particulars, is an essential. I know that you will not mind this from me as I have your interest at heart. Sincerely yours, Wm. Osler.*"

Frantically, Cushing offered to resign. Osler calmed him and for a while he made an effort to keep his temper in check. In this one respect, however, the man who otherwise disciplined himself so severely never learned control.

Frequently, in gathering material for this chapter from those who knew him, I have encountered stories of these outbursts. Some of these tales have the ring of truth. Others, which recount how the great man was brilliantly told off by some subordinate, have obviously been invented by the victim to poultice his *amour-propre.* Quite often, it seems, those who most resent him will not admit his claim to greatness, while conversely his admirers will not admit that he had faults. They are in effect saying that if he has faults, he isn't great, or if he is great, he can't have faults—a point of view which is peculiarly American, for only here do we insist that a great man must in addition be a paragon.

It was at this point in Cushing's career that he began to demonstrate his ability to do a vast amount of work in addition to that which was required of him. He gave lectures at other institutions—and for the very first one forgot to pack his dress trousers. He wrote papers—and found writing very hard work. He is famous now for his literary style, but writing never came easily to him. He made draft after draft of each article and speech, writing each one out himself in his crabbed hand, the misspelled words standing out from the page.

In 1902 he and the Puss Cat were at long last married. The wedding took place in Cleveland, and afterward they settled down in the house next to the Oslers, where Cushing had been keeping bachelor quarters. Kate had waited for him for ten years. A short time after they were married she wrote to Dr. Kirke, "How do you make him take care of himself when he has a cold and how old is he?"

Cushing was in the midst of domestic felicity, which he rather took for granted. The Puss Cat was ornamental as well as useful. She had the long, willowy lines of the "Gibson girl," an open, serious face and an unmistakable look of good breeding. Cushing could be proud of her in any society, which was a matter of importance to him. She subjugated herself to his will with grace, and why shouldn't she? She had served a long apprenticeship. She took over the management of their home, which suited him perfectly, so that he could live, as someone put it, "like a guest in his own house." In 1903 she completed the portrait of domestic perfection by presenting him with a son, William Harvey Cushing, the first of their five children.

Marriage gave Cushing the sense of establishment he had always craved, and one begins to see in him less of the brilliant young virtuoso and more of the mature scientist. He was steadying down. Pyrotechnics were giving way to growth, and there was tremendous vitality in the growth.

His work in the operating room absorbed him, and he was developing what his great biographer, John F. Fulton, calls the "fastidious ritual" of his operating technique. The infinite pains he took with his cases were both the admiration and despair of his colleagues. He seemed never to tire. He could stand perfectly still, holding a piece of cotton to a tiny bleeding point for half an hour if necessary. He could support the hot, damp air of the operating room long after his team was exhausted, and then, before taking off his gown or even his rubber gloves, he would write out detailed notes of the operation, illustrating them with his excellent pen-and-ink sketches.

In the early days of his brain tumor operation the mortality rate was somewhere around an appalling ninety-five percent. He had no assurance but his own faith in himself that he could ever bring that figure down. He made no attempt to conceal it from the medical world, for in order to carry out his idea that the medical profession should be educated in the symptoms and treatment of brain tumors, he began to publish accounts of all his cases.

In addition to his operating schedule, Cushing adopted Halsted's practice of supporting his operating work with laboratory research. He also interested himself in new methods for the control of bleeding (perforce, since it was one of the main problems of brain surgery), in the circulation of the cerebrospinal fluid, in blood transfusions (introduced by Crile in 1909) and in the pituitary, that mysterious gland which governs, among other things, the growth of the body, and which was at this time thought to be inaccessible to surgery. He began his collecting of books on medical history, which was so to enrich his later days. All these interests, and many more besides, he carried along with him through his busy day.

Meanwhile, his mortality rate was going rapidly down. By 1910 it had been reduced to eleven deaths in one hundred operations, a startling change which impressed the medical profession of two continents. Young doctors were beginning now to seek him out as once he had himself sought out Halsted.

One of these young medical men was Dr. William Sharpe, who reported for duty on New Year's Day in 1911. It was typical of Cushing that Sharpe found him on this holiday, at eight o'clock in the morning, working in the laboratory on an anesthetized dog. Sharpe tells the story in a delightful book of reminiscences—how Cushing, without stopping work, told him to go at once to Washington and perform an autopsy on a pituitary giant whose funeral was scheduled for two o'clock that afternoon. Sharpe was instructed to give fifty dollars to the Polish priest who had arranged for the autopsy and to bring back the giant's pituitary, thyroid, parathyroids and adrenals, heart, lungs, kidneys, pancreas, testicles and brain—a fairly clean sweeping which Sharpe was instructed to store in the laboratory icebox.

Sharpe rushed to Washington and located the undertaker's parlor, which turned out to be a single big room with a partition across one end. There were—or should have been—three hours in which to do the job. The priest was right on hand to receive the fifty dollars, but he had not gotten the family's permission for the autopsy, which disturbed Sharpe somewhat. Sharpe was led behind the partition, and there, in an out-size coffin, lay the seven-foot-three-and-a-half-inch corpse, all dressed up for the funeral in formal attire, including a boiled shirt. The undertaker and Sharpe together couldn't lift him out of the huge coffin. The priest refused to help. The only thing Sharpe could do was to pull the boiled shirt over the dead man's face and go to work right there.

He made a long incision and collected the heart and other assorted organs. Then he went fishing blindly for the thyroid and parathyroids, for he didn't dare make an incision which would show above the collar. It was working under difficulties, and one o'clock came before Sharpe could begin the operation for the removal of the pituitary, which was the most important item on the list.

The funeral guests were beginning to gather on the other side of the partition and Sharpe could hear them asking why they couldn't see the body. By this time the priest was frantic. Then Sharpe remembered that the sawing of the skull, which was necessary to reach the pituitary gland, would be a noisy business. He worked furiously and the people, who were only a few feet from him, were demanding to know what the strange sounds meant. Two o'clock came. The crowd had increased and their voices were angry. The priest went off to find a taxi. The whole nightmare business had, Sharpe said, turned into "the most difficult operation of my entire life"—an autopsy in a coffin. He finished at last, crammed the various organs into his black bag and ran like mad for the waiting taxi, which pulled away from the curb just as someone threw a rock at him.

Back at Johns Hopkins, he put his treasure in the icebox and phoned Cushing that the job was done. That night, when Sharpe was sleeping the good sleep of sound achievement, someone shook his shoulder roughly.

"I opened my eyes," Sharpe says, "and saw Dr. Cushing standing beside the bed. He was angry.

" 'I thought I told you to get every ductless gland in that man's body.'

" 'Yes, Dr. Cushing, I did.'

" 'You did not. You missed the left parathyroid body.'

"I told him of the difficulty of the autopsy. In fact, I told him I had never seen a parathyroid gland in all my life.

"He became more and more annoyed. 'When I tell you to do a job,' he said, 'you are to do it.' He told me I had chosen the wrong profession for my life's work, and climaxed his tirade by saying that I was discharged from his service."

Dr. Sharpe was not discharged, however, for after one of these outbursts Cushing was often in a mood of serene affability. Cushing was a creative genius suffering, as this type of mind always does, from strains, tensions and mental anguish about which the non-creative temperament knows nothing. These tempests of his were his way of clearing the atmosphere of the static electricity created by the friction of his own nerves.

Cushing's spectacular rise in the field of neurosurgery had brought him many opportunities to transfer to other institutions. He declined them, though sometimes with regret. Then, in 1910, when he was forty-one years old, he accepted the senior chair of surgery at the newly founded Peter Bent Brigham Hospital in Boston, and subsequently the Moseley Professorship of Surgery at the Harvard Medical School as well. When he accepted the appointment at Peter Bent Brigham, the hospital was only a set of incomplete plans on paper, and Cushing stayed on at Johns Hopkins, making frequent trips to Boston to follow progress there. The slowness of it annoyed him exceedingly—in fact, he fussed and fumed so much that the Trustees, in self-defense, voted him funds for a trip to Europe, but as he had just returned from Europe, he declined.

Two years passed before he could begin work in Boston, and when it came time to pack up and leave Baltimore, the Puss Cat, who was in Little Boar's Head with the children, left the move surprisingly to him. "Shall I," the new chief of surgery wrote to her, "bring the grass rugs in the cellar?" He arrived in Boston in September, 1912, bringing an entourage of young doctors with him. The advent of the new chief at Peter Bent Brigham was an event in the medical world. He took command with no hesitation at all.

In his new post he ruled with an iron hand from which the velvet glove was often missing. He believed in autocracy; authority was his natural element. This brought him into frequent conflict with the administrators of the hospital, and he did not always emerge the victor. His working day began in his office shortly after eight o'clock. There he munched buttered toast, of which he was exceedingly fond, while he wrote letters and worked on his papers and lectures until time to begin his rounds or go to the operating room. He operated three or four times a week, and the members of his staff were inclined to feel that he had a special fondness for scheduling an operation on Saturday afternoon. He seemed not to know the meaning of the word holiday.

After he had finished operating and writing his detailed notes, he had tea and more buttered toast before returning to his office and more work. He sometimes wrote as many as ten thousand words in a day, which is a good deal more than most professional writers produce. At home after dinner he would retire to his study and work again, though frequently this evening work had to do with his book collecting, which was interesting him more and more. Whatever it was he was doing, the whole house had to be muted, for it was a cardinal rule that he was never to be disturbed.

He had made great progress since the days when he had chosen to specialize in neurosurgery. Then he had lost nearly every case of brain tumor which had come to his operating table. By 1915 he had reduced that appalling record to an average mortality of a little more than eight percent—and this in spite of the fact that he performed many reoperations, which often entailed considerable risk. At this same time mortality rates in other parts of the world were substantially higher. They are often quoted as being thirty-eight to fifty percent and for the sake of a good story it is too bad that the statement cannot be left at that. Actually, the bases on which they were compiled, though they seem simple enough, were not the same. Nevertheless, the figures do indicate that Cushing was getting vastly superior results.

By this time Cushing was generally conceded to be the

world's leading neurological surgeon, and his fame was spreading beyond medical circles. There is something essentially dramatic about the idea of an operation on the brain. Some of Cushing's results seemed like miracles. Occasionally it happened, for example, that a patient whose hand and arm were paralyzed when he was wheeled into the operating room would be able to shake hands with Cushing before he was wheeled out again. Understandably, his patients adored him and regarded him as only a little less powerful than God.

Even his failures frequently had a dramatic quality, notably one which occurred at about this period in his career. The patient was under local anesthesia only and was perfectly conscious. Cushing incised the scalp and turned back the bone flap with his usual scrupulous attention to detail, while everyone in the operating room watched with close attention. As soon as the flap was turned back, the tumor was visible. It was about the size of a golf ball, firm in texture, and as they watched, it began slowly to extrude itself from the surrounding brain. Cushing removed it without the least difficulty. There remained, however, what appeared to be the stem on which the tumor had grown. Cushing, anxious to remove that also, seized it in his forceps and cut it off. He had been mistaken; it was not a stem, but a small artery, which at once began to pour out blood. At that stage in the development of his operating technique there was nothing he could do. Everyone in the operating room realized instantly that the mistake was a fatal one. There was a tense and horrified stillness. Then Cushing laid down his instrument. He walked to the side of the operating table, leaned over the conscious man, who was, without knowing it, rapidly bleeding to death, and said, "You must not worry now. In a very few minutes you are going to feel better."

Cushing was in the full stride of his career and nearing its peak when war broke out. In 1915 he interrupted his work at Peter Bent Brigham to go abroad with a volunteer unit from

Harvard to work with the wounded at the American hospital at Neuilly-sur-Seine. His tour of duty lasted for three months, and on his return crossing he stood at the rail for an hour gazing at floating debris of the *Lusitania*, which had been sunk two days earlier.

A month after the United States declared war—an event which had for some time seemed inevitable to Cushing—he was once more on his way to Europe. In France he sometimes operated for sixteen hours at a stretch, always in the midst of confusion or worse. He preferred to do one case well, rather than several in a slap-dash fashion. He simply refused to be hurried, and when the cases began to pile up, he let them be handled by other surgeons as best they could. His operating costume was a rubber apron, and when the floors were wet, or when there were no floors at all, he wore rubber boots. He wrote of "the unusual experience, for me, of operating with a strange anesthetist using chloroform and a so-called 'clean-up' sister." He abandoned chloroform for ether, and ether for local anesthesia, which he used for the rest of his life. He arranged a huge magnet to draw shell fragments out of head wounds, a spectacular form of surgery which attracted much attention. Sometimes as many as fifty people crowded into his cramped quarters to watch him perform.

Fastidious by nature, he was disturbed by his physical discomforts, but he made a joke of them. "We can manage to circumvent the rats," he wrote, "and the imperfect drainage and the dark tents; but we can't keep ahead of the holes in our socks. Roger says he favors a purse-string suture and subsequent trimming with scissors borrowed from the operating room."

In a lull he went to see Crile, who was operating at Saint Rémy. Crile told him he didn't know the day of the week or the month, and didn't care. He felt, he told Cushing, like a savage, and was astonished to find he liked it. Cushing had somewhat the same reaction to the war: ". . . the savage in you makes you adore it with its squalor and wastefulness and danger and strife and glorious noise. You feel that, after all, this is what men were intended for . . ."

Cushing had a deep-rooted conviction that army rules and regulations should not apply to him, an attitude which brought him into serious trouble. Once, when he was with a unit under British command, he was so amused by one of the tommies' letters that he copied part of it and sent it to the Puss Cat, forgetting that his own letters were being censored. He was severely reprimanded, but he made a joke of the whole affair and later enclosed a paper written by a British officer in a letter home. This time his clash with authority might have resulted in the court-martial which threatened him, had not a high British officer suggested to American headquarters that Cushing be immediately transferred to them.

Shortly after his return to duty he fell ill of a mysterious malady which caused numbness and unsteadiness in his legs. He was put to bed, where he amused himself by plotting the progress of the war with pins and a ball of wool until the malady spread to his hands. For a while he was afraid he could never operate again. He grew better slowly and in time his hands regained their normal dexterity, but the circulation in his legs and feet was permanently impaired. He returned to Boston at the end of the war with his understanding of brain surgery much broadened by his war experiences, but he had passed forever his physical prime.

The years which followed were filled with hard work, though he did not operate quite so often now. His legs continued to give him trouble—so much, in fact, that he was in constant pain for days at a stretch. Only those who knew him well ever guessed what effort the long hours of standing on the tile floor of the operating room sometimes cost him. But though he was tired more often, he never shortened the elaborate ritual of the operation, and when, as often happened these days, distinguished visitors came to watch him at work, he seemed inclined to prolong and elaborate his technique. He wore glasses to operate, and he had grown thinner than ever. He seemed to live in flashes of brilliance, vivacity, anger or wit, and at other times he was taciturn and disinclined toward friendliness. Both the highlights and the shadows of his personality had grown more pronounced.

At home Cushing was as much of an autocrat as at the hospital, for it was part of his nature that where he loved deeply he demanded complete subjugation to his will. Toward his oldest son, Bill, who was at Andover preparing for Yale, Cushing was an iron disciplinarian. Bill often felt that his father was more stern and demanding than other fathers. The boy was too much of an individualist to give in without a struggle; he resented being coerced, and there was constant discord between them. Summer vacations, when Bill was at home with his father while Kate and the other children were at Little Boar's Head, were particularly trying times. Cushing's letters to the Puss Cat are full of complaints about the behavior of their son. "Bill," he wrote on one occasion, "blew in last night an hour late for dinner with that defiant look of his. I told him what I thought of it and subsequently apologized, but he was still sulking this morning and got up an hour late . . ." The big house with the two of them alone in it was full of anger and bitterness.

At times they seemed to be close to hatred. Bill made it a point of honor to defy his father in a hundred little ways. The father's nature was such that he had to possess; the boy would not be possessed. Cushing, alone in his study late at night after one of his outbursts, brooded about the boy's stubborn willfulness. He was both lonely and unhappy.

Cushing always expected others to conform to him, not he to them, and he failed to comprehend the boy's point of view. Bill was in a constant state of revolt. By the time he was ready to go to Yale, the two of them could scarcely be together at all without anger on one side and sullenness on the other. But when Bill was in New Haven the friction lessened. Cushing remembered his own college days with nostalgia and sentiment. He remembered, too, the many disagreements he himself had had with his own father, and he made up his mind to make a fresh start with Bill. It was all the easier to do because they were separated. Cushing began to advise rather than scold, and a winter-sunshine warmth crept into his letters to his son. The great man, who had never once, in a long life, failed to get anything he really wanted, was making a wistful, even a humble, plea for his son's love.

At first Bill hardly knew how to respond to these advances, but he was more mature now and not so dependent on his father. Moreover, he began to realize that his professors regarded Dr. Harvey Cushing as one of the great men of the generation, which made him see his father in a new light. He discovered that his father was famous in nearly every country on the globe. He discovered that the great men of the college faculty were interested in him because he was Cushing's son, and that he shone, to an extent, by reflected glory. Exploring these surprising new ideas cautiously, he began to feel proud of such a father. Then suddenly the floodgates of his affection, which he had so long willfully kept closed, burst open and he wrote to his father, "Thanks for your letter . . . I have something more I want to say to you. You have often told me that I was selfish and didn't think of anything but my own personal pleasure. I always meekly agreed and then went upstairs and stormed around, bemoaning my fate in having a parent who wasn't so lenient as some others. I am just beginning to realize that you have always done the right thing . . . Perhaps I have come to the turning point . . ."

He had indeed reached the turning point, and though the disagreements between father and son were not quite ended, after this they touched the surface only and the love between them grew deep and strong.

One Saturday morning in June, 1926, Cushing entered his

operating room, silent, cold and withdrawn as always. And as always on his appearance, the atmosphere was on the instant charged with purpose. The patient was wheeled in, a woman whose eyesight had been destroyed by a tumor, and Cushing went to work. The operation was long and arduous. Cushing worked steadily for close to three hours. Everything was accomplished but the closing of the wound, which Cushing, unlike some other surgeons, invariably did himself. Suddenly he turned to his first assistant, Dr. Leo Davidoff, and, asking him to finish, quickly left the operating room.

Much later in the day Dr. Davidoff discovered that, just as Cushing had been about to leave his office to go to the operating room, he had received word that Bill had been killed in an automobile accident.

The shadows were beginning to lengthen and Cushing knew it. He was in pain more and more frequently, and the long hospital corridors were too long to walk through without stopping to rest. He made these pauses seem as though they were intended to emphasize some point in his conversation, and few guessed that he was actually suffering.

His operating technique was as brilliant as ever—in fact, he had gradually refined it to such an extent that operations which formerly required three or four hours now had to be allotted five or even six. Frequently there were distinguished visitors present; doctors came from all over the world to watch him operate. He welcomed them, for there was much of the showman in him. He was as aware of the fine lines of his profile as any actor, and with the years his showmanship had acquired the subtlety of art which conceals art. But though he dramatized both himself and his operations, only those who disliked him beyond the point of rationality (and there were quite a few) ever claimed that he sacrificed the quality of his work to gain a theatrical effect.

This leaning toward the dramatic might not have been so palatable had he not relieved it with humor. Dr. Bronson Ray tells how, one evening when Cushing was to sail for Europe, he delayed so long over a pleasant dinner with friends that he was in danger of missing his boat. One of the party telephoned the pier that Cushing was on his way and asked that the sailing be delayed for him if possible. When Cushing and Dr. Ray reached the pier they were relieved to see that one gangplank was still down. Then they discovered that the police had cleared a broad aisle for them through the crowd. As soon as Cushing, who had been almost running, saw that, he slowed down to a slow walk and, smiling, passed like a king through the cheering crowd.

In 1925, when Cushing was in Atlantic City attending meetings of the American Medical Association, he stopped to watch a demonstration of a diathermy machine cutting up, with an electric current, a piece of beef. The use of electricity in surgery was not new, but it had never been applied to surgery of the brain, and Cushing walked away from the demonstration deep in thought. When he returned to Boston he sent for Dr. W. T. Bovie, a physicist, and asked him to develop two currents which could be used in brain work, one which would cut tissue and one which would coagulate points of bleeding.

If these two currents could be made to function properly they would be of great value, for many tumors could not be removed because they bled profusely, and most of the time consumed in brain operations was given to the slow process of arresting the flow of blood. Dr. Bovie was installed in a laboratory up the street from the hospital, where he went to work, and Cushing joined him whenever he could find the time.

While operating one morning some time later, Cushing uncovered a tumor of the type for which the electric currents were being developed. He closed the flap of skull and sent the patient back to the ward, but he was not satisfied and that afternoon he suddenly decided to send the patient to the operating room again and see what he could accomplish with his untried electrical apparatus. He didn't know it but it was an historic occasion—October of 1926. No one who was there ever forgot it, for the customary discipline of the operating room, the tense silence, the long-familiar ritual, went completely to pieces and something very like chaos took its place.

The homemade apparatus had to be wheeled to the hospital from the laboratory a block away, bumping and jolting as it came. By the time it arrived, various of its parts had shaken loose and it had to be overhauled while everyone stood around and waited. All this was very hard on Cushing's nerves, for he was feeling in advance the strain of the unaccustomed procedures. He fussed and fumed. Everyone around him was filled with apprehension about the coming operation. The electrical contraption was put into working condition at last, but no one really trusted it. Someone suggested that a blood donor be sent for, just in case, and presently a student arrived who had been typed to fill the role. They put him on a chair in the corner, out of the way. Like everyone else present, he promptly fell prey to the jitters.

The patient was wheeled in. He was exceedingly apprehensive and thoroughly upset by being rolled off to the operating room for the second time in one day. While he was being calmed, a delegation of French visitors arrived and had to be dealt with. They all had colds in their heads. The operating room never did quiet down, but somehow the patient's scalp was anesthetized with morphine—the only anesthetic he was to have—and the skull flap was turned back. The great moment had come. The electrical apparatus was pushed into place. The Frenchmen crowded around, coughing. Bovie, who was not a surgeon and seemed never to have heard about asepsis, leaned over the patient's open head.

Then Cushing picked up the electric instrument. There was a silence so profound that those present could hear their own blood pounding in their ears. Tension and suspense were at their worst, when over in the corner there was a thud. The student blood donor had fallen off his chair in a dead faint.

At the same moment it was discovered that the patient had taken a turn for the worse and was sinking rapidly. Suddenly it was all too much for Cushing's first assistant, a young English surgeon who had been on Cushing's service only two or three days. He probably thought all Cushing's operations were going to be like this one, for he announced in tones of desperation that he couldn't go on.

Everything came to a stop once more. Someone sent out to find Cushing's regular assistant, who was somewhere around the huge hospital. He was found and came on the run. Everyone stood about, waiting, while he scrubbed up and got into his operating clothes, to the accompaniment of Gallic coughs. Meanwhile the patient had been revived—rather miraculously, it would seem.

The tale goes on and on. In his notes Cushing called it a three-ring circus, but the electric cutting current and the cautery worked magnificently, and in the weeks which followed, Cushing called in for reoperation many patients whose tumors could not be removed with the former technique. His mortality rate went up a little as a result, but he had inaugurated—amidst some of the wildest hours ever known in an operating room—a new era in brain surgery.

In the few brain operations that were performed before Cushing's time, the technique was crude in the extreme. Two or three days before the operation the patient's head was shaved, then scoured with green soap and ether or a mixture of ether and turpentine. Then it was wrapped in towels soaked in disinfectant, which were not removed until the operation was about to begin. The patient was given chloroform, and the point at which the skull was to be entered, which was determined by guesswork, was then marked. One old textbook recommends that this be done by hammering in a tack. A band, to act as a tourniquet, was tied around the head, for the scalp bleeds exceedingly freely, but it had slight effect. The incision in the scalp was made, and, struggling to keep the gory flood from impeding his work, the surgeon attacked the skull.

Continental surgeons went at this part of the work briskly with hammer and chisel, but English and American surgeons preferred to use the trephine, an instrument which cut a neat round hole and left intact a "button" of bone. This button the surgeon laid carefully aside in a warm antiseptic solution, to be replaced later as the climax of the operation—and thereafter it might or might not grow into place.

When Dr. Keen did the first brain tumor operation, he used a trephine to make a hole an inch and a half across. This was considered enormous, but the opening proved to be too small and had to be enlarged twice with bone nippers until it measured two and a half by three inches. The next step was to incise the dura, the tough membrane sheath under the bone, and to expose the brain itself.

A great deal of the success of this famous operation was sheer luck. Keen opened the skull at approximately the point where the tumor was, though without the aid of X-ray he could not be sure of the location. The tumor lay on the surface of the brain, where Keen saw it immediately when the button of bone was removed. He put his little finger under it and found that it was firm in substance and that he was able to lift it out with "as little difficulty as one scoops an egg out of its shell." His patient lived for thirty years wearing a skullcap with a sheet of metal in the lining to cover the hole in his head, but if the operation had not turned out to be comparatively simple, or if his patient had died, other doctors might not have dared to repeat his experiment.

Nothing could define more dramatically Cushing's contribution to brain surgery than the contrast between Keen's operation and a modern operation for brain tumor, substantially every important phase of which was originated or developed by Cushing. Recently I watched an operation for brain tumor at Mount Sinai Hospital in New York. The surgeon was one of Cushing's students, Dr. Leo Davidoff; the anesthetist, Dr. Arthur Rosenthal. The following are notes I wrote during the operation, and since I am not a surgeon, they are necessarily from the layman's point of view.

Mon. Jan 31 '55

Brain Tumor Operation at Mt. Sinai

Operating surgeon—Dr Leo M. Davidoff
Anesthetist—Dr Arthur Rosenthal
Assistant Supervisor, 9th floor O.R. Miss Media Marella

The operation is scheduled for one-thirty. It is now one-fifteen & I have just arrived on the 9th floor. I have been given a gown & cap (gray green) & mask. The anesthetic is being given. This is not the op room but an alcove off corridor. Patient is woman, about forty. Head completely shaved gives her doll-without-wig look.

Dr. D just appeared—gowned & masked. We shook hands. Indicated anesthetist by patient's head. Dr Arthur Rosenthal. We acknowledge intro. with eyes. Wouldn't recognize either without caps & masks or they me. Just 3 pairs eyes.

Dr D held up 3 X-ray plates. "I'll show you where we are going in" (left side of head). "I'm afraid we have something serious here. Malignancy." Pointed to shadowy area on film. I glanced at patient who was being strapped to table. Hand hanging over edge is beautiful & sensitive.

Dr D gone to scrub up. Writing this on edge of stretcher cart. Bad desk. Patient now strapped to table. Anesthetic is mixture nitrous oxide & pentothal. Tube through her mouth into trachea held with adhesive adds to something-not-human look. Pentothal bottle on high standard at table foot dripping through tube into needle.

Cleaning head now. Alcohol & ether judging by smell. They are fixing chrome racks over patient. Getting ready to wheel table to op. room.

In op. room. Green tile floor & walls. Many wires & tubes on floor to step over. Huge dome light over op table—greenish glass—dim—no glare. Room shadowy outside of light area.

Two floodlights on standards suddenly go on. Startling. Focused on patient & unbelievably brilliant. Her bald head being painted with scarlet antiseptic. Color effect incredibly beautiful. Scarlet, white, parchment skin, 3 surgeons' hands in 3 shades chrome yellow gloves. Putting cotton in her ear.

Draping patient now—several layers—gray-green sheets over racks make flat-topped tent such as children playing house construct. Anesthetist is sitting on stool beside her, charts on his knees.

Patient's face has disappeared under green-gray drape. Nothing visible but site of op.

Instrument nurse standing on high stool putting trays of instruments on racks over patient. Tall table with rows of instruments behind her. O.R. personnel besides Dr D, 2 assistants, instrument nurse, colored orderly kept on jump adjusting floods every time Dr D moves.

Dr D has just indicated where I am to stand—directly behind him to his left. Think he is left-handed but uses them so interchangably, can't be sure.

Missed marking of skull getting myself adjusted. Think done by scratching scalp. Everyone working very rapidly now. Dr D has scalpel in hand.

Incision being made. 2:00 o'clock. Assistants press edges together with both hands as cut lengthens. Hemostats flash as they move through air to doctor's hand. They are going on bottom of incision only. Scissor-shaped, a fringe of them hanging down. Assistant gathers them in bunches of five & fastens them with clamps.

Incredibly little blood though remember from war days how profusely scalp bleeds.

Upper edge of wound edged with clips—prevents bleeding.

Put on with pincers. Nurse hands out pincers with clip in nose.

Blood draining down drape—scarlet on gray-green incredibly brilliant in white light. White gauze around incision almost blinding. Dr D picks up most of instruments himself from tray where nurse has put them. That business novelists love so of nurse slapping *instruments into doctor's outheld hand doesn't go here.*

Incision complete. My heels made clicking noise when I moved, so took shoes off & carried them to corner. Dr D boring hole in skull, bit in hand. Medieval-looking instrument—except that it is chrome. Almost soundless as it goes into bone. Ass't drips liquid on bit as it turns. More holes being bored. They outline flap of bone to be turned back. Using bone-nipping instrument. Sound is like breaking chicken bone.

Whole business has deceptively casual look—comes of everyone knowing exactly what to do, I suppose.

Dr D is inserting a long, slightly curved instrument from one hole to another. To protect brain from saw obviously, for he is now inserting saw—thin wire saw, about 2 ft long. Pulling saw back & forth now.

Sawing finished. Messy business at that but still surprised loss of blood so slight.

Skull flap now being turned back time 2:28.

Electric cautery apparatus makes buzzing sound. Suction instrument, on tube from wall outlet, runs intermittently cleaning up bits of blood. D picks up various shaped pieces of what I take to be fibrin from time to time & applies them to bleeding point. Stuff made from active agent of blood clots, I believe. Effect in stopping ooze of blood miraculous.

Tumor in evidence. Dr D, "Here is the tumor. Malignant."

The part I can see is oblong, crinkled, rather yielding when touched by instrument.

Clips being used to stop bleeding as D cuts down adjacent to tumor. He has turned to explain they were invented by Cushing. "Cushing clips, they are called."

Op. exceedingly interesting at this point. Great temptation to get too close. You forget there is anything human under the drapes.

Tumor is at upper edge of exposed dura. He is going down now on either side. Electric cautery—or knife—can't see which—buzzing steadily. Op room tense now. Nothing dramatic—just a feel in the air.

2:50. Plasma bottle hanging on standard beside pentothal now.

He is getting ready now to take out part of tumor. It is beginning to emerge. Suction & electrocautery going all the time.

3:02. Everyone much tenser now. I am standing on stool looking directly down. Tumor nearly out.

3:04. Piece of tumor lifted free. Dr. D drops it on tray. Instrument nurse instantly puts it in glass jar.

No, that was only a big piece of tumor about one inch by three-fourths. More to come. What an evil *thing. Covered as it is with blood, it looks same color as surrounding brain but even so, it looks like an interloper.*

Another piece out. 3:14. Into jar.

Is that all? Yes. Dr D is working now to stop bleeding with fibrin & cautery. A long, slow process—tiny bleeding points. He is inspecting walls of cavity carefully as he works. Everyone has relaxed from tension of a moment ago.

Suddenly Dr D turned around & looked at me. (He seems to know all the time exactly where I am standing.) "It is always a surprise when you think you have a malignant tumor & it turns out to be benign. That is the situation here. This tumor is benign."

When *did he know?* How *did he know?*

The real work is over now. Change of mood in room very noticeable. No one has heaved a sigh, but that is how it feels.

The stillness of the patient suddenly strikes me—no sleep looks so still. You forget she is human with that fringe of hemostats hanging from her scalp.

3:37. Tying sutures at one end of cavity—black silk, they seem to be. Sutures have cup-hook-shaped needles on each one.

They are taking gauze cover off bone flap—3:45.

Still working on stopping bleeding & cleaning up blood with suction tube.

Dr D is putting bone flap back in place—like a trap door.

3:52. Flap has beveled edges so it doesn't drop onto brain.

4:06. Scalp laid back in place. The black suture threads are flying—Dr D working on one side, an assistant on the other. Lots of bleeding now. This is bloodiest part of op. I try to estimate how much loss there has been by looking at swabs & red cascade down the drape sheet & figure it as a cup or a little more. Asked anesthetist who said loss of blood was about two pints! Time to get back into my shoes . . .

Cushing first attempted to control scalp bleeding with an elastic bandage around the head. This was never satisfactory, and he abandoned it in favor of injecting the scalp with a blood vessel constrictor and ringing the incision with hemostats. He was exceedingly expert at inserting the saw from hole to hole to cut the bone flap, a process by no means as simple as it appears. Bleeding from the bone he controlled with a substance called bone wax, which was developed by an English surgeon a good many years ago.

I have been told that Cushing used a good deal of saline solution to keep the exposed brain moist during the operation. He never went to such extremes in this respect as the English brain surgeon, Sir Percy Sargent, whom the eminent American neurologist, Dr. John H. Nichols, recalls having watched operate in rubber boots and a rubber apron with the operating room floor an inch deep in water.

Once inside the skull, Cushing took such pains that there was usually little loss of blood. The clips to which Dr. Davidoff referred were invented by Cushing in 1910, to stop bleeding from vessels which could not be ligatured. Sometimes he used small pieces of muscle to arrest capillary bleeding, or held a piece of cotton against the vessel with infinite patience until the bleeding had stopped. He helped to develop fibrin, which is a derivative of the agent that causes blood to clot and is absorbed and can be left in the wound. Cushing was the first to use a suction instrument for the removal of tumors which are too soft to be handled in any other way.

Tumors vary greatly. Some are malignant, some benign. Some grow rapidly, some develop very slowly. Some are compact, some soft and shapeless as jellyfish. Cushing was the first to differentiate between the various types.

Even today it is not possible to remove all brain tumors, and some can be removed only partially. There is always danger that one which has apparently been removed will grow back again, and one which has been partially cut away is certain to do so. When a surgeon discovers a growth which he knows is malignant and will recur, no matter what he does or how often he does it, what course should he follow? He cannot answer that question wholly from his store of surgical knowledge, for it lies largely in the realm of philosophy, of morality in the broader sense and of religion.

To make his dilemma clearer, imagine the case of a comparatively young man who has a fast-growing malignant tumor of the brain. The malignant nature of the growth is discovered in the operating room and verified on the spot by microscopic examination. The surgeon cannot remove all of it. He is faced with four choices. First, he can remove a substantial quantity, close the wound and plan to perform repeated operations to take out some of the growth each time. The patient is doomed in any event, and though the first operation may restore normal functions for a short time, subsequent ones are not likely to stave off mental deterioration.

Second, the surgeon can resort to the course which was common before the radical removal of brain tumors was attempted—which is to say, he can leave a sort of trap door through which the growth can expand. Such cases were once not uncommon in our big hospitals, men and women with huge excrescences on their heads, their normal functions gone—human vegetables, the living dead.

The third possibility is to remove a considerable amount of the tumor—perhaps a piece the size of a small orange—leaving a cavity, then close the wound completely. The usual result of this is that the patient is returned to life for a month or two, but during that time the tumor is rapidly filling up the cavity. Then it begins to press against the skull, and when that happens death is mercifully swift.

The fourth possibility is to do nothing at all, to admit defeat at once and to close the incision without disturbing the malignant growth. Some surgeons do, in fact, prefer to take this course. But there is something else to consider. If no attempt is made to operate, how is surgical knowledge to advance? Victor Horsley, the great English surgeon, once said in such a situation, "If I don't do this operation, the men who come after me will never learn how." The argument, though grim, is valid.

Faced with the dilemma of whether to shorten life and be merciful or whether to prolong it, whatever the cost, surgeons have never reached an agreement. Indeed, as we all know, the dilemma is not peculiar to brain surgery, and in a time when one death in five results from a malignant growth, the question is not an academic one. It skirts close to the edge of the issue of euthanasia, and there are legal pitfalls by the way. Under the circumstances, there will probably be no general agreement in the near future, and each surgeon will continue to do what he does now, which is to follow his conscience and his guiding intellect, making his decision afresh with each new case, and helped to arrive at it, perhaps, by the patient's family or even by the patient himself.

Because Cushing had, as Osler said, opened a new book of surgery, he was faced with the problem of what to do in cases of malignant growths more often than other surgeons. He seems to have decided consistently in favor of operating in order to advance his knowledge. On one case, in fact, he chose to operate sixteen times. Whether or not he chose the right course can only be a matter of individual opinion.

The extent to which a brain tumor can dominate and disrupt the lives of a family is told in a little book, by John Gunther, called *Death Be Not Proud.* It tells the human side of the story and it is one of the most moving books of our generation.

In these later postwar years Cushing's sense of humor sharpened, as though he felt a greater need to offset the grimness of his hard-working life and his growing physical disability. There was, for example, the occasion on which a distinguished Philadelphia doctor named Chevalier Jackson was expected to attend a dinner before going to speak at a meeting of the Harvard Medical Society. Just before the dinner, which had been arranged by Cushing, Jackson sent word that he never attended functions of this sort before making a speech and didn't intend to make an exception. It was too late to call off the dinner. Cushing telephoned to his resident at the hospital, telling him that he was to hurry over to the place where the dinner was to be held, for it was to be his job to impersonate Jackson. The resident arrived, somewhat breathlessly, and was duly presented to the assembled company. Afterward, when the bona fide Jackson appeared to make his speech, there was considerable bewilderment, which Cushing enjoyed thoroughly.

He was quite as capable of appreciating a joke on himself as though it were on another person. In 1929, Cushing arrived at his sixtieth birthday. It was a Saturday morning, and after operating, Cushing was invited to go to the surgical laboratory, where his staff and associates had gathered to pay him tribute. For a while proceedings stayed on a note of high solemnity. Then Dr. McKenzie, a former assistant who had come from

Toronto for the occasion, rose and presented Cushing with a lurid tie. There was a great deal of laughter, for it was well known that bright-colored ties were Cushing's only sartorial idiosyncrasy. When the laughter died down McKenzie read a poem entitled, "The Tie That Blinds."

Some may long for the soothing touch
Of lavender, cream and mauve,
But the ties I wear must possess the glare
Of a red hot kitchen stove.
The books I read and the life I lead,
Are sensible, sane and mild,
I like calm hats and I don't wear spats
But I want my neckties wild.

That was only the first stanza. Cushing retired, bearing the tie, and returned wearing it. Then he made a speech in which he said that, though the tie gave him horizontal mystagmus, he was honored to be its possessor, and that, in truth, most of his ties were gifts from grateful patients.

Cushing hated formal social functions, and he had to be coerced by Kate and the girls before he would appear at one. On one occasion he reluctantly put on white tie and tails to escort them to an affair at one of the hotels. When they arrived he saw them safely through the revolving door, but he kept on going around until he was disgorged into the street again, where he rapidly faded from view.

In 1930 his daughter Betsey married James Roosevelt, and Cushing wrote to a friend, "The town is full of Delanos, Roosevelts and motorcycle policemen and detectives. Our front yard looks like a circus and I feel like Mr. Ringling—the wedding ringling."

Ill health continued to plague Cushing, but he did not alter his schedule in the least, and the burden of his work was more and more of a strain on him. He was tired most of the time, and irritable, and he smoked incessantly. Finally the circulatory condition of his legs and feet drove him into a hospital bed, where he proved himself a most difficult and unreasonable patient. Not one of Cushing's contemporaries could do anything with him, but fortunately there was a junior house officer named Meagher who, surprisingly, was not in the least afraid of Cushing and was able to match Cushing's bad temper with quick Irish wit. Bullied by this junior, who was devoted to him, Cushing grew slowly well enough to return to his hospital duties.

In May of 1931, he performed his two-thousandth brain tumor operation, surrounded by moving-picture cameras and searchlights. He was sixty-two, but his creative mind was as active as ever. The next year he identified a previously unknown disease, pituitary basophilism, which came to be called Cushing's Disease.

Cushing himself had set the age of retirement for the chief of surgery at Peter Bent Brigham Hospital at sixty-three, but when he reached that age he was by no means ready to relinquish work. Many other positions were open to him, but he put off making any final decision. On August 17, 1932, he performed his last operation, and the next day he sailed for Europe. When he returned to the hospital he found his successor, Dr. E. C. Cutler, already installed in his old suite of offices, and though Cushing was fond of Cutler and knew that he had taken over, finding someone else actually at home in his own familiar habitat disturbed him greatly. Cutler, who understood Cushing's temperament, deliberately refrained from consulting Cushing about the running of the department, knowing full well that if he did, Cushing could not help trying to take control. Undoubtedly Cutler was wise, but Cushing was deeply wounded, and he watched Cutler making changes in the established order with great unhappiness. Cutler had given him a tiny office off the laboratory, and here Cushing bleakly pursued his work, entering and leaving the hospital by the students' door.

Unhappy as he was at Peter Bent Brigham, he could not bear to tear himself away from the scenes of his great triumphs. Finally, however, he accepted the offer of the Sterling Chair at Yale, with the title of professor of neurology. When President Angell announced the appointment to an assembly of alumni at the commencement exercises, there was a storm of applause.

The unhappiness of breaking old ties had literally eaten into Cushing's vitals, for he had developed a stomach ulcer. Once the move to New Haven had been made, however, and the family had settled into the pleasant house which Kate found for them, Cushing reveled in his return to his beloved university. He continued to write and to lecture, but he had more time for his book collecting and for his friends. His ready wit—and his bad puns—illumine these declining years. His pictures show him alert and smiling. He gained a little weight, and the tired, intense look disappeared, so that he actually seemed to have grown younger. Even his illnesses he accepted with reasonable placidity. Once when he had to have an operation on his foot for the old circulatory trouble, under a local anesthetic, he watched the performance with so much interest and made so many suggestions that, when he was forced to have another, the surgeon saw to it that the anesthetic was a general one.

His second retirement—from the Sterling Professorship—came when he was sixty-seven years old, but he continued to busy himself with literary-surgical affairs and his own collection of books on medical history. His seventieth birthday was marked by a celebration which he thoroughly enjoyed, and messages came to him from all over the world. The honors he had received in his long life fill nearly four pages of fine type. Among them are twenty-two degrees and many decorations, including the Distinguished Service Medal. His books number fifteen, including his great life of Osler and the *Bio-Bibliography of Vesalius* on which he was working when he died.

One evening when he was at work on his writing, he attempted to lift a heavy folio volume of Vesalius and was seized with an attack of pain around his heart. The next day the pain was much worse and he was moved to the hospital. Three days later, on October 7, 1939, he died. At the autopsy it was discovered that he had a small tumor in his brain.

The Revolution

"Quae prosunt omnibus artes."

—Motto of the Surgeons' Company

The men who have made outstanding contributions to surgery have been geniuses in many varying ways, unlike one another as individuals and dissimilar in their personal histories. On casual inspection, no common denominator is evident in their greatness. Personalities as unlike as Paré and Cushing, Vesalius and Lister, and backgrounds as different as those of Harvey and McDowell, Hunter and Halsted, would seem at first glance to contain no similarities. Nevertheless, inquiring minds ranging from the poet's to the scientist's have searched for common characteristics among the great. In a measure they have found them and in doing so thrown light on the traits which have made these men great.

Diderot believed that genius depends on enthusiasm and deep emotion, Matthew Arnold that it is largely a matter of energy; Thomas Carlyle described it as "the transcendent capacity for taking trouble." Scientists hunt genius with the intelligence quotient, preserve it in numerical formulae and arrive at the conclusion that the intelligence of scientists—surgeons are in this category—is equaled only by the philosophers', but that in the quality of persistence none can compete with them. And finally there is the complacent summary of genius made in 1775 by the Abbé Du Bois, who stated that "genius consists of a happy arrangement of the organs." When we know more about the physiological determination of character, we may discover that he was right.

Of the eight heroes of this book, the five about whose boyhoods we have detailed information had an unusual interest in natural sciences and the anatomy of birds and animals. The twig was early bent. All eight chose medical careers without further vacillation as soon as they had become aware of the real nature of the work. Once launched on their careers, all undertook research projects which they pursued, in spite of other demands on their time, with exceptional energy and perseverance. This ability to cope with exacting research undertakings and at the same time to fulfill the ordinary demands of their professions is one of the most striking characteristics of gifted men.

In addition to their vast and systematic industry, these men all possessed a high degree of intellectual curiosity. Their primary aim was not scholarship, their preoccupation was with the unknown. In every case the unknown concerned some factor encountered in their daily work about which their colleagues had not the imagination to be curious; for another attribute of outstanding men is that described by Cicero as the ability to make themselves strangers to the familiar.

Through their prodigious work these men accumulated a vast store of fact and concept, and in this complex their minds were quick to perceive significant relationships; for another mark of the superior intellect seems to be the power to abstract similarities from a stockpile of dissimilar memories.

Their work was powered by nervous tension which, when deflected by frustration, broke down into irritability, eccentricity or moods of black despair. In spite of brief intervals when the belt seemed to have slipped off the flywheel of their control, these men had an unshakable faith in the value of their work and in its ultimate success, and for its sake they would willingly sacrifice the happiness of others. Some of these men thoroughly enjoyed their fame, but as none of them worked for wealth, so also none of them worked for glory, but rather for the sake of what Kant called "*Ding an Sich*," the "thing itself."

Surgery will always produce great men to solve its problems. It is producing them today, but from the beginning of this century the trend of developments in the field of surgery has been in a direction that makes them less conspicuous. In the operating room, surgery has become more and more enmeshed with sciences which lie outside the surgeon's special field of knowledge. Today perhaps ten of these sciences play a more or less direct part in the procedure of the operation, and though the surgeon is still the focal point, other techniques have to a degree deflected his limelight. Surgery has lost its isolation.

In the laboratory, research in the sciences which contribute to the advance of surgery has passed beyond the range of the simple equipment which formerly the surgeon could buy with his own funds and operate without assistance in his spare time. Scientific equipment has become so costly that it can only be financed by institutions, research techniques so complicated as to require full-time technicians, and the object of the research so recondite as to require the skills of various trained scientists. As a research worker the surgeon has lost his isolation and become one of a team. There the spotlight of publicity cannot so easily pick him out. It has, in fact, shifted from the worker to his work, and the popular acclaim formerly accorded the exceptional surgeon is now accorded the exceptional drug, or what is loosely termed a drug. Insulin, penicillin, heparin and other such tools of modern surgery are all better known than their discoverers. In medicine, a similar shift of the spotlight from person to product is taking place, though Salk, whose public acclaim has not yet equaled either Lister's or Cushing's, may in time prove to be an exception, if for no other reason than that the vaccine bears his name.

Well before the start of the century the elaboration of research was beginning to create a vast new problem of financing. Deans of medical schools, who had tended to look on laboratories as the exasperatingly expensive playthings of their prima donna chiefs of surgery, found that they must raise huge sums for these laboratories if their schools were to keep abreast of the times, and that the school, hospital and laboratory must function as a unit. About the turn of the century, the financial demands of the new research were almost wholly met by a few men of great wealth. Johns Hopkins, Peter Bent Brigham, Rockefeller, Carnegie, Harkness and others made huge gifts either directly or through foundations created for the purpose. Later, when the financial burden could no longer be carried largely by a few individual fortunes, funds were raised through appeals to the public at large, but though today such funds amount to a huge total, they cannot equal the growing demands of medical research. A partial solution has appeared even as the financial skies have grown threatening, for large corporations have begun to make grants for research. Drug houses, manufacturers of electrical equipment and, more recently, cigarette manufacturers are sponsoring research not only in laboratories of their own but in the universities as well —a development in which there is much hope for the future.

The horse-and-buggy surgeon who carried a spade on his rounds to dig himself out of the mud and operated on an ironing board or a leaf from the extension table had become an anachronism before the end of the century's first decade. Events in his world moved rapidly. In 1901, Landsteiner described three of the blood groups—a discovery which made blood transfusion safe—the Rockefeller Institute was opened and the Nobel Prize was founded. That same year adrenalin was isolated and the Riva Rocci blood-pressure apparatus was introduced by Cushing. In 1902 the Carnegie Institute was founded. In 1904 the negative pressure chamber for thoracic surgery was developed. In 1905 (the year in which the Wright brothers made their first successful flight) novocaine was discovered. In 1906 a pituitary tumor was removed successfully for the first time. In 1908 the Model T Ford brought country doctors into closer touch with city hospitals.

In 1909, a fact known to Vesalius was resurrected from the dust of centuries and became the basis for modern chest surgery. It was that respiration could be maintained indefinitely by air introduced through the trachea under positive pressure. In 1910 the fourth blood type was discovered, and Crile published an important work on the prevention of shock. That year Flexner presented his report on medical education which made the startling disclosure that there were 155 medical schools in this country—more than in the whole rest of the world—but that most of them existed for private profit and only a third were affiliated with universities. The end result was the raising of educational standards, the blasting out of existence of the proprietary schools, with the consequent reduction of the number of schools (by 1923) to eighty. In 1911, Cushing invented silver clips for brain hemostasis, the previous method of control having been largely saline solution.

When the First World War broke out it proved to be, from a surgical point of view, different from any previous war.

Governments had learned well the lesson forced on them by the Nightingale-inspired women of the Crimean and Civil Wars, and from the start they acknowledged their full responsibility for the care and rehabilitation of the wounded. At the same time the enormous numbers of the wounded created a crisis that made demands upon the resources of the whole medical profession. For the first time surgeons realized that battlefield surgery involved more than surgical techniques.

Nothing could show more clearly the interdependence of surgery and other sciences, and the reliance of surgery on laboratory work, than the surgical battle with the bacillus of gas gangrene. It frequently occurred that, when a wounded man was carried into a base hospital and the surgeon removed the dressing which had been put on in the front-line dressing station a day or perhaps two days earlier, he heard a faint hiss of escaping gas. He could see that the skin around the wound was puffy, and when he pressed it, he heard a crackling sound. Those symptoms told him that he was faced with a case of gas gangrene. One wounded man out of every three was infected, and in the early days of the war most of them died, for there was no known cure.

Under the microscope the germs of gas gangrene could be seen clustering in grayish-white colonies surrounded by bubbles of gas. Each microorganism was straight, fat and blunt-nosed, and reproduced with great rapidity simply by bisecting itself. William Henry Welch—that same Welch who befriended Halsted—discovered the microorganisms of gas gangrene, having been led to look for them (according to a story which has no authority but hearsay) by curiosity after a corpse had exploded at a funeral.

The bacillus of gas gangrene was subsequently named after Welch—bacillus welchii, or, in common usage, b-welchii. These microorganisms grow harmlessly in the intestines of humans and animals, and they are found in great numbers in plowed fields. Gas gangrene had made its appearance in other wars, but not in such great strength, for the battleground of the First World War was cultivated land.

Surgeons attacked b-welchii with a technique called debridement, the cutting away of damaged tissue and muscle. If the injury was in an arm or a leg the most successful attack seemed to be to amputate at once—a return to the pre-Lister method of attacking septicemia. Sometimes this radical surgery was successful, sometimes not, and surgeons did not understand the reason for either the success or the failure until after the beginning of the Second World War.

The rate of gas gangrene infection in the Second World War was the same as in the first, about one wounded man out of every three. That was a far worse record than in previous wars. Then British surgeons discovered that when gas and swelling were present in wounds, those wounds all, without exception, contained dead tissue. It was in this dead tissue that b-welchii bred. Debridement saved the patient if the infected tissue could be cut away before the gas infection had time to force its way into healthy parts of the body. It failed if surgery was too long delayed. The answer was plain—the surgeon must move as close to the fighting lines as he could and, armed with scalpel, antitoxin and the sulphanilamides, must operate as fast as he could get the wounded men to his table. As soon as this happened, the death rate from b-welchii infection dropped, and fewer limbs had to be sacrificed.

The formidable resources of American and British laboratories were by this time focused on the habits of the blunt-nosed organism, and it was discovered that it could not tolerate oxygen. This in turn completed the enlightenment as to why so many more wounds were infected with gas gangrene in the two world wars than in any other wars in history. The reason was that the wounds themselves were of a new type, caused by high explosives which hurled metal fragments deep into the body, so deep in fact that the lips of the wound frequently closed behind them, shutting out the air. The fragments had picked up the microorganisms from the mud on the soldiers' clothes and transplanted them to a spot where they were safe from oxygen, safe to multiply in the ready-made culture of destroyed tissue unless the surgeon's knife could reach them before their deadly work began.

The result of these discoveries was that only about one percent of the wounded men contaminated with b-welchii developed cases of gas gangrene, and few of these ended fatally. B-welchii is still with us, and probably always will be, but it has ceased to be the great killer of the modern battlefield.

The medical resources of Europe were so damaged by the First World War, and their finances so drained, that leadership in surgery and its allied sciences shifted to the United States. Four new fields of surgery have been developed in this century, and it is in this country that the greater part of those developments has taken place. These new fields are surgery of the brain, thoracic surgery, vascular surgery and surgery of the heart. The first of these includes the special type of brain surgery—still very much in the experimental stage—which is called psycho-surgery, and aims at relieving emotional stress. Thoracic surgery has brought new hope to patients with cancer of the lungs. Vascular surgery is accomplishing miracles by repairing faulty circulation in various ways, including rerouting of the blood supply through newly joined arteries and replacement of diseased parts of arteries with sections of plastic tubing or with artery drawn from "artery banks."

Heart surgery is a tale of wonder. In 1882 a research-minded doctor, thinking years ahead of his times, made a small wound in the heart of a rabbit and stitched it together again. The rabbit survived. Other experiments followed, and some of the more imaginative surgeons began to dream of the possibility of some day being able to stitch together wounds in the human heart, wounds which in those days were always fatal. Surgeons of the old school were horrified at the idea. The German surgeon Billroth, rallying the opposition to something which had not so far occurred, thundered a warning: "The surgeon who would attempt to suture a wound in the heart would lose the respect of his colleagues."

Angry words have never permanently halted progress, and once the possibility of stitching up wounded hearts had taken possession of surgeons' minds, it was inevitable that someone would try to do it. And as often happens when the time is ripe, not one man but three attempted to suture a heart wound at almost the same time.

There is some uncertainty about who was actually the first. It may have been Cappelen of Christiania in 1895, though the credit is usually given to Farina of Rome, who in 1896 stitched up a dagger wound in the heart. Both these attempts at heart suture failed. Then, in September of that same year, Louis Rehn of Frankfort received a patient with a stab wound in the right side of the heart. The man was a poor risk, for his wound was thirty-six hours old before he was brought to Rehn's operating table, but in spite of the delay the suturing was successful and the patient lived to become an exhibit at a German medical meeting.

The idea that the heart is frail and delicate is a myth. Actually, it is a tough, thick organ, mostly made up of muscle, which holds stitches well. It is surrounded by a strong protecting bag called the pericardium, which the surgeon must cut open before he can get at the heart to stitch the wound. Frequently, when the heart is wounded, this bag fills rapidly with blood which cannot escape, and as it fills, with the whole force of the circulation driving the blood, the heart is more and more compressed, and less and less able to carry out its work. When the surgeon opens the pericardium to reach the heart, the pressure is released as the blood pours out, and the heart begins to leap wildly in an effort to reestablish its normal action. If the wound is in the left ventricle, or if a coronary artery has been opened, the heart's blood spurts out—high enough to strike the surgeon in the face if he is not careful—

and pours, foaming, over the patient's chest. The red deluge completely hides the heart from view. Rudolph Matas, writing with feeling from his own experience, has described what happens then: "The operator must thrust his fingers into the pericardial sac through the swirl of blood and endeavor to locate the wound . . . or he must grasp the heart with his whole hand and drag the bleeding, writhing organ . . . out . . . where, by gradually relaxing his grasp, the seat of the hemorrhage will certainly be identified and the suture readily applied."

Wounds in hearts are not always so dramatic—it depends on the location and nature of the wound—and the technique has changed somewhat, but as wounds of this character are always emergencies, they are handled—and with success—by hospitals' resident surgeons. Ten years after the first successful suturing of the heart, the operation was being performed without failure forty or fifty percent of the time. Today the percentage of failure in the operation is so small that it does not cause any great concern.

The difficulty of performing a most delicate operation through blood which sometimes amounted to a torrent made surgeons dream of the possibility of operating inside a quiescent heart, one which had been temporarily drained of blood. It was a dream seemingly as wild as any ever imagined, for aside from the hemorrhage there is the difficulty of executing minute, precise techniques on a handful of muscle which will not stay still and which may be in violent, agitated motion.

As soon as the technique of suturing the heart was conquered, the old die-hards of the profession who had said that could not be done retreated behind a new barrier and began to defend it with mighty rhetoric. This time their battle cry was that to touch the heart *with a knife* would be criminal folly.

In the meantime, surgeons were perfecting the technique of a daring operation close to the heart, involving two of the large arteries. When a child is born, the artery called the aorta, which is the main life stream, is connected by a small tube or duct to an artery which carries used blood to the lungs to receive from them a fresh supply of oxygen. Before the child is born these two arteries are connected, because the child gets oxygen from its mother, not from its own lungs. Normally, the connecting duct with which it is born shrivels up and disappears within a few days. Occasionally, however, this fails to happen and the duct remains open. Then, part of the blood in the aorta, which should be on its way to nourish the body, is detoured for a second, useless trip through the lungs.

The amount of oxygenated blood which is sidetracked in this way depends on the size of the duct. Sometimes it is so little as to make no difference and the person never discovers he has this abnormality. Occasionally as much as seventy percent of the blood is diverted. Doctors call this condition ductus arteriosus, and it is one of the most common defects with which we may chance to be born. Less than twenty years ago, those who had it in serious form were doomed to early death.

In 1939, Dr. R. E. Gross of Boston succeeded in tying off the duct which diverted the oxygenated blood. Later he improved on his own operation, and instead of merely tying off the duct, he removed a section of it so that there would be no danger of its reopening. Today this delicate operation has become routine and has saved the lives of thousands of children.

With such success behind them, surgeons grew bolder. In June of 1949 there appeared the announcement that Doctors Bailey, Gover and O'Neill of Philadelphia had opened the heart and operated on the mitral valve within, and that they had performed the operation successfully not once but several times. The condition for which this bold operation was devised is known as mitral stenosis, a narrowing of the valve which controls the blood flow from the left auricle into the left ventricle. This blood comes from the lungs, where it has taken on its load of oxygen, and if the valve opening is too narrow, blood backs up in the lungs and presses on the walls of the auricle, stretching them dangerously.

In the operation, to clear away the obstruction in the valve, the surgeon cuts a small hole in the side of the heart and inserts a finger to which a small knife blade is fastened. The finger feels for the valve, the knife cuts away the obstruction and the blood flows normally once more. Since 1949 the form of that operation also has been changed somewhat and the operation is now fairly common.

Faulty heart valves are the cause of most forms of fatal heart disease, and they cannot always be repaired. In 1952, Dr. Charles Hufnaegel succeeded in removing the valve which controls the flow of blood into the aorta and replacing it with a valve made of plastic. The operation involved cutting away about four inches of the aorta, through which the main blood supply of the body flows from the heart at the rate of seven pints a minute. The operation was performed on a middle-aged woman, already weakened by years of a badly functioning heart, and it was a success.

At the University of Minnesota, Dr. Lillehei and his associates experimented on animals in the technique of operating on a heart drained of blood, or, in surgical language, in a "dry field." Their first human patient was a thirteen-month-old boy who had an opening between two of the chambers of his heart. In order to drain the heart, the child's circulatory system had to be connected with that of another person having the same type of blood, so that the other's heart and lungs could do the work for both.

The "donor" chosen was the child's father. They lay on two operating tables side by side; oxygenated blood from the main artery in the father's thigh was routed into a pump and from there to a tube inserted into an artery in the baby's chest. From there it flowed through the child's body, detouring the heart, and out again through a second set of tubes and pumps, into a vein in the father's thigh. The father's heart and lungs had taken over all the work.

The child's heart continued to beat throughout the operation, for the supply of blood the heart itself used was not shut off. The operation, which was finished in seventeen and a half minutes, was successful in correcting the malformation, though the child died a few days after the operation from pneumonia.

The technique of rerouting the blood flow through the circulation of another person is called controlled cross-transfusion, and because it entails a serious risk for the donor, surgeons began at once to look for a safer means of achieving the same end. In 1955, after many further experiments, this same Minnesota team substituted the lung of a dog to accomplish the oxygenation. Their first human patient was a thirteen-year-old boy who had been in an accident which had torn three holes in the wall that separates the chambers of the heart. His blood flowed through these holes, destroying the balance of his circulatory system.

In preparing for the operation, surgeons removed a lung from an anesthetized dog. (These laboratory dogs are handled with as much consideration as human patients, and when it is necessary to sacrifice their lives to save human lives, they are painlessly put to death, as this one was.) The dog's lung was suspended in a plastic container and connected with plastic tubes to a pump. The boy's chest was opened and the great vein, which ordinarily carries blood to the heart, was connected to a tube leading to the dog's lung. The lung, inside its container, which was kept supplied with oxygen, received the dark venous blood and filled it with oxygen. From the lung the blood, now bright red, flowed to the bottom of the container, from there into the pump and so into a tube which directed it into the boy's aorta. In this way the boy's heart was drained of blood for twenty minutes, in which time the surgeons successfully finished their repairs. The ideal method would be a completely mechanical contrivance for the oxygenation of the blood, and today progress is being made in several research centers upon the development of such a contrivance.

Another approach to the dry field essential for certain operations on the heart and arteries is "frozen sleep," a temporary hibernation which is called "hypothermia." The patient is anesthetized in the usual way and placed in ice, or on a rubber mattress through which ice water flows, until his temperature drops fifteen or twenty degrees below normal. Frozen sleep is the outcome of research done by Dr. W. G. Bigelow of Toronto, and the physiological principle on which it is based is a simple one. Body cells need oxygen to keep them alive, oxygen which the blood stream gives to them before returning to the lungs for a fresh supply. If the cells were to be deprived of their oxygen, they would die, but not all at once; for, though we speak of "instant death," in reality the body dies by stages. Deprived of oxygen, the brain begins to die within minutes, and cells in other parts of the body die, each in its own time, until at last the whole organism has ceased to live. Cells which are cooled below normal temperature, however, do not need as much oxygen as they must have at normal temperatures; like the cells of a hibernating animal, they are then in a state of partially suspended function.

In this state of frozen sleep oxygen-carrying blood can be withheld from the brain for approximately fifteen minutes without fear of the mental impairment which would follow the death of some of the cells. Blood can be withheld from other parts of the body for as long as an hour at these low body temperatures. Cold has become the anesthesia, and in the fifteen minutes' leeway allowed the surgeon before the brain is endangered, there is time to perform many types of operations on the heart or arteries. During this time the heart may be completely drained of blood to give the surgeon the dry field which he needs. Hypothermia is accepted by the body with less protest than other forms of anesthesia because it is merely the extension of a natural process, and so it reduces the danger of shock. The technique holds out great promise for the future.

One of the obstacles to heart surgery is the weakened condition in which most patients with heart difficulties come to the operating room. Anesthetizing adds another burden to the system of a person who may already be a poor risk. In 1954, Dr. Frank Glenn, chief surgeon of New York Hospital, and Dr. Joseph F. Artusio, Jr., anesthetist, found an answer to the problem which was new to major surgery. Their patient was a woman of thirty-seven who was suffering from a narrowing of the mitral valve in her heart following rheumatic fever. She had been a semi-invalid for years. She was given the anesthetic in the usual way—barbiturates, thiopenthal sodium, then nitrous oxide, oxygen and ether—until she had lost consciousness. But then, instead of holding her in that state, Dr. Artusio gave her oxygen until she had returned to the threshold of consciousness. He kept her close to that border line.

She was in what is known as the analgesic stage. Analgesia means absence of pain. She could turn her head, answer questions, do what Dr. Artusio told her to do, but she was in a state similar to the ether frolic revelers of a century earlier, who sometimes hurt themselves severely without feeling pain. While Dr. Artusio held her skillfully in this conscious but painless state, Dr. Glenn proceeded with the operation. Those who were present say it was a moving sight: the young woman with her chest open and her heart in plain view, answering Dr. Artusio when he spoke to her—cheerfully, docilely and without any sign of fear. Her recovery was prompt and complete, and she can recall nothing of the scene in the operating room.

Important discoveries which advance surgery once were made at the rate of about one every century. Now they occur every few years. What has this ever more swift advance actually accomplished for mankind? In answering that broad question it is not possible to separate the effects of surgery from those of medicine, for though over the years surgeons and physicians have more and more tended to specialize, the arts they practice have become increasingly united. The most striking gain has been in the extension of life. People live longer. In Shakespeare's time the average person lived to be thirty-three years old; today the average length of life is over sixty-seven years.

That is the average age to which babies born today may be expected to live. In 1850 the baby's life expectancy at birth was thirty-five years, a little more than half what it is now. By 1900 only a little more than twelve years had been added, bringing his life expectancy then to forty-seven years, but in the next half-century twenty years were added, an enormous increase in his life expectancy.

In older people the hope for life has not lengthened so dramatically. For example, a forty-year-old person today can look forward to only a little over three more years of life than the forty-year-old in 1900. But though the gains for older people are not so striking as they are for babies, they are nevertheless great enough to create some new problems, not only for the physician but for state governments, which are faced with an increasing number of old people who must be cared for in institutions. Geriatrics, the care of the aged, is steadily becoming a more important medical specialty. The lengthening out of life has made some important changes in surgical work also, for greater numbers of people reach the time of life in which they are more subject to cancer and to the wearing out of the mechanism of circulation.

THE CONTROL OF SHOCK

Democritus's Well

". . . Nor do I doubt that many things still lie hidden in Democritus's well that are destined to be drawn into the light by the indefatagable dillegence of coming ages."

—William Harvey

Ever since the middle of the nineteenth century, the physical condition that had come to be spoken of as "shock" had been of growing concern to surgeons. They did not know what shock was or what caused it, but they recognized it when they saw it in a puzzling set of symptoms which appeared with distressing frequency during or after an operation or following an accident. In 1870, Hermann Eberhard Fischer described these symptoms in a youth who had been brought into the hospital after being struck in the abdomen by the pole of a carriage. "As you see he is lying very quietly without paying any attention to events around him. His face is drawn and peculiarly elongated, the forehead wrinkled, and the nostrils dilated. His weary, lusterless eyes are deeply sunken in their sockets. They are half covered by the eyelids and are surrounded by broad, dark rings . . . The patient looks dully and vacantly into the distance. His skin and visible mucous surfaces have a marble-like pallor; his hands and lips are somewhat blue. Large drops of sweat are hanging down from his forehead and eyebrows. The temperature of his whole body seems considerably below normal . . . The patient frowns only in response to very painful sensations and makes slow defensive movements. He does not raise his limbs spontaneously, but on urgent and repeated requests will move them slightly. If the limbs are lifted they fall back listlessly . . . The pulse is hardly palpable, irregular, unequal and very fast. The arteries are narrow and of low tension . . . But withal he is completely conscious . . ."

These symptoms were completely identical with those which surgeons frequently observed during or following an operation. Surgeons knew that shock was most likely to appear in connection with a prolonged operation or a serious accident, especially when there had been considerable loss of blood. On the other hand, shock not infrequently appeared when the operation was minor or the accident damage slight, and this seeming contradiction, which was the first of a long series, baffled them. In either case, the patient very frequently died, growing colder and colder, his pulse flickering slowly out as though death were coming to him by stages, but remaining conscious almost to the end.

A great many mid-nineteenth-century surgeons took shock for granted, considering it inevitable, as most of them still regarded infection and pain. But toward the end of the century, when the victories over infection and pain became clearer and clearer, surgeons gave more attention to the problem of shock. The inquiries then made into the nature of shock were largely confined to what they were able to observe, for they lacked the sort of laboratory equipment which in the present century has produced so many startling revelations. Each observation they made tended to produce more evidence of contradictions. The doctors discovered that, though the hands and feet of a person in shock were usually cold, sometimes they were normally warm. Sometimes there was sweating, sometimes not—and so on through what the doctors now call the syndrome of shock. By 1900 they had learned little more than that shock was not always easy to recognize but that it was probably present far more often than had previously been thought.

To this scant knowledge they added the conviction that there might be an exceedingly complicated set of physiological conditions present in shock, all related in one way or another to a general breakdown of the circulatory system. They discovered, however, that when they attempted to restore the circulation with alcohol and other stimulants, they were more apt to kill the patient than cure him—another apparent contradiction of physiology which they could not understand. There was no practical, generally available blood-pressure apparatus to throw light on what was happening to the circulation, but doctors, keeping in mind the typical cold hands and the thin, rapid pulse, put their fingers on the arteries of patients in shock and found them soft and relaxed, as though the system did not have enough blood in it to distend them properly. But if the blood supply was not enough for the hands and feet, why was not the brain also short of blood? Obviously, enough blood reached it so that its functions were not seriously impaired, for shock patients usually remained conscious up to death. What mysterious controls were at work inside the body to cut down the blood supply in one part and preserve it in another? There was no answer.

At the turn of the century, the Cleveland surgeon, Dr. George Crile, realized that shock was responsible for more deaths in connection with surgery than any other single factor. Crile was an able scientist, in addition to being one of the country's leading surgeons, and he had the conviction, which was uncommon in his day, that the laboratory was a necessary adjunct of the operating room. He began a series of experiments, using dogs for his subjects and employing homemade equipment for taking blood-pressure readings.

His first step was to confirm the belief that there was a rapid and severe fall in blood pressure during shock. This convinced him that the problem of controlling shock was largely a question of how to keep the blood pressure at normal levels, and he directed his experiments with that in view. First he too tried all the ordinary stimulants, including alcohol, but he found that they actually seemed to hasten death. In 1901, Takamine isolated adrenalin and Crile found that by injecting it into the blood stream of his dogs he could raise blood pressure, but only for a brief time. (By repeated injections he actually kept the circulation system of a decapitated dog working for eleven hours.) That same year Cushing returned from his European studies bringing with him an instrument for reading blood pressure, called the Riva Rocci apparatus, which was a vast improvement over the one Crile had been using. Cushing, it will be remembered, had introduced the charting of pulse and respiration during operations, and to these Crile now added the reading of blood pressure. It was universally adopted, though not without some plaints from old-time surgeons who did not know either how to read the instrument or what the readings signified, and from this time on, surgeons could tell with some exactness when a patient on the operating table was beginning to show signs of shock.

About the same time it occurred to Crile that blood pressure might be controlled by air pressure on the body, and after various unsuccessful experiments in an effort to create a pressurized room for shock patients, he invented one of the strangest medical gadgets ever seen, an inflated rubber suit. The patient was put into the suit, and air was blown in to build up the desired pressure. The contraption was clumsy and impractical, and in it the patient rather resembled the figure in the Tyre Michelin ads, but perhaps the strangest thing about it was that it actually worked, and Crile used it on his shock patients from 1902 until 1907.

In the meantime he had been carrying on another line of research. As far back as 1898, Crile had discovered that blood transfusions raised the blood pressure of his experimental dogs. Crile had great difficulty when he first tried the technique on his dogs. Then in 1901, Landsteiner discovered the differences in human blood types, bringing human blood transfusion within the range of possibility. Crile tried his first transfusion of human blood on a woman patient in 1905, but though the transfusion appeared to be successful, the woman died. He tried again a year later. His patient, a twenty-three-year-old Russian man, was in desperate straits, and his despairing family was anxious to have Crile try any means at all to save him. The call came to Crile in the middle of the night, and taking his wife, Grace Crile, with him, he hurried through the gas-lit corridors of St. Alexis Hospital to the operating room. The patient and his brother, who was to act as donor, were waiting there. Crile cut the donor's radial artery and sutured it end-to-end to one of the patient's veins. Grace Crile wrote an account of what followed during the next tense hour.

"When the Chief and I entered the operating room the unconscious patient was on the operating table, his sturdy brother, the donor, beside him, their heads in opposite directions. I had never seen death. The contracted features, the deep orbital spaces, the greenish pallor of the patient, to me signified death. The feet were stiff and marble-like, and the countenance livid in contrast to his auburn hair.

"I stood at the foot of the operating table and witnessed the miracle of resurrection. I saw the livid pallor slowly take on a pinkish tinge. I watched the barely perceptible sighing respiration become established to a normal rhythm, and heard the nurse report that the pulse could be felt at last. Involuntary movements followed, then restlessness, consciousness, and finally, recognition. So suffused with blood did the patient become that his cheeks, his lips, even his ears, took on a rose glow, his eyes resumed a normal expression, and he began to talk and jest almost like a man intoxicated.

"Meanwhile, the donor, a large man of ruddy complexion, seemed to have shrunk to half his size. He was white, hollow-eyed and sighing. Cold perspiration stood on his brow. Constantly he asked for water. There was, of course, no knowledge as to how much blood could be taken from a given donor, nor was there any method of measuring the amount that was being given. Suddenly, with a deep diaphragmatic effort for air, the donor crumpled before my eyes. He was unconscious. He had been bled too low!

"The Chief said, 'Leave the room, Grace.' As I left I saw them tilting the donor in a head-down position and swiftly preparing resuscitation measures. Back and forth, in those dim, gaslit halls of St. Alexis I paced, knowing it was really a human experiment that I had witnessed, but believing it was the opening of a new epoch. I returned in time to see the donor wheeled away for a good meal and a nephrectomy performed on the recipient, after which he was placed in the pneumatic suit to ensure the maintenance of the blood pressure."

Crile's work in the study of shock resulted in a number of important advances. One was the discovery that the functions of the heart, like those of the brain, are not disturbed by shock. The heart beats faster during shock, but otherwise it continues to work as in health. Crile concluded that since the failure of the circulation did not originate in the heart, then it must be that the breakdown came in the outlying blood vessels remote from the heart, a theory which would explain the coldness of the hands and feet while the heart remained normal.

Another of Crile's contributions to the battle against shock was the development of a combination of general and local anesthesia—known as anociassociation blocking—which reduced the likelihood of shock by reducing the patient's anxiety and fear. By what he described as "gentleness," both toward the patient's troubled mind and in the handling of his body tissues, Crile made an enormous reduction in operative mortality.

These discoveries, in addition to his great work in developing blood transfusion, were the first scientific attack on shock, though blood transfusions were not in general use for another thirty years. Crile had approached the problem from two directions simultaneously and evolved both a prevention and a cure. Neither was infallible, but Crile's was the first victory, these the first weapons, in the attack on shock.

When the First World War broke out in 1914, it was apparent from the first days of battle that shock would be a major problem—a problem on a gigantic scale. Europe became a great laboratory for the study of shock, and surgeons, working with the wounded, noticed a curious thing. The blood of men in shock was thick—so thick, in fact, that it flowed sluggishly through their bodies like a slow-moving stream. Every wounded man was a shock victim, but when the familiar symptoms showed themselves, there was little the surgeons could do. Transfusions would have saved lives, but few surgeons were familiar with the complicated technique for giving them which was then in use. Even had they been, the collecting, typing and administering of fresh blood when the wounded were literally pouring into the inadequate hospitals was out of the question.

Doctors and nurses did their best to keep the men warm as long as the supplies of blankets held out, for warmth sometimes helped a little in the early stages of shock. That was all they could do. But with hundreds of cases around them, they learned to recognize almost at a glance the various stages of shock and to tell when shock had progressed to a point of no return. When a wounded man reached this stage, they knew he would not recover, and they spoke of it as the point at which the trend became "irreversible." There was nothing they could do but name it. Hundreds of men died who should not have died; men whose wounds were slight died conscious, with that strange, thick blood creeping sluggishly through their veins.

In this crisis men in the laboratories went to work with renewed vigor. Nothing that anyone had yet discovered had thrown any real light on what happens to a body in shock, but a research scientist named Walter B. Cannon made a wild inferential leap in the dark and guessed that there might be some sort of poison, some toxic agent, at work in the blood of persons in shock which might be at least partly responsible for the changes in the circulation. There was nothing which could be called real evidence to support his idea, and no way of testing the truth of his scientific brain wave, but in point of fact he had struck very near the mark.

That inspired guess, and the posing of other searching questions about what exactly it is that happens to the outlying blood vessels during shock, was about all the real progress which came out of the First World War. A few wrong guesses were hazarded also, such as the one which was translated down from the higher echelons of the laboratories to the hospital where I was a frightened, starched and under-age probation nurse, and rendered up to us in the form of positive fact that particles of fat, loose in the blood stream, were the sole and absolute cause of shock. This dictum was even elaborated into the explanation that the warmth treatment for shock was designed to melt these bits of fat!

Progress, however, cannot always be measured in tangible

terms. Throughout the war years surgeons and scientists alike were becoming more familiar with various phases of the central problem—a necessary precursor to solving it—and coming to realize that shock was an even more complicated physical state than had been thought. New equipment and refinement of methods were increasing the effectiveness of the work at the same time that the work was becoming more searching and subtle. When the war came to an end the laborers in the laboratories inevitably slackened their efforts a little, especially since this was to be the last of all wars and shock henceforward would be confined to the numerically less important civilian cases. Nevertheless, there was progress in the period between the wars. As it was of a highly technical nature, the following is an outrageously simplified review of it which does some violence to chronology in order to make the complicated story clear.

While surgeons were using blood transfusions to fight shock whenever practicable—and finding them effective in the majority of cases—scientists had begun to inquire into the structure of the blood itself, and to take it apart into its separate elements. Part of this process was to put it into a centrifuge and whirl it at a speed that made the heavy part of the blood settle to the bottom, leaving a thin, brownish liquid. This liquid was pure blood plasma.

The fact that blood plasma became thick during shock meant that some of the fluid in the blood, the plasma, had mysteriously escaped from the circulatory system. Blood transfusions replaced this lost fluid and restored the normal balance of the blood until nature had time to recover herself and take over her duties. But transfusions added more of the thick part—the red and white cells—than was really necessary. Why not add only the plasma?

This was tried experimentally on animals in shock, and in 1918 it was found to be successful. By the middle of the 1930s, plasma was being used with success for human beings. Plasma has certain advantages over whole blood, especially in times of emergency. It does not have to be typed and so it can be used without danger on anyone. It keeps longer than whole blood (about two years), but on the other hand it is easily damaged either by heat or cold, and for some reason not fully understood to this day, it is not always as successful in treating shock as whole blood. Nevertheless, under conditions which make the use of whole blood impossible, it is capable of saving lives on a large scale.

Another drawback to the use of plasma is that it is bulky to handle. In 1934, Earl William Flosdorf and his research team perfected a method of freezing and drying plasma. The end product was a flaky, brownish-white substance which can be converted back into plasma instantly by adding sterile water. Dry plasma keeps five years, it is not damaged by heat or cold and it can be shipped in small, non-breakable containers. It is, in short, almost the ideal material with which to attack shock in war or mass disaster.

Meanwhile, scientists were asking what happens to that fluid which vanishes from the blood in state of shock. How does it escape from the circulatory system and where does it go? Blood plasma, it was discovered, contains protein molecules which have in themselves the mysterious power to hold fluid in the blood. It is these protein molecules which maintain the correct fluid balance of the blood, or, to use the technical term, the correct osmotic pressure. When a person is in shock some changes takes place in the small blood vessels called the capillaries. We do not know exactly what it is that happens, but the result is that the capillaries, instead of holding the protein molecules inside themselves, allow the molecules to escape through their walls into the surrounding tissues. When this occurs there are not enough molecules left in the capillaries to hold the fluid in the blood, and that too escapes, leaving behind the familiar thick blood of shock.

When the fluid has made its escape there is actually less

blood left behind in the circulation "tree." That which remains is not enough to keep the circulation "full" or to supply the demands of all the parts of the body. This is why the arteries of a person in shock feel soft and relaxed and why the blood pressure sinks, sometimes so low that it is impossible to make a reading. The thick blood is harder to move through the veins, the heart must work faster to drive it, and so we find the rapid pulse of shock.

When the blood supply is not sufficient for the needs of the body, a remarkable thing happens. Nature takes command in the emergency and, using the network of nerves which surrounds the capillaries as a control mechanism, begins to shrink some of them in order to lessen their capacity to hold blood. It is an amazing process, for the capillaries which are shut down, or partially shut down, are those in parts of the body which are not necessary to maintain the vital functions of life. This is why, in shock, the hands and feet grow cold before the rest of the body feels the lack of blood. Long ago it was observed that a person in shock remained conscious almost to the end. With the new understanding of the mechanism of shock, it became plain that nature preserves the vital function of the brain at the cost of less important functions. And not only the brain, but, as Crile discovered, the heart also is safeguarded. Shock sets off an alarm in the body, nature drops her customary pursuits and rushes to protect the stronghold of life itself. Today we know that the process is far more delicately selective than even Crile suspected, for nature preserves all the vital organs, guarding their supply of blood almost in the order of their importance to life.

By the time the Second World War again intensified the interest of surgeons and laboratory scientists in the problem of shock, they were almost ready to cope with it on a large scale both on the battlefields and in civilian bombings. While the armies were fighting, research workers were improving their methods for producing shock experimentally in animals and perfecting their techniques for measuring the effects of shock. Irreversible shock—that percentage of shock which for unexplained reasons does not yield to transfusions—was given intensive study. Those still mysterious cases of shock in which no serious hemorrhage or severe accident was involved came in for renewed attention.

And always the problem of shock seemed to grow more and more complex. If loss of blood was not involved in a certain percentage of cases, what was the unknown factor? In 1944, Dr. Robert Chambers and Dr. Benjamin W. Zweifach injected the blood of rats which were in a state of shock into the blood of healthy rats. The healthy rats at once showed symptoms of shock, and the only possible explanation was that Dr. Cannon's inspired guess of years gone by had been correct and that some toxic agent appears in the blood of persons in a state of shock. What the toxic agent—or possibly agents—might be was not known, but the discovery that something of the sort existed was an important step.

This time, with the whole of Europe and the Pacific for a laboratory, scientists and doctors began to make distinctions between different kinds of shock. They saw differences between wound shock and burn shock, surgical and medical shock. During the bombings they placed those injured by falling rubble into the new category of crush shock, and the surgeons began to adapt the treatment to the special needs of each category.

During the Second World War dried plasma went up into the front lines and into the fighting with the troops. Plasma bottles hung from the roofs of ambulances carrying wounded men to the rear. The Red Cross collected thirteen million pints of blood from volunteers, and whole blood, which is still desirable when it can be obtained, was flown to Europe at the rate of a thousand pints a day.

During the Korean campaign, blood was collected at a base in California, where it was typed, and type O, which can be used safely on almost anyone, was segregated. A special air service flew the whole blood, under refrigeration, to blood banks in Japan. It arrived when it was only six days old. From Japan it was delivered to the fighting area by helicopter. Only type O blood went to the foremost lines.

Research into the nature, the cause, the prevention and the care of shock still goes on. Today we know that shock is involved in most deaths. A certain percentage of all heart disease cases show symptoms of shock, and shock may appear in cases of septicemia, pneumonia and other diseases. At the present time the precautions against shock in operating rooms are routine. The plasma bottle hangs on a standard above the operating table, and blood substance is replaced in proportion to its loss by bleeding.

We do not yet know what the toxic agent is which is present in the blood stream during shock. One theory, put forward by Dr. Jacob Fine of Harvard, is that this agent may be the bacteria ordinarily imprisoned harmlessly in the stomach, which, escaping during shock, run a riot of destruction. Another theory is that the unknown factor may be certain chemicals which Dr. Zweifach and Dr. Ephraim Shorr have shown are released into the system during shock.

The treatment of shock has changed greatly in recent years. Transfusions are still the main reliance, but now the transfusion, instead of being given intravenously, is sometimes given directly into the artery, an advance in technique which saved many lives in Korea. Antibiotics are also used to treat shock. Dr. Fine's theory has not been proven according to stern scientific standards, but without doubt the resistance of the system to infection is lowered during shock, and whatever may be the reason, the antibiotics are saving lives.

At the present time a great deal of work is being done with drugs that act directly on the circulatory system, work which is dependent to a degree on some surprising recent discoveries in the well-explored field of anatomy. The effect of these drugs is either to forestall or counteract the harmful behavior of the circulatory system in time of shock. Some of these drugs are still in the experimental stage, but others have come out of the laboratories and are now in use by surgeons in cases where transfusions have failed. They are perhaps the most hopeful development in the fight to halt the progress of irreversible shock.

But the strangest of all the recent discoveries is that laboratory rats (those martyrs of science) can be trained to withstand a degree of shock to which an untrained rat would succumb. This idea stirs the imagination with thoughts of strange possibilities, though what the usefulness and what the implications of that discovery may be, we do not yet know.

In the event of atomic war, with the mass injuries which would certainly ensue, shock would become a problem on a gigantic scale. Our present methods of combating it with transfusions and injections would be both cumbersome and too slow. Science is looking ahead to the development of a drug which can be taken by mouth and produced in sufficient quantity to be available in the event of mass disaster. That is not thought to be impossible.

Science is still interested in that small percentage of cases of irreversible shock which do not yield to any modern method of treatment. But the main battle has been won. The fourth great barrier to the advance of surgery has gone down. To the control of hemorrhage, the control of infection and the control of pain has been added the control of shock. As in the case of the other controls, much work still remains to be done. The clearing of these four barriers will be worked on for an indefinite time, as new knowledge and finer scientific equipment come to the aid of the workers, but this is the work which follows victory.

Almost every discovery brings about some change in the surgeon's work. Antibiotics, for example, are currently reducing the need for certain types of surgery, and for a variety of other reasons a number of operations which were once common have become unnecessary. Over the years, the finest surgical techniques have gone through a long, evolutionary process of becoming outmoded. But even as the need for the older types of surgery is being reduced or eliminated, new and different demands are constantly being made on the surgeon's skill. This has been markedly true in our times with the opening of the new surgical fields, and it is as true of the work of the surgical specialist as of the practice of the more general surgeon. The old days when a surgeon at the end of his life practiced the same sort of surgery he learned in medical school are gone forever, for in surgery the only changeless thing is change.

PARTIAL BIBLIOGRAPHY

GENERAL HISTORY

Castiglioni, Arturo, A History of Medicine. 1947.

Garrison, Fielding Hudson, An Introduction to the History of Medicine. 1929.

Graham, Harvey (Pseud), Isaac Harvey Flack, Surgeons All. 1939.

Leonardo, Richard Anthony, History of Surgery. 1895.

Major, Ralph H., A History of Medicine. 1954.

Sigerist, Henry E., A History of Medicine. 1951.

VESALIUS, ANDREAS

Boerhaave, Hermann and Albinus, The Life and Work of Andreas Vesalius. 1930.

Cushing, Harvey Williams, a Bio-Bibliography of Andreas Vesalius. 1943.

Garrison, Fielding Hudson, In Defence of Vesalius. 1916.

Piersol, George Arthur, Andreas Vesalius and His Time. 1915–16.

Vesalius, Andreas, De Humani Corporis Fabrica. 1543.

PARÉ, AMBROISE

Broussais, Maxence, Ambroise Paré, Sa Vie, Son Oeuvre. 1900.

Doe, Janet, A Bibliography of the Works of Ambroise Paré. 1937.

M.E., Ambroise Paré Est-Il Mort Catholique? Bulletin Commission Historique de la Mayerne, Laval, Series 2. 1890.

Packard, Francis Randolph, Life and Times of Ambroise Paré. 1921.

Paget, Stephen, Ambroise Paré and His Times. 1897.

Paré, Ambroise, Apology and Treatise of Ambroise Paré Containing the Voyages Made into Divers Places with Many of His Writings upon Surgery, edited and with introduction by Geoffrey Langdon Keynes. 1951.

Paré, Ambroise, Method of Curing Wounds by Gun-Shot. Also by Arrows and Darts, with Their Accidents . . . Faithfully done into English out of the French Copies by Walter Hamond, Chirurgien. 1617.

Paré, Ambroise, Relation due Siège de Metz, en 1552.

PARTIAL BIBLIOGRAPHY

HARVEY, WILLIAM

Aubrey, John, Memoirs of the Celebrated Dr. Harvey. 1813.
Da Costa, Jacob Mendes, Harvey and his Discovery. 1879.
Harvey, William, De Motu Cordis. 1643.
Keynes, Geoffrey Langdon, The Personality of William Harvey. 1949.

HUNTER, JOHN

Foot, Jesse, The Life of John Hunter. 1794.
Gilchrest, Edgar Lorrington, Hunter, the Founder of Scientific Surgery. 1933.
Gray, Ernest Alfred, Portrait of a Surgeon. 1952.
Hunter, John, A Treatise on the Blood, Inflammation and Gunshot Wounds. 1796.
Paget, Stephen, John Hunter, Man of Science and Surgeon. 1898.
Power, D'Arcy, John Hunter, a Martyr to Science. 1925.

MCDOWELL, EPHRAIM

Gross, Samuel David, Memorial Oration in Honor of Ephraim McDowell. 1879.
McDowell, Ephraim, Observation on Diseased Ovaria. 1819.
McDowell, Ephraim, Three Cases of Extirpation of Diseased Ovaria. 1817.
Schachner, August, Ephraim McDowell, "Father of the Ovariotomy" and Founder of Abdominal Surgery. 1921.
Valentine, Mary Thompson, The Biography of Ephraim McDowell. 1890.

THE ANESTHETISTS

Morton, Elizabeth Whitman, The Discovery of Anesthesia, McClure's Magazine, September, 1896.
Colton, Gardner Quincy, Anesthesia, Who Made and Developed This Great Discovery? 1886.
Robinson, Victor, Victory Over Pain. 1946.
Duncum, Barbara M., The Development of Inhalation Anaesthesia. 1947.

LISTER, JOSEPH

Ashurst, Paston Cooper Astley, The Centenary of Lister, a Tale of Sepsis and Antisepsis. 1927.
Godlee, John Rickman, Lord Lister. 1917.
Johnson and Johnson, Lister and the Ligature, a Land-

mark in the History of Modern Surgery. Compiled by research readers of the scientific department. 1925.

Lister, Joseph, On the Antiseptic Principle in the Practice of Surgery. 1867.

Lister, Joseph, On a New Method of Treating Compound Fracture, Abscess, etc., with Observations on the Conditions of Suppuration. 1867.

Power, D'Arcy, A Mirror for Surgeons. 1939.

HALSTED, WILLIAM STEWART

Finney, J. M. T., Personal Appreciation of Dr. Halsted. Bulletin of the Johns Hopkins Hospital. 1925.

Heuer, George J., Dr. Halsted. Bulletin of the Johns Hopkins Hospital, Vol. 90, supp. 1952.

Matas, Rudolph, In Memoriam—William Stewart Halsted—an Appreciation. Bulletin of the Johns Hopkins Hospital. 1925.

MacCallum, W. G., William Stewart Halsted. Johns Hopkins Press. 1930.

CUSHING, HARVEY

Bulletin of the New York Academy of Medicine, Harvey Cushing as We Knew Him. A symposium. 1954.

Fulton, John F., Harvey Cushing, a Biography. 1946.

Sachs, Ernest, Diagnosis and Treatment of Brain Tumors. 1931.

Sharpe, William, Brain Surgeon. 1952.

Thomson, Elizabeth H. T., Harvey Cushing, Surgeon, Author, Artist. 1950.

THE REVOLUTION

Bauer, Louis H., editor, Seventy-Five Years of Medical Progress. 1954.

Dickinson, Frank G., and *Walker, Everett L.,* Mortality Trends in the United States, 1900–1948. The Journal of the American Medical Association. Bulletin 92. 1952.

Harkins, Henry H., Fifty Years of Surgery. Quarterly Review of Surgery, 8, 1. 1951.

Heyd, Charles G., The Evolution of Modern Surgery. American Journal of Surgery, new series, 51. 1951.

Matas, Rudolph, Surgical Operations Fifty Years Ago. American Journal of Surgery, new series, 51. 1951.

Sava, George, The Way of a Surgeon. 1947.

Wiggers, Carl J., Physiology of Shock. 1950.

INDEX

Abbott, Gilbert, 144–145, 146
abdominal surgery, 114–120
Académie des Sciences (Paris), 130, 180
Adair, Robin, 91
adrenalin, 272, 290
Alexandria, Medical Center in, 8
almshouses, 110
American Medical Association, 252
amputations, 54
  in Middle Ages, 28, 39, 40
  mortality rate following, 162–163
Anatomy
  comparative, 62, 95
  improved knowledge of, 54, 55, 78
  pathological, 78, 107
  scant knowledge of, in early times, 9
Anderson, Thomas, 180, 182
anesthesia, 134–155
  cocaine, 204–205
  combination of general and local, 293
  ether, 132
  local, 203, 204–205, 247
  refrigeration, 128
Angell, James R., 266
angina pectoris, 98
animal magnetism, 129–130
Anjou, Duc de, 46
anociassociation blocking, 293
antibiotics, 299
antiseptics, 181–185
appendix, gangrenous, 123
apprentice system, 108
Arnold, Matthew, 269
Artusio, Dr. Joseph F., vi, 282
Arundel, Earl of, 68–69
aseptic principle, 196
Avicenna (Arabian physician), 9

Babylon, 5
bacillus welchii, 273–275
bacteriology, 197, 202
barber-surgeons, 29, 33, 38, 39, 40, 42
Barber-Surgeons Company, 29, 77–78
Bell, John, 113, 159–160
Belle Isle, 91, 92
Bellevue Hospital (New York), 110, 200, 201, 203–204
Bergmann, Ernst von, 195
Bezoar stones, 44–45
Bigelow, Dr. W. G., 281
Blood
  coagulation of, 178
  discovery of the circulation of the, 56, 58, 62–63, 64, 65, 69–70, 75
  plasma, 295–296
  poisoning, 159, 160, 162, 170, 171, 172
  transfusions, 241, 272, 291–292, 293, 295, 299, 300
Boniface VIII, Pope, 12
Bourg Hersent, France, 32
Bovie, Dr. W. T., 252, 253
brain tumors, 237, 241, 245, 252–253, 263–265, 267
Brigham, Peter Bent, 271
British Museum, 64
Brown, Elizabeth, *see* Harvey, Mrs. William
Brown, Dr. Lancelot, 61
Buchanan, Janet, 82–83
b-welchii, 273–275

Caesarian section, 54, 55, 114
Caius College (Cambridge), 57
Calcar, Jan Stephan van, 21, 22, 23, 24
Cannon, Walter B., 294
capillaries, 63, 76, 296, 297
Cappelen of Christiania, 276
carbolic acid, 182–185, 187, 190, 195, 197, 212
carbolic poisoning, 183
carbon dioxide, 135
Carlisle, Thomas, 181, 269
Carnegie, Andrew, 271
Carnegie Foundation, 110
Carnegie Institute, 272
catgut ligatures, 187–188, 210
cauterization, 28, 167
Chambers, Dr. Robert, 298
Chambers Street Hospital (New York City), 203
Charing Cross Hospital, 213
Charity Hospital (New York City), 203

Index

Charles I, King (England), 66–68, 70, 71–72
Charles V, Emperor, 25, 39
Charles IX, King, 44, 45
charms, 53
Chauliac, Guy de, 163
Chelsea Hospital, 88
Cheselden, Dr., 88, 133
childbearing, 129
chloroform, 146, 148–149, 197, 247, 254
cocaine, 204–207, 209, 210, 216, 217
Code of Hammurabi, 5
Codman, Amory, 232
Coligny, Admiral, 43, 45, 46, 47, 49
Collège de Saint Côme, 30, 39, 42
College of Philadelphia, 109, 113
College of Physicians and Surgeons (Columbia University), 200, 202, 203
Colombo, Realdo, 24, 25
Colt, Samuel, 136–137
Colton, Gardner Quincy, 139, 154
Colton Dental Association, 154
Columbia University, 109, 200
Columbus, Christopher, 10
Congress, U. S., 151–152
"corpse poisoning," 88
corpuscles, 76
country doctors, 110–111
Crawford, Jane Todd, 116–120, 122
Crile, Dr. George, 164, 241, 247, 272, 290–293, 297
Crile, Grace, 291–292
Crowell, Katherine, *see* Cushing, Mrs. Harvey
Crusades, knights of the, 12
Cushing, Betsey, 264
Cushing, Harvey, 23, 24, 101, 164, 210, 213, 214, 216, 222–223, 224–267, 268, 271, 272, 290
Cushing, Mrs. Harvey, 230, 232, 234, 240, 244, 248, 249, 264, 266
Cushing, Dr. Henry Kirke, 227–230, 240
Cushing, William Harvey, 240, 249, 250, 251
Cushing's Disease, 265
Cutler, Dr. E. C., 265
cysts, ovarian, 114–122
Danville, Kentucky, 113, 115, 117
Danvilliers, siege of, 40
Dark Ages, 7
Darwin, Charles, 133
Davidoff, Dr. Leon M., vi, 251, 256–260
Davy, Humphry, 134–136
Death Be Not Proud (Gunther), 263
debridement technique, 274
De Quincey, 208
Diderot, 269
disease, scant knowledge of, in early times, 6–7, 53
dissections, experimental in 1500's, 16
Douglas, Martha Jane, 82, 83
drug addiction, 205–208, 209, 210, 211, 217, 234
DuBois, Abbé, 269
ductus arteriosus, 278
Dupuytren, Guillaume, 127, 133

Earl's Court, 93–95, 97, 101, 102, 103
Edgehill, Battle of, 70
Edinburgh, University of, 109, 112, 114, 115, 121, 131, 163, 168, 169, 171, 173, 176, 177, 178, 188, 190, 191
Edward IV, King (England), 29
Elizabeth I, Queen, 57, 61
Ent, Dr., 72, 73, 74
Erichsen, Sir John, 194
erysipelas, 159, 175, 201
ether, 137–138, 140–148, 150, 152, 155, 197, 231–232, 247, 256, 282
"Exercises on the Generation of Animals" (Harvey), 73

Fabricius, Dr., 59–60
Faculté de Médecine (Paris), 15, 38, 50
Farina of Rome, 276
Feast of Saint Bartholomew, 45
Ferguson, William, 132
fibrin, 258, 261
Fine, Dr. Jacob, 299
Fischer, Hermann Eberhard, 288
Flexner report, 110, 272
Flosdorf, Earl William, 296
Flourens (physiologist), 146

INDEX

François II, King, 43, 44
Franklin, Benjamin, 130
French Institute, 150
Frost, Eben, 143, 145
"frozen sleep," 281
Fulton, John F., 241

Galilei (Galileo), 66
Galen, 8, 9, 12, 15, 16, 17, 18, 22, 23, 24, 38, 40, 52
Gangrene
  gas, 273–275
  hospital, 159, 160, 167–168, 175, 178, 183, 195
Garrison, Fielding, 53
gas gangrene, 273–275
geriatrics, 283
Glasgow Infirmary, 179–180, 187, 188, 194
Glasgow, Scotland, 81, 82, 188
Glasgow, University of, 179, 188
Glenn, Dr. Frank, 282
gloves, rubber, 182
Godlee, Richman, 188
Goodyear Rubber Company, 212
Graham, Harvey, 77
Gray, Stephen, 129
Greece, ancient, 5–6, 8
Gross, Dr. R. F., 164, 278
Guinterius, *see* Günther, Johann
Guise, Duc de, 46, 47, 48
gun cotton, discovery of, 142
gunshot wounds, treatment of, 38
Günther, Johann, 19
Gunther, John, 263

Halsted, William Stewart, 164, 198, 199–217, 233–234, 235, 237, 241, 242, 268, 273
Halsted, Mrs. William Stewart, 211–215
Hammurabi, Code of, 5
Hampstead Church, 74
Hampton, Caroline, *see* Halsted, Mrs. William Stewart
Harkness, E. S., 271
Hartford Hospital, 220
Harvard Medical School, 140, 230, 244
Harvard University, 109
Harvey, Eliab, 74
Harvey, Perry, 227
Harvey, William, 56, 57–58, 164, 185, 225, 268, 287
Harvey, Mrs. William, 61
heart surgery, 275–282
hemorrhage, control of, 3–123
hemostasis, 75, 198
Henri of Navarre, 45
Henri II, King, 39, 40, 43
Henry VIII, King (England), 10, 29
herbs, as pain-killers, 127, 128
Hickman, Henry Hill, 135, 136
High Hampton, North Carolina, 214
Hofmann, Caspar, 69–70
Holmes, Oliver Wendell, 148, 150
Holy Land, 26
Home, Anne, *see* Hunter, Mrs. John
Home, Everard, 106
home surgery, 195
Hopkins, Johns, 207, 271
Horsley, Victor, 262
"Hospital diseases," 162, 163, 171, 172, 176, 177, 179, 180, 185
Hospital for Incurables (Venice), 21
hospital gangrene, 159, 160, 167–168, 175, 178, 183, 195
Hospitals, *see also* names of hospitals
  in Mexico, 110
  in Middle Ages, 30–31
  in nineteenth century, 160–163
  in the U. S., 110
Hôtel Dieu (Paris), 33, 34, 37, 161
Hufnaegel, Dr. Charles, 279
Huguenots, 45, 49
Humani Corporis Fabrica, De (Vesalius), 19, 20, 23, 24, 25, 54
Humphreys, Dr. Alexander, 114
Hunter chancre, 97
Hunter, James, 81, 82, 83
Hunter, John, 78, 79–107, 114, 115, 121, 133, 211, 230, 268
Hunter, Mrs. John, 97–98, 102, 103, 105, 106,
Hunter, William, 81–91, 95, 96, 97, 98, 102
Hunter, Dr. William, 213
Hunterian Museum, 94

Index

Huxley, Aldous, 206
hypnotism, 131–132
hypothermia, 281

Immigrant Hospital (New York City), 203
India, 131
Infection, control of, 159–283
insulin, 271
Italy, 20, 66

Jackson, Charles Thomas, 139, 140, 141, 142, 147, 150–155
Jackson, Chevalier, 263
James I, King (England), 61, 66
Jefferson Medical College (Philadelphia), 237
Jenner, Edward, 99
Johns Hopkins (Baltimore), 207, 208, 209, 212–213, 233–238, 243, 244
Jonson, Ben, 106

Kant, Immanuel, 270
Keen, Dr. W. W., 237, 255
Kelly, Howard, 209, 233
Kilbride, Scotland, 81, 90
King's College (London), 190, 191–193
King's College (New York City), 109
King's Hospital (London), 193
King's School (Canterbury), 57
Kircher, Athanasius, 76
Knapp, George, 119
Koch, Robert, 165

Lafayette, Marquis de, 130
Landsteiner, Karl, 272, 291
Leeuwenhoek, Anton van, 76, 162
Lennox, Duke of, 66
life expectancy, 283
ligatures, 28, 40, 54, 75, 186–187, 196
  catgut, 187–188, 210
Lillehei, Dr., 279
Lincoln, Abraham, 223
Lister, Joseph, 53, 164, 165–193, 194–195, 210, 268, 271
Lister, Mrs. Joseph, 169–170, 176, 179, 188, 190, 191, 192, 193
Lister, Joseph Jackson, 165–166, 188
Liston, Robert, 146, 164, 167, 168
London, England, 29, 70–71, 76–77, 83, 87, 109, 185, 190
Long, Crawford Williamson, 137–138, 151
Long Island Medical School, 219
Louis XII, King (France), 10
Louvain, France, 11, 19, 20
Loyola, Ignatius, 21
Luke, Saint, 59
Lumley, Lord, 63
Lusitania, 247
Luther, Martin, 10
Lyons, Archbishop of, 51

Macbeth, 53–54
magic, 53, 130
Major, Ralph, 196
Malpighi, Marcello, 76
mandragora, 127
Marella, Media, 256
Marie Antoinette, 130
Maryland, University of, 122
Massachusetts General Hospital, 140, 144, 145, 147, 151, 152, 154, 230–231, 232–233
Massachusetts Medical Society, 146–147
Matas, Rudolph, 277
Mayos, the, 164, 221
Mazelin, Jeanne, 38, 50, 51
McBride, Thomas, 204
McDowell, Ephraim, 111, 112–123, 132, 268
McDowell, James, 119
McLean Asylum, 154
medical schools, 109–110, 219, 272
Medical Society of Paris, 149
Medical Use of Snow, The (Severino), 128
Medici, Catherine de, 43, 44, 45, 46, 47
medicine men, 5
Medico-Chirurgical Review, 121
mercuric chloride, 212
Merton College, 71
mescalin, 206
Mesmer, Franz Anton, 129–131
mesmerism, 131
Mexico, University of, 110
Middle Ages, 12, 29, 76
Minnesota, University of, 279

mitral stenosis, 278
Montejon, Monsieur, 34
Montfaçon, 18, 49, 85
Morgan, John, 109, 121
morphine, 253
Morse, Samuel B., 142
Morton, Mrs. Elizabeth, 141–142, 151, 152
Morton, Remember, 139
Morton, William Thomas Green, 139, 140–147, 150–155
Motion of the Heart, The (Harvey), 65
Mount Sinai Hospital (New York), vi, 256
mutilations, by primitive men, 4–5

neurosurgery, 237, 244–246, 254–255
New York Academy of Medicine, vi, 223
New York Hospital, 110, 201, 230, 282
Nichols, Dr. John H., vi, 260
Nightingale, Florence, 161
nitrous oxide, 134–140, 142, 148, 154, 256, 282
Nobel Prize, 272
novocaine, 272

O'Brien, the giant, 99–102
opium, intravenous injection of, 128
Osler, William, 209, 211, 233, 234, 235, 238, 239, 240, 262, 266
osteomyelitis, 191
ovarian cysts, 114–115, 117–120
ovariotomy, 120, 121, 122, 132
Oxford, England, 70–72
Oxford University, 71, 89

Padua, University of, vi, 21, 22, 24, 26, 58–61, 69
Paget, Stephen, 103
pain, control of, 127–155
palliatives
  in Middle Ages, 31, 127
  search for, 127
Paré, Ambroise, 26, 31, 32, 51, 52, 54, 57, 75, 103, 128, 161, 179, 188, 268
Paris, France, 4, 11–14, 15, 17, 18, 19, 20, 21, 22, 26, 33, 37, 42, 45, 49, 51, 109, 130
Parr, Thomas, 68
Pasteur, Louis, 165, 180, 182, 186
penicillin, 271
Pennsylvania Hospital, 110
pentothal, 256
pesthouses, 30, 69
Peter Bent Brigham Hospital (Boston), 244, 246, 265, 266
Philadelphia, Pennsylvania, 109, 192
Phillips Academy, 199
Physicians
  evolution of, 7
  number of, in U. S., 109
Physick, Dr., 121
physiology, 55, 78
plague, 30, 66, 69, 76
plasma, blood, 295–296, 298
plastic surgery, 54
Polk, James, 122
prehistoric man, 4–5
Presbyterian Hospital (New York City), 203
Priestly, Joseph, 134
primitive man, 4–5
psycho-surgery, 275
puerperal fever, 170
putrefaction, 180
Puységur, Count de, 131
pyemia, 159, 175

quacks, 29
Quakers, 166

Raleigh, Sir Walter, 66
Ray, Dr. Bronson, vi, 251, 252
Red Cross, 298
Reed, Walter, 210
Rehn, Louis, 276
Renaissance, 8, 9, 19, 20, 29, 35, 53, 55
Resurrectionists, 85–87, 168
Reynolds, Sir Joshua, 103–104, 105
Rhazes (Persian physician), 9, 20
rituals, primitive, 4–5
Riva Rocci apparatus, 272, 290
Robinson, Dr. Victor, 136, 142
Rockefeller, John D., 271
Rockefeller Institute, 272

Roentgen, William, 233
Roosevelt, James, 264
Roosevelt Hospital (New York City), 202
Rosenthal, Dr. Arnold, 256
Rousselet, Jacqueline, 30
Royal College of Physicians, vi, 61, 73, 74
Royal College of Surgeons, vi, 101, 104, 106, 168
Royal Society, 96, 193
rubber gloves, 182
Rush, Benjamin, 109, 121

St. Alexis Hospital (Cleveland), 291, 292
Saint André des Arts, 51
Saint Anthony's fire, 175
Saint Bartholomew's Hospital (London), 61, 77, 88
Saint George's Hospital (London), 82, 90, 105
Saint Innocents cemetery, 18
St. Luke's Hospital (New York), 153
Saint Martin's-in-the-Fields, 106
Saint Thomas' Hospital (London), 77, 161, 173
Salerno, medical school at, 8
Salk, Jonas E., 271
Sargent, Sir Percy, 260
Scotland, 79, 189
Semmelweis, Ignaz, 170–171, 173, 192
septic diseases, 159–162, 167, 178, 181
Seven Years War, 91
Severino, Marco Aurelio, 128
Shakespeare, William, 57, 63, 65, 123, 283
Sharpe, Dr. William, 242–244
Shelly, Sarah, *see* McDowell, Mrs. Ephraim
Shippen, William, 109, 121
Shock
  control of, 287–301
  irreversible, 294, 298, 300
  syndrome of, 289
Shorr, Dr. Ephraim, 299
Simpson, James Young, 146, 168
"sleeping sponge," 127, 128
smallpox, 99
Smith, Dr. Alban, 119
Smith, Dr. J. H., 154
Smith, Oliver Cotton, 219–222
Smith, Mrs. Oliver Cotton, 220
Society of Friends, 166, 169
somnambulistic trance, 131
Spanish Armada, 57
spermatozoa, discovery of, 76
steam sterilizer, 196
sterilization, 196
Stevenson, Robert Louis, 102
Stewart, John, 191
Stuart, Mary, 43
superstition, 52, 53, 54, 65
surgeons, evolution of, 7
"surgical stink," 172
Sylvius, Jacobus, 12, 14, 15, 17, 19, 22, 24, 37, 38
Syme, Agnes, *see* Lister, Mrs. Joseph
Syme, James, 132, 168, 169, 171, 179, 188–189
syphilis, 97

Tagliacozzi, 54
Takamine, Jokichi, 290
thoracic surgery, 275
Titian, 21, 26
Tournai, college of, 15
tourniquets, 54, 75
transfusions, blood, 241, 272, 291–292, 293, 295, 299, 300
Treatise on the Blood, Inflammation and Gunshot Wounds (Hunter), 92
trepanation (trephining), 4–5, 237
trephine, 255
Trinity College, 71
tuberculosis, 80, 83, 90
tumors, brain, 237, 241, 245, 252–253, 263–265, 267
Turner, Daniel, 108

University College of London, 166–167, 168

vascular surgery, 275
Venable, James M., 137–138, 151
venereal disease, 97
Venice, Italy, 21, 69

Vesalius, Andreas, 9, 10–27, 28, 37, 43, 52, 54, 58, 59, 60, 85, 199, 266–267, 268, 272
Victoria, Queen, 146, 193
Victory over Pain (Robinson), 136
Vienna, Austria, 68, 130, 131, 170
Virgil, 66

Warren, Dr. John Collins, 144–145, 146–147
Washington, George, 130, 223
Waterman, Clarabel, *see* Smith, Mrs. Oliver Cotton
Welch, William, 201–202, 203, 207, 208, 209, 211, 213, 215, 233, 273
Wellcome Historical Medical Museum, vi, 166, 191
Wells, Horace, 138–140, 147, 148–149, 151, 154, 155
Wesel, André, *see* Vesalius, Andreas
Westminster Abbey, 106, 193
Wilderness Road, 113
witch doctors, 5
Wright brothers, 272

X-ray, discovery of, 233

Yale University, vi, 108, 109, 199, 200, 222, 227–230, 249, 266
yellow fever, 109

Zante, island of, 26–27
Zweifach, Dr. Benjamin W., 298, 299

ABOUT THE AUTHOR

AGATHA YOUNG spent four years in Washington during the Second World War as a dollar-a-year consultant to the War Department and to the War Manpower Commission. She was for many years a designer for the theatre, and taught at the famous Yale School of Drama. She has written both fiction and non-fiction, some of the latter under the name of Agnes Brooks Young.

Research for this book was pursued in many medical libraries, among them the New York Academy of Medicine and the Royal College of Surgeons in London. The work took Agatha Young into a number of medical centers, both ancient and modern, ranging from the University of Padua, Italy, which flourished as a medical school in the Renaissance, to the Western Reserve School of Medicine, where an experiment in new methods of medical teaching is taking place. She became familiar with a number of hospitals and with the scenes in their operating rooms.

Agatha Young is from Cleveland, Ohio, but she now divides her time between Cleveland and New York City.